LONDON

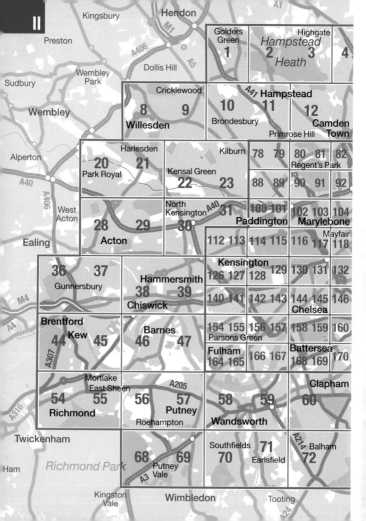

Key to map pages

Atlas pages at 3½ inches to 1 mile are shown in blue

Central London atlas pages at 7 inches to 1 mile are shown in red (See page 77)

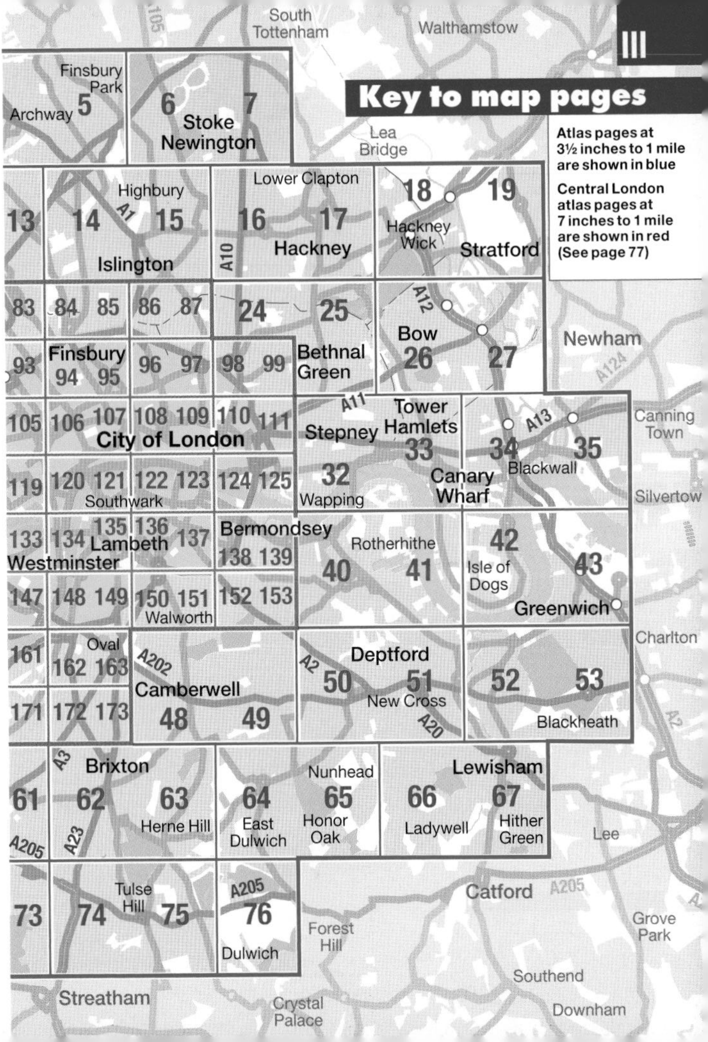
South Tottenham
Walthamstow
105
Finsbury Park
Archway
5
6
7
Stoke Newington
Lea Bridge
Highbury
A1
13
14
15
Islington
Lower Clapton
16
17
A10
Hackney
18
19
Hackney Wick
Stratford
83
84
85
86
87
24
25
A12
Bow
26
27
Newham
A124
93
Finsbury
94
95
96
97
98
99
Bethnal Green
A11
Tower Hamlets
105
106
107
108
109
110
111
City of London
Stepney
33
A13
34
35
Canning Town
Blackwall
119
120
121
122
123
124
125
32
Southwark
Wapping
Canary Wharf
Silvertown
133
134
135
136
137
Lambeth
Westminster
Bermondsey
138
139
Rotherhithe
40
41
42
Isle of Dogs
43
147
148
149
150
151
152
153
Walworth
Greenwich
161
Oval
162
163
A202
Camberwell
Deptford
A2
50
51
New Cross
52
53
Charlton
171
172
173
48
49
A20
Blackheath
A2
A3
Brixton
61
62
63
Herne Hill
64
East Dulwich
Nunhead
65
Honor Oak
Lewisham
66
Ladywell
67
Hither Green
Lee
A205
A23
Tulse Hill
73
74
75
A205
76
Dulwich
Forest Hill
Catford
A205
Grove Park
Southend
Streatham
Crystal Palace
Downham

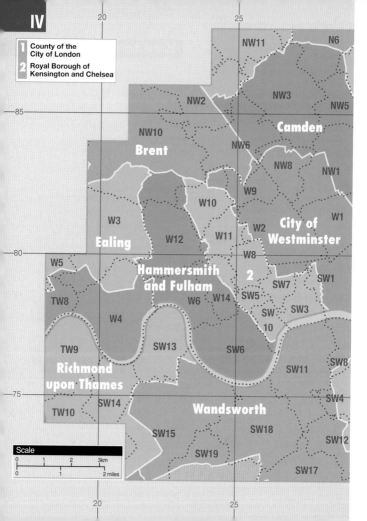

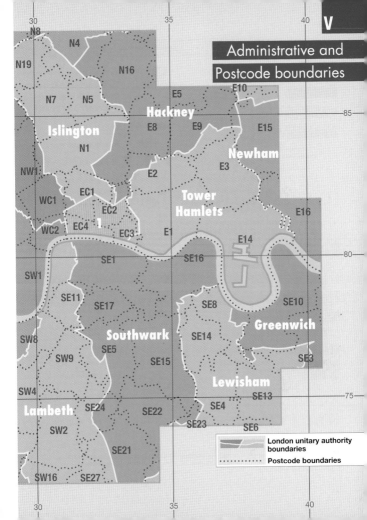

Administrative and
Postcode boundaries

London unitary authority boundaries
Postcode boundaries

VI

Key to map symbols

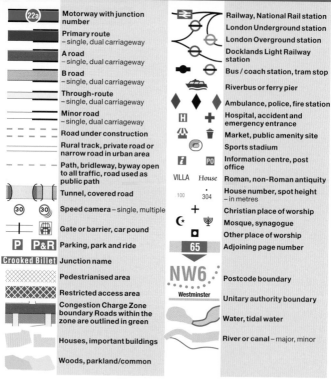

Motorway with junction number

Primary route
– single, dual carriageway

A road
– single, dual carriageway

B road
– single, dual carriageway

Through-route
– single, dual carriageway

Minor road
– single, dual carriageway

Road under construction

Rural track, private road or narrow road in urban area

Path, bridleway, byway open to all traffic, road used as public path

Tunnel, covered road

Speed camera – single, multiple

Gate or barrier, car pound

Parking, park and ride

Crooked Billet Junction name

Pedestrianised area

Restricted access area

Congestion Charge Zone boundary Roads within the zone are outlined in green

Houses, important buildings

Woods, parkland/common

Railway, National Rail station

London Underground station

London Overground station

Docklands Light Railway station

Bus / coach station, tram stop

Riverbus or ferry pier

Ambulance, police, fire station

Hospital, accident and emergency entrance

Market, public amenity site

Sports stadium

Information centre, post office

VILLA   House   Roman, non-Roman antiquity

100   304   House number, spot height – in metres

Christian place of worship

Mosque, synagogue

Other place of worship

65   Adjoining page number

NW6   Postcode boundary

Westminster   Unitary authority boundary

Water, tidal water

River or canal – major, minor

The map scale on the pages numbered in blue is 3½ inches to 1 mile
5.52 cm to 1 km • 1: 18 103

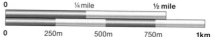

0   ¼ mile   ½ mile

0   250m   500m   750m   1km

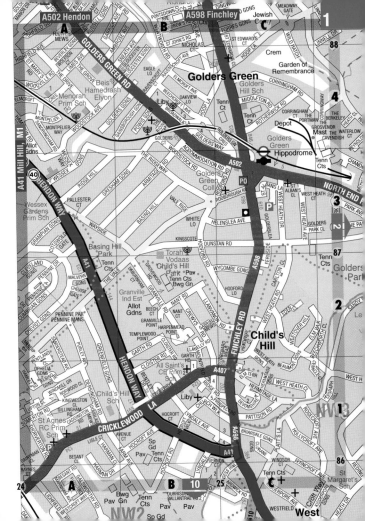

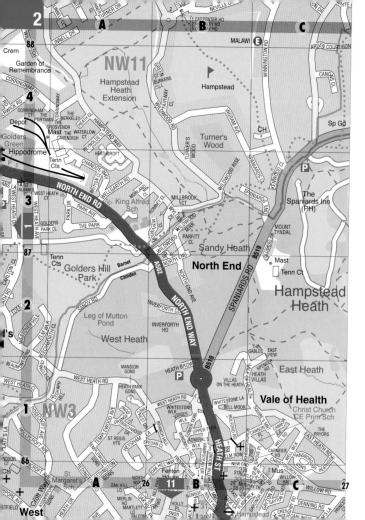

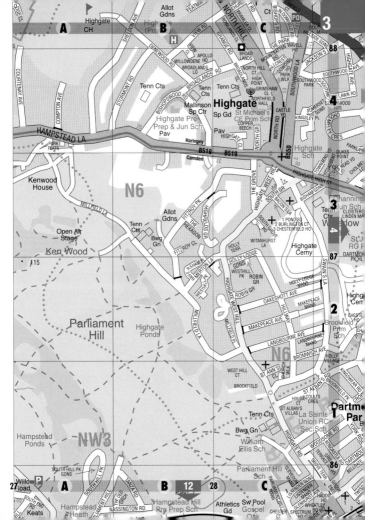

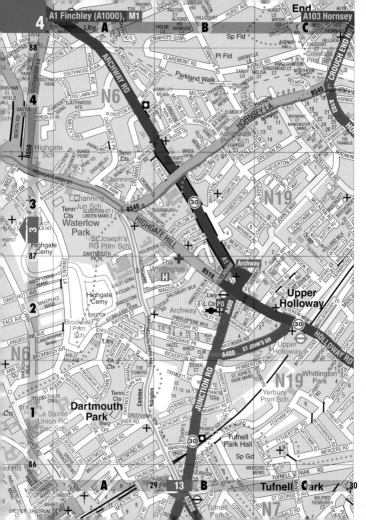

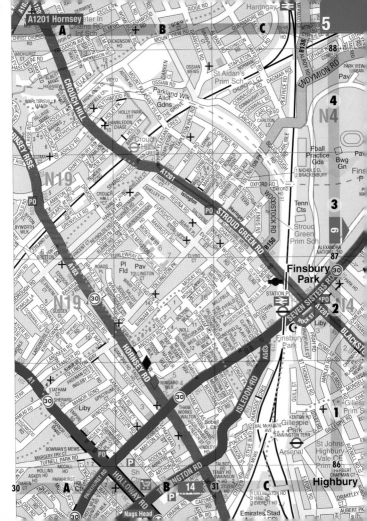

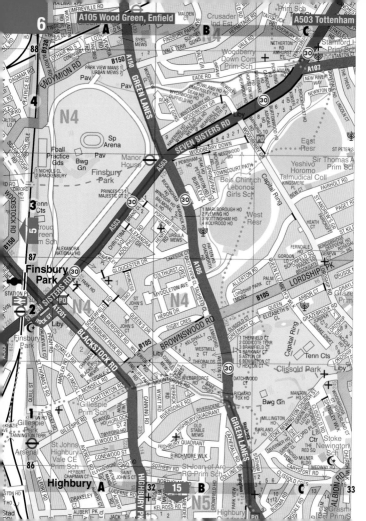

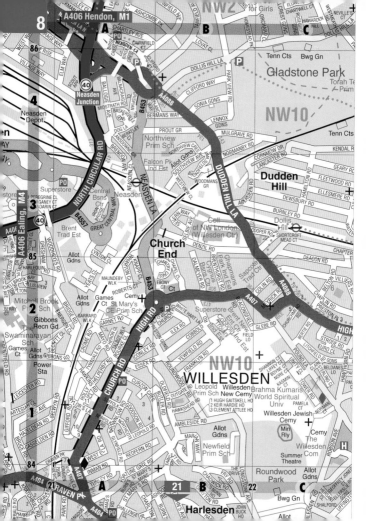

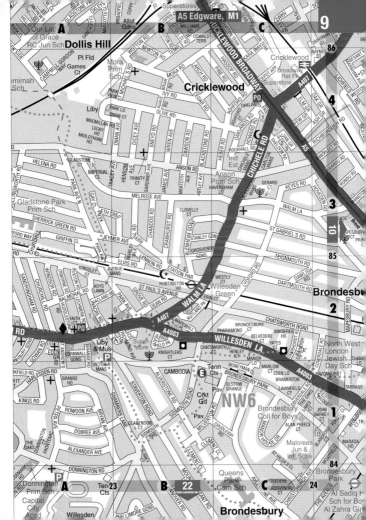

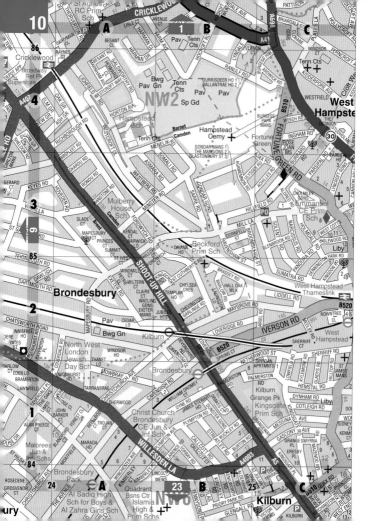

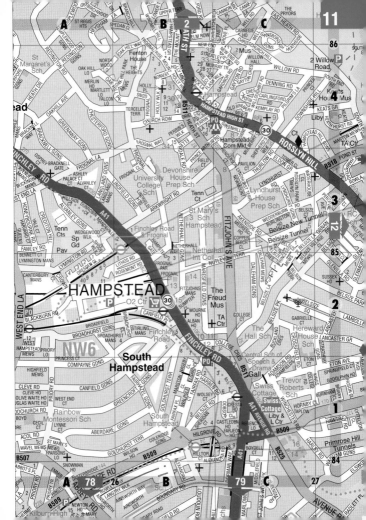

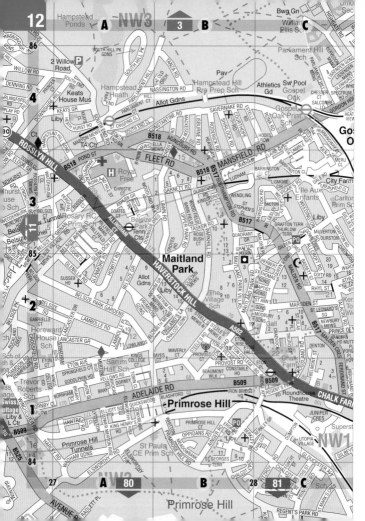

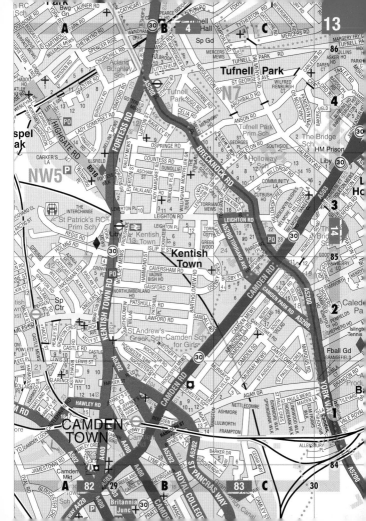

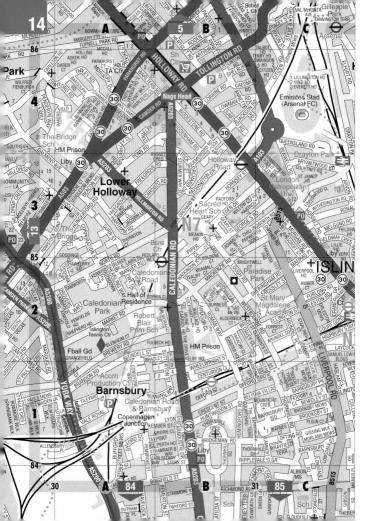

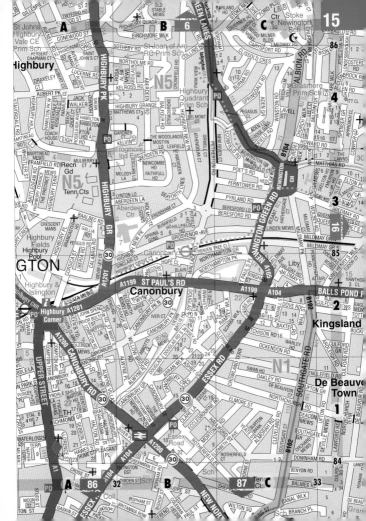

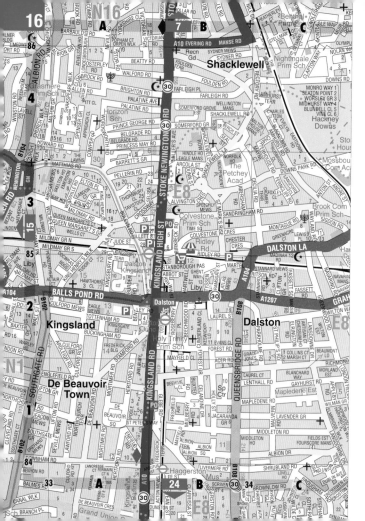

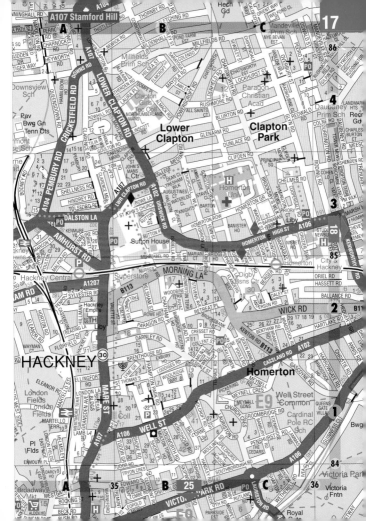

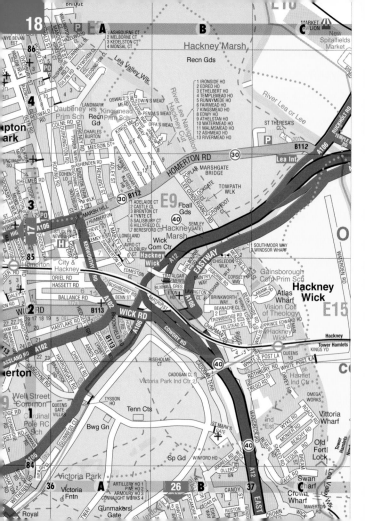

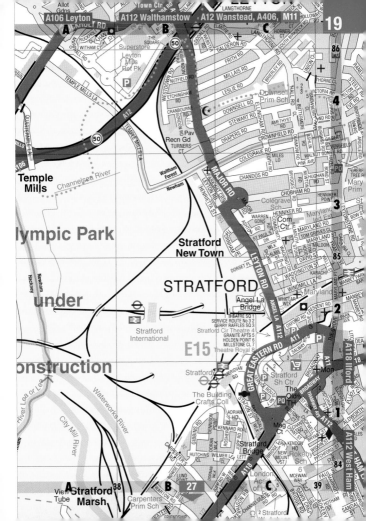

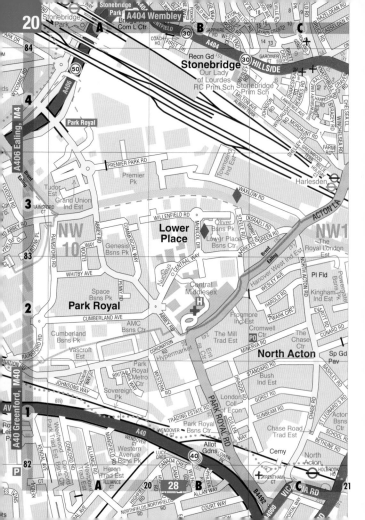

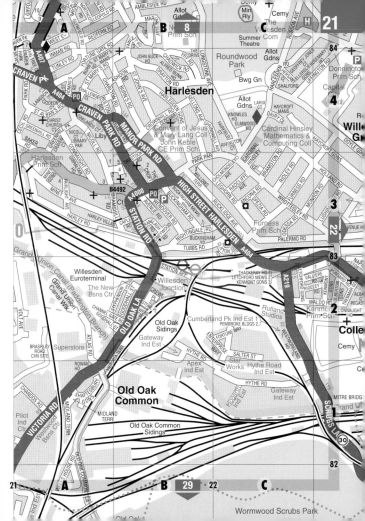

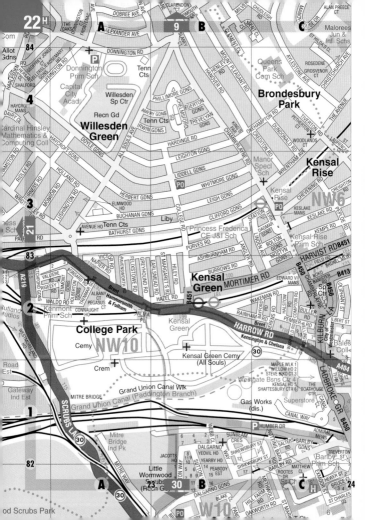

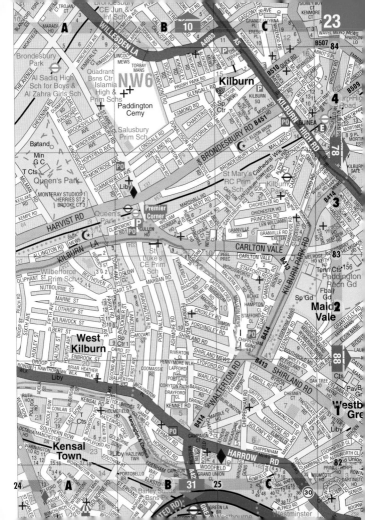

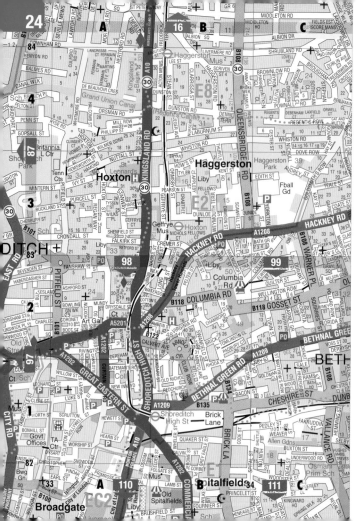

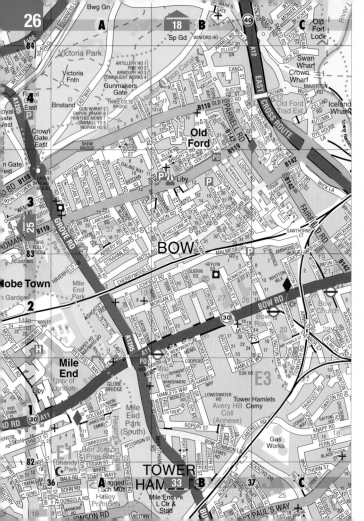

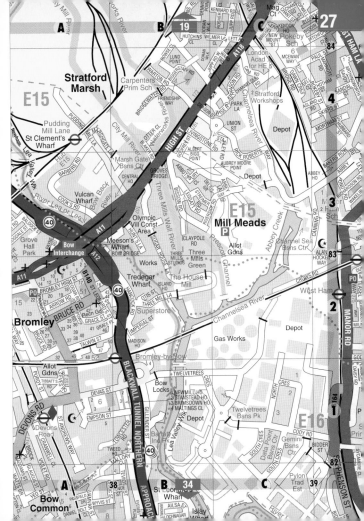

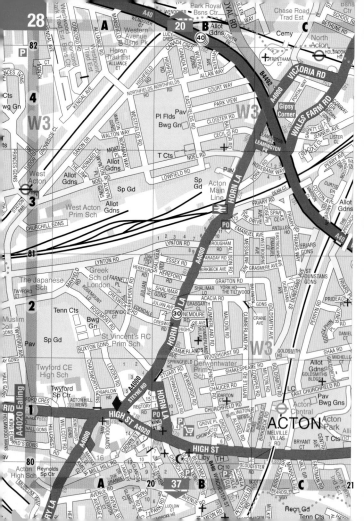

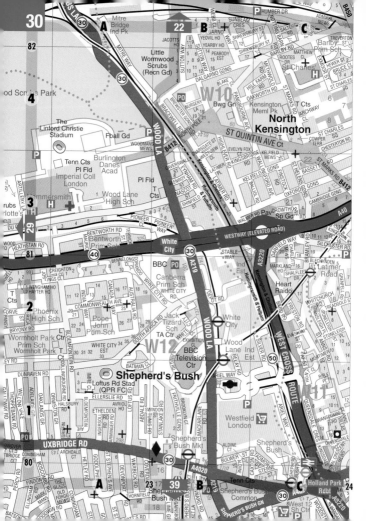

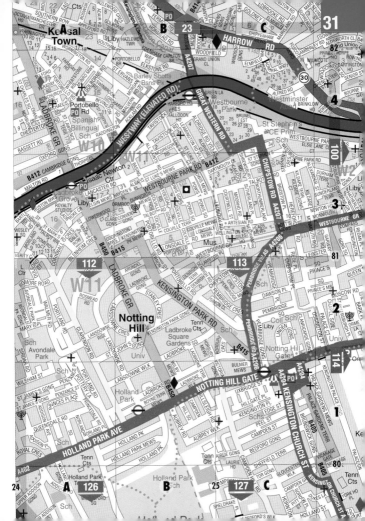

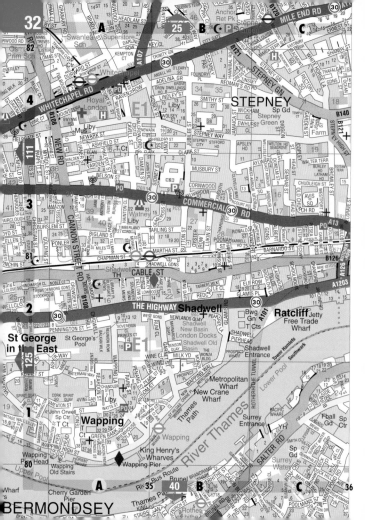

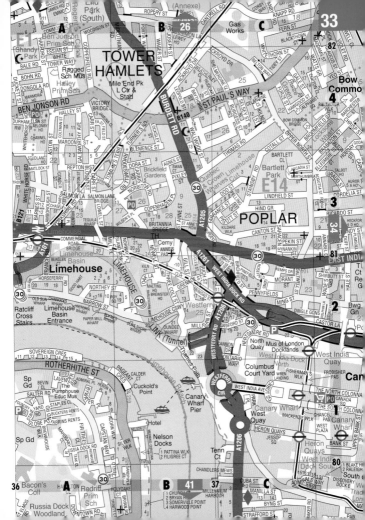

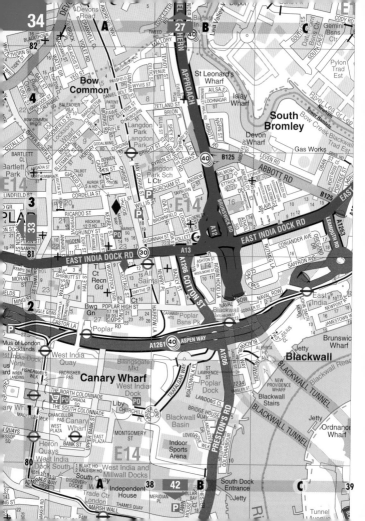

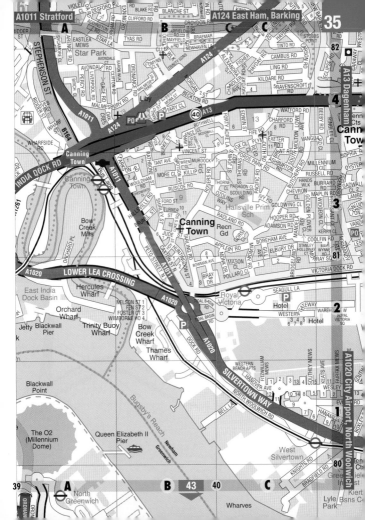

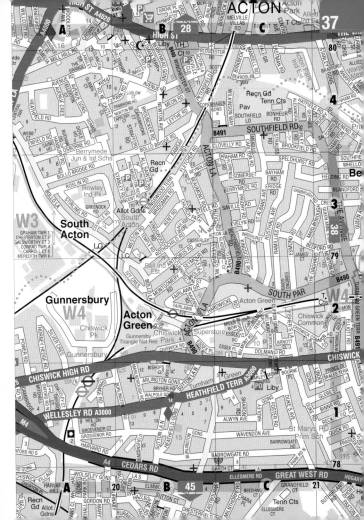

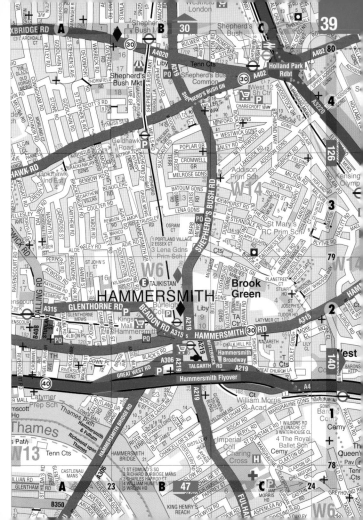

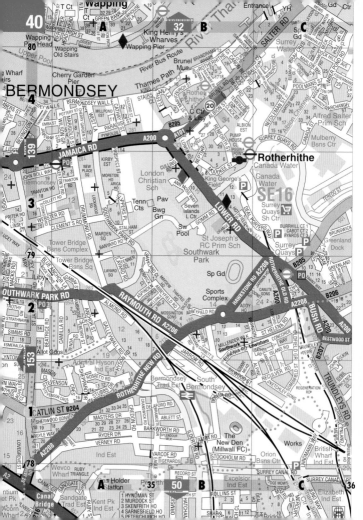

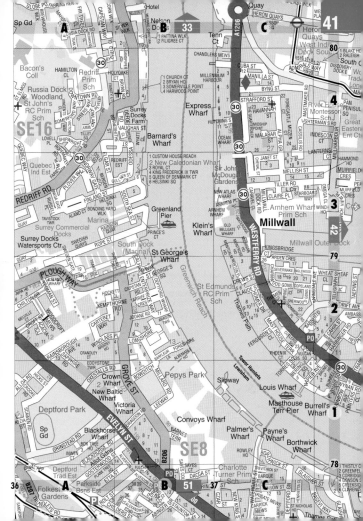

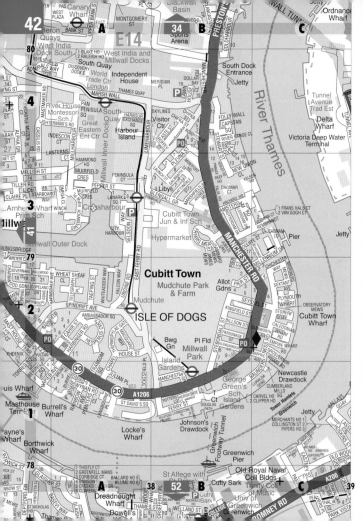

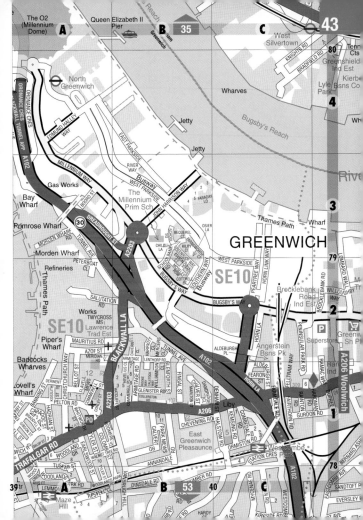

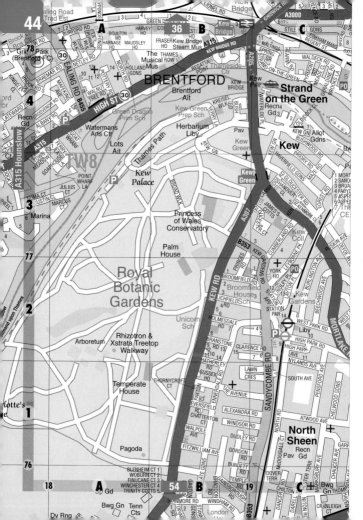

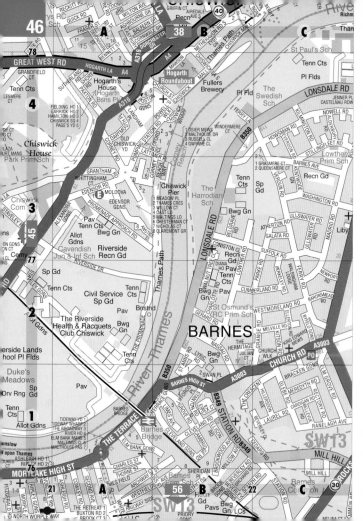

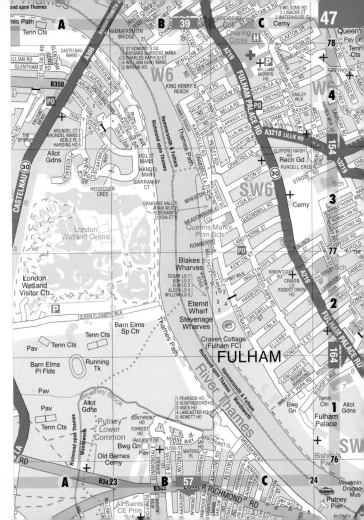

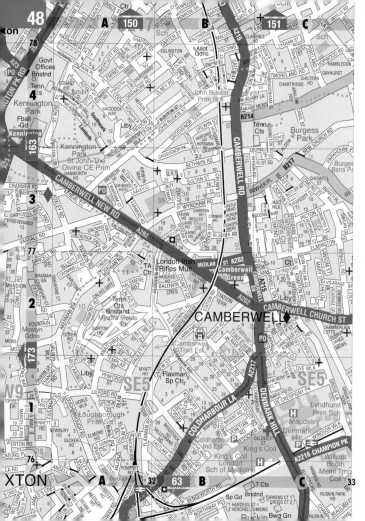

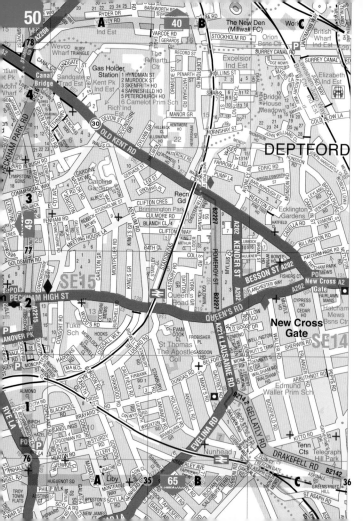

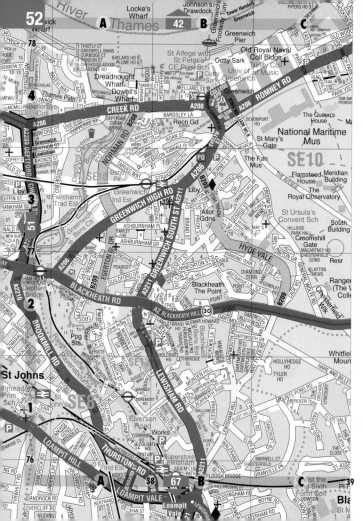

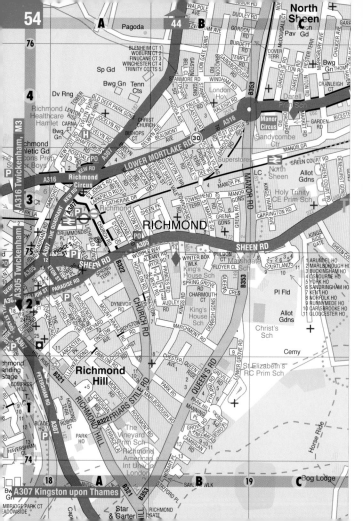

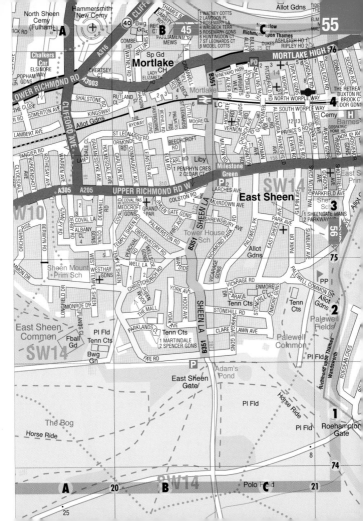

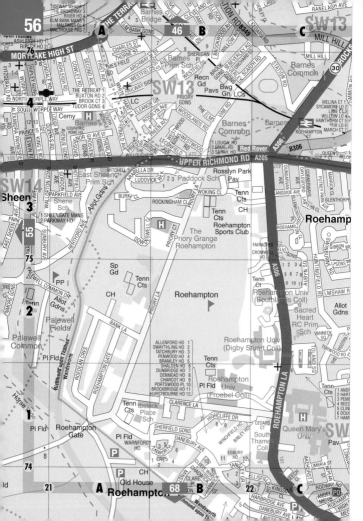

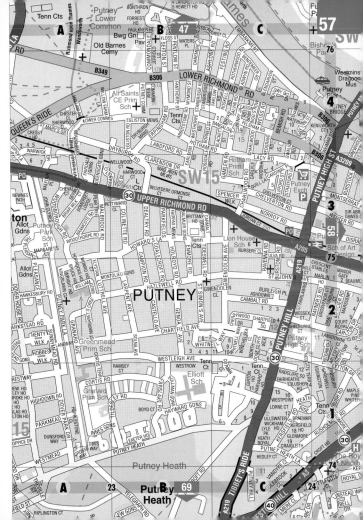

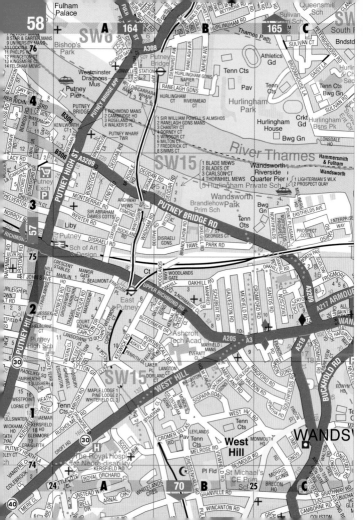

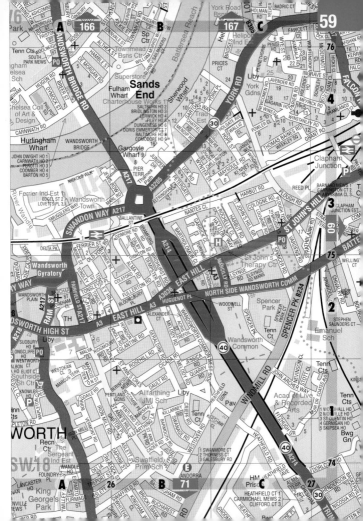

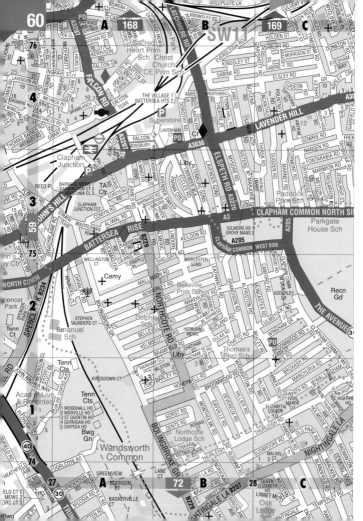

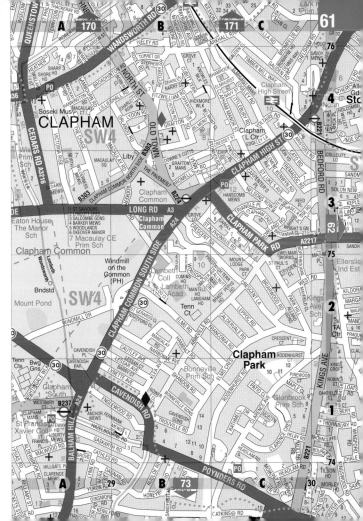

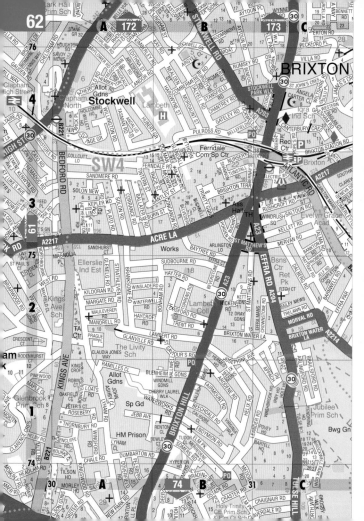

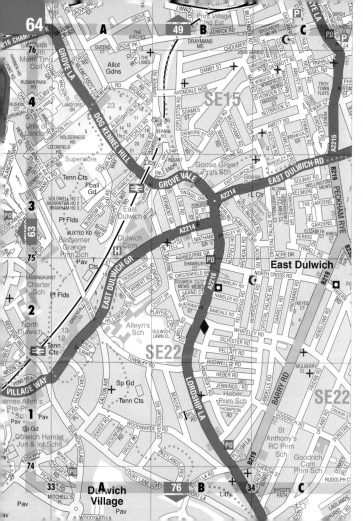

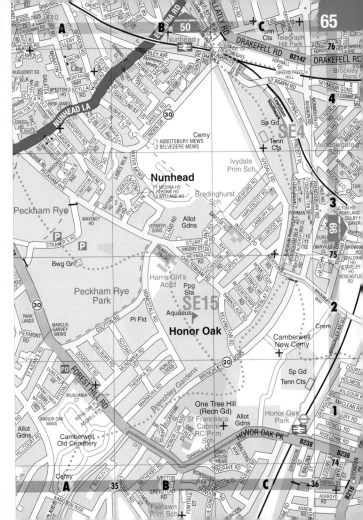

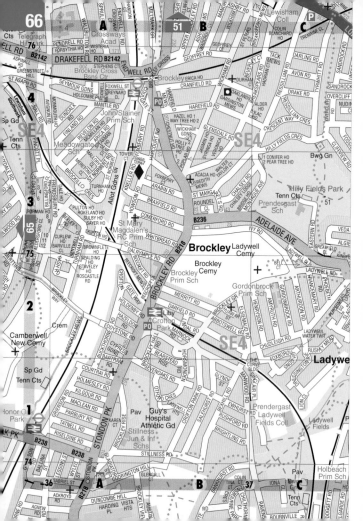

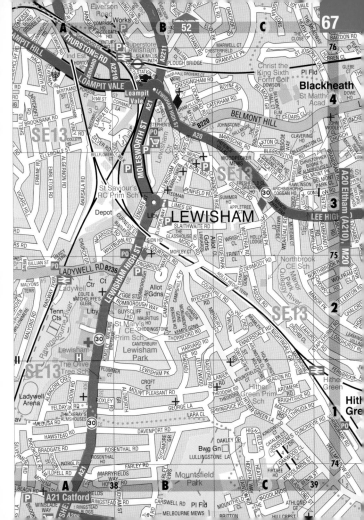

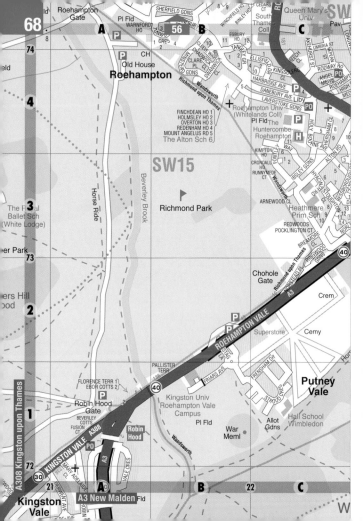

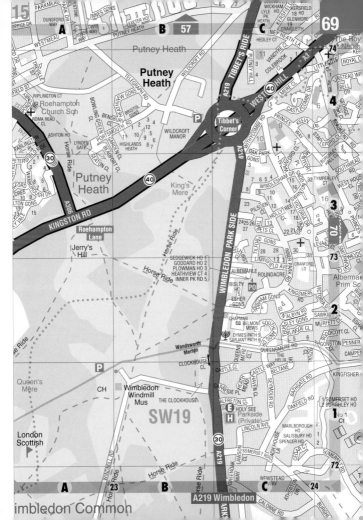

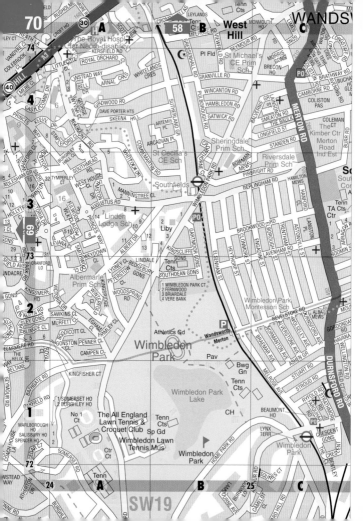

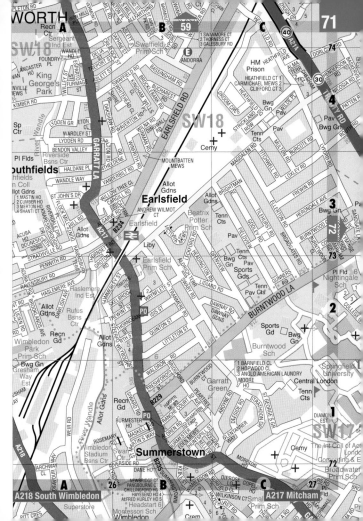

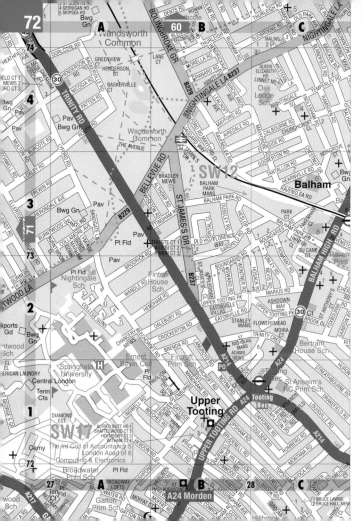

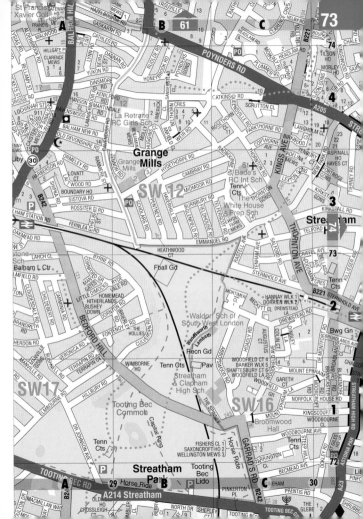

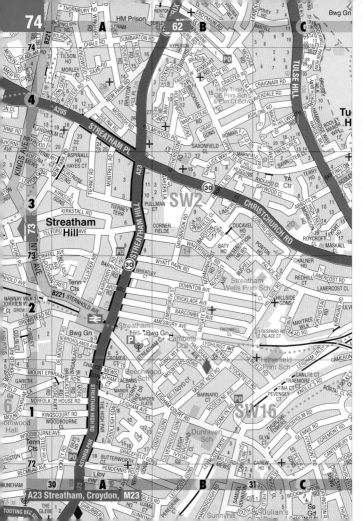

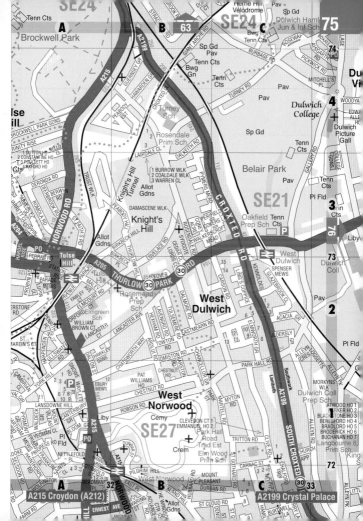

Key to central London map pages

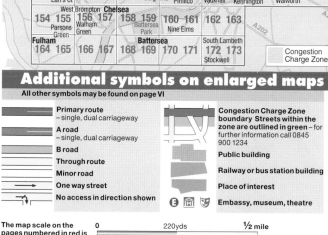

78 79 St John's Wood	Primrose Hill **80 81** Regent's Park	**82 83** Somers Town	**Islington 84 85** King's Cross	**86 87**
Maida Vale **88 89** Westbourne Green	Lisson Grove **90 91**	**92 93** Bloomsbury	St Pancras **Finsbury** **94 95**	**Shoreditch 96 97**	**Bethnal Green 98 99**
Paddington 100 101	**Marylebone 102 103**	Fitzrovia **104 105**	Holborn **106 107** St Giles	**City 108 109**	**110 111** Whitechapel
Notting Hill **112 113**	Bayswater **114 115** Kensington	**116 117** Hyde Park	Mayfair **118 119** St James	Strand **120 121** South Bank	**122 123** **Southwark**	**124 125** St George in the East
Kensington 126 127 Holland Pk West	Kensington Gardens **128 129**	Knightsbridge **130 131** Brompton	Green Park **132 133**	Waterloo **134 135**	The Borough **136 137**	**138 139** **Bermondsey**
West Kensington **140 141** Earl's Ct	South Kensington **142 143**	**Westminster 144 145** Belgravia	Victoria **146 147** Pimlico	**Lambeth 148 149** Vauxhall Kennington	Newington **150 151** Walworth	**152 153**
West Brompton **154 155** Parsons Green	**Chelsea 156 157** Walham Green	**158 159** Battersea Park	**160 161** Nine Elms	**162 163**		
Fulham 164 165	**Battersea 166 167**	**168 169**	**170 171**	South Lambeth **172 173** Stockwell		

Congestion Charge Zone

Additional symbols on enlarged maps

All other symbols may be found on page VI

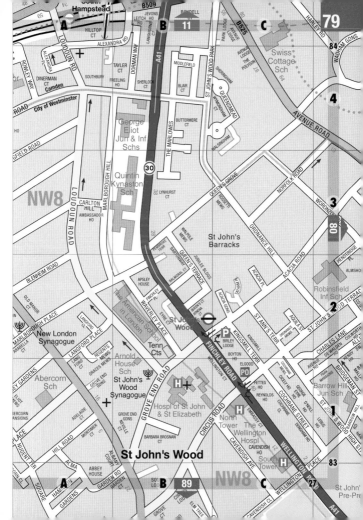

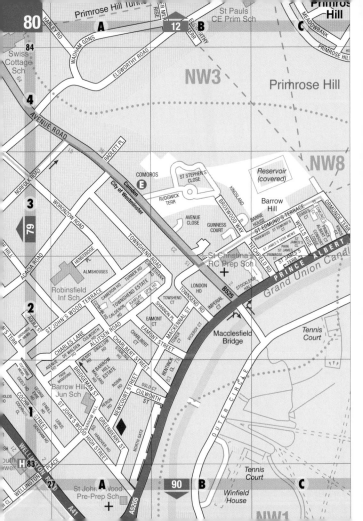

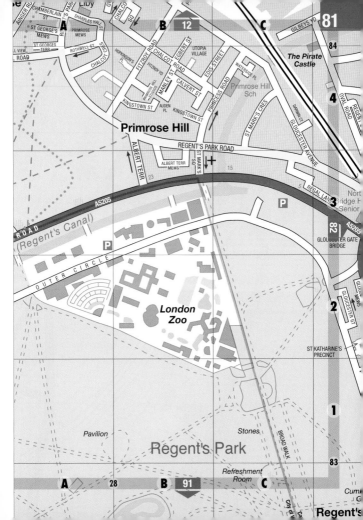

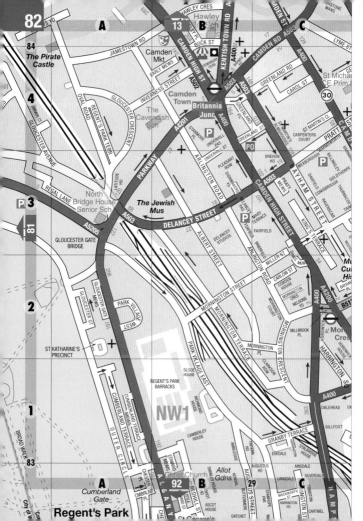

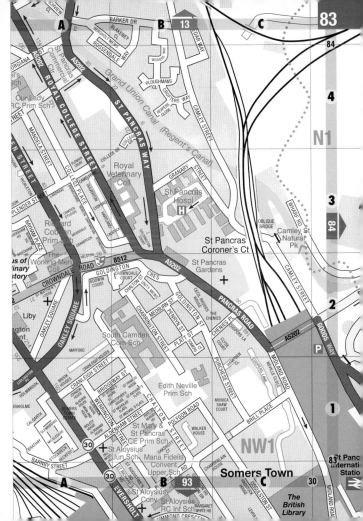

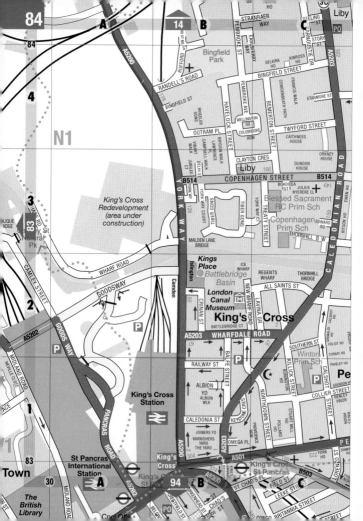

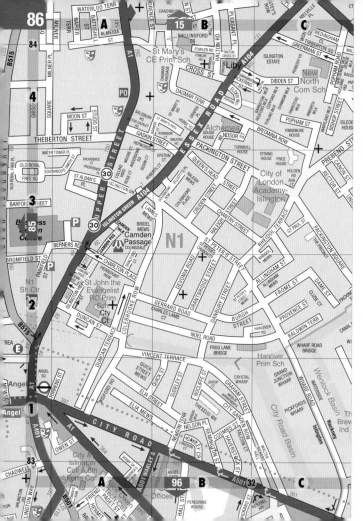

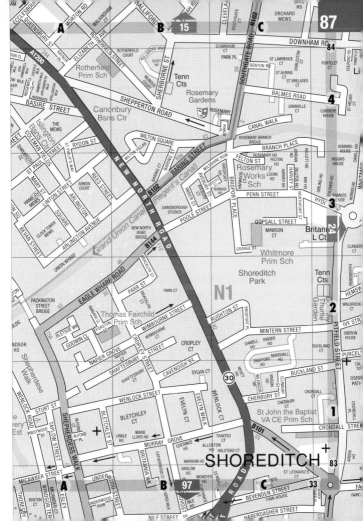

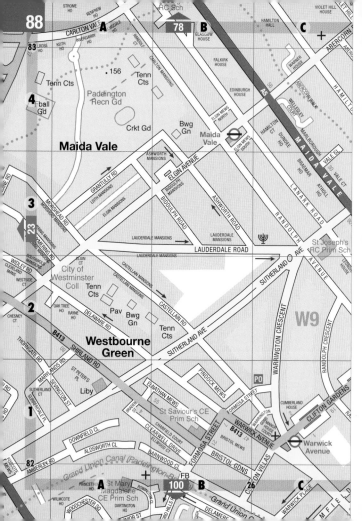

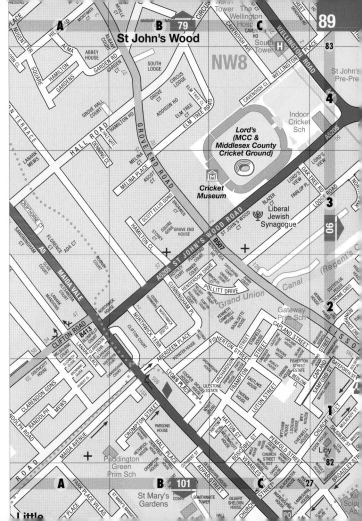

St John's Wood

NW8

83

HILL

MORTIMER CT

NEVILLE CT

BARBARA CASTLE CT

CAVENDISH AVE

CAVENDISH HO

South
Tower

H

4

AS205

St John's
Pre-Pre

NUGENT TER

ALMA

ABBEY
HOUSE

GARDEN RD

SOUTH
LODGE

CIRCUS
LODGE

ADDISON HO

ELM TREE CT

ELM TREE
ELM TREE RD

Lord's
(MCC &
Middlesex County
Cricket Ground)

WELLINGTON ROAD

CAVENDISH PL

HAMILTON
GARDENS

GROVE
GARDEN

CIRCUS
RD

GROVE
CT

HAMILTON HO

Indoor
Cricket
Sch

HALL ROAD

DENNING CL

PARK CL

HAMILTON CL

MELINA CT

ASCOT CT

Cricket
Museum

BLAZER
CT

LORD'S
VIEW

OAKTREE RD

LORD'S VIEW

FAIRLOP PL

LODGE ROAD

3

TERRACE

LANARK MEWS

CROPTHORNE CT

FLORENCE
CT

ADA CT

SANDRINGHAM
CT

CLIVE
COURT

SCOTT ELLIS GDNS

SQUIRE
GDNS

BRONWEN CT

GROVE END
HOUSE

HAMILTON CL

STOREY

Liberal
Jewish
Synagogue

ST JOHN'S WOOD

06

(Regent's

AS205

MAIDA VALE

A5

ALEXANDRA
COURT

LANARK
COURT

PRIORY
COURT

NORTHWICK
HOUSE

ST JOHN'S WOOD ROAD

B507

HENDERSON DRIVE

POLLITT DRIVE

CUNNINGHAM PL

Grand Union

Canal

Gateway
Prim Sch

2

CLIFTON ROAD

B413

MELBOURNE
COURT

LANARK PLACE

CLIFTON
COURT

NORTHWICK
TERR

CLIFTON
COURT

ABERDEEN PLACE

POYNTER HOUSE

CAPLAND STREET

KENNETH
CAMPBELL HO

CAPLAND STREET

STANHOPE
STREET

FISHERTON
STREET
ESTATE

FISHERTON STREET

SO

1

CLARENDON GDNS

RANDOLPH MEWS

LYONS PLACE

CROMPTON STREET

PARSONS
HOUSE

HALL PLACE

FRAMPTON
STREET

ORCHARDSON
STREET

LILESTONE
ESTATE

LUTON STREET

CHURCH
STREET EST

BROADLEY

CHURCH

SALISBURY ST

EDEN HOUSE

Liby

82

RANDOLPH ROAD

MAIDA AVENUE

Paddington
Green
Prim Sch

HATTON ST

PENFOLD STREET

BOSCOBEL ST

ADPAR STREET

VENABLES
STREET

PO

27

St Mary's
Gardens

BRAITHWAITE
TOWER

GILBERT
SHELDON
HOUSE

Little

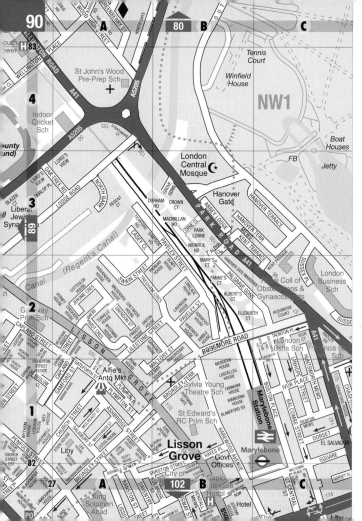

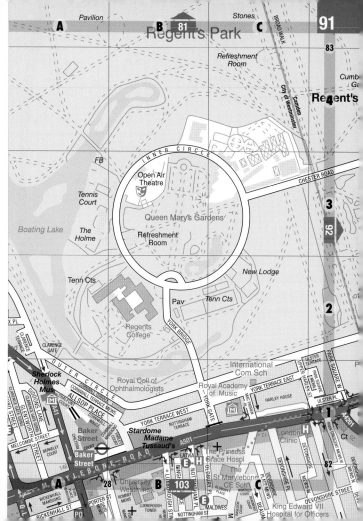

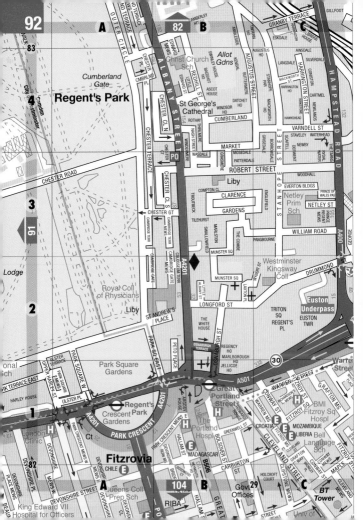

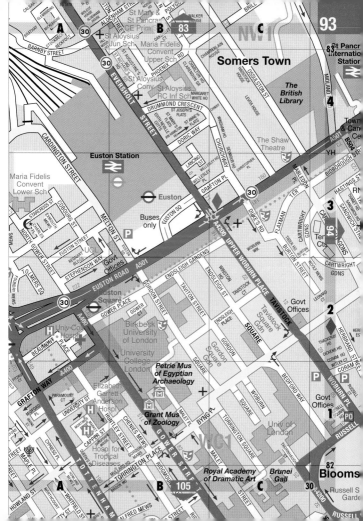

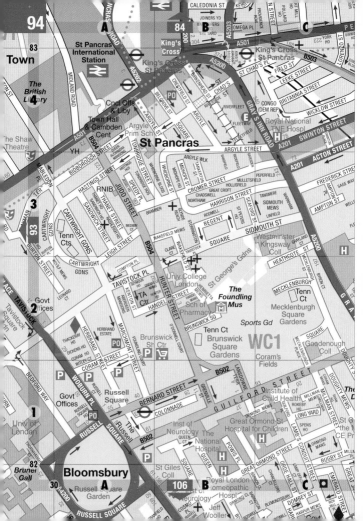

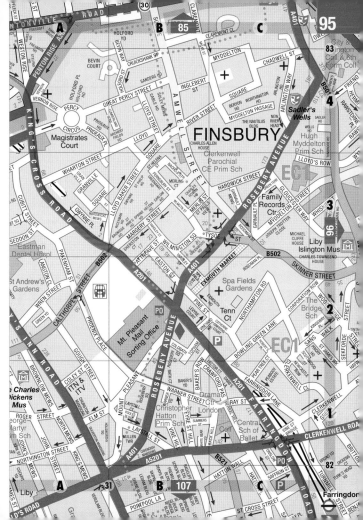

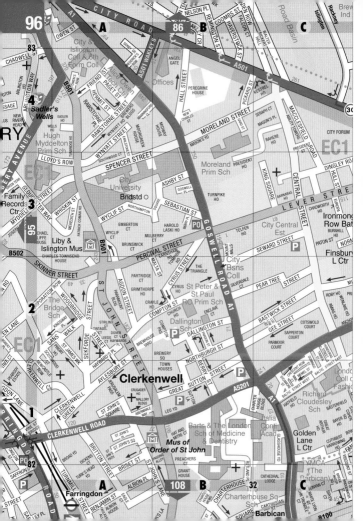

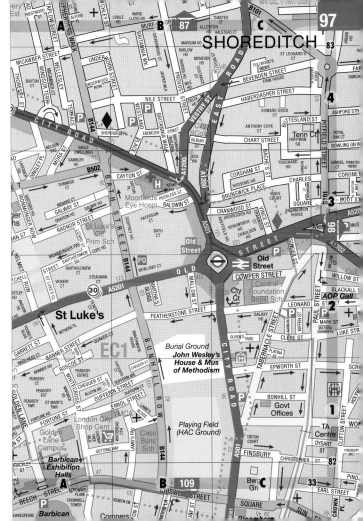

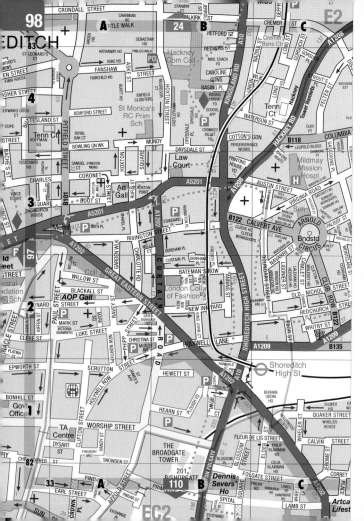

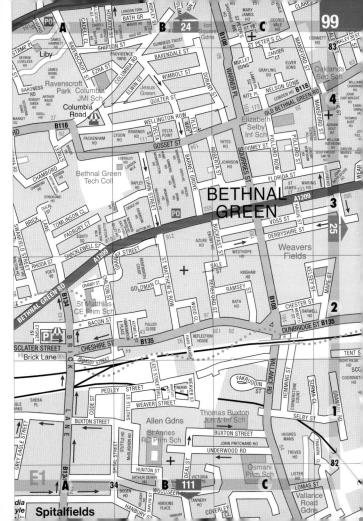

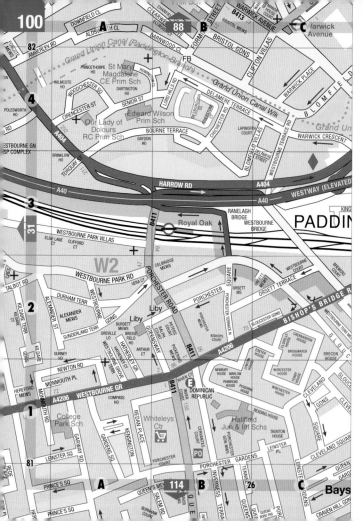

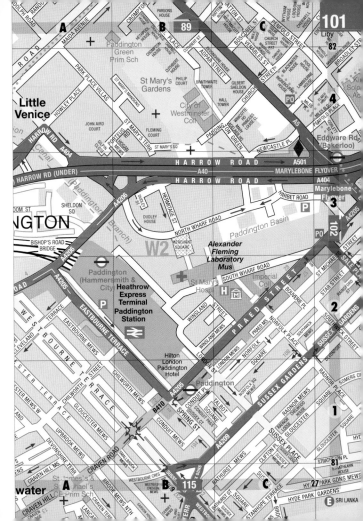

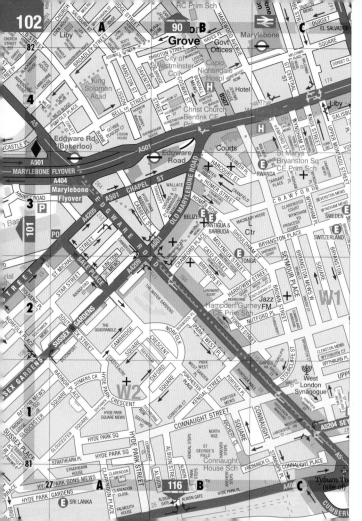

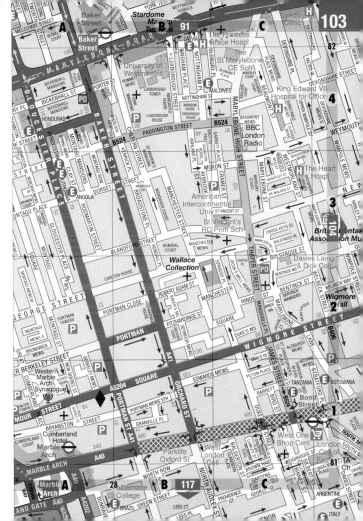

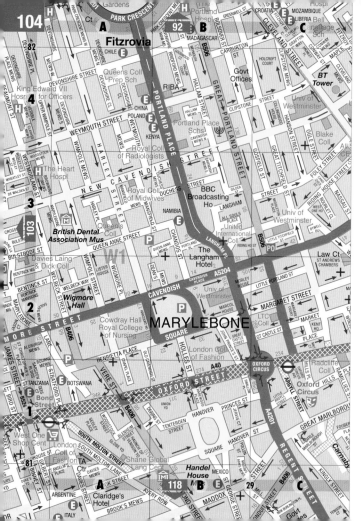

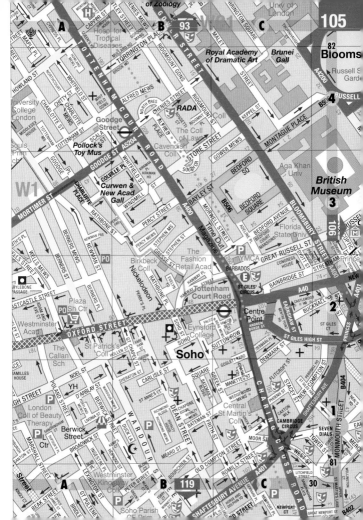

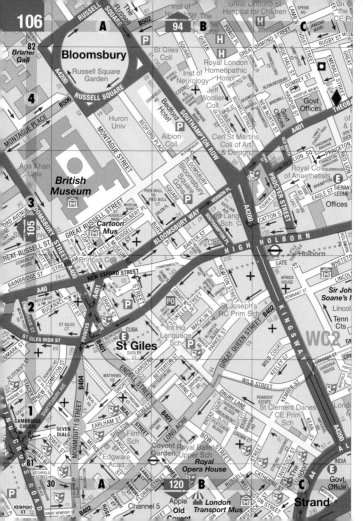

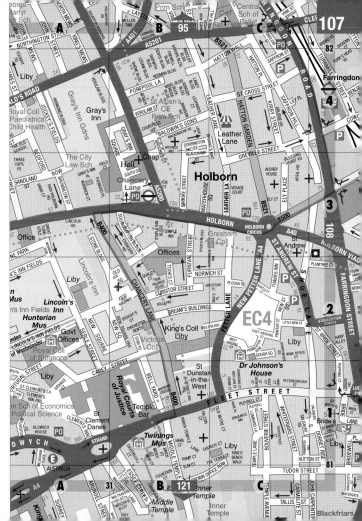

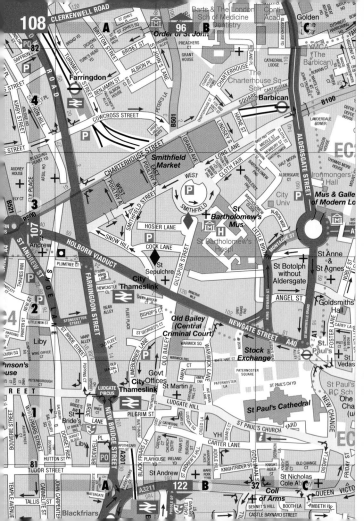

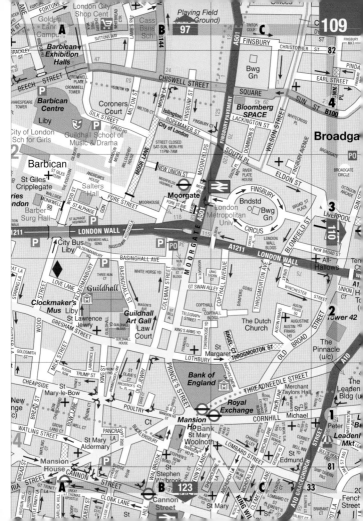

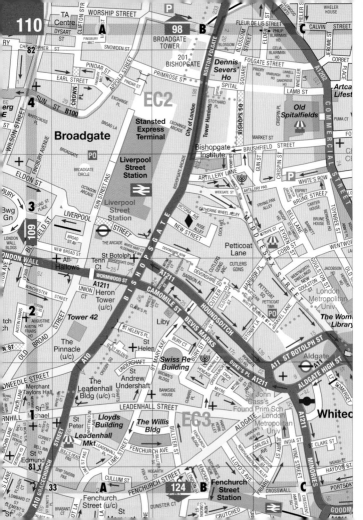

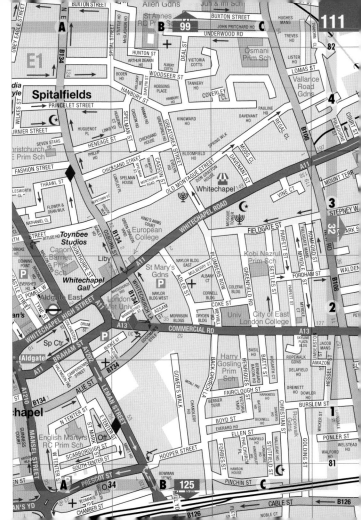

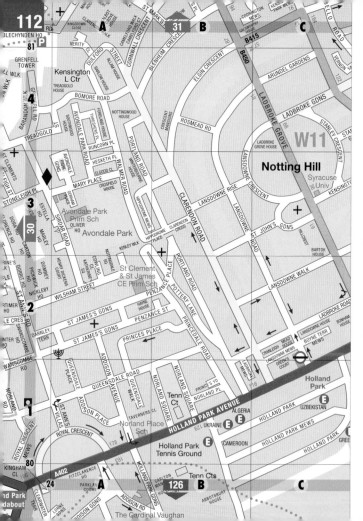

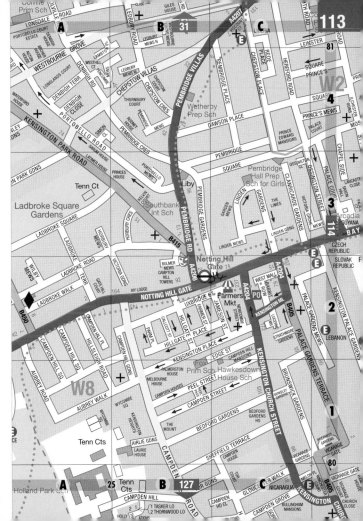

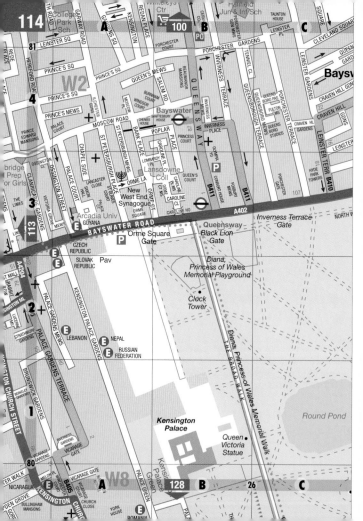

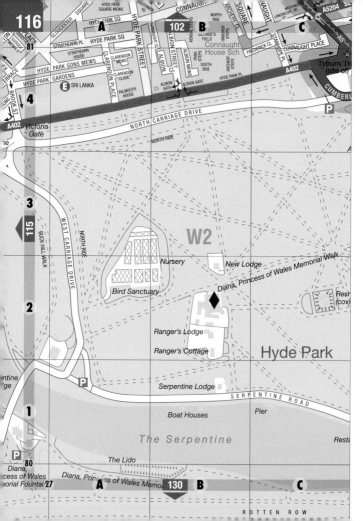

GLOUCESTER SQUARE

HYDE PARK SQUARE MEWS

CONNAUGHT

A5204

HYDE PARK SQ

A

NORTH RISE

SQUARE

C

81

STRATHEARN PL

HYDE PARK STREET

HYDE PARK STREET

ALBION STREET

102

B

GEORGE'S FIELD

ARCHERY CL

FREDERICK CL

Connaught
House Sch

STANHOPE

CONNAUGHT PLACE

STRATHEARN
HOUSE

CLARENDON
MEWS

ALBION MEWS

ALBION STREET

HANOVER STEPS

ARCHERY
STEPS

A402

Tyburn Tree
(site of)

HYDE PARK GDNS MEWS

CLARENDON
PLACE

SOUTH
RISE

HYDE PARK GARDENS

CLARENDON
CLOSE

E SRI LANKA

FALMOUTH
HOUSE

25

ALBION
GATE

ALBION GATE

ALBION GATE

HYDE PARK PL

CUMBERLA

4

P

BROOK ST

A402

NORTH CARRIAGE DRIVE

Victoria
Gate

NORTH RIDE

3

115

BUCK HILL WALK

WEST CARRIAGE DRIVE

NORTH RIDE

W2

Nursery

New Lodge

Diana, Princess of Wales Memorial Walk

Bird Sanctuary

Resr
(cov)

2

◆

Ranger's Lodge

Ranger's Cottage

Hyde Park

P

Serpentine Lodge

SERPENTINE ROAD

ntine
ge

1

Boat Houses

Pier

The Serpentine

Resta

P

80

Diana,
cess of Wales
orial Fountain

27

The Lido

A

Diana, Princess of Wales Memor

130

B

▼

C

ROTTEN ROW

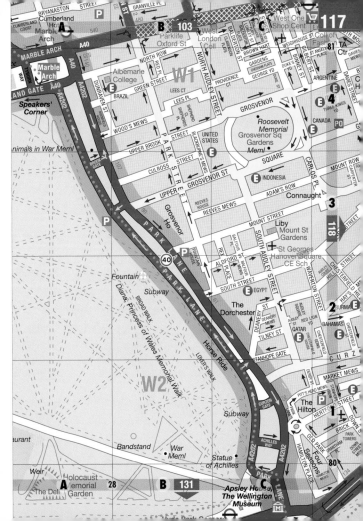

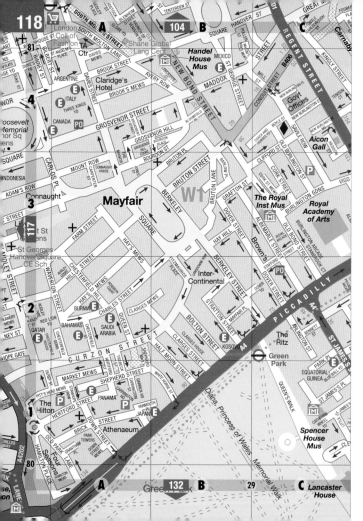

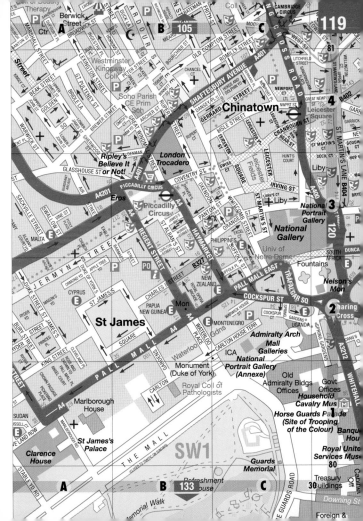

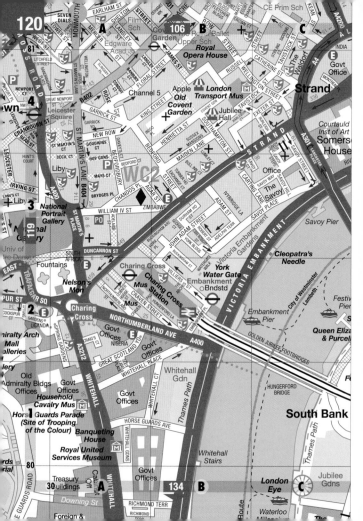

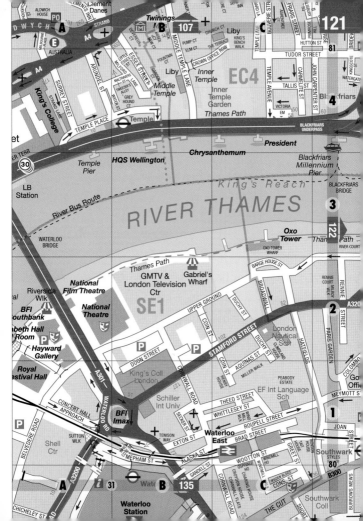

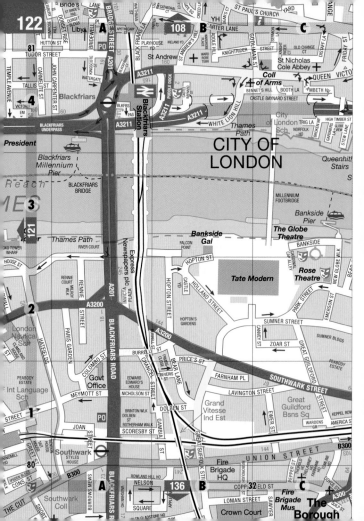

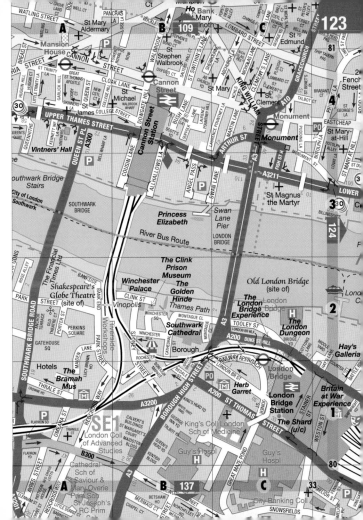

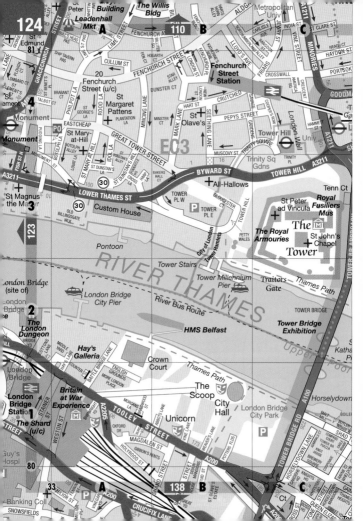

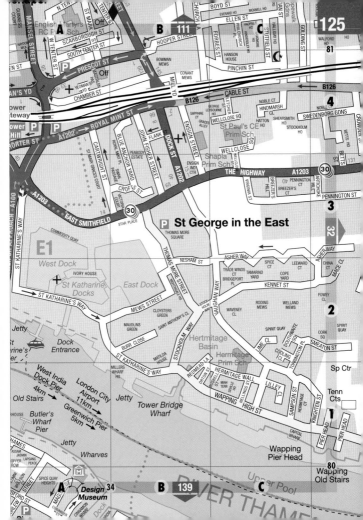

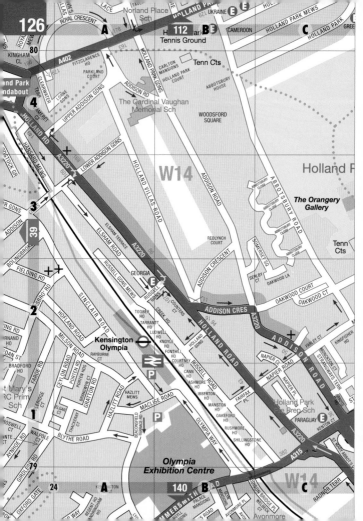

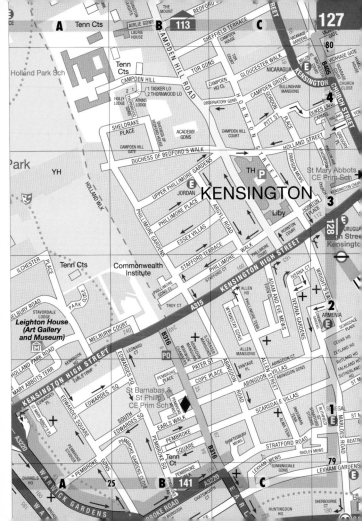

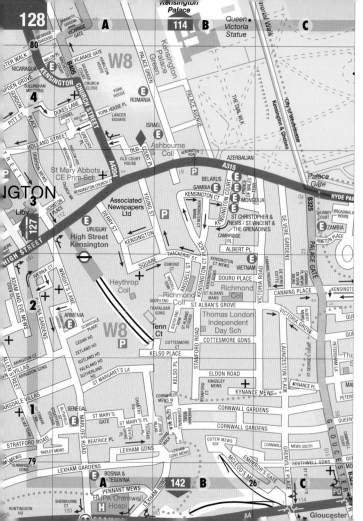

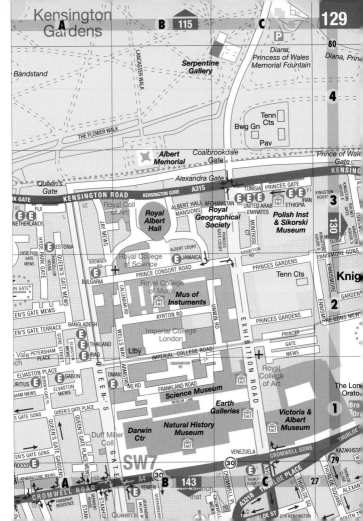

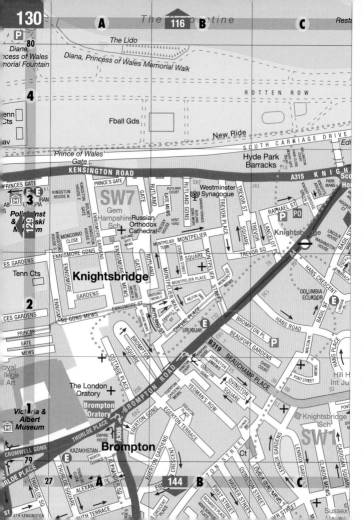

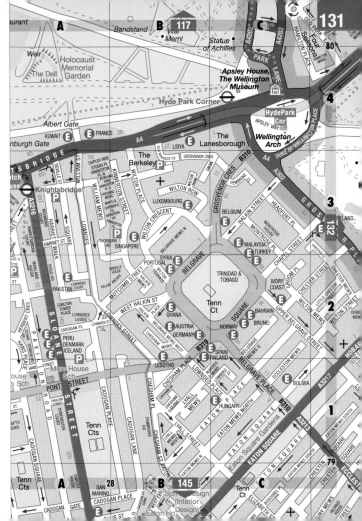

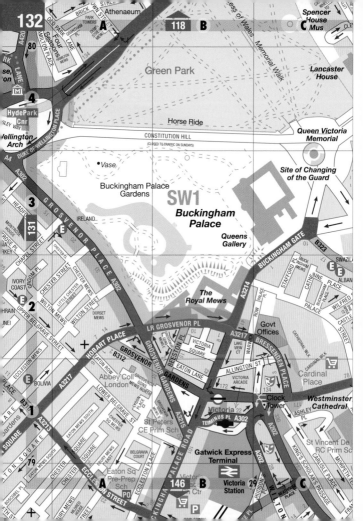

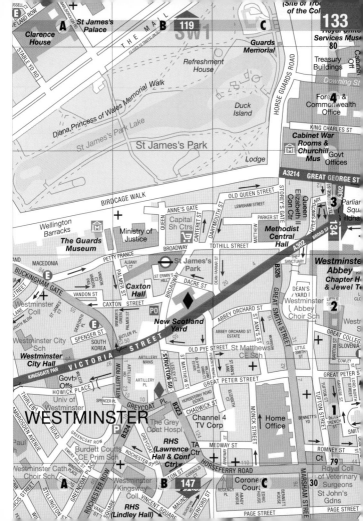

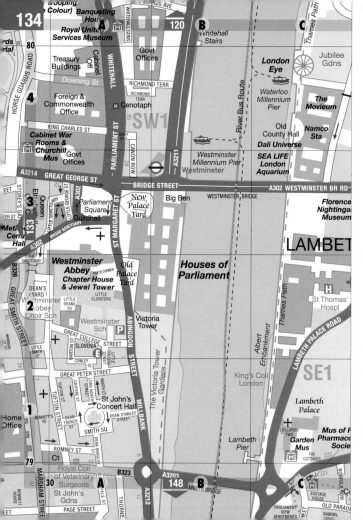

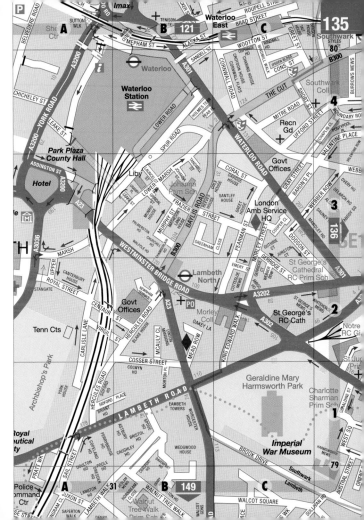

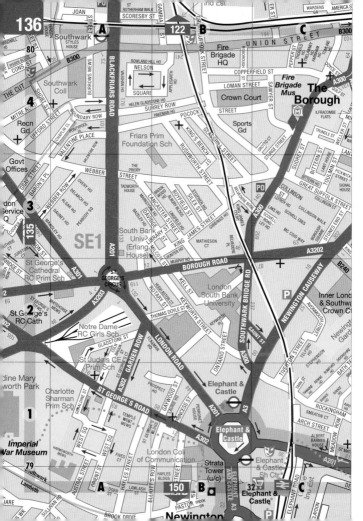

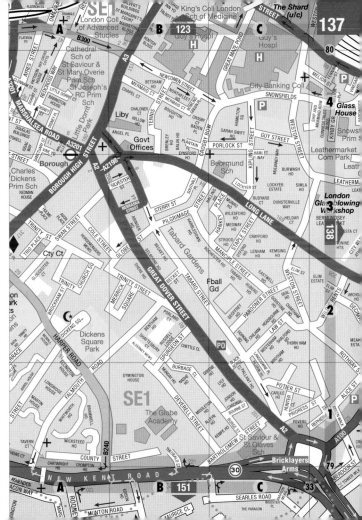

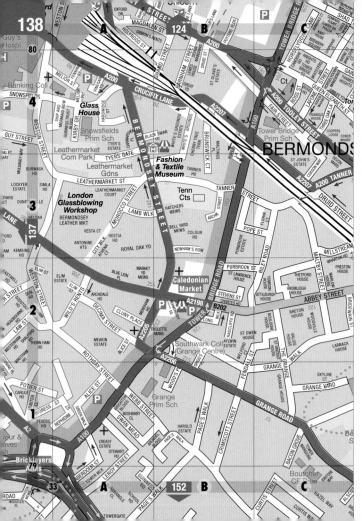

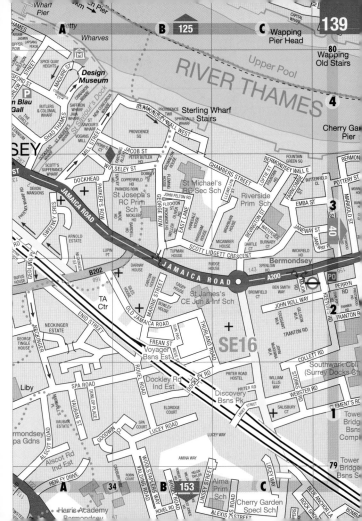

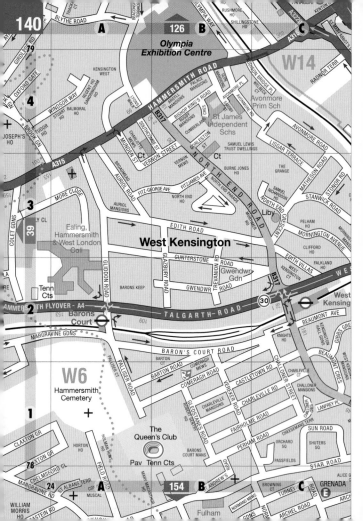

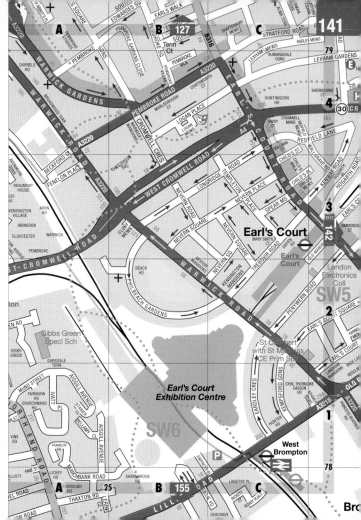

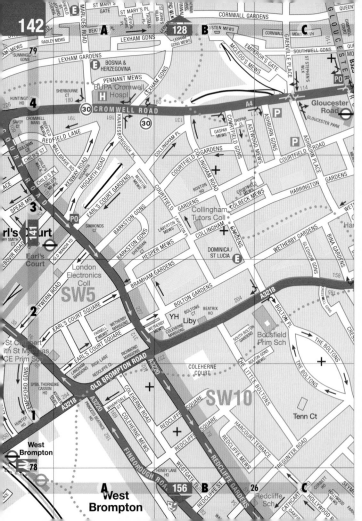

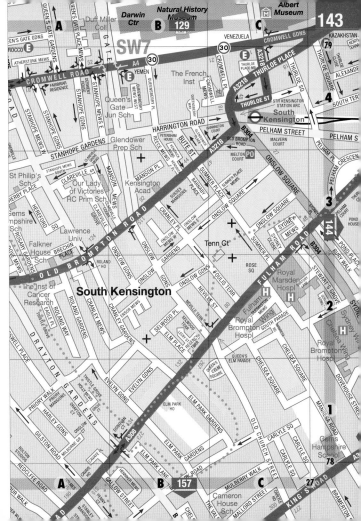

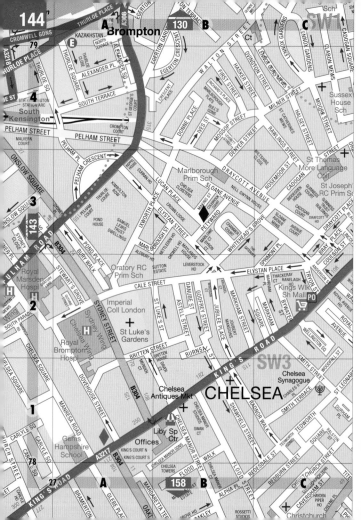

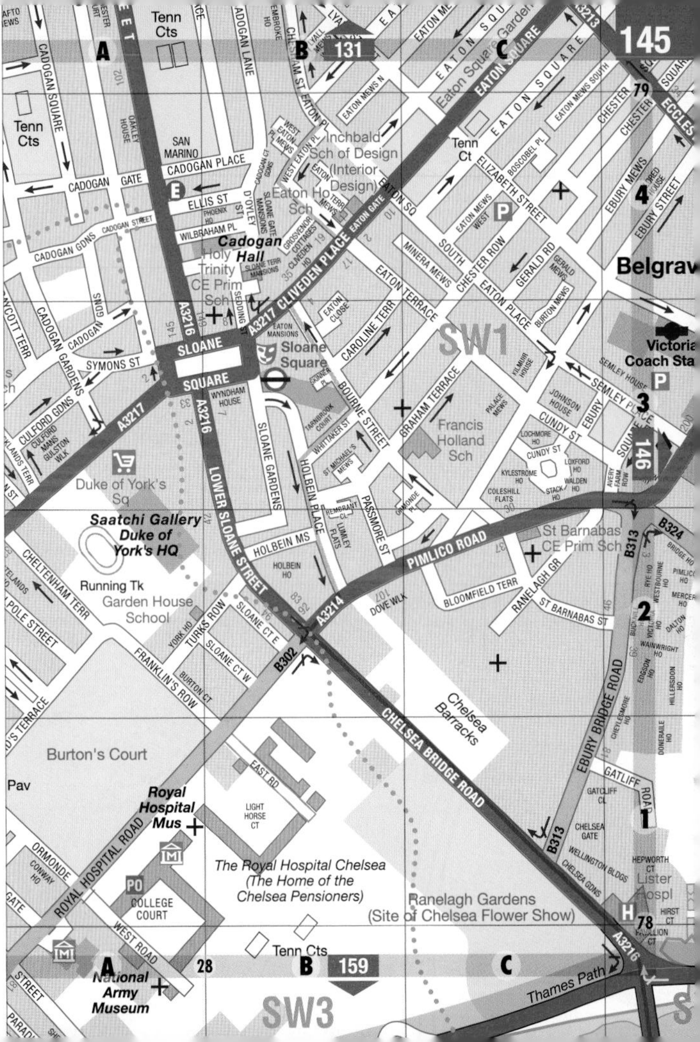

A
B
C
131
Tenn Cts
CADOGAN SQUARE
CADOGAN LANE
CADOGAN PLACE
CADOGAN GATE
CADOGAN STREET
CADOGAN GDNS
CADOGAN GARDENS
OAKLEY HOUSE
SAN MARINO
ELLIS ST
WILBRAHAM PL
PHOENIX HO
D'OYLEY ST
Cadogan Hall
Holy Trinity CE Prim Sch
SEDDING ST
SLOANE SQUARE
A3216
A3217
CLIVEDEN PLACE
EATON GATE
EATON SQUARE
Eaton Square Gardens
EATON MEWS N
EATON MEWS SOUTH
WEST EATON PL
WEST EATON PL MEWS
Inchbald Sch of Design (Interior Design)
Eaton Ho Sch
SLOANE GATE MANSIONS
GROSVENOR COTTAGES
CLIVEDEN HO
SLOANE TERR MANSIONS
EATON MANSIONS
Sloane Square
EATON CLOSE
CAROLINE TERR
EATON TERRACE
MINERA MEWS
SOUTH EATON PL
CHESTER ROW
EATON PLACE
GERALD RD
GERALD MEWS
BURTON MEWS
ELIZABETH STREET
BOSCOBEL PL
EATON MEWS WEST
Tenn Ct
CHESTER SQ
CHESTER ST
ECCLESTON ST
EBURY MEWS
EBURY STREET
Belgravia
Victoria Coach Sta
SEMLEY HOUSE
SEMLEY PLACE
EBURY SQUARE
SW1
KILMUIR HOUSE
JOHNSON HOUSE
CUNDY ST
LOCHMORE HO
LOXFORD HO
KYLESTROME HO
WALDEN HO
STACK HO
COLESHILL FLATS
AVERY FARM ROW
146
Francis Holland Sch
PALACE MEWS
GRAHAM TERRACE
BOURNE STREET
SKINNER PL
TARNBROOK COURT
WHITTAKER ST
ST MICHAEL'S MEWS
SYMONS ST
CULFORD GDNS
CULFORD MANS
GULSTON WLK
WYNDHAM HOUSE
SLOANE GARDENS
HOLBEIN PLACE
HOLBEIN MS
HOLBEIN HO
REMBRANT CL
LUMLEY FLATS
PASSMORE ST
ORMONDE PL
Duke of York's Sq
Saatchi Gallery
Duke of York's HQ
Running Tk
Garden House School
CHELTENHAM TERR
LOWER SLOANE STREET
PIMLICO ROAD
A3214
St Barnabas CE Prim Sch
RANELAGH GR
BLOOMFIELD TERR
ST BARNABAS ST
DOVE WLK
B313
B324
BRIDGE HO
PIMLICO HO
RYE HO
WESTBOURNE HO
MERCER HO
DALTON HO
WAINWRIGHT HO
EDGSON HO
HILLERSDON HO
CHEYLESMORE HO
DONERAILE HO
EBURY BRIDGE ROAD
GATLIFF ROAD
GATCLIFF CL
CHELSEA GATE
WELLINGTON BLDGS
CHELSEA GDNS
HEPWORTH CT
Lister Hospl
HIRST CT
PAVILION CT
TURKS ROW
YORK HO
SLOANE CT E
SLOANE CT W
BURTON CT
FRANKLIN'S ROW
B302
CHELSEA BRIDGE ROAD
Chelsea Barracks
Burton's Court
Pav
Royal Hospital Mus
EAST RD
LIGHT HORSE CT
The Royal Hospital Chelsea (The Home of the Chelsea Pensioners)
Ranelagh Gardens (Site of Chelsea Flower Show)
ROYAL HOSPITAL ROAD
ORMONDE GATE
CONWAY HO
PO
COLLEGE COURT
WEST ROAD
National Army Museum
Tenn Cts
159
SW3
Thames Path
A3216
1
2
3
4
28
78
79

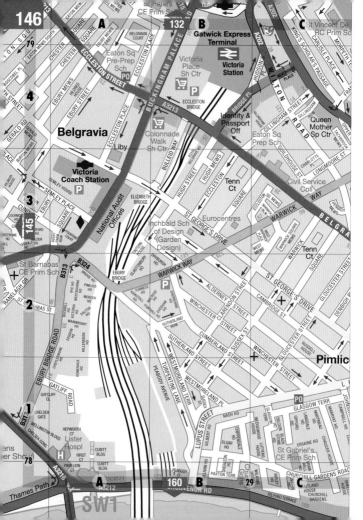

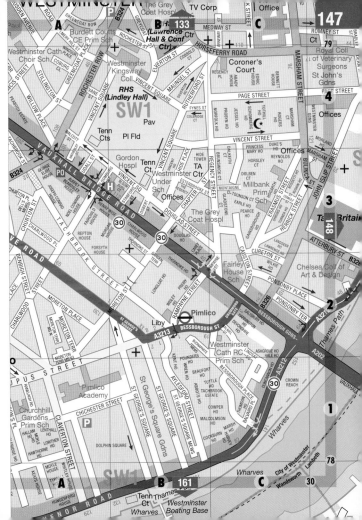

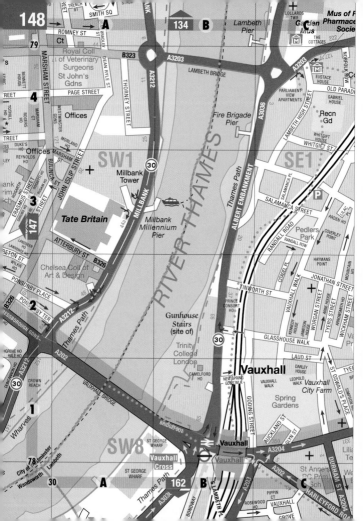

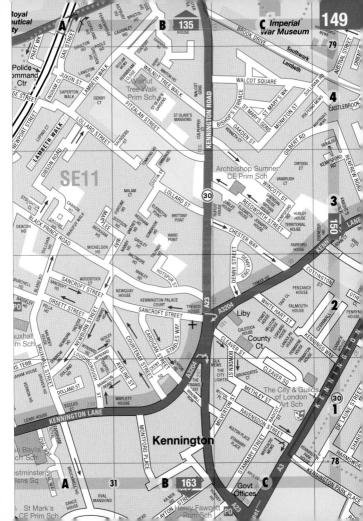

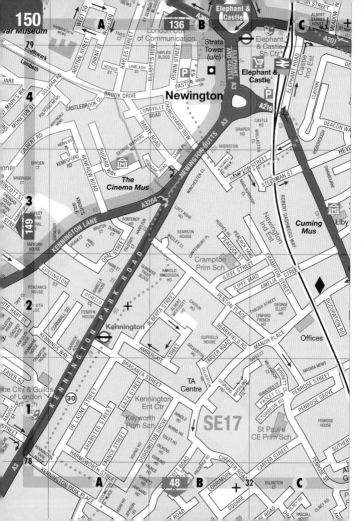

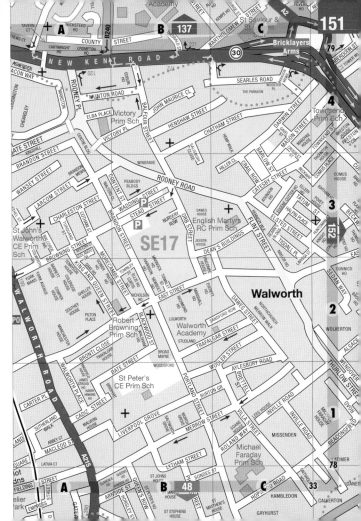

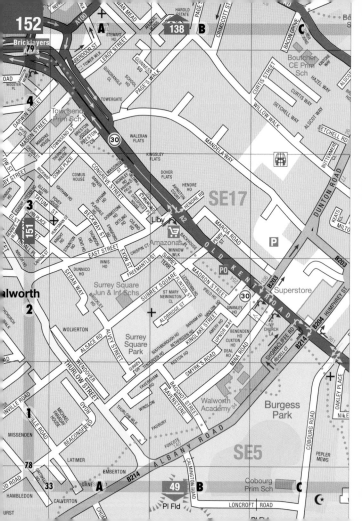

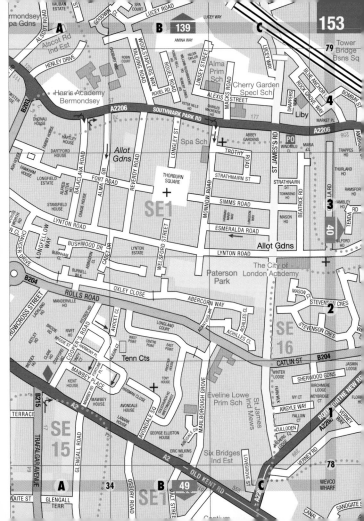

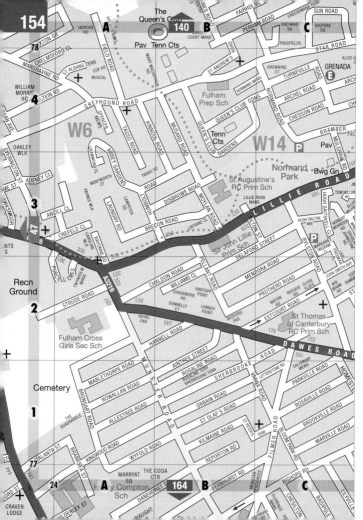

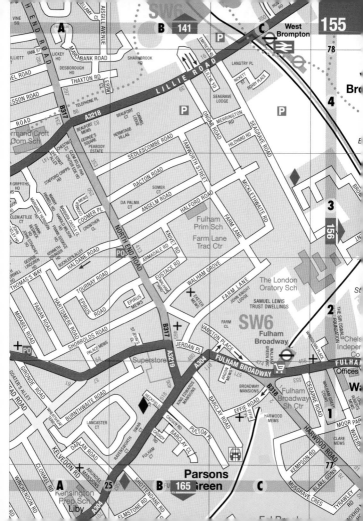

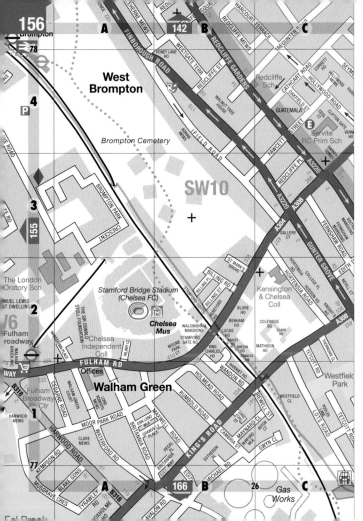

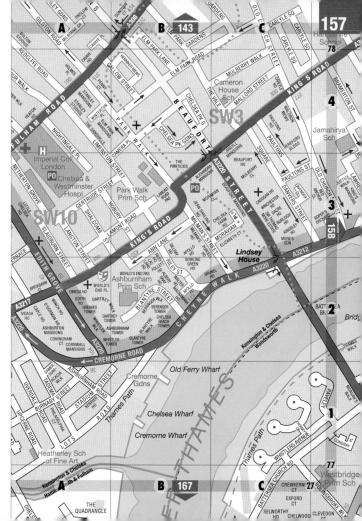

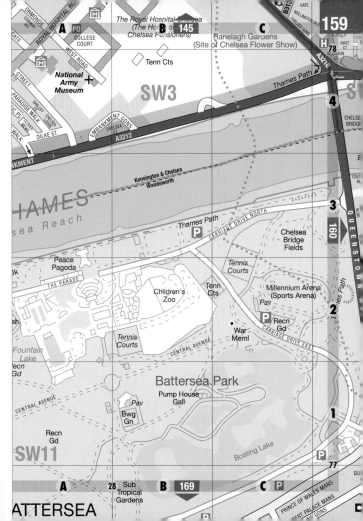

A ORMONDE

ROYAL HOSPITAL RD

A PO
COLLEGE
COURT

WEST ROAD

The Royal Hospital Chelsea (The Home of the Chelsea Pensioners) **145**

B

C Ranelagh Gardens
(Site of Chelsea Flower Show)

GATE WELLINGTON

CHELSEA BRIDGE GDNS

159

H HIRST
78 CT
A3216

National
Army
Museum

Tenn Cts

SW3

4

CHELSEA
BRIDGE

SHELLEY

DILKE ST

EMBANKMENT GDNS

CHELSEA
A3212

EMBANKMENT

Thames Path

CENTRAL
BL

Kensington & Chelsea
Wandsworth

THAMES
sea Reach

Thames Path **P**

CARRIAGE DRIVE NORTH

3

QUEENSTOWN

BLDGS

160

Chelsea
Bridge
Fields

Peace
Pagoda

THE PARADE

Tennis
Courts

Children's
Zoo

Tenn
Cts

Millennium Arena
(Sports Arena)
Pav

P Recn
Gd

2

Thames Path

Fountain
Lake

Tennis
Courts

CENTRAL AVENUE

War
Meml

CARRIAGE DRIVE EAST

Recn
Gd

Battersea Park

CENTRAL AVENUE

Pump House
Gall

1

Pav

Bwg
Gn

P

77

Recn
Gd

SW11

Boating Lake

P

A
28 Sub
Tropical
Gardens

B **169**

C **P**

PRINCE OF WALES MANS

BATTERSEA

ALBERT PALACE MANS

QUI

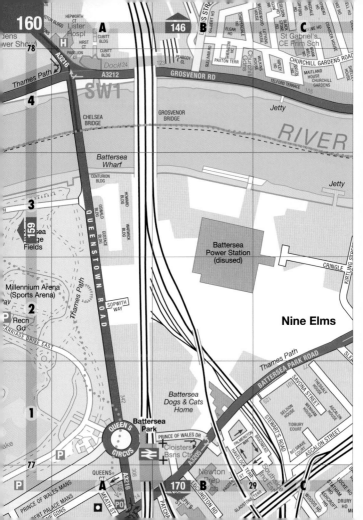

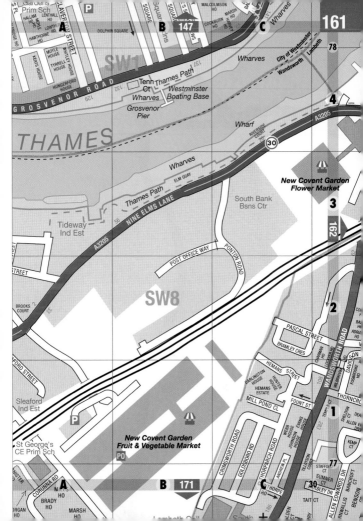

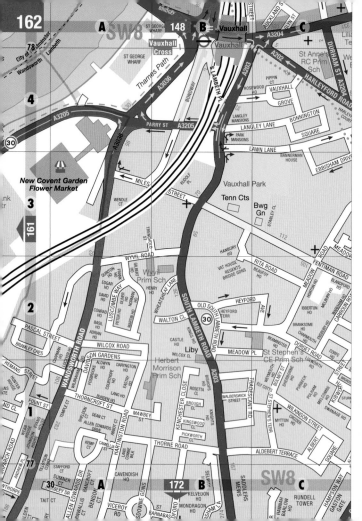

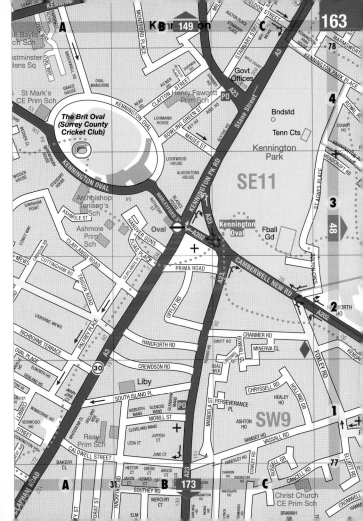

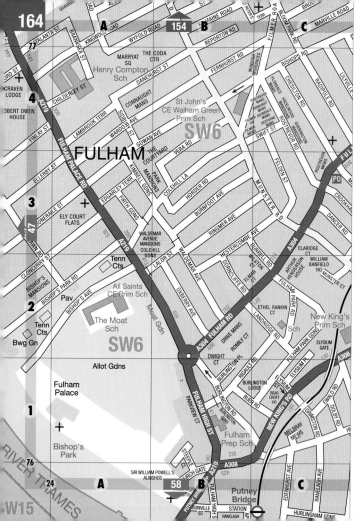

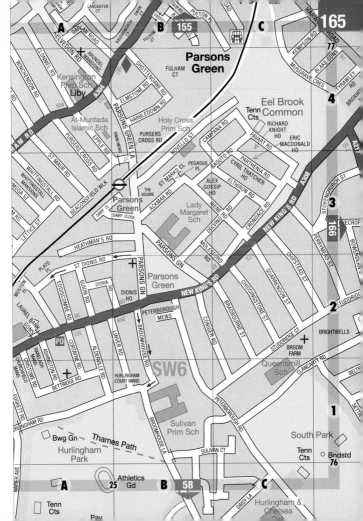

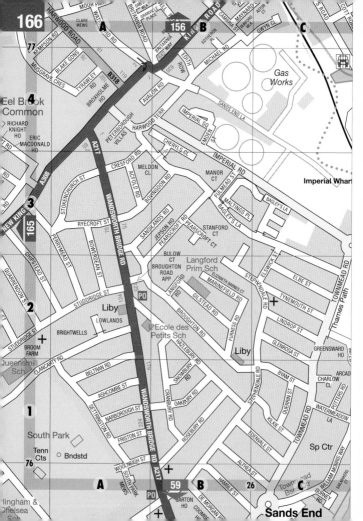

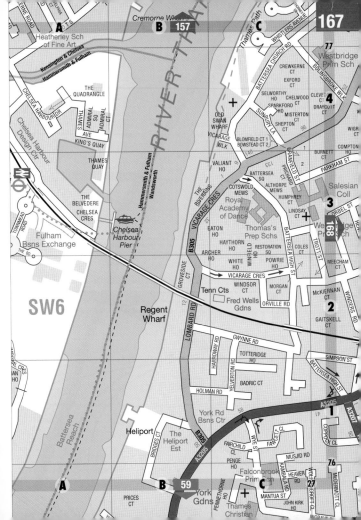

Cremorne Wharf

A 157 **B** **C**

Thames Path

Heatherley Sch
of Fine Art

Kensington & Chelsea
Hammersmith & Fulham

77 Westbridge Prim Sch

CREWKERNE CT

THE QUADRANGLE

EXFORD CT

BATTERSEA CHURCH RD

BOLINGBROKE WLK

SELWORTHY HO

CHELWOOD CT

CLEVED CT

4

CHELSEA HARBOUR DR

ADMIRAL AVE

THAMES AVE

ADMIRAL SQ

ADMIRAL CT

OLD SWAN WHARF

SPARKFORD HO

MISTERTON CT

DRAYCOTT CT

WIGR CT

Chelsea Harbour Design Ctr

VICARAGE WLK

SHEPTON CT

BLOMFIELD CT 1
BOWSTEAD CT 2

COMPTON CT

BURNETT CT

PARKHAM ST

KING'S QUAY

THAMES QUAY

VALIANT HO

BATTERSEA SQ

PRIORAD

CRANFIELD ST

133

THE BELVEDERE
CHELSEA CRES

THE RIVERSIDE

COTSWOLD MEWS

ALTHORPE MEWS

Salesian Coll

3

Chelsea Harbour Pier

VICARAGE CRES

Royal Academy of Dance

HUMPHREY CT

ORBEL ST

168 Westbridge Prim Sch

Fulham Bsns Exchange

EATON HO

Thomas's Prep Schs

LINDSAY CT

TOMMEAD ROAD

THE BD

HAYTHORN HO

ARCHER HO

RESTORATION SQ

WINFIELD HO

COLES CT

BATTERSEA HIGH ST

TROTT ST

MEECHAM CT

WHITE HO

POWRIE HO

GROVESIDE CT

B305

VICARAGE CRES

SW6

Tenn Cts

WINDSOR CT

MORGAN CT

McKIERNAN CT

Regent Wharf

Fred Wells Gdns

ORVILLE RD

GAITSKELL CT

2

LOMBARD RD

GWYNNE RD

SIMPSON ST

HARROWAY RD

TOTTERIDGE HO

YELVERTON RD

BADRIC CT

BATTERSEA HIGH ST

HOLMAN RD

A3205

A3207

1

Battersea Reach

Heliport

BRIDGES CT

The Heliport Est

B305

York Rd Bsns Ctr

WEST ST

FAWCETT CL

COPPOCK CL

FAIRCHILD CL

76

PENNETHORNE HO

PENGE CL

MUSJID RD

HEAVER CT

KAMBALA RD

27

WOLSEY CROFT

McDERMOTT RD

A **B** 59 **C**

PRICES CT

York Gdns

MANTUA ST

Falconbrook Prim Sch

JOHN KIRK HO

Thames Christian

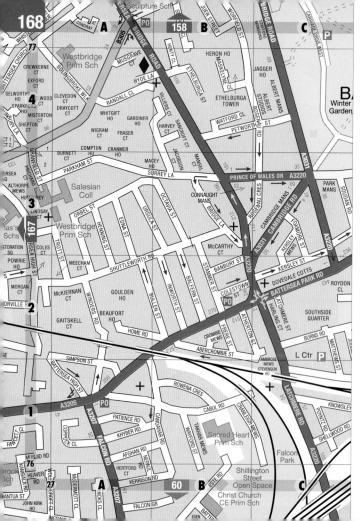

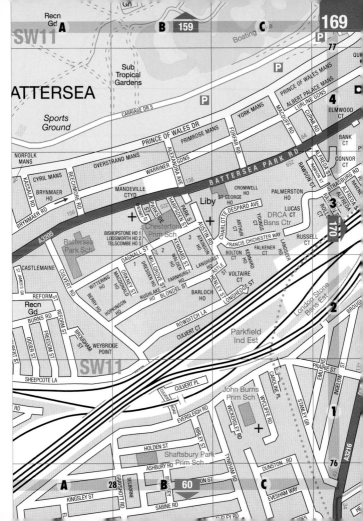

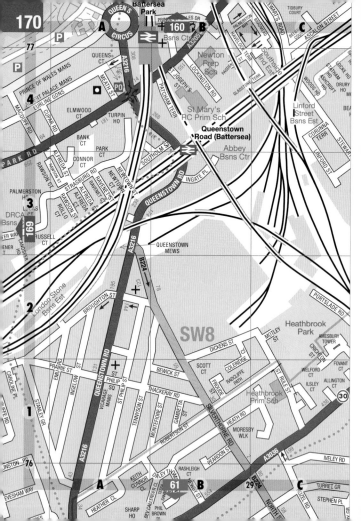

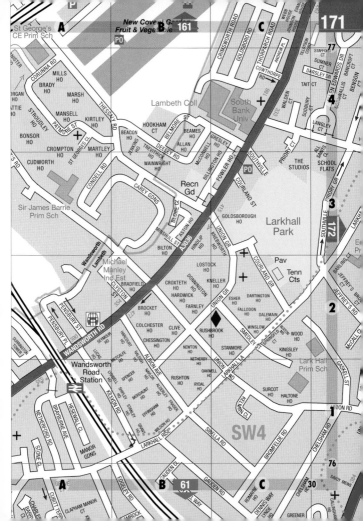

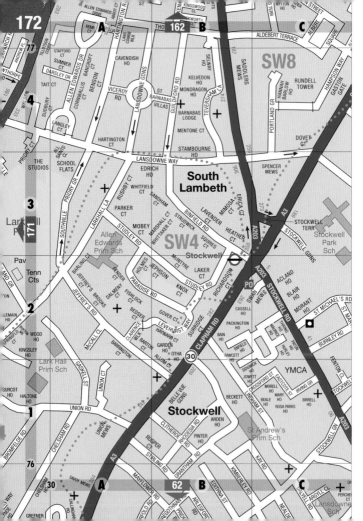

Index

Church Rd **6** Beckenham BR2..........**53** C6 **228** C6

Place name	**Location number**	**Locality, town or village**	**Postcode district**	**Standard scale reference**	**Enlarged scale reference**
May be abbreviated on the map	Present when a number indicates the place's position in a crowded area of mapping	Shown when more than one place (outside London postal districts) has the same name	District for the indexed place	Page number and grid reference for the standard mapping	Page number and grid reference for the central London enlarged mapping, underlined in red

Public and commercial buildings are highlighted in magenta.
Places of interest are highlighted in blue with a star★
Cities, towns and villages are listed in CAPITAL LETTERS

Abbreviations used in the index

Acad	**Academy**	Ct	**Court**	Int	**International**	Prom	**Promenade**
App	**Approach**	Ctr	**Centre**	Intc	**Interchange**	RC	**Roman Catholic**
Arc	**Arcade**	Crkt	**Cricket**	Jun	**Junior**	Rd	**Road**
Art Gall	**Art Gallery**	Ctry Pk	**Country Park**	Junc	**Junction**	Rdbt	**Roundabout**
Ave	**Avenue**	Cty	**County**	La	**Lane**	Ret Pk	**Retail Park**
Bglws	**Bungalows**	Ctyd	**Courtyard**	L Ctr	**Leisure Centre**	Sch	**School**
Bldgs	**Buildings**	Dr	**Drive**	Liby	**Library**	Sec	**Secondary**
Bsns Ctr	**Business Centre**	Ent Ctr	**Enterprise Centre**	Mans	**Mansions**	Sh Ctr	**Shopping Centre**
Bsns Pk	**Business Park**	Ent Pk	**Enterprise Park**	Mdw/s	**Meadow/s**	Sp	**Sports**
Bvd	**Boulevard**	Est	**Estate**	Meml	**Memorial**	Specl	**Special**
Cath	**Cathedral, Catholic**	Ex Ctr	**Exhibition Centre**	Mid	**Middle**	Sports Ctr	**Sports Centre**
CE	**Church of England**	Ex Hall	**Exhibition Hall**	Mix	**Mixed**	Sq	**Square**
Cemy	**Cemetery**	Fst	**First**	Mkt	**Market**	St	**Street, Saint**
Cir	**Circus**	Gdn	**Garden**	Mon	**Monument**	Sta	**Station**
Circ	**Circle**	Gdns	**Gardens**	Mus	**Museum**	Stad	**Stadium**
Cl	**Close**	Gn	**Green**	Obsy	**Observatory**	Tech	**Technical Technology**
Cnr	**Corner**	Gr	**Grove**	Orch	**Orchard**	Terr	**Terrace**
Coll	**College**	Gram	**Grammar**	Par	**Parade**	Trad Est	**Trading Estate**
Com	**Community**	Her Ctr	**Heritage Centre**	Pas	**Passage**	Twr/s	**Tower/s**
Comm	**Common**	Ho	**House**	Pav	**Pavilion**	Univ	**University**
Comp	**Comprehensive**	Hospl	**Hospital**	Pk	**Park**	Wlk	**Walk**
Con Ctr	**Conference Centre**	Hts	**Heights**	Pl	**Place**	Yd	**Yard**
Cotts	**Cottages**	Ind Est	**Industrial Estate**	Prec	**Precinct**		
Cres	**Crescent**	Inf	**Infant**	Prep	**Preparatory**		
Cswy	**Causeway**	Inst	**Institute**	Prim	**Primary**		

176 Gall★ NW5.....12 C2
201 Bishopgate
EC2.............110 B4

A

Abady Ho SW1.....147 C4
Abberley Mews 9
SW4...............61 A4
Abbess Cl SW2.....75 A3
Abbeville Mews 8
SW4...............61 B2
Abbeville Rd SW4...61 B2
Abbey Bsns Ctr
SW8...............170 B4
Abbey Coll London
SW1..............132 A1
Abbey Ct
10 Bedford Pk
W12.................38 A3
Camberwell SE17...151 A1
St John's Wood
NW8..............78 C2
Abbeyfield Rd
SE16...............40 B2
Abbey Gdns
10 Bermondsey
SE16..............153 C4
St John's Wood
NW8...............79 A1
West Kensington
W6................154 A3
Abbey Ho NW8.....89 A4
Abbey La E15.......27 C3
Abbey Lo NW8......90 B3
Abbey Orchard St
SW1...............133 C2
Abbey Orchard Street
Est SW1...........133 C2
Abbey Rd
St John's Wood
NW8..............78 C2
Wembley NW10....20 A3
Abbey St SE1......138 C2
Abbot Cl SW8.....162 A1
Abbot Ho 14 E14...34 A2
Abbotsbury Ho
Kensington W14....126 C3
Mill Meads E15.....27 B3
Abbotsbury Ho
W14..............126 B4
Abbotsbury Mews
SE15..............65 B4
Abbotsbury Rd
W14..............126 C3
Abbotshade Rd 18
SE16...............32 C1
Abbots Ho
Kensington W14....126 C1
Pimlico SW1.......147 B1
Abbots La SE1.....124 B1
Abbot's Pl NW6....78 A4
Abbot St E8........16 B2
Abbotstone Ho 4
E5.................7 C2
Abbotstone Rd
SW15...............57 B4
Abbotswell Rd
SE4................66 B2
Abbotswood Rd
London SE22.......64 A3
Streatham SW16...73 C1
Abbott Ho SW12...72 B4
Abbott Rd E14.....34 C3

Abbotts Cl N1......15 B2
Abbotts Wharf 4
E14................33 C3
Abchurch La EC2,
EC4...............123 C4
Abchurch Yd EC4...123 B4
Abdale Rd W12.....30 A1
Abel Ho 7 SE11...163 B4
Aberavon Rd E3....26 A2
Abercorn Cl NW8...88 C4
Abercorn Mans
NW8................79 A1
Abercorn Mews 10
TW10...............54 B3
Abercorn Pl NW8...78 C1
Abercorn Sch
NW8................79 A1
Abercorn Way
SE1...............153 B2
Abercorn Wlk
NW8................88 C4
Abercrombie Ho 8
W12................30 A2
Abercrombie St
SW11..............168 B2
Aberdale Ct 22
SE16...............40 C4
Aberdare Gdns
NW6................11 A1
Aberdeen Ct
Canonbury N5......15 B3
Paddington W2.....89 B1
Aberdeen Ctr N5...15 B3
Aberdeen La N5.....15 B3
Aberdeen Mans
WC1................94 A2
Aberdeen Pk N5....15 B3
Aberdeen Pk N5....15 B2
Aberdeen Rd
Canonbury N5......15 B4
Dudden Hill NW10..8 B3
Aberdeen Terr
SE3................52 C1
Aberdour St SE1...152 A4
Aberfeldy Ho SE5...48 A3
Aberfeldy St E14...34 B3
Abersham Rd E8....16 B3
Ability Plaza 8 E8..16 B1
Ability Twrs EC1....96 C4
Abingdon W14.....141 A3
Abingdon Cl
Fulham SE1,SE5....153 A2
Kentish Town NW1..13 C2
Abingdon Ct SW8..127 C1
Abingdon Gdns
W8................127 C1
Abingdon Ho
E2.............24 B1 98 C2
Abingdon Mans
W8................127 C1
Abingdon Rd W8...127 C1
Abingdon St SW1...134 A2
Abingdon Villas
W8................127 C1
Abinger Gr SE8.....51 B4
Abinger Ho SE1....137 B3
Abinger Mews W9...23 C1
Abinger Rd W4......38 A3
Ablett St SE16......40 B1
Abney Gdns 5 N16..7 B2
Abney Park
Cemetery★
N16................7 A2
Abney Park Ct N16..7 B2
Aborfield 6 NW5...13 B3
Aboyne Rd SW17...71 C1

Abyssinia Cl SW11..60 A3
Abyssinia Rd
SW11..............60 A3
Acacia Cl SE8......41 A2
Acacia Gdns NW8...79 C2
Acacia Gr SE21.....75 C2
Acacia Ho
Brockley SE4.......66 B3
Stoke Newington N16..6 C2
Acacia Pl NW8.....79 C2
Acacia Rd
Acton W3...........28 B2
St John's Wood
NW8................79 C2
Acacia Wlk SW10..157 A1
Academy Ct 13 E2..25 B2
Academy Gdns
W8................127 B4
Academy Sch The 9
NW3................11 C4
Academy The 2
N19...............4 C3
Acad of Live &
Recorded Arts
SW18..............59 C1
Acanthus Dr SE1...153 B2
Acanthus Rd
SW11...............60 C4
Accommodation Rd
NW11..............1 B3
Acer Cl 2 NW2.....9 C4
Acer Rd E8.........16 B1
Acfold Rd SW6.....166 A3
Achilles Cl SE1....153 C2
Achilles Ho 19 E2..25 A3
Achilles St SE14....51 A3
Achilles Way W1...117 C1
Acklam Rd W10....31 B4
Ackmar Rd SW6....165 B3
Ackroyd Dr E3......33 C4
Acland Burghley Sch
NW5................13 A4
Acland Cres SE5....63 C4
Acland Ho SW9....172 C2
Acland Rd NW2.....9 A2
Acol Ct 3 NW6....10 C1
Acol Rd NW6.......11 A1
Acorn Ct 5 E3......26 C3
Acorn Gdns W3....28 C4
Acorn Par 7 SE15..50 A3
Acorn Production Ctr
N7................14 A1
Acorns The 21
SW19...............69 C3
Acorn Wharf SE15..49 C4
Acorn Wlk SE16....33 A1
Acre Dr SE22.......64 C3
Acre La SW2........62 B3
Acris St SW18......59 B2
ACTON..............28 C1
Acton Bsns Ctr
NW10...............20 C1
Acton Central Ind Est
6 W3..............28 A1
Acton Central Sta
W3................28 C1
Acton Ctr 16 W3...28 C1
Acton Green W4....37 B3
Acton High Sch
W3................36 C4
Acton Hill Mews
W3................28 A1
Acton Ho
5 Acton W3........28 B3
18 Haggerston E8...24 B4

Acton La
Acton Green W4....37 B3
Harlesden NW10....20 C3
W3................37 B3
Acton Main Line Sta
W3................28 B3
Acton Mews E8.....24 B4
Acton Park Ind Est
W3................37 B4
Acton St WC1......94 C3
Acton Town Sta
W3................36 C4
Acton Vale Ind Pk
W3................29 B1
Acton & West London
Coll 18 W3........28 A1
Acuba Ho SW18....71 A3
Acuba Rd SW18....71 A2
Ada Ct
Islington N1.......86 C3
St John's Wood W9..89 A3
Ada Gdns E14......34 C3
Ada Gdns E15......27 C4
Adair Ho SW3......158 B4
Adair Rd W10......23 A1
Adair Twr 7 W10...23 A1
Ada Kennedy Ct 6
SE10..............52 B3
Adam Ct SE11.....150 A3
Adam & Eve Ct
W1...............105 A2
Adam & Eve Mews
W8................127 C2
Adamfields Ind 5
SE16...............40 C4
Adams Gardens Est 5
SE16...............40 B4
Adams Ho 3 E14...34 C3
Adams Mews
SW17...............72 B2
Adamson Rd
Hampstead NW3....11 C1
Newham E16.......35 C3
Adams Pl N7......14 B3
Adam's Row W1...117 C3
Adam St WC2......120 B3
Adam Wlk SW6....47 B3
Ada Pl E2..........24 C4
Ada Rd SE5........49 A3
Ada Wlk SW16,
SW2................74 B2
Adderley Gr SW11..60 C2
Adderley St E14....34 B3
Addey Ho SE8.....51 B3
Addey & Stanhope
Sch 11 SE14.......51 C2
Addington Ct 7
SW14...............55 C4
Addington Ho 18
SW9...............173 A1
Addington Rd E3...26 C2
Addington Sq SE5..48 C3
Addington Sq SE5..48 C3
Addington St SE1..135 A3
Addis Ho 18 E1...32 B4
Addison Ave
W11.........31 A1 112 A1
Addison Bridge Pl
W14..............140 C4
Addison Cres
W14..............126 B2
Addison Gdns
W14................39 C3
Addison Gr W4.....38 A3
Addison Ho NW8...89 B3
Addison Park Mans 16
W14................39 C4

176–Adr 175

Addison Pl
W11.........31 A1 112 A1
Addison Prim Sch
W14................39 C3
Addison Rd W14...126 C2
Addison Rd E14...108 B1
Addlestone Ho 4
W10...............30 B4
Addy Ho SE16......40 B2
Adela Ho 9 W6....39 B1
Adelaide Ave SE4..66 C3
Adelaide Cl SW9...62 C3
Adelaide Ct
Hackney E5........18 A3
St John's Wood
NW8................79 A1
Adelaide Gr W12...29 C1
Adelaide Rd
Primrose Hill NW3..12 A1
Richmond TW9.....54 B3
2 Wandsworth
SW18...............58 C2
Adelaide St WC2...120 A3
Adela St W10......23 A1
Adelina Gr E1......32 B4
Adelina Mews
SW12...............73 C3
Adeline Pl WC1....105 C3
Adelphi Ct 20
SE16...............40 C4
Adelphi Terr WC2..120 B3
Adeney Cl W6......47 C4
Aden Gr N16.......15 C4
Aden Ho 15 E1....32 C4
Aden Lo N16.......15 C4
Adie Rd W6........39 B3
Adisham Ho 4 E5..17 A3
Adler St E1........111 B2
Adley St E5........18 A3
Admiral Ct
Chelsea SW10.....167 A4
Marylebone W1....103 B3
Admiral Hyson Ind Est
SE16................40 A1
Admiral Mews
W10................22 C1
Admiral Pl SE16...33 A1
Admirals Ct
Bermondsey SE1...124 C1
52 Putney SW19...69 C3
Admirals Gate
SE10...............52 A2
Admiral Sq SW10..167 A4
Admiral St SE8....51 C2
Admirals Way E14..41 C4
Admiral's Wlk NW3..2 B1
Admiralty Arch★
SW1...............119 C2
Admiralty Cl 1
SE8................51 C2
Adolphus Rd N4...6 A3
Adolphus St SE8...51 B3
Adpar St W2......101 B4
Adrian Bolt Ho 2
E2.................25 A2
Adrian Ho
Islington N1.......85 A3
South Lambeth
SW8...............162 A2
Stratford E15......19 C1
Adrian Mews
SW10..............156 B4

Adriatic Bldg 18
E14 .... 33 A2
Adriatic Ho 13 E1 ... 25 C1
Adron Ho 18 SE16 ... 40 B2
Adstock Ho 5 N1 ... 15 A1
Adventurers Ct 17
E14 .... 34 C2
Adys Lawn NW2 ..... 9 A2
Adys Rd SE15 ...... 64 B4
Aegean Apts 7
E16 .... 35 C2
Aegon Ho 8 E14 .. 42 A3
Affleck St N1 ...... 85 A1
Afghan Rd SW11 ... 168 A1
Africa Ho WC2 ..... 106 C2
Afsil Ho EC1 ...... 107 C3
Aga Khan Univ
WC1 .... 105 C3
Agamemnon Rd
NW6 .... 10 B3
Agar Gr NW1 ...... 13 C1
Agar Pl NW1 ...... 13 B1
Agar St WC2 ...... 120 B3
Agate Rd W6 ...... 39 B3
Agatha Cl E14 ..... 32 B1
Agave Rd NW2 ...... 9 B4
Agdon St EC1 ...... 96 A2
Agincourt Rd NW3 .. 12 B4
Agnes Ct 11 SW18 .. 59 C3
Agnes Ho 13 W11 .. 30 C2
Agnes Rd W3 ...... 38 B4
Agnes St E14 ...... 33 B3
Aicon Gall★ SW1 .. 118 C4
Aigburth Mans 5
SW9 .... 163 B1
Ailsa St E14 ...... 34 B4
Ainger Rd NW3 ..... 12 B1
Ainsdale NW1 ...... 92 C4
Ainsdale Dr SE1 ... 153 B1
Ainsley St 2 ...... 25 A2
Ainslie Wlk 8
SW12 .... 73 A4
Ainsty St 20 SE16 .. 40 B4
Ainsworth Cl SE5 .. 49 A1
Ainsworth Est
NW8 .... 78 B3
Ainsworth Ho NW8 .. 78 B3
Ainsworth Rd E9 ... 17 B1
Ainsworth Way
NW8 .... 78 C4
Aintree St SW6 .... 154 B2
Aird Ho SE1 ...... 136 C1
Airdrie Cl N1 ..... 14 B1
Airedale Ave W4 ... 38 B1
Airedale Ave S W4 .. 38 B1
Airedale Rd SW12 .. 72 B4
Airlie Gdns
W8 ..... 31 C1 113 B1
Air St W1 .... 119 A3
Aisgill Ave SW5 ... 141 A1
Aiten Ho 20 E14 ... 33 B3
Aitken Cl E8 ...... 24 C4
Ajax Ho 15 E2 .... 25 A3
Ajax Rd NW6 ...... 10 C3
Akbar Ho 7 E14 ... 42 A2
Akehurst St SW15 .. 68 C4
Akenside 3
NW3 .... 11 C3
Akenside Rd NW3 ... 11 C3
Akerman Rd SW9 ... 48 A2
Akintaro Ho 7
SE8 .... 51 B4

Alamaro Lo 5
SE10 .... 43 B3
Aland Ct SE16 ..... 41 A3
Alan Preece Ct
NW6 .... 9 C1
Alaska Bldg 12
SE13 .... 52 A2
Alaska Ho 10 E14 .. 121 B1
Alaska St SE1 .... 121 B1
Albacore Cres
SE13 .... 67 A1
Alba Mews SW18,
SW19 .... 70 C2
Alban Ho
Hampstead NW3 .... 11 B2
New Cross SE14 ... 51 B2
Albans Cl SW16 ... 74 A1
Albany W1 .... 118 C3
Albany Cl SW14 ... 55 A3
Albany Ct
College Pk NW10 .. 22 A2
NW8 .... 79 B1
Westminster SW1 .. 133 B2
8 Whitechapel E1 . 111 B2
Albany Ctyd W1 ... 119 A3
Albany Ho 8 TW8 .. 44 A4
Albany Mews
Camberwell SE5 ... 48 B4
Islington N1 ..... 14 C1
Albany Par 4
TW8 .... 44 A4
Albany Pas 12
TW10 .... 54 A2
Albany Rd
Camberwell SE5 ... 49 A4
Richmond TW10 ... 54 A2
Albany St NW1 .... 92 B4
Albany Terr 6
TW10 .... 54 B2
Alba Pl W11 ...... 31 B3
Albemarle SW19 ... 69 C2
Albemarle Coll
W1 .... 117 A4
Albemarle Ho
2 Brixton SW2 ... 62 C4
Rotherhithe SE8 .. 41 B2
Albemarle Mans
NW3 .... 11 A4
Albemarle Prim Sch
SW19 .... 70 A2
Albemarle St W1 .. 118 C3
Albemarle Way
EC1 .... 96 A1
Alberta Ct 1
TW10 .... 54 B2
Alberta Ho E14 ... 34 B1
Alberta St SE17 .. 150 B2
Albert Ave SW8 ... 162 C1
Albert Barnes Ho
SE1 .... 136 C1
Albert Bigg Point
E15 .... 27 B4
Albert Bridge Rd
SW11 .... 158 C1
Albert Cl 9 E9 ... 25 A4
Albert Cotts 2
E1 .... 111 B4
Albert Ct
Knightsbridge
SW7 .... 129 B3
9 Putney SW19 ... 70 A3
Albert Dr SW19 ... 70 A3
Albert Emb SE1 ... 148 B3

Albert Gate Ct
SW1 .... 130 C3
Albert Gdns E1 ... 32 C3
Albert Gray Ho
SW10 .... 157 B2
Albert Hall Mans
SW7 .... 129 B3
Albert Mans
Battersea SW11 ... 168 C4
Hornsey N8 ...... 5 A4
Albert Meml★
SW7 .... 129 B3
Albert Mews W8 ... 128 C2
Albert Palace Mans
SW11 .... 169 C4
Albert Rd
Finsbury Pk N4 .. 5 B4
Kilburn NW6 ..... 23 B3
Richmond TW10 ... 54 B2
Albert's Coll N1 .. 90 B2
Albert Sq SW8 ... 162 C1
Albert St NW1 .... 82 B3
Albert Starr Ho 7
SE8 .... 40 C2
Albert Studios
SW11 .... 168 C4
Albert Terr
Camden Town
NW1 .... 81 B3
Stonebridge NW10 . 20 B4
Albert Terr Mews
NW1 .... 81 B3
Albert Way SE15 .. 50 A3
Albion Ave SW8 ... 171 B1
Albion Cl W2 ..... 116 B4
Albion Coll WC1 .. 106 B3
Albion Ct 6 W6 ... 39 A2
Albion Dr E8 ..... 16 C1
Albion Est SE16 .. 40 B4
Albion Gate W2 ... 116 B4
Albion Gdns 1
W6 .... 39 A2
Albion Gr N16 .... 16 A4
Albion Ho
17 Deptford SE8 .. 51 C3
EC1 .... 108 A4
Albion Mews
Bayswater W2 .... 116 B4
6 Hammersmith
W6 .... 39 A2
Islington N1 ..... 85 B4
Albion Pl
Broadgate EC2 ... 109 C3
Clerkenwell EC1 .. 108 A4
Hammersmith W6 .. 39 A2
Albion Prim Sch 34
SE16 .... 40 B4
Albion Rd N16 .... 15 C4
Albion Riverside
SW11 .... 158 A2
Albion Sq E8 ..... 16 B1
Albion St
Bayswater W2 .... 116 B4
Rotherhithe SE16 . 40 B4
Albion Terr E8 ... 16 B1
Albion Way
Barbican EC2 .... 108 C3
Lewisham SE13 ... 67 B3
Albion Wlk N1 .... 84 B1
Albion Works Studios
18 E8 .... 16 C3
Albion Yd N1 ..... 84 B1
Albon Ho SW18 ... 59 A1

Albrighton Rd SE5,
SE22 .... 64 A4
Albury Bldgs SE1 .. 136 B3
Albury Ct SE8 .... 51 C4
Albury Lo 7 SW2 .. 74 B4
Albury St SE8 .... 51 C4
Albyn Rd SE8 ..... 51 C2
Alchemea Coll of
Audio Engineering
N1 .... 86 B4
Alconbury Rd E5 .. 7 C2
Aldbourne Rd
W12 .... 29 C1
Aldbridge St SE17 . 152 B2
Aldburgh Mews
W1 .... 103 C2
Aldbury Ho SW3 ... 144 A3
Aldebert Terr
SW8 .... 162 C1
Aldeburgh Cl E5 .. 7 C2
Aldeburgh Pl SE10 . 43 C2
Aldeburgh St SE10 . 43 C1
Aldenham Ho N1 ... 83 A1
Aldenham St NW1 .. 83 B1
Alden Ho E8 ...... 25 A4
Aldensley Rd W6 .. 39 A3
Alderbrook Prim Sch
SW12 .... 61 A1
Alderbrook Rd
SW12 .... 61 A1
Alderbury Rd
SW13 .... 46 C4
Aldergrove Ho 3
E5 .... 7 C2
Alder Ho
Camberwell SE15 .. 49 B4
1 Maitland Pk
NW3 .... 12 B2
St Johns SE4 .... 66 C4
Alderley Ho 36
SW8 .... 171 B1
Alder Lo SW6 ..... 47 C2
Aldermanbury
EC2 .... 109 A2
Aldermanbury Sq
EC2 .... 109 A3
Alderman's Wlk
EC2 .... 110 A3
Alder Mews 12 N19 . 4 B2
Alderney Ho 20
N1 .... 15 B2
Alderney Mews
SE1 .... 137 B2
Alderney Rd EL ... 25 C1
Alderney St SW1 .. 146 B2
Alder Rd SW14 .... 55 C4
Aldersford Cl SE4 . 65 C3
Aldersgate Ct
EC1 .... 108 C3
Aldersgate St EC1 . 108 C3
Aldershot Rd NW6 . 23 B4
Alderson St W10 .. 23 A1
Alderton Rd SE24 . 63 B4
Alderville Rd
SW6 .... 165 A2
Alderwick Ct N7 .. 14 B2
Aldford St W1 .... 117 C2
Aldgate EC3 ...... 110 B1
Aldgate East Sta
E1 .... 111 A2
Aldgate High St
EC3 .... 110 C1
Aldgate Sta EC3 .. 110 C1
Aldham Ho SE4 ... 51 B2
Aldine Ct W12 .... 30 B1
Aldine St W12 .... 39 B4

Aldington Ct 1
E8 .... 16 C1
Aldred Rd NW6 .... 10 C3
Aldren Rd SW17 ... 71 B1
Aldrich Terr SW18 . 71 B2
Aldrick Ho N1 .... 85 A2
Aldridge Ct W11 .. 31 B4
Aldridge Rd Villas
W11 .... 31 B4
Aldsworth Cl W9 .. 88 A1
Aldwich Ho WC2 ... 107 A1
Aldworth Gr SE13 . 67 B1
Aldwych WC2 ..... 107 A1
Aldwych Bldgs
WC2 .... 106 B2
Aldwyn Ho SW8 ... 162 A1
Alexander Ave
NW10 .... 9 A1
Alexander Ct
SW13 .... 59 B2
Alexander Fleming
Laboratory Mus★
W2 .... 101 C2
Alexander Ho 15
E14 .... 41 C3
Alexander Mews 2
W2 .... 100 A2
Alexander Pl SW7 . 144 A4
Alexander Sq
SW3 .... 144 A4
Alexander St 2 W2 . 31 C3
Alexandra Ave
SW11 .... 169 B3
Alexandra Cl SE8 . 51 B4
Alexandra Cotts
SE14 .... 51 B2
Alexandra Ct
Paddington W9 ... 89 A2
4 Shacklewell N16 . 16 B4
5 Shepherd's Bush
W12 .... 38 C4
Alexandra Gdns
W4 .... 46 A3
Alexandra Gr N4 .. 6 A3
Alexandra Ho 13
W6 .... 39 B1
Alexandra Mans
Chelsea SW3 ..... 157 B3
Cricklewood NW2 .. 9 C3
6 Hampstead NW6 . 10 C3
Shepherd's Bush
W12 .... 30 B1
Alexandra National
Ho N4 .... 6 A2
Alexandra Pl NW8 . 79 A4
Alexandra Rd
Acton W4 .... 37 C4
Hampstead NW8 ... 11 C1
Mortlake SW14 ... 55 C4
Richmond TW9 .... 44 B1
Alexandra St
6 Deptford SE14 .. 51 A3
Newham E16 ..... 35 C4
Alex Gossip Ho
SW6 .... 165 A3
Alexis St SE16 ... 153 C4
Alfearn Rd E5 .... 17 B4
Alfie's Antique Mkt★
NW8 .... 90 A1
Alford Ct N1 ..... 87 A1
Alford Pl N1 ..... 87 A1
Alfreda Ct SW11 .. 170 A3
Alfreda St SW11 .. 170 A3
Alfred Butt Ho
SW17 .... 72 B1

Alfred Cl W4 . . . . .37 C2
Alfred Ho E9 . . . . .18 A3
Alfred Mews W1,
WC1 . . . .**105** B4
Alfred Nunn Ho
NW10 . . . . .21 B4
Alfred Pl WC1 . . . .**105** B4
Alfred Rd
Acton W3 . . . . .28 B1
Paddington W2 . . . . . . .31 C4
Alfred Salter Ho
SE1 . . . .**153** A3
Alfred Salter Prim
Sch SE16 . . . . .40 C4
Alfred St E3 . . . . .26 B2
Alfreton Cl SW19 . . . . .69 C1
Alfriston Rd SW11 . . . .60 B2
Algar Ho SE1 . . . .**136** A3
Algarve Rd SW18 . . . . .71 A3
Algernon Rd
Kilburn NW6 . . . . .23 C4
Lewisham SE13 . . . . . . .67 A3
Algiers Rd SE13 . . . . . .66 C3
Alice Gilliott Ct
W14 . . . .**155** A4
Alice La E3 . . . . .26 B4
Alice Owen Tech Ctr
EC1 . . . . .96 A4
Alice Shepherd Ho
E14 . . . . .42 B4
Alice St SE1 . . . .**138** A1
Alice Walker Cl ⑧
SE24 . . . . .63 A3
Alie St E1 . . . .**111** A1
Aliwal Rd SW11 . . . . . .60 A3
Alkerden Rd W4 . . . . . .38 A1
Alkham Rd N16 . . . . . . .7 B2
Allam Ho
W11 . . . .**112** A4
Allanbridge N16 . . . . . .7 A4
Allan Ho SW8 . . . .**171** B4
Allard Gdns SW4 . . . . .61 C2
Allardyce St SW4,
SW9 . . . . .62 B3
Allbrook Ho ④
SW15 . . . . .68 C4
Allcroft Rd NW5 . . . . . .12 C2
Allendale Cl SE5 . . . . . .48 C2
Allen Edwards Dr
SW8 . . . .**172** A4
Allen Edwards Prim
Sch SW4 . . . .**172** A3
Allenford Ho
SW15 . . . . .56 B1
All England Lawn
Tennis & Croquet
Club The SW19 . . . . . .70 A1
Allen Ho W8 . . . .**127** C2
Allen Mans W8 . . . . . .**127** C2
Allen Rd
Old Ford E3 . . . . .26 B3
Stoke Newington
N16 . . . . .16 A4
Allensbury Pl ⑦
⑦ Camden Town
NW1 . . . . .13 C1
Camden Town NW1 . . .14 A1
Allen St W8 . . . .**127** C1
Allenswood ⑫
SW19 . . . . .70 A3
Allerdale Ho ⑲ N4 . . . .6 B4
Allerton Ho N1 . . . . . .**87** C1
Allerton Rd N16 . . . . . .6 B2
Allerton St N1 . . . . . . .97 C4
Allerton Wlk ⑪ N7 . . .5 B2

Allestree Rd SW6 . . . .**154** A1
Alleyn Cres SE21 . . . . .75 C2
Alleyn Ho
Bermondsey SE1 . . . .**137** B1
St Luke's EC1 . . . . .97 A1
Alleyn Pk SE21 . . . . . . .76 A1
Alleyn Rd SE21 . . . . . .76 A1
Alleyn's Sch SE22 . . . .64 A2
Allfarthing JMI Sch
SW18 . . . . .59 B1
Allfarthing La
SW18 . . . . .59 B1
Allgood St ⑩ E2 . . . . .24 B3
Allhallows La EC4 . . .**123** B3
Alliance Ct W3 . . . . . . .28 A4
Alliance Rd W3 . . . . . . .29 A4
Allied End Est W3 . . . . .29 A1
Allied Way W3 . . . . .38 A4
Allingham Mans W3 . .12 A3
Allingham Mews
N1 . . . .**86** C2
Allingham St N1 . . . . .**86** C2
Allington Ct ⑥
SW8 . . . .**170** C1
Allington Rd W10 . . . . .23 A3
Allington St ④ SW1 . .**132** B1
Allison Cl SE10 . . . . . .52 B2
Allison Gr SE21 . . . . . .76 A3
Allison Rd W3 . . . . .28 B2
Alliston Ho ⑰
E2 . . . . .24 B2 99 A3
Allitsen Rd NW8 . . . . .**80** A2
All Nations Ho ⑩
E8 . . . . .17 A1
Allnutt Way SW4 . . . . .61 C2
Allom Ct ⑬ SW4 . . . .**172** B1
Allonby Ho E14 . . . . . .33 A4
Alloway Rd E3 . . . . . . .26 A2
Allport Ho SE5 . . . . . . .63 C4
Allport Mews ㊹
E1 . . . . .25 B1
All Saints Ct
Lower Clapton E5 . . . .17 B4
⑯ Shadwell E1 . . . . . .32 B2
All Saints Dr SE3 . . . . .53 B1
All Saints Ho ②
W11 . . . . .31 B4
All Saints Pas
SW18 . . . . .58 C2
All Saints Rd W11 . . . .31 B3
All Saints' Rd W3 . . . . .37 B3
All Saints St N1 . . . . .**84** C2
All Saints Sta E14 . . . .34 A2
Allsop Pl NW1 . . . .**91** A1
All Souls Ave
NW10 . . . . .22 A4
All Souls CE Prim Sch
W1 . . . .**104** C3
All Souls Pl W1 . . . . . .**104** B3
Alma Birk Ho ④
NW6 . . . . .10 B1
Almack Rd E5 . . . . .17 B4
Alma Gr SE1 . . . .**153** A3
Alma Pl ⑦ NW8 . . . . .44 A4
Alma Pl NW10 . . . . . . .22 A2

Alma Prim Sch ㉒
SE16 . . . .**153** C4
Alma Rd SW18 . . . . . . .59 B2
Alma Sq NW8 . . . .**89** A4
Alma St
Camden Town
NW5 . . . . .13 A2
Stratford New Town
E15 . . . . .19 C2
Alma Terr
Earl's Court W8 . . . . .**127** C1
Wandsworth SW18 . . . .71 C4
Almeida St ⑩ N1 . . . . .15 A1
Almeric Rd SW11 . . . . .60 B3
Almington St N4 . . . . . .5 B3
Almond Ave W5 . . . . . .36 A3
Almond Cl SE15 . . . . . .49 C1
Almond Ho SE4 . . . . . .51 B1
Almond Rd SE16 . . . . .40 A2
Almorah Rd N1 . . . . . . .15 C1
Al-Muntada Islamic
Sch SW6 . . . .**165** A4
Alperton St W10 . . . . . .23 B1
Alphabet Sq E3 . . . . . .33 C4
Alpha Cl NW8 . . . .**90** B3
Alpha Ct ⑧ NW5 . . . . .13 A2
Alpha Gr E14 . . . . .41 C4
Alpha Ho
⑩ Brixton SW4 . . . . .62 B3
Kilburn NW6 . . . . .23 C3
Lisson Gr NW8 . . . . . .**90** B1
Alpha Pl
Chelsea SW3 . . . .**158** B4
Kilburn NW6 . . . . .23 C3
Alpha Rd SE14 . . . . . . .51 B2
Alpha St SE15 . . . . . . .49 C1
Alpine Gr ⑦ E9 . . . . . .17 B1
Alpine Rd SE16 . . . . . .40 C1
Alroy Rd N4 . . . . .5 C4
Alsace Rd SE17 . . . . .**152** A2
Al Sadiq High Sch for
Boys & Al Zahra Girls
Sch NW6 . . . . .23 A4
Alscot Rd SE1 . . . . . .**139** A1
Alscot Road Ind Est
SE1 . . . .**139** A1
Alscot Way SE1 . . . . .**152** C4
Altair Ct N1 . . . . .15 C2
Altenburg Gdns
SW11 . . . . .60 B3
Althea St SW6 . . . . . . .59 A4
Althorpe Mews
SW11 . . . .**167** C3
Althorp Rd SW17 . . . . .72 B3
Altima Ct SE22 . . . . . . .64 C3
Alton Ho ③ E3 . . . . . . .27 A2
Alton Rd
Richmond TW10,
TW9 . . . . .54 A3
Roehampton SW15 . . . .68 C3
Alton St E14 . . . . .34 A4
Alumni Ct SE1 . . . . . .**139** A4
Alvanley Ct NW3 . . . . .11 A3
Alvanley Gdns
NW6 . . . . .11 A3
Alverstone Ave SW18,
SW19 . . . . .70 C2
Alverstone Ho ⑪
SE11 . . . .**163** B3
Alverstone Rd NW2 . . .9 B1
Alverton St SE8 . . . . . .51 B4
Alvey St SE17 . . . .**152** A2
Alvington Cres E8 . . . .16 B3
Alwyn Ave W4 . . . . .37 C1

Alwyne La N1 . . . . .15 A1
Alwyne Pl N1 . . . . .15 B1
Alwyne Rd N1 . . . . .15 B1
Alwyne Sq N1 . . . . .15 B2
Alwyne Villas N1 . . . . .15 A1
Alwyn Gdns W3 . . . . . .28 A3
Alzette Ho ⑪ E2 . . . . .25 C3
Aman Dalvi Ho ⑨
W6 . . . . .70 A4
Amazonas St ⑧ **152** B3
Amazon St E1 . . . . .32 A3
Ambassador Ct ⑨
NW6 . . . . .10 C3
Ambassador Ho
NW8 . . . .**79** A3
Ambassador Sq
E14 . . . . .42 A2
Amber Ct N7 . . . . .14 C2
Ambergate St
SE17 . . . .**150** B2
Amberley Ct ②
SW9 . . . . .63 A4
Amberley Rd W9 . . . . .31 C4
Amber Wharf ㉖
E2 . . . . .24 B4
Ambler Prim Sch ②
N4 . . . . .6 A2
Ambler Rd N4 . . . . .6 A1
Ambleside ⑬ Putney SW19 . . . . . . .70 A3
Regent's Pk NW1 . . . .**82** B1
Ambleside Cl E9 . . . . .17 B3
Ambleside Point ①
SE15 . . . . .50 B3
Ambleside Rd
NW10 . . . . .8 B1
Ambrosden Ave
SW1 . . . .**133** A1
Ambrose Ho ⑨
E14 . . . . .33 C4
Ambrose Mews
SW11 . . . .**168** C2
Ambrose St SE16 . . . . .40 A2
Ambrose Wlk ㉓ E3 . .26 C3
Amelia Cl W3 . . . . .37 A4
Amelia Ho ⑤ W6 . . . . .39 B1
Amelia St SE17 . . . . . .**150** C2
Amen Cnr EC4 . . . . . .**108** B1
Amen Ct EC4 . . . .**108** B1
American
Intercontinental Univ
W1 . . . .**103** C3
American Sch in
London The NW8 . . .**79** B2
American Univ in
London The ⑧ N1 . . .5 B1
America Sq EC3 . . . .**124** C4
America St SE1 . . . . .**122** C1
Amerland Rd
SW18 . . . . .58 B1
Amersham Gr
SE14 . . . . .51 B3
Amersham Rd
SE14 . . . . .51 B3
Amersham Vale SE14,
SE8 . . . . .51 B3
Amery Gdns NW10 . . .22 A4
Amery Ho SE17 . . . . .**152** B2
Amesbury Ave
SW2 . . . . .74 B2
Amesbury Twr ④
SW8 . . . .**170** C2
Ames Cotts ⑮ E3 . . . .33 A4
Ames Ho ⑯ E2 . . . . . .25 C3

Amethyst Rd E15 . . . . .19 C4
Amhurst Ct N4 . . . . .6 C4
Amhurst Par N16 . . . . . .7 B4
Amhurst Pk N16, N16 .7 A4
Amhurst Rd E8 . . . .
N16 . . . . .16 C4
Amhurst Terr E8 . . . . . .16 C4
Amias Ho EC1 . . . . . . .96 C2
Amiel St ⑱ E1 . . . . . . .25 B1
Amies St SW11 . . . . . . .60 B4
Amigo Ho SE1 . . . . . .**135** C2
Amina Way SE16 . . . .**139** B1
Amner Rd SW11 . . . . . .60 C1
Amor Rd W6 . . . . .39 B3
Amory Ho N1 . . . .**85** A2
Amott Rd SE15 . . . . . . .64 C4
Amoy Pl E14 . . . . .33 C2
Ampton Pl WC1 . . . . . .94 C3
Ampton St WC1 . . . . . .94 C3
Amstel Ct ⑫ SE15 . . . .49 B3
Amsterdam Rd
E14 . . . . .42 B3
Amundsen Ct ⑦
E14 . . . . .41 C1
Amwell St EC1 . . . . . . .95 B4
Amyruth Rd SE4 . . . . . .66 C2
Anatola Rd N19 . . . . . . .4 B2
Anchorage Point ①
E14 . . . . .41 C4
Anchor Ho EC1 . . . . . .96 C2
Anchor Mews
SW12 . . . . .61 A1
Anchor Ret Pk E1 . . . .25 B1
Anchor St SE16 . . . . . .40 A2
Anchor Terr SE1 . . . .**123** A2
Anchor Yd EC1 . . . . . .97 A2
Ancill Cl W6 . . . .**154** A3
Ancona Rd NW10 . . . . .21 C3
Andalus Rd SW9 . . . . .62 A4
Andaman Ho ③
E1 . . . . .33 A4
Andersens Wharf ⑨
E14 . . . . .33 B3
Anderson Ho ⑩ 28 C3
Anderson Ho ⑩
E14 . . . . .34 B2
Anderson Rd E9 . . . . . .17 C2
Andersons Sq N1 . . . .**86** A3
Anderson St SW3 . . .**144** C2
Anderton Cl SE5 . . . . . .63 C4
Andover Ho ⑤ N7 . . . .5 B2
Andover Pl NW6 . . . . .78 A1
Andover Rd N7 . . . . .5 B2
Andoversford Ct ②
SE15 . . . . .49 A4
Andre St E8 . . . . .16 C3
Andrew Borde St
WC2 . . . .**105** C2
Andrewes Ho EC2 . . .**109** A3
Andrew Ho
New Cross SE4 . . . . . .51 B1
Putney SW15 . . . . .56 C2
Andrew Logan's
Glasshouse[*]
SE1 . . . .**138** A4
Andrew Marvell Ho ⑫
N16 . . . . .16 A4
Andrew Pl SW8 . . . . .**171** C4
Andrew Reed Ho ⑧
SW18 . . . . .70 A4
Andrews Crosse
WC2 . . . .**107** B1
Andrew's Rd E8 . . . . . .25 A4
Andrew St E14 . . . . . . .34 B3

Andrews Wharf 14
E8 . . . . .25 A4
Andrews Wlk SE17 . .48 A4
Andrew Wilmot Ct
SW18 . . . . .71 B3
Anfield Cl SW12 . .73 B4
Angel E1 . . . . .86 B1
Angela Carter Cl
SW9 . . . . .62 C4
Angela Davis Ind Est
20 SW9 . . . . .63 A3
Angel Ct
Broadgate EC2 . . . .109 C2
St James SW1 . . . .119 A1
8 Willesden NW2 . . .8 C2
Angel Gate EC1 . . . .96 B4
Angel Ho N1 . . . . . . .85 C1
Angelina Ho 2
SE15 . . . . .49 C2
Angelis Appartments
N1 . . . . .86 B1
Angel La E15 . . . . . . .19 C2
Angell Park Gdns 9
SW9 . . . . .62 C4
Angell Rd SW9 . . . . .63 A4
Angel Mews
Finsbury N1 . . . . . . .85 C1
Putney SW15 . . . . . . .68 C4
Stepney E1 . . . . .32 A2
Angel Pas EC4 . . . .123 B3
Angel Pl SE1 . . . . . .137 B4
Angel Sq N1 . . . . . . .85 C1
Angel St EC1 . . . . . .108 C2
Angel Sta EC1 . . . . . .85 C1
Angel Wlk W6 . . . . . .39 B2
Angerstein Bsns Pk
SE10 . . . . .43 C2
Angerstein La SE3 . .53 B2
Anglebury 5 W2 . . .31 C3
Anglers La NW5 . . . .13 A2
Anglesey Ho 13
E14 . . . . .33 C3
Anglia Ho 15 E14 . . .33 A3
Anglo American
Laundry SW17 . . . . .71 B1
Anglo Rd 18 E3 . . . . .26 B3
Angrave Ct 8 E8 . . . .24 B4
Angrave Pas 5 E8 . .24 B4
Angus Ho 12
SW12 . . . . .73 C4
Angus St SE14 . . . . .51 A3
Anhalt Rd SW11 . . . .158 B1
Animals in War
Meml* W1 . . . . .117 A4
Anley Rd W14 . . . . . .39 C4
Annabel Cl E14 . . . . .34 A3
Anna Cl E8 . . . . .24 B4
Annandale Rd
Chiswick W4 . . . . . . .38 A1
Greenwich SE10 . . . .43 B1
Anne Goodman Ho 3
E1 . . . . .32 B3
Anne Kerr Ct 15
SW15 . . . . .57 C1
Anne's Ct NW8 . . . . .90 B1
Annesley Ho 15
SW9 . . . . .173 B4
Annesley Wlk N19 . . .4 B2
Annette Cres 18

Annette Ct 17
N7 . . . . .5 B1
Annette Rd N7 . . . . . .14 B4
Annie Besant Cl
E3 . . . . .26 B4

Anning St
EC2 . . . . .24 A1 98 B2
Annis Rd E9 . . . . .18 A2
Ann St SW10 . . . . . .157 B3
Ann Moss Way
SE16 . . . . .40 B3
Ann's Cl SW1 . . . . . .131 B3
Ann's Pl E1 . . . . .110 C3
Ansdell Rd SE15 . . . .50 B1
Ansdell St W8 . . . . .128 B2
Ansdell Terr W8 . . . .128 B2
Ansell Ho E1 . . . . . . .32 B4
Ansell Rd SW17 . . . .72 B1
Anselm Rd SW6 . . . .155 B3
Ansleigh Pl W11 . . . .30 C2
Anson Ho
Pimlico SW1 . . . . . .160 C4
1 Tower Hamlets
E1 . . . . .26 A1
Anson Prim Sch
NW2 . . . . .9 C3
Anson Rd
Cricklewood NW2 . . . .9 B3
Tufnell Pk N7 . . . . . .13 C4
Anstey Ct 3 W3 . . . . .37 A4
Anstey Ho 7 E9 . . . . .25 B4
Anstey Rd SE15 . . . .64 C4
Anstice Cl W4 . . . . . .46 A3
Antenor Ho 11 E2 . . .25 A3
Anthony Cope Ct
N1 . . . . .97 C4
Anthony Ho NW8 . . . .90 A1
Anthony St E1 . . . . . .32 A3
Antilles Bay 19
E14 . . . . .42 B4
Antill Rd E3 . . . . .26 A2
Antill Terr 5 E1 . . . . .32 C3
Antonine Hts 8 SE1 138 A3
Anton St E8 . . . . .16 C3
Antony Ho
4 Deptford SE14 . . .50 C3
2 Rotherhithe
SE16 . . . . .40 B2
Antrim Gr NW3 . . . . .12 B2
Antrim Ho SW11 . . . .60 C4
Antrim Mans NW3 . . .12 A2
Antrim Rd NW3 . . . . .12 B2
Antrobus Rd W4 . . . .37 B3
AOP Gall* EC2 . . . . .98 A2
Apex Ind Est
N19 . . . . .21 B1
Aphrodite Ct 11
E14 . . . . .41 C2
Apollo Bldg 2
E14 . . . . .41 C2
Apollo Ho
Chelsea SW10 . . . . .157 B3
32 Hackney E2 . . . . .25 A3
Highgate N6 . . . . .3 C4
Apollo Ind Bsns Ctr 20
SE8 . . . . .50 C4
Apollo Pl SW10 . . . .157 B2
Apollo Studios 13
NW5 . . . . .13 B3
Apothecary St
EC4 . . . . .108 A1
Appach Rd SW2 . . . .62 C1
Appleby Ct 3 W3 . . . .37 B4
Appleby Rd
Hackney E8 . . . . .16 C1
Newham E16 . . . . . . .35 C3
Appleby St E2 . . . . . .24 B3
Appledore Cl SW12 .72 B2
Appleford 8 NW5 . . .13 B3

Appleford Ho 6
W10 . . . . .23 A1
Appleford Rd W10 . . .23 A1
Applegarth Ho
Borough The SE1 . .136 A4
9 Camberwell
SE5 . . . . .49 C3
Applegarth Rd
W14 . . . . .39 C3
Apple Mkt* WC2 . . .120 B4
Appleshaw Ho 4
SE5 . . . . .64 A4
Appleton Ct 30 E8 . .17 A3
Appleton Rd E22 . . . .8 B4
Apple Tree Yd
SW1 . . . . .119 A2
Appold St EC2 . . . . .110 A4
Appollo Ct 7
SW9 . . . . .173 B4
Apprentice Way 5
E5 . . . . .17 A4
Approach Cl N16 . . . .16 A4
Approach Rd E2 . . . .25 B3
Approach The 3 . . . .28 C3
April Ct 30 E2 . . . . . .24 C3
April St E8 . . . . .16 B4
Apsley Ho
Stepney E1 . . . . .32 B4
St John's Wood
NW8 . . . . .79 B2
Apsley Ho, The
Wellington Mus*
SW1 . . . . .131 C4
Apsley Way W1 . . . .131 C4
Aquila St NW8 . . . . . .79 C2
Aquinas St SE1 . . . .121 C1
Arabella Ct NW8 . . . .79 A2
Arabella Dr SW15 . . .56 A3
Arabian Ho 3 E1 . . . .26 A1
Arabin Rd SE4 . . . . . .66 B3
Aragon Twr SE8 . . . .41 B2
Arakan Ho 4 N16 . . . .15 C4
Aral Ho 14 E1 . . . . . .25 C1
Arapiles Ho 6
E14 . . . . .34 C3
Arbery Rd E3 . . . . . . .26 A3
Arbon Ct N1 . . . . . . .87 A3
Arbor Ct N16 . . . . .6 C2
Arborfield Cl SW2 . . .74 B3
Arborfield Ho 7
E14 . . . . .33 C2
Arbour Ho 3 E1 . . . . .32 C3
Arbour Sq E1 . . . . . . .32 C3
Arbuthnot Rd
SE14 . . . . .50 C1
Arbutus St E8 . . . . . .24 B4
Arcade The
Broadgate EC2 . . . .110 A3
1 Tufnell Pk N7 . . . . .14 A2
Arcadian Ho SW6 . . .167 A1
Arcadian Pl SW18 . . .70 B4
Arcadia St E14 . . . . . .33 C3
Arcadia Univ W2 . . .114 A3
Archangel St SE16 . . .40 C4
Archbishop Coggan
Ho SE13 . . . . .67 C3
Archbishop's Pl 1
SW2 . . . . .74 B4
Archbishop Sumner
CE Prim Sch
SE11 . . . . .149 C3
Archbishop Tenison's
Sch SE11 . . . . .163 A1
Archdale Ct W12 . . . .30 A1
Archdale Ho SE1 . . . .138 A2
Archdale Rd SE22 . . .64 B3

Archel Rd W14 . . . . .154 C4
Archer Ho
1 Battersea
SW11 . . . . .167 C2
24 Hoxton N1 . . . . . .24 A4
1 New Cross SE14 . . .51 A2
Notting Hill
W11 . . . . .31 B2 113 A4
Archers Lo 22
SE16 . . . . .153 C1
Archer Sq SE14 . . . . .51 A4
Archer St W1 . . . . . .119 B4
Archery Cl W2 . . . . . .102 B1
Archery Fields Ho
WC1 . . . . .95 B4
Archery Stps W2 . . .116 A4
Arches The WC2 . . . .120 B2
Archibald Mews
W1 . . . . .118 A3
Archibald Rd N7 . . . . .13 C4
Archibald St E3 . . . . .26 C2
Archie St SE1 . . . . . .138 B3
Arch St SE1 . . . . .136 C1
Archway N19 . . . . .4 B2
Archway Bsns Ctr 5
N19 . . . . .4 C1
Archway Cl
North Kensington
W10 . . . . .30 C4
2 Upper Holloway
N19 . . . . .4 B2
Archway Hts 5
N19 . . . . .4 B3
Archway L Ctr N19 . .4 B2
Archway Mews
SW15 . . . . .58 A3
Archway Rd N6 . . . . . .4 A4
Archway St SW13 . .
SW14 . . . . .56 A4
Arcola St E8 . . . . .16 B3
Arctic St NW5 . . . . . .13 A3
Ardbeg Rd SE24 . . . .63 C2
Arden 17 SW19 . . . . .69 C3
Arden Cres E14 . . . . .41 C2
Arden Ho
8 Hoxton N1 . . . . . . .24 A3
20 Stockwell SW9 . .172 B1
Vauxhall SE11 . . . . .148 C3
Ardent Ho 30 E3 . . . .26 A3
Ardilaun Rd N5 . . . . .15 B4
Ardleigh Rd N1 . . . . .16 A2
Ardlui Rd SE27 . . . . .75 B2
Ardmere Rd SE13 . . .67 C1
Ardshiel Cl 8
SW15 . . . . .57 C4
Ardwell Rd SW2 . . . .74 A2
Ardwick Rd NW2 . . . .10 C4
Ares Ct 16 E14 . . . . . .41 C2
Arethusa Ho 8
E14 . . . . .42 A2
Argo Bsns Ctr 24
NW6 . . . . .23 C2
Argon Mews SW6 . .155 C1
Argos Ct 2 SW9 . . . .173 B4
Argos Ho 8 E2 . . . . . .25 A3
Argosy Ho
Fitzrovia W1 . . . . . . .92 B1
Rotherhithe SE8 . . . .41 A2
Argyle Ho E14 . . . . . .42 B3
Argyle Mans 4
NW2 . . . . .9 C2
Argyle Pl W6 . . . . . . .39 A2
Argyle Prim Sch
WC1 . . . . .94 A4
Argyle Rd E1 . . . . . . .25 C1

Argyle Sq WC1 . . . . .94 B4
Argyle St WC1 . . . . .94 B4
Argyle Way SE16 . . .153 C1
Argyle Wlk WC1 . . . .94 B3
Argyll Cl SW9 . . . . . .62 B4
Argyll Ct 12 SW2 . . .74 A4
Argyll Mans
Chelsea SW3 . . . . . .157 C4
West Kensington
W14 . . . . .140 B4
Argyll Rd W8 . . . . . .127 C3
Argyll St W1 . . . . . . .104 C1
Arica Ho SE16 . . . . . .40 A3
Arica Rd SE4 . . . . . . .66 A4
Ariel Ct
5 Hammersmith
W12 . . . . .39 B4
Newington SE11 . . . .150 A3
Ariel Rd NW6 . . . . . . .10 C2
Ariel Way W12 . . . . . .30 B1
Aristotle Rd SW4 . . . .61 C4
Arizona Bldg 10
SE13 . . . . .52 A2
Arkansas Ho 21
N19 . . . . .4 C4
Ark Ct N16 . . . . .7 B2
Arklow Ho SE17 . . . .48 C4
Arklow Rd SE14 . . . . .51 B4
Arklow Road Trad Est
SE14 . . . . .51 B4
Arkwright Ho 23
SW2 . . . . .74 A4
Arkwright Mans 1
NW3 . . . . .11 B3
Arlesey Cl SW15 . . . .58 A2
Arlesford Rd SW9 . . .62 A4
Arlidge Ho EC1 . . . . .107 C4
Arlingford Rd
SW2 . . . . .62 C1
Arlington Ave N1 . . . .87 A3
Arlington Cl SE13 . . .67 C2
Arlington Ct 13
W3 . . . . .28 A1
Arlington Gdns
W4 . . . . .37 B1
Arlington Ho
3 Deptford SE8 . . . .51 B4
Finsbury EC1 . . . . . . .95 C4
1 Shepherd's Bush
W12 . . . . .30 A1
Arlington Lo 2 SW2 . .62 B3
Arlington Park Mans
4 W4 . . . . .37 B1
Arlington Pl 7
SE10 . . . . .52 B3
Arlington Rd NW1 . . .82 B3
Arlington Sq N1 . . . . .87 A3
Arlington St SW1 . . .118 C2
Arlington Way EC1 . . .95 C4
Armada Ct 11 SE8 . . .51 C4
Armadale Rd
SW6 . . . . .155 B3
Armada St 18 SE8 . . .51 C4
Armagh Rd E3 . . . . . .26 B4
Arminger Rd W12 . . .30 A1
Armitage Ho
NW1 . . . . .102 B4
Armitage Rd
Golders Green
NW11 . . . . .1 B3
Greenwich SE10 . . . .43 B1
Armour Ho N1 . . . . . .14 B2
Armoury Ho E3 . . . . .26 A4
Armoury Rd SE8 . . . .52 A1

Armoury Way
SW18 ....58 C2

Armsby Ho 🔢 E1 ...32 B4

Armstrong Ho 🔢
SW15 ....57 C1

Armstrong Rd
East Acton W3 .....29 B1
Knightsbridge SW7 129 B1
🔟 Willesden NW10 ...8 A1
Arnal Cres SW18 ...70 A4
Arncliffe NW6 ......78 B3

Arndale Wlk 🔢
SW18 ....59 A2

Arne Ho SE11 ...148 C2
Arne St WC2 .....106 B1
Arneway St SW1 ..133 C1
Arnewood Cl
SW15 ....68 C3

Arngask Rd SE6 ...67 C4

Arnhem Pl E14 ....41 C3
Arnhem Way 🔢
SE22 ....64 A2

Arnhem Wharf
E14 ....41 C3

Arnhem Wharf Prim
Sch E14 ....41 C3

Arnold Cir
E2 ......24 B2 98 C3
Arnold Est SE1 ...139 A3

Arnold Ho
Newington SE17 ..150 B1
🔢 Stoke Newington
N16 ....7 A1

Arnold House Sch
NW8 ....79 B1

Arnold Rd E3 ......26 C2
Arnot Ho 🔢 SE5 ...48 B3
Arnot Cl W14 .....37 C2
Arnould Ave SE5 ...63 C3

Arnside Ho 🔢
SE17 ....48 C4

Arnside St SE17 ...48 C4
Arodene Rd SW2 ..62 B1
Arragon Rd SW18 .70 C3

Arran Ho
🔢 Canary Wharf
E14 ....34 B1

Arran Wlk N1 .....15 B1
Arrol Ho SE1 .....137 A1
Arrowe Ct 🔢 E5 ...17 A4
Arrow Ho 🔢 N1 ...24 A4
Arrow Rd E3 ......27 A2
Arrowsmith Ho
SE11 ....148 C2

Arsenal Sta N5 ....5 C1
Arta Ho 🔢 E1 ....32 B3
Artcadia Lifestyle*
EC2 ....110 C4

Artemis Ct 🔢 E14 .41 C2
Artemis Pl SW18 ..70 B4
Artesian Rd W2 ...31 C3
Arthur Ct
Battersea SW11 ..169 C3
🔟 North Kensington
W10 ....30 C3
Paddington W2 ..100 A2

Arthur Deakin Ho 🔢
E1 ....111 B4

Arthurdon Rd SE4 .66 C2
Arthur Henderson Ho
🔢 Crouch End N19 ..4 C4
🔢 Fulham SW6 ....164 C2
Arthur Newton Ho 🔢
SW11 ....59 C4
Arthur Rd N7 ......14 B4
Arthur St EC4 ....123 C4

Arthur Wade Ho 🔢
E2 ....24 B2 99 A4

Artichoke Hill 🔢
E1 ....32 A2

Artichoke Mews 🔢
SE5 ....48 C2

Artichoke Pl SE5 ..48 C2

Artillery Ho
🔢 Bow E3 ....26 A4
Westminster SW1 ..133 B1

Artillery La
Broadgate E1 .....110 B3
North Kensington
W12 ....29 C3

Artillery Pas E1 ...110 B3
Artillery Pl SW1 ..133 B1

Artillery Row
SW1 ....133 B1

Artisan Ct E8 .....16 C2
Artisan Mews 🔢
NW10 ....22 C2

Artisan Quarter 🔟
NW10 ....22 C2

Artizan St E1 .....110 B2
Arton Wilson Ho 🔢
SW15 ....56 C2

Arts Educational Sch
The 🔢 W4 ....38 A2

Arundel Bldgs
SE1 ....138 B1

Arundel Cl SW11 ..60 A2

Arundel Ct
Barnes SW13 ......47 A4
Chelsea SW3 .....144 B2
Putney SW15 .....57 C2

Arundel Gdns
W11 ......31 B2 112 C4

Arundel Gr N16 ...16 A3

Arundel Ho
Islington N1 ......86 B4
Richmond TW10 ...54 C2
🔢 South Acton W3 .37 A4

Arundel Lo 🔢 N19 ..5 A2

Arundel Mans
Barnes SW13 ......47 A4
Fulham SW6 .....165 A4
Arundel Pl N1, N7 ..14 C2
Arundel Sq N7 ....14 C2
Arundel St WC2 ..121 A4

Arundel Terr
SW13 ....47 A4

Arungford Mews 🔢
SW2 ....62 C2

Arvon Rd N5 .....14 C3
Asaph Ho SE14 ....51 B2
Ascalon Ct 🔟 SW2 .74 B4
Ascalon Ho SW8 ..160 C1
Ascalon St SW8 ..160 C1
Ascham St NW5 ...13 B3

Ascot Ct
🔢 Brixton SW4 ....62 A3
St John's Wood
NW8 ....89 B3

Ascot Ho
🔢 Acton Green
W4 ....37 B1
Regent's Pk NW1 ..92 B4
🔢 Paddington W9 ..31 C4
Ascott Ave W5 ....36 A4

Ashbourne Coll
W8 ....128 A3

Ashbridge Ct E5 ...18 A4

Ashbourne Gr
Chiswick W4 ......38 A1
East Dulwich SE22 .64 B3

Ashbridge Ct 🔢
W6 ....39 A3

Ashbridge St NW8 .90 A1
Ashbrook Rd N19 ...4 C2

Ashburn Gdns
SW7 ....142 C4

Ashburnham Gr
SE10 ....52 A3

Ashburnham Pl
SE10 ....52 A3

Ashburnham Prim Sch
SW10 ....157 B2

Ashburnham Rd
Chelsea SW10 ....157 A1
Kensal Rise NW10 .22 B3

Ashburnham Retreat 🔢
SE10 ....52 A3

Ashburnham Twr
SW10 ....157 B2

Ashburn Pl SW7 ..142 C3

Ashburton Mans
SW10 ....157 A2

Ashburton Rd E16 .35 C3
Ashby Ct NW8 .....89 C2
Ashby Gr N1 ......15 B1

Ashby Ho
🔢 Brixton SW9 ....48 A1
🔢 Islington N1 ....15 B1

Ashby Mews 🔢
Clapham Pk
SW2 ....62 A2
New Cross SE4 ....51 B1
Ashby Rd SE4 .....51 B1
Ashby St EC1 .....96 B3

Ashchurch Ct 🔢
W12 ....38 C3

Ashchurch Gr
W12 ....38 C3

Ashchurch Park Villas
W12 ....38 C3

Ashchurch Terr
W12 ....38 C3

Ashcombe Ct 🔢
SW15 ....58 A2

Ashcombe Ho 🔢
E3 ....27 A2

Ashcombe St
SW6 ....166 A1
Ashcroft Ho SW8 .170 C4
Ashcroft Rd E3 ....26 A2
Ashcroft Sq 🔢 W6 .39 B2
Ashcroft Tech Acad
SW15 ....58 B2

Ash Ct
Clapham SW11 ...60 C2
Marylebone W1 ..102 C2
🔢 Rotherhithe
SE16 ....33 A1
Upper Holloway N19 ..4 B2
Ashdale Ho N4 .....6 C4
Ashdene 🔢 SE15 ..49 B3
Ashdon Rd NW10 ..21 B4
Ashdown Cres
NW5 ....12 C3
Ashdown Ct SE22 .76 C3
Ashdown Ho 🔢
SW1 ....72 C4
Ashdown Way
SW17 ....72 C2
Ashdown Wlk 🔢
E14 ....41 C2
Ashenden SE17 ...151 A4

Ashenden Rd E5 ...18 A3
Ashen Gr SW19 ....70 C2
Ashentree Ct EC4 107 C1
Asher Way E1 ....125 C3
Ashfield Ho 🔢 N5 ..15 B3
Ashfield Rd W3 ....29 B1
Ashfield St
E1 ....32 B4
🔢 Whitechapel E1 ..32 A4
Ashfield Yd 🔢 E1 .32 B4
Ashford Ho
🔢 Brixton SW9 ....63 A3
🔢 Deptford SE8 ....51 B4
Ashford Rd NW2 ....9 C4
Ashford St
N1 ......24 A2 98 A4
Ash Gr
Cricklewood NW2 ..10 A4
Ealing W5 ....36 A3
Hackney E8 ....25 A4
Ashgrove Ct 🔢
W9 ....31 C4
Ashgrove Ho SW1 147 C2
Ash Ho
🔢 Canary Wharf
E14 ....42 B4
Fulham SE1 ......153 A3
Ashington 🔢 NW5 .12 C2
Ashington Ho 🔢
E1 ....25 A1
Ashington Rd
SW6 ....165 A1
Ashleigh Ho SW14 .56 A4
Ashleigh Rd SW14 .56 A4
Ashley Cres SW11 .60 C4
Ashley Ct
Hampstead NW3 ...11 A3
🔢 Kingsland N16 ...16 A3
Ashley Pl SW1 ....132 C1
Ashley Rd
Hornsey N19 ....5 A4
Richmond TW9 ....54 A4
Ash Lo SW6 ....47 C2
Ashlone Rd SW15 ..57 C4
Ashmead Bsns Ctr 🔢
E16 ....27 C1
Ashmead Ho 🔢 E9 .18 A3
Ashmead Mews 🔢
SE8 ....51 C1
Ashmead Prim Sch
SE8 ....51 C1
Ashmead Rd SE8 ..51 C1
Ashmere Gr 🔢 SW2,
SW4 ....62 A3
Ashmere Ho 🔢
SW2 ....62 A3
Ashmill St NW8 ..102 A4
Ashmole Prim Sch
SW8 ....163 A3
Ashmole St SW8 ..163 A3
Ashmore NW1 ......13 C1
Ashmore Ho W14 126 B1
Ashmore Rd W9 ...23 B2
Ashmount Prim Sch
N19 ....4 C4
Ashmount Rd N19 ...4 C4
Ashness Rd SW11 .60 B2
Ashpark Ho 🔢
E14 ....33 A3
Ashtead Ct 🔢
SW19 ....69 C3
Ashtead Rd E5 .....7 C4

Ashton Ho
🔢 Kennington
SW9 ....163 C1
Roehampton SW15 .69 A3
Ashton Rd E15 .....19 C3
Ashton St E14 .....34 B2
Ashurst Lo 🔢 N5 ...15 A3
Ashwin St E8 ......16 B2
Ashworth Cl SE5 ..48 C1
Ashworth Mans
W9 ....88 B3
Ashworth Rd W9 ..88 B3
Aske Ho 🔢
N1 ....24 A2 98 A4
Aske St N1 ..24 A2 98 A4
Askew Cres W12 ..38 C4
Askew Mans 🔢
W12 ....38 C4
Askew Rd W12 ....38 C4
Askham Ct W12 ...29 C1
Askham Rd W12 ...29 C1
Askill Dr SW15 ....58 A2
Asland Rd E15 .....27 C4
Aslett St SW18 ....71 B4
Asmara Rd NW2 ...10 A3
Asolando Dr SE17 151 A3
Aspect Ho 🔢 E14 ..42 B4
Aspen Cl
Ealing W5 ....36 A4
🔢 Upper Holloway
N19 ....4 B2
Aspen Ct
🔟 Acton W3 ....28 B3
🔢 Hackney E8 .....16 C3
Richmond TW9 ....44 C3
Aspen Gdns 🔢
W6 ....39 A1
Aspen Ho
🔢 Deptford SE15 ..50 B4
🔢 Maitland Pk
NW3 ....12 B2
Richmond TW9 ....44 C3
Aspenlea Rd W6 ..47 C4
Aspen Way E14 ...34 B2
Aspern Gr NW3 ...12 A3
Aspinall Ho SW12 .74 A3
Aspinall Rd SE4 ...65 C4
Aspinden Rd SE16 .40 A2
Aspire Bld 🔟
SW15 ....58 B2
Aspley Rd SW18 ...59 A2
Assam St E1 ......111 B2
Assata Mews N1 ...15 A2
Assembly Pas E1 ..32 B4
Assisi Ct SW12 ....72 B3
Astbury Bsns Pk 🔢
SE15 ....50 B2
Astbury Ho SE11 .135 B1
Astbury Rd SE15 ..50 B2
Astell St SW3 ....144 B2
Aster Ho 🔢 SE3 ..53 B1
Astey's Row 🔢 N1 .15 B1
Astle St SW11 ....169 C2
Astley Ave NW2 ....9 B3
Astley Ho
Fulham SE1 ......153 A2
🔢 Paddington W2 ..31 C4
Aston Ct N4 ....6 B2
Aston Ho
Notting Hill
W11 ......31 B2 113 A4

Aston Ho continued
South Lambeth
SW8 . . . . **171** B3
Aston St E14 . . . . 33 A4
Astonville St
SW18 . . . . 70 C3
Astor Ct SW6 . . . . **156** C1
Astoria Mans 18
SW16 . . . . 74 A1
Astoria Par SW16 . . 74 A1
Astoria Wlk SW9 . . 62 C4
Astra Ho
4 Bow E3 . . . . 26 B2
Hornsey N4 . . . . 5 B4
Astrop Mews W6 . . 39 B3
Astrop Terr W6 . . . 39 B4
Astwood Mews
SW7 . . . . **142** C4
Asylum Rd SE15 . . 50 A3
Atalanta St
SW6 . . . . 47 C3 **154** A1
Atheldene Rd
SW18 . . . . 71 B3
Athelstan Gdns
NW6 . . . . 10 A1
Athelstane Gr E3 . . 26 B3
Athelstane Mews
N4 . . . . 5 C3
Athelstan Gdns 8
NW6 . . . . 10 A1
Athelstan Ho
Hackney Wick E9 . . . 18 B3
Stoke Newington
N16 . . . . 16 A4
Athena Ct
Bermondsey SE1 . . **138** A3
St John's Wood
NW8 . . . . 79 B2
Athenia Ho 7 E14 . . 34 C3
Athenlay Rd SE15 . . 65 C2
Athenoeum Ct N5 . . 15 B4
Athens Gdns W9 . . 23 C1
Atherden Rd E5 . . . 17 B4
Atherfield Ct
SW18 . . . . 59 A1
Atherfold Rd SW9 . . 62 A4
Atherstone Ct W2 **100** B4
Atherstone Mews
SW7 . . . . **143** A4
Atherton St SW13 . . 46 C3
Atherton St SW11 **168** B2
Athlone Cl 24 E5 . . 17 A3
Athlone Ho
16 Camden Town
NW5 . . . . 12 C2
9 Stepney E1 . . . . . 32 B3
Athlone Rd SW2 . . 74 C4
Athlone St NW5 . . . 12 C2
Athol Ct 15 N4 . . . . 5 B2
Atholl Ho W9 . . . . . 88 C3
Athol St E14 . . . . . 34 B3
Atkins Ct 13 E3 . . . 26 B4
Atkins Lo W8 . . . **127** B4
Atkinson Ho
Battersea SW11 . . **169** B3
16 Hackney E2 . . . . 24 C3
Walworth SE17 . . . **151** C3
Atkins Rd SW4,
SW12 . . . . 73 C4
Atlanta Bldg 7
SE13 . . . . 52 A2
Atlantic Ct 13 E14 . . 34 C2
Atlantic Ho
5 Putney SW15 . . . 58 B2
4 Tower Hamlets
E1 . . . . 33 A4

Atlantic Rd SW2, SW9,
SE24 . . . . 62 C3
Atlas Mews
Dalston E8 . . . . 16 B2
Islington N7 . . . . . . 14 B2
Atlas Rd NW10 . . . . 21 A2
Atney Rd SW15 . . . 58 A3
Atterbury St SW1 **148** A3
Attilburgh Ho SE1 **138** C2
Attlee Ho 1 . . . . . **111** A3
Attneave St WC1 . . 95 B3
Atwater Ct SW2 . . . 74 B3
Atwell Rd 6 SE15 . . 49 C1
Atwood Av TW9 . . . 44 C1
Atwood Ho SE21 . . 76 A1
Atwood Rd W6 . . . 39 A2
Aubert Ct N5 . . . . . 15 A4
Aubert Pk N5 . . . . . 15 A4
Aubert Rd N5 . . . . . 15 A4
Aubrey Beardsley Ho
SW1 . . . . **147** A3
Aubrey Mans
NW1 . . . . **102** A4
Aubrey Moore Point
E15 . . . . 27 B3
Aubrey Pl NW8 . . . **78** C1
Aubrey Rd
W14 . . . . 31 B1 **113** A1
Aubrey Wlk
W14 . . . . 31 B1 **113** A1
Auburn Cl SE14 . . . 51 A3
Aubyn Sq SW15 . . 56 C2
Auckland Ho 11
W12 . . . . 30 A2
Auckland Rd
SW11 . . . . 60 A3
Auckland St SE11 **148** C1
Auden Pl NW1 . . . . 81 B4
Audley Cl 8 SW11 . . 60 C4
Audley Ct W1 . . . **118** A2
Audley Dr TW10 . . 54 B2
Audley Sq W1 . . . **117** C2
Audley St W1 . . . . **117** C2
Audrey Ho EC1 . . . **107** C3
Audrey St E2 . . . . . 24 C3
Augusta St E14 . . . 34 A3
Augustine Ho
Broadgate EC2 . . . **109** C2
New Cross SE4 . . . . 51 B2
Augustine Rd W14 . . 39 C3
Augustines Ct E9 . . 17 B3
Augustus Cl W12 . . 39 A3
Augustus Ct
8 Putney SW19 . . . 70 A3
Streatham SW16 . . 73 C2
Augustus Ho NW1 . 92 C4
Augustus Rd
Putney SW19 . . . . . 69 C3
Putney SW19 . . . . . 70 A3
Augustus St NW1 . 92 B4
Aulton Pl SE11 . . . **149** C1
Aura Ho 3 TW9 . . . 45 A2
Auriga Mews N1 . . 15 C3
Auriol Mans W14 **140** A3
Auriol Rd W14 . . . **140** A3
Aurora Bldg 4
E14 . . . . 34 B1
Aurora Ho E14 . . . . 34 A3
Austen Ho 5 NW6 . 23 C2
Austin Friars EC2 **109** C2
Austin Friars Ho
EC2 . . . . **109** C2
Austin Friars Sq
EC2 . . . . **109** C2
Austin Ho
6 Brixton SW2 . . . 62 B2

Austin Ho continued
1 New Cross SE14 . . 51 B3
Austin Rd SW11 . . **169** B3
Austins Ct SE15 . . 64 C4
Austin St E2 . . 24 B2 98 C3
Australia Rd W12 . . 30 A2
Austral St SE11 . . **150** A4
Autumn Rise 9
SW4 . . . . 37 C1
Autumn St E3 . . . . 26 C4
Avalon Rd SW6 . . **166** A4
Avebury Ct N1 . . . . 87 B3
Avebury St N1 . . . . 87 B3
Aveline St SE11 . . **149** B1
Aveling Ho 12 N19 . . 4 B1
Ave Maria La EC4 . **108** B1
Avenell Mans N5 . . . 6 A1
Avenell Rd N5 . . . . . 6 A1
Avenfield Ho W1 . **117** A4
Avening Rd SW18 . . 70 C4
Avening Terr
SW18 . . . . 70 C4
Avenue Cl NW8 . . . 80 B3
Avenue Cres W3 . . 37 A4
Avenue Ct
Chelsea SW3 . . . . **144** C3
Willesden NW2 . . . . . 1 A1
Avenue Gdns
Mortlake SW14 . . . 56 A4
South Acton W3 . . . 37 A4
Avenue Ho
St John's Wood
NW8 . . . . 80 A1
Upper Clapton N16 . . 7 C2
Willesden Green
NW10 . . . . 22 A3
Avenue Lo 12
NW8 . . . . 11 C1
Avenue Mans
Clapham SW11 . . . 60 A3
Hampstead NW3 . . . 11 A3
Willesden NW2 . . . . 9 A2
Avenue Park Rd SE21,
SE27 . . . . 75 C2
Avenue The
Bedford Pk W4 . . . . 38 A3
Brondesbury Pk
NW6 . . . . 22 C4
Clapham SW4 . . . . 60 C2
Greenwich SE10 . . . 52 C3
Richmond TW9 . . . 44 B1
Wandsworth SW18,
SW12 . . . . 72 B4
Avenue Rd NW8 . . . 47 C4
Avery Farm Row
SW1 . . . . **146** A3
Avery Hill Coll (Mile
End Annexe) E3 . . 26 B1
Avery Row W1 . . . **118** B4
Aviary Cl E16 . . . . . 35 B4
Avignon Rd SE4 . . . 65 C4
Avingdor Ct 10
W3 . . . . 28 B1
Avington Ct SE1 . . **152** B3
Avis Sq E1 . . . . 32 C3
Avocet Cl SE1 . . . . **153** B2
Avon Ct
1 Acton W3 . . . . . 28 B3
6 Putney SW15 . . . 58 A2
Avondale Ct E16 . . . 35 A4

Avondale Ho
11 Bermondsey
SE1 . . . . **153** B1
6 Mortlake SW14 . . 55 C4
Avondale Mans
SW6 . . . . **164** C4
Avondale Park Gdns
W11 . . . . . . 31 A2 **112** A3
Avondale Park Prim
Sch W11 . . 31 A2 **112** A3
Avondale Park Rd
W11 . . . . . . 31 A2 **112** A3
Avondale Rd
Mortlake SW14 . . . 55 C4
Newham E16 . . . . . 35 A4
Avondale Rise
SE15 . . . . 64 B4
Avondale Sq SE1 **153** B1
Avon Ho
2 Islington N1 . . . . 14 C1
10 Stoke Newington
N16 . . . . 15 C4
West Kensington
W14 . . . . **141** A3
Avonhurst Ho
NW6 . . . . 10 A1
Avonley Rd SE14 . . 50 B3
Avonmore Gdns
W14 . . . . **141** A3
Avonmore Pl
W14 . . . . **140** B4
Avonmore Prim Sch
W14 . . . . **140** B4
Avonmore Rd
W14 . . . . **140** C4
Avon Pl SE1 . . . . . **137** A3
Avon Rd SE4 . . . . . 66 C4
Avriol Ho W12 . . . . 30 A1
Avro Ct E9 . . . . 18 A3
Axford Ho SW2 . . . 75 A3
Axis Ct SE10 . . . . . 53 A4
Axminster Rd N7 . . . 5 B1
Aybrook St W1 . . . **103** B3
Aycliffe Rd W12 . . . 29 C1
Aylesbury Ho 15
SE15 . . . . 49 C4
Aylesbury Rd
SE17 . . . . **151** C1
Aylesbury St EC1 . . 96 A1
Aylesford Ho SE1 **137** C3
Aylesford St SW1 **147** B1
Aylesham Sh Ctr
SE15 . . . . 49 C2
Aylestone Ave
NW6 . . . . 22 C4
Aylmer Ho SE10 . . . 42 C1
Aylmer Rd W12 . . . 38 B4
Aylton Est 28 SE16 . 40 B4
Aylward St E1 . . . . 32 C3
Aylwin Est SE1 . . **138** B2
Aynhoe Mans W14 . 39 C3
Aynhoe Rd W14 . . . 39 C3
Ayres St SE1 . . . . **137** A4
Ayrsome Rd N16 . . . 7 A1
Ayrton Gould Ho 9
E2 . . . . 25 C2
Ayrton Rd SW7 . . **129** B2
Aysgarth Rd SE21 . . 76 A4
Ayshford Ho E1 . . . 25 A2
Ayston Ho 10 SE8 . . 40 C2
Aytoun Ct 9 SW9 **173** A1
Aytoun Pl SW9 . . **173** A1
Aytoun Rd SW9 . . **173** A1
Azalea Ho SE14 . . . 51 B3

Azania Mews NW5 . . 13 A2
Azenby Rd SE15 . . . 49 B1
Azof St SE10 . . . . . 43 A2
Azov Ho 10 E1 . . . . 26 A1
Aztec Ct 8 N16 . . . 16 A2
Azure Ho 28
E2 . . . . 24 C2 99 B3

B

Baalbec Rd N5 . . . . 15 A3
Babington Ct
WC1 . . . . **106** B3
Babington Ho
SE1 . . . . **137** A4
Babmaes St SW1 . **119** B3
Bacchus Wlk 12
N1 . . . . 24 A3
Bache's St N1 . . . . 97 C3
Back Church La
E1 . . . . **111** B1
Back Hill EC1 . . . . . 95 C1
Backhouse Pl SE1 **152** B3
Back La NW3 . . . . . 11 B4
Bacon Gr SE1 . . . **138** C1
Bacon's Coll SE16 . . 41 A4
Bacon's La N6 . . . . . 3 C3
Bacon St E2 . 24 B1 99 A2
Bacton NW5 . . . . . . 12 C3
Bacton St E2 . . . . . 25 B2
Baddeley Ho
SE11 . . . . **149** A2
Baddow Wlk N1 . . . 86 C4
Baden Pl SE1 . . . . **137** B4
Badminton Ct 9
N4 . . . . 6 B4
Badminton Ho
SE22 . . . . 64 A3
Badminton Mews 6
E16 . . . . 35 C1
Badric Ct SW11 . . . 60 C1
Badsworth Rd 3
SE5 . . . . 48 B2
Bagley's La SW6 . . 166 B3
Bagnigge Ho WC1 . . 95 B3
Bagshot Ho NW1 . . 92 B4
Bagshot St SE17 . . **152** B1
Baildon 27 E2 . . . . 25 B3
Baildon St SE8 . . . 51 B3
Bailey Ct 9 W12 . . 38 C4
Bailey Ho 10 SE18 **156** B2
Bailey Mews
Brixton SW2 . . . . . 62 C2
Chiswick W4 . . . . . 45 A4
Bainbridge St
WC1 . . . . **105** C2
Bain Ho 13 SW9 . . **172** B2
Baird Ho 20 W12 . . 30 A2
Baird St EC1 . . . . . 97 A2
Baizdon Rd SE3 . . . 53 A1
Baker Ho 12 E3 . . . 27 A2
Baker Rd NW10 . . . 21 A4
Bakers Field N7 . . . 14 A4
Bakers Hall Ct
EC3 . . . . **124** B3
Baker's Mews W1 **103** B2
Bakers Pas 22
NW3 . . . . 11 B4
Bakers Rents 13
E2 . . . . 24 B2 98 C3
Baker's Row E15 . . 27 C3
Baker's Row EC1 . . 95 B1
Baker St W1 . . . . **103** A4
Baker Street W1 . **103** A4

Baker Street Sta
NW1 . . . . **91** A1
Baker's Yd EC1 . . . . **95** B1
Bakery Cl SW9 . . . . . **163** A1
Balaclava Rd SE1 . . . **153** A3
Balchier Rd SE22 . . . **65** A1
Balcombe Ho
Lisson Gr NW1 . . . . . **90** C2
⑤ Streatham SW2 . . . **74** B3
Balcombe St NW1 . . . **90** C1
Balcorne St E9 . . . . . **17** C1
Balderton Flats
W1 . . . . **103** C1
Balderton St W1 . . . **103** C1
Baldock Ho **31**
SE5 . . . . **48** B1
Baldock St E3 . . . . . . **27** A3
Baldrey Ho **1**
SE10 . . . . **43** B1
Baldwin Cres SE5 . . **48** B2
Baldwin Ho **13**
SW2 . . . . **74** C3
Baldwin Rd SW11 . . **60** C1
Baldwin's Gdns
EC1 . . . . **107** B4
Baldwin St EC1 . . . . . **97** B3
Baldwin Terr N1 . . . . **86** C2
Baldwyns Gdns W3 . **28** C2
Balearic Apts **3**
E16 . . . . **35** C2
Bale Rd E1 . . . . **33** A4
Bales Coll W10 . . . . . **22** C2
Balfern Gr W4 . . . . . . **38** A1
Balfern St SW11 . . . **168** B2
Balfe St N1 . . . . **84** B1
Balfour Ho **4**
W10 . . . . **30** C4
Balfour Mews W1 **117** C2
Balfour Pl
Mayfair W1 . . . . . . **117** C3
Putney SW15 . . . . . **57** A3
Balfour Rd
Highbury N5 . . . . . . **15** B4
North Acton W3 . . . **28** B4
Balfour St SE17 . . . **151** B4
Balfron Twr **4**
E14 . . . . **34** B3
BALHAM **72** C3
Balham Gr SW12 . . . **72** C4
Balham High Rd SW12,
SW17 . . . . **72** C3
Balham Hill SW12 . . **61** A1
Balham L Ctr
SW12 . . . . **73** A2
Balham New Rd
SW12 . . . . **73** A2
Balham Park Mans
SW12 . . . . **72** C3
Balham Park Rd SW12,
SW17 . . . . **72** B3
Balham Sta Rd SW12 **73** A3
Balham Station Rd
SW12 . . . . **73** A3
Balin Ho SE1 . . . . . . **137** B4
Balkan Wlk E1 . . . . . . **32** A2
Balladier Wlk E14 . . **34** A4
Ballance Rd E9 . . . . . **18** A2
Ballantine St
SW18 . . . . **59** B3
Ballantrae Ho
NW2 . . . . **10** B4
Ballard Ho SE10 . . . . **52** A4
Ballast Quay SE10 . . **42** C1
Ballater Rd SW2,
SW4 . . . . **62** A3
Ball Ct EC3 . . . . **109** C1

Ballin Ct **14** E14 . . . . **42** B4
Ballingdon Rd
SW11 . . . . **60** C1
Ballinger Point **15**
E3 . . . . **27** A2
Balliol Ho **11**
SW15 . . . . **57** C1
Balliol Rd W10 . . . . . **30** C3
Ballogie Ave NW10 . . **8** A4
Ballow Cl **13** SE5 . . . **49** A3
Ball's Pond Pl **3**
N1 . . . . **15** C2
Ball's Pond Rd N1 . . **16** A2
Balman Ho **3**
SE16 . . . . **40** C2
Balmer Rd E3 . . . . . . **26** B3
Balmes Rd N1 . . . . . . **87** C4
Balmoral Cl **1**
SW15 . . . . **57** C1
Balmoral Ct
21 Rotherhithe
SE16 . . . . **32** C1
St John's Wood
NW8 . . . . **79** B2
Balmoral Gr N7 . . . . **14** B2
Balmoral Ho
1 Isle of Dogs
E14 . . . . **42** A3
Stoke Newington N4 . **6** B3
West Kensington
W14 . . . . **140** A4
Balmoral Mews
W12 . . . . **38** B3
Balmoral Rd NW2 . . . **9** A2
Balmore Cl E14 . . . . . **34** B3
Balmore St N19 . . . . . **4** A2
Balmuir Gdns
SW15 . . . . **57** B3
Balnacraig Ave
NW10 . . . . **8** A4
Balniel Gate SW1 **147** C2
Balsam Ho **3** E14 . . **34** A2
Baltic Apts **5** E16 . . **35** C2
Baltic Ho **7** SE5 . . . **48** B1
Baltic St E E C1 . . . . **96** C1
Baltic St W EC1 . . . . **96** C1
Baltimore Ho
Clapham SW18 . . . . **59** B3
Kennington SE11 . **149** B2
Balvaird Pl SW1 . . . **147** C1
Balvernie Gr SW18 . **70** C4
Bamber Rd **5**
SE15 . . . . **49** B2
Bamborough Gdns **11**
W12 . . . . **39** B4
Banbury Ct WC2 . . . **120** A4
Banbury Ho **5** E9 . . **17** C1
Banbury Rd E9 . . . . . **17** C1
Banbury St **3**
SW11 . . . . **168** B2
Bancroft Ct SW8 . . . **172** A4
Bancroft Ho **1** E1 . . **25** B1
Bancroft Rd E1 . . . . . **25** C1
Banfield Rd SE15 . . . **65** A4
Bangabandhu Prim Sch
3 . . . . **25** B2
Bangalore St
SW15 . . . . **57** C4
Banim St W6 . . . . **39** A2
Banister Ho
Hackney E9 . . . . **17** C3
Nine Elms SW8 . . . **171** A4
9 West Kilburn
W10 . . . . **23** A2
Banister Rd W10 . . . **22** C2

Bank Ct SW11 . . . . . **170** A4
Bank End SE1 . . . . . **123** A2
Bank La SW15 . . . . . . **56** A2
Bank of England ★
EC2 . . . . **109** B1
Bank of England
Mus ★ EC2 . . . . **109** B1
Bank's Ho SE1 . . . . . **136** C1
Bankside
Borough The SE1 . . **122** C3
Borough The SE1 . . **123** A2
Bankside Ave **1**
SE13 . . . . **67** B4
Bankside Gall ★
SE1 . . . . **122** B3
Bankside Ho EC3 . . **110** B1
Bankside Pier
SE1 . . . . **122** C3
Bank St E14 . . . . **34** A1
Bank Sta EC3 . . . . . **109** C1
Bank The N6 . . . . **4** A3
Bankton Rd SW2 . . . **62** C3
Banner Ct **5** SE16 . . **40** B2
Banner Ho EC1 . . . . . **97** A1
Bannerman Ho
SW8 . . . . **162** C3
Banner St EC1 . . . . . . **97** A2
Banning Ho **8**
SW19 . . . . **69** C3
Banning St SE10 . . . . **43** A1
Bannister Cl SW2 . . . **74** C3
Bannister Ho **28**
SE14 . . . . **50** C4
Banqueting Ho ★
SW1 . . . . **120** A1
Banstead Ct
East Acton W12 . . . **29** B2
Stoke Newington N4 . **5** B3
Banstead St SE15 . . . **65** B4
Bantock Ho **8**
W10 . . . . **23** A2
Bantry Ho **3** E1 . . . . **25** C1
Bantry St SE5 . . . . . . **48** C3
Banville Ho SW8 . . . **163** A1
Banyan Ho **3**
NW3 . . . . **11** A2
Banyard Rd SE16 . . . **40** A3
Baptist Gdns NW5 . . **12** C2
Barandon Wlk **6**
W11 . . . . **30** C2
Barbara Brosnan Ct
NW8 . . . . **79** B1
Barbara Castle Cl
SW6 . . . . **155** A3
Barbara Rudolph Ct
6 N19 . . . . **5** A4
Barbauld Rd N16 . . . . **7** A1
Barber Beaumont Ho
21 E1 . . . . **25** C2
Barbers Rd E15 . . . . . **27** A3
BARBICAN **109** A3
Barbican ★ EC2 . . . **109** A3
Barbican Ctr ★
EC2 . . . . **109** A4
Barb Mews W6 . . . . . **39** B3
Barbon Alley EC3 . . **110** B2
Barbon Cl WC1 . . . . **106** C4
Barbrook Ho E9 . . . . **17** B2
Barchard St SW18 . . **59** A2
Barchester St E14 . . . **34** A4
Barclay Cl SW6 . . . . **155** B1
Barclay Ho **20** E9 . . . **17** B1
Barclay Rd SW6 . . . **155** C1
Barcombe Ave
SW2 . . . . **74** B2

Bardell Ho **17** SE1 . **139** B3
Bardolph Ho
Richmond TW9 . . . . **54** B4
Tufnell Pk N7 . . . . . . **14** A4
Bard Ho NW1 . . . . . . **30** C2
Bardsey Pl **41** E1 . . . **25** B1
Bardsey Wlk **5**
N1 . . . . **15** B2
Bardsley Ho **6**
SE10 . . . . **52** B4
Bardsley La SE10 . . . **52** B4
Barents Ho **10** E1 . . . **25** C1
Barfett St W10 . . . . . **23** B1
Barford Ho **23** E3 . . **26** B3
Barford St N1 . . . . . . **85** C3
Barforth Rd SE15 . . . **65** B4
Barge House St
SE1 . . . . **121** C2
Barge La **10** E3 . . . . **26** B4
Barham Ho SE17 . . . **152** B2
Baring Ct N1 . . . . **87** B3
Baring Ho **19** E14 . . **33** C3
Baring St N1 . . . . **87** B3
Barker Cl TW9 . . . . . **45** A2
Barker Dr NW1 . . . . . **13** C1
Barker Ho
Dulwich SE21 . . . . . **76** A1
Walworth SE17 . . . **152** A3
Barker Mews SW4 . . **61** A3
Barker St SW10 . . . . **156** C4
Barker Wlk SW16 . . . **73** C1
Bark Pl W2 . . . . **114** A4
Barkston Gdns
SW5 . . . . **142** A3
Barkway Ct N4 . . . . . . **6** B2
Barkwith Ho **27**
SE14 . . . . **50** C4
Barkworth Ho
SE16 . . . . **40** B1
Barlborough St
SE14 . . . . **50** C3
Barlby Gdns W10 . . . **22** C1
Barlby Prim Sch
W10 . . . . **22** C1
Barlby Rd W10 . . . . . **30** C4
Barleycorn Way
E14 . . . . **33** B2
Barley Mow Pas
Chiswick W4 . . . . . . **37** B1
Clerkenwell EC1 . . . **108** B3
Barley Shotts Bsns Pk
W10 . . . . **31** B4
Barling **6** NW1 . . . . **13** A1
Barling Ct **1**
SW4 . . . . **172** A2
Barlings Ho **2**
SE4 . . . . **65** C3
Barloch Ho **14**
SW11 . . . . **169** B2
Barlow Ho
14 Bermondsey
SE16 . . . . **40** A2
Notting Hill
W11 . . . . . . **31** A2 **112** A4
Shoreditch N1 . . . . . **97** B4
Barlow Pl W1 . . . . . **118** B3
Barlow Rd
Acton W3 . . . . **28** A1
Brondesbury NW6 . . **10** B2
Barlow St SE17 . . . . **151** C3
Barmouth Ho **6** N7 . **5** B2
Barmouth Rd
SW18 . . . . **59** B1
Barnabas Ho EC1 . . . **96** C3
Barnabas Lo SW8 . . **172** B4

Barnabas Rd E9 . . . . **17** C3
Barnaby Pl SW7 . . . **143** B3
Barnard Ct SW16 . . . **74** B1
Barnard Ho **17** E2 . . **25** A2
Barnard Lo **10** W9 . . **31** C4
Barnard Mews
SW11 . . . . **60** A3
Barnardo Gdns **1**
E1 . . . . **32** C2
Barnardo St E1 . . . . . **32** C3
Barnard Rd SW11 . . . **60** A3
Barnard's Inn EC4 **107** C2
Barnbrough NW1 . . . **82** C3
Barnby St NW1 . . . . . **93** A4
Barn Cl **18** NW5 . . . . **13** C3
Barn Elms Sp Ctr
SW15 . . . . **47** B2
Barnersbury Ho
N7 . . . . **14** A4
BARNES **46** B2
Barnes Ave SW13 . . . **46** C3
Barnes Bridge Sta
SW13 . . . . **46** A1
Barnes Common ★
SW13 . . . . **56** C4
Barnes Ct N1 . . . . **14** C1
Barnes High St
SW13 . . . . **46** B1
Barnes Ho
14 Bethnal Green
E2 . . . . **25** B3
Camden Town NW1 . **82** B4
4 Deptford SE14 . . **50** C4
Hornsey N19 . . . . **5** A4
Barnes Hospl
SW14 . . . . **56** A4
Barnes Prim Sch
SW13 . . . . **56** B4
Barnes St E14 . . . . . . **33** A3
Barnes Sta SW13 . . . **56** C4
Barnes Terr SE8 . . . . **41** B1
Barnet Gr
E2 . . . . **24** C2 **99** B3
Barnet Ho **55** SE5 . . **48** B1
Barnett St **18** E1 . . . **32** A3
Barn Field NW3 . . . . **12** B3
Barnfield Cl
London N4 . . . . **5** A4
Wandsworth SW17 . . **71** B1
Barnfield Pl E14 . . . . **41** C2
Barnham St SE1 . . . **138** B4
BARNSBURY **14** A1
Barnsbury Gr N7 . . . **14** B1
Barnsbury Ho **12**
SW4 . . . . **61** C1
Barnsbury Pk N1 . . . **14** C1
Barnsbury Rd N1 . . . **85** B3
Barnsbury Sq N1 . . . **14** C1
Barnsbury St N1 . . . **14** C1
Barnsbury Terr N1 . . **14** B1
Barnsdale Ave
E14 . . . . **41** C2
Barnsdale Rd W9 . . . **23** B1
Barnsley St E1 . . . . . **25** A1
Barn St N16 . . . . **7** A2
Barnstaple La
SE13 . . . . **67** B3
Barnston Wlk N1 . . . **86** C4
Barnwell Ho **1**
SE5 . . . . **49** A2
Barnwell Rd SW2 . . . **62** C2
Barnwood Cl W9 . . . **88** B1
Baron Cl N1 . . . . **85** B2

Baroness Rd **5**
E2 . . . . 24 B2 **99** A4
Barons Court Mans
W14 . . . . 140 B1
Baron's Court Rd
W14 . . . . 140 B2
Barons Court Sta
W14 . . . . 140 A2
Barons Gate **13**
W4 . . . . 37 B3
Barons Keep W14 140 A2
Barons Lo **9** E14 . . 42 B2
Baronsmead Rd
SW13 . . . . 46 C2
Baronsmede W5 . . 36 B4
Baron's Pl SE1 . . 135 C3
Baron St N1 . . . . . 85 B2
Baron Wlk E16 . . . . 35 B4
Barque Mews SE8 . 51 C4
Barradell Ho **18**
W14 . . . . 39 C3
Barratt Ho **15** N1 . . 15 A1
Barratt Ind Pk E3 . . 27 B1
Barret Ho NW6 . . . 23 C4
Barrett Ct **2**
NW10 . . . . 21 A3
Barrett's Gr N16 . . 16 A3
Barretts Green Rd
NW10 . . . . 20 C3
Barrett St W1 . . 103 C1
Barrhill Rd SW2 . . 74 A2
Barriedale SE14 . . 51 A1
Barrie Ho
Acton W3 . . . . 37 B4
Bayswater W2 . . . 115 A3
Primrose Hill NW8 . 80 B3
8 Stoke Newington
N16 . . . . 7 A1
Barrington Cl
NW5 . . . . 12 C3
Barrington Ct
6 Acton W3 . . . . . 37 A4
Kentish Town NW5 . 12 C3
31 South Lambeth
SW9 . . . . 172 B1
Barrington Rd
SW9 . . . . 63 A4
Barrowgate Ho
W4 . . . . 37 C1
Barrowgate Rd
W4 . . . . 37 C1
Barrow Hill Est
NW8 . . . . 80 A1
Barrow Hill Jun Sch
NW8 . . . . 80 A1
Barrow Hill Rd
NW8 . . . . 80 A1
Barry Ct SW4 . . . . 61 B1
Barry Ho **4** SE16 . . 40 A1
Barry Lo **4** 5 B4
Barry Par SE22 . . . 64 C3
Barry Rd SE22 . . . . 64 C2
Barset Rd SE15 . . . 65 B4
Barston Rd SE27 . . 75 B1
Barstow Cres SW2 . 74 B3
Bartell Ho SW2 . . . 62 C1
Barter St WC1 . . 106 B3
Bartholomew Cl
Barbican EC1 . . . 108 C3
Wandsworth SW18 . 59 B3
Bartholomew Ct
16 Blackwall E14 . . 34 C2
St Luke's EC1 . . . . 97 A2

Bartholomew Ho **22**
SE5 . . . . 48 B1
Bartholomew La
EC2 . . . . 109 C1
Bartholomew Pas
EC1 . . . . 108 B3
Bartholomew Pl
EC1 . . . . 108 C3
Bartholomew Rd
NW5 . . . . 13 B2
Bartholomew Sq
18 Bethnal Green
E1 . . . . 25 A1
St Luke's EC1 . . . . 97 A2
Bartholomew St
SE1 . . . . 137 C1
Bartholomew Villas
NW5 . . . . 13 B2
Bartok Ho
W11 . . . . . 31 B2 112 C3
Barton Cl
Hackney E9 . . . . . . 17 B3
Peckham SE15 . . . . 65 A4
Barton Ct
6 South Lambeth
SW4 . . . . 172 A2
West Kensington
W14 . . . . 140 B2
Barton Ho
5 Bromley E3 . . . 27 A2
Islington N1 . . . . . . 15 A1
Sands End SW6 . . . 59 A4
Barton Rd W14 . . 140 B1
Barton St SW1 . . 134 A2
Bartonway NW8 . . 79 B2
Bartram Rd SE4 . . 66 A1
Bartrip St E9 . . . . . 18 B2
Barts & The London
Sch of Medicine &
Dentistry EC1 . . . 96 B1
Barville Cl SE4 . . . 66 A3
Barwell Ho **7**
E2 . . . . 24 C1 99 C2
Barwick Ho **7** W3 . . 37 B4
Bascome St **13**
SW2 . . . . 62 C1
Base Apartments **9**
N1 . . . . 15 B1
Baseline Business
Studios **18** W11 . . 30 C2
Basevi Way SE8 . . 52 A4
Bashley Rd NW10 . 20 C1
Basildon Ct **4** . . 103 C4
Basil Ho
South Lambeth
SW8 . . . . 162 A2
22 Whitechapel E1 111 C2
Basil Mans SW1 130 C3
Basil St
Knightsbridge
SW1 . . . . 130 C3
Knightsbridge SW1,
SW3 . . . . 130 C2
Basin App **20** E14 . . 33 A3
Basing Ct **13** SE15 . 49 B2
Basingdon Way
SE5 . . . . 63 C3
Basinghall Ave
EC2 . . . . 109 B2
Basinghall St EC2 109 B2
Basing Ho **14** 5 A3
Basing House Yd **22**
E2 . . . . 24 A2 98 B4

Basing Pl E2 . 24 A2 **98** B4
Basing St W11 . . . . 31 B3
Basire St N1 . . . . . 87 A4
Baskerville Ct
SW18 . . . . 72 A4
Baskerville Gdns
NW10 . . . . 8 A4
Baskerville Rd
SW18 . . . . 72 A4
Baslow Wlk E5 . . . 17 C4
Basnett Rd **9**
SW11 . . . . 60 C4
Basque Ct **21** SE16 . 40 C4
Bassano St SE22 . . 64 B2
Bassein Park Rd
W12 . . . . 38 B4
Bassett House Sch **20**
W10 . . . . 30 C3
Bassett Rd W10 . . 30 C3
Bassett St NW5 . . . 12 C2
Bassingbourn Ho **3**
N1 . . . . 15 A1
Bassingham Rd
SW18 . . . . 71 B4
Bassishaw Highwalk
EC2 . . . . 109 B3
Basswood Cl **8**
SE15 . . . . 65 A4
Basterfield Ho EC1 96 C1
Bastion Highwalk
EC2 . . . . 108 C3
Bastwick St EC1 . . 96 C2
Basuto Rd SW6 . . 165 C3
Batavia Ho **1**
SE14 . . . . 51 A3
Batavia Mews **3**
SE14 . . . . 51 A3
Batavia Rd SE14 . . 51 A3
Batchelor St N1 . . . 85 C3
Bateman Ho **8**
SE17 . . . . 48 A4
Bateman's Bldgs
W1 . . . . 105 B1
Bateman's Row
EC2 . . . . . . 24 A1 98 B2
Bateman St W1 . . 105 B1
Bate St **10** E14 . . . . 33 B2
Bath Cl SE15 . . . . . 50 A3
Bath Ct
Finsbury EC1 . . . . . 97 B3
3 Forest Hill SE26 . 76 C1
Holborn EC1 . . . . . 95 B1
Bathgate Ho **8**
SW9 . . . . 48 A2
Bathgate Rd SW19 . 69 C1
Bath Gr E2 . . . . . . 24 C3
Bath Ho
Bethnal Green
E2 . . . . 24 C1 99 C2
Borough The SE1 . 137 A2
Bath Pl
14 Hammersmith
W6 . . . . 39 B1
5 Shoreditch
EC2 . . . . . . 24 A2 98 A3
Bath Rd W4 . . . . . . 38 A2
Bath St EC1 . . . . . . 97 B3
Bath Terr SE1 . . . 136 C2
Bathurst Gdns
NW10 . . . . 22 A3
Bathurst Ho **2**
W12 . . . . 30 A2
Bathurst Mews
W2 . . . . 115 C4
Bathurst St W2 . . 115 C4
Batley Pl **3** N16 . . . . 7 B1

Batley Rd N16 . . . . . 7 B1
Batman Cl W12 . . . 30 A1
Batoum Gdns W6 . 39 B3
Batson Ho **2** E1 . . 111 C1
Batson St W12 . . . 38 C4
Batten Ho
7 London SW4 . . 61 B2
10 West Kilburn
W10 . . . . 23 A2
Batten St SW11 . . . 60 A4
BATTERSEA 169 A4
Battersea Bridge Rd
SW11 . . . . 158 A1
Battersea Bsns Ctr
SW11 . . . . 60 C4
Battersea Church Rd
SW11 . . . . 167 B1
Battersea Dogs & Cats
Home SW8 . . . . . 160 B1
Battersea High St
SW11 . . . . 167 B1
Battersea Hts
SW11 . . . . 60 B4
Battersea Park★ . . 159 B1
Battersea Park Rd
SW11, SW8 . . . . 169 A3
Battersea Park Sch
SW11 . . . . 169 B3
Battersea Park Sta
SW8 . . . . 160 A1
Battersea Power
Station(dis) SW8 160 B4
Battersea Rise
SW11 . . . . 60 A3
Battishill St **9** N1 . 15 A1
Battlebridge Ct
NW1 . . . . 84 B2
Battle Bridge La
SE1 . . . . 124 A1
Battledean Rd N5 . 15 A3
Battle Ho **8** SE15 . . 49 C4
Batty St E1 . . . . . 111 C2
Baty Ho SW2 . . . . . 74 B3
Baulk The SW18 . . 70 C4
Bavaria Rd N19 . . . 5 A2
Bavent Rd SE5 . . . 48 B1
Bawdale Rd SE22 . . 64 B2
Bawtree Rd SE14 . . 51 A3
Baxendale St
E2 . . . . 24 C2 99 B4
Baxter Ho **11** E3 . . . 27 A2
Baxter Rd N1 . . . . . 15 C2
Baycliffe Ho **8** E9 . 17 C2
Bay Ct
Ealing W5 . . . . 36 A3
7 Stepney E1 . . . . 25 C1
Bayer Ho EC1 . . . . 96 C1
Bayes Ct NW3 . . . . 12 B1
Bayfield Ho **8**
SE4 . . . . 65 C3
Bayford Rd NW10 . 22 C2
Bayford St Ind Ctr **8**
E8 . . . . 17 A1
Bayford St **8** E8 . . 17 A1
Bayham Pl NW1 . . 83 A3
Bayham Rd W4 . . . 37 C3
Bayham St NW1 . . 82 C3
Bayhurst Ho N4 . . . 6 B4
Bayley St WC1 . . 105 B3
Baylis Rd SE1 . . . 135 B3
Baynes Mews **2**
NW3 . . . . 11 C2
Baynes St NW1 . . . 13 B1

Bayon Ho **27** N19 . . . 4 C4
Bayonne Rd W6 . . 154 A3
Bayston Rd N16 . . . 7 B1
BAYSWATER . . . 114 C4
Bayswater Rd W2 115 B3
Bayswater Sta
W2 . . . . 115 A3
Bayswater Sta
W2 . . . . 114 B4
Bayton Ct **2** E8 . . . 16 C1
Baytree Rd SW2 . . 62 B3
Bazalgette Ho
NW8 . . . . 89 C2
Bazeley Ho SE1 . . 136 A3
Bazely St E14 . . . . 34 B2
BBC Television Ctr
W12 . . . . 30 B1
Beach Ho SW5 . . 141 B2
Beachy Rd E3 . . . . 18 C1
Beaconfield Terrace
Rd W14 . . . . 126 A1
Beacon Gate SE14 . 65 C4
Beacon Hill N7 . . . 14 A3
Beacon Ho
11 Camberwell
SE5 . . . . 49 A3
4 Isle Of Dogs E14 . 42 A1
South Lambeth
SW8 . . . . 171 B4
Beacon Rd SE13 . . 67 C1
Beaconsfield Cl
Acton Green W4 . . . 37 B1
Greenwich SE3 . . . 53 C4
Beaconsfield Rd
Acton W4 . . . . 37 C3
Greenwich SE3 . . . 53 C3
Walworth SE17 . . . 152 A1
Willesden NW10 . . . 8 B2
Beaconsfield Wlk
SW6 . . . . 165 A3
Beadon Rd W6 . . . 39 B2
Beak St W1 . . . . . 119 A4
Beale Ho **7** SW9 . 172 C1
Beale Rd E3 . . . . . 26 B4
Beames Ho SW8 . 171 B4
Beames Rd NW10 . 20 C4
Beaminster Ho
SE5 . . . . 162 C2
Beamish Ho **7**
SE16 . . . . 40 B2
Beanacre Cl E9 . . . 18 B2
Bear Alley EC4 . . 108 A2
Bear Croft Ho **6**
SW6 . . . . 164 C1
Beardsley Way
W3 . . . . 37 C4
Bear Gdns SE1 . . 122 C2
Bear La SE1 . . . . 122 B1
Bear St WC2 . . . . 119 C4
Bearstead Rise
SE4 . . . . 66 B2
Beaton Cl SE15 . . . 49 B2
Beatrice Ho
2 Brixton SW2 . . 62 B2
4 Hammersmith
W6 . . . . 39 B1
2 Stepney E1 . . . . 32 C4
Beatrice Pl W8 . . 128 A1
Beatrice Rd
Bermondsey SE1 . . 153 C3
Finsbury Pk N4 . . . . 5 C4
2 Richmond TW10 . 54 B2
Beatrice Tate Sch **13**
E2 . . . . 25 A2

Beatrice Webb Ho **4**
E3 . . . . 26 A3
Beatrix Ho SW5 . . **142** B2
Beatrix Potter Prim
Sch SW18 . . . . 71 B3
Beatson Wlk **23**
SE16 . . . . 32 C1
Beattie Ho SW8 . . **171** A4
Beatty Ho **10** E14 . . 41 A4
Beatty Rd N16 . . . . . 16 A4
Beauchamp Cl **17**
W4 . . . . 37 B3
Beauchamp Pl
SW3 . . . . **130** B1
Beauchamp Rd
SW11 . . . . 60 B3
Beauchamp St
EC1 . . . . **107** B3
Beauchamp Terr
SW15 . . . . 57 A4
Beauclerc Rd W6 . . 39 A3
Beauclerk Ho **10**
SW16 . . . . 74 A1
Beaufort Cl SW19 . . 69 A4
Beaufort Ct SW5 . . **141** B3
Beaufort Gdns
SW3 . . . . **130** B2
Beaufort Ho
Battersea SW11 . . **168** A2
Chelsea SW3 . . . . **157** C3
20 Millwall E14 . . 41 C4
Pimlico SW1 . . . . **147** B1
Beaufort Mans
SW3 . . . . **157** C3
Beaufort Mews
SW6 . . . . **155** A4
Beaufort St SW3 . . **157** B4
Beaufoy Ho
South Lambeth
SW8 . . . . **162** C2
3 West Norwood
SE27 . . . . 75 A1
Beaufoy Rd **11**
SW8 . . . . 61 A4
Beaufoy Wlk SE11 **149** A3
Beaulieu Cl SE5 . . . 63 C4
Beaulieu Pl W4 . . . 37 B3
Beaumaris Mans
W2 . . . . **114** B4
Beaumaris Twr **2**
W3 . . . . 37 A4
Beaumont SW15 . . . 58 A2
Beaumont Ave
Richmond TW9 . . . . 54 B4
West Kensington
W14 . . . . **140** C2
Beaumont Bldgs
WC2 . . . . **106** B1
Beaumont Cres
W14 . . . . **140** C1
Beaumont Ct
10 Acton Green
W4 . . . . 37 B1
Marylebone W1 . . **103** C4
1 Mile End E1 . . . 26 A2
Beaumont Gdns
NW3 . . . . 1 C1
Beaumont Gr **1** E1 25 C1
Beaumont Ho
1 Streatham
SW2 . . . . 74 A3
West Kensington
W14 . . . . **141** A4
Wimbledon SW19 . . 70 C1
Beaumont Lo E8 . . 16 C2

Beaumont Pl NW1, WC1,
W1 . . . . **93** A2
Beaumont Rd
Putney SW15,
SW19 . . . . 70 A4
South Acton W4 . . . 37 B3
Beaumont Rise N19 . 4 C3
Beaumont Sq **1** E1 32 C4
Beaumont St W1 . . **103** C4
Beaumont Wlk
NW3 . . . . 12 B1
Beauvale **5**
NW1 . . . . 12 C1
Beauval Rd SE22 . . 64 B1
Beavis Ho N16 . . . . . 7 A1
Beavor La W6 . . . . . 38 C1
Beccles St E14 . . . . 33 B3
Beck Cl SE13 . . . . . 52 A2
Beckers The N16 . . 16 C4
Becket Ho SE1 . . . **137** B3
Becket St SE1 . . . . **137** B2
Beckett Cl
Streatham SW16 . . . 73 C2
Willesden NW10 . . . 8 A2
Beckett Ho
28 London SW9 . **172** B1
11 Stepney E1 . . . 32 B4
Beckfoot NW1 . . . . 83 A1
Beckford Cl W14 . . **141** A3
Beckford Ho **10**
N16 . . . . 16 A3
Beckford Prim Sch
NW6 . . . . 10 B3
Beckham Ho
SE11 . . . . **149** A3
Beck Ho N16 . . . . . . 7 A1
Beckington **18**
NW5 . . . . 12 C2
Beckley Ho **5**
E3 . . . . 26 B1
Becklow Gdns
Chiswick W12 . . . . . 38 B4
7 Shepherd's Bush
W12 . . . . 38 C4
Becklow Mews **7**
W12 . . . . 38 C4
Becklow Rd W12 . . 38 B4
Beck Rd E8 . . . . 25 A4
Beckton Rd E16 . . . 35 B4
Beckway St SE17 **152** A3
Beckwith Ho **22**
E2 . . . . 25 A3
Beckwith Rd SE24 . . 63 C2
Bective Pl SW15 . . . 58 B3
Bective Rd SW15 . . 58 B3
Bedale St SE1 . . . **123** B1
Bedefield WC1 . . . . 94 B3
Bede Ho
London SE14 . . . . 51 B2
5 Putney SW15 . . . 57 C1
Bedford Ave WC1 **105** C3
Bedfordbury WC2 **120** A3
Bedford Cl W4 . . . . 46 B4
Bedford Cnr **3**
W4 . . . . 38 A2
Bedford Court Mans
WC1 . . . . **105** C3
Bedford Ct
8 Richmond TW9 . 54 B3
St James WC2 . . . **120** A3
Bedford Gardens Ho
W8 . . . . **31** C1
Bedford Gdns
W8 . . . . 31 C1 **113** C1
Bedford Ho
2 Acton W4 . . . . . 38 A2
3 Stockwell SW4 . . 62 A3

BEDFORD PARK . . **38** A3
Bedford Park Cnr **5**
W4 . . . . 38 A2
Bedford Park Mans **4**
W4 . . . . 37 C2
Bedford Pas SW6 . **154** B2
Bedford Pl WC1 . . **106** A4
Bedford Rd
Acton W4 . . . . 38 A3
7 Stockwell SW2,
SW4 . . . . 62 A3
Bedford Row
WC1 . . . . **107** A3
Bedford Sq WC1 . . **105** C3
Bedford St WC2 . . **120** B3
Bedford Way WC1 . 93 C1
Bedgebury Gdns
SW19 . . . . 70 A2
Bedlam Mews
SE11 . . . . **149** B4
Bedlow Cl NW8 . . . 89 C1
Bedser Cl SE11 . . . **163** A4
Bedser Ct **7** SW4 **172** A2
Bedwell Ho **8**
SW9 . . . . **173** B1
Beech Ave W3 . . . . 29 A1
Beech Cl
Deptford SE8 . . . . 51 B4
Putney SW15 . . . . 68 C4
Beechcroft Ave
NW11 . . . . 1 B4
Beechcroft Ct **3**
Golders Green
NW11 . . . . 1 B4
Greenwich SE3 . . . 53 C2
Beechcroft Ct SE5 **173** B1
Beechcroft Rd
Mortlake SW14 . . . 55 B4
Upper Tooting
SW17 . . . . 72 A2
Beechcroft Way
N19 . . . . 4 C3
Beech Ct
Child's Hill NW2 . . . 1 B2
Marylebone W1 . . **102** C2
4 Notting Hill W2 . **31** C4
7 Rotherhithe
SE16 . . . . 33 A1
Beechdale Rd
SW2 . . . . 62 B1
Beechdene **4**
SE15 . . . . 50 A2
Beeches Rd SW17 . 72 B1
Beeches The **1**
N19 . . . . 5 A3
Beechey Ho **31** E1 . 32 A1
Beech Gdns W5 . . . 36 A3
Beech Ho
6 Maitland Pk
NW3 . . . . 12 B2
22 Rotherhithe
SE16 . . . . 40 B4
6 Stoke Newington
N16 . . . . 6 C2
Beechmore Rd
SW11 . . . . 169 A3
Beech St EC2 . . . . **109** A4
Beech Tree Cl N1 . **14** C1
Beechwood Ave
TW9 . . . . 44 C2
Beechwood Ct
Chiswick W4 . . . . 45 C4
Stamford Hill N16 . 7 A4
Beechwood Gr
W3 . . . . 29 A2

Beechwood Ho **28**
E2 . . . . 24 C3
Beechwood Rd E8 . 16 B2
Beechworth Cl
NW3 . . . . 1 C2
Beecroft La SE4 . . 66 A2
Beecroft Mews
SE4 . . . . 66 A2
Beecroft Rd SE4 . . 66 A2
Beehive Cl E8 . . . . 16 B1
Beehive Pl SW9 . . 62 C4
Beeston Cl **5** E8 . . 16 C3
Beeston Pl SW1 . . **132** B2
Beeston's Ho SE15 . 65 A4
Beethoven St W10 . 23 A2
Begbie Ho SW9 . . **173** A2
Begonia Wlk W12 . 29 B3
Beira St SW12 . . . 73 A4
Beis Chinuch Lebonos
Girls Sch N4 . . . . . 6 B4
Beis Hamedrash Elyon
NW11 . . . . 1 A4
Beis Malka Girls Sch
N16 . . . . 7 B3
Beis Rochel d'Satmar
Girls Sch **1** N16 . . 7 A4
Bekesbourne St **1**
E14 . . . . 33 A3
Beldanes Lo NW10 . 8 C1
Belenoyd Ct SW16 . 74 B1
Belfast Rd N16 . . . 7 B2
Belfont Wlk N7 . . . 14 A4
Belford Ho **7** E8 . . 24 B4
Belfort Rd SE15 . . 50 B1
Belfry Cl **33** SE16 . 40 A1
Belgrade Ho N16 . . 16 A4
Belgrade Rd N16 . . 16 A4
Belgrave Cl **1** W3 . 37 B4
Belgrave Ct **8**
Acton Green
W4 . . . . 37 B1
2 Limehouse E14 . 33 B2
Nine Elms SW8 . . **160** C1
Belgrave Gdns
Kilburn NW8 . . . . **78** C3
St John's Wood
NW8 . . . . **78** C3
Belgrave Mans
NW8 . . . . **78** C3
Belgrave Mews N
SW1 . . . . **131** B3
Belgrave Mews S
SW1 . . . . **131** C2
Belgrave Mews W
SW1 . . . . **131** B2
Belgrave Pl SW1 . **131** C1
Belgrave Rd
Barnes SW13 . . . . 46 B3
Westminster SW1 . **146** C3
Belgrave Sq SW1 . **131** B2
Belgrave St E1 . . . 32 C3
Belgrave Yd SW1 . **132** A1
BELGRAVIA **146** A4
Belgrave Ct SW1 . **132** A1
Belgravia Ho **11**
SW4 . . . . 61 C1
Belgravia Ct SW1 . 94 B4
Belham Wlk **13**
SE5 . . . . 48 C2
Belinda Rd **8**
SW9 . . . . 63 A4
Belitha Villas N1 . . 14 C1
Bellamy Cl
11 Millwall E14 . . 41 C4
West Kensington
SW5 . . . . **141** A1

Bellamy's Ct **16**
SE16 . . . . 32 C1
Bellamy St SW12 . 73 A4
Bellasis Ave SW2 . 74 A2
Bell Ct SE13 . . . . 66 C2
Bell Dr SW18 . . . . 70 A4
Bellefields Rd
SW9 . . . . 62 B4
Bellenden Prim Sch
5 SE15 . . . . 64 C4
Bellenden Rd
SE15 . . . . 49 B1
Bellenden Rd Ret Pk
SE15 . . . . 49 C2
Bellendon Road Bsns
Ctr SE15 . . . . 49 B1
Bellerbys Coll SE8 . 51 C4
Belleville Prim Sch
SW11 . . . . 60 B2
Belleville Rd SW11 . 60 B2
Belle Vue Gdns
SW9 . . . . **172** B1
Bellevue Pl E1 . . . 25 B1
Bellevue Rd
Barnes SW13 . . . . 46 C1
Upper Tooting
SW17 . . . . 72 B3
Bell Flats **1** NW2 . 8 C2
Bellflower Ct SE13 . 67 A3
Bellgate Mews
NW5 . . . . 4 A1
Bellgrave Lo **9**
W4 . . . . 37 A1
Bell Ho
Greenwich SE10 . . 52 B4
3 Streatham SW4 . 74 A4
Bellina Mews NW5 . 13 B4
Bell Ind Est **2** W4 . 37 B2
Bell Inn Yd EC3 . . **109** C1
Bell La
Newham E16 . . . . 35 C1
Spitalfields E1 . . . **110** C3
Bell Language Sch
W1 . . . . **92** C1
Bellmaker Ct **13**
E3 . . . . 33 C4
Bell Moor NW3 . . . 2 B1
Bello Cl SE24, SW2 . 75 A3
Bellot Gdns **1**
SE10 . . . . 43 A1
Bellot St SE10 . . . 43 A1
Bell St NW1 . . . . . **102** A4
Bell Wharf La
EC4 . . . . **123** A4
Bellwood Rd SE15 . 65 C3
Bell Yard Mews
SE1 . . . . **138** B3
Bell Yd WC2 . . . . **107** B1
Belmont Cl SW4 . . 61 B4
Belmont Ct
Highbury N5 . . . . 15 B4
6 Stamford Hill N16 . 7 A3
Belmont Gr
Chiswick W4 . . . . 37 C2
Lewisham SE13 . . 67 C4
Belmont Hall Ct
SE13 . . . . 67 C4
Belmont Hill SE13 . 67 C4
Belmont Mews
SW19 . . . . 69 C2
Belmont Prim Sch **10**
W4 . . . . 37 C2

Belmont Rd
Clapham SW4.........**61** B4
London W4.............**37** C2
Belmont St NW1....**12** C2
Belmont Terr W4....**37** C2
Belmore Ho N7......**13** C3
Belmore La N7.......**13** C3
Belmore St SW8....**171** B4
Beloe Cl SW18......**56** C3
Belper Ct E9 E5......**17** C4
Belsham St E9 ....**17** B2
Belsize Ave NW3....**11** C3
Belsize Court Garages
 1 NW3..............**11** C3
Belsize Cres NW3...**11** C2
Belsize Gr NW3.....**12** A2
Belsize La NW3......**11** C3
Belsize Mews
 NW3.................**11** C3
Belsize Park Gdns
 NW3.................**12** A3
Belsize Park Mews 11
 NW3.................**11** C2
Belsize Park Sta
 NW3.................**12** A3
Belsize Pk NW3.....**11** C2
Belsize Pl NW3......**11** C3
Belsize Rd NW6....**78** B4
Belsize Sq NW3.....**11** C2
Belsize Terr NW3...**11** C2
Beltane Dr SW19....**69** C1
Belthorn Cres
 SW12................**73** C4
Belton Rd NW2.......**9** A2
Belton Way E3.......**33** C4
Beltran Rd SW6....**166** A1
Belvedere Bldgs
 SE1.................**136** B3
Belvedere Ct
 Brandesbury NW2.....**9** C2
 7 Clapham Pk SW4..**61** C1
 Putney SW15...........**57** C2
 33 Shoreditch N1....**24** A4
Belvedere Htss
 NW8................**90** A2
Belvedere Mews
 SE15................**65** B4
Belvedere Pl
 Brixton SW2..........**62** B3
 Lambeth SE1........**136** B3
Belvedere Rd SE1...**121** A1
Belvedere The
 SW10...............**167** A3
Belvoir Lo SE22....**76** C4
Belvoir Rd SE22....**76** C4
Bembridge Cl
 NW6.................**10** A1
Bembridge Ho
 5 Deptford SE8....**41** B2
 Wandsworth SW18...**59** A4
Bemerton St N1....**84** C4
Bemish Rd SW15...**57** C4
Benabo Ct E8 ......**16** C3
Benbow Ct W6......**39** A3
Benbow Ho 12
 SE8.................**51** C4
Benbow Rd W6.....**39** A3
Benbow St SE8....**51** C4
Bence Ho SE8 ......**41** A2
Bendall Mews
 NW1................**102** B4

Benden Ho SE13.....**67** B2
Bendon Valley
 SW18................**71** A4
Benedict Rd SW9....**62** B4
Benenden Ho
 SE17................**152** B2
Ben Ezra Ct SE17..**151** A3
Benfleet Ct E8 E8....**24** B4
Bengal Ct EC3......**109** C1
Bengal Ho E1........**32** C4
Bengeworth Rd
 SE5.................**63** B4
Benham Cl SW11....**59** C4
Benham Ho SW10..**156** B2
Benham's Pl 11
 NW3.................**11** B4
Benhill Rd SE5......**48** C2
Benington Ct N4.....**6** B2
Benjamin Cl E8......**25** A4
Benjamin Franklin
 House 1 SW1...**120** A2
Benjamin Ho 12
 W3...................**28** A1
Benjamin Mews
 SW12................**73** B4
Ben Jonson Ct 3
 N1...................**24** A3
Ben Jonson Prim Sch
 E1...................**26** A1
Ben Jonson Rd E1..**33** A4
Benledi Rd E14.....**34** C3
Bennelong Cl W12..**30** A3
Bennerley Rd
 SW11................**60** B2
Bennet's Hill EC4...**122** B4
Bennett Ct
 Hampstead NW6.....**11** A2
 Lower Holloway N7...**5** B1
 7 South Acton W3...**37** A4
Bennett Gr SE13....**52** A2
Bennett Ho
 3 Streatham
 SW4..................**73** C4
 Westminster SW1...**147** C4
Bennett St
 Chiswick W4..........**38** A1
 St James SW1......**118** C2
Bennett's Yd SW1..**133** C1
Benn Ho E2......**24** C2 **99** B3
Benn St E9.........**18** A2
Benns Wlk 3
 TW9..................**54** A3
Bensbury Cl SW15..**69** B4
Ben Smith Way 3
 SE16...............**139** C2
Benson Ct
 South Lambeth
 SW8................**172** A4
 1 Tufnell Pk N19....**13** B4
Benson Ho
 Lambeth SE1.......**121** C1
 Shoreditch
 E2.............**24** B1 **98** C2
Benson Quay E1....**32** B2
Benthal Ct N16......**7** C1
Benthal Prim Sch
 N16....................**7** C1
Benthal Rd N16......**7** C1
Bentham Ct 11 N1..**15** B1
Bentham Ho SE1...**137** C2
Bentham Rd E9 .....**17** C2
Bentinck Cl NW8....**80** B1
Bentinck Ho 4
 W12.................**30** A2
Bentinck Mans
 W1..................**103** C2

Bentinck Mews
 W1..................**103** C2
Bentinck St W1....**103** C2
Bentley Ct SW19....**70** C1
Bentley Cl SE13....**67** B3
Bentley Dr NW2....**10** B1
Bentley Ho
 6 Bow E3.........**26** C2
 7 Camberwell SE5...**49** A2
Bentley Rd N1......**16** A2
Bentworth Ct 11
 E2.............**24** C1 **99** B2
Bentworth Prim Sch
 W12.................**30** A3
Bentworth Rd
 W12.................**30** A3
Benwell Rd N7......**14** C3
Benwick Cl SE16....**40** A2
Benworth St E3.....**26** B2
Benyon Ho EC1.....**95** C4
Benyon Rd N1......**87** C4
Benyon Wharf 31
 E8...................**24** A4
Beormund Sch
 SE1.................**137** C3
Bequerel Ct SE10...**43** B3
Berber Pl 1 E14...**33** C2
Berber Rd SW11....**60** B2
Berebinder Ho 21
 E3....................**26** B3
Berenger Twr
 SW10...............**157** B2
Berenger Wlk
 SW10...............**157** B2
Berens Rd NW10...**22** C2
Beresford Ct E9....**18** A3
Beresford Ho
 Dulwich SE21.......**76** A1
 15 Stockwell SW2...**62** C3
Beresford Lo N4....**15** C3
Beresford Rd N5....**15** C3
Beresford Terr 3
 N5...................**15** B3
Bere St E1..........**32** C2
Berestede Rd 4
 W6...................**38** B1
Bergen Ho SE5....**48** B1
Bergen Sq SE16....**41** A3
Berger Prim Sch 30
 E9...................**17** C2
Berger Rd E9.......**17** C2
Berghem Mews
 W14.................**39** C3
Bergholt Cres N16...**7** A4
Bergholt Mews 4
 NW1.................**13** B1
Berglen Ct E14.....**33** A2
Bering Sq E14......**41** C1
Berisford Mews
 SW18................**59** B1
Berkeley Ct
 1 Golders Green
 NW11...............**1** C4
 Marylebone NW1....**91** A1
 Willesden NW10......**8** A4
Berkeley Gdns
 W8.............**31** C1 **113** C1
Berkeley Ho
 17 Bow E3........**26** B2
 2 Deptford SE8....**41** B1
Berkeley Mews
 W1..................**103** A1
Berkeley Rd SW13..**46** C2
Berkeley Sq W1...**118** B3
Berkeley St W1....**118** B2

Bentinck Mews
 W1..................**103** C2
Berkeley The NW11..**2** A4
Berkeley Wlk 1 N7...**5** B2
Berkley Gr NW1....**12** C1
Berkley Rd NW1...**12** B1
Berkshire Ho
 WC2................**106** A2
Berkshire Rd E9...**18** B2
Bermans Way
 NW10.................**8** A4
BERMONDSEY....**40** A4
Bermondsey Leather
 Mkt SE1..........**138** A3
Bermondsey Sq
 SE1.................**138** B2
Bermondsey St
 SE1.................**138** B2
Bermondsey Sta
 SE16................**40** A3
Bermondsey Trad Est
 SE16................**40** B1
Bermondsey Wall E
 SE16................**40** B4
Bermondsey Wall W
 SE1, SE16..........**139** B4
Bernard Angell Ho 1
 SE10.................**52** C4
Bernard Cassidy St 2
 E16...................**35** B4
Bernard Ho E1....**110** C3
Bernard Shaw Ct 5
 NW1.................**13** B1
Bernard Shaw Ho 2
 NW10.................**20** C4
Bernard St WC1....**94** B1
Bernay's Gr SW9...**62** B3
Berners Ho N1......**85** B2
Berners Mews
 W1..................**105** A3
Berners Pl W1.....**105** A2
Berners Rd N1......**86** A3
Berners St W1.....**105** A2
Berner Terr 27 E1..**111** C1
Bernhard Baron Ho 2
 E1...................**111** C1
Bernhardt Cres
 NW8.................**90** A2
Bernie Grant Ho 40
 E9...................**17** B1
Bernwood Ho 6
 N4....................**6** C4
Berridge Mews
 NW6.................**10** C3
Berriman Rd N7......**5** B1
Berry Cotts 2 E14..**33** A3
Berry Ct SW9........**62** C4
Berryfield Rd
 SE17................**150** B2
Berry Ho
 10 Battersea
 SW11...............**169** A2
 25 Bethnal Green
 E1...................**25** A1
Berrymead Gdns
 W3...................**37** B4
Berrymede Inf Sch
 W3...................**37** A4
Berrymede Jun Sch
 W3...................**37** A4
Berrymede Rd W4..**37** C3
Berry Pl EC1........**96** B3
Berry St EC1........**96** B1
Berry Way W5......**36** A3
Bertha Neubergh Ho
 4 SE5..............**48** B2
Berthon St SE8....**51** C4
Bertie Rd NW10.....**8** C2
Bertram St N19....**4** A2

Bertrand Ho 11
 SW16................**74** A1
Bertrand St SE13...**67** A4
Bertrum House Sch
 SW17................**72** C2
Berwick St W1....**105** A1
Berwick Street Mkt*
 W1..................**105** A1
Berwyn Rd
 Mortlake SW14,
 TW10.................**55** A3
 Streatham SE24.....**75** A3
Beryl Rd W6.........**39** C1
Besant Cl NW2.......**1** A1
Besant Ct N1........**15** C3
Besant Ho NW8....**78** C3
Besant Pl SE22....**64** B3
Besant Rd NW2.....**10** A4
Besant Wlk N7.......**5** B2
Besford Ho 20 E2..**24** C3
Bessant Dr TW9....**45** A2
Bessborough Gdns
 SW1.................**147** C2
Bessborough Pl
 SW1.................**147** C2
Bessborough St
 SW1.................**147** B2
Bessemer Ct 7
 NW1.................**13** B1
Bessemer Grange
 Prim Sch SE5....**64** A3
Bessemer Park Ind
 Est SE24..........**63** A3
Bessemer Rd SE5...**48** B1
Bessingham Wlk
 SE4...................**65** C2
Besson St SE14.....**50** C2
Bessy St E2.........**25** B2
Bestwood St SE8...**40** C2
Beswick Mews 11
 NW6.................**11** A2
Beta Pl 20 SW4....**62** B3
Betchworth Ho 8
 N7....................**13** C3
Bethersden Ho
 SE17................**152** B2
Bethlehem Ho 11
 E14...................**33** B2
BETHNAL GREEN..**25** A2
Bethnal Green Rd
 Bethnal Green
 E2..............**24** C2 **99** B3
 Spitalfields
 E1.............**24** B1 **99** A2
Bethnal Green Sta
 Bethnal Green E1....**25** B1
 Bethnal Green E2....**25** B2
Bethnal Green Tech
 Coll 50 E2....**24** B2 **99** A3
Bethune Rd
 North Acton NW10...**20** C1
 Stamford Hill N16....**7** A4
Bethwin Rd SE5....**48** B3
Betsham Ho SE1...**137** B4
Betterton Ho
 WC2................**106** B1
Betterton St WC2..**106** B1
Bettridge Rd SW6..**165** A1
Betts Ho E1.........**32** A2
Betts St E1..........**32** A2
Betty Layward Prim
 Sch 1 N16.......**6** C1

Betty May Gray Ho **2**
E14 . . . . 42 B2
Bevan St N1 . . . . 87 A3
Bev Callender Cl **4**
SW8 . . . . 61 A4
Bevenden St N1 . . . . 97 C4
Beveridge Rd **1**
NW10 . . . . 8 A1
Beverley Cl
Barnes SW13 . . . . . . 46 C1
6 Wandsworth
SW11 . . . . 59 C3
Beverley Cotts
SW15 . . . . 68 A1
Beverley Ct
9 Acton Green
W4 . . . . 37 B2
8 Acton W12 . . . . . 38 A4
Brockley SE4 . . . . . . 66 B4
Islington N5 . . . . 15 A2
Beverley Gdns
Barnes SW13 . . . . . . 56 B4
Hendon NW11 . . . . . . 1 A4
Beverley Lo **6**
TW10 . . . . 54 A2
Beverley Path **5**
SW13 . . . . 46 B1
Beverley Rd
Barnes SW13 . . . . . . 56 B4
Chiswick W4 . . . . 38 B1
Beversbrook Rd
N19 . . . . 4 C2
Beverstone Rd
SW2 . . . . 62 B2
Beverston Mews
NW1 . . . . 102 C3
Bevin Cl SE16 . . . . . 33 A1
Bevin Ct WC1 . . . . . . 95 A4
Bevington Prim Sch
18 W10 . . . . 31 A4
Bevington Rd W10 . . 31 A4
Bevington St
SE16 . . . . 139 C3
Bevin Ho
18 Bethnal Green
E2 . . . . 25 B2
8 Bow E3 . . . . 26 C2
Bevin Sq SW17 . . . . . 72 B1
Bevin Way WC1 . . . . 95 B4
Bevis Marks EC3 . . 110 B2
Bew Ct SE21 . . . . . . 76 C4
Bewdley Ho N4 . . . . . 6 B4
Bewdley St N1 . . . . . 14 C1
Bewick Mews
SE15 . . . . 50 A3
Bewick St SW8 . . . . 170 B1
Bewley Ct SW2 . . . . . 62 B1
Bewley Ho **7** E1 . . . 32 A2
Bewley St E1 . . . . . . 32 A2
Bexhill Rd
Catford SE4 . . . . 66 B1
Mortlake SW14 . . . . . 55 B4
Bexley Ho SE4 . . . . . 66 A3
BFI Imax (Cinema)
SE1 . . . . 121 B1
BFI Southbank *
SE1 . . . . 121 A2
Bianca Rd SE1,
SE15 . . . . 49 C4
Bicester Rd TW9 . . . 54 C4
Bickenhall Mans
W1 . . . . 103 A4
Bickenhall St W1 . . 103 A4
Bickerton Rd N19 . . . 4 B2
Bicknell Ho **24** E1 . 111 C1
Bicknell Rd SE5 . . . . 63 B4

Bicknor Ho **2** E5 . . 17 A3
Bidborough St N1,
WC1 . . . . 94 A3
Biddenham Ho **18**
SE16 . . . . 40 C2
Bidder St E16 . . . . . 35 A4
Biddesden Ho
SW3 . . . . 144 C3
Biddestone Rd N7 . . 14 B4
Biddulph Mans
W9 . . . . 88 B3
Biddulph Rd W9 . . . . 88 B3
Bidwell St SE15 . . . . 50 A2
Big Ben * SW1 . . . 134 B3
Biggerstaff Rd
E15 . . . . 27 B4
Biggerstaff St N4 . . . 5 C2
Bigg's Row SW15 . . . 57 C4
Biggs Sq **9** E9 . . . . 18 B2
Bigland Green Prim
Sch **31** E1 . . . . . . 32 A3
Bigland St E1 . . . . . 32 A3
Bilberry Ho **13** E3 . 33 C4
Billie Holiday Ct
NW10 . . . . 20 C3
Billingford Cl SE4 . . 65 C3
Billing Ho **7** E1 . . . 32 B3
Billingley W1 . . . . . . 82 C3
Billing Pl SW10 . . . 156 B2
Billing Rd SW10 . . . 156 B2
Billingsgate Mkt
E14 . . . . 34 A1
Billing St SW10 . . . 156 B2
Billington Ho
SW8 . . . . 171 C3
Billington Rd SE14 . . 50 C3
Billiter Sq EC3 . . . . 110 B1
Billiter St EC3 . . . . 110 B1
Billson St E14 . . . . . 42 B2
Bilton Ho SW8 . . . . 171 B3
Bilton Twrs W1 . . . . 103 A1
Bina Gdns SW5 . . . 142 C3
Binbrook Ho **3**
W10 . . . . 30 B4
Binden Rd W12 . . . . 38 B3
Binfield Ct SE5 . . . . 48 B1
Binfield Rd SW4 . . . 172 B3
Bingfield St N1 . . . . 84 C4
Bingham Pl W1 . . . . 103 B4
Bingham St N1 . . . . . 15 C2
Binley Ho SW15 . . . 56 B1
Binney St W1 . . . . . 103 C1
Binnie Ct SE10 . . . . 52 A3
Binnie Ho SE1 . . . . 136 C1
Binns Rd W4 . . . . . . 38 A1
Binns Terr **3** W4 . . 38 A1
Binstead Ho SW18 . . 59 A1
Binyon Ho **8** N16 . . 16 A4
Birbeck Ho **4** N19 . . 4 C3
Bircham Path SE4 . . 65 C3
Birch Cl
Newham E16 . . . . . . 35 A4
Peckham SE15 . . . . 49 C1
Upper Holloway N19 . 4 B2
Birchdown Ho **12**
E3 . . . . 27 A2
Birches The SE5 . . . 49 A1
Birchfield Ho **3**
E14 . . . . 33 C2
Birchfield St E14 . . . 33 C2
Birchgrove Ho
TW9 . . . . 45 A3
Birch Ho
New Cross Gate
SE14 . . . . 51 B2
8 Tulse Hill SW2 . 62 C1

Birchington Ct **2**
NW6 . . . . 78 A4
Birchington Ho **1**
E5 . . . . 17 A3
Birchington Rd
NW6 . . . . 23 C4
Birchin La EC3 . . . 109 C1
Birchlands Ave
SW12 . . . . 72 B4
Birchmere Lo **18**
SE16 . . . . 40 A1
Birchmere Row
SE3 . . . . 53 B1
Birchmore Wlk N5 . . 6 B1
Birch Vale Ct NW8 . 89 C2
Birchwood Dr NW3 . . 2 A1
Birdcage Wlk
SW1 . . . . 133 B3
Birdhurst Rd
SW18 . . . . 59 B2
Bird In Bush Rd
SE15 . . . . 49 C3
Bird In Hand Yd **24**
NW3 . . . . 11 B4
Birdsall Ho **5** SE5 . 64 A4
Birdsfield La **2**
E3 . . . . 26 B4
Bird St W1 . . . . 103 C1
Birdwood Ave **4**
SE13 . . . . 67 C1
Birkbeck Ave **3** W3 28 B2
Birkbeck Coll W1 . . 105 B2
Birkbeck Ct **3** W3 . 28 C1
Birkbeck Gr W3 . . . . 37 C4
Birkbeck Hill SE21 . . 75 A3
Birkbeck Mews **5**
E8 . . . . 16 B3
Birkbeck Pl SE21 . . . 75 B2
Birkbeck Rd
Acton W3 . . . . 28 C1
Dalston E8 . . . . 16 B3
Birkbeck St E2 . . . . . 25 A2
Birkbeck Univ of
London W1 . . . . . . 93 B2
Birkdale Cl **30**
SE16 . . . . 40 A1
Birkenhead Ho **11**
N7 . . . . 14 C3
Birkenhead St
WC1 . . . . 94 B4
Birkwood Cl SW12 . . 73 C4
Birley Lo NW8 . . . . . 79 C2
Birley St SW11 . . . 169 B1
Birnam Rd N4 . . . . . . 5 B2
Birrell Ho **9** SW9 . 172 C1
Birse Cres NW10 . . . 8 A4
Birtwhistle Ho **5**
E3 . . . . 26 B4
Biscay Ho **11** E1 . . . 25 C1
Biscay Rd W6 . . . . . . 39 C1
Biscoe Way SE13 . . . 67 C4
Biscott Ho **3** E3 . . . 27 A1
Bisham Gdns N6 . . . . 3 C3
Bishop Challoner
Collegiate Sch **20**
E1 . . . . 32 B3
Bishop **20** SW2 . . 62 C2
Bishop Duppa's
Almshouses **7**
TW10 . . . . 54 A2
Bishop King's Rd
W14 . . . . 140 B4
Bishop's Ave SW6 . 164 A2
Bishop's Bridge Rd
W2 . . . . 100 C2
Bishops Cl W4 . . . . . 37 B1

Bishop's Cl N19 . . . . . 4 B1
Bishops Ct
15 Bayswater W2 . 100 B2
Richmond TW9 . . . . . 54 A4
Bishop's Ct
Holborn EC4 . . . . . 108 A2
Holborn WC2 . . . . . 107 B2
Bishopsdale Ho **6**
NW6 . . . . 23 C4
Bishopsgate EC2 . . 110 A2
Bishopsgate Arc
E1 . . . . 110 B3
Bishopsgate
Churchyard EC2 . . 110 A2
Bishopsgate Inst
EC2 . . . . 110 B3
Bishops Ho SW8 . . 162 B1
Bishop's Mans
SW6 . . . . 47 C1
Bishops Mead SE5 . . 48 B3
Bishop's Park Rd
SW6 . . . . 47 C1
Bishops Rd SW6 . . 164 C4
Bishops Sq E1 . . . . 110 B4
Bishop St N1 . . . . . . 86 C4
Bishop's Terr
SE11 . . . . 149 C4
Bishopstone Ho **1**
SW11 . . . . 169 B2
Bishop's Way E2 . . . 25 B3
Bishopswood Rd
N6 . . . . 3 B4
Bishop Wilfred Wood
Cl SE15 . . . . 49 C1
Bisley Ho SW19 . . . . 69 C2
Bissextile Ho SE13 . . 52 A1
Bisson Rd E15 . . . . . 27 B3
Bittern Ho **7** SE8 . . 51 C4
Bittern Ho SE1 . . . 136 C3
Bittern St SE1 . . . . 136 C3
Blackall St
EC2 . . . . 24 A1 98 A2
Blackburn Ct **21**
SW2 . . . . 62 C1
Blackburn's Mews
W1 . . . . 117 B3
Blackburn Rd
NW6 . . . . 11 A2
Blackdown Ho E8 . . . 16 C4
Blackett St SW15 . . . 57 C4
Blackfriars Bridge
EC4 . . . . 122 A3
Blackfriars Ct
EC4 . . . . 122 A4
Black Friars La
EC4 . . . . 108 A1
Blackfriars Pas
EC4 . . . . 122 A4
Blackfriars Pier
EC4 . . . . 122 A4
Blackfriars Rd
SE1 . . . . 122 A1
Blackfriars Underpass
EC4 . . . . 121 C4
Blackheath * SE3 . . 53 A2
Blackheath Ave
SE3 . . . . 53 A3
Blackheath Bsns Est
SE10 . . . . 52 B2
Blackheath Gr SE3 . . 53 B1
Blackheath High Jun
Sch SE3 . . . . 53 B1
Blackheath High Sch
SE3 . . . . 53 C3
Blackheath Hill
SE10 . . . . 52 B2

Blackheath Prep Sch
SE3 . . . . 53 C2
Blackheath Rd
SE10 . . . . 52 A2
Blackheath Rise
SE13 . . . . 52 A1
BLACKHEATH
VALE 53 B1
Blackheath Vale
SE3 . . . . 53 A1
Blackheath Village
SE3 . . . . 53 B1
Black Horse Ct
SE1 . . . . 137 C2
Blackhorse Rd
SE8 . . . . 51 A4
Blacklands Terr
SW3 . . . . 145 A3
Black Lion La W6 . . . 38 C2
Black Lion Mews **4**
W6 . . . . 38 C2
Blackmore Ho
Islington N1 . . . . 85 A3
2 Wandsworth
SW18 . . . . 59 C3
Blackmore Twr **1**
W3 . . . . 37 B3
Blackpool Rd
SE15 . . . . 50 A1
Black Prince Rd SE1,
SE11 . . . . 149 A3
Black Roof Ho **9**
SE5 . . . . 48 A2
Black's Rd W6 . . . . . 39 B2
Blackstock Ho **2**
N5 . . . . 6 A1
Blackstock Mews
N4 . . . . 6 A1
Blackstock Rd N4,
N5 . . . . 6 A2
Blackstone Ho
Dulwich SE21 . . . . . 76 A1
Pimlico SW1 . . . . . 146 C1
Blackstone Rd NW2 . 9 B4
Black Swan Yd
SE1 . . . . 138 A4
Blackthorn Ct
20 Camberwell
SE5 . . . . 49 B3
4 Leyton E15 . . . 19 C4
Blackthorn St E3 . . . 26 C1
Blacktree Mews **11**
SW9 . . . . 62 C4
BLACKWALL 34 C2
Blackwall Sta E14 . . 34 B2
Blackwall Trad Est
SE10 . . . . 34 C2
Blackwall Tunnel E14,
SE10 . . . . 34 C4
Blackwall Tunnel App
E14, E3 . . . . 27 B1
Blackwall Tunnel
Northern Approach
E14, E3 . . . . 27 B1
Blackwall Way
E14 . . . . 34 B2
Blackwater Ho
NW8 . . . . 101 C4
Blackwater St
SE22 . . . . 64 B2
Blackwell Cl **16** E5 . 17 C4
Blackwell Ho **3**
SW4 . . . . 61 C1

Blackwood Ho **11**
  E1 . . . . 25 A1
Blackwood St
  SE17 . . . . 151 B2
Blade Mews SW15 . . 58 B3
Bladen Ho **4** E1 . . . 32 C3
Blades Ct
  4 Hammersmith
  W6 . . . . 39 A1
  Putney SW15 . . . . . . 58 B3
Blades Ho
  SE11 . . . . 163 B3
Blades Lo **10** SW2 . . 62 C1
Blagdon Rd SE13 . . . 67 A1
Blagrove Rd **1**
  W10 . . . . 31 B4
Blair Cl N1 . . . . 15 B2
Blair Ct NW8 . . . . . . 79 B4
Blairderry Rd SW2 . . 74 A2
Blairgowrie Ct **13**
  E14 . . . . 34 C3
Blair Ho SW9 . . . . . 172 C2
Blair St E14 . . . . 34 C3
Blake Coll W1 . . . . . 104 C4
Blake Ct
  8 Bermondsey
  SE16 . . . . 40 A1
  Kilburn NW6 . . . . 23 C2
Blake Gdns SW6 . . . 166 A4
Blake Ho
  2 Deptford SE8 . . . 51 C4
  Isle Of Dogs E14 . . . 42 A4
  1 Kentish Town
  N19 . . . . 13 C3
  Lambeth SE11 . . . . . 135 B2
  14 Stoke Newington
  N16 . . . . 16 A4
Blake Mews **15**
  TW9 . . . . 44 C2
Blakemore Rd
  SW16 . . . . 74 A1
Blakeney Cl
  5 Camden Town
  NW1 . . . . 13 C1
  4 Dalston E8 . . . . . 16 C3
Blakenham Ct
  W12 . . . . 29 C1
Blaker Rd E15 . . . . . . 27 B4
Blakes Cl W10 . . . . . 30 B4
Blake's Rd SE15 . . . . 49 A3
Blanca Ho **11** N1 . . . 24 A3
Blanchard Way E8 . . 16 C2
Blanch Cl SE15 . . . . . 50 B3
Blanchedowne
  SE5 . . . . 63 C3
Blandfield Rd
  SW12 . . . . 72 C4
Blandford Ct
  Brondesbury Pk
  NW6 . . . . 10 A1
  6 De Beauvoir Town
  N1 . . . . 16 A1
Blandford Ho
  SW8 . . . . 162 C2
Blandford Rd W4 . . . 38 A3
Blandford Sq NW1 . . 90 B1
Blandford St W1 . . . 103 B3
Bland Ho SE11 . . . . 149 A2
Blantyre St SW10 . . 157 B2
Blantyre Twr
  SW10 . . . . 157 B2
Blantyre Wlk
  SW10 . . . . 157 B2
Blashford NW3 . . . . . 12 B1

Blasker Wlk **8**
  E14 . . . . 42 A1
Blaxland Ho **12**
  W12 . . . . 30 A2
Blazer Ct NW8 . . . . . 89 C3
Blechynden Ho **17**
  W10 . . . . 30 C3
Blechynden St
  W10 . . . . 30 C2
Bleeding Heart Yd
  EC1 . . . . 107 C3
Blemundsbury
  WC1 . . . . 106 C4
Blendworth Point **4**
  SW15 . . . . 69 A3
Blenheim **25** SW19 . 69 C3
Blenheim Cres
  Notting Hill W11 . . . 31 A3
  Notting Hill
  W11 . . . . 31 A2 112 B4
Blenheim Ct
  Barnsbury N7 . . . . . . 14 A2
  Richmond TW9 . . . . . 54 B4
  7 Rotherhithe
  SE16 . . . . 32 C1
  Upper Holloway N19 . . 5 A2
Blenheim Gdns
  Clapham Pk SW2 . . 62 B1
  Dollis Hill NW2 . . . . . . 9 B3
Blenheim Gr SE15 . . 49 C1
Blenheim Pas
  NW8 . . . . 78 C2
Blenheim Rd
  Acton W4 . . . . 38 A3
  St John's Wood
  NW8 . . . . 79 A2
Blenheim St W1 . . . 104 A1
Blenheim Terr
  NW8 . . . . 78 C2
Blenkarne Rd
  SW11 . . . . 60 B1
Blessed Sacrament
  RC Prim Sch N1 . . . 84 C3
Blessington Cl
  SE13 . . . . 67 C4
Blessington Rd
  SE13 . . . . 67 C3
Bletchley Ct N1 . . . . 87 B1
Bletchley St N1 . . . . 87 A1
Bletsoe Wlk N1 . . . . 87 A2
Blick Ho **1** SE16 . . . 40 B3
Blincoe Cl SW19 . . . 69 C2
Blissett St SE10 . . . . 52 B2
Bliss Mews **14**
  W10 . . . . 23 A2
Blisworth Ho **2**
  E2 . . . . 24 C4
Blithfield St W8 . . . 128 A1
Bloemfontein Ave
  W12 . . . . 30 A1
Bloemfontein Rd
  W12 . . . . 30 A2
Blomfield Ct
  Battersea SW11 . . . 167 C4
  Paddington W9 . . . . . 89 A2
Blomfield Ho **4**
  E14 . . . . 34 A2
Blomfield Mans **3**
  W12 . . . . 30 B1
Blomfield Rd W9 . . . 100 C4
Blomfield St EC2 . . . 109 C3
Blomfield Villas
  W9 . . . . 100 C4
Blondel St SW11 . . . 169 B2
Blondin St E3 . . . . . . 26 C3

Bloomburg St
  SW1 . . . . 147 A3
Bloomfield Ho **13**
  E1 . . . . 111 B3
Bloomfield Pl W1 . . 118 B4
Bloomfield Terr
  SW1 . . . . 145 C2
Bloom Gr SE27 . . . . . 75 A1
Bloom Park Rd
  SW6 . . . . 154 C1
Bloomsbury Space*
  EC1 . . . . 109 C4
BLOOMSBURY 106 A4
Bloomsbury Ct
  WC1 . . . . 106 B3
Bloomsbury Ho **10**
  SW4 . . . . 61 C1
Bloomsbury
  International
  Language Sch
  WC1 . . . . 106 B3
Bloomsbury Pl
  London SW18 . . . . . . 59 B2
  St Giles WC1 . . . . . . 106 B3
Bloomsbury Sq
  WC1 . . . . 106 B3
Bloomsbury St
  WC1 . . . . 105 C3
Bloomsbury Way
  WC1 . . . . 106 B3
Blore Cl SW8 . . . . . . 171 B3
Blore Ct W1 . . . . 119 B4
Blore Ho SW10 . . . . 156 B2
Blossom Cl W5 . . . . . 36 A4
Blossom Pl
  E1 . . . . 24 A1 98 B1
Blossom St
  E1 . . . . 24 A1 98 B1
Blount St E14 . . . . . . 33 A3
Blucher Rd SE5 . . . . 48 B3
Blue Anchor Alley **1**
  TW9 . . . . 54 A3
Blue Anchor La
  SE16 . . . . 40 A2
Blue Anchor Yd
  E1 . . . . 125 B4
Blue Ball Yd SW1 . . 118 C1
Bluebell Cl **8** E9 . . 25 B4
Blue Gate Fields Jun
  & Inf Schs **23** E1 . . 32 B2
Bluegate Mews
  E1 . . . . 32 A2
Blue Lion Pl SE1 . . . 138 A2
Brigstlet Apartments
  13 SW12 . . . . 73 A4
Blundell Cl E8 . . . . . . 16 C4
Blundell St N7 . . . . . 14 A2
Blurton Rd E5 . . . . . . 17 C4
Blyth Cl E14 . . . . 42 C2
Blythe Ho **8**
  SE11 . . . . 163 C4
Blythe Mews **2**
  W14 . . . . 39 C3
Blythendale Ho **14**
  E2 . . . . 24 C3
Blythe Rd W14 . . . . 126 A1
Blythe St E2 . . . . 25 A2
Blyth's Wharf E14 . . 33 A2
Blythwood Rd N4 . . . . 5 A4
BMI Fitzroy Square
  Hospl w1 . . . . 92 C1
Bnois Jerusalem Girls
  Sch **2** N16 . . . . . . 6 C4
Boades Mews **3**
  NW3 . . . . 11 C4
Boadicea St N1 . . . . 84 C3

Boardwalk Pl E14 . . 34 B1
Boarley Ho SE17 . . . 152 A3
Boathouse Ctr The
  W10 . . . . 22 C1
Boathouse Wlk **23**
  SE15 . . . . 49 B3
Boat Lifter Way **11**
  SE16 . . . . 41 A2
Bobbin Cl SW4 . . . . . 61 B3
Bob Marley Way **1**
  SE24 . . . . 62 C3
Boby Foundation
  Sch **4** N16 . . . . . . 7 B4
Bocking St E8 . . . . . . 25 A4
Boddicott Cl SW19 . 70 A2
Boddington Gdns
  W3 . . . . 36 C4
Bodington Ho **2**
  SE14 . . . . 50 B2
Bodeney Ho **10**
  SE5 . . . . 49 A2
Boden Ho **6** E1 . . . 111 B4
Bodington Ct **2**
  W12 . . . . 39 C4
Bodley Manor Way
  SE24 . . . . 74 C4
Bodmin St SW18 . . . 70 C3
Bodney Rd E5, E8 . . 17 A3
Bogart Ct E14 **3** . . 33 C2
Bohemia Pl **1** E8 . . 17 A2
Bohn Rd E1 . . . . 33 A4
Boileau Rd SW13 . . . 47 A4
Boilerhouse SE1 . . . 124 C1
Boisseau Ho **31** E1 . 32 B4
Bolden St SE8 . . . . . . 52 A1
Boldero Pl NW8 . . . . 90 A1
Boleyn Rd N16 . . . . . 16 A3
Bolina Rd SE16 . . . . . 40 B1
Bolingbroke Gr
  SW11 . . . . 60 B1
Bolingbroke Rd
  W14 . . . . 39 C3
Bolingbroke Wlk
  SW11 . . . . 168 A4
Bollo Bridge Rd
  W3 . . . . 37 B4
Bollo Ct **2** W3 . . . . 37 B3
Bollo La W3 . . . . 37 A3
Bolney Gate **3** SW7 130 A3
Bolney St SW8 . . . . 162 C1
Bolsover St W1 . . . . . 92 B1
Bolt Ct EC4 . . . . 107 C1
Bolton Cres SE5 . . . . 48 A3
Bolton Ct SW11 . . . 169 C3
Bolton Gdns
  Kensal Rise NW10 . . 22 C3
  South Kensington
  SW5 . . . . 142 B2
Bolton Gdns Mews
  SW10 . . . . 142 C2
Bolton Ho **5** SE10 . 43 A1
Bolton Pl SW5 . . . . . 142 C2
Bolton Rd
  Chiswick W4 . . . . 45 B3
  Harlesden NW10 . . . 21 A4
  1 Kensal Rise
  NW8 . . . . 78 B3
Boltons Cl SW5 . . . . 142 B2
Boltons Ct SW5 . . . . 142 B2
Bolton St W1 . . . . . . 118 B2
Boltons The
  SW10 . . . . 142 C2
Bolton Studios
  SW10 . . . . 143 A1
Bolton Wlk N7 . . . . . . 5 B2
Bombay Ct **8**
  SE16 . . . . 40 B4
Bombay St SE16 . . . . 40 A2

Bomore Rd
  W11 . . . . . . 31 A2 112 A4
Bonar Rd SE15 . . . . . 49 C3
Bonchurch Rd
  W10 . . . . 31 A4
Bond Ct EC4 . . . . . . 109 B1
Bond Ho N1 **4** NW6 . 23 C3
Bonding Yard Wlk
  SE16 . . . . 41 A3
Bond St **4** 37 C2
Bond Street Sta
  W1 . . . . 103 C1
Bondway SW8 . . . . . 162 B4
Bonfield Rd SE13 . . . 67 B3
Bonham Ho
  W11 . . . . 31 B1 112 C2
Bonham Rd SW2 . . . 62 B2
Bonheur Rd W4 . . . . 37 C4
Bonhill St EC2 . . . . . 97 C1
Boningham Ho N1 . . 84 C1
Bonita Mews SE15 . . 65 C4
Bonner Ho **3**
  SW15 . . . . 56 C2
Bonner Prim Sch **30**
  E2 . . . . 25 B2
Bonner Rd E2 . . . . . . 25 B3
Bonner St E2 . . . . . . 25 B3
Bonneville Gdns
  SW4 . . . . 61 B1
Bonneville Prim Sch
  SW4 . . . . 61 B1
Bonnington Sq
  SW8 . . . . 162 C4
Bonny St NW1 . . . . . 13 B1
Bonsor Ho SW8 . . . 171 A4
Bonsor St SE5 . . . . . 49 A3
Bonthron Ho
  SW15 . . . . 47 B1
Booker Cl **11** E3 . . . 33 B4
Boord St SE10 . . . . . 43 A3
Boothby Rd N19 . . . . 4 C2
Booth Cl **10** E9 . . . 25 A4
Booth Ho **2** SW2 . . 74 C4
Booth La EC4 . . . . . . 122 C4
Booth's Pl W1 . . . . . 105 A3
Booth Ho N1 . . 24 A2 98 A3
Bordon Wlk **8**
  SW15 . . . . 68 C4
Boreas Wlk N1 . . . . . 86 B1
Boreham Ave E16 . . 35 C3
Boreman Ho **11**
  SE10 . . . . 52 B4
Borland Rd SE15 . . . 65 B3
Borneo St SW15 . . . 57 B4
Borough High St
  SE1 . . . . 123 B2
Borough Mkt*
  SE1 . . . . 123 B1
Borough Rd SE1 . . . 136 B2
Borough Sq SE1 . . . 136 C3
Borough Sta SE1 . . . 137 A3
BOROUGH THE . . . 136 C4
Borrett Cl SE17 . . . . 150 C1
Borrodaile Rd
  SW18 . . . . 59 A1
Borrowdale NW1 . . . 92 C3
Borthwick St SE8 . . . 41 C1
Boscastle Rd NW5 . . . 4 A1
Boscobel Ho
  E8 . . . . 17 A2
Boscobel Pl SW1 . . 145 C4
Boscobel St NW8 . . . 89 C1
Boscombe Cl E5 . . . 18 A3
Boscombe Rd
  W12 . . . . 38 C4
Boss Ho SE1 . . . . . . 138 C4

Boss St SE1 . . . . 138 C4
Boston Gdns W4 . . . . 46 A4
Boston Ho
24 Camberwell
SE5 . . . . 48 B1
Earl's Ct SW5 . . . . . 142 B3
Lisson Gr NW1 . . . . . 90 C2
Boston Pl NW1 . . . . . 90 C1
Bosun Cl 22 E14 . . . . 41 C4
Boswell Ct
Bloomsbury WC1 . . 106 B4
9 Hammersmith
W14 . . . . 39 C3
Boswell Ho WC1 . . . 106 B4
Boswell St WC1 . . . . 106 B4
Bosworth Ho 4
W10 . . . . 23 A1
Bosworth Rd W10 . . 23 A1
Bothwell Cl E16 . . . . 35 B4
Bothwell St 4 W6 . . 47 C4
Botolph Alley EC3 124 A4
Botolph La EC3 . . . . 124 A4
Bott's Mews W2 . . . . 31 C3
Boughton Ho SE1 137 B4
Boulcott St E1 . . . . . 32 C3
Boulevard The
Chelsea SW6 . . . . . 167 A3
4 Upper Tooting
SW17 . . . . 72 C2
Boulogne Ho SE1 138 C2
Boulter Ho 4
SE14 . . . . 50 B2
Boulton Ho TW8 . . . 36 A1
Boundaries Mans 3
SW12 . . . . 72 C3
Boundaries Rd
SW12 . . . . 72 C3
Boundary Ho
Balham SW12 . . . . . 73 A3
1 Camberwell SE5 . 48 B3
15 Notting Hill W11 30 C1
Boundary La SE17 . . 48 B4
Boundary Pas
E2 . . . . 24 B1 98 C2
Boundary Rd NW8 . 79 A4
Boundary Road Est
NW8 . . . . 78 C3
Boundary Row
SE1 . . . . 136 A4
Boundary St
E2 . . . . 24 B1 98 C2
Bourchier St W1 . . . 119 B4
Bourdon Pl W1 . . . . 118 B4
Bourdon St W1 . . . . 118 B3
Bourke Cl
London SW4 . . . . . . 62 A1
Willesden NW10 . . . . 8 A2
Bourlet Cl W1 . . . . . 104 C3
Bourne Ct W4 . . . . . 45 B4
Bourne Ho 5
SW4 . . . . 61 B3
Bourne Mews W1 103 C1
Bournemouth Cl
SE15 . . . . 49 C1
Bournemouth Rd
SE15 . . . . 49 C1
Bourne Pl W4 . . . . . 37 C1
Bourne St SW1 . . . . 145 B3
Bourne Terr W2 . . . 100 B4
Bousfield Prim Sch
SW10 . . . . 142 C2
Bousfield Rd SE14 . 50 C1
Boutcher CE Prim Sch
SE1 . . . . 152 C4
Boutflower Rd
SW11 . . . . 60 A3

Bouverie Mews
N16 . . . . 7 A2
Bouverie Pl W2 . . . 101 C2
Bouverie Rd N16 . . . 7 A2
Bouverie St EC4 . . . 107 C1
Bovingdon Cl
N19 . . . . 4 B2
Bovingdon Rd
SW6 . . . . 166 B3
Bowater Cl SW2 . . . 62 A1
Bowater Ho EC1 . . . 97 A1
Bow Brook The 20
E2 . . . . 25 C3
Bow Church Sta
E3 . . . . 26 C2
BOW COMMON . . . 34 A4
Bow Common La
E3 . . . . 26 B1
Bowden Ho 2 E3 . . 27 A2
Bowden St SE11 . . . 149 C1
Bowditch SE8 . . . . . 41 B1
Bowen Ct 2 N5 . . . 15 A4
Bowen Dr SE21 . . . . 76 A1
Bowen St E14 . . . . . 34 A3
Bower Ave SE3 . . . . 53 A3
Bowerdean St
SW6 . . . . 166 A3
Bowerman Ave
SE14 . . . . 51 A4
Bowerman Ct 4
N19 . . . . 4 C2
Bower St E1 . . . . 32 C3
Bowes-Lyon Hall 13
E16 . . . . 35 C1
Bowfell Rd W6 . . . . . 47 B4
Bowhill Cl SW9 . . . . 163 C2
Bow Ho 1 E3 . . . . . 26 C2
Bowie Cl SW4 . . . . . 73 C4
Bow La EC2, EC4 . . . 109 A1
Bowland Ho N4 . . . . . 6 B4
Bowland Rd SW4 . . 61 C3
Bowland Yd SW1 . . 131 A3
Bowl Ct EC2 . . . 24 A1 98 B1
Bowles Rd 1 SE1 . . 49 C4
Bowley Ho 6
SE16 . . . . 139 B2
Bowling Green Cl
SW19 . . . . 69 A4
Bowling Green Ho
SW10 . . . . 157 B2
Bowling Green La
EC1 . . . . 95 C2
Bowling Green St
SE11 . . . . 163 B4
Bowling Green Wlk
N1 . . . . 24 A2 98 A4
Bowman Ave E16 . . 35 B2
Bowman Mews
St George in E
E1 . . . . 125 B4
Wandsworth SW18 . 70 B3
Bowman's Mews
N7 . . . . 5 A1
Bowman's Pl N7 . . . 5 A1
Bowmore Wlk
NW1 . . . . 13 C1
Bowness Cl 8 E8 . . 16 B2
Bowness Ho SE15 . 50 B3
Bowood Rd SW11 . . 60 C2
Bow Rd E3 . . . . 26 C2
Bow Road Sta E3 . . 26 C2

Bowry Ho 14 E14 . . 33 B4
Bow Sec Sch 12
E3 . . . . 26 B3
Bowsprit Point 1
E14 . . . . 41 C3
Bow St WC2 . . . . . . 106 B1
Bowstead Ct
SW11 . . . . 167 C3
Bow Triangle Bsns Ctr
13 E3 . . . . 26 C1
Bowyer Ho
27 Shoreditch N1 . . 24 A4
Wandsworth SW18 . 59 A1
Bowyer Pl SE5 . . . . 48 B3
Bowyer St 15 SE5 . . 48 B3
Boxall Rd SE21 . . . . 64 A1
Boxley Ho 8 E5 . . . 17 A3
Boxmoor Ho
14 Hackney E2 . . . 24 C4
9 Shepherd's Bush
W11 . . . . 30 C1
Box Tree Ho SE8 . . 41 A1
Boxworth Gr N1 . . . 85 A4
Boyce Ho 4 W10 . . 23 B2
Boyd St E1 . . . . 111 C1
Boydell Ct NW8 . . . 11 C1
Boyfield St SE1 . . . 136 B3
Boyle St 4 W1 . . . . 118 C4
Boyne Ct NW10 . . . . 8 C1
Boyne Rd SE13 . . . . 67 C4
Boyne Terr Mews
W11 . . . . 31 B1 112 C2
Boyson Rd 10
SE17 . . . . 48 C4
Boyton Cl N1 . . . . . . 15 C2
Boyton Ho
Kennington SE11 . . 149 B1
St John's Wood
NW8 . . . . 79 C2
Brabant Ct EC3 . . . 124 A4
Brabazon St E14 . . . 34 A4
Brabner Ho 3
E2 . . . . 24 C2 99 B4
Braburn Gr SE15 . . 50 B1
Bracer Ho 1 N1 . . . 24 A3
Bracewell Rd W10 . 30 B4
Bracey Mews 1 N4 . 5 A2
Bracey St N4 . . . . . . 5 A2
Bracken Ave
SW12 . . . . 72 C4
Brackenbury N4 . . . . 5 B3
Brackenbury Gdns
W6 . . . . 39 A3
Brackenbury Prim Sch
4 W6 . . . . 39 A3
Brackenbury Rd
W6 . . . . 39 A3
Bracken Gdns
SW13 . . . . 46 C1
Bracken Ho 15 E3 . 33 C4
Brackley Ct NW8 . . . 89 C2
Brackley Rd W4 . . . 38 A1
Brackley St EC1 . . . 109 A4
Brackley Terr 6
W4 . . . . 38 A1
Bracklyn Ct N1 . . . . 87 B2
Bracklyn St N1 . . . . 87 B2
Bracknell Gate
NW3 . . . . 11 A3
Bracknell Gdns
NW3 . . . . 11 A4
Bracknell Way
NW3 . . . . 11 A4

Bradbeer Ho 24
E2 . . . . 25 B2
Bradbourne St
SW6 . . . . 165 C2
Bradbury Ct 2
SE3 . . . . 53 C3
Bradbury Ho 11 . . 111 A2
Bradbury St 28
N16 . . . . 16 A3
Braddon Ho 11 . . . . 78 B1
Braddon Rd TW9 . . 54 B4
Braddyll St SE10 . . . 43 A1
Bradenham
SE17 . . . . 48 C4
Bradenham Cl
SE17 . . . . 48 C4
Braden St W9 . . . . . 88 A1
Bradfield Ct 14
NW1 . . . . 13 A1
Bradfield Ho 4
SW8 . . . . 171 B2
Bradford Ho 4
W14 . . . . 39 A4
Bradford Rd W3 . . . 38 A4
Bradgate Rd SE6 . . 67 A1
Brading Rd SW2 . . . 74 B4
Brading Terr W12 . . 38 C3
Bradiston Rd W9 . . 23 B2
Bradley Cl N7 . . . . . 14 B2
Bradley Ho
Bermondsey SE16 . 40 A2
5 Bromley E3 . . . . 27 A2
Bradley Mews
SW12 . . . . 73 A4
Bradley's Cl N1 . . . . 85 C2
Bradlow Ho 25
SE5 . . . . 48 C4
Bradmead SW8 . . . 160 C1
Bradmore Park Rd
W6 . . . . 39 A2
Brad St SE1 . . . . . . 121 C1
Bradstock Ho E9 . . 18 A1
Bradstock Rd E9 . . 17 C2
Bradwell Ho 8
NW6 . . . . 78 A3
Bradwell St 24 E1 . . 25 C2
Brady Ho
London SW4 . . . . . . 61 C2
South Lambeth
SW8 . . . . 171 A4
Brady St E1 . . . . 25 A1
Braefoot Ct SW15 . 57 C2
Braemar SW15 . . . . 57 C1
Braemar Ave SW19 73 C2
Braemar Ho W9 . . . 88 C3
Braemar Mans
W8 . . . . 128 B1
Braes St N1 . . . . 15 A1
Braganza St SE17 . 150 A1
Braham St E1 . . . . . 111 A2
Brahma Kumaris
World Spiritual Univ
NW10 . . . . 8 C1
Braid Ave W3 . . . . . 29 A3
Braid Ho SE10 . . . . . 52 B2
Braidwood St SE1 124 A1
Brailsford Rd SW2 . 62 C1
Braintree Ho 6
E1 . . . . 25 B1
Braintree St E2 . . . . 25 B2
Braithwaite Ho
EC1 . . . . 97 B2
Braithwaite Twr
W2 . . . . 101 B4
Bramah Gn SW9 . . 173 C4

Bos-Bra 187

Bramah Mus of Tea &
Coffee The*
SE1 . . . . 123 A1
Bramall Ct N7 . . . . . 14 B2
Bramber WC1 . . . . . 94 A3
Bramber Ct TW8 . . . 36 A2
Bramber Rd W14 . . 154 C4
Brambledown 8
N4 . . . . 5 A4
Bramble Gdns
W12 . . . . 29 B2
Bramble Ho 16 E3 . 33 C4
Brambling Ct 25
SE8 . . . . 51 B4
Bramcote Gr SE16 . 40 B1
Bramcote Rd
SW15 . . . . 57 A3
Bramerton NW6 . . . . 9 C1
Bramerton St
SW3 . . . . 158 A4
Bramfield Ct N4 . . . . 6 B2
Bramfield Rd
SW11 . . . . 60 B1
Bramford Rd
SW18 . . . . 59 B3
Bramham Gdns
SW5 . . . . 142 B2
Bramham Ho SE22 . 64 A3
Bramlands Cl
SW11 . . . . 60 A4
Bramley Cres
SW8 . . . . 161 C2
Bramley Ct SE13 . . 67 C2
Bramley Ho
10 North Kensington
W10 . . . . 30 C3
Roehampton SW15 . 56 B1
Bramley Rd W10 . . . 30 C3
Brampton WC1 . . . . 106 C3
Bramshaw Rd E9 . . 17 C2
Bramshill Gdns
NW5 . . . . 4 A1
Bramshill Rd
NW10 . . . . 21 B3
Bramshurst NW8 . . 78 B3
Bramston Rd
Harlesden NW10 . . . 21 C3
Wandsworth SW17 . 71 B1
Bramwell Ho
Borough The SE1 . . 137 A1
Chelsea SW1 . . . . . 160 C4
Bramwell Mews
N1 . . . . 85 A4
Brancaster Ho
22 Globe Town E1 . . 25 C2
Islington N5 . . . . 15 A3
Brancaster Rd
SW16 . . . . 74 A1
Branch Hill NW3 . . . . 2 B1
Branch Pl N1 . . . . . . 87 C4
Branch Rd E14 . . . . 33 A2
Branch St SE15 . . . . 49 A3
Brand Cl N4 . . . . 6 A3
Brandon Lo 13 W4 . 37 B1
Brandon Mews
Barbican EC2 . . . . . 109 B4
Walworth SE17 . . . . 151 A3
Brandon Rd N7 . . . . 14 A1
Brandon St SE17 . . 151 A3
Brandlehow Prim Sch
SW15 . . . . 58 B3
Brandlehow Rd
SW15 . . . . 58 B3
Brandon Mews
Barbican EC2 . . . . . 109 B4
Walworth SE17 . . . . 151 A3

Brandrams Wharf
SE16 . . . . .40 B4
Brandreth Rd
SW17 . . . . .73 A2
Brand St SE10 . . . . . .52 B3
Brangton Rd SE11 149 A1
Brangwyn Ct W14 126 A1
Branksea St SW6 154 A1
Branksome Ho
SW8 . . . . 162 C2
Branksome Rd
SW2 . . . . .62 A2
Bransby Ct 4 N16 . .16 A4
Branscombe NW1 . .83 A3
Branscombe St
SE13 . . . . .67 A4
Bransdale Cl NW6 .23 C4
Branstone Ct 9
TW9 . . . . .44 B2
Branstone Rd TW9 . .44 B2
Branston Ho N7 . . . .14 C3
Brantwood Ho 9
SE5 . . . . .48 B3
Brantwood Rd
SE24 . . . . .63 B2
Brasenose Dr
SW13 . . . . .47 B4
Brashley Road Cvn
Site NW10 . . . . .21 A2
Brassey Ho 1 E14 . .42 A2
Brassey Rd NW6 . . . .10 B2
Brassey Sq SW11 . . .60 C4
Brassie Ave W3 . . . .29 A3
Brass Talley Alley 51
SE16 . . . . .40 C4
Brathay NW1 . . . . . . .83 A1
Brathway Rd
SW18 . . . . .70 C4
Bratley St 11
E1 . . . . .24 C1 99 B1
Bravington Pl W9 . .23 B1
Bravington Rd W9 . .23 B1
Braxfield Ho 12
SE17 . . . . .48 A4
Braxfield Rd SE4 . . .66 B3
Bray NW3 . . . . .12 A1
Brayard's Rd SE15 . .50 A1
Braybrook St W12 . .29 B3
Brayburne Ave
SW4 . . . . 171 A1
Bray Cres SE16 . . . . .40 C4
Braydon Rd N16 . . . .7 C3
Bray Dr E16 . . . . .35 B2
Brayfield Terr N1 . . .14 C1
Brayford Sq 6 E1 . .32 B3
Bray Pl SW3 . . . . . . 144 C3
Bread St EC2, EC4 109 A1
Breakspeare SE21 . .76 B1
Breakspears Mews
SE4 . . . . .51 C1
Breakspears Rd
SE4 . . . . .66 C4
Breamore Ct 16
W10 . . . . .23 A1
Breamore Cl
SW15 . . . . .69 A3
Breamore Ho 21
SE15 . . . . .49 C3
Bream's Bldgs
EC4 . . . . 107 B2
Bream St E3 . . . . . . .18 C1
Breasley Cl SW15 . .57 A3
Brechin Pl SW7 . . . 143 A3

Brecknock Prim Sch
18 N7 . . . . .13 C2
Brecknock Rd N19 . .13 C3
Brecon Ho
Stamford Hill N16. . . .7 B3
Wandsworth SW18 . . .70 C4
Brecon Rd W6 . . . . 154 B3
Bredel Ho 4 E14 . . .33 C4
Bredgar SE13 . . . . . .67 A2
Bredgar Rd N19 . . . .4 B2
Bredinghurst SE22 . .76 C4
Bredinghurst Sch
SE15 . . . . .65 C3
Bredin Ho SW10 . . 156 B2
Breer St SW6 . . . . . .59 A4
Breezer's Ct 22
E1 . . . . 125 C3
Breezer's Hill E1 . . 125 C3
Brehon Ho NW1 . . . .82 C3
Bremans Row 1
SW18 . . . . .71 B2
Bremner Rd SW7 . . 129 A2
Brenchley Gdns SE15,
SE22, SE23 . . . . .65 C1
Brenda Rd SW17 . . .72 B2
Brendon Ave NW10 . .8 A4
Brendon Ho NW1 . . 103 B4
Brendon St W1 . . . 102 B2
Brenley Ho SE1 . . . 137 B4
Brennands Ct 13
N19 . . . . .4 B1
Brent Adult Comm
Education Service
Coll 10 NW10 . . . . .20 C4
Brentford Fountain L
Ctr W4 . . . . .36 C1
Brent Ho 18 E9 . . . .17 B2
Brenthouse Rd E9 . .17 B2
Brenthurst Rd
NW10 . . . . .8 B2
Brent Mus* NW10 . . .9 A2
Brent New Ent Ctr
NW10 . . . . .8 B2
Brenton Ct 7 E9 . . .18 A3
Brenton St E14 . . . .33 A3
Brent Rd E16 . . . . . .35 C4
Brent Trad Est
NW10 . . . . .8 A3
Brentwick Gdns
TW8 . . . . .36 A2
Brereton Ho 4
SW2 . . . . .74 C4
Bressenden Pl
SW1 . . . . 132 C2
Breton Ho
Bermondsey SE1 . . . 138 C2
St Luke's EC2 . . . . . . .97 A1
Brett Cl N16 . . . . .7 A2
Brett Cres NW10 . . .20 C4
Brettell St SE17 . . . 151 C1
Brett Ho 1 SW15 . . .69 C4
Brett House Cl 2
SW15 . . . . .69 C4
Brettinghurst 3
SE1 . . . . 153 B1
Bretton Ho N19 . . . . .5 A3
Brett Pas 28 E8 . . . .17 A3
Brett Rd E8 . . . . .17 A3
Brewers Bldgs EC1 96 A4
Brewers Ct W2 . . . 100 C2
Brewer's Gn SW1 . 133 B2
Brewers Hall Gdns
EC2 . . . . 109 A3
Brewer St W1 . . . . 119 A4

Brewery Ind Est The
N1 . . . . .87 A1
Brewery Rd N7 . . . . .14 A2
Brewery Sq
Bermondsey SE1 . . . 124 C1
Clerkenwell EC1 . . . . .96 B2
Brewhouse La
Putney SW15 . . . . . . .58 A4
Wapping E1 . . . . .32 A1
Brewhouse Wlk
SE16 . . . . .33 A1
Brewhouse Yd EC1 .96 A2
Brewster Gdns
W10 . . . . .30 B4
Brewster Ho
Bermondsey SE1 . . . 153 A4
Poplar E14 . . . . .33 B2
Briant Ho SE1 . . . . 135 A1
Briant St SE14 . . . . .50 C3
Briar Ct
7 Bow E3 . . . . .26 C3
6 Dalston E8 . . . . . .16 B1
Briardale SW19 . . . .70 B3
Briardale Gdns
NW3 . . . . .1 C1
Briardale Ho 12
N16 . . . . .7 A3
Briar Rd NW2 . . . . . . .9 B4
Briar Wlk
Putney SW15 . . . . . . .57 A3
West Kilburn W10 . . .23 A1
Briarwood Rd
SW4 . . . . .61 C2
Briary Cl NW3 . . . . .12 A1
Briary Ct 10 E16 . . .35 B3
Brickbarn Cl
SW10 . . . . 157 A2
Brick Ct EC4 . . . . . 107 B1
Brick Farm Cl
TW9 . . . . .45 A2
Brick La
Shoreditch
E2 . . . . .24 B2 99 A3
Spitalfields
E1 . . . . .24 B1 99 A1
Brick Lane Mkt★
E2 . . . . .99 A2
Bricklayers Arms
SE1 . . . . 137 C1
Brick St W1 . . . . . . 118 A1
Brickworth Ho 28
SW9 . . . . 173 C4
Brideale Cl SE15 . . .49 B4
Bride Ct EC4 . . . . . 108 A1
Bride La EC4 . . . . . 108 A1
Bridel Mews N1 . . . .86 A3
Bride St N7 . . . . .14 B2
Bridewain St SE1 . 138 C2
Bridewell Pl
Holborn EC4 . . . . . . 108 A1
20 Wapping E1 . . . .32 A1
Bridford Mews
W1 . . . . 104 B4
Bridge Acad The
E2 . . . . .24 B4
Bridge App NW1 . . .12 C1
Bridge Ave W6 . . . . .39 B1
Bridge Avenue Mans
1 W6 . . . . .39 B1
Bridge Cl 1 W10 . . .30 C3
Bridge Ct
7 Blackwall E14 . . . .34 C2
7 Willesden NW10 . . .8 A1
Bridge Field Ho 2
W2 . . . . 100 A2
Bridgefoot SE1 . . . 148 B1

Bridge Gdns N16 . .15 C4
Bridge Ho
Brockley SE4 . . . . . . .66 B3
1 Camden Town
NW1 . . . . .12 C1
Homerton E9 . . . . . . .17 C3
Bridge House Quay
E14 . . . . .34 B1
Bridge La SW11 . . 168 B3
Bridgeland Rd
E16 . . . . .35 C2
Bridgeman Ho 11
N1 . . . . .86 A3
Bridgeman Rd N1 . .14 B1
Bridgeman St
NW8 . . . . .80 A1
Bridge Meadows
SE14 . . . . .50 C4
Bridgend Rd SW18 .59 B3
Bridge Ho 9 E1 . . . .32 A3
Bridge Pk 7
SW18 . . . . .58 C2
Bridge Rd SW1 . . . 146 B4
Bridgeport Pl 4
E1 . . . . 125 C2
Bridge Rd
Stratford Marsh
E15 . . . . .27 C4
Willesden NW10 . . . . .8 A2
Bridge Sch The
Clerkenwell EC1 . . . . .96 A2
Lower Holloway N7 . .14 A3
Bridge St SW11 . . 167 B1
1 Richmond TW10 . .54 A2
5 SE5 . . . . .48 B3
Bridge St
Chiswick W4 . . . . . . .37 C2
Bridge Terr E15 . . . .19 C1
7 Bridgeview 2 W6 .39 B1
Bridgewater Rd
E15 . . . . .27 B4
Bridgewater Sq
EC2 . . . . 108 C4
Bridgewater St
EC2 . . . . 108 C4
Bridgeway St NW1 .83 A1
Bridge Wharf 18
E2 . . . . .25 C3
Bridgford St SW17 .
SW18 . . . . .71 B1
Bridgman Rd W4 . . .37 B3
Bridgnorth Ho 10
SE15 . . . . .49 C4
Bridgwater Ho
W2 . . . . 100 C2
Bridle La W1 . . . . . 119 A4
Bridlington Ho
SW18 . . . . .59 B3
Brief St SE5 . . . . . . .48 A2
Brierfield NW1 . . . . .82 C3
Brierley Rd
Leyton E11 . . . . .19 C4
Upper Tooting
SW12 . . . . .73 B2
Brierly Gdns 2 E2 . .25 B3
Brigade St SE3 . . . . .53 B1
Briggeford Cl 5 E5 . .7 C2
Briggs Ho 22
E2 . . . . .24 B2 99 A4
Brightling Rd SE4 . .66 B1

Brightlingsea Pl 5
E14 . . . . .33 B2
Brightman Rd
SW18 . . . . .71 C3
Brighton Bldgs
SE1 . . . . 138 A1
Brighton Ct SW15 . .58 B1
Brighton Gr SE14 . .51 A2
Brighton Ho 7
SE5 . . . . .48 C2
Brighton Rd N16 . . .16 A4
Brighton Terr
SW9 . . . . .62 B3
Brightside Rd
SE13 . . . . .67 C1
Bright St E14 . . . . . .34 A4
Brightwell Ct N7 . . .14 B3
Brightwells 1
SW6 . . . . 166 A2
Brig Mews SE8 . . . . .51 C4
Brigstock Ho SE5 . . .48 B1
Brill Pl NW1 . . . . . . .83 C1
Brindley Ho
9 Notting Hill W2 . . .31 C4
22 Streatham SW12 .74 A4
Brindley St SE14 . . .51 B2
Brine Ho 8 E3 . . . . .26 A3
Brinklow Ho W2 . . 100 A3
Brinkworth Way
E9 . . . . .18 B2
Brinsley Ho 7 E1 . . .32 B3
Brinsley St 35 E1 . . .32 A3
Brinton Wlk SE1 . . 122 A1
Brion Pl E14 . . . . . . .34 B4
Brisbane Ho 3
W12 . . . . .30 A2
Brisbane St SE5 . . . .48 C3
Briset St EC1 . . . . . . .96 A1
Briset Way N7 . . . . . .5 B2
Bristol Gdns
Putney SW15 . . . . . . .69 B4
Westbourne Green
W9 . . . . .88 B1
Bristol Ho SE11 . . 135 B1
Bristol Mews W9 . . .88 B1
Bristowe Cl 2
SW2 . . . . .62 C1
Britannia Building
N1 . . . . .97 B4
Britannia Cl SW4 . . .61 C3
Britannia Gate 11
E16 . . . . .35 C1
Britannia Junc
NW1 . . . . .82 B4
Britannia L Ctr N1 .24 A4
Britannia Rd
23 Millwall E14 . . . . .41 C2
Walham Green
SW6 . . . . 156 A1
Britannia Row N1 . .86 C4
Britannia St WC1 . . .94 C4
Britannia Way
NW10 . . . . .20 A1
Britannia Wlk N1 . . .97 B4
British Coll of
Osteopathic
Medicine NW3 . . . .11 B2
British Dental
Association Mus★
W1 . . . . 104 C3
British Gr W4 . . . . . .38 B1
British Grove Pas 2
W4 . . . . .38 B1
British Grove S 3
W4 . . . . .38 B1

British Library The ★ WC1 . . . . 93 C4
British Mus ★ WC1 . . . . 106 A3
British Optical Association Mus ★ SW1 . . . . 120 A2
British St E3 . . . . 26 B2
British Wharf Ind Est SE14 . . . . 50 C4
Britley Ho 16 E14 . . . 33 B3
Brit Oval The (Surrey Cnty Crkt Club) SE11 . . . . 163 A3
Brittage Rd 11 NW10 . . . . 8 A1
Brittany Ho SW15 . . 57 B3
Brittany Point SE11 . . . . 149 B3
Britten Cl NW11 . . . 2 A3
Britten Ho SW3 . . . 144 A2
Britten St SW3 . . . 144 A2
Britton St EC1 . . . . 96 A1
BRIXTON 62 C4
Brixton Day Coll 6 SW9 . . . . 62 B4
Brixton Hill SW2 . . 62 B1
Brixton Hill Ct 5 SW2 . . . . 62 B2
Brixton Hill Pl SW2 . . . . 74 A4
Brixton Mkt ★ SW9 . . . . 62 C3
Brixton Oval 7 SW2 . . . . 62 C3
Brixton Rd SW9 . . 173 B2
Brixton Rec Ctr SW9 . . . . 62 C4
Brixton Sta SW9 . . . 62 C3
Brixton Station Rd SW9 . . . . 62 C4
Brixton Water La SW2 . . . . 62 B2
Broadbent Cl N6 . . . 4 A3
Broadbent St W1 . . 118 A4
Broadbridge Cl SE3 . . . . 53 C3
Broad Common Est N16 . . . . 7 C3
Broad Ct WC2 . . . 106 B1
Broadfield NW6 . . . 11 A2
Broadfield La NW1 . . . . 14 A1
Broadfields Way NW10 . . . . 8 B3
Broadford Ho 27 E1 . . . . 26 A1
BROADGATE . . . 110 A4
Broadgate EC2 . . . 110 A4
Broadgate Circ EC2 . . . . 110 A4
Broadgates Ct SE11 . . . . 149 C1
Broadgates Rd SW18 . . . . 71 C3
Broadgate Twr The EC2 . . . . 98 B1
Broadhinton Rd SW4 . . . . 61 B4
Broadhurst Cl
Hampstead NW6 . . 11 B2
9 Richmond TW10 . 54 B2
Broadhurst Gdns NW6 . . . . 11 A2
Broadhurst Mans NW6 . . . . 11 A2

Broad La EC2 . . . . 110 A4
Broadlands N6 . . . . 3 C4
Broadlands Ave SW16 . . . . 74 A2
Broadlands Cl
Highgate N6 . . . . 3 C4
Streatham SW16 . . 74 A2
Broadlands Ct TW9 . . . . 44 C3
Broadlands Lo N6 . . 3 B4
Broadlands Mans 2 SW16 . . . . 74 A2
Broadlands Rd N6 . . 3 B4
Broadley St NW8 . . 102 A4
Broadley Terr NW1 . . . . 90 B1
Broadmayne SE17 151 B2
Broadmead W14 . . . 140 A3
Broadoak Ct 8 SW9 . . . . 62 C4
Broadoak Ho 11 NW6 . . . . 78 B3
Broad St Ave EC2 . . 110 A3
Broad Sanctuary SW1 . . . . 134 A3
Broadstone Ho 8 SW8 . . . . 162 C1
Broadstone Pl W1 . . . . 103 B3
Broad Street Pl EC2 . . . . 109 C3
Broadwalk Ho SW7 . . . . 128 C3
Broadwalk La NW11 . 1 B4
Broadwall SE1 . . . 121 C2
Broadway
Stratford E15 . . . 19 C1
Westminster SW1 . 133 B2
Broadway Arc 8 W6 . . . . 39 B2
Broadway Ctr The 6 W6 . . . . 39 B2
Broadway Ho 2 E8 . . . . 25 A4
Broadway Mans SW6 . . . . 155 C1
Broadway Market E8 . . . . 25 A4
Broadway Market Mews 21 E8 . . . . 24 C4
Broadway Mews E5 . 7 B4
Broadway Mkt 18 E8 . 25 A4
Broadway Ret Pk NW2 . . . . 9 C2
Broadway The
Barnes SW13 . . . 46 A1
South Acton W3 . . 36 C4
Broadway Wlk 4 E14 . . . . 41 C3
Broadwick St W1 . . 105 A1
Broad Wlk
Mayfair W1 . . . . 117 B2
Regent's Pk NW1 . 81 C1
Richmond TW9 . . 44 B3
Broad Wlk The W8 . . . . 114 B1
Broadwood Terr W14 . . . . 141 A4
Broad Yd EC1 . . . . 96 A1
Brocas Cl NW3 . . . 12 A1
Brockbridge Ho 5 SW15 . . . . 56 B1
Brocket Ho 16 SW8 . . . . 171 B2
Brockham Dr SW2 . 74 B4

Brockham Ho
Camden Town NW1 . . . . 83 A3
11 Streatham SW2 . 74 B4
Brockham St SE1 . 137 A2
Brockhurst Ho N4 . . 6 C4
Brockill Cres SE4 . . 66 A3
Brocklebank Rd SW18 . . . . 71 B4
Brocklehurst Road Ind Est SE7 . . . . 43 C2
Brocklehurst St SE14 . . . . 50 C3
BROCKLEY 66 B3
Brockley Cross SE4 . . . . 66 B4
Brockley Cross Bsns Ctr SE4 . . . . 66 A4
Brockley Gdns SE4 . . . . 51 B1
Brockley Gr SE4 . . 66 B2
Brockley Hall Rd SE4 . . . . 66 A2
Brockley Ho SE17 152 A2
Brockley Mews SE4 . . . . 66 A2
Brockley Prim Sch SE4 . . . . 66 B2
Brockley Rd SE4 . . 66 B2
Brockley Sta SE4 . . 66 A4
Brockley Way SE4 . 66 A2
Brockmer Ho 5 E1 . . . . 32 A2
Brock Pl E3 . . . . . 27 A1
Brock St SE15 . . . 65 B4
Brockweir 28 E2 . . . 25 B3
Brockwell Ct 2 SW2 . . . . 62 C2
Brockwell Ho SE11 . . . . 163 A4
Brockwell Lido SE24 . . . . 63 A1
Brockwell Park ★ SE24 . . . . 63 A1
Brockwell Park Gdns SE24 . . . . 75 A4
Brockwell Park Row SW2 . . . . 62 C1
Broderick Ho SE21 . . . . 76 A1
Brodia Rd N16 . . . . 7 A1
Brodick Ho 12 E3 . . 26 B3
Brodie Ho SE1 . . . 153 A2
Brodie St SE1 . . . 153 A2
Brodlove La E1 . . . 32 C2
Brodrick Rd SW17 . 72 A2
Brody Ho E1 . . . . 110 C3
Broken Wharf EC4 . . . . 122 C4
Brokesley St E3 . . . 26 B2
Broke Wlk
Hackney E8 . . . . 24 B4
11 Hackney E8 . . . 24 C4
Bromar Rd SE5 . . . 64 A4
Bromehead St E1 . . . . 32 B3
Bromell's Rd SW4 . 61 B3
Bromfelde Rd SW4 . . . . 171 C1
Bromfield Ct 20 SE16 . . . . 139 C2
Bromfield St N1 . . . 85 C2
Bromleigh Ho SE1 . . . . 138 C2
BROMLEY E3 . . . . 27 A2

Bromley-by-Bow Sta E3 . . . . 98 A2
Bromley Hall Rd E14 . . . . 34 B4
Bromley High St E3 . . . . 27 A2
Bromley Ho 3 E3 . . 28 B3
Bromley Lo 2 W3 . . 28 B3
Bromley Pl W1 . . . 104 C4
Bromley St E1 . . . . 32 C3
BROMPTON 130 A1
Brompton Arc SW1 . . . . 131 A3
Brompton Oratory SW3 . . . . 130 A1
Brompton Park Cres SW6 . . . . 156 A3
Brompton Pl SW3 . 130 B2
Brompton Rd SW3 . . . . 130 A1
Brompton Sq SW3 . . . . 130 A2
Bromstone Ho 19 SW9 . . . . 173 B3
Bromwich Ave N6 . . 3 C2
Bromwich Ho 3 TW10 . . . . 54 A1
Bromyard Ave W3 . 29 A2
Bromyard Ho
Acton W3 . . . . . 29 A1
8 Peckham SE15 . . 50 A3
Bron Ct NW6 . . . . 23 C4
BRONDESBURY . . 10 A1
Brondesbury Coll for Boys 12 NW6 . . . 10 A1
Brondesbury Ct NW2 . . . . 9 C2
Brondesbury Mews 11 NW6 . . . . 10 B1
BRONDESBURY PARK 22 C4
Brondesbury Park Sta NW6 . . . . 23 A4
Brondesbury Pk NW2 . . . . 9 C1
Brondesbury Rd NW6 . . . . 23 B3
Brondesbury Sta NW6 . . . . 10 B1
Brondesbury Villas NW6 . . . . 23 B3
Bronsart Rd SW6 . . 154 A1
Bronte Ct 3 W14 . . 39 C3
Bronte Ho
6 Stoke Newington N16 . . . . 16 A3
Bronti Cl SE17 . . . 151 A2
Bronwen Ct NW8 . . 89 B3
Bronze St SE8 . . . . 51 C3
Brookbank Rd SE13 . . . . 67 A4
Brook Cl SW17 . . . 72 C2
Brook Com Prim Sch E8 . . . . 16 B3
Brook Cotts SW14 . . 56 A4
Brookdale Rd SE6 . . 67 A1
Brook Dr SE11 . . . 150 A4
Brooke Ct W10 . . . 23 A3
Brooke Ho 4 SE14 . . . . 51 A2
Brooke Rd E5, N16 . 7 C1
Brookes Ct EC1 . . . 107 B4
Brooke's Mkt EC1 . 107 C4
Brooke St EC1 . . . 107 B3
Brookfield
Dartmouth Pk N6 . 3 C1

Brookfield continued
1 Finsbury Pk N4 . . 5 C2
Brookfield Ho 23 E2 . . . . 25 A3
Brookfield Pk NW5 . 4 A1
Brookfield Prim Sch N19 . . . . 4 A2
Brookfield Rd
Acton W4 . . . . . 37 C4
Homerton E9 . . . 18 A2
Brookgate N16 . . . . 6 C2
Brook Gate W1 . . . 117 A3
Brook Gdns SW13 . 56 B4
Brook Gn W6 . . . . 39 C2
BROOK GREEN 11 W14 . . . . 39 C3
Brook Green Flats 11 W14 . . . . 39 C3
Brook Ho
3 Clapham Pk SW4 . . . . 61 B2
Ealing W13 . . . . 36 C4
4 Hammersmith W6 . . . . 39 B2
Marylebone WC1 . 105 B4
Brook Hos NW1 . . . 83 A1
Brooklands Ave SW18 . . . . 71 A2
Brooklands Court Apartments 3 NW6 . . . . 10 B1
Brooklands Ct 2 NW6 . . . . 10 B1
Brooklyn Ct W12 . . 30 B1
Brooksmarsh Ind Est SE10 . . . . 52 A3
Brook Mews N W2 . . . . 115 C4
Brookmill Rd SE8 . . 51 C2
Brooksbank Ho 7 E9 . . . . 17 B2
Brooksbank St 9 E9 . . . . 17 B2
Brooksby Ho 4 N1 . . . . 14 C1
Brooksby Mews N1 . . . . 14 C1
Brooksby St N1 . . . 14 C1
Brooksby's Wlk E9 . 17 C3
Brooks Ct
3 London SW4 . . 172 A2
Nine Elms SW8 . . 161 A2
Brookside Rd N19 . . 4 C2
Brooks Ho 6 SW2 . . 74 C3
Brookside Rd N19 . . 4 C2
Brooks La W4 . . . . 44 C4
Brook's Mews W1 . 118 A4
Brooks Rd W4 . . . . 36 C1
Brook St
Bayswater W2 . . . 115 C4
Mayfair W1 . . . . 118 A4
Brookstone Ct SE15 . . . . 65 A3
Brooksville Ave NW6 . . . . 23 A4
Brookville Rd SW6 . 154 C1
Brookwood Ave SW13 . . . . 46 B1
Brookwood Ho SE1 . . . . 136 B3
Brookwood Rd SW18 . . . . 70 C3
Broome Ct 3 TW9 . . . . 44 C2
Broome Ho 7 E5 . . 17 A3

Broome Way SE5 ....48 C3
Broom Farm SW6 165 C2
Broomfield **7**
　NW1 ....12 C1
Broomfield Ho
　SE17 ....44 B2
Broomfield House Sch
　TW9 ....44 B2
Broomfield Rd
　TW9 ....44 B2
Broomfield St E14 ..34 A4
Broomgrove Rd
　SW9 ....173 A1
Broomhill Rd
　SW18 ....58 C2
Broomhouse La
　SW6 ....58 C2
Broomhouse Rd
　SW6 ....165 B2
Broomsleigh St
　NW6 ....10 B3
Broomwood Hall
　(Lower Sch) **5**
　SW12 ....60 D1
Broomwood Hall Sch
　(Lower Sch)
　SW16 ....73 C1
Broomwood Hall Sch
　(Upper Sch) **3**
　SW12 ....72 C4
Broomwood Rd
　SW11 ....60 C2
Brougham Rd
　Acton W3 ....28 A3
　Hackney E8 ....24 C4
Brougham St
　SW11 ....169 A2
Brough Cl SW8 ....162 B1
Broughton Dr **9**
　SW9 ....63 A3
Broughton Rd
　SW6 ....166 B2
Broughton Road App
　2 SW6 ....166 A2
Broughton St
　SW8 ....170 A2
Brouncker Rd W3 ..37 B4
Browne Ho **5** SE8 ..51 C3
Brownfield St E14 ..34 B3
Brownflete Ho
　SE4 ....66 A3
Brown Hart Gdns
　W1 ....117 C4
Browning Ho **7**
　W1 ....89 A1
Browning Ct W14 ..154 C4
Browning Ho
　1 London SE14 .....51 A2
　7 Shepherd's Bush
　W12 ....30 B3
　10 Stoke Newington
　N16 ....16 A4
Browning Mews
　W1 ....103 C3
Browning St SE17 151 A3
Brownlow Ho **10**
　SE16 ....139 B3
Brownlow Mews
　WC1 ....95 A1
Brownlow Rd
　Hackney E8 ....24 C4
　Willesden NW10 ....8 A1
Brownlow St WC1 107 A3
Brown's Bldgs
　EC3 ....110 B1

Brown St W1 ....102 C2
Brownswood Rd N4 ..6 B2
Broxash Rd SW11 ...60 C1
Broxbourne Ho **1**
　E27 ....27 A1
Broxholme Ho
　SW6 ....166 A4
Broxholm Rd SE27,
　SW16 ....74 C1
Broxwood Way
　NW8 ....80 B3
Bruce Cl W10 ......30 C4
Bruce Glasier Ho **13**
　N19 ....4 C4
Bruce Ho
　4 Clapham Pk
　SW4 ....61 C1
　5 North Kensington
　W10 ....30 C4
　Putney SW15 .....57 A2
Bruce Rd E3 ....27 A2
Bruckner St W10 ...23 B2
Bruges Pl **18** NW1 ..13 C1
Brune Ho **1** 110 C3
Brunei Gall*
　WC1 ....105 C4
Brunel Cl **3** SE19 ..23 B2
Brunel Est W2 .....31 C4
Brunel Ho
　Chelsea SW10 ....157 C2
　4 Gospel Oak NW5 ..13 A4
　New Cross SE8 ....41 A2
　6 Streatham SW2 ..74 A4
Brunel Mews
　NW10 ....22 C2
Brunel Mus* **6** SE16 40 B4
Brunel St E16 ......35 B3
Brune St E1 ....110 C3
Brunlees Ho **1** ...137 A1
Brunswick Ct **8** E8 ..16 C2
　Bermondsey SE1 ...138 B4
　Finsbury EC1 ......96 A3
　Westminster SW1 ..147 C3
Brunswick Gdns
　W8 ....31 C1 113 C1
Brunswick Ho
　4 Haggerston E2 ..24 B3
　Lisson Gr NW1 ....90 C2
Brunswick Mews
　W1 ....103 A2
Brunswick Park Prim
　Sch **2** SE5 ....48 C3
Brunswick Pk SE5 ..49 A2
Brunswick Pl N1 ...97 C3
Brunswick Quay
　SE16 ....40 C3
Brunswick Rd E14 ..34 B3
Brunswick Sh Ctr
　WC1 ....94 B2
Brunswick St **6** ...94 B2
Brunswick Villas **3**
　SE5 ....49 A2
Brunton Pl E14 ....33 A3
Brushfield St E1 ...110 C4
Brussels Rd SW11 ..59 C3
Bruton La W1 ......118 B3
Bruton Pl W1 ......118 B3
Bruton St W1 ......118 B3
Brutus Ct SE11 ....150 A3
Bryan Ave NW10 ....9 A1
Bryan Ct W1 ......102 C2

Bryan Ho SE16 .....41 B4
Bryan Rd SE16 .....41 B4
Bryanston Ct W1 ...102 C2
Bryanston Ho **12**
　SE15 ....49 B2
Bryanston Mans
　W1 ....102 C4
Bryanston Mews E
　W1 ....102 C2
Bryanston Mews W
　W1 ....102 C2
Bryanston Pl W1 ...102 C2
Bryanston Sq W1 ...102 C2
Bryanston St W1 ...103 A1
Bryant Ct
　Acton W3 ....28 C1
　Haggerston E2 ....24 B3
Bryce Ho **25** SE14 ..50 C4
Brydale Ho **2**
　SE16 ....40 C2
Brydges Pl WC2 ...120 A3
Brydges Rd E15 ....19 C3
Brydon Wlk N1 ....84 B4
Bryer Ct EC2 ......108 C4
Bryett Rd N7 ......5 A1
Bryher Ho W1 .....37 B1
Brymay Cl E3 ......26 C3
Brymon Ct W1 .....103 A3
Brynmaer Ho
　SW11 ....169 A3
Brynmaer Rd
　SW11 ....169 A3
Bryony Rd W12 ....29 C2
B T Twr* W1 ......104 C4
Buccleuch Ho E5 ...7 C4
Buchanan Ct **10**
　SE16 ....40 C2
Buchanan Gdns
　NW10 ....22 A3
Buchan Ho
　Dulwich SE21 .....76 A1
　Wandsworth SW18 ..70 C4
Buchan Rd SE15 ...65 B4
Bucharest Rd
　SW18 ....71 B4
Buckfast St
　E2 ....24 C2 99 B3
Buck Hill Wlk W2 ..115 C3
Buckhold Rd
　SW18 ....58 C1
Buckhurst Ho **8**
　N7 ....13 C3
Buckhurst St E1 ...25 A1
Buckingham Ave
　SW1 ....120 B3
Buckingham Gate
　SW1 ....133 A2
Buckingham Ho
　Finsbury Pk N4 ....6 B3
　Richmond TW10 ...54 C2
Buckingham Mans
　NW6 ....11 A3
Buckingham Mews
　Harlesden NW10 ...21 B3
　7 Kingsland N1 ...16 A2
　Westminster SW1 ..132 C2
Buckingham Pal*
　SW1 ....132 C2

Buckingham Rd
　Harlesden NW10 ...21 B3
　Kingsland N1 ......16 A2
Buckingham St
　WC2 ....120 B3
Buckingham Yd
　NW10 ....21 B3
Buckland Cres
　NW3 ....11 C2
Buckland Ct **6** N1 ..24 A3
Buckland Ho **3**
　N1 ....14 C1
Buckland St N1 ....87 C1
Buckland Wlk **2**
　W3 ....37 B4
Buckler's Alley
　SW6 ....155 A2
Bucklersbury EC2,
　EC4 ....109 B1
Buckle St
　19 Whitechapel
　E1 ....111 B2
　Whitechapel E1 ...111 A2
Buckley Ct **5**
　NW6 ....10 B1
Buckley Rd NW6 ...10 B1
Buckmaster Cl **1**
　N7 ....62 C4
Buckmaster Ho
　3 ....14 B4
Buckmaster Rd
　SW11 ....60 A3
Bucknall St WC1 ...106 A2
Bucknell Cl SW2 ...62 B3
Buckner Rd SW2 ...62 B3
Buckridge Bldg
　EC1 ....107 B4
Buckshead Ho **19**
　W2 ....31 C4
Buck St NW1 .....13 A1
Buckstone Cl SE23 ..65 B1
Buckters Rents
　SE16 ....33 A1
Buckthorne Rd
　SE4 ....66 A2
Budge Row EC4 ...109 B1
Budge's Wlk W2 ...115 A2
Budleigh Ho **19**
　SE15 ....49 C3
Buer Rd SW6 ......164 B1
Bugsby's Way
　SE10 ....43 B2
Buick Ho **4** E3 ....26 C1
Building Crafts Coll
　The E15 ....19 C1
Bulbarrow NW8 ...78 B3
Bulinca St SW1 ....147 C3
Bullace Row SE5 ...48 C2
Bullards Pl **3** E2 ...25 C2
Bulleid Way SW1 ..146 B3
Bullen Ho **18** E1 ...25 A1
Bullen St SW11 ....168 B2
Buller Cl SE15 .....49 C3
Buller Rd NW10 ...22 C2
Bullfinch Ct **4**
　SE21 ....75 C2
Bullingham Mans
　W8 ....127 C4
Bull Inn Ct WC2 ...120 B3
Bullivant St **9**
　E14 ....34 B2
Bulls Alley SW14 ...45 C1
Bull's Gdns SW3 ...144 B4
Bull Yd SE15 ......49 C2

Bulmer Mews
　W11 ....31 C1 113 B2
Bulow Ct **3** SW6 ..166 B2
Bulstrode Pl W1 ...103 C3
Bulstrode St W1 ...103 C2
Bulwer St W12 ....30 B1
Bunbury Ho SE15 ..49 C3
Bunhill Row EC1 ...97 B1
Bunhouse Pl SW1 145 C2
Bunkers Hill NW11 ..2 B4
Bunning Ho N7 ....14 A4
Bunning Way N7 ...14 B1
Bunsen Ho **2** E3 ..26 A3
Bunsen St **3** E3 ...26 A3
Bunyan Ct EC2 ....108 C4
Buonaparte Mews
　SW1 ....147 B2
Burbage Cl SE1 ...137 B1
Burbage Ho
　16 Deptford SE14 ..50 C4
　Shoreditch N1 .....87 C3
Burbage Rd SE21,
　SE24 ....75 C4
Burbage Sch **34**
　N1 ....24 A3
Burcham St E14 ...34 B3
Burchell Ho **1** SE11 149 A2
Burchell Rd SE15 ..50 A2
Burcher Gale Gr **5**
　SE15 ....49 B3
Burcote Rd SW18 ..71 C4
Burden Ho SW8 ...162 A1
Burdenshott Ave
　TW10 ....55 A3
Burder Cl N1 ......16 A2
Burder Rd N1 .....16 A2
Burdett Coutts &
　Townshend CE Prim
　Sch SW1 ....147 C3
Burdett Mews **4**
　W2 ....100 A2
Burdett Rd
　Richmond TW9 ....54 B4
　Tower Hamlets E3 ..33 B4
Burdon Ct **3** E8 ...16 C2
Burford Ct SE8 ....51 C4
Burford Ho
　1 Brentford TW8 ..36 A1
　5 South Lambeth
　SW9 ....173 A1
Burford Rd
　Brentford TW8 ....36 A1
　5 Stratford Marsh
　E15 ....27 C4
Burford Wlk SW6 ..156 B1
Burgate Ct **3**
　SW9 ....62 C4
Burges Gr SW13 ...47 A3
Burgess Bsns Pk
　SE5 ....48 C3
Burgess Hill NW2 ..10 C4
Burgess Ho **9**
　SE5 ....48 B3
Burgess Park Mans
　NW10 ....10 C4
Burgess St E14 ....33 C4
Burge St SE1 ......137 C1
Burgh House &
　Hampstead Mus*
　NW3 ....12 B4
Burghley Hall Cl
　SW19 ....70 A3
Burghley Ho SW19 ..70 A1
Burghley Rd NW5 ..13 A4
Burghley Twr W3 ..29 B2
Burgh St N1 ......86 B2

Burgon St EC4.....108 B1
Burgos Gr SE10......52 A2
Burgoyne Rd SW9..62 B4
Burhan Uddin Ho
  E1............24 B1 98 C1
Buriton Ho
  SW15...............69 A3
Burke Cl SW15......56 A3
Burke Ho ▓ SW11...59 C3
Burland Rd SW11..60 B2
Burleigh Coll W6...39 B2
Burleigh Ho
  Chelsea SW1 ....157 C3
  ▓ North Kensington
  W10.................30 C4
Burleigh Pl SW15..57 C2
Burleigh St WC2...120 C4
Burley Ho E1.......32 C3
Burlington Arc
  W1................118 C3
Burlington Ave
  TW9................24 C1
Burlington Cl W9...23 C1
Burlington Ct
  Chiswick W4.......45 B3
  Highgate N6........3 C3
Burlington Danes
  Acad W12...........30 A3
Burlington Gdns
  Acton Green W4....37 B1
  Acton W3...........28 B1
  ▓ Fulham SW6....164 B1
  Marylebone W1...118 C3
Burlington Ho
  NW3.................11 C3
Burlington La W4...45 C3
Burlington Lodge
  SW6................164 B1
Burlington Mews
  Acton W3...........28 B1
  ▓ Putney SW15....58 B3
Burlington Pl
  SW6................164 B1
Burlington Rd
  Acton Green W4....37 B1
  Fulham SW6.......164 B1
Burma Rd N16.......15 C4
Burmarsh ▓ NW5...12 C2
Burmester Ho
  SW17...............71 B1
Burmester Rd
  SW17...............71 B1
Burnaby Cres W4...45 B4
Burnaby Ct
  SE16...............139 C3
Burnaby Gdns W4..45 A4
Burnaby St SW10..157 A1
Burnand Ho ▓
  W14.................39 C3
Burnbury Rd SW12.73 B3
Burne Jones Ho
  W14................140 B3
Burnell Ho ▓
  SW2.................74 C3
Burnell Wlk SE1...153 A2
Burness Cl N7........14 B2
Burne St NW1......102 A4
Burnett Cl E9........17 B3
Burnett Ho ▓
  SE13................52 B1
Burney St SE10.....52 B3
Burnfoot Ave
  SW6................164 B3
Burnham NW3......12 A1

Burnham Cl SE1...153 A3
Burnham Ct W2....114 A4
Burnham Est ▓
  E2..................25 B2
Burnhill Ho EC1....96 C3
Burnley Rd
  London SW9.......172 C2
  Willesden NW10....8 B2
Burns Ho ▓
  ▓ Bethnal Green
  E2..................25 B2
  ▓ Islington N7.....14 B2
  Kennington SE17...150 B1
  ▓ Stoke Newington
  N16.................16 A4
Burn's Ho NW10....21 B4
Burnside Cl SE16...32 C1
Burns Rd SW11......59 A4
Bursar's Rd SW3..144 B2
Burnthwaite Rd
  SW6................155 A1
Burntwood Cl
  SW18...............72 A3
Burntwood Ct
  SW17...............71 B1
Burntwood Grange Rd
  SW18...............72 A3
Burntwood La
  SW17...............71 C2
Burntwood Sch
  SW17...............71 C2
Buross St E1.........32 A3
Burrage Ct ▓
  SE16...............40 C2
Burrard Ho ▓ E2...25 B3
Burrard Rd NW6...10 C4
Burr Cl E1..........125 B2
Burrell St SE1......122 A2
Burrell's Wharf Sq
  E14.................42 A1
Burrhill Ct SE16....40 C3
Burrow Ho ▓
  SW9................173 A1
Burrow Rd SE22....64 A3
Burrows Mews
  SE1................136 A4
Burrows Rd NW10..22 B2
Burrow Wlk SE21..75 B4
Burr Rd SW18.......70 C4
Bursar St SE1......124 A1
Burslem St E1......111 C1
Burstock Rd SW15.57 C3
Burston Rd SW15..57 C2
Burtley Cl N4.........6 B3
Burton Bank N1....15 C1
Burton Ct SW3....145 A2
Burton Gr SE17....151 B1
Burton Ho
  ▓ Bermondsey
  SE1................40 A4
  Brixton SE5........48 A1
Burton Lo ▓
  SW15...............58 B2
Burton Mews
  SW1................145 C3
Burton Pl WC1.....93 C3
Burton Rd
  ▓ Brixton SW9...173 B2
  Brixton SW9.......48 A1
  Brondesbury NW6..10 A1
  Burtons Ct E15....19 C1
  Brixton SW9........48 A1
Burtonwood Ho N4..6 C4

Burtt Ho ▓
  N1.........24 A2 98 A4
Burwash Ho SE1...137 C3
Burwell Cl ▓ E1....32 A3
Burwell Rd E5......16 C4
Burwell Wlk E3....26 C1
Burwood Ho ▓
  SW9................63 A3
Bury Cl SE16........32 C1
Bury Ct EC3........110 B2
Bury PI WC1........106 B3
Bury St
  St James SW1....119 A2
  Whitechapel EC3..110 B2
Bury Wlk SW3.....144 A2
Busbridge Ho ▓
  E14.................33 C4
Busby Mews ▓
  NW1.................13 C2
Busby PI NW5......13 C2
Bushbaby Cl SE1..138 A1
Bushberry Rd E9...18 A2
Bush Cotts ▓
  SW18...............58 C2
Bush Ct ▓ W12....39 C4
Bushell Cl SW2....74 B2
Bushell St E1......125 C2
Bushey Down
  SW12...............73 A2
Bushey Hall SE5....48 B2
Bushey Hill Rd
  SE5.................49 B2
Bushfield Ho N5....15 B3
Bush Ind Est
  N19.................4 C1
Bush La EC4.......123 B4
Bushnell Rd SW17..73 A1
Bush Rd
  Bermondsey SE8...40 C2
  Hackney E8.........25 A4
  Richmond TW9.....44 B4
Bushwood Dr SE1..153 A3
Bushwood Rd
  TW9.................44 C4
Business Design Ctr★
  N1..................85 C3
Buspace Studios ▓
  W10.................23 A1
Butcher Row E14...32 C3
Butchers Rd E16...35 C3
Bute Gdns W6.......39 C2
Bute House Prep Sch
  ▓ W6...............39 C2
Bute St SW7.......143 B4
Bute Wlk ▓ N1....15 C2
Butfield Ho ▓ E9..17 B2
Butler Ho
  ▓ Bethnal Green
  E2..................25 B2
  ▓ Brixton SW9....48 A2
  ▓ Poplar E14......33 B3
Butler Rd NW10...8 B1
Butler Rd NW10....8 B1
Butlers & Colonial
  Wharf SE1........139 A4
Butler St E2.........25 B2
Butler's Wharf W
  SE1................124 C1
Butley Ct ▓ E3.....26 A3
Butterfield Cl ▓
  SE16...............40 A4
Butterfly Wlk ▓
  SE5.................48 C2
Buttermere Cl SW1.92 B4

Buttermere Cl
  Bermondsey SE1..152 C3
  Leyton E11.........19 C4
Buttermere Ct
  NW8.................79 B4
Buttermere Dr
  SW15...............58 A2
Buttermere Ho ▓
  E3..................26 B2
Buttermere Wlk ▓
  E8..................16 B2
Butterwick W6.....39 B2
Butterworth Ct
  SW16...............74 A1
Buttesland St N1...97 C4
Buxhall Cres E9....18 B2
Buxted Rd
  Camberwell SE22..64 A3
  Dalston E8.........16 B1
Buxton Ct N1.......97 A4
Buxton Gdns W3...28 A2
Buxton Ho ▓
  SW11...............59 C3
Buxton Mews
  SW4................171 C2
Buxton Rd
  Mortlake SW14....56 A4
  Upper Holloway N19..4 C3
  Willesden NW2....9 B2
Buxton St
  E1............24 B1 99 A1
Byam Shaw Sch of Art
  ▓ N19................4 C2
Byam St SW6.......166 C1
Byards Ct SE16.....40 C3
Byas Ho ▓ E3......26 B2
Byefield Cl SE16....41 A4
Byelands Cl ▓
  SE16...............32 C1
Bye The W3.........29 A3
Byeway The SW13..46 B2
Byfeld Gdns SW13..46 C2
Bygrove Prim Sch
  E14.................34 A3
Bygrove St E14.....34 A3
Byng Pl WC1.......93 B1
Byng St E14........41 C4
Byrne Ho ▓ SW2..62 B2
Byrne Rd SW12....73 A2
Byron Cl E8.........24 C4
Byron Ct
  Chelsea SW3.....144 B3
  Dulwich SE21......76 C3
  ▓ Hampstead NW6..11 B1
  Paddington W9....23 C1
  St Pancras WC1...94 C2
Byron Mews
  Hampstead NW3...12 A4
  ▓ Maida Vale W9..23 C1
Byron St E14........34 B3
Bythorn St SW9....62 B3
Byward St EC3.....124 B3
Bywater PI SE16...33 A1
Bywater St SW3...144 C2
Bywell PI W1......104 C3
Byworth Wlk N19...5 A3

C

Cabbell St NW1...102 A3
Cabinet Off SW1...134 A4
Cabinet War Rooms &
  Churchill Mus★
  SW1................133 C4
Cable Ho WC1.......95 B4

Bur–Cal 191

Cable PI SE10.......52 B2
Cable St E1..........32 A2
Cabot Ct SE16......40 C3
Cabot Sq E14.......33 C1
Cabul Rd SW11....168 B1
Cactus Cl SE5.......49 A1
Cactus Wlk W12...29 B3
Cadbury Way ▓
  SE16...............153 B3
Caddington Rd
  NW2.................1 A1
Cadell Cl E2.........24 B3
Cadell Ho ▓ E2....24 B3
Cade Rd SE10......52 C2
Cader Rd SW18....59 B1
Cadet Dr SE1.......153 A2
Cade Tyler Ho ▓
  SE10...............52 B2
Cadiz St SE17......151 A1
Cadman Cl SW9....48 A3
Cadmore Ho ▓
  N1..................15 A1
Cadmus Cl ▓
  SW4................61 C4
Cadmus Ct ▓
  SW9................173 B4
Cadnam Point ▓
  SW15...............69 A3
Cadogan Cl E9.....18 B1
Cadogan Ct SW3..144 C3
Cadogan Ct Gdns
  SW1................145 B4
Cadogan Gate
  SW1................145 A4
Cadogan Gdns
  SW3................145 A3
Cadogan Hall★
  SW1................145 C4
Cadogan La SW1..131 B1
Cadogan Pl SW1...131 B1
Cadogan Sq SW1..131 A1
Cadogan St SW3...144 C3
Cadogan Terr E9...18 B1
Caedmon Rd N7....14 B4
Caernarvon Ho
  W2................100 C2
Caesar Ct ▓ E2....25 C3
Cahill St EC1........97 A1
Cahir St E14........42 A2
Caine Ho W3.......37 A4
Caird St W10.......23 B2
Cairns Ho ▓ N7...14 B4
Cairns Rd SW11....60 A2
Caister Ho N7.......14 B2
Caistor Ho ▓
  SW12...............73 A4
Caistor Mews
  SW12...............73 A4
Caistor Rd SW12...73 A4
Caithness Ho N1....84 C4
Caithness Rd W14..39 C3
Calabria Rd N5.....15 A3
Calais Gdns SE5....48 A2
Calais St SE5.......48 A2
Calbourne Rd
  SW12...............72 C4
Calcraft Ho ▓ E2..25 B3
Caldecot Ct SE5....48 B1
Caldecot Rd SE5...48 B1
Calder Ct SE16.....33 B1
Calderon Ho NW8..80 A2

Calderon Pl 20
W10 . . . . 30 B4
Caldervale Rd
SW4 . . . . 61 C2
Caldew St SE5 . . . . . . 48 B3
Caldwell St SW9 . . 163 A1
Caldy Wlk N1 . . . . . . 15 A2
Caleb St SE1 . . . . . 137 A4
Caledonia Ho 8
E14 . . . . 33 A3
Caledonian Market
SE1 . . . . 138 B2
Caledonian Rd
Islington N1 . . . . 84 C3
Lower Holloway N7 . 14 B2
Caledonian Road &
Barnsbury Sta N7 . 14 B1
Caledonian Road Sta
N7 . . . . 14 B2
Caledonian Sq 6
NW1 . . . . 13 C2
Caledonian Wharf Rd
E14 . . . . 42 C2
Caledonia St N1 . . . 84 B1
Cale St SW3 . . . . . 144 A2
Caletock Way
SE10 . . . . 43 B1
Calgarth NW1 . . . . . 83 A2
Calgary Ct 12 SE16 . 40 B4
Caliban Twr 9 N1 . . 24 A3
Calico Ho 4 SW11 . 59 B4
Calico Row 5
SW11 . . . . 59 B4
Calidore Cl 20 SW2 . 62 B1
California Bldg 2
SE13 . . . . 52 A2
Callaby Terr 11
N1 . . . . 15 C2
Callahan Cotts 8
E1 . . . . 32 B4
Callan Sch The
W1 . . . . 105 A2
Callcott Ct N16 . . . . 10 B1
Callcott Rd NW6 . . . 10 B1
Callcott St
W8 . . . . . . 31 C1 113 B2
Callendar Rd
SW7 . . . . 129 B2
Callingham Cl 13
E14 . . . . 33 B4
Callingham Ho 1
SW4 . . . . 172 A2
Callow St SW3 . . . 157 B4
Calmington Rd
SE5 . . . . 49 A4
Calshot Ho N1 . . . . 84 C2
Calshot St N1 . . . . . 84 C1
Calstock NW1 . . . . . 83 B3
Calstock Ho SE11 . 149 C2
Calthorpe St WC1 . 95 A2
Calton Ave SE21 . . . 64 A1
Calver 11 NW5 . . . . 13 A4
Calverley Gr N19 . . 4 C3
Calvert Ave
E2 . . . . 24 B2 98 C3
Calvert Ct
1 London N19 . . . . . 4 B3
5 Richmond TW9 . . 54 B4
Calvert Ho 9 W12 . . 30 A2
Calverton SE5 . . . . . 49 A4
Calvert Rd SE10 . . . 43 B1
Calvert's Bldgs
SE1 . . . . 123 B1
Calvert St NW1 . . . . 81 B4

Calvin St E1 . . 24 B1 98 C1
Calypso Cres 6
SE15 . . . . 49 B3
Calypso Way SE8 . . 41 B2
Cambalt Ho 3
SW15 . . . . 57 C2
Cambalt Rd SW15 . . 57 C2
Camber Ho 7
SE15 . . . . 50 B4
Camberley Ho
NW1 . . . . 82 B1
CAMBERWELL 48 B2
Camberwell Bsns Ctr
SE5 . . . . 48 C3
Camberwell Church
St SE5 . . . . 48 C2
Camberwell Coll of
Arts
1 Camberwell
SE5 . . . . 49 A2
28 Camberwell
SE15 . . . . 49 B3
Camberwell Glebe
SE5 . . . . 49 A2
Camberwell Gn
SE5 . . . . 48 C2
Camberwell Gr
SE5 . . . . 49 A1
Camberwell Green
SE5 . . . . 48 B2
Camberwell New Rd
SW9 . . . . 48 A3
Camberwell Rd
SE5 . . . . 48 B3
Camberwell Station
Rd SE5 . . . . 48 B2
Camberwell Trad Est
SE5 . . . . 48 C2
Camborne Rd
SW18 . . . . 70 C4
Cambourne Mews 6
W11 . . . . 31 A3
Cambria Ho 14
E14 . . . . 33 A3
Cambria Lo 3
SW15 . . . . 58 B2
Cambrian Cl SE27 . 75 A1
Cambrian Rd
TW10 . . . . 54 B1
Cambria Rd SE5 . . . 63 B4
Cambria St SW6 . . 156 B1
Cambridge Ave
NW6 . . . . 23 C3
Cambridge Cir
WC2 . . . . 105 C1
Cambridge Cotts
TW9 . . . . 44 C4
Cambridge Cres 2
E2 . . . . 25 A3
Cambridge Ct
2 Bethnal Green
E2 . . . . 25 A3
2 Hammersmith
W6 . . . . 39 B2
3 Kilburn NW6 . . . 23 C3
Marylebone W2 . . 102 A3
Stamford Hill N16 . . 7 A4
Cambridge Gate
NW1 . . . . 92 A2
Cambridge Gate
Mews NW1 . . . . 92 B2
Cambridge Gdns
Kilburn NW6 . . . . . . 23 C3

Cambridge Gdns
continued
North Kensington
W10 . . . . 31 A3
Cambridge Gr W6 . 39 A2
Cambridge Heath Rd
E1, E2 . . . . 25 A1
Cambridge Heath Sta
E2 . . . . 25 A2
Cambridge Ho
SW6 . . . . 58 A4
Cambridge Mans
SW11 . . . . 168 C3
Cambridge Pas 8
E9 . . . . 17 B1
Cambridge Pl W8 128 B3
Cambridge Rd
Barnes SW13 . . . . . . 46 B1
Battersea SW11 . . 168 C3
Kilburn NW6 . . . . . . 23 C2
Richmond TW9 . . . . 44 C3
Cambridge Rd N
W4 . . . . 37 A1
Cambridge Rd S 7
W4 . . . . 37 A1
Cambridge Sch 15
W6 . . . . 39 A2
Cambridge Sq
W2 . . . . 102 A2
Cambridge St
SW1 . . . . 146 C2
Cambridge Terr
NW1 . . . . 92 A3
Cambridge Terr Mews
NW1 . . . . 92 B3
Cambus Rd E16 . . . 35 C4
Cam Ct 2 SE15 . . . 49 B4
Camden Coll of
English 8 NW1 . . 12 C1
Camden Gdns
NW1 . . . . 13 A1
Camden High St
NW1 . . . . 82 C3
Camden Ho 6
SE8 . . . . 41 B1
Camdenhurst St
E14 . . . . 33 A3
Camden Lock Pl
NW1 . . . . 13 A1
Camden Mews
NW1 . . . . 13 C2
Camden Park Rd
NW1 . . . . 13 C2
Camden Pas * N1 . 86 A3
Camden Rd NW1 . . 82 B4
Camden Road Sta
NW1 . . . . 13 B1
Camden Row SE3 . 53 A1
Camden Sch for Girls
The NW5 . . . . 13 B2
Camden Sq NW1 . . 13 C2
Camden St NW1 . . . 83 A3
Camden Studios
NW1 . . . . 83 A3
Camden Terr 17
NW1 . . . . 13 C2
CAMDEN TOWN . . 13 A1
Camden Town Sta
NW1 . . . . 82 B4
Camden Wlk N1 . . 86 A3
Cameford Ct 20
SW12 . . . . 74 A4
Camelford NW1 . . . 83 A3

Camelford Ct 15
W11 . . . . 31 A3
Camelford Ho
SE1 . . . . 148 B1
Camelford Wlk 13
W11 . . . . 31 A3
Camellia Ho SE8 . . 51 B3
Camellia St SW8 . 162 A1
Camelot Ho 15
NW1 . . . . 13 C2
Camelot Prim Sch
SE15 . . . . 50 A4
Camera Pl SW10 . 157 B4
Camera Press Gall
The * SE1 . . . . 138 C4
Cameret Ct 6
W11 . . . . 39 C4
Cameron Ct 3
SW19 . . . . 70 A3
Cameron Ho
SE5 . . . . 48 B3
St John's Wood
NW8 . . . . 90 A1
Cameron House Sch
SW10 . . . . 157 B4
Cameron Pl SW16 . 74 C2
Camerton Cl 8
E8 . . . . 16 B2
Camilla Rd SE16 . . 40 A2
Camlet St
E2 . . . . 24 B1 98 C2
Camley St Natural
Pk * NW1 . . . . 83 C3
Camley St N1 . . . . . 83 C3
Camomile St EC3 . 110 B2
Campaign Ct W9 . . 23 B1
Campana Rd SW6 . 165 C4
Campbell Ct
Dulwich SE21 . . . . . 76 C3
South Kensington
SW7 . . . . 128 C1
Campbell Gordon Way
NW2 . . . . 9 A4
Campbell Ho
Paddington W2 . . . . 89 B1
Pimlico SW1 . . . . . 146 C1
30 Shepherd's Bush
W12 . . . . 30 A2
Campbell Rd E3 . . . 26 C2
Campbell Wlk N1 . . 84 B4
Campdale Rd N7 . . . 4 C1
Campden Gr W8 . . 127 C4
Campden Hill W8 . 127 B4
Campden Hill Ct
W8 . . . . 127 C4
Campden Hill Gate
W8 . . . . 127 B4
Campden Hill Gdns
W8 . . . . . . 31 C1 113 B2
Campden Hill Mans
W8 . . . . 113 C2
Campden Hill Pl
W14 . . . . . . 31 B1 113 A2
Campden Hill Rd
W8 . . . . 127 B4
Campden Hill Sq
W14 . . . . . . 31 B1 113 A2
Campden Ho 4
W8 . . . . 127 B4
Campden Hos
W8 . . . . . . 31 C1 113 B1
Campden House Cl
W8 . . . . 127 C4
Campden St
W8 . . . . . . 31 C1 113 B1
Campen Cl SW19 . . 70 A2

Camperdown St
E1 . . . . 111 A1
Campion Ho 16
N16 . . . . 16 A3
Campion Rd SW15 . 57 B2
Camplin St SE14 . . 50 C3
Campshill Pl SE13 . 67 B2
Campshill Rd SE13 . 67 B2
Campton Hill Twrs
W8 . . . . 113 B2
Cam Rd E15 . . . . . . 27 C4
Camsey Ho 8
SW2 . . . . 62 B2
Canada Cres W3 . . 20 B1
Canada Gdns SE13 . 67 B2
Canada Rd W3 . . . . 28 B4
Canada Sq E14 . . . . 34 A1
Canada St SE16 . . . 40 C4
Canada Water Sta
SE16 . . . . 40 C3
Canada Way W12 . . 30 A2
Canal App SE8 . . . . 51 A4
Canal Bldg N1 . . . . 86 C2
Canal Bridge SE15 . 49 C4
Canal Bvd 7 NW1 . 13 C2
Canal Cl
Mile End E1 . . . . 26 A1
North Kensington
W10 . . . . 22 C1
Canal Gr SE15 . . . . 50 A4
Canal Head Public Sq
1 SE15 . . . . 49 C2
Canal Path E2 22 . . 24 A4
Canalside Studios 20
N1 . . . . 24 A4
Canal St SE5 . . . . . 48 C4
Canal Way W10 . . . 22 C1
Canal Wlk N1 . . . . . 87 C4
CANARY WHARF . . 34 A1
Canary Wharf 5
E14 . . . . 34 A1
Canary Wharf Pier
(River Bus) E14 . . 33 B1
Canary Wharf Sta
E14 . . . . 34 A1
Canary Wharf Sta
(DLR) E14 . . . . 33 C1
Canberra Prim Sch
E16 . . . . 35 C4
Canbury Mews
SE26 . . . . 76 C1
Cancell Rd SW9 . . 173 C4
Candahar Rd
SW11 . . . . 168 B1
Candida Ct 9
NW1 . . . . 13 A1
Candishe Ho SE1 . 138 C4
Candle Gr SE15 . . . 65 A4
Candlemakers 24
SW11 . . . . 59 C4
Candover St W1 . . 104 C3
Candy St E3 . . . . . . 26 B4
Canfield Gdns
NW6 . . . . 11 A1
Canfield Pl NW6 . . 11 B2
Canford Rd SW11 . 60 C2
Canham Rd W3 . . . 38 A4
Cann Ho W14 . . . . 126 B1
Canning Cross
SE5 . . . . 49 A1
Canning Ho 23
W12 . . . . 30 A2
Canning Pas W8 . . 128 C2
Canning Pl W8 . . . 128 C2
Canning Pl Mews
W8 . . . . 128 C2

Canning Rd N5 . . . . 6 A1
Cannington **14**
NW5 . . . . 12 C2
CANNING TOWN . . 35 B3
Canning Town
E16 . . . . 35 A3
Canning Town Sta
E16 . . . . 35 A3
Cannock Ho N4 . . . . . . 6 C4
Cannon Dr 🡒 E14 . . 33 C2
Cannon Hill NW6 . . 10 C3
Cannon Ho SE11 . . 149 A3
Cannon La NW3 . . . . . 2 C1
Cannon PI NW3 . . . . . 2 C1
Cannon St EC4 . . . . 123 A4
Cannon Street Rd
E1 . . . . 32 A3
Cannon Street Sta
EC4 . . . . 123 B4
Cannon Wharf Bsns
Ctr 🡒 SE8 . . . . . . 41 A2
Canon Barnett Prim
Sch E1 . . . . 111 A2
Canon Beck Rd
SE16 . . . . 40 B4
CANONBURY 15 B2
Canonbury Bsns Ctr
N1 . . . . 87 A4
Canonbury Cres
N1 . . . . 15 B1
Canonbury Ct 🡒
N1 . . . . 15 B1
Canonbury Gr N1 . . 15 B1
Canonbury Hts 🖪
N1 . . . . 15 C2
Canonbury La N1 . . 15 A1
Canonbury Pk N
N1 . . . . 15 B2
Canonbury Pk S
N1 . . . . 15 B2
Canonbury PI N1 . . 15 A2
Canonbury Prim Sch
🖪 N1 . . . . 15 B1
Canonbury Rd N1 . . 15 A1
Canonbury Sq N1 . . 15 A1
Canonbury St N1 . . 15 B1
Canonbury Sta N1,
N5 . . . . 15 B3
Canonbury Villas
N1 . . . . 15 A1
Canonbury Yd E **28**
N1 . . . . 15 B3
Canon Murnane Rd
SE1 . . . . 138 C1
Canon Row SW1 . . 134 A3
Canons Cl N2 . . . . 2 C4
Canon St N1 . . . . . . 86 C3
Canrobert St E2 . . . 25 A2
Cantelowes Rd
NW1 . . . . 13 C2
Canterbury SE13 . . 67 B2
Canterbury Cl **16**
SE5 . . . . 48 B1
Canterbury Cres
SW9 . . . . 62 C4
Canterbury Ct
Acton W3 . . . . 29 A1
Kilburn NW6 . . . . . 23 C3
Canterbury Gr SE27,
SW16 . . . . 75 B2
Canterbury Ho
🔸 Bromley E3 . . . . 27 A2
Lambeth SE1 . . . . 135 A2
Canterbury Ind Pk 🖪
SE15 . . . . 50 B4

Canterbury Mans
NW6 . . . . 11 A2
Canterbury PI
SE17 . . . . 150 B3
Canterbury Rd
NW6 . . . . 23 C3
Canterbury Terr
NW6 . . . . 23 C3
Cantium Ret Pk
SE1 . . . . 49 C4
Canton St E14 . . . . 33 C3
Cantrell Rd E3 . . . . 26 C1
Canute Ct SW16 . . 74 C1
Canute Gdns SE16 . 40 C2
Canvey St SE1 . . . 122 C2
Cape Henry Ct **15**
E14 . . . . 34 C2
Capel Ho N16 . . . . 15 C2
Capel Lo 🔸
🔸 Richmond TW9 . . 44 B2
🔟 Streatham SW2 . 74 B4
Capener's Cl SW1 131 B3
Capern Rd SW18 . . 71 B3
Capio Nightingale
Hospl NW1 . . . . . 102 B4
Capital City Acad
NW10 . . . . 22 A4
Capital East Apts 🟦
E16 . . . . 35 C2
Capital Interchange
Way TW8 . . . . 36 C1
Capital Sh Ctrs
SW1 . . . . 133 B3
Capital Wharf **14**
E1 . . . . 125 C1
Capland Ho NW8 . . 89 C2
Capland St NW8 . . 89 C2
Caple Ho SW10 . . 157 A2
Caple Rd NW10 . . . 21 B3
Capper St WC1 . . . 93 A1
Capstan Ho 🔟 E14 42 B2
Capstan Rd SE8 . . 41 B2
Capstan Sq E14 . . 42 B4
Capstan Way SE16 . 33 A1
Capulet Mews 🔟
E16 . . . . 35 C1
Caradoc Cl W2 . . . 31 C3
Caradoc St SE10 . . 43 A1
Cara Ho 🔟 N1 . . . . 14 C1
Caranday Villas 🔸
W11 . . . . 30 C1
Caravel Cl E14 . . . 41 C3
Caravel Mews 🔟
SE8 . . . . 51 C4
Caraway Hts E14 . . 34 B2
Carbery Ave W3 . . 36 B4
Carbis Rd E14 . . . . 33 B3
Carbroke Ho 🔟
E9 . . . . 25 B4
Carburton St W1 . . 92 B1
Cardale St 🔟 E14 . 42 B3
Carden Rd SE15 . . 65 A4
Cardiff Ho 🟨 SE15 . 49 C4
Cardigan Rd
Barnes SW13 . . . 46 C1
Bow E3 . . . . 26 B3
Richmond TW10 . . 54 A1
Cardigan St SE11 149 B2
Cardigan Wlk **19**
N1 . . . . 15 B1
Cardinal Bourne St
SE1 . . . . 137 C1
Cardinal Cap Alley
SE1 . . . . 122 C3
Cardinal Hinsley Cl
NW10 . . . . 21 C3

Cardinal Hinsley
  Mathematics &
  Computing Coll
NW10 . . . . 21 C4
Cardinal PI SW15 . 57 C3
Cardinal Pole RC Sch
London E9 . . . . . . 17 C1
London E9 . . . . . . 18 A3
Cardinals Way N19 . 4 C3
Cardinal Vaughan
  Meml Sch The
W14 . . . . 126 A4
Cardinal Wlk
SW1 . . . . 132 C1
Cardine Mews
SE15 . . . . 50 A3
Cardington St
NW1 . . . . 93 A3
Cardozo Rd N7 . . . 14 A3
Cardross St W6 . . . 39 A3
Cardwell Rd 🔟
N7 . . . . 14 A4
Career Ct **11** SE16 . 40 C4
Carew Cl N7 . . . . . . 5 B2
Carew Ct 🔟 SE14 . 50 C4
Carew St SE5 . . . . 48 B1
Carew St SE5 . . . . 48 B1
Carey Ct 🟨 SE5 . . 48 B3
Carey Gdns SW8 . 171 B3
Carey La EC2 . . . 108 C2
Carey PI SW1 . . . 147 B3
Carey St WC2 . . . 107 A1
Carfax PI SW4 . . . 61 C3
Carfree Cl 🔟 N1 . . 14 C1
Cargill Rd SW18 . . 71 B3
Carinthia Ct 🟨
SE8 . . . . 41 A2
Carisbrooke Ct
Acton W3 . . . . 37 B4
🔟 Streatham SW16 74 B1
Carisbrooke Gdns
SE15 . . . . 49 B3
Carisbrooke Ho
TW10 . . . . 54 C2
Carker's La
  Crouch End N19 . . . 4 C4
  Gospel Oak NW5 . . 13 A3
Carleton Gdns
N19 . . . . 13 B3
Carleton Rd N7 . . . 13 C4
Carlile Cl E3 . . . . . 26 B3
Carlile Ho SE1 . . . 137 C1
Carlingford Rd
NW3 . . . . 11 C4
Carlisle Ave
  Acton W3 . . . . 29 A3
  Whitechapel EC3 . 110 C1
Carlisle Ho 🔟 NW5 . 4 B1
Carlisle La SE1 . . 135 A2
Carlisle PI SW1 . . 132 C1
Carlisle Rd
  Finsbury Pk N4 . . . 5 C4
  Kilburn NW6 . . . . 23 A4
Carlisle St W1 . . . 105 B1
Carlisle Wlk **8** E8 . 16 B2
Carlos PI W1 . . . . 118 A3
Carlow St NW1 . . . 82 C2
Carlson Ct SW15 . . 58 B3
Carlton Cl NW3 . . . 1 C2
Carlton Ct
  Brixton SW9 . . . . 48 A2
  Kilburn NW6 . . . . 78 B2
  🔟 Willesden NW2 . 9 B2
Carlton Dr SW15 . . 58 A2

Carlton Gdns
SW1 . . . . 119 B1
Carlton Gr SE15 . . 50 A2
Carlton Hill NW8 . . 78 C2
Carlton Ho
  🔸 Kilburn NW6 . . 23 B3
  Kilburn NW6 . . . . 23 C3
  Marylebone W1 . 115 A1
Carlton House Terr
SW1 . . . . 119 C2
Carlton Lo 🟨 N4 . . 5 C4
Carlton Mans
  Brixton SW9 . . . . 62 C3
  Cricklewood NW2 . 9 C3
  Kensington W14 . 126 A4
  Maida Vale W9 . . 88 B4
  🔟 South Hampstead
    NW6 . . . . 10 C1
  Stamford Hill N16 . 7 B3
Carlton Prim Sch
NW5 . . . . 12 C3
Carlton Rd
  Acton W4 . . . . . . 37 C4
  Finsbury Pk N4 . . . 5 C4
  Mortlake SW14 . . 55 B3
Carlton Sq E1 . . . 25 C1
Carlton St SW1 . . 119 B3
Carltons The 🔟
SW15 . . . . 58 A2
Carlton Tower PI
SW1 . . . . 131 A2
Carlton Vale NW6 . 23 C3
Carlton Vale Inf Sch
🔟 NW6 . . . . 23 B2
Carlyle Ho
  🔟 Camberwell
    SE5 . . . . 48 B3
  Chelsea SW3 . . . 157 C4
  🔟 Stoke Newington
    N16 . . . . 7 A1
Carlyle Mans
SW3 . . . . 158 A3
Carlyle Mews **24**
E1 . . . . 25 C1
Carlyle PI SW15 . . 57 C3
Carlyle Rd 🟦
NW10 . . . . 20 C4
Carlyle's Ho *
SW3 . . . . 158 A3
Carlyle Sq SW3 . . 143 C1
Carmalt Gdns
SW15 . . . . 57 B3
Carmarthen Ho 🟨
SW15 . . . . 69 B4
Carmarthen PI
SE1 . . . . 138 A4
Carmel Ct W8 . . . 128 A4
Carmelite St EC4 . 121 C4
Carmel Lo SW6 . . 155 B4
Carmen St E14 . . . 34 A3
Carmichael Cl 🔟
SW11 . . . . 59 C4
Carmichael Ct 🔟
SW13 . . . . 46 B1
Carmichael Ho 🔟
E14 . . . . 34 B2
Carmichael Mews
SW18 . . . . 71 C4
Carminia Rd SW17 73 A2
Carnaby St * W1 . 104 C1
Carnac St SE21,
SE27 . . . . 75 C1
Carna Ct TW9 . . . . 54 A4
Carnegie Ho NW3 . 2 C1
Carnegie PI SW19 . 69 C1
Carnegie St N1 . . . 85 A3

Carnicot Ho 🟨
SE15 . . . . 50 A2
Carnoustie Dr N1 . 14 B1
Carnwath Ho SW6 . 59 A4
Carnwath Rd SW6 . 59 A4
Caroline Cl
  Bayswater W2 . . 114 B3
  Streatham SW16 . 74 B1
Caroline Gdns
E2 . . . . 24 A2 98 B4
Caroline Ho
  🔸 Bayswater W2 . 114 B3
  🔸 Hammersmith
    W6 . . . . 39 B1
Caroline Martyn Ho 🟨
N19 . . . . 4 C4
Caroline PI
  Bayswater W2 . . 114 B3
  Clapham SW11 . . 169 C1
Caroline PI Mews
W2 . . . . 114 B3
Caroline St E1 . . . 32 C3
Caroline Terr
SW1 . . . . 145 B3
Caroline Wlk W6 . 154 A3
Carol St NW1 . . . . 82 C4
Caronia Ct 🟦
SE16 . . . . 41 A2
Carpenter Ho
  🔟 Tower Hamlets
    E14 . . . . 33 C4
  🔟 Tufnell Pk N19 . 13 C4
Carpenters Ct
NW1 . . . . 82 C4
Carpenter's PI
SW4 . . . . 61 C3
Carpenters Prim Sch
E15 . . . . 27 B4
Carpenter St W1 . 118 A3
Carradale Ho 🟨
E14 . . . . 34 B3
Carrara Cl 🔟 SW9 . 63 A3
Carrara Wharf
SW6 . . . . 58 A4
Carriage Dr E
SW11 . . . . 159 C2
Carriage Drive E
SW11 . . . . 159 C2
Carriage Dr N
  Battersea SW8,
    SW11 . . . . 158 C2
  Battersea SW8,
    SW11 . . . . 159 C3
Carriage Dr S
SW11 . . . . 169 B4
Carriage Dr W
SW11 . . . . 158 C1
Carrick Ho
  Islington N7 . . . . 14 B2
  Kennington SE11 . 150 A2
Carrick Mews SE8 . 51 C4
Carrington Ct
SW11 . . . . 60 A3
Carrington Ho
W1 . . . . 118 A1
Carrington Lo 🔣
TW10 . . . . 54 A2
Carrington Rd
TW10 . . . . 54 C3
Carrington St W1 . 118 A1
Carrol Cl NW5 . . . 13 A4

Carroll Ct
Acton W3 . . . . 37 A3
4 Shacklewell E5 . . . 7 C1
Carroll Ho W12 . . . . 115 B4
Carron Cl E14 . . . . . . 34 A3
Carroun Rd SW8 . . 162 C2
Carr St 5 E14 . . . . . 33 A3
Carslake Rd SW15 . . 57 B1
Carson Rd
Dulwich SE21 . . . . . 75 C2
Newham E16 . . . . . . 35 C4
Carter Cl E14 . . . . . . 108 B1
Carter Ct EC4 . . . . . . 108 B1
Carteret Ho 9
W12 . . . . 30 A2
Carteret St SW1 . . . 133 B3
Carteret Way SE8 . . 41 A2
Carter Ho
11 London SW2 . . . . 62 C2
Spitalfields E1 . . . . 110 C3
Carter La EC4 . . . . . 108 B1
Carter Pl SE17 . . . . . 151 A1
Carters Cl 2 NW5 . . 13 C2
Carter's Yd SW18 . . 58 C2
Carthew Rd W6 . . . . 39 A3
Carthew Villas W6 . . 39 A3
Carthusian St EC1 . 108 C4
Cartier Circ E14 . . . . 34 B1
Carting La WC2 . . . . 120 B3
Cartmel NW1 . . . . . . 92 C4
Carton Ho
4 Bermondsey
SE16 . . . . 139 B2
5 Shepherd's Bush
W11 . . . . 30 C2
Cartoon Mus The ★
WC1 . . . . 106 A3
Cartwright Gdns
WC1 . . . . 94 A3
Cartwright Ho
SE1 . . . . 137 A1
Cartwright St E1 . . 125 A3
Cartwright Way
SW13 . . . . 47 A3
Carvel Ho E14 . . . . . . 42 B1
Carver Cl 13 W4 . . . . 37 B3
Carver Rd SE24 . . . . 63 B1
Carville Cres TW8 . . 36 A2
Caryl Ho 5 SW19 . . 69 C3
Carysfort Rd N16 . . 15 C4
Casby Ho 7 SE16 . 139 B2
Casella Rd SE14 . . . 50 C3
Casey Cl NW8 . . . . . . 90 B3
Casino Ave SE24 . . . 63 C2
Caspian Ho 10 E1 . . 32 C4
Caspian St SE5 . . . . 48 C3
Cassandra Ct 7
NW2 . . . . 9 B2
Cass Bsns Sch EC1 . 97 B1
Cassell Ho 3
SW9 . . . . 172 B2
Casserley Ho W4 . . . 37 C3
Cass Ho 23 E9 . . . . . 17 C2
Cassidy Rd SW6 . . . 155 B1
Cassilis Rd E14 . . . . 41 C4
Cassinghurst SE24 . 63 C2
Cassland Rd E9 . . . . 17 C1
Casson Ho 11 E1 . . . 111 B4
Casson St E1 . . . . . . 111 B3
Castalia Sq 12 E14 . 42 B4
Castellain Mans
W9 . . . . 88 A2
Castell Ho 11 SE8 . . 51 C3

Castello Ave SW15 . . 57 B2
Castelnau SW13 . . . . 47 A3
Castelnau Gdns
SW13 . . . . 47 A4
Castelnau Mans
SW13 . . . . 47 A4
Castelnau Row
SW13 . . . . 47 A4
Casterbridge
Kilburn NW6 . . . . . . 78 B4
3 Notting Hill W11 . 31 C3
Casterton St 8 E8 . . 17 A2
Castleacre W2 . . . . 102 A1
Castle Baynard St
EC4 . . . . 122 C4
Castlebrook Cl
SE11 . . . . 150 A4
Castle Cl
12 Acton W3 . . . . . . 37 A4
Homerton E9 . . . . . . 18 A3
South Acton W3 . . . 37 A4
Wimbledon SW19 . . 69 C1
Castlecombe Dr
SW19 . . . . 69 C4
Castle Ct EC3 . . . . . 109 C1
Castleden Ho
NW6 . . . . 11 C1
Castleford Ct NW8 . 89 C2
Castlefrank Ho 20
N1 . . . . 24 A2 98 B4
Castlegate TW9 . . . . 54 B4
Castlehaven Rd
NW1 . . . . 13 A1
Castle Ho
SE1 . . . . 151 A4
Newington SE1 . . . 150 C4
South Lambeth
SW8 . . . . 162 B2
Castle Ind Est
SE17 . . . . 150 C4
Castle La SW1 . . . . 132 C2
Castlemaine 8
SW11 . . . . 169 A2
Castlemaine St 2
E1 . . . . 32 A4
Castle Mead SE5 . . . 48 B3
Castle Mews NW1 . . 13 A2
Castle Pl
8 Acton W4 . . . . . . 38 A2
Camden Town NW1 . 13 A2
Castle Rd NW1 . . . . . 13 A2
Castlereagh St
W1 . . . . 102 C2
Castleton Ho 3
E14 . . . . 42 B2
Castletown Rd
W14 . . . . 140 B1
Castleview Cl N4 . . . 6 B2
Castle Way SW19 . . . 69 C1
Castlewood Ho
WC1 . . . . 105 C2
Castle Yd
Highgate N6 . . . . 3 C4
Lambeth SE1 . . . . . 122 B2
Castor La E14 . . . . . . 34 A2
Catalpa Ct SE13 . . . 67 C1
Caterham Rd SE13 . 67 C4
Catesby Ho 25 E9 . . 17 B1
Catesby St SE17 . . . 151 C3
Cathay Ho SE16 . . . 40 A4
Cathay St SE16 . . . . 40 A4
Cathcart Hill N19 . . . 4 B1
Cathcart Rd SW10 . 156 C4
Cathcart St NW5 . . . 13 A2
Cathedral Ct EC4 . . 108 B1
Cathedral Lo 4 EC1 108 C4

Cathedral Sch of St Saviour & St Mary Overie Prim Sch
SE1 . . . . 137 A4
Cathedral St SE1 . . 123 B2
Cathedral Wlk
SW1 . . . . 132 C2
Catherall Rd N5,
N16 . . . . 6 B1
Catherine Baird Ct 12
SW12 . . . . 73 A4
Catherine Dr TW9 . . 54 A3
Catherine Gr SE10 . . 52 A2
Catherine Griffiths Ct
EC1 . . . . 95 C2
Catherine Ho 10
N1 . . . . 24 A4
Catherine Pl SW1 . 132 C2
Catherine St WC2 . 120 C4
Catherine Wheel Alley
E1 . . . . 110 B3
Catherine Wheel Yd
SW1 . . . . 118 C1
Catherwood Ct N1 . . 87 B1
Cathles Rd SW12 . . . 61 A1
Cathnor Rd W12 . . . . 39 A4
Catlin St SE16 . . . . . 40 A1
Catman Ho N4 . . . . . . 5 B3
Cato Rd SW4 . . . . 61 C3
Cator St
Camberwell SE15 . . 49 B3
Camberwell SE15 . . 49 B4
Cato St W1 . . . . 102 B2
Catton St WC1 . . . . 106 C3
Caughley Ho
SE11 . . . . 135 B1
Caulfield Ct 15
NW1 . . . . 13 B1
Caulfield Rd SE15 . . 50 A1
Causeway The
SW18 . . . . 59 A2
Causton Cotts 3
E14 . . . . 33 A3
Causton Ho SE5 . . . 48 B3
Causton Rd N6 . . . . . . 4 A4
Causton St SW1 . . . 147 C2
Cautley Ave SW4 . . . 61 B2
Cavalry Gdns
SW15 . . . . 58 B2
Cavave Ho SW10 . . 157 A4
Cavaye Pl SW10 . . . 143 A1
Cavell Ct 5 N19 . . . . 4 B2
Cavell Ho 8 N1 . . . . . 24 A4
Cavell St E1 . . . . 32 A4
Cavendish Ave
NW8 . . . . 79 C1
Cavendish Cl
Brondesbury NW6 . . 10 B2
5 Putney SW15 . . . 58 A2
St John's Wood
NW8 . . . . 89 C3
Cavendish Coll
WC1 . . . . 105 B4
Cavendish Ct EC2 . 110 B2
Cavendish Gdns
SW4 . . . . 61 B1
Cavendish Ho
South Lambeth
SW8 . . . . 172 A4
St John's Wood
NW8 . . . . 79 C1
Cavendish Jun & Inf
Sch W4 . . . . 46 A3
Cavendish Mans
2 Clapham Pk
SW12 . . . . 61 B1

Cavendish Mans
continued
Hackney E5 . . . . 17 B3
Holborn EC1 . . . . . . 95 B1
8 West Hampstead
NW6 . . . . 10 C3
Cavendish Mews N
W1 . . . . 104 B4
Cavendish Mews S
W1 . . . . 104 B3
Cavendish Par
SW4 . . . . 61 A1
Cavendish Pl
Balham SW4 . . . . . . 61 A1
Brondesbury NW2 . . 9 C2
Marylebone W1 . . . 104 B2
Cavendish Rd
Brondesbury NW6 . . 10 B1
Chiswick W4 . . . . . . 45 B2
Clapham Pk SW12 . . 61 B1
Clapham SW12 . . . . 61 A1
Cavendish Sch E4 . . . 1 C1
Cavendish Sch The
NW1 . . . . 82 B4
Cavendish Sq W1 . . 104 B2
Cavendish St N1 . . . . 87 B1
Cavendish The
NW11 . . . . 2 B4
Caversham Ho 7
SE15 . . . . 49 C4
Caversham Rd
NW5 . . . . 13 B2
Caversham St
SW3 . . . . 158 C4
Cavour Ho SE17 . . . 150 B2
Cawdor Cres E3 . . . . 26 C2
Caxton Gr E3 . . . . . . 26 C2
Caxton Hall ★
SW1 . . . . 133 B2
Caxton Rd W12 . . . . 39 C4
Caxton St E16 . . . . . 35 B3
Caxton St SW1 . . . . 133 B2
Caxton St N E16 . . . 35 B3
Caxton Wlk WC2 . . 105 C1
Cayford Ho 3
NW3 . . . . 12 B3
Cayley Prim Sch 2
E14 . . . . 33 A3
Cayton Pl EC1 . . . . . 97 B3
Cayton St EC1 . . . . . 97 B3
Cazenove Mans 1
N16 . . . . 7 C2
Cazenove Rd N16 . . . 7 C2
Cecil Ct
Chelsea SW10 . . . . 156 C4
South Hampstead
NW6 . . . . 11 A1
St James WC2 . . . . 120 A3
Cecilia Rd E8 . . . . . . 16 C3
Cecil Mans 2
SW17 . . . . 72 C2
Cecil Rd
Acton W3 . . . . 28 B4
Harlesden NW10 . . . 21 A4
Cecil Rhodes Ho
NW1 . . . . 83 B2
Cedar Cl
Old Ford E3 . . . . 26 B4
West Norwood
SE21 . . . . 75 B2
Cedar Ct
Islington N1 . . . . . . 15 B1
Marylebone W1 . . . 102 B2
Mortlake SW14 . . . . 55 B3
Wimbledon SW19 . . 69 C1

Cedar Gr W5 . . . . 36 A3
Cedar Ho
16 Cubitt Town
E14 . . . . 42 B4
Kensington W8 . . . 128 A2
New Cross Gate
SE14 . . . . 50 C2
5 Richmond TW9 . . 45 A2
Rotherhithe
SE16 . . . . 40 C4
Cedar Lo
Brondesbury NW2 . . 10 B2
Fulham SW6 . . . . . . 47 C2
Cedar Rd NW2 . . . . . . 9 B4
Cedars Cl SE13 . . . . 67 C4
Cedars Ct SW15 . . . . 56 C1
Cedars Ho 17 SW2 . 62 B3
Cedars Mews SW4 . 61 A3
Cedars Rd
Barnes SW13 . . . . . . 46 C1
Clapham SW4 . . . . . 61 A3
Cedars The E9 . . . . . 17 C1
Cedar Terr TW9 . . . . 54 A3
Cedar Way NW1 . . . . 83 B4
Cedra Ct N16 . . . . 7 C3
Cedric Chambers
NW8 . . . . 89 B2
Celandine Cl E3,
E14 . . . . 33 C4
Celandine Dr E8 . . . 16 B1
Celbridge Mews
W2 . . . . 100 B2
Celestial Gdns
SE13 . . . . 67 C3
Celia Blairman Ho
E1 . . . . 110 C4
Celia Ct 7 TW9 . . . . 45 A2
Celia Ho 10 N1 . . . . 24 A3
Celia Rd N19 . . . . 13 B4
Celtic St E14 . . . . . . 34 A4
Cenacle Cl NW3 . . . . 1 C1
Cenotaph ★ SW1 . . 134 A4
Centaur Ct 3
TW8 . . . . 36 A1
Centaur St SE1 . . . . 135 A2
Central Ave SW11 . 159 A1
Central Bsns Ctr
NW10 . . . . 8 A3
Central Foundation
Boys' Sch EC2 . . . . 97 C2
Central Foundation
Lower Girls Sch The
10 E3 . . . . 26 A2
Central Foundation
Upper Girls Sch The
22 E3 . . . . 26 B2
Central Ho E15 . . . . . 27 B3
Central Middlesex
Hospl NW10 . . . . . . 20 B2
Central Par W3 . . . . . 37 A4
Central St Martins
Coll EC1 . . . . 95 C1
Central St Martin's
Coll of Art & Design
W1 . . . . 105 C1
Central St Martins
Coll of Art & Design
(The London Inst)
WC1 . . . . 106 C3
Central Sch of Ballet
EC1 . . . . 95 C1
Central Sch of Speech
& Drama NW3 . . . . 11 C1
Central St EC1 . . . . . 96 C3
Central Way NW10 . . 20 B2

Centre Acad 2
SW11 ....59 C3
Centre Ave W3 ....28 C1
Centre Bldg SE17 151 A4
Centre Hts 5
NW3 ....11 C1
Centre Point 3
SE1 ....153 B2
Centre Point Ho
WC2 ....105 C2
Centurion Bldg
SW8 ....160 A3
Centurion Cl N7 ...18 B3
Centurion La E3 ...26 B3
Century Ho SE13 ..52 A1
Cephas Ave E1 ....25 B1
Cephas Ho 8
E1 ....25 B1
Cephas St E1 .....25 B1
Cerise Rd SE15 ...49 C2
Cerney Mews W2. 115 B4
Cervantes Ct 12
W2 ....100 B1
Cester St E2 ......24 C4
Ceylon Rd
6 Hammersmith
W14 ....39 C3
Kensington W14 . 126 A1
Chabot Dr SE15 ...65 A4
Chadacre Ho 10
SW9 ....63 A3
Chadbourn St E14 .34 A4
Chadston Ho 17
N1 ....15 A1
Chadswell WC1 ...94 B3
Chadwell St EC1 ..95 C4
Chadwick Cl SW15 .68 B4
Chadwick Rd
Harlesden NW10 ..21 B4
Peckham SE15 ....49 B1
Chadwick St SW1. 133 B1
Chadworth Ho
Finsbury EC1 .....96 C3
Finsbury Pk N4 ....6 B3
Chagford Ho
5 Bromley E3 ....27 A2
Marylebone NW1 ..90 C1
Chagford St NW1 ..91 A1
Chalbury Ho 8
SW9 ....62 B3
Chalbury Wlk N1 ..85 B2
Chalcot Cres NW1 .81 A4
Chalcot Gdns NW3 .12 B2
Chalcot Mews
SW16 ....74 A1
Chalcot Rd NW1 ...81 B4
Chalcot Sch 21
NW1 ....13 A1
Chalcot Sq NW1 ..12 C1
Chaldon Rd SW6 . 154 B2
Chale Rd SW2 .....62 A1
Chalfont Ct NW1 ..91 A1
Chalfont Ho 2
SE16 ....40 A3
Chalford NW3 .....11 B2
Chalford Ct 15
SW15 ....57 C1
Chalkers Cnr TW9 .55 A4
Chalk Farm Sta
NW3 ....12 C1
Chalk Hill Rd W6 ..39 C2
Chalkwell Ho 10
E1 ....32 C3
Challenge Cl
NW10 ....21 A4

Challenger Ho 7
E14 ....33 A2
Challice Way SW2 .74 B3
Challoner Cres
W14 ....140 C1
Challoner Mans
W14 ....140 C1
Chalmers Ho 14
SW11 ....59 B4
Chalmer's Wlk 14
SE17 ....48 A4
Chalner Ho SW2 ..74 C3
Chaloner Ct SE1 . 137 B4
Chalsey Lodge
E14 ....34 B3
Chalsey Rd SE4 ...66 B3
Chalton Ho NW1 . 83 A1
Chalton St NW1 ...83 A1
Chamberlain Cotts
SE5 ....48 C2
Chamberlain Ho 6
E1 ....32 B2
Chamberlain St 17
NW1 ....12 B1
Chamberlayne Mans
3 NW10 ....22 C2
Chamberlayne Rd
NW10 ....22 B4
Chambers La NW10 .9 B1
Chambers Rd N7 ..14 A4
Chambers St
SE16 ....139 C3
Chamber St E1 .. 125 A4
Chambon Pl 7
W6 ....38 C2
Chambord Ho 2
E2 ....24 B2 99 A3
Chambord St
E2 ....24 B2 99 A3
Champion Gr SE5 .63 C4
Champion Hill SE5 .63 C4
Champion Pk SE5 .48 C1
Champlain Ho 28
W12 ....30 A2
Chancel Ct W1 .. 119 B4
Chancellor Gr
SE21 ....75 B1
Chancellor Ho
South Kensington
SW7 ....129 A2
20 Wapping E1 ...32 A1
Chancellor Pas
E14 ....33 C1
Chancellors' Ct
WC1 ....106 C1
Chancellor's Rd
W6 ....39 B1
Chancellors St W6 .39 B1
Chancellors Wharf 21
W6 ....39 B1
Chancel St SE1 .. 122 A1
Chancery Bldgs 14
E1 ....18 A2
Chancery Ho
WC2 ....107 B3
Chancery La EC4 . 107 B2
Chancery Lane Sta
.............107 B2
Chancery Mews
SW17 ....72 A2
Chance St
E2 ....24 B1 98 C2
Chandler Ave E16 .35 C4
Chandlers Mews
E14 ....41 C4
Chandler St E1 ...32 A1

Chandlers Way 11
SE24 ....74 C4
Chandler Way
SE15 ....49 B3
Chandlery Ho 28
E1 ....111 B1
Chandos Pl WC2. 120 A3
Chandos Rd
Cricklewood NW2 ..9 B4
Old Oak Comm
NW10 ....21 A1
Stratford New Town
E15 ....19 C4
Chandos St W1 .. 104 B3
Chandos Way
NW11 ....1 C3
Change Alley EC3 109 C1
Channel Gate Rd
NW10 ....21 A2
Channel Ho E14 ..33 A4
Channel Sea Bsns Ctr
E15 ....27 C4
Channelsea Rd
E15 ....27 C4
Channing Jun Sch
..............3 C3
Channing Sch N6 ..4 A3
Chantrey Rd SW9 .62 B4
Chantry Cl W9 ....23 B1
Chantry Cres SW6 .58 A4
Chantry Sq W8 .. 128 A1
Chantry St N1 ....86 B3
Chant Sq E15 ....19 C1
Chant St E15 .....19 C1
Chapel Ct SE1 ... 137 B4
Chapel House St
E14 ....42 A1
Chapel Mkt* N1 ..85 B2
Chapel Pl
Islington N1 .....85 C2
Marylebone W1 .. 104 A1
12 Shoreditch
EC2 ......24 A2 98 A3
Chapel Side W2 . 114 A3
Chapel St
Paddington NW1 . 102 A3
Westminster SW1 131 C3
Chapleton Ho
SW2 ....62 C2
Chaplin Cl SE1 .. 136 A4
Chaplin Ho 6
SW9 ....62 C3
Chaplin Rd NW2 ...8 C2
Chaplow Cl SW6 . 166 C1
Chapman Ho
20 Stepney E1 ...32 A3
2 West Norwood
SE27 ....75 A1
Chapman Rd E9 ..18 B2
Chapmans Park Ind
Est NW10 ....8 B2
Chapman Sq
SW19 ....69 C2
Chapman St E1 ...32 A2
Chapone Pl W1 .. 105 B1
Chapter Cl 16 W4 .37 B3
Chapter House &
Jewel Twr*
SW1 ....134 A2
Chapter Rd
Kennington SE17 150 B1
Willesden NW2 ....8 C3
Chapter St SW1 . 147 B3
Chara Pl W4 .....45 C4

Charcot Ho SW15 .56 B1
Charcroft Ct 11
W14 ....39 C4
Chard Ho 7 N7 ....5 B2
Chardin Ho 30
SW9 ....173 C4
Chardin Rd 8 W4 .38 A2
Chardmore Rd N16 .7 C3
Charecroft Way
W12 ....39 C4
Charfield Ct W9 ...88 B1
Charford Rd E16 ..35 C4
Chargrove Cl 24
SE16 ....40 C4
Charing Cross
SW1 ....120 A2
Charing Cross Hospl
W6 ....39 C1
Charing Cross Rd
WC2 ....105 C2
Charing Cross Sta
WC2 ....120 B2
Charing Ho SE1 . 135 C4
Chariot Cl 3 E3 ...26 C4
Charlbert Ct NW8 .80 A2
Charlbert St NW8 .80 A2
Charles Allen Ho
EC1 ....95 C4
Charles Auffray Ho 30
E1 ....32 B4
Charles Barry Cl
SW4 ....61 B4
Charles Burton Ct
E5 ....18 A4
Charles Coveney Rd
SE15 ....49 B2
Charles Darwin Ho 8
E2 ....25 A2
Charles Dickens Ho 1
E2 ....25 A2
Charles Dickens Mus
The* WC1 ......95 A1
Charles Dickens Prim
Sch SE1 ......136 C3
Charles Edward
Brooke Sch 11
SW9 ....48 A2
Charles Edward
Brooke Sch (Dennen
Site) 10 SE5 ....48 A2
Charles Flemwell
Mews 7 E16 ....35 C1
Charles Haller St 2
SW2 ....74 C4
Charles Harrod Ct
SW13 ....47 B4
Charles Hobson Ho 4
NW10 ....8 A1
Charles Hocking Ho
8 W3 ....37 B4
Charles II Pl SW3 144 C1
Charles II St SW1 119 B2
Charles La NW8 ...80 A2
Charles Lamb Ct
N1 ....86 B2
Charles Mackenzie Ho
7 SE16 ....153 C4
Charles Pl NW1 ...93 A3
Charles Rowan Ho
WC1 ....95 B3
Charles Sq N1 ....97 C3
Charles St
Barnes SW13 ....46 A1
Mayfair W1 .... 118 A2
Charleston St
SE17 ....151 A3

Charles Townsend Ho
EC1 ....96 A2
Charles Utton Ct
E8 ....16 C4
Charlesworth Ho 6
E14 ....33 C3
Charleville Ct
SW5 ....140 C1
Charleville Mans
W14 ....140 B1
Charleville Rd
W14 ....140 C1
Charlie Chaplin Ho
W6 ....38 C2
Charlotte Despard
Ave SW11 .....169 C3
Charlotte Ho 12
W6 ....39 B1
Charlotte Mews
Marylebone W1 . 105 A4
North Kensington
W10 ....30 C3
West Kensington
W14 ....140 A4
Charlotte Pl
Marylebone W1 . 105 A3
Westminster SW1 146 C3
Charlotte Rd
Barnes SW13 ....46 B2
Shoreditch
EC2 ......24 A1 98 A2
Charlotte Row
SW4 ....61 B4
Charlotte Sharman
Prim Sch SE1 .. 136 A1
Charlotte Sq 5
TW10 ....54 B1
Charlotte St W1 . 105 A4
Charlotte Terr N1 .85 C2
Charlotte Turner Prim
Sch SE8 ....51 C4
Charlton Ct
22 Hackney E2 ...24 B4
17 Kentish Town N7 .13 C3
Charlton Ho
5 Brentford TW8 ..44 A4
Somers Town NW1 .93 B4
Charlton King's Rd
NW5 ....13 C3
Charlton Pl N1 ....86 A2
Charlton Rd NW10 .21 A4
Charlton Way SE10,
SE3 ....53 A2
Charlwood Ho
Richmond TW9 ...45 A3
1 Streatham SW2 .74 B3
Westminster SW1 147 B3
Charlwood Pl
SW1 ....147 A3
Charlwood Rd
SW15 ....57 C3
Charlwood St
SW1 ....147 A2
Charlwood Terr 5
SW15 ....57 C3
Charman Ho
16 London SW2 ...62 C1
South Lambeth
SW8 ....162 A2
Charmian Ho 19
N1 ....24 A3
Charmouth Ct
TW10 ....54 B2

Charmouth Ho
  SW8 . . . . **162** C2
Charnock Ho **22**
  W12 . . . . .30 A2
Charnwood Gdns
  E14 . . . . .41 C2
Charrington Ho **41**
  E1 . . . . .25 B1
Charrington St
  NW1 . . . . .83 B2
Charter Bldgs **14**
  SE10 . . . . .52 A2
Charter Ct
  Finsbury Pk N4 . . . . . .5 C3
  Marylebone W1 . . . .**102** B3
Charter Ho W2 **C1** 100 B1
Charterhouse Bldgs
  EC1 . . . . .97 A1
Charterhouse Mews
  EC1 . . . .**108** B4
Charterhouse Rd
  E8 . . . . .16 C3
Charterhouse Sq
  EC1 . . . .**108** B4
Charterhouse Square
  Sch The EC1 . . . . . .**108** B4
Charterhouse St
  EC1 . . . .**108** A3
Charterhouse Works
  SW18 . . . . .59 B3
Charteris Rd
  Finsbury Pk N4 . . . . . .5 C3
  Kilburn NW6 . . . . . . .23 B4
Charteris Sports Ctr
  NW6 . . . . .23 C4
Charter Sch SE24 . . .63 C2
Chartes Ho SE1 . . . .**138** C2
Chartfield Ave
  SW15 . . . . .57 B2
Chartfield Sq
  SW15 . . . . .57 C2
Chartham Ct **12**
  SW9 . . . . .62 C4
Chartham Ho SE1 . .**75** A1
Chartham Rd SE27 . .75 A1
Chart House The **5**
  E14 . . . . .42 A1
Chartridge SE17 . . . .48 C4
Chart St N1 . . . . .97 C4
Chartwell **25**
  SW19 . . . . .69 C3
Chase Ct SW3 . . . . .130 C1
Chase Ctr The
  NW10 . . . . .20 C2
Chaseley Ct W4 . . . .37 A1
Chaseley St E14 . . . .33 A3
Chasemore Ho
  SW6 . . . .**154** B2
Chase Rd NW10 . . . .20 C1
Chase Road Trad Est
  NW10 . . . . .20 C1
Chase The NW10 . . .61 A4
Chater Ho **6** E2 . . . . .25 C2
Chatfield Rd SW11 . .59 B4
Chatham Ct SW11 . .60 B2
Chatham Ho **7**
  SE5 . . . . .49 A1
Chatham Pl E9 . . . . .17 B2
Chatham Rd SW11 . .60 B2
Chatham St SE17 . .**151** C4
Chatsworth Ct
  Brondesbury NW2 . . .9 C2
  Clapton Pk E5 . . . . .17 C4
  Earl's Ct W8 . . . . . .**141** B4

Chatsworth Est E5 . .**17** C4
Chatsworth Gdns
  W3 . . . . .28 A1
Chatsworth Lo **1**
  W4 . . . . .37 C1
Chatsworth Rd
  Brondesbury NW2 . . .9 C2
  Chiswick W4 . . . . . . .45 B4
  Clapton Pk E5 . . . . .17 C4
Chatsworth Way
  SE27 . . . . .75 B1
Chattenden Ho **4**
  N4 . . . . .6 C4
Chatterton Rd N4 . . .6 A1
Chatto Rd SW11 . . . .60 B2
Chaucer Ave TW9 . . .44 C1
Chaucer Ct **7**
  N16 . . . . .16 A4
Chaucer Dr SE1 . . . .**153** A3
Chaucer Ho SW1 . .**146** C1
Chaucer Rd
  Acton W3 . . . . .28 B1
  Herne Hill SE24 . . . .63 A2
Chaulden Ho EC1 . . .97 C3
Cheadle Ct NW8 . . . .89 C2
Cheadle Ho **9**
  E14 . . . . .33 B3
Cheam St **8** SE15 . . .65 A4
Cheapside EC2 . . . .**109** A1
Chearsley SE17 . . . .**151** A4
Cheddington Ho **9**
  E2 . . . . .24 C4
Chedworth Cl E16 . . .35 B3
Chedworth Ho **2**
  E5 . . . . .7 C2
Cheesemans Terr
  W14 . . . . .140 C1
Chelmer Rd E9 . . . . .17 C3
Chelmsford Cl W6 . .47 C4
Chelmsford Ho **5**
  N7 . . . . .14 B4
Chelmsford Sq
  NW10 . . . . .22 B4
Chelsea Antiques
  Mkt* SW3 . . . . .144 B1
Chelsea Barracks*
  SW1 . . . . .145 C1
Chelsea Bridge
  SW1 . . . . .160 A4
Chelsea Bridge Rd
  SW1 . . . . .145 C2
Chelsea Cl NW10 . . .20 C4
Chelsea Cloisters
  SW3 . . . . .144 B3
Chelsea Coll of Art &
  Design SW1 . . . . . .148 A2
Chelsea Cres
  Brondesbury NW2 . .10 B2
  Chelsea SW10 . . . .167 A3
Chelsea Emb
  SW3 . . . . .158 A3
Chelsea Farm Ho
  SW10 . . . . .157 C3
Chelsea Gate
  SW1 . . . . .145 C1
Chelsea Gdns
  SW1 . . . . .145 C1
Chelsea Harbour
  Design Ctr SW10 .167 A4
Chelsea Harbour Dr
  SW10 . . . . .167 A4

Chelsea Harbour Pier
  SW10 . . . . .167 B3
Chelsea Ind Coll
  SW6 . . . . .156 A1
Chelsea Lo SW3 . . .159 A4
Chelsea Manor Ct
  SW3 . . . . .158 B4
Chelsea Manor Gdns
  SW3 . . . . .144 B1
Chelsea Manor St
  SW3 . . . . .144 B1
Chelsea Manor
  Studios SW3 . . . . .144 B1
Chelsea Mus*
  SW6 . . . . .156 B2
Chelsea Park Gdns
  SW3 . . . . .157 B4
Chelsea Physic Gdn*
  SW1 . . . . .158 C4
Chelsea Reach Twr
  SW10 . . . . .157 B2
Chelsea Sp Ctr
  SW3 . . . . .144 B1
Chelsea Sq SW3 . . .143 C1
Chelsea Twrs
  SW3 . . . . .158 B4
Chelsea &
  Westminster Hospl
  SW10 . . . . .157 A3
Chelsfield Ho
  SE17 . . . . .152 A3
Chelsfield Point **3**
  E9 . . . . .18 A1
Chelsham Ho **1**
  SW4 . . . . .61 C4
Chelsham Rd SW4 . .61 C4
Cheltenham Pl
  10 Acton W3 . . . . . .28 A1
  Acton W3 . . . . .37 A4
  1 South Acton W3 . .37 B4
Cheltenham Rd
  SE15 . . . . .65 B2
Cheltenham Terr
  SW3 . . . . .145 A2
Chelverton Ct
  SW15 . . . . .57 C3
Chelverton Rd
  SW15 . . . . .57 C3
Chelwood Ct
  SW11 . . . . .167 C4
Chelwood Ho
  TW9 . . . . .44 C1
Chelwood Ho W2 . .101 C1
Chenappa Cl **4**
  E13 . . . . .27 A1
Chenies Ho W2 . . . .114 A4
Chenies Mews
  WC1 . . . . .93 B1
Chenies Pl NW1 . . . .83 C2
Chenies St WC1 . . . .105 B4
Chenies The NW1 . . .83 C2
Cheniston Gdns
  W8 . . . . .128 A2
Chepstow Cl
  SW15 . . . . .58 A2
Chepstow Cres
  W11 . . . . .31 C2 113 B4
Chepstow Ct
  W11 . . . . .31 C2 113 B4
Chepstow Pl
  W2 . . . . . .31 C2 113 C4
Chepstow Rd W2 . . .31 C3
Chepstow Villas
  W11 . . . . .31 C2 113 B4
Chequers Ct EC1 . . . .97 B1
Chequers Ho NW8 . .90 A2
Chequer St EC1 . . . .97 A1

Cherbury Ct N1 . . . . .87 C1
Cherbury St N1 . . . . .87 C1
Cheriton Ho **5** 57 A3
Cheriton Sq SW17 . .72 C2
Cherry Ct **7** SW2 . . .74 C4
Cherry Ct
  Acton W3 . . . . .29 A1
  5 Rotherhithe
  SE16 . . . . .33 A1
Cherry Garden Ho **7**
  SE16 . . . . .40 A4
Cherry Garden Sch **12**
  SE16 . . . . .153 C4
Cherry Garden St
  SE16 . . . . .40 A4
Cherry Laurel Wlk
  SW2 . . . . .62 B1
Cherry Tree Ct **11**
  E9 . . . . .25 B4
Cherry Tree Ct
  1 Camden Town
  NW1 . . . . .13 B1
  11 Peckham SE15 . .50 A2
Cherry Tree Dr
  SW16 . . . . .74 A1
Cherrytree Ho **8**
  W10 . . . . .22 C2
Cherry Tree Ho
  SE14 . . . . .51 B1
Cherry Trees Sch The
  E3 **22** 26 C2
Cherry Tree Terr
  SE1 . . . . .138 C4
Cherry Tree Wlk
  EC1 . . . . .97 A1
Cherrywood Cl E3 . .26 A2
Cherrywood Dr
  SW15 . . . . .57 C2
Chertsey St SW14 . .55 A4
Chertsey Ho **37**
  E2 . . . . .24 B2 **98** C3
Cherwell Ho NW8 . . .89 C1
Cheryls Cl SW6 . . . .166 B4
Chesham Cl SW1 . .131 B1
Chesham Ct SW18 . .71 C4
Chesham Flats
  W1 . . . . .117 C4
Chesham Ho SW1 . .131 B1
Chesham Mews
  SW1 . . . . .131 B2
Chesham Pl SW1 . .131 B1
Chesham St SW1 . .131 B1
Cheshire St
  E2 . . . . .24 B1 99 A2
Chesholm Rd N16 . . .7 A1
Cheshunt Ho **9**
  NW6 . . . . .78 A3
Chesil Ct
  17 Bethnal Green
  E2 . . . . .25 B3
  Chelsea SW3 . . . . .158 B4
Chesilton Rd SW6 . .164 C4
Chesney Ct W9 . . . . .23 C1
Chesney Ho SE13 . . .67 C3
Chesney St SW11 . .169 B3
Chessington Ho **10**
  SW8 . . . . .171 B2
Chesson Rd W14 . . .155 A4
Chessum Ho E8 . . . .16 C2
Chester Ave TW10 . .54 B1
Chester Cl
  Barnes SW13 . . . . . .57 A4
  Knightsbridge SW1 132 A3
  Richmond TW10 . . . .54 B1
Chester Close N
  NW1 . . . . .92 B4

Chester Close S
  NW1 . . . . .92 B3
Chester Cres E8 . . . .16 B3
Chester Ct
  Bermondsey SE8 . . .40 C1
  4 Camberwell SE5 . .48 C3
  Gospel Oak NW5 . . .12 C4
  Regent's Pk NW1 . . .92 B3
Chesterfield Ct
  SE13 . . . . .67 B4
Chesterfield Gdns
  Greenwich SE10 . . .52 C3
  Mayfair W1 . . . . . . .118 A2
Chesterfield Gr
  SE22 . . . . .64 B2
Chesterfield Hill
  W1 . . . . .118 A2
Chesterfield Ho
  Highgate N6 . . . . .3 C3
  Mayfair W1 . . . . . . .117 C2
Chesterfield Rd
  W4 . . . . .45 B4
Chesterfield St
  W1 . . . . .118 A2
Chesterfield Way
  SE15 . . . . .50 B3
Chesterford Gdns
  NW3 . . . . .11 A4
Chester Gate NW1 . .92 B3
Chester Ho
  Dartmouth Pk N19 . . .4 A2
  1 Deptford SE8 . . . .51 B4
Chesterman Ct
  W4 . . . . .46 A3
Chester Mews
  SW1 . . . . .132 A2
  1 Chester Pl NW1 . .92 A4
Chester Rd
  Dartmouth Pk N19 . . .4 A2
  Regent's Pk NW1 . . .92 A4
Chester Row SW1 . .145 C4
Chester Sq SW1 . . .146 A4
Chester Sq Mews
  SW1 . . . . .132 A1
Chester St
  Bethnal Green
  E2 . . . . .24 C1 99 C3
  Westminster SW1 .131 C2
Chester Terr NW1 . . .92 A4
Chesterton Cl
  SW18 . . . . .58 C2
Chesterton Ct W3 . . .37 A3
Chesterton Ho
  20 Battersea
  SW11 . . . . .59 C4
  3 Kensal Town
  W10 . . . . .23 A1
Chesterton Prim Sch
  SW11 . . . . .169 B3
Chesterton Rd
  W10 . . . . .31 A4
Chesterton Sq
  W8 . . . . .141 B3
Chester Way SE11 . .149 C3
Chestnut Alley
  SW6 . . . . .155 A3
Chestnut Ave **11**
  SW14 . . . . .55 C4
Chestnut Cl
  New Cross Gate
  SE14 . . . . .51 B2
  1 Stoke Newington
  N16 . . . . .6 C2
Chestnut Ct SW6 . .155 A4
Chestnut Gr SW12 . .72 C3

Chestnut Grove Sch
⑧ SW12 ....72 C3

Chestnut Ho
❶ Acton W4 ....38 A2
Brockley SE4 ....66 B4
❼ Maitland Pk
NW3 ....12 B2
West Norwood
SE27 ....75 B1

Chestnut Rd SE21,
SE27 ....75 B1

Chestnuts The ❶
N5 ....15 A4
Chettle Cl SE11 ....137 B2
Chetwode Ho NW8 ..90 A2
Chetwode Rd
SW17 ....72 B1
Chetwynd Rd NW5 ..13 A4
Cheval Ct SW15 .....57 A3
Cheval Pl SW7 .....130 B2
Cheval St E14 ....41 C3
Chevening Rd
Cubitt Town SE10 ...43 B1
Kilburn NW6 ....23 A4

Cheverell Ho ㉕
E2 ....24 C3
Cheverton Rd N19 ...4 C3
Chevet St E9 ....18 A3
Chevington NW2 ....10 B2
Cheviot Cl SE16 ....50 B3
Cheviot Ct ❶ SE14 .50 B3
Cheviot Gate NW2 ...1 A2
Cheviot Gdns NW2 ...1 A2
Cheviot Ho N16 .....7 B3
Chevron Cl E16 .....35 C3
Cheylesmore Ho
SW1 ....146 A2
Cheyne Ct SW3 ....158 C4
Cheyne Gdns
SW3 ....158 B3
Cheyne Mews
SW3 ....158 B3
Cheyne Pl SW3 ....158 C4
Cheyne Row SW3 ...158 A3
Cheyne Wlk
SW10 ....157 B2
Cheyney Ho ❷ E9 ..17 C2
Chichele Mans
NW2 ....9 C3
Chichele Rd NW2 ...9 C3
Chicheley St SE1 ..135 A4
Chichester Ct ❷
NW1 ....13 B1
Chichester Ho
NW6 ....23 C3
Chichester Rd
Bayswater W2 ......100 B4
Kilburn NW6 ....23 C3
Chichester Rents
WC2 ....107 B2
Chichester St
SW1 ....147 A1
Chichester Way
E14 ....42 C2
Chicksand Ho ❶❹
E1 ....111 B4
Chicksand St E1 ...111 A3
Chicksand Street
E1 ....111 A3
Chiddingstone
SE13 ....67 B2
Chiddingstone St
SW6 ....165 C2
Chigwell Ct ❶ E9 ..18 A2
Chigwell Hill E1 ....32 A2
Chiham Ho ❺
SE15 ....50 B4

Chilcombe Ho ❻
SW15 ....68 C4
Chilcot Cl ⑬ E14 ...34 A3
Childebert Rd
SW17 ....73 A2
Childeric Prim Sch
SE14 ....51 A3
Childeric Rd SE14 ..51 A3
Childerley St
SW6 ....164 A4
Childers St SE8 .....51 B4
Child La SE10 ......43 B3
Childrens House
Upper Sch ⑬ N1 ..16 A2
CHILD'S HILL 1 C2
Child's Hill Sch
NW2 ....1 A1
Child's Mews
SW5 ....141 C3
Child's Pl SW5 .....141 C3
Child's St SW5 .....141 C3
Child's Wlk SW5 ...141 C3
Chilham Ct ⑬
SW9 ....62 C4
Chilham Ho ❺
SE1 ....137 C2
Chillington Dr
SW11 ....59 C3
Chillingworth Rd
N7 ....14 C3
Chiltern Ct
⑮ Deptford SE14 ...50 B3
Marylebone NW1 ...91 A1
Chiltern Ho
Camberwell SE17 ...48 C4
❹ Kensal Town
W10 ....31 A4
❺ Stamford Hill N16 .7 B3
Chiltern Rd E3 .....26 C1
Chiltern St W1 .....103 B4
Chilton Gr SE8 .....41 A2
Chilton Rd TW9 ....54 C4
Chilton St
E2 ....24 B1 99 A2
Chilver St SE10 ....43 B1
Chilworth Ct ⑧
SW19 ....69 C3
Chilworth Mews
W2 ....101 B1
Chilworth St W2 ...101 A1
Chimney Ct ㉓ E1 ..32 A1
China Ct ❶ E1 .....32 A1
China Hall Mews ⑱
SE16 ....40 B3
China Mews ⑰
SW2 ....74 B4
Chindit Ho ⑩ N16 .15 C4
Ching Ct WC2 ......106 A1
Chinnocks Wharf
E14 ....33 A2
Chipka St E14 .....42 B4
Chipley St SE14 ....51 A3
Chippendale Ho
SW1 ....146 B1
Chippendale Gdns
NW6 ....23 C2
Chippenham Mews
W9 ....23 C1
Chippenham Rd
W9 ....23 C1
Chip St SW4 ....61 C3
Chipstead Ho ❹
SW2 ....74 A3
Chipstead St SW6 .165 C2
Chirk Ct SE4 ....51 B1
Chisenhale Prim Sch
⑱ E3 ....26 A3

Chisenhale Rd E3 ...26 A3
Chisholm Ct ❶
W6 ....38 C1
Chisholm Rd ⑬
TW10 ....54 B1
Chisledon Wlk E9 ..18 B2
Chislehurst Rd ❶
TW10 ....54 A2
Chislet ❽ NW5 .....12 C2
Chiswell St
Barbican EC1 ......109 B4
Camberwell SE5 ....48 C3
CHISWICK 38 B1
Chiswick & Bedford
Park Prep Sch ❶
W4 ....38 A2
Chiswick Common Rd
W4 ....37 C2
Chiswick Com Sch
W4 ....45 C3
Chiswick Green
Studios ❶ W4 ....37 B2
Chiswick High Rd
W4 ....38 A2
Chiswick High Rd
(North Circular Rd)
W4 ....36 C1
Chiswick Ho❋ W4 ..45 C4
Chiswick La W4 ....38 A1
Chiswick La S W4 ..46 A4
Chiswick Mall W4 ..38 B1
Chiswick Park Sta
W4 ....37 B2
Chiswick Pier W4 ..46 B3
Chiswick Pl W4 ....37 A2
Chiswick Plaza
W4 ....45 A4
Chiswick Quay W4 .45 B2
Chiswick Rd W4 ...37 B2
Chiswick Rdbt W4 ..36 C1
Chiswick Sq W4 ....46 A4
Chiswick Sta W4 ...45 B3
Chiswick Staithe
W4 ....45 B2
Chiswick Terr ❻
W4 ....37 B2
Chiswick Village
W4 ....45 A4
Chiswick Wharf
W4 ....46 B4
Chitty St W1 ......105 A4
Chivalry Rd SW11 ..60 A2
Chivelston ㉗
SW19 ....69 C2
Chobham Gdns
SW19 ....69 C2
Chobham Rd E15 ...19 C3
Cholmeley Cres N6 .4 A4
Cholmeley Lo N6 ...4 A3
Cholmeley Pk N6 ...4 A4
Cholmley Gdns
NW6 ....10 C3
Cholmondeley Ave
NW10 ....21 C3
Chopin's Ct ⑱ E1 ..32 A1
Chopwell Cl E15 ...19 C1
Choumert Gr SE15 .49 C1
Choumert Mews
SE15 ....49 C1
Choumert Rd SE15 .49 B1
Choumert Sq ❹
SE15 ....49 C1
Chow Sq ❷ E8 ....16 B3
Chrisp Ho SE10 ....53 A4
Chrisp St E14 ......34 A3

Christ Church
TW9 ....54 A4
Christchurch Ave
NW6 ....10 A1
Christ Church
Bentinck CE Prim
Sch NW1 ....102 B4
Christ Church
Brondesbury CE Jun
& Inf Sch NW6 ....10 B1
Christchurch CE Prim
Sch SW3 ....158 C4
Christ Church CE
Prim Sch
Battersea SW11 ....60 A4
Cubitt Town SE10 ..43 A1
Christ Church CE
Prim Sch,
Hampstead NW3 ...2 C1
Christchurch CE Sch
E1 ....111 A3
Christ Church
❶ Brondesbury Pk
NW6 ....10 A1
Harlesden NW10 ...21 A4
Christchurch Hill
NW3 ....11 C4
Christchurch Ho ❷
SW2 ....74 A3
Christchurch Pas
NW3 ....2 B1
Christchurch Rd
Mortlake SW14 ....55 B2
Streatham SW2 ....74 C3
Christ Church Sch
NW1 ....92 B4
Christchurch Sq ❷
E9 ....25 B4
Christchurch St
SW3 ....158 C4
Christ Church
Streatham CE Prim
Sch ❷ SW2 ....74 C3
Christchurch Terr
SW3 ....158 C4
Christchurch Way
SE10 ....43 A1
Christian Ct SE16 ..33 B1
Christian St E1 ....111 C1
Christie Ct
Maitland Pk NW3 ..12 A3
❷ Upper Holloway
N19 ....5 A2
Christie Ho ❷
SE10 ....43 B1
Christie Rd E9 .....18 A2
Christina Sq N4 ....6 A3
Christina St
EC2 ....24 A1 98 A2
Christopher Boone's
Almshouses SE13 ..67 C3
Christopher Cl
SE16 ....40 C4
Christopher France
Ho ❻ E1 ....26 A2
Christopher Hatton
Prim Sch EC1 .....95 B1
Christopher Lo ❷
N6 ....4 C4
Christopher Pl
NW1 ....93 C3
Christopher St EC2 .97 C1
Christ's Sch TW10 .54 C2
Christ the King RC
Prim Sch N4 .....5 B2

Christ the King Sixth
Form Coll SE13 ...67 C4
Chryssell Rd SW9 .163 C1
Chubworthy St ❺
SE14 ....51 A4
Chudleigh Rd
Hampstead NW6 ...9 C1
Leonee SE4 ....66 C2
Chudleigh St E1 ...32 C3
Chumleigh Gdns
SE5 ....49 A4
Chumleigh St SE5 ..49 A4
Church App SE21 ..75 C1
Church Ave
Camden Town
NW1 ....13 A2
Mortlake SW14 ....55 C4
Church Cl W8 ......128 A4
Church Cres E9 ....17 C1
Churchcroft Cl
SW12 ....72 C4
Church Ct
Holborn EC4 ....107 C1
Rotherhithe SE16 ..41 B4
Churchdale Ct ❶
W4 ....37 A1
Church End E4 .....108 B1
Church Entry EC4 .108 B1
Church Estate
Almshouses ❽
TW9 ....54 B3
Churchfield Ho
W2 ....89 B1
Churchfield Mans
SW6 ....165 A1
Churchfield Rd
W3 ....28 B1
Churchfields SE10 ..52 B4
Church Garth ❹
N19 ....4 C2
Church Gate SW6 ..58 A4
Church Gn ❹
SW9 ....173 C2
Church Gr SE13 ....67 A2
Churchhill Gardens
Prim Sch SW1 ....147 A1
Church Ho EC1 ...96 B2
Churchill Ct
Finsbury Pk N4 ....5 C4
Peckham SE15 .....49 C1
Willesden NW2 ....9 A3
Churchill Gdns
SW1 ....160 C4
Churchill Gdns Rd
SW1 ....160 C4
Churchill Pl E14 ...34 A1
Churchill Rd
Gospel Oak NW5 ..13 A4
Willesden NW2 ....9 A2
Churchill Wlk E9 ...17 B3
Church Mead SE5 ..48 B3
Churchmead Rd
NW10 ....8 C2
Church Path W4 ...37 B3
Church Pl SW1 ....119 A3
Church Rd
Acton W3 ....37 B4
Barnes SW13 ......46 C2
㉔ Canonbury N1 ..15 B2
Richmond TW10,
TW9 ....54 A2
Willesden NW10 ...8 A1
Church Row NW3 ..11 B4

Church St
Chiswick W4 . . . . **46** B4
Lisson Gr NW8 . . . . . . **90** A1

Church Street Est
NW8 . . . . **89** C1

Church Studios 16
NW1 . . . . **13** C2

Churchward Ho
Camberwell SE17 . . . . **48** A4
West Kensington
SW5 . . . . **141** A1

Churchway NW1 . . . . **93** C4

Church Wlk
Barnes SW13 . . . . **46** C2
Canonbury N16 . . . . . . **15** C4
Child's Hill NW2 . . . . . . **1** A3
Dartmouth Pk N6 . . . . . **3** C1

Churchyard Row
SE11 . . . . **150** B4

Churnfield 2 N4 . . . . **5** C2

Churston Cl 16
SW2 . . . . **74** C3

Churston Mans
WC1 . . . . **95** A1

Churton Pl
Brentford W4 . . . . **45** A4
Pimlico SW1V **147** A3

Churton St SW1 . . . **147** A3

Chute Ho 17 SW9 . . **173** B1

Chuter Ede Ho
SW6 . . . . **155** A3

Cicada Rd SW18 . . . . **59** B2

Cicely Ho NW8 . . . . . **79** C1

Cicely Rd SE15 . . . . . **49** C2

Cinema Mus The ★
SE11 . . . . **150** A3

Cinnabar Wharf
Central 18 E1 . . . . **125** C2

Cinnabar Wharf East
18 E1 . . . . **125** C2

Cinnabar Wharf West
17 E1 . . . . **125** C2

Cinnamon Cl 8
SE15 . . . . **49** B3

Cinnamon Row 8
SW11 . . . . **59** B4

Cinnamon St E1 . . . . **32** A1

Cinnamon Wharf
SE1 . . . . **139** A4

Circle Ho 16 E14 . . . . **34** C3

Circle The SE1 . . . . **139** A4

Circus Lo NW8 . . . . . **79** B4

Circus Mews W1 . . **102** C4

Circus Pl EC2 . . . . . **109** C3

Circus Rd NW8 . . . . . **79** B1

Circus St SE10 . . . . . **52** B3

Cirencester St
W2 . . . . **100** A4

Cissbury Ho 6
SE26 . . . . **76** C1

Citadel Pl SE11 . . . . **148** C2

Citizen Ho N7 . . . . . . **14** C4

Citizen Rd N7 . . . . . . **14** C4

Citron Terr 4
SE15 . . . . **65** A4

Citrus Ho 14 SE8 . . . **41** B1

City Banking Coll
SE1 . . . . **137** C4

City Bsns Coll EC1 . . **96** B3

City Bsns St 33
SE16 . . . . **40** B4

City Central Est
EC1 . . . . **96** C3

City Coll N1 . . . . **97** B4

City Coll of London
The WC1 . . . . **107** A3

City Forum EC1 . . . . . **96** C4

City Garden Row
N1 . . . . **86** B1

City Gate E1 . . . . **25** B1

City & Guilds of
London Art Sch The
SE11 . . . . **149** C1

City & Hackney Ctr for
Mental Health
(Hospl) E9 . . . . **18** A3

City Hall ★ SE1 . . . **124** B2

City Harbour E14 . . . . **42** A3

City & Islington 6th
Form Coll EC1 . . . . **96** A4

City & Islington Coll
(Ctr for Applied
Sciences) EC1 . . . . **96** A4

City & Islington Coll
(Ctr for Bsns, Arts &
Technology) N7 . . . . **14** A4

City & Islington Coll
(Ctr for Health,
Social & Child Care)
7 N7 . . . . **14** B4

City & Islington Coll
(Ctr for Lifelong
Learning) 3 N4 . . . . **6** A2

City Law Sch The
EC1 . . . . **107** A3

City Lights The
SE11 . . . . **149** C1

CITY OF
LONDON **122** B4

City of London Acad-
Islington N1 . . . . . . **86** C3

City of London Acad
The SE1 . . . . **153** C2

City of London
Information Ctr ★
EC4 . . . . **108** B1

City of London Sch
EC4 . . . . **122** C4

City of London Sch
for Girls EC2 . . . . . **109** A4

City of Westminster
Coll W2 . . . . **101** B4

City of Westminster
Coll, Cosway Street
Ctr NW1 . . . . **102** B4

City of Westminster
Coll, Maida Vale Ctr
1 W9 . . . . **88** A3

City of Westminster
Coll, Queens Park
Ctr 10 W9 . . . . **23** C2

City Rd EC1 . . . . **97** A4

City Thameslink Sta
EC4 . . . . **108** A1

City University EC1 . . **96** A3

City Wlk SE1 . . . . . . **138** A3

Civil Service Coll
SW1 . . . . **146** C3

Clabon Mews
SW1 . . . . **144** C4

Clack St SE16 . . . . . . **40** B4

Claire Ct NW2 . . . . . . **10** A2

Claire Pl E14 . . . . **41** C3

Clancarty Rd SW6 . . **165** C1

Clandon Cl W3 . . . . . . **37** A4

Clandon St SE8 . . . . . **51** C1

Clanfield Ho 12
SW15 . . . . **68** C3

Clanricarde Gdns
W2 . . . . . . **31** C2 **113** C3

CLAPHAM **61** A4

Clapham Common ★
SW4 . . . . **61** A3

Clapham Common
North Side SW4 . . . . **60** C3

Clapham Common
South Side SW4 . . . . **61** B2

Clapham Common Sta
SW4 . . . . **61** B3

Clapham Common
West Side
Clapham SW4,
SW11 . . . . **60** B3
Clapham SW11 . . . . . . **60** C2

Clapham Computer &
Secretarial Coll 1
SW11 . . . . **60** B2

Clapham Court Terr
2 SW4 . . . . **62** A2

Clapham Cres
SW4 . . . . **61** C3

Clapham Ct 8
SW4 . . . . **61** C3

Clapham High St
SW4 . . . . **61** C3

Clapham High Street
Sta SW4 . . . . **61** C4

Clapham Junction Est
SW11 . . . . **60** A3

Clapham Junction Sta
SW11 . . . . **60** A3

Clapham L Ctr
SW4 . . . . **61** C4

Clapham Manor Ct 1
SW4 . . . . **61** B4

Clapham Manor Prim
Sch 8 SW4 . . . . **61** B4

Clapham Manor St
SW4 . . . . **61** C4

Clapham Mans
SW4 . . . . **61** A1

Clapham North Bsns
Ctr 10 SW4 . . . . **61** C4

Clapham North Sta
SW4 . . . . **62** A4

CLAPHAM PARK **61** C2

Clapham Park Rd
SW4 . . . . **61** C3

Clapham Park Terr 4
SW2 . . . . **62** A2

Clapham Rd SW9 . . . **163** A1

Clapham South Sta
SW4 . . . . **61** A1

Clapton Comm E5 . . . . **7** C4

Clapton Girls Tec Coll
E5 . . . . **17** C4

Clapton Pas E5 . . . . . **17** B3

Clapton Sq E5 . . . . . . **17** B3

Clapton Terr E5 . . . . . **17** C4

Clara Grant Ho 16
E14 . . . . **42** A3

Clare Ct WC1 . . . . **94** B3

Claredale Ho 3
E2 . . . . **25** A3

Claredale St E2 . . . . . **24** C3

Clare Gdns W11 . . . . . **31** A3

Clare Ho
Bermondsey SE1 . . . . **153** A2
6 Old Ford E3 . . . . . . **26** B4

Clare La N1 . . . . **15** B1

Clare Lawn Ave
SW14 . . . . **55** C2

Clare Mews SW6 . . . **156** A1

Clare Mkt WC2 . . . . . **107** A1

Claremont 4
SW15 . . . . **58** A2

Claremont Cl
Finsbury N1 . . . . **85** C1
4 Streatham SW2 . . . **74** B3

Claremont Ct 1
W9 . . . . **23** B2

Claremont Gr W4 . . . . **46** A3

Claremont Rd
Highgate N6 . . . . **4** B4
West Kilburn W9 . . . . . **23** B2

Claremont Sq N1 . . . . **85** C1

Claremont St SE10 . . **52** A4

Clarence Ave SW4 . . **61** C1

Clarence Cres
SW4 . . . . **61** C1

Clarence Ct 10
W6 . . . . **39** C2

Clarence Gate
NW1 . . . . **91** A2

Clarence Gate Gdns
NW1 . . . . **91** A1

Clarence Gdns
NW1 . . . . **92** B3

Clarence Ho SE17 . . . **48** B4

Clarence Ho ★
SW1 . . . . **119** A1

Clarence La SW15 . . . **56** B1

Clarence Mews
Balham SW12 . . . . **73** A4
Hackney E5 . . . . **17** A3
1 Rotherhithe
SE16 . . . . **32** C1

Clarence Pl 21 E5 . . . **17** A3

Clarence Rd
Brentford W4 . . . . **36** C1
Brondesbury NW6 . . . . **10** B1
Greenwich SE8 . . . . . . **52** A4
Lower Clapton E5 . . . . **17** A3
Richmond TW9 . . . . . . **44** C2

Clarence St 5
TW9 . . . . **54** A3

Clarence Terr
NW1 . . . . **91** A2

Clarence Way
NW1 . . . . **13** A1

Clarence Wlk 9
SW4 . . . . **172** A2

Clarendon Cl
Bayswater W2 . . . . . . **116** A4
38 Hackney E9 . . . . . . **17** B1

Clarendon Cross
W11 . . . . . . **31** A2 **112** B3

Clarendon Ct
Paddington W9 . . . . . . **89** A2
1 Richmond TW9 . . . . . **44** C2
Willesden NW2 . . . . . . **9** B1

Clarendon Dr
SW15 . . . . **57** B3

Clarendon Flats
W1 . . . . **103** C1

Clarendon Gdns
W9 . . . . **89** A1

Clarendon Gr NW1 . . **93** B4

Clarendon Ho
NW1 . . . . **83** A1

Clarendon Mews
W2 . . . . **116** A4

Clarendon Pl W2 . . . **116** A4

Clarendon Rd
W11 . . . . . . **31** A2 **112** B3

Clarendon Rise
SE13 . . . . **67** B3

Clarendon St
SW1 . . . . **146** B2

Clarendon Terr
W9 . . . . **89** A2

Clarendon Wlk 11
W11 . . . . **31** A3

Clare Pl SW15 . . . . . . **68** B4

Clare Rd
New Cross Gate
SE14 . . . . **51** B2
Willesden NW10 . . . . . . **8** C1

Clare St E2 . . . . **25** A3

Clareville Ct SW7 . . . **143** A3

Clareville Gr SW7 . . . **143** A3

Clareville Grove Mews
SW7 . . . . **143** A3

Clareville St SW7 . . . **143** A3

Clarewood Ct W1 . . . **102** C3

Clarewood Wlk
SW9 . . . . **62** C3

Clarges Ho W1 . . . . . **118** A2

Clarges Mews
W1 . . . . **118** A2

Clarges St W1 . . . . . **118** A2

Clariat Ct W3 . . . . **36** C4

Claribel Rd SW9 . . . . **48** A1

Claridge Ct SW6 . . . **164** C3

Clarissa Ho 7 E14 . . **34** A3

Clarissa St E8 . . . . . . **24** B4

Clarke Ho 2 SW4 . . . **61** B4

Clarke Path N16 . . . . . **7** C3

Clarkes Mews W1 . . **103** C4

Clark Ho SW10 . . . . . **156** C2

Clark Lawrence Ct 11
SW11 . . . . **59** C4

Clarkson Rd E16 . . . . . **35** B3

Clarkson Row
NW1 . . . . **82** C1

Clarkson St E2 . . . . . . **25** A2

Clark's Pl EC2 . . . . . **110** A2

Clark St E1 . . . . **32** B4

Classic Mans 33
E9 . . . . **17** B1

Classinghall Ho 14
SW15 . . . . **57** C1

Claude Rd SE15 . . . . . **50** A1

Claude St E14 . . . . . . **41** C2

Claudia Jones Way
SW2 . . . . **62** A1

Claudia Pl SW19 . . . . **70** A3

Clavell St 3 SE10 . . . **52** B4

Claverdale Rd
SW2 . . . . **74** C4

Clavering Ave
SW13 . . . . **47** A4

Clavering Ho SE13 . . **67** C3

Claverton St SW1 . . . **147** A1

Clave St E1 . . . . **32** B1

Claxton Gr
W6 . . . . **39** C1 **140** A1

Claybank Gr SE13 . . . **67** A4

Claybrook Rd W6 . . . . **47** C4

Claydon SE17 . . . . . . **150** C4

Clayhall Ct 8 E3 . . . . **26** B3

Claylands Pl SW8 . . . **163** B2

Claylands Rd
SW8 . . . . **163** A3

Claypole Rd E15 . . . . . **27** B3

Claypons Ave
TW8 . . . . **36** A2

Claypons Hospl
W5 . . . . **36** A3

Claypons La TW8 . . . . **36** A1

Clays Ct N16 . . . . **7** B3

Clay Ct W1 . . . . **103** A3
Clayton Cres N1 . . . **84** C3
Clayton Ct N16 . . . . . . 7 C4
Clayton Ho 22 E9 . . . . .17 B1
Clayton Mews
SE10 . . . . .52 C2
Clayton Rd SE15 . . . .49 C2
Clayton St SE11 . . . . **163** B4
Clearbrook Way 10
E1 . . . . .32 B3
Clear Water Ho 9
TW10 . . . . .54 A2
Clearwater Terr 4
W11 . . . . .39 B4
Clearwell Dr W9 . . . .88 B1
Cleaver Ho 6
Cleaver Sq SE11 . . . **149** C1
Cleaver St SE11 . . . . **149** C2
Cleeve Ho 11
E2 . . . . .24 A2 **98** B3
Cleeve Way SW15 . . .68 B4
Cleeve Workshops 14
E2 . . . . .24 A2 **98** B3
Clegg St 16 E1 . . . . . . .32 A1
Cleland Ho 19 E2 . . . .25 B3
Clematis St W12 . . . . .29 C2
Clem Atlee Par
SW6 . . . . **155** A3
Clem Attlee Ct
SW6 . . . . **155** A3
Clemence St E14 . . .33 B4
Clement Ave SW4 . . .61 C3
Clement Ct
Acton W3 . . . . .37 C2
Hampstead NW6 . . . . . .10 C3
Clement Danes Ho 3
W12 . . . . .30 A3
Clement Ho
14 Deptford SE8 . . . .41 A2
17 North Kensington
W10 . . . . .30 B4
Clements Ave 1
E16 . . . . .35 C2
Clements Inn
WC2 . . . . **107** A1
Clements Inn Pas
WC2 . . . . **107** A1
Clement's La EC2,
EC4 . . . . **123** C4
Clement's Rd SE16 . .40 A3
Clemson Ho 8 E8 . .24 B4
Clennam St SE1 . . . **137** A4
Clenston Mews
W1 . . . . **102** C2
Clent Ho 4 N16 . . . . . .7 B3
Cleopatra's Needle*
WC2 . . . . **120** C3
Clephane Rd 13
N1 . . . . .15 B2
Clephane Rd N N1 . .15 C2
Clephane Rd S N1 . .15 C2
Clere Pl EC2 . . . . . . .97 C2
Clere St EC2 . . . . .97 C2
CLERKENWELL 96 A1
Clerkenwell Cl
EC1 . . . . .95 C1
Clerkenwell Gn
EC1 . . . . .96 A1
Clerkenwell Parochial
CE Prim Sch EC1 . .95 B3
Clerkenwell Rd
EC1 . . . . .96 A1
Clermont Rd E9 . . . .25 B4

Clevedon Ct
Battersea SW11 . . . . . **168** A4
Dulwich SE21 . . . . .75 C1
Clevedon Mans
NW5 . . . . .12 C4
Cleve Ho NW6 . . . . . .11 A1
Cleveland Ave W4 . .38 B2
Cleveland Ct W1 . . . .93 A1
Cleveland Gdns
Barnes SW13 . . . . .46 B1
Paddington W2 . . . . . . **100** C1
Cleveland Gr 39
E1 . . . . .25 B1
Cleveland Mans
8 Brixton SW9 . . . . . . **163** B1
8 Brondesbury
NW6 . . . . .10 B1
Paddington W9 . . . . . . .23 C1
Cleveland Mews
W1 . . . . **104** C4
Cleveland Pl SW1 . **119** A2
Cleveland Rd
Barnes SW13 . . . . .46 B1
Islington N1 . . . . .15 C1
14 South Acton W3 . . .37 B3
Cleveland Row
SW1 . . . . **119** A1
Cleveland Sq W2 . . **100** C1
Cleveland St W1 . . . .92 C1
Cleveland Terr
W2 . . . . **101** A2
Cleveland Way E1 . .25 B1
Clevendon Cl N16 . . .7 B1
Cleve Rd NW6 . . . . . .11 A1
Cleverly Cotts
W12 . . . . .29 B1
Cleverly Est W12 . . .29 C2
Cley Ho SE4 . . . . .65 C3
Clichy Ho 25 E1 . . . . .32 B4
Clifden Mews E5 . . .17 C3
Clifden Rd E5 . . . . . .17 C3
Cliff Ct 14 NW1 . . . . .13 C2
Cliffe Ho 4 SE10 . . .43 B1
Clifford Ave
Mortlake SW14 . . . . . . .45 B1
Mortlake SW14,
TW9 . . . . .55 A4
Clifford Ct
Bayswater W2 . . . . . . **100** A3
Wandsworth SW18 . . .71 C4
Willesden NW10 . . . . . . .8 A4
Clifford Dr SW9 . . . .63 A3
Clifford Gdns
NW10 . . . . .22 B3
Clifford Haigh Ho
SW6 . . . . .47 C3
Clifford Ho W14 . . . **140** C3
Clifford's Inn Pas
EC4 . . . . **107** B1
Clifford St W1 . . . . . **118** C3
Clifford Way NW10 . . .8 B4
Cliff Rd NW1 . . . . .13 C2
Cliff Road Studios 13
NW1 . . . . .13 C2
Cliffsend Ho 9
SW9 . . . . **173** C3
Cliff Terr SE8 . . . . . .51 C1
Cliffview Rd SE13 . .66 C4
Cliff Villas NW1 . . . .13 C2
Cliff Wlk E16 . . . . . . .35 B4
Clifton Ave W12 . . . .29 B1
Clifton Cres SE15 . .50 A3
Clifton Ct
Finsbury Pk N4 . . . . .5 C4
Paddington NW8 . . . . .89 B2
Peckham SE15 . . . . . . .50 A3

Clifton Ct continued
Putney SW15 . . . . .57 C2
Clifton Gate
SW10 . . . . **156** C4
Clifton Gdns
Chiswick W4 . . . . .37 C2
Paddington W9 . . . . . .88 C1
Clifton Gr 22 E8 . . .16 C2
Clifton Hill NW8 . . . .78 C3
Clifton Ho 21 98 C2
Clifton Mans 4
SW9 . . . . .62 C3
Clifton Pl
Paddington W2 . . . . . . **101** C1
Rotherhithe SE16 . . . . .40 B4
Clifton Rd
Harlesden NW10 . . . . . .21 C3
Newham E16 . . . . .35 A4
Paddington W9 . . . . . .89 A2
Clifton St
EC2 . . . . .24 A1 **98** A1
Clifton Terr N4 . . . . . .5 C2
Clifton Villas W9 . . **100** C4
Clifton Way SE15 . . .50 B3
Climsland Ho SE1 **121** C2
Clinch Ct 17 E16 . . .35 C4
Cline Ho SW15 . . . . .56 C2
Clinger Ct N1 . . . . . .24 A4
Clink Prison Mus
The* SE1 . . . . **123** B2
Clink St SE1 . . . . . . **123** B2
Clinton Rd E3 . . . . . .26 B2
Clipper Appts 12
E14 . . . . .52 B4
Clipper Cl 3 SE16 . .40 C4
Clipper Ho 14 . . . . . .42 B1
Clipper Way SE13 . .67 B3
Clipstone Ho 10
SW15 . . . . .56 C2
Clipstone Mews
W1 . . . . **104** C4
Clipstone St W1 . . . **104** C4
Clissold Cres N16 . .15 C4
Clissold Ct N4 . . . . . . .6 B2
Clissold Ho 4 N16 . . .6 C3
Clissold Rd N16 . . . . .6 C1
Clitheroe Rd SW9 . **172** B1
Clive Ct W9 . . . . .89 A2
Cliveden Ho SW1 . . **145** B4
Cliveden Pl SW1 . . **145** B4
Clive Ho
10 Clapham SW8 . . **171** B2
Greenwich SE10 . . . . . .52 B4
Clive Rd SE21,
SE27 . . . . .75 C1
Cloak La EC4 . . . . . **123** B4
Clochar Ct NW10 . .21 B4
Clock Ho N16 . . . . . . .7 B4
Clockhouse Cl
SW19 . . . . .69 B2
Clockhouse Pl
SW15 . . . . .58 A1
Clockhouse The
SW19 . . . . .69 B2
Clockmakers Mus*
EC2 . . . . **109** A2
Clock Tower Mews
N1 . . . . .87 A3
Clock Tower Pl 11
N7 . . . . .14 A2
Clock View Cres 2
N7 . . . . .13 C2
Cloister Rd
Acton W3 . . . . .28 B4

Cloister Rd continued
Child's Hill NW2 . . . . . . 1 B2
Cloisters Ct N6 . . . . . .4 A3
Cloisters The 22
SW9 . . . . **173** C3
Clonbrock Rd N16 . .16 A4
Clone Ct 4 W12 . . . .38 A3
Cloncurry St SW6 . .47 C1
Clonmel Rd SW6 . . **154** C1
Clonmore St SW18 .70 B3
Clorane Gdns NW3 . .1 C1
Close The
Lewisham SE3 . . . . .52 C1
Mortlake TW9 . . . . .55 A4
Cloth Ct EC1 . . . . . . **108** B3
Cloth Fair EC1 . . . . **108** B3
Clothier St EC3 . . . **110** B2
Cloth St EC1 . . . . . . **108** C4
Cloudesdale Rd
SW17 . . . . .73 A2
Cloudesley Mans
N1 . . . . .85 C3
Cloudesley Pl N1 . .85 C3
Cloudesley Rd N1 . .85 B3
Cloudesley Sq N1 . .85 C3
Cloudesley St N1 . .85 C3
Clove Cres E14 . . . . .34 C2
Clovelly Ct NW2 . . . . .9 B3
Clovelly Ho 2 W2 . **100** C2
Clovelly Rd W4 . . . . .37 C4
Clovelly Way E1 . . . .32 B3
Clover Mews
SW3 . . . . **159** A4
Clowes Ho 3
SW4 . . . . .62 A3
Clowns Mus* E8 . . .24 B4
Cloysters Gn E1 . . **125** B2
Club Row E2 . . . . . . **98** C2
Clunbury St N1 . . . . .87 C1
Clunie Ho SW1 . . . **131** A2
Cluny Mews SW5 . **141** B3
Cluny Pl SE1 . . . . . **138** A2
Cluse Ct N1 . . . . .86 C2
Clutton St E14 . . . . .34 A4
Clyde Ct NW1 . . . . . .83 C2
Clyde Flats SW6 . . **154** C2
Clyston Cr SW8 . . . **171** A2
Clyde Ct NW1 . . . . . .83 C2
Clydesdale Gdns
TW10 . . . . .55 A3
Clydesdale Ho 4
W11 . . . . .31 B3
Clydesdale Rd
W11 . . . . .31 B3
Clyde St SE8 . . . . . . .51 B4
Clynes Ho 3 E2 . . . .25 C2
Clyro Ct N4 . . . . .5 B3
Clyston St SW8 . . . **171** A2
Coach & Horses Yd
W1 . . . . **118** C4
Coach House La
Highbury N5 . . . . .15 A4
Wimbledon SW19 . . . . .69 C1
Coach House Mews
SE23 . . . . .65 C1
Coach House Yd 5
NW3 . . . . .11 C4
Coachmaker Mews 5
SW9 . . . . .62 A4
Coalbrook Mans 3
SW12 . . . . .73 A3
Coaldale Wlk SE21 .75 B4
Coalecroft Rd
SW15 . . . . .57 B2
Coalport Ho SE11 . **149** B4
Coatbridge Ho 8
N1 . . . . .14 B1
Coates Ave SW18 . .60 A1

Coates Ct NW3 . . . . .12 A3
Coate St E2 . . . . .24 C3
Cobb Ct W4 . . . . .45 A4
Cobbett St SW8 . . . **163** A1
Cobble La N1 . . . . . . .15 A1
Cobble Mews N4,
N5 . . . . .6 B1
Cobbold Ct SW1 . . **147** B4
Cobbold Ind Est
NW10 . . . . .8 B2
Cobbold Mews
W12 . . . . .38 B4
Cobbold Rd
Bedford Pk W12 . . . . . .38 B4
Willesden NW10 . . . . . . .8 B2
Cobb's Hall 1
SW6 . . . . .47 C4
Cobb St E1 . . . . **110** C3
Cobden Bldgs
WC1 . . . . .94 C4
Cobden Ho
1 Bethnal Green
E2 . . . . .24 C2 **99** C4
Regent's Pk NW1 . . . .82 C2
Cobham Cl SW11 . . .60 A1
Cobham Mews 3
NW1 . . . . .13 C1
Coborn Mews 9
E3 . . . . .26 B2
Coborn Rd E3 . . . . . .26 B2
Coborn St E3 . . . . . .26 B2
Cobourg Prim Sch
SE5 . . . . .49 B4
Cobourg Rd SE5 . . .49 B4
Cobourg St NW1 . . .93 A3
Coburg Cl SW1 . . . **147** A4
Coburg Cres SW2 . .74 C3
Coburg Dwellings 11
E1 . . . . .32 B2
Cochrane Cl NW8 . .79 C1
Cochrane Ho 15
E14 . . . . .41 C4
Cochrane Mews
NW8 . . . . .79 C1
Cochrane St NW8 . .79 C1
Cock Hill E1 . . . . . . **110** B3
Cock La EC1 . . . . . . **108** B3
Cockpit Yd WC1 . . . **107** A4
Cockspur Ct SW1 . **119** C2
Cockspur St SW1 . **119** C2
Coda Ctr The
SW6 . . . . **164** B4
Code St E1 . . . . .24 B1 **99** A1
Codicote Ho 22
SE8 . . . . .40 C2
Codicote Terr N4 . . . .6 B2
Codling Cl 12 E1 . . **125** C2
Codrington Ct 5
SE16 . . . . .33 A1
Codrington Ho 7
E1 . . . . .25 A1
Codrington Mews
W11 . . . . .31 A3
Cody Rd E16 . . . . . . .27 C1
Coffey St SE8 . . . . . .51 C3
Cohen Lo E5 . . . . . . .18 A3
Coin St SE1 . . . . . . **121** B2
Coity Rd NW5 . . . . . .12 C2
Coke St E1 . . . . **111** B2
Cokers La SE21 . . . .75 C3
Coke St E1 . . . . **111** C2

Colas Mews **7**
NW6 . . . . .23 C4
Colbeck Mews
SW5 . . . . .142 B3
Colberg Pl **16** 7 B4
Colbert **1** E5 . . . . . . .49 B2
Colborne Ho **8**
E14 . . . . .33 C2
Colchester Ho **17**
SW8 . . . . .171 B2
Colchester St E1 . . .111 A2
Coldbath Sq EC1 . . . .95 B2
Coldbath St SE13 . . . .52 A1
Cold Blow La SE14 . . .50 C4
Coldharbour E14 . . . .34 B1
Coldharbour Ind Est
SE5 . . . . .48 B1
Coldharbour La
SW9 . . . . .63 A4
Coldharbour Pl
SE5 . . . . .48 C1
Coldstream Gdns
SW18 . . . . .58 B1
Colebeck Mews
N1 . . . . .15 A2
Colebert Ave E1 . . . . .25 B1
Colebert Ho **21** E1 . . .25 B1
Colebrook Cl
SW19 . . . . .69 C4
Colebrook Ct
SW3 . . . . .144 B3
Colebrooke Pl N1 . . .86 B3
Colebrooke Row
Islington N1 . . . . . . .84 B4
Islington N1 . . . . . . .86 A2
Islington N1 . . . . . . .86 B3
Colebrook Ho **1**
E14 . . . . .34 A3
Coleby Path **21**
SE5 . . . . .48 C3
Colechurch Ho **2**
SE1 . . . . .153 B1
Colefax Bldg **13**
E1 . . . . .111 C2
Coleford Rd SW18 . . .59 B2
Colegrave Rd E15 . . .19 C3
Colegrave Sch
E15 . . . . .19 C3
Colegrove Rd
SE15 . . . . .49 B4
Coleherne Ct
SW10 . . . . .142 B1
Coleherne Mans
SW5 . . . . .142 B2
Coleherne Mews
SW10 . . . . .142 A1
Coleherne Rd
SW10 . . . . .142 A1
Colehill Gdns
SW6 . . . . .164 A3
Colehill La SW6 . . . .164 B3
Cole Ho SE1 . . . . . . .135 C3
Coleman Ct SW18 . . .70 C4
Coleman Fields
N1 . . . . .87 A4
Coleman Mans N19 . .5 A4
Coleman Rd SE5 . . . .49 A3
Coleman St EC2 . . . .109 B2
Coleman Street Bldgs
EC2 . . . . .109 B2
Colenso Rd E5 . . . . . .17 B4
Coleraine Rd SE3 . . .53 B4
Coleridge CI SW8 . . .170 B1
Coleridge Ct W14 . . .39 C3

Coleridge Gdns
NW6 . . . . .11 B1
Coleridge Ho
Pimlico SW1 . . . . . .147 A1
Walworth SE17 . . . .151 A2
Coleridge Prim Sch
N8 . . . . .4 C4
Coleridge Rd N4,
N7 . . . . .5 C2
Coleridge Sq
SW10 . . . . .156 C2
Coles Ct SW11 . . . . .167 C3
Coleshill Flats
SW1 . . . . .145 C3
Cole St SE1 . . . . .137 A3
Colestown St
SW11 . . . . .168 B2
Colet Gdns W14 . . . .39 C2
Colet Ho SE17 . . . . .150 B1
Colette Ct **5** SE16 . . .40 C4
Coley St WC1 . . . . . . .95 A1
Colfe & Hatchcliffe's
Glebe SE13 . . . . . . .67 A2
Colgate Ho SE13 . . . .52 A1
Colin Blanchard Ho
SE4 . . . . .51 C1
Colin Ct SW16 . . . . . .73 C2
Colinette Rd SW15 . .57 B3
Colin Rd NW10 . . . . . .8 C2
Colinsdale N1 . . . . . .86 A3
Colin Winter Ho **45**
E1 . . . . .25 B1
Coliston Pas SW18 . . .70 C4
Coliston Rd SW18 . . .70 C4
Collamore Ave
SW18 . . . . .72 A3
Collard **7** NW1 . . . . . .13 A1
Collcutt Lo SW4 . . . .62 A3
College App SE10 . . .52 B4
College Cl E5 . . . . . . .17 B3
College Cres **3** . . .11 C2
College Cross **1** . .14 C1
College Ct
Chelsea SW3 . . . . . .145 A1
3 Hammersmith
W6 . . . . .39 B1
Hampstead NW3 . . . .11 C2
College Gdns
Dulwich SE21 . . . . . .76 A3
Upper Tooting
SW17 . . . . .72 A2
College Gr **11** NW1 . .83 B4
College Green Ct
SW9 . . . . .63 A4
College Hill EC4 . . . .123 A4
College La NW5 . . . .13 A4
College Mews **5**
SW18 . . . . .59 A2
COLLEGE PARK . . .22 A2
College Park Cl
SE13 . . . . .67 C3
College Park Sch **20**
W2 . . . . .100 A1
College Pl
Camden Town
NW1 . . . . .83 A3
Chelsea SW10 . . . . .156 C2
College Rd
Dulwich SE19,
SE21 . . . . .76 A2
Kensal Green NW10 . .22 B3
College Terr E3 . . . . .26 B2
College Terr **5**
NW3 . . . . .11 C2
Collent Ho **19** E9 . . .17 B2
Collent St E9 . . . . . . .17 B2

Collerston Ho
SE10 . . . . .43 B1
Collette Ho N16 . . . . . .7 B3
Collett Ho SE13 . . . .67 A4
Collett Rd SE16 . . . .139 C2
Colley Ho **7** N7 . . . .13 C3
Collier St N1 . . . . . . .84 C1
Collingbourne Rd
W12 . . . . .30 A1
Collingham Gdns
SW5 . . . . .142 B3
Collingham Pl
SW5 . . . . .142 B4
Collingham Rd
SW5 . . . . .142 B3
Collingham Tutors
Coll SW5 . . . . .142 B3
Collington St SE10 . .42 C1
Collingwood Ho
27 Bethnal Green
E1 . . . . .25 A1
Marylebone W1 . . . .104 C4
Collingwood St E1 . .25 A1
Collins Ct E8 . . . . . . .16 C2
Collins Ho
9 Cubitt Town
E14 . . . . .42 B3
4 Poplar E14 . . . . .34 B2
Collinson Ct **11**
SE15 . . . . .49 C3
Collinson Ho **14**
SE15 . . . . .49 C3
Collinson St SE1 . . . .136 C3
Collinson Wlk
SE1 . . . . .136 C3
Collins Rd N5, N16 . .15 B4
Collins Sq SE3 . . . . . .53 B1
Collins St SE3 . . . . . .53 A1
Collins Yd N1 . . . . . . .86 A3
Collinson Pl N16 . . . .7 A3
Coll of Arms*
EC4 . . . . .122 C4
Coll of Central
London The
EC2 . . . . .24 A1 98 A2
Coll of Law The
(Bloomsbury)
EC1 . . . . .105 A4
Coll of Law The
(Moorgate) EC1 . . . .97 B1
Coll of NW London
NW6 . . . . .23 C4
Coll of NW London
(Willesden Centre)
NW10 . . . . .8 B3
Coll of Optometrists
The SW1 . . . . .120 A2
Coll Sharp Ct **22**
E2 . . . . .24 B2 98 C4
Coll's Rd SE15 . . . . . .50 B2
Collyer Pl SE15 . . . . .49 C2
Colmans Wharf **5**
E14 . . . . .34 A4
Colmar Cl **8** E1 . . . .25 C1
Colne Ho NW8 . . . . . .89 C1
Colne Rd E5 . . . . .18 A4
Cologne Rd SW11 . . .59 C3
Colombo St SE1 . . . .122 A1
Colonel St SE1 . . . . .122 C1
Colombo St SE1 . . . .122 A1
Colonial Dr W4 . . . . .37 B2
Colonnade WC1 . . . . .94 B1
Colonnade Ho SE3 . .53 B1

Colonnades The **6**
E8 . . . . .17 A2
Colonnade The **12**
SE8 . . . . .41 B2
Colonnade Wlk SW Ctr
SW1 . . . . .146 B4
Colorado Bldg **9**
SE13 . . . . .52 A2
Colosseum Terr
NW1 . . . . .92 B2
Colour Ho SE1 . . . . .138 C3
Colstead Ho **27** E1 . .25 A1
Colston Rd SW14 . . .55 B3
Colthurst Cres N4 . . .6 B2
Coltman Ho SE10 . . .52 B4
Coltman St E14 . . . . .33 A4
Columba Ho SE14 . . .51 B2
Columbas Dr NW3 . . .2 C3
Columbia Ho E3 . . . .26 C2
Columbia Point
SE16 . . . . .40 B3
Columbia Prim Sch **12**
E2 . . . . .24 B2 99 A4
Columbia Rd
9 Hackney E2 . . . .24 C3
Shoreditch
E2 . . . . .24 B2 98 C4
Columbia Road
Flower Mkt*
E2 . . . . .24 B2 99 A4
Colverson Ho **14**
E1 . . . . .32 B4
Colvestone Cres
E8 . . . . .16 B3
Colvestone Prim Sch
E8 . . . . .16 B3
Colville Ho
22 Bethnal Green
E2 . . . . .25 B3
Notting Hill W11 . . . .31 B3
Colville Mews
W11 . . . . .31 B3
Colville Pl W1 . . . . . .105 A3
Colville Prim Sch **53**
W11 . . . . .31 B3
Colville Rd
Notting Hill W11 . . . .31 B3
South Acton W3 . . . . .37 A3
Colville Sq W11 . . . . .31 B3
Colville Terr W11 . . . .31 B3
Colwall Ho **18**
SW9 . . . . .173 A1
Colwell Rd SE22 . . . .64 B2
Colwick Cl N6 . . . . . . .4 C4
Colwith Rd W6 . . . . . .47 B4
Colworth Gr SE17 . . .151 A3
Colwyn Ho SE1 . . . .135 B1
Colyton Rd SE22 . . . .65 A2
Combe Ave SE3 . . . . .53 B3
Combedale Rd
SE10 . . . . .43 C1
Combe Ho
Mortlake SW14 . . . . .45 B1
20 Paddington W2 . .31 C4
Combemartin Rd
SW18 . . . . .70 A3
Combe Mews **4**
SE3 . . . . .53 B3
Comber Gr SE5 . . . . .48 B3
Comber Grove Prim
Sch SE5 . . . . .48 B3
Comber Ho SE5 . . . .48 B3
Combermere Rd
SW9 . . . . .62 B4

Combe The NW1 . . . .92 B3
Com Coll Hackney
The **17** E8 . . . . . . .25 A4
Comeragh Mews
W14 . . . . .140 B1
Comeragh Rd
W14 . . . . .140 B1
Comerford Rd SE4 . .66 B3
Comet Pl SE8 . . . . . . .51 C3
Comet St SE8 . . . . . . .51 C3
Comfort St **6**
SE15 . . . . .49 A4
Comins Ho SW4 . . . .61 B2
Commercial Rd
Stepney E1 . . . . .32 B3
Whitechapel E1 . . . .111 C2
Commercial St
E1 . . . . .110 C4
Commercial Way
Peckham SE15 . . . . .49 C3
Wembley NW10 . . . . .20 A3
Commerell Pl
SE10 . . . . .43 B1
Commerell St
SE10 . . . . .43 A1
Commodity Quay
E1 . . . . .125 A3
Commodore Ct
SE8 . . . . .51 C2
Commodore Ho **7**
E14 . . . . .34 B2
Commodore St E1 . . .26 A1
Commodale
SW15 . . . . .57 B4
Common Rd SW13 . .56 C4
Common View
SW15 . . . . .57 B4
Commonwealth Ave
25 W12 . . . . .30 A2
Commonwealth Ho
WC1 . . . . .106 B2
Community La N7 . . .13 C3
Community Rd
E15 . . . . .19 C3
Como Rd SE23 . . . . . .65 C2
Comodore Ho
SW18 . . . . .59 B3
Compania Bldg **12**
E1 . . . . .32 C2
Compass Ct SE1 . . . .124 C1
Compass Ho
Bayswater W2 . . . . .100 A1
London SE8 . . . . .52 A2
Compass Point **16**
E14 . . . . .33 C2
Compayne Gdns
NW6 . . . . .11 A1
Compton Ave
Islington N1 . . . . . . .15 A2
London N6 . . . . .3 A4
Compton Cl
Camberwell SE15 . . .49 B3
Regent's Pk NW1 . . .92 B3
Compton Cres W4 . . .45 B4
Compton Ho
SW11 . . . . .168 A4
Compton Pas EC1 . . .96 B2
Compton Pl WC1 . . . .94 A2
Compton Rd
Islington N1 . . . . . . .15 A2
Kensal Green NW10 . .22 C2
Compton Terr N1 . . .15 A2
Comus Ho SE17 . . . .152 A3
Comus Pl SE17 . . . . .152 A3
Comyn Rd SW11 . . . .60 A3
Comyns Cl E16 . . . . .35 B4

Conant Ho SE11....48 A4
Conant Mews 1
E1....125 B4
Concanon Rd SW2,
SW4....62 B3
Concert Hall App
SE1....121 A1
Concord Bsns Ctr
W3....28 A4
Concorde Way
SE16....40 C2
Concordia Wharf 10
E14....34 B1
Concord Rd W3....20 A1
Condell Rd SW8..171 A3
Conder St E14....33 A3
Condray Pl SW11 158 A1
Conduit Ct WC2....120 A4
Conduit Ho SE10....52 C2
Conduit Mews
W2....101 B1
Conduit Pas W2...101 B1
Conduit Pl W2....101 B1
Conduit St W1....118 C4
Conewood St N5....6 A1
Coney Acre SE21....75 B3
Coney Way SW8....163 A3
Congers Ho SE5....51 C1
Congress Ho WC1 105 C2
Congreve Ho 10
N16....16 A3
Congreve St SE17 152 A3
Conifer Ct 23
SW19....69 C3
Conifer Gdns
SW16....74 B1
Conifer Ho SE14....51 A2
Coniger Rd SW6..165 B2
Coningham Ct
SW10....157 A2
Coningham Mews
W12....29 C1
Coningham Rd
W12....39 A4
Coningsby Rd N4....6 A4
Conington Rd
SE13....52 B1
Conisbrough NW1..82 C3
Coniston NW1....92 C4
Coniston Cl
Barnes SW13....46 B3
Chiswick W4....45 B3
Coniston Ct
Marylebone W2..102 B1
6 Rotherhithe
SE16....40 C4
Coniston Way N7..14 A1
Coniston Ho
1 Bow E3....26 B2
18 Camberwell SE5..48 B3
Coniston Wlk E9....17 B3
Conlan St W10....23 A1
Conley Rd NW10....8 A2
Conley St SE10....43 A1
Connaught Ave
SW14....55 B3
Connaught Cl W2..102 B1
Connaught Ho
College Pk NW10....22 A2
Mayfair W1....118 A3
Connaught House Sch
W2....102 C1
Connaught Lo N4....5 C4
Connaught Mans
Battersea SW11..168 B3
1 Brixton SW9....62 C3

Connaught Mans
continued
15 Canonbury N16...15 C4
Fulham SW6....164 A4
Connaught Pl W2 102 C1
Connaught Rd
Finsbury Pk N4....5 C4
Harlesden NW10....21 B3
Richmond TW10....54 B2
Connaught Sq
W2....102 C1
Connaught St W2 102 B1
Connaught Works
E3....26 A3
Connell Ct 6
SE14....50 C4
Connor Ct SW11..170 A3
Connor St E9....25 C4
Conrad Ho
8 Limehouse
SE16....33 A2
South Lambeth
SW8....162 A2
12 Stoke Newington
N16....16 A3
Conrad Twr W3....37 A3
Consort Ho W2...114 B3
Consort Lo NW8....80 C3
Consort Rd SE15....50 A1
Cons St SE1....135 C4
Constable Ct 11
SE16....40 A1
Constable Ho
28 Millwall E14....41 C4
Primrose Hill NW3..12 B1
Constable Wlk
SE21....76 A1
Constant Ho 6
E14....34 A2
Constantine Ho
SW2....74 C3
Constantine Rd
NW3....12 A4
Constitution Hill
W1....132 B4
Consul Ho 6 E3....26 C1
Content St SE17..151 B3
Convent Gdns
W11....31 B3
Convent of Jesus &
Mary Language Coll
NW10....21 B4
Convent of Jesus &
Mary RC Inf Sch 9
NW2....9 B2
Conway Gr W3....28 C4
Conway Ho
Chelsea SW3....145 A1
4 Millwall E14....42 A2
6 Streatham SW2..74 A3
Conway Mews W1..92 C1
Conway St W1....92 C1
Conybeare NW3....12 A1
Conyer St 21 E3....26 A3
Cookham Cres
SE16....40 C4
Cookham Ho
E2....24 B1 98 C2
Cook's Rd
Camberwell SE17..48 A4
Stratford Marsh E15..27 A3
Coomassie Rd W9..23 B1
Coombe Ho 18 N7..13 C3
Coombe Rd W4....38 A1
Coomber Ho SW6..59 A4
Coombs St N1....86 B1

Coomer Mews
SW6....155 A3
Coomer Pl SW6...155 A3
Cooperage The
SE1....124 C1
Cooper Cl SE1....135 C3
Cooper Ho NW8....89 B1
Cooper Rd NW10....8 B4
Coopersale Rd E9 17 C3
Coopers Cl E1....25 B1
Coopers Ct
3 Acton W3....28 B1
Tower Hamlets E3..26 B1
Coopers La NW1...83 C1
Coopers Lo SE1...138 C4
Cooper's Rd SE1..153 A2
Coopers Row
EC3....124 C4
Cooper St 10 E16...35 B4
Coopers Yd N1....15 A1
Cope Ho EC1....97 A3
Copeland Dr E14..41 C2
Copeland Ho
SE11....135 A1
Copeland Rd SE15 50 A1
Copenhagen Gdns
W4....37 C4
Copenhagen Ho
N1....85 B3
Copenhagen Pl
E14....33 B3
Copenhagen Prim Sch
N1....84 C3
Cope Pl W8....127 B1
Cope St SE16....40 C2
Copford Wlk N1....86 C4
Copleston Rd
SE15....64 B4
Copley Cl 15 SE17..48 A4
Copley St E1....32 C4
Coppedhall 2
SE21....75 C2
Copperas St SE8..52 A4
Copper Beech N6....3 C4
Copperbeech Cl
NW3....11 C3
Copperfield Ho 12
SE1....139 B3
Copperfield Rd E3 33 A4
Copperfields Ct
W3....36 C4
Copperfield St
SE1....136 C4
Copper Mews 2
W4....37 B3
Copper Row SE1..124 C1
Coppin Ho SW2....75 A3
Coppock Cl SW11 168 A1
Copse Ct SW15....58 A2
Copthall Ave EC2 109 C2
Copthall Bldgs
EC2....109 C2
Copthall Cl EC2..109 B2
Copthorne Ave
SW12....73 C4
Coptic St WC1....106 A3
Copton Cl E3....33 C4
Coral Apts 6 E16..35 C2
Coral Ho 5 E1....26 A1
Coral Row 1
SW11....59 B4
Coral St SE1....135 C3
Coram Ho
Bloomsbury WC1...94 A3

Coram Ho continued
8 Chiswick W4....38 A1
Coram Mans WC1..94 C1
Coram St WC1....94 A1
Corbden Cl SE15...49 B2
Corbet Ct EC3....109 C1
Corbet Ho N1....85 B3
Corbet Pl E1....110 C4
Corbett Ho W10..156 C4
Corbett's La SE16..40 B2
Corbetts Pas 8
SE16....40 B2
Corbidge Ct SE8...52 A4
Corbiere Ho 5
N1....24 A4
Corbin Ho 7 E3....27 A2
Corbridge Cres E2..25 A3
Corbyn St N4, N19..5 A3
Corby Rd NW10....20 C3
Corby Way E3....26 C1
Cordelia Cl SE24...63 A3
Cordelia Ho 26 N1..24 A3
Cordelia St E14....34 A3
Cording St E14....34 A4
Cordwainers Ct 11
E9....17 B1
Corfe Ho SW8....162 C2
Corfe Lodge 15
SE21....75 C2
Corfe Twr 6 W3....37 B4
Corfield St E2....25 A2
Coriander Ave E14..34 C3
Coriander Ct SE1 139 A4
Corinne Rd N19....13 B4
Cork St Mews W1 118 C3
Cork Sq E1....32 A1
Cork St W1....118 C3
Corlett St NW1....102 A4
Cormont Rd SE5...48 A2
Cormorant Ct
30 Deptford SE8....51 B4
11 Dulwich SE21...75 C2
Cornbury Ho 6
SE8....51 B4
Cornelia St N7....14 B2
Corneli Bldg 7
E1....111 B2
Corner Fielde
SW2....74 B3
Corner Gn SE3....53 C1
Corner House St
WC2....120 A2
Cornerstone Ct 6
E1....24 C1 99 C1
Cornerways SW15..56 C3
Corney Rd W4....46 A4
Corney Reach Way
W4....46 A3
Cornflower Terr
SE22....65 A1
Cornford Gr SW12..73 A2
Cornhill EC3....109 C1
Cornick Ho 7
SE16....40 A3
Cornish Ho
7 Camberwell
SE17....48 A4
Cornmill La SE13...67 B4
Cornmow Dr NW10..8 C3
Cornwall Ave E2....25 B2
Cornwall Cres
W11....31 A3
Cornwall Flats
SE1....135 C4

Cornwall Gdns
Kensington SW7...128 B1
Willesden NW10....9 A2
Cornwall Gdns Wlk
SW7....128 B1
Cornwall Gr W4....38 A1
Cornwall Ho
Marylebone NW1....91 A1
1 Putney SW15....69 B4
Cornwallis Ct
SW8....172 A4
Cornwallis Ho 26
W12....30 A2
Cornwallis Rd N19..5 A2
Cornwallis Sq
3 Finsbury Park N4..5 C2
London N19....5 A2
Cornwall Mans
Chelsea SW10....157 A2
Marylebone NW1...91 A1
Cornwall Mews S
SW7....128 C1
Cornwall Mews W 1
SW7....128 B1
Cornwall Rd
Finsbury Pk N4....5 C4
Lambeth SE1....135 C4
Cornwall Sq SE11 150 A2
Cornwall St 4 E1...32 A2
Cornwall Terr
NW1....91 A1
Cornwall Terrace
Mews NW1....91 A1
Cornwood Dr E1...32 B3
Coronation Ave
N16....16 B4
Coronation Ct 10
W10....30 B4
Coronet St
N1....24 A2 98 A3
Corporation Row
EC1....95 C2
Corporation St N7 14 A3
Corpus Christi RC
Prim Sch SW2....62 B2
Corrance Rd SW2,
SW4....62 A3
Corringham Ct
NW11....1 C4
Corringham Ho 11
E1....32 C3
Corringham Rd
NW11....1 C4
Corringway NW11...2 A4
Corry Dr SW9....63 A3
Corry Ho 2 E14....34 A2
Corsham St N1....97 C3
Corsica St N5....15 A2
Corsley Way E9....18 B2
Cortayne Rd SW6 165 A2
Cortis Rd SW15....57 A1
Cortis Terr SW15...57 A1
Corunna Rd SW8 171 A4
Corunna Terr
SW8....170 C4
Corvette Sq 5
SE10....52 C4
Coryton Path W9...23 B1
Cosbycote Ave
SE24....63 B2
Cosgrove Ho 11
E2....24 C4
Cosmo Pl WC1....106 B4
Cosmur Cl W12....38 B3

Cossall Wlk SE15 ....50 A2
Cossar Mews 🔟
SW2 ....62 C2
Cosser St SE1 ....135 B2
Costa St SE15 ......49 C1
Coston Wlk 4
SE4 ....65 C3
Cosway Mans
NW1 ....102 B4
Cosway St NW1 ...102 B4
Cotall St E14 ....33 C4
Cotes Ho NW8 ....90 A1
Cotham St SE17 ...151 A3
Cotherstone Rd
SW2 ....74 B3
Cotleigh Rd NW6 ...10 C1
Cotman Cl SW15 ....57 C2
Cotman Ho 8 .....80 A2
Cotrill Gdns E8 ......17 A2
Cotswold Ct EC1 ...96 C2
Cotswold Gate
NW2 ....1 A3
Cotswold Ho 5
N15 ....5 A2
Cotswold Mews
SW11 ....167 C3
Cottage Gn SE5 ....48 C3
Cottage Gr SW9 ....62 A4
Cottage Pl SW3 ...130 A1
Cottage St E14 ......34 A2
Cottages The SE1 134 C1
Cottage Wlk 2 N16 ..7 B1
Cottenham Ho 5
N19 ....5 A2
Cottesbrook St 9
SE14 ....51 A3
Cottesloe Ho NW8 .90 A2
Cottesloe Mews
SE1 ....135 C2
Cottesmore Ct
W8 ....128 B2
Cottesmore Gdns
W8 ....128 B2
Cottingham Rd
SW8 ....163 A2
Cottington St
SE11 ....150 A2
Cotton Ave W3 ......28 C3
Cotton Ho
Bedford Pk W12 ....38 B4
1 Streatham SW2 .74 A4
South Lambeth
SW11 ....170 C4
Cotton's Gdns
E2 ....24 A2 98 B4
Cottons La SE1 ...123 C2
Cotton St E14 ....34 B2
Cottrell Ct SE10 ....43 B2
Couchman Ho 8
SW4 ....61 B1
Coulgate St SE4 ....66 A4
Coulsdon Ho 5
SW2 ....74 A3
Coulson St SW3 ...144 C2
Coulter Rd W6 ....39 A3
Coults Cres NW5 ....3 C1
Councillor St SE5 ..48 B3
Counters Ct W14 ..126 B2
Counter St SE1 ....124 A1
Countess Rd NW5 ..13 B3
Countisbury Ho
SE26 ....76 C1
County Gr SE5 ......48 B2
County Ho
🗒 Herne Hill SE24 ..63 A3

County Ho continued
9 South Lambeth
SW9 ....173 B4
County St SE1 .....137 A1
Courier Ho 🗒
SW2 ....74 C4
Courland Gr SW8 171 C3
Courland St SW8 .171 C3
Courtauld Ho 🗒2
Courtauld Inst of Art*
WC2 ....120 C4
Courtauld Rd N19 ...5 A3
Courtenay Ave 5 ...3 A4
Courtenay Sq
SE11 ....149 B1
Courtenay St
SE11 ....149 B2
Courtfield Gdns
SW5 ....142 B3
Courtfield Ho EC1 107 B4
Courtfield Mews
SW7 ....142 B3
Courtfield Rd
SW7 ....142 C3
Court Gdns N7 ....14 C2
Courthill Rd SE13 ..67 B3
Courthope Ho
7 Rotherhithe
SE16 ....40 B3
South Lambeth
SW8 ....162 A1
Courthope Rd
NW3 ....12 B4
Court La SE21 ....76 B4
Courtlands TW10 ...54 C2
Courtlands Ave
TW9 ....45 A1
Court Lane Gdns
SE21 ....76 A4
Court Mans 8 ...46 B2
Courtmead Cl
SE24 ....63 B1
Courtnell St W2 .....31 C3
Courtney Ct N7 .....14 C3
Courtney Ho W14 126 B2
Courtney Rd N7 ....14 C3
Courtrai Rd SE23 ..66 A1
Court Royal SW15 .58 A2
Court St 3 E1 ......32 A4
Courtville Ho 12
W10 ....23 A2
Court Way W3 ....28 B4
Courtyard The
Fulham SW6 ....164 A3
Islington N1 ....14 C1
7 Wandsworth
SW18 ....59 C3
Cousin La EC4 .....123 B3
Couzens Ho 8 E3 .33 B4
Coval Gdns SW14 ..55 A3
Coval La SW14 ......55 A3
Coval Pas SW14 ....55 B3
Coval Rd SW14 ......55 B3
Covell Ct 16 SE8 ...51 C3
Covent Garden Sta
WC2 ....106 B1
Coventry Cl NW6 ...23 C4
Coventry Rd E1 .....25 A1
Coventry St W1 ....119 B3
Coverdale Rd
Brondesbury NW2 ..10 A2
Hammersmith W12 .39 A4
Hampstead NW6 .....9 C1
Coverham Ho 5
SE4 ....65 C3

Coverley Cl E1 .....111 C4
Coverley Point
SE11 ....148 C3
Cowcross St EC1 .108 A4
Cowdenbeath Path
N1 ....84 C4
Cowdray Hall Royal
Coll of Nursing
W1 ....104 A2
Cowdray Ho 22
SE22 ....64 A4
Cowdry Rd E9 ....18 B2
Cowley Rd
Brixton SW9 ....173 C4
East Acton W3 ......29 B1
Mortlake SW14 .....56 A4
Cowley St SW1 ....134 A1
Cowling Cl
W11 ....31 A1 112 A2
Cowper Ho
Pimlico SW1 ....147 C1
Walworth SE17 ....151 A2
Cowper Rd
Acton W3 ....28 C1
Stoke Newington
N16 ....7 A1
Cowper's Ct EC3 ..109 C1
Cowper St EC1,EC2 .97 C2
Cowper Terr W10 ...30 C4
Cowthorpe Rd
SW8 ....171 C4
Cox Ho W6 ....154 A4
Coxson Way SE1 ..138 C3
Coysh Ct 8 SW15 ..58 A2
Crabtree Cl E2 ......24 B3
Crabtree Hall SW6 .47 B3
Crabtree La SW6 ...47 C3
Craddock St NW5 ..12 C2
Cragie Ho SE1 .....153 A3
Craigleith SW15 ....57 C1
Craignair Rd SW2 ..74 C4
Craig's Ct SW1 ....120 A2
Crail Row SE17 ....151 C3
Cramer St W1 ......103 C3
Crammond Cl W6 .154 A3
Crampton Prim Sch
SE17 ....150 C2
Crampton St SE17 150 C2
Cranbourn Alley
WC2 ....119 C4
Cranbourne Ct
SW11 ....158 B2
Cranbourne Rd
E15 ....19 B4
Cranbourn Ho 6
SE16 ....40 A4
Cranbourn Pas 5
SE16 ....40 A4
Cranbourn St
WC2 ....119 C4
Cranbrook NW1 ....83 A3
Cranbrook Ho 5
E5 ....17 A3
Cranbrook Rd
Chiswick W4 ....38 A1
St Johns SE8 ....51 C2
Cranbrook St 2 E2 .25 C3
Cranbury Rd SW6 166 B1
Crandale Ho 8
E5 ....17 A3
Crandley Ct SE8 ....41 A2
Crane Ave W3 ....28 B2
Crane Ct
7 Acton W12 ....38 A4
Holborn EC4 ....107 C1

Crane Gr N7 ....14 C2
Crane Ho
24 Bow E3 ....26 A3
16 Peckham SE15 ..49 B2
Crane Mead SE16 ..40 C2
Crane St
Greenwich SE10 ....42 C1
8 Peckham SE15 ...49 B2
Cranfield Ct NW1 102 B3
Cranfield Ho WC1 106 B4
Cranfield Rd SE4 ..66 B4
Cranford Cotts 8
E1 ....32 C2
Cranford Lo SW19 .69 C2
Cranford St E1 ......32 C2
Cranhurst Rd NW2 ..9 B3
Cranleigh
W11 ....31 B1 112 C2
Cranleigh Ct
Richmond TW9 ......54 C4
4 Stamford Hill N16 ..7 A3
Cranleigh Hos
NW1 ....83 A1
Cranleigh Mews
SW11 ....168 C1
Cranleigh St NW1 ..83 A1
Cranley Gdns
SW7 ....143 B2
Cranley Mews
SW7 ....143 A2
Cranley Pl SW7 ...143 B3
Cranmer Ct SW3 ..144 B3
Cranmer Ho
SW11 ....168 A4
Cranmer Rd SW9 163 C2
Cranswick Rd
SE16 ....40 A1
Cranwell Cl E3 ......27 A1
Cranwich Rd N16 .....7 A4
Cranwood Ct EC1 ..97 C3
Cranwood St EC1 ..97 C3
Cranworth Gdns
SW9 ....173 B4
Cranworth Ho 6
N7 ....14 B4
Craster Rd SW2 ....74 B4
Craston Ho 2 SE5 .49 A1
Craven Cl N16 ....7 C4
Craven Cottage
(Fulham FC) SW6 ..47 C2
Craven Hill W2 ....115 A4
Craven Hill Gdns
W2 ....114 C4
Craven Hill Mews
W2 ....115 A4
Craven Ho 2
SW14 ....55 C4
Craven Lo
Bayswater W2 .....115 A4
Fulham SW6 ....47 C2
Craven Mews 6
SW11 ....169 B1
Craven Park Mews
NW10 ....21 A4
Craven Park Rd
NW10 ....21 A4
Craven Pas SW1 ..120 A2
Craven Pk NW10 ...21 A4
Craven Rd
Paddington W2 ....101 A1
Stonebridge NW10 .20 C4
Craven St WC2 ....120 A2
Craven Terr W2 ...115 A4
Craven Wlk E5, N16 .7 A4

Crawford Bldgs
NW1 ....102 B3
Crawford Mews
W1 ....102 C3
Crawford Pas EC1 ..95 C1
Crawford Pl W1 ...102 B3
Crawford Place
Dwellings NW1 ...102 B3
Crawford Prim Sch
E16 ....35 B3
Crawford Prim Sch
SE5 ....48 B2
Crawford Rd SE5 ..48 B1
Crawford St W1 ...102 C3
Crawshay Ct SW9 173 C4
Crawshay Ho 13
N16 ....15 C4
Crawthew Gr SE22 .64 B3
Crayford Ho
Bermondsey SE1 ..137 C3
5 Lower Holloway
N7 ....14 A4
Crayford Rd N7 .....14 A4
Crayle Ho EC1 ....96 B2
Crealock St SW18 ..59 A1
Creasy Est SE1 ....138 A1
Crebor St SE22 .....64 C1
Credenhill Ho 2
SE15 ....50 A3
Crediton Hill NW6 ..11 A3
Crediton Rd NW10 .22 C4
Credon Rd SE16 ....40 A1
Creechurch La
EC3 ....110 B1
Creechurch Pl
EC3 ....110 B1
Creed Ct 5 E1 ......26 A2
Creed Ho SE15 ......65 A4
Creed La EC4 ....108 B1
Creek Ho W14 .....126 B2
Creek Rd SE10,
SE8 ....52 A4
Creek Road Ind Est
SE8 ....52 A4
Creekside SE8 ......52 A3
Creekside Foyer
SE8 ....52 A4
Crefeld Cl W6 ......154 A3
Creighton Cl W12 ..30 A2
Creighton Rd NW6 .22 C3
Cremer Bsns Ctr 8
E2 ....24 B3
Cremer St E2 ....24 B3
Cremorne Rd
SW10 ....157 B2
Creon Ct 3 SW9 ..173 B4
Crescent EC3 ......124 C4
Crescent Arc 1
SE10 ....52 B4
Crescent Court Bsns
Ctr 11 E16 ....27 C1
Crescent Ct SW4 ..61 C2
Crescent Gdns
SW19 ....70 C1
Crescent Gr SW4 ..61 B3
Crescent Ho SE13 .52 A1
Crescent La SW4 ..61 C2
Crescent Mans
Islington N5 ....15 A3
Notting Hill
W11 ....31 A2 112 B4
Crescent Pl SW3 ..144 B4
Crescent Row EC1 .96 C1
Crescent St N1 ......14 B1

Crescent Stables
SW15 . . . . 58 A2
Crescent The
Acton W3 . . . . 29 A3
Barnes SW13 . . . . . 46 C1
Wimbledon SW19 . . 70 C1
Crescent Way SE4 . . 66 C4
Crescent Wood Rd
SE21, SE26 . . . . . . 76 C1
Cresford Rd SW6 . 166 A3
Cressage Ho 9
TW8 . . . . 44 A4
Cressall Ho 14
E14 . . . . 41 C3
Cresset Ho 8 E9 . . 17 B2
Cresset Rd E9 . . . . 17 B2
Cresset St SW4 . . . 61 C4
Cressfield Cl NW5 . 12 C3
Cressida Rd N19 . . . 4 C3
Cressingham Rd
SE13 . . . . 67 B4
Cressington Cl 4
N16 . . . . 16 A3
Cresswell Gdns
SW5 . . . . 142 C2
Cresswell Pl
SW10 . . . . 143 A2
Cressy Ct
Hammersmith W6 . 39 A3
8 Stepney E1 . . . . 32 B4
38 Stepney E1 . . . 32 B4
Cressy Ho SW13 . . 57 A4
Cressy Hos 7 E1 . . 32 B4
Cressy Pl E1 . . . . . 32 B4
Cressy Rd NW3 . . . 12 B4
Cresta Ho
7 Bow E3 . . . . 26 C1
Hampstead NW6 . . 11 C1
Crestfield St
WC1 . . . . 94 B4
Crestview NW5 . . . . 4 A1
Crestway SW15 . . . 57 A1
Creswick Ct W3 . . . 28 A2
Creswick Rd W3 . . 28 A2
Creswick Wlk 1
E3 . . . . 26 C2

Cripplegate St
EC1 . . . . 109 A4
Crispe Ho N1 . . . . 85 A3
Crispian Cl NW10 . . 8 A4
Crispin Cl SE17 . . 152 A3
Crispin Pl E1 . . . . 110 C4
Crispin St E1 . . . . 110 C3
Crisp Rd W6 . . . . . 39 B1
Cristowe Rd SW6 . 165 A1
Criterion Mews
N19 . . . . 4 C2
Crockerton Rd
SW17 . . . . 72 B2
Croft Ct SE13 . . . . 67 B1
Croftdown Rd NW5 . 4 A1
Crofters Ct 9 SE8 . 41 A2
Crofters Way NW1 . 83 B4
Croft Ho
Putney SW15 . . . . 58 A1
1 West Kilburn
W10 . . . . 23 A2
Crofton Ave W4 . . . 45 C3
Crofton Gate Way
SE4 . . . . 66 A2
Crofton Park Rd
SE4 . . . . 66 B1
Crofton Park Sta
SE4 . . . . 66 A2
Crofton Rd SE5 . . . 49 A1
Crofton Terr
Homerton E5 . . . . 18 A3
Richmond TW9 . . . 54 B3
Crofts Ho 21 E2 . . 24 C3
Crofts St E1 . . . . 125 B3
Croft St SE8 . . . . . 41 A2
Croft The NW10 . . . 21 B3
Crogsland Rd
NW1 . . . . 12 C1
Cromartie Rd N19 . . 4 C4
Cromarty Ho 8
E1 . . . . 33 A4
Crombie Mews 5
SW11 . . . . 168 B2
Cromdale Ct N16 . . 7 B4
Cromer Ct
Streatham SW16 . . 74 A1
Wandsworth SW18 . 58 B1
Crome Rd NW10 . . . 8 A2
Cromer St WC1 . . . 94 B3
Cromer Terr E8 . . . 16 C3
Cromer Villas Rd
SW18 . . . . 58 A1
Cromford Path 1
E5 . . . . 17 C4
Cromford Rd
SW18 . . . . 58 C2
Crompton Ct SW3 . 144 A4
Crompton Ho
Borough The SE1 . 137 A1
Paddington W2 . . . 89 B1
South Lambeth
SW8 . . . . 171 A3
Crompton St W2 . . 89 B1
Cromwell Ave
Hammersmith W6 . 39 A2
Highgate N6 . . . . . 4 A3
Cromwell Cl
Acton W3 . . . . 28 B1
2 Gunnersbury W4 . 37 A1
Cromwell Cres
SW5 . . . . 141 B4
Cromwell Ctr
NW10 . . . . 20 C2
Cromwell Gdns
SW7 . . . . 129 C1
Cromwell Gr W6 . . 39 B3

Cromwell Ho
Battersea SW11 . . 169 C3
Putney SW15 . . . . 56 C3
Cromwell Hospl
(BUPA) SW5 . . . . 142 A4
Cromwell Lo 49
E1 . . . . 25 B1
Cromwell Mans
SW5 . . . . 141 C4
Cromwell Mews
SW7 . . . . 143 C4
Cromwell Pl
5 Acton W3 . . . . . 28 B1
Barbican EC1 . . . 109 A4
Highgate N6 . . . . . 4 A3
Mortlake SW14 . . . 55 B4
South Kensington
SW7 . . . . 143 C4
Cromwell Rd
Brixton SW9 . . . . . 48 A2
South Kensington
SW7 . . . . 143 A4
Cromwell Twr
EC2 . . . . 109 A4
Crondace Rd
SW6 . . . . 165 C3
Crondall Ct 7 N1 . . 24 A3
Crondall Ho SW15 . 68 C3
Crondall Pl 18 N1 . 24 A3
Crondall St N1 . . . 24 A3
Crone Ct 5 NW6 . . 23 B3
Cronin St SE15 . . . 49 B3
Crooked Billet Yd 18
E2 . . . . . . 24 A2 98 B4
Crooke Rd SE8 . . . 41 A1
Crookham Rd
SW6 . . . . 164 C3
Croom's Hill SE10 . 52 C3
Croom's Hill Gr
SE10 . . . . 52 B3
Cropley Ct N1 . . . . 87 B2
Cropley St N1 . . . . 87 B2
Cropthorne Ct W9 . 89 A3
Crosby Ct SE1 . . . 137 B4
Crosby Ho 10 E14 . 42 B3
Crosby Row SE1 . . 137 B4
Crosby Sq EC3 . . . 110 A2
Crosby Wlk
3 Dalston E8 . . . . 16 B2
Streatham SE24 . . 74 C4
Crosfield Ct 3
W10 . . . . 30 C3
Crosfield Ho
W11 . . . . 31 A2 112 A3
Crosland Pl 5
SW11 . . . . 60 C4
Crossbow Ho 15
N1 . . . . 24 A4
Cross Cl SE15 . . . . 50 A1
Cross Ct SE5 . . . . 63 C4
Crossfield Rd
NW3 . . . . 11 C2
Crossfield St SE8 . 51 C3
Crossford St SW9 . 172 C1
Crossharbour Sta
E14 . . . . 42 A3
Cross Keys Cl W1 . 103 C3
Cross La EC3 . . . . 124 A3
Crossleigh Ct 3
SE14 . . . . 51 B3
Crosslet St SE17 . . 151 C4
Crosslet Vale SE10 . 52 A2
Crossley St N7 . . . 14 C2
Crossman Hos 15
SW12 . . . . 74 A4

Crossmount Ho 13
SE5 . . . . 48 B3
Cross Rd SE5 . . . . 49 A1
Cross St
Islington N1 . . . . . 86 B4
Mortlake SW13 . . . 56 A4
Crossthwaite Ave SE5,
SE24 . . . . 63 C3
Crosstrees Ho 2
E14 . . . . 41 C3
Crosswall EC3 . . . 124 C4
Crossway SE8, N16 . 16 A3
Crossway SE4 . . . . 51 A1
Crossways Acad
SE4 . . . . 51 A1
Croston St E8 . . . . 24 C4
Crouch End Hill N8 . 4 C4
Crouch Hall Ct N19 . 5 A3
Crouch Hill N4, N8,
N19 . . . . 5 A4
Crouch Hill Sta N4 . 5 B4
Crouchmans Cl SE21,
SE26 . . . . 76 C1
Crowder St E1 . . . . 32 A2
Crowfield Ho N5 . . 15 B4
Crowfoot Cl E9 . . . 18 B3
Crowhurst Cl
SW9 . . . . 173 C2
Crowhurst Ho 21
SW9 . . . . 173 A1
Crowland Ho NW8 . 78 C3
Crowland Terr N1 . 15 C1
Crowline Wlk 1
N1 . . . . 15 B2
Crown Cl
Bow E3 . . . . 26 C4
Hampstead NW6 . . 11 A2
Crown Close Bsns Ctr
122 E3 . . . . 26 C4
Crown Ct
City of London
EC4 . . . . 109 A1
4 Putney SW15 . . 57 C3
St Giles WC2 . . . 106 B1
St John's Wood
NW8 . . . . 90 B3
Crowndale Ct NW1 . 83 B2
Crowndale Rd
NW1 . . . . 83 A2
Crownfield Rd
E15 . . . . 19 C4
Crowngate Ho 33
E3 . . . . 26 B3
Crownleigh Ct
SW2 . . . . 62 C2
Crown Lo SW3 . . . 144 B3
Crown Mews 9
E1 . . . . 32 C4
Crown Office Row
EC4 . . . . 121 B4
Crown Pas SW1 . . 119 A1
Crown Pl
Broadgate EC2 . . 110 A4
Kentish Town NW5 . 13 A2
Crown Reach
SW1 . . . . 147 C1
Crown St
Acton W3 . . . . 28 A1
Camberwell SE5 . . 48 B3
Crownstone Ct 1
SW2 . . . . 62 C2
Crownstone Rd
SW2 . . . . 62 C2

Crown Terr TW9 . . . 54 B3
Crows Rd E3, E15 . 27 C2
Crowther Ave
TW8 . . . . 36 A2
Crowther Cl SW6 . 155 A3
Crowthorne Cl
SW18 . . . . 70 B3
Crowthorne Rd
W10 . . . . 30 C3
Croxley Rd W9 . . . 23 B2
Croxted Cl SE21 . . 75 B4
Croxted Rd SE21,
SE24 . . . . 75 C3
Croxteth Ho 8
SW8 . . . . 171 B2
Croydon Ho SE1 . . 135 C4
Crozier Ho SW8 . . 162 C1
Crozier Terr E9 . . . 17 C3
Crucifix La SE1 . . 138 C4
Cruden Ho
15 Bow E3 . . . . . 26 B3
1 Camberwell
SE17 . . . . 48 A4
Cruden St N1 . . . . 86 B3
Cruickshank St
WC1 . . . . 95 B4
Cruikshank Ho
NW8 . . . . 80 B2
Crusader Ho EC1 . . 96 A1
Crusoe Mews N16 . 6 C2
Crutched Friars
EC3 . . . . 124 B4
Crystal Palace Rd
SE22 . . . . 64 C2
Crystal Wharf N1 . . 86 B1
Cuba St E14 . . . . . 41 C4
Cubitt Bldg SW1 . . 146 A1
Cubitt St WC1 . . . . 95 A3
Cubitt Terr SW4 . . 61 B4
CUBITT TOWN . . . 42 B2
Cubitt Town Jun & Inf
Sch E14 . . . . 42 B3
Cuddington SE17 . 151 A4
Cudworth Ho
SW8 . . . . 171 A3
Cudworth St E1 . . . 25 A1
Cuffley Ho 3 W10 . 30 B4
Cuff Point 2
E2 . . . . . . 24 B2 98 C4
Culand Ho SE17 . . 152 A3
Culford Gdns
SW3 . . . . 145 A3
Culford Gr N1 . . . . 16 A2
Culford Mans
SW3 . . . . 145 A3
Culford Mews N1 . 16 A2
Culford Rd
Kingsland N1 . . . . 16 A2
Shoreditch N1 . . . 24 A4
Culham Ho
2 Paddington W2 . 31 C4
21 Shoreditch
E2 . . . . . . 24 B2 98 C4
Cullen Ho W9 . . . . 23 B3
Cullen Way NW10 . 20 B1
Culling Rd SE16 . . 40 B3
Cullingworth Rd
NW10 . . . . 9 A3
Culloden Cl 51
SE16 . . . . 153 C1
Culloden Prim Sch 18
E14 . . . . 34 B3
Cullum St EC3 . . . 124 A4

Culmore Rd SE15..50 B3
Culmstock Rd
SW11.............60 C2
Culpepper Ct
SE11...........149 B4
Culross Bldgs
NW1.............84 A2
Culross St W1...117 B3
Culver Ct SW18...59 A1
Culverden Rd
SW12............73 B2
Culverhouse WC1 106 C3
Culverhouse Gdns
SW16...........74 B1
Culvert Ct E1 N7...14 B3
Culvert Ct SW11..169 B2
Culvert PI SW11..169 B1
Culvert Rd SW11..169 A2
Culworth Ho NW8..80 A1
Culworth St NW8..80 A1
Cumber Ho SW18..70 C3
Cumberland Ave
NW10...........20 A2
Cumberland Bsns Pk
NW10...........20 A2
Cumberland Cl..16 B2
Cumberland Cres
W14............140 B4
Cumberland Ct
W1.............103 A1
Cumberland Gate
W1.............117 A4
Cumberland Gdns
WC1............95 B4
Cumberland Ho
Paddington W9...88 C1
1 Putney SW15...69 B4
Cumberland Mans
Marylebone W1..102 C2
7 West Hampstead
NW6............10 C3
Cumberland Market
NW1............92 B4
Cumberland Mills Sq
E14............42 C1
Cumberland Park Ind
Est NW10........21 C2
Cumberland Pk
W3.............28 B2
Cumberland PI
NW1............92 A4
Cumberland Rd
Acton W3........28 B2
Barnes SW13....46 C2
Richmond TW9...44 C3
Cumberland St
SW1............146 B2
Cumberland Terr
NW1............82 A1
Cumberland Terrace
Mews NW1.......82 A1
Cumberland Villas
W3.............28 B2
Cumberland Wharf 12
SE16...........40 B4
Cumbrian Gdns
NW2............1 A2
Cuming Mus*
SE17...........150 C3
Cumming St N1...85 A1
Cumnor Cl 6
SW9............173 A2
Cunard PI EC3...110 B1
Cunard Rd NW10..20 C2

Cunard Wlk 3
SE16...........41 A2
Cundy St SW1...145 C3
Cunningham Ct
W2.............89 B1
Cunningham Ho 16
SE5............48 C3
Cunningham Ho
NW4............89 B2
Cunnington St W4..37 B2
Cupar Rd SW11...169 C4
Cureton St SW1...147 C3
Curlew Ho
Brockley SE4.....66 A3
7 Peckham SE15..49 B2
Curlew St SE1...139 A4
Curness St SE13...67 B3
Curran Ho SW3...144 A3
Curricle St W3...29 A1
Currie Ho 13
SW12...........73 C4
Cursitor St EC4...107 B2
Curtain PI
EC2........24 A1 98 B2
Curtain Rd
EC2........24 A1 98 B2
Curtis Dr W3....28 C3
Curtis Ho SE17...151 B2
Curtis St SE1...152 C4
Curtis Way SE1...152 C4
Curve Bldg The
SE4............66 B2
Curve The W12...29 C2
Curwen & New Acad
Gall* W1.......105 B3
Curwen Rd W12...38 C4
Curzon Cres NW10..8 A1
Curzon Gate W1...117 C1
Curzon Sq W1...117 C1
Curzon St W1...118 A2
Custance Ho N1...87 B1
Custance St N1...97 B4
Custom House
EC3............124 A3
Custom House Reach
SE16...........41 B3
Cutbush Ho N7...13 C3
Cutcombe Rd SE5..48 B1
Cuthbert Harrowing
Ho EC1..........96 C1
Cuthbert Ho W2...101 B4
Cuthbert St W2....89 B1
Cuthill Wlk 3 SE5..48 C2
Cutlers Gdns EC2..110 B2
Cutlers Gdns Arc
EC2............110 B2
Cutlers Sq E14...41 C2
Cutlers St EC2...110 B2
Cut The SE1.....135 C4
Cutty Sark* SE10..52 B4
Cutty Sark Ho 4
E14............42 A2
Cutty Sark Ret
Development
SE10...........52 B4
Cutty Sark Sta
SE10...........52 B4
Cuxton Ho SE17...152 B2
Cyclops Mews 12
E14............41 C2
Cygnet Ho NW8...78 C4
Cygnet House N 18
E14............34 A3
Cygnet House S 17
E14............34 A3

Cygnet St
E1........24 B1 99 A2
Cygnus Bsns Ctr
NW10...........21 B1
Cynthia St N1...85 A1
Cyntra PI 8 E8...17 A1
Cypress CI 9 E5...17 C2
Cypress Ct 8 E11...19 C4
Cypress Gdns SE4..66 A2
Cypress Ho SE14..50 C2
Cypress PI W1....93 A1
Cypress PI 23 E2..25 B3
Cypress St E3....26 B3
Cyprus PI 24 E2..25 B3
Cyprus St E2....25 B3
Cyrena Rd SE22...64 B2
Cyril Jackson Prim
Sch (North Bldg) 34
E14............33 B2
Cyril Jackson Prim
Sch (South Bldg) 35
E14............33 B2
Cyril Mans SW11..169 A3
Cyril Thatcher Ho
SW6............165 C3
Cyrus Ho EC1....96 B2
Cyrus St EC1....96 B2
Czar St SE8.....51 C4

D

Dabb's La EC1...95 C1
Dabin Cres SE10...52 B2
Dacca St SE8....51 B4
Dace Rd E3.....26 C4
Dacre Ho SW3...157 C3
Dacre St SW1...133 B2
Daffodil St W12...29 B2
Dafforne Rd SW17..72 C1
Dagmar Ct E14...42 B3
Dagmar Gdns
NW10...........22 C3
Dagmar Pas N1...86 B4
Dagmar Rd
Camberwell SE5...49 A2
Finsbury Pk N4...5 C4
Dagmar Terr N1...86 B4
Dagnall St SW11..169 B3
Dagnan Rd SW12..73 B3
Dagobert Ho 27
E1.............32 B4
Daimler Ho 6 E3..26 C1
Dainton Ho 22 W2..31 C4
Dairy Ho W2.....18 B2
Dairy CI NW10....21 C4
Dairyman CI NW2..1 A1
Daisy Dormer Ct 11
SW9............62 B3
Daisy La SW6....58 C4
Dakin PI 6 E1...33 A4
Dakota bldg 6
SE8............52 A2
Dalberg Rd SW2..62 C2
Dalbury Ho 6
SW9............62 B3
Dalby Rd SW18...59 B3
Dalby St NW5....13 A2
Dalebury Rd SW17..72 B2
Dale Croft N4....6 B1
Dalehead NW1...82 C1
Daleham Gdns
NW3............11 C2
Daleham Mews
NW3............11 C2
Dale Ho
London SE4.....66 A3

Dale Ho continued
St John's Wood
NW8............78 C4
Dalemain Ho 5
E8.............16 C1
Dalemain Mews 2
E16............35 C1
Dale Rd
Camberwell SE17..48 A4
Gospel Oak NW5..12 C3
Dale Row W11....31 A3
Dale St W4.......38 A1
Daley Ho 6 W12..30 A3
Daley St E9.....17 C2
Daley Thompson Way
7 SW8..........61 A4
Dalgarno Gdns
W10............22 B1
Dalgarno Way
W10............22 B1
Daling Way E3...26 A3
Dalkeith Ct SW1..147 C3
Dalkeith Ho 6
SW9............48 A2
Dalkeith Rd SE21..75 B4
Dalling Rd W6....39 A2
Dallington Sch
EC1............96 B2
Dallington St EC1..96 B2
Dalmeny Ave N7..13 C4
Dalmeny Avenue Est
3 N7...........13 C4
Dalmeny Ct 2
SW4............172 A2
Dalmeny Rd N7...13 C4
Dalmeyer Rd NW10..8 B2
Dalmore Rd SE21..75 B2
Dalrymple Rd SE4..66 A3
DALSTON.......16 C2
Dalston Jct E8...16 B2
Dalston Junction Sta
E8.............16 B2
Dalston Kingsland Sta
E8.............16 B3
Dalston La E8....16 C3
Dalton Ho
7 Balham SW12..73 A4
19 Bow E3.......26 A3
16 Deptford SE14..50 C4
Dalton St SE27...75 A1
Dalwood St SE5...49 A2
Dalyell Rd SW9...62 B4
Damascene Wlk
SE21...........75 B2
Damer Ho 5
TW10...........54 B1
Damer Terr SW10..157 A1
Dame St N1.....86 C2
Damien Ct 12 E1..32 A3
Damien St E1....32 A3
Damory Ho 1
SE16...........40 B2
Dan Bryant Ho 5
SW12...........73 C4
Danbury St N1...86 B2
Danby Ho
23 Hackney E9...17 B1
3 West Kilburn
W10............23 B2
Danby St SE15...64 B4
Dancer Rd
Fulham SW6....164 C3
Richmond TW9...54 C4
Dandridge Cl SE10..43 B1

Dandridge Ho E1..110 C4
Danebury 18 W10..30 B4
Danebury Ave
SW15...........56 B1
Danecroft Rd
SE24...........63 C2
Dane Ho 18 SE5...48 B1
Danehurst St
SW6............164 A4
Danemere St
SW15...........57 B4
Dane PI E3......26 B3
Danes Ct NW8...80 C3
Danesdale Rd E9..18 A2
Danesfield SE5...49 A4
Danes Ho W10...30 B4
Dane St WC1....106 C3
Daneville Rd SE5..48 C2
Daniel Bolt Cl E14..34 A4
Daniel Ct W3....29 A2
Daniel Gdns SE15..49 B3
Daniell Ho N1...87 C2
Daniel's Rd SE15..65 B4
Dan Leno Wlk
SW6............156 A1
Dansey PI W1...119 B4
Dante PI SE11...150 A4
Dante Rd SE11...150 A4
Danube Ct 13
SE15...........49 B3
Danube St SW3...144 B2
Danvers Ho 35 E1 111 C1
Danvers St SW3...157 C3
Da Palma Ct SW6..155 B3
Daphne St SW18..59 B1
Daplyn St 3 E1...111 B4
D'arblay St W1...105 A1
Darcy Ho E8.....25 A4
Darell Prim Sch
TW9............54 C4
Darell Rd TW9...54 C4
Daren Ct N7.....14 A4
Darent Ho NW8...101 C4
Darenth Rd N16...7 B3
Darfield NW1....82 C3
Darfield Rd SE4...66 B2
Darfield Way W10..30 C2
Darfur St 3 SW15..57 C4
Darien Ho
16 London SW11..59 C4
1 Stepney E1....32 C4
Darien Rd SW11..59 C4
Daring Ho 26 E3..26 A3
Darlan Rd SW6...155 A1
Darley Ho SE11...148 C1
Darley Rd SW11..60 B1
Darling Rd SE4...66 C4
Darling Row E1...25 A1
Darnall Ho 4
SE10...........52 B2
Darnay Ho 8
SE16...........139 B2
Darnell Ho 9
SE10...........52 B2
Darnley Ho 7 E14..33 A3
Darnley Rd E9...17 B2
Darnley Terr 12
W11...........31 A1
Darrell Rd SE22...64 C2
Darren Cl N4....5 A4
Darsley Dr SW8..172 A4
Dartford Ho SE1..153 A4
Dartford St SE17..48 B4
Dartington NW1...83 A3

Dartington Ho
Bayswater W2 .... **100** A4
7 London SE10 .. **171** C2
Dartle Ct SE16 **139** C3
Dartmoor Wlk 18
E14 .... 41 C2
Dartmouth Cl W11..31 C3
Dartmouth Ct
SE10 .... 52 B2
Dartmouth Gr
SE10 .... 52 B2
Dartmouth Hill
SE10 .... 52 B2
Dartmouth Ho
Dartmouth Pk N19 ....4 A2
Lewisham SE10 ..... 52 B2
DARTMOUTH PARK 4 A1
Dartmouth Park Ave
NW5 .... 4 A1
Dartmouth Park Hill
N19 .... 4 A1
NW5 .... 4 A1
Dartmouth Park Rd
NW5 .... 4 A2
Dartmouth Pl W4...46 A4
Dartmouth Row
SE10 .... 52 B2
Dartmouth St
SW1 .... **133** C3
Dartmouth Terr
SE10 .... 52 B2
Darton Ct W3 ....28 B1
Dartrey Twr
SW10 .... **157** B2
Dartrey Wlk
SW10 .... **157** A2
Dart St W10 ....23 B2
Darville Rd N16 .....7 B1
Darwen Pl E2 ....25 A4
Darwin Ct NW1 ....82 B4
Darwin Ctr* SW7 **129** B1
Darwin Ho 8
SE13 .... 52 B1
Darwin St SE17..**152** A4
Daryngton Ho
SW8 .... **162** A1
Dashwood Ho
SE21 .... 76 B1
Data Point Bsns Ctr
E16 .... 27 C1
Datchelor Pl 14
SE5 .... 48 C2
Datchet Ho NW1 .. 92 B4
Datchett Ho 46
E2 .... 24 B2 **98** C3
Datchwood Ct N1 ..6 B1
Datchworth Ho 8
N1 .... 15 A1
Date St SE17 .... **151** B1
Daubeney Prim Sch
E5 .... 18 A4
Daubeney Rd E5....18 A4
Daubeney Twr 2
SE8 .... 41 B1
Dault Rd SW18....59 B1
Dauney Ho SE1..**136** A3
Dave Adams Ho 8
E3 .... 26 B3
Davenant Ho 20
E1 .... **111** C4
Davenant Rd N19....4 C2
Davenant St E1 .. **111** C3
Davenport Ho
SE11 .... **135** B3

Davenport Mews 6
W12 .... 30 A1
Davenport Rd SE6..67 B1
Daventry St NW1 ..**102** A4
Dave Porter Hts
SW19 .... 70 A4
Daver Ct SW3 .... **144** B1
Davern Cl SE10....43 B2
Davey Cl N7 ....14 B2
Davey Rd E9 ....18 C1
Davey's Ct WC2....**120** A4
Davey St SE15....49 B4
David Devine Ho 7
E8 .... 16 C3
David Game Coll
SW7 .... **143** B3
Davidge Ho SE1.. **135** C3
Davidge St SE1 .. **136** B3
David Hewitt Ho 2
E3 .... 34 A4
David Ho
8 Putney SW15 ..56 C2
South Lambeth
SW8 .... **162** A2
David Mews W1 .. **103** A4
Davidson Gdns
SW8 .... **162** A2
Davidson Ho 7
N19 .... 13 B4
David St E15 .... 19 C3
Davies Laing & Dick
Coll W1 .... **103** C2
Davies Mews W1 ..**118** A4
Davies St W1 .... **118** A4
Davina Ho
Brondesbury NW2 ..10 B2
7 Hackney E5 ....17 A3
Da Vinci Ct 19
SE16 .... 40 A1
Davis Ho 52 W12 ..30 A2
Davis Rd W3 .... 38 B4
Davisville Rd W12..38 C4
Dawes Ho SE17 .. **151** B3
Dawes Rd SW6 .. **154** C2
Dawes St SE17 .. **151** C2
Dawlish Ave SW18..71 A2
Dawlish Rd NW2 ....9 C2
Dawnay Gdns
SW18 .... 71 C2
Dawnay Rd SW17,
SW18 .... 71 C2
Dawn Cres E15....27 C4
Dawson Ho
22 Bethnal Green
E2 .... 25 B2
Camberwell SE5..49 A2
Dawson Pl
W2 .... 31 C2 **113** C4
Dawson Rd NW2 .. 9 B4
Dawson St E2 .... 24 B3
Day Ho 2 SE5 .... 48 B3
Daylesford Ave
SW15 .... 56 C3
Daynor Ho 4
NW6 .... 23 C4
Daysbrook Rd
SW2 .... 74 B3
Dayton Gr SE15..50 B2
Deacon Ho SE11..**149** A3
Deacon Mews N1 ..15 C1
Deacon Rd NW2 ....8 C2
Deacon Way SE17 **151** A4
Deal Ho
Deptford SE15 ....50 C4
Walworth SE17.. **152** B2

Deal Porters Way
SE16 .... 40 C2
Deal St E1 .... **111** B4
Dealtry Rd SW15..57 B3
Deal Wlk 8 SW9 **163** C1
Dean Bradley St
SW1 .... **134** A1
Dean Cl
Hackney E9 ....17 B3
Rotherhithe SE16..32 C1
Dean Coll of London
4 N7 .... 5 B1
Deancross St E1....32 B3
Dean Ct
Acton W3 .... 28 C3
South Lambeth
SW8 .... **162** A1
Deanery Mews
W1 .... **117** C2
Deanery St W1 .. **117** C2
Dean Farrar St
SW1 .... **133** C2
Deanhill Ct 2
SW14 .... 55 A3
Deanhill Rd SW14..55 A3
Dean Ho
London N4 .... 6 B4
New Cross SE14..51 B3
Stamford Hill N16..7 B3
18 Stepney E1 ....32 B3
Dean Rd NW2 .... 9 B2
Dean Ryle St SW1 **148** A4
Dean's Bldgs
SE17 .... **151** C3
Deans Cl W4 .... 45 A4
Dean's Ct EC4 .. **108** B1
Dean's Gateway 20
SE10 .... 51 C2
Deanshanger Ho 21
SE8 .... 40 C2
Dean's Mews W1 ..**104** B2
Dean St W1 .... **105** B1
Dean Stanley St
SW1 .... **134** A1
Dean's Yd SW1 .. **133** C2
Dean Trench St
SW1 .... **134** A1
Dearmer Ho 6
SW2 .... 74 C4
Deason St E15....27 B4
Deauville Ct
14 London SW4 ..61 B1
4 Rotherhithe
SE16 .... 40 C4
Deauville Mans 13
SW4 .... 61 B1
De Barowe Mews
5 Highbury N5 ..15 A4
1 London N5.....15 A3
Debdale Ho 20
N1 .... 24 A4
De Beauvoir Cres
N1 .... 24 A4
De Beauvoir Ct N1 ..15 C1
De Beauvoir Pl 5
N1 .... 16 A2
De Beauvoir Prim Sch
15 N1 .... 16 A2
De Beauvoir Rd
N1 .... 16 A1
De Beauvoir Sq
N1 .... 16 A1
DE BEAUVOIR TOWN 16 A1
Debenham Ct E8..24 C4
Debnams Rd SE16..40 B2
Decima St SE1 .. **138** A2

Deck Cl SE16.....32 C1
De Crespigny Pk
SE5 .... 48 C1
Deeley Rd SW8 .. **171** B4
Deepdale N4 .... 6 A1
Deepdene Gdns
SW2 .... 74 B4
Deepdene Ho SE5..63 C3
Deepdene Lo 6
SW2 .... 74 B4
Deepdene Mans
SW6 .... **164** C4
Deepdene Rd SE5,
SE24 .... 63 B3
Deerbrook Rd SE24,
SW2 .... 75 A3
Dee Rd TW9 ....54 B3
Deerdale Rd SE24..63 B3
Deerhurst Ho 6
SE15 .... 49 C4
Deerhurst Rd NW2 ..9 C2
Deer Lo SW6 ....58 A4
Deeside Rd SW17..71 C1
Dee St E14 .... 34 B3
Defoe Ave TW9 ..44 C3
Defoe Ho
Barbican EC2 .. **108** C4
8 Stoke Newington
N16 .... 7 A1
Defoe Pl EC2 .. **108** C4
Defoe Rd
Rotherhithe SE16..41 B4
Stoke Newington N16..7 A1
De Gama Pl 3
E14 .... 41 C1
Dekker Ho 18 SE5..48 C3
Dekker Rd SE21..64 A1
Delafield Ho 28
E1 .... **111** C1
Delaford Rd SE16..40 A1
Delaford St SW6.. **154** B3
Delamere Ho 4 N4 ..6 C4
Delamere Rd W5..36 A4
Delamere St W2 .. **100** C3
Delamere Terr
W2 .... **100** B4
Delancey Pas NW1 **82** B3
Delancey St NW1..**82** B3
Delancey Studios
NW1 .... **82** B3
Delany Ho SE10..52 B4
Delarch Ho SE1 .. **136** A3
De Laune St SE17 **150** A1
Delaware Rd W9 .. **88** A2
Delawyk Cres
SE24 .... 63 C1
Delft Way 2 SE22 ..64 A2
Delhi St N1 .... 84 B3
Delia St SW18 .... 71 A4
Delius Gr E15 .... 27 B3
Dellafield N4 ....5 C2
Dell Cl E15 .... 27 C4
Dellow Ho 6 E1 ..32 A2
Dellow St E1 .... 32 A2
Dell's Mews SW1 **147** A3
Deloraine Ho SE8..51 C2
Deloraine St SE8..51 C2
Delorme St W6 .... 47 C4
Delta Bldg 7 E14 ..34 B3
Delta Ho N1 .... **97** B4
Delta Pk SW18 .... 59 A3
Delta Point 5
E2 .... 24 C2 **99** B4
Delta St 6
E2 .... 24 C2 **99** B4

Delverton Ho
SE17 .... **150** B2
Delverton Rd
SE17 .... **150** B1
Delvino Rd SW6 .. **165** C3
De Montfort Ct 5
SW16 .... 74 A1
De Montfort Rd
SW16 .... 74 A2
De Morgan Rd
SW6 .... 59 A4
Dempster Rd
SW18 .... 59 B2
Denbigh Cl
W11 .... 31 B2 **113** A4
Denbigh Gdns
TW10 .... 54 B2
Denbigh Ho
Knightsbridge
SW1 .... **131** A2
7 Notting Hill W11..31 B3
Notting Hill
W11 .... 31 B2 **113** A4
Denbigh Mews
SW1 .... **146** C3
Denbigh Pl SW1..**146** C2
Denbigh Rd
W11 .... 31 B2 **113** A4
8 London W13....**147** A2
Denbigh St
SW1 .... **147** A2
Denbigh Terr
W11 .... 31 B2 **113** A4
Denbury Ho 48 E3..27 A2
Denby Ct SE11 .. **149** A4
Dence Ho 18
E2 .... 24 C2 **99** B3
Denchworth Ho 14
SW9 .... **173** B1
Dene Cl SE4 .... 66 A3
Denehurst Gdns
Acton W3 .... 28 A1
Richmond TW10 .. 54 C3
Dene Mans 1
NW6 .... 10 C2
Denesmead SE24..63 B2
Denewood Ho 4
SW16 .... 3 B4
Dengie Wlk N1 .. **86** C4
Denham Ho 22
W12 .... 30 A2
Denham St SE10..43 C1
Denholme Rd W9..23 B2
Denland Ho SW8..**163** A1
Denman Ho N1....16 A2
Denman Rd SE15..49 B1
Denmark Gr N1....**85** B2
Denmark Hill SE5..48 C1
Denmark Hill Sta
SE5 .... 48 C1
Denmark Mans 14
SE5 .... 48 B1
Denmark Pl
2 Bromley E3....26 C2
Soho WC2 .... **105** C2
Denmark Rd
Camberwell SE5..48 B1
Kilburn NW6 .... 23 B3
Denmark St WC2..**105** C2
Denmead Ho
SW15 .... 56 B1
Denne Terr E8 .... 24 B4
Dennett's Gr SE14..50 C1
Dennett's Rd SE14..50 B2
Denning Cl NW8..**89** A3

Denning Mews
SW12................60 C1
Denning Point E1 111 A2
Denning Rd NW3....11 C4
Dennington Park
Mansions 12
NW6................10 C3
Dennington Park Rd
NW6................10 C3
Dennis Ct SE10.....52 B2
Dennis Ho 4 E3...26 B3
Dennison Point
E15.................19 B1
Dennis Severs'
House* E1.......110 B4
Dennis Way SW4...61 C4
Denny Cres SE11..149 C2
Denny St SE11.....149 C2
Densham Ho NW8..79 C1
Denstone Ho 5
SE15................49 C4
Dent Ho SE17.....152 A3
Denton NW1.........12 C2
Denton St SW18....59 A1
Dents Rd SW11.....60 B1
Denver Rd N16......7 A4
Denyer Ho 1
NW5................13 A4
Denyer St SW3...144 B4
Denys Bldg EC1...107 B4
Denzil Rd NW10....8 B3
Deodar Rd SW15...58 A3
Depot App NW2....9 C4
Depot Rd W12......30 B2
Depot St SE5.......48 C4
DEPTFORD..........50 C3
Deptford Bridge
SE8................51 C2
Deptford Bridge Sta
SE8................51 C2
Deptford Broadway
SE8, SE14..........51 C2
Deptford Church St
SE8................51 C3
Deptford Ferry Rd 20
E14................41 C2
Deptford Gn SE8..51 C4
Deptford Green Sch
SE14................51 B3
Deptford Green Sch
(Annex) 12 SE14..51 A3
Deptford High St
SE8................51 C3
Deptford Park Prim
Sch 8 SE8.........41 A1
Deptford Sta SE8..51 C3
Deptford Trad Est
SE8................51 A4
Deptford Wharf
SE8................41 B2
De Quincey Mews 3
E16................35 C1
Derby Ct E5........17 C4
Derby Gate SW1..134 A4
Derby Ho SE11....149 B4
Derby Rd
Mortlake SW14...55 C4
South Hackney E9..25 C4
Derbyshire St
E2.............24 C2 99 C3
Derby St W1......117 C1
Dereham Ho 7
SE4................65 C3

Dereham Pl
EC2............24 A1 98 B2
Derek Walcott Cl
SE24................63 A2
Dericote St E8.....25 A4
Dering St W1......104 B1
Dermody Gdns
SE13................67 C2
Dermody Rd SE13..67 C2
Deronda Rd SE24,
SW2................74 C3
Derrick Ho 13
SW2................74 C3
Derrycombe Ho 18
W2.................31 C4
Derry St W8.......128 A3
Dersingham Rd
NW2.................1 A1
Derwent NW1......92 C3
Derwent Ct
2 Hammersmith
W6..................38 C2
8 Rotherhithe
SE16................40 C4
Derwent Gr SE22...64 B3
Derwent Ho
South Kensington
SW7...............143 A4
Tower Hamlets E3..26 B1
Derwent St SE10...43 A1
Derwentwater Mans
2 W3................28 B1
Derwentwater Prim
Sch W3.............28 A1
Derwentwater Rd
W3.................28 B1
Desborough Cl
W2.................100 B4
Desborough Ho
W14...............155 A4
Desenfans Rd
SE21................64 A1
Design Mus* SE1 139 A4
Desmond St SE14..51 A4
Despard Row W2...74 C2
Despard Rd N19....4 B3
Desvignes Dr SE13 .67 C1
Dethick Ct E3......26 A4
Detling Ho SE17...152 A3
Devas St E3........27 A1
Deventer Cres 8
SE22................64 A2
De Vere Cotts W8 128 C2
De Vere Gdns W8 128 C3
Deverell St SE1...137 B1
De Vere Mews
W8................128 C2
Devereux Ct WC2..107 B1
Devereux Ho 7
SW15................56 C2
Devereux La SW13..47 A3
Devereux Rd
SW11................60 B1
Devitt Ho 5 E14....34 A2
Devizes St N1......87 C3
Devonhurst Pl 4
W4..................37 C1
Devonia Rd N1.....86 B2
Devon Mans SE1..138 B4
Devonport 2
W2..................102 A2
Devonport Ho
Greenwich SE10....52 B4
2 Paddington W2..31 C4
Devonport Rd
W12.................39 A4
Devonport St E1...32 C3

Devonshire Cl
W1.................104 A4
Devonshire Ct
14 Balham SW12...73 A4
6 Richmond TW9..44 B2
Devonshire Dr
SE10................52 A2
Devonshire Gdns
W4..................45 B3
Devonshire Gr
SE15................50 A4
Devonshire Hall 11
E9..................17 B2
Devonshire Ho
Brondesbury NW6..10 B2
Newington SE1.....137 C2
2 Putney SW15....69 B4
Westminster SW1 147 C2
Devonshire House
Prep Sch SW3....11 B3
Devonshire Mews 7
W4..................38 A1
Devonshire Mews N
W1.................104 A4
Devonshire Mews S
W1.................104 A4
Devonshire Mews W
W1.................103 C4
Devonshire Pl
Child's Hill NW2.....1 C1
Kensington W8....128 A1
Marylebone W1...103 C4
Devonshire Place
Mews W1...........103 C4
Devonshire Rd
W4..................38 A1
Devonshire Row
EC2................110 B3
Devonshire Row
Mews W1...........92 B1
Devonshire Sq
EC2................110 B2
Devonshire St
Chiswick W4........38 A1
Marylebone W1...104 A4
Devons Rd E3......27 A1
Devons Road Sta
E3...................27 A1
Devon St SE15.....50 A4
De Walden Ho
NW8................80 A2
De Walden St W1 103 C3
Dewar St SE15.....64 C4
Dewberry St E14...34 B4
Dewey Rd N1.......85 B2
Dewhurst Rd W14..39 C3
Dewsbury Ct 6
W4..................37 B2
Dewsbury Rd NW10..8 C3
Dewsbury Terr
NW1.................82 B4
D'eynsford Rd SE5..48 C2
Dhonau Ho SE16..153 A4
Diadem Ct W1....105 B2
Dial Wlk The W8..128 B4
Diamond Est
SW17................72 A1
Diamond Ho 22
E3...................26 A3
Diamond St SE15...49 A3
Diamond Terr
SE10................52 B2
Diana 27 SE8......51 B4

Diana Ho
Barnes SW13.......46 B2
4 Brixton SW2.....62 B2
Diana, Princess of
Wales Mml
Fountain*
W2................129 C4
Diana, Princess of
Wales Mml Wlk
W2................114 C1
Dibden Ho 8 SE5..49 A3
Dibden St N1........86 C4
Dibdin Ho W9.......78 A1
Dicey Ave NW2.....9 B3
Dickens Ct EC1.....96 A1
Dickens Ho
Bloomsbury WC1....94 A2
Kennington SE17..150 B1
Kilburn NW6.......23 C2
Paddington NW8...89 C2
Dickenson Rd N8....5 A4
Dickens Sq SE1...137 A2
Dickens St SW8....170 B2
Dickinson Ho 18
E2.............24 C2 99 B3
Dicksee Ho NW8...89 B1
Dick Shepherd Ct 17
SW2................62 C1
Dickson Ho 4 E1...32 A3
Didbin Ho N7......14 B2
Digby Bsns Ctr E9..17 C2
Digby Cres N4.......6 B2
Digby Mans W6....39 B1
Digby Rd E9.........17 C2
Digby St E2..........25 B2
Diggon St E1.......32 C4
Dighton Ct SE17...48 B4
Dighton Rd SW18..59 B3
Dignum St N1......85 B2
Digswell St N7......14 C2
Dilke St SW3......159 A4
Dilston Gr SE16....40 B2
Dilton Gdns SW15..69 A3
Dimes Pl 6 W6....39 A2
Dimson Cres E3....26 C2
Dinerman Ct NW8..79 A4
Dingle Gdns E14...33 C2
Dingley La SW16...73 C2
Dingley Pl EC1......97 A3
Dingley Rd EC1......96 A3
Dingwall Rd SW18..71 B4
Dinmont Ho 27 E2..25 A3
Dinmont St 11 E2..25 A3
Dinmore Ho 6 E9..25 B4
Dinnington Ho 14
E1...................25 A1
Dinsdale Rd SE3....53 B4
Dinsmore Rd
SW12................73 A4
Dinton Ho NW8....90 A2
Dinwiddy Ho N1....84 C1
Dionis Ho SW6....165 B2
Disbrowe Rd W6..154 B3
Discovery Bsns Pk 9
E16................35 C1
Discovery Dock E
E14..................42 A4
Discovery Ho 1
E14..................34 B2
Disney Pl SE1.....137 A4
Disney St SE1.....137 A4
Disraeli Cl 1 W4...37 C2
Disraeli Gdns
SW15................58 B3
Disraeli Rd
Acton NW10........20 C3

Disraeli Rd continued
Putney SW15........58 A3
Diss St E2......24 B2 98 C4
Distaff La EC4.....122 C4
Distillery La W6....39 B1
Distillery Rd W6....39 B1
Distillery Wlk 14
TW8.................44 A4
Distin St SE11.....149 B3
Ditchburn St E14...34 B2
Ditton Ho 10 E5...17 A3
Divis Way SW15....57 A1
Dixon Clark Ct N1...15 A2
Dixon Ho 20 NW10..30 C3
Dixon Rd SE14......51 A2
Dixon's Alley 16
SE16................40 A4
Dixon Way 9
NW10.................8 A1
Dobree Ave NW10...9 A1
Dobson Cl NW6....11 C1
Dobson Ho 18
SE14................50 C4
Doby Ct EC4......123 A4
Dockers Tanner Rd 5
E14..................41 C2
Dockhead SE1.....139 A3
Dockhead Wharf
SE1................139 A4
Dock Hill Ave
SE16................40 C4
Docklands Ct 20
E14..................33 B3
Docklands Visitor
Ctr* E14...........42 B4
Dockley Rd SE16 .139 B1
Dockley Road Ind Est
SE16...............139 B1
Dock Offices 12
SE16................40 B3
Dock Rd E16........35 B2
Dock St E1........125 B4
Doctor Spurstowe
Almshouses 9
E8...................17 A2
Docura Ho N7.......5 B2
Docwras Bldgs N1..16 A2
Dodbrooke Rd
SE27................75 A1
Dodd Ho 10 SE16...40 A2
Doddington Gr
SE17................150 B1
Doddington Pl 4
SE17................48 A4
Dodson St SE1...135 C3
Dod St E14.........33 C3
Dog & Duck Yd
WC1...............106 A4
Dog Kennel Hill
SE22................64 A4
Dog Kennel Hill Sch
22 SE22..............64 A4
Dog La NW10........8 A4
Dolben Ct SW1...147 C3
Dolben St SE1.....122 B1
Dolby Rd SW6....164 C1
Doleman Ho 16
SE10................52 A2
Dolland Ho SE11 .149 A1
Dolland St SE11 .149 A1
Dollar Bay E14....42 B4
DOLLIS HILL.........9 A4
Dollis Hill Sta NW2..8 C3
Dolman Rd W4.....37 C2
Dolman St SW4....62 B3

Dolphin Cl **2**
SE16 . . . . .40 C4
Dolphin Ct N7 . . . . . .13 C4
Dolphin La E14 . . . . .34 A2
Dolphin Sch SW11 . .60 B2
Dolphin Sq SW1 . . .147 A1
Dolphin Twr **21**
SE8 . . . . .51 B4
Dombey Ho
8 Bermondsey
SE1 . . . .**139** B3
3 Shepherd's Bush
W11 . . . . .30 C1
Dombey St WC1 . . .106 C4
Domelton Ho
SW18 . . . . .59 B3
Domett Cl SE5 . . . . .63 C3
Domfe Pl E5 . . . . . . .17 C4
Domfred Rd E21 . . .96 C1
Dominion St EC2 . .109 C4
Donaghue Cotts **11**
E14 . . . . .33 A4
Donaldson Rd
NW6 . . . . .23 B4
Donegal Ho **2** E1 . . .25 B1
Donegal St N1 . . . . .85 A1
Doneraile Ho
SW1 . . . . .146 A1
Doneraile St SW6 . .47 C2
Dongola Rd E1 . . . . .33 A4
Don Gratton Ho **23**
E1 . . . . .111 B3
Donkey Alley SE22 . .64 C1
Donkin Ho **13**
SE16 . . . . .40 A2
Donne Ct SE24 . . . . .63 B1
Donne Ho
18 Canonbury N16 . .15 C4
3 Deptford SE14 . .50 C4
2 Poplar E14 . . . . . .33 C3
Donnelly Ct SW6 . . .154 A2
Donne Pl SW3 . . . . .144 B4
Donnington
11 Camden Town
NW1 . . . . .13 A1
Willesden NW10 . . . .9 A1
Donnington Ho **12**
SW8 . . . . .171 B2
Donnington Prim Sch
NW10 . . . . .22 A4
Donnington Rd
NW10 . . . . .22 A4
Donovan Ct SW7 . . .143 B1
Donovan Ho **4** E1 . . .32 B2
Don Phelan Ho **23**
SE5 . . . . .48 C2
Doon St SE1 . . . . . .121 B2
Doradus Ct **20**
SW19 . . . . .69 C3
Dora Ho
11 Shepherd's Bush
W11 . . . . .30 C2
1 Tower Hamlets
E14 . . . . .33 B3
Dorando Cl W12 . . . .30 A2
Doran Wlk
Stratford E15 . . . . . .19 B1
Stratford Marsh E15 .27 B4
Dora St E14 . . . . . . .33 B3
Dorcas Ct **9**
SW18 . . . . .59 C3
Dorchester Ct
1 De Beauvoir Town
N1 . . . . .16 A1
Herne Hill SE24 . . . . .63 B2
Knightsbridge SW1 . .131 A1

Dorchester Ct
continued
5 Streatham SW16 . .74 A2
Dorchester Dr
SE24 . . . . .63 B2
Dorchester Gr W4 . . .38 B1
Dorchester Ho
TW9 . . . . .45 A3
Dordrecht Rd W3 . . .29 A1
Doria Rd SW6 . . . . .165 A2
Doric Ho **7** E2 . . . . . .25 C3
Doric Way NW1 . . . .93 B4
Doris Emmerton Ct
SW18 . . . . .59 B3
Dorking Cl SE8 . . . . .51 B4
Dorking Ho SE1 . . . .137 C2
Dorland Ct SW15 . . .58 B1
Dorlcote Rd SW18 . . .72 A4
Dorleston Ct N1 . . . .87 C4
Dorman Way NW8 . .79 B4
Dormay St SW18 . . . .59 A2
Dormstone Ho
SE17 . . . . .152 A3
Dornberg Cl SE3 . . . .53 C3
Dorncliffe Rd
SW6 . . . . .164 B2
Dorney NW3 . . . . . . .12 A1
Dorney Ho SW15 . . . .58 A4
Dornfell St NW6 . . . .10 B3
Dornoch Ho **2** E3 . . .26 B3
Dornton Rd SW12,
SW17 . . . . .73 B2
Dorothy Charrington
Ho **1** SE22 . . . . . . .64 C2
Dorothy Rd SW11 . . .60 B4
Dorrell Pl **18** SW9 . . .62 C4
Dorrien Wlk SW16 . .73 C2
Dorrington Point **20**
E3 . . . . .27 A2
Dorrington St
EC1 . . . . .107 B4
Dorrit Ho **2** W11 . . . .30 C1
Dorrit St SE1 . . . . . .137 A4
Dorset Bldgs EC4 . .108 A1
Dorset Cl NW1 . . . . .102 C4
Dorset Ct **3** N1 . . . . .16 A1
Dorset Mans **2**
W6 . . . . .47 C4
Dorset Mews
SW1 . . . . .132 A2
Dorset Pl E15 . . . . . .19 C2
Dorset Rd SW8 . . . .162 C2
Dorset Rise EC4 . . . .108 A1
Dorset Sq NW1 . . . . .90 C1
Dorset St W1 . . . . . .103 A3
Dorton Cl **3** SE15 . . .49 A3
Dorville Cres W6 . . . .39 A3
Doughty Ct **1** E1 . . . .32 A1
Doughty Mews
WC1 . . . . .94 C1
Doughty St WC1 . . . .94 C1
Douglas Bldgs
SE1 . . . . .137 A4
Douglas Ct **5**
NW6 . . . . .10 C1
Douglas Gracey Ho **1**
SW18 . . . . .70 A4
Douglas Ho
Putney SW15 . . . . . . .56 C1
Westminster SW1 . .147 B3
Douglas Johnstone
Ho **4** SW6 . . . . . . .154 C3
Douglas Mews
NW2 . . . . .1 A1
Douglas Path E14 . . .42 B1

Douglas Rd
Islington N1 . . . . .15 B1
Kilburn NW6 . . . . . . .23 B4
5 Newham E16 . . . . .35 C4
Douglas Rd N N1 . . .15 B2
Douglas Rd S N1 . . .15 B2
Douglas St SW1 . . .147 B3
Douglas Waite Ho
NW6 . . . . .11 A1
Douglas Way SE8 . . .51 B3
Doulton Ho SE11 . . .149 A4
Doulton Mews **4**
NW6 . . . . .11 A2
Dounesforth Gdns
SW18 . . . . .71 A3
Douro Pl W8 . . . . . .128 B2
Douro St E3 . . . . . . .26 C3
Douthwaite Sq **1**
E1 . . . . .125 C2
Dovecote Gdns **3**
SW14 . . . . .55 C4
Dove Ct EC2 . . . . . .109 B1
Dovedale Cotts **6**
SW11 . . . . .168 C2
Dovedale Ho N16 . . . .6 C4
Dovedale Rd SE22 . .65 A1
Dovehouse St
SW3 . . . . .144 A1
Dove Mews SW7 . . .143 A2
Dovercourt Rd
SE22 . . . . .64 B1
Dover Ct
Clerkenwell EC1 . . . . .96 A2
17 Greenwich SE10 . .52 A2
Dover Flats **1** SE1 . .152 B3
Dover Ho
Brixton SE5 . . . . .48 A2
11 Deptford SE15 . . .50 B4
Dover House Rd
SW15 . . . . .57 A2
Dover Mans **18**
SW9 . . . . .62 C4
Dover Park Dr
SW15 . . . . .57 A1
Dover St W1 . . . . . .118 C2
Dover Terr **19** TW9 . .44 C1
Dover Yd W1 . . . . . .118 C2
Doves Yd N1 . . . . . . .85 B3
Dovet Ct SW8 . . . . .172 C4
Doveton Ho **7** E1 . . .25 B1
Doveton St **6** E1 . . .25 B1
Dowdeny Cl **2** SE5 . .49 A2
Dowdeswell Cl
SW15 . . . . .56 A3
Dowding Ho N6 . . . . . .3 C4
Dowell Ho SE21 . . . .76 B1
Dowes Ho **13**
SW16 . . . . .74 A1
Dowgate Hill EC4 . .123 B4
Dowland St W10 . . . .23 A2
Dowlas St SE5 . . . . .49 A3
Dowlen Ct **14** E14 . . .41 C4
Dowler Ho **2** E1 . . .111 C1
Downbarton Ho **9**
SW9 . . . . .173 B4
Downbury Mews **18**
SW18 . . . . .58 C2
Downend Ct **1**
SE15 . . . . .49 A4

Downer's Cotts
SW4 . . . . .61 B3
Downey Ho **6** E1 . . . .25 C1
Downfield Cl W9 . . . .88 A1
Downham Ct **1**
N1 . . . . .15 C1
Downham Rd N1 . . . .15 C1
Downing Ho
North Kensington
W10 . . . . .30 C3
4 Putney SW15 . . . . .56 C2
Downing St*
SW1 . . . . .134 A4
Down Pl W6 . . . . . . .39 A1
Down St Mews
W1 . . . . .118 A1
Downs Ct **10** E8 . . . .17 A3
Downsell Prim Sch
E15 . . . . .19 C4
Downsell Rd E15 . . . .19 C4
Downshire Hill
NW3 . . . . .11 C4
Downside **2**
SW15 . . . . .58 A2
Downside Cres
NW3 . . . . .12 A3
Downs La **2** E5 . . . .17 A4
Downs Park Rd E5,
E8 . . . . .16 C3
Downs Rd E5, N16 . .16 C4
Down St W1 . . . . . . .118 A1
Downsview Sch
E5 . . . . .17 A4
Downton Ave SW2 . .74 B2
Downtown Rd
SE16 . . . . .41 A4
Dowrey St N1 . . . . . .85 B4
Dowson Cl SE5 . . . . .63 C3
Dowson Ct SE13 . . . .67 C4
Dowson Ho **6** E1 . . .32 C3
Doyce St SE1 . . . . . .136 C4
Doyle Gdns NW10 . . .22 A4
Doyle Ho W3 . . . . . . .37 A4
D'Oyley St SW1 . . . .145 B4
Doynton St N19 . . . . .4 A2
Draco St SE17 . . . . . .48 B4
Dragon Ct WC2 . . . .106 B2
Dragon Rd SE15 . . . .49 A4
Dragon Yd WC1 . . . .106 B2
Dragoon Rd SE8 . . . .41 B1
Dragor Rd NW10 . . . .20 B1
Drake Cl SE16 . . . . . .40 C4
Drake Croft N16 . . . . .6 C2
Drake Ct **5** W12 . . . .39 A4
Drakefell Rd SE4,
SE14 . . . . .65 C4
Drakefield Rd
SW17 . . . . .72 C1
Drake Ho
2 Limehouse E14 . . .33 A2
20 Stepney E1 . . . . . .32 B4
Drakeley Ct N5 . . . . . .15 A4
Drake Rd SE4 . . . . . .66 C4
Drakes Ctyd NW6 . . .10 B1
Drakes Ct WC1 . . . .106 C3
Drama Ctr London
EC1 . . . . .95 C1
Draper Ho **1** SE1 . .150 B4
Draper Pl N1 . . . . . . .86 B4
Drapers Almshouses **5**
E3 . . . . .26 C2
Drapers Gdns
EC2 . . . . .109 C2
Drapers Rd E15 . . . . .19 C4
Drappers Way **8**
SE16 . . . . .153 C4

Draycott Ave SW3 . .144 B3
Draycott Cl SE5 . . . . .48 C3
Draycott Ct SW11 . .168 A4
Draycott Pl SW3 . . .144 C3
Draycott Terr
SW3 . . . . .145 A3
Drayford Cl W9 . . . . .23 B1
Dray Gdns SW2 . . . . .62 B2
Draymans Ct **4**
SW9 . . . . .62 B4
Draymans Mews
SE15 . . . . .49 B1
Drayson Mews
W8 . . . . .127 C3
Drayton Cl SW13 . . .143 A1
Drayton Gdns
SW10 . . . . .143 A1
Drayton Ho **14**
SE5 . . . . .48 C3
Drayton Park Mews
12 N5 . . . . .14 C3
Drayton Park Prim
Sch **15** N5 . . . . . . .14 C3
Drayton Park Sta
N5 . . . . .14 C3
Drayton Pk N5, N7 . .14 C4
Drayton Rd NW10 . . .21 B4
DRCA Business Pk
SW11 . . . . .169 C3
Dreadnought St
SE10 . . . . .43 A3
Dresden Cl NW6 . . . .11 A2
Dresden Ho
4 Clapham
SW11 . . . . .169 B2
Lambeth SE11 . . . . .149 A4
Dresden Rd N19 . . . . .4 C3
Dressington Ave
SE4 . . . . .66 C1
Drewett Ho **3** E1 . . .111 C1
Drew Ho **15** SW16 . .74 A1
Drewstead La
SW16 . . . . .73 C2
Drewstead Rd
SW16 . . . . .73 C2
Driffield Rd **3** E3 . . .26 A3
Driftway Ho **19** E3 . . .26 B3
Drinkwater Ho **11**
SE5 . . . . .48 C3
Drive Mans **1**
SW6 . . . . .164 B2
Drive The
Acton W3 . . . . .28 B3
Harlesden NW10 . . . .21 B4
Hendon NW11 . . . . . . .1 A4
Islington N7 . . . . .5 A1
Dr Johnson Ave
SW17 . . . . .73 A1
Dr Johnson's House*
EC4 . . . . .107 C2
Droitwich Cl SE26 . . .76 C1
Dromore Rd SW15 . .58 A1
Dron Ho **11** E1 . . . . .32 B4
Droop St W10 . . . . . .23 A1
Drovers Ct SE13 . . . .67 B4
Drovers Pl SE15 . . . .50 A3
Drovers Way N4 . . . . .6 B2
Druce Rd SE21 . . . . .64 A1
Druid St SE1 . . . . . .138 C3
Drummer Lo N7 * 5 B1
Drummond Cres
NW1 . . . . .93 B4

Drummond Gate
  SW1 . . . . **147** C2
Drummond Ho **13**
  E2 . . . . 24 B4
Drummond Rd
  SE16 . . . . .40 A3
Drummond Pl
  TW9 . . . . .54 A3
Drummond St
  NW1 . . . . **92** C2
Drum St E1 . . . . **111** A2
Drury Ho SW8 . . . . . **170** C4
Drury La WC2 . . . . . **106** B1
Dryad St SE15 . . . . . **50** A4
Dryburgh Ho SW1 . **146** B2
Dryburgh Mans
  SW15 . . . . .57 B4
Dryburgh Rd
  SW15 . . . . .57 B4
Dryden Bldg **10**
  E1 . . . . **111** B2
Dryden Cl SW4 . . . . . .61 C2
Dryden Ct SE11 . . . . **149** C3
Dryden Ho
  6 Camberwell
    SE5 . . . . .49 A2
  13 Stoke Newington
    N16 . . . . .7 A1
Dryden St WC2 . . . . **106** B1
Dryfield Wlk **3**
  SE8 . . . . .51 C4
Drysdale Flats **3**
  E8 . . . . .16 B3
Drysdale Ho **16**
  E2 . . . . 24 A2 **98** B4
Drysdale Pl
  N1 . . . . 24 A2 **98** B4
Drysdale St
  N1 . . . . 24 A2 **98** B4
Dublin Ave E8 . . . . . .24 C4
Ducal St E2 . . . . 24 **99** A3
Ducane Cl **6** W12 . .30 B3
Du Cane Ct SW12 . . .72 C3
Du Cane Rd W12 . . . . .29 C3
Ducavel Ho SW2 . . . .74 B3
Duchess Mews
  W1 . . . . **104** B3
Duchess of Bedford
  Ho W8 . . . . **127** B4
Duchess of Bedford's
  Wlk W8 . . . . **127** B3
Duchess St W1 . . . . **104** B3
Duchy St SE1 . . . . . **121** C2
Ducie Ho **5** SW15 . .57 B2
Ducie St SW4 . . . . . . .62 B3
Duckett St E1 . . . . . . .33 A4
Duck La W1 . . . . **105** B1
Du Cros Rd W3 . . . . . .29 A1
DUDDEN HILL 8 C3
Dudden Hill La
  NW10 . . . . .8 B3
Dudley Ct
  Marylebone W1 . . . **102** C1
  St Giles WC2 . . . . . **106** A2
Dudley Ho
  13 Brixton SW9 . . **173** B4
  Paddington W2 . . . **101** B3
Dudley Mews **14**
  SW2 . . . . .62 C1
Dudley Rd
  Kilburn NW6 . . . . . . .23 B3
  Richmond TW9 . . . . . .44 B1
Dudley St W2 . . . . . **101** B3

Dudmaston Mews
  SW3 . . . . **143** C2
Duffell Ho SE11 . . . **149** A1
Dufferin Ave EC1 . . . **97** B1
Dufferin Ct EC1 . . . . **97** B1
Dufferin St EC1 . . . . **97** A1
Duff Miller Coll
  SW7 . . . . **129** A1
Duff St **4** E14 . . . . . . .34 A3
Dufour's Pl W1 . . . . **105** A1
Dugard Way SE11 . . **150** A3
Dugdale Ho **10** N7 . .13 C3
Duke Humphrey Rd
  SE3 . . . . .53 A1
Duke of Wellington Pl
  SW1, W1 . . . . **131** C4
Duke of York's Sq
  SW3 . . . . **145** A3
Duke of York St
  SW1 . . . . **119** A2
Duke Rd W4 . . . . .37 C1
Duke St St James's
  SW1 . . . . **119** A2
Duke's Ave W4 . . . . . .37 C1
Dukes Ct
  Dulwich SE22 . . . . . .76 C3
  East Dulwich SE22 . . .65 A2
  Lewisham SE13 . . . . .52 B1
  Mortlake SW14 . . . . .45 C1
Dukes Gate **4** W4 . .37 B2
Duke's Head Yd N6 . .4 A3
Duke's Ho SW1 . . . . **147** C4
Duke Shore Wharf
  E14 . . . . .33 B2
Dukes La W8 . . . . . **128** A4
Duke's Mews W1 . . **103** C2
Duke's Pl EC3 . . . . . **110** B1
Dukes Point N6 . . . . . .4 A3
Duke's Rd WC1 . . . . . **93** C3
Duke St W1 . . . . **103** C1
Duke Street Mans
  W1 . . . . **103** C1
Duke's Yd W1 . . . . . **117** C4
Dulas St N4 . . . . .5 B3
Dulford St
  W11 . . . . . . 31 A2 **112** A4
Dulka Rd SW11 . . . . . .60 B2
Dulverton NW1 . . . . **83** A3
Dulverton Mans
  WC1 . . . . .95 A1
DULWICH 76 A1
Dulwich Coll SE21 . . .76 A1
Dulwich Coll Prep Sch
  SE21 . . . . .76 A1
Dulwich Com Hospl
  SE22 . . . . .76 C3
Dulwich Comm
  SE21 . . . . .76 A3
Dulwich Hamlet Jun
  Sch SE21 . . . . .76 A3
Dulwich Lawn Cl
  SE22 . . . . .64 B2
Dulwich L Ctr
  SE22 . . . . .64 A2
Dulwich Mead
  SE24 . . . . .63 B1
Dulwich Mews
  1 East Dulwich
    SE22 . . . . .64 B3
  SE22 . . . . .64 A3
Dulwich Oaks The
  SE21 . . . . .76 A4
Dulwich Picture Gall★
  SE21 . . . . .76 A4

Dulwich Rd SE24 . . . .63 A1
DULWICH
  VILLAGE 76 A4
Dulwich Village
  SE21 . . . . .76 A4
Dulwich Village CE Inf
  Sch SE21 . . . . .64 A1
Dumain Ct SE11 . . . **150** A3
Du Maurier Ho **2**
  NW3 . . . . .12 B3
Dumbarton Ct **7**
  SW2 . . . . .74 A4
Dumbarton Rd
  SW2 . . . . .62 A1
Dumont Rd N16 . . . . . .7 A1
Dumphreys Ho **5**
  SW4 . . . . .73 C4
Dumpton Pl NW1 . . . **81** C4
Dunbar St SE27 . . . . .75 B1
Dunbar Wharf **20**
  E14 . . . . .33 B2
Dunboyne Rd
  NW3 . . . . .12 B3
Dunbridge Ho
  SW15 . . . . .56 B1
Dunbridge St
  E2 . . . . 24 C1 **99** C2
Duncan Ct **3** E14 . . .34 B4
Duncan Gr W3 . . . . . .29 A3
Duncan Ho
  SW1 . . . . .12 B1
Duncannon Ho
  SW1 . . . . **147** C1
Duncannon St
  WC2 . . . . **120** A3
Duncan Rd
  Hackney E8 . . . . .25 A4
  Richmond TW9 . . . . . .54 A4
Duncan St N1 . . . . . **86** A2
Duncan Terr N1 . . . . **86** A2
Dunch St **21** E1 . . . .32 A3
Duncombe Ho **7**
  SW19 . . . . .69 C3
Duncombe Prim Sch
  N19 . . . . .5 A3
Duncombe Rd N19 . . .4 C3
Duncrievie Rd
  SE13 . . . . .67 C1
Dundalk Ho **2** E1 . .32 B3
Dundalk Rd SE4 . . . . .66 A4
Dundas Ho **12** E2 . .25 B3
Dundas Rd SE15 . . . . .50 B1
Dundee Ct **38** E1 . . .32 A1
Dundee Ho W9 . . . . . **88** C4
Dundee St E1 . . . . . . .32 A1
Dundee Wharf
  E14 . . . . .33 B2
Dundonald Rd
  NW10 . . . . .22 C4
Dundry Ho **8**
  SE26 . . . . .76 C1
Dunelm Gr SE27 . . . . .75 B1
Dunelm St E1 . . . . . . .32 C3
Dunford Rd N7 . . . . . .14 B4
Dungarvan Ave
  SW15 . . . . .56 C3
Dungeness Ho
  SW18 . . . . .59 B3
Dunhill Point **12**
  SW15 . . . . .69 A3
Dunkeld Ho **15**
  E14 . . . . .34 C3
Dunlace Rd E5 . . . . . . .17 C4
Dunlin Ho **12** SE21 . .75 C2

Dunlin Ho **13** SE16 . .40 C2
Dunloe Ct **7** E2 . . . . .24 B3
Dunloe St E2 . . . . .24 B3
Dunlop Pl SE16 . . . . **139** A1
Dunmore Point **15**
  E2 . . . . 24 B2 **98** C3
Dunmore Rd NW6 . . .23 A4
Dunmow Ho SE11 . . **149** A2
Dunmow Rd E15 . . . . .19 C4
Dunmow Wlk N1 . . . **86** C4
Dunnage Cres
  SE16 . . . . .41 A2
Dunne Mews **11**
  NW5 . . . . .13 B3
Dunnet Ho **27** E3 . . .26 B3
Dunnico Ho SE17 . . **152** A2
Dunnock Ct **11**
  SE21 . . . . .75 C2
Dunn's Pas WC1 . . . **106** B2
Dunn St E8 . . . . .16 B3
Dunollie Pl NW5 . . . . .13 B3
Dunollie Rd NW5 . . . .13 B3
Dunoon Ho N1 . . . . . **84** C3
Dunraven Ho **12**
  TW9 . . . . .44 B2
Dunraven Rd W12 . . .29 C1
Dunraven Sch
  SW16 . . . . .74 A1
Dunraven St W1 . . . **117** A4
Dunrobin Ct NW3 . . .11 A3
Dunsany Rd W14 . . . .39 C3
Dunsfold Ho **4**
  SW2 . . . . .74 B4
Dunsford Way
  SW15 . . . . .57 A1
Dunsmure Rd N16 . . . .7 A3
Dunstable Ct **3**
  SE3 . . . . .53 C3
Dunstable Mews
  W1 . . . . **103** C4
Dunstable Rd TW10,
  TW9 . . . . .54 A3
Dunstall Ho **9**
  SE15 . . . . .49 C2
Dunstan Ho SE4 . . . . .51 B1
Dunstan Hos **5**
  E1 . . . . .32 B4
Dunstan Rd NW11 . . .1 C3
Dunstan's Gr SE22 . . .65 A1
Dunstan's Rd SE22 . . .64 C1
Dunster Ct EC3 . . . . **124** B4
Dunster Gdns
  NW6 . . . . .10 B1
Dunsterville Way
  SE1 . . . . **137** C3
Dunston Rd
  Clapham SW11 . . . . **169** C1
  Hackney E8 . . . . .24 B4
Dunston St E8 . . . . . . .24 B4
Dunton Ho **14**
  SW16 . . . . .74 A1
Dunton Rd SE1 . . . . **152** C3
Duntshill Rd SW18 . . .71 A3
Dunworth Mews
  W11 . . . . .31 B3
Duplex Ride SW1 . . **131** A3
Durand Gdns
  SW9 . . . . **173** A3
Durand Prim Sch
  SW9 . . . . **173** A4
Durant St
  E2 . . . . 24 C2 **99** B4
Durban Ho **28**
  W12 . . . . .30 A2
Durdans Ho **3**
  NW1 . . . . .13 B1

Durfey Pl SE5 . . . . . . .48 C3
Durford Cres
  SW15 . . . . .69 A3
Durham Ct
  Brockley SE4 . . . . . . .66 A3
  4 Kilburn NW6 . . . .23 C3
Durham Ho
  7 Dartmouth Pk
    NW5 . . . . .4 B1
  Lisson Gr NW8 . . . . **90** B3
Durham House St
  WC2 . . . . **120** B3
Durham Pl SW3 . . . **144** C1
Durham Rd N4, N7 . . .5 B2
Durham Row E1 . . . . .33 A4
Durham St SE11 . . . **162** C4
Durham Terr W2 . . . **100** A2
Durley Rd N16 . . . . . . .7 A4
Durlock Ho **10**
  SW9 . . . . **173** B4
Durlston Rd E5 . . . . . . .7 C2
Durnford St
  SE10 . . . . .52 B4
Durnsford Ave SW18,
  SW19 . . . . .70 C2
Durnsford Rd SW18,
  SW19 . . . . .70 C2
Durrell Rd SW6 . . . . **164** C3
Durrels Ho W14 . . . **141** A4
Durrington Rd E5 . . . .18 A4
Durrington Twr **3**
  SW8 . . . . **171** A2
Durrisdeer Ho
  NW2 . . . . .10 B4
Durston NW5 . . . . . . .12 C3
Durward St E1 . . . . . . .32 A4
Durweston Mews
  W1 . . . . **103** A4
Durweston St W1 . . **103** A3
Dutch Yd SW18 . . . . . .58 C2
Dutton Ho SW2 . . . . .75 A3
Dutton St SE10 . . . . . .52 B2
Dwight Ct **3** SW6 . **164** B2
Dycer Ho **19** E9 . . . .17 C2
Dye House La E3 . . . . .26 C4
Dyer Ho SE4 . . . . .51 A1
Dyer's Bldgs EC1 . . **107** B3
Dyer's La SW15 . . . . . .57 A3
Dykes Ct **13** SW2 . . .74 B3
Dylan Rd **2** SE24 . . .63 A3
Dylways SE5 . . . . .63 C3
Dymchurch Ho **12**
  E5 . . . . .17 A3
Dymes Path SW19 . . .69 C2
Dymock St SW6 . . . . .59 A4
Dyne Rd NW6 . . . . . . .10 B1
Dynevor Rd
  Richmond TW10 . . . .54 A2
  Shacklewell N16 . . . . .7 B1
Dynham Rd NW6 . . . .10 C1
Dyott St
  Soho WC1 . . . . **105** C2
  St Giles WC1, WC2 . **106** A2
Dysart St
  EC2 . . . . 24 A1 **98** A1
Dyson Ho **3** SE10 . .43 B1

E

Eade Rd N4 . . . . .6 B4
Eagle Cl SE16 . . . . . . .40 B1
Eagle Ct
  10 Dulwich SE21 . . .75 C2
  Holborn EC1 . . . . . . **108** A4

Eagle Dwellings
EC1 . . . . **97** A4
Eagle Ho
22 Bethnal Green
E1 . . . . **25** A1
Finsbury Pk N7 . . . . **5** B1
Eagle Hts 10 SW11 . . **60** A4
Eagle Mans N16 . . . . **16** B3
Eagle Mews N1 . . . . **16** A2
Eagle Pl
South Kensington
SW7 . . . . **143** A2
St James SW1 . . . . . . **119** A3
Eagle Wharf SE1 . . . **106** C3
Eagle Wharf Rd
N1 . . . . **87** A2
Eagle Works
E1 . . . . **24** B1 **99** A1
Eagling Cl E3 . . . . **26** C2
Ealing, Hammersmith
& West London Coll
W14 . . . . **140** A2
Eamann Casey Ho
SW9 . . . . **173** C3
Eamont Ct NW8 . . . . . **80** B2
Eamont St NW8 . . . . . **80** B2
Eardley Cres SW5 . . **141** C1
Earldom Rd SW15 . . **57** B3
Earle Ho SW1 . . . . . **147** C3
Earlham St WC2 . . . **106** A1
Earl Ho NW1 . . . . **90** B1
Earlom Ho WC1 . . . . **95** B3
Earl Rd SW14 . . . . . . **55** B3
EARL'S COURT **141** C3
Earl's Court Ex Ctr★
SW5 . . . . **141** B1
Earl's Court Gdns
SW5 . . . . **142** A3
Earl's Court Rd SW5,
W8 . . . . **141** C4
Earl's Court Sq
SW5 . . . . **142** A2
Earl's Court Sta
SW5 . . . . **141** C3
Earlsferry Way N1 . . **14** A1
EARLSFIELD **71** B3
Earlsfield Prim Sch
SW18 . . . . **71** B2
Earlsfield Rd
SW18 . . . . **71** B3
Earlsfield Sta
SW18 . . . . **71** B3
Earlsmead Rd
NW10 . . . . **22** B2
Earl St EC2 . . . . **110** A4
Earls Terr W8 . . . . . **127** A1
Earlsthorpe Mews 3
SW12 . . . . **60** C1
Earlstoke St EC1 . . . **96** A4
Earlston Gr E9 . . . . . **25** A4
Earls Wlk W8 . . . . . **127** B1
Earlswood Cl 10
SE10 . . . . **43** A1
Earlswood Ho 2
SW2 . . . . **74** B3
Earlswood St SE10 . . **43** A1
Early Mews NW1 . . . **82** B4
Earnshaw Ho EC1 . . . **96** B3
Earnshaw St W1,
WC2 . . . . **105** C2
Earsby St W14 . . . . **140** B4
Earth Galleries★
SW7 . . . . **129** C1

Eashing Point 5
SW15 . . . . **69** A3
Easleys Mews W1 **103** C2
EAST ACTON **29** A1
East Acton Arc
W3 . . . . **29** B3
East Acton Ct W3 . . . **29** A2
East Acton La W3 . . . **29** A2
East Acton Prim Sch
W3 . . . . **29** A2
East Acton Sta
W12 . . . . **29** B3
East Arbour St E1 . . **32** C3
East Bank N16 . . . . . . **7** A4
East Block 5 E1 . . . . **32** C2
Eastbourne Ave
W3 . . . . **28** C3
Eastbourne Gdns
SW14 . . . . **55** B4
Eastbourne Mews
W2 . . . . **101** A2
Eastbourne Rd
W4 . . . . **45** B4
Eastbourne Terr
W2 . . . . **101** A2
Eastbury Gr W4 . . . . **38** A1
Eastbury Terr E1 . . . **25** C1
Eastcastle St W1 . . **105** A2
Eastcheap EC3 . . . . **124** A4
East Churchfield Rd
W3 . . . . **28** C1
Eastcote St SW9 . . **172** C1
East Cross Route
Bow E3 . . . . **26** C4
Hackney Wick E9 . . . **18** B3
Eastdown Ho E8 . . . . **16** C4
Eastdown Pk SE13 . . **67** C3
EAST DULWICH **64** C2
East Dulwich Gr
SE22 . . . . **64** A2
East Dulwich Rd SE15,
SE22 . . . . **64** C3
East Dulwich Sta
SE22 . . . . **64** A3
East End Computing &
Bsns Coll 20 E1 . . . **32** A3
Eastern Rd SE4 . . . . **66** C3
East Ferry Rd E14 . . **42** A2
Eastfields Ave
SW18 . . . . **58** C3
Eastfields Rd W3 . . . **28** B4
Eastfield St E14 . . . . **33** A4
East Harding St
EC4 . . . . **107** C2
East Heath Rd NW3 . . **2** C1
East India Bldgs 6
E14 . . . . **33** C2
East India Ct 7
SE16 . . . . **40** B4
East India Dock
Basin★ E14 . . . . . . **35** A2
East India Dock Rd
E14 . . . . **34** A2
East India Dock Road
Tunnel 7 E14 . . . . . **34** C2
East India St E14 . . . **34** C2
East La 15 SE16 . . **139** B3
Eastlake Ho NW8 . . . **89** C1
Eastlake Rd SE5 . . . **48** B1
Eastlands Cres
SE21 . . . . **64** B1
Eastleigh Wlk 9
SW15 . . . . **68** C4
Eastman Dental Hospl
WC1 . . . . **94** C2

Eastman Rd 7
W3 . . . . **61** B1
Eastmearn Rd SE21,
SE27 . . . . **75** B2
East Mount St E1 . . . **32** A4
Eastney St SE10 . . . **42** C1
Easton Ho 5 SE27 . . **75** A1
Easton St WC1 . . . . . **95** B2
East Parkside
SE10 . . . . **43** B4
East Pas EC1 . . . . . **108** C4
East Plaza E14 . . . . . **34** A1
East Point 4 SE1 . . **153** B2
East Poultry Ave
EC1 . . . . **108** A3
East Putney Sta
SW15 . . . . **58** A2
East Rd
Chelsea SW1 . . . . . . **145** B1
Shoreditch N1 . . . . . **97** C4
East Row W10 . . . . . **23** A1
Eastry Ho SW8 . . . . **162** A1
EAST SHEEN **55** C3
East Sheen Ave
SW14 . . . . **55** C3
East Sheen Prim Sch
SW14 . . . . **56** A3
East Smithfield
E1 . . . . **125** A3
East St SE17 . . . . . . **151** B2
East Surrey Gr
SE15 . . . . **49** B3
East Tenter St E1 . . **111** A1
Eastvale W3 . . . . **29** B1
East View NW3 . . . . . . **2** C1
Eastway E3, E9 . . . . . **26** A4
Eastwell Ho SE1 . . . **137** C2
Eastwick Ct 2
SW19 . . . . **69** C3
Eastwood Cl 2
N7 . . . . **14** C3
Eaton Cl SW1 . . . . . **145** B3
Eaton Dr SW9 . . . . . **63** A3
Eaton Gate SW1 . . . **145** B4
Eaton Ho
Battersea SW11 . . . **167** C3
20 Limehouse E14 . . **33** B2
Eaton House Sch
SW1 . . . . **145** B4
Eaton House The
Manor Sch SW4 . . . **61** A3
Eaton La SW1 . . . . . **132** B1
Eaton Mans SW1 . . **145** B3
Eaton Mews N
SW1 . . . . **131** C1
Eaton Mews S
SW1 . . . . **132** A1
Eaton Mews W
SW1 . . . . **145** C4
Eaton Pl SW1 . . . . . **131** C1
Eaton Row SW1 . . . **132** A1
Eaton Sq SW1 . . . . . **131** C1
Eaton Sq Pre-Prep
Sch SW1 . . . . **146** A4
Eaton Sq Prep Sch
SW1 . . . . **146** C3
Eaton Terr
Belgravia SW1 . . . . **145** C4
Bow E3 . . . . **26** A2
Eaton Terr Mews
SW1 . . . . **145** B4
Eatonville Rd
SW17 . . . . **72** B2
Eatonville Villas
SW17 . . . . **72** B2

Ebbisham Dr SW8 **162** C3
Ebbsfleet Rd NW2 . . **10** A4
Ebenezer Ho
SE11 . . . . **150** A3
Ebenezer Mussel Ho
5 E2 . . . . **25** B3
Ebenezer St N1 . . . . . **97** B4
Ebley Cl SE15 . . . . . . **49** B4
Ebner St SW18 . . . . . **59** A2
Ebony Ct NW10 . . . . . **8** B2
Ebony Ho
27 Bethnal Green
E2 . . . . **24** C2 **99** B3
16 West Hampstead
NW3 . . . . **11** A2
Ebor Cotts SW15 . . . **68** A1
Ebor St E1,
E2 . . . . **24** B1 **98** C2
Eburne Rd N7 . . . . **5** A1
Ebury Bridge Rd
SW1 . . . . **145** C1
Ebury Mews
Belgravia SW1 . . . . **146** A4
West Norwood
SE27 . . . . **75** A1
Ebury Mews E
SW1 . . . . **132** A1
Ebury Sq SW1 . . . . . **145** C3
Ebury St SW1 . . . . . **146** A4
Ecclesbourne Rd
N1 . . . . **15** B1
Eccles Ct SE11 . . . . **149** A1
Eccles Rd SW11 . . . . **60** B3
Eccleston Ho 1
SW2 . . . . **62** C1
Eccleston Mews
SW1 . . . . **131** C1
Eccleston Pl SW1 . . **146** A4
Eccleston Sq
SW1 . . . . **146** B3
Eccleston Sq Mews
SW1 . . . . **146** C3
Eccleston St SW1 . . **146** A4
Eckford St N1 . . . . . . **85** B2
Eckstein Rd SW11 . . **60** A3
Edans Ct W12 . . . . . **38** B4
Edbrooke Rd W9 . . . . **23** C1
Eddisbury Ho 7
SE26 . . . . **76** C1
Eddiscombe Rd
SW6 . . . . **165** A2
Eddison Ct N19 . . . . . **5** A2
Eddystone Rd SE4 . . **66** A2
Eddystone Twr
SE8 . . . . **41** A1
Edenbridge Cl 28
SE16 . . . . **40** A1
Edenbridge Rd E9 . . **17** C1
Eden Cl
Child's Hill NW3 . . . . . **1** C2
Kensington W8 . . . . **127** C2
Edendale Rd SW2 . . . **28** A2
Eden Gr
Islington N7 . . . . **14** B3
Willesden NW10 . . . . . **9** A2
Edenham Way
W10 . . . . **31** B4
Eden High Sch 9
W6 . . . . **38** C1
Eden Ho
15 Battersea
SW11 . . . . **60** A4
Lisson Gr NW8 . . . . . **90** A1
Edenhurst Ave
SW6 . . . . **58** B4
Eden Lodge NW6 . . . **9** C1

Eden Mews SW17 . . **71** B1
Edensmuir Ct SE3 . . **53** C3
Edensor Gdns W4 . . **46** A3
Edensor Rd W4 . . . . . **46** A3
Edenvale St SW6 . . **166** C1
Eden Way E3 . . . . **26** B4
Edgar Ho
Homerton E9 . . . . . . **18** A3
South Lambeth
SW8 . . . . **162** A2
Edgar Kail Way
SE22 . . . . **64** A3
Edgarley Terr
SW6 . . . . **164** A3
Edgar Rd E3 . . . . **27** A2
Edgar Wallace Cl 4
SE15 . . . . **49** A3
Edgcott Ho 2
W10 . . . . **30** B4
Edgecombe Ho
4 London SE5 . . . . . **49** A1
Putney SW19 . . . . **70** A4
Edgecote Cl 7
W3 . . . . **28** B1
Edgehill Ho 4
SW9 . . . . **48** A1
Edgeley La SW4 . . . . **61** C4
Edgeley Rd SW4 . . . . **61** C4
Edgel St SW18 . . . . . **59** A3
Edge St
W8 . . . . **31** C1 **113** C2
Edgeworth Ho
NW8 . . . . **78** C4
Edgson Ho SW1 . . . **146** A2
Edgware Acad
WC2 . . . . **106** B1
Edgware Rd W1, W2,
NW1, NW8 . . . . **102** A3
Edgware Road Sta
(Bakerloo) NW1 **102** A3
Edgware Road Sta
(Met, Distr, Circle)
NW1 . . . . **102** B3
Edinburgh Cl 7
E2 . . . . **25** B3
Edinburgh Ct 10
SE16 . . . . **32** C1
Edinburgh Ho
3 Acton W3 . . . . **28** C3
Maida Vale W9 . . . . . **88** B4
Edington 20 NW5 . . . **12** C2
Edison Bldg 7
E14 . . . . **41** C4
Edison Ct SE10 . . . . **43** B3
Edison Ho SE1 . . . . **151** B4
Edis St NW1 . . . . **81** C4
Editha Mans
SW10 . . . . **156** C3
Edith Cavell Cl 2
N19 . . . . **5** A4
Edith Gr SW10 . . . . **157** A2
Edith Ho 6 W6 . . . . . **39** B1
Edithna St SW9 . . . . . **62** A4
Edith Neville Cotts
NW1 . . . . **93** B4
Edith Neville Prim
Sch NW1 . . . . **83** B1
Edith Ramsay Ho 2
E1 . . . . **33** A4
Edith Rd
Stratford New Town
E15 . . . . **19** C3
West Kensington
W14 . . . . **140** B3

Edith Row SW6 . . . . . **166** B4
Edith St E2 . . . . .24 C3
Edith Summerskill Ho
SW6 . . . . **154** C2
Edith Terr SW10 . . . **156** C2
Edith Villas W14 . . . **140** C2
Edith Yd SW10 . . . . **157** A2
Edmeston Ct E9 . . . . .18 A2
Edmond Ct SE14 . . . . .50 B2
Edmonton Ct **5**
SE16 . . . . .40 B3
Edmund Halley Way
SE10 . . . . .43 A4
Edmund Ho
Kennington SE17 . . **150** B1
New Cross Gate
SE14 . . . . .51 B2
Edmundsbury Ct Est
18 SW9 . . . . .62 B3
Edmund St SE5 . . . . . .48 C3
Edmund Waller Prim
Sch SE14 . . . . .51 A1
Ednam Ho SE15 . . . . .49 C4
Edna St SW11 . . . . . **168** A3
Edred Ho E9 . . . . .18 A4
Edrich Ho SW4 . . . . **172** A3
Edric Ho SW1 . . . . . **147** C4
Edric Rd SE14 . . . . . . .50 C3
Edridge Ho **9**
SE27 . . . . .75 A1
Edward Alleyn Ho
SE21 . . . . .76 A4
Edward Ct **2** E16 . . .35 C4
Edward Dodd Ct
N1 . . . . **97** C4
Edward Edward's Ho
SE1 . . . . **122** A1
Edwardes Pl W8 . . . **127** A1
Edwardes Sq W8 . . . **127** A1
Edward Friend Ho **6**
N16 . . . . .7 A1
Edward Ho
Paddington W2 . . . . .**89** B1
Vauxhall SE11 . . . . . **149** A2
Edward Kennedy Ho
18 W10 . . . . .23 A1
Edward Mann Cl **13**
E1 . . . . .32 C3
Edward Mews
NW1 . . . .**82** B1
Edward Pl SE8 . . . . . .51 B4
Edward Robinson Ho
3 SE14 . . . . .50 C3
Edward's Cotts **11**
N1 . . . . .15 A1
Edward's La N1 . . . . . .7 A2
Edwards Mews
Islington N1 . . . . .14 C1
Marylebone W1 . . . **103** B1
Edward Sq
Islington N1 . . . . **84** C3
11 Rotherhithe
SE16 . . . . .33 A1
Edward St SE14 . . . . .51 B3
Edward VII Mans
NW10 . . . . .22 C2
Edward Wilson Prim
Sch **2** W2 . . . . **100** A4
Edwin Ho SE15 . . . . . .49 C3
Edwin's Mead E9 . . . . .18 A4
Edwin St
Bethnal Green E1 . . .25 B1
Newham E16 . . . . . . .35 C4
Edwy Ho E9 . . . . .18 B4

Edwyn Ho SW18 . . . . .59 A1
Effie Pl SW6 . . . . **155** C1
Effie Rd SW6 . . . . . . **155** C1
Effingham Ho **37**
SW8 . . . . **171** B1
Effra Ct SW2 . . . . .62 B2
Effra Par SW2 . . . . . . .62 C2
Effra Rd SW2 . . . . .62 C2
Effra Rd SW2 . . . . .62 C2
Effra Road Ret Pk
SW2 . . . . .62 C2
EF International
Language Sch
SE1 . . . . **121** C1
Egbert Ho E9 . . . . . . .18 A3
Egbert St NW1 . . . . . .**81** B4
Egbury Ho SW15 . . . . .56 B1
Egerton Cres
SW3 . . . . **144** B4
Egerton Ct **6**
TW10 . . . . .54 A2
Egerton Dr SE10 . . . . .52 A2
Egerton Gdns
Knightsbridge
SW3 . . . . **130** A1
Willesden NW10 . . . . .22 B4
Egerton Gdns Mews
SW3 . . . . **130** B1
Egerton Ho W4 . . . . . .45 B4
Egerton Pl SW3 . . . . **130** B1
Egerton Rd N16 . . . . . .7 B4
Egerton Terr SW3 . . **130** B1
Egham Cl SW19 . . . . . .70 A2
Eglantine Rd
SW18 . . . . .59 B2
Eglington Ct SE17 . . .48 B4
Egliston Mews
SW15 . . . . .57 B4
Egliston Rd SW15 . . . .57 B4
Egmont St SE14 . . . . .50 C3
Egremont Ho
SE13 . . . . .52 A1
Egremont Rd SE27 . . .74 C1
Egret Ho **11** SE16 . . .40 C2
Eider Ct **39** SE8 . . . .51 B4
Elaine Ct **18** NW3 . . .12 B2
Elaine Ho N4 . . . . .5 A3
Elam Cl SE5 . . . . .48 A1
Elam St SE5 . . . . .48 A1
Elan Ct E1 . . . . .32 A4
Eland Rd SW11 . . . . . .60 B4
Elba Pl SE17 . . . . **151** A4
Elbe St SW6 . . . . **166** C2
Elborough
SW18 . . . . .70 C3
Elbury Dr E16 . . . . . . .35 C3
Elcho St SW11 . . . . . **158** B1
Elcot Ave SE15 . . . . . .50 A3
Elderberry Rd W5 . . . .36 A4
Elderfield Ho **4**
E14 . . . . .33 C2
Elderfield Rd E5 . . . . .17 B4
Elder St E1 . . . . .24 B1 **98** C1
Elder Wlk
Islington N1 . . . .**86** B4
2 Lewisham SE13 . . .67 B4
Eldon Ho SW9 . . . . . . .63 A4
Eldon Rd W8 . . . . . . **128** B1
Eldon St EC2 . . . . . . **109** C3
Eldon Way NW10 . . . . .20 A3
Eldridge Ct SE16 . . . **139** B1
Eleanor Cl SE16 . . . . .40 C4
Eleanor Gr **12** E2 . . .24 C4

Eleanor Gr SW13 . . . .56 A4
Eleanor Ho
18 Hammersmith
W6 . . . . .39 B1
1 Kentish Town
NW5 . . . . .13 B3
Eleanor Palmer Prim
Sch **12** NW5 . . . . . . .13 B4
Eleanor Rathbone Ho
6 N6 . . . . .4 C4
Eleanor Rd E8 . . . . . . .17 A1
Eleanor St E3 . . . . . . .26 C2
Electra Ct **6** NW2 . . .9 B2
Electric Ave SW9 . . . . .62 C3
Electric Ho **13** E3 . . .26 C2
Electric La **2**
SW9 . . . . .62 C3
Electric Mans **1**
SW9 . . . . .62 C3
Elephant & Castle
Newington SE1 . . . **136** B1
Newington SE1 . . . **150** B4
Elephant & Castle Sh
Ctr SE1 . . . . **150** C4
Elephant & Castle Sta
Lambeth SE1 . . . . . **136** B1
Newington SE17 . . **150** C4
Elephant La SE16 . . . .40 B4
Elephant Rd SE17 . . **150** C4
Elfindale Rd SE24 . . . .63 B2
Elfort Rd N5 . . . . .14 C4
Elf Row E1 . . . . .32 B2
Elgar Ave W5 . . . . .36 A4
Elgar Cl SE8 . . . . .51 C3
Elgar Ct W14 . . . . . . **126** A1
Elgar Ho
Pimlico SW1 . . . . . . **146** B1
South Hampstead
NW6 . . . . .11 B1
Elgar St SE16 . . . . . . .41 A3
Elgin Ave
Hammersmith
W12 . . . . .39 A3
Westbourne Green
W9 . . . .**88** B4
Elgin Cl W12 . . . . .39 A4
Elgin Cres
W11 . . . . . . .31 A2 **112** A4
Elgin Ct W9 . . . .**88** A2
Elgin Ho **6** E14 . . . . .34 A3
Elgin Mans W9 . . . . . .**88** B3
Elgin Mews W11 . . . . .31 A3
Elgin Mews N W9 . . . .**88** B4
Elgin Mews S W9 . . . .**88** B4
Elgo Cl
W11 . . . . . . .31 A1 **112** A1
Elgood Ho NW8 . . . . .**79** C1
Elham Ho **5** E5 . . . . .17 A3
Elia Mews N1 . . . .**86** A1
Elias Pl SW8 . . . . **163** B3
Elia St N1 . . . .**86** A1
Elim Est SE1 . . . . **138** A2
Elim St SE1 . . . . **138** A2
Eliot Cotts SE3 . . . . . .53 A1
Eliot Ct SW18 . . . . . . .59 A1
Eliot Gdns SW15 . . . . .56 C3
Eliot Hill SE13 . . . . . . .52 B1
Eliot Ho **10** TW10 . . .54 B1
Eliot Mews NW8 . . . . .78 C1
Eliot Pk SE13 . . . . .52 B1
Eliot Rd SE13 . . . . . . .53 A1
Eliot Vale SE3 . . . . . . .52 C1
Elizabeth Ave
Islington N1 . . . . .15 C1
Shoreditch N1 . . . . . .**87** A4

Elizabeth Barnes Ct
5 SW6 . . . . **166** B2
Elizabeth Blount Ct **4**
E14 . . . . .33 A3
Elizabeth Cl
Paddington W9 . . . . .**89** A1
12 Poplar E14 . . . . .34 A3
Elizabeth Cooper Lo
SW12 . . . . .60 C1
Elizabeth Cotts **5**
TW9 . . . . .44 C2
Elizabeth Ct
Chelsea SW10 . . . . **157** C3
East Dulwich SE22 . . .64 C3
Marylebone NW8 . . . .**90** B2
Westminster SW1 . . **133** C1
Elizabeth Finn Ho **1**
W12 . . . . .38 C3
Elizabeth Garrett
Anderson Hospl
NW1 . . . .**93** A1
Elizabeth Garrett
Anderson Language
Coll N1 . . . .**85** A1
Elizabeth Gdns
W3 . . . . .29 B1
Elizabeth Ho
18 Hammersmith
W6 . . . . .39 B1
Lambeth SE11 . . . . **149** C3
Elizabeth Ind Est
SE14 . . . . .50 C4
Elizabeth Kenny Ho
N1 . . . . .15 B2
Elizabeth Mews
28 Hackney E2 . . . . .24 C3
Maitland Pk NW3 . . . .12 B2
Elizabeth Selby Inf
Sch **12** E2 . . .24 C2 **99** C4
Elizabeth Sq **3**
SE16 . . . . .33 A2
Elizabeth St SW1 . . **145** C4
Elkington Point
SE11 . . . . **149** B3
Elkstone Rd W10 . . . . .31 B4
Ellacombe Ho **1**
SW2 . . . . .74 C4
Ellaline Rd W6 . . . . . . .47 C4
Elland Ho **18** E14 . . .33 B3
Elland Rd SE15 . . . . . .65 B3
Ella Rd N4, N8 . . . . . . .5 A4
Ellenborough Ho **5**
W12 . . . . .30 A2
Ellenborough Pl
SW15 . . . . .56 C3
Ellen St E1 . . . . **111** C1
Ellen Wilkinson Ho
7 Globe Town E2 . . .25 C2
West Brompton
SW6 . . . . **155** A3
Ellerby St SW6 . . . . . .47 C2
Ellerdale Cl **15**
NW3 . . . . .11 B4
Ellerdale Rd NW3 . . . .11 B3
Ellerdale St SE13 . . . .67 A4
Ellerker Gdns
TW10 . . . . .54 A1
Ellerslie Gdns
NW10 . . . . .21 C4
Ellerslie Ind Est
SW2 . . . . .62 A2
Ellerslie Rd W12 . . . . .30 A1
Ellerton Ct W3 . . . . . . .37 A4
Ellerton Rd
Barnes SW13 . . . . . . .46 C2

Ellerton Rd continued
Wandsworth SW17,
SW18 . . . . .71 C3
Ellery Cl **5** NW10 . . .21 B3
Ellery Ho SE17 . . . . . **151** C3
Ellery St SE15 . . . . . . .50 A1
Ellesmere Ct W4 . . . . .45 C4
Ellesmere Rd
Bow E3 . . . . .26 A3
Chiswick W4 . . . . .45 C4
Willesden NW10 . . . . .8 C3
Ellesmere St E14 . . . .34 A3
Ellingfort Rd E8 . . . . . .17 A1
Ellingham Rd
Leyton E15 . . . . .19 C4
Shepherd's Bush
W12 . . . . .38 C4
Ellington Ho SE1 . . . **137** A1
Ellington St N7 . . . . . **14** C2
Elliott Rd
Acton W4 . . . . .38 A2
Brixton SW9 . . . . .48 A2
Elliott Sch SW15 . . . . .57 B1
Elliott's Pl N1 . . . . **86** B3
Elliott Sq NW3 . . . . . . .12 A1
Elliott's Row SE11 . . **150** B4
Ellis Cl NW10 . . . . .9 B2
Ellisfield Dr SW15 . . . .68 C4
Ellis Franklin Ct
NW8 . . . .**78** C2
Ellis Ho SE17 . . . . . . **151** B2
Ellison Ho **1** SE13 . . .52 B1
Ellison Rd SW13 . . . . .46 B1
Ellis St SW1 . . . . **145** B4
Ellsworth St E2 . . . . . .25 A2
Ellwood Ct **1** W9 . . .**88** B1
Elmar Ct SW6 . . . . . . **164** B2
Elm Bank Gdns
SW13 . . . . .46 A1
Elm Bank Mans
SW13 . . . . .46 A1
Elmbourne Rd
SW17 . . . . .73 A1
Elmbridge Wlk E8 . . . .16 C1
Elm Cl N19 . . . . .4 B2
Elmcourt Rd SE21,
SE27 . . . . .75 B2
Elm Court Sch
SE27 . . . . .75 B2
Elm Cres W5 . . . . .36 A4
Elmcroft N6 . . . . .4 B4
Elmcroft Ave NW11 . . .1 B4
Elmcroft Cres
NW11 . . . . .1 A4
Elmcroft St E5 . . . . . . .17 B4
Elm Ct
Brixton SW9 . . . . . . **173** B4
Lewisham SE13 . . . . .67 C4
42 Notting Hill W2 . . .31 C4
Strand EC4 . . . . **121** B4
Elmer Ho NW1 . . . . . **102** A4
Elmfield Ho
6 Canonbury N5 . . . .15 B3
Paddington W9 . . . . .23 C1
Elmfield Mans **5**
SW17 . . . . .72 C2
Elmfield Rd SW17 . . . .73 A2
Elmfield Way W9 . . . . .31 C4
Elm Friars Wlk
NW1 . . . . .13 C1
Elm Gn W3 . . . . .29 A3
Elm Gr
Cricklewood NW2 . . . .9 C4
Peckham SE15 . . . . . .49 C1

Elmgreen Sch The
SE27 . . . . **75** A2
Elm Grove Rd
Barnes SW13 . . . . **46** C1
Ealing W5 . . . . **36** A4
Elm Ho 🔳 E14 . . . . . . **42** B4
Elmhurst Mans
SW4 . . . . **61** C4
Elmhurst St SW4 . . . . **61** C2
Elmhurst Villas
SE15 . . . . **65** B3
Elmington Rd SE5 . . . **48** C3
Elmira St SE13 . . . . . . **67** A4
Elm Lo SW6 . . . . **47** C2
Elmore Ho SW9 . . . . . **48** A1
Elmore St N1 . . . . **15** C1
Elm Park Ho
SW10 . . . . **143** B1
Elm Park Rd
SW10 . . . . **143** B1
Elm Park La SW3 . . . **143** B1
Elm Park Mans
SW10 . . . . **157** A4
Elm Park Rd SW3 . . . **157** B4
Elm Pk SW2 . . . . **74** B4
Elm Pl SW7 . . . . **143** B2
Elm Quay SW8 . . . . . **161** B3
Elm Rd SW14 . . . . **55** B3
Elm Row NW3 . . . . **2** B1
Elms Cres SW4 . . . . . . **61** C1
Elmshaw Rd SW15 . . . **56** C2
Elmslie Point 🔳
E3 . . . . **33** B4
Elms Mews W2 . . . . **115** B4
Elms Rd SW4 . . . . **61** B2
Elm St WC1 . . . . **95** A1
Elms The
Barnes SW13 . . . . **56** B4
🔳 Harlesden
NW10 . . . . **21** A3
Elmstone Rd SW6 . . **165** B4
Elm Terr NW2 . . . . **1** C1
Elmton Ct NW8 . . . . . **89** B2
Elm Tree Cl NW8 . . . . **89** B4
Elm Tree Ct
SE5 🔳 Camberwell
SE5 . . . . **48** B2
St John's Wood
NW8 . . . . **89** B4
Elm Tree Rd NW8 . . . **89** B4
Elm Way NW10 . . . . . . **8** A4
Elm Wlk NW3 . . . . **1** C2
Elmwood Ct
SW11 . . . . **170** A4
Elm Wood Prim Sch
SE27 . . . . **75** C1
Elmwood Rd
Chiswick W4 . . . . **45** B4
Herne Hill SE24 . . . . . **63** C2
Elmworth Gr SE21 . . . **75** C2
Elnathan Mews
W9 . . . . **88** B1
Elphinstone St N5 . . . **15** A4
Elrington Rd E8 . . . . . **16** C2
Elsa St E1 . . . . **33** A4
Elsdale Ho 🔳 E9 . . . . **17** B1
Elsdale St E9 . . . . **17** B1
Elsden Mews E2 . . . . . **25** B3
Elsenham St SW18,
SW19 . . . . **70** B2
Elsfield NW5 . . . . **13** A3
Elsham Rd W14 . . . . **126** A3
Elsham Terr W14 . . . **126** A3
Elsiemaud Rd SE4 . . . **66** B2
Elsie Rd SE22 . . . . **64** B3

Elsinore Gdns NW2 . . **1** A1
Elsinore Ho
🔳 Camberwell
SE5 . . . . **48** B1
Islington N1 . . . . **85** B3
Elsinore Way TW9 . . . **55** A4
Elsley Rd SW11 . . . . . **60** C4
Elsley Sch 🔳
SW11 . . . . **72** A2
Elspeth Rd SW11 . . . . **60** B3
Elstead Ho 🔳
SW2 . . . . **74** B4
Elsted St SE17 . . . . . **151** C3
Elstow Grange
NW6 . . . . **9** C1
Elswick Rd SE13 . . . . **52** A1
Elswick St SW6 . . . . **166** C2
Elsworthy Rd NW3 . . . **80** A4
Elsworthy Rise
NW3 . . . . **12** A1
Elsworthy Terr
NW3 . . . . **12** A1
Elsynge Rd SW18 . . . **59** C2
Elsynge Road Mans
SW18 . . . . **59** C2
Elthiron Rd SW6 . . . **165** C3
Elthorne Rd N19 . . . . . **4** C2
Elthruda Rd SE13 . . . **67** C1
Elton Ho 🔳 E3 . . . . . . **26** B4
Elton Pl N16 . . . . **16** A3
Elton 🔳 N16 . . . . **16** A3
Eltringham St
SW18 . . . . **59** B3
Elvaston Mews
SW7 . . . . **129** A2
Elvaston Pl SW7 . . . **129** A2
Elveden Ho 🔳
SW9 . . . . **63** A3
Elver Gdns 🔳
E2 . . . . **24** C2 **99** C4
Elverson Rd SE8 . . . . **52** A1
Elverson Rd Sta
SE8 . . . . **52** A1
Elverton St SW1 . . . **147** B4
Elvin Ho 🔳 E9 . . . . . . **17** B2
Elwin St E2 . . . **24** C2 **99** B4
Elwood Ho N5 . . . . **6** A1
Elwood St N4, N5 . . . . **6** A1
Elworth Ho SW8 . . . **163** A1
Ely Cotts SW8 . . . . . **162** C1
Ely Court Flats
SW6 . . . . **164** A3
Ely Ct
Holborn EC1 . . . . . . **107** C3
🔳 Maida Vale NW6 . . **23** C2
Ely Pl EC1 . . . . **107** C3
Elysium Gate 🔳
SW6 . . . . **164** C2
Elysium Pl N1 . . . . . **164** C1
Elysium St SW6 . . . . **164** C1
Elystan Ct SW15 . . . . **57** A2
Elystan Pl SW3 . . . . **144** C2
Elystan St SW3 . . . . **144** B3
Elystan Wlk N1 . . . . . **85** B3
Emanuel Ave W3 . . . . **28** B3
Emanuel Ct W3 . . . . . **28** C3
Emanuel Sch 🔳
SW11 . . . . **60** A2
Embankment
SW15 . . . . **47** C1
Embankment Gdns
SW3 . . . . **159** A4
Embankment Pier
WC2 . . . . **120** B2

Embankment Pl
WC2 . . . . **120** B2
Embankment Sta
WC2 . . . . **120** B2
Embassy Ct NW8 . . . . **79** C1
Embassy Ho 🔳
NW6 . . . . **10** C1
Ember Ct 🔳 W12 . . . . **38** A3
Emberton SE5 . . . . . . **49** A4
Emberton Ct EC1 . . . . **96** A3
Embleton Rd SE13 . . . **67** A3
Emden St SW6 . . . . . **166** B4
Emerald Ho 🔳
NW10 . . . . **20** C4
Emerald Rd NW10 . . . **20** C4
Emerald St WC1 . . . **106** C4
Emerson Ho N16 . . . . **16** A3
Emerson St SE1 . . . . **122** C2
Emery Hill St
SW1 . . . . **133** A1
Emery St SE1 . . . . . . **135** C2
Emily St 🔳 E16 . . . . . **35** B3
Emirates Stad
(Arsenal FC) N7 . . . . **14** C4
Emlyn Gdns 🔳
W12 . . . . **38** A3
Emlyn Rd W12 . . . . . . **38** B3
Emmanuel Ho
Dulwich SE21 . . . . . . **75** C1
Lambeth SE11 . . . . . **149** B3
Emmanuel Rd
SW12 . . . . **73** C3
Emma St E2 . . . . **25** A3
Emminster 🔳 NW6 . . **78** A4
Emmott Cl E1 . . . . **26** A1
Emperor's Gate
SW7 . . . . **142** C4
Empingham Ho 🔳
SE8 . . . . **40** C2
Empire Ho SW3 . . . **130** A1
Empire Sq N19 . . . . . . **5** A1
Empire Wharf E3 . . . . **26** A4
Empire Wharf Rd
E14 . . . . **42** C2
Empress Mews 🔳
SE5 . . . . **48** B1
Empress Pl SW5 . . . **141** B1
Empress St SE17 . . . **48** B4
Empson St E3 . . . . . . **27** A1
Emsworth St SW2 . . . **74** B2
Emu Rd SW8 . . . . . . **170** A1
Enard Ho 🔳 E3 . . . . . . **26** B3
Enbrook St W10 . . . . . **23** A2
Enclave Ct EC1 . . . . . **96** B2
Endell St WC2 . . . . . **106** A1
Enderby St SE10 . . . . **43** A1
Endlesham Ct 🔳
SW12 . . . . **72** C4
Endlesham Rd
SW12 . . . . **72** C4
Endsleigh Gdns
WC1 . . . . **93** B2
Endsleigh Mans 🔳
SW16 . . . . **74** A1
Endsleigh Pl WC1 . . . **93** C2
Endsleigh St WC1 . . . **93** C2
Endwell Rd SE4 . . . . . **51** A1
Endymion Rd
Harringay N4 . . . . **6** A4
Tulse Hill SW2 . . . . . . **62** B1
Energen Cl NW10 . . . . **8** A2
Enfield Cloisters 🔳
N1 . . . . **24** A2 **98** A4
Enfield Ho 🔳
SW9 . . . . **172** B2

Enfield Rd
De Beauvoir Town E8,
N1 . . . . **16** A1
South Acton W3 . . . . . **37** A4
Enford St W1 . . . . . . **102** C4
Engadine St SW18 . . . **70** C3
Engate St SE13 . . . . . **67** B3
England's La NW3 . . . **12** B2
Englefield NW1 . . . . . **92** C3
Englefield Rd N1 . . . . **16** A1
Englewood Rd
SW12 . . . . **61** B1
English Gardening
Sch The SW3 . . . . . **158** C4
English Grounds
SE1 . . . . **124** A1
English Martyrs RC
Prim Sch
Walworth SE17 . . . . **151** C3
Whitechapel E1 . . . . **111** A1
English St E3 . . . . **26** B1
Enid St SE16 . . . . . . **139** A2
Enid Stacy Ho 🔳
N19 . . . . **5** A3
Enmore Ct SW14 . . . . **55** C2
Enmore Gdns
SW14 . . . . **55** C2
Enmore Rd SW15 . . . **57** B3
Ennerdale Ho 🔳
N4 . . . . **6** B4
Ennerdale Rd TW9 . . . **44** B1
Ennersdale Rd
SE13 . . . . **67** C2
Ennis Ho 🔳 E14 . . . . . **34** A3
Ennismore Ave
W4 . . . . **38** B2
Ennismore Gdns
SW7 . . . . **130** A3
Ennismore Gdns
Mews SW7 . . . . **130** A2
Ennismore Mews
SW7 . . . . **130** A2
Ennismore St
SW7 . . . . **130** A2
Ennis Rd N4 . . . . **5** C3
Ensbury Ho SW8 . . . **162** C2
Ensign Ct 🔳 E1 . . . . **125** C3
Ensign Ho 🔳 E14 . . . **41** C4
Ensign St E1 . . . . . . **125** B4
Ensor Mews SW7 . . . **143** B2
Enterprise Ho 🔳
E9 . . . . **17** B1
Enterprise Way
College Pk NW10 . . . . **21** C2
Wandsworth SW18 . . . **58** C3
Enterprise Way
SE8 . . . . **41** B2
Epirus Mews SW6 . . **155** B2
Epirus Rd SW6 . . . . . **155** A2
Epping Cl E14 . . . . . . **41** C2
Epping Ho 🔳 E5 . . . . . **7** C2
Epping Pl N1 . . . . **14** C2
Epple Rd SW6 . . . . . **165** A4
Epstein Ct N1 . . . . **86** B3
Epworth St EC2 . . . . . **97** C1
Equity Sq 🔳
E2 . . . . **24** B2 **99** A3
Erasmus St SW1 . . . **147** C3
Erconwald St W12 . . . **29** B3
Eresby Ho SW7 . . . . **130** B3
Eresby Pl NW6 . . . . . **10** C1
Erica Ct SW4 . . . . . . **172** B3
Erica Ho SE4 . . . . **66** B4
Erica St W12 . . . . **29** C2
Ericcson Cl SW18 . . . **58** C2

Eric Fletcher Ct 🔳
N1 . . . . **15** B1
Eric Macdonald Ho
SW6 . . . . **165** C3
Eric Rd NW10 . . . . **8** B2
Ericson Ho
London SE13 . . . . **67** C3
Stamford Hill N16 . . . . **7** B3
Eric St E3 . . . . **26** B1
Eric Wilkins Ho 🔳
SE1 . . . . **153** B1
Eridge Ho SE22 . . . . . **64** B4
Eridge House Sch 🔳
SW6 . . . . **164** C2
Eridge Rd W4 . . . . . . **37** C3
Erin Ct NW2 . . . . **9** B2
Erlanger Rd SE14 . . . **50** C1
Ermine Rd SE13 . . . . **67** A3
Ernest Bevin Coll
SW17 . . . . **72** A2
Ernest Gdns W4 . . . . **45** A4
Ernest Simmonds Ho
SE14 . . . . **50** B1
Ernest St E1 . . . . **25** C1
Ernshaw Pl SW15 . . . **58** A2
Eros (Shaftesbury
Meml)* N1 . . . . **119** B3
Erpingham Rd
SW15 . . . . **57** B4
Errington Rd W9 . . . . **23** B1
Errol St EC1 . . . . **97** A1
Erskine Ho SW1 . . . . **146** C1
Erskine Rd NW3 . . . . **12** B1
Escuan Lo N5 . . . . . . **15** B3
Esher Gdns SW19 . . . **69** C2
Esher Ho 🔳 SW8 . . . **171** C2
Eskdale NW1 . . . . **82** C1
Esk Ho E3 . . . . **26** B1
Esme Ho SW15 . . . . . **56** B3
Esmeralda Rd
SE1 . . . . **153** C3
Esmond Ct W8 . . . . . **128** B2
Esmond Gdns W4 . . . **37** C2
Esmond Rd
Acton W4 . . . . **37** C3
Kilburn NW6 . . . . **23** B4
Esmond St SW15 . . . . **58** A3
Esparto St SW18 . . . . **71** A4
Espirit Ct E1 . . . . **110** C3
Espirit Ho 🔳
SW15 . . . . **58** A2
Essendine Mans
W9 . . . . **23** C2
Essendine Prim Sch 🔳
W9 . . . . **23** C2
Essendine Rd W9 . . . . **23** C2
Essex Ct
Barnes SW13 . . . . . . **46** B1
Hammersmith W6 . . . **39** B3
Holborn EC4 . . . . . . **107** B1
Essex Ho 🔳 E14 . . . . **34** A3
Essex Park Mews
W3 . . . . **29** A1
Essex Pl W4 . . . . **37** B2
Essex Place Sq 🔳
W4 . . . . **37** C2
Essex Rd
Acton W3 . . . . **28** B2
Chiswick W4 . . . . **37** C2
Islington N1 . . . . **86** B4
Willesden NW10 . . . . . **8** A1
Essex Road Sta N1 . . **15** B1
Essex St WC2 . . . . . . **121** B4
Essex Villas W8 . . . . **127** B3

Essian St E1 . . . . 33 A4
Essington SW15 . . . . 58 A1
Estcourt Rd SW6 . . 154 C2
Estella Ho ⑩ W11 . . 30 C2
Estelle Rd NW3 . . . . 12 B4
Esterbrooke St
SW1 . . . . 147 B3
Este Rd SW11 . . . . . . 60 A4
Estoria Cl ㉒ SW2 . . 74 C4
Etal Ho N1 . . . . 15 A1
Etcham St
E15 . . . . 19 B4
Eternit Wlk SW6 . . . 47 C2
Ethelbert Ho E9 . . . . 18 A4
Ethelbert St SW12 . . 73 A3
Ethelburga St
SW11 . . . . 168 B4
Ethelburga Twr
SW11 . . . . 168 B4
Ethelden Rd W12 . . 30 A1
Ethel Rankin Ct ⑧
SW6 . . . . 164 C2
Ethel St SE17 . . . . . 151 A3
Ethelworth Ct ④
SW2 . . . . 74 C3
Etherow St SE22 . . . 76 C4
Ethnard Rd SE15 . . . 50 A4
Eton Ave NW3 . . . . . . 12 A1
Eton Cl SW18 . . . . . . 71 A4
Eton College Rd
NW3 . . . . 12 B2
Eton Ct NW3 . . . . 11 C1
Eton Garages ⑪
NW3 . . . . 12 A2
Eton Ho
Hackney E9 . . . . 18 B2
Highbury N5 . . . . . . 15 A4
Eton Pl NW1 . . . . 12 C1
Eton Rd NW3 . . . . 12 B2
Eton Rise NW3 . . . . . . 12 B2
Eton St TW10 . . . . . . 54 A2
Eton Villas NW3 . . . . 12 B2
Etta St SE8 . . . . 51 A4
Ettrick St E14 . . . . . . 34 B3
Eugene Cotter Ho
SE17 . . . . 151 C3
Eugenia Rd SE16 . . . 40 B2
Eurocentres SW1 . . 146 B3
Euro CI NW10 . . . . 8 C3
Eurolink Bsns Ctr
SW2 . . . . 62 C2
Europa PI EC1 . . . . . 96 C3
European Coll ⑬
E1 . . . . 111 B2
Eustace Bldg
SW8 . . . . 160 A3
Eustace Ho SE11 . . 148 C4
Eustace Rd SW6 . . 155 B2
Euston Rd NW1 . . . . 93 A2
Euston Sq NW1 . . . . 93 B3
Euston Square Sta
WC1 . . . . 93 A2
Euston St NW1 . . . . 93 A3
Euston Sta NW1 . . . . 93 B3
Euston Underpass
NW1 . . . . 92 C2
Evan Cook Cl SE15 . 50 B2
Evandale Rd SW9 . 173 C2
Evangelist Rd
NW5 . . . . 13 A4
Evans Cl E8 . . . . 16 B2

Evans Ho
㉞ Shepherd's Bush
W12 . . . . 30 A2
South Lambeth
SW8 . . . . 161 C1
Evelina Mans ⑦
SE5 . . . . 48 C3
Evelina Rd SE15 . . . 50 B1
Eveline Lowe Prim
Sch ㉓ SE1 . . . . . . 153 C1
Evelyn Ct
Marylebone W1 . . 102 C1
Shacklewell E8 . . . 16 C4
Shoreditch N1 . . . . 87 B1
Evelyn Denington Ct
② N1 . . . . 15 A1
Evelyn Fox Ct W10 . 30 B4
Evelyn Gdns
Richmond TW9 . . . 54 A3
South Kensington
SW7 . . . . 143 B1
Evelyn Ho
Bedford Pk W12 . . 38 B4
③ Brixton SW2 . . . 62 B2
⑱ Spitalfields E1 . 111 B3
Evelyn St
Greenwich SE10 . . 52 B4
SE8 . . . . 41 A1
Evelyn Terr TW9 . . . 54 A4
Evelyn Wlk N1 . . . . . . 87 B1
Evelyn Yd W1 . . . . . 105 B2
Evenwood Cl
SW15 . . . . 58 A2
Everard Ho ⑬ E1 . . 111 C1
Everatt Cl SW18 . . . 58 B2
Everdon Rd SW13 . . 46 C4
Everest PI E14 . . . . . 34 B4
Everett Ho
Islington N7 . . . . . . 14 C4
Walworth SE17 . . . 151 B2
Evergreen Sq ⑨
E8 . . . . 16 B1
Everilda St N1 . . . . . . 85 A3
Evering Rd E5, N16 . . 7 C1
Everington St W6 . . 47 C4
Everitt Rd NW10 . . . 20 C2
Everleigh St N4 . . . . . 5 B3
Eversfield Rd TW9 . . 44 B1
Evershed Ho E1 . . . 111 A2
Evershed Wlk W4 . . 37 C2
Evershot Rd N4 . . . . . 5 B3
Eversleigh Rd
SW11 . . . . 169 B1
Eversley Ho ⑫
E2 . . . . 24 C2 99 B3
Everthorpe Rd
SE15 . . . . 64 B4
Everton Bldgs
NW1 . . . . 92 C3
Evesham Ct ⑧
TW10 . . . . 54 B1
Evesham Ho
① Bethnal Green
E2 . . . . 25 B3
Pimlico SW1 . . . . . 146 B2
St John's Wood
NW8 . . . . 78 C3
Evesham St W11 . . . 30 C2
Evesham Way
SW11 . . . . 60 C4
Evesham Wlk
Brixton SW9 . . . . . 173 B2

Evesham Wlk continued
Camberwell SE5 . . . 48 C1
Ewald Rd SW6 . . . . 164 C1
Ewart PI ⑱ E3 . . . . . 26 B3
Ewe CI N7 . . . . 14 A2
Ewen Cres SW2 . . . . 74 C4
Ewen Henderson Ct
⑩ SE14 . . . . 51 A3
Ewen Ho N1 . . . . 84 C3
Ewer St SE1 . . . . . . 122 C1
Ewhurst ① SW15 . . 57 C1
Ewhurst Cl E1 . . . . . . 32 B4
Ewhurst Rd SE4 . . . . 66 B1
Exbury Ho
Hackney E9 . . . . 17 B2
⑨ London SW9 . . . 62 B3
Excel Cl WC2 . . . . . 119 C3
Excelsior Gdns
SE13 . . . . 52 B1
Excelsior Ind Est
SE15 . . . . 50 B4
Exchange Arc
EC2 . . . . 110 B4
Exchange Ct WC2 . 120 B3
Exchange Mans ②
NW11 . . . . 1 B4
Exchange PI EC2 . . 110 A4
Exeter Ho
Paddington W2 . . 100 C2
⑪ Peckham SE15 . 49 C4
Putney SW15 . . . . . 57 B1
Exeter Mans NW2 . . 10 A2
Exeter Mews
Fulham SW6 . . . . . 155 B2
⑯ Hampstead NW6 . 11 A2
Exeter Rd
Brondesbury NW2 . 10 A2
Newham E16 . . . . . 35 C4
Exeter St WC2 . . . . 120 C4
Exeter Way ②
SE14 . . . . 51 B3
Exford Ct SW11 . . . 167 C4
Exhibition Cl W12 . . 30 B2
Exhibition Rd
SW7 . . . . 129 C2
Exmoor Ho ㉘ E3 . . 26 A3
Exmoor St W10 . . . . 30 C4
Exmouth Ho
Clerkenwell EC1 . . . 95 C2
⑯ Millwall E14 . . . 42 A2
Exmouth Market
EC1 . . . . 95 C2
Exmouth Mews
NW1 . . . . 93 A3
Exmouth PI E8 . . . . . 17 A1
Exmouth St E1 . . . . . 32 B3
Exonbury NW8 . . . . . 78 B3
Exon St SE17 . . . . . 152 A3
Explorers Ct ⑤
E14 . . . . 34 C2
Express Wharf ⑩
E14 . . . . 41 C4
Exton St SE1 . . . . . 121 B1
Eynella Rd SE21 . . . 76 B4
Eynham Rd W12 . . . 30 B3
Eynsford Coll W1 . 105 B2
Eynsford Ho
Borough The SE1 . 137 B4
⑫ Deptford SE15 . . 50 B4
Walworth SE17 . . . 152 A3
Eyot Gdns W6 . . . . . 38 B1
Eyot Green W4 . . . . . 38 B1
Eyre Ct NW8 . . . . 79 B2
Eyre St Hill EC1 . . . . 95 B1
Eythorne Rd SW9 . 173 C3

Ezra St E2 . . . . 24 B2 99 A4

F
Fabian Rd SW6 . . . 155 A2
Fabyc Ho TW9 . . . . . 44 C3
Fairacres SW15 . . . . 56 C3
Fairbairn Gn ①
SW9 . . . . 48 A2
Fairbriar Residence
SW7 . . . . 143 A4
Fairbridge Rd N19 . . . 4 C2
Fairburn Ct SW15 . . 58 A2
Fairburn Ho
⑨ Stamford Hill
N16 . . . . 7 A3
West Kensington
SW5 . . . . 141 A1
Fairby Ho SE1 . . . . 153 A4
Faircharm Trad Est
SE8 . . . . 52 A3
Fairchild Cl ⑥
SW11 . . . . 167 C1
Fairchild Ho
⑬ Hackney E9 . . . . 17 B2
Pimlico SW1 . . . . . 147 A3
⑤ Shoreditch
N1 . . . . 24 A2 98 A4
Fairchild PI
EC2 . . . . 24 A1 98 B1
Fairchild St
EC2 . . . . 24 A1 98 B1
Fairclough St E1 . . 111 C1
Faircourt NW3 . . . . . 12 B2
Faircroft N16 . . . . 6 C3
Fairdale Gdns
SW15 . . . . 57 A3
Fairdene Ct N7 . . . . . 14 A2
Fairfax Ho
⑪ Brixton SW9 . . 173 C1
⑤ Putney SW15 . . 56 C2
Fairfax Mews
SW15 . . . . 57 B3
Fairfax PI
Kensington W14 . . 126 B1
South Hampstead
NW6 . . . . 11 B1
Fairfax Rd
Acton W4 . . . . 38 A3
South Hampstead
NW6 . . . . 11 B1
Fairfield
Camden Town NW1 . 82 C3
④ Stepney E1 . . . . . 32 B4
Fairfield Ct
Harlesden NW10 . . 21 C4
⑭ London SW18 . . 59 A2
Fairfield Dr SW18 . . 59 A2
Fairfield Rd E3 . . . . . 26 C3
Fairfield St SW18 . . 59 A2
Fairfoot Rd E3 . . . . . 26 C1
Fairford Ho SE11 . . 149 C3
Fairhazel Gdns
NW6 . . . . 11 B1
Fairheathe SW15 . . . 57 C1
Fairholme Rd
W14 . . . . 140 B1
Fairholt Cl N16 . . . . . . 7 A3
Fairholt Rd N16 . . . . . 6 C3
Fairholt St SW7 . . . 130 B2
Fairhurst ④ NW6 . . . 11 B2
Fairlawn Ave W4 . . . 37 B2
Fairlawn Ct ⑧ W4 . . 37 B2

Fairlawn Mans
SE14 . . . . 50 C2
Fairlawns SW15 . . . . 57 C2
Fairlead Ho ⑥
E14 . . . . 41 C3
Fairley House Sch
SW1 . . . . 147 C2
Fairlie Ct
⑨ Bromley E3 . . . . 27 A2
⑩ Tufnell Pk N7 . . 13 C4
Fairlight Ave
NW10 . . . . 21 A3
Fairlight Ct ④
NW10 . . . . 21 A3
Fairlop PI NW8 . . . . . 89 C3
Fairmead Ho E9 . . . . 18 A4
Fairmead Rd N7,
N19 . . . . 5 A2
Fairmont Ave E14 . . 34 C1
Fairmont Ho ①
E3 . . . . 26 C1
Fairmount Rd
SW2 . . . . 62 B1
Fair St SE1 . . . . 138 C4
Fairstead Wlk N1 . . . 86 C4
Fairthorn Rd SE7,
SE10 . . . . 43 C1
Fairview Ho ⑭
SW2 . . . . 74 B4
Fairview Pl SW2 . . . 74 B4
Fairwall Ho ⑧
SE5 . . . . 49 A2
Fairway Cl NW11 . . . . 2 A4
Fairway Ct ⑬
SE16 . . . . 40 C4
Fairway The W3 . . . . 29 A3
Fairweather Ho
N7 . . . . 14 A4
Faith Ct NW2 . . . . 9 A2
Faithfull Ho N5 . . . . . 15 B3
Fakruddin St
E1 . . . . 24 C1 99 C1
Falconberg Ct
W1 . . . . 105 C2
Falconberg Mews
W1 . . . . 105 C2
Falconbrook Prim Sch
㉛ SW11 . . . . 59 C4
Falcon Cl
Chiswick W4 . . . . . . 45 B4
Lambeth SE1 . . . . . 122 B2
Falcon Ct
⑨ Dulwich SE21 . . 75 C2
Holborn EC4 . . . . . 107 B1
Islington N1 . . . . . . 86 B1
Falcon Gr SW11 . . . . 60 A4
Falcon Ho ⑭ SE15 . 49 B2
Falcon La SW11 . . . . 60 A4
Falcon Lo
⑫ Paddington W9 . 31 C4
West Hampstead
NW3 . . . . 11 A4
Falcon Pk Ind Est
NW10 . . . . 8 A3
Falcon Point SE1 . . 122 B3
Falcon Rd SW11 . . . . 60 A4
Falcons Pre Prep Sch
The ⑩ W4 . . . . 45 B4
Falcons Prep Sch for
Boys The ㉞ TW9 . . 54 A3
Falcon Terr SW11 . . 60 A4
Falcon Way E14 . . . . 42 A2
Falcomwood Ct
SE3 . . . . 53 B1
Falkener Ct SW11 . 169 C3

Falkirk Ct 11 SE16 . . .32 C1
Falkirk Ho W9. . . . 88 B4
Falkirk St N1. . . . .24 A3
Falkland Ho
  Kensington W8. . .128 A1
  West Kensington
  W14 . . . . . 140 C2
Falkland Pl 2
  NW5. . . . . . .13 B3
Falkland Rd NW5. . .13 B3
Falkner House Sch
  SW7 . . . . . . 143 A2
Fallodon Ho
  6 London SW8. . 171 C2
  Paddington W11. . .31 B4
Fallow Ct 20 SE16. . 153 C4
Fallowfield N4 . . . . 5 B2
Falmouth Ho
  Bayswater W2 . . . 116 A4
  Kennington SE11. . 149 C2
Falmouth Rd SE1. . 137 A1
Falmouth St E15. . . 19 C3
Falstaff Ct SE11. . .150 A3
Falstaff Ho 18 N1. . .24 A3
Fane St W14 . . . .155 A4
Fan Mus The*
  SE10 . . . . . . .52 B3
Fanet St EC1. . . . .97 A1
Fanshaw St
  N1. . . . . .24 A2 98 A4
Fanthorpe St
  SW15 . . . . . . .57 B4
Faraday Ho
  2 Balham SW12. . .73 A4
  6 Gospel Oak NW5. . .13 A4
  Kensal Town W10. . .31 A4
  4 Poplar E14 . . . 33 B2
Faraday Lo SE10. . .43 B3
Faraday Rd
  Acton W3 . . . . 28 B2
  Kensal Town W10 . . .31 A4
Fareham Ho 19
  SW15 . . . . . . .68 C3
Fareham St W1. . . 105 B2
Farjeon Ho NW6. . .11 C1
Farleigh Pl N16. . .16 B4
Farleigh Rd N16. . .16 B4
Farley Ct
  Kensington W14. . 126 C2
  Marylebone NW1. . .91 B1
Farlington Pl
  SW15 . . . . . . .69 A4
Farlow Rd SW15. . .57 A4
Farlton Rd SW18 . . .71 A4
Farm Ct SW6. . . .155 C2
Farmdale Rd SE10. .43 C1
Farmer Ho 4
  SE16 . . . . . . .40 A3
Farmers Mkt*
  W8 . . . . 113 C2
Farmers Rd SE5. . .48 A3
Farmer St
  W8. . . . .31 C1 113 B2
Farm La SW6. . . .155 C2
Farm Lane Trad Ctr
  SW6 . . . . . . .155 C3
Farmleigh Ho
  SW9 . . . . .63 A2
Farm Pl
  W8. . . . .31 C1 113 B2
Farm Rd NW10. . . .20 C4
Farm St W1. . . . .118 A3
Farnaby Ho 2
  W10 . . . . .23 B2

Farnborough Ho 1
  SW15 . . . . . . .68 C3
Farncombe St
  SE16 . . . . . . 139 C3
Farndale Ho 3
  NW6 . . . . .78 A4
Farnell Mews
  SW5 . . . . 142 A2
Farnell Pl W3. . . . 28 A2
Farnfield Ho 12
  SW2. . . . . . . .62 B2
Farnham Ct 2 N16. .7 A3
Farnham Ho
  Borough The SE1. . 122 C1
  Marylebone NW1. . .90 B1
Farnham Pl SE1. . 122 B1
Farnham Royal
  SE11. . . . . . . 149 A1
Farnhurst Ho 7
  SW11 . . . . . . 169 B2
Farningham Ho 9
  N4 . . . . 6 C4
Farnley Ho 13
  SW8 . . . . 171 B2
Farnsworth Ct
  SE10 . . . . . . .43 B3
Farnworth Ho 5
  E14 . . . . .42 C2
Faroe Rd W14 . . . .39 C3
Farquhar Rd SW19. .70 C1
Farrance St E14. . . 33 C3
Farrant Ho 14
  SW11 . . . . . . .59 C4
Farrell Ho E1. . . . 32 B3
Farrer Ho SE8. . . . 51 C3
Farriers Mews
  SE15 . . . . . . .65 B4
Farrier St NW1. . . 13 B1
Farrier Wlk SW10. .156 C4
Farringdon La EC1. . 95 C1
Farringdon Rd EC1. . 95 C1
Farringdon St
  EC4 . . . . 108 A2
Farringdon Sta
  EC1 . . . . 108 A4
Farrins Rents
  SE16 . . . . 33 A1
Farrow La SE14. . . .50 B3
Farrow Pl SE16. . . .41 A3
Farthingale Wlk
  E15 . . . . .19 C1
Farthing Alley 8
  SE1 . . . . 139 B3
Farthing Fields 8
  E1 . . . . .32 A1
Fashion Retail Acad
  The W1 . . . . . 105 B2
Fashion St E1. . . .111 A3
Fashion & Textile
  Mus* SE1. . . . . 138 C4
Fassett Rd E8. . . . 16 C2
Fassett Sq E8. . . . 16 C2
Fauconberg Ct
  W4 . . . . 45 B4
Fauconberg Rd
  W4 . . . . 45 B4
Faulkner Ho SW15. .47 B1
Faulkner's Alley
  EC1 . . . . 108 A4
Faulkner St SE14. . .50 B2
Faunce Ho 1
  SE17 . . . . . . 149 A4
Faunce St SE17. . .150 A1
Favart Rd SW6. . . 165 C3

Faversham Ho
  Camden Town
  NW1. . . . . . . .83 A3
  Walworth SE17. . . 152 A1
Fawcett Cl SW11. . 167 C1
Fawcett Est E5. . . . 7 C3
Fawcett Ho 25
  SW9 . . . . 172 B2
Fawcett Rd NW10. . .8 B1
Fawcett St SW10. . 156 C4
Fawe Park Rd
  SW15 . . . . . . .58 B3
Fawe St E14. . . . . 34 A4
Fawkham Ho SE1. . 153 A3
Fawley Ct SE27. . . 75 A2
Fawley Lo 2 E14. . .42 C2
Fawley Rd NW6. . . 11 A3
Fawnbrake Ave
  SE24 . . . . . . .63 B2
Fayetville Ho 29
  N19 . . . . 5 A3
Faygate Rd SW2. . .74 B2
Fazerley Ct 49 W2. . .31 C4
Fearnley Ho SE5. . . 49 A1
Fearon St SE10. . . .43 C1
Feathers Pl SE10. . .52 C4
Featherstone St
  EC1 . . . . .97 B2
Featley Rd SW9. . . 63 A4
Felbridge Ho 21
  SE22 . . . . . . .64 A4
Felday Rd SE13. . . .67 A1
Felden St SW6. . . 164 C3
Feldman Cl N16. . . . 7 C3
Felgate Mews 4
  W6 . . . . 39 A2
Felix St 18 E2. . . .25 A3
Felixstowe Rd
  NW10 . . . . . . .22 A2
Fellbrigg Rd SE22. . 64 B2
Fellbrigg St 21 E1. . .25 A1
Fell Ho 11 N19. . . . 4 B1
Fellows Ct E2. . . . 24 B3
Fellows Rd NW3. . . 12 A1
Fells Haugh 6
  W3 . . . . 28 B3
Felltram Way SE7. . .43 C1
Felmersham Cl 2
  SW4 . . . . .61 C3
Felsberg Rd SW2. . .74 A4
Felsham Ho 5
  SW15 . . . . . . .57 C4
Felsham Mews 14
  SW15 . . . . . . .57 C4
Felsham Rd SW15. . 58 B2
Felstead St E9. . . . 18 B2
Felstead Wharf
  E14 . . . . .42 B1
Felton Ho N1. . . . .87 C3
Felton St N1. . . . . 87 C3
Fenchurch Ave
  EC3 . . . . 110 A1
Fenchurch Bldgs
  EC3 . . . . 110 B1
Fenchurch Pl 6
  EC3 . . . . 124 B4
Fenchurch St EC3. . 124 A4
Fenchurch Street Sta
  EC3 . . . . 124 B4
Fendall St SE1. . . .138 B1
Fender Ct 5 SW4. . 172 A2
Fendt Cl 8 E16. . . .35 B3
Fenelon Pl W14. . . 141 A3
Fenham Rd SE15. . .50 A3
Fenner Cl SE16. . . 40 A2
Fenner Ho 28 E1. . .32 A1

Fenner Sq 9
  SW11 . . . . . . .59 C4
Fenning St SE1. . . 138 A4
Fenn St E9. . . . . 17 B3
Fen St E16. . . . . .35 B2
Fenstanton 3 N4. . .5 C3
Fenstanton Prim Sch
  20 SW2 . . . . . .74 C3
Fentiman Rd SW8 162 C2
Fenton Cl
  11 Dalston E8. . .16 B2
  South Lambeth
  SW9 . . . . 172 C1
Fenton Ho SE14. . . 51 A3
Fenton House*
  NW3 . . . . 2 B1
Fentons SE3. . . . . 53 B3
Fenton St E1. . . . .32 A3
Fenwick Gr SE15. . .64 C4
Fenwick Pl SW9. . . 62 A4
Fenwick Rd SE15. . .64 C4
Ferdinand Ho 1
  NW1 . . . . .13 A1
Ferdinand Pl NW1. . 12 C1
Ferdinand St NW1. . 12 C1
Ferguson Dr W3. . . 28 C3
Ferguson Ho SE10. . 52 B2
Ferguson's Cl E14. . .41 C2
Fergus Rd N5. . . . 15 A3
Fermain Ct E N1. . . 24 A4
Fermain Ct N N1. . . 24 A4
Fermain Ct W N1. . .24 A4
Fermoy Rd W9. . . . 23 B1
Fernbank Mews
  SW12 . . . . . . .61 B1
Fern Cl 3 N1. . . . .24 A3
Ferncliff Rd E8. . . .16 C3
Ferncroft Ave
  NW3 . . . . .10 C4
Fern Ct SE14. . . . .50 C1
Ferndale Com Sp Ctr
  SW9 . . . . .62 B3
Ferndale Ct 3
  SE3 . . . . .53 B3
Ferndale Ho N16. . .6 C3
Ferndale Rd SW4,
  SW9 . . . . .62 B3
Ferndene Rd SE24. .63 B3
Ferndown Lo 17
  E14 . . . . .42 B3
Fernhead Rd W9. . .23 B2
Fernhill Ho E5. . . . 7 C2
Fernholme Rd
  SE15 . . . . . . .65 C2
Fernhurst Rd
  SW6 . . . . 164 B4
Fernie Ho SE22. . . .64 B4
Fernlea Rd SW12. . .73 A3
Fernleigh Cl W9. . . 23 B2
Fernsbury St WC1. . 95 B3
Fernshaw Mans
  SW10 . . . . . . 156 C3
Fernshaw Rd
  SW10 . . . . . . 156 C3
Fernside NW11. . . . 1 C3
Fernside Rd SW12. .72 C4
Fern St E3. . . . . .26 C1
Fernthorpe Rd
  SW16 . . . . . . .73 C1
Fern Wlk 18 SE16. .153 C1
Fernwood SW19. . . 70 B3
Ferrey Mews 9
  SW9 . . . . 173 B1
Ferriby Cl N1. . . . .14 C1
Ferrier Ind Est
  SW18 . . . . . . .59 A3

Ferrier Point 6
  E16 . . . . .35 C4
Ferrier St SW18. . . 59 A3
Ferrings SE21. . . . 76 A1
Ferris Rd SE22. . . .64 C3
Ferrybridge Ho
  SE11 . . . . . . 135 A1
Ferry La
  Barnes SW13. . . 46 B4
  Brentford TW8. . . 44 A4
  Richmond TW9. . . 44 B4
Ferry Rd SW13. . . .46 C2
Ferry Sq 1 TW8. . .44 A4
Ferry St E14. . . . .42 B1
Festing Rd SW15. . .57 C4
Festival Ct 5 E8. . .16 B1
Festival Pier SE1. . 120 C2
Fetter La EC4. . . . 107 C2
Fettes Ho NW8. . . .79 C1
Ffinch St SE8. . . . .51 C3
Field Ct
  Hampstead NW3. . 11 B3
  Holborn WC1. . . 107 A3
  Lower Holloway N7. . .14 A3
  Wimbledon SW19. . .70 C1
Fieldgate Mans 2
  E1 . . . . 111 C3
Fieldgate St E1. . . 111 C3
Field Ho NW10. . . 22 C2
Fieldhouse Rd
  SW12 . . . . . . .73 B3
Fielding Ho
  Chiswick W4. . . . 46 A4
  6 Kilburn NW6. . .23 C2
  St John's Wood
  NW8 . . . . .78 C4
Fielding Mews
  SW13 . . . . . . .47 A4
Fielding Rd
  Acton W4 . . . . .38 A3
  Hammersmith W14. . .39 C3
Fielding St SE17. . . 48 B4
Fields Est E8. . . . .16 C1
Fields Lo NW10. . . .8 B2
Fields St WC1. . . . 94 C4
Fieldsway Ho N5. . .14 C3
Fieldview SW17,
  SW18 . . . . . . .71 C3
Fieldview Ct 2
  N5 . . . . 15 A3
Fieldway Cres N5,
  N7 . . . . .14 C3
Fife Rd
  Mortlake SW14. . . 55 B2
  Newham E16. . . . 35 C4
Fife Terr N1. . . . . 85 A2
Fifth Ave W10. . . . 23 A2
Fig Tree Cl NW10. . .21 A4
Filey Ave N16. . . . 7 C3
Filey Ho SW18. . . .59 B3
Filigree Ct SE16. . . 33 B1
Filmer Ho SW6. . . 164 B4
Filmer Mews
  SW6 . . . . 164 B4
Filmer Rd SW6. . . 154 C1
Filton Ct 14 SE14. . 50 B3
Finborough Rd
  SW10 . . . . . . 156 B4
Finchdean Ho
  SW15 . . . . . . .68 B4
Finch Ho 1 SE8. . .52 A4

Finch La EC2, EC3 .... 109 C1
Finchley PI NW8 .... 79 B2
Finchley Ho
 Hampstead NW3 ....11 B2
 St John's Wood
 NW8 .... 79 B2
Finchley Road &
 Frognal Sta NW3 ..11 B3
Finchley Road Sta
 NW3 ....11 B2
Finch Lo 19 NW9 ...31 C4
Finch Mews 3
SE15 .... 49 B2
Finch's Ct 11 E14 ...34 A2
Findhorn St 5
E14 .... 34 B3
Findon Cl SW18 ...58 C1
Findon Rd W12...38 C4
Fineran Ct 18
SW11 .... 59 C3
Fingal St SE10...43 B1
Fingest Ho 90 A2 NW8
Finland Rd SE4...66 A4
Finland St SE16 ...41 A3
Finlay St SW6 ...47 C2
Finley Ct 21 SE5 ...48 B3
Finmere Ho 1 N4...6 B4
Finnemore Ho N1...86 C4
Finn Ho N1...97 C4
Finnis St E2...25 A1
FINSBURY 95 C4
Finsbury Ave EC2 109 C3
Finsbury Cir EC2 109 C3
Finsbury Ct EC2...109 B4
Finsbury L Ctr EC1...96 C3
Finsbury Market
 EC2 .... 110 A4
Finsbury Mkt 5
 EC2 .... 24 A1 98 A1
FINSBURY PARK 5 C2
Finsbury Park N4,
 N5 .... 6 A2
Finsbury Park Sta
 N4 .... 5 C2
Finsbury Pavement
 EC2 .... 109 C4
Finsbury Sq EC2 109 C4
Finsbury St EC2...109 B4
Finsen Rd SE5...63 B4
Finstock Rd W10 ...30 C3
Finton House Sch
 SW17 .... 72 B2
Finucane Ct 3 TW9 64 B4
Finwhale Ho E14 ...42 A3
Fiona Ct 19 NW6 ...23 B3
Firbank Rd SE15...50 A1
Fircroft N1...86 B4
Fircroft Prim Sch
 SW17 .... 72 B1
Fircroft Rd SW17 ...72 B1
Fire Brigade Pier
 SE1 .... 148 B4
Firecrest Dr NW3...2 A1
Firle Ho 7 W10 ...30 B4
Fir Lo SW15 ...57 A3
Firmston Ho 9
SW14 .... 55 C4
Firs Ave SW14 ...55 B3
Firsby Rd N16 ...7 C3
First Ave
 East Acton W3 ...29 B1
 Mortlake SW14 ...56 A4
 West Kilburn W10...23 B1
First St SW3...144 B4

Firth Gdns SW6 .... 164 A3
Fir Tree Ho 11
 SE14 .... 50 B3
Fir Trees Cl SE16...33 A1
Fisher Ho
 Islington N1 .... 85 B3
 5 Shadwell E1 ...32 B2
 2 Tufnell Pk N19 ...4 B1
Fishermans Dr
 SE16 .... 40 C4
Fisher St
 Holborn WC1 ...106 C3
 Newham E16 ...35 C4
Fisherton St NW8 89 C2
Fisherton Street Est
 NW8 .... 89 C1
Fishlock Ct 6
SW4 .... 172 A2
Fish St Hill EC3 ...123 C3
Fitch Ct SW2...62 C2
Fitzalan St SE11...149 B4
Fitzclarence Ho
 W11 .... 126 A4
Fitz-George Ave
 W14 .... 140 A3
Fitzgerald Ave
 SW14 .... 56 A4
Fitzgerald Ho
 13 Brixton SW9 ...173 B1
 14 Poplar E14 ...34 A3
Fitzgerald Rd
 SW14 .... 55 C4
Fitzhardinge Ho
 W1 .... 103 B2
Fitzhardinge St
 W1 .... 103 B2
Fitzherbert Ho 3
 TW10 .... 54 B1
Fitzhugh Gr SW18 59 C1
Fitzjames Ave
 W14 .... 140 B3
Fitzjohn's Ave
 NW3 .... 11 C3
Fitzjohns Mans
 NW3 .... 11 B2
Fitzjohns Prim Sch 4
 NW3 .... 11 C3
Fitzmaurice Ho 9
 SE16 .... 40 A2
Fitzmaurice PI
 W1 .... 118 B2
Fitzroy Cres 4
 W4 .... 45 C3
Fitzroy Ho
 12 Bermondsey SE1 ...153 A2
 7 Tower Hamlets
 E14 .... 33 B3
Fitzroy Mews W1 ...92 C1
Fitzroy Pk N6 ...3 B3
Fitzroy Rd NW1...81 B4
Fitzroy Sq W1 ...92 C1
Fitzroy St W1 ...92 C1
Fitzroy Yd NW1 ...81 B4
Fitzwarren Gdns
 N19 .... 4 B3
Fitzwilliam Ave
 TW9 .... 44 B1

Fitzwilliam Mews
 E16 .... 35 C1
Fitzwilliam Rd
 SW4 .... 61 B4
Five Cts SE11 ...136 A1
Fiveways Rd SW9 173 C1
Flamborough Ho 2
 SE15 .... 49 C2
Flamborough St
 E14 .... 33 A3
Flamingo Ct 2
 SE8 .... 51 C3
Flamsteed Ct 15
 SE13 .... 52 A2
Flamsteed Ho* ...
Flanchford Rd
 W12 .... 38 B3
Flanders Ho N16 ...7 A1
Flanders Mans 1
 W4 .... 38 B2
Flanders Rd W4...38 A2
Flanders Way E9 ...17 C2
Flank St 1 E1 ...125 B4
Flansham Ho 2
 E14 .... 33 B3
Flask Cotts 4
 NW3 .... 11 C4
Flask Wlk NW3 ...11 C4
Flatiron Sq SE1...123 A1
Flatiron Yd SE1...123 A1
Flavell Mews SE10...43 A1
Flaxman Ho
 6 Chiswick W4 ...38 A1
 Newington SE1 ...136 B2
Flaxman Rd SE5 ...48 A1
Flaxman Sp Ctr
 SE5 .... 48 B1
Flaxman Terr WC1 ...93 C3
Flecker Ho 6 SE5 ...48 C3
Fleece Wlk N7 ...14 A2
Fleet Ct 1 W12 ...38 A3
Fleet Prim Sch 18
 NW3 .... 12 B3
Fleet Rd NW3 ...12 B3
Fleet Sq WC1...94 B3
Fleet St EC4 ...107 C1
Fleet Street Hill 10
 E1 .... 24 C1 99 B1
Fleetway WC1 ...94 B4
Fleet Wood 6 N16 ...7 B2
Fleetwood Rd
 NW10 .... 8 C3
Fleetwood St N16 ...7 A2
Fleming Cl 4 W9 ...23 C1
Fleming Ct W2 ...101 B4
Fleming Ho
 6 Bermondsey
 SE16 .... 139 B3
 Finsbury Pk N4 ...6 B3
Fleming Rd SE17 ...48 A4
Fletcher Bldgs
 WC2 .... 106 B1
Fletcher Ho
 8 Brixton SW2 ...62 C2
 6 Limehouse E14 ...33 A2
Fletcher Path 7
 SE8 .... 51 C3
Fletcher Rd W4 ...37 B3

Fletcher St 16 E1 125 C4
Fleur De Lis St
 E1 .... 24 B1 98 C1
Fleur Gates 5
 SW19 .... 69 C4
Flinders Ho 28 E1 ...32 A1
Flinton St SE17 ...152 B2
Flint St 7 SE17 ...151 C3
Flitcroft St WC2 ...105 C1
Flitton Ho 5 N1 ...15 A1
Flock Mill PI
 SW18 .... 71 A3
Flodden Rd SE5 ...48 B2
Flood St SW3...158 B4
Flood Wlk SW3 ...158 B4
Flora Cl E14 ...34 A3
Flora Gardens Prim
 Sch 7 W6 ...39 A2
Flora Gdns 2 W6 ...39 A2
Floral St WC2 ...120 A4
Florence Ct W9 ...89 A3
Florence Gdns W4..45 B4
Florence Ho
 20 Bermondsey
 SE16 .... 40 A1
 2 Brixton SW2 ...62 B2
 16 Shepherd's Bush
 W11 .... 30 C2
 3 Wandsworth
 SW18 .... 59 C3
Florence Mans
 SW6 .... 164 C4
Florence Nightingale
 Ho 4 N1 ...15 B2
Florence Nightingale
 Mus* SE1 ...135 A3
Florence Rd
 Acton W4 ...38 C3
 Finsbury Pk N4 ...5 C4
 New Cross Gate
 SE14 .... 51 B2
Florence St N1 ...15 A1
Florence Terr
 Kingston u T SW15 ...68 A1
 New Cross Gate
 SE14 .... 51 B2
Florence Way
 SW12 .... 72 B3
Flores Ho 15 E1 ...32 C4
Florfield Rd E8 ...17 A2
Florian SE5 ...49 A2
Florian Rd SW15 ...58 A3
Florida St
 E2 .... 24 C2 99 C3
Florida State Univ
 WC1 .... 105 C3
Florin Ct SE1 ...138 C3
Floris PI 7 SW4 ...61 B4
Florys Ct 7 SW19 ...70 A3
Floss St SW15 ...47 B1
Flower & Dean Wlk
 E1 .... 111 A3
Flowersmead
 SW17 .... 72 C2
Flowers Mews 5
 N19 .... 4 B2
Flower Wlk The
 SW7 .... 129 A4
Floyer Cl TW10 ...54 B2
Flynn Ct 13 E14 ...33 B2
Foley Ho 19 E14 ...32 B3
Foley St W1 ...104 C3
Folgate St E1 ...110 C4
Foliot Ho N1 ...84 C2
Foliot St W12 ...29 B3
Follett Ho SW10 ...157 B2

Follett St E14 ...34 B3
Folly Wall E14...42 B4
Fonda Ct 14 E14 ...33 C2
Fontarabia Rd
 SW11 .... 60 C3
Fontenelle SE5 ...49 A2
Fontenoy Ho
 SE11 .... 150 A3
Fontenoy Rd SW12,
 SW17 .... 73 B2
Fonthill
 Kensington W14 ...126 B2
 Pimlico SW1 ...146 B2
Fonthill Mews N4 ...5 B2
Fonthill Rd N4 ...5 C2
Fontley Way SW15...68 C4
Footpath The
 SW15 .... 56 C2
Forber Ho 2 E2 ...25 B2
Forbes Ho 2 W4 ...36 C1
Forbes St E1 ...111 C1
Forburg Rd N16 ...7 C3
Ford Cl 3 E3 ...26 A3
Fordcombe 13
 NW5 .... 12 C2
Fordham Ho 11
 SE14 .... 51 A3
Fordham St 13 E1 ...111 C2
Fordingley Rd W9...23 B2
Ford Rd E3 ...26 B3
Fords Park Rd E16...35 C3
Ford Sq E1 ...32 A4
Ford St
 Bow E3 ...26 A3
 Canning Town E16 ...35 B3
Fordwych Ct NW2 ...10 A2
Fordwych Rd NW2...10 A3
Forecastle Ct E14 ...41 C4
Foreign &
 Commonwealth
 Office SW1 ...134 A4
Foreland Ho
 W11 .... 31 A2 112 A4
Foreshore SE8 ...41 B2
Fore St EC2 ...109 A3
Fore St Ave EC2 ...109 B3
Forest Cl NW6 ...10 A1
Forester Rd SE15 ...65 A3
Forest Gr E8 ...16 B2
Forest Hill Rd
 SE22 .... 65 A1
Forest Rd
 Dalston E8 ...16 B2
 Richmond TW9 ...44 C3
Fore Street Ave ...
Forest Way 8 N19 ...4 B2
Forfar Rd SW11 ...169 C4
Forge PI NW1 ...12 C2
Forman Ho SE4 ...65 C3
Formby Ct 9 N7 ...14 C3
Formosa Ho 1 E1...26 A1
Formosa St W9 ...88 B1
Formunt Cl E16 ...35 B4
Forrest Ct N7 ...14 C2
Forrest Ho SW15 ...47 B1
Forset Ct W1 ...102 B2
Forset St W1 ...102 B2
Forster Rd SW2 ...74 A4
Forston St N1 ...87 A2
Forsyth Gdns SE17...48 A4
Forsyth Ho
 14 Hackney E9 ...17 B1
 Pimlico SW1 ...147 A3
Forsythia Ho SE4...66 A4

Fortescue Ave **1**
E8 .... 17 A1
Fortess Gr NW5 ..... 13 B3
Fortess Rd NW5 ..... 13 B4
Fortess Wlk NW5 .... 13 A3
Forthbridge Rd
SW11 .... 60 C3
Forth Ho **12** E3 .... 26 B3
Forties The **3**
NW5 .... 13 B3
Fortior Ct N6 .... 4 B4
Fortnam Rd N19 ...... 4 C2
Fort Rd SE1 .... 153 A3
Fortrose Cl E14 ...... 34 C3
Fortrose Gdns SW12,
SW2 .... 74 A3
Fort St E1 .... 110 B3
Fortuna Cl N7 .... 14 B2
Fortune Ct **3** E8 .. 16 B1
Fortune Gate Rd
NW10 .... 21 A4
Fortune Green Rd
NW6 .... 10 C4
Fortune Ho
Lambeth SE11 ..... 149 B3
St Luke's EC1 ...... 97 A1
Fortune St EC1 ...... 97 A1
Fortune Way
NW10 .... 21 C2
Forty Acre La E16 ... 35 C4
Forum Cl **7** E3 .... 26 C4

Forward Bsns Ctr The
3 E16 .... 27 C1
Fosbroke Ho
SW8 .... 162 A1
Fosbury Ho **7**
SW9 .... 62 B3
Fosbury Mews
W2 .... 31 C3
Foscote Mews W9 ... 31 C4
Foskett Rd SW6 .... 165 A1
Fossil Rd SE13 ...... 66 C4
Foster Ct
6 Camden Town
NW1 .... 13 B1
Canning Town E16 ... 35 B2
Foster Ho SE14 ..... 51 B2
Foster La EC2 ...... 108 C2
Foster Rd
Acton W3 .... 29 A2
Chiswick W4 .... 37 C1
Foubert's Pl W1 ... 104 C1
Foulden Rd N16 .... 16 B4
Foulden Terr N16 ... 16 B4
Foulis Terr SW7 ... 143 C2
Foulser Rd SW17 ... 72 C1
Foundary Ho **6**
E14 .... 34 A4
Founders Ct EC2 .. 109 B2
Founders Ho **1**
SW1 .... 147 B2
Foundling Ct WC1 .. 94 A2
Foundling Mus The*
WC1 .... 94 B2
Foundry Cl SE16 .... 33 A1
Foundry Mews
NW1 .... 93 A2
Foundry Pl
Stepney E1 .... 32 B4
Wandsworth SW18 .. 71 A4
Fountain Ct
Belgravia SW1 .... 146 A3
14 Shepherd's Bush
W11 .... 39 C4
Strand EC4 .... 121 B4
Fountain Green Sq **5**
SE16 .... 139 C3

Fountain Ho
13 Bermondsey
SE16 .... 139 C3
3 Brondesbury Pk
NW6 .... 10 A1
Mayfair W1 .... 117 B2
Fountain Mews
5 Highbury N5 ... 15 B4
Maitland Pk NW3 ... 12 B2
Fountain Pl SW9 .. 173 C3
Fountayne Rd N16 .. 7 C2
Fount St SW8 ..... 161 C1
Fournier St E1 .... 111 A4
Fourscore Mans
E8 .... 16 C1
Four Seasons Cl
E3 .... 26 C3
Fourth Ave W10 .... 23 A2
Fovant Ct **5** SW8 170 C1
Fowey Cl E1 .... 32 A1
Fowey Ho SE11 .... 149 C2
Fowler Cl SW11 .... 59 C4
Fowler Ho
5 Camberwell
SE5 .... 49 A1
Islington N1 .... 86 B4
South Lambeth
SW8 .... 171 C3
Fowler Rd N1 .... 86 B4
Fownes St SW11 ... 60 A4
Fox and Knot St
EC1 .... 108 B4
Foxberry Ct SE4 .... 66 B3
Foxberry Rd SE4 ... 66 A4
Foxborough Gdns
SE4 .... 66 C2
Foxbourne Rd
SW17 .... 72 C2
Fox Cl
Bethnal Green E1 ... 25 B1
Newham E16 .... 35 C4
Foxcombe Rd **6**
SW15 .... 68 C3
Foxcote SE5 .... 152 B1
Foxcroft WC1 .... 85 A1
Fox Ct EC1 .... 107 B3
Foxfield NW1 .... 82 B3
Foxglove St W12 ... 29 B2
Foxham Rd N19 ..... 4 C1
Fox Ho **2** SW11 .. 59 C3
Foxley Cl E8 .... 16 C3
Foxley Ho **4** E3 .. 27 A2
Foxley Rd SW9 ..... 48 A3
Foxley Sq **3** SW9 48 A2
Foxmore St SW11 168 C3
Fox Prim Sch
W8 .... 31 C1 113 B1
Fox Rd E16 .... 35 B4
Fox's Yd E2 ... 24 B1 99 A2
Foxwell Mews SE4 .. 66 A4
Foxwell St SE4 ...... 66 A4
Foyle Rd SE3 .... 53 B4
Fradel Lo N16 .... 7 C3
Framfield Rd N5 .... 15 A3
Frampton NW1 ...... 13 C1
Frampton Ct **3**
W3 .... 37 B4
Frampton Ho NW8 . 89 C1
Frampton Park Rd
E9 .... 17 B1
Frampton St NW8 .. 89 C1
Francemary Rd
SE4 .... 66 C2
Franche Court Rd
SW17 .... 71 B1

Francis Chichester
Way SW11 .... 169 C3
Francis Cl **6** E14 . 42 C2
Francis Ct **12** SE14 50 C4
Francis Ho
Harlesden NW10 .... 21 B4
11 Shoreditch N1 . 24 A4
Walham Green
SW10 .... 156 B2
Francis Holland Sch
Belgravia SW1 .... 145 C3
Marylebone NW1 ... 90 C2
Francis Snary Lo **1**
SW18 .... 58 C2
Francis St SW1 .... 147 A4
Francis Terr N19 .... 4 B1
Francis Terrace Mews
12 N19 .... 4 B1
Francis Wlk N1 ..... 84 C4
Franconia Rd SW4 . 61 C2
Frank Barnes Sch **13**
NW3 .... 11 C1
Frank Beswick Ho
SW6 .... 155 A3
Frank Dixon Cl
SE21 .... 76 A3
Frank Dixon Way
SE21 .... 76 A3
Frankfurt Rd SE24 . 63 B2
Frankham Ho **8**
SE8 .... 51 C3
Frankham St SE8 ... 51 C3
Frank Ho SW8 .... 162 A2
Frankland Cl SE16 . 40 A2
Frankland Ho **4**
SW12 .... 73 A4
Frankland Rd
SW7 .... 129 B1
Franklin Bldg **5**
E14 .... 41 C4
Franklin Cl
Greenwich SE13 .... 52 A2
West Norwood
SE27 .... 75 A1
Franklin Ho
New Cross SE14 .... 51 A1
10 Wapping E1 ... 32 A1
Franklin Pl SE13 ... 52 A2
Franklin Sq SW5 . 141 A1
Franklin's Row
SW3 .... 145 A2
Franklin St **13** E3 . 27 A2
Franklyn Rd NW10 . 8 B2
Frank Soskice Ho
SW6 .... 155 A3
Frank Whymark Ho **4**
SE16 .... 40 B4
Frans Hals Ct E14 . 42 C3
Fraserburgh Ho **20**
E3 .... 26 B3
Fraser Ct SW11 ... 168 A4
Fraser Ho
Brentford TW8 ...... 36 B1
1 Clapham SW8 . 171 B1
Fraser Regnart Ct **12**
NW5 .... 12 B3
Fraser St W4 .... 38 A1
Frazier St SE1 .... 135 B3
Frean St SE16 .... 139 B2
Frearson Ho **5**
WC1 .... 95 A4
Freda Corbett Cl **10**
SE15 .... 49 C3
Frederica St **4**
N7 .... 14 B1
Frederick Blg N1 ... 16 A2

Frederick Charrington
Ho **4** E1 .... 25 B1
Frederick Cl W2 .. 116 C4
Frederick Cres
SW9 .... 48 A3
Frederick Ct SW6 . 58 A4
Frederick's Pl
EC2 .... 109 B1
Frederick Sq **11**
SE16 .... 33 A2
Frederick's Row
EC1 .... 96 A4
Frederick St WC1 .. 94 C3
Frederick Terr E8 .. 16 B1
Frederic Mews
SW1 .... 131 B3
Freedom St SW11 169 A2
Freegrove Rd N7 ... 14 A3
Freeling Ho NW8 ... 79 B4
Freeling St **7** N1 . 14 B1
Freeman Ho **13**
SW2 .... 74 A4
Freemantle St
SE17 .... 152 A2
Freemens Hos **1**
SW9 .... 62 B3
Freke Rd SW11 .... 60 C4
Fremantle Ho **14**
E1 .... 25 A1
Fremont St E9 ...... 25 B4
French Inst The
SW7 .... 143 B4
French Pl
E1 .... 24 A1 98 B2
Frendsbury Rd
SE4 .... 66 A3
Frensham Ct N5 ... 15 B3
Frensham Dr
SW15 .... 68 C2
Frensham St SE15 . 49 C4
Frere St **6** SW11 168 B2
Freshfield Ave E8 .. 16 B1
Freshfield Cl SE13 . 67 C3
Freshford St SW17,
SW18 .... 71 B1
Freston Rd W10,
W11 .... 30 C2
Freswick Ho **6**
SE8 .... 41 B2
Freud Mus The*
NW3 .... 11 B2
Frewell Bldg EC1 . 107 B4
Frewin Rd SW18 ... 71 C3
Friar Mews SE27 ... 75 A1
Friars Ave
Putney SW15 .... 58 A2
Roehampton SW15 . 68 B1
Friars Cl SE1 ...... 122 B1
Friars Gdns W3 .... 28 C3
Friars Mead E14 ... 42 B3
Friars Place La
W3 .... 28 C2
Friars Prim
Foundation Sch
SE1 .... 136 B3
Friars Stile Pl **9**
TW10 .... 54 A1
Friars Stile Rd
TW10 .... 54 A1
Friar St EC4 ...... 108 B1
Friars Way W3 ...... 28 C3
Friary Park Ct **12**
W3 .... 28 B3
Friary Rd
Acton W3 .... 28 C3
Peckham SE15 ...... 49 C3

Friday Grove Mews **11**
SW12 .... 73 B4
Friday St EC4 .... 122 C4
Frideswide Pl
NW5 .... 13 B3
Friendly Pl **16**
SE13 .... 52 A2
Friendly St SE8 .... 51 C2
Friendly Street Mews
3 SE8 .... 51 C1
Friendship Way
E15 .... 27 B4
Friend St EC1 ...... 96 A4
Frigate Ho **4** E14 . 42 B2
Frigate Mews SE8 . 51 C4
Frimley Cl SW19 ... 70 A2
Frimley Way E1 .... 25 C1
Frinstead Ho **1**
W10 .... 30 C2
Friston St SW6 ... 166 A1
Frith Ho
Bethnal Green
E2 .... 24 C2 99 B3
Paddington NW8 .. 89 C1
Frith Rd E11 .... 19 C4
Frith St W1 .... 105 B1
Frithville Ct **2**
W12 .... 30 B1
Frithville Gdns
W12 .... 30 B1
Frobisher Ct
3 Greenwich
SE10 .... 52 C4
3 Shepherd's Bush
W12 .... 39 B4
Frobisher Ho **27**
E1 .... 32 A1
Frobisher Pas E14 . 33 C1
Frobisher Pl SE14 . 50 B2
Frobisher St SE10 . 53 A4
Frogley Rd SE22 ... 64 B3
Frogmore SW18 ... 58 C2
Frogmore Est
NW10 .... 20 B2
Frogmore Ind Est
N5 .... 15 B4
Frognal NW3 .... 11 B3
Frognal Cl NW3 .... 11 B3
Frognal Ct NW3 .... 11 B2
Frognal Gdns
NW3 .... 11 B4
Frognal La NW3 ... 11 A3
Frognal Par NW3 .. 11 B2
Frognal Rise NW3 . 11 B4
Frognal Way NW3 . 11 B4
Frome Ho SE15 .... 65 B3
Frome St N1 .... 86 C2
Fromow's Cnr **4**
W4 .... 37 B1
Frontenac NW10 .... 9 A1
Frostic Wlk E1 .... 111 A3
Froude St SW8 ... 170 B1
Frye Ct **5** E3 ...... 26 B2
Frying Pan Alley
E1 .... 110 C3
Fulbeck Ho N7 ..... 14 B2
Fulbourne St **1**
E1 .... 32 A4
Fulcher Ho
3 Deptford SE8 .. 41 B1
10 Shoreditch N1 . 24 A4

Fulford Mans **3**
N19 . . . . 5 A1
Fulford St SE16 . . . .40 A4
FULHAM 47 C1
Fulham Broadway
SW6 . . . . .155 C1
Fulham Broadway Sh
Ctr SW6 . . . . .155 C1
Fulham Broadway Sta
SW6 . . . . .155 C2
Fulham Bsns
Exchange SW6 . .167 A3
Fulham Cross Girls
Sec Sch SW6 . . . .154 A1
Fulham Ct SW6 . . .165 B4
Fulham High St
SW6 . . . . .164 B1
Fulham Pal★ 164 A1
Fulham Palace Rd SW6,
W6 . . . . .47 C4
Fulham Park Gdns
SW6 . . . . .164 C2
Fulham Park Rd
SW6 . . . . .164 C2
Fulham Prep Sch
6 Fulham SW6 . .164 B1
Fulham W14 . . . . . .154 A4
Fulham Prim Sch
SW6 . . . . .155 B3
Fulham Rd
Chelsea SW10 . . . .157 A4
Fulham SW6 . . . . .165 A4
Fuller Cl **4**
E2 . . . . .24 C1 99 B2
Fullers Ho **5** . . . .
Fullerton Rd SW18 .59 B2
Fullwood's Mews
N1 . . . . .97 C4
Fulmar Ct **5** SE21 .75 C2
Fulmar Ho
12 Bermondsey
SE16 . . . . .40 C2
Marylebone NW8 . . . .90 B1
Fulmead St SW6 . .166 B3
Fulneck **1** E1 . . . . . .32 B4
Fulthorp Rd SE3 . . .53 C1
Fulton Mews W2 . .114 C4
Fulwood Pl WC1 . .107 A3
Fulwood Wlk
SW19 . . . . .70 A3
Furber St W6 . . . . . .39 A3
Furley Ho **7** SE15 . .49 C3
Furley Rd SE15 . . . .49 C3
Furlong Rd N7 . . . .14 C2
Furmage St SW18 . .71 A4
Furness Ho SW1 . . .146 A2
Furness Lo **4**
SW14 . . . . .55 A3
Furness Prim Sch
NW10 . . . . .21 C3
Furness Rd
Harlesden NW10 . . .21 C3
Sands End SW6 . . .166 B2
Furnival St EC4 . . .107 B2
Furrow La E9 . . . . . .17 B3
Fursecroft W1 . . . .102 C2
Furze St E3 . . . . . . .33 C4
Fusion Ct SW15 . . . .68 A1
Futters Cl **1**
NW10 . . . . .21 A3
Fyfield N4 . . . . .5 C2
Fyfield Rd **5** SW9 .62 C4

Fynes St SW1 . . . . .147 B4

G

Gable Ho **12** W4 . . . .38 A2
Gables Cl SE5 . . . . .49 A2
Gables The
3 Clapham SW4 . . .61 B4
Hampstead NW3 . . . .2 C1
Gabriel Ho **11** SE11 .148 C4
Gabrielle Ct **8** NW3 .11 C2
Gaddesden Ho EC1 .97 C3
Gadsden Ho
8 Homerton E9 . . . .17 C2
8 Kensal Town
W10 . . . . .23 A1
Gagarin Ho SW11 . .59 C4
Gage Rd E16 . . . . . .35 A4
Gage St WC1 . . . . .106 B4
Gainford Ho **18** E2 . .25 A2
Gainford St N1 . . . . .85 B4
Gainsborough Ct
5 Bermondsey
SE16 . . . . .40 A1
Dulwich SE21 . . . . . .76 A2
Shepherd's Bush
W12 . . . . .39 B4
Gainsborough Gdns
Golders Green
NW11 . . . . .1 B4
Hampstead NW3 . . . .2 C1
Gainsborough Ho
Finsbury Pk N4 . . . . .5 B3
1 Hampstead NW3 .11 B4
6 Limehouse E14 . . .33 A2
Westminster SW1 . .147 C3
Gainsborough Prim
Sch E9 . . . . .18 C2
Gainsborough Rd
Bedford Pk W4 . . . . .38 B2
Richmond TW9 . . . . .54 B4
Gainsborough St **3**
E9 . . . . .18 B2
Gainsborough Studios
N1 . . . . .87 B3
Gainsford St SE1 . .139 A4
Gairloch Ho **2** . . . . . .
Gairloch Rd SE5 . . .49 A1
Gaisford St NW5 . . .13 B2
Gaitskell Ct SW11 .168 A2
Gaitskell Ho SE17 . .48 C4
Gaitskell Way SE1 .136 C4
Galata Rd SW13 . . .46 C3
Galatea Sq SE15 . . .65 A4
Galaxy Bldg **6**
E14 . . . . .41 C2
Galaxy Ho EC2 . . . .97 C4
Galbraith St E14 . . .42 B3
Gale Ho **10** SW2 . . . .62 B2
Galena Ho **4** W6 . . .39 A2
Galen Pl WC1 . . . . .106 B3
Galesbury Rd
SW18 . . . . .59 B1
Gales Gdns E2 . . . . .25 A2
Gale St E3 . . . . .33 C4
Galgate Cl **4**
SW19 . . . . .70 A3
Galleon Cl SE16 . . . .40 C4
Galleon Ho **8** E14 . .42 B2

Galleries of Modern
London★ EC1 . . . .108 C3
Gallery Ct SW10 . . .156 C3
Gallery Rd SE21 . . . .75 C3
Galleywall Rd
SE16 . . . . .40 A2
Galleywall Road Trad
Est **5** SE16 . . . . . . .40 A1
Galleywood Ho **11**
W10 . . . . .30 B4
Gallia Rd N5 . . . . . . .15 A3
Galloway Rd W12 . .29 C1
Galsworthy Ave
E14 . . . . .33 A4
Galsworthy Ct W3 . .37 A3
Galsworthy Ho **4**
W11 . . . . .31 A3
Galsworthy Rd
NW2 . . . . .10 A4
Galton St W10 . . . . .23 A2
Galveston Ho **2**
E1 . . . . .26 A1
Galveston Rd
SW15 . . . . .58 B2
Galway Cl **28** SE16 .40 A1
Galway Ho
Finsbury EC1 . . . . . .97 A3
1 Stepney E1 . . . . .32 C4
Galway St EC1 . . . . .97 A3
Gambetta St **3**
SW8 . . . . .170 B1
Gambia St SE1 . . . .122 B1
Gambier Ho **5** EC1 .97 A3
Gamlen Rd SW15 . . .57 C3
Gandolfi St **6**
SE15 . . . . .49 A4
Ganley Ct **11** . . . . . .
SW11 . . . . .59 C4
Gannet Ct **5** SE21 .75 C2
Gannet Ho SE15 . . . .49 B2
Ganton St W1 . . . . .105 A1
Garand Ct **2** N7 . . . .14 B3
Garbett Ho **2** . . . . . .
SE17 . . . . .48 A4
Garbutt Pl W1 . . . . .103 C3
Garden Ct
4 Richmond TW9 .44 B2
12 South Acton W4 .37 B3
St John's Wood
NW8 . . . . .89 B4
Strand EC4 . . . . . . .121 B4
Garden Flats
SW16 . . . . .74 A1
Garden Ho **12**
SW9 . . . . .172 B2
Garden House Sch
SW3 . . . . .145 A2
Garden Mews
W2 . . . . .31 C2 113 C3
Garden Mus★ . . . . . .
SE1 . . . . .134 C1
Garden Pl **28** E2 . . . .24 B4
Garden Rd
Richmond TW9 . . . . .54 C4
St John's Wood
NW8 . . . . .89 B3
Garden Row SE1 . .136 A2
Garden Royal **10**
SW15 . . . . .57 C1
Gardens The
East Dulwich SE22 . .64 C3
Stamford Hill N16 . . .7 B4

Garden Terr
Knightsbridge
SW7 . . . . .130 B3
Pimlico SW1 . . . . . .147 B2
Garden Wlk
EC2 . . . . .24 A1 98 A2
Gardiner Ave NW2 . .9 B3
Gardiner Ct NW10 . .20 C4
Gardiner Ho
SW11 . . . . .168 A4
Gardiners La E4 . . .122 C4
Gardnor Mans **7**
NW3 . . . . .11 B4
Gardnor Rd NW3 . . .11 C4
Gard St EC1 . . . . . . .96 B4
Gareth Ct SW16 . . . .73 C1
Garfield Ho **2**
W2 . . . . .102 C1
Garfield Mews **7** . . . . .
SW11 . . . . .60 C4
Garfield Rd SW11 . .60 C4
Garford St E14 . . . . .33 C2
Garland Ct **12** E14 . .33 C2
Garland Ho N16 . . . . .6 C1
Garland Rd SE18 . . .76 A2
Garlick Hill EC4 . . .123 A4
Garlinge Ho **9** . . . . . .
SW9 . . . . .173 B4
Garlinge Rd NW2 . .10 B2
Garnault Mews
EC1 . . . . .95 C3
Garnault Pl EC1 . . . .95 C3
Garner St E2 . . . . . . .24 C3
Garner Rd NW10 . . . .8 A2
Garnet Rd NW10 . . . .8 A2
Garnet St E1 . . . . . . .32 B2
Garnett Ho **5** . . . . . .
NW3 . . . . .12 B3
Garnett Rd NW3 . . . .12 B3
Garnham Cl **2** N16 . .7 B2
Garnham St **1** N16 . .7 B2
Garnies Cl SE15 . . . .49 B3
Garrad's Rd SW16 . .73 C1
Garrard Wlk NW10 . .8 A2
Garratt Ho **8** N16 . . .7 A3
Garratt La SW18 . . .71 A3
Garratt Park Sec
Spec1 Sch **8**
SW18 . . . . .71 A2
Garraway Ct SW13 .47 B3
Garraway Ho SE21 . .76 B1
Garrett Cl W3 . . . . . .28 C4
Garrett Ho **5** . . . . . .
W12 . . . . .30 A3
Garrett St EC1 . . . . .97 A2
Garrick Cl SW18 . . .59 B3
Garrick Ho
Chiswick W4 . . . . . . .46 A4
Mayfair W1 . . . . . . .118 A1
Garrick Rd TW9 . . . .44 C1
Garrick St WC2 . . . .120 A4
Garrick Yd WC2 . . . .120 A4
Garsdale Terr
SW5 . . . . .141 A2
Garsington Mews
SE4 . . . . .66 B4
Garson Ho **10** . . . . . .
W2 . . . . .115 B4
Garston Ho **6** N1 . . .15 A1
Garter Way SE16 . . .40 C4
Garth Ct W4 . . . . . . .45 C4
Garth Ho NW2 . . . . . .1 B2
Garth Rd
Child's Hill NW2 . . . . .1 B2
3 Chiswick W4 . . . .37 C1
Gartmoor Gdns
SW19 . . . . .70 B3
Garton Ho **6** N6 . . . . .4 C4
Garton Pl SW18 . . . .59 B1

Gartons Way
SW11 . . . . .59 A4
Garway Rd W2 . . . .100 A1
Gascoigne Pl **17**
E2 . . . . .24 B2 98 C3
Gascony Ave NW6 . .10 C1
Gascoyne Ho **2**
E9 . . . . .17 C1
Gascoyne Rd E9 . . .17 C1
Gaselee St E14 . . . . .34 B2
Gasholder Pl
SE11 . . . . .149 A1
Gaskarth Rd SW12 .61 A1
Gaskell St SW4 . . . .172 A2
Gaskin Ho N16 . . . . .6 C1
Gaskin St N1 . . . . . .86 A4
Gaspar Cl SW7 . . . .142 B4
Gaspar Mews
SW5 . . . . .142 B4
Gasson Ho **2** . . . . . .
SE14 . . . . .50 C4
Gastein Rd W6 . . . . .47 C4
Gastigny Ho EC1 . . .97 A3
Gaston Bell Cl
TW9 . . . . .54 B4
Gaston Gate SW8 . .172 C4
Gataker Ho **5** . . . . . .
SE16 . . . . .40 A3
Gataker St **6**
SE16 . . . . .40 A3
Gatcliff Cl SW1 . . . .145 C1
Gatcombe Ho **20**
SE22 . . . . .64 A4
Gatcombe Rd
8 Newham E16 . . .35 C1
Tufnell Pk N19 . . . . . .4 C1
Gatefield Ct SE15 . .64 C4
Gateforth St NW8 . .90 A1
Gate Hill Ct
W11 . . . . .31 B1 113 A2
Gatehouse Sch **20**
E2 . . . . .25 C3
Gatehouse Sq
SE1 . . . . .123 A2
Gateley Ho **6** SE4 . .65 C3
Gateley Rd SW9 . . . .62 B4
Gate Mews SW7 . . .130 B3
Gatesborough St
EC2 . . . . .24 A1 98 A2
Gates Ct SE17 . . . .150 C2
Gateside Rd SW17 . .72 B1
Gate St WC2 . . . . . .106 C2
Gateway SE17 . . . . .48 B4
Gateway Arc N1 . . . .86 A2
Gateway Ho SW12 . .61 A1
Gateway Ind Est
NW10 . . . . .21 C1
Gateway Mews **4**
E8 . . . . .16 B3
Gateway Prim Sch
NW8 . . . . .89 C2
Gateways The
SW3 . . . . .144 B3
Gateway Trad Est
NW10 . . . . .21 B2
Gathorne St **19** E2 . .25 C3
Gatliff Rd SW1 . . . .146 A1
Gatonby St SE15 . . .49 B2
Gatwick Ho **3** E14 . .33 B3
Gatwick Rd SW18 . .70 B4
Gauden Cl SW4 . . . .61 C4
Gauden Rd SW4 . . . .61 C4
Gaugin Ct **10** SE16 .40 A1
Gaunt St SE1 . . . . . .136 C2
Gautrey Rd SE15 . . .50 B1

Gavel St SE17 .... **151** C4
Gaverick Mews **3**
E14 .... 41 C2
Gaviller Pl **3** E5 .. 17 A4
Gawber St F2 ...... 25 B3
Gawthorne Ct E3 .. 26 C3
Gay Cl NW2 .... 9 A3
Gaydon Ho W2 ... 100 A4
Gayfere St SW1... **134** A1
Gayford Rd W12 ... 38 B4
Gay Ho N16 .... 16 A3
Gayhurst SE17 .... 152 A3
Gayhurst Ho NW8 . **90** B2
Gayhurst Prim Sch **5**
E8 .... 16 C1
Gayhurst Rd E8 ... 16 C1
Gaymead NW8 .... **78** B3
Gay Rd E15 .... 27 C3
Gaysley Ho SE11 . **149** B3
Gay St SW15 .... 57 C4
Gayton Cres NW3... 11 C4
Gayton Ho E3 ..... 26 C1
Gayton Rd NW3 ... 11 C4
Gayville Rd SW11..60 B1
Gaywood Cl SW2 ..74 C3
Gaywood St SE1 .. **136** B1
Gaza St SE17 ...... **150** A1
Gaze Ho N1 **4** 24 C3
Gean Ct **3** E11 .... 19 C4
Geary Ho N7 ...... 14 B3
Geary Rd NW10.... 8 C3
Geary St N7 .... 14 B3
Gedling Ho SE22 .. 64 B4
Gedling Pl SE1 ... **139** A2
Gees Ct W1 .... **104** A1
Gee St EC1 .... 96 C2
Geffrye Ct N1 ..... 24 A3
Geffrye Mus* **3**
E2 .... 24 B3
Geffrye St E2 ...... 24 B3
Geldart Rd SE15 .. 50 A3
Geldeston Rd E5 .. 7 C2
Gellatly Rd SE14 .. 50 C1
Gemini Bsns Ctr
E16 ....**3**
Gemini Ho **3**
E3 .... 26 C4
Gems Hampshire Sch
(Main Sch) SW7 **144** A1
Gems Hampshire Sch
(The Early Years)
SW7 .... **143** A3
General Wolfe Rd
SE10 .... 52 C2
Genesis Bsns Pk
NW10.............. 20 A3
Geneva Ct
1 Putney SW15 ... 57 C2
Stoke Newington N16 .. 6 C3
Geneva Dr SW9 ... 62 C3
Genoa Ave SW15 . 57 B2
Genoa Ho **1** E1 ... 25 C1
Geoffrey Cl SE5 .. 48 B1
Geoffrey Ct SE4 ... 66 B4
Geoffrey Ho SE1 . **137** C2
Geoffrey Jones Ct
NW10.............. 21 C4
Geoffrey Rd SE4 .. 66 B4
George Beard Rd **11**
SE8 .... 41 B2
George Beare Lo **3**
SW4 .... 61 B2
George Belt Ho **3**
E2 .... 25 C2
George Ct WC2 ... **120** B3
George Downing Est
N16 .... 7 B2

George Eliot Ho
SW1 .... **147** A3
George Eliot Jun & Inf
Schs NW8........ 79 B4
George Elliot Ho
SE17 .... **150** C2
George Elliston Ho **13**
SE1 .... **153** B1
George Eyre Ho
NW8 .... 79 C1
George Green's Sch
E14 .... 42 B1
George Inn Yd
SE1 .... **123** B1
George La SE13 ... 67 B1
George Lansbury Ho
1 Bow E3 .... 26 B2
3 Willesden NW10.. 8 A1
George Lashwood Ct
1 SW9 .... 62 B3
George Leybourne Ho
1 E1 .... **125** C4
George Lindgren Ho
SW6 .... **155** A2
George Loveless Ho
2 E2 .... 24 B2 **99** A4
George Mathers Rd
SE11 .... **150** A4
George Mews
27 Brixton SW9 .. **173** B1
1 .... 92 C3
George Peabody Ct
NW1 .... **102** A4
George Row SE16 **139** B3
George's Rd N7 ... 14 B3
George's Sq SW6 **155** A4
George St
5 Canning Town
E16 .... 35 B3
Marylebone W1 ... **103** A2
George Tingle Ho
SE1 .... **139** A2
Georgette Pl SE10 . **52** B3
George Vale Ho **58**
E2 .... 24 C3
George Walter Ho **11**
SE16 .... 40 B2
George Wyver Cl
SW18 .... 70 A4
George Yd
City of London
EC3 .... **109** C1
Mayfair W1 .... **117** C4
Georgiana St NW1.. 83 A4
Georgian Ct **2** E9 .. 25 B4
Georgina Gdns **16**
E2 .... 24 B2 **99** A4
Geraldine Rd
Brentford W4 ...... 44 C4
Wandsworth SW18 .. 59 B2
Geraldine St SE11 **136** A1
Gerald Mews
SW1 .... **145** C4
Gerald Rd SW1 ... **145** C4
Gerard Ct NW2 ... 9 C3
Gerards Cl SE16 .. 40 B1
Gernigan Ho
SW18 .... 59 C1
Gernon Rd E3 ..... 26 A3
Gerrard Ho **3**
SE5 .... 49 C3
Gerrard Pl N1 ..... **119** C4
Gerrard Rd N1 .... 86 B2
Gerrard St W1 .... **119** C4
Gerridge St SE1 .. **135** C2

Gerridge St SE1 .. **135** C2
Gerry Raffles Sq
E15 .... 19 C2
Gertrude St SW10 **157** A3
Gervase St SE15 .. 50 A3
Getters Talmud Torah
SE1 .... **139** A2
Ghent Way E8 ..... 16 B2
Giant Arches Rd
SE24 .... 63 B1
Gibbings Ho **1** SE1 **136** B3
Gibbins Rd E15 ... 19 B1
Gibbon Ho NW8 .. **89** C1
Gibbon Rd
Acton W3 .... 29 A2
Nunhead SE15 ..... 50 B1
Gibbons Rd NW10 . 8 A2
Gibbon's Rents
SE1 .... **124** A1
Gibbon Wlk SW15 . 56 C3
Gibbs Gn W14 ... **141** A2
Gibbs Green Rd
W14 .... **140** C2
Gibbs Green Specl
Sch W14 .... **141** A2
Gibbs Ho **5** SW12.. 73 A4
Gibraltar Ho
NW10.............. 21 A3
Gibraltar Wlk **28**
E2 .... 24 B2 **99** A3
Gibson Cl E1 ...... 25 B1
Gibson Gdns N16.. 7 B2
Gibson Rd SE11 .. **149** A3
Gibson Sq N1 ...... 85 C4
Gibson St SE10 ... 43 A1
Gideon Rd SW11 .. 60 C4
Giesbach Rd N19 .. 4 C2
Giffen Square Mkt*
SE8 .... 51 C3
Giffin St SE8 ...... 51 C3
Gifford Ho
3 Clapham SW4 .. 61 C3
Greenwich SE10 ... 42 C1
Pimlico SW1 ..... **146** C1
Gifford Rd NW10 .. 8 A1
Gifford St N1 ...... 14 A1
Gilbert Ho
Barbican EC2 .... **109** A3
Deptford SE8 .... 51 C4
3 Globe Town E2 .. 25 C2
Pimlico SW1 ..... **146** B1
Gilbert Pl WC1 ... **106** A3
Gilbert Rd SE11 .. **149** C4
Gilbert Sheldon Ho
W2 .... **101** C4
Gilbertson Ho **10**
E14 .... 41 C3
Gilbert St W1 ..... **103** C1
Gilbeys Yd NW1 .. 12 C1
Gilby Ho **5** E9 .... 17 C2
Gilda Cres N16 ... 7 C3
Gilda St W1 .... **104** B3
Gilden Cres NW5 .. 12 C3
Giles Ho
3 Bermondsey
SE16 .... **139** B2
Notting Hill W11 .. 31 C3
Gilesmead SE5 ... 48 C2
Gilkes Cres SE21 . 64 A1
Gilkes Pl SE21 .... 64 A1
Gillam Ho **3** SE16 . 40 B2
Gill Ave E16 .... 35 C3
Gillender St E3 ... 27 B1

Gillespie Prim Sch
N5................ 6 A1
Gillespie Rd N4, N5 .. 6 A1
Gillett Pl **2** N16 .. 16 A3
Gillett Rd E15 ..... 16 A3
Gillett St E8 ...... 16 A3
Gillfoot NW1 ...... 82 C1
Gillian St SE13 ... 67 A2
Gillies Ho **6** NW6 . 11 A2
Gilling Ct **5** NW3 .. 12 A2
Gillingham Ho
SW1 .... **146** C4
Gillingham Mews
SW1 .... **146** C4
Gillingham Row
SW1 .... **146** C4
Gillingham St
SW1 .... **146** C4
Gillison Wlk **19**
SE16 .... **139** C2
Gillman Ho **22** E2 .. 24 C3
Gillray Ho SW10 . **157** B3
Gill St E14 .... 33 B2
Gilmore Ho SW4 .. 60 B3
Gilmore Rd SE13 .. 67 C3
Gilpin Ave SW14 .. 55 C3
Gilpin Cl W2 ..... **101** A4
Gilpin Rd E5 ...... 18 A4
Gilray Ho W2 ..... **115** B4
Gilstead Rd SW6 **166** B2
Gilston Rd SW10 **143** A1
Giltspur St EC1 ... **108** B2
Gilwell Ct E5 ..... 17 A4
Gipsy Cnr W3 ..... 28 C3
Gipsy La SW15 ... 57 A4
Giraud St E14 ..... 34 A3
Girdlers Rd W14 .. 39 C2
Girdlestone Wlk
N19................ 4 C2
Girdwood Rd SW18,
SW19 .... 70 A4
Girling Ho **9** N1 .. 24 A4
Gironde Rd SW6 .. **155** A1
Girton Ho SW15 .. 57 C1
Girton Villas **6**
W10 .... 30 C3
Gisburn Ho **22**
SE15 .... 49 C3
Gissing Wlk N1 ... 14 C1
Glade The W12 ... 39 A4
Gladding Terr N16 .. 7 A2
Gladsmuir Rd N19 .. 4 B3
Gladstone Ct
Westminster SW1 . **147** C3
Willesden NW10.. 9 A3
Gladstone Ho **10**
E14 .... 33 C3
Gladstone Park Sch
NW10.............. 9 A4
Gladstone Rd W4.. 37 C3
Gladstone St SE1 **136** A2
Gladstone Terr
3 SW8 .... **170** B4
Gladwin Ho NW1 .. 83 A1
Gladwyn Rd SW15 .. 57 C4
Gladys Rd NW6 ... 10 C1
Glaisher St SE8 .. 52 A4
Glamis Ct W3 ..... 37 A4
Glamis Est **3** E1 .. 32 C2
Glamis Pl E1 ...... 32 B2
Glamis Rd E1 ..... 32 B2
Glanville Ho **4**
SW12 .... 73 B4
Glanville Rd SW2.. 62 A2
Glasbury Ho **5**
SW9 .... 62 B3

Glaserton Rd N16 .. 7 A4
Glasgow Ho W9 ... **78** B1
Glasgow Terr
SW1 .... **146** C1
Glasshill St SE1 .. **136** B4
Glasshouse Fields
E1................. 32 C2
Glasshouse St
W1 .... **119** A3
Glasshouse The
SE13 .... 67 B3
Glasshouse Wlk
SE11 .... **148** C2
Glasshouse Yd
EC1................ 96 C1
Glass St **4** E2..... 25 A1
Glastonbury Ct **12**
SE14 .... 50 B3
Glastonbury Ho
SW1 .... **146** A2
Glastonbury Pl **22**
E1................. 32 B3
Glastonbury St
NW6 .... 10 B3
Glaucus St E3 ..... 33 A4
Glazbury Rd W14 **140** B2
Glazebrook Cl
SE21 .... 75 C2
Glebe Cl **1** W4.... 38 A1
Glebe Ho **8** SE16.. 40 A3
Glebelands Cl SE5.. 64 A4
Glebe Pl SW3 .... **158** A4
Glebe Rd
Barnes SW13 ..... 46 C1
Dalston E8 .... 16 B1
Willesden NW10.. 8 C2
Glebe St W4 ...... 38 A1
Gledhow Gdns
SW5 .... **142** C3
Gledstanes Rd
W14 .... **140** B1
Glegg Pl **3** SW15 . 57 C3
Glenaffric Ave E14 .. 42 C2
Glen Albyn Rd
SW19 .... 69 C2
Glenalmond Ho **2**
SW15 .... 57 C1
Glenarm Rd E5.... 17 C4
Glenbrook Prim Sch
SW4 .... 61 C1
Glenbrook Rd
NW6 .... 10 C3
Glenburnie Rd
SW17 .... 72 B1
Glencoe Mans **6**
SW9 .... **163** B1
Glendall St SW9 .. 62 B3
Glendarvon St
SW15 .... 57 C4
Glendower Gdns **3**
SW14 .... 55 C4
Glendower Pl
SW7 .... **143** B4
Glendower Prep Sch
SW7 .... **143** B4
Glendower Rd
SW14 .... 55 C4
Glendown Ho **2**
E8................. 16 C3
Glendun Ct W3 ... 29 A2
Glendun Rd W3 ... 29 A2
Gleneagles Cl **21**
SE16 .... 40 A1
Glenelg Rd SW2.. 62 A2

Glenfield Rd SW12...73 B3
Glenfinlas Way
SE5..................48 A3
Glenforth St SE10 .43 B1
Glengall Gr SE15..49 C2
Glengall Pass 2
NW6.................23 C4
Glengall Rd
 Camberwell SE15...49 B4
 Kilburn NW6.......23 C4
Glengall Terr SE15..49 B4
Glengarnock Ave
E14..................42 B2
Glengarry Rd SE22..64 B2
Glenhurst Ave
NW5..................12 C4
Glenilla Rd NW3....12 A2
Glenister Rd SE10..43 B1
Glenkerry Ho 1
E14..................34 B3
Glenloch Ct 2
NW3..................12 A2
Glenloch Rd NW3 ..12 A3
Glenluce Rd SE3...53 C4
Glenmore SW15....57 C1
Glenmore Ho 6
TW10................54 A1
Glenmore Rd NW3..12 A2
Glennie Ct SE21...76 C3
Glennie Ho SE10...52 B2
Glennie Rd SE27,
SW16................74 C1
Glenridding NW1...83 A1
Glenrosa St SW6 .166 C2
Glenroy St W12.....30 B3
Glensdale Rd SE4..66 B4
Glenshaw Mans 7
SW9................163 B1
Glentanner Way
SW17................71 C1
Glentham Gdns
SW13................47 A4
Glentham Rd
SW13................47 A4
Glenthorne Mews
W6...................39 A2
Glenthorne Rd
W6...................39 A2
Glenthorpe SW15..56 C3
Glentworth St
NW1.................91 A1
Glenville Gr SE8 ..51 B3
Glenville Mews
SW18................70 C4
Glenworth Ave
E14..................42 C2
Gliddon Rd W14 .140 A2
Globe Acad The
SE1................137 B1
Globe Pond Rd
SE16................33 A1
Globe Prim Sch 57
E2...................25 B2
Globe Rd E1, E2...25 B1
Globe St SE1......137 B3
Globe Terr 8 E2 ..25 B2
Globe Theatre The★
SE1................122 C3
GLOBE TOWN.....25 C2
Globe View EC4 ..122 C4
Globe Yd W1......104 A1
Gloucester Arc 4
SW7................141 A3
Gloucester Ave
NW1..................81 C4

Gloucester Cir
SE10................52 B3
Gloucester Cres
NW1.................82 A4
Gloucester Ct 4
 Borough The SE1 .137 A2
 City of London EC3 .124 B3
 Dulwich SE22.......76 C3
 Golders Green NW11 ..1 B4
 Richmond TW9......44 C3
Gloucester Dr N4...6 A2
Gloucester Gate
NW1.................82 A2
Gloucester Gate
Mews NW1.........82 A2
Gloucester Gdns
 Golders Green
 NW11...............1 B4
 Paddington W2 ..100 C2
Gloucester Ho
 Kilburn NW6.......23 C3
 Richmond TW10 ...54 C2
Gloucester Mews
W2.................101 A1
Gloucester Mews W
W2.................101 A1
Gloucester Pk
SW7................142 C4
Gloucester Pl W1 .103 B4
Gloucester Pl Mews
W1.................103 B3
Gloucester Prim Sch
SE15................49 A3
Gloucester Rd
 Acton W3...........37 B4
 South Hampstead
 SW7................142 C4
Gloucester Road Sta
6 SW7..............142 C4
Gloucester Sq
 6 Hackney E2.....24 C4
 Paddington W2 ..102 A1
Gloucester St
SW1................146 C2
Gloucester Terr
W2.................101 A1
Gloucester Way
EC1..................95 C3
Gloucester Wlk
W8.................127 C4
Glover Ho
 London SE15......65 A3
 2 South Hampstead
 NW6................11 B1
Glycena Rd SW11 ..60 B4
Glyn Ct SE27......74 C1
Glynde Mews
SW3................130 B1
Glynde Reach WC1 .94 B3
Glynde St SE4.....66 B1
Glynfield Rd NW10 ..8 A1
Glyn Mans W14 ..140 B4
Glyn Rd E5..........17 C4
Glyn St SE11......148 C1
Goater's Alley
SW6................155 A1
Goat Wharf TW8...44 A4
Godalming Rd E14..34 A4
Goddard Ho SW19 .69 C2
Godfrey Ho EC1 ...97 B3
Godfrey St
 Chelsea SW3 ....144 B2
 Mill Meads E15....27 B3
Goding St SE11 ..148 B1

Godley Rd SW18...71 C3
Godliman St EC4 .122 C4
Godman Rd SE15..50 A1
Godolphin Ho
 Primrose Hill NW3 ..12 A1
 7 Streatham SW2 ..74 C3
Godolphin & Latymer
 Sch 10 W6.........39 A2
Godolphin Pl W3 ..28 C2
Godolphin Rd
W12..................39 A4
Godson St N1......85 B2
Godstone Ct 1 N16..7 A3
Godwin Ho SE1 ..137 C2
Godwin Cl N1......87 A2
Godwin Ct NW1 ...83 A2
Godwin Ho
 2 Haggerston E2 ..24 B3
 Kilburn NW6.......78 A2
Goffers Ho SE3....53 A1
Goffers Rd SE3,
SE13.................53 A1
Goffton Ho 14
SW9................173 A1
Golborne Gdns
 5 Kensal Town
 W10................23 A1
 West Kilburn W10 ..23 B1
Golborne Mews 9
W10..................31 A4
Golborne Rd W10...31 A4
Golden Cross Mews
2 W11..............31 B3
Golden Hinde The★
SE1................123 B2
Golden La EC1....97 A1
Golden Lane Campus
EC1..................96 C1
Golden Lane L Ctr
EC1..................96 C1
Golden Plover Cl 8
E16..................35 C3
Golden Sq W1.....119 A4
Golders Ct NW11 ...1 B4
Golders Gdns NW11 .1 B4
GOLDERS GREEN ..1 C4
Golders Green Coll
NW11.................1 C3
Golders Green Cres
NW11.................1 C3
Golders Green Rd
NW11.................1 A4
Golders Green Sta
NW11.................1 C3
Golders Hill Sch
NW11.................1 C4
Golderslea NW11 ...1 C3
Golders Park Cl
NW11.................1 C3
Golders Way NW11..1 B4
Goldhawk Ind Est
W6...................39 A3
Goldhawk Mews 2
W12..................39 A4
Goldhawk Rd W12 .38 C3
Goldhawk Road Sta
W12..................39 B4
Goldhurst Terr
NW6..................11 B1
Goldie Ho N19......4 C4
Golding St E1.....111 C1
Goldington Cres
NW1..................83 B2

Goldington Ct
NW1..................83 B3
Goldington St
NW1..................83 B2
Goldman Cl
E2...................24 C1 99 B2
Goldney Rd W9....23 C1
Goldsboro Rd
SW8................161 C1
Goldsborough Ho
SW8................171 C3
Goldsmith Ave W3.28 C2
Goldsmith Cl
WC1.................106 B2
Goldsmith Ho W3 .28 C2
Goldsmith Rd
 Acton W3...........28 C1
 Peckham SE15.....49 C2
Goldsmiths Bldgs
W3...................28 C1
Goldsmiths Coll, Univ
 of London SE14 ..51 A2
Goldsmith's Pl 6
NW6..................78 A3
Goldsmith's Row
E2...................24 C3
Goldsmith's Sq 17
E2...................24 C3
Goldsmith St EC2 .109 A2
Goldthorpe NW1...82 C3
Goldwell Ho SE22 .64 A3
Goldwin Cl SE14...50 B2
Goldwing Cl E16....35 C3
Gomm Rd SE16....40 B3
Gondar Gdns NW6 .10 B3
Gondar Mans NW6 .10 B3
Gonson St SE8.....52 A4
Gonston Cl SW19 ..70 A2
Gonville Ho 6
SW15................57 C1
Gonville St SW6 ...47 C4
Gooch Ho EC1 ...107 B4
Goodall Ho 10 SE4.65 C3
Goodenough Coll
WC1..................94 C2
Goodfaith Ho 18
E14..................34 A2
Goodge Pl W1 ...105 A3
Goodge St W1 ...105 B3
Goodge Street Sta
W1..................105 B4
Goodhall St NW10 .21 B2
Good Hart Pl E14 ..33 A2
Goodhope Ho 17
E14..................34 A2
Goodinge Cl N7 ...14 A2
Goodinge Rd N7 ..14 A2
Goodman Cres
SW2..................73 C2
Goodman's Stile 1
E1...................111 B2
Goodman's Yd E1,
EC3.................124 C4
Goodrich Ct 9
W10..................30 C3
Goodrich Ho
 20 Bethnal Green
 E2...................25 B3
 Stamford Hill N16....7 A4
Goodrich Rd SE22 .64 C1
Good Shepherd RC
 Prim Sch The
 W12..................38 B4

Goodson Rd NW10 ..8 A1
Goodspeed Ho 20
E14..................34 A2
Goodsway NW1ᴺ ..84 A2
Goodway Gdns
E14..................34 C3
Goodwill Ho 22
E14..................34 A2
Goodwin Cl SE16 .139 A1
Goodwin Ho 2
SE15.................65 A4
Goodwins Ct WC2 .120 A4
Goodwin St N4......5 C2
Goodwood Cl W1 .104 B4
Goodwood Ho 3
W4...................37 B1
Goodwood Mans 3
SW9..................62 C4
Goodwood Rd
SE14.................51 A3
Goose Green Prim
 Sch SE22...........64 B3
Goose Green Trad Est
SE22.................64 C3
Gophir La EC4 ....123 B4
Gopsall St N1......87 C3
Gordon Ave SW14 .56 A3
Gordonbrook Prim
 Sch SE4.............66 A3
Gordonbrook Rd
SE4..................66 C2
Gordon Ct 5 W12 .30 B3
Gordon Gr SE5....48 A1
Gordon Ho 7 E1 ..32 B2
Gordon Hospl
SW1................147 B3
Gordon House Rd
NW5..................12 C4
Gordon Mans WC1 .93 B1
Gordon Pl W8 ....127 C4
Gordon Rd
 Chiswick W4.......45 A4
 Leyton E15..........19 B4
 Peckham SE15.....50 A1
 Richmond TW9......44 B1
Gordon Sq WC1...93 C2
Gordon St WC1....93 B2
Gorefield Ho NW6 .23 C3
Gorefield Pl NW6 ..23 C3
Gore Rd E9..........25 B4
Gore St SW7 .....129 A2
Gorham Ho 2
SW4..................61 B1
Gorham Pl
W11.................31 A2 112 A3
Goring St EC3 ....110 B2
Gorleston St W14 .140 B4
Gorse Cl E16.......35 C3
Gorsefield Ho 6
E14..................33 C2
Gorst Rd
 London SW11......60 B1
 North Acton NW10 .20 C1
Gorsuch Pl 1
E2...................24 B2 98 C4
Gorsuch St
E2...................24 B2 98 C4
Gosberton Rd
SW12.................72 C3
Gosfield St W1....104 C3
Gosford Ho 2ᴱ3 E3..26 B3
Goslett Yd WC2...105 C1

Gosling Ho 2 E1 . . . . 32 B2
Gosling Way SW9 . . 173 B4
Gospatric Home Ho
SW14 . . . . .56 A4
GOSPEL OAK 12 C4
Gospel Oak Prim Sch
NW5 . . . . .12 C4
Gospel Oak Sta
NW5 . . . . .12 C4
Gosport Ho 9
SW15 . . . . .68 C3
Gosset St E2 . . . . 24 C2 99 B4
Gosterwood St
SE8 . . . . .51 A4
Goswell Pl EC1 . . . . . 96 B3
Goswell Rd EC1 . . . . 96 B4
Gothic Ct 17 SE5 . . . 48 B3
Gottfried Mews
NW5 . . . . .13 B4
Gough Ho N1 . . . . . . 86 B4
Gough Sq EC4 . . . . . 107 C2
Gough St WC1 . . . . . 95 A1
Goulden Ho SW11 . . 168 A2
Gouldman Ho 33
E1 . . . . .25 B1
Gould Terr 2 E8 . . . . 17 A3
Goulston St E1 . . . . . 110 C2
Goulton Rd E5 . . . . . 17 A4
Govan St E2 . . . . 24 C4
Gover Ct 8 SW4 . . . 172 B2
Gowan Ave SW6 . . . 164 A4
Gowan Ho 2
E2 . . . . 24 B2 99 A3
Gower Cl SW4 . . . . . . 61 B1
Gower Ct WC1 . . . . . 93 B2
Gower Ho SE17 . . . . 151 A2
Gower Mews
WC1 . . . . 105 C4
Gower Pl NW1,
WC1 . . . . 93 B2
Gower Sch The 4
N7 . . . . .14 A2
Gower St WC1 . . . . . . 93 B1
Gower's Wlk E1 . . . . 111 B1
Gowrie Rd SW11 . . . .60 C4
Gracechurch St EC2,
EC4 . . . . 123 C4
Gracefield Gdns
SW16 . . . . .74 A1
Gracehill 2 E1 . . . . . .32 B4
Grace Ho SE11 . . . . 162 C4
Grace Jones Cl E8 . . 16 C2
Graces Mews NW8 . . 79 A1
Grace's Mews SE5 . . 49 A1
Grace's Rd SE5 . . . . . 49 A1
Grace St E3 . . . . .27 A2
Graemesdyke Ave
SW14 . . . . .55 A3
Grafton Cres NW1 . . 13 A2
Grafton Ct 10 E8 . . . 16 C3
Grafton Ho
10 Bow E3 . . . . 26 C2
2 Deptford SE8 . . . . 41 B1
Grafton Mans SW4 . . 61 B3
Grafton Mews W1 . . 92 C1
Grafton Prim Sch 5
N7 . . . . .5 B1
Grafton Rd
Acton W3 . . . . 28 B2
Gospel Oak NW5 . . . 12 C3
Grafton Sq SW4 . . . . 61 B4

Grafton St W1 . . . . . 118 B3
Grafton Terr NW5 . . . 12 C3
Grafton Way W1 . . . . 93 A1
Grafton Yd NW5 . . . . 13 A2
Graham Ct 5
SE14 . . . . .50 C4
Graham Ho
5 Balham SW12 . . . .73 A4
6 Tufnell Pk N19 . . . 13 C3
Graham Mans 2
E8 . . . . .17 A2
Graham Rd
Acton W4 . . . . 37 C3
Dalston E8 . . . . 16 C2
Graham St N1 . . . . . . 86 B1
Graham Terr SW1 . . 145 C3
Graham Twr W3 . . . . 37 A3
Grainger Ct 2
SE5 . . . . .48 B3
Grampian Gdns
NW2 . . . . .1 A3
Grampians The 10
W14 . . . . .39 C4
Granard Ave SW15 . . 57 A2
Granard Ho 20 E9 . . . 17 C2
Granard Prim Sch
SW15 . . . . .57 A1
Granard Rd SW11,
SW12 . . . . .72 B4
Granary Rd E1 . . . . . . 25 A1
Granary Sq N1 . . . . . 14 C2
Granary St NW1 . . . . 83 B3
Granary The SE8 . . . . 51 C3
Granby Pl SE1 . . . . . 135 B3
Granby St
Bethnal Green
E2 . . . . 24 C1 99 B2
Shoreditch
E2 . . . . 24 B1 99 A2
Granby Terr NW1 . . . 82 C1
Grand Ave EC1 . . . . 108 B4
Grandfield Ct W4 . . . 45 C4
Grandison Rd
SW11 . . . . .60 B2
Grand Junction Wharf
N1 . . . . .86 C1
Grand Par SW14 . . . . 55 B3
Grand Union Cl
W9 . . . . .31 B4
Grand Union Cres
E8 . . . . .24 C4
Grand Union Ind Est
NW10 . . . . .20 A3
Grand Vitesse Ind Est
SE1 . . . . 122 B1
Granfield St
SW11 . . . . 167 C3
Grangecourt Rd
N16 . . . . .7 A3
Grange Ct
Peckham SE15 . . . . . 49 B1
Strand WC2 . . . . 107 A1
1 Willesden NW10 . . .8 A4
Grangefield NW1 . . . 14 A1
Grange Gdns NW3 . . .2 A1
Grange Gr N1 . . . . . . 15 B2
Grange Ho
Bermondsey SE1 . . . 138 C1
Willesden NW10 . . . . .8 C1
Grange La SE21 . . . . . 76 B2
Grangemill 11
NW5 . . . . .13 A4
GRANGE MILLS 73 B3
Grange Mills
SW12 . . . . .73 B3
Grange Pl NW6 . . . . . 10 C1

Grange Prim Sch
SE1 . . . . 138 A1
Grange Rd
Barnes SW13 . . . . . . 46 C2
Bermondsey SE1 . . . 138 C1
Gunnersbury W4 . . . 37 A1
Willesden NW10 . . . . .9 A2
Grange St N1 . . . . . . 87 C3
Grange The
Bermondsey SE1 . . . 138 C1
7 Gunnersbury W4 . 37 A1
Hammersmith W12 . 39 A3
10 Maitland Pk
NW3 . . . . 12 B2
South Acton W3 . . . . 37 A4
West Kensington
W14 . . . . 140 C3
Grangeway NW6 . . . . 10 C1
Grange Wlk SE1 . . . 138 C1
Grange Yd SE1 . . . . . 138 C1
Granite Apts E15 . . . 19 C2
Grannary The
SE16 . . . . .40 B4
Gransden Ave E8 . . . 17 A1
Gransden Ho 1
SE8 . . . . .41 B1
Gransden Rd W12 . . . 38 B4
Grantbridge St N1 . . 86 B2
Grantham Ct 7
SE16 . . . . .40 C4
Grantham Ho 12
SE15 . . . . .49 C4
Grantham Pl W1 . . . 118 A1
Grantham Rd
Chiswick W4 . . . . 46 A3
South Lambeth
SW9 . . . . 172 B1
Grantley Ho
2 Deptford SE14 . . . 50 C4
5 Putney SW19 . . . . 69 C3
Grantully Rd W9 . . . . 88 A3
Granville Ct
8 Deptford SE14 . . . 51 A3
Shoreditch N1 . . . . . 87 C4
Granville Gr SE13 . . . 67 B4
Granville Ho 10
E14 . . . . 33 C3
Granville Ind Est
NW2 . . . . .1 B2
Granville Mans 8
W12 . . . . .39 B4
Granville Pk SE13 . . .67 C4
Granville Pl
Marylebone W1 . . . . 103 B1
Walham Green
SW6 . . . . 156 A1
Granville Point
NW2 . . . . .1 B2
Granville Rd
Child's Hill NW2 . . . . .1 B2
Kilburn NW6 . . . . 23 C3
Wandsworth SW18 . . 70 B4
Granville Sq
3 Camberwell
SE15 . . . . .49 A3
Finsbury WC1 . . . . . . 95 A3
Granville St WC1 . . . 95 A3

Grape St WC2 . . . . . 106 A2
Grasgarth Cl SW3 . . . 28 B2
Grasmere NW1 . . . . . 92 B3
Grasmere Ave W3 . . . 28 C2
Grasmere Ct
SW13 . . . . .46 C4
Grasmere Ho 20
N16 . . . . .15 C4
Grasmere Point 2
SE15 . . . . .50 B3
Grasmere Rd
N16 . . . . .15 C4
Grateley Ho 10
SW15 . . . . .69 A3
Gratton Rd W14 . . . 126 A1
Graveley Ho 7
SE8 . . . . .41 A2
Gravel La E1 . . . . . . 110 C2
Gravesend Rd
W12 . . . . .29 C2
Grayfriars Pas
EC1 . . . . 108 B2
Gray Ho SE17 . . . . . 151 A2
Grayland Ct WC1 . . . 94 C3
Grayling Rd N16 . . . . .6 C2
Grayling Sq
E2 . . . . 24 C2 99 C4
Grayshott Rd
SW11 . . . . .60 C4
Gray's Inn PI WC1 . . 107 A3
Gray's Inn Rd WC1 . . 95 A2
Gray's Inn Sq
WC1 . . . . 107 A4
Grayson Ho EC1 . . . . 97 A3
Gray St SE1 . . . . 135 C3
Grayswood Point 14
SW15 . . . . .68 C3
Gray's Yd W1 . . . . . . 103 C2
Grazebrook Rd N16 . . 6 C2
Great Arthur Ho
EC1 . . . . 96 C1
Great Bell Alley
EC2 . . . . 109 B2
Great Castle St
W1 . . . . 104 C2
Great Central St
NW1 . . . . 102 C4
Great Chapel St
W1 . . . . 105 B2
Great Chart St
SW11 . . . . .59 B3
Great Chertsey Rd
SW14,W4 . . . . 45 C2
Great Church La
W6 . . . . .39 C1
Great College St
SW1 . . . . 134 A2
Great Croft WC1 . . . . 94 B3
Great Cross Ave
SE3 . . . . .53 A3
Great Cumberland
Mews W1 . . . . 102 C1
Great Cumberland PI
W1 . . . . 103 A1
Great Dover St
SE1 . . . . 137 B2
Great Eastern Bldgs
10 E8 . . . . 17 A2
Great Eastern Ent Ctr
E14 . . . . .42 A4
Great Eastern Pier
E14 . . . . .41 C1
Great Eastern Rd
E15 . . . . 19 C2

Great Eastern St
EC2 . . . . 24 A1 98 A2
Great Eastern Wharf
SW11 . . . . 158 C2
Great Field 7
NW5 . . . . .13 B3
Greatfield Cl
London SE6 . . . . 66 C3
4 Tufnell Pk N19 . . . 13 B4
Great George St
SW1 . . . . 134 A3
Great Guildford Bsns
Sq SE1 . . . . 122 C1
Great Guildford St
SE1 . . . . 122 C1
Greatham Wlk 8
SW15 . . . . .68 C3
Great James St
WC1 . . . . 106 C4
Great Marlborough St
W1 . . . . 104 C1
Great Maze Pond
SE1 . . . . 137 C4
Great Newport St
WC2 . . . . 120 A4
Greatorex Ho 11
E1 . . . . 111 B4
Greatorex St E1 . . . . 111 B4
Great Ormond St
Hospl for Children
WC1 . . . . 94 C1
Great Ormond St
WC1 . . . . 94 C1
Great Percy St
WC1 . . . . 95 B4
Great Peter St
SW1 . . . . 133 C1
Great Portland St
W1 . . . . 104 B4
Great Portland Street
Sta W1 . . . . 92 B1
Great Pulteney St
W1 . . . . 119 A4
Great Queen St
WC2 . . . . 106 B2
Great Russell Mans
WC1 . . . . 106 A3
Great Russell St
WC1 . . . . 106 A3
Great St Helen's
EC3 . . . . 110 A2
Great St Thomas
Apostle EC4 . . . . 123 A4
Great Scotland Yd
SW1,WC2 . . . . 120 A2
Great Smith St
SW1 . . . . 133 C2
Great Spilmans
SE22 . . . . .64 A2
Great Suffolk St
SE1 . . . . 122 B1
Great Sutton St
EC1 . . . . 96 B1
Great Swan Alley
EC2 . . . . 109 B2
Great Titchfield St
W1 . . . . 104 C3
Great Tower St
EC3 . . . . 124 A4
Great Trinity La
EC4 . . . . 123 A4
Great Turnstile
WC2 . . . . 107 A3

Great Western Rd W2,
W9 .... 31 B4
Great West Rd W4,
W6 .... 45 C4
**Great West Road
Cedars Rd** W4 ...... 45 B4
**Great West Road
Hogarth La** W4 .... 46 A4
Great Winchester St
EC2 .... 109 C2
Great Windmill St
W1 .... 119 B4
Great Yd SE1 ...... 138 B4
Greaves Cotts 16
E14 .... 33 A4
Greaves Twr
SW10 .... 157 A2
Grebe Ct 18 E14 ... 42 B4
Greek Ct W1 ...... 105 C1
Greek Sch of London
W3 .... 28 A2
Greek St W1 ...... 105 C1
Greenacre Ct E8 ... 16 C3
Greenacre Sq 23
SE16 .... 40 C4
Green Arbour Ct
EC1 .... 108 A2
Greenaway Gdns
NW3 .... 11 A4
Greenaway Ho
Finsbury WC1 .... 95 B3
St John's Wood
NW8 .... 78 C4
Green Bank E1 ..... 32 A1
Greenberry St
NW8 .... 80 A1
Green Cl NW11 ...... 2 B4
Greencoat Pl
SW1 .... 147 A4
Greencoat Row
SW1 .... 133 A1
Greencourt Ho 23
E1 .... 25 C1
Greencroft Gdns
NW6 .... 11 B1
Green Ct 2 NW10 .... 8 A4
Green Dale SE22 ... 64 A2
Greendale Cl SE22 .. 64 A2
Green Dragon Ct
SE1 .... 123 B1
Green Dragon Ho
WC1 .... 106 B2
Green Dragon La
TW8 .... 36 B1
*Green Dragon Prim
Sch* TW8 .... 44 A4
Green Dragon Yd 24
E1 .... 111 B3
Greene Ct 20 SE14 . 50 C4
Greene Ho SE1 ... 137 B1
Greenend Rd W4 ... 38 A4
Green Ho 3
SW4 .... 61 C4
Greenfell Mans
SE8 .... 52 A4
Greenfield Gdns
NW2 .... 1 A1
Greenfield Ho 28
SW19 .... 69 C3
Greenfield Rd E1 . 111 C2
Greenham Cl SE1 . 135 B3
Greenham Ho 5
E9 .... 25 B4

Greenheath Bsns Ctr
3 E2 .... 25 A1
Greenhill NW3 .... 11 C4
Greenhill Pk
NW10 .... 21 A4
Greenhill Rd
NW10 .... 21 A4
Greenhill's Rents
EC1 .... 108 A4
Greenhills Terr 15
N1 .... 15 C2
Green Ho The 5
SW19 .... 70 A3
Green Hundred Rd
SE15 .... 49 C4
Greening Ho SE13 . 67 C3
Greenland Ho
Bermondsey SE8 .. 40 C1
4 *Mile End* E1 ...... 26 A1
Greenland Mews
SE8 .... 40 C1
Greenland Pl NW1 . 82 B4
Greenland Quay
SE16 .... 40 C2
Greenland Rd
NW1 .... 82 C4
Greenland St NW1 . 82 B4
Green Lanes N4, N8,
N15 .... 6 A4
Greenleaf Cl 8
SW2 .... 74 C4
Green Link Wlk
TW9 .... 45 A2
Greenman St N1 ... 86 C4
Greenock Rd 11
W3 .... 37 B3
Green Park SW1,
W1 .... 132 B4
Green Park Sta
W1 .... 118 C2
Greenroof Way
SE10 .... 43 B3
Greens Ct W1 .... 119 B4
Green's Ct
W11 .... 31 B1 112 C1
Greenside Prim Sch
W12 .... 38 C4
Greenside Rd W12 . 38 C4
Greenstead Gdns
SW15 .... 57 A2
Greenstreet Hill
SE4 .... 65 C4
Greensward Ho
SW6 .... 166 C2
Green Terr EC1 .... 95 C3
Green The W3 ..... 29 A3
Greenview Cl W3 .. 29 A1
Greenview Ct
East Dulwich SE22 . 64 C3
Wandsworth SW18 . 72 A4
Greenway Cl N4 .... 6 B2
Greenwell St W1 .. 92 B1
GREENWICH 43 C3
Greenwich Acad
SE10 .... 52 A2
Greenwich Bsns Ctr
SE10 .... 52 B3
Greenwich Bsns Pk
SE10 .... 52 B3
Greenwich Church St
SE10 .... 52 B4
Greenwich Coll 17
SE10 .... 52 B3

Greenwich Ct 11
E1 .... 32 A3
Greenwich High Rd
SE10 .... 52 A3
Greenwich Ho
SE13 .... 67 C1
Greenwich Ind Est
SE10 .... 52 A3
Greenwich Mkt 2
SE10 .... 52 B4
Greenwich Park St
SE10 .... 53 A3
Greenwich Park St
SE10 .... 52 C4
Greenwich Quay
SE8 .... 52 A4
Greenwich South St
SE10 .... 52 B2
Greenwich Sta
SE10 .... 52 A3
Greenwich View Pl
E14 .... 42 A3
Green Wlk SE1 ... 138 A1
Greenwood 8
SW19 .... 69 C4
Greenwood Ho
Finsbury WC1 ..... 95 B3
8 *Nunhead* SE4 ... 65 C3
Greenwood Pl
NW5 .... 13 A3
Greenwood Rd E8 . 16 C2
Greenwood Terr
NW10 .... 20 C3
Green Yd WC1 ..... 95 A2
Greet Ho SE1 .... 135 C3
Greet St SE1 ..... 121 C1
Gregor Mews SE3 . 53 C3
Gregory Ho M8 . 128 A4
Grenada Ho 18
E14 .... 33 B2
Grenade St E14 .... 33 B2
Grena Gdns TW9 ... 54 B3
Grena Rd TW10,
TW9 .... 54 B3
Grendon Ho
22 *Hackney* E9 .... 17 B1
Pentonville N1 .... 84 C1
Grendon St NW8 ... 90 A2
Grenfell Ho SE5 ... 48 B3
Grenfell Rd W11 ... 30 C2
Grenfell Twr 5
W11 .... 30 C2
Grenfell Wlk 4
W11 .... 30 C2
Grenier Apartments
1 SE15 .... 50 A3
Grenville Ho
2 *Bow* E3 .... 26 A3
4 *Deptford* SE8 .... 51 C4
Grenville Lo N6 .... 4 B4
Grenville Mans
WC1 .... 94 A2
Grenville Mews
SW7 .... 142 C3
Grenville Pl SW7 . 142 C4
Grenville Rd N19 ... 5 A3
Gresham Almshouses
3 SW9 .... 62 B3
Gresham Coll EC1 107 C3
Gresham Gdns
NW11 .... 1 A3
Gresham Pl 2 N19 .. 4 C2

Gresham Rd SW9 .. 62 C4
Gresham St EC2 .. 109 A2
Gresham Way
SW19 .... 70 C1
Gresham Way Est
SW19 .... 71 A1
Gresley Ho SW8 . 171 C4
Gresley Rd N19 .... 4 B4
Gressenhall Rd
SW18 .... 70 B4
Gresse St W1 .... 105 B2
Greswell St SW6 .. 47 C2
Greta Ho SE3 ..... 53 B4
Greville Hall NW6 . 78 B2
Greville Ho
Knightsbridge
SW1 .... 131 B2
Putney SW15 .... 58 A2
Greville Lo 2 W2 . 100 A2
Greville Mews 5
NW6 .... 78 A3
Greville Pl NW6 ... 78 B2
Greville Rd
Kilburn NW6 .... 78 B2
Richmond TW10 .... 54 B1
Greville St EC1 .. 107 C4
**Grey Coat Hospital
The**
SW1 .... 147 B3
SW1 .... 133 B1
Greycoat Pl SW1 . 133 B1
Greycoat St SW1 . 133 B1
Grey Eagle St
E1 .... 24 B1 99 A1
Greyfriars 8 SE26 . 76 C1
Greyfriars Ho SE3 . 53 B4
Grey Ho 27 W12 ... 30 A2
Greyhound Ct
WC2 .... 121 B4
Greyhound Rd
College Pk NW10 .. 22 A2
Fulham W6 .... 154 A4
Greyladies Gdns
SE10 .... 52 B1
Greystoke Ho
SE15 .... 49 C4
Greystoke Pl EC4 107 C2
Grey Turner Ho
W12 .... 29 C3
Griffon Ho 3
SW11 .... 60 A4
Grigg's Pl SE1 .... 138 B1
Grimaldi Ho N1 ... 84 C2
Grimsby St
8 *Bethnal Green*
E2 .... 24 C1 99 A2
Shoreditch
E2 .... 24 B1 99 A2
Grimsel Path SE5 . 48 A3
Grimshaw Cl N6 .... 3 C4
Grimston Rd SW6 152 A1
Grinthorpe Ho
EC1 .... 96 A2
Grindal Cl SE15 ... 65 B4
Grindall Ho 28 E1 . 25 A1

Grindal St SE1 .... 135 B3
Grindley Ho 3
E3 .... 33 B4
*Grinling Gibbons Prim
Sch* 32 SE8 .... 51 B4
Grinling Pl SE8 .... 51 C4
Grinstead Rd SE8 . 41 A1
Grisedale NW1 ..... 92 C4
Grittleton Rd W9 .. 23 C1
Groombridge Rd
E9 .... 17 C1
Groom Cres SW18 . 71 C4
Groome Ho SE11 . 149 A3
Groom Pl SW1 ... 131 C2
Grosse Way SW15 . 57 A1
Grosvenor Ave
Canonbury N5 ...... 15 B3
Mortlake SW14 .... 56 A4
Richmond TW10 ... 54 A2
Grosvenor Bridge
SW1 .... 160 B3
Grosvenor Cotts
SW1 .... 145 A4
**Grosvenor Court
Mans** W2 .... 102 C1
Grosvenor Cres
SW1 .... 131 C3
Grosvenor Cres Mews
SW1 .... 131 B3
Grosvenor Ct
Brondesbury Pk
NW6 .... 22 C4
Gunnersbury W4 ... 37 A1
22 *Poplar* E14 ..... 33 A3
Putney SW15 ...... 58 A2
Grosvenor Gdns
Cricklewood NW2 ... 9 C3
Mortlake SW14 .... 56 A4
Westminster SW1 132 B1
Grosvenor Gdns Mews
E SW1 .... 132 A1
Grosvenor Gdns Mews
N SW1 .... 132 A1
Grosvenor Gdns Mews
S SW1 .... 132 B1
Grosvenor Hill
W1 .... 118 A4
Grosvenor Hill Ct
W1 .... 118 A4
Grosvenor Ho E5 ... 7 C3
Grosvenor Park
SE5 .... 48 B3
Grosvenor Pier
SW1 .... 161 B4
Grosvenor Pl
SW1 .... 132 A3
Grosvenor Rd
Acton Green W4 ... 37 B1
Pimlico SW1 .... 161 A4
Richmond TW10 .... 54 A2
Grosvenor Residences
1 W14 .... 39 C3
Grosvenor Sq W1 117 C4
Grosvenor St W1 . 118 A4
Grosvenor The
NW11 .... 2 A4
Grosvenor Wharf Rd
E14 .... 42 C2
Grote's Bldgs SE3 . 53 A1
Grote's Pl SE3 ..... 53 A1
Groton Rd SW18 ... 71 A2
Grotto Ct SE1 .... 136 C4
Grotto Pas W1 ... 103 B4

Grove Crescent Rd
E15 . . . . .19 C2
Grove Ct
Camberwell SE5 . . . . .49 A1
Clapham SW4 . . . . . .61 B4
South Kensington
SW10 . . . . .143 A1
St John's Wood
NW8 . . . . .89 B4
Grovedale Rd N19 . . . .4 C2
Grove Dwellings
E1 . . . . .32 B4
Grove End NW5 . . . . . .13 A4
Grove End Gdns
NW8 . . . . .79 A1
Grove End Ho
NW8 . . . . .89 B3
Grove End Rd NW8 . . .89 B3
Grove Gdns NW8 . . . .90 B3
Grove Hall Ct
Bow E3 . . . . .26 C3
St John's Wood
NW8 . . . . .89 A4
Grove Hill Rd SE5 . . . .64 A4
Grove Ho
Blackheath SE3 . . . . .53 B1
Chelsea SW3 . . . . . .158 B4
Go La SE5 . . . . .64 A4
Groveland Ct EC4 . . .109 A1
Grovelands Cl SE5 . . .49 A1
Grove Lane Terr
SE5 . . . . .64 A4
Groveley Ho N4 . . . . . .6 B4
Grove Lo SW4 . . . . . . .61 B3
Grove Mans
London SW4 . . . . . . .60 B3
2 Shepherd's Bush
W6 . . . . .39 B4
3 Stamford Hill N16 . .7 C3
Grove Mews W6 . . . . .39 B3
GROVE PARK W4 . . . .45 B2
Grove Park Bridge
W4 . . . . .45 B3
Grove Park Gdns
W4 . . . . .45 A3
Grove Park Mews
W4 . . . . .45 B3
Grove Park Prim Sch
W4 . . . . .45 B3
Grove Park Rd W4 . . .45 A3
Grove Park Terr
W4 . . . . .45 A4
Grove Pk SE5 . . . . .49 A1
Grove Pl
Acton W3 . . . . .28 B1
Balham SW12 . . . . . .61 A1
Hampstead NW3 . . . . .2 C1
Grover Ct SE13 . . . . . .52 A1
Grover Ho
4 London SW4 . . . . .61 B2
Vauxhall SE11 . . . . .149 A1
Groveside Ct
SW11 . . . . .167 B2
Grove St SE8 . . . . .41 B1
Grove Terr NW5 . . . . .13 A4
Grove Terrace Mews
NW5 . . . . .4 A1
Grove The
Dulwich SE21 . . . . . .76 C3
Hendon NW11 . . . . . . .1 A4

Grove The continued
Highgate N6 . . . . .3 C3
Stroud Green N4 . . . . .5 B4
Grove Vale SE22 . . . . .64 B3
Groveway SW9 . . . . .173 A3
Grovewood
TW9 . . . . .44 C2
Grovewood Ho
NW2 . . . . .1 B2
Grummant Rd
SE15 . . . . .49 B2
Grundy St E14 . . . . . . .34 A3
Guardian Angels RC
Prim Sch **3** E3 . . . .26 A2
Guards Mus The★
SW1 . . . . .133 A3
Gubyon Ave SE24 . . . .63 A2
Guilden Dr E5 . . . . . . .17 A4
Guerin Sq E3 . . . . .26 B2
Guernsey Gr SE24 . . . .75 B4
Guernsey Ho
N1 . . . . .15 B2
Guernsey Rd 11
N1 . . . . .15 B2
Guildford Gr SE10 . . . .52 A2
Guildford Ho 8
SE5 . . . . .48 B1
Guildford Rd SW8 . . .172 B4
Guildhall Art Gall★
EC2 . . . . .109 A2
Guildhall Ho EC2 . . . .109 B2
Guildhall Sch Music &
Drama EC2 . . . . . .109 A4
Guildhall Yd EC2 . . . .109 A2
Guildhouse St
SW1 . . . . .146 C3
Guilford Pl WC1 . . . . . .94 C1
Guilford St WC1 . . . . .94 B1
Guillemot Ct 20
SE8 . . . . .51 B4
Guinness Cl E9 . . . . . .18 A1
Guinness Ct
Chelsea SW3 . . . . . .144 C3
Finsbury EC1 . . . . . . .97 A3
Primrose Hill NW8 . . .80 B3
Whitechapel E1 . . . . .111 A1
Guinness Sq SE1 . . . .152 A4
Guinness Trust Bldgs
Bermondsey SE1 . . . .138 A4
7 Bethnal Green
E2 . . . . .24 C3
Chelsea SW3 . . . . . .144 C3
Hammersmith W6 . . . .39 B1
Kennington SE11 . . . .150 A2
Guion Rd SW6 . . . . . .165 A2
Gujarat Ho 11 N16 . . . .7 A1
Gulland Wlk 21 N1 . . .15 B2
Gullane Ho 24 E3 . . . . .26 B3
Gulliver St SE16 . . . . . .41 B3
Gulston Wlk SW3 . . . .145 A3
Gunmakers La E3 . . . . .26 A4
GUNNERSBURY 37 A2
Gunnersbury Avenue
(North Circular Rd)
W3 . . . . .36 C3
Gunnersbury Cl **8**
W4 . . . . .37 A1
Gunnersbury Cres
W3 . . . . .36 C4
Gunnersbury Ct 9
W3 . . . . .37 A4
Gunnersbury Dr
W5 . . . . .36 B4
Gunnersbury Gdns
W3 . . . . .36 C4

Gunnersbury La
W3 . . . . .36 C4
Gunnersbury Mews 6
W4 . . . . .37 A1
Gunnersbury Park
W3 . . . . .36 C3
Gunnersbury Park
Mus★ W3 . . . . .36 C3
Gunnersbury Sta
W4 . . . . .37 A1
Gunnersbury Triangle
Nat Res★ W12 . . . . .37 B2
Gunners Rd SW18 . . . .71 C2
Gunpowder Sq
EC4 . . . . .107 C2
Gun St E1 . . . . .110 C3
Gunstor Rd N16 . . . . . .16 A4
Gunter Gr SW6 . . . . . .156 C2
Gunterstone Rd
W14 . . . . .140 B2
Gunthorpe St E1 . . . . .111 A2
Gunwhale Cl SE16 . . . .32 C1
Gun Wharf
Old Ford E3 . . . . .26 A4
Wapping E1 . . . . . . .125 B2
Gurdon Ho 7 E14 . . . . .33 C3
Gurdon Rd SE7 . . . . . .43 C1
Gurney Ho
1 Bayswater W2 . . .100 A2
14 Bethnal Green
E2 . . . . .24 C3
Gurney Rd SW6 . . . . . .59 B4
Guthrie Ct SE1 . . . . . .135 C3
Guthrie St SW3 . . . . . .144 A2
Gutter La EC2 . . . . . . .108 C2
Guyscliff Rd SE13 . . . . .67 B2
Guy's Hospl SE1 . . . . .137 C4
Guy's Sq SE1 . . . . . . .137 C4
Gwalior Rd SW15 . . . . .57 C4
Gwendolen Ave
SW15 . . . . .57 C2
Gwendolen Cl
SW15 . . . . .57 C2
Gwendwr Rd W14 . . . .140 B2
Gwent Ct 18 SE16 . . . . .32 C1
Gwilym Maries Ho 11
E2 . . . . .25 A2
Gwyn Cl SW6 . . . . . . .156 C1
Gwynne Cl W4 . . . . . . .46 B4
Gwynne Ho
Finsbury WC1 . . . . . . .95 B3
6 Streatham SW2 . . .74 B3
Whitechapel E1 . . . . . .32 A4
Gwynne Pl WC1 . . . . . .95 A3
Gwynne Rd SW11 . . . .167 C2
Gye Ho 2 SW4 . . . . . . .62 A3
Gylcote Cl SE5 . . . . . . .63 C3

H

Haarlem Rd 12
W14 . . . . .39 C3
Haberdasher Pl 4
N1 . . . . .24 A2
Haberdashers' Aske's
Hatcham Coll
SE4 . . . . .51 A1
Haberdasher St
N1 . . . . .97 C4
Hackford Rd SW9 . . . .173 A4
Hackford Wlk
SW9 . . . . .173 B3
HACKNEY 17 A2
Hackney Central Sta
E8 . . . . .17 A2

Hackney Com Coll 53
N1 . . . . .24 A2
Hackney Downs Sta
E8 . . . . .17 A3
Hackney Empire
E8 . . . . .17 A2
Hackney Free &
Parochial CE Sec Sch
16 E9 . . . . .17 C2
Hackney Gr E8 . . . . . . .17 A2
Hackney Rd E2 . . . . . . .24 C3
HACKNEY WICK 18 C2
Hackney Wick Sta
E9 . . . . .18 C2
Hackney Wick Sta
E8 . . . . .18 C2
Hackworth Point 24
E3 . . . . .27 A2
Haddo Ho
Gospel Oak NW5 . . . .13 A4
Greenwich SE10 . . . . .52 A4
Haddon Ct W3 . . . . . . .29 B2
Haddo St SE10 . . . . . . .52 B4
Haden Ct N4 . . . . .5 C2
Hadfield Ho 37
E1 . . . . .111 C1
Hadleigh Cl 11 E1 . . . . .25 B1
Hadleigh Ho 10 E1 . . . .25 B1
Hadleigh St E2 . . . . . . .25 B2
Hadley Ct N16 . . . . .7 C3
Hadley Gdns W4 . . . . .37 C1
Hadley St NW1 . . . . . . .13 A2
Hadlow Ho SE17 . . . . .152 B2
Hadrian Cl 8 E3 . . . . . .26 C4
Hadrian Ct SE11 . . . . .150 A3
Hadrian Est 8 E2 . . . . . .24 C3
Hadrian St SE10 . . . . . .43 A1
Hadstock Ho NW1 . . . .93 C4
Hadyn Park Ct 8
W12 . . . . .38 C4
Hadyn Park Rd
W12 . . . . .38 C4
Hafer Rd SW11 . . . . . . .60 B3
Haggard Rd TW1 . . . . .54 C1
HAGGERSTON 24 B3
Haggerston Rd E8 . . . . .24 B4
Haggerston Sch **35**
E2 . . . . .24 B3
Haggerston Studios
E8 . . . . .24 B3
Hague Prim Sch 29
E2 . . . . .25 A1
Hague St 30
E2 . . . . .24 C2 99 C3
Haig Ho 7 E2 . . . . .24 C3
Hailsham Ave SW2 . . .74 B2
Hainford Cl SE4 . . . . . .65 C3
Haining Cl 3 W4 . . . . . .36 C1
Hainton Cl E1 . . . . .32 A3
Halcomb St N1 . . . . . . .24 A4
Halcrow St 1 E1 . . . . . .32 A4
Haldane Pl SW18 . . . . .71 A3
Haldane Rd SW6 . . . . .155 A3
Haldon Rd SW18 . . . . . .58 B1
Hale Ho SW1 . . . . .147 C2
Hales Ho 3 SW12 . . . . .73 A4
Hales Prior N1 . . . . .84 C1
Hales St SE8 . . . . .51 C3
Hale St E14 . . . . .34 A2
Halesworth Rd
SE13 . . . . .67 A4
Half Moon Cres
N1 . . . . .85 A2
Half Moon Ct EC1 . . . .108 C3

Half Moon La
SE24 . . . . .63 B1
Halfmoon Pas 6 E1 . . .111 A1
Half Moon St W1 . . . . .118 B1
Halford Ho 9
SW15 . . . . .57 C2
Halford Rd
Richmond TW10 . . . . .54 A2
West Brompton
SW6 . . . . .155 B3
Haliday Ho N1 . . . . .15 C2
Haliday Wlk 5 N1 . . . . .15 C2
Halidon Cl E9 . . . . .17 B3
Haliwell Ho 10
NW6 . . . . .78 A3
Halkett Ho 11 E2 . . . . . .25 B4
Halkin Arc SW1 . . . . . .131 A2
Halkin Mews SW1 . . . .131 B2
Halkin Pl SW1 . . . . . . .131 B2
Halkin St SW1 . . . . . . .131 C3
Hall Ct SW11 . . . . .104 B2
Hallam Ho
17 London SW9 . . . .173 B4
Pimlico SW1 . . . . . . .147 A1
Hallam Mews W1 . . . . .104 B4
Hallam Rd SW13 . . . . . .57 A4
Hallam St W1 . . . . .104 B4
Halley Gdns SE13 . . . . .67 C3
Halley Ho
18 Bethnal Green
E2 . . . . .24 C3
5 Cubitt Town
SE10 . . . . .43 B1
Halley Prim Sch
E14 . . . . .33 A4
Halley St E14 . . . . .33 A4
Hallfield Jun & Inf
Schs W2 . . . . .100 B1
Hall Gate NW8 . . . . . . .89 A4
Halliday Ho 40 E1 . . . .111 C1
Halliford St N1 . . . . . . .15 C1
Halling Ho SE1 . . . . . .137 C3
Hallings Wharf
Studios **2** E15 . . . .27 C4
Halliwell Ct 4
SE22 . . . . .64 C2
Halliwell Rd SW2 . . . . .62 B1
Hall Oak Wlk NW6 . . . .10 B2
Hall Pl W2 . . . . .89 B1
Hall Rd
Leyton E15 . . . . .19 C4
St John's Wood
NW8 . . . . .89 A4
Hall Sch The NW3 . . . .11 C2
Hall Sch Wimbledon
SW15 . . . . .68 C1
Hall St EC1 . . . . .96 B4
Hallsville Prim Sch
E16 . . . . .35 C3
Hallsville Rd E16 . . . . . .35 B3
Hall Twr W2 . . . . .101 C4
Halpin Pl SE17 . . . . . . .151 C3
Halsbury Ho 7 N7 . . . . .14 B4
Halsbury Rd W12 . . . . .30 A1
Halsey St SW3 . . . . . . .144 C4
Halsmere Rd SE5 . . . . .48 A2
Halstead Ct N1 . . . . . . .87 C1
Halston Cl SW11 . . . . . .60 B1
Halstow 12 NW5 . . . . . .12 C2
Halstow Prim Sch 3
SE10 . . . . .43 C1
Halstow Rd
Greenwich SE3,
SE10 . . . . .43 C1

Halstow Rd *continued*
Kensal Green NW10 . . **22** C2
Halton Cross St
N1 . . . . **86** B4
Haltone Ho **1**
SW4 . . . . **171** C1
Halton Ho **22** N1 . . **15** A1
Halton Mans N1 . . . . **15** A1
Halton Pl N1 . . . . . . **86** C4
Halton Rd N1 . . . . . . **86** B4
Halyard Ho E14 . . . . **42** B3
Hambalt Rd SW4 . . . **61** B2
Hambledon Ct SE17 . . **48** C4
Hambledon Chase
N4 . . . . **5** A4
Hambledon Ho E5 . . **17** A4
Hambledon Pl
SE21 . . . . **76** B3
Hambledon Rd
SW18 . . . . **70** B4
Hamble St SW6 . . . . **59** A4
Hambley Ho **5**
SE16 . . . . **40** A2
Hamblyn Ct N16 . . . . **7** B4
Hambridge Way
SW2 . . . . **74** C4
Hambrook Ct **13**
NW5 . . . . **13** A4
Hamers Ho **19**
SW2 . . . . **74** C4
Hamilton Cl
Rotherhithe SE16 . . . **41** A4
St John's Wood
NW8 . . . . **89** B3
Hamilton Ct W9 . . . . **88** C4
Hamilton Gdns
NW8 . . . . **89** A4
Hamilton Hall
NW8 . . . . **78** C1
Hamilton Ho
23 Bow E3 . . . . **26** B2
Chiswick W4 . . . . . . **46** A4
Kensington W8 . . . . **128** A4
1 Poplar E14 . . . . . **33** B2
Putney SW15 . . . . . . **56** C2
10 Richmond TW9 . . **44** C2
St John's Wood
NW8 . . . . **89** A4
Hamilton La N5 . . . . **15** A4
Hamilton Lo **37** E1 . . **25** B1
Hamilton Mews
W1 . . . . **132** A4
Hamilton Pk N5 . . . . **15** A4
Hamilton Pk W N5 . . **15** A4
Hamilton Pl W1 . . . **117** C1
Hamilton Terr
NW8 . . . . **89** A4
Hamlet Ct
1 Hammersmith
W6 . . . . **38** C2
Kennington SE11 . . . **150** A2
Hamlet Gdns W6 . . . **38** C2
Hamlet Ind Ctr E9 . . **18** C1
Hamlet Sq NW2 . . . . **1** A1
Hamlets Way E3 . . . . **26** B1
Hamlet The SE5 . . . . **63** C4
Hamlet Way SE1 . . . **137** C4

Hammelton Gn **2**
SW9 . . . . **48** A2
Hammersley Ho **1**
SE14 . . . . **50** B3
HAMMERSMITH . . . **39** B2
Hammersmith Bridge
Rd W6, SW13 . . . . . **39** B1
Hammersmith
Broadway
Hammersmith W6 . . . **39** B1
8 Hammersmith
W6 . . . . **39** B1
Hammersmith Flyover
W6 . . . . **39** B1
Hammersmith Gr
W6 . . . . **39** B3
Hammersmith Hospl
W12 . . . . **30** A3
Hammersmith Rd
Hammersmith W6 . . . **39** C2
Kensington W14 . . . **140** B4
Hammersmith Sta
W6 . . . . **39** B2
Hammersmith Terr **6**
W6 . . . . **38** C1
Hammett St EC3 . . . **124** C4
Hammond Ho
10 Deptford SE14 . . **50** B3
Millwall E14 . . . . . . **42** A3
Hammond Lo **6**
W9 . . . . **31** C4
Hammond St NW5 . . **13** B2
Hammond Sq N1 . . . **24** A3
Hampden Cl NW1 . . **83** C2
Hampden Gurney CE
Prim Sch W1 . . . . . **102** B2
Hampden Gurney St
W1 . . . . **102** C1
Hampden Rd N19 . . . **4** C2
Hampshire Ct **8**
SW13 . . . . **46** B1
Hampshire Hog La
3 Hammersmith
W6 . . . . **39** A2
11 Hammersmith
W6 . . . . **39** A2
Hampshire St
NW5 . . . . **13** C2
Hampson Way
SW8 . . . . **172** C4
HAMPSTEAD **11** B2
Hampstead Coll of
Fine Arts &
Humanities **12**
NW3 . . . . **12** A2
Hampstead Com
Mkt* NW3 . . . . **11** C4
Hampstead Gate
NW3 . . . . **11** B3
Hampstead Gn
NW3 . . . . **12** A3
Hampstead Gr NW3 . **2** B1
Hampstead Heath*
NW3 . . . . **2** C3
Hampstead Heath Pre
Prep Sch NW3 . . . . **12** B4
Hampstead Heath Sta
NW3 . . . . **12** A4
Hampstead High St
3 NW3 . . . . **11** B2
Hampstead High St
NW3 . . . . **11** C4
Hampstead Hill Gdns
NW3 . . . . **12** A3
Hampstead Hill Sch
1 NW3 . . . . **12** A3

Hampstead La N6 . . . **3** A4
Hampstead Parochial
CE Prim Sch **30**
NW3 . . . . **11** B4
Hampstead Rd
NW1 . . . . **92** C4
Hampstead Sch
NW2 . . . . **10** A4
Hampstead Sq **1**
NW3 . . . . **2** B1
Hampstead Sta
NW3 . . . . **11** B4
Hampstead West **4**
NW6 . . . . **10** C2
Hampstead Wlk **4**
E3 . . . . **26** B4
Hampton Cl NW6 . . . **23** C2
Hampton Ct
1 Islington N1 . . . . **15** A2
10 Rotherhithe
SE16 . . . . **32** C1
Hampton St SE1 . . . **150** B3
Hamstead Gates **1**
NW5 . . . . **13** A2
Ham Yd W1 . . . . . . **119** B4
Hana Mews E5 . . . . . **17** A3
Hanbury Ho
8 Bethnal Green
E1 . . . . **111** B4
South Lambeth
SW8 . . . . **162** B3
Hanbury Mews N1 . . **87** A3
Hanbury Rd W3 . . . . **37** A4
Hanbury St E1 . . . . **111** A4
Hancock Nunn Ho **4**
NW3 . . . . **12** B1
Hancock Rd E3 . . . . **27** B2
Handa Wlk **3** N1 . . **15** B2
Hand Ct WC1 . . . . . **107** A3
Handel House
Museum* W1 . . . . **118** B4
Handel Mans
Barnes SW13 . . . . . **47** B3
Bloomsbury WC1 . . . **94** B2
Handel St WC1 . . . . **94** B2
Handforth Rd
SW9 . . . . **163** B2
Handley Rd E9 . . . . . **25** B4
Hands Wlk E16 . . . . **35** C3
Hanford Cl SW18 . . . **70** C3
Hankey Pl SE1 . . . . **137** C3
Hanley Ct N4 . . . . . . **5** B3
Hanley Gdns N4 . . . . **5** B3
Hanley Rd N4, N19 . . **5** A3
Hanmer Wlk N7 . . . . **5** B2
Hannah Mary Way **1**
SE1 . . . . **153** C3
Hannay La N8 . . . . . . **4** C4
Hannay Wlk SW16 . . **73** C2
Hannell Rd SW6 . . . **154** B2
Hannen Ho SE5 . . . . **63** C4
Hannen Rd SE27 . . . **75** A1
Hannibal Rd E1 . . . . **32** B4
Hannington Rd
SW4 . . . . **61** A4
Hanover Ave E16 . . . **35** C1
Hanover Cl TW9 . . . . **44** C3
Hanover Ct
Shepherd's Bush
W12 . . . . **29** C1
Stamford Hill N16 . . . **7** B4
Hanover Gate Mans
NW1 . . . . **90** B2
Hanover Gdns
SE11 . . . . **163** B3
Hanover Ho NW8 . . . **80** A1

Hanover Mans **5**
SW2 . . . . **62** C2
Hanover Pk SE15 . . . **49** C2
Hanover Pl
16 Bow E3 . . . . **26** B2
St Giles WC2 . . . . . **106** B1
Hanover Prim Sch
N1 . . . . **86** C2
Hanover Rd NW10 . . **22** B4
Hanover Sq W1 . . . **104** B1
Hanover St W1 . . . . **104** B1
Hanover Stps W2 . . **102** B1
Hanover Terr NW1 . . **90** C3
Hanover Terrace
Mews NW1 . . . . **90** B3
Hanover West Ind Est
NW10 . . . . **20** C2
Hanover Yd N1 . . . . **86** C2
Hansard Mews
W14 . . . . **39** C4
Hanscomb Mews
SW4 . . . . **61** B3
Hans Cres SW1 . . . **130** C2
Hansler Ct **14**
SW19 . . . . **70** A3
Hansler Rd SE22 . . . **64** B2
Hanson Cl
Balham SW12 . . . . . **73** A3
Mortlake SW14 . . . . **55** B4
Hanson Ho **2** E1 . . **125** C4
Hanson St W1 . . . . **104** C4
Hans Pl SW1 . . . . . **130** C2
Hans Rd SW3 . . . . . **130** C2
Hans St SW1 . . . . . **131** A1
Hanway Ho **25**
SW9 . . . . **173** C4
Hanway Pl W1 . . . . **105** B2
Hanway St W1 . . . . **105** B2
Hanworth Ho SE5 . . **48** A3
Harben Rd NW6 . . . . **11** B1
Harberson Rd
SW12 . . . . **73** A3
Harberton Rd N19 . . **4** B3
Harbet Rd W2 . . . . . **101** C3
Harbinger Prim Sch
11 E14 . . . . **42** A2
Harbinger Rd E14 . . **42** A2
Harbin Ho **3** SW2 . . **74** C3
Harbledown Ho
SE1 . . . . **137** B3
Harbledown Rd
SW6 . . . . **165** B4
Harbord Cl
Camberwell SE15 . . . **49** A3
London SE5 . . . . . . **48** C1
Harbord Ho **6**
SE16 . . . . **40** C2
Harbord St SW6 . . . **47** C2
Harbour Ave
SW10 . . . . **167** A3
Harbour Exchange Sq
E14 . . . . **42** A4
Harbour Rd SE5 . . . . **63** B4
Harbridge Ave
SW15 . . . . **68** C4
Harbut Rd SW11 . . . **59** C3
Harcombe Rd N16 . . **7** A1
Harcourt Ho
27 Clapham SW8 . . **171** B2
Marylebone W1 . . . . **104** A2
4 Willesden NW10 . . **9** A2
Harcourt Rd SE4 . . . **66** B4
Harcourt St W1 . . . . **102** B3
Harcourt Terr
SW10 . . . . **142** B1

Hardcastle Ho
5 New Cross Gate
SE14 . . . . **51** A2
8 Peckham SE15 . . **49** C2
Hardel Rise SW2 . . . **75** A3
Hardel Wlk SW2,
SW9 . . . . **74** C3
Harden Ho SE5 . . . . **49** A1
Harders Rd SE15 . . . **50** A1
Hardess St SE24 . . . **63** B4
Hardham Ho **5**
SW2 . . . . **62** C2
Harding Cl SE17 . . . **48** B4
Hardinge Rd
NW10 . . . . **22** B4
Hardinge St E1 . . . . **32** B3
Harding Ho SW13 . . **47** A4
Hardington **2**
NW1 . . . . **12** C1
Hardwicke Ho **14**
E3 . . . . **27** A2
Hardwicke Mews
WC1 . . . . **95** A3
Hardwicke Rd W4 . . **37** C2
Hardwick Ho
14 London SW8 . . . **171** B2
Marylebone NW8 . . . **90** B2
Hardwick St EC1 . . . **95** C3
Hardwick's Way
SW18 . . . . **58** C2
Hardwidge St SE1 . . **138** A4
Hardy Ave **4** E16 . . **35** C1
Hardy Cl SE16 . . . . . **40** C4
Hardy Cotts **2**
SE10 . . . . **52** C4
Hardy Ct SE3 . . . . . **53** B4
Hardy Rd SE3 . . . . . **53** B4
Hare and Billet Rd
SE3 . . . . **52** C1
Harecourt Rd N1 . . . **15** B2
Hare Ct EC4 . . . . . **107** B1
Haredale Ho **24**
SE16 . . . . **139** B3
Haredale Rd SE24 . . **63** B3
Harefield Mews
SE4 . . . . **66** B4
Harefield Rd SE4 . . . **66** B4
Hare Marsh
E2 . . . . **24** C1 **99** B2
Hare Pl EC4 . . . . . **107** C1
Hare Row E2 . . . . . . **25** A3
Hare Wlk N1 . . . . . . **24** A3
Harewood Ave
NW1 . . . . **90** B1
Harewood Pl W1 . . **104** B1
Harewood Row
NW1 . . . . **102** B4
Harfield Gdns **1**
SE5 . . . . **64** A4
Harfleur Ct SE11 . . . **150** A3
Harford Ho
Camberwell SE5 . . . **48** B4
Notting Hill W11 . . . **31** B4
Harford Mews **6**
N19 . . . . **4** C1
Harford St E1 . . . . . **26** A1
Hargrave Mans **3**
N19 . . . . **4** C2
Hargrave Park Prim
Sch **17** N19 . . . . . . **4** B2
Hargrave Pk N19 . . . **4** B2
Hargrave Pl N7 . . . . **13** C3
Hargrave Rd N19 . . . **4** B2
Hargraves Ho **14**
W12 . . . . **30** A2
Hargwyne St SW9 . . **62** B4

Harkness Ho 30
E1 .... 111 C1
Harlech Twr 5
W3 .... 37 B4
Harlescott Rd
SE15 .... 65 C3
HARLESDEN 21 B4
Harlesden Gdns
NW10 .... 21 B4
Harlesden Plaza 2
NW10 .... 21 B3
Harlesden Prim Sch
NW10 .... 21 A4
Harlesden Rd
NW10 .... 21 C4
Harlesden Sta
NW10 .... 20 C3
Harleyford Ct
SW8 .... 162 C4
Harleyford Manor 8
W3 .... 28 B1
Harleyford Rd
SE11 .... 149 A2
Harleyford St
SE11 .... 163 B3
Harley Gdns
SW10 .... 143 A1
Harley Gr 12 E3 ..... 26 B2
Harley Ho NW1 ..... 91 C1
Harley Pl W1 ...... 104 A3
Harley Rd
Hampstead NW3 ..... 11 C1
Harlesden NW10 ..... 21 A3
Harley St W1 ...... 104 A3
Harley Villas
NW10 .... 21 A3
Harling Ct 3
SW11 .... 168 C2
Harlowe Ho 13 E8 .. 24 B4
Harlynwood 17
SE5 .... 48 B3
Harman Cl
10 Bermondsey
SE1 .... 153 B1
Harman Dr NW2 ..... 10 A4
Harmon Ho 7 SE8 .. 41 B2
Harmood Gr NW1 ... 13 A1
Harmood Ho 2
NW1 .... 13 A1
Harmood St NW1 ... 13 A1
Harmsworth St
SE17 .... 150 A1
Harold Ho 16 E2 ... 25 C1
Harold Ct 14 SE16 .. 40 C4
Harold Est SE1 .... 138 B1
Harold Ho 16 E2 ... 25 C1
Harold Laski Ho
EC1 .... 96 B3
Harold Maddison Ho
SE17 .... 150 B2
Harold Rd NW10 ... 20 C2
Harold Wilson Ho
SW6 .... 155 A3
Harp Alley EC4 ... 108 A2
Harpenden Rd SE27,
SW16 .... 75 A2
Harpenmead Point
NW2 .... 1 B2
Harper Ho 3 SW9 . 63 A4
Harper Mews
SW17 .... 137 A2
Harp La EC3 ...... 124 A3
Harpley Sq E1 ..... 25 C1

Harpsden St
SW11 .... 169 B3
Harpur Mews
WC1 .... 106 C4
Harpur St WC1 .... 106 C4
Harrier Ho 9
SW11 .... 60 A4
Harriet Cl E8 ...... 24 C4
Harriet Ho SW6 ... 156 B1
Harriet St SW1 ... 131 A3
Harriet Tubman Cl 21
SW2 .... 74 C4
Harriet Wlk SW1 .. 131 A3
Harrington Ct
South Kensington
SW7 .... 143 C4
3 West Kilburn W9 .. 23 B2
Harrington Gdns
SW7 .... 142 C3
Harrington Ho
Regent's Pk NW1 ... 92 C4
Westminster SW1 .. 147 C2
Harrington Rd
SW7 .... 143 B4
Harrington Sq
NW1 .... 82 C1
Harrington St NW1 . 92 C4
Harriott Cl SE10 ... 43 B2
Harriott Ho 11 E1 . 32 B3
Harris Acad at
Peckham SE15 ..... 49 B2
Harris Acad
Bermondsey SE1 ... 153 A4
Harris Girl's Acad
SE15 .... 65 B2
Harris Ho
5 Bow E3 .... 26 C2
7 Brixton SW9 ..... 62 C4
Harrison Ho SE17 .. 151 B2
Harrison Rd NW10 . 20 C4
Harrisons Ct 1
SE14 .... 50 C4
Harrison St WC1 ... 94 B3
Harris St SE5 ...... 48 C3
Harrodian Sch The
SW13 .... 46 B3
Harrogate Ct 2
SE26 .... 76 C1
Harrold Ho
NW3 .... 11 B1
Harroway Rd
SW11 .... 167 C2
Harrowby St W1 ... 102 B2
Harrowgate Ho 22
E9 .... 17 C2
Harrowgate Rd E9 . 18 A1
Harrow La E14 ..... 34 B2
Harrow Pl E1 ...... 110 B2
Harrow Rd
Little Venice W2 ... 101 A3
Westbourne Green W2,
W9 .... 23 C1
Harry Gosling Prim
Sch 41 E1 .... 111 C1
Harry Hinkins Ho
SE17 .... 151 A1
Harry Lambourn Ho
10 SE15 .... 50 A3
Hartfield Terr E3 ... 26 C3
Hartham Cl N7 ..... 14 A3
Hartham Rd N7 .... 14 A3
Hart Ho SW2 ...... 74 C3
Hartington Ct
Chiswick W4 ...... 45 A3

Hartington Ct continued
South Lambeth
SW8 .... 172 A4
Hartington Rd
Chiswick W4 ...... 45 B2
South Lambeth
SW8 .... 162 A1
Hartismere Rd
SW6 .... 155 A2
Hartlake Rd E9 .... 18 A2
Hartland NW1 ...... 83 A3
Hartland Rd
Camden Town
NW1 .... 13 A1
Kilburn NW6 ...... 23 B4
Hartley Ho
Bermondsey SE1 ... 153 A4
Putney SW15 ...... 56 C2
Hartley St E2 ...... 25 B2
Hartnoll Ho 4 N7 .. 14 C3
Hartnoll St N7 ..... 14 B3
Harton Lodge 8
SE8 .... 51 C2
Harton St SE8 ..... 51 C2
Hartopp Ct 20 N16 . 7 A1
Hartopp Point
SW6 .... 154 B2
Hartshorn Alley
EC3 .... 110 B1
Hart's La SE14 ..... 51 A2
Hart St EC3 .... 124 B4
Hartswood Ho 10
SW2 .... 74 A3
Hartswood Rd
W12 .... 38 B3
Hartwell Cl 17
SW2 .... 74 B3
Hartwell Ct SE22 .. 64 C3
Hartwell St E8 ..... 16 B2
Harvard Ct NW6 ... 11 A3
Harvard Hill W4 ... 45 A4
Harvard Ho
3 Camberwell
SE17 .... 48 A4
4 Putney SW15 .... 57 C1
Harvard Mans 18
SW11 .... 59 C3
Harvard Rd
2 Acton Green
W4 .... 37 B1
Gunnersbury W4 ... 37 A1
Lewisham SE13 .... 67 B2
Harvey Ct SW11 ... 168 B4
Harvey Ho
1 Bethnal Green
E1 .... 25 A1
Brentford TW8 .... 36 A1
Pimlico SW1 ..... 147 C1
Shoreditch N1 ..... 87 C3
Harvey Lo 9 W9 .. 31 C4
Harvey Point 7
E16 .... 35 C4
Harvey Rd 13 SE5 . 48 C2
Harvey St N1 ...... 87 C3
Harvington Wlk
E8 .... 16 C1
Harvist Rd NW6 ... 23 A3
Harwood Ct
Putney SW15 ...... 57 B3
Shoreditch N1 ..... 87 C3
Harwood Point
SE16 .... 41 B4
Harwood Rd SW6 . 156 A1
Harwood Terr
SW6 .... 166 A4

Hascombe Ho 11
SW15 .... 69 A3
Hascombe Terr 2
SE5 .... 48 C1
Haselrigge Rd
SW4 .... 61 C3
Hasker St SW3 .... 144 B4
Haslam Cl N1 ..... 14 C1
Haslam Ho 16 N1 . 15 B1
Haslam St SE15 ... 49 B2
Haslemere Ave
SW18 .... 71 A2
Haslemere Ct 5
N16 .... 7 A3
Haslemere Ind Est
SW18 .... 71 A2
Haslemere Rd N8 .. 5 A4
Hassard St E2 ..... 24 B3
Hassett Rd E9 ..... 18 A2
Hassop Rd NW2 .... 9 C4
Hastings Cl 17
SE15 .... 49 C3
Hastings Ho 18
W12 .... 30 A2
Hastings Hos WC1 . 94 A3
Hastings St WC1 ... 94 A3
Hatcham Park Mews
SE14 .... 50 C2
Hatcham Park Rd
SE14 .... 50 C2
Hatchard Rd N19 .. 5 A2
Hatchers Mews
SE1 .... 138 B3
Hatcliffe Almshouses
8 SE10 .... 43 A1
Hatcliffe St SE10 .. 43 B1
Hatfield Cl SE14 ... 50 C3
Hatfield Ct SE3 .... 53 C3
Hatfield Ho EC1 ... 96 C1
Hatfield Rd W4 .... 37 C4
Hatfields SE1 ..... 121 C2
Hathaway Ho 8
N1 .... 24 A2 98 A4
Hatherley Ct 6
W2 .... 100 A2
Hatherley Gr W2 .. 100 A2
Hatherley Rd TW9 . 44 B2
Hatherley St SW1 . 147 A3
Hathersage Rd N1 . 15 C3
Hathersley Ho 3
SW2 .... 74 C4
Hathorne Cl 3
SE15 .... 50 A1
Hathway Ho 3
SE15 .... 50 B1
Hathway St 4
SE15 .... 50 B1
Hatley Rd N4, N7 .. 5 B2
Hat & Mitre Ct EC1 . 96 B1
Hatstone Ct 2
NW3 .... 11 B3
Hatteraick St 9
SE16 .... 40 B4
Hatton Gdn EC1 ... 107 C4
Hatton Ho 11 E1 .. 125 C4
Hatton Pl EC1 .... 107 C4
Hatton Row NW8 .. 89 C1
Hatton St NW8 .... 89 C1
Hatton Wall EC1 .. 107 C4
Haunch of Venison Yd
W1 .... 104 A1
Hauteville Court Gdns
2 W6 .... 38 B3

Havana Rd SW18,
SW19 .... 70 C2
Havannah St E14 .. 41 C4
Havelock Cl 13
W12 .... 30 A2
Havelock Ct 8
SE15 .... 50 A3
Havelock St N1 .... 84 B4
Havelock Terr
SW8 .... 160 B1
Haven Cl SW19 ... 69 C1
Havenpool NW8 ... 78 B3
Haven St 18 NW1 . 13 A1
Haven The TW9 ... 54 C4
Havercourt 3
NW3 .... 12 A2
Haverfield Gdns
TW9 .... 44 C3
Haverfield Rd E3 .. 26 A2
Haverhill Rd SW12 . 73 B3
Havering 8 NW1 ... 13 A1
Havering St E1 .... 32 C3
Haversham Lo NW2 . 9 C3
Haversham Pl N6 .. 3 B2
Haverstock Hill
NW3 .... 12 B2
Haverstock Rd
NW5 .... 12 C3
Haverstock Sch 22
NW5 .... 12 C2
Haverstock St N1 .. 86 B1
Havil St SE5 ...... 49 A2
Havisham Ho 25
SE16 .... 139 B3
Hawarden Gr SE24 . 75 B4
Hawberry Lo N7 ... 14 A2
Hawes St N1 ...... 15 A1
Hawgood St E3 .... 33 C4
Hawke Ho 20 E1 .. 25 C1
Hawke Pl 22 SE16 . 40 C4
Hawkesbury Rd
SW15 .... 57 A2
Hawkesbown House
Sch 30 ..... 31 C1 113 C1
Hawkesworth Ho 5
SW4 .... 61 B1
Hawke Twr 4
SE14 .... 51 A4
Hawk Ho 7 SW11 . 60 A4
Hawkins Ho 6
SE8 .... 51 C4
Hawkins Rd NW10 . 8 A1
Hawkley Gdns
SE27 .... 75 A2
Hawkridge 19
NW5 .... 12 C2
Hawkshaw Cl 23
SW2 .... 74 A4
Hawkshead NW1 ... 92 C4
Hawkshead Rd
Acton W4 .... 38 A4
Willesden NW10 .... 8 B1
Hawkslade Rd
SE15 .... 65 C2
Hawksley Rd N16 .. 7 A1
Hawks Mews 10
SE10 .... 52 B3
Hawksmoor Mews
E1 .... 32 A2
Hawksmoor Pl 2
E2 .... 24 C1 99 B2
Hawksmoor St 5
W6 .... 47 C4

Hawkstone Rd
SE16 . . . . 40 B2
Hawkwell Wlk N1 . 87 A4
Hawley Cres NW1 . .13 A1
Hawley Inf Sch 28
NW1 . . . . .13 A1
Hawley Mews 4
NW1 . . . . .13 A1
Hawley Rd 8
NW1 . . . . .13 A1
Hawley St NW1 . . . .13 A1
Haworth Ho 7
SW2 . . . . .62 C1
Hawstead Rd SE6. .67 A1
Hawthorn Ct
Putney SW15 . . . . . .57 A4
Richmond TW9 . . . . .45 A2
Hawthorne Ave E3 . .26 B4
Hawthorne Cl N1 . . .16 A2
Hawthorne Ho
SW1 . . . . 147 A1
Hawthorn Ho SE14 .51 B2
Hawthorn Rd NW10. .8 C1
Hawthorn Wlk
W10 . . . . .23 A1
Hawtrey Rd NW3 . . .12 A1
Haycroft Gdns
NW10 . . . . .22 A4
Haycroft Mans
NW1 . . . . .21 C4
Haycroft Rd SW2 . .62 A2
Hay Currie St E14 . .34 A3
Hayday Rd E16 . . . . .35 C4
Hayden Piper Ho
SW3 . . . . 158 C4
Hayden's Pl W11 . . .31 B3
Haydon St EL,EC3 124 C4
Haydon Way SW11 .59 C3
Haydon Wlk E1. . . . 111 A1
Hayes Ct
22 Camberwell
SE5 . . . . .48 B3
Streatham SW12 . . .74 A3
Hayes Gr SE15,
SE22. . . . . .64 B3
Hayes Pl NW1 . . . . .90 B1
Hayfield Pas E1 . . . .25 B1
Hayfield Yd 3 E1. . .25 B1
Hay Hill W1 . . . . . . 118 B3
Hayhurst N1 . . . . . .86 B4
Hayles Bldgs
SE11. . . . . 150 B4
Hayles St SE11 . . . 150 A4
Hayling Cl 2 N16 . .16 A3
Haymans Point
SE11 . . . . 148 C2
Haymarket SW1 . . . 119 B3
Haymerle Ho 6
SE15 . . . . .49 C3
Haymerle Rd SE15 .49 C4
Haymerle Sch 17
SE15 . . . . .49 C4
Hayne Ho
W11 . . . . . . .31 A1 112 A2
Haynes Ho 3 E9 . . .17 C2
Hayne St EC1 . . . . 108 B4
Hay's Galleria★
SE1 . . . . 124 A2
Hay's La SE1 . . . . . 124 A2
Hay's Mews W1 . . . 118 A2
Hay St E2 . . . . .24 C4
Hayter Ho W12 . . . .29 C2
Hayter Rd SW2 . . . .62 B2

Haythorn Ho
SW11 . . . . 167 C3
Hayton Ct 11 E8 . . .16 B2
Hayward Ct 14
SW4 . . . . 172 B2
Hayward Gallery★
SE1 . . . . 121 A2
Hayward Gdns
SW15 . . . . .57 B1
Hayward Ho N1 . . . .85 B2
Haywards Pl EC1 . . .96 A2
Hayward's Pl EC1. . .96 A2
Haywood Lo 2
N7. . . . . .13 C3
Hazelbourne Rd
SW12 . . . . .61 A1
Hazel Cl
Peckham SE15 . . . . .49 C1
Upper Holloway N19 . .4 B2
Hazel Ct 3 SE16 . . .33 A1
Hazeldon Rd SE4 . .66 A2
Hazel Ho
London SE4. . . . . . .66 B4
12 Maitland Pk
NW3 . . . . .12 B2
Hazellville Rd N19. . .4 C3
Hazelmere Ct 10
SW2 . . . . .74 B3
Hazelmere Rd
NW6 . . . . .23 B4
Hazel Rd NW10 . . . .22 B2
Hazel Way SE1 . . . 152 C4
Hazelwood Cl W5 . .36 A4
Hazelwood Ho 11
SE8 . . . . .41 A2
Hazelwood Mans
SW6 . . . . 164 C4
Hazlebury Rd
SW6 . . . . 166 B2
Hazledene Rd W4 . .45 B4
Hazlewell Rd
SW15 . . . . .57 B2
Hazlewood Cres
W10 . . . . .23 A1
Hazlewood Twr
W10 . . . . .23 B1
Hazlitt Mews
W14 . . . . 126 A1
Hazlitt Rd W14 . . . 126 A1
Headbourne Ho
SE1 . . . . 137 C2
Headcorn 10 NW5. .12 C2
Headfort Pl SW1 . . 131 C3
Headington Rd
SW18 . . . . .71 B2
Headlam Rd SW4 . .73 C4
Headlam St E1 . . . . .25 A1
Heads Mews W11 . .31 C3
Heald St SE14 . . . . .51 C2
Healey St NW1 . . . .13 A2
Healy Ho 2 E3 . . . .26 C1
Heanor Ct 5 E5 . . .17 C4
Hearne Rd W4 . . . . .44 C4
Hearn's Bldgs
SE17 . . . . 151 C3
Hearnshaw St 1
E14 . . . . .33 A3
Hearn St
EC2 . . . . .24 A1 98 B1
Hearnville Rd
SW12 . . . . .72 C3
Heart Hospl The
W1 . . . . 103 C3
Heart Raido W11 . .30 C2

Heathbrook Prim Sch
11 SW4 . . . . 170 C4
Heath Brow NW3 . . .2 B1
Heath Cl NW11 . . . . .2 A4
Heathcote Point 25
E9 . . . . .17 C2
Heathcote St WC1 . .94 C3
Heathcroft NW11 . . .2 A3
Heath Ct
2 Hampstead
NW3 . . . . .11 B2
Stoke Newington N16 . .6 C3
Heath Dr SW11 . . . .11 A4
Heather Cl SW8 . . . .61 A4
Heather Ct SW4 . . 172 B3
Heather Ho 11 E14 .34 B3
Heatherley Ct N16. . .7 C1
Heatherley Sch of
Fine Art SW10 . . . 157 A1
Heather Lo N16 . . . . .7 A3
Heather Wlk W10. . .23 A1
Heathfield Ave
SW18 . . . . .71 C4
Heathfield Ct
3 Bow E3 . . . . .26 C3
6 Chiswick W4 . . . .37 C1
Wandsworth SW18 .71 C4
Heathfield Gdns
Acton Green W4 . . . .37 B1
Blackheath SE3 . . . .53 A1
Wandsworth SW18 .59 C1
Heathfield Ho SE3 . .53 A1
Heathfield House Sch
16 W4. . . . . .37 B1
Heathfield Pk NW2 . .9 B2
Heathfield Rd
Acton W3 . . . . .37 A4
Wandsworth SW18 .59 C1
Heathfield Sq
SW18 . . . . .71 C4
Heathfield Terr
W4 . . . . .37 C1
Heathgate Pl NW3. .12 B4
Heath House Prep
Sch 1 SE8 . . . . . . .53 B1
Heath Hurst Rd
NW3 . . . . .12 A4
Heath La SE3 . . . . . .52 C1
Heathland Rd N16. . .7 A3
Heath Mans
5 Hampstead
NW3 . . . . .11 B4
Putney SW15 . . . . . .57 C1
Heathman's Rd
SW6 . . . . 165 A3
Heath Mead SW19 .69 C1
Heathmere Prim Sch
SW15 . . . . .68 C3
Heath Park Gdns
NW3 . . . . .2 A1
Heathpool Ct 8
E1 . . . . .25 A1
Heath Rd SW8. . . . 170 B1
Heath Rise SW15 . .57 C1
Heath Royal SW15 .57 C1
Heathshott 3
TW10 . . . . .54 A1
Heathside NW11 . .11 C4
Heathside Prep Sch
22 NW3 . . . . .11 B4
5 NW3 . . . . .2 B1
Heathstan Rd W12 .29 C3
Heath View NW5. . .12 C4
Heathview Ct
SW19 . . . . .69 C2

Heathview Gdns
SW15 . . . . .69 B4
Heath Villas SW3 . .11 B4
Heathville Rd N4,
N19 . . . . .5 A4
Heathwall St
SW11 . . . . .60 B4
Heathway SE3 . . . . .53 C3
Heathway Ct NW3. . .1 C2
Heathwood Ct
SW12 . . . . .73 B3
Heaton Ho
Chelsea SW10 . . . . 157 A4
2 Peckham SE15 . . .50 A1
Heaton Rd SE15 . . .50 A1
Heaven Tree Cl
N1. . . . . .15 B3
Heaver Rd 22
SW11 . . . . .59 C4
Hebden Ct 24 E2 . .24 B4
Hebdon Rd SW17 . .72 A1
Heber Prim Sch
SE22 . . . . .64 B1
Heber Rd
Cricklewood NW2 . . .9 C4
East Dulwich SE22 . .64 B1
Heckfield Pl SW6. . 155 B1
Heckford Ho E14 . . .34 A3
Heckford St E1 . . . .32 C2
Hector Cl
1 London SW9 . . . 173 B4
Putney SW15 . . . . . .57 B4
Hector Ho 6 E2 . . . .25 A3
Heddington Gr N7. . .14 B3
Heddon St W1. . . . 118 C4
Hedger's Gr 11 E9 . .18 A2
Hedger St SE11. . . 150 A4
Hedingham Cl 6 6
N1 . . . . .15 B1
Hedley Ct SW15 . . .57 C1
Hedley Ho E14 . . . .42 B3
Hedley Row N5,
N16. . . . . .15 C3
Hedsor Ho
2 E2 . . . . 24 B1 98 C2
Heidegger Cres
SW13 . . . . .47 A3
Heights The NW3 . .11 B4
Heiron St SE17 . . . .48 A4
Helby Rd SW4 . . . . .61 C1
Heldar Ct SE1 . . . . 137 C3
Helena Rd NW10 . . . .9 A3
Helena Sq SE16. . . .33 A2
Helen Gladstone Ho
SE1 . . . . 136 A4
Helen Ho 6 E2 . . . .25 A3
Helen Mackay Ho 10
E14 . . . . .34 C3
Helen Peele Cotts 7
SE16 . . . . .40 B3
Helenslea Ave
NW11 . . . . .1 C3
Helen's Pl E2 . . . . . .25 B2
Helen Taylor Ho 6
SE16 . . . . 153 B4
Heliport Ind Est
SW11 . . . . 167 B1
Helix Ct 17 W11 . . .30 C1
Helix Gdns SW2 . . .62 B1
Helix Rd SW2. . . . . .62 B1
Helix The SW19 . . .69 C2
Hellings St E1 . . . . 125 C1
Helmet Row EC1 . . .97 A2

Helmsdale Ho
NW6 . . . . .78 A1
Helmsley Pl E8 . . . .17 A1
Helmsley St 7 E8 . .17 A1
Helperby Rd NW10 . .8 A1
Helsby Ct NW8 . . . .89 B2
Helsinki Sq SE16 . . .41 A3
Helston NW1 . . . . . .83 A2
Helston Ho SE11. . 149 C2
Hemans Est SW8 . 161 C1
Hemans St SW8 . . 161 C1
Hemberton Rd
SW9 . . . . .62 A4
Hemingford Rd N1 .85 A4
Hemlock Rd W12. . .29 B2
Hemming St
E1 . . . . 24 C1 99 C1
Hemmingway Cl
NW5 . . . . .12 C4
Hemp Wlk SE17 . . 151 C4
Hemstal Rd NW6 . . .10 C1
Hemsworth Ct N1 . .24 A3
Hemsworth St N1 . .24 A3
Hemus Pl SW3 . . . 144 B1
Henchman St W12. .29 B3
Henderson Ct
8 Deptford SE14 . . .50 C4
Hampstead NW3 . . .11 C3
Wandsworth SW18 . .72 A4
Henderson Dr
NW8 . . . . .89 B2
Henderson Rd
SW18 . . . . .72 A4
Hendham Rd
SW17 . . . . .72 B2
Hendre Ho SE1. . . 152 B3
Hendre Rd SE1 . . . 152 B3
Hendrick Ave
SW12 . . . . .72 B4
Heneage La EC3. . 110 B1
Heneage Pl EC3 . . 110 B1
Heneage St E1 . . . 111 A4
Henfield Cl N19 . . . .4 C3
Henley Cl SE16 . . . .40 B4
Henley Ct
Brondesbury NW2 . . .9 C2
Peckham SE15 . . . . .64 C4
Henley Dr SE1 . . . . 153 A4
Henley Ho
E2 . . . . 24 B1 99 A2
Henley Prior N1. . . .84 C1
Henley Rd NW10 . . .22 B4
Henley St SW11 . . 169 C2
Henniker Mews
SW3 . . . . 157 B4
Henniker Rd E15 . . .19 C3
Henning St SW11 . 168 A3
Henrietta Cl SE8. . .51 C4
Henrietta Ho 11
W6 . . . . .39 B1
Henrietta Mews
WC1 . . . . .94 B2
Henrietta Pl W1 . . 104 A2
Henrietta St
Strand WC2 . . . . . . 120 B4
Stratford New Town
E15 . . . . .19 B3
Henriques St E1 . . 111 C2
Henry Cavendish Prim
Sch 2 SW12 . . . . .73 B3
Henry Compton Sch
SW6 . . . . 154 A4
Henry Dent Cl SE5 .63 C4
Henry Dickens Ct
W11 . . . . . . .31 A1 112 A2

Henry Fawcett Prim
Sch 15 SE11 . . . . 163 B4
Henry Ho
Lambeth SE1 . . . . . . 121 C1
South Lambeth
SW8 . . . . 162 A2
St John's Wood
NW8 . . . . 80 A2
Henry Jackson Ho 6
SW15 . . . . 57 C4
Henry Jackson Rd
SW15 . . . . 57 C4
Henry Rd N4 . . . . 6 B3
Henryson Rd SE4 . . . 66 C2
Henry Wise Ho
SW1 . . . . 147 A3
Henshall Point 1
E3 . . . . 27 A2
Henshall St N1 . . . . 15 C2
Henshaw St SE17 . . 151 B4
Hensley Point 23
E9 . . . . 17 C2
Henslowe Rd SE22 . . 64 C2
Henslow Ho 12
SE15 . . . . 49 C3
Henson Ave NW2 . . . 9 B3
Henson Ct 3 N5 . . . 15 B4
Henstridge Pl
NW8 . . . . 80 A3
Henty Cl SW11 . . . . 168 B4
Henty Wlk SW15 . . . 57 A2
Hepburn Mews
SW11 . . . . 60 B2
Hepplestone Cl 6
SW15 . . . . 57 A1
Hepscott Rd E9 . . . . 18 C1
Hepworth Ct
Chelsea SW1 . . . . 146 A1
Islington N1 . . . . . . 86 A4
Hera Ct 15 E14 . . . . . 41 C2
Heralds Pl SE11 . . . 150 A4
Herald St E2 . . . . . . 25 A1
Herbal Hill EC1 . . . . 95 C1
Herbert Chapman Ct
N5 . . . . 15 A4
Herbert Cres
SW1 . . . . 131 A2
Herbert Gdns
Chiswick W4 . . . . . 45 A4
Willesden Green
NW10 . . . . 22 A3
Herbert Ho E1 . . . . 110 C2
Herbert Mews 13
SW2 . . . . 62 C1
Herbert Morrison Ho
SW6 . . . . 154 C3
Herbert Morrison
Prim Sch SW8 . . . 162 A1
Herbert St NW5 . . . . 12 C2
Herbrand Est WC1 . . 94 A2
Herbrand St WC1 . . . 94 A2
Hercules Ct 7
SE14 . . . . 51 A4
Hercules Pl N7 . . . . 5 A1
Hercules Rd SE1 . . . 135 A1
Hercules St N7 . . . . 5 A1
Hereford Bldgs
SW3 . . . . 157 C4
Hereford Ho
1 Brixton SW2 . . . . 62 C3
2 Camberwell SE5 . . 48 B1
Knightsbridge SW3 . 130 B2
Walham Green
SW10 . . . . 156 B2
Hereford Mans 15
W2 . . . . 31 C3

Hereford Mews 11
W2 . . . . 31 C3
Hereford Pl SE14 . . . 51 B3
Hereford Rd
Acton W3 . . . . 28 B2
Bayswater
W2 . . . . 31 C2 113 C4
Hereford Retreat 5
SE15 . . . . 49 C3
Hereford Sq SW7 . . 143 A3
Hereford St
E2 . . . . 24 C1 99 B2
Hereward House Sch
NW3 . . . . 11 C2
Heritage Cl SW9 . . . 63 A4
Heritage Ct SE8 . . . 40 C1
Heritage Ho 22
SW19 . . . . 69 C3
Hermes Cl 9 W9 . . . 23 C1
Hermes Ct 12
SW9 . . . . 173 B4
Hermes St N1 . . . . . 85 B1
Hermitage
2 Child's Hill NW2 . . 1 C1
3 Wapping E1 . . . . 125 C1
Hermitage Gdns
NW2 . . . . 1 C1
Hermitage La NW2 . . 1 C1
Hermitage Prim Sch
10 E1 . . . . 125 C2
Hermitage Row 8
E8 . . . . 16 C3
Hermitage The
Barnes SW13 . . . . . 46 B2
Richmond TW10 . . . 54 A2
Hermitage Villas
SW6 . . . . 155 B4
Hermitage Wall
E1 . . . . 125 C1
Hermit Pl NW6 . . . . 78 A3
Hermit St EC1 . . . . . 96 A4
Herndon Rd SW18 . . 59 B2
HERNE HILL 63 B2
Herne Hill Ho
SE24 . . . . 63 A1
Herne Hill Mans
SE24 . . . . 63 B1
Herne Hill Rd
SE24 . . . . 63 B3
Herne Hill Sta
SE24 . . . . 63 B1
Herne Hill Velodrome
SE24 . . . . 63 C2
Herne Pl SE24 . . . . . 63 A2
Heron Cl NW10 . . . . 8 A2
Heron Ct
1 Cubitt Town
E14 . . . . 42 B3
2 Dulwich SE21 . . . 75 C2
Herondale Ave
SW18 . . . . 72 A3
Heron Dr N4 . . . . . . 6 B2
Herongate N1 . . . . . 87 A4
Heron Ho
Battersea SW11 . . . 168 B4
Peckham SE15 . . . . 49 B2
St John's Wood
NW8 . . . . 80 A1
Heron Pl
Marylebone W1 . . . 103 C2
Rotherhithe SE16 . . 33 A1
Heron Quays E14 . . . 33 C1

Heron Quays Sta
E14 . . . . 33 C1
Heron Rd SE24 . . . . 63 B3
Heron Trad Est
W3 . . . . 28 A4
Herrick Ho
5 Camberwell
SE5 . . . . 48 C3
7 Canonbury N16 . . 15 C4
Herrick Rd N5 . . . . . 6 B1
Herrick St SW1 . . . 147 C3
Herries St W10 . . . . 23 A3
Hersant Cl NW10 . . . 21 C4
Herschell's Mews
SE5 . . . . 63 B4
Hersham Cl SW15 . . 68 C4
Hershell Ct 1
SW14 . . . . 55 A3
Hertford Ave
SW14 . . . . 56 A3
Hertford Ct 18
SW11 . . . . 60 A4
Hertford Lo 10
SW19 . . . . 70 A3
Hertford Pl W1 . . . . 93 A1
Hertford Rd N1 . . . . 24 A4
Hertford St W1 . . . 118 A1
Hertmitage The 5
SE13 . . . . 52 B1
Hertslet Rd N7 . . . . 5 B1
Hertsmere Rd E14 . . 33 C2
Hesewall Cl SW4 . . 171 A1
Hesketh Pl
W11 . . . . . . 31 A2 112 A3
Heslop Ct 1
SW12 . . . . 72 C3
Heslop Rd SW12 . . . 72 B3
Hesper Mews
SW5 . . . . 142 A3
Hesperus Cres
E14 . . . . 42 A2
Hessel St E1 . . . . . . 32 A3
Hestercombe Ave
SW6 . . . . 164 B3
Hester Rd SW11 . . . 158 A1
Hester Terr TW9 . . . 54 C4
Hestia Ho 1 SE1 . . 138 A3
Heston Ho
Gunnersbury W4 . . . 37 A1
8 St Johns SE8 . . . . 51 C2
Heston St SE14 . . . . 51 C2
Hetherington Rd
SW4 . . . . 62 A3
Hethpool Ho W2 . . . 89 B1
Hetley Rd W12 . . . . 39 A4
Hetty Rees Ct 3
N19 . . . . 5 A4
Hevelius Cl SE10 . . . 43 B1
Hever Ho SE15 . . . . 50 C4
Heversham Ho
SE15 . . . . 50 B4
Heward Ct SE13 . . . 52 B1
Hewer Ho 6 SW4 . . 61 B2
Hewer St W10 . . . . . 30 C4
Hewett Ho 1
EC2 . . . . 24 A1 98 B1
Hewison St E3 . . . . . 26 B3
Hewlett Rd E3 . . . . . 26 A3
Hewling Ho 7
N16 . . . . 16 A3
Hexagon The N6 . . . 3 B3
Hexham Rd SE27 . . . 75 B2
Hexton Ct N4 . . . . . . 6 B2
Heybridge 7 NW1 . . 13 A2

Heydon Ho 8
SE14 . . . . 50 B2
Heyford Ave SW8 . . 162 B2
Heyford Terr
SW8 . . . . 162 B2
Heygate St SE17 . . . 151 B4
Heylyn Sq E3 . . . . . 26 B2
Heysham La NW3 . . . 2 A1
Heythorp St SW18 . . 70 B2
Heythrop Coll W8 . . 128 A2
Heywood Ho
1 Deptford SE14 . . . 50 C4
8 Tulse Hill SW2 . . . 62 C1
Heyworth Rd E5 . . . 17 A4
Hibbert Ho 18 E14 . 41 C3
Hibbert St SW11 . . . 59 B4
Hichisson Rd SE15 . . 65 B2
Hicken Rd SW2 . . . . 62 B2
Hickes Ho 6 NW6 . . 11 C1
Hickey's Almshouses
7 TW9 . . . . 54 B3
Hickin Cl SE7 . . . . . 43 A2
Hickin St 2 E14 . . . . 42 B3
Hickleton N1 . . . . . . 83 A3
Hickling Ho 8
SE16 . . . . 40 A3
Hickmore Wlk
SW4 . . . . 61 B4
Hicks Cl SW11 . . . . 60 A4
Hicks St SE8 . . . . . . 41 A1
Hide Pl SW1 . . . . . 147 B3
Hide Twr SW1 . . . . 147 B3
Hieover SE21 . . . . . 75 B2
Higgins Ho 7 N1 . . . 24 A4
Higginson Ho 2
NW3 . . . . 12 B1
Higgs Ind Est 5
SE24 . . . . 63 A4
Highbridge Ct 12
SE14 . . . . 50 B3
High Bridge Wharf
SE10 . . . . 42 C1
Highbury Mans 21
N1 . . . . 15 A1
HIGHBURY 15 A4
Highbury Cnr N5 . . . 15 A2
Highbury Corner
N5 . . . . 15 A2
Highbury Cres N5 . . 14 C2
Highbury Fields Sch
4 N5 . . . . 15 A3
Highbury Gr N5 . . . . 15 B3
Highbury Grange
N5 . . . . 15 B4
Highbury Grove Ct
N5 . . . . 15 A1
Highbury Grove Sch
7 N5 . . . . 15 B4
Highbury Hill N5 . . . 15 A4
Highbury & Islington
Sta N1 . . . . 15 A2
Highbury New Pk
N5 . . . . 15 B4
Highbury Pk N5 . . . . 15 A4
Highbury Pl N5 . . . . 15 A2
Highbury Pool N5 . . 15 A2
Highbury Quadrant
N5 . . . . 6 B1
Highbury Quadrant
Prim Sch N5 . . . . . 15 B4
Highbury Station Rd
N1 . . . . 14 C2
Highbury Terr N5 . . . 15 A3
Highbury Terrace
Mews N5 . . . . 15 A3
Highcliffe Dr
SW15 . . . . 56 B1

Highcroft Rd N19 . . . 5 A4
Highcross Way 4
SW15 . . . . 68 C3
Highdown Rd
SW15 . . . . 57 A1
Highfield Ave NW11 . 1 A4
Highfield Cl SE13 . . . 67 C1
Highfield Mews
NW6 . . . . 11 A1
Highfield Rd W3 . . . . 28 B4
Highfields Gr N6 . . . 3 B3
HIGHGATE 3 C4
Highgate Archway
N6 . . . . 4 B3
Highgate Ave N6 . . . 4 A4
Highgate Cemetery *
N19 . . . . 4 A2
Highgate Cl N6 . . . . 3 C4
Highgate High St
N6 . . . . 3 C4
Highgate Hill N19 . . 4 B3
Highgate Ho 4
SE26 . . . . 76 C1
Highgate Pre-Prep &
Jun Sch N6 . . . . . . 3 A4
Highgate Rd NW5 . . 13 A4
Highgate Sch N6 . . . 3 C4
Highgate West Hill
Highgate N6 . . . . . . 3 C3
London N6 . . . . 3 C2
Highgrove Point 2
NW3 . . . . 11 B4
High Holborn
WC1 . . . . 106 C3
High Holborn Ho
WC1 . . . . 107 A3
Highlands Ave W3 . . 28 B2
Highlands Cl N4 . . . . 5 A4
Highlands Heath
SW15 . . . . 69 B4
Highlever Rd W10 . . 30 B4
High London St 6
N6 . . . . 4 C4
Highmore Rd SE3 . . 53 A3
High Mount 1 N4 . . . 5 A4
High Park Ave
TW9 . . . . 44 C2
High Park Rd TW9 . . 44 C2
High Par The
SW16 . . . . 74 A1
High Point Ho 6
E14 . . . . 27 A3
High Rd NW10 . . . . . 8 C2
Highshore Rd
SE15 . . . . 49 B1
Highshore Sch 10
SE15 . . . . 49 B2
High St
Acton W3 . . . . 28 A1
Brentford TW8 . . . . 44 A4
Stratford Marsh E15 . 27 B4
High Street Harlesden
NW10 . . . . 21 B3
High Street
Kensington Sta
W8 . . . . 128 A3
High The SW16 . . . . 74 A1
High Timber St
EC4 . . . . 122 C4
High Trees SW2 . . . 74 C3
Hightrees Ho
SW12 . . . . 60 C1
Highview N8 . . . . . . 5 A4
Highview Ct 2
SW19 . . . . 70 A3

High View Prim Sch
　1 SW11 ....59 C3
Highway Bsns Pk The
　7 E1 ....32 C2
Highway The **E** The
　2 E1 ....32 B2
Highway Trad Ctr The
　8 E1 ....32 C2
Highwood Cl SE22 ..76 C3
Highwood Rd N19 .....5 A1
Highworth St
　NW1 ....**102** B4
Hilary Cl SW6 ....156 A2
Hilary Rd W12 ....29 B2
Hilborough Ct **1**
　E8 ....24 B4
Hilborough Rd **1**
　E8 ....16 B1
Hilda Terr **2**
　SW9 ....**173** C2
Hilditch Ho **7**
　TW10 ....54 B1
Hildred Ho SW1 ..146 A4
Hildreth St **3**
　SW12 ....73 A3
Hildreth Street Mews
　2 SW12 ....73 A3
Hiley Rd NW10 ....22 B2
Hilgrove Rd NW6 ...11 B1
Hillary Ct **13** W12 ...39 B4
Hillbeck Cl
　Deptford SE15 ....50 B3
　Deptford SE15 ....50 B4
Hillbrow **7** TW10 ..54 A1
Hillbury Rd SW17 ...73 A1
Hillcourt Rd SE22 ...65 A1
Hillcrest
　Camberwell SE24 ...63 C3
　Highgate N6 ....3 C4
　Notting Hill
　W11 ....31 B2 **112** C3
Hillcrest Ct NW2 ....10 A3
Hillcrest Rd W3 ....28 A1
Hill Ct
　Hampstead NW3 ...12 A4
　Putney SW15 ....57 C2
Hilldrop Cres **1** N7 ..13 C3
Hilldrop La N7 ....13 C3
Hilldrop Rd N7 ....13 C3
Hillersdon Ave
　SW13 ....46 C1
Hillersdon Ho
　SW1 ....**146** A2
Hillery Cl SE17 ....**151** C3
Hill Farm Rd W10 ...30 C4
Hillfield Ct NW3 .....12 A3
Hillfield Ho N5 ....15 B3
Hillfield Mans
　NW3 ....12 A3
Hillfield Rd NW6 ...10 C3
Hillgate **7**
　Balham SW12 ....73 A4
　Kensington
　W8 ....31 C1 **113** B2
Hillgate St
　W8 ....31 C1 **113** B2
Hill House
　International Jun
　Sch SW1 ....**131** A1
Hilliard Ho **1** E1 ....32 A1
Hilliard's Ct E1 ......32 B1
Hillier Ho **1** NW1 ...14 A4
Hillier Rd SW11 .....60 B1
Hillingdon St SE17..48 A4

Hill Lo SW11 ....59 C3
Hillman Dr **12**
　NW10 ....22 B1
Hillman St E8 ....17 A2
Hillmarton Rd N7 ...14 A3
Hillmead Dr SW9 ....63 A3
Hill Mead Prim Sch
　SW9 ....63 A3
Hillrise Ct SE13 .....67 C4
Hill Rd NW8 ....79 A1
Hillrise Mans N19 ....5 A4
Hillrise Rd N19 ....5 A4
Hillsboro Rd SE22 ..64 A2
Hillsborough Ct **6**
　NW6 ....78 A3
Hillside
　Greenwich SE10 ...52 C3
　Stonebridge NW10..20 C4
Hillside Cl NW8 ....**78** B2
Hillside Ct NW3 ....11 A3
Hillside Gdns SW2 ..74 C2
Hillside Rd SW2 ....74 C2
Hillsleigh Rd
　W14 ......31 B1 **113** A2
Hills Pl W1 ....**104** C1
Hill St W1 ....**118** A2
Hillstone Ct **3** E3 ..27 A1
Hilltop Ct
　12 London SW18 ...59 C3
　South Hampstead
　NW8 ....11 B1
Hilltop Ho **7** N6 ....4 C4
Hilltop Rd NW6 ......10 C1
Hill View NW1 ....**81** A4
Hill Wood Ho NW1 ..83 B1
Hillworth Rd SW2 ...74 C4
Hillyard St SW9 ...**173** B3
Hillyfield Cl E3 ....18 A3
Hilly Fields Cres
　SE4 ....66 C4
Hilsea Point **7**
　SW15 ....69 A3
Hilsea St E5 ....17 B4
Hilton Ho
　Lower Holloway
　N7 ....14 A4
　9 Nunhead SE4 ....65 C3
Hilversum Cres **10**
　SE22 ....64 A2
Hinckley Rd SE15 ...64 C3
Hind Ct EC4 ....**107** C1
Hinde Mews W1 ...**103** C2
Hinde St W1 ....**103** C2
Hind Gr E14 ....33 C3
Hindhead Point **6**
　SW15 ....69 A3
Hind Ho
　3 Deptford SE14 ...50 C4
　Islington N7 ....14 C4
Hindle Ho E8 ....16 B3
Hindley Ho N7 ....5 B1
Hindlip Ho SW8 ...**171** B3
Hindmans Rd
　SE22 ....64 C2
Hindmarsh Cl E1 ..**125** C4
Hindrey Rd E5 ....17 A3
Hinstock Mews N4 ...78 A4
Hinton Rd SE24 ....63 A4
Hippodrome Mews
　W11 ......31 A2 **112** A3
Hippodrome Pl
　W11 ......31 A2 **112** A3
Hirst Ct SW1 ....**146** A1
Hitchin Sq **2** E3 ....26 A3
Hithe Gr **15** SE16 ...40 B3

Hitherfield Prim Sch
　SW16 ....74 C2
Hitherfield Rd SW16,
　SW27 ....74 C1
Hither Green La
　SE13 ....67 C1
Hither Green Prim
　Sch SE13 ....67 C1
Hitherlands SW12 ..73 A2
HM Prison
　Wormwood Scrubs
　W12 ....29 C3
Hoadly Rd SW16 ....73 C2
Hobart Pl SW1 .....**132** A2
Hobbes Wlk SW15 ..57 A2
Hobb's Ct SE1 .....**139** A4
Hobbs' Pl N1 ....24 A4
Hobday St E14 ....34 A3
Hobson's Pl **7** E1 .**111** B4
Hobury St SW10 ...**157** B3
Hocker St **4**
　E2 ....28 A2 **98** C3
Hockett Cl SE8 ....41 B2
Hockley Ho **8** E9 ...17 B2
Hockliffe Ho **5**
　W10 ....30 B4
Hockney Ct **1**
　SE16 ....40 A1
Hockworth Ho **7**
　N16 ....7 A3
Hocroft Ave NW2 ....1 B1
Hocroft Ct NW2 ....1 B1
Hocroft Rd NW2 ......1 B1
Hocroft Wlk NW2 ...1 C1
Hodford Lo NW11 ....1 C2
Hodford Rd NW11 ....1 C3
Hodister Cl **28** SE5 .48 B3
Hodnet Gr SE16 .....40 B2
Hoffman Sq N1 ....97 C4
Hofland Rd W14 ...**126** A2
Hogan Mews **2**
　W2 ....**101** B4
Hogan Way E5 ....7 C2
Hogarth Bsns Pk
　W4 ....46 A4
Hogarth Ct
　8 Camden Town
　NW1 ....13 B1
　City of London EC3.**124** B4
　24 Whitechapel E1 .**111** C1
Hogarth Ho SW1 ..**147** C3
Hogarth Ind Est
　NW10 ....21 C1
Hogarth La W4 ....46 A4
Hogarth Pl SW5 ...**142** A3
Hogarth Rd SW5 ..**142** A3
Hogarth Roundabout
　W4 ....46 A4
Hogarth's House *
Holbeach Mews **1**
　SW12 ....73 A3
Holbeck Row SE15 .49 C3
Holbein Ho SW1 ...**145** B2
Holbein Mews
　SW1 ....**145** B2
Holbein Pl SW1 ...**145** B3
Holberton Gdns
　NW10 ....22 A2
HOLBORN **107** C3
Holborn Cir EC1 ..**107** C3
Holborn **1**
　W12 ....30 A3

Holborn Pl WC1 ...**106** C3
Holborn Sta WC1 .**106** C3
Holborn Viaduct
　EC1 ....**108** A3
Holbrook Cl N19 ......4 A3
Holbrooke Ct **7** 14 A4
Holbrook Ho
　Acton W3 ....28 C4
　5 Streatham SW2 .74 B3
Holcombe Ho
　SW9 ....62 A4
Holcombe Pl SE4 ...66 A4
Holcombe St W6 ....39 A2
Holcroft Ct W1 ....**104** C4
Holcroft Ho
　Battersea SW11 ....59 C4
　Lewisham SE10 ....52 B2
Holcroft Rd E9 ....17 B1
Holdenby Rd SE4 ...66 A2
Holden Ho
　12 Deptford SE8 ....51 C3
　Islington N1 ....86 C3
Holden Point E15 ...19 C2
Holden St SW11 ...**169** B1
Holdernesse Rd **8**
　SW17 ....72 C2
Holderness Ho
　SE5 ....64 A4
Holdsworth Ho **5**
　SW2 ....74 C4
Holford Ho
　6 Bermondsey
　SE16 ....40 A2
　Finsbury WC1 ......95 A4
Holford Pl WC1 .....95 A4
Holford Rd NW3 ......2 B1
Holford St WC1 ......95 B4
Holford Yd WC1 .....85 B1
Holgate Ave SW11 .59 C4
Holland Gdns
　Brentford TW8 .....44 A4
　Kensington W14 .**126** B2
Holland Gr SW9 ...**163** C1
Holland Park
　W11 ......31 B1 **112** C1
Holland Park Ave
　W11 ....31 A1 **112** B1
Holland Park Ct
　W14 ....**126** B1
Holland Park Gdns
　W14 ....**126** A4
Holland Park Mews
　W11 ......31 B1 **112** C1
Holland Park Prim
　Prep Sch W14 ...**126** C1
Holland Park Rd
　W14 ....**127** A1
Holland Park Rdbt
　W12 ....39 C4
Holland Park Sch
　W8 ....**127** A4
Holland Park Sta
　W11 ......31 B1 **112** C1
Holland Pas N1 .....86 C4
Holland Pl W8 .....**128** A4
Holland Rd
　West Kensington
　W14 ....**126** B2
　Willesden Green
　NW10 ....22 A3
Holland Rise Ho
　SW9 ....**163** A1
Holland St
　Kensington W8 ...**127** C4
　Lambeth SE1 .....**122** B2

Holland Villas Rd
　W14 ....**126** A3
Holland Wlk
　Kensington W14...**127** A3
　Upper Holloway N19 ..4 C3
Hollar Rd N16 ....7 B1
Holles St **1**
　W1 ....**104** B2
Holles Ho **5** SW9 ..**172** B1
Holles St W1 ....**104** B2
Holley Rd W3 ....38 A4
Holliday Sq **6**
　SW11 ....59 C4
Hollies The SW12 ...73 A4
Hollies Way **1**
　SW12 ....72 C4
Hollingbourne Rd
　SE24 ....63 B2
Hollins Ho N7 ....14 A4
Hollisfield WC1 .....**94** B3
Holloway Rd
　Lower Holloway
　N7 ....14 B3
　Upper Holloway N19 .4 C2
Holloway Road Sta
　N7 ....14 B3
Holloway Sch N7 ...13 C3
Holly Berry La **8**
　NW3 ....11 B4
Hollybush Gdns
　E2 ....25 A2
Holly Bush Hill **4**
　NW3 ....11 B4
Hollybush Ho **23**
　E2 ....25 A2
Hollybush Pl E2 .....25 A2
Holly Bush Steps **6**
　NW3 ....11 B4
Holly Bush Vale **11**
　NW3 ....11 B4
Holly Cl NW10 ....8 A1
Hollycroft Ave NW3 ..1 C1
Hollydale Prim Sch
　SE15 ....50 B1
Hollydale Rd SE15 .50 B1
Hollydene
　Hither Green SE13..67 C1
　6 Peckham SE15 ...50 A2
Holly Gr SE15 ....49 C1
Hollyhedge Ho
　SE3 ....52 C1
Holly Hill NW3 ......11 B4
Holly Lodge SW12 .11 C1
Holly Lodge Gdns
　N6 ....3 C3
Holly Lodge Mans
　N6 ....3 C2
Holly Mews SW10 .**143** A1
Holly Mount NW3 ..11 B4
Hollymount Cl **9**
　SE10 ....52 B2
Holly Park Est N4 ....5 B4
Holly Pk N4 ....5 B4
Holly Pl NW3 ....11 B4
Holly Rd **4** W4 ....37 C2
Holly St E8 ....16 B1
Holly Terr N6 ....3 C3
Hollytree Cl SW19 ..69 C3
Holly Tree Ho SE4 ..66 B4
Holly Village N6 ......4 A2
Holly Wlk NW3 ......11 B4
Hollywood Lofts
　E1 ....24 B1 **98** C1

Hollywood Mews
SW10 ..... **156** C4
Hollywood Rd
SW10 ..... **156** C4
Holman Ho **2** E2...25 C2
Holman Hunt Ho
W14 ..... **140** A1
Holman Rd SW11. **167** B1
Holmbrook NW1... **83** A1
Holmbury Ct SW17 .72 B1
Holmbury Ho SW9 .63 A2
Holmbush Rd
SW15 ..... 58 A1
Holmcote Gdns
N5 ..... 15 B3
Holmdale Rd NW6. 10 C3
Holmdene Ave
SE24 ..... 63 B2
Holmead Rd SW6. **156** B1
Holmefield Ct **4**
NW3 ..... 12 A2
Holmefield Ho
W10 ..... 23 A1
Holmes Cl SE22 ... 64 C3
Holmes Ct
1 South Acton
W4 ..... 37 B3
18 South Lambeth
SW4 ..... **172** A2
Holmesdale Ave
SW14 ..... 55 A3
Holmesdale Ho **12**
NW6 ..... 23 C4
Holmesdale Rd
Highgate N6 ..... 4 A4
Richmond TW9 ....44 B2
Holmesley Rd
SE23 ..... 66 A1
Holmes Pl SW10. **157** A4
Holmes Rd NW5 ..13 A3
Holmes Terr SE1. **135** B4
Holmewood Gdns
SW2 ..... 74 B4
Holmewood Rd
SW2 ..... 74 B4
Holmhurst SE13 .. 67 C1
Holmleigh Prim Sch
N16 ..... 7 A3
Holmleigh Rd N16... 7 A3
Holm Oak Cl SW15 .58 B1
Holmsbury Ho **6**
N7 ..... 13 C3
Holmsdale Ho **24**
E14 ..... 34 A2
Holmside Ct SW12..60 C1
Holmside Rd
SW12 ..... 60 C1
Holmsley Ho
SW15 ..... 68 B4
Holm Wlk SE3 .... 53 C1
Holmwood Ct **3**
N16 ..... 7 B4
Holocaust Meml
Gdn* W2 ..... **131** A4
Holroyd Rd SW15 . 57 B2
Holsgrove Ct W3 ..29 A1
Holst Mans SW13 ..47 B3
Holsworthy Ho **49**
E3 ..... 27 A2
Holsworthy Sq
WC1 ..... 5 A1
Holt Ct SE10 ..... 52 B4
Holt Ho SW2 ..... 62 C1
Holton St E1 ..... 25 C1
Holwood Pl **7**
SW4 ..... 61 C3

Holybourne Ave
SW15 ..... 68 C4
Holy Cross Prim Sch
SW6 ..... **165** B4
Holy Family RC Prim
Sch **22** E14 ..... 33 C2
Holy Ghost RC Prim
Sch **4** SW12 ..... 72 C4
Holyhead Cl E3...26 C2
Holyoake Ct SE16...41 B4
Holyoak Rd SE11. **150** B3
Holyport Rd SW6. 47 C3
Holyrood Ho N4... 6 B3
Holyrood Mews
5 Greenwich SE7...43 C1
6 Newham E16....35 C1
Holyrood St SE1. **124** A1
Holy Trinity CE Prim
Sch
Belgravia SW1..... **145** B4
Dalston E8 ..... 16 B2
14 Hampstead NW3 .11 B2
Richmond TW10....54 C3
Streatham SW2 ....74 B4
Holy Trinity & Saint
Silas CE Prim Sch
NW1 ..... 13 A1
Holywell Cl
33 Bermondsey
SE16 ..... 40 A1
2 Greenwich SE3...53 C4
Holywell La
EC2 ..... 24 A1 **98** B2
Holywell Row
EC2 ..... 24 A1 **98** A1
Homan Ho **6** SW4 .73 C4
Homecross Ho **7**
W4 ..... 37 C2
Homefield Rd W4. 38 B1
Homefield St **14**
N1 ..... 24 A3
Homeleigh Ct **8**
SW16 ..... 74 A1
Homeleigh Rd
SE15 ..... 65 C2
Homemead SW12 .73 A2
Home Office SW1 **133** C1
Home Park Rd
SW19 ..... 70 B1
Home Rd SW11... **168** A2
Homer Dr E14 .... 41 C2
Homer Rd E9 ..... 18 A2
Homer Row W1.. **102** B3
Homer St W1 ..... **102** B3
HOMERTON 17 C1
Homerton Gr E9... 17 C3
Homerton High St
E9 ..... 17 C3
Homerton Rd E9 .. 18 B3
Homerton Row E9 .17 B3
Homerton Terr **1**
E9 ..... 17 B2
Homerton Terr E9 .17 B2
Homerton University
Hospl E9 ..... 17 C3
Homestall Rd
SE22 ..... 65 B2
Homestead Rd
SW6 ..... **155** A1
Homewoods **2**
SW12 ..... 73 B4
Homildon Ho **10**
SE26 ..... 76 C1
Honduras St EC1.. **96** C2
Honeybourne Rd
NW6 ..... 11 A3

Honeybrook Rd SW12,
SW4 ..... 73 B4
Honeyfield N4..... 5 C2
Honey La EC2 .... **109** A1
Honey Lane Ho
SW10 ..... **156** B4
Honeyman Cl NW6 ..9 C1
Honeywell Jun & Inf
Schs SW11 ..... 60 B1
Honeywell Rd
SW11 ..... 60 B1
Honeywood Ho **5**
SE15 ..... 49 C2
Honeywood Rd
NW10 ..... 21 B3
Honiton Gdns **1**
SE15 ..... 50 B1
Honiton Ho **20** SE5 .48 B1
Honiton Rd NW6 .. 23 B3
HONOR OAK 65 B2
Honor Oak Park Sta
SE23 ..... 65 C1
Honor Oak Pk
SE23 ..... 65 C1
Honor Oak Rise
SE23 ..... 65 B2
Honwell Ho **2**
W2 ..... 31 C4
Hood Ave SW14 .. 55 B2
Hood Ct N7 ..... 5 B1
Hood Ho **17** SE5 .. 48 C3
Hooke Ct SE10.... 52 B2
Hooke Ho **23** E3 .. 26 A3
Hookham Ct SW8. **171** B4
Hooks Cl SE15.... 50 A2
Hooper Ho **9**
SW18 ..... 58 B2
Hooper Rd E16 ... 35 C3
Hooper's St SW11 ..1 B4
Hooper's Mews **4**
W3 ..... 28 B1
Hooper St E1 .... **111** B1
Hoop La NW11 .... 1 C4
Hope Cl
2 Brentford TW8 .36 A1
Canonbury N1..... 15 B2
Hopefield Ave
NW6 ..... 23 A3
Hope Gdns **10** W3 .37 A4
Hope St SW11 .... 59 C4
Hopetown St E1 . **111** A3
Hopewell St **5** SE5..48 C3
Hop Gdns WC2 .. **120** A3
Hopgood St **5**
W12 ..... 30 B1
Hopkins Ho **7**
E14 ..... 33 C3
Hopkinson Ho **1**
SW11 ..... **169** B2
Hopkinson's Pl
NW1 ..... **81** B4
Hopkins St W1 .. **105** B1
Hopping La N1 ... 15 A2
Hop St SE10 ..... 43 B2
Hopton Ho **5**
SW9 ..... 48 A1
Hopton's Gdns
SE1 ..... **122** B2
Hopton St SE1.... **122** B2
Hopwood Cl SW17..71 B1
Hopwood Rd SE17..48 C4
Horace Rd Wlk E8 ..16 C1
Horatio Ho **11** E14..34 B1
Horatio Pl **9** E14..34 B1
Horatio St **11** E2...24 B3

Horbury Cres
W11 ..... 31 C2 **113** B3
Horbury Mews
W11 ..... 31 B2 **113** A3
Horder Rd SW6.. **164** B3
Hordle Prom E **15**
SE15 ..... 49 B3
Hordle Prom N **4**
SE15 ..... 49 B3
Hordle Prom S **7**
SE15 ..... 49 B3
Horizon Bldg **2**
E14 ..... 33 C2
Horizon Ind Est
SE15 ..... 49 C3
Horizon Sch N16 ..16 A4
Horle Wlk SE5.... 48 A1
Hormead Rd W9... 23 B1
Hornbeam Cl
SE11 ..... **149** B4
Hornbeam Ho **2**
NW3 ..... 12 B2
Hornbeam Sq **6**
E3 ..... 26 B4
Hornblower Cl **2**
SE16 ..... 41 A2
Hornby Cl NW3 ... 11 C1
Hornby Ho **6**
SE11 ..... **163** C4
Horndean Cl **2**
SW15 ..... 68 C3
Horne Way SW15 .. 47 B1
Horn La
Acton W3 ..... 28 B3
Greenwich SE10...43 C2
Horn Link Way
SE10 ..... 43 C2
Hornsby House Sch
SW12 ..... 72 C3
Hornsey La N6 .... 4 B4
Hornsey Lane Gdns
N6 ..... 4 B4
Hornsey Rd N7, N19 ..5 B3
Hornsey Rise
N19 ..... 5 A4
Hornsey Rise Gdns
N19 ..... 5 A4
Hornsey St N7 ... 14 B3
Hornshay St SE15. 50 B4
Hornton Ct W8 .. **127** C3
Hornton Pl W8 .. **127** C3
Hornton St W8 .. **127** C4
Horrocks Ho
SW15 ..... 57 A2
Horse & Dolphin Yd
W1 ..... **119** C4
Horseferry Pl
SE10 ..... 52 B4
Horseferry Rd
Limehouse E14....33 A2
Westminster SW1 . **147** C4
Horse Guards Ave
SW1 ..... **120** A1
Horse Guards Par*
SW1 ..... **119** C1
Horse Guards Rd
SW1 ..... **133** C4
Horsell Rd N5.... 14 C3
Horselydown La
SE1 ..... **124** C1
Horselydown Mans
SE1 ..... **138** C4
Horsemongers Mews
SE1 ..... **137** A3

Horsendon Ho **11**
N7 ..... 13 C3
Horseshoe Cl E14 ..42 B1
Horse Yd N1 ..... **86** B4
Horsfield Ho **13**
N1 ..... 15 B1
Horsford Rd SW2..62 B2
Horsley Ct SW1... **147** C3
Horsley St **3** SE17..48 C4
Horsman Ho SE5.. 48 B4
Horsman St SE5.. 48 B4
Horsmonden Rd
SE4 ..... 66 B1
Horston Ho N4 .... 6 B4
Hortensia Ho
SW10 ..... **156** C2
Hortensia Rd
SW10 ..... **156** C2
Horticultural Pl **6**
W4 ..... 37 C1
Horton Ave NW2 ..10 A4
Horton Ho
South Lambeth
SE8 ..... 51 B4
West Kensington
W14 ..... **140** A1
Horton Rd E8 .... 17 A2
Horton St **4** SE13..67 A4
Horwood Ho
2 Bethnal Green
E2 ..... 25 A2
Marylebone NW8 .. **90** B2
Hosack Rd SW12,
SW17 ..... 72 C2
Hosier La EC1 ... **108** B3
Hoskins St SE10.. 42 C1
Hospl for Tropical
Diseases NW1... **93** A1
Hospl of St John & St
Elizabeth NW8 .. **79** B1
Hotham Prim Sch
SW15 ..... 57 C3
Hotham Rd SW15..57 B4
Hothfield Pl SE16..40 B3
Hotspur St SE11. **149** B2
Houblon Rd TW10..54 A2
Houghton Cl **10**
E8 ..... 16 B2
Houghton Sq SW9..62 A4
Houghton St WC2 **107** A1
Houndsditch EC3. **110** B2
Household Cavalry
Mus* SW1..... **120** A1
Houseman Way **20**
SE5 ..... 48 C3
House Mill The*
E3 ..... 27 B2
Houses of
Parliament*
SW1 ..... **134** B2
Hoveden Rd NW2..10 A3
Howard Bldg
SW8 ..... **160** A3
Howard Cl
Acton W3 ..... 28 A3
Cricklewood NW2..10 A4
Howard Ct
Lewisham SE10 ... 52 B2
Peckham SE15 ... 64 C4
Howard Ho
6 Brixton SW9 .... 62 C4
14 Deptford SE8... 51 B4

Howard Ho continued
Fitzrovia W1 . . . . **92** B1
Howard Mews N5 . . .**15** A4
Howard Rd
Canonbury N16. . . . . . .**15** C4
Cricklewood NW2. . . . . . .**9** C4
Howard's La SW15. . . .**57** B3
Howbury Rd SE15 . . .**65** B4
Howcroft Ho 3
E3 . . . .**26** B2
Howden St SE15. . . . .**64** C4
Howell Ho 6 N7 . . . .**13** C3
Howell Wlk SE1 . . . .**150** B3
Howgate Rd SW14. . .**55** C4
Howick PI SW1 . . . .**133** A1
Howie St SW11 . . . .**158** A1
Howitt CI
6 Maitland Pk
NW3 . . . .**12** A2
Stoke Newington
N16 . . . .**16** A4
Howitt Rd NW3 . . . . .**12** A2
Howland Ho 5
SW16 . . . .**74** A1
Howland Mews E
W1 . . . .**105** A4
Howland St W1 . . . .**105** A4
Howland Way
SE16 . . . .**41** A4
Howletts Rd SE24 . . .**63** B1
Howley PI W2 . . . . .**101** A4
Howsman Rd
SW13 . . . .**46** C4
Howson Rd SE4 . . . . .**66** A3
Howson Terr
TW10 . . . .**54** A1
How's St E2 . . . .**24** B3
HOXTON **24** A3
Hoxton Mkt 10
N1 . . . .**24 A3 98 A3**
Hoxton Point
EC1 . . . .**24 A3 98 A3**
Hoxton Sq
N1 . . . .**24 A3 98 A3**
Hoxton St N1 . . . .**24** A3
Hoxton Sta E2 . . . . . .**24** B3
Hoylake Rd W3 . . . . . .**29** A3
Hoyland CI 4
SE15 . . . .**50** A3
Hoy St E16 . . . .**35** B3
Hub Buildings The 3
SW12 . . . .**73** A3
Hub CI E15 . . . .**27** A3
Huberd Ho 5 SE1 . .**137** C2
Hubert Gr SW9 . . . . . .**62** A4
Hubert Ho 3 SW1 . . .**90** A1
Hucknall Ct NW8 . . . .**89** B2
Huddart St 6 E3 . . . .**33** B4
Huddleston CI E2 . . . .**25** B3
Huddlestone Rd
NW2 . . . .**9** A2
Huddleston Rd N7 . .**13** B4
Hudson CI 13 W12. . .**30** A2
Hudson Ct 1 E14 . . .**41** C1
Hudson Ho
Chelsea SW10 . . . . . .**156** C2
5 Notting Hill W11 . .**31** A3

Hugh Astor Ct
SE1 . . . .**136** B2
Hugh Dalton Ave
SW6 . . . .**154** C3
Hughenden Ho
NW8 . . . .**90** A2
Hughenden Terr
E15 . . . .**19** B4
Hughes Ho
26 Bethnal Green
E2 . . . .**25** B2
Camberwell SE5 . . . . . .**48** B2
19 Deptford SE8 . . . .**51** C4
Newington SE17 . . . . .**150** B3
Hughes Mans
E1 . . . .**24 C1 99 C1**
Hughes Terr 6
E16 . . . .**35** B4
Hugh Gaitskell CI
SW6 . . . .**154** C3
Hugh Gaitskell Ho
Stoke Newington
N16 . . . .**7** B2
Willesden NW10 . . . .**8** B1
Hugh Mews SW1 . . .**146** B3
Hugh Morgan Ho 5
SW4 . . . .**61** C4
Hugh Platt Ho 22
E2 . . . .**25** A3
Hugh St SW1 . . . . . .**146** B3
Hugo Ho SW1 . . . . . .**131** A2
Hugon Rd SW6 . . . . . .**59** A4
Hugo Rd N19. . . . .**13** B4
Huguenot Ct 7
E1 . . . .**111** B4
Huguenot PI
London SW18 . . . .**59** B2
Spitalfields E1 . . . .**111** A4
Huguenot Sq SE15 . .**65** A4
Hullbridge Mews
N1 . . . .**87** B4
Hull CI SE16 . . . .**32** C1
Hull Ct SE5 . . . .**48** C1
Hull St EC1 . . . .**96** C3
Hulme PI SE1 . . . . . .**137** A3
Humber Dr W10 . . . . .**22** C1
Humber Rd SE3 . . . . .**53** B4
Humberton CI E9 . . . .**18** A3
Humbolt Rd W6 . . . .**154** A3
Hume Ct N1 . . . .**15** A1
Hume Ho 14 W11 . . . .**30** C1
Humphrey Ct
SW11 . . . .**167** C3
Humphrey St SE1 . .**152** C2
Humphry Ho 19
SW15 . . . .**57** C2
Hungerford Bridge
WC2 . . . .**120** C2
Hungerford Ho
SW1 . . . .**161** A4
Hungerford La
WC2 . . . .**120** B2
Hungerford Prim Sch
10 N7 . . . .**13** C2
Hungerford Rd
12 Camden Town
N7 . . . .**13** C2
Lower Holloway N7 . . . . .**14** A2
Hungerford St 21
E1 . . . .**32** A3
Hunsdon Rd SE14 . . .**50** C3
Hunslett St 28 E2 . . .**25** B3
Hunstanton Ho

Hunt CI W11. . . . .**30** C1
Hunter CI
Borough SE1 . . . . . .**137** C1
Upper Tooting
SW12 . . . .**72** C3
**Huntercombe-
Roehampton Hospl**
The SW15 . . . .**68** C4
Hunter Ct
15 London SE5 . . . . . .**63** C3
27 Streatham SW2 . .**74** C4
Hunter Ho
Bloomsbury WC1 . . . . .**94** B2
Lambeth SE1 . . . .**136** B3
South Lambeth
SW8 . . . .**161** C1
1 Tufnell Pk N19 . . . . .**4** B1
West Brompton
SW5 . . . .**141** C1
Hunter Lo 9 W9 . . . .**31** C4
Hunter St WC1 . . . . . .**94** B2
Huntingdon Ct
SW14 . . . .**55** B4
Huntingdon Gdns
W4 . . . .**45** B3
Huntingdon Ho
SW5 . . . .**141** C4
Huntingdon St
Canning Town E16 . . . .**35** B3
Islington N1 . . . .**14** B1
Huntingfield Rd
SW15 . . . .**56** C2
Huntingford Ho
SW15 . . . .**47** B1
Huntington Ho
NW2 . . . .**9** B2
Huntley St WC1 . . . . .**93** B1
Hunton St E1 . . . . . .**111** B4
Hunts CI SE3 . . . .**53** C1
Hunt's Ct WC2 . . . . .**119** C3
Huntshaw Ho 37
E3 . . . .**27** A2
Hunt's La E15 . . . .**27** B3
Huntsman St
SE17 . . . .**152** A3
Huntspill St SW17 . . .**71** B1
Hunts Slip Rd
SE21 . . . .**76** A2
Hurdwick Ho 20
NW1 . . . .**82** C2
Hurdwick PI NW1. . . .**82** C2
Hurleston Ho 11
SE8 . . . .**41** B1
Hurley Cres SE16 . . .**40** C4
Hurley Ho
Lambeth SE11 . . . . . .**149** C3
34 Shoreditch
E2 . . . .**24 B2 98 C3**
Hurley Lo SE22 . . . . .**65** B1
**Hurlingham &
Chelsea Sec Sch**
SW6 . . . .**58** C4
**Hurlingham Court
Mans** SW6 . . . .**165** B1
Hurlingham Gdns
SW6 . . . .**58** B4
Hurlingham Rd
SW6 . . . .**165** A1

Hurlingham Sch
SW15 . . . .**58** B3
Hurlingham Sq
SW6 . . . .**59** A4
Hurlock Ho 5 N5 . . . .**6** A1
Hurlock St N5 . . . .**6** A1
Huron Rd SW17 . . . . .**72** C1
Huron Univ WC1 . . .**106** A4
Hurstbourne Ho
SW15 . . . .**56** B1
Hurstdene Gdns
N15 . . . .**7** A4
Hurst Ho WC1 . . . . . .**85** A1
Hurst St SE24 . . . .**63** A1
Hurstway Wlk 2
W11 . . . .**30** C2
Husborne Ho 8
SE8 . . . .**41** A2
Huson CI NW3. . . . . . .**12** A1
Hutching's St E14 . . .**41** C4
Hutching's Wharf 1
E14 . . . .**41** C4
Hutchins CI E15 . . . . .**19** B1
Hutchins Ho 3
SW4 . . . .**73** C4
Hutchinson Ho 9
SE14 . . . .**50** B3
Hutton Ct 5 N4 . . . . . .**5** B4
Hutton Ho 19
E2 . . . .**24 C2 99 B3**
Hutton St EC4 . . . . .**107** C1
Huxbear St SE4 . . . . .**66** B2
Huxley Ho
4 London SW9 . . . .**172** C2
Paddington NW8 . . . . . .**89** C2
Huxley St W10 . . . . . .**23** A2
Hyacinth Rd SW15 . .**68** C3
Hyde Farm Mews
SW12 . . . .**73** C3
Hyde La SW11 . . . . .**168** A4
Hyde Park * W2 . . .**116** C3
Hyde Park Cnr
SW1 . . . .**131** C4
Hyde Park Corner Sta
SW1 . . . .**131** C4
Hyde Park Cres
W2 . . . .**102** A1
Hyde Park Gate Mews
SW7 . . . .**129** A3
Hyde Park Gdns
W2 . . . .**115** C4
Hyde Park Gdns Mews
W2 . . . .**116** A4
Hyde Park Mans
NW1 . . . .**102** B3
Hyde Park PI W2 . . .**116** B4
Hyde Park Sq W2 . .**102** A1
**Hyde Park Square
Mews** W2 . . . .**102** A1
Hyde Park St W2 . . .**102** A1
Hyde Park Twrs
W2 . . . .**114** C3
Hyde Rd
Richmond TW10 . . . . . .**54** B2
Shoreditch N1 . . . .**24** A4
Hyde's PI 11 N1 . . . . .**15** A1
Hyde St SE8 . . . .**51** C4
Hydethorpe Rd
SW12 . . . .**73** B3
Hyde Vale SE10 . . . . .**52** B3
Hylda Ct NW5 . . . .**3** C1
Hyndman Ho 4
N19 . . . .**13** C4
Hyndman St SE15 . . .**50** A4
Hyperion Ho
27 Bow E3 . . . .**26** A3

Hyperion Ho continued
Streatham SW2 . . . .**74** B4
Hyson Rd SE16 . . . . . .**40** A1
Hythe Ho 14 SE16 . . .**40** B4
Hythe Rd NW10. . . . . .**21** C1
Hythe Road Ind Est
NW10 . . . .**21** C1

I

Ian Hamilton Ho
NW1 . . . .**93** B4
Ian Mikardo Sch 8
E3 . . . .**27** A2
Ibberton Ho
Kensington W14 . . . .**126** B1
South Lambeth
SW8 . . . .**162** C2
Ibbotson Ave E16 . . .**35** B3
Ibbott St 12 E1 . . . . . .**25** B1
Iberia Ho 17 N19 . . . . .**4** C4
Ibis Ct 18 SE8 . . . .**51** B4
Ibis La W4 . . . .**45** B2
Ibsley Gdns SW15 . . .**68** C3
Ibstock Place Sch
SW15 . . . .**56** A1
Icarus Ho 22 E3 . . . . .**26** B2
Iceland Rd E3 . . . .**26** C4
Iceland Wharf
SE16 . . . .**41** A2
Iceni Ct 23 E3 . . . .**26** B4
Ice Wharf NW1 . . . . . .**84** B2
Idaho Bldg 7
SE13 . . . .**52** A2
Ida St E14 . . . .**34** B3
**Identity & Passport
Office** SW1 . . . . . .**146** B3
Idmiston Rd SE27, . . .
SE27 . . . .**75** B2
Idol La EC3 . . . .**124** A3
Idonia St SE8 . . . .**51** C3
Iffley Ho 9
E2 . . . .**24 B2 98 C3**
Iffley Rd W6. . . . .**39** A3
Ifield Ho SE17 . . . . .**152** B2
Ifield Rd SW10 . . . . .**156** B4
Ifor Evans PI E1 . . . . .**25** C1
Ightham Ho SE17 . . .**152** A3
Ikon Ho 21 E1 . . . .**32** B2
Ilbert St W10 . . . .**23** A2
Ilchester Gdns
W2 . . . .**114** A4
Ilchester Mans
W8 . . . .**127** B2
Ilchester PI W14 . . . .**127** A2
Ildersly Gr SE21 . . . . .**75** C2
Ilderton Prim Sch
SE16 . . . .**40** B1
Ilderton Rd SE15, . . .
SE16 . . . .**50** B4
Ilex Rd NW10 . . . .**8** B2
Ilford Ho 14 N1 . . . . . .**15** C2
Ilfracombe Flats
SE1 . . . .**137** A4
Iliffe St SE17 . . . .**150** B2
Iliffe Yd SE17 . . . . . .**150** B2
Ilkeston Ct 7 E5 . . . . .**17** C4
Ilminster Gdns
SW11 . . . .**60** A3
Ilsley Ct 8 SW8 . . . .**170** C1
Imber St N1 . . . .**87** B3
Imperial Ave 5
N16 . . . .**16** A4
Imperial CI NW2 . . . . .**9** A3

Imperial College London (Charing Cross) W6 ....39 C1
Imperial College London (Chelsea & Westminster) SW10 ...157 A3
Imperial College London (Hammersmith) W12 ....30 A3
Imperial College London (Royal Brompton) SW3 ..144 A2
Imperial College London (South Kensington) SW7 ....129 B2
Imperial College London (St Mary's) W2 ....101 C2
Imperial Cres SW6 ....167 A1
Imperial Ct NW8 ..80 B2
Imperial Ho
1 Bow E3 ....26 A3
2 Poplar E14 .....33 B2
Strand WC2 .....107 B1
Imperial Rd SW6 ..166 B3
Imperial Sq SW6 ..166 B3
Imperial Twrs 3
NW3 ....11 B2
Imperial War Mus★
SE1, SE11 ....135 C1
Imperial Wharf Sta
SW10 ....167 B3
Imre Cl W12........30 A1
Inchbald Sch of Design (Garden Design) SW1 ...146 B3
Inchbald Sch of Design (Interior Design) SW1 ...145 B4
Independent Pl E8 ..16 B3
Indescon Ct E14 ....42 A4
Indiana Bldg 7
SE8 ....51 C2
India St EC3 .....110 C1
India Way W12 ....30 A2
Indigo Mews N16......6 C1
Indoor Sports Arena
E14 ....34 B1
Indus Ct 1 SE16 ..49 B3
Ingate Pl SW8 ....170 B3
Ingelow Ho W8 ..128 A4
Ingersoll Rd W12 ..30 A1
Ingestre Pl W1 ..105 A1
Ingestre Rd NW5 ..13 A4
Ingham Rd NW6 ...10 C4
Inglebert St EC1 ....95 B4
Ingleborough St
SW9 ....173 B2
Ingleby Rd N7 ....5 A1
Inglefield Sq 12
E1 ....32 A1
Ingle Ho 3 SW12 ..73 C3
Inglesham Wlk E9 ..18 B2
Ingleside Gr SE3 ..53 B4
Inglethorpe Ho 6
E5 ....7 C2
Inglethorpe St
SW6 ....47 C2
Ingleton St SW9 ..173 B2

Inglewood Cl E14....41 C2
Inglewood Mans 11
........................10 C3
Inglewood Rd
NW6 ....10 C3
Inglis St 1 SW15 ..57 B2
Inglis St SE5 ....48 A2
Ingram Ave NW11 ....2 B4
Ingram Ho 3 E3 ....33 B4
Ingram Lo 8 SW4 ..61 C1
Ingrave St SW11 ..60 A4
Ingrebourne Ho
........................101 C4
Ingress St 4 W4 ....38 A1
Inigo Pl WC2 .....120 A4
Inkerman Rd NW5 ..13 A2
Inkerman Terr
W8 ....127 C1
Inkster Ho 9
SW11 ....60 A4
Inman Rd
Harlesden NW10 ....21 A4
Wandsworth SW18 ..71 B4
Inner Circ NW1.....91 B4
Inner Park Rd
SW19 ....69 C2
Inner Temple★
EC4 ....121 B4
Inner Temple La
EC4 ....107 B1
Innes Gdns SW15 ..57 A1
Innisfree Ho NW2 ....9 C2
Innis Ho SE17 ....152 A2
Insley Ho 15 E3 ....27 A2
Institute of Cancer Research The
SW7 ....143 A2
Institute PI 18 E8 ..17 A3
Inst of Child Health
WC1 ....94 C1
Inst of Neurology
Bloomsbury WC1 ..106 B4
St Pancras WC1 ....94 B1
Int Coll of Accountancy The
SW17 ....72 B1
Interchange The
NW5 ....13 A3
International Com Sch
W1 ....91 C1
International House Language Sch
WC2 ....106 B2
International Sch of London's........36 C2
Inver Ct
1 Bayswater W2 ..100 B1
4 Hammersmith
W6 ....38 C3
Inverforth Cl NW3 ..2 B2
Inverforth Ho NW3 ..2 B2
Invergarry Ho
NW6 ....78 A1
Invermead Cl W6 ..38 C2
Inverness Gdns
W8 ....114 A1
Inverness Mews
W2 ....114 B4
Inverness Pl W2 ..114 B4
Inverness St NW1 ..82 B4
Inverness Terr
W2 ....114 B4
Inverton Rd SE15 ..65 C3
Invicta 1 E3 ....33 C4
Invicta Plaza SE1 ..122 A2

Invicta Prim Sch
SE3 ....53 C3
Invicta Rd SE3, SE7 ..53 C4
Inville Rd SE17 ...151 C1
Inwen Ct SE8 ......41 A1
Inwood Ct 12 NW1..13 B1
Inwood Ho 16
SE22 ....64 A4
Inworth St SW11 ..168 B2
Inworth Wlk N1 ....86 C4
Ion Ct 8 E2 ....24 C3
Ionian Bldg 19
E14 ....33 A2
Ionian Ho 22 E1 ....25 C1
Ipsden Bldgs SE1 ..135 C4
Ipswich Ho SE4 ....65 C2
Iqra Ind Sch SW9 ..62 C3
Irby Ho SW2 ....62 C1
Ireland Yd EC4 ....108 B1
Irene Rd SW6 .....165 C3
Ireton Ho 22 SW9 ..173 C1
Ireton St 12 E3 ....26 C1
Iris Ct 8 SE15 .....50 A1
Iroko Ho 7 NW3 ..11 A2
Iron Bridge Cl
NW10 ....8 A3
Iron Bridge Ho
NW3 ....12 B1
Irongate Ho EC3 ..110 B2
Iron Mill Pl SW18 ..59 A1
Iron Mill Rd SW18 ..59 A1
Ironmonger La
EC2 ....109 B1
Ironmonger Pas
EC1 ....97 A3
Ironmonger Row
EC1 ....97 A3
Ironmonger Row Baths EC1 ....97 A3
Ironmongers Pl
E14 ....41 C2
Ironmonger's Pl 22
E14 ....41 C2
Ironside Cl SE16 ..40 C4
Ironside Ho E9 .....18 A4
Ironworks 8 E3 ....26 C4
Irvine Ct W1 ....93 A1
Irvine Ho N7 ....14 B2
Irving Gr SW9 ....172 C1
Irving Ho SE17 ...150 A1
Irving Mews N1 ....15 B2
Irving Rd W14 .....39 C3
Irving St WC2 ....119 C3
Irwell Est 80 SE16 ..40 B4
Irwin Gdns NW10 ..22 A4
Isabella 4 3
TW10 ....54 B1
Isabella Ho
19 Hammersmith
W6 ....39 B1
Kennington SE11 ..150 A2
Isabella Mews 1
E8 ....16 A2
Isabella Rd E9 .....17 B3
Isabel St SW9 ....173 A4
Isambard Mews
E14 ....42 B3
Isambard Pl SE16 ..32 C1
Iseldon Ct N7 ......14 A4
Isel Way 4 SE22 ..64 A2
Isis Cl SW15 ....57 B3
Isis Ct W4 ....45 A3
Isis Ho NW8 ....89 C1
Isis St SW18 ....71 B2
Islamia Girls' High
Sch NW6 ....23 A4

Islamia Prim Sch
NW6 ....23 A4
Islamic Coll for Advanced Studies 2
NW10 ....9 A2
Island Gardens Sta
E14 ....42 B1
Island Ho E14 .....27 B2
Island Rd SE16 ....40 C2
Island Row E14 ....33 B3
Islay Wlk 17 N1 ....15 B2
Isleden Ho N1 .....86 C4
Isledon Rd N4, N7 ..5 C1
ISLE OF DOGS 42 B2
ISLINGTON 14 C2
Islington Arts & Media Sch 8 N4 ..5 B2
Islington Bsns Ctr
N1 ....87 A4
Islington Est 1 N1 ..86 C4
Islington Gn N1 ....86 A3
Islington High St
N1 ....86 A2
Islington Mus★
WC1 ....96 A3
Islington Park Mews
N1 ....15 A1
Islington Park St
N1 ....15 A1
Islington Tennis Ctr
N7 ....14 A2
Islip St NW5 ....13 B3
Isokon Flats 3
NW3 ....12 B3
Issac Way SE1 ...137 A4
Italia Conti Acad of Theatre Arts EC1 ..96 C1
Ivanhoe Ho
11 Balham SW12 ..73 A4
3 Bow E3 ....26 A3
Ivanhoe Rd SE5 ...64 B4
Ivatt Pl W14 .....141 A1
Iveagh Cl E9 ....25 C4
Iveagh Ct EC3 ....110 C1
Iveagh Ho
3 Brixton SW9 ....48 A1
Chelsea SW10 ...157 A2
Ivebury Ct 8 W10 ..30 B3
Iveley Rd SW4 ...170 C1
Iver Ct N1 ....15 B2
Iverna Ct W8 .....127 C2
Iverna Gdns W8 ..127 C2
Iverson Rd NW6 ..10 C2
Ives Rd E16 ....35 A4
Ives St SW3 ......144 B4
Ivimey St E2 ....24 C2
Ivinghoe Ho N7 ..13 C3
Ivor Ct NW1 ....90 C2
Ivories The N1 .....15 B1
Ivor Mayor Lo
SW12 ....60 C1
Ivor Pl NW1 ....90 C1
Ivor St NW1 ....13 B1
Ivory Ho
1 London SW11 ..59 B4
St George in t East
........................125 A2
Ivory Sq 15 SW18 ..59 B4
Ivybridge Ho 18
SE22 ....64 A4
Ivybridge La WC2 ..120 B3
Ivy Cres W4 ....37 B2
Ivy Ct 11 SE16 ...153 C1

Ivydale Prim Sch
SE15 ....65 C3
Ivydale Rd SE15 ..65 C3
Ivyday Gr SW16 ..74 B1
Ivy Ho Lo W8 ...31 C1
Ivymount Rd SE27 ..74 C1
Ivy Rd
Brockley SE4 ......66 C3
Cricklewood NW2 ..9 B4
Newham E16 ......35 C3
Ivy St N1 ....24 A3
Ixworth Pl SW3 ..144 A3

J

Jacaranda Gr E8 ..16 B1
Jackman Ho 24
........................32 A1
Jackman St E8 .....25 A4
Jackson Cl E9 .....17 C1
Jackson Ho 16
........................59 C4
Jackson Rd N7 ....14 B4
Jackson's La N6 ....4 A4
Jack Taylor Sch
NW8 ....78 C4
Jack Tizard Sch
........................38 C2
Jack Walker Ct
N5 ....15 A4
Jacobin Lo N7 ....14 A3
Jacob Mans 13 E1 ..32 A3
Jacobson Ct
........................168 B3
Jacobson Ho 1 ..110 C2
Jacob St SE1 .....139 B4
Jacob's Well Mews
W1 ....103 C2
Jacotts Ho W10 ..22 B1
Jacqueline Ho 8
E1 ....32 C4
Jacques Prevert Sch
3 W6 ....39 C2
Jaggard Way
SW12 ....72 B4
Jagger Ho SW11 ..168 C4
Jago Wlk SE5 .....48 C3
Jamahirya Sch
SW3 ....158 A4
Jamaica Rd
Bermondsey SE1 ..139 B3
Bermondsey SE16 ..40 A3
Jamaica St E1 .....32 B4
James Allen's Girls'
Sch 22 SE22 ......64 A2
James Allen's Pre-Prep Sch SE21 ..63 C1
James Allen's Prep
Sch 18 SE22 ......64 A2
James Anderson Ct 2
E2 ....24 A3
James Ave NW2 ....9 B3
James Brine Ho 6
E2 ....24 82 pre-comes... 24 B2 99 B4
James Campbell Ho
2 E2 ....25 B3
James Collins Cl
W9 ....23 B1
James Docherty Ho
4 E2 ....25 B3
James Hammett Ho
9 E2 ....24 B3

James Ho
Mile End E1......26 A1
33 Rotherhithe
SE16............40 C4
James Joyce Wlk 7
SE24............63 A3
James Leicester Hall
of Residence N7 ..14 A2
James Lind Ho
SE8............41 B2
James Middleton Ho
20 E2............25 A2
Jameson Ct E2...25 B3
Jameson Ho SE11 148 C2
Jameson Pl 11 W3..37 B4
Jameson St
W8 ...31 C1 113 C2
James's Cotts
TW9............44 C3
James St
Marylebone W1 .. 103 C1
Strand WC2 ...... 120 B4
James Stewart Ho
NW6............10 B1
James Stroud Ho
SE17...........151 A1
Jamestown Rd
NW1............82 A4
Jamestown Way
E14............34 C2
James Voller Way 30
E1.............32 B3
James Wolfe Prim
Sch 10 SE10 ....52 B3
Jamiatul Ummah Sch
40 E1...........32 A3
Jamuna Cl E14 ...33 A4
Jane E1...........32 A3
Janet St E14 .....41 C3
Janeway Pl 2
SE16 ......40 A4
Janeway St SE16 139 C3
Jansen Ho 5
SW15 ....56 C2
Jansen Wlk SW11 .59 C3
Japan Cres N4 ....5 B3
Jardine Rd E1....32 C2
Jarman Ho
Bermondsey SE16 ..40 C2
13 Stepney E1 ....32 B4
Jarrett Cl SW7 ...75 A3
Jarrow Rd SE16 ...40 B1
Jarrow Way E9 ...18 A4
Jarvis Ho 3 SE15 ..49 C2
Jarvis Rd SE22 ...64 A3
Jasmin SE1 ......125 A1
Jasmine Sq 3 E3 .26 B4
Jasmin Ho SE4 ...66 B4
Jasmin Lo 17 SE16..40 A1
Jason Ct
2 London SW9...173 B4
Marylebone W1 .. 103 C2
Jasper Wlk N1....97 B4
Java Wharf SE1 .. 139 A4
Jay Ho SW15.....47 B1
Jay Mews SW7 .. 129 A3
Jean Darling Ho
SW10...........157 B3
Jean Pardies Ho 28
E1.............32 B4
Jebb Ave SW2....62 A1
Jebb St E3........26 C3
Jedburgh St SW11..60 C3
Jeddo Mews W12 ..38 B4

Jeddo Rd W12.....38 B4
Jefferson Bldg 3
E14............41 C4
Jeffrey's Ct 2
SW4 .... 172 A2
Jeffrey's Pl NW1 ..13 B1
Jeffrey's Rd SW4 172 A2
Jeffrey's St NW1 ..13 B1
Jeff Wooller Coll
WC1...........106 B4
Jeger Ave E2.....24 B4
Jelf Rd SW2......62 C2
Jellicoe Ho
5 Bethnal Green
E2.............24 C3
Fitzrovia NW1 ....92 B1
11 Putney SW15 ...57 C2
Jemotts Ct 5
SE14...........50 C4
Jenkins Ho SW8 . 171 B4
Jenkinson Ho 12
E2.............25 C2
Jenner Ave W3 ...28 C4
Jenner Ho SE3 ...53 A4
Jenner Pl SW13 ...47 A4
Jenner Rd N16 ....7 B1
Jennifer Ho SE11 149 C3
Jennings Ho SE10..42 C1
Jennings Rd SE22 .64 B1
Jenson Ho 8 E3 ..26 C1
Jephson Ct 17
SW4 ....172 B1
Jephson Ho 6
SE17............48 A4
Jephson St SE5...48 C2
Jephtha Rd SW18..58 C1
Jerdan Pl SW6 .. 155 B2
Jeremiah St 11
E14............34 A3
Jeremy Bentham Ho
24 E2 ....24 C2 99 C3
Jermyn St SW1 .. 119 A2
Jerningham Ct
SE14...........51 A2
Jerningham Rd
SE14...........51 A2
Jerome Cres NW8 .90 A2
Jerome Ho NW1 .. 102 B4
Jerome St
E1 ....24 B1 98 C1
Jerome Twr 8
W3............37 A4
Jerrard St SE13...67 A4
Jerrold Lo SW15 ..57 A4
Jerrold St N1....24 A3
Jersey Ho 15 N1 ..15 B2
Jersey Rd N1....15 B2
Jersey St E2 .....25 A2
Jerusalem Pas
.............96 A1
Jervis Bay Ho 9
E14............34 C3
Jervis Ct
2 Greenwich
SE10...........52 B2
Marylebone W1 .. 104 B1
Jessel Ho
St Pancras WC1 ...94 A3
Westminster SW1 . 147 C4
Jessica Blythe La 4
Jessie Duffett Ho 1
SE5............48 B3
Jesson Ho SE17 . 151 B3
Jessop Ct N1.....86 B1

Jessop Ho 9 W4...37 C2
Jessop Sq E14....33 C1
Jeston Ho 10 SE27..75 A1
Jethou Ho 16 N1 ..15 B2
Jevons Ho 9
.............11 C1
Jewell Ho 9
Jewish Mus The *
NW1............82 B3
Jewry St EC3 .... 110 C1
Jews Row SW18 ..59 B3
Jeymer Ave NW2 ..9 B3
Jeypore Rd SW18..59 B1
Jim Griffiths Ho
SW6 ....155 A3
Jim Veal Dr 3
N7............14 A2
Joanna Ho 7 W6 ..39 B1
Joan St SE1 ..... 122 A1
Jocelin Ho N1 ....85 A3
Jocelyn Rd TW9 ..54 A4
Jocelyn St SE15 ..49 C2
Jockey's Fields
WC1...........107 A4
Jodane St SE8 ...41 B2
Jodrell Rd E3 ....26 B4
Johanna Prim Sch
SE1............135 B3
Johanna St SE1 . 135 B3
John Adam St
WC2...........120 B3
John Aird Ct W2. 101 A4
John Archer Way
SW18...........59 C1
John Ball Prim Sch
SE3............53 A1
John Barker Ct
NW6............10 A1
John Betts' Ho
W12............38 B3
John Betts Prim Sch
W6............38 C3
John Bond Ho 3
E3 ....26 B3
John Brent Ho 8
SE8............40 C2
John Buck Ho
NW10...........21 B4
John Burns Prim Sch
17 SW11 .... 169 C1
John Campbell Rd
N16...........16 A3
John Carpenter St
EC4...........122 A4
John Cartwright Ho
7 E2............25 A2
John Clynes Ct
SW15...........57 A3
John Conwey Ho 2
SW2............62 C1
John Dee Ho 5
SW14...........55 C4
John Donne Prim Sch
18 SE15 ....50 A2
John Dwight Ho
SW6............59 A4
John Fearon Wlk 5
W10............23 A2
John Felton Rd 10
SE16...........139 B3
John Fielden Ho 10
E2.............25 A2
John Fisher St E1 125 B4

John F Kennedy Specl
Sch 6 E15 ....27 C4
John Harris Ho
SE15...........64 C4
John Harrison Way
SE10............43 B3
John Islip St SW1 148 A3
John Keall Ho 5
SW15...........57 C4
John Keble CE Prim
Sch NW10......21 B4
John Kennedy Ct
N1.............15 C2
John Kennedy Ho
6
N1.............15 C2
John Kennedy Lo 2
N1.............15 C2
John King Ct 5
N19............
John Kirk Ho
21 Battersea
SW11...........59 C4
5 Streatham SW16 ..74 A1
John Knight Lo
SW6 ....155 C2
John McDonald Ho 3
E14............42 B3
John McKenna Wlk 17
SE16...........139 C2
John Maurice Cl
SE17...........151 B4
John Nettleford Ho 4
E2.............25 A2
John Orwell Sports
Ctr E1..........32 A1
John Parker Sq 7
SW11...........59 C4
John Parry Ct 2
N1.............24 A3
John Paul II Sch 8
SW19...........69 C4
John Penn Ho SE8..51 B3
John Penn St
SE13...........52 A2
John Perryn Prim Sch
W3............29 A3
John Prince's St
W1............104 B2
John Pritchard Ho 10
E1 ....24 C1 99 C1
John Ratcliffe Ho 6
NW6...........23 C2
John Rennie Wlk 1
E1.............32 B1
John Roan Sch
SE3 ....53 A3
John Roll Way
SE16...........139 C2
John Ruskin Prim Sch
SE5............48 B4
John Ruskin St
SE5............48 B4
John Scurr Ho 18
E14............33 A3
John Scurr Prim Sch
48 E1 ....25 B1
John Silkin La SE8 .40 C1
John's Mews WC1 ..95 A1
John Smith Ave
SW6 ....154 C2
John Smith Mews
E14............34 C2
Johnson Cl E8...24 C4
Johnson Ct 10
SW18...........59 C3

Johnson Ho
Belgravia SW1 ... **145** C3
23 Bethnal Green
E2 ....24 C2 **99** C3
Somers Town NW1.. **83** A1
South Lambeth
SW8 .... **161** C1
Johnson Lo 12 W9 .31 C4
Johnson Rd NW10..20 C4
Johnsons Ct EC4 . **107** C1
Johnson's Pl SW1 **146** C1
Johnson St E1 ...32 B3
Johnsons Way
NW10...........20 A1
John Spencer Sq
N1.............15 A2
John's Pl E1 .....32 A3
John St WC1 .....95 A1
John Stainer Prim
Sch 66 A4
Johnston Cl SW9 **173** A3
Johnstone Ho
SE13...........67 C4
John Strachey Ho
SW6 ....155 A3
John Trundle Ct
EC4...........108 C4
John Tucker Ho 3
E14............41 C3
John Wesley's House
& Mus of
Methodism *
EC1............97 C2
John Wheatley Ho
14 London N19......4 C4
West Brompton
SW6 ....155 A3
John Williams Cl
SE14............50 C4
Joiners Arms Yd 5
SE5............48 C2
Joiner St SE1 ... **123** C1
Joiners Yd N1....84 B1
Jolles Ho 9 E3 ...27 A2
Jonathan St
SE11...........148 C2
Jones Ho
4 South Bromley
E14............34 C3
Stamford Hill N16...7 A3
Jones St W1.... **118** A3
Jones Wlk
TW10...........54 B1
Jonson Ho
Borough The SE1 . **137** C1
16 Canonbury N1. ..15 C4
Jordan Ct SW15 ..57 C3
Jordan Ho
12 London SE4....65 C3
Shoreditch N1 ....87 C3
Jordans Ho NW8 . **90** A1
Joscoyne Ho 5
E1.............32 A3
Joseph Ave W3 ...28 C3
Joseph Conrad Ho
SW1...........147 A3
Joseph Ct N16 ....7 A4
Joseph Hardcastle Cl
SE14...........50 C3
Josephine Ave
SW2............62 B2
Joseph Irwin Ho 11
E14............33 B2
Joseph Powell Cl 1
SW12...........61 B1

Joseph Priestley Ho
12 E2 ....25 A2
Joseph St E3 ....26 B1
Joseph Trotter Cl
EC1 ....95 C3
Joshua St E14 ....34 B3
Joslings Cl W12 ....29 C2
Josseline Ct **8** E3 .....26 A3
Joubert Mans
SW3 ....144 B2
Joubert St SW11 ....169 A2
Jowett Ho **27**
SW9 ....172 B1
Jowett St SE15 ....49 B3
Jubet Ho **9** N16 ....15 C4
Jubilee Bldgs NW8 ......79 B2
Jubilee Cl
NW10 ....21 B3
Jubilee Cres E14 ....42 B3
Jubilee Ct N1 ....14 A2
Jubilee Hall Mkt★
WC2 ....120 B4
Jubilee Ho SE11 ....149 C3
Jubilee Hts NW2 ....10 B2
Jubilee JMI Sch
N16 ....7 C3
Jubilee Mans **10**
E1 ....32 B3
Jubilee Prim Sch
SW2 ....62 C1
Jubilee St E1 ....32 B4
Jubilee The **2**
SE10 ....52 A3
Judd St WC1 ....94 A3
Jude St E16 ....35 B3
Judges' Wlk NW3 ....2 B1
Juer St SW11 ....158 B1
Julian Ave W3 ....28 A2
Julian Ct SW13 ....46 B2
Julian Pl E14 ....42 A1
Julia St NW5 ....12 C3
Juliet Ho **1** N1 ....24 A3
Julius Ct TW8 ....44 A3
Julius Ho **8** E14 ....34 C3
Julius Nyerere Cl
N1 ....84 C3
Junction App
Battersea SW11 ....60 A4
Lewisham SE13 ....67 B4
Junction Mews
W2 ....102 A2
Junction Pl W2 ....101 C2
Junction Rd N19 ....4 B1
Juniper Cres NW1 ....12 C1
Juniper Ct N16 ....6 C2
Juniper Dr SW18 ....59 B3
Juniper Ho
6 Peckham SE14,
SE15 ....50 B3
9 Richmond TW9 ....45 A2
Juniper St **16** E1 .....32 B2
Juno Ct **11** SW9 .....163 B1
Juno Ho **2** E3 ....26 C4
Juno Way SE14 ....50 C4
Juno Way Ind Est
SE14 ....50 C4
Jupiter Ct **10**
SW9 ....163 B1
Jupiter Way N7 ....14 B2
Jupp Rd E15 ....19 C1
Jupp Rd W E15 ....27 C4
Jura Ho SE16 ....41 A2
Jurston Ct SE1 ....135 C3
Justice Wlk SW3 ....158 A3

Justines Pl E2 ....25 C2
Jutland Cl N19 ....5 A3
Jutland Ho **4** SE5 ....48 B1
Juxon St SE11 ....149 A4

K

Kambala Rd SW11 ....59 C4
Kara Way SW2 ....74 B4
Karen Ct
3 Camberwell
SE5 ....64 A4
Forest Hill SE23 ....66 A1
Karen Ho **7** N16 ....16 A4
Kasmin Ct NW10 ....8 C1
Kassala Rd SW11 ....169 A3
Katherine Cl **3**
SE16 ....32 C1
Katherine Ho **18**
W10 ....23 A1
Katherine Sq
W11 ....31 A1 112 A2
Kathleen Ave W3 ....28 A4
Kathleen Rd SW11 ......60 B4
Kay Rd SW9 ....172 C1
Kay St E2 ....24 C3
Kean Ho **8** SE17 ......48 A4
Kean St WC2 ....106 C1
Keats Cl
Bermondsey SE1 ....152 C3
Hampstead NW3 ....12 A4
Keats Gr NW3 ....12 A4
Keats Ho
22 Bethnal Green
E2 ....25 A3
30 Camberwell SE5 ..48 B3
Stockwell SW1 ....161 A4
Keats House Mus★
NW3 ....12 A4
Keats Pl EC2 ....109 B3
Keble Ho **4** SW15 ....57 C1
Keble Pl SW13 ....47 A4
Kedelston Ct E5 ....18 A4
Kedge Ho **6** E14 ......41 C3
Kedleston Wlk **21**
E2 ....25 A2
Keel Cl SE16 ....32 C1
Keel Ct **8** E14 ....34 C2
Keeley St WC2 ....106 C1
Keeling Ho **4** E2 ......25 A3
Keelson Ho **9**
E14 ....41 C3
Keen's Yd N1 ....15 A2
Keeper Wharf **1** E1 ..32 C2
Keepier Wharf **18**
E1 ....32 C2
Keep The SE3 ....53 C1
Keeton's Rd SE16 ....40 A3
Keevil Dr SW19 ....70 A4
Keighley Cl N7 ....14 A4
Keildon Rd SW11 ....60 B3
Keir Hardie Ho
Fulham W6 ....47 C4
17 Upper Holloway
N19 ....4 C4
Willesden NW10 ....9 A1
Keir Hardy Prim Sch
E16 ....35 C4
Keith Connor Cl **5**
SW8 ....61 A4
Keith Gr W12 ....29 C1
Keith Ho NW6 ....78 A1
Kelby Ho N7 ....14 B2
Kelfield Ct **1** W10 ....30 C3

Kelfield Gdns W10 ......30 C3
Kelfield Mews
W10 ....30 C3
Kellett Ho N1 ....87 C3
Kellett Rd SW2 ....62 C3
Kellow Ho **11** SE1 ..137 B4
Kell St SE1 ....136 B2
Kelly Ave SE15 ....49 B2
Kelly Ct **18** E14 ....33 C2
Kelly Mews **9** W9 ....23 B1
Kelly St NW1 ....13 A2
Kelman Cl SW4 ....171 C1
Kelmore Gr SE22 ....64 C3
Kelmscott Gdns
W12 ....38 C3
Kelmscott House★
W6 ....39 A2
Kelmscott Rd
SW11 ....60 B2
Kelross Rd N5 ....15 B4
Kelsall Mews TW9 ......45 A2
Kelsey St E2 ....24 C1 99 C2
Kelshall Ct N4 ....6 B2
Kelson Ho E14 ....42 B3
Kelso Pl W8 ....128 B2
Kelvedon Ho SW8 ......172 B4
Kelvedon Rd SW6 ......155 A1
Kelvin Ct
Chiswick W4 ....45 B3
Notting Hill
W11 ....31 C2 113 B3
Kelvington Rd
SE15 ....65 C2
Kelvin Ho **5** E14 ....42 A2
Kelyway Ho **20**
SW2 ....74 C4
Kember St N1 ....14 B1
Kemble Ho SW9 ....63 A4
Kemble St WC2 ....106 C1
Kemerton Rd SE5 ....63 B4
Kemey's St E9 ....18 A3
Kemp Ct SW8 ....162 A1
Kempe Ho SE1 ....137 C1
Kempe Rd NW6 ....22 C3
Kemp Ho
Finsbury EC1 ....97 B3
17 Globe Town E2 ...25 C3
Kemps Way **5**
SE22 ....64 A2
Kemplay Rd NW3 ....11 C4
Kemp's Ct W1 ....105 B1
Kemps Dr E14 ....33 C2
Kempsford Gdns
SW5 ....141 C1
Kempsford Rd
Lambeth SE11 ....149 C3
Newington SE11 ....150 A3
Kemps Rd SW6 ....165 B2
Kempson Rd SW6 ......155 C1
Kempthorne Rd
SE8 ....41 B2
Kempton Ct E1 ....32 A4
Kempton Ct **13**
N1 ....24 A4
Kemsing Ho SE1 ....137 C3
Kemsing Rd SE10 ....43 C1
Kemsley SE13 ....67 A2
Kenbrook Ho
Kensington W14 ....127 A1
5 Kentish Town
NW5 ....13 B3
Kenbury Gdns **10**
SE5 ....48 B1
Kenbury Mans **18**
SE5 ....48 B1
Kenbury St SE5 ....48 B1

Kenchester Cl
SW8 ....162 B1
Kendal NW1 ....92 B4
Kendal Ave W3 ....28 A4
Kendal Cl SW9 ....48 A3
Kendal Ct SE5 ....48 A3
Kendal Ct NW2 ....10 A3
Kendal Ho
32 Hackney E9 ....17 B1
Islington N1 ....85 A2
Kendall Ct **6**
SW19 ....70 C4
Kendall Pl W1 ....103 B3
Kendall Pl SW15 ....58 B2
Kendal Rd NW10 ....8 C4
Kendal St W2 ....102 B1
Kendal Stps W2 ....102 B1
Kender Prim Sch
SE14 ....50 B2
Kender St SE14 ....50 B2
Kendoa Rd **1**
SW4 ....61 C3
Kendon Ho E15 ....19 C1
Kendrick Ct **12**
SE15 ....50 A2
Kendrick Mews
SW7 ....143 B3
Kendrick Pl SW7 ....143 B3
Kenford Rd
SW12 ....73 A4
Kenilworth Ct
SW6 ....58 A4
Kenilworth Rd
Bow E3 ....26 A3
Kilburn NW6 ....23 B4
Kenley Wlk
W11 ....31 A2 112 A3
Kenmont Gdns
NW10 ....22 A2
Kenmont Prim Sch
NW10 ....22 A2
Kenmore Ct TW9 ....44 C3
Kenmore Cl NW6 ....10 C1
Kenmure Rd E8 ....17 A3
Kenmure Yd E8 ....17 A3
Kennacraig Cl **6**
E16 ....35 C1
Kennard Ho **12**
SW11 ....169 C3
Kennard Rd E15 ....19 C1
Kennard St
SW11 ....169 B3
Kennedy Cox Ho **9**
E16 ....35 B4
Kennedy Ho SE11 ......148 C2
Kennedy Wlk
SE17 ....151 C3
Kennet Cl SW11 ....59 C3
Kennet Ct **7** W9 ....31 C4
Kenneth Campbell Ho
NW8 ....89 C2
Kenneth Cres NW2 ....9 A3
Kenneth Ct SE11 ....149 C4
Kennet Ho NW8 ....89 C1
Kenneth Younger Ho
SW6 ....155 A3
Kennet Rd W9 ....23 B1
Kennet St E1 ....125 C2
Kennett Wharf La
EC4 ....123 A4
Kenning Ho **5** N1 ......24 A4
Kenning St **16**
SE16 ....40 B4
Kennings Way
SE11 ....149 C2
KENNINGTON 149 B1

Kennington Ent Ctr
SE17 ....150 A1
Kennington La
SE11 ....149 A1
Kennington Oval
SE11 ....163 A3
Kennington Palace Ct
SE11 ....149 B2
Kennington Park
Gdns SE17 ....48 A4
Kennington Park Ho
SE11 ....149 C1
Kennington Park Pl
SE11 ....48 A4
Kennington Park Rd
SE11 ....150 A2
Kennington Rd
SE1 ....135 B3
Kennington Sta
SE17 ....150 A2
Kennoldes SE21 ....75 C2
Kenrick Pl W1 ....103 B3
KENSAL GREEN 22 B2
Kensal Green Cemy
(All Souls)★
NW10 ....22 B2
Kensal Green Sta
NW10 ....22 C2
Kensal Ho W10 ....22 C1
Kensal Rd W10 ....23 A1
KENSAL RISE 22 C3
Kensal Rise Prim Sch
NW6 ....23 B4
Kensal Rise Sta
NW10 ....22 C3
KENSAL TOWN 23 A1
KENSINGTON 127 C2
Kensington Acad
SW6 ....156 A1
Kensington & Chelsea
Coll
Chelsea SW10 ....156 C2
14 Notting Hill
W10 ....31 A4
Kensington Church Ct
W8 ....128 A3
Kensington Church St
W8 ....31 C1 113 C1
Kensington Church
Wlk W8 ....128 A3
Kensington Court
Mans W8 ....128 B2
Kensington Court
Mews W8 ....128 B2
Kensington Court Pl
W8 ....128 B2
Kensington Ct
W8 ....128 B3
Kensington Ct Gdns
W8 ....128 B2
Kensington Gardens★
W2 ....115 A1
Kensington Gate
W8 ....128 C2
Kensington Gdns Sq
W2 ....100 A1
Kensington Gore
SW7 ....129 B3
Kensington Hall Gdns
W14 ....140 C2
Kensington High St
W8 ....127 C2
Kensington Ho **3**
NW5 ....13 B3

Kensington Hts
W8 . . . . .31 C1 113 B1
Kensington L Ctr
W11 . . . . . . 31 A2 112 A4
Kensington Mall
W8 . . . . .31 C1 113 C2
Kensington Mans
SW5 . . . . 141 C2
Kensington Olympia
Sta W14. . . . . 126 A2
Kensington Pal★
W8 . . . . 114 B1
Kensington Palace
Gdns W8 . . . . . . 114 A2
Kensington Park Gdns
W11 . . . . . . .31 B1 113 A1
Kensington Park
Mews W11 . . . . . . 31 B3
Kensington Park Rd
W11 . . . . . .31 B2 113 A4
Kensington Pl
W8 . . . . .31 C1 113 B1
Kensington Prep Sch
SW6 . . . . 165 A4
Kensington Rd
SW7 . . . . 129 A3
Kensington Sq
W8 . . . . 128 A3
Kensington Village
W14 . . . . 141 A3
Kensington W
W14 . . . . 140 A4
Kensworth Ho EC1 . . 97 C3
Kent CI 8 E2 . . . . . . 24 B3
Kent Ho
Camberwell SE1 . . . 153 A1
13 Chiswick W4 . . . . . 38 A1
Marylebone W1 . . . . 104 C2
Pimlico SW1 . . . . . . 147 B1
Richmond TW10 . . . . 54 C2
Kentish Bldgs
SE1 . . . . 123 B1
KENTISH TOWN . . 13 B2
Kentish Town CE Prim
Sch 15 NW5 . . . . . . 13 B3
Kentish Town City
Farm★ NW5 . . . . . . 12 C3
Kentish Town Rd
NW1 . . . . 13 B2
Kentish Town Sta
NW5 . . . . 13 B3
Kentish Town West
Sta NW5 . . . . 13 A2
Kentmere Ho SE15 . 50 B4
Kenton CI W14 . . . . 126 C1
Kenton Ho
20 Globe Town E1 . . 25 B1
Highbury N5 . . . . 5 C1
Kenton Rd E9 . . . . . 17 C2
Kenton St WC1 . . . . 94 A2
Kent Pas NW1 . . . . . 90 C2
Kent Pk Ind Est
SE15 . . . . 50 A4
Kent Rd
Richmond TW9 . . . . 44 C3
South Acton W4 . . . 37 B3
Kent St E2 . . . . 24 B3
Kent Terr NW1 . . . . 90 B3
Kentwell CI SE4 . . . . 66 A3
Kentwode Gn
SW13 . . . . 46 C3
Kent Yard SW7 . . . . 130 B3
Kenway Rd SW5 . . . 142 A3

Ken Wilson Ho 19
E2 . . . . 24 C3
Kenwood CI NW3 . . . 2 C3
Kenwood Ho 15
SW9 . . . . 63 A3
Kenwood Ho★
NW3 . . . . 3 A1
Kenworthy Rd E9 . . . 18 A2
Kenwrick Ho N1 . . . . 85 A3
Kenwyn Rd SW4 . . . 61 C3
Kenyon Ho 31 SE5 . . 48 B3
Kenyon St SW6 . . . . 47 C2
Kepler Ho 9 SE10 . . 43 B1
Kepler Rd SW2,
SW4 . . . . 62 A3
Keppel Ho
Brompton SW3 . . . . 144 A3
3 Deptford SE8 . . . . 41 B1
Keppel Row SE1 . . . 122 C1
Keppel St WC1 . . . . 105 C4
Kerbela St 3
E2 . . . . 24 C1 99 B3
Kerbey St E14 . . . . . 34 A3
Kerfield Cres SE5 . . 48 C2
Kerfield Pl SE5 . . . . 48 C2
Kerridge Ct 10 N1 . . 16 A2
Kerrington Ho 1
W12 . . . . 39 B4
Kerrison Rd
Battersea SW11 . . . . 60 A4
Mill Meads E15 . . . . 27 C4
Kerry N7 . . . . 14 A2
Kerry Ho 5 E1 . . . . . 32 B3
Kerry Path SE8 . . . . 51 B4
Kerscott Ho 10 E3 . . 27 A2
Kersfield Ho SW15 . 57 C1
Kersfield Rd SW15 . 57 C1
Kershaw CI SW18 . . 59 C1
Kershaw Ho 7
SE27 . . . . 75 A1

Kersley Mews
SW11 . . . . 168 C3
Kersley Rd N16 . . . . . 7 A1
Kersley St SW11 . . . 168 C2
Kerslake Mans
NW10 . . . . 22 C3
Keslake Rd NW6 . . . 22 C3
Keston Ho SE17 . . . 152 B2
Keston Rd SE15 . . . 64 C4
Kestrel Ave SE24 . . 63 B2
Kestrel Ho
4 Battersea
SW11 . . . . 60 A4
Finsbury EC1 . . . . . . 96 C4
Kestrel Pl SE14 . . . . 51 A4
Keswick Broadway 1
SW15 . . . . 58 B2
Keswick Ct 2
SE22 . . . . 64 C2
Keswick Ho 8
SE5 . . . . 48 B2
Keswick Hts 6
SW15 . . . . 58 A2
Keswick Rd SW15 . . 58 A2
Kett Gdns SW2 . . . . 62 B2
Kettleby Ho SW9 . . . 63 A4
Ketton Ho 11 W10 . . 22 B1
Kevan Ho SE5 . . . . . 48 B3
KEW 44 C4
Kew Bridge TW8 . . . 36 B1
Kew Bridge Ct 4
W4 . . . . 36 C1

Kew Bridge
Distribution Ctr
TW8 . . . . 36 B1
Kew Bridge Rd
TW8 . . . . 36 B1
Kew Bridge Sta
TW8 . . . . 36 B1
Kew Bridge Steam
Mus★ TW8 . . . . 36 B1
Kew Coll TW9 . . . . . 44 C3
Kew Foot Rd TW9 . . 54 A4
Kew Gardens Rd
TW9 . . . . 44 C2
Kew Gardens (Royal
Botanic)★ TW9 . . . . 44 A3
Kew Gardens Sta
TW9 . . . . 44 C2
Kew Gn TW9 . . . . . . 44 B4
Kew Green TW9 . . . 44 C4
Kew Green Prep Sch
TW9 . . . . 44 A4
Kew Lo 11 TW9 . . . . 44 B2
Kew Pal★ TW9 . . . . 44 A3
Kew Pier TW9 . . . . . 44 C4
Kew Rd TW9, W4 . . . 44 B4
Kew Ret Pk TW9 . . . 45 A2
Kew Riverside Prim
Sch TW9 . . . . 45 A1
Key Ct E1 . . . . 125 C4
Keyes Ct SE22 . . . . 64 C2
Keyes Rd NW2 . . . . . 9 C3
Keyham Ho 10 W2 . 31 C4
Key Ho 9 SE11 . . . . 163 B4
Keymer Rd SW2 . . . 74 B2
Keynsham Ho 2
N4 . . . . 6 B4
Keystone Cres N1 . . 84 B1
Keyworth Cl E5 . . . . 18 A4
Keyworth Pl SE1 . . . 136 B2
Keyworth Prim Sch
SE17 . . . . 150 B2
Keyworth St SE1 . . . 136 B2
Kezia St SE8 . . . . . . 41 A1
Khyber Rd SW11 . . . 168 A1
Kibworth St SW8 . . 162 C1
Kickbroooke Gdns
SE3 . . . . 53 C2
Kidderpore Ave
NW3 . . . . 10 C4
Kidderpore Gdns
NW3 . . . . 10 C4
Kiffen St EC2 . . . . . 97 C2
Kilbrennan Ho 6
E14 . . . . 34 B3
KILBURN 23 C4
Kilburn Gate NW6 . . 78 A2
Kilburn High Rd
NW6 . . . . 23 C4
Kilburn High Road Sta
NW6 . . . . 78 A3
Kilburn Ho 18 W9 . . 23 B2
Kilburn La W10 . . . . 23 A3
Kilburn Park Rd
NW6 . . . . 23 C2
Kilburn Park Sch 10
NW6 . . . . 78 A3
Kilburn Park Sta
NW6 . . . . 78 A2
Kilburn Pl NW6 . . . . 23 C4
Kilburn Priory
NW6 . . . . 78 A3
Kilburn Sq NW6 . . . 23 C4
Kilburn Sta NW2 . . . 10 B2
Kilburn Vale NW6 . . 78 A3

Kilburn Vale Est 13
NW6 . . . . 23 C4
Kilby Ct SE10 . . . . . 43 B3
Kildare Ct W2 . . . . . 31 C3
Kildare Gdns W2 . . . 31 C3
Kildare Rd E16 . . . . 35 C4
Kildare Terr W2 . . . . 31 C3
Kildare Wlk E14 . . . 33 C3
Kildoran Rd SW2 . . . 62 A2
Kildare Ho 3 E14 . . 33 C3
Kilgour Rd SE23 . . . 66 A1
Kilkie St SW6 . . . . . 166 C1
Killarney Rd SW18 . 59 B1
Killick St N1 . . . . . . 84 C1
Killieser Ave SW2 . . 74 A2
Killip CI E16 . . . . . . 35 B3
Killoran Ho 2 E14 . . 42 B3
Killowen Rd E9 . . . . 17 C2
Killyon Rd SW8 . . . . 171 B1
Kilmaine Rd SW6 . . 154 B1
Kilmarsh Rd W6 . . . 39 B2
Kilmington Rd
SW13 . . . . 46 C4
Kilmore Ho 17 E14 . 34 A3
Kilmuir Ho 1 SW1 . 145 C3
Kilmuir Rd SW1 . . . 145 C3
Kiln Ct E14 . . . . 33 B2
Kilner Ho 5 SE11 . . 163 B4
Kilner St E14 . . . . . 33 C4
Kiln Pl NW5 . . . . . . 12 C3
Kiloh Ct 11 SW11 . . 60 A4
Kilpatrick Ct N16 . . . 7 B3
Kilpeck Ho 9 N4 . . . . 6 B4
Kilravock St W10 . . . 23 A2
Kilronan 3 W3 . . . . 28 C3
Kimbell Gdns
SW6 . . . . 164 A3
Kimber Ctr The
SW18 . . . . 70 C4
Kimberley Ave
SE15 . . . . 65 B4
Kimberley Ho 6
E14 . . . . 42 B3
Kimberley Rd
Kilburn NW6 . . . . . . 23 A4
Stockwell SW9 . . . . 62 A4
Kimber Rd SW18 . . . 71 A4
Kimble Ho
Lisson Gr NW8 . . . . 90 B2
11 Lower Holloway
N7 . . . . 14 A3
Kimbolton Row
SW3 . . . . 144 A3
Kimpton Ct 12 SE5 . 48 C2
Kimpton Ho SW15 . 68 C4
Kimpton Rd SE5 . . . 48 C2
Kinburn St SE16 . . . 40 C4
Kincaid Rd SE15 . . . 50 A3
Kincardine Gdns
W9 . . . . 23 C1
Kindell Ho 4
SW14 . . . . 55 C4
Kinder Ho N1 . . . . . 87 C2
Kindersley Ho 18
E1 . . . . 111 C1
Kinder St 10 E1 . . . 32 A3
Kinefold Ho N7 . . . . 14 A2
Kinfauns Rd SW2 . . 74 C2
King Alfred Sch
NW11 . . . . 1 A2
King Arthur Cl
SE15 . . . . 50 B3
King Charles Ct 16
SE17 . . . . 48 A4
King Charles Ho
SW6 . . . . 156 B2

King Charles St
SW1 . . . . 134 A4
King Charles Terr 11
E1 . . . . 32 A2
King Charles Wlk 6
SW19 . . . . 70 A3
King David La E11 . . 32 B2
Kingdom St W2 . . . 100 C3
Kingdon Ho 8
E14 . . . . 42 B3
Kingdon Rd NW6 . . . 10 C2
Kingdown Cl W10 . . 30 C3
King Edward Mans 8
E8 . . . . 25 A4
King Edward Mews
SW13 . . . . 46 C2
King Edwards Mans
SW6 . . . . 155 B1
King Edward's Rd
E9 . . . . 25 B4
King Edward St
EC1 . . . . 108 C2
King Edward The
Third Mews 2
SE16 . . . . 40 A4
King Edward VII Hospl
for Officers W1 . . . 103 C4
King Edward Wlk
SE1 . . . . 135 C2
King Fahed Acad
W3 . . . . 29 B2
Kingfield St E14 . . . 42 B2
Kingfisher
11 Battersea
SW11 . . . . 60 A4
17 Cubitt Town E14 . 42 B4
Putney SW19 . . . . . . 70 A2
Kingfisher Ho
4 Battersea
SW18 . . . . 59 B4
Peckham SE15 . . . . 49 B2
West Kensington
W14 . . . . 126 C2
Kingfisher Mews
SE13 . . . . 67 A2
Kingfisher Sq 19
SE8 . . . . 51 B4
King Frederick IX Twr
SE16 . . . . 41 B3
King George Sq
TW10 . . . . 54 B1
King George St
SE10 . . . . 52 B3
Kingham Cl
3 Shepherd's Bush
W11 . . . . 39 C4
Wandsworth SW18 . 71 B4
Kingham Ind Est
NW10 . . . . 20 C2
King Henry's Rd
NW3 . . . . 12 A1
King Henry's Reach
W6 . . . . 47 B4
King Henry St N16 . 16 A3
King Henry's Wlk
N1 . . . . 16 A2
King Henry's Yd 5
N16 . . . . 16 A3
King Henry Terr 10
E1 . . . . 32 A2
King Ho 5 W12 . . . . 30 A3
Kinghorn St EC1 . . . 108 C3
King James St
SE1 . . . . 136 B3
King James St
SE1 . . . . 136 B3

King John Ct
EC2 . . . . 24 A1 98 B1
King John St E1 . . . . 32 C4
Kinglake St SE17 . 152 B2
Kingly Ct W1 . . . . . . 119 A4
Kingly St W1 . . . . . . 118 C4
King & Queen St
SE17 . . . . 151 A2
King's Arms Ct E1 . 111 B3
King's Arms Yd
EC2 . . . . 109 B2
Kings Ave SW4 . . . 62 A1
Kings Avenue Sch
SW4 . . . . 62 C2
King's Bench St
SE1 . . . . 136 B4
King's Bench Wlk
EC4 . . . . 107 C1
Kingsbridge N1 . . 6 C3
Kingsbridge Ave
W3 . . . . 36 B4
Kingsbridge Ct
E14 . . . . 41 C2
Kingsbridge Rd
W10 . . . . 30 B3
Kingsbury Rd N1 . 16 A2
Kingsbury Terr N1 . 16 A2
Kingsclere Ct
SW15 . . . . 68 C4
Kingscliffe Gdns
SW19 . . . . 70 B3
King's Coll SE24 . 63 C1
Kings College Ct
NW3 . . . . 12 A1
King's College Hospl
SE5 . . . . 48 B1
Kings College Rd
NW3 . . . . 11 C1
King's Coll London
(Denmark Hill
Campus) SE5 . . . 48 B1
King's Coll London
School of Medicine
SE1 . . . . 123 C1
King's Coll London
(Strand Campus)
WC2 . . . . 121 A4
King's Coll London (St
Thomas' Campus)
SE1 . . . . 134 C2
King's Coll London
(Waterloo Campus)
SE1 . . . . 121 B1
Kingscote NW11 . . 1 B3
Kingscote W4 . . . 37 C3
Kingscote St EC4 . 122 A4
King's Court N
SW3 . . . . 144 A1
Kingscourt Rd
SW16 . . . . 74 A1
King's Court S
SW3 . . . . 144 A1
King's Cres N4, N5 . . 6 B1
Kingscroft SW4 . . 62 A1
Kingscroft Rd
NW2 . . . . 10 B2
KING'S CROSS . . . 84 C2
King's Cross WC1 . 94 B4
King's Cross Bridge
WC1 . . . . 94 B4
King's Cross Rd
WC1 . . . . 95 A3
King's Cross, St
Pancras N1 . . . . . 94 A4
King's Cross Sta
N1 . . . . 84 B1

Kings Ct
6 Barnsbury N7 . . 14 B1
Chiswick W6 . . . . . 38 C2
East Dulwich SE22 . 64 C3
Primrose Hill NW8 . 80 C3
16 Putney SW15 . . . 68 C4
Kingsdale Gdns
W11 . . . . 30 C1
Kingsdale Sch
SE21 . . . . 76 A1
Kingsdown Ave
W3 . . . . 29 A1
Kingsdown Cl
20 Deptford SE16 . . 40 A1
8 Notting Hill W11 . 31 A3
Kingsdown Ct
SW11 . . . . 60 A1
Kingsdown Ho 1
E8 . . . . 16 C3
Kingsdown Rd
N19 . . . . 5 A2
Kingsfield Ho 18
N16 . . . . 16 A3
Kingsford St NW5 . 12 B3
Kingsgate Est N1 . . 16 A2
Kingsgate Ho 20
SW9 . . . . 173 C4
Kingsgate Par
SW1 . . . . 133 A1
Kingsgate PI NW6 . 10 C1
Kingsgate Prim Sch
NW6 . . . . 10 C1
Kingsgate Rd
NW6 . . . . 10 C1
King's Gdns 6
NW6 . . . . 10 C1
King's Gr 8
3 Hammersmith
W12 . . . . 38 C3
Willesden NW10 . . . 22 B4
Kings PI W4 . . . . . . 37 B2
Kings PI* N1 . . . . . 84 B2
King's PI SE1 . . . . 136 C3
King Sq EC1 . . . . . . 96 C3
King's Quay SW10 167 A4
Kings Rd
Richmond TW10,
TW9 . . . . 54 B2
Willesden NW10 . . . 9 A1
King's Rd
Chelsea SW3 . . . . 144 B1
Chelsea SW10 . . . 157 B3
Mortlake SW14 . . . . 55 C4
Kings Ride Gate
TW10 . . . . 54 C2
Kingsridge SW19 . 70 A2
King's Scholars' Pas
SW1 . . . . 146 C4
King St
Acton W3 . . . . 28 B1
Hammersmith W6 . . 38 C2
St James SW1 . . . . 119 A2
Strand WC2 . . . . . 120 A4
Whitechapel EC2 . . 109 A1
King Stairs Cl
SE16 . . . . 40 A4
King's Terr NW1 . . 82 C3
Kingston Ho 4
NW6 . . . . 10 A1
Kingston Ho E
SW7 . . . . 130 A3
Kingston Ho N
SW7 . . . . 130 A3
Kingston Ho S
SW7 . . . . 130 A3
Kingston Rd SW15,
SW19 . . . . 69 A3

Kingsley Mews
Kensington W8 . . . 128 B1
15 St George in East
E1 . . . . 32 A2
Kingsley PI N6 . . . 3 C4
Kingsley Rd NW6 . 23 B4
Kingsley St SW11 . 60 B4
Kings Mall Sh Ctr
W6 . . . . 39 B2
King's Mans SW3 158 A3
Kingsmead TW10 . . 54 B1
Kingsmead Ho E9 . 18 A4
Kingsmead Prim Sch
E9 . . . . 18 A4
Kingsmead Rd
SW2 . . . . 74 C2
King's Mead Way E5,
E9 . . . . 18 A4
Kingsmere Cl 13
SW15 . . . . 57 C4
Kingsmere PI N16 . 6 C3
Kingsmere Rd
SW19 . . . . 69 C2
King's Mews
1 Clapham Pk
SW4 . . . . 62 A2
Gray's Inn WC1 . . . 95 A1
Kingsmill NW8 . . 79 C2
Kingsmill Terr
NW8 . . . . 79 C2
Kingsnorth Ho 12
W10 . . . . 30 C3
King Solomon Acad
NW1 . . . . 102 A4
King's Par 5
3 Hammersmith
W12 . . . . 38 C3
Willesden NW10 . . . 22 B4
Kings PI W4 . . . . . . 37 B2
Kings PI* N1 . . . . . 84 B2
King's PI SE1 . . . . 136 C3
King Sq EC1 . . . . . . 96 C3

Kingston Univ
(Roehampton Vale)
SW15 . . . . 68 B1
Kingston Vale
SW15 . . . . 68 B1
Kingstown St NW1 81 B4
King Street Cloisters
6 . . . . 39 A2
King Street Coll 10
W12 . . . . 39 B2
Kingswater PI
SW11 . . . . 158 A1
Kingsway
Mortlake SW14,
TW9 . . . . 55 A4
St Giles WC2 . . . 106 C2
Kingsway Coll 17
. . . . 13 A2
Kingsway Mans
WC1 . . . . 106 C4
Kingsway PI EC1 . 96 A2
Kingswear Rd NW5 4 B1
Kings Well 25
NW3 . . . . 11 B4
Kingswood 4
E2 . . . . 25 B2
Kingswood Ave
NW6 . . . . 23 A3
Kingswood Cl
SW8 . . . . 162 B1
Kingswood Ct
Hither Green SE13 67 C1
7 Richmond TW10 54 B2
Kings Wood Ct 4
NW6 . . . . 10 C1
Kingswood Rd
South Acton W4 . . 37 B3
Streatham SW2 . . . 74 A4
Kingswood Terr
W4 . . . . 37 B3
Kings Yd E15 . . . . 18 C2
Kington Ho 18
NW6 . . . . 78 B3
Kingward Ho E1 . 111 B4
Kingweston Ct N2 1 A1
Kinloch St N7 . . . . 5 B1
Kinnaird Ave W4 . 45 B3
Kinnear Rd W12 . . 38 B4
Kinnerton PI N
SW1 . . . . 131 A3
Kinnerton PI S
SW1 . . . . 131 A3
Kinnerton St SW1 131 B3
Kinnerton Yd
SW1 . . . . 131 B3
Kinnoull Mans 10
E5 . . . . 17 A4
Kinnoul Rd W6 . . 154 A4
Kinross Ho N1 . . . 84 C4
Kinsale Rd SE15 . . 64 C4
Kinsham Ho 5
E2 . . . . 24 C1 99 C2
Kintore Way SE1 . 152 C4
Kintyre Ct 17 SW2 74 A4
Kintyre Ho 6 E14 34 B1
Kinver Ho N4 . . . . 6 C4
Kipling Ho 29 SE5 . 48 B3

Kipling St SE1 . . . 137 C4
Kipling Twr 3 W3 . 37 B3
Kirby Est SE16 . . . 40 A3
Kirby Gr SE1 . . . . 138 A4
Kirby Rd EC1 . . . . 107 C4
Kirkeby Bldg EC1 . 107 B3
Kirkland Wlk 3
E8 . . . . 16 B2
Kirkley Ho N16 . . . 7 A3
Kirkman Ho W1 . . 105 B3
Kirkman PI W1 . . . 105 B3
Kirkmichael Rd
E14 . . . . 34 B3
Kirkside Rd SE3 . . 53 C4
Kirk's PI E14 . . . . 94 A1
Kirkstall Gdns
SW2 . . . . 74 A3
Kirkstall Ho SW1 146 A2
Kirkstall Rd SW2 . 74 A3
Kirkstead Ct E5 . . 18 A4
Kirkstone NW1 . . . 92 C4
Kirkwall PI E2 . . . 25 B2
Kirkwood Rd SE15 50 A1
Kirtley Ho SW8 . . 171 A4
Kirtling St SW8 . . 160 C2
Kirton Cl W4 . . . . 37 C2
Kirton Gdns 26
E2 . . . . 24 B2 99 A3
Kirwin Way SE5 . . 48 A3
Kitcat Terr E3 . . . 26 C2
Kite Ho 5 SW11 . . 60 A4
Kite PI 9
E2 . . . . 24 C2 99 C4
Kitson Rd
Barnes SW13 . . . . 46 C2
Camberwell SE5 . . 48 B3
Kittiwake Ct 26
SE8 . . . . 51 B4
Kitto Rd SE14 . . . 50 C1
Kiver Rd N19 . . . . 5 A2
Klea Ave SW4 . . . 61 B1
Kleffens Ct 2 SE3 . 53 B3
Kleine Wharf 30
N1 . . . . 24 A4
Knapp Cl NW10 . . 8 A2
Knapp Rd E3 . . . . 26 C1
Knaresborough Dr
SW18 . . . . 71 A3
Knaresborough Ho
N4 . . . . 6 B4
Knaresborough PI
SW5 . . . . 142 A4
Knatchbull Rd
Brixton SE5 . . . . . 48 A2
Stonebridge NW10 . 20 C4
Knebworth Ho
South Lambeth
SW8 . . . . 171 C3
2 Stoke Newington
N16 . . . . 16 A4
Knebworth Rd 3
E8 . . . . 16 C1
Kneller Ho 3
SW8 . . . . 171 C2
Kneller Rd SE4 . . 66 A3
Knighten St E1 . . . 32 A1
Knighthead Point 25
E14 . . . . 41 C4
Knightleas Ct NW2 9 B2
Knightrider Ct
EC4 . . . . 122 C4
Knightrider St
EC4 . . . . 122 B4

Knights Arc SW1 . . **130** C3
Knight's Ave W5 . . . .**36** A4
KNIGHTSBRIDGE
. . . . **130** A2
Knightsbridge SW1,
SW7 . . . . **130** C3
Knightsbridge Ct
SW1 . . . . **131** A3
Knightsbridge Gn
SW1 . . . . **130** C3
Knightsbridge Sch
SW11 . . . . **130** C2
Knightsbridge Sta
SW1 . . . . **131** A3
Knightsbridge Under
Sch SW7 . . . . **143** A3
Knights Cl E9 . . . .**17** B3
Knights Ho
Bermondsey SE1 . . **138** C4
South Lambeth
SW8 . . . . **162** B1
West Kensington
SW5 . . . . **140** C2
Knight's Ho SW10 . . **156** C2
Knights Rd E16 . . . . . .**43** C4
Knight's Wlk SE11 . . **150** A3
Knightswood Ct N6 . . .**4** C4
Knivet Rd SW6 . . . . . **155** B3
Knoll Ho NW8 . . . .**78** C2
Knoll Rd SW18 . . . . . **59** C2
Knolly's Cl SE27,
SW16 . . . . **74** C1
Knolly's Rd SE27,
SW16 . . . . **74** C1
Knot Ho SE1 . . . . **124** C1
Knottisford St E2 . . . . **25** B2
Knowlden Ho E1 . . . . **32** B2
Knowle Cl SW9 . . . . . **62** C4
Knowledge Point Sch
E7 . . . . **14** B2
Knowles Hill Cres
SE13 . . . . **67** C2
Knowles Ho
Wandsworth
SW18 . . . . **59** A1
Willesden Green
NW10 . . . . **21** C4
Knowles Wlk SW4 . . . **61** B4
Knowlton Ho SW9 . . . **173** C4
Knowsley Rd
SW11 . . . . **168** C1
Knox Ct SW4 . . . . **172** B2
Knox Ho SW15 . . . . . . **47** B1
Knox St W1 . . . . **102** C4
Knoyle Ho W14 . . . . . **126** B2
Knoyle St SE14 . . . . . **51** A4
Kobi Nazrul Prim Sch
E1 . . . . **111** C2
Kossuth St SE10 . . . . **43** A1
Kotree Way SE16 . . . . **139** C2
Kramer Mews
SW5 . . . . **142** A1
Kreedman Wlk E8
. . . .**16** C3
Kreisel Wlk TW9 . . . . . **44** B4
Kylemore Ct E4
. . . . **145** C3
W12 . . . . **38** C4
Kylemore Rd NW6 . . .**10** C1
Kylestrome Ho
SW1 . . . . **145** C3

Kynance Mews
SW7 . . . . **128** B1
Kynance Pl SW7 . . . . **128** C1
Kynaston Ho 7
SW2 . . . . **74** B3
Kynaston Rd N16 . . . . .**7** A1
Kyrle Rd SW11 . . . . . **60** C1
Kyverdale Rd N16 . . . . .**7** B3

L

Laburnham Ct NW2 . . **1** B2
Laburnum Cl 5
SE15 . . . . **50** B3
Laburnum Ct 26
E2 . . . .**24** B4
Laburnum Ho
New Cross SE4 . . . . . **51** B1
6 Stoke Newington
. . . .**6** C2
Laburnum St E2 . . . . . **24** B4
Lacey Ho 7 SE13 . . . . **52** B1
Lacey Mews 9 E3 . . . .**26** C3
Lacine Ct 12 SE16 . . . **40** C4
Lackington St
EC2 . . . . **109** C4
Lackland Ho SE1 . . . **153** A2
Lacland Ho SW10 . . . **157** B2
Lacon Rd SE22 . . . . . . **64** C3
Lacy Rd SW15 . . . . . . **57** C3
Ladbroke Cres
W11 . . . . **31** A3
Ladbroke Gdns
W11 . . . . **31** A2 **112** C4
Ladbroke Gr
Kensal Town W10 . . **31** A4
Notting Hill
W11 . . . . **31** B2 **112** C4
Ladbroke Grove Ho
W11 . . . . **31** B2
Ladbroke Grove Sta
W10 . . . .**31** A3
Ladbroke Ho E1 . . . . **111** A3
Ladbroke Mews
W11 . . . . **31** A1 **112** B1
Ladbroke Rd
W11 . . . . **31** B1 **112** C4
Ladbroke Sq
W11 . . . . **31** B2 **113** A3
Ladbroke Terr
W11 . . . . **31** B1 **113** A3
Ladbroke Wlk
W11 . . . . **31** B1 **113** A2
Ladlands SE22 . . . . . . **76** C4
Ladybower Ct 8
E5 . . . . **17** C4
Ladycroft Rd SE13 . . . **67** A4
Lady Elizabeth Ho
SW14 . . . . **55** B4
Ladyfern Ho 19 E3 . . .**33** C4
Lady Florence Ctyd 5
SE8 . . . . **51** C3
Lady Margaret Rd
NW5 . . . . **13** B3
Lady Margaret Sch
SW6 . . . . **165** B3
Lady Somerset Rd
NW5 . . . . **13** A4
LADYWELL **66** C1
Ladywell Arena
SE13 . . . . **67** A1
Ladywell Cl SE4 . . . . . **66** B3
Ladywell Hts SE4 . . . . **66** B1
Ladywell Rd SE13 . . . . **67** A2
Ladywell Sta SE13 . . . **67** A2

Ladywell Water Twr
SE4 . . . . **66** C2
Lafitte Ho 22 N19 . . . . .**4** C4
Lafone Ho 11 SW2 . . .**74** A4
Lafone St SE1 . . . . . . **138** C4
Lagado Mews
SE16 . . . . **32** C1
Lagonda Ho 6 E3 . . . .**26** C1
Lagonier Ho EC1 . . . . **97** A3
Laindon Ho 6 N16 . . . .**7** B3
Laing Ho SE5 . . . . **48** B3
Lainson St SW18 . . . . **70** C4
Lairdale Cl SE21 . . . . . **75** B4
Laird Ho SE5 . . . . **48** B3
Lairs Cl N7 . . . . **14** A2
Laitwood Rd
SW12 . . . . **73** A3
Lakanal 8 SE5 . . . . . . **49** A2
Lake Ho SE1 . . . . **136** C3
Laker Ct SW4 . . . . . . **172** B2
Laker Pl SW15 . . . . . . **58** A1
Lakeside Ct N4 . . . .**6** B3
Lakeside Rd W14 . . . . **39** C3
Lakeview 23 E3 . . . . . **25** C3
Lake View Ct
SW1 . . . . **132** B2
Lakis Cl NW3 . . . . **11** B4
Laleham Ho
E2 . . . . **24** B1 **98** C2
Lalor St SW6 . . . . **164** B2
Lambard Ho 4
SE10 . . . . **52** B3
Lamb Ct 18 E14 . . . . . . **33** A2
Lamberhurst Ho 14
SE15 . . . . **50** B4
Lambert Ave TW9 . . . .**55** A4
Lambert Ho
10 Brixton SW9 . . . **173** B1
11 Crouch End N19 . . .**4** C4
Lambert Rd SW2 . . . . **62** B2
Lambert St N1 . . . . . . **14** C1
LAMBETH **134** C3
Lambeth Acad
SW4 . . . . **61** B2
Lambeth Coll
SW4 . . . . **74** A1
Lambeth Coll (Brixton
Ctr) SW2 . . . .**62** B2
Lambeth Coll
(Clapham Ctr)
SW4 . . . . **61** B2
Lambeth Coll
(Vauxhall Ctr)
SW8 . . . . **171** B4
Lambeth Ct 8
SW18 . . . . **58** C2
Lambeth High St
SE1 . . . . **148** C4
Lambeth Hill EC4 . . . . **122** C4
Lambeth Hospl
SE11 . . . . **149** B1
Lambeth North Sta
SE1 . . . . **135** B2
Lambeth Pal* **134** C2
Lambeth Palace Rd
SE1 . . . . **134** C2
Lambeth Pier SE1 . . . **134** B1
Lambeth Rd SE11 . . . **135** C1
Lambeth Twrs
SE11 . . . . **135** B1
Lambeth Wlk
SE11 . . . . **149** A4
Lambfold Ho N7 . . . . . **14** A2

Lamb Ho
28 Camberwell
SE5 . . . . **48** B3
8 Camberwell SE5 . . **48** C2
Greenwich SE10 . . . . **52** B4
Lamb La E8 . . . .**17** A1
Lamble St NW5 . . . . . . **12** C4
Lamb Office Ct
WC1 . . . . **106** A4
Lambolle Mews 3
NW3 . . . . **12** A2
Lambolle Rd NW3 . . . .**12** A2
Lambourn Cl 9
NW5 . . . . **13** B4
Lambourne Gr
SE16 . . . . **40** C1
Lambourne Ho
NW8 . . . . **101** C4
Lambourn Rd SW4 . . . **61** A4
Lambrook Ho 15
SE15 . . . . **49** C2
Lambrook Terr
SW6 . . . . **164** A4
Lamb's Bldgs EC1 . . . . **97** B1
Lamb's Conduit Pas
WC1 . . . . **106** C4
Lamb's Conduit St
WC1 . . . . **94** C1
Lamb's Mews N1 . . . . **86** A3
Lamb's Pas EC1 . . . . . **97** B1
Lamb St E1 . . . . **110** C4
Lambton Ct 2 N19 . . . . .**5** A3
Lambton Mews 4
N19 . . . .**5** A3
Lambton Pl
W11 . . . . **31** B2 **113** A4
Lambton Rd N19 . . . .**5** A3
Lamb Wlk SE1 . . . . . . **138** A3
Lamerton Lo 10
TW9 . . . . **44** B2
Lamerton St 2
SE8 . . . . **51** C4
Lamington St 3
W6 . . . . **39** A2
Lamlash St SE11 . . . . **150** A4
Lamley Ho SE10 . . . . . **52** A3
Lammas Rd E9 . . . . . . **17** C1
Lammermoor Rd
SW12 . . . . **73** A4
Lamont Rd SW10 . . . . **157** B3
Lamont Rd Pas
SW10 . . . . **157** B3
Lampard Gr N16 . . . .**7** B3
Lampern Sq 8
E2 . . . . **24** C2 **99** C4
Lampeter Sq W6 . . . . **154** A3
Lamplighter Cl 34
E1 . . . .**25** B1
Lampson Ho 2
N19 . . . .**13** B4
Lanark Ho 12 SE1 . . . **153** B1
Lanark Mans
Paddington W9 . . . . . **89** A2
12 Shepherd's Bush
W12 . . . . **39** B4
Lanark Mews NW8 . . .**89** A3
Lanark Pl W9 . . . .**89** A2
Lanark Rd W9 . . . . **88** C3
Lanark Sq E14 . . . .**42** A3
Lanbury Rd SE15 . . . . **65** C3
Lancashire Ct W1 . . . **118** B4
Lancaster Ave SE21,
SE27 . . . .**75** B2
Lancaster Cl
13 De Beauvoir Town
N1 . . . .**16** A1
Kensington W2 . . . . **114** A3

Lancaster Cotts 1
TW10 . . . . **54** A1
Lancaster Ct
Bayswater W2 . . . . . **115** A4
Parsons Green
SW6 . . . . **155** A1
West Norwood
SE27 . . . .**75** A2
Lancaster Dr
Canary Wharf E14 . . **34** B1
Maitland Pk NW3 . . . .**12** A2
Lancaster Gate
W2 . . . . **115** A4
Lancaster Gate Sta
W2 . . . . **115** B4
Lancaster Gr NW3 . . . . **12** A2
Lancaster hall 14
E16 . . . .**35** C1
Lancaster Ho
SW15 . . . . **47** B1
Lancaster Lo 2
W11 . . . . **31** A3
Lancaster Mews
Bayswater W2 . . . . . **115** A4
2 Richmond TW10 . . .**54** A1
3 Wandsworth
SW18 . . . . **59** A2
Lancaster Pk
TW10 . . . . **54** A2
Lancaster Pl WC2 . . . **120** C3
Lancaster Rd
Dudden Hill NW10 . . . .**8** C3
Finsbury Pk N4 . . . .**5** C4
Notting Hill W11 . . . . .**31** A3
Lancaster St SE1 . . . **136** B3
Lancaster Stables 10
NW3 . . . . **12** A2
Lancaster Terr
W2 . . . . **115** B4
Lancaster Wlk
W2 . . . . **115** A2
Lancefield Ho
SE15 . . . . **65** A4
Lancefield St W10 . . . .**23** B2
Lancell St N16 . . . .**7** A2
Lancelot Pl SW7 . . . . **130** C3
Lancer Sq W8 . . . . . . **128** A4
Lanchester Ct W2 . . . **102** C1
Lanchester Way
SE14 . . . . **50** C2
Lancing St NW1 . . . . . .**93** B3
Lancresse Ct N1 . . . . . **24** A4
Landale Ct SE10 . . . . . **52** B2
Landale Ho 13
SE16 . . . . **40** B3
Landcroft Rd SE22 . . . **64** B1
Landells Rd SE22 . . . . **64** C1
Landford Rd SW15 . . . **57** B4
Landin Ho 1 E14 . . . . . **33** C3
Landleys Field 21
N7 . . . .**13** C3
Landmann Ho 16
SE16 . . . . **40** A2
Landmann Way
SE14 . . . . **40** C1
Landmark Hts E5 . . . . **18** A4
Landon Pl SW1 . . . . . **130** C2
Landons Cl E14 . . . . . . **34** B1
Landon Wlk 16
E14 . . . .**34** A2
Landor Ct N16 . . . . **16** A3
Landor Ho 7 SE5 . . . . **48** C3

Landor Rd SW9......62 A4
Landor Wlk 11
 W12.............38 C4
Landrake NW1...83 A3
Landridge Rd
 SW6............164 C2
Landseer Ct SW11..169 C3
Landseer Ho
 Battersea SW11...169 C3
 Paddington NW8....89 C2
 Westminster SW1...147 C3
Landseer Rd N19...5 B2
Landulph Ho
 SE11............149 C2
Landward Ct W1...102 B2
Lane Cl SW11......74 B4
Lanercost Cl SW2..74 C2
Lanercost Rd SW2..74 C2
Lane The NW8.....78 C1
Laneway SW15.....57 A2
Laney Bldg EC1....107 B4
Lanfranc Rd E3....26 A3
Lanfrey Pl W14...140 C1
Langbourne Ave N6..3 C2
Langbourne Ho 7
 SW2............62 C2
Langbourne Mans
 N6.............3 C2
Langbourne Pl
 E14............42 A1
Langbourne Prim Sch
 SE21...........76 A1
Langdale NW1.....92 C4
Langdale Cl
 Camberwell SE17...48 B4
 Mortlake SW14.....55 A3
Langdale Ho SW1..146 C1
Langdale Rd SE10..52 B3
Langdale St 25 E1..32 A3
Langdon Ct
 Finsbury EC1.....86 B1
 Harlesden NW10...21 A4
Langdon Ho 3
 E14............34 B3
Langdon Park Rd
 N6.............4 B4
Langdon Park Sch
 E14............34 B3
Langdon Park Sta
 E14............34 B3
Langdon Pk L Ctr
 E14............34 B3
Langdon Pk Sta
 E14............34 A4
Langdon Pl SW14..55 B4
Langdon Way 16
 SE1...........153 C3
Langford Cl
 Shacklewell E8....16 C3
 St John's Wood
 NW8...........79 A2
Langford Ct NW8..79 A1
Langford Gn SE5..64 A4
Langford Ho 5
 SE8............51 C4
Langford Prim Sch
 SW6............166 B2
Langford Rd 4
 SW6............166 B2
Langham Ct 4
 SW15...........57 C2
Langham Ho SW4..61 B2
Langham Mans
 SW5............142 A1

Langham Pl
 Chiswick W4.....46 A4
 Fitzrovia W1....104 B3
Langham St W1...104 B3
Lang Ho
 South Lambeth
 SW8...........162 A1
 13 Tufnell Pk N19...4 B1
Langholm Cl
 SW12...........73 C4
Langhorne Ct 10
 NW8............11 C1
Langhurst Ho 11
 SW11...........169 B2
Langland Gdns
 NW3............11 A3
Langland Ho 10
 SE5............48 C3
Langland Mans
 NW3............11 A3
Langler Rd NW10..22 B3
Langley Ct
 South Lambeth
 SW8...........172 A4
 Strand WC2....120 A4
Langley Dr W3....37 A4
Langley Ho
 11 Lower Clapton
 E5.............17 A3
 36 Paddington W2..31 C4
Langley La SW8...162 B4
Langley Mans
 SW8...........162 B4
Langley St WC2...106 A1
Langmead Ho 14
 E3.............27 A2
Langmore Ho 10
 E1.............111 C1
Langport Ho 1
 SW9............48 A1
Langridge 13 NW5..12 C2
Langroyd Rd
 SW17...........72 B2
Langside Ave
 SW15...........56 C3
Lang St E1.......25 B1
Langston Hughes Cl
 8 SE24........63 A3
Langthorn Ct EC2.109 C2
Langthorne Lo 30
 SW2............74 C4
Langthorne St
 SW6............47 C3
Langton Cl WC1...95 A2
Langton Ct SW15..58 B1
Langton Ho SE11..149 A4
Langton Pl SW18..70 C3
Langton Rd SW9..48 A3
Langton St SW10..157 A3
Langton Way SE3..53 C3
Langtry Pl SW6...155 C4
Langtry Rd NW8...78 A3
Langtry Wlk NW8..78 C3
Lanhill Rd W9....23 C1
Lanier Rd SE13...67 C1
Lanner Ho 2
 SW11...........60 A4
Lannoy Point
 SW6...........154 B2
Lanrick Rd E14...34 C3
Lansbury Gdns 1
 E14............34 C3
Lansbury Lawrence
 Prim Sch 24 E14..34 A3
Lanscombe Wlk
 SW8...........162 A1

Lansdell Ho 9
 SW2............62 C1
Lansdowne Coll
 W2............114 A3
Lansdowne Cres
 W11........31 A2 112 B3
Lansdowne Dr E8..16 C1
Lansdowne Gdns
 SW8...........172 A4
Lansdowne Gr
 NW10...........8 A4
Lansdowne Hill
 SE27...........75 A1
Lansdowne Ho
 W11........31 B1 112 C2
Lansdowne Mews
 W11........31 B1 112 C2
Lansdowne Pl
 SE1...........137 C2
Lansdowne Rd
 W11........31 A2 112 B3
Lansdowne Rise
 W11........31 A2 112 B3
Lansdowne Row
 W1............118 B2
Lansdowne Sch 5
 SW9............62 B4
Lansdowne Terr
 WC1............94 B1
Lansdowne Way SW4,
 SW8...........172 B2
Lansdowne Wlk
 W11........31 B1 112 C2
Lansdowne Wood Cl
 11 SE27.........75 A1
Lanson Ho 10
 SW8............48 B1
Lantern Cl SW15..56 C3
Lantern Ho E14...41 C4
Lanterns Ct E14..41 C3
Lant Ho SE1.....136 C3
Lantry Ct 1 W3..28 A1
Lant St SE1.....137 A3
Lanvanor Rd SE15..50 B1
Lanyard Ho 4 SE8..41 B2
Lapford Cl W9....23 B1
Lapsang SE1.....125 A1
Lapwing Twr 31
 SE8............51 B4
Lapworth Ct W2..100 B4
Lara Cl SE13......67 B1
Larch Ave W3.....29 A1
Larch Cl
 Balham SW12......73 A2
 Deptford SE8.....51 B4
 10 Upper Holloway
 N19............4 B2
Larch Ct 41 W2...31 C4
Larches Ave SW14..55 C3
Larchfield Ho 2
 N5.............15 B3
Larch Ho 28 SE16..40 B4
Larchmore Ct N19..5 A2
Larch Rd NW2.....9 B4
Larcom St SE17...151 A3
Larden Rd W3.....38 A4
La Retraite RC Girls
 Sch SW12........73 B4
Larissa St SE17...151 C3
Larix Ct NW10....21 C4
Larkfield Rd TW9..54 A3
Larkhall La SW4..172 A3
Larkhall Rise
 SW4...........171 B1
Lark Row E2.....25 B4

Larmenier & Sacred
 Heart RC Prim Sch
 4 W6...........39 C2
Larnaca Ho SE1..138 C2
Larnach Rd W6...47 C4
Larpent Ave SW15..57 B2
La Saint Union RC Sec
 Sch NW5.........4 A1
Lascelles Ho NW1..90 B1
Lassell St SE10..42 C1
Lasseter Pl SE3..53 B4
Latchmere Rd
 SW11...........168 C1
Latchmere St 5
 SW11...........168 C2
Latham Ho E1....32 C3
Latham Ho E1....32 C3
Lathom Rd E6....152 A1
Latimer Ho
 11 Homerton E9....17 C2
 Notting Hill
 W11........31 B2 113 A3
Latimer Ind Est 1
 W10............30 B3
Latimer Pl W10...30 B3
Latimer Rd W10...30 B3
Latimer Road Sta
 W10............30 B3
Latitude Ho NW1..82 A3
Latona Rd SE15...49 C4
Latvia Ct SE17...151 A1
Latymer Ct W6...39 C2
Latymer Upper Sch 14
 W6............38 C2
Lauderdale Mans
 W9.............88 B3
Lauderdale Rd W9..88 B3
Lauderdale Twr
 EC2...........108 C4
Laud St SE11.....148 C2
Laughton Ho 11
 SW2............62 C1
Launcelot St SE1..135 B3
Launceston Pl
 W8............128 C1
Launch St E14...42 B3
Laundress La N16..7 C1
Laundry Rd W6...154 A3
Laura Pl E5......17 B4
Laurel Bank Gdns 3
 SW6............165 A2
Laurel Cl 11 N19..4 B2
Laurel Ct
 Dalston E8......16 B1
 2 Putney SW15....57 C2
 3 Rotherhithe
 SE16...........33 A1
Laurel Ho
 7 Deptford SE8....51 B4
 3 Hamstead NW3...11 A2
Laurel Rd SW13...46 C1
Laurel St E8......16 B2
Laurence Mews 12
 W12............38 C4
Laurence Pountney
 Hill EC4........123 B4
Laurence Pountney La
 EC4...........123 C4
Laurie Gr SE14...51 A2
Laurie Ho
 Newington SE1...136 B1
 Notting Hill
 W8.........31 C1 113 B1
Laurier Rd NW5...4 A1

Lauriston Ho 6
 E9.............17 C1
Lauriston Lo N5..15 B2
Lauriston Prim Sch 6
 E9.............25 C4
Lauriston Rd E9..17 C1
Lausanne Rd SE15..50 B2
Lavell St N16.....15 C4
Lavender Cl SW3..157 C3
Lavender Ct SW4..172 B3
Lavender Gdns
 SW11...........60 B3
Lavender Gr E8...16 C1
Lavender Hill
 SW11...........60 C4
Lavender Ho
 19 Rotherhithe SW9..45 A3
 4 Rotherhithe
 SE16...........32 C1
Lavender Rd
 Battersea SW11...59 C4
 Rotherhithe SE16..33 A1
Lavender Sweep
 SW11...........60 B3
Lavender Terr 12
 SW11...........60 A4
Lavender Wlk
 SW11...........60 B3
Lavendon Ho NW8..90 B2
Lavengro Rd SE27..75 B2
Lavenham Rd
 SW18...........70 C3
Lavers Rd N16.....7 A1
Laverstoke Gdns
 SW15...........68 C4
Laverton Mews
 SW5...........142 B3
Laverton Pl SW5..142 B3
Lavina Gr N1.....84 C2
Lavington Cl E9...18 B2
Lavington St SE1..122 B1
Lawdale Jun Sch 22
 E2.............24 C2 99 C4
Lawford Rd
 Chiswick W4.....45 B3
 De Beauvoir Town
 N1............16 A1
 Kentish Town NW5..13 B2
Lawford's Wharf 18
 NW1............13 B1
Lawless Ho 6 E14..34 B2
Lawless St E14...34 A2
Lawley St E5.....17 B4
Lawman Ct 2
 TW9............44 B2
Lawn Cres TW9...44 C1
Lawnfield Ct NW6..9 C1
Lawn House Cl
 E14............42 B4
Lawn La SW8.....162 C4
Lawn Rd NW3.....12 B3
Lawns The N16...16 A3
Lawrence Ave
 NW10...........20 C4
Lawrence Bldgs 1
 N16............7 B1
Lawrence Cl
 Bow E3..........26 C3
 6 Shepherd's Bush
 W12............30 A2
Lawrence Ct
 South Acton
 W3.............37 B3
 Stoke Newington N16..7 B1

Lawrence Ho
20 Camden Town
NW1 . . . . **13** A1
Westminster SW1 . **147** C3
Lawrence La EC2 . **109** A2
Lawrence Mans
SW3 . . . . **158** A3
Lawrence Ho N1 . . . **84** B4
Lawrence St
Canning Town E16 . . **35** B4
Chelsea SW3 . . . . . . **158** A3
Lawrence Trad Est
SE10 . . . . **43** A2
Lawrence Univ
SW7 . . . . **143** A3
Lawson Cl SW19 . . **69** C1
Lawson Ct N4 . . . . . . **5** B3
Lawson Ho **17**
W12 . . . . **30** A2
Law St SE1 . . . . . . **137** C2
Lawton Rd E3 . . . . . **26** A2
Laxfield Ct E8 . . . . **24** C4
Laxley Cl SE5 . . . . . **48** A3
Laxton Path **1**
SE4 . . . . **65** C3
Laxton Pl NW1 . . . . **92** B2
Layard Rd SE16 . . . . **40** A2
Layard Sq SE16 . . . . **40** A2
Laybourne Ho **18**
E14 . . . . **41** C4
Laycock Prim Sch **5**
N1 . . . . **15** A2
Laycock St N1 . . . . **14** C2
Layfield Ho **9**
SE10 . . . . **43** C1
Laystall Ct EC1 . . . **95** B1
Laystall St EC1 . . . **95** B1
Layton Pl TW9 . . . . **44** C2
Lazar Wlk **2** N7 . . . . **5** B2
Leabank Sq E9 . . . **18** C2
Leabourne Rd N16 . **7** C4
Leacroft Ave
SW12 . . . . **72** B4
Lea Ct **3** W12 . . . . **38** A4
Leadenhall Mkt★
EC3 . . . . **110** A1
Leadenhall Pl
EC3 . . . . **110** A1
Leadenhall St
EC3 . . . . **110** A1
Leadenham Ct **18**
E3 . . . . **26** C1
Lea Ho NW8 . . . . . . **90** A1
Leahurst Rd SE13 . . **67** C2
Lea Int E9 . . . . **18** C3
Leake St
Lambeth SE1 . . . . . **135** B3
South Bank SE1 . . . **135** A4
Leamington Ct
4 Forest Hill
SE26 . . . . **76** C1
North Acton W3 . . . **28** C4
Leamington Ho **4**
W11 . . . . **31** B4
Leamington Pk
W3 . . . . **28** C4
Leamington Rd Villas
W11 . . . . **31** B4
Leamore St W6 . . . **39** B2
Leamouth Rd E14 . **34** C3
Leander Ct
27 Hackney E9 . . . . **17** B1
St Johns SE8 . . . . . . **51** C2
Leander Rd SW2 . . **62** C1

Leary Ho SE11 . . . **149** A1
Lea Sq **22** E3 . . . . . **26** B4
Leatherdale St
32 Bethnal Green
E1 . . . . **25** B1
11 Globe Town E1 . . **25** C1
Leatherhead Cl N16 . **7** B3
Leather La EC1 . . . **107** C4
Leather La
EC1 . . . . **107** C4
Leathermarket Ct
SE1 . . . . **138** A3
Leathermarket St
SE1 . . . . **138** A3
Leather Rd SE16 . . . **40** C2
Leathwaite Rd
SW11 . . . . **60** B2
Leathwell Rd SE8 . . **52** A1
Lebanon Gdns
SW18 . . . . **58** C1
Lebanon Rd SW18 . **58** C2
Lebus Ho NW8 . . . . **80** A1
Lechmere Rd NW2 . . **9** A2
Leckford Rd SW18 . . **71** B3
Leckhampton Pl **2**
SW2 . . . . **74** C4
Leconfield Ave SW13,
SW15 . . . . **56** B4
Leconfield Ho SE5 . **64** A4
Leconfield Rd N5 . . **15** C4
Lector Ct EC1 . . . . . **95** C1
Leda Ct **8** SW9 . . . **163** B1
Ledam Bldg EC1 . . **107** B4
Ledbury Ho **12**
SE22 . . . . **64** A4
Ledbury Mews N
W11 . . . . **31** C3
Ledbury Mews W
W11 . . . . . **31** C2 **113** B4
Ledbury Rd W11 . . . **31** C3
Ledbury St SE15 . . . **49** C3
Ledo Ho **1** N16 . . . **15** C4
Lee Conservancy Rd
E9 . . . . **18** B3
Lee Ct SE13 . . . . . . **67** C3
Leeds Ct EC1 . . . . . **96** A2
Lee Ho **8** N19 . . . . **13** C3
Leeke St WC1 . . . . . **94** C4
Leeland Way NW10 . . **8** B4
Leerdam Dr E14 . . . **42** B3
Lees Ct W1 . . . . . . **117** B4
Lees Pl W1 . . . . . . **117** B4
Leeson Rd **1**
SE24 . . . . **62** C3
Lees Pl W1 . . . . . . **117** B4
Lee St E8 . . . . **24** B4
Lee Ct N16 . . . . **15** C4
Leeve Ho **7** W9 . . . **23** B2
Leeward Ct **3** E1 . **125** C2
Leeway SE8 . . . . **41** B1
Lefevre Wlk E3 . . . . **26** C4
Leffern Rd W12 . . . **38** C4
Leff Ho **9** NW6 . . . **10** A1
Lefroy Ho SE1 . . . . **136** C3
Lefroy Rd W12 . . . . **38** B4
Legard Rd N5 . . . . . . **6** A1
Leggatt Rd E15 . . . . **27** B3
Legge St SE13 . . . . **67** B2
Leghorn Rd NW10 . . **21** C3
Legion Cl N1 . . . . . . **14** C1
Legion Terr E3 . . . . **26** C4

Leicester Ct
46 Paddington W2 . . **31** C4
St James WC2 . . . . **119** C4
Leicester Ho
4 Brixton SW9 . . . . **63** A4
5 Putney SW15 . . . **69** B4
Leicester Pl WC2 . **119** C4
Leicester Sq★ WC2
. . . . **119** C3
Leicester Square Sta
WC2 . . . . **119** C4
Leicester St WC2 . **119** C4
Leigham Ave
SW16 . . . . **74** A1
Leigham Cl **5**
SW16 . . . . **74** B1
Leigham Hall **3**
SW16 . . . . **74** A1
Leigham Hall Par **2**
SW16 . . . . **74** A1
Leigham Vale SE27,
SW16, SW2 . . . . **74** C2
Leigh Ct **29** SW2 . . **62** C1
Leighfield Ho **5** N4 . **6** B4
Leigh Gdns NW10 . . **22** B3
Leigh Ho **4** SW15 . **56** C2
Leigh Orchard Cl
SW16 . . . . **74** B1
Leigh Pl EC1 . . . . . **107** B4
Leigh Rd N5 . . . . . . **15** A4
Leigh St WC1 . . . . . **94** A3
Leighton Cres
NW5 . . . . **13** B3
Leighton Gdns
NW10 . . . . **22** B3
Leighton Gr NW5 . . **13** B3
**Leighton House (Art
Gall & Mus)★**
W14 . . . . **127** A2
Leighton Pl NW5 . . **13** B3
Leighton Rd NW5 . . **13** B3
Leinster Ave SW14 . **55** B3
Leinster Gdns W2 . **114** C4
Leinster Mews
W2 . . . . **114** C4
Leinster Pl W2 . . . . **100** C1
Leinster Sq W2 . . . **100** A1
Leinster Terr W2 . . **114** C4
Leitch Ho **8** NW8 . . **11** C1
Leithcote Path
SW16 . . . . **74** B1
Leith Ho
7 Kentish Town
N7 . . . . **13** C3
17 Streatham SW2 . **74** B4
Leith Mans W9 . . . . **88** A3
Leith Yd **3** NW6 . . . **23** C4
Lelitia Cl E8 . . . . . . **24** C4
Leman St E1 . . . . . **111** A1
Le Moal Ho **28** E1 . **32** B4
Lemsford Ct N4 . . . . **6** B2
**Lena Gardens Prim
Sch** W6 . . . . **39** B3
Lena Gdns W6 . . . . **39** B3
Lendal Terr **7**
SW4 . . . . **61** C4
Len Freeman Pl
SW6 . . . . **154** C3
Lenham **11** NW5 . . . **12** C2
10 Streatham SW2 . **74** B3
Lenham Ho SE1 . . . **137** C3
Lennon Rd NW2 . . . . **9** B3
Lennox Gdns
Knightsbridge
SW1 . . . . **130** C1
Willesden NW10 . . . . **8** B4

Lennox Gdns Mews
SW1 . . . . **144** C4
Lennox Ho **10** E9 . . **17** B2
Lennox Rd N4, N7 . . . **5** C2
Lenthall Ho SW1 . . **147** B2
Lenthall Rd E8 . . . . **16** C1
Lenthorp Rd SE10 . **43** B2
Lenton Rise TW9 . . **54** A4
Len Williams Ct
NW6 . . . . **23** C3
Leonard Ct
Bloomsbury WC1 . . . **94** A2
Kensington W8 . . . . **127** B2
Leonard Day Ho **3**
NW5 . . . . **13** A2
Leonard Pl **6** N16 . . **16** A4
Leonard St EC2 . . . . **97** C2
Leonora Ho W9 . . . . **88** C2
Leontine Cl SE15 . . **50** A3
Leopards Ct EC1 . . **107** B4
Leopold Bldgs **14**
E2 . . . . **24** B2 **98** C4
Leopold Mews E9 . **25** B4
Leopold Prim Sch
NW10 . . . . **8** B1
Leopold Rd NW10 . . **8** A1
Leopold St E3 . . . . . **33** B4
Leopold Wlk SE11 . **148** C1
Leo St SE15 . . . . . . **50** A3
Leo Yd EC1 . . . . **96** B1
Leppoc Rd SW4 . . . **61** C2
Leroy St SE1 . . . . . **152** A4
Lerry Cl W14 . . . . . **155** A4
Lerwick Ho SW18 . . **59** B3
Lesley Ct SW1 . . . . **133** B1
Leslie Prince Ct **5**
SE5 . . . . **48** C3
Leslie Rd E11 . . . . . **19** C4
Lessar Ave SW4 . . . **61** B1
Lessar Ct SW4 . . . . **61** B1
Lester Ct **42** E3 . . . . **27** A2
Leswin Pl N16 . . . . . **7** B1
Leswin Rd N16 . . . . . **7** B1
Letchford Gdns
NW10 . . . . **21** C2
Letchford Mews
NW10 . . . . **21** C2
Letchmore Ho **7**
W10 . . . . **22** B1
Lethaby Ho **15**
SW4 . . . . **62** B3
Lethbridge Cl
SE13 . . . . **52** B1
Letterstone Rd
SW6 . . . . **154** C1
Lettice St SW6 . . . . **165** A3
Lett Rd E15 . . . . **19** C1
Lettsom St SE5 . . . . **49** A1
Levana Cl SW19 . . . **70** A3
Levant Ho **17** E1 . . . **25** C1
Levehurst Way SW4,
SW9 . . . . **172** B2
Leven Rd E14 . . . . . **34** C3
Lever Ct **15** E9 . . . . **17** C2
Leverett St SW3 . . **144** B4
Leverington Pl N1 . **97** C3
Lever St EC1 . . . . . . **96** C3
Leverstock Ho
SW3 . . . . **144** B2
Leverton Pl NW5 . . **13** B3
Leverton St NW5 . . **13** B3
Levison Way **2**
N19 . . . . **4** C3
Levita Ho NW1 . . . . **93** C4
Leyne Ct EC1 . . . . . **95** B2

Lewesdon Cl **13**
SW19 . . . . **69** C3
Lewes Ho
Bermondsey SE1 . . **138** B4
Peckham SE15 . . . . **49** C4
Leweston Pl N16 . . . **7** B4
Lewey Ho E3 . . . . . . **26** B1
Lewin Rd SW14 . . . . **55** C4
Lewis Ct **6** SE16 . . **40** A1
Lewis Gr SE13 . . . . . **67** B4
LEWISHAM **67** B3
**Lewisham Bridge
Prim Sch** **3** SE13 . **67** A4
Lewisham Bsns Ctr
SE14 . . . . **50** C4
**Lewisham Coll
(Deptford Campus)**
23 SE8 . . . . **51** C2
**Lewisham Coll
(Lewisham Way
Campus)** SE4 . . . . **51** C1
Lewisham Ctr
SE13 . . . . **67** B4
Lewisham High St
SE13 . . . . **67** A2
Lewisham Hill
SE13 . . . . **52** B1
Lewisham Hospl
SE13 . . . . **67** A2
Lewisham Pk SE13 . **67** B1
Lewisham Rd SE13 . **52** B1
Lewisham Sta SE13 **67** B3
Lewisham St SW1 . **133** C3
Lewisham Sta
SE13 . . . . **67** B4
Lewisham Way SE4,
SE14 . . . . **51** B2
Lewis Pl E8 . . . . **16** C3
Lewis Silkin Ho **9**
SE15 . . . . **50** B4
Lewis St NW1 . . . . . **13** A2
Lexden Rd W3 . . . . **28** A1
Lexfield Ho N5 . . . . **15** B4
**Lexham Gardens
Mews** W8 . . . . **128** B1
Lexham Gdns W8 . **142** C4
Lexham Mews
W8 . . . . **141** C4
Lexham Wlk W8 . . . **128** B1
Lexington St W1 . . **119** A4
Lexton Gdns SW12 . **73** C3
Leyborne Pk TW9 . . **44** C2
Leyburn Ho **20**
SE15 . . . . **50** B4
Leyburne Rd **6**
NW1 . . . . **13** A1
Leybourne St **5**
NW1 . . . . **13** A1
Leyden Mans **7**
N19 . . . . **5** A4
Leyden St E1 . . . . . **110** C3
Leydon Cl
Rotherhithe SE16 . . **32** C1
SE16 . . . . **32** C1
Ley Ho SE1 . . . . . . **136** C3
Leyland Ho **6** E14 . **34** A2
Leylands SW18 . . . . **58** B1
Leylang Rd SE14 . . . **50** C3
Leys Ct **3** SW9 . . . **173** B1
Leysdown Ho
SE17 . . . . **152** B2
Leysfield Rd W12 . . **38** C4
Leythe Rd W3 . . . . . **37** B4
LEYTON **19** C4
Leyton Mill Ret Pk
E10 . . . . **19** C4

Leyton Mills E10 . . . . . . **19** B4
Leyton Rd E15 . . . . **19** C2
Liardet St SE14 . . . . . . **51** A4
Liberia Rd N5 . . . . **15** C3
Liberty Mews
 SW12 . . . . **61** A1
Liberty St SW9 . . . . . **173** A3
Libra Rd 🔢 E3 . . . . . . **26** B3
Library Mans 🔢
 W12 . . . . **39** B4
Library Par NW10 . . . . **21** A4
Library Pl E1 . . . . **32** A2
Library St SE1 . . . . . . **136** B3
Lichfield Ct TW9 . . . . . **54** A3
Lichfield Gdns TW10,
 TW9 . . . . **54** A2
Lichfield Ho 🔢
 SE5 . . . . **48** B1
Lichfield Rd
 Mile End E3 . . . . **26** A2
 Richmond TW9 . . . . . . **44** B2
 West Hampstead
 NW2 . . . . **10** A4
Lichfield Terr 🔢
 TW9 . . . . **54** A2
Lickey Ho W14 . . . . . **155** A4
Lidcote Gdns 🔢
 SW9 . . . . **173** A1
Liddell Gdns
 NW10 . . . . **22** B3
Liddell Rd NW6 . . . . . **10** C2
Lidfield Rd N16 . . . . . **15** C4
Lidgate Rd 🔢
 SE15 . . . . **49** B3
Lidiard Rd SW18 . . . . . **71** B2
Lidlington Pl NW1 . . . **83** A1
Lido The W2 . . . . . **116** A1
Lidyard Rd N19 . . . . . **4** B3
Liffey Ct NW10 . . . . **8** C1
Liffords Pl SW13 . . . . . **46** B1
Lifford St SW15 . . . . . **57** C3
Lighter Cl 🔢 SE16 . . . . **41** A2
Lighterman Mews 🔢
 E1 . . . . **32** C3
Lighterman's Rd
 E14 . . . . **42** A4
Lighterman's Wlk
 SW18 . . . . **58** C3
Light Horse Ct
 SW1 . . . . **145** B1
Ligonier St
 E2 . . . . **24** B1 **98** C2
Lilac Ho SE4 . . . . **66** B4
Lilac Pl SE11 . . . . **148** C3
Lilac St W12 . . . . **29** C2
Lilestone Est NW8 . . . **89** C1
Lilestone Ho NW8 🔢
 . . . . **89** C1
Lilestone St NW8 . . . . **90** A2
Lilford Ho 🔢 SE5 . . . . **48** B1
Lilford Rd SE5 . . . . **48** A1
Lilian Baylis Ho
 N1 . . . . **15** B2
Lilian Baylis Tech Sch
 SE11 . . . . **149** A1
Lilian Cl 🔢 N16 . . . . . **7** A1
Lilian Ave W3 . . . . **36** C4
Lillian Cl 🔢 N16 . . . . **7** A1
Lillian Rd SW13 . . . . . **47** A4
Lillie Ho N5 . . . . **14** C3
Lillie Rd SW6 . . . . . . **154** C3
Lillie Road Mans
 SW6 . . . . **154** B3
Lillieshall Rd SW4 . . . **61** B4
Lill St SW6 . . . . **155** B4
Lillington Ho N7 . . . . . **14** C4
Lily Cl W14 . . . . **39** C2

Lily Pl EC1 . . . . **107** C4
Lilyville Rd SW6 . . . . **164** C4
Limborough Ho 🔢
 E14 . . . . **33** C4
Limburg Rd SW11 . . . **60** A3
Limeburner La
 EC4 . . . . **108** A2
Lime Cl E1 . . . . **125** C2
Lime Ct SW15 . . . . **57** A4
Lime Gr W12 . . . . **39** B4
Limeharbour E14 . . . . **42** A4
Lime Ho 🔢 TW9 . . . . . **45** A2
LIMEHOUSE **33** A2
Limehouse Cswy
 E14 . . . . **33** B2
Limehouse Ct 🔢
 E14 . . . . **33** C3
Lime House Ct 🔢
 E14 . . . . **33** B3
Limehouse Cut 🔢
 E14 . . . . **34** A4
Limehouse Fields Est
 🔢 E14 . . . . **33** A4
Limehouse Link
 (Tunnel) E14 . . . . . **33** B2
Limehouse Sta
 E14 . . . . **33** A3
Limekiln Wharf 🔢
 E14 . . . . **33** B2
Limerick Cl SW12 . . **73** B4
Limerick Ct 🔢
 SW12 . . . . **73** B4
Limerston St
 SW10 . . . . **157** A3
Lime St Pas EC3 . . . **124** A4
Limes Ave
 Barnes SW13 . . . . **46** B1
 Golders Green NW11 . . **1** A4
Limes Ct NW6 . . . . **9** C1
Limes Field Rd
 SW14 . . . . **56** A4
Limesford Rd
 SE15 . . . . **65** C3
Limes Gdns SW18 . . . **58** C1
Limes Gr SE13 . . . . . . **67** B3
Lime St EC3 . . . . **110** A1
Limes The
 Camberwell SE5 . . . . . **64** A4
 Kensington
 W2 . . . . . . **31** C2 **113** C3
Limes Wlk SE15 . . . . . **65** B3
Limetree Ct SW2 . . . **74** B3
Lime Tree Ct 🔢
 SW19 . . . . **69** C2
Limpsfield Ave
 SW19 . . . . **69** C2
Limscott Ho 🔢 E3 . . . **27** A2
Linacre Cl SE15 . . . . . **65** A4
Linacre Ct W6 . . . . **39** C1
Linacre Rd NW2 . . . . . **9** A2
Linale Ho N1 . . . . **87** B1
Linberry Wlk 🔢
 SE8 . . . . **41** B2
Lincoln Ave SW19 . . . **69** C1
Lincoln Ct 🔢 N16 . . . . **6** C4
Lincoln Ho
 Bloomsbury WC1 . . . **107** A3
 🔢 Dartmouth Pk
 NW5 . . . . **4** B1
 Knightsbridge SW1 . **130** C3
Lincoln Mews
 NW6 . . . . **23** B4
Lincoln's Inn★
 WC2 . . . . **107** A2

Lincoln's Inn Fields
 WC2 . . . . **107** A2
Lincoln St SW3 . . . . **144** C3
Lindale SW19 . . . . **70** A2
Lindal Rd SE4 . . . . **66** B2
Linden Ave NW10 . . . **22** C3
Linden Ct
 🔢 Battersea
 SW8 . . . . **59** C3
 🔢 Shepherd's Bush
 W12 . . . . **30** B1
Linden Gdns
 Chiswick W4 . . . . **37** C1
 Notting Hill
 W2 . . . . **31** C2 **113** C3
Linden Gr SE15 . . . . . **65** B4
Linden Ho 🔢 SE8 . . . . **51** B4
Linden Lodge Sch
 SW19 . . . . **70** A3
Linden Mans N6 . . . . . **4** A3
Linden Mews
 Kensington
 W2 . . . . **31** C2 **113** C3
 Stoke Newington N1 . **15** C3
Lindens The W4 . . . . . **45** B2
Lindfield Gdns
 NW3 . . . . **11** B3
Lindfield Hts NW3 . . . **11** B3
Lindfield St E14 . . . . . **33** C3
Lindisfarne Way
 E9 . . . . **18** A4
Lindley Ho
 🔢 Peckham SE15 . . . **49** C3
 🔢 Stepney E1 . . . . . . **32** B4
Lindley Pl TW9 . . . . . **44** C2
Lindley St E1 . . . . **32** B4
Lindore Rd SW11 . . . **60** B3
Lindo St SE15 . . . . **50** B1
Lindrop St SW6 . . . . **166** C2
Lindsay Ct SW11 . . . **167** C3
Lindsay Sq SW1 . . . **147** C2
Lindsell St 🔢
 SE10 . . . . **52** B2
Lindsey Ho★
 SW10 . . . . **157** C2
Lindsey Mews 🔢
 N1 . . . . **15** B1
Lindsey St EC1 . . . . **108** B4
Lind St SE8 . . . . **52** A1
Linfield WC1 . . . . **94** C3
Linford Christie
 Stadium The
 W12 . . . . **30** A4
Linford Ho 🔢 E2 . . . . **24** C4
Linford St SW8 . . . . **170** C3
Linford Street Bsns
 Est SW8 . . . . **170** C4
Lingard Ho 🔢 E14 . . . **42** B3
Lingards Rd SE13 . . . **67** B3
Lingfield Ho
 🔢 Acton Green
 W4 . . . . **37** B1
 Lambeth SE1 . . . . . . **136** B3
Lingham St SW9 . . . **172** C1
Ling Rd E16 . . . . **35** C4
Ling's Coppice
 SE21 . . . . **75** C2
Lingwell Rd SW17 . . . **72** A1
Lingwood Rd E5 . . . . . **7** C4
Linhope St NW1 . . . . . **90** C1
Linkenholt Mans 🔢
 W6 . . . . **38** B2
Link St E9 . . . . **17** B3
Links Yd
 🔢 Spitalfields E1 . . . **111** B4

Links Yd continued
 Spitalfields E1 . . . . . **111** A4
Link The W3 . . . . **28** A3
Linkway N4 . . . . **6** B4
Linkwood Wlk
 NW1 . . . . **13** C1
Linnell Ho
 Spitalfields E1 . . . . . **110** C4
 St John's Wood
 NW8 . . . . **78** C4
Linnell Rd SE5 . . . . . . **49** A1
Linnet Mews
 SW12 . . . . **72** C4
Linom Rd SW4 . . . . . . **62** A3
Linscott Rd E5 . . . . . . **17** B4
Linsey St
 Bermondsey SE16 . . . **153** B4
 Bermondsey SE16 . . . **139** C1
Linstead Ho 🔢
 E1 . . . . **111** C1
Linstead St 🔢
 NW6 . . . . **10** C1
Linstead Way SW18,
 SW19 . . . . **70** A4
Lintaine Cl W6 . . . . . **154** B3
Linthorpe Rd N16 . . . . **7** A4
Linton Ho
 Lower Holloway
 N7 . . . . **14** B4
 🔢 Tower Hamlets
 E3 . . . . **33** C4
Linton St N1 . . . . **87** A3
Linver Rd SW6 . . . . . **165** B2
Linwood Cl SE5 . . . . . **49** B1
Lion Cl SE4 . . . . **66** C1
Lionel Ho 🔢 W10 . . . . **31** A4
Lionel Mans 🔢
 W14 . . . . **39** C3
Lionel Mews 🔢
 W10 . . . . **31** A4
Lionel Road N
 TW8 . . . . **36** A2
Lionel Road Prim Sch
 TW8 . . . . **36** A2
Lionel Road S
 TW8 . . . . **36** B1
Lion Gate Gdns
 TW9 . . . . **54** B4
Lion Gate Mews
 SW18 . . . . **70** C4
Lion House Sch
 SW15 . . . . **57** C3
Lion Mills 🔢 E2 . . . . . **24** C3
Lion Yd SW4 . . . . **61** C3
Lipton Rd 🔢 E1 . . . . . **32** C3
Lisburne Rd NW3 . . . . **12** B4
Lisford St SE15 . . . . . . **49** B2
Lisgar Terr W14 . . . . **140** C4
Liskeard Gdns SE3 . . **53** C2
Liskeard Ho SE11 . . . **149** C2
Lisle Ct NW2 . . . . **1** A1
Lisle St WC2 . . . . . . **119** C4
Lismore Cir NW5 . . . . **12** C3
Lismore Wlk 🔢
 N1 . . . . **15** B2
Lissenden Gdns
 NW5 . . . . **4** A1
Lissenden Mans
 NW5 . . . . **4** A1
Lisson Cotts NW1 . . **102** B4
Lisson Gr NW1,
 NW8 . . . . **90** A2
LISSON GROVE **90** B1
Lisson Ho NW1 . . . . **102** A4
Lisson St NW1 . . . . . **102** A4

Lister Cl W3 . . . . **28** C4
Lister Ct N16 . . . . **7** A2
Lister Ho
 Greenwich SE3 . . . . . . **53** A4
 Marylebone W1 . . . **104** A2
 Spitalfields E1 . . . . . **111** C4
Lister Hospl SW1 . . . **146** A1
Lister Mews N7 . . . . . **14** B4
Liston Rd SW4 . . . . . . **61** B4
Listowel Cl 🔢
 SW9 . . . . **163** C2
Listria Lo N16 . . . . **7** B2
Listria Pk N16 . . . . **7** B2
Litcham Ho 🔢 E1 . . . **25** C2
Litchfield Gdns
 NW10 . . . . **8** C2
Litchfield St WC2 . . **119** C4
Lithos Rd NW3 . . . . . . **11** B2
Little Albany St
 NW1 . . . . **92** B2
Little Argyll St
 W1 . . . . **104** C1
Little Boltons The
 SW10 . . . . **142** B1
Little Britain EC1 . . **108** C3
Littlebury Rd SW4 . . . **61** C4
Little Chelsea Ho
 SW10 . . . . **157** A3
Little Chester St
 SW1 . . . . **132** A2
Little Cloisters
 SW1 . . . . **134** A2
Little College St
 SW1 . . . . **134** A2
Little Combe Cl 🔢
 SW15 . . . . **57** C1
Littlecote Cl SW19 . . . **70** A4
Little Cottage Pl
 SE10 . . . . **52** A3
Little Deans Yd
 SW1 . . . . **134** A2
Little Dimocks
 SW12 . . . . **73** A2
Little Dorrit Ct
 SE1 . . . . **137** A4
Little Edward St
 NW1 . . . . **92** B4
Little Essex St
 WC2 . . . . **121** B4
Littlefield Cl N19 . . . . **13** B4
Little George St
 SW1 . . . . **134** A3
Little Green St
 NW5 . . . . **13** A4
Little Marlborough St
 W1 . . . . **104** C1
Little Newport St
 WC2 . . . . **119** C4
Little New St EC4 . . **107** C2
Little Portland St
 W1 . . . . **104** C2
Little Russell St
 WC1 . . . . **106** A3
Little St James's St
 SW1 . . . . **118** C1
Little St Leonards
 SW14 . . . . **55** B4
Little Sanctuary
 SW1 . . . . **134** A3
Little Smith St
 SW1 . . . . **133** C2
Little Somerset St
 E1 . . . . **110** C1

Little Titchfield St
W1 . . . . **104** C3
Littleton St SW18 . . . . **71** B2
Little Trinity La
EC4 . . . . **123** A4
Little Turnstile
WC1 . . . . **106** C3
LITTLE VENICE █ . . **101** A4
Little Venice* █
W9 . . . . **100** C4
Littlewood SE13 . . . . . **67** B1
Livermere Ct █
E8 . . . . **24** B4
Livermere Rd E8 . . . . . **24** B4
Liverpool Gr SE17 **151** B1
Liverpool Ho N7 . . . . **14** C2
Liverpool Rd
Islington N1 . . . . **85** C3
Islington N1, N7 . . . **14** C1
Newham E16 . . . . . . **35** A4
Liverpool St EC2 . . . **110** A3
Liverpool Street Sta
EC2 . . . . **110** A3
Livesey Pl SE15 . . . . . **49** C4
Livingstone Ho █
SE5 . . . . **48** B3
Livingstone Lo █
W9 . . . . **31** C4
Livingstone Pl E14 . . **42** B1
Livingstone Rd
█ Battersea
SW11 . . . . **59** C4
Mill Meads E15 . . . . . **27** B4
Livity Sch The
SW2 . . . . **62** A2
Livonia St W1 . . . . . **105** A1
Lizard St EC1 . . . . . . **97** A3
Llandovery Ho █
E14 . . . . **42** B4
Llanelly Rd NW2 . . . . **1** B2
Llanvanor Rd NW2 . . **1** B2
Llewellyn Ho █
N19 . . . . **4** B1
Llewellyn St SE16 **139** C3
L'ile aux Enfants
NW5 . . . . **12** C3
Lloyd Baker St
WC1 . . . . **95** B3
Lloyd Ct
Ladywell SE13 . . . . . . **67** A2
█ West Norwood
SE27 . . . . **75** A1
Lloyd Ho N16 . . . . **6** C1
Lloyd's Ave EC3 . . . **110** B1
Lloyd's Bldg*
EC3 . . . . **110** A1
Lloyd's Pl SE3 . . . . . **53** A1
Lloyd St WC1 . . . . . . **95** B4
Lloyd's Row EC1 . . . . **96** A3
Lloyd St WC1 . . . . . . **95** B4
Lloyd Villas SE4 . . . . **51** C1
Lloyd Williamson Sch
█ W10 . . . . **31** A4
Loampit Hill SE13 . . **52** A1
Loampit Vale SE13 . . **67** B3
Loanda Cl █ E8 . . . . . **24** B4
Loats Rd SW2 . . . . . . **62** A1
Locarno Rd █ W3 . . . **28** B1
Lochaline St W6 . . . . **47** B4
Lochbie █ N4 . . . . **5** A4
Lochinvar St
SW12 . . . . **73** A4
Lochmore Ho
SW1 . . . . **145** C3

Lochnagar St E14 . . **34** B4
Lockbridge Ct █
W9 . . . . **31** C4
Locke Ho
Nine Elms SW8 . . . . **170** C4
Stamford Hill N16 . . . **7** B3
Lockesfield Pl E14 . . **42** A1
Lockgate Ct EC19 . . . **18** B3
Lockhart Cl N7 . . . . . **14** B2
Lockhart St E3 . . . . . **26** B1
Lockhurst St E5 . . . . **17** C4
Lockington Rd
SW8 . . . . **170** A4
Lockmead Rd
SE13 . . . . **67** B4
Lock Mews █
N1 . . . . **13** C2
Lockside E14 . . . . **33** A2
Locksley St E14 . . . . **33** B4
Lock View Ct █
E14 . . . . **33** A2
Lockwood Ho █
SE11 . . . . **163** B3
Lockwood Sq
SE16 . . . . **40** A3
Lockyer Est SE1 . . . **137** C3
Lockyer Ho
█ Greenwich
SE10 . . . . **43** B1
█ Putney SW15 . . . . **57** C4
South Lambeth
SW8 . . . . **162** A2
Lockyer St SE1 . . . . **137** C3
Locton Gn █ E3 . . . . . **26** B4
Loddiges Ho █ E9 . . **17** B1
Loddiges Rd E9 . . . . **17** B1
Loddon Ho NW8 . . . . **89** C1
Loder St SE15 . . . . . . **50** B3
Lodge Ave SW14 . . . . **56** A4
Lodge Rd NW8 . . . . . **90** A3
Lodge The █ W4 . . . . **38** A3
Lodore St E14 . . . . . . **34** B3
Lodsworth Ho
SW11 . . . . **169** B3
Loftie St SE16 . . . . . **139** C3
Lofting Ho █ N1 . . . **14** C1
Lofting Rd N1 . . . . . **14** C1
Lofts on the Park █
E9 . . . . **17** C2
Loftus Rd W12 . . . . . **30** A1
Loftus Rd (Queens
Park Rangers FC)
W12 . . . . **30** A1
Logan Mews W8 . . **141** B4
Logan Pl W8 . . . . . **141** B4
Loggetts SE21 . . . . . **76** A2
Lohmann Ho █
SE11 . . . . **163** B4
Lolesworth Cl E1 **111** A3
Lollard St SE11 . . . **149** B3
Lollards Twr SE1 . . **134** C1
Loman St SE1 . . . . . **136** B4
Lomas Dr █ E8 . . . . . **16** B1
Loman St E1 . . . . . . **111** C4
Lombard Ct
█ Acton W3 . . . . **28** A1
City of London EC3 **123** C4
Lombard La EC4 . . **107** C1
Lombard Rd
SW11 . . . . **167** B2
Lombard St EC3 . . . **109** C1
Lombardy Pl W2 . . **114** B3
Lomley Ho
SW2 . . . . **62** C1
Lomond Gr SE5 . . . . . **48** C3

Lomond Ho █
SE5 . . . . **48** C2
Loncroft Rd SE5 . . . . **49** A4
Londesborough Ho █
N16 . . . . **16** A4
Londesborough Rd
N16 . . . . **16** A4
London Acad for
Higher Education
The E15 . . . . **27** C4
London Acad of
Computing &
Electronics SW17 . . **72** B1
London Bridge EC4,
SE1 . . . . **123** C3
London Bridge City
Pier SE1 . . . . **124** A2
London Bridge
Experience The
SE1 . . . . **123** C2
London Bridge Hospl
SE1 . . . . **123** C2
London Bridge St
SE1 . . . . **123** C1
London Bridge Sta
SE1 . . . . **123** C1
London Bridge Wlk
SE1 . . . . **123** C2
London Britannia Coll
N1 . . . . **97** B4
London Business Sch
NW1 . . . . **90** C2
London Canal Mus*
N1 . . . . **84** B2
London Central
Mosque* NW8 . . . . **90** B3
London Chest Hospl
E2 . . . . **25** B3
London Christian Sch
SE16 . . . . **40** B3
London City Sch Ctr
EC1 . . . . **97** A1
London Clinic (Hospl)
NW1 . . . . **91** C1
London Coll of
Advanced Studies
SE1 . . . . **123** B1
London Coll of Beauty
Therapy W1 . . . . . . **105** A1
London Coll of Bsns &
Computer Studies █
SW4 . . . . **61** C3
London Coll of
Communication (Sch
of Printing &
Publishing) SE1 **136** B1
London Coll of
Economics &
Science NW10 . . . . . **20** B1
London Coll of
Fashion (Curtain Rd)
EC2 . . . . . . **24** A1 **98** B2
London Coll of
Fashion (Golden La)
EC1 . . . . **96** C1
London Coll of
Fashion (John
Prince's St) W1 . . **104** A1
London Coll of
Fashion (Lime
Grove) █ W6 . . . . . **39** B4
London Coll of
Fashion (Mare St)
E8 . . . . **17** B1

London Coll of
International
Business Studies
WC1 . . . . **106** B3
London Ct █
SW12 . . . . **58** C2
London Dungeon
The* SE1 . . . . **123** C2
London Electronics
Coll SW5 . . . . **142** A2
London Eye
(Millennium
Wheel)* SE1 . . . . **134** C4
London Fields East
Side E8 . . . . **17** A1
London Fields Prim
Sch E8 . . . . **25** A4
London Fields Sta
E8 . . . . **17** A1
London Fields West
Side E8 . . . . **16** C1
London Fire Brigade
Mus* SE1 . . . . **136** C4
London Glassblowing
Workshop SE1 . . **138** A3
London Ho NW8 . . . . **38** C2
London Ho TW9 . . . . **54** B4
London Ho NW8 . . . . **80** B2
London Hospital
Dental Inst █ E1 . . **32** A4
London Independent
Hospl The E1 . . . . . **32** C4
London International
Film Sch W2 . . . . . **106** A1
London Irish Rifles
Mus* SE1 . . . . **138** A2
London La E8 . . . . . . **17** A1
London Meridian Coll
█ N7 . . . . **5** C2
London Metrocity Coll
█ E3 . . . . **26** C2
London Metropolitan
Univ
Islington N7 . . . . . . **14** C3
London Metropolitan
Univ (Central Ho) █
E1 . . . . **111** B2
London Metropolitan
Univ (Commercial
Rd) █ E1 . . . . **111** C2
London Metropolitan
Univ (Ladbroke Ho)
█ N5 . . . . **15** A3
London Metropolitan
Univ (Moorgate)
EC2 . . . . **109** C3
London Metropolitan
Univ (Tower Hill)
EC3 . . . . **124** C4
London Metropolitan
Univ (Spring Ho) █
N7 . . . . **14** C2
London Mews W2 **101** C2
London Nautical Sch
SE1 . . . . **121** C2
London Oratory Sch
The SW6 . . . . **155** C2
London Oratory The*
SW7 . . . . **130** A1
London Rd SE1 . . . **136** B2
London Sch of
Economics &
Political Science
WC2 . . . . **107** A1

London South Bank
Univ SE1 . . . . **136** B2
London St
City of London
EC3 . . . . **124** B4
Paddington W2 . . . **101** B1
London Stile █
W4 . . . . **36** C1
London Stock
Exchange* EC2 **108** C2
London Terr █ E2 . . **24** C3
London Transport
Mus* WC2 . . . . . . **120** B4
London Trocadero*
W1 . . . . **119** B3
London Wall EC2 . . **109** C3
London Wall Bldgs
EC2 . . . . **109** C3
London Wetland Ctr*
SW13 . . . . **47** A3
London Wetland
Visitor Ctr*
SW13 . . . . **47** A2
London Wharf █
E2 . . . . **25** A4
London Zoo*
NW1 . . . . **81** B2
Long Acre WC2 . . . **106** B1
Longbeach Rd
SW11 . . . . **60** B4
Longberrys NW2 . . . . **1** B2
Longbridge Way
SE13 . . . . **67** B2
Longcliffe Ho
SW18 . . . . **59** A2
Long Dr W3 . . . . **29** A3
Longfellow Way
SE1 . . . . **153** A3
Longfield Dr
SW14 . . . . **55** A2
Longfield Est SE1 **153** A3
Longfield St SW18 . . **70** C4
Longford Ct
█ Bedford Pk
W12 . . . . **38** A4
█ Clapton Pk E5 . . . **17** C4
Longford Ho █
E1 . . . . **32** B3
Longford St NW1 . . . **92** B2
Longford Wlk █
SW2 . . . . **74** C4
Longhope Cl SE15 . . **49** B4
Longhurst Ho █
W9 . . . . **23** B2
Long La
Bermondsey SE1 . . **137** C3
Holborn EC1 . . . . . **108** B4
Longland Ct
Bermondsey SE1 . . **153** B2
Hackney E9 . . . . **18** A3
Longlands Ct
W11 . . . . . . **31** B2 **113** A4
Longleat Ho SW1 . . **147** B2
Longleigh Ho █
SE5 . . . . **49** A2
Longlents Ho █
NW10 . . . . **20** C4
Longley Ho █
N19 . . . . **13** B4
Longley St SE1 . . . . **153** C3
Longman Ho
█ Globe Town E2 . . **25** C3
█ Shoreditch E8 . . . **24** B4
Long Meadow █
N7 . . . . **13** C3

Longmoor Point 14
SW15 . . . . 69 A3
Longmore St
SW1 . . . . 146 C3
Longnor Rd E1 . . . . . . 25 C2
Long Pond Rd SE3 . . 53 A2
Long Rd SW4 . . . . 61 B3
Longridge Ho
SE1 . . . . 137 A1
Longridge Rd
SW5 . . . . 141 C3
Longs Ct 2 TW9 . . . . 54 B3
Long's Ct 11 . . . . . . 119 C3
Longshore SE8 . . . . . 41 B2
Long St E2 . . 24 B2 98 C4
Longstaff Cres
SW18 . . . . 70 C4
Longstaff Rd
SW18 . . . . 58 C1
Longstone Ave
NW10 . . . . 21 B4
Longthorne Ho 13
E3 . . . . 26 C2
Longthorpe Ct 9
W6 . . . . 38 C2
Longville Rd SE11 150 B4
Long Wlk SE1 . . . . . 138 B2
Longwood Dr
SW15 . . . . 56 C1
Long Yd WC1 . . . . . . 94 C1
Lonsdale Ave
Fulham SW6 . . . . . . 58 C4
6 Stoke Newington
N4 . . . . 6 B2
Lonsdale Mews
Notting Hill W11 . . . 31 B3
4 Richmond TW9 . . 44 C2
Lonsdale Pl N1 . . . . 14 C1
Lonsdale Rd
Barnes SW13 . . . . . 46 B3
Chiswick W4 . . . . . . 38 B2
Kilburn NW6 . . . . . . 23 B4
Notting Hill W11 . . . 31 B3
Lonsdale Sq
Islington N1 . . . . . . 14 C1
Islington N1 . . . . . . 85 C4
Lopez Ho 3 SW9 . . 62 A4
Loraine Rd
Chiswick W4 . . . . . . 45 A4
Islington N7 . . . . . . 14 B4
Lord David Pitt Ho 8
SE24 . . . . 62 C3
Lorden Wlk 11
E2 . . . . 24 C2 99 B3
Lord Hills Rd W2 100 B4
Lord Holland La 5
SW9 . . . . 173 C2
Lord Napier Pl
W6 . . . . 38 C1
Lord North St
SW1 . . . . 134 A1
Lord Roberts Mews
SW6 . . . . 156 A1
Lords Cl SE21 . . . . . 75 B1
Lord's Cricket Mus*
NW8 . . . . 89 C3
Lordship Gr N16 . . . . 6 C2
Lordship Ho 3 N16 . . 6 C2
Lordship La SE22 . . 64 B1
Lordship Park Mews
N16 . . . . 6 B2
Lordship Pk N16 . . . . 6 C2
Lordship Rd N16's 158 A3
Lordship Rd N16 . . . . 6 C2
Lordship Terr N16 . . . 6 C2

Lord's Indoor Cricket
Sch NW8 . . . . 90 A4
Lord's (MCC &
Middlesex Cty
Cricket Ground)★
NW8 . . . . 89 C4
Lord's View NW8 . . 89 C3
Loreburn Ho 2
N7 . . . . 14 B4
Lorenzo St N1,
WC1 . . . . 94 C4
Loris Rd W6 . . . . . . 39 B3
Lorn Ct SW9 . . . . . 173 B2
Lorne Cl NW8 . . . . . 90 B3
Lorne Ct SW11 . . . . 57 C1
Lorne Gdns 5
W11 . . . . 39 C4
Lorne Ho
Hornsey N4 . . . . 5 B4
7 Tower Hamlets
E1 . . . . 33 A4
Lorne Rd
Finsbury Pk N4 . . . . . 5 B3
3 Richmond TW10 . 54 B2
Lorn Rd SW9 . . . . . 173 B2
Lorraine Ct 10
NW1 . . . . 13 A1
Lorrimore 14
SE17 . . . . 48 A4
Lorrimore Sq
SE17 . . . . 48 A4
Lorton Ho 9 NW6 . . 23 C4
Lostock Ho 6
SW8 . . . . 171 B2
Lothair Rd 8 N4 . . . . 6 A4
Lothbury EC2 . . . . . 109 B2
Lothian Rd SW9 . . . 48 A2
Lothrop St W10 . . . . 23 A2
Lots Rd SW10 . . . . 157 A1
Loudoun Rd NW8 . . 79 A3
Loughborough Ct 7
SW9 . . . . 63 A4
Loughborough
Junction Sta
SW9 . . . . 63 A4
Loughborough Pk
SW9 . . . . 63 A3
Loughborough Prim
Sch SW9 . . . . 48 A1
Loughborough Rd SE5,
SW9 . . . . 48 A1
Loughborough St
SE11 . . . . 149 A1
Lough Rd N7 . . . . . . 14 B2
Louisa Ct E9 . . . . . . 25 C4
Louisa Gdns E1 . . . . 25 C1
Louisa Ho SW15 . . . 56 B3
Louisa St E1 . . . . . . 25 C1
Louise Bennett Cl 7
SE24 . . . . 63 A3
Louise De Marillac Ho
3 E1 . . . . 32 B4
Louise White Ho 1
N19 . . . . 4 C3
Louisville Rd
SW17 . . . . 72 C1
Louvaine Rd SW11 . 59 C3
Lovat Cl NW2 . . . . . 12A A3
Lovatt Ct SW12 . . . . 73 A3
Loveday Ho 2
SW2 . . . . 74 C3
Lovegrove St SE1 . . 49 C4
Lovegrove Wlk
E14 . . . . 34 B1
Love La EC2 . . . . . . 109 A2
Lovelace Ho 12 E8 . . 24 B4

Lovelace Rd SE21 . . 75 B3
Lovelinch Cl SE15 . . 50 B4
Lovell Ho E8 . . . . . . 24 C4
Lovell Pl SE16 . . . . . 41 A3
Loveridge Mews
NW6 . . . . 10 B2
Loveridge Rd NW6 . 10 B2
Lover's Wlk W1 . . . 117 B1
Lovette Ho 4 E3 . . . 26 C2
Lovetts Pl SW18 . . . 59 A3
Love Wlk SE5 . . . . . 48 C1
Low Cross Wood La
SE21 . . . . 76 B1
Lowden Rd SE24 . . . 63 B3
Lowder Ho 6 E1 . . . 32 A1
Lowe Ave E16 . . . . . 35 C4
Lowell St E14 . . . . . 33 A3
Lowell St E14 . . . . . 33 A3
Lower Addison Gdns
W14 . . . . 126 A3
Lower Belgrave St
SW1 . . . . 132 A1
LOWER CLAPTON 17 B4
Lower Clapton Rd
E5 . . . . 17 B4
Lower Clarendon Wlk
8 W11 . . . . 31 A3
Lower Comm S
SW15 . . . . 57 A4
Lower Grosvenor Pl
SW1 . . . . 132 B2
Lower Grove Rd
TW10 . . . . 54 B2
LOWER
HOLLOWAY 14 A3
Lower James St
W1 . . . . 119 A4
Lower John St
W1 . . . . 119 A4
Lower Lea Crossing
E14, E16 . . . . 35 A2
Lower Mall W6 . . . . 39 A1
Lower Marsh SE1 . . 135 B3
Lower Merton Rise
NW3 . . . . 12 A1
Lower Mortlake Rd
TW9 . . . . 54 B4
Lower Pk
Acton W3 . . . . 20 B1
5 Putney SW15 . . . 57 C2
LOWER PLACE 20 B3
Lower Place Bsns Ctr
NW10 . . . . 20 B3
Lower Richmond Rd
Mortlake SW14,
TW9 . . . . 55 A4
Putney SW15 . . . . . 57 B4
Lower Robert St
WC2 . . . . 120 B3
Lower Sloane St
SW1 . . . . 145 B2
Lower Terr NW3 . . . . 2 B1
Lower Thames St
EC3 . . . . 124 A3
Lowerwood Ct
W11 . . . . 31 A3
Loweswater Ho
E3 . . . . 26 B1
Lowfield Rd
Dagenham W3 . . . . 28 B3
Hampstead NW6 . . . 10 C1
Lowlands NW3 . . . . 12 A2
Lowman Rd N7 . . . . 14 B4
Lowndes Cl SW1 . . 131 C1

Lowndes Ct
Knightsbridge
SW1 . . . . 131 A2
Marylebone W1 . . . 104 C1
Lowndes Lo SW1 . . 131 A2
Lowndes Pl SW1 . . 131 B1
Lowndes Sq SW1 . . 131 A3
Lowndes St SW1 . . 131 B2
Lowood Ho 12 E1 . . 32 B2
Lowood St E1 . . . . . 32 A2
Lowry Ct 3 SE16 . . 40 A1
Lowth Rd SE5 . . . . . 48 B1
Loxford Ho SW1 . . 145 C3
Loxham St WC1 . . . 94 B3
Loxley Rd SW18 . . . 71 C3
LTC Coll London
W1 . . . . 104 C2
Lubavitch Boys Prim
Sch 6 E5 . . . . 7 C3
Lubavitch Girls Prim
Sch 8 N16 . . . . 7 B4
Lubavitch House Sch
(Jun Boys) 1 E5 . . . 7 B4
Lubbock Ho 21
E14 . . . . 34 A2
Lubbock St SE14 . . 50 B3
Lucan Ho N1 . . . . . 87 C3
Lucan Pl SW3 . . . . 144 B3
Lucas Ct SW11 . . . 169 C3
Lucas Ho
8 Clapham SW8 . . 171 A2
Walham Green
SW10 . . . . 156 B2
Lucas St SE4, SE8 . . 51 C2
Lucas Vale Prim Sch
SE8 . . . . 51 C2
Lucerne Mews
W8 . . . . 31 C1 113 C2
Lucerne Rd N5 . . . . 15 A4
Lucey Rd SE16 . . . 139 B1
Lucey Way SE16 . . 153 C4
Lucien Rd SW18 . . . 71 A2
Lucraft Ho 12 SW2 . 74 A4
Lucy Ashe Ho
SE17 . . . . 150 B3
Lucy Brown Ho
SE1 . . . . 123 A1
Lucy Cres W3 . . . . . 20 B1
Ludgate Broadway
EC4 . . . . 108 B1
Ludgate Cir EC4 . . 108 A1
Ludgate Hill EC4 . . 108 B1
Ludgate Sq EC4 . . 108 B1
Ludham NW5 . . . . . 12 B3
Ludlow Ct W3 . . . . . 37 B4
Ludlow St EC1 . . . . 96 C2
Ludovick Wlk
SW15 . . . . 56 A3
Ludwell Ho W14 . . 126 B2
Ludwick Mews
SE14 . . . . 51 A3
Lugard Ho 2 W12 . . 30 A1
Lugard Rd SE15 . . . 50 A2
Luke Ho 8 E1 . . . . . 32 A3
Luke St EC2 . . 24 A1 98 A2
Lukin St E1 . . . . 32 B3

Lullingstone Ho 20
SE15 . . . . 50 B4
Lullingstone La
SE13 . . . . 67 C1
Lullington Rd
Dalston N19 . . . . . . 4 A2
Lulworth
Camden Town
NW1 . . . . 13 C1
Walworth SE17 . . . 151 B2
Lulworth Ho SW8 162 C1
Lulworth Rd SE15 . . 50 A1
Lumiere Ct 7
SW17 . . . . 72 C2
Lumina Bldg 1
E14 . . . . 34 B1
Lumley Ct WC2 . . . 120 B3
Lumley Flats SW1 145 B2
Lumley St W1 . . . . 103 C1
Lumsden Ho 78 B3
Lunan Ho 14 E3 . . . 26 B3
Lund Point E15 . . . . 27 B4
Lundy Wlk 1 N1 . . . 15 B2
Lupin Cl SW2 . . . . . 75 A2
Lupino Ct SE11 . . . 149 A4
Lupin Point SE1 . . 139 A3
Lupton St NW5 . . . . 13 B4
Lupus St SW1 . . . . 147 A1
Luralda Gdns E14 . . 42 C1
Lurgan Ave W6 . . . . 47 C4
Lurline Gdns
SW11 . . . . 169 C4
Luscombe Ho
SW18 . . . . 58 B2
Luscombe Way
SW8 . . . . 162 A2
Lusher Ho SW15 . . . 57 C1
Lushington Rd
NW10 . . . . 22 A3
Lushington Terr 11
E8 . . . . 16 C3
Luton Pl SE10 . . . . . 52 B3
Luton St NW8 . . . . . 89 C1
Luttrell Ave SW15 . . 57 A2
Lutyens Ho W1 . . . 146 C1
Luxborough Ho
W1 . . . . 103 B4
Luxborough St
W1 . . . . 103 B4
Luxborough Twr
W1 . . . . 103 B4
Luxemburg Gdns
W6 . . . . 39 C2
Luxford St SE16 . . . 40 C2
Luxmore St SE4 . . . 51 B2
Luxor St SE5 . . . . . . 63 B4
Lyall Mews SW1 . . 131 B1
Lyall Mews W
SW1 . . . . 131 B1
Lyall St SW1 . . . . . 131 B1
Lyal Rd E3 . . . . 26 A3
Lyceum Flr 10 SE22 . 74 A4
Lycett Pl 3 W12 . . . 38 C4
Lycott Gr SE22 . . . . 64 B2
Lydden Gr SW18 . . . 71 A4
Lydden Rd SW18 . . . 71 A4
Lydford NW1 . . . . . . 83 A3
Lydford Cl 22 N16 . . 16 A3
Lydford Rd
Brondesbury NW2 . . 9 C2
Paddington W9 . . . . 23 B1
Lydgate Ho 8
N16 . . . . 16 A3
Lydhurst Ave SW2 . 74 B2

Lydney Cl
Camberwell SE15....49 A3
Putney SW19........70 A2
Lydon Rd SW4.......61 B4
Lydwell Ho **20**
SW8................**171** B1
Lyford Rd SW18....72 A3
Lygoe Ho 18 N6....4 C4
Lygon Ho 2
E2............24 C2 **99** B4
Lygon Pl SW1....**132** A1
Lyham Cl SW2......62 A1
Lyham Rd SW2.....62 A1
Lyle Pk SW15.......57 C1
Lyly Ho SE1.......**137** C1
Lyme Gr E9........17 B1
Lyme Grove Ho **2**
E9................17 B1
Lyme St NW1....82 C4 ⑭
Lyminge Gdns SW17,
SW18.............72 A3
Lymington Mans
NW6...............11 A2
Lymington Rd
NW6...............11 A2
Lympstone Gdns
SE15..............49 C3
Lynbrook Gr SE15..49 A3
Lynch Wlk 2 SE8...51 B4
Lyncott Cres SW4..61 A3
Lyncourt SE3.......52 C1
Lyndale Gdns
NW6...............10 C3
Lyncroft Mans 4
NW6...............10 C3
Lyndale NW2.......1 B1
Lyndale Ave NW2....1 B1
Lyndale CI SE3......53 B4
Lynde Ho 2 SW4....61 C4
Lynden Gate SW15..69 A4
Lyndhurst Gdns
NW3...............11 C3
Lyndhurst Gr SE5,
SE15..............49 B1
Lyndhurst Ho 4
SW15..............68 C4
Lyndhurst House Prep
Sch NW3...........11 C3
Lyndhurst Lo 8
E14................42 C2
Lyndhurst Rd NW3..11 C3
Lyndhurst Sch
SE5...............48 C1
Lyndhurst Sq SE15..49 B2
Lyndhurst Terr
NW3...............11 C3
Lyndhurst Way
SE15..............49 B1
Lynette Ave SW4...61 B1
Lynford French Ho 7
SE17.............**150** C2
Lyngham Ct 10 N4....5 A4
Lynhurst Ct NW8...79 B3
Lyn Mews 13 E3....26 B2
Lynmouth Rd N16....7 B3
Lynne Ct NW6......11 A1
Lynnett Ct E9.......18 A2
Lyn Ho SE15.......49 C4
Lynn Rd SW12......73 A4
Lynton Cl NW10.....8 B3
Lynton Ct 5 W3....28 B3
Lynton Est 16 SE1..**153** B3
Lynton Ho 16 W2...**100** B1

Lynton Lo N5........15 A3
Lynton Mans SE1..**135** B2
Lynton Rd
Acton W3...........28 A2
Bermondsey SE1.....49 A3
Paddington NW8....**153** A3
Lynton Terr 3 W3...28 B3
Lynx Terr SW19.....70 C1
Lyon Ho NW8.......90 A1
Lyons Pl NW8......89 B1
Lyon St N1.........14 B1
Lyons Wlk W14....**140** A4
Lyric Rd SW13......46 B2
Lysander Gr N19....4 C3
Lysander Ho 10
E2................25 A3
Lysander Mews
N19...............4 C3
Lysia Ct SW6......47 C3
Lysias Rd SW12.....61 A1
Lysia St SW6......47 C3
Lysons Wlk SW15...56 C2
Lytcott Gr SE22....64 C2
Lytham St SE17....**151** B1
Lyttelton Cl NW3...12 A1
Lyttelton Ho 22 E9..17 B1
Lytten Ct 5 W12...38 C4
Lyttleton Ho 16 E9..17 B1
Lytton Ct WC1.....**106** B3
Lytton Gr SW15.....58 A1

M

Mabel Thornton Ho **12**
N16...............15 C4
Mabledon Pl NW1,
WC1...............93 C3
Mablethorpe Rd
SW6..............**154** A1
Mabley St E9.......18 A3
MacArthur Ho 4
SW2................74 A4
Macartney Ho
SE10..............52 C3
Macaulay CE Prim
Sch SW4...........61 A3
Macaulay Ct SW4...61 A4
Macaulay Ho 4
2 Kensal Town
W10...............31 A4
10 Stoke Newington
N16................7 A1
Macaulay Rd SW4..61 A3
Macaulay Sq SW4...61 A3
Macauley Mews
SE13..............52 B1
McAuley Cl SE1....**135** B2
Macaulay Mews
SE13..............52 B1
McAusland Ho 8
E3................26 B3
Macbeth Ho 4
N1................24 A3
Macbeth St W6.....39 A1
McBride Ho 9 E3...26 B3
McCall Cl SW4.....**172** A2
McCall Ho 10 N7....14 A4
Mccarthy Ct
SW11.............**168** B3
Macclesfield Rd
EC1................96 C4
Macclesfield St
W1................**119** C4
McCoid Way SE1....**136** B3
McConnell Ho
SW8..............**171** B3
McCormick Ho 7
SW2................74 C3

McCrone Mews 3
NW3...............11 C2
McCullum Rd E3....26 B4
McDermott Cl
SW11..............60 A4
McDermott Rd
SE15..............64 C4
Macdonald Ho 3
SW11.............**169** B2
Macdonald Rd N19...4 B2
McDougall Ct
TW9................44 C1
McDougall Ho
E2............24 C2 **99** B4
McDowall Cl E16....35 B4
McDowall Rd SE5....48 B2
Macduff Rd SW11..**169** C4
Mace Cl E1.........32 A1
Mace St E2........25 C3
McEwan Way E15...27 C4
Macey Ho
Battersea SW11....**168** A3
10 Greenwich SE10..52 B4
Macfarlane Rd
W12................30 B1
McGlashon Ho 19
E1...........24 C1 **99** B1
McGregor Ct 3
N1................24 A2 **98** B4
McGregor Rd W11..31 B4
Machell Rd SE15....65 B4
McIndoe Ct N1.....87 B4
McIntosh Ho 11
SE16...............40 B2
McIntyre Ct 19
SW4..............**172** B2
Mackay Ho 33
W12................30 A2
Mackay Rd SW4....61 A4
McKenna Ho 3
E3................26 B4
Mackennal St NW8...80 B2
Mackenzie Cl **7**
W12................30 A2
Mackenzie Rd N7...14 B2
Mackenzie Wlk
E14................33 C1
McKerrell Rd SE15..49 C2
Mackeson Rd
NW3................12 B4
Mackie Ho 18
SW2................74 C4
Mackie Rd SW2.....74 C4
McKiernan Ct 2
SW11.............**168** A2
McKinnon Wood Ho
E2............24 C2 **99** B3
Mackintosh La E9...17 C3
Macklin St WC2...**106** B2
Mackonochie Ho
EC1...............**107** B4
Mackrow Wlk 1
E14................34 B2
Macks Rd SE16....**153** C4
Mackworth Ho
NW1...............92 C4
Mackworth St
NW1...............92 C4
Mac Laren Mews
SW15..............57 B3
Maclean Rd SE23..66 A1

Mcleod Ct SE21....76 C3
McLeod's Mews
SW7..............**142** B4
Macleod St SE17..**151** A1
Maclise Rd W14...**126** A1
McManus Ho 7
SW11..............59 C4
Mcmillan Ho SW4..44 A4
Macmillan Ho
Cricklewood NW3....9 B2
Lisson Gr NW8.....90 B3
McMillan St SE8....51 C4
Mcmorran Ho
N7.................14 A4
McNair Ho
SE15..............50 A2
Macnamara Ho
SW10.............**157** B2
Mcneil Rd SE5......49 A1
McNicol Dr NW10...20 B3
Maconochies Rd 9
E14................42 A1
Macquarie Way
E14................42 A2
Macready Ho W1..**102** B3
Macready Pl **2**
N7.................14 A4
Macroom Ho W9....23 B2
Macroom Rd W9....23 B2
Mac's Pl EC4......**107** C2
Madame Tussaud's ★
NW1..............**91** B1
Madani Girls Sch 36
E1................32 A3
Maddams St E3.....27 A1
Maddocks Ho 3
E1................32 A2
Maddock Way
SE17.............**148** A4
Maddox St W1....**118** B4
Madinah Rd
7 Dalston E8.....16 C2
London E8.........16 C3
Madison Ho E3.....27 B2
Madras Pl N7......14 C2
Madrid Rd SW13....46 C3
Madron St SE1....**152** B3
Mafeking Ave
TW8................44 A4
Magdala Ave N19....4 B2
Magdalene Cl **7**
SE15..............50 A1
Magdalene Ho **7**
SW15..............57 C1
Magdalen Pas E1..**125** A4
Magdalen Rd
SW18...............71 B3
Magdalen St SE1..**124** A1
Magee St SE11....**163** B4
Magellan Ho **16**
E1................25 C1
Magellan Pl 25
E14................41 C2
Magnolia Ct
Richmond TW9......45 A2
Wandsworth SW11....60 B1
Magnolia Ho 13
SE8................51 B4
Magnolia Pl SW4....62 A2
Magnolia Rd W4....45 A4
Magnolia Wharf
W4................45 A4
Magpie Ho 7 E3...26 B4
Magpie Pl SE14.....51 A4
Magri Wlk 22 E1....32 B4
Maguire St SE1....**139** A4

Mahatma Gandhi Ind
Est **1** SE24........63 A3
Mahogany Cl SE16..33 A1
Mahoney Ho SE14..51 B2
Maida Ave W2......89 A1
MAIDA VALE........88 A4
Maida Vale W9.....88 B4
Maida Vale Sta
W9................88 B3
Maiden La
Borough The SE1...**123** A2
Camden Town NW1...13 C1
Strand WC2.......**120** B4
Maidenstone Hill
SE10..............52 B2
Maidstone Bldgs
SE1...............**123** B1
Maidstone Ho **4**
E14................34 A3
Mail Coach Yd **23**
E2............24 A2 **98** B4
Main Yd E15........19 C2
Maismore St SE15..49 C4
Maitland Cl 3
SW4................61 B3
Maitland Ct W2....**115** B4
Maitland Ho
Chelsea SW1.....**160** C4
16 South Hackney
E2................25 B3
MAITLAND PARK....12 B2
Maitland Park Rd
NW3...............12 B2
Maitland Park Villas
NW3...............12 B2
Maitland Pl E5......17 A4
Majestic Ct N4......6 A3
Major Cl SW9.......63 A4
Majorie Mews **6**
E1................32 C3
Major Rd E15.......19 C3
Makepeace Ave N6...3 C2
Makepeace Mans
N6.................3 C2
Makins St SW3....**144** B3
Malabar Ct 20
W12................30 A2
Malabar St E14....41 C4
Malam Ct SE11...**149** B3
Malam Gdns **3**
E14................34 A2
Malay Ho 2 E1....32 B1
Malbrook Rd
SW15..............57 A3
Malcolm Ho 13 N1..24 A3
Malcolm Pl E2.....25 B1
Malcolm Rd E1.....25 B1
Malcolmson Ho
SW1..............**147** C1
Malden Cres NW1..12 C2
Malden Pl NW5.....12 C3
Malden Rd NW5.....12 C2
Malden Cl
Camberwell SE5....49 A4
Shoreditch N1.....87 A4
Stratford New Town
E15................19 C3
Maldon Rd W3.....28 B2
Malet Pl WC1......93 B1
Malet St WC1.....**105** C4
Maley Ave SE27....75 A2
Malfort Rd SE5.....64 A4
Mallams 2 SW9....63 A3
Mallard Cl
Hackney E9.........18 A2
Kilburn NW6........23 C4
Mallams Mews 1
SW9................63 A3

Mallard Cl
- **1** Hackney E9 . . . . . . 18 B2
- Kilburn NW6 . . . . . . 23 C4

Mallard Ho
- **8** Camberwell
- SE15 . . . . 49 B2
- St John's Wood
- NW8 . . . . . . 80 A1

Mallard Point 6
- E3 . . . . . 26 C2

Mallet Ho 11
- SW15 . . . . 56 C2

Mallet Rd SE13 . . . 67 C1
Mall Galleries ★
- SW1 . . . . 119 C2

Malling SE13 . . . 67 A2
Mallinson Rd
- SW11 . . . . 60 B2
- N6 . . . . 3 B4

Mallon Gdns E1 . . 111 A3
Mallord St SW3 . . 157 C4
Mallory Bldgs EC1 . 96 A1
Mallory Cl SE4 . . 66 A3
Mallory St NW8 . . 90 B2
Mallow Ct SE13 . . 52 B1
Mallow St EC1 . . 97 B2
Mall Rd W6 . . . 39 A1
Mall Studios 9
- NW3 . . . . 12 B3

Mall The
- Mortlake SW14 . . 55 B2
- St James SW1 . . 119 B1

Malmesbury 32 . . 25 B3
Malmesbury Prim Sch
- E3 . . . . 26 B2

Malmesbury Rd
- Bow E3 . . . . 26 B3
- Newham E16 . . 35 A4

Malmesbury Terr
- E16 . . . . 35 B4

Malmsey Ho SE11 . 149 A2
Malmsmead Ho
- E9 . . . . 18 A3

Malorees Jun & Inf
- Schs NW6 . . . 9 C1

Malpas Rd
- Hackney E8 . . 17 A2
- New Cross SE4 . 51 B1

Malta St EC1 . . 96 B2
Maltby St SE1 . . 138 C2
Malthouse Dr W4 . 46 B4
Malthouse Pas
- SW13 . . . 46 A1

Malting Ho E14 . . 33 B2
Maltings Cl SW13 . 46 A1
Maltings Lo SW13 . 46 A1
Maltings Pl
- Bermondsey SE1 . 138 B4
- Parsons Green
- SW6 . . . 166 B3

Malt Mill SE1 . . 124 C1
Malton Mews 1
- W10 . . . . 31 A3

Malton Rd W10 . . 31 A3
Maltravers St
- WC2 . . . . 121 B4

Malt St SE1 . . 49 C4
Malva Cl SW18 . . 59 A2
Malvern Cl W10 . . 31 B4
Malvern Ct
- **7** Shepherd's Bush
- SW11 . . . . 38 C4
- South Kensington
- SW7 . . . . 143 C4

Malvern Gdns NW2 . . 1 A2
Malvern Ho
- London N16 . . . 7 B3
- SE17 . . . . 151 A1

Malvern Mews
- NW6 . . . . 23 C2

Malvern Pl NW6 . . 23 B2
Malvern Rd
- Dalston E8 . . . 16 C1
- Maida Vale NW6 . . 23 C2
- Upper Holloway N19 . 4 C3

Malvern Terr N1 . . 85 B4
Malwood Rd
- SW12 . . . . 61 A1

Malyons Rd SE13 . . 67 A2
Malyons Terr SE13 . 67 A2
Managers St 8
- E14 . . . . 34 B1

Manaton Cl SE15 . . 65 A4
Manbre Rd W6 . . 47 B4
Manchester Dr
- W10 . . . . 23 A1

Manchester Gr
- E14 . . . . 42 B1

Manchester Ho
- SE17 . . . . 151 A2

Manchester Mans
- N19 . . . . 4 C4

Manchester Mews
- W1 . . . . 103 B3

Manchester Rd
- E14 . . . . 42 B3

Manchester Sq
- W1 . . . . 103 C2

Manchester St
- W1 . . . . 103 B3

Manchuria Rd
- SW11 . . . . 60 C1

Manciple St SE1 . . 137 C2
Mandalay Ho 6
- N16 . . . . 15 C4

Mandalay Rd SW4 . 61 B2
Mandarin Ct 5
- SE8 . . . . 51 C4

Mandela Cl 36
- W12 . . . . 30 A2

Mandela Ho 18
- E2 . . . . 24 B2 98 C4

Mandela Rd E16 . . 35 C3
Mandela St
- Camden Town
- NW1 . . . . 83 A4
- Kennington SW9 . . 163 B1

Mandela Way 5 SE1 . 152 B4
Mandeville Ho
- SE1 . . . . 153 A2

Mandeville Cl 5
- SE3 . . . . 53 B3

Mandeville Ct
- NW3 . . . . 11 A3

Mandeville Ctyd
- SW11 . . . . 169 B3

Mandeville Ho B
- SW4 . . . . 61 B2

Mandeville Pl W1 . . 103 C2
Mandrake Rd
- SW17 . . . . 72 B1

Mandrell Rd SW2 . . 62 A2
Manette St W1 . . 105 C1
Manfred Ct 7
- SW15 . . . . 58 B2

Manfred Rd SW15 . 58 B2
Manger Rd N7 . . 14 A2
Manilla St E14 . . 41 C4
Manitoba Ct 29
- SE16 . . . . 40 B4

Manley Ct N16 . . . 7 B1
Manley Ho SE11 . . 149 B2
Manley St NW1 . . 81 B4
Mannebey Prior N1 . 85 A1
Mannering Ho 16
- SW2 . . . . 62 B2

Manningford Cl
- EC1 . . . . 96 A4

Manning Ho 3
- W11 . . . . 31 A3

Manning Pl TW10 . . 54 B1
Manningtree Cl
- SW19 . . . . 70 A3

Manningtree St 2
- E1 . . . . 111 B2

Manny Shinwell Ho
- SW6 . . . . 155 A3

Manor Ave SE4 . . 51 B1
Manor Circus TW9 . 54 C4
Manor Ct
- **7** Brixton SW2 . . 62 B2
- Camberwell SE15 . 49 B2
- Gunnersbury W3 . . 36 C2
- Parsons Green
- SW6 . . . . 166 B3
- Streatham SW16 . . 74 A1

Manorfield Cl 3
- N19 . . . . 13 B4

Manorfield Prim Sch
- **8** E14 . . . . 34 A4

Manor Gdns
- **8** Chiswick W4 . . 38 A1
- Clapham SW4 . . 171 A1
- Gunnersbury W3 . . 36 C2
- Richmond TW10,
- TW9 . . . . 54 B3
- Upper Holloway N7 . 5 A1

Manor Gr
- Deptford SE15 . . 50 B4
- Richmond TW9 . . 54 C4

Manor Gt SE15 . . 58 A2
Manor Ho NW1 . . 102 B4
Manor House Ct
- W9 . . . . 88 C1

Manor House Dr
- NW6 . . . . 9 C1

Manor House Sta
- N4 . . . . 6 A2

Manor Lo NW2 . . 9 C2
Manor Mans
- **7** Hampstead
- NW3 . . . . 12 A2
- Tufnell Pk N7 . . 5 A1

Manor Mews
- New Cross SE4 . . 51 A1
- Paddington NW6 . . 23 C3

Manor Oak Mans
- SE22 . . . . 65 A1

Manor Par N16 . . 7 B2
Manor Park Rd
- SE13 . . . . 67 C3

Manor Park Rd
- NW10 . . . . 21 B4

Manor Pl TW9 . . 54 B3
Manor Pl SE17 . . 150 C2
Manor Rd
- Richmond TW10,
- TW9 . . . . 54 B3
- Stamford Hill N16 . . 7 A3

Manor Specl Sch
- NW10 . . . . 22 B4

Manor Street Est
- SW3 . . . . 158 B4

Manor The W1 . . 118 A3
Manor Way W3 . . 36 C2
Manresa Rd SW3 . 144 A1

Mansel Ct SW11 . . 168 B3
Mansell Ho SW8 . . 171 A4
Mansell Rd W3 . . 37 C4
Mansell St E1 . . 111 A1
Manse Rd N16 . . 7 B1
Mansfield Ct 27
- E2 . . . . 24 B4

Mansfield Ho
- SW15 . . . . 57 C1

Mansfield Mews
- W1 . . . . 104 A3

Mansfield Pl 28
- NW3 . . . . 11 B4

Mansfield Rd
- Acton W3 . . . 20 A1
- Maitland Pk NW3 . . 12 B4

Mansfield St W1 . . 104 A3
Mansford St E2 . . 24 C3
Mansion Cl SW9 . . 173 C4
Mansion Gdns NW3 . 2 A1
Mansion Ho ★
- EC4 . . . . 109 B1

Mansion House Pl EC3,
- EC4 . . . . 109 B1

Mansion House St
- EC2 . . . . 109 B1

Mansion House Sta
- EC4 . . . . 123 A4

Mansions The
- NW6 . . . . 10 B3

Manson Mews
- SW7 . . . . 143 B3

Manson Pl SW7 . . 143 B3
Manston NW1 . . 13 B1
Manstone Rd NW2 . 10 A3
Manston Ho W14 . . 126 B1
Mantell Ho SW4 . . 61 B2
Mantle Rd SE4 . . 66 A4
Manton Ho N16 . . 6 C1
Mantua St 22
- SW11 . . . . 59 C4

Mantus Cl E1 . . 25 B1
Mantus Rd E1 . . 25 B1
Manville Gdns
- SW17 . . . . 73 A1

Manville Rd SW17 . 73 A1
Manwood Rd SE4 . . 66 B1
Many Gates SW12 . 73 A2
Mapesbury Ct
- NW2 . . . . 10 A3

Mapesbury Rd
- NW2 . . . . 10 A2

Mapeshill Pl NW2 . . 9 B2
Mapes Ho 7 NW6 . 10 A1
Mape St E2 . . 25 A1
Maple Ave W3 . . 29 A1
Maple Ct 3 NW2 . . 9 C4
Maplecroft Est E8 . 16 C1
Maplecroft Rd E8 . 16 C1
Maple Ho
- **5** Maitland Pk
- NW3 . . . . 12 B2
- **5** New Cross SE8 . 51 B3
- **4** Richmond TW9 . 45 A2

Maple Leaf Sq 27
- SE16 . . . . 40 C4

Maple Lo SW15 . . 58 A1
Maple Mews NW6 . 78 A2
Maple Pl W1 . . 93 A1
Maples Pl E1 . . 32 A4
Maple St
- **5** Bethnal Green
- E2 . . . . 25 A3
- Fitzrovia W1 . . 93 A1

Maplestead Rd
- SW2 . . . . 74 B4

Mapleton Cres
- SW18 . . . . 59 A1

Mapleton Rd
- SW18 . . . . 59 A1

Maple Wlk W10 . . 22 C1
Maplin St E3 . . 26 B2
Marada Ho NW6 . . 10 A1
Marais W4 . . . 45 B3
Marban Rd W9 . . 23 B2
Marble Arch ★
- W1 . . . . 117 A4

Marble Arch Sta
- W1 . . . . 103 A1

Marble Cl W3 . . 28 A1
Marbleford Ct 4
- N6 . . . . 4 C4

Marble Ho W9 . . 23 B1
Marcella Rd SW9 . . 173 B1
Marchant Ho 13
- SW2 . . . . 62 B2

Marchant St SE14 . 51 A4
Marchbank Rd
- W14 . . . . 155 A4

March Ct SW15 . . 57 A3
Marchmont Rd
- TW10 . . . . 54 B2

Marchmont St
- WC1 . . . . 94 A2

Marchwood Cl 9
- SE5 . . . . 49 A3

Marcia Rd SE1 . . 152 B3
Marcilly Rd SW18 . 59 C2
Marcol Ho W1 . . 104 B2
Marcon Ct 28 E8 . . 17 A3
Marcon Pl E8 . . 17 A3
Marco Rd W6 . . 39 B3
Marcus Ct TW8 . . 44 A3
Marcus Garvey Mews
- SE22 . . . . 65 A2

Marcus Garvey Way
- **9** SE24 . . . . 62 C3

Marcus Ho 14
- SE15 . . . . 49 B2

Marcus St SW18 . . 59 A1
Marcus Terr SW18 . 59 A1
Marden Ho E8 . . 17 A3
Marden Sq SE16 . . 40 A3
Mardyke Ho SE17 . 151 C4
Maresfield Gdns
- NW3 . . . . 11 B2

Mare St E8 . . 17 A1
Margaret Bondfield
- Ho
- **6** Bow E3 . . 26 A3
- **22** Kentish Town N7 . 13 C3

Margaret Ct W1 . . 104 C2
Margaret Herbison Ho
- SW6 . . . . 155 A3

Margaret Ho 10
- W6 . . . . 39 B1

Margaret Ingram Cl
- SW6 . . . . 154 C3

Margaret Mcmillan
- Ho 10 N19 . . 4 C4

Margaret Rd N16 . . 7 B3
Margaret Rutherford
- Pl 8 SW12 . . 73 B3

Margaret St W1 . . 104 C2
Margaretta Terr
- SW3 . . . . 158 B4

Margaret White Ho
- NW1 . . . . 93 B4

Margate Rd SW2 . . . .62 A2
Margery Fry Ct N7. . . .5 A1
Margery St WC1 . . . . .95 B3
Margravine Gdns
　Hammersmith W6 . . . .39 C1
　West Kensington
　W14 . . . . .140 A2
Margravine Rd
　W6 . . . . .154 A4
Marham Gdns SW17,
　SW18 . . . . .72 A3
Maria Cl 18 SE1 . . . . .153 C4
Maria Fidelis Convent
　Sch (Lower) W1 93 A3
Maria Fidelis Convent
　Sch (Upper) W1 93 B4
Marian Ct E9 . . . . . . .17 B3
Marian Pl E2 . . . . . . .25 A3
Marian Sq E2 . . . . . . .25 A3
Marian Way NW10 . . . .8 B1
Maria Terr E1 . . . . . . .25 C1
Maribor 18 SE10 . . . . .52 B3
Marie Curie SE5 . . . .49 A2
Marie Lloyd 18
　SW9 . . . . .62 B3
Marie Lloyd Gdns 11
　N19 . . . . .5 A4
Marie Lloyd Ho N1 . .87 B1
Marie Stopes Ct 8
　N19 . . . . .5 A4
Marigold St SE16. . . .40 A4
Marina Ct 12 E3 . . . .26 C2
Marina Point 4
　E14 . . . . .42 A3
Marinefield Rd
　SW6 . . . . .166 B2
Marinel Ho 22 SE5. .48 B3
Mariners Mews
　E14 . . . . .42 C2
Marine Twr 20
　SE8 . . . . .51 B4
Marion Richardson
　Prim Sch 17 E1. . . .32 C3
Marischal Rd SE13. .67 C4
Maritime Greenwich
　Coll 18 SE8 . . . . . .51 C3
Maritime Ho 6
　SW4 . . . . .61 B4
Maritime Quay 5
　E14 . . . . .41 C1
Maritime St E3. . . . .26 B1
Marius Mans 3
　SW17 . . . . .72 C2
Marius Rd SW17. . . .72 C2
Marjorie Gr SW11 . .60 B3
Market Ct W1 . . . . .104 C2
Market La W12 . . . . .39 B4
Market Mews W1 . .118 A1
Market Pl
　1 Acton W3 . . . . . . .28 B1
　1 Bermondsey
　SE16. . . . . .40 A2
　Marylebone W1 . . . .104 C2
Market Rd
　Barnsbury N7 . . . . . .14 A2
　Richmond TW9 . . . . .54 C4
Market Sq E14 . . . . .34 A3
Market St E1 . . . . . .110 C4
Market Studios 14
　W12 . . . . .39 B4
Market Way E14. . . .34 A3

Market Yd Mews
　SE1. . . . . .138 A2
Markham Pl SW3 . .144 C2
Markham Sq SW3 . .144 C2
Markham St SW3 . .144 B2
Mark Ho 8 E3 . . . . . .27 A2
Mark La EC3 . . . . . .124 B4
Markland Ho W10 . .30 C2
Mark Mans W12 . . . .38 C4
Marksbury Ave 54 C4
Mark Sq EC2 . .24 A1 98 A2
Mark St EC2. .24 A1 98 A2
Markstone Ho
　SE1. . . . . .136 A3
Markyate Ho 6
　W10 . . . . .22 B1
Marland Ho SW1 . .131 A2
Marlborough
　11 Putney SW19 . . . .69 C3
　St John's Wood NW8 . .88 C4
Marlborough Ave 3
　E8 . . . . .24 C4
Marlborough Cl
　SE17. . . . . .150 B3
Marlborough Cres
　W4 . . . . .38 A3
Marlborough Ct
　Kensington W8 . . . .141 B4
　Marylebone W1 . . . .104 C1
Marlborough Flats
　SW3 . . . . .144 B4
Marlborough Gr
　SE1. . . . . .153 B1
Marlborough Hill
　NW8 . . . . .79 A3
Marlborough Ho
　Marylebone NW1 . . . .92 B2
　Richmond TW10 . . . .54 C2
　Stoke Newington N4 . .6 B3
Marlborough Ho
　SW1 . . . . .119 A1
Marlborough Lo
　10 Stepney E1 . . . . .25 B1
　St John's Wood
　NW8 . . . . .78 C1
Marlborough Mans 1
　NW6 . . . . .10 C3
Marlborough Mews 2
　SW2 . . . . .62 B3
Marlborough Pl
　NW8 . . . . .79 A2
Marlborough Prim
　Sch SW3 . . . . .144 B3
Marlborough Rd
　Acton Green W4 . . . .37 B1
　Richmond TW10 . . . .54 B1
　St James SW1 . . . . .119 A1
Marlborough St
　SW3 . . . . .144 B3
Marlborough Trad Est
　TW9 . . . . .45 A2
Marlborough Yd
　N19 . . . . .4 C2
Marlbury NW8. . . . . .78 B3
Marley Ho 14 W11. .30 C2
Marley Wlk NW2 . . . .9 B3
Marlin Ho SW15 . . . .58 A2
Marloes Rd W8. . . .128 A1
Marlow Bsns Ctr 2
　SE14 . . . . .51 A3
Marlowe Ct SW3 . .144 B3

Marlowe Ho 18
　N16 . . . . .16 A4
Marlowes The
　NW8 . . . . .79 B4
Marlow Ho
　Bermondsey SE1 . . .138 C2
　18 Kensington W2 . .100 B1
　44 Spitalfields
　E2 . . . . .24 B2 98 C3
Marlow Studio
　Workshops 43
　E2 . . . . .24 B2 98 C3
Marlow Way SE16 . .40 C4
Marl Rd SW18 . . . . .59 B3
Marlstone Ho 2 . . . .92 B3
Marlston NW1 . . . . . .92 B3
Marmara Apts 3
　E16 . . . . .35 C2
Marmion Ho 13
　SW12 . . . . .73 A4
Marmion Mews 4
　SW11 . . . . .60 C4
Marmion Rd SW11. .60 C3
Marmont Rd SE15 . .49 C2
Marmora Ho E1 . . . .33 A4
Marmora Rd SE22 . .65 B1
Marner Prim Sch 6
　E3 . . . . .27 A1
Marne St W10 . . . . .23 A2
Marney Rd SW11 . . .60 C3
Marnfield Cres
　SW2 . . . . .74 B3
Marnham Ave
　NW2 . . . . .10 A4
Marnock Ho SE17 . .151 B2
Marnock Rd SE4. . . .66 B2
Maroon St E14 . . . . .33 A4
Marquess Rd N1 . . . .15 C2
Marquess Rd S 18
　N1 . . . . .5 B3
Marquis Rd
　Finsbury Pk N4. . . . . .5 C3
　Kentish Town NW1 . .13 C2
Marrick Cl SW15 . . .56 C3
Marrick Ho 10
　NW6 . . . . .78 B3
Marriott Rd N4 . . . . .5 B3
Marryat Ct 12 W6. .39 A2
Marryat Ho SW1 . . .146 C1
Marryat Sq SW6 . . .164 A4
Marsala Rd SE13 . . .67 A3
Marsalis Ho 3 E3 . . .26 C2
Marsden Rd SE15. . .64 B4
Marsden St NW5 . . .12 C2
Marshall Cl SW18. .59 B1
Marshall Ct SW4 . .172 B3
Marshall Ho
　Paddington NW6 . . . .23 B3
　Shoreditch N1. . . . . .87 C2
　Walworth SE17. . . . .152 B2
Marshall Rd E10. . . .19 A4
Marshall St L Ctr
　W1 . . . . .105 A1
Marshall St W1 . . . .105 A1
Marshalsea Rd
　SE1. . . . . .137 A4
Marsham St SW1 . .133 C1
Marsh Ct
　11 Putney SW19 . . . .69 C3
　Westminster SW1 . . .147 C4
Marsh Gate Bsns Ctr
　E15 . . . . .27 B3

Marshgate Sch
　TW10 . . . . .54 B2
Marsh Hill E9 . . . . . .18 A3
Marsh Ho
　Nine Elms SW8. . . . .171 A4
　Pimlico SW1 . . . . . . .147 C1
Marsh St E14. . . . . .42 A2
Marsh Wall E14 . . . .42 A4
Marshwood Ho 10
　NW6 . . . . .23 C4
Marsland Cl SE17. .150 B1
Marsom Ho N1 . . . . .87 B1
Marston SE17 . . . . .151 A4
Marston Cl NW6. . . .11 B1
Marston Ho 22
　SW9 . . . . .173 C1
Marsworth Ho 8
　E2 . . . . .24 C4
Martaban Rd N16. . . .7 B2
Martello St E8. . . . . .17 A1
Martello Terr E8. . . .17 A1
Martell Rd SE21 . . . .75 C1
Martel Pl E8 . . . . . . .16 B2
Martha's Bldgs
　EC1. . . . . .97 B2
Martha St E1 . . . . . .32 B3
Martin Ct 18 E14 . . . .42 B4
Martindale SW14. . . .55 B2
Martindale Ave 2
　E16 . . . . .35 C2
Martindale Ho 22
　E14 . . . . .34 A2
Martindale Rd
　SW12 . . . . .73 A4
Martineau Ho
　SW1 . . . . .146 C1
Martineau Mews
　N5 . . . . .15 A4
Martineau Rd N5. . . .15 A4
Martin Ho
　Newington SE1. . . . .137 A1
　South Lambeth
　SW8 . . . . .162 A2
Martin La EC4 . . . . .123 C4
Martlett Ct WC2 . . .106 B1
Martlett Lo NW3. . . .11 A4
Martley Ho SW8 . . . .171 A4
Martock Ct 10
　SE15. . . . . .50 A2
Marton Rd 2 N16. . . .7 A1
Marvel Ho 5 SE5. . . .48 C3
Marville Rd SW6. . .154 C1
Marvin St 8 E8 . . . . .17 A2
Marwell Ct SE3 . . . . .52 C1
Mary Adelaide Cl
　SW15 . . . . .68 A1
Mary Adelaide Ho
　W2 . . . . .101 C4
Mary Ann Bldgs
　SE8 . . . . .51 C4
Mary Datchelor Cl
　SE5 . . . . .48 C2
Mary Dine Ct
　SW8 . . . . .163 A1
Mary Gn NW8 . . . . . .78 B4
Mary Ho
　6 Hammersmith
　W6 . . . . .39 B1
　8 Stockwell SW9 . . .172 C1
Mary James Ho 32
　E2 . . . . .24 C3
Mary Jones Ho 20
　E14 . . . . .33 C2
Maryland Rd
　Paddington W9 . . . . .23 C1

Maryland Rd *continued*
　Stratford New Town
　E15 . . . . .19 C3
Marylands Rd W9 . .88 A1
Maryland Wlk N1. . .86 C4
Mary Lawrenson Pl 1
　SE3 . . . . .53 C3
MARYLEBONE 104 B2
Marylebone Flyover
　NW1 . . . . .102 A3
Marylebone High St
　W1 . . . . .103 C4
Marylebone La
　W1 . . . . .103 C2
Marylebone Mews
　W1 . . . . .104 A3
Marylebone Pas
　W1 . . . . .105 A2
Marylebone Rd
　NW1 . . . . .103 A4
Marylebone St
　W1 . . . . .103 C3
Marylebone Sta
　NW1 . . . . .90 C1
Marylee Way
　SE11. . . . . .149 A3
Mary McArthur Ho 12
　N19 . . . . .4 C4
Mary Macarthur Ho
　18 Globe Town E2 . . .25 C2
　W14 . . . . .154 A4
Maryon Mews
　NW3 . . . . .12 A4
Mary Pl
　W11 . . . . . . .31 A2 112 A3
Mary's Ct NW8 . . . . .90 B2
Mary Secole Cl 21
　E8 . . . . .24 B4
Mary Smith Ct
　SW5 . . . . .141 C3
Mary St
　6 Canning Town
　E16 . . . . .35 B4
　Shoreditch N1. . . . . .87 A3
Mary Terr NW1 . . . . .82 C3
Mary Wharrie Ho 4
　NW3 . . . . .12 B1
Masbro' Rd W14. . . .39 C3
Mascotte Rd 2
　SW15 . . . . .57 C3
Masefield Ct N5. . . .15 B4
Masefield Ho 4
　NW6 . . . . .23 C2
Mashie Rd W3. . . . . .29 A3
Maskall Cl SW2 . . . .74 C3
Maskell Rd SW17. . .71 B1
Maskelyne Cl
　SW11 . . . . .168 B4
Mason Cl
　Bermondsey SE16 . .153 C2
　Newham E16 . . . . . .35 C2
Mason Ho
　6 Bermondsey
　SE1 . . . . .153 C3
　18 Hackney E9. . . . .17 B1
Mason's Arms Mews
　W1 . . . . .118 B4
Mason's Ave EC2 . .109 B2
Mason's Pl EC1 . . . . .96 C4
Mason St SE17 . . . .151 C4
Mason's Yd
　Finsbury EC1 . . . . . . .96 A4
　St James SW1 . . . . .119 A2
Massie Rd E8 . . . . . .16 C2
Massinger St SE17 . .152 A3

Massingham St
E1 . . . . .25 C1
Mast Ct **17** SE16 . . . . .41 A2
Masterman Ho **1**
SE5 . . . . .48 C3
Masters Dr SE16 . . . .40 A1
Masters Lo **24** E1 . . . .32 B3
Master's St **18** E1 . . . .32 C4
Mast House Terr
E14 . . . . .41 C2
Mastin Ho SW18 . . . . .70 C3
Mastmaker Rd
E14 . . . . .41 C4
Matara Mews
SE17 . . . . .150 C1
Matching Ct **14** E3 . .26 C2
Matham Gr SE22 . . . .64 B3
Matheson Lang Ho
SE1 . . . . .135 B3
Matheson Rd
W14 . . . . .139 C2
Mathews Yd WC2 . . .106 A1
Mathieson Ct SE1 . .136 B3
Mathison Ho
SW10 . . . . .156 C2
Matilda Gdns **10**
E3 . . . . .26 C3
Matilda Ho E1 . . . . . .125 B2
Matilda St N1 . . . . . . .85 A4
Matlock Cl SE24 . . . . .63 B3
Matlock Ct
7 Herne Hill SE5 . . .63 C3
St John's Wood
NW8 . . . . .78 C2
Matlock St E14 . . . . . .33 A3
Maton Ho SW6 . . . . .154 C2
Matson Ho
9 Bermondsey
SE16 . . . . .40 A3
16 Homerton E9 . . . . .17 C2
Matthew Cl W10 . . . . .22 C1
Matthew Parker St
SW1 . . . . .133 C3
Matthews Ct N5 . . . . .15 B4
Matthews Ho **3**
E14 . . . . .33 C4
Matthews St
SW11 . . . . .168 C2
Matthias Ct **12**
TW10 . . . . .54 A1
Matthias Ho **2**
N16 . . . . .16 A3
Matthias Rd N16 . . . .16 A3
Mattingly Way **3**
SE15 . . . . .49 B3
Maude Ho **8** E2 . . . .24 C3
Maude Rd SE5 . . . . . . .49 A2
Maudlins Gn E1 . . . .125 B2
Maudsley Ho TW8 . . .36 A1
Maudslay Hospl
SE5 . . . . .48 B3
Maud Wilkes Cl **10**
NW5 . . . . .13 B3
Maud St E16 . . . . .35 B4
Maugham Ct **5**
W3 . . . . .37 B3
Mauleverer Rd
SW2 . . . . .62 A2
Maundeby Wlk
NW10 . . . . .8 A2
Maunsel St SW1 . . . .147 B4
Maurer Ct **2** SE10 . .43 B3
Mauretania Bldg **11**
E1 . . . . .32 C2
Maurice Ct **4** E1 . . .26 A2

Maurice Ho **1**
SW9 . . . . .172 C2
Maurice St W12 . . . . .30 A3
Mauritius Rd SE10 . . .43 A2
Maury Rd N16 . . . . . . .7 C1
Maverton Rd E3 . . . . .26 C4
Mavor Ho N1 . . . . . . .85 A3
Mawbey Ho SE1 . . . .153 A1
Mawbey Pl SE1 . . . . .153 A1
Mawbey Rd SE1 . . . .153 A1
Mawbey St SW8 . . . .162 A1
Mawdley Ho SE1 . . . .135 C3
Mawson Ct N1 . . . . . .87 C3
Mawson Ho EC1 . . . .107 B4
Mawson La W4 . . . . . .46 B4
Maxden Ct SE15 . . . . .64 C4
Maxted Rd SE15 . . . . .64 B4
Maxwell Ct SE21 . . . . .76 C3
Maxwell Rd SW6 . . . .156 B1
Maya Cl SE15 . . . . . . .50 A1
Mayall Rd SE24 . . . . . .63 A2
Maybury Ct W1 . . . . .103 C3
Maybury Gdns
NW10 . . . . .9 A2
Maybury Mews N6 . . .4 B4
Maydew Ho **11** SE16 .40 B2
Maydwell Ho **5**
E14 . . . . .33 C4
MAYFAIR 118 A3
Mayfair Pl W1 . . . . . .118 B2
Mayfield Cl
Clapham Pk SW4 . . . . .61 C2
Dalston E8 . . . . .16 B1
Mayfield Ho
1 Bethnal Green
E2 . . . . .25 A3
Stamford Hill N16 . . . . . .7 A4
Mayfield Mans
SW15 . . . . .58 B2
Mayfield Rd
Acton W3 . . . . .28 A2
Bedford Pk W12 . . . . .38 A4
Dalston E8 . . . . .16 B1
Mayflower Cl SE16 . .40 C2
Mayflower Prim Sch
22 E14 . . . . .34 A3
Mayflower Rd
SW9 . . . . .62 A4
Mayflower St **1**
SE16 . . . . .40 B4
Mayford NW1 . . . . . . .83 A2
Mayford Cl SW12 . . . .72 B4
Mayford Rd SW12 . . .72 C4
Maygood Ho N1 . . . . .85 B2
Maygood St N1 . . . . . .85 B2
Maygrove Rd NW6 . . .10 B2
Mayhew Ct **2** SE5 . .63 C3
Maylands Ho
SW3 . . . . .144 B3
Maylie Ho **4** SE16 . .40 A4
Maynard Cl SW6 . . . .156 B1
Maynard Ho E1 . . . . . .26 A2
Maynards Quay E1 . . .32 B2
Mayne Ct E8 . . . . .16 C4
Mayo Ho **10** E1 . . . . .32 B4
Mayola Rd E5 . . . . . . .17 B4
Mayo Rd NW10 . . . . . . .8 A2
May's Buildings Mews
SE10 . . . . .52 C3
Mays Ct WC2 . . . . . . .120 A3
May's Ct SE10 . . . . . . .52 C3
Maysoule Rd
SW11 . . . . .59 C3
May St W14 . . . . .141 A1

Mayston Mews **3**
SE10 . . . . .43 C1
Maythorne Cotts
SE13 . . . . .67 C1
Mayton St N7 . . . . .5 B1
May Tree Ho SE4 . . . .66 B4
Maytree Wlk SW2 . . . .74 C2
Mayward Ho **7**
SE5 . . . . .49 A2
Maze Hill SE10,
SE3 . . . . .53 A4
Maze Hill Lodge **1**
SE10 . . . . .52 C4
Maze Hill Sta
SE10 . . . . .53 A4
Mazenod Ave
NW6 . . . . .10 C1
Maze Rd TW9 . . . . . . .44 C3
Mead Cl **3** NW1 . . . .12 C1
Meadcroft Rd
SE17 . . . . .48 A4
Meade Cl W4 . . . . .44 C4
Meader Ct SE14 . . . . .50 C3
Mead Ho
W11 . . . . .31 B1 112 C2
Mead Lo W4 . . . . .37 C4
Meadowbank NW3 . .12 B1
Meadow Bank **8**
SW15 . . . . .58 B2
Meadowbank Cl
SW6 . . . . .47 B3
Meadow Cl E9 . . . . . . .18 B3
Meadowcroft **8**
W4 . . . . .45 A4
Meadowgate Sch
SE4 . . . . .66 A4
Meadow Mews
SW8 . . . . .162 C3
Meadow Pl
Chiswick W4 . . . . .46 A3
South Lambeth
SW8 . . . . .162 B2
Meadow Row SE1 . . .136 C1
Meadow Row SE1 . . .136 C1
Mead Pl E9 . . . . .17 B2
Mead Row SE1 . . . . . .135 B2
Meadway The SE3 . . . .52 C1
Meakin Est SE1 . . . . .138 A2
Meakin Ho N7 . . . . . . .14 B3
Meard St W1 . . . . .105 B1
Meath Cres E1, E2 . . .25 C2
Meath Ho SE24 . . . . . .63 A1
Meath St SW11 . . . . .170 A4
Mecklenburgh Pl
WC1 . . . . .94 C2
Mecklenburgh Sq
WC1 . . . . .94 C2
Mecklenburgh St
WC1 . . . . .94 C2
Medburn St NW1 . . . .83 B2
Medcroft Gdns
SW14 . . . . .55 B3
Medfield St SW15 . . . .69 A4
Medhurst Cl **10** E3 . .26 A3
Median Rd E5 . . . . . . .17 B3
Medina Ct N7 . . . . .5 C1
Medina Gr N7 . . . . .5 C1
Medina Ho SE15 . . . . .65 B3
Medina Rd N7 . . . . .5 C1
Medlar St SE5 . . . . . . .48 B2
Medley Rd NW6 . . . . .10 C2
Medora Rd SW2 . . . . .74 B4
Medresco Ho
NW3 . . . . .11 C3
Medusa Ho SE6,
SE13 . . . . .67 A1

Medway Bldgs E3 . .26 A3
Medway Ct WC1 . . . . .94 A3
Medway Ho
Bermondsey SE1 . . . .137 C3
Paddington NW8 . . . .102 A4
Stoke Newington
N16 . . . . .15 C4
Medway Mews **59**
E3 . . . . .26 A3
Medway Rd E3 . . . . . .26 A3
Medway St SW1 . . . .133 C1
Medwin St SW4 . . . . .62 B3
Meecham Ct **1**
SW11 . . . . .168 A2
Meeson St E5 . . . . . . .18 A4
Meeting House Alley
7 E1 . . . . .32 A1
Meeting House La
SE15 . . . . .50 A3
Mehetabel Rd E9 . . . .17 B3
Melba Way SE13 . . . . .52 A2
Melbourne Ct
Hackney E5 . . . . .18 A4
Paddington W9 . . . . . .89 A2
Melbourne Gr
SE22 . . . . .64 B3
Melbourne Ho
W8 . . . . .31 C1 113 B1
Melbourne Mews
SW9 . . . . .173 B3
Melbourne Pl
WC2 . . . . .107 A1
Melbourne Sq **2**
SW9 . . . . .173 B3
Melbray Mews **11**
SW6 . . . . .164 C1
Melbreak Ho **10**
SE22 . . . . .64 A4
Melbury Ct W8 . . . . .127 A2
Melbury Dr SE5 . . . . .49 A3
Melbury Ho SW8 . . . .162 C2
Melbury Rd W14 . . . .127 A2
Melchester **3**
W11 . . . . .31 B3
Melchester Ho **1**
N19 . . . . .4 C1
Melcombe Ct
NW1 . . . . .102 C4
Melcombe Ho
SW8 . . . . .162 C1
Melcombe Pl
NW1 . . . . .102 C4
Melcombe Prim Sch
3 W6 . . . . .47 C4
Melcombe St NW1 . . .91 A1
Melcombe St NW6 . .166 B4
Melford Ct
Bermondsey SE1 . . . .138 B2
Dulwich SE22 . . . . . . .76 C4
Melford Rd SE21,
SE22 . . . . .76 C4
Melgund Rd N5 . . . . . .14 C3
Melina Ct
Putney SW15 . . . . .56 C4
St John's Wood
NW8 . . . . .89 B3
Melina Pl NW8 . . . . . .89 B3
Melina Rd W12 . . . . . .39 A4
Melior Pl SE1 . . . . . . .138 A4
Melior St SE1 . . . . . . .138 A4
Melisa Ct N6 . . . . .4 C4
Mellington Ct **2**
N16 . . . . .7 C1
Mellis Ave TW9 . . . . . .45 A2
Mellish Ho **2** E1 . . . .32 A3
Mellish St E14 . . . . . . .41 C3

Mellitus St W12 . . . . .29 B3
Mell St **6** SE10 . . . . .43 A1
Melody La N5 . . . . . . .15 B3
Melody Rd SW18 . . . . .59 B2
Melon Pl W8 . . . . .127 C4
Melon Rd SE15 . . . . . .49 C2
Melrose Ave
Cricklewood NW2 . . . . .9 B3
Wimbledon SW19 . . . . .70 C1
Melrose Ct SW18 . . . .58 B1
Melrose Gdns W6 . . . .39 B3
Melrose Ho
Maida Vale NW6 . . . . .23 C2
Pimlico SW1 . . . . .146 B2
Melrose Rd
1 Barnes SW13 . . . .46 B1
Wandsworth SW18 . . .58 B1
Melrose Terr W6 . . . . .39 B3
Melton Ct SW7 . . . . . .143 C3
Melton Ho E5 . . . . .7 C2
Melton St NW1 . . . . . .93 B3
Melville Court Flats
W12 . . . . .39 A4
Melville Ct
4 Brentford W4 . . . .36 C1
Rotherhithe SE8 . . . . . .41 A2
Melville Ho SE10 . . . . .52 B2
Melville Pl **4** N1 . . . .15 B1
Melville Rd SW13 . . . .46 C2
Melville Villas Rd
W3 . . . . .28 C1
Melvin Ct **11** TW9 . .44 C2
Melwood Ho **3**
E1 . . . . .32 A3
Melyn Cl N7 . . . . .13 B4
Memel Ct EC1 . . . . . . .96 C1
Memel St EC1 . . . . . . .96 C1
Menai Pl **2** E3 . . . . . .26 C3
Menard Ct EC1 . . . . . .97 A3
Mendham Ho SE1 . .138 A2
Mendip Ct
8 Battersea
SW11 . . . . .59 B4
Deptford SE14 . . . . . . .50 B4
Mendip Dr NW2,
NW11 . . . . .1 A2
Mendip Ho **2** N4 . . . .6 C4
Mendip Hos **12** E2 . .25 B2
Mendip Rd SW11 . . . .59 B4
Mendora Rd SW6 . . .154 C2
Menelik Rd NW2 . . . . .10 B4
Menorah Prim Sch
NW11 . . . . .1 A4
Menotti St **8**
E2 . . . . .24 C1 99 C2
Menteath Ho **9**
E14 . . . . .33 C3
Mentmore Terr E8 . . .17 A1
Mentone Ct SW8 . . . .172 B4
Meon Rd W3 . . . . .37 B4
Mepham St SE1 . . . . .121 B1
Merbury Ct SE13 . . . . .67 C2
Mercator Pl **4**
E14 . . . . .41 C1
Mercator Rd SE13 . . .67 C3
Merceron Ho **3**
E2 . . . . .25 B2
Merceron St E1 . . . . . .25 A1
Mercer's Cotts **8**
E1 . . . . .33 A3
Mercers Mews N7 . . .13 C4
Mercers Pl W6 . . . . . .39 C2
Mercers Rd N19 . . . . . .4 C1

Mercer St WC2....106 A1
Merchant Ct E1......32 B1
Merchants Ho
　SE10..............42 C1
Merchant Sq W2 101 B3
Merchant St E3 ....26 B2
Merchant Taylors
　Hall* EC3........109 C1
Merchon Ho N7....13 B4
Mercia Gr SE13....67 B3
Mercia Ho **9** SE5 ..48 B1
Mercie Ct SE22....76 C3
Mercier Rd SW15..58 A2
Mercury Ct
　2 Brixton SW9 173 B4
　3 Millwall E14 ....41 C2
Mercury Ho **5** E3 ..26 C4
Mercury Way SE4 ..50 C4
Mercy Terr SE13 ....67 A2
Mere CI SW15,
　SW19..............69 C4
Meredith Ave NW2 ..9 B3
Meredith Ho **17**
　N16..............16 A3
Meredith Mews
　SE4..............66 B3
Meredith St EC1....96 A3
Meredith Twr W3 ....37 A3
Meredyth Rd
　SW13..............46 C1
Meretone CI SE4 ..66 A3
Mereton Mans **6**
　SE8..............51 C2
Mereworth Ho **5**
　SE15..............50 B4
Merganser Ct **17**
　SE8..............51 B4
Meridan St SE13...67 C3
Meriden Ct SW3....144 A1
Meriden Ho **25** N1..24 A4
Meridian Building*
　SE10..............52 C3
Meridian Ho SE10 ..43 A2
Meridian PI E14 ....42 B4
Meridian Prim Sch **9**
　SE10..............52 C3
Meridian Sq E15...19 C1
Merivale Rd SW15..58 A3
Merlin Ho
　7 Chiswick W4 ....37 C1
　West Hampstead
　　NW3............11 A4
Merlin Sch The **11**
　SW15..............58 A2
Merlins Ct WC1....95 B3
Merlin St EC1......95 B3
Mermaid Ct
　Bermondsey SE1 ..137 B4
　Rotherhithe SE16..33 B1
Mermaid Ho **8**
　E14..............34 B2
Mermaid Twr **8**
　SE8..............51 B4
Meroe Ct N16 ......7 A2
Merredene St
　SW2..............62 B1
Merriam Ave **2**
　E8..............18 B2
Merricks Ct **5**
　SW14..............55 A3
Merrick Sq SE1....137 B2
Merrington Rd
　SW6..............155 C4
Merritt Rd SE4 ....66 B2

Merrivale NW1......83 A3
Merrow St SE17 ....151 B1
Merrow Wlk SE17 ..151 C2
Merryfield SE3 ....53 B1
Merryweather Ct **13**
　N19................4 B1
Mersey Ho **17** N7 ....14 C3
Merston Ho
　SE18..............59 A1
Merthyr Terr
　SW13..............47 A4
Merton Ave W4 ....38 B2
Merton Ho SW18 ..70 C3
Merton La N6 ......3 B2
Merton Rd SW18 ..70 C4
Merton Rise NW3 ..12 A1
Merton Road Ind Est
　SW18..............70 C4
Mertins Rd SE15...65 C2
Meru CI NW5........12 C3
Mervan Rd SW2 ....62 C3
Messaline Ave W3..28 B3
Messina Ave NW6..10 C1
Messiter Ho N1 ....85 A3
Metcalfe Ho **28**
　SW8..............171 B2
Meteor St SW11....60 C3
Methley Ho **8** N7 ....5 B2
Methley St SE11...149 C1
Methodist Central
　Hall* SW1........133 C3
Methwold Rd W10..30 C4
Metropolis
　Apartments **5**
　SW12..............73 A3
Metropolitan Benefit
　Societies
　Almshouses **9**
　N1..............16 A2
Metropolitan Bsns Ctr
　9 N1..............16 A1
Metropolitan CI **23**
　E14..............33 C4
Mews St E1........125 B2
Mews The
　Shoreditch N1......87 A4
　1 Upper Holloway
　　N19............5 A3
Mexborough NW1 ..82 C3
Mexfield Rd SW15..58 B2
Meyer Ho **1**
　SW12..............73 A4
Meymott St SE1 ....122 A1
Meynell Cres E9 ..17 C1
Meynell Gdns E9 ..17 C1
Meynell Rd E9 ....17 C1
Meyrick Ho **8**
　E14..............33 C4
Meyrick Rd
　Battersea SW11....60 A4
　Willesden NW10....8 C2
Miah Terr **1** E1 ....125 C1
Micawber Ct N1 ....97 A4
Micawber Ho **21**
　SE16..............139 C3
Micawber St N1....97 A4
Michael Cliffe Ho
　EC1..............95 C3
Michael Faraday Ho
　SE17..............151 C1
Michael Faraday Prim
　Sch SE17..........151 C1
Michael Manley Ind
　Est **23** SW8........171 A2
Michael Rd SW6...166 B4

Michael Tippett Sch
　The SE24..........63 B3
Michelangelo Ct **4**
　SE16..............40 A1
Michelle Ct W3 ....28 C2
Michels Almshouses
　1 N5..............15 A3
Michelsdale Dr **3**
　TW9..............54 A3
Michelson Ho
　SE11..............149 A3
Michel's Row **1**
　TW9..............54 A3
Michigan Ho E14 ..41 C3
Mickledore NW1 ....83 A1
Micklethwaite Rd
　SW6..............155 C3
Mickleton Ho **2**
　W2...............31 C4
Middlefield NW8 ..79 B4
Middle Row W10 ..23 A1
Middle Row Prim Sch
　21 W10............23 A1
Middlesex Ct **5**
　W4...............38 B2
Middlesex Ho **2** W1 105 A4
Middlesex Pas
　EC1..............108 B3
Middlesex St E1...110 C2
Middlesex Univ
　(Archway Campus)
　10 N19............108 C4
Middle Temple*
　EC4..............121 B4
Middle Temple La
　EC4..............121 B4
Middleton Dr
　SE16..............40 C4
Middleton Gr N7 ..14 A3
Middleton Ho
　Dalston E8........16 B1
　Newington SE1...137 B1
Middleton Mews
　N7...............14 A3
Middleton PI W1...104 C3
Middleton Rd
　Dalston E8........16 B1
　Golders Green NW11..1 C4
Middleton St E2 ..25 A2
Middleton Way
　SE13..............67 C3
Middle Yd SE1....124 A2
Midford PI W1 ......93 A1
Midhope Ho WC1...94 B3
Midhope St WC1...94 B3
Midhurst Ct N8 ....5 A4
Midhurst Ho **6**
　E14..............33 B3
Midhurst Way E5..16 C4
Midland PI E14 ....42 B1
Midland Rd NW1...94 A4
Midland Terr
　NW10..............21 A2
Midlothian Ho NW2 ..9 A4
Midlothian Rd E3..26 B1
Midmoor Rd SW12..73 B3
Midship CI SE16 ..32 C1
Midship Point E14..41 C4
Midstrath Rd NW10..8 A4
Midway Ho EC1 ....96 B4
Midwood CI NW2 ..9 A4
Milborne Ho **11** E9..17 B2

Milborne St E9 ....17 B2
Milbrook Ct NW3 ....2 B3
Milcote St SE1....136 B3
Mildmay Ave N1...15 C2
Mildmay Ct N1....15 C3
Mildmay Gr N N1...15 C3
Mildmay Gr S N1...15 C3
Mildmay Ho **6**
　SW15..............57 B2
Mildmay Mission
　Hospl E2..........98 C3
Mildmay Pk N1....15 C3
Mildmay Rd N1....16 A3
Mildmay St N1....15 C2
MILE END..........26 A1
Mile End Hospl E2..25 C2
Mile End Park L Ctr **1**
　E3...............33 B4
Mile End PI E1 ....25 C1
Mile End Rd E1, E3..25 C1
Mile End Sta E3 ..26 B2
Miles Bldgs NW1 ..102 A4
Miles Coverdale Prim
　Sch **1** W12........39 C4
Miles Ct E1........32 A3
Miles Ho **5** SE10 ..43 A1
Miles Lo E15......19 C3
Miles PI NW8......101 C4
Miles St SW8......162 B3
Milestone Green
　SW14..............55 C3
Milfoil St W12 ....29 C2
Milford Ct **3** N16 ..7 A3
Milford La WC2....121 B4
Milford Mews
　SW16..............74 B1
Milk St EC2........109 A2
Milkwell Yd **7**
　SE5..............48 B2
Milkwood Rd SE24..63 A3
Mill Yd E1..........32 B2
Millais Rd E11.....19 C4
Milland Ho **1**
　SW15..............68 C3
Millard CI **1** N16..16 A3
Millbank SW1......148 A3
Millbank Prim Sch
　SW1..............147 C3
Millbrooke Ct **7**
　SW15..............58 A2
Millbrook Ho **4**
　SE15..............49 C4
Millbrook Rd SW9..63 A4
Millender Wlk
　SE16..............40 B2
Millennium Bridge*
　SE1, EC4..........122 C3
Millennium City Acad
　W1...............104 B3
Millennium Dr
　E14..............42 C2
Millennium Harbour
　E14..............41 C4
Millennium PI **7**
　E2...............25 A3
Millennium Prim Sch
　SE10..............43 B3
Millennium Sq
　SE1..............139 A4
Millennium Way
　SE10..............43 A3
Miller Ho **19** SW2 ..74 A4
Miller's Ave E8,
　N16..............16 B3

Miller's Ct **1** W4 ..38 B1
Miller St NW1......82 C2
Miller's Terr **1** E8..16 B3
Miller's Way W6 ..39 B4
Millers Wharf Ho
　E1...............125 B1
Miller Wlk SE1 ....121 C1
Millfield La N6 ......3 B2
Millfield PI N6......3 C2
Millfields Com Sch
　E5...............17 B4
Millgrove St **6**
　SW11..............169 B2
Millharbour E14 ..42 A4
Mill Hill SW13 ....56 C4
Mill Hill Gr **11** W3..28 A1
Mill Hill Rd
　Barnes SW13......46 C1
　South Acton W3...37 A4
Mill Hill Terr **5**
　W3...............28 A1
Mill Ho **4** SE13 ....67 B4
Milligan St E14 ....33 B2
Milliners Ho SW18..58 C3
Millington Ho N16..6 C1
Mill La NW6........10 C3
Millman Ct WC1 ..94 C1
Millman Mews
　WC1..............94 C1
Millman PI WC1 ..95 A1
Millman St WC1 ..94 C1
Millmark Gr SE14..51 A1
MILL MEADS........27 C3
Millner Ct SE4 ....51 B1
Mill Pl E14........33 A3
Mill Pond CI SW8 161 C1
Millpond Est SE16..40 A4
Mill Row N1........24 A4
Mills Ct EC2........24 A2
Mills Gr **1** E14 ....34 B4
Mills Ho SW8......171 A4
Millshott CI SW6 ..47 B2
Mills Row W4......37 C2
Mill St
　Bermondsey SE1 ..139 A4
　Mayfair W1........118 C4
Millstone CI E15...19 C2
Millstream Ho **14**
　SE16..............40 A4
Millstream Rd
　SE1..............138 C3
Mill Trad Est The
　NW10..............20 B2
MILLWALL..........41 C3
Millwall Dock Rd
　E14..............41 C3
Millwood St **10**
　W10..............31 A4
Mill Yd E1........125 B4
Milman Rd NW6 ..23 A3
Milman's Ho
　SW10..............157 B3
Milman's St SW10 157 B3
Milner Bldg N16...6 C2
Milner Ho **1**
　SW11..............59 C4
Milner Pl N1......85 C4
Milner Sq N1......15 A1
Milner St SW3....144 C4
Milnthorpe Rd W4..45 C4
Milo Rd SE22......64 B1
Milroy Wlk SE1....122 A2
Milson Rd W14...126 A2
Milsted Ho **25** E5 ..17 A3

Milton Ave
Becontree NW10 . . . . .20 C4
Crouch End N6 . . . . 4 B4
Stonebridge NW10. . . 20 B4
Milton Cl SE1 . . . . . 152 C3
Milton Court Rd
SE14. . . . . .51 A4
Milton Ct
Fulham SW6. . . . . 58 A4
St Luke's EC2 . . . . . 109 B4
9 Wandsworth
SW18 . . . . .58 C2
Milton Gr N16. . . . . . .16 A4
Milton Ho
19 Bethnal Green
E2. . . . . .25 B2
2 Camberwell SE5 . . 48 C3
Milton House Mans
E8. . . . . .16 B4
Milton Pk N6. . . . . 4 B4
Milton Pl 3 N7 . . . . 14 C3
Milton Rd
Acton W3 . . . . .28 C1
Crouch End N6 . . . . . . 4 B4
Mortlake SW14 . . . . . .55 A4
Tulse Hill SE24 . . . . . .63 A2
Milton St EC1, EC2 109 B4
Milverton NW5. . . . . .12 C3
Milverton Rd NW6. . . . 9 B1
Milverton St SE11 149 C1
Milward St E1. . . . . . .32 A4
Mimosa Ct SW4 . . . 172 B3
Mimosa St SW6 . . . 165 A3
Mina Rd SE17 . . . . . 152 A2
Minchin Ho 10
E14 . . . . .33 C3
Mincing La EC3 . . . . 124 A4
Minera Mews
SW1 . . . . 145 C4
Minerva Cl SW9 . . . 163 C2
Minerva Rd NW10 . . .20 C2
Minerva St E2 . . . . . .25 A3
Minerva Wlk EC1 . . 108 B2
Minet Ave NW10. . . . .21 A3
Minet Ho 20 E1 . . . 111 B1
Minet Rd SE5, SW9. . .48 A1
Minford Gdns
W14 . . . . .39 C4
Mingard Wlk N7. . . . . 5 B1
Ming St E14. . . . . . . .33 C2
Minnow Wlk SE17 152 B3
Minshull St SW8. . 171 B3
Minson Rd E9 . . . . . .25 C4
Minstead Gdns
SW15 . . . . 68 B4
Minster Ct EC3 . . . . 124 A4
Minster Rd NW2. . . . .10 A3
Mint Bsns Pk 12
E16 . . . . .35 C4
Mintern St N1. . . . . . 87 C2
Minton Ho SE11 . . . 149 B4
Minton Mews 3
NW6 . . . . .11 A2
Mint St SE1 . . . . 137 A4
Mirabel Rd SW6 . . . 155 A2
Miranda Cl 11 E1. . . .32 B4
Miranda Ho 17 N1. . .24 A3
Miranda Rd N19 . . . . .4 B3
Missenden SE17. . . 151 C1
Missenden Ho
NW8 . . . . .90 A2
Mission Pl SE15. . . . .49 C2
Mission Sq 13
TW8 . . . . .44 A4

Mission The
13 Bermondsey
SE16. . . . . .40 A4
14 Poplar E14 . . . . .33 B3
Misterton Ct
SW11 . . . . 167 C3
Mistral SE5. . . . . .49 A2
Mitali Pas 21 E1. . . 111 B1
Mitcham Ho 9
SE5. . . . . .48 B2
Mitchell Brook Prim
Sch NW10 . . . . 8 A2
Mitchell Ct SW14 . . .56 A3
Mitchell Ho
Gunnersbury W4 . . . .37 A1
6 Islington N1. . . . . 15 A1
7 Shepherd's Bush
W12. . . . . .30 A2
Mitchell's Pl SE21 . . .76 A4
Mitchell St EC1. . . . .97 A2
Mitchison Rd N1 . . . .15 C2
Mitford Rd N19. . . . . . 5 A2
Mitre Bridge Ind Pk
W10 . . . . .22 A1
Mitre Rd SE1 . . . . . 135 C4
Mitre Sq EC3 . . . . . 110 B1
Mitre St EC3 . . . . . . 110 B1
Mitre The 8 E14 . . . .33 B2
Mitre Way W10. . . . . .30 B4
Mizzen Ct E14 . . . . . .41 C4
Moatfield NW6 . . . . . .10 A1
Moat Pl
Acton W3 . . . . .28 A3
Stockwell SW9 . . . . . .62 B4
Moat Sch The 7
SW6 . . . . 164 A2
Moberly Rd SW4 . . . .73 C4
Mobey St SW4 . . . . 172 A3
Mocatta Ho 9 E1 . . .25 A1
Modbury Gdns
NW5 . . . . .12 C2
Modder Pl SW15 . . . .57 C3
Model Cotts SW14. . .55 B4
Modling Ho 8 E2 . . .25 C3
Moelwyn Hughes Ct
N7. . . . . 13 C3
Moffat Ho 24 SE5. . .48 B3
Mohawk Ho 33 E3. . .26 A3
Moira Ct SW17 . . . . . .72 C2
Moira Ho 13 SW9. . 173 B4
Molasses Ho 1
SW11 . . . . .59 B4
Molasses Row 2
SW11 . . . . .59 B4
Mole Ct 2 W12 . . . . .38 A4
Mole Ho NW8 . . . . . .89 C1
Molesey Ho
E2. . . . . 24 B1 98 C2
Molesford Rd
SW6 . . . . 165 B3
Molesworth Ho 9
SE17. . . . . .48 A4
Molesworth St
SE13. . . . . .67 B4
Molly Huggins Cl
SW12 . . . . .73 B4
Molton Ho N1. . . . . . 85 A3
Molyneux Ho W1 . . 102 B2
Molyneux St W1. . . 102 B3
Mona Rd SE15. . . . . .50 B1
Mona St E16 . . . . . . .35 B4
Monck's Row
SW18 . . . . .58 B1
Monck St SW1 . . . . 133 C1
Monckton Ct W14 126 C2
Monclar Rd SE5 . . . . .63 C3

Moncorvo Cl SW7 130 A3
Moncrieff St SE15. . . .49 C1
Mondragon Ho
SW8 . . . . 172 B4
Monet Ct 15 SE16. . .40 A1
Moneyer Ho N1 . . . . 97 B4
Monica Shaw Ct
NW1 . . . . 83 C1
Monier Rd E3. . . . . . .18 C1
Monkbretton Ho
E2. . . . . 24 C2 99 B3
Monk Ct W12. . . . . . .29 C1
Monk Dr E16. . . . . . .35 C2
Monkridge 3 N8. . . .4 C4
Monksfield N4 . . . . . . 5 C2
Monkswell Ho
E2. . . . . 24 C2 99 B3
Monkton Ho
26 Bermondsey
SE16. . . . . .40 C4
27 Hackney E5. . . . .17 A3
Monkton St SE11 . . 149 C4
Monkwell Sq EC2 . . 109 A3
Monmouth Cl W4. . .37 C3
Monmouth Gr
TW8 . . . . .36 A2
Monmouth Ho
5 Camden Town
NW5 . . . . .13 A2
Wandsworth SW18 . .58 C1
Monmouth Pl W2 . 100 A1
Monmouth Rd W2. .31 C3
Monmouth St
WC2 . . . . 106 A1
Monnery Rd N19 . . . .4 B1
Monroe Dr SW14 . . . .55 A2
Monroe Ho
10 Crouch End N19 . . . 4 C4
Lisson Gr NW8 . . . . .90 B3
Monro Ho
11 Hampstead
NW3 . . . . .11 B4
Putney SW15 . . . . . . .57 A2
Monsal Ct E5. . . . . . .18 A4
Monsell Ct 4 N4. . . . .6 A1
Monsell Rd N4, N5. . . 6 A1
Monson Rd
Deptford SE14. . . . . .50 C3
Willesden Green
NW10. . . . . .22 A3
Montagu Ct W1 . . . 103 A3
Montague Ave
SE4 . . . . .66 C3
Montague Cl SE1 . 123 B2
Montague Pl WC1 105 C4
Montague Rd
Richmond TW10 . . . .54 A1
Shacklewell E8. . . . . .16 C3
Montague Sq SE15 .50 B3
Montague St
Bloomsbury WC1 . . . 106 A4
City of London EC1 108 C3
Montagu Mans
W1 . . . . 103 A4
Montagu Mews N
W1 . . . . 103 A3
Montagu Mews S
W1 . . . . 103 A2
Montagu Mews W
W1 . . . . 103 A2
Montagu Pl W1. . . . 103 A3
Montagu Row W1 . 103 A3
Montagu Sq W1. . . 103 A3
Montagu St W1. . . . 103 A2

Montague Cl
SW1 . . . . 147 C3
Montana Bldg 4
SE13. . . . . .52 A2
Montana Rd SW17 . .72 C1
Montcalm Ho E14 . . .41 C3
Montclare St
E2. . . . . 24 B1 98 C2
Monteagle Ct 27
N1. . . . . .24 A3
Monteagle Way
Nunhead SE15 . . . . . .65 A4
Shacklewell E5. . . . . . 7 C1
Montefiore Ct 2
N16. . . . . 7 B3
Montefiore St
SW8 . . . . 170 B1
Montego Cl 10
SW2 . . . . .62 C3
Montem Prim Sch
N7. . . . . 5 B1
Montem St N4 . . . . . . 5 B3
Monteray Studios
W10 . . . . .23 A3
Montesquieu Terr 3
E16. . . . . .35 B3
Montford Pl SE11. . 149 B1
Montfort Ho
4 Bethnal Green
E2. . . . . .25 B2
Cubitt Town E14 . . . . .42 B3
Montfort Pl SW19 . .69 C3
Montgomery Ct
W4 . . . . .45 B4
Montgomery Ho 5
SE14 . . . . .55 C4
Montgomery Lo 32
E1 . . . . .25 B1
Montgomery Rd
W4 . . . . .37 B2
Montgomery St
E14 . . . . .34 A1
Montholme Rd
SW11 . . . . .60 B1
Monthope Rd 17
E1 . . . . 111 B3
Montolieu Gdns
SW15 . . . . .57 A2
Montpelier Gr
NW5 . . . . .13 B3
Montpelier Mews
SW7 . . . . 130 B2
Montpelier Pl
Knightsbridge
SW7 . . . . 130 B2
21 Stepney E1. . . . .32 B3
Montpelier Rd
SE15. . . . . .50 A2
Montpelier Rise
NW11 . . . . .1 A4
Montpelier Row
SE3 . . . . .53 B1
Montpelier Sq
SW7 . . . . 130 B3
Montpelier St
SW7 . . . . 130 B2
Montpelier Terr
SW7 . . . . 130 B3
Montpelier Vale
SE3 . . . . .53 B1
Montpelier Way
NW11 . . . . .1 A4
Montpelier Wlk
SW7 . . . . 130 B2
Montreal Pl WC2 . . 120 C4
Montrell Rd SW2. . . .74 A3

Montrose Ave
NW6 . . . . .23 A3
Montrose Ct SW7 129 C3
Montrose Ho
Belgravia SW1 . . . 131 C3
Millwall E14 . . . . . . .41 C3
Montrose Pl SW1 . 131 C3
Montrose Villas 5
W6 . . . . .38 C1
Montserrat Rd
SW15 . . . . .58 A3
Monument* EC3 123 C3
Monument Gdns
SE13 . . . . .67 B2
Monument St EC3 123 C4
Monument Sta
EC3 . . . . 123 C4
Monza Bldg The
E1 . . . . .32 B2
Monza St E1 . . . . . . .32 B2
Moodkee St SE16. . . .40 B3
Moody Rd SE15. . . . .49 B2
Moody St E1 . . . . . . .25 C2
Moon St N1. . . . . . . .86 A4
Moorcroft Rd
SW16 . . . . .74 A1
Moore Ct SW14. . . . .55 B4
Moore Ct N1 . . . . . . 86 A3
Moore Ho
18 Bethnal Green
E2. . . . . .25 B2
7 Shadwell SE10 . . .43 B1
2 Wandsworth SW17 .71 C1
Moore Park Ct
SW6 . . . . 156 B2
Moore Park Rd
SW6 . . . . 156 A1
Moore St SW3 . . . . 144 C4
Moorfields EC2. . . . 109 B3
Moorfields Eye Hospl
EC1 . . . . 97 B3
Moorfields Highwalk
EC2 . . . . 109 B3
Moorgate EC2 . . . . 109 B3
Moorgate PI 2 EC2 109 B2
Moorgate Sta
EC2 . . . . 109 B3
Moorgreen Ho
EC1 . . . . 96 A4
Moorhouse EC2 . . . 109 B3
Mooring Ho 3
W2 . . . . .31 C3
Moor La EC2. . . . . . 109 B3
Moorland Rd SW9 . .63 A3
Moor PI EC2. . . . . . 109 B3
Moor St W1 . . . . . . 105 C1
Morant Ho SW9 . . . 172 C2
Morant St E14 . . . . . .33 C2
Mora Prim Sch
NW2 . . . . 9 B4
Mora Rd NW2 . . . . . . 9 B4
Mora St EC1 . . . . . . 97 A3
Morat St SW9 . . . . 173 A4
Moravian Cl SW3 157 C3
Moravian Pl
SW10 . . . . 157 C3
Moravian St 19 E2. .25 B2
Moray Ho 11 E1. . . .26 A1
Moray Mews N4, N7. . 5 B2
Moray Rd N4, N7. . . . 5 B2
Mordaunt Ho
4 Becontree
NW10 . . . . .20 C4

Mordaunt Ho continued
34 Clapham SW8 ... 171 B1
Mordaunt Rd
NW10 ..... 20 C4
Mordaunt St SW9 .. 62 B4
Morden Hill SE13 .. 52 B1
Morden Ho 10
SW2 ...... 62 C1
Morden La SE13 .... 52 B2
Morden Mount Prim
Sch 1 SE13 ...... 52 A1
Morden Rd SE3 .... 53 C1
Morden Road Mews
SE3 ...... 53 C1
Morden St SE13 .... 52 A2
Morden Wharf Rd
SE10 ...... 43 A3
Mordern Ho NW1 .. 90 B1
Morecambe Cl 3
E1 ...... 32 C4
Morecambe St
SE17 ...... 151 A2
More Cl
Canning Town E16 .. 35 B3
West Kensington
W14 ...... 140 A3
Moredown Ho 3
E8 ...... 16 C3
More House Sch
SW1 ...... 131 A1
Moreland Ct 3
NW2 ...... 1 C1
Moreland Prim Sch
EC1 ...... 96 B3
Moreland St EC1 .. 96 B4
Morella Rd SW11,
SW12 ...... 72 B4
Morell Ho 5 SW9 172 C1
More London Pl
SE1 ...... 124 A1
Moresby Wlk 6
SW8 ...... 170 B1
More's Gdn SW3 .. 157 C3
Moreton Ho SE16 .. 40 A3
Moreton Pl SW1 .. 147 A2
Moreton St SW1 .. 147 B2
Moreton Terr
SW1 ...... 147 A2
Moreton Terr Mews N
SW1 ...... 147 A2
Moreton Terr Mews S
SW1 ...... 147 A2
Moreton Twr 3
W3 ...... 28 A1
Morgan Ct 5
SW11 ...... 167 C2
Morgan Ho
Nine Elms SW8 .. 171 A4
Pimlico SW1 ...... 147 A3
Morgan Rd
Islington N7 ...... 14 C3
Notting Hill W10 .. 31 B4
Morgan's La SE1 .. 124 A1
Morgan St
Canning Town E16 .. 35 B4
Globe Town E3 .... 25 C2
Morgan's Wlk
SW11 ...... 158 A1
Moriarty Cl N7 .... 14 A4
Morie St SW18 .... 59 A2
Morkyns Wlk SE21.. 76 A1
Morland Cl NW11.... 2 A3
Morland Ct 12 .... 39 A4
Morland East E8 .. 16 C1

Morland Ho
Kilburn NW6 ...... 23 C4
Notting Hill W11.... 31 A3
Somers Town NW1 .. 83 A1
Westminster SW1 .. 148 A4
Morland Mews N1.. 14 C1
Morley Cell SE1 .. 135 C2
Morley Ct SE13 .... 67 B3
Morley Ho
Stoke Newington
N16 ...... 7 C2
Streatham SW2 .... 74 A4
W1 ...... 104 B2
Morley Rd SE13 .... 67 B3
Morna Rd SE5 ...... 48 B1
Morning La E9 ...... 17 B2
Morningside Prim Sch
17 E9 ...... 17 B2
Mornington Ave
W14 ...... 140 C3
Mornington Avenue
Mans W14 ...... 140 C3
Mornington Cres
Camden Town NW1 .. 82 C2
NW1 ...... 82 C2
Mornington Crescent
Sta NW1 ...... 82 C2
Mornington Ct
NW1 ...... 82 C2
Mornington Gr E3 .. 26 C2
Mornington Mews 2
SE5 ...... 48 B2
Mornington Pl
4 New Cross SE8.. 51 B3
Regent's Pk NW1 .. 82 C2
Mornington Rd SE14,
SE8 ...... 51 B3
Mornington St
NW1 ...... 82 B2
Mornington Terr
NW1 ...... 82 B2
Morocco St SE1 .. 138 A3
Morpeth Gr E9 ...... 25 C4
Morpeth Rd E9 ...... 25 C4
Morpeth Sch E2 .... 25 B2
Morpeth St E2 ...... 25 C2
Morpeth Terr
SW1 ...... 146 C4
Morrel Ct 11 E2 .. 24 C3
Morris Blitz Ct 2
E2 ...... 16 B4
Morris Ct 3 SE5 .. 63 C3
Morris Gdns SW18.. 70 C4
Morris Ho
17 Bethnal Green
E2 ...... 25 B2
Lisson Gr NW8 .... 90 A1
1 Stockwell SW4 .. 62 A3
10 Tufnell Pk N19.. 13 B4
Morrish Rd SW2 .. 74 A4
Morrison Bldgs 3
E1 ...... 111 B2
Morrison Ho SW2 .. 74 C3
Morrison St SW11 .. 60 C4
Morris Pl N4 ...... 5 C2
Morris Rd E14 ...... 34 A4
Morriss Ho 7
SE16 ...... 40 A4
Morris St E1 ...... 32 A3
Morshead Mans
W9 ...... 23 C2
Morshead Rd W9 .. 23 C2
Mortain Ho 10
SE16 ...... 40 A2
Morten Cl SW4 .... 61 C1

Mortimer Cl
1 Child's Hill NW2 .. 1 B1
Streatham SW16 .. 73 C2
Mortimer Cres
NW6 ...... 78 B3
Mortimer Ct NW8 .. 79 A1
Mortimer Est NW6.. 78 A3
Mortimer Ho
9 Shepherd's Bush
W12 ...... 30 A1
West Kensington
W14 ...... 140 B3
Mortimer Lo 11
SW19 ...... 70 A3
Mortimer Market
WC1 ...... 93 A1
Mortimer Pl NW6.. 78 A3
Mortimer Rd
De Beauvoir Town
N1 ...... 16 A1
Kensal Green N10.. 22 B2
Mortimer Sq W11 .. 30 C2
Mortimer St W1 .. 105 A3
Mortimer Terr
NW5 ...... 13 A4
MORTLAKE 55 B4
Mortlake High St
SW14 ...... 55 C4
Mortlake Ho 7
W4 ...... 37 B2
Mortlake Rd SW14,
TW9 ...... 44 C2
Mortlake Sta
SW14 ...... 55 B4
Mortlake Terr
TW9 ...... 44 C3
Mortlock Cl SE15 .. 50 A2
Morton Cl 20 E1 .. 32 B3
Morton Ho SE17 .. 48 A4
Morton Mews
SW5 ...... 142 A3
Morton Pl SE1 .. 135 B1
Morton Rd N1 ...... 15 B1
Morval Rd SW2 .... 62 C2
Morven Rd SW17 .. 72 B1
Morville Ho SW18 .. 59 C1
Morville St E3 ...... 26 C3
Morwell St WC1 .. 105 C3
Moscow Pl W2 ...... 114 A4
Moscow Rd W2 .... 114 A4
Mosedale NW1 ...... 92 B3
Moseley Row SE10.. 43 B2
Mosque Tower 20
E1 ...... 111 C3
Mossbourne Com
Acad E8 ...... 17 A3
Mossbury Rd
SW11 ...... 60 A4
Moss Cl E1 ...... 111 C4
Mossford St E3 .... 26 B1
Mossington Gdns
SE16 ...... 40 B2
Mossop St SW3 .. 144 B4
Mostyn Gdns
NW10 ...... 22 C3
Mostyn Gr E3 ...... 26 C3
Mostyn Lo N5 ...... 15 B4
Mostyn Rd SW9 .. 173 C3
Motcomb St SW1 .. 131 B2
Mothers Sq The 12
E5 ...... 17 A4
Motley Ave
EC2 ...... 24 A1 98 A2
Motley St SW8 .. 170 C2
Moules Ct SE5 .... 48 B3
Moulins Rd E9 ...... 17 B1

Moulsford Ho
5 Lower Holloway
N7 ...... 13 C3
2 Paddington W2 .. 31 C4
Mounsey Ho 13
W10 ...... 23 A2
Mount Adon Pk SE21,
SE22 ...... 76 C4
Mountague Pl 2
E14 ...... 34 B2
Mountain Ho
SE11 ...... 148 C2
Mount Angelus Rd
SW15 ...... 68 B4
Mount Ararat Rd
TW10 ...... 54 A2
Mountbatten Ho
N6 ...... 3 C4
Mountbatten Mews
SW18 ...... 71 B3
Mount Carmel 3
N7 ...... 14 B3
Mount Carmel RC
Tech Coll For Girls 6
N19 ...... 4 C3
Mountearl Gdns SW16,
SW2 ...... 74 B1
Mount Ephraim La
SW16 ...... 73 C1
Mount Ephraim Rd
SW16 ...... 73 C1
Mountfield Ct
SE13 ...... 67 C1
Mount Ford St E1 .. 111 B2
Mountfort Cres
N1 ...... 14 C1
Mountfort Terr 1
N1 ...... 14 C1
Mountgrove Rd N5 .. 6 B1
Mountjoy Ho EC2 .. 108 C3
Mount Lodge SW4 .. 61 C3
Mount Mills EC1 .... 96 B3
Mount Nod Rd SW16,
SW2 ...... 74 B1
Mount Pl 7 W3 .... 28 A1
Mount Pleasant
WC1 ...... 95 B3
Mount Pleasant Cres
N4 ...... 5 B4
Mount Pleasant Rd
Lewisham SE13 .... 67 B1
Willesden NW10 .... 22 B4
Mount Pleasant Villas
N4 ...... 5 B4
Mount Rd SW18,
SW19 ...... 71 A2
Mount Row 4 W1 .. 118 A3
Mounts Pond Rd SE3,
SE13 ...... 52 C1
Mount Sq The 3
NW3 ...... 2 B1
Mount St W1 ...... 117 C2
Mount Terr E1 ...... 32 A4
Mount Tyndal NW3 .. 2 C3
Mount Vernon
NW3 ...... 11 B4
Mountview 4
SW16 ...... 74 B1
Mountview Cl
NW11 ...... 2 B3
Mount Villas SE27 .. 75 A1

Mourne Ho NW3 ... 11 B2
Movieum The *
SE1 ...... 134 C4
Mowatt Cl N19 ...... 4 C3
Mowbray Rd NW6 .. 10 A1
Mowlem Prim Sch 30
E2 ...... 25 B3
Mowll St SW9 .. 163 B1
Moxon St W1 ...... 103 B3
Moye Cl 10 E2 ...... 24 C3
Moylan Rd W6 .... 154 A3
Moyle Ho SW1 .... 161 A4
Moyne Ho 16 SW9 .. 63 A3
Mozart St W10 ...... 23 B2
Mudchute Pk &
Farm * E14 ...... 42 B2
Mudie Ho 3 SW2 .. 74 A4
Mudlarks Blvd 3
SE10 ...... 43 B3
Muirdown Ave
SW14 ...... 55 C3
Muir Dr SW18 ...... 60 A1
Muirfield W3 ...... 29 A3
Muirfield Cl 22
SE16 ...... 40 A1
Muirfield Cres
E14 ...... 42 A3
Muir Rd E5 ...... 7 C1
Mulberry Bsns Ctr
SE16 ...... 40 C4
Mulberry Cl
Chelsea SW3 .. 157 C3
East Dulwich SE22 .. 64 C1
Hampstead NW3 .. 11 C4
Mulberry Ct
Finsbury EC1 ...... 96 B3
Islington N5 ...... 15 A3
1 Leyton E11 ...... 19 C4
10 Paddington W9 .. 23 B2
Mulberry Ho
6 Bethnal Green
E2 ...... 25 B2
8 Deptford SE8.. 51 B4
Mulberry House Sch
NW2 ...... 10 A3
Mulberry Mews
SE14 ...... 51 B2
Mulberry Pl W6 .. 38 C1
Mulberry Rd E8 .. 16 B1
Mulberry Sch for Girls
18 Stepney E1 ...... 32 A3
St George in East
E1 ...... 32 A2
Mulberry St 7
E1 ...... 111 B2
Mulberry Wlk
SW3 ...... 157 C4
Mulgrave Rd
West Kensington
W14 ...... 154 C4
Willesden NW10 .... 8 B4
Mulkern Rd N19 .... 4 C3
Mullard Ho WC1 .. 105 B4
Mullen Twr EC1 .... 95 B1
Mullens Ho 7
SW15 ...... 57 B2
Mullet Gdns 7
E2 ...... 24 C2 99 C4
Mulletsfield WC1 .. 94 B3
Mull Ho 9 E3 ...... 26 B3
Mullins Path
SW14 ...... 55 C4
Mulready St NW8 .. 90 A1

Multi Way W3 . . . . .38 A4
Multon Ho E9 . . . . . . .17 B1
Multon Rd SW18 . . . .71 C4
Mulvaney Way
SE1 . . . . .137 C3
Mumford Rd SE24 . .63 A2
Muncaster Rd
SW11 . . . . .60 C2
Mundania Ct SE22 . .65 A1
Mundania Rd SE22 . .65 A1
Munday Ho SE1 . . . .137 B1
Munday Rd E16 . . . .35 C2
Munden Ho E5 . . . . .18 A3
Munden St W14 . . . .140 A4
Mund St W14 . . . . .141 A1
Mundy Ho W10 . . . .22 C2
Mundy St
N1 . . . .24 A2 98 B4
Munro Ho
Bermondsey SE1 . . .137 C3
Lambeth SE1 . . . . .135 B3
Munro Mews W10 . . .31 A4
Munster Ct SW6 . . . .164 C3
Munster Rd SW6 . . .154 B2
Munster Residences
SW6 . . . . .164 B4
Munster Sq NW1 . . . .92 B3
Munton Rd SE1 . . . .151 A4
Murchison Ho 1
W10 . . . . .31 A4
Murdoch Ho 4
SE16 . . . . .40 B3
Murdock Cl E16 . . . .35 B3
Murdock St SE15 . . . .50 A4
Muriel St N1 . . . . . . .85 A4
Murphy Ho SE1 . . . .136 B2
Murphy St SE1 . . . .135 B3
Murray Gr N1 . . . . . .87 B1
Murray Mews
NW1 . . . . .13 C1
Murray St NW1 . . . .13 C1
Murray Terr NW3 . . .11 C4
Musard Rd W6 . . . .154 B4
Musbury St E1 . . . . .32 B3
Muscal W6 . . . . . .154 A4
Muscatel Pl SE5 . . . .49 A2
Muschamp Rd
SE15 . . . . .64 B4
Muscott Ho 12 E2 . . .24 C4
Muscovy St EC3 . . . .124 B4
Museum & Galleries
of Modern London*
EC2 . . . . .108 C2
Museum Ho 3 E2 . . .25 B2
Museum La SW7 . . . .129 B1
Museum Mans
WC1 . . . . .106 A3
Museum of Brands,
Packaging &
Advertising*
W11 . . . . .31 B3
Museum of Childhood
(V&A)* E2 . . . . . .25 B2
Museum of Culinary
History &
Alimentation*
NW1 . . . . .83 A2
Museum of
Instruments*
SW7 . . . . .129 B2
Museum of London*
EC2 . . . . .108 C3
Museum of London
Docklands* E14 . .33 C2

Museum of the Order
of St John* EC1 . . .96 A1
Museum St WC1 . . . .106 A2
Museum Way W3 . . . .36 C4
Musgrave Cres
SW6 . . . . .165 C4
Musgrave Ct
SW11 . . . . .168 A4
Musgrove Ho 9 E9 . . .17 C2
Musgrove Rd SE14 . .51 A2
Musical Mus The*
TW8 . . . . .44 B4
Musjid Rd 7
SW11 . . . . .167 C1
Mus of the Royal
Pharmaceutical
Society* SE1 . . . .148 C4
Mustow Pl 2
SW6 . . . . .165 A2
Mutrix Rd NW6 . . . .23 C4
Mutton Pl NW1 . . . .12 C2
Myatt Garden Prim
Sch SE4 . . . . .51 B1
Myatt Ho 50 SE5 . . .48 A1
Myatt Rd SW9 . . . . .48 A2
Myatts Field Ct
SE5 . . . . .48 B2
Mycenae Rd SE3 . . . .53 C4
Myddelton Pas
EC1 . . . . .95 C4
Myddelton Sq EC1 . . .95 C4
Myddelton Sq EC1 . . .95 C3
Myddelton Ave N4 . . . .6 B2
Myers Ho 5 SE5 . . . .48 B3
Mylius Cl SE14 . . . . .50 B2
Mylne Cl W6 . . . . . .38 C1
Mylne St EC1 . . . . . .85 B1
Mynterne Ct 16
SW19 . . . . .69 C3
Myrdle Ct 14 E1 . . . .111 C2
Myrdle St E1 . . . . . .111 C2
Myron Pl SE13 . . . . .67 B4
Myrtle Ho SE14 . . . .50 C2
Myrtle Rd W3 . . . . . .28 B1
Myrtle Wlk 20 N1 . . . .24 A3
Mysore Rd SW11 . . . .60 B3
Myton Rd SE21 . . . . .75 C1
Mytton Ho SW8 . . . .162 C1

N

N1 Shopping Ctr
N1 . . . . .85 C2
Nags Head N7 . . . . .14 B4
Nags Head Ct EC1 . . .97 A1
Nags Head Sh Ctr The
N7 . . . . .14 B4
Naima Jewish Prep
Sch 4 NW6 . . . . .78 A2
Nainby Ho SE11 . . . .149 B3
Nairne Gr SE5 . . . . .63 C3
Nairn St E14 . . . . . .34 B4
Naldera Gdns SE3 . . .53 C4
Nalton Ho 4 NW6 . . .11 B1
Namco Sta* SE1 . . . .134 C4
Nankin St E14 . . . . .33 C3
Nansen Rd SW11 . . . .60 C4
Nant Ct NW2 . . . . . . .1 B2
Nantes Cl SW18 . . . .59 B3
Nant Rd NW2 . . . . . . .1 B2
Nant St E2 . . . . .25 A2
Naoroji St WC1 . . . .95 B3

Napier Ave
Deptford E14 . . . . . .41 C1
Fulham SW6 . . . . . .58 B4
Napier Cl
New Cross SE14,
SE8 . . . . .51 B3
West Kensington
W14 . . . . .126 C2
Napier Ct
Fulham SW6 . . . . . .58 B4
Shoreditch N1 . . . . .87 B2
Napier Gr N1 . . . . . .87 A2
Napier Ho SE17 . . . .48 A4
Napier Pl W14 . . . .126 C1
Napier Rd
College Pk NW10 . . . .22 A2
Kensington W14 . . . .126 C1
Napier Terr N1 . . . . .15 A1
Narbonne Ave
SW4 . . . . .61 B2
Narborough St
SW6 . . . . .166 A1
Narcissus Rd NW6 . . .10 C3
Narford Rd E5 . . . . . .7 C2
Narrow St
8 Acton W3 . . . . . .28 A1
Limehouse E14 . . . . .33 A2
Nascot St W12 . . . . .30 B3
Naseby Cl NW6 . . . . .11 B1
Nashe Ho SE1 . . . .137 B1
Nash Ho
5 Millwall E14 . . . .41 C3
Pimlico SW1 . . . . .146 B1
Nash Rd SE4 . . . . . .66 A2
Nasmyth St W6 . . . .39 A3
Nassau Rd SW13 . . . .46 B2
Nassau St W1 . . . . .104 C3
Nassington Rd
NW3 . . . . .12 B4
Nathan Ho SE11 . . . .149 C3
Nathaniel Cl E1 . . . .111 A3
National Archives The
TW9 . . . . .45 A3
National Army Mus*
SW3 . . . . .159 A4
National Gallery*
W1 . . . . .119 C3
National Hospl for
Neurology &
Neurosurgery
WC1 . . . . .94 B1
National Maritime
Mus* SE10 . . . . . .52 C4
National Portrait
Gallery* W1 . . . . .119 C3
National Portrait
Gallery (Annexe)*
SW1 . . . . .119 C2
National Theatre*
SE1 . . . . .121 A2
Natural History Mus*
SW7 . . . . .129 B1
Nautilus Bldg The
EC1 . . . . .95 C4
Naval Row E14 . . . . .34 B2
Navarino Gr E8 . . . . .16 C2
Navarino Mans E8 . . .16 C2
Navarino Rd E8 . . . . .16 C2
Navarre St
E2 . . . . . . .24 B1 98 C2
Navenby Wlk 13
E3 . . . . .26 C1
Navy St SW4 . . . . . .61 C4
Naxos Bldg 9 E14 . . .41 C4

Naylor Bldg W 4
E1 . . . . .111 B2
Naylor Ho
53 Clapham SW8 . . .171 B1
Walworth SE17 . . . .151 C2
5 West Kilburn
W10 . . . . .23 B2
Naylor Rd SE15 . . . .50 A3
Nazareth Cl SE15 . . . .50 A1
Nazrul St E2 . . . .24 B2 98 C4
Nealden St SW9 . . . .62 B4
Neal St WC2 . . . . . .106 A1
Neal's Yd WC2 . . . .106 A1
Neasden Cl NW10 . . . .8 A3
Neasden Junc
NW10 . . . . .8 A4
Neasden La NW10 . . . .8 A3
Neasden La N
NW10 . . . . .8 A4
Neasden Sta NW10 . . .8 A3
Neathouse Pl
SW1 . . . . .146 C4
Nebraska Bldg 1
SE13 . . . . .52 A2
Nebraska St SE1 . . .137 B3
Neckinger SE16 . . . .139 C2
Neckinger Est
SE16 . . . . .139 A2
Neckinger St SE1 . . .139 A3
Nectarine Way
SE13 . . . . .52 A1
Nedahall Ct 4
NW11 . . . . .1 B4
Needham Ho
SE11 . . . . .149 B3
Needham Rd W11 . . .31 C3
Needleman St
SE16 . . . . .40 C4
Needwood Ho N4 . . . .6 B3
Neilson-Terry Ct 9
SW9 . . . . .62 B3
Neil Wates Cres 3
SW2 . . . . .74 C3
Nella Rd W6 . . . . . .47 C4
Nelldale Rd SE16 . . . .40 B2
Nell Gwynn Ho
SW3 . . . . .144 B3
Nelson Cl 2 NW6 . . .23 C2
Nelson Ct SE16 . . . .33 B1
Nelson Docks
SE16 . . . . .33 B1
Nelson Gdns
E2 . . . . . . .24 C2 99 C4
Nelson Pas EC1 . . . .97 A4
Nelson Pl N1 . . . . . .86 B1
Nelson Rd SE10 . . . .52 B4
Nelson's Monument*
WC2 . . . . .120 A2
Nelson Sq SE1 . . . .136 A4
Nelsons Row 4
SW4 . . . . .61 C3
Nelson St
Canning Town E16 . . .35 B2
Stepney E1 . . . . . . .32 A3
Nelsons Yd NW1 . . . .82 C2
Nelson Terr N1 . . . . .86 B1
Nemoure Rd W3 . . . .28 B2
Nepaul Rd 17
SW11 . . . . .60 A4
Nepean St SW15 . . . .68 C4
Neptune Ct 11 E14 . .41 C2
Neptune Ho
2 Rotherhithe
SE16 . . . . .40 B3
11 Stoke Newington
N16 . . . . .16 A3
Neptune St SE16 . . . .40 B3

Nesham Ho 14 N1 . . .24 A4
Nesham St E1 . . . . .125 B2
Ness St 9 SE16 . . . .139 B2
Nestor Ho 18 E2 . . . .25 A3
Netheravon Rd
W4 . . . . .38 B1
Netheravon Rd S
W4 . . . . .38 B1
Netherby Ho 23
SW8 . . . . .171 B1
Nethercombe Ho 3
SE3 . . . . .53 C4
Nethercott Ho 27
E3 . . . . .27 A2
Netherfield Rd
SW17 . . . . .72 C1
Netherford Rd
SW4 . . . . .171 A1
Netherhall Gdns
NW3 . . . . .11 B3
Netherhall Int Coll
NW3 . . . . .11 B2
Netherhall Way
NW3 . . . . .11 B3
Netherleigh Cl N6 . . . .4 A3
Netherton Gr
SW10 . . . . .157 A3
Netherwood Rd
W14 . . . . .39 C4
Netherwood St
NW6 . . . . .10 C2
Netley 5 SE5 . . . . . .49 A2
Netley Prim Sch
NW1 . . . . .92 C3
Netley Rd TW8 . . . . .44 A4
Netley St NW1 . . . . .92 C3
Nettlecombe Ho 1 . . .13 C1
Nettleden Ho
SW3 . . . . .144 B3
Nettleton Rd SE14 . . .50 C2
Nevada St SE10 . . . .52 B4
Nevena Ct 3 SW2 . . .62 C2
Nevern Mans
SW5 . . . . .141 B2
Nevern Pl SW5 . . . .141 C3
Nevern Rd SW5 . . . .141 B3
Nevern Sq SW5 . . . .141 C3
Nevil Ho 7 SW9 . . . .48 A1
Nevill Ct SW10 . . . .156 C2
Neville Cl
Acton W3 . . . . .37 B4
Paddington NW6 . . . .23 B3
Peckham SE15 . . . . .49 C2
Somers Town NW1 . . .83 C1
Neville Ct 10
SW18 . . . . .72 A4
Neville Gill Cl
SW18 . . . . .59 A1
Neville Rd NW6 . . . .23 B3
Neville St SW7 . . . .143 B2
Neville Terr SW7 . . . .143 B2
Nevill Rd N16 . . . . . .7 A1
Nevinson Cl SW18 . . .59 C1
Nevis Rd SW17 . . . . .72 C2
Nevitt Ho N1 . . . . . . .87 C1
Newall Ho SE1 . . . .137 A2
Newark Cres
NW10 . . . . .20 C2
Newark Ho 3
SW9 . . . . .48 A1
Newark St E1 . . . . . .32 A4
New Atlas Wharf
E14 . . . . .41 C3

New Bentham Ct **10**
  N1 . . . . **15** B1
Newbery Ho N1 . . . . . **15** B1
Newbold Cotts **4**
  E1 . . . . **32** B3
Newbolt Ho SE17 . **151** B2
New Bond St W1 . **118** B4
New Bridge St
  EC4 . . . . **108** A1
New Broad St
  EC2 . . . . **110** A3
New Brons Ctr The
  NW10 . . . . **21** B2
Newburgh Rd W3 . . **28** B1
Newburgh St W1 . **105** A1
New Burlington Mews
  W1 . . . . **118** C4
New Burlington Pl
  W1 . . . . **118** C4
New Burlington St
  W1 . . . . **118** C4
Newburn Ho SE11 **149** A2
Newburn St SE11 **149** A2
Newbury Ct E5 . . . . . **18** A3
Newbury Ho
  Brixton SW9 . . . . . **48** A1
  14 Kensington W2 . **100** B1
Newbury Mews
  NW5 . . . . **12** C2
Newbury St EC1 . . **108** C4
New Butt La SE8 . . **51** C3
Newby Ho **14** **92** C4
Newby Pl E14 . . . . . **34** B2
Newby St SW8 . . . . . **61** A4
New Caledonian
  Mkt★ SE1 . . . . . . **138** B2
New Caledonian
  Wharf SE16 . . . . . **41** B3
New Campden Ct **1**
  NW3 . . . . **11** B4
Newcastle Cl EC4 **108** A2
Newcastle Ct EC4 **123** A4
Newcastle Ho W1 **103** B4
Newcastle Pl W2 . **101** C4
Newcastle Row
  EC1 . . . . **95** C1
New Cavendish St
  W1 . . . . **104** A3
New Change EC4 **108** C1
New Charles St
  EC1 . . . . **96** B4
New Church Rd
  25 Camberwell
  SE5 . . . . **48** B3
  Camberwell SE5 . . **48** C4
New College Ct **6**
  NW3 . . . . **11** B2
New College Mews **7**
  N1 . . . . **14** C1
New College Par **1**
  NW3 . . . . **11** C3
Newcombe Ho N5 . . **15** B3
Newcombe St
  W8 . . . . **31** C1 **113** C2
Newcomen Ho **5**
  NW5 . . . . **13** A4
Newcomen Rd
  SW11 . . . . **59** C4
Newcomen St
  SE1 . . . . **137** B4
New Compton St
  WC2 . . . . **106** A1
New Concordia Wharf
  SE1 . . . . **139** A4

Newcourt Ho **2**
  E2 . . . . **25** A2
Newcourt St NW8 . . **80** A1
New Covent Garden
  Flower Market★
  SW8 . . . . **162** A3
New Covent Garden
  Fruit & Vegetable
  Mkt★ SW8 . . . . . **161** B1
New Crane Pl E1 . . **32** B1
New Crescent Yd **1**
  NW10 . . . . **21** B3
NEW CROSS **51** B2
New Cross SE14 . . **51** B3
NEW CROSS
  GATE **50** C2
New Cross Gate
  SE14 . . . . **51** A2
New Cross Rd
  SE14 . . . . **51** A2
New Cross Sta
  SE14 . . . . **51** B3
New Ct
  City of London
  EC4 . . . . **107** B1
  22 Hampstead NW3 . **11** B4
  Stoke Newington N16 . **6** C3
New Den (Millwall
  FC) The SE16 . . . . **40** B1
Newdigate Ho **5**
  E14 . . . . **33** B3
Newell St E14 . . . . . **33** B3
New End NW3 . . . . . **2** B1
New End Prim Sch **13**
  NW3 . . . . **11** B4
New End Sq NW3 . . **11** C4
Newent Cl SE15 . . . **49** A3
New Fetter La
  EC4 . . . . **107** C2
Newfield Prim Sch
  N16 . . . . **8** B1
Newgate St EC1 . . **108** B2
New Globe Wlk
  SE1 . . . . **122** C2
New Goulston St
  E1 . . . . **110** C2
Newham Sixth Form
  Coll (Stratford Ctr)
  7 E15 . . . . **19** C1
Newham's Row
  SE1 . . . . **138** B3
Newhaven La **1**
  E16 . . . . **35** C4
New Hope Christian
  Sch **38** SE22 . . . . . **64** B3
NEWINGTON . . . **150** B4
Newington Barrow
  Way N7 . . . . **5** B1
Newington Butts SE1,
  SE11 . . . . **150** B3
Newington Cswy
  SE1 . . . . **136** C2
Newington Gn
  N16 . . . . **15** C3
Newington Green
  Mans N16 . . . . **15** C3
Newington Green
  Prim Sch N16 . . **15** C3
Newington Green Rd
  N1 . . . . **15** C3
Newington Ind Est
  SE17 . . . . **150** C3
New Inn Broadway
  EC2 . . . . **24** A1 **98** B2

New Inn Sq
  EC2 . . . . **24** A1 **98** B2
New Inn St
  EC2 . . . . **24** A1 **98** B2
New Inn Yd
  EC2 . . . . **24** A1 **98** B2
New James Ct
  SE15 . . . . **65** A4
New King's Prim Sch
  12 SW6 . . . . **165** A2
New King's Rd
  SW6 . . . . **165** C3
New King St SE8 . . **51** C4
Newland Ct EC1 . . . **97** B2
Newland Ho **17**
  SE14 . . . . **50** C4
Newlands NW1 . . . . **92** C4
Newlands Quay E1 . **32** B2
New London St
  EC3 . . . . **124** B4
Newlyn NW1 . . . . . . **83** A3
Newman Pas W1 . **105** A3
Newman's Ct EC3 **109** C1
Newman's Row
  WC2 . . . . **107** A3
Newmill Ho E3 . . . . **27** B1
Newmount NW3 . . . **11** C3
New Mount St E15 . **19** C1
Newnes Path
  SW15 . . . . **57** A3
Newnham Ho **9**
  SW15 . . . . **57** C1
Newnham Terr
  SE1 . . . . **135** B2
New North Com Sch
  N1 . . . . **86** C4
New North Pl
  EC2 . . . . **24** A1 **98** A2
New North Rd N1 . . **87** B2
New North Road
  Bridge N1 . . . . **87** A2
New North St
  WC1 . . . . **106** C4
Newnton Cl N4 . . . . **6** C4
New Oxford St
  WC1 . . . . **106** A2
New Palace Yd
  SW1 . . . . **134** A3
New Park Ct **28**
  SW2 . . . . **74** A4
New Park Par **14**
  SW2 . . . . **74** A4
New Park Rd SW2 . **74** A4
New Place Sq
  SE16 . . . . **40** A3
Newport Ave E14 . . **34** C2
Newport Ct WC2 . . **119** C4
Newport Ho **2** E3 . . **26** A2
Newport Pl WC2 . . **119** C4
Newport Rd SW13 . **46** C2
Newport St SE11 . **149** A4
New Priory Ct **9**
  NW6 . . . . **10** C1
New Providence
  Wharf E14 . . . . . . **34** C1
Newquay Ho SE11 **149** B2
New Quebec St
  W1 . . . . **103** A1
New Rd E1 . . . . **32** A4
New River Ct N5 . . . **15** C4
New River Way N4 . . **6** C4
New Row WC2 . . . **120** A4
New St Sq EC4 . . . **107** C2

New Scotland Yard★
  SW1 . . . . **133** B2
New Shepherd's Bush
  Mkt★ **6** W12 . . . . **39** B4
New Spring Gdns Wlk
  SE11 . . . . **148** B1
New Sq WC2 . . . . . **107** A2
New Square Pas
  WC2 . . . . **107** A2
New St EC2 . . . . . . **110** B3
Newstead Ho N1 . . **85** C2
Newton Ave W3 . . . **37** B4
Newton Gr W4 . . . . . **38** A2
Newton Ho
  22 Clapham SW8 . **171** B2
  Paddington NW8 . . . **78** B4
  1 Stepney E1 . . . . . **32** A2
Newton Point **1**
  E16 . . . . **35** B3
Newton Prep Sch
  SW8 . . . . **170** B4
Newton Rd
  Acton W3 . . . . **37** B4
  Kensington W2 . . . . **100** A1
  Stratford New Town
  E15 . . . . **19** C3
Newton St WC2 . . **106** B2
Newton's Yd **14**
  SW18 . . . . **58** C2
New Tower Bldgs **21**
  E1 . . . . **32** A1
Newtown Ct
  Battersea SW11 . . **170** A3
  Clapham SW4 . . . . . **61** A2
New Union Cl E14 . **42** B3
New Union St
  EC2 . . . . **109** B3
New Wharf Rd N1 . . **84** C2
Niagara Cl N1 . . . . . **87** A2
Niagara Ct **6**
  SE16 . . . . **40** B3
Nicholas Ct
  Chiswick W4 . . . . . . **46** A3
  Golders Green NW11 . . **1** C4
Nicholas Ho **2**
  SW15 . . . . **56** C2
Nicholas La EC2,
  EC4 . . . . **123** C4
Nicholas Pas EC3 **123** C4
Nicholas Rd
  Bethnal Green E1 . . **25** B1
  20 Shepherd's Bush
  W11 . . . . **30** C2
Nicholay Rd N19 . . . **4** C3
Nicholl Ho N4 . . . . . . **6** B3
Nicholl St E2 . . . . . . **24** C4
Nichols Cl N4 . . . . . . **5** C2
Nichols Ct E2 . . . . . **24** B3
Nicholson Ho
  SE17 . . . . **151** B2
Nicholson St SE1 **122** A1
Nicklenby Ho
  SE17 . . . . **151** B2
  7 Shepherd's Bush
  W11 . . . . **30** C1
Nickols Wlk SW18 . **59** A3
Nicoll Ct NW10 . . . . **21** A4
Nicoll Rd NW10 . . . . **21** A4
Nicosia Rd SW18 . . **72** A4
Nigel Bldg EC1 . . . **107** B4
Nigel Playfair Ave
  W6 . . . . **39** A1
Nigel Rd SE15 . . . . . **64** C4
Nightingale Cl W4 . **45** B4

Nightingale Ct
  14 Cubitt Town
  E14 . . . . **42** B3
  Finsbury Pk N4 . . . . . **5** B2
Nightingale Gr
  SE13 . . . . **67** C2
Nightingale Ho
  21 Hoxton E1 . . . . **24** A4
  North Kensington
  W12 . . . . **30** B3
  37 St George in East
  E1 . . . . **125** B2
Nightingale La SW11,
  SW12 . . . . **60** C1
Nightingale Lo **5**
  W9 . . . . **31** C4
Nightingale Mans **7**
  SW12 . . . . **60** C1
Nightingale Mews
  11 Bow E3 . . . . . . **26** A3
  Newington SE11 . . **150** A4
Nightingale Pl
  SW10 . . . . **157** A4
Nightingale Prim Sch
  SW12 . . . . **73** A4
Nightingale Rd
  22 Canonbury N1 . . **15** B2
  Dagenham NW10 . . . **21** B3
Nightingale Sch
  SW17 . . . . **72** A2
Nightingale Sq
  SW12 . . . . **72** C4
Nightingale Wlk SW18,
  SW4 . . . . **61** A1
Nile Cl N16 . . . . **7** B1
Nile Ho N1 . . . . **97** B4
Nile St N1 . . . . **97** B4
Nile Terr SE1,
  SE15 . . . . **153** A1
Nimegen Way **8**
  SE22 . . . . **64** A2
Nimrod Pas **4** N1 . . **16** A2
NINE ELMS **160** C2
Nine Elms La
  SW8 . . . . **161** B3
Nisbet Ho E9 . . . . . . **17** C3
Niton Rd TW9 . . . . . **54** C4
Niton St SW6 . . . . . **47** C3
No 2 Willow Rd★
  NW3 . . . . **12** A4
Nobel Ho **8** SE5 . . . **48** B1
Noble Ct E1 . . . . **32** A2
Noble St EC2 . . . . . **108** C2
Noel Coward Ho
  SW1 . . . . **147** A3
Noel Ho **3** NW3 . . . **11** C1
Noel Rd
  Acton W3 . . . . **28** A3
  Islington N1 . . . . **86** B2
Noel St W1 . . . . **105** A1
Noko NW10 . . . . **22** C2
Nolan Way E5 . . . . . **16** C4
Noll Ho N7 . . . . **5** B2
Norbiton Rd E14 . . . **33** B3
Norbroke St W12 . . **29** B2
Norburn St W10 . . . **31** A4
Norcombe Ho **2**
  N19 . . . . **4** C1
Norcott Rd N16 . . . . **7** C1
Norcroft Gdns
  SE22 . . . . **76** C4
Norden Ho **22** E2 . . **25** A2
Nore Ct NW10 . . . . . **8** C1
Norfolk Cres W2 . . **102** B2

Norfolk Ho
City of London
EC4 . . . . 122 C4
Greenwich SE3 . . . . 53 A4
4 Putney SW15 . . . 69 B4
Richmond TW10 . . . 54 C2
Shacklewell E8 . . . . 16 B4
St Johns SE8 . . . . . 51 C2
Westminster SW1 . 147 C4
Norfolk House Rd
SW16 . . . . 74 A1
Norfolk Mans
Battersea SW11 . . 169 A3
10 Wandsworth
SW18 . . . . 58 C2
Norfolk Mews 12
W10 . . . . 31 A4
Norfolk Pl W2 . . . 101 C2
Norfolk Rd
St Johns Wood
NW8 . . . . 79 C3
Willesden NW10 . . . . 8 A1
Norfolk Row SE1,
SE11 . . . . 148 C4
Norfolk Sq W2 . . . 101 C2
Norfolk Sq Mews
W2 . . . . 101 C1
Norgrove St SW12 . 72 C4
Norland Ho 13
W11 . . . . 30 C1
Norland Pl
W11 . . . . . 31 A1 112 B1
Norland Place Sch
W11 . . . . 31 A1 112 B1
Norland Rd 18
W11 . . . . 30 C1
Norland Sq
W11 . . . . . 31 A1 112 B1
Norley Vale SW15 . . 68 C3
Norman Butler Ho 16
W10 . . . . 23 A1
Normanby Cl
SW15 . . . . 58 B2
Normanby Rd NW10 . 8 B4
Norman Ct
Dulwich SE22 . . . . . 76 C4
Finsbury Pk N4 . . . . . 5 C4
Willesden NW10 . . . . 8 C1
Normand Croft Com
Sch W14 . . . . . . 155 A4
Normand Mews
W14 . . . . 154 B4
Normand Rd W14 154 C4
Normanhurst Ho 8
E14 . . . . 42 B4
Normandy Rd
SW9 . . . . 173 B3
Norman Gr E3 . . . . 26 A3
Norman Ho 5 SW8 162 A2
Normanhurst Rd
SW2 . . . . 74 C2
Norman Rd SE10 . . 52 A3
Norman St EC1 . . . 97 A3
Normanton Ave SW18,
SW19 . . . . 70 C2
Normanton Ho 6
SW4 . . . . 61 B1
Norman Way W3 . . 28 A3
Norris Ho
12 Hoxton N1 . . . . 24 A4
8 South Hackney
E9 . . . . 25 B4
Norris St SW1 . . . 119 B3
Norroy Rd SW15 . . 57 C3
Norse Ho 18 SE5 . . 48 B1
Norstead Pl SW15 . 68 C2

NORTH ACTON . . . 20 C2
North Acton Rd
W10 . . . . 20 C2
North Acton Sta
W3 . . . . 28 C4
Northampton Gr
N1 . . . . 15 C3
Northampton Pk
N1 . . . . 15 C2
Northampton Rd
EC1 . . . . 95 C2
Northampton Sq
EC1 . . . . 96 A3
Northampton St
N1 . . . . 15 B1
North Audley St
W1 . . . . 117 B4
North Ave 5 W9 . . 23 C1
Northaw Ho 4
W10 . . . . 22 B1
North Bank NW8 . . 90 A3
North Block 11 E1 . 32 B2
Northbourne Ho 21
E5 . . . . 17 A3
Northbourne Rd
SW4 . . . . 61 C2
North Bridge House
Sch 18 NW3 . . . . 11 C2
North Bridge House
Senior Sch NW1 . . 82 A3
Northbrook CE Sch
SE12 . . . . 67 C2
Northburgh St EC1 . 96 B2
North Carriage Dr
W2 . . . . 116 B4
Northchurch
SE17 . . . . 151 C2
Northchurch Ho 19
E2 . . . . 24 C4
Northchurch Rd
N1 . . . . 15 C1
Northchurch Terr
N1 . . . . 16 A1
North Circular Rd NW2,
NW10 . . . . 8 A3
North Colonnade The
E14 . . . . 34 A1
Northcote Lodge Sch
SW11 . . . . 60 B1
Northcote Rd
Wandsworth SW11 . 60 B2
Willesden NW10 . . . . 8 C1
Northcourt W1 . . . 105 A4
North Cres
Marylebone WC1 . . 105 B4
Newham E16 . . . . 27 C1
Northcroft Ct 8
W12 . . . . 38 C4
North Cross Rd
SE22 . . . . 64 C2
North Ct SW1 . . . . 134 A1
Northdown St N1 . . 84 C1
North Dulwich Sta
SE21 . . . . 63 C2
NORTH END 2 B2
North End Ho
NW3 . . . . 2 B2
North End Cres
W14 . . . . 140 C3
North End Ho
W14 . . . . 140 B3
North End Par
W14 . . . . 140 B3
North End Rd
Golders Green
NW11 . . . . 2 A3

North End Rd continued
West Kensington
W14 . . . . 141 A1
North End Way
NW3 . . . . 2 B2
Northern Hts N8 . . . 4 C4
Northesk Ho 6
E1 . . . . 25 A1
North Eyot Gdns 5
W6 . . . . 38 B1
Northey St E14 . . . 33 A2
Northfield Hall N6 . . 3 C4
Northfield Ho 8
SE15 . . . . 49 C4
Northfield Rd N16 . . 7 A4
Northfields SW18 . . 58 C3
Northfields Prospect
SW18 . . . . 58 C3
Northfields Rd W3 . 28 B4
Northfleet Ho
SE1 . . . . 137 B4
North Flower Wlk
W2 . . . . 115 B3
North Gate NW8 . . 80 A1
Northgate Ct 14
SW9 . . . . 62 C4
North Gower St
NW1 . . . . 93 A3
North Gr N6 . . . . . . 3 C4
North Greenwich Sta
SE10 . . . . 43 A4
North Hill N6 . . . . . 3 C4
North Ho 3 SE8 . . 41 B1
Northiam WC1 . . . 94 B3
Northiam St E9 . . . 25 A4
Northington St
WC1 . . . . 95 A1
NORTH
KENSINGTON . . . 31 A4
Northlands St SE5 . 48 B1
Northleigh Ho 36
E3 . . . . 27 A2
North Lo SW4 . . . . 61 A3
North Lodge Cl
SW15 . . . . 57 C2
North London Science
Ctr 2 N1 . . . . . . 14 C1
North Mews WC1 . . 95 A1
Northolme Rd N5 . . 15 B4
North Pas SW18 . . 58 C2
Northpoint Sq 8
NW1 . . . . 13 C2
North Pole Rd
W10 . . . . 30 B4
Northport St N1 . . . 87 C3
North Rd
Barnsbury N7 . . . . 14 A2
Brentford TW8 . . . 44 A4
Highgate N6 . . . . . . 3 C4
Richmond TW9 . . . 44 C1
North Ride 2 W2 . 116 A3
North Rise W2 . . . 102 B1
North Row W1 . . . 117 B4
NORTH SHEEN . . . 44 C1
North Sheen Sta
TW10 . . . . 54 C3
North Side
Wandsworth Comm
SW18 . . . . 59 C2
North St SW4 . . . . 61 B4
Northstead Rd
SW2 . . . . 74 C2
North Tenter St
E1 . . . . 111 A1
North Terr SW3 . . 130 A1

Northumberland Alley
EC3 . . . . 110 B1
Northumberland Ave
WC2 . . . . 120 A2
Northumberland Ho
NW5 . . . . 13 B2
Northumberland
Mans E5 . . . . 17 B4
Northumberland Pl
W2 . . . . 31 C3
Northumberland St
WC2 . . . . 120 A2
Northumbria Ct 10
TW9 . . . . 54 A3
Northumbria St
E14 . . . . 33 C3
North Verbena Gdns
2 W6 . . . . 38 C1
Northview 7 N7 . . . 5 A1
Northview Cres
NW10 . . . . 8 B4
Northview Prim Sch
NW10 . . . . 8 B4
North Villas NW1 . . 13 C2
Northway Rd SE5 . . 63 C4
Northways Par 2
NW3 . . . . 11 C1
North Wlk W2 . . . 114 C3
Northwest Pl N1 . . 85 C2
North Wharf Rd
W2 . . . . 101 B3
Northwick Cl NW8 . 89 B2
Northwick Ho
NW8 . . . . 89 A2
Northwick Terr
NW8 . . . . 89 B2
North Wlk W2 . . . 114 C3
Northwold Prim Sch
E5 . . . . 7 C2
Northwold Rd E5,
N16 . . . . 7 C2
North Wood Lo
NW3 . . . . 11 A4
Northwood Ho
SE27 . . . . 75 C1
North Worple Way
SW14 . . . . 55 C4
Norton Folgate
E1 . . . . 110 B4
Norton Ho
14 Globe Town E2 . 25 C3
8 Stepney E1 . . . . 32 A3
18 Stockwell SW9 . 173 A1
Norval Gn 6 SW9 . 173 C2
Norvic Ho 6 SE5 . . 48 B1
Norway Gate SE16 . 41 A3
Norway Pl E14 . . . 33 B3
Norway St SE10 . . 52 A4
Norwich Ho 6
E14 . . . . 34 A3
12 Norwich St EC4 . 107 B2
Norwood Cl NW2 . . 1 A1
Norwood Ho 25
E14 . . . . 34 A2
Norwood Rd SE24,
SE27 . . . . 75 A3
Notley St SE5 . . . . 48 C3
Notre Dame RC Girls
Sch SE1 . . . . 136 B1
Notting Barn Rd
W10 . . . . 22 C1
Nottingdale Sq
W11 . . . . . 31 A1 112 A1
Nottingham Ct
WC2 . . . . 106 A1

Nottingham Ho
53 Camberwell
SE5 . . . . 48 B1
Stoke Newington N4 . 6 B3
Nottingham Pl
W1 . . . . 103 B4
Nottingham Rd
SW17 . . . . 72 B3
Nottingham St
W1 . . . . 103 B4
Nottingham Terr
NW1 . . . . 91 B1
NOTTING HILL . . . 112 C3
Notting Hill Gate
W11 . . . . . 31 C1 113 B2
SE5 . . . . 31 C1 113 A2
Notting Hill Gate Sta
W11 . . . . . 31 C1 113 B2
Notting Hill Prep Sch
W11 . . . . 31 A2
Nottingwood Ho
W11 . . . . . 31 A2 112 A4
Nova Bldg 1 E14 . 41 C2
Nova Ct E 3 E14 . 34 B1
Nova Ct W 4 E14 . 34 B1
Novello St SW6 . . 165 B3
Nowell Rd SW13 . . 46 C4
Noyna Rd SW17 . . 72 B1
Nucleus NW10 . . . 20 B2
Nuding Cl SE13 . . . 66 C4
Nuffield Lo 14 W9 . 31 C4
Nugent Ct 3 N19 . . 5 A3
Nugent Rd N19 . . . 5 A3
Nugent Terr NW8 . 79 A1
Nun Ct EC2 . . . . . 109 B2
NUNHEAD 65 B3
Nunhead Cres
SE15 . . . . 65 A4
Nunhead Gn SE15 . 65 A4
Nunhead Gr SE15 . 65 B4
Nunhead La SE15 . 65 A4
Nunhead Sta SE15 . 50 B1
Nursery Cl
New Cross SE4 . . . 51 B1
Putney SW15 . . . . 57 C3
Nursery La
North Kensington
W10 . . . . 30 B4
Shoreditch E2 . . . 24 B4
Nursery Rd
Hackney E9 . . . . . 17 B2
Stockwell SW9 . . . 62 B3
Nursery Row
SE17 . . . . 151 B3
Nutbourne St W10 . 23 A2
Nutbrook St SE15 . 64 C4
Nutcroft Rd SE15 . 50 A3
Nutfield Rd
East Dulwich SE22 . 64 B3
Leyton E15 . . . . . 19 B4
Nutford Pl W1 . . . 102 C2
Nuthurst Ave SW2 . 74 B2
Nutley Terr NW3 . . 11 C2
Nutmeg La E14 . . . 34 C3
Nuttall St N1 . . . . 24 A3
Nutt St SE15 . . . . 49 B3
Nye Bevan Ho
SW6 . . . . 154 C2
Nye's Wharf SE1,
SE15 . . . . 49 C4
Nylands Ave TW9 . 44 C1
Nynehead St SE14 . 51 A3
Nyton Cl N19 . . . . . 5 A3

O

O2 Ctr NW6 .... 11 B2
O2 Millennium Dome
The★ SE10 .... 35 A1
Oakbury Rd SW6 .... 166 B1
Oakcourt 17 SE15 .... 49 B3
Oak Cres E16 .... 35 A4
Oakcroft SE13 .... 53 C2
Oakcroft Rd SE13 ... 52 C1
Oakdale Ct N19 .... 5 A2
Oakdale Rd SE15 ... 65 B4
Oakdene 3 SE5 ...... 48 C2
Oakdene Ho 16 N16 .. 7 A3
Oakden St SE11 .... 149 C4
Oakeford Ho W14 .. 126 B1
Oakend Ho 10 N4 ..... 6 C4
Oakeshott Ave N6 ... 3 C2
Oakey La SE1 ...... 135 B2
Oakfield Ct
Clapham Pk SW4 .... 62 A1
Finsbury Pk N8 .... 5 A4
Oakfield Prep Sch
SE21 .... 75 C3
Oakfield Rd
Finsbury Pk N4 .... 5 C4
Wimbledon SW19 .... 69 C1
Oakford Rd NW5 .... 13 B4
Oak Gr NW2 .... 10 A4
Oakham Ho 5
W10 .... 22 B1
Oakhill Ave NW3 ... 11 A4
Oakhill Ct
Honor Oak SE23 .... 65 B1
Putney SW15 .... 58 B2
Oak Hill Lo NW3 .... 11 A4
Oakhill Park Mews
NW3 .... 11 B4
Oak Hill Pk NW3 ... 11 A4
Oakhill Pl SW15 .... 58 C2
Oakhill Rd SW15 ... 58 B2
Oak Hill Way NW3 .. 11 B4
Oak Ho
13 Cubitt Town
E14 .... 42 B4
2 Maitland Pk
NW3 .... 12 B2
2 Richmond TW9 ... 45 A2
2 Stoke Newington
N16 .... 6 C2
Oakhurst Gr SE22 ... 64 C3
Oakington Rd W9 ... 23 C1
Oakington Way N8 .. 5 A4
Oak La E14 .... 33 B2
Oaklands Ct
Dagenham NW10 .... 21 A4
5 Shepherd's Bush
W12 .... 30 A1
Oaklands Gr W12 ... 29 C1
Oaklands Ho SE4 ... 66 B4
Oaklands Mews 1
NW2 .... 9 C4
Oaklands Pas NW2 .. 9 C4
Oaklands Pl 8
SW4 .... 61 C3
Oaklands Rd
Cricklewood NW2 .... 9 C4
Mortlake SW14 ..... 55 C4
Oaklands Sec Sch 51
E2 .... 25 A2

Oakley Cres EC1 .... 86 B1
Oakley Dr SE13 ..... 67 C1
Oakley Gdns SW3 . 158 B4
Oakley Ho SW1 .... 145 A4
Oakley Pl SE1 ...... 152 C1
Oakley Rd N1 .... 15 C1
Oakley Sq NW1 .... 83 A2
Oakley St SW3 ..... 158 A4
Oakley Wlk W6 ..... 47 C4
Oak Lodge 14
SE21 .... 75 C2
Oak Lodge Sch
SW12 .... 72 C4
Oakman Ho 20
SW19 .... 69 C3
Oakmead Rd
SW12 .... 73 A3
Oak Park Gdns
SW19 .... 69 C3
Oak Park Mews
N16 .... 7 B1
Oakshaw Rd SW18 . 71 A4
Oakshott Ct NW1 .... 83 B1
Oaks Sh Ctr The
W3 .... 28 B1
Oaks The
Brondesbury Pk
NW6 .... 9 C1
Willesden NW10 ...... 9 A1
Oak Tree Ct
Acton W3 .... 28 A2
8 Clapham Pk SW4 . 62 A2
Oak Tree Ho W9 .... 88 A2
Oak Tree Rd NW8 .. 90 A3
Oakview Lo NW11 ... 1 B4
Oak Village NW5 .... 12 C4
Oak Way W3 .... 29 A1
Oakwell Ho 4
SW8 .... 171 B1
Oakwood Cl SE13 .. 67 C1
Oakwood Ct W14 .. 126 C2
Oakwood La W14 .. 126 C2
Oakworth Rd W10 .. 30 C4
Oast Ct 3 E14 ...... 33 B2
Oat La EC2 .... 109 A2
Oatlands Ct 3
SW19 .... 69 C3
Oatwell Ho SW3 ... 144 B3
Oban Ho E14 .... 34 C3
Oban St E14 .... 34 C3
Oberon Ho 5 N1 ... 24 A3
Oberstein Rd 12
SW11 .... 59 C3
Oborne Cl SE24 .... 63 A2
O'Brian Ho 15 E1 .. 25 C2
Observatory Gdns
W8 .... 127 C4
Observatory Mews
E14 .... 42 C2
Observatory Rd
Kensington SW7 ... 129 B1
Mortlake SW14 ..... 55 B3
Occupation Rd
SE17 .... 150 C2
Ocean St E1 .... 32 C4
Ocean Wharf E14 .. 41 C4
Ockbrook 3 E1 ..... 32 B4
Ockendon Rd N1 ... 15 C2
Ockley Rd SW16 ... 74 A1
Octagon Arc EC2 .. 110 A3
Octagon The W3 ... 10 C4
Octavia Ho W10 ... 23 A1
Octavia Mews 1
W9 .... 23 B1
Octavia St SW11 .. 168 B3

Octavius St SE8 .... 51 C3
Odell Wlk SE13 .... 67 B4
Odeon Ct
Dagenham NW10 ... 21 A4
1 Newham E16 ..... 35 C4
Odessa Rd NW10 .. 21 C3
Odessa St SE16 ... 41 B3
Odette Duval Ho 2
E1 .... 32 B4
Odger St SW11 .... 169 A2
Odhams Wlk WC2 . 106 B1
Odin Ho 6 SE5 ..... 48 B1
O'Donnell Ct WC1 .. 94 B2
O'Driscoll Ho 4
W12 .... 30 A3
Offa's Mead E9 .... 18 A4
Offenbach Ho 12
E2 .... 25 C3
Offerton Rd SW4 ... 61 B3
Offham Ho SE17 .. 152 A3
Offley Ho 10 E9 .... 17 C2
Offley Rd SW9 .... 163 B2
Offord Rd N1 .... 14 B1
Offord St N1 .... 14 B1
Ogilvie Ho 12 E1 .. 32 C3
Oglander Rd SE15 . 64 B4
Ogle St W1 .... 104 C4
O'Gorman Ho
SW10 .... 157 A2
Ohio Bldg 13 SE13 . 52 A2
Oil Mill La W6 ...... 38 C1
Okeham Ho
N16 .... 10 C4
Okeover Manor
SW4 .... 61 A3
Olaf St W11 .... 30 C2
Old Bailey EC4 .... 108 B1
Old Bailey (Central
Criminal Court)★
EC4 .... 108 B2
Old Barrack Yd
SW1 .... 131 B3
Old Bellgate Wharf
E14 .... 41 C3
Old Bethnal Green Rd
E2 .... 25 A2
Old Billingsgate Wlk
EC3 .... 124 A3
Old Bldgs WC2 .... 107 B2
Old Bond St W1 ... 118 C3
Old Brewery Mews
NW3 .... 11 C4
Old Broad St EC2 . 109 C2
Old Brompton Rd SW5,
SW7 .... 143 A3
Old Burlington St
W1 .... 118 C3
Oldbury Ct E9 ...... 18 A3
Oldbury Pl W1 .... 103 C4
Old Castle St E1 .. 111 A2
Old Cavendish St
W1 .... 104 A1
Old Change Ct
EC4 .... 108 C1
Old Chiswick Yd
W4 .... 46 A4
Old Church Rd E1 .. 32 C3
Old Church St
SW3 .... 143 C1
Old Compton St
W1 .... 105 B1
Old Court Ho W8 .. 128 A3
Old Court Pl W8 ... 128 A3
Old Covent Gdn★
WC2 .... 120 B4
Old Cty H★ SE1 ... 134 C4

Old Dairy Mews
5 Balham SW12 .... 72 C3
4 Camden Town
NW5 .... 13 A2
Old Deer Park Gdns
TW9 .... 54 A4
Old Devonshire Rd
SW12 .... 73 A4
Old Dock Cl TW9 ... 44 C4
Oldfield Gr SE16 ... 40 C2
Oldfield Ho 14 W4 . 38 A1
Oldfield Mews N6 ... 4 B4
Oldfield Rd
Bedford Pk W3,
W12 .... 38 B4
Stoke Newington N16 . 7 A1
Willesden NW10 ..... 8 B1
Old Fish St Hill
EC4 .... 122 C4
Old Fleet La EC4 .. 108 A2
OLD FORD 26 B4
Old Ford Prim Sch 38
E3 .... 26 B4
Old Ford Rd E2, E3 . 25 C3
Old Ford Trad Est
E3 .... 26 C4
Old Forge Mews
W12 .... 39 A4
Old Forge Rd N19 .. 4 C2
Old Gloucester St
WC1 .... 106 B4
Oldham Terr W3 ... 28 B1
Oldhill St N16 .... 7 C3
Old Hospital Cl SW12,
SW17 .... 72 B3
Olding Ho 6
SW12 .... 73 B4
Old Jamaica Bsns Est
23 SE16 .... 139 B1
Old Jamaica Rd
SE16 .... 139 B2
Old James St SE15 . 65 A4
Old Jewry EC2 .... 109 B1
Old Kent Rd
Deptford SE1,
SE15 .... 152 B4
Walworth SE1 ..... 152 B2
Old Laundry The 14
SW18 .... 59 C3
Old Manor Ct NW8 . 79 A2
Old Manor Yd
SW5 .... 142 A3
Old Market Sq 1
E2 .... 24 B2 99 A4
Old Marylebone Rd
NW1 .... 102 B3
Old Mitre Ct EC4 .. 107 C1
Old Montague St
E1 .... 111 B3
Old Nichol St
E2 .... 24 B1 98 C2
Old North St WC1 . 106 C4
Old Oak
COMMON 21 B1
Old Oak Common La
NW10 .... 21 A1
Old Oak La NW10 .. 21 A2
Old Oak Prim Sch
W12 .... 29 C3
Old Oak Rd W3 .... 29 B2
Old Orch The NW3 . 12 B4
Old Palace Prim Sch
E3 .... 27 A2
Old Paradise St
SE11 .... 148 C4

Old Park Ave
SW12 .... 60 C1
Old Park La W1 ... 118 A1
Old Pearson St
SE10 .... 52 A3
Old Pye St SW1 ... 133 B2
Old Pye Street Est
SW1 .... 133 B1
Old Quebec St
W1 .... 103 A1
Old Queen St
SW1 .... 133 C3
Oldridge Rd SW12 . 73 A4
Old Royal Free Pl
N1 .... 85 C3
Old Royal Free Sq
N1 .... 85 C3
Old School Sq 12
E14 .... 33 C3
Old School The
WC1 .... 107 A4
Old Seacoal La
EC4 .... 108 A1
Old South Lambeth
Rd SW8 .... 162 B2
Old Spitalfields Mkt★
E1 .... 111 A4
Old St EC1 .... 97 C2
Old St E1 .... 107 B2
Old Stable Mews
N5 .... 6 B1
Old Street Sta EC1 . 97 C2
Old Sun Wharf
E14 .... 33 A2
Old Swan Wharf
SW11 .... 167 C4
Old Theatre Ct
SE1 .... 123 A2
Old Town SW4 ..... 61 B3
Old Vicarage Sch 13
TW10 .... 54 A1
Old Woolwich Rd
SE10 .... 42 C1
Old York Rd SW18 . 59 A2
Olga Prim Sch 82
E3 .... 26 A3
Olga St 20 E3 ...... 26 A3
Oliphant St W10 ... 23 A2
Olive Blythe Ho 14
W10 .... 23 A1
Oliver Bsns Pk
NW10 .... 20 B3
Oliver Cl W4 .... 45 A4
Olive Rd NW2 .... 9 B4
Oliver Goldsmith Prim
Sch 51 SE5 .... 49 B2
Oliver Ho
22 Bermondsey
SE16 .... 139 B3
Notting Hill
W11 .... 31 A2 112 A3
South Lambeth
SW8 .... 162 A2
Oliver House Prep
Sch 18 SW4 .... 61 A1
Oliver Mews SE15 . 49 C1
Oliver's Yd EC1 .... 97 C2
Olive Tree Ho 7
SE15 .... 50 B4
Olive Tree Sch The
SE13 .... 67 C1
Olivette St 1
SW15 .... 57 C3
Olive Waite Ho
NW6 .... 11 A1

Ollerton Gn E3 . . . . . . 26 B4
Ollgar Cl W12 . . . . 29 B1
Olliffe St E14 . . . . 42 B3
Olmar St SE1 . . . . 49 C4
Olney Ho NW8 . . . . . . 90 B2
Olney Rd SE17 . . . . . . 48 A4
Olympia Ex Ctr★
W14 . . . . 126 B1
Olympian Ct 8
E14 . . . . 41 C3
Olympia Way
W14 . . . . 126 B1
Olympia Yd W2 . . . . . 114 B3
Olympic Ho 10
W10 . . . . 30 B3
Olympus Sq E5 . . . . 7 C1
Oman Ave NW2 . . . . 9 B4
Oman Ct NW4 . . . . 9 A4
Ombersley Ho N4 . . . . . 6 B4
Omeara St SE1 . . . . . . 123 A1
Omega Cl E14 . . . . 42 A3
Omega Ho SW10 . . . . 157 A2
Omega Pl N1 . . . . 84 B1
Omega St SE14 . . . . . . 51 C2
Omega Works E3 . . . 18 C1
Ommaney Rd
SE14 . . . . 51 A2
Omnibus Bsns Ctr
N7 . . . . 14 A3
Ondine Rd SE15 . . . . . 64 B3
Onedin Point 10
E1 . . . . 125 C3
Onega Gate SE16 . . . . 41 A3
O'Neill Ho NW8 . . . . . 79 C1
One Tree Cl SE23 . . . . 65 B1
Ongar Ho 16 N1 . . . . . 15 C2
Ongar Rd SW6 . . . . . 155 C4
Onslow Ave NW10 . . . 54 A2
Onslow Avenue Mans
10 TW10 . . . . 54 A2
Onslow Cl W9 . . . . 23 B2
Onslow Ct SW10 . . . . 143 A1
Onslow Gdns
SW7 . . . . 143 B3
Onslow Lo 28 SW2 . . 74 C4
Onslow Mews E
SW7 . . . . 143 B3
Onslow Mews W
SW7 . . . . 143 B3
Onslow Rd TW10 . . . . 54 A1
Onslow Sq SW7 . . . . . 143 C3
Onslow St EC1 . . . . . . 95 C1
Ontario St SE1 . . . . . 136 B2
Ontario Way E14 . . . . 33 C2
Opal St SE11 . . . . 150 A2
Open Air Theatre,
Regent's Pk★
NW1 . . . . 91 B3
Openview SW17,
SW18 . . . . 71 C2
Opera Ct 17 N19 . . . . . 4 C1
Operating Theatre
Mus & Herb Garret
The★ SE1 . . . . 123 C1
Ophelia Gdns NW2 . . . 1 A1
Ophir Terr SE15 . . . . . 49 C2
Opie Ho NW8 . . . . 80 B2
Oppenheim Rd
SE13 . . . . 52 B1
Oppidan Apartments
NW6 . . . . 11 A1
Oppidans Rd NW3 . . . 12 B1
Orange Pl SE16 . . . . . 40 B3
Orangery Gallery
The★ W8 . . . . 126 C3
Orange St WC2 . . . . . 119 C3

Orange Yd WC2 . . . . . 105 C1
Oransay Rd 22 N1 . . 15 B2
Oratory La SW3 . . . . . 143 C2
Oratory RC Prim Sch
SW3 . . . . 144 A2
Orbain Rd SW6 . . . . . 154 B1
Orbel St SW11 . . . . . . 168 A3
Orb St SE17 . . . . 151 B3
Orchard Cl
Honor Oak SE23 . . . . . 65 B1
21 Islington N1 . . . . . . 15 B1
Kensal Town W10 . . . 31 A4
Orchard Cl
Barnes SW13 . . . . 56 B4
Marylebone W1 . . . . 103 B2
Orchard Dr SE3 . . . . . 52 A2
Orchard Hill Lo SE13 . . 52 A2
Orchard Ho
Camberwell SE5 . . . . . 48 B2
11 Rotherhithe
SE16 . . . . 40 B3
Shepherd's Bush
W12 . . . . 29 C1
Orchard House Sch 18
W4 . . . . 37 C2
Orchard Mead Ho
NW11 . . . . 1 C2
Orchard Mews N1 . . . 15 C1
Orchard Pl E14 . . . . . 35 A2
Orchard Prim Sch 41
E9 . . . . 17 B1
Orchard Rd
Highgate N6 . . . . 4 A4
Richmond TW9 . . . . . 54 C4
Orchard Rise
TW10 . . . . 55 A3
Orchardson Ho
NW8 . . . . 89 C1
Orchardson St
NW8 . . . . 89 C1
Orchard Sq W14 . . . . 140 C1
Orchard St W1 . . . . . . 103 C2
Orchard The
Acton Green W4 . . . . . 37 C2
Lewisham SE3 . . . . . . 52 C1
Orchid Cl SE13 . . . . . . 67 C2
Orchid St W12 . . . . . . 29 C2
Orde Hall St WC1 . . . 106 C4
Orde Ho 10 N16 . . . . 15 C4
Ordell Ct 18 E3 . . . . . 26 B3
Ordell Rd E3 . . . . 26 B3
Ordnance Cres
SE10 . . . . 43 A4
Ordnance Hill
NW8 . . . . 79 C3
Ordnance Mews
NW8 . . . . 79 C2
Ordnance Rd E16 . . . . 35 B4
Oregano Dr E14 . . . . . 34 C3
Oregon Bldg 3
SE13 . . . . 52 A2
Orestes Mews 1
NW6 . . . . 10 C3
Orford Ct SE27 . . . . . . 75 A2
Oriana Ho 7 E14 . . . . 33 B2
Oriel Ct NW3 . . . . 11 B4
Oriel Dr SW13 . . . . . . 47 B4
Oriel Rd
Hackney E9 . . . . 18 A2
Homerton E9 . . . . 17 C2
Orient St SE11 . . . . . . 150 A4
Orion Bsns Ctr
SE14 . . . . 40 C1
Orion Ho 20 E1 . . . . . 25 A1
Orion Point 5
E14 . . . . 41 C2

Orkney Ho N1 . . . . . . 84 C4
Orkney St SW11 . . . . 169 B2
Orlando Rd SW4 . . . . 61 B4
Orleston Mews N7 . . 14 C2
Orleston Rd N7 . . . . . 14 C2
Orlop St SE10 . . . . . . 43 A1
Orme Ct W2 . . . . 114 A3
Orme Ct Mews
W2 . . . . 114 B3
Orme Ho 8 E8 . . . . . 24 B4
Orme La W2 . . . . 114 A3
Ormeley Rd SW12 . . 73 A3
Ormerod Ho 3
SW9 . . . . 62 A4
Orme Sq W2 . . . . 114 A3
Ormiston Gr W12 . . . 30 A1
Ormiston Rd SE10 . . 43 C1
Ormond Cl WC1 . . . . 106 B4
Ormonde Ct SW15 . . 57 B3
Ormonde Gate
SW3 . . . . 145 A1
Ormonde Mans
WC1 . . . . 106 B4
Ormonde Pl SW1 . . . 145 C3
Ormonde Rd
SW14 . . . . 55 B4
Ormonde Terr
NW8 . . . . 80 C3
Ormond Ho 7 N16 . . 6 C2
Ormond Mans
WC1 . . . . 94 C1
Ormond Mews
WC1 . . . . 94 B1
Ormond Rd N4, N19 . 5 A3
Ormond Yd SW1 . . . 119 A2
Ormrod Ct W11 . . . . . 31 B3
Ormsby Lo 7 W4 . . . 38 A3
Ormsby Pl N16 . . . . . 7 B1
Ormsby St E2 . . . . . . 24 B3
Ormside St SE15 . . . . 50 B4
Ornan Rd NW3 . . . . . 12 A3
Orpen Ho SW5 . . . . . 141 C3
Orpen Wlk N16 . . . . . 7 A1
Orpheus Ho 29 N19 . 4 C4
Orpheus St SE5 . . . . 48 C2
Orsett Mews W2 . . . 100 C2
Orsett St SE11 . . . . . . 149 A2
Orsett Terr W2 . . . . . 100 C2
Orsman Rd N1 . . . . . . 24 A4
Orton St E1 . . . . 125 B1
Orville Rd SW11 . . . . 167 C2
Orwell Ct
Hackney E8 . . . . 24 C4
Highbury N5 . . . . 15 B4
Orwell Ho W12 . . . . . 29 C2
Osbaldeston Rd
N16 . . . . 7 C3
Osbert St SW1 . . . . . 147 B3
Osborn Cl E8 . . . . 24 C4
Osborne Rd
Finsbury Pk N4 . . . . . 5 C3
Hackney E9 . . . . 18 B2
South Acton W3 . . . . 37 A4
Willesden NW2 . . . . . 9 A2
Osborn St E1 . . . . . . 111 A4
Osbourne Ho
TW10 . . . . 54 C2
Oscar Faber Pl 8
N1 . . . . 16 A1
Oscar St SE8 . . . . 51 C1
Oseney Cres NW5 . . 13 C2
Osier Ct E1 . . . . 25 C1
Osier La SE10 . . . . . . 43 B3
Osier Mews W4 . . . . 46 B4
Osiers Rd SW18 . . . . 58 C3
Osier St E1 . . . . 25 B1

Oslo Ct NW8 . . . . 80 A1
Oslo Ho 2 SE5 . . . . . 48 B1
Oslo Sq SE16 . . . . . . 41 A3
Oslow Cl W10 . . . . . . 23 B2
Osman Prim Sch
E1 . . . . 111 C4
Osman Rd W6 . . . . . . 39 B3
Osmington Ho
SW8 . . . . 163 A1
Osmund St W12 . . . . 29 B4
Osnaburgh St NW1 . 92 B2
Osnaburgh Terr
NW1 . . . . 92 B2
Osprey Ct SW3 . . . . . 11 A3
Osprey Ho
Camberwell SE15 . . . . 49 B2
3 Limehouse E14 . . . 33 A2
Ospringe Ho SE1 . . . 121 C1
Ospringe Rd NW5 . . 13 B4
Osram Ct W6 . . . . . . 39 B3
Osric Path 5 N1 . . . . 24 A3
Ossian Mews N4 . . . 5 B4
Ossian Rd N4 . . . . . . 5 B4
Ossington Bldgs
W1 . . . . 103 B3
Ossington Cl
W2 . . . . 31 C2 113 C3
Ossington St W2 . . . 114 A3
Ossory Rd SE1 . . . . . 49 C4
Ossulston St NW1 . . 83 C2
Ostade Rd SW2 . . . . 74 B4
Osten Mews SW7 . . . 128 B1
Osterley Ho 5
E14 . . . . 34 A3
Osterley Rd N16 . . . . 16 A4
Oswald Bldg SW8 . . 160 A3
Oswald's Mead E9 . . 18 A4
Osward Rd SW12,
SW17 . . . . 72 B2
Oswell Ho 9 E1 . . . . 32 A1
Oswin St SE11 . . . . . . 150 B4
Oswyth Rd SE5 . . . . . 49 A1
Otford Cres SE4 . . . . 66 B1
Otford Ho
Bermondsey SE1 . . . 137 C3
6 Deptford SE15 . . . 50 B4
Otha Ho 13 SW9 . . . 172 B2
Othello Cl SE11 . . . . . 150 A2
Otis St E3 . . . . 27 B2
Otley Ho N5 . . . . 6 A1
Ottaway Ct E5 . . . . . 7 C1
Ottaway St E5 . . . . . . 7 C1
Otterburn Ho 17
SE5 . . . . 48 B3
Otter Cl E15 . . . . 27 B4
Otto St SE17 . . . . 48 A4
Our Lady of Dolours
RC Prim Sch 1
W2 . . . . 100 A4
Our Lady of Lourdes
RC Prim Sch
1 Lewisham SE13 . . 67 C4
London NW10 . . . . . . 20 C3
Our Lady of Victories
RC Prim Sch
7 Putney SW15 . . . 57 C3
South Kensington
SW7 . . . . 143 A3
Our Lady Queen of
Heaven RC Prim Sch
10 SW19 . . . . 69 C4
Our Lady RC Prim Sch
Camden Town
NW1 . . . . 83 A4
28 Poplar E14 . . . . . 33 B3

Our Lady & St Joseph
RC Prim Sch 14
N1 . . . . 16 A2
Our Lady's Convent
RC High Sch 3
N15 . . . . 7 A4
Ouseley Rd SW12 . . 72 B3
Outer Circ NW8 . . . . 81 A1
Outgate Rd NW10 . . 8 B1
Outram Pl N1 . . . . . . 84 B4
Outwich St EC3 . . . . 110 B2
Outwood Ho 3
SW2 . . . . 74 B4
Oval Mans SE11 . . . . 163 A4
Oval Pl SW8 . . . . 163 A2
Oval Rd NW1 . . . . . . 82 A4
Oval Sta SE11 . . . . . . 163 B3
Oval The E2 . . . . 25 A3
Oval Way SE11 . . . . . 149 A1
Overbury Ho 5
E5 . . . . 17 C4
Overbury St E5 . . . . . 17 C4
Overcliff Rd SE13 . . . 66 C4
Overhill Rd SE21,
SE22 . . . . 76 C4
Overlea Rd E5 . . . . . . 7 C4
Oversley Ho 17
W2 . . . . 31 C4
Overstone Ho 19
E14 . . . . 33 C3
Overstone Rd W6 . . 39 B2
Overstrand Mans
SW11 . . . . 169 B3
Overton Ho SW15 . . 68 B4
Overton Rd SW9 . . . 173 C1
Overy Ho SE1 . . . . . . 136 A3
Ovex Cl E14 . . . . 42 B4
Ovington Ct SW3 . . . 130 B1
Ovington Gdns
SW3 . . . . 130 B1
Ovington Mews
SW3 . . . . 130 B1
Ovington Sq SW3 . . 130 B1
Ovington St SW3 . . . 144 B4
Owen Ho 11 N19 . . . 13 B4
Owen's Ct EC1 . . . . . 96 A4
Owen's Row EC1 . . . 96 A4
Owen St EC1 . . . . 86 A1
Owgan Cl SE5 . . . . . . 48 C3
Oxberry Ave SW6 . . 164 B2
Oxbridge Ct 8
W4 . . . . 37 A1
Oxendon St SW1,
W1 . . . . 119 B3
Oxenford St SE15 . . 64 B4
Oxenham Ho 13
SE8 . . . . 51 C4
Oxenholme NW1 . . . 83 A1
Oxestalls Rd SE8 . . . 41 A1
Oxford & Cambridge
Mans NW1 . . . . 102 B3
Oxford Cir W1 . . . . . 104 C1
Oxford Circus Ave
W1 . . . . 104 C1
Oxford Circus Sta
W1 . . . . 104 C1
Oxford Ct
City of London
EC4 . . . . 123 B4
Gunnersbury W4 . . . 37 A1
48 Paddington W2 . . 31 C4
Oxford Dr SE1 . . . . . 124 A1
Oxford Gardens Prim
Sch 21 W10 . . . . . . 30 C3

Oxford Gate W6 . . . .**39** C2
Oxford Gdns
  Brentford W4 . . . . . .**44** C4
  North Kensington
  W10 . . . .**30** C3
Oxford Ho N4 . . . .**5** C3
Oxford Rd
  Finsbury Pk N4 . . . . . .**5** C3
  Paddington NW6 . . . .**23** C3
  Putney SW15 . . . .**58** A3
  Stratford E15 . . . .**19** C2
Oxford Rd N W4 . . . . .**37** A1
Oxford Rd S W4 . . . . .**37** A1
Oxford Sq W2 . . . .**102** B1
Oxford St W1 . . . .**104** B1
Oxley Cl SE1 . . . .**153** A2
Oxonian St SE22 . . . . .**64** B3
Oxo Tower Wharf
  SE1 . . . .**121** C3
Oxo Twr★ SE1 . . . . . .**121** C3
Oxted CT N16 . . . .**7** A3
Oyster Row E1 . . . .**32** B3
Ozolins Way E16 . . . . .**35** C3

P

Pablo Neruda Cl 4
  SE24 . . . .**63** A3
Pace Pl E1 . . . .**32** A3
Pacific Ho 15 E1. . . . . .**25** C1
Pacific Rd E16 . . . .**35** C3
Pacific Wharf
  SE16 . . . .**32** C1
Packenham Ho
  24 Crouch End N19 . . .**4** C4
  Spitalfields
  E2 . . . .**24 B2 99** A4
Packington Sq N1. .**86** C4
Packington St N1 . .**86** B3
Padbury SE17 . . . .**152** B1
Padbury Ct 3
  E2 . . . .**24** B2 **99** A4
Padbury Ho NW8 . . .**90** B2
Paddenswick Ct 2
  W6 . . . .**39** A3
Paddenswick Rd
  W6 . . . .**38** C3
PADDINGTON **100** C3
Paddington Acad 7
  W9 . . . .**23** C2
Paddington Gn
  W2 . . . .**101** B4
Paddington Green
  Prim Sch NW8 . . .**89** B1
Paddington St
  W1 . . . .**103** B4
Paddington Sta
  W2 . . . .**101** B2
Paddock Cl SE3 . . . .**53** C1
Paddock Prim Sch
  SW11 . . . .**60** C3
Paddock Sch
  SW15 . . . .**56** B3
Paddock Way 11
  SW15 . . . .**69** B4
Padfield Rd SE5 . . . .**63** B4
Padstone Ho 30
  E3 . . . .**27** A2
Padstow Ho 12
  E14 . . . .**33** B2
Pagden St SW8. .**170** B4
Pageant Cres
  SE16 . . . .**33** B1

Pageantmaster Ct
  EC4 . . . .**108** A1
Page Ho SE10 . . . . . .**52** B4
Page St SW1 . . . .**147** C4
Page's Wlk SE1. . . .**138** B1
Page's Yd W4 . . . .**46** A4
Paget Ho 16 E2 . . . . . .**25** B2
Paget Rd N16 . . . .**6** C3
Paget St EC1 . . . .**96** A4
Pagham Ho 8
  W10 . . . .**22** B1
Pagnell St SE14 . . . .**51** B3
Pagoda Ave TW9 . . . .**54** B4
Pagoda Gdns SE3 . .**52** C1
Pagoda Gr SE27 . . . .**75** B2
Paine Ct SE3 . . . .**53** B4
Painsthorpe Rd 3
  N16 . . . .**7** A1
Painswick Ct 1
  SE15 . . . .**49** B3
Painters Mews
  SE16 . . . .**153** C4
Pakeman Ho SE1 . .**136** B4
Pakeman Prim Sch 5
  Pakeman St N7. . . . . . .**5** B1
Pakenham Cl
  SW12 . . . .**72** C3
Pakenham St WC1 . .**95** A2
Palace Ave W8 . .**128** B4
Palace Cl 4 E9 . . . . . .**18** B2
Palace Ct
  Hampstead NW3 . . . .**11** A3
  Kensington W2 . . . . .**114** A3
  Streatham SW2 . . . . . .**74** C2
Palace Garden Mews
  W8 . . . .**31** C1 **113** C2
Palace Gate W8 . .**128** C3
Palace Gdns Mews
  W8 . . . .**114** B3
Palace Gn W8 . . . . .**114** A1
Palace Mans W14 .**140** B4
Palace Mews
  Belgravia SW1 . . . . .**145** C3
  Fulham SW6 . . . .**155** A2
Palace Pl SW1 . . . .**132** C2
Palace Rd SE27, SW16,
  SW2 . . . .**74** C2
Palace St SW1 . . . .**132** C2
Palatine Ave N16 . . .**16** A4
Palatine Rd N16 . . . .**16** A4
Palazzo Apartments
  11 N1 . . . .**16** A1
Palemead Cl SW6 . .**47** C2
Palermo Rd NW10 . .**21** C3
Palewell Common Dr
  SW14 . . . .**55** D2
Palewell Pk SW14 . .**55** C2
Palfrey Pl SW8 . . . .**163** A2
Palgrave Gdns
  NW1 . . . .**90** B2
Palgrave Ho
  7 Camberwell
  SE5 . . . .**48** B3
  4 Maitland Pk
  NW3 . . . .**12** B3
Palgrave Rd W12 . . .**38** B3
Palissy St 35
  E2 . . . .**24** B2 **98** C3
Pallant Ho SE1 . . . .**137** C1
Pallester Ct NW11 . . .**1** A3
Palliser Ct W14 . . . .**140** A1
Palliser Ho
  2 Greenwich
  SE10 . . . .**52** C4
  21 Stepney E1 . . . . . .**25** C1

Palliser Rd W14 . .**140** A1
Pallister Terr
  SW15 . . . .**68** B2
Pall Mall SW1 . . . .**119** B1
Pall Mall E SW1 . . .**119** C2
Pall Mall Pl SW1 . .**119** A1
Palm Ct
  18 Camberwell
  SE15 . . . .**49** B3
  Stoke Newington N16 . .**6** C2
Palmer Ho
  6 Deptford SE14 . . . .**50** C3
  8 Kentish Town
  NW5 . . . .**13** B4
  9 Tufnell Pk N19 . . . . .**4** B1
Palmer Pl N7 . . . .**14** C3
Palmers Rd
  Globe Town E2 . . . . . .**25** C3
  Mortlake SW14 . . . . . .**55** B4
Palmer St SW1 . . . .**133** B2
Palmerston Ct 22
  E3 . . . .**25** C3
Palmerston Ho
  Battersea SW11 . . . .**169** C3
  Kensington
  W8 . . . .**31** C1 **113** B1
Palmerston Rd
  Acton Green W3 . . . .**37** B3
  Brondesbury NW6 . . .**10** B1
  Hampstead NW6 . . . .**10** C1
  Mortlake SW14 . . . . . .**55** B3
Palmerston Way
  SW8 . . . .**160** B1
Palm Gr W5 . . . .**36** A3
Palm Tree Ho 2
  SE14 . . . .**50** C3
Pamela Ct NW10 . . . . .**8** C1
Pamela Ho 14 E8 . . . .**24** B4
Pamlion Ct N4 . . . .**5** A4
Panama Ho 6 E1 . . . .**32** C4
Pancras La EC2 . . . .**109** B1
Pancras Rd NW1 . . . .**83** C2
Pandian Way 3
  NW5 . . . .**13** C2
Pandora Rd NW6 . . . .**10** C2
Pangbourne NW1 . . . .**92** C3
Pangbourne Ave
  W10 . . . .**30** B4
Pangbourne Ho 4
  N7 . . . .**14** A3
Pankhurst Cl 7
  SE14 . . . .**50** C3
Pankhurst Ho 2
  NW10 . . . .**30** B3
Panmure Cl N5. . . . . .**15** A4
Pan Peninsula Sq
  E14 . . . .**42** A4
Pansy Gdns W12 . . .**29** C2
Panton St SW1 . . . .**119** B3
Panyer Alley EC2 . .**108** C2
Paper Mill Wharf
  E14 . . . .**33** A2
Papworth Gdns
  N7 . . . .**14** B3
Papworth Way
  SW2 . . . .**74** C4
Parade Mans 19
  SE5 . . . .**48** B1
Parade Mews SE27,
  SW2 . . . .**75** A2
Parade The SW11 . .**159** A2
Paradise Pas N7 . . . .**14** C3
Paradise Rd
  Richmond TW10 . . . . .**54** A2

Paradise Rd continued
  South Lambeth
  SW4 . . . .**172** A2
Paradise Row E2. . . .**25** A2
Paradise St SE16 . . .**40** A4
Paradise Wlk
  SW3 . . . .**159** A4
Paragon Christian
  Acad E5 . . . .**17** C4
Paragon Cl E16 . . . . .**35** C3
Paragon Ho SE3 . . . .**53** B1
Paragon Mews
  SE1 . . . .**151** C4
Paragon Pl SE3 . . . . .**53** B1
Paragon Rd E9 . . . . .**17** B2
Paragon The
  Kidbrooke SE3 . . . . . .**53** C1
  Walworth SE17. . . . .**151** C4
Paramount Bldg
  EC1 . . . .**96** A2
Paramount Ct
  WC1 . . . .**93** A1
Parbury Rd SE23 . . . .**66** A1
Pardoner St SE1 . . .**137** C2
Pardon St EC1 . . . . . .**96** B2
Parfett St E1 . . . . . .**111** C2
Parfitt Cl NW11 . . . . . .**2** B3
Parfrey St W6 . . . . . .**47** B4
Paris Gdn SE1 . . . . .**122** A2
Paris Ho 13 E2 . . . . . .**25** A3
Park Ave
  Golders Green
  NW11 . . . .**2** A3
  Mortlake SW14 . . . . . .**55** C3
  Willesden NW2 . . . .**9** B2
Park Ave N NW10 . . . . .**9** A3
Park Cl
  Kensington W14 . . . .**127** A2
  13 South Hackney
  E9 . . . .**25** B4
Park Cres W1 . . . .**92** A1
Park Crescent Mews E
  W1 . . . .**92** B1
Park Crescent Mews W
  W1 . . . .**92** A1
Park Ct
  Battersea SW11 . . . .**170** A4
  Clapham Pk SW4 . . . .**61** C2
  Dulwich SE21 . . . .**75** C1
  12 Hammersmith
  W6 . . . .**38** C2
  Upper Tooting
  SW12 . . . .**72** C3
Park Dr
  Acton W3 . . . .**36** C3
  Golders Green NW11. . .**2** A3
  Mortlake SW14 . . . . . .**55** C3
Park Dwellings 5
  NW3 . . . .**12** B3
Park End NW3 . . . . . .**12** A4
Parker Ct
  Shoreditch N1 . . . . . .**87** A4
  South Lambeth
  SW4 . . . .**172** A3
Parke Rd SW13 . . . . .**46** C2
Parker Mews
  WC2 . . . .**106** B2
Parkers Row 18
  SE16 . . . .**139** B3
Parker's Row SE1 .**139** A3
Parkfield Ave
  SW14 . . . .**56** A3
Parkfield Ct SE14. . . .**51** B2

Parkfield Ind Est
  SW11 . . . .**169** C2
Parkfield Rd
  New Cross SE14. . . . . .**51** B2
  Willesden NW10 . . . . . .**9** A1
Parkfields SW15 . . . .**57** B3
Parkfield St N1. . . . . .**85** C2
Park Flats N6 . . . .**3** A4
Parkgate Gdns
  SW14 . . . .**55** C2
Parkgate House Sch
  SW11 . . . .**60** C3
Parkgate Mews N6 . . .**4** B4
Parkgate Rd
  SW11 . . . .**158** B1
Park Hall SE21 . . . . . .**52** C3
Park Hall Rd SE21 . . .**75** C1
Park Hall Road Trad
  Est SE21 . . . .**75** C1
Parkham St SW11 . .**168** A3
Park Heights Ct 2
  E14 . . . .**33** B3
Park Hill
  Clapham Pk SW4 . . . .**61** C2
  Richmond TW10 . . . . .**54** B1
Park Hill Ct SW17 . . .**72** B1
Parkhill Rd NW3 . . . .**12** B3
Park Hill Wlk 10
  NW3 . . . .**12** B3
Park Ho
  3 Camberwell
  SE5 . . . .**48** C2
  Finsbury Pk N4 . . . . . .**6** A2
  8 Hackney E9 . . . .**17** B1
  Richmond TW10 . . . . .**54** A1
Parkholme Rd E8. . . .**16** C2
Parkhouse St SE5 . . .**48** C3
Parkhurst Ct N7 . . . .**14** A4
Parkhurst Rd N7 . . . .**14** A4
Parkinson Ct
  Finsbury N1 . . . .**97** B3
  Shoreditch EC1. . . . . .**97** C4
Parkinson Ho 6
  E9 . . . .**17** B1
Park La
  Mayfair W1 . . . .**117** B3
  Mill Meads E15. . . . . .**27** C4
Parkland Ct W14 . .**126** A4
Parkland Gdns 12
  SW19 . . . .**69** C3
Parklands
  East Dulwich SE22 . . .**65** A2
  Highgate N6 . . . .**4** A4
Parklands Cl
  SW14 . . . .**55** B2
Park Lea Ct N16 . . . . . .**7** A4
Parklife Oxford St
  W1 . . . .**103** B1
Park Lo
  11 South Hampstead
  NW8 . . . .**11** C1
  18 Wapping E1. . . . . .**32** A1
  Willesden NW2 . . . .**9** B4
Park Lofts 5 SW4 . . .**62** A2
Park Lorne NW8. . . . .**90** B3
Park Mans
  Battersea SW11. . . . .**168** C3
  Bedford Pk W6 . . . . . .**38** B3
  Fulham SW6 . . . .**164** B3
  Knightsbridge SW1 . .**130** C3
  St John's Wood
  NW8 . . . .**80** A1
  Vauxhall SW8 . . . . . .**162** B4
Parkmead SW15 . . . .**57** A1
Park Mews
  Greenwich SE10. . . . .**43** B1

Park Mews continued
Kensal Rise W10 . . . . .23 A3
Park Par
Acton W3 . . . . .36 C3
Dagenham NW10 . . . .21 B3
Park Piazza 3
SE13 . . . . .67 C1
Park Pl
Canary Wharf E14 . . .33 C1
Gunnersbury W3 . . . .36 C2
Shoreditch N1 . . . . . .87 C4
St James SW1 . . . . . .118 C2
Park Place Dr W3 . . .36 C3
Park Place Ho 8
SE10 . . . . .52 C4
Park Place Villas
W2 . . . .**101** A4
Park Rd
Chiswick W4 . . . . .45 C4
Dagenham NW10 . . . .21 A4
Lisson Gr NW1,
NW8 . . . .**90** B2
Richmond TW10 . . . . .54 B1
Park Rd E W3 . . . . . . .37 B4
Park Rd N
Chiswick W4 . . . . .37 C1
South Acton W3 . . . . .37 A4
Park Road E 1
W3 . . . . .37 A4
Park Row SE10 . . . . .52 C4
Park Royal NW10 . . .20 A2
Park Royal NW10 . . .20 A2
Park Royal Bsns Ctr
NW10 . . . . .20 B1
Park Royal Metro Ctr
NW10 . . . . .20 A1
Park Royal Rd NW10,
W3 . . . . .20 B1
Park S SW11 . . . . . .**169** B3
Park St James
NW8 . . . .**80** C3
Park Sheen 3
SW14 . . . . .55 A3
Parkshot TW9 . . . . . .54 A3
Parkside
East Acton W3 . . . . . .29 A1
Greenwich SE3 . . . . . .53 B3
Park Side NW2 . . . . . . .9 A4
Parkside Bsns Est
SE8 . . . . .51 A4
Parkside Cres N7 . . . . .5 C1
Parkside Est E9 . . . . .25 C4
Parkside (Private)
Hospl NW10 . . . . . . .21 A3
Parkside St SW11 . .**169** B3
Park Sq E NW1 . . . . .**92** B2
Park Square Mews
NW1 . . . .**92** A1
Park Sq W NW1 . . . .**92** A1
Park St
Borough The SE1 . . .**123** A2
Mayfair W1 . . . .**117** B3
Parkstead Rd
SW15 . . . . .57 A2
Parkstone Rd 5
SE15 . . . . .49 C1
Park Stps W2 . . . . . .**116** B4
Park The NW11 . . . . . .2 A3
Parkthorne Rd
SW12 . . . . .73 C4
Park Twrs W1 . . . . . .**118** A1
Park View
Dagenham W3 . . . . . .28 B4
Highbury N5 . . . . .15 B4
Willesden NW2 . . . . . . .9 B4
Parkview Ct SW6 . .**164** B1

Park View Ct
SW18 . . . . .58 C1
Park View Ho
SE24 . . . . .63 A1
Park View Mans N4 . .6 A4
Park View Mews 1
SW9 . . . .**172** C2
Park View Rd NW10 . .8 B4
Parkville Rd
NW1 . . . .**82** B1
Park Village E
NW1 . . . .**82** A2
Park Village W
NW1 . . . .**82** A2
Parkville Rd SW6 . .**154** C1
Park Vista SE10 . . . .52 C4
Park Walk Prim Sch
SW10 . . . .**157** B3
Parkwat Cres E15 . . .19 B3
Parkway NW1 . . . . . .**82** A3
Park Way W3 . . . . . . .36 C2
Parkway Ho SW14 . . .55 C3
Park West W2 . . . . . .**102** B1
Park West PI W1,
W2 . . . .**102** B2
Park Wlk
Chelsea SW10 . . . . .**157** B4
Highgate N6 . . . . .3 C4
Parkwood NW8 . . . . .**80** C3
Parkwood Prim Sch
1 N4 . . . . .6 A2
Parliament Ct
NW3 . . . . .12 A4
Parliament Hill
NW3 . . . . .12 A4
Parliament Hill Mans
NW5 . . . . .12 C4
Parliament Hill Sch
NW5 . . . . .12 C3
Parliament Mews
SW14 . . . . .45 B1
Parliament Sq*
SW1 . . . .**134** A3
Parliament St
SW1 . . . .**134** A4
**Parliament View
Apartments**
SE11 . . . .**148** C4
Parma Cres SW11 . . .60 B3
Parminter Ind Est 3
E2 . . . . .25 A3
Parmiter St E2 . . . . . .25 A3
Parmoor Ct EC1 . . . .**96** C2
Parnell Cl W12 . . . . .39 A3
Parnell Ho WC1 . . . .**105** C2
Parnell Rd E3 . . . . . .26 B4
Parnham St E14 . . . . .33 A3
Parolles Rd N19 . . . .4 B3
Parr Ct N1 . . . . .87 B2
Parrington Ho 1
SW4 . . . . .61 C1
Parr PI W4 . . . . .38 B2
Parr St N1 . . . . .87 B2
Parry Ho 32 E1 . . . . .32 A1
Parry Rd W10 . . . . . .23 A2
Parry St SW8 . . . . . .**162** B4
Parsifal Coll 1
NW3 . . . . .10 C4
Parsifal Ho NW3 . . . .10 C4
Parsifal Rd NW6 . . . .10 C3
Parsonage St E14 . . .42 B2
Parsons Gn SW6 . . . .**165** B3
**PARSONS
GREEN** **165** B4
Parsons Green La
SW6 . . . .**165** B4
Parsons Green Sta
SW6 . . . .**165** B3

Parsons Ho
Paddington W2 . . . . .**89** B1
21 Streatham SW12 . .74 A4
Parsons Lo NW6 . . . .11 A1
Parthenia Rd
SW6 . . . .**165** C3
Partington Cl N19 . . .4 C3
Parton Lo 6 E8 . . . . .16 B2
Partridge Ct EC1 . . .**96** A2
Partridge Ho 22
E3 . . . . .26 B3
Pascall Ho SE17 . . . .48 B4
Pascal St SW8 . . . . .**161** C2
Pascoe Rd SE13 . . . .67 C2
Pasley Cl SE17 . . . . .**150** C1
Passfield Dr E14 . . . .34 A4
Passfields W14 . . . .**140** C1
Passing Alley EC1 . . .**96** B1
Passmore St SW1 . . .**145** B3
Pastor St SE1,
SE11 . . . .**150** B4
Patcham Terr
SW8 . . . .**170** B4
Patent Ho E14 . . . . . .34 A4
Paternoster La
EC4 . . . .**108** B2
Paternoster Sq
EC4 . . . .**108** B2
Pater St W8 . . . .**127** B1
Patience Rd
SW11 . . . .**168** A1
Patience Villas
SE13 . . . . .67 C4
Patio Cl SW4 . . . . . .61 C1
Patmore Ho 6
N16 . . . . .16 A3
Patmore St SW8 . . .**171** A4
Patmos Rd SW9 . . . .48 A2
Paton Cl E3 . . . . .26 C2
Paton Ho 2 SW9 . . .**172** C2
Paton St EC1 . . . .**96** A3
Patrick Coman Ho
EC1 . . . .**96** A3
Patrick Connolly Gdns
4 E3 . . . . .27 A2
Patriot Sq E2 . . . . . . .25 A3
Patrol PI SE6 . . . . . . .67 A1
Pat Shaw Ho 2
E1 . . . . .25 C1
Patshull PI NW5 . . . .13 B2
Patshull Rd NW5 . . . .13 B2
Patten Ho N4 . . . . . . .6 B3
Patten Rd SW18 . . . .72 A4
Patterdale NW1 . . . . .**92** B3
Patterdale Rd
SE15 . . . . .50 B3
Pattina Wlk SE16 . . . .33 A1
Pattinson Point 10
E16 . . . . .35 C4
Pattison Ho
Borough The SE1 . . .**137** A4
1 Stepney E1 . . . . . .32 C3
Pattison Rd NW2 . . . .1 C1
Pat Williams Ho
SE27 . . . . .75 B1
Paul Daisley Ct 2
NW6 . . . . .10 A1
Paulet Rd SE5 . . . . . .48 B2
Pauline Ho 21 E1 . . .**111** C4
Paul Julius Cl E14 . . .34 C2
Paul St EC2 . . . . .24 A1 **98** A2
Paultons Ho SW3 . . .**157** C4
Paultons Sq SW3 . . .**157** C4
Paultons St SW3 . . .**157** C3
Pauntley Ho 6 N19 . .4 B3

Pauntley St 4 N19 . . .4 B3
Pavan Ct 25 E2 . . . . .25 B2
Paveley Dr SW11 . . .**158** A1
Paveley Ho N1 . . . . . .**84** C1
Paveley St NW8 . . . . .**90** B2
Pavement The
Brentford W5 . . . . . . .36 A3
Clapham SW4 . . . . . . .61 B3
Pavilion Ct
7 Hampstead
NW3 . . . . .11 B4
Hampstead NW3 . . . .11 A4
3 Paddington NW6 . .23 C2
Pavilion Mans 10
SW9 . . . . .62 B3
Pavilion Rd SW1 . . .**131** A1
Pavilion Sq SW17 . . .72 B1
Pavilion St SW1 . . . .**131** A1
Pavilion Terr 8
W12 . . . . .30 B3
Pavillion Ct SW1 . . .**160** A4
Pavitt Ct NW10 . . . . .8 C1
Paxton Cl TW9 . . . . .44 B1
Paxton Ho SE17 . . . .**151** A2
Paxton Rd W4 . . . . . .46 A4
Paymal Ho 88 E1 . . .32 B4
Payne Ho N1 . . . .**85** A3
Payne Rd E3 . . . . . . .27 A3
Paynesfield Ave
SW14 . . . . .55 C4
Payne St SE8 . . . . . . .51 B4
Paynes Wlk W6 . . . .**154** A3
Peabody Ave
SW1 . . . .**146** B1
Peabody Bldgs
6 Camberwell
SE5 . . . . .48 C2
Walworth SE17 . . . .**151** B3
Peabody Cl SE1 . . . .**160** B4
Peabody Ct
9 Camberwell
SE5 . . . . .48 C2
St Luke's EC1 . . . . . .**97** A1
Peabody Est
18 Bethnal Green
E2 . . . . .25 A3
Borough The SE1 . . .**122** C1
Fulham SW6 . . . . . .**155** A4
17 Hammersmith
W6 . . . . .39 B1
Holborn EC1 . . . .**95** C1
Lambeth SE1 . . . . . .**121** C1
North Kensington
W10 . . . . .30 B4
4 Ratcliff E1 . . . . . . .32 C2
7 St George in East
E1 . . . .**125** B4
St Luke's EC1 . . . . . .**97** A1
Strand WC2 . . . .**106** C1
Streatham SE24 . . . .75 B4
Westminster SW1 . . .**147** A4
Peabody Hill SE21 . . .75 B3
Peabody Sq SE1 . . . .**136** A3
Peabody Twr EC1 . . .**97** A1
Peabody Yd N1 . . . . .**86** C4
Peace Pagoda*
SW3 . . . .**159** A2
Peach Rd W10 . . . . . .23 A2
Peachum Rd SE3 . . . .53 B4
Peach Walk Mews 24
E3 . . . . .25 C3
Peacock St SE17 . . . .**150** B3
Peacock Yd SE17 . . . .**150** B3
Peak Ho N4 . . . . .6 B3

Pearce Ho
Camden Town N19 . . .4 B1
7 Streatham SW2 . . .74 A4
Westminster N1 . . . .**147** C3
Pear Cl SE14 . . . . . . .51 A3
Pear Ct 3 SE15 . . . . .49 B3
Peardon St SW8 . . . .**170** B1
Pearfield Ho 1
N5 . . . . .15 B3
Pearl St E1 . . . . .32 A1
Pearmain Ho 9
SE13 . . . . .52 B1
Pearman St SE1 . . . .**135** C3
Pear PI SE1 . . . .**135** B4
Pearscroft Rd
SW6 . . . .**166** B3
Pearse St 3 SE15 . . .49 A4
Pearson Cl 4 SE5 . . .48 B2
Pearson Ho SW15 . . .47 B1
Pearson's Ave SE8,
SE14 . . . . .51 C2
Pearson St E2 . . . . . .24 B3
Peartree Ave
SW17 . . . . .71 B1
Pear Tree Cl 23
E2 . . . . .24 B4
Pear Tree Ct
Holborn EC1 . . . .**95** C1
Putney SW15 . . . . . . .57 A3
Pear Tree Ho SE4 . . .66 B3
Peartree La E1 . . . . . .32 B2
Peartree St EC1 . . . . .**96** C2
Peartree Way
SE10 . . . . .43 C2
Peary PI 2 E2 . . . . . .25 B2
Peckarmans Wood
SE21, SE26 . . . . .75 C1
Peckett Sq 3 N5 . . . .15 A4
Peckford PI SW9 . . .**173** C1
PECKHAM 49 C2
Peckham Gr SE15 . . .49 A3
Peckham High St
SE15 . . . . .49 C2
Peckham Hill St
SE15 . . . . .49 C3
Peckham Park Prim
Sch 28 SE15 . . . . . . .49 C3
Peckham Park Rd
SE15 . . . . .49 C3
Peckham Rd SE5 . . . .49 A2
Peckham Rye
East Dulwich SE22 . . .64 C3
Peckham SE15,
SE22 . . . . .65 A3
Peckham Rye Sta
SE15 . . . . .49 C1
Peckwater Ho 2
NW5 . . . . .13 C2
Peckwater St NW5 . . .13 B3
Pedlars Wlk N7 . . . . .14 A3
Pedley St E1 . . . . . . .24 B1 **99** A1
Pedro St E5 . . . . .17 C4
Pedworth Gdns 4
SE16 . . . . .40 B2
Peel Gr E2 . . . . .25 B3
Peel Pass
W8 . . . . .31 C1 **113** B1
Peel Prec NW6 . . . . .23 C3
Peel Wlk 1 W8 . .31 C1 **113** B1
Peerless St EC1 . . . . .**97** B3
Pegasus Cl N16 . . . . .15 C4

Pegasus Ct
11 Acton W3 . . . . .28 B3
Brentford TW8 . . . . . . .36 B1
College Pk NW10 . . . . .22 A2
Pegasus Ho 9 E15 . . . .76 A3
Pegwell Ho 10 E5 . . . .17 A3
Pekin Cl E14 . . . . .33 C3
Pekoe SE1 . . . . .125 A1
Peldon Ct TW10 . . . . . .54 B2
Pelham Cl SE5 . . . . . . .49 A1
Pelham Cres SW7 . **144** A3
Pelham Ct SW3 . . . . .144 A3
Pelham Ho W14 . . . .140 C3
Pelham Pl SW7 . . . . .144 A3
Pelham Wlk SW7 . . . .143 C4
Pelican Ho 8 SE8 . .41 B2
Pelican Pas 3 E1 . . .25 B1
Pelier St SE17 . . . . .48 B4
Pella Ho SE11 . . . . . .149 A2
Pellant Rd SW6 . . . . .154 B2
Pellatt Rd SE22 . . . . . .64 B2
Pellerin Rd N16 . . . . . .16 A3
Pellew Ho 15 E1 . . . . .25 A1
Pelling St E14 . . . . .33 C3
Pelter St E2 . . . .24 B2 98 C4
Pelton Rd SE10 . . . . . . .43 A1
Pember Rd NW10 . . . . .22 C2
Pemberton Ct 18
E1 . . . . .25 C2
Pemberton Gdns
N19 . . . . .4 B1
Pemberton Pl 2
E8 . . . . .17 A1
Pemberton Row
EC4 . . . . .107 C2
Pemberton Terr
N19 . . . . .4 B1
Pembridge Cres
W11 . . . . .31 C2 113 B4
Pembridge Gdns
W2 . . . . . .31 C2 113 C3
Pembridge Hall Prep
Sch for Girls
W2 . . . . . .31 C2 113 C3
Pembridge Mews
W11 . . . . .31 C2 113 B4
Pembridge Pl
Notting Hill
W2 . . . . . .31 C2 113 C4
1 Wandsworth
SW11 . . . . .58 C2
Pembridge Rd
W11 . . . . .31 C2 113 C3
Pembridge Sq
W2 . . . . . .31 C2 113 C3
Pembridge Villas
W11 . . . . .31 C2 113 B4
Pembroke W14 . . . .141 A3
Pembroke Ave N1 . . .84 B4
Pembroke Bldgs
NW10 . . . . .21 C2
Pembroke Cl
SW1 . . . . .131 C3
Pembroke Gdns
W8 . . . . .141 A4
Pembroke Gdns Cl
W8 . . . . .127 B1
Pembroke Ho
Acton W3 . . . . .37 B4
Chelsea SW1 . . . . . . .145 A4
5 Clapham Pk SW2 . .62 A2
17 Kensington W2 . .100 B1
Putney SW15 . . . . .56 C2

Pembroke Lo 2
SW16 . . . . .74 B1
Pembroke Mews
6 Bow E3 . . . . .26 A2
Kensington W8 . . . . . .127 B1
Pembroke Pl W8 . . . .127 B1
Pembroke Rd W8 . **141** B4
Pembroke Sq W8 . . .127 B1
Pembroke St N1 . . . . .84 B4
Pembroke Studios
W8 . . . . .127 A1
Pembroke Terr
NW8 . . . . .79 B3
Pembroke Villas
W8 . . . . .141 B4
Pembroke Wlk
W8 . . . . .141 B4
Pembury Cl E5 . . . . . . .17 A3
Pembury Ho SE5 . . . . .49 A1
Pembury Pl 16 E5,
E8 . . . . .17 A3
Pembury Rd E5 . . . . . . .17 A3
Pemell Cl 30 E1 . . . . . .25 B1
Pemell Ho 31 E1 . . . . .25 B1
Penally Pl N1 . . . . .87 C4
Penang St E1 . . . . .32 A1
Penarth Ctr The
SE15 . . . . .50 B4
Penarth St SE15 . . . . . .50 B4
Pencombe Mews
W11 . . . . . .31 B2 113 A4
Pencraig Way
SE15 . . . . .50 A4
Penda's Mead E9 . . . . .18 A4
Pendennis Ho 15
SE8 . . . . .41 A2
Penderyn Way N7 . . . .13 C4
Pendle Ho 18
SE26 . . . . .76 C1
Pendley Ho 18 E2 . .24 C4
Pendrell Ho WC2 . . .105 C1
Pendrell Rd SE4 . . . . . .51 A1
Penelope Ho 20
SW9 . . . . .173 B3
Penfield Lo 7 W9 . . .31 C4
Penfields Ho N7 . . . . . .14 A2
Penford Pl NW1 . . . .102 A4
Penford St NW8 . . . . .89 C1
Penford St SE5 . . . . . . .48 A1
Penhurst Mans
SW6 . . . . .164 C4
Peninsula Ct E14 . . . . .42 A3
Peninsular Park Rd
SE7 . . . . .43 C2
Penmayne Ho
SE11 . . . . .149 C2
Penn Almshouses 1
SE10 . . . . .52 B2
Pennant Mews
W8 . . . . .142 A4
Pennard Mans 8
W12 . . . . .39 B4
Pennard Rd W12 . . . . .39 B4
Pennethorne Ho
N11 . . . . .15 C2
Penner Cl SW19 . . . . . .70 A2
Pennethorne Cl
E9 . . . . .25 B4
Pennethorne Ho
SW11 . . . . .59 C4
Pennethorne Rd
SE15 . . . . .50 A3
Penn Ho NW8 . . . . .90 A1
Pennine Ho NW2 . . . . .1 A2
Pennine Mans NW2 . .1 A2

Pennine Par NW2 . . .1 A2
Pennington Ct
4 Rotherhithe
SE16 . . . . .33 A1
22 St George in t East
E1 . . . . .125 C2
Pennington St E1 . . .125 C3
Penn Rd N7 . . . . .14 A4
Penn St N1 . . . . .87 C3
Penny Ct SW10 . . . . .157 A4
Pennyfields E14 . . . . . .33 C2
Pennyford Ct NW8 . .89 B2
Penny Mews
SW12 . . . . .73 A4
Pennymore Wlk
W9 . . . . .23 B1
Penny Rd NW10 . . . . .20 A2
Penpoll Rd E8 . . . . .17 A2
Penrhyn Cres
SW14 . . . . .55 B3
Penrith Cl SW15 . . . . . .58 A2
Penrith Pl SE27 . . . . . .75 A2
Penrose Gr SE17 . . .150 C1
Penrose Ho SE17 . . .150 C1
Penrose Rd SE17 . . .150 C1
Penrose St SE17 . . . .150 C2
Penryn Ho SE11 . . . .150 A2
Penryn St NW1 . . . . . .83 B2
Penry St SE1 . . . . . . .152 B3
Pensbury Pl SW8 . . .171 A2
Pensbury St SW8 . . .171 A2
Pensford Ave TW9 . . .44 C1
Penshurst 2 NW5 . .12 C2
Penshurst Ho 1
SE15 . . . . .50 B4
Penshurst Rd E9 . . . . .17 C1
Pentland Cl NW11 . . . .1 A2
Pentland Gdns
SW18 . . . . .59 B1
Pentland Ho
7 Camden Town
NW5 . . . . .12 C2
2 Stamford Hill N16 . .7 B3
Pentland Rd 1
NW6 . . . . .23 C2
Pentland St SW18 . . .59 B1
Pentlow St SW15 . . . .57 B4
Pentney Rd SW12 . . . .73 B3
Penton Gr N1 . . . . .85 B1
Penton Ho N1 . . . . .85 B1
Penton Pl SE17 . . . . .150 C2
Penton Rise WC1 . . . .95 A4
Penton St N1 . . . . .85 B1
PENTONVILLE 85 A1
Pentonville Rd
WC1 . . . . .84 C1
Pentridge St SE15 . . .49 B3
Penwith Rd SW18 . . .71 A2
Penwood Ho 6
SW15 . . . . .56 B1
Penywern Rd
SW5 . . . . .141 C2
Penzance Ho
SE11 . . . . .149 C2
Penzance Pl W11 . . . .31 A1 112 B2
Penzance St
W11 . . . . . .31 A1 112 B2
Peony Gdns W12 . . . . .29 C2
Peperfield WC1 . . . . . .94 C3
Pepler Ho 17 W10 . .23 A1
Pepler Mews SE1 . . .152 C1
Peploe Rd NW6 . . . . . .22 C3
Peppermead Sq
SE13 . . . . .66 C2
Pepper St
Borough The SE1 . . .136 C4

Pepper St continued
Millwall E14 . . . . .42 A3
Peppie CE14 . . . . .42 A2
Pepys Cres 2 E16 . .35 C1
Pepys Ent Ctr 13
SE8 . . . . .41 B2
Pepys Ho
14 Bethnal Green
E2 . . . . .25 B2
Clapham Pk SW4 . . . .61 C2
Pepys Rd SE14 . . . . . .50 C1
Pepys St EC3 . . . . . .124 B4
Perceval Ave NW3 . .12 A3
Percheron Ct 3
SW9 . . . . .62 B4
Perch St E8 . . . . .16 B4
Percival Rd SW14 . . . .55 B3
Percival St EC1 . . . . . .96 B3
Percy Cir WC1 . . . . . . .95 A4
Percy Laurie Ho 4
SW15 . . . . .57 C3
Percy Mews W1 . . . .105 B3
Percy Pas W1 . . . . . .105 B3
Percy Rd
Newham E16 . . . . .35 A4
Shepherd's Bush
W12 . . . . .38 C4
Percy St W1 . . . . . . .105 B3
Peregrine Ho
6 Battersea
SW11 . . . . .60 A4
Finsbury EC1 . . . . .96 B4
Perham Rd W14 . . . .140 B1
Perifield SE21 . . . . .75 B3
Perkins Ho 18 E14 . .33 B4
Perkins Rents
SW1 . . . . .133 B1
Perkins Sq SE1 . . . . .123 A2
Perley Ho 9 E3 . . . .33 B4
Perotti Ho SW6 . . . . . .59 A4
Perran Rd SW2 SE24,
. . . .
Perren St NW5 . . . . . .13 A2
Perrers Rd W6 . . . . . . .39 A2
Perring Est E3 . . . . . . .33 C4
Perrin's Ct 20 NW3 .11 B4
Perrin's La NW3 . . . . .11 B4
Perrin's Wlk NW3 . . .11 B4
Perronet Ho SE1 . . . .136 B1
Perry Ave W3 . . . . . . .28 C3
Perry Ct 6 E14 . . . . . .41 C1
Perry Ho 24 SW2 . . . .74 A4
Perrymead St
SW6 . . . . .166 A3
Perryn Ho W3 . . . . .29 A2
Perryn Rd
Acton W3 . . . . .28 C2
1 Bermondsey
SE16 . . . . .40 A3
Perry's Pl W1 . . . . . .105 B2
Perrywood Ho 17
E5 . . . . .17 A3
Perseverance Works
17 E2 . . . . .24 A2 98 B4
Perth Ct 5 SE5 . . . . . .63 C3
Perth Ho N1 . . . . .14 B1
Perth Rd N4 . . . . .5 C3
Petchey Acad The
. . . .
Peter Ave NW10 . . . . . .9 A1
Peter Best Ho 1
E1 . . . . .32 A3
Peterboat Cl SE10 . . .43 A2
Peterborough Ct
EC4 . . . . .107 C1

Peterborough Mews
SW6 . . . . .165 B2
Peterborough Rd
SW6 . . . . .58 C4
Peterborough Villas
SW6 . . . . .166 A4
Peter Butler Ho 9
SE1 . . . . .139 B3
Peterchurch Ho
SE15 . . . . .50 A4
Petergate SW11 . . . . . .59 B3
Peter Heathfield Ho
4 E15 . . . . .27 C4
Peter Hills Ho 6
SE16 . . . . .153 B4
Peter Hills Sch 42
. . . . .33 C1
Peter Ho SW8 . . . . . .162 A2
Peter James Ent Ctr
NW10 . . . . .20 B2
Peterley Bsns Ctr 41
E2 . . . . .25 A3
Peters Ct 9 W2 . . . .100 B2
Peter's Ct SW4 . . . . . .62 A1
Petersfield Rd W3 . . . .37 B4
Petersfield Rise
SW15 . . . . .69 A3
Petersham Ho
SW7 . . . . .143 B4
Petersham La
SW7 . . . . .128 C2
Petersham Mews
SW7 . . . . .129 A1
Petersham Pl
SW7 . . . . .129 A2
Peter's La EC1 . . . . . .108 B4
Peter St W1 . . . . .119 B4
Peterstow Cl
SW19 . . . . .70 A2
Petherton Ct
NW10 . . . . .22 C4
Petherton Ho N4 . . . . . .6 B3
Petherton Rd N5 . . . . .15 B3
Petiver Cl 26 E9 . . . .17 B1
Petley Rd W6 . . . . .47 C3
Peto Pl NW1 . . . . .92 B2
Peto St N E16 . . . . .35 B3
Petrel Ct 8 SE21 . . . .75 C2
Petrie Ho NW2 . . . . . . .10 A2
Petrie Mus of
Egyptian
Archaeology★
WC1 . . . . .93 B1
Petros Gdns 1
NW3 . . . . .11 B2
Petticoat Lane Mkt★
EC2 . . . . .110 C3
Petticoat Sq E1 . . . . .110 C2
Petticoat Twr E1 . . . .110 C2
Pettiward Cl SW15 . . .57 B3
Petty France SW1 . . .133 A2
Petty Wales EC3 . . . .124 B3
Petworth Ho 18
SE22 . . . . .64 A4
Petworth St
SW11 . . . . .168 B4
Petyt Pl SW3 . . . . . .158 A3
Petyward SW3 . . . . . .144 B3
Pevensey Ct
4 South Acton
W3 . . . . .37 A4
West Norwood
SW16 . . . . .74 C1
Pevensey Ho 5
E1 . . . . .33 A4
Peveril Ho SE1 . . . .137 C1

Pewsham Ho N4 ..... 6 B3
Peyton Pl SE10 ..... 52 B3
Pharamond N4 ..... 9 C2
Phelps Ho **11**
SW15 ..... 57 C4
Phelp St SE17 ..... 48 C4
Phene St SW3 ..... 158 B4
Philadelphia Ct
SW10 ..... 157 A1
Philbeach Gdns
SW5 ..... 141 B2
Phil Brown Pl **3**
SW8 ..... 61 A4
Philchurch Pl **30**
E1 ..... 111 C1
Philia Ho **4** NW1 ..... 13 B1
Philip Blairman Ho
E1 ..... 24 B1 98 C1
Philip Ct W2 ..... 101 B4
Philip Ho **5** NW6 ..... 78 A3
Philip Turner Est **26**
E9 ..... 17 B1
Philip Wlk SE15 ..... 64 C4
Phillimore Ct W8 ..... 127 C3
Phillimore Gardens Cl **1**
W8 ..... 127 B2
Phillimore Gdns
Kensington W8 ..... 127 B3
Willesden NW10 ..... 22 B4
Phillimore Pl W8 ..... 127 B3
Phillimore Terr
W8 ..... 127 C2
Phillimore Wlk
W8 ..... 127 C2
Phillip Ho E1 ..... 111 A3
Phillipp St N1 ..... 24 A4
Philpot La EC3 ..... 124 A4
Philpot Sq SW6 ..... 59 A4
Philpot St E1 ..... 32 A3
Philsom Mans **6**
E1 ..... 111 C2
Phipps Ho **10** W12 ..... 30 A2
Phipp St
EC2 ..... 24 A1 98 A2
Phoebeth Rd SE4 ..... 66 C2
Phoenix Bsns Ctr **22**
E3 ..... 33 C4
Phoenix Cl **3** E8 ..... 24 B4
Phoenix Ct
4 Brentford TW8 ..... 36 A1
2 Deptford SE14 ..... 51 A4
Millwall E14 ..... 41 C2
Phoenix High Sch
W12 ..... 29 C3
Phoenix Ho SW1 ..... 145 B4
Phoenix Lodge Mans
1 W6 ..... 39 B2
Phoenix Pl WC1 ..... 95 A2
Phoenix Rd NW1 ..... 93 B4
Phoenix Sch The **12**
NW3 ..... 11 B2
Phoenix Sec & Prim
Sch **32** E3 ..... 26 B2
Phoenix St WC2 ..... 105 C1
Phoenix Wharf Rd
SE1 ..... 139 A3
Phyllis Hodges Ho
NW1 ..... 83 B1
Physic Pl SW3 ..... 158 C4
Piccadilly W1 ..... 118 C2
Piccadilly Arc
SW1 ..... 118 C2
Piccadilly Cir*
W1 ..... 119 B3
Piccadilly Circus Sta
SW1 ..... 119 B3

Piccadilly Ct **5**
N7 ..... 14 B2
Piccadilly Pl W1 ..... 119 A3
Pickard St EC1 ..... 96 B4
Pickering Cl E9 ..... 17 C1
Pickering Ho
8 Kensington
W2 ..... 100 B1
Stoke Newington N4 ..... 6 C4
Pickering Mews **7**
W2 ..... 100 B2
Pickering Pl SW1 ..... 119 A1
Pickering St N1 ..... 86 B4
Pickets St SW12 ..... 73 A4
Pickfords Wharf
N1 ..... 86 C1
Pickwick Ho
27 Bermondsey
SE16 ..... 139 B3
3 Shepherd's Bush
W11 ..... 30 C1
Pickwick Rd SE21 ..... 76 A4
Pickwick St SE1 ..... 136 C3
Pickworth Cl
SW8 ..... 162 B1
Picton Ho **1** SW4 ..... 74 A4
Picton Pl W1 ..... 103 C1
Picton St SE5 ..... 48 C3
Picture Ho **8**
SW16 ..... 74 A3
Pied Bull Ct WC1 ..... 106 B3
Pied Bull Yd WC1 ..... 106 B3
Pier Head E1 ..... 32 A1
Pierhead Wharf **37**
E1 ..... 32 A1
Pier Ho SW3 ..... 158 B3
Piermont Rd SE22 ..... 65 A2
Pierpoint Bldg **4**
E14 ..... 41 C4
Pierrepoint Rd
W3 ..... 28 A2
Pierrepoint Row
N1 ..... 86 A2
Pier St E14 ..... 42 B2
Pier Terr SW18 ..... 59 B3
Piggott Ho **2** E2 ..... 25 C3
Pigott St E14 ..... 33 C3
Pilgrimage St
SE1 ..... 137 B3
Pilgrim Ho SE1 ..... 137 B1
Pilgrims Cloisters **10**
SE5 ..... 49 A3
Pilgrims Ct SE3 ..... 53 C2
Pilgrim's La NW3 ..... 11 C4
Pilgrims Mews **12**
E14 ..... 34 C2
Pilgrim's Pl **6**
NW3 ..... 11 C4
Pilgrim St EC4 ..... 108 A1
Pilgrims Way N19 ..... 4 C3
Pilgrims Way Prim
Sch **22** SE15 ..... 50 B4
Pilkington Rd **4**
SE15 ..... 50 A1
Pilot Ind Ctr NW10 ..... 21 A1
Pilsden Cl SW19 ..... 69 C3
Pilton Pl SE17 ..... 151 A2
Pimlico Sta SW1 ..... 147 B2
PIMLICO 146 C1
Pimlico Acad
SW1 ..... 147 A1
Pimlico Sch SW1 ..... 145 C2
Pimlico Wlk **1**
N1 ..... 24 A2 98 A4
Pinchin St E1 ..... 125 C4

Pincombe Ho
SE17 ..... 151 B2
Pincott Pl SE4 ..... 65 C4
Pindar St EC2 ..... 110 A4
Pindock Mews W9 ..... 88 B1
Pine Apple Ct
SW1 ..... 132 C2
Pine Ave E15 ..... 19 C3
Pine Cl **1** N19 ..... 4 B2
Pinedene **8** SE15 ..... 50 A2
Pinefield Cl E14 ..... 33 C2
Pine Gr N4, N19 ..... 5 B2
Pine Ho
Bow E3 ..... 26 A4
21 Rotherhithe
SE16 ..... 40 B4
Pinehurst Ct **6**
W11 ..... 31 B3
Pinelands **7**
E2 ..... 53 B3
Pine Lo SW15 ..... 58 A1
Pine Rd NW2 ..... 9 C4
Pines Ct E14 ..... 41 C3
Pine St EC1 ..... 95 B2
Pine Tree Ho SE14 ..... 50 C3
Pine Tree Way **1**
SE13 ..... 67 A4
Pinewood Ct SW4 ..... 61 C1
Pinkham Mans
W4 ..... 36 C1
Pinnace Ho E14 ..... 42 B3
Pinnacle Ho EC3 ..... 124 A3
Pinnacle The **7**
N1 ..... 15 C2
Pinner Ct NW8 ..... 89 B2
Pinner Ho **30** SE5 ..... 48 B1
Pintail Ct **8** SE8 ..... 51 B4
Pinter Ho **30** SW9 ..... 172 B1
Pioneer Cl
10 Bow Common E14 ..... 34 A4
London W12 ..... 30 A3
Pioneer St SE15 ..... 49 C2
Pioneer Way W12 ..... 30 B3
Piper Cl N7 ..... 14 B3
Pipers Ho SE10 ..... 42 C1
Pippin Ho **17** W10 ..... 30 C2
Pirate Castle The*
NW1 ..... 13 C1
Pirbright Rd SW18 ..... 70 C3
Pitcairn Ho **1** E9 ..... 17 B1
Pitfield Ho N5 ..... 15 B3
Pitfield St N1 ..... 24 A3
Pitman Ho **4** SE8 ..... 51 C2
Pitman St SE5 ..... 48 B3
Pitmaston Ho **2**
SE13 ..... 52 B1
Pitsea Pl E1 ..... 32 C3
Pitsea St E1 ..... 32 C3
Pitt Ho **4** SW11 ..... 59 C3
Pitt's Head Mews
W1 ..... 117 C1
Pitt St W8 ..... 127 C4
Pixley St E14 ..... 33 B3
Planetree Ct W6 ..... 39 C2
Plane Tree Ho
SE14 ..... 50 B3
Plantain Pl SE1 ..... 137 B4
Plantation La EC3 ..... 124 A4
Plantation The
SE3 ..... 53 C1
Platehouse The **3**
E14 ..... 42 A1
Platina St EC2 ..... 97 C2
Plato Pl **1** SW6 ..... 165 A2
Plato Rd SW2 ..... 62 A3
Platt's La NW3 ..... 1 C1

Platt St NW1 ..... 83 B2
Plaxdale Ho SE17 ..... 152 A1
Playfair St W6 ..... 39 B1
Playfield Cres
SE22 ..... 64 B2
Playford Rd
Finsbury Pk N4 ..... 5 B2
Finsbury Pk N4 ..... 5 C2
Playhouse Yd EC4 ..... 108 A1
Plaza Sh Ctr W1 ..... 105 A2
Pleasance Rd
SW15 ..... 57 A2
Pleasance The
SW15 ..... 57 A3
Pleasant Pl N1 ..... 15 A1
Pleasant Row NW1 ..... 82 B3
Plender St NW1 ..... 83 A3
Plender St NW1 ..... 83 A3
Pleshey Rd N7 ..... 13 C4
Plevna St E14 ..... 42 B3
Pleydell Ave W6 ..... 38 B2
Pleydell Ct EC4 ..... 107 C1
Pleydell St EC4 ..... 107 C1
Plimsoll Cl E14 ..... 34 A3
Plimsoll Rd N4 ..... 6 A1
Plough Cl EC3 ..... 123 C4
Plough La SE22 ..... 64 B1
Ploughmans Cl
NW1 ..... 83 B4
Plough Mews **3**
SW11 ..... 59 C3
Plough Pl EC4 ..... 107 C2
Plough Rd SW11 ..... 59 C3
Plough St **16** E1 ..... 111 B2
Plough Terr SW11 ..... 59 C3
Plough Way SE16 ..... 41 A2
Plough Yd
EC2 ..... 24 A1 98 B1
Plover Ho **4** SW9 ..... 163 B2
Plover Way SE16 ..... 41 A3
Plowman Ho
SW19 ..... 69 C2
Plumbers Row E1 ..... 111 C2
Plumbridge St **7**
SE10 ..... 52 B2
Plume Ho SE10 ..... 52 A4
Plummer Ct SE13 ..... 67 A1
Plummer Rd SW4 ..... 73 C4
Plumtree Ct EC4 ..... 108 A2
Plymouth Ho **20**
SE10 ..... 52 A2
Plymouth Rd E16 ..... 35 C4
Plymouth Wharf
E14 ..... 42 C2
Plympton Ave
NW6 ..... 10 B1
Plympton Pl NW1 ..... 90 A1
Plympton Rd NW6 ..... 10 B1
Plympton St NW8 ..... 90 A1
Pocklington Ct
SW15 ..... 68 C3
Pocklington Lo **6**
W12 ..... 38 C3
Pocock St SE1 ..... 136 B4
Podmore Rd SW18 ..... 59 B3
Poets Cnr* SW1 ..... 134 A2
Poets Mews **8**
SE24 ..... 63 A2
Poet's Rd N5 ..... 15 C3
Point Cl SE10 ..... 52 B2
Pointer Sch The
SE3 ..... 53 C3
Pointers Cl E14 ..... 42 A1
Point Hill SE10 ..... 52 B2
Point Ho SE10 ..... 52 B2

Point Pleasant
SW18 ..... 58 C3
Point Wharf La
TW8 ..... 44 A3
Poland Ho **3** E15 ..... 27 C4
Poland St W1 ..... 105 A1
Polesworth Ho **4**
W2 ..... 31 C4
Polish Inst & Sikorski
Mus* SW7 ..... 129 C3
Polish Univ Abroad **18**
W6 ..... 38 C2
Pollard Cl
Islington N7 ..... 14 B4
Newham E16 ..... 35 C2
Pollard Ho N1 ..... 84 C1
Pollard Row
E2 ..... 24 C2 99 C4
Pollard St
E2 ..... 24 C2 99 C4
Pollen St W1 ..... 104 B1
Pollitt Dr NW8 ..... 89 C2
Pollock Ho W10 ..... 23 A1
Pollock's Toy Mus*
W1 ..... 105 A4
Polperro Mans **3**
NW6 ..... 10 C3
Polperro Mews
SE11 ..... 150 A4
Polygon Rd NW1 ..... 83 B1
Polygon The
1 Clapham SW4 ..... 61 B3
St John's Wood
NW8 ..... 79 C4
Pomell Way E1 ..... 111 A2
Pomeroy Ct W11 ..... 31 A3
Pomeroy Ho **8**
E2 ..... 25 C3
Pomeroy St SE15 ..... 50 B2
Pomfret Rd SE5 ..... 63 A4
Pomoja La N19 ..... 5 A2
Pomona Ho **6**
SE8 ..... 41 A2
Pond Cl SE3 ..... 53 C1
Pond Cotts SE21 ..... 76 A3
Ponder St **5** N7 ..... 14 B1
Pondfield Ho **4**
N5 ..... 15 B3
Pond Ho SW3 ..... 144 A3
Pond Mead SE21 ..... 63 C1
Pond Pl SW3 ..... 144 A3
Pond Rd SE3 ..... 53 B1
Pond Sq N6 ..... 3 C3
Pond St NW3 ..... 12 A3
Ponler St E1 ..... 32 A3
Ponsard Rd NW10 ..... 22 A2
Ponsford St E9 ..... 17 B2
Ponsonby Ho **13**
E2 ..... 25 B3
Ponsonby Pl SW1 ..... 147 C2
Ponsonby Rd
SW15 ..... 69 A4
Ponsonby Terr
SW1 ..... 147 C2
Ponton Ho SW2 ..... 74 C3
Ponton Rd SW8 ..... 161 C3
Pont St Mews
SW1 ..... 130 C1
Pont St SW1 ..... 131 A1
Pontypool Pl SE1 ..... 136 A4
Poole Ho SE11 ..... 135 A1
Poole Rd E9 ..... 17 C2
Pooles Bldgs EC1 ..... 95 B1

Pooles La SW10 ... **156** C1
Pooles Park Prim Sch
🔟 N4 .... 5 B2
Pooles Pk N4 .... 5 C2
Poole St N1 .... **87** B3
Pooley Ho E1 ...... **25** C2
Pool Ho NW8 ..... **101** C4
Poolmans St SE16 .. **40** C4
Poonah St E1 ...... **32** B3
Pope Ho
🔽 Bermondsey
SE16 .... **40** A2
🔾 Camberwell SE5 .. **48** C3
Pope John Prim Sch
W12 .... **30** A2
Pope's Head Alley
EC3 .... **109** C1
Pope's La N5 .... 5 A3
Pope's Rd SW9 ..... **62** C4
Pope St SE1 .... **138** B3
Popham Ct N16 ...... 7 A1
Popham Gdns
TW9 .... 54 C4
Popham Rd N1 .... **86** C4
Popham St
Islington N1 ...... **86** B4
Shoreditch N1 .... **86** C4
POPLAR **33** C3
Poplar Bath St 🔟
E14 .... 34 A2
Poplar Bsns Pk
E14 .... 34 B2
Poplar Cl E9 .... 18 B3
Poplar Ct 🔢 SW16 .. **74** B1
Poplar Gr W6 ...... 39 B4
Poplar High St
E14 .... 34 A2
Poplar Ho
Brockley SE4 ...... 66 B3
🔟 Rotherhithe
SE16 .... 40 C4
Poplar Mews 🔾
W12 .... 30 B1
Poplar Pl W2 .... **114** B4
Poplar Rd SE24 .... 63 B3
Poplar Sta E14 ..... 34 A2
Poplars The NW5 .. 13 B3
Poplar Wlk SE24 ... 63 B3
Poppins Ct EC4 ... **108** A1
Porchester Ctw2 🔟 **100** B1
Porchester Gate
W2 .... **114** C3
Porchester Gdn Mews
W2 .... **100** B1
Porchester Gdns
W2 .... **114** B4
Porchester Ho 🔢
E1 .... 32 A3
Porchester Mews
W2 .... **100** B3
Porchester Pl W2 **102** B1
Porchester Rd
W2 .... **100** B2
Porchester Sq
W2 .... **100** B2
Porchester Terr
W2 .... **114** C4
Porchester Terr N
W2 .... **100** B2
Porden Rd SW2 .... **62** B3
Porland Ct SE1 ... **137** B2
Porlock Ho 🔢
SE26 .... 76 C1
Porlock St SE1 ... **137** C4

Porson Ct SE13 ..... **67** A4
Portal Cl SE27 .... **74** C1
Portal Way W3 .... 28 C4
Portbury Cl 🔢
SE15 .... 49 C2
Portchester Cl
SE24 .... 63 C3
Portelet Ct 🔟 N1 .. 24 A4
Portelet Rd E1 .... 25 C2
Porten Hos W14 .. **126** A1
Porten Rd W14 ... **126** A1
Porter Sq N19 ...... 5 A3
Porter St
Borough The SE1 .. **123** A2
Marylebone W1 ... **103** A4
Porteus Rd W2 ... **101** A4
Portfleet Pl 🔢 N1 .. 24 A4
Portgate Cl W9 .... 23 B1
Port Ho 🔢 SW11 .. 59 B4
Port House The 🔟
E14 .... 42 A1
Portia Way E3 ...... 26 B1
Porticos The SW3 **157** B3
Portinscale Rd
SW15 .... 58 B2
Portishead Ho 🔽
W2 .... 31 C4
Portland Ave N16 .. 7 B4
Portland Ct
🔽 De Beauvoir Town
N1 .... 16 A1
🔟 Deptford SE14 .. 51 A4
Portland Gr SW8 . **172** C4
Portland Ho 🔟
SW2 .... 74 C3
Portland Hospl for
Women & Children
The W1 .... 92 B1
Portland Mews
W1 .... **105** A1
Portland Pl W1 ... **104** B3
Portland Place Sch
W1 .... **104** B4
Portland Rd
Notting Hill
W11 .... 31 A1 **112** B3
Notting Hill
W11 .... 31 A2 **112** A3
Portland Rise N4 ... 6 B3
Portland Sq 🔢 E1 .. 32 A1
Portland St SE17 . **151** B1
Portland Village
W6 .... 39 B3
Portman Ave
SW14 .... 55 C4
Portman Cl W1 ... **103** B2
Portman Gate
NW1 .... 90 B1
Portman Hts 🔟
NW3 .... 1 C1
Portman Mews S
W1 .... **103** B1
Portman Pl E2 ...... 25 B2
Portman Sq W1 ... **103** B2
Portman St W1 ... **103** B1
Portman Twrs
W1 .... **103** A2
Portnall Rd W9 .... 23 B2
Portobello Ct Est
W11 .... 31 B3
Portobello Mews
W11 .... 31 C2 **113** B3
Portobello Rd
W11 .... 31 B2 **113** A4

Portobello Road
Mkt* W10 .... 31 A4
Portpool La EC1 .. **107** B4
Portree St E14 ..... 34 C3
Port Royal Pl 🔢
N16 .... 16 A3
Portsea Hall W2 .. **102** B1
Portsea Pl W2 ... **102** B1
Portsea Mews
W2 .... **102** B1
Portsea Pl W2 ... **102** B1
Portslade Rd
SW8 .... **170** C2
Portsmouth Rd
SW15 .... 69 A3
Portsmouth St
WC2 .... **107** A1
Portsoken St E1,
EC3 .... **124** C4
Portswood Pl
SW15 .... 56 B1
Portugal St WC2 . **107** A1
Poseidon Ct 🔢
E14 .... 41 C2
Postern The EC2 . **109** A3
Post Office Way
SW8 .... **161** B2
Potier St SE1 ..... **137** C1
Potterne Cl 🔢
SW19 .... 69 C4
Potters Cl 🔢 SE15 .. 49 A3
Potters Fields
SE1 .... **124** B1
Potters Lo E14 ..... 42 B1
Potters Rd SW6 ... **166** C1
Pottery La
W11 .... 31 A1 **112** B2
Pottery Rd TW8 .... 44 A4
Pottery St SE16 .... 40 A4
Pott St E2 .... 25 A2
Poullett Ho SW2 ... 75 A3
Poulton Cl E8 ...... 17 A2
Poultry EC2 ...... **109** B1
Pound La NW10 .... 8 C2
Pountney Rd
SW11 .... 60 C4
Povey Ho
Tulse Hill SW2 .... 62 C1
Walworth SE17 .. **152** A3
Powell's Wlk W4 .. 46 B4
Powergate Bsns Pk
NW10 .... 20 C2
Power Ho 🔟 TW9 .. 44 C2
Power Ho The W4 . 38 B2
Power Rd W4 ...... 36 C2
Powerscroft Rd
E5 .... 17 B4
Powis Gdns
Golders Green
NW11 .... 1 B4
Notting Hill W11 .. 31 B3
Powis Ho WC2 ... **106** B2
Powis Mews W11 .. 31 B3
Powis Pl WC1 .... 94 B1
Powis Rd E3 .... 27 A2
Powis Sq W11 ..... 31 B3
Powis Terr W11 .... 31 B3
Powlesland Ct 🔢
E14 .... 33 A3
Powlett Ho NW1 .. 13 A2
Powlett Pl NW1 ... 13 A1
Pownall Rd E8 ..... 24 C4
Powrie Ho 🔢
SW11 .... **167** C2
Poynder Ct 🔢 N7 . 14 A3

Poynders Ct 🔢
SW4 .... 61 B1
Poynders Gdns
SW12 .... 73 B4
Poynders Rd SW12,
SW4 .... 73 C4
Poynings Rd N19 .. 4 B1
Poynter Ho
Paddington W2 .. 89 B2
🔟 Shepherd's Bush
W11 .... 30 C1
Poyntz Rd SW11 . **168** C1
Poyser St E2 ...... 25 A3
Praed Mews W2 .. **101** C2
Praed St W2 ..... **101** C2
Prague Pl SW2 .... 62 A2
Prah Rd N4 .... 5 C2
Prairie St SW8 ... **170** A1
Pratt Mews NW1 .. 82 C3
Pratt St NW1 ..... 82 C4
Pratt Wlk SE1,
SE11 .... **149** A4
Preachers Ct EC1 . 96 B1
Prebend Gdns W4,
W6 .... 38 B2
Prebend Mans 🔢
W4 .... 38 B2
Prebend St N1 .... 86 C4
Precinct The
Islington N1 ...... 86 C3
Islington N5 ...... 15 A3
Premier Corner
NW6 .... 23 B3
Premier Ho 🔢 N1 . 15 A1
Premier Park Rd
NW10 .... 20 A3
Premier Pk NW10 . 20 A3
Premier Pl 🔢 E14 . 33 C2
Prendergarp Ho 🔽
SW4 .... 73 C4
Prendergast Ladywell
Fields Coll SE4 .. 66 C1
Prendergast Sch
SE4 .... 66 C3
Prescot St E1 .... **125** A4
Prescott Ho 🔢
SE17 .... 48 A4
Prescott Pl SW4 .. 61 C3
Presentation Mews
SW2 .... 74 B3
President Dr E1 .... 32 A1
President Ho EC1 .. 96 B3
President St EC1 .. 96 C4
Prestage Way 🔢
E14 .... 34 B2
Prested Rd SW11 .. 60 A3
Preston Cl SE1 ... **152** A4
Preston Gdns NW10 .8 A2
Preston Ho
Bermondsey SE1 . **138** C2
Walworth SE1 ... **152** A4
Preston Pl
Richmond TW10 .. 54 A2
Willesden NW2 .... 8 C2
Preston's Rd E14 .. 34 B1
Prestwich Terr
SW4 .... 61 C2
Prestwood Ho 🔢
SE16 .... 40 A3
Prestwood St N1 .. 87 A1
Priam Ho 🔢 E2 ... 25 A3
Price Cl SW17 ..... 72 B1
Price Ho N1 .... 86 C3
Prices Ct SW11 .... 59 C4
Price's St SE1 .... **122** B2
Price's Yd N1 ..... 85 A3

Prichard Ct
Battersea SW11 ... **167** C3
Islington N7 ...... 14 B3
Prideaux Ho WC1 .. 95 A4
Prideaux Pl
Acton W3 .... 28 C2
St Pancras WC1 ... 95 A4
Prideaux Rd SW9 .. 62 A4
Pride Ct N1 .... 85 C2
Priestley Cl N16 .... 7 B4
Priestley Ho
🔢 Camden Town
NW5 .... 13 A2
St Luke's EC1 ..... 97 A2
Priestman Point 🔢
E3 .... 27 A2
Priests Bridge
SW14 .... 56 A4
Priest's Ct EC2 .. **108** C2
Prima Rd SW9 ... **163** B2
Primrose Cl 🔾 E3 .. 26 C3
Primrose Ct
🔢 Child's Hill NW2 .1 B1
Primrose Hill NW8 . 80 C3
🔢 Streatham SW12 .73 C4
Primrose Gdns
NW3 .... 12 A2
PRIMROSE HILL .. 12 B1
Primrose Hill EC4 **107** C1
Primrose Hill Ct
NW3 .... 12 B1
Primrose Hill Rd NW1,
NW3 .... 12 B1
Primrose Hill Sch
NW1 .... 81 C4
Primrose Hill Studios
NW1 .... 81 B4
Primrose Ho
🔽 Peckham SE15 ..49 C2
🔢 Richmond TW9 ..44 B2
Primrose Mans
SW11 .... **169** B4
Primrose Mews 🔢
NW1 .... 12 B1
Primrose Sq E9 ... 25 B4
Primrose St EC2 . **110** B4
Primrose Wlk 🔢
SE14 .... 51 A3
Prince Of Wales Dr
SW11 .... 59 C4
Prince Albert Ct
NW8 .... 80 C3
Prince Albert Rd
NW8 .... 80 C3
Prince Arthur Ct 🔢
NW3 .... 11 B4
Prince Arthur Mews
🔢 NW3 .... 11 B4
Prince Arthur Rd
NW3 .... 11 B3
Prince Charles Rd
SE3 .... 53 B2
Prince Consort Ho
SE1 .... **148** B2
Prince Consort Rd
SW7 .... **129** B2
Princedale Rd
W11 .... 31 A1 **112** B2
Prince Edward Mans
W2 .... 31 C3 **113** C4
Prince Edward Rd
E9 .... 18 B2
Prince George Rd
N16 .... 16 A4
Princelet St E1 ... **111** A4
Prince of Orange La
🔢 SE10 .... 52 B3

Prince of Wales Dr
SW11 . . . .**169 B4**
Prince of Wales Mans
Battersea SW11 . . . . . .**169 C4**
Clapham SW4 . . . .**61 A2**
Prince of Wales Pas
NW1 . . . .**92 C3**
Prince of Wales Rd
Blackheath Vale
SE3 . . . .**53 B2**
Camden Town NW5 . .**12 C2**
Prince Of Wales Terr
Chiswick W4 . . . .**38 A1**
Kensington W8 . . . .**128 B3**
Prince Regent Ct **2**
SE16 . . . .**33 A1**
Prince Regent Mews
NW1 . . . .**92 C3**
Princes Arc SW1 . .**119 A2**
Princes Ave W3 . . . .**36 C3**
Princes Cir WC2 . . .**106 A2**
Princes Cl N4 . . . .**6 A3**
Princes Coll WC1 . .**106 A2**
Princes Court Bsns
Ctr **14** E1 . . . .**125 C4**
Princes Ct
Brondesbury NW2 . . .**10 A3**
Hampstead NW3 . . . .**11 C4**
Stepney E1 . . . .**32 A2**
Prince's St SE16 . . . . . .**41 B4**
Prince's Gate
SW7 . . . .**130 A3**
Princes Gate Ct
SW7 . . . .**129 C3**
Princes Gate Mews
SW7 . . . .**129 C2**
Princes Gdns
SW7 . . . .**129 C2**
Princes Ho
W11 . . . .**31 C2 113 B3**
Prince's Mews
1 Hammersmith
W6 . . . .**39 A1**
Kensington W2 . . . . .**114 A4**
Princes Pl
Notting Hill
W11 . . . .**31 A1 112 A2**
St James SW1 . . . . . .**119 A2**
Princes Rd
Kew TW9 . . . .**44 B2**
Richmond TW10 . . . . .**54 B2**
Prince's Rd SW14 . .**55 C4**
Princes Rise SE13 . . .**52 B1**
Princes Riverside Rd
7 SE16 . . . .**32 C1**
Princess Alexandra
School of Nursing
The **3** E1 . . . .**32 A4**
Princess Alice Ho **7**
W10 . . . .**22 B1**
Princess Beatrice Ho
SW10 . . . .**142 A1**
Princess Cres N4 . . . . .**6 A2**
Princess Ct
Hampstead NW6 . . . .**11 A1**
Kensington W2 . . . . .**114 B4**
Marylebone W1 . . . .**102 C3**
Princess Frederica CE
Jun & Inf Sch
NW10 . . . .**22 B3**
Princess Grace Hospl
The W1 . . . .**91 B1**
Princess Louise Cl
W2 . . . .**101 C4**

Princess Mary Ho
SW1 . . . .**147 C3**
Princess May Prim
Sch **6** N16 . . . .**16 B4**
Princess May Rd
N16 . . . .**16 A4**
Princess Mews
NW3 . . . .**11 C2**
Prince's Sq W2 . . . .**114 A4**
Princess Rd
Camden Town NW1 . .**81 C4**
Paddington NW6 . . . .**23 C3**
Princess St SE1 . . . .**136 B1**
Princes St W1 . . . . . .**104 B1**

Prince's St
City of London
EC2 . . . .**109 B1**
Richmond TW10,
TW9 . . . .**54 A2**
Prince St SE8 . . . .**51 B4**
Princes Way
Acton W3 . . . .**36 C3**
Putney SW15,
SW19 . . . .**70 A3**
Princes Yd
W11 . . . .**31 A1 112 B1**
Princethorpe Ho
W2 . . . .**100 A4**
Princeton Ct **2**
SW15 . . . .**57 C4**
Princeton Mans
WC1 . . . .**106 C3**
Princeton St WC1 .**106 C4**
Principal Sq E9 . . . . .**17 C3**
Printers Mews E3 . . .**26 A4**
Printer St EC4 . . . . . .**107 C2**
Printing House Yd **16**
E2 . . . .**24 A2 98 B3**
Printon Ho **11** E3 . . . .**33 B4**
Print Village Ind Est
SE15 . . . .**49 B1**
Prior Bolton St N1 . .**15 A2**
Prioress Ho **2** E3 . . . .**27 A2**
Prioress Rd SE27 . . . .**75 A1**
Prioress St SE1 . . . .**137 C1**
Priors Lo **4** TW10 . . . .**54 A1**
Prior St SE10 . . . .**52 B3**
Prior Weston Prim
Sch EC1 . . . .**97 B2**
Priory Ave W4 . . . .**38 A3**
Priory Ct
City of London
EC4 . . . .**108 B1**
Homerton E9 . . . .**17 C3**
Nunhead SE15 . . . . . .**65 B3**
Roehampton SW15 . .**56 B3**
South Lambeth
SW8 . . . .**171 C4**

Priory Gdns
Barnes SW13 . . . .**56 B4**
6 Chiswick W4 . . . . . .**38 A2**
Priory Gn N1 . . . .**84 C2**
Priory Gr SW8 . . . . .**172 A3**
Priory Ho
Clerkenwell EC1 . . . . .**96 A2**
Pimlico SW1 . . . .**147 B2**
Spitalfields E1 . . . . . .**110 C4**
Priory Hospl Grange
Roehampton
SW15 . . . .**56 B3**
Priory Hts N1 . . . .**85 A2**
Priory La SW15 . . . . . .**56 B2**
Priory Lo **2** W4 . . . . . .**36 C1**
Priory Mans
17 Maitland Pk
NW3 . . . .**12 B2**

Priory Mans continued
South Kensington
SW10 . . . .**143 A1**
Priory Park Rd
NW6 . . . .**23 B4**
Priory Rd
Bedford Pk W4 . . . . . .**37 C3**
Hampstead NW6 . . . .**11 A1**
Richmond TW9 . . . . . .**44 C3**
Priory St **16** E3 . . . . .**27 A2**
Priory Terr NW6 . . . . .**78 A4**
Priory The SE1 . . . . .**136 A3**
Priory Wlk SW10 . . .**143 A1**
Pritchard Ho **33**
E2 . . . .**24 C3**
Pritchard's Rd E2 . .**24 C3**
Priter Rd SE16 . . . . .**139 C1**
Priter Road Hostel **18**
SE16 . . . .**139 C1**
Probert Rd SW2 . . . .**62 C2**
Probyn Ho SW1 . . . .**147 C4**
Probyn Rd SW2 . . . . .**75 A2**
Procter Ho **12** SE5 . .**48 C3**
Procter St WC1 . . . .**106 C3**
Proctor Ho **5**
SE1 . . . .**153 B1**
Prome Ho **3** N16 . . . .**15 C4**
Promenade Approach
Rd W4 . . . .**46 A3**
Promenade The
W4 . . . .**46 A2**
Prospect Cotts
SW18 . . . .**58 C3**
Prospect Ho
1 Dalston E8 . . . . . .**16 B2**
Islington N1 . . . .**85 B1**
Newington SE1 . . . .**136 B1**
10 North Kensington
W10 . . . .**23 A1**
Prospect House Sch
13 SW15 . . . .**69 C4**
Prospect Pl
5 Child's Hill NW2 . .**1 B1**
2 Chiswick W4 . . . . . .**37 C1**
6 Deptford SE8 . . . . .**51 B4**
7 Hampstead NW3 . .**11 B4**
5 Lower Holloway
N7 . . . .**14 A4**
Wapping E1 . . . .**32 B1**
Prospect Quay
SW18 . . . .**58 C3**
Prospect Rd NW2 . . .**1 C1**
Prospect St SE16 . . .**40 A4**
Prospect Wharf
E1 . . . .**32 B2**
Prospero Rd N19 . . . .**4 C3**
Prothero Rd SW6 . .**154 C2**
Proud Ho **10** E1 . . . . .**32 A3**
Prout Gr NW10 . . . .**8 B4**
Provence St N1 . . . . . .**86 C2**
Providence Cl E9 . . .**25 C4**
Providence Ct
Islington N1 . . . .**86 A3**
Mayfair W1 . . . .**117 C4**
Providence Ho
N1 . . . .**84 C1**
Providence Row
N1 . . . .**84 B1**
Providence Row Cl **20**
E2 . . . .**25 A2**
Providence Sq **38**
SE1 . . . .**139 B4**
Providence Yd **1**
E2 . . . .**24 C2 99 B4**
Provost Ct NW3 . . . . .**12 B2**
Provost Rd NW3 . . . .**12 B1**
Provost St N1 . . . .**97 B4**

Prowse Pl NW1 . . . . . .**13 B1**
Prudent Pas EC2 . . .**109 A1**
Prusom's Island **8**
E1 . . . .**32 B1**
Prusom St E1 . . . .**32 A1**
Pryors The NW3 . . . . . .**2 C1**
Pudding La EC3 . . . .**123 C4**
Pudding Mill La
E15 . . . .**27 A4**
Pudding Mill Lane Sta
E15 . . . .**27 A4**
Puddle Dock EC4 . .**122 B4**
Pugin Ct N1 . . . .**14 C1**
Pulborough Rd
SW18 . . . .**70 B4**
Pulham Ho SW8 . . .**162 C1**
Pullman Ct SW2 . . . .**74 B3**
Pullman Gdns
SW15 . . . .**57 B1**
Pulross Rd SW9 . . . . .**62 B4**
Pulteney Cl **20** E3 . . .**26 B4**
Pulteney Terr N1 . . . .**85 A4**
Pulton Ho SE4 . . . . . .**66 A3**
Pulton Pl SW6 . . . . .**155 B1**
Puma Ct E1 . . . .**110 C4**
Pump Ct EC4 . . . .**107 B1**
Pump Ho Cl SE16 . . .**40 B4**
Pumphouse
Educational Mus
The* SE16 . . . .**33 A1**
Pump House Gall*
SW11 . . . .**159 B1**
Pumping Ho **3**
E14 . . . .**34 C2**
Pumping Station Rd
W4 . . . .**46 A4**
Pump La SE14 . . . .**50 B3**
Punderson's Gdns
E2 . . . .**25 A2**
Purbeck Ho SW8 . .**162 C1**
Purbrook Est SE1 . .**138 B3**
Purbrook Ho **2**
SW15 . . . .**69 A3**
Purbrook St SE1 . . .**138 B2**
Purcell Cres SW6 . .**154 A2**
Purcell Ho SW10 . . .**157 B3**
Purcell Mews **2**
NW10 . . . .**8 A1**
Purcell St N1 . . . .**24 A3**
Purchese St NW1 . . .**83 C1**
Purday Ho W10 . . . . . .**23 B2**
Purdon Ho **11**
SE15 . . . .**49 C2**
Purdy St E3 . . . .**27 A1**
Purley Ave NW2 . . . . . .**1 A2**
Purley Pl N1 . . . .**15 A1**
Purser Ho **3** SW2 . . .**62 C1**
Pursers Cross Rd
SW6 . . . .**165 A4**
Purves Rd NW10 . . . .**22 B3**
Pusey Ho **24** E14 . . . .**33 C3**
Puteaux Ho **6** E2 . . .**25 C3**
PUTNEY **57 B2**
Putney Bridge App
SW6 . . . .**58 A4**
Putney Bridge Rd
SW15 . . . .**58 B3**
Putney Bridge Sta
SW6 . . . .**58 A3**
Putney Comm
SW15 . . . .**57 B3**
Putney Exchange
Shopping Ctr
SW15 . . . .**57 C3**
PUTNEY HEATH **57 B1**

Putney Heath
SW15 . . . .**57 B1**
Putney Heath La
SW15 . . . .**57 C1**
Putney High Sch
SW15 . . . .**57 C2**
Putney High St
SW15 . . . .**58 A3**
Putney Hill
12 Putney SW15 . . . . .**69 B4**
Putney SW15 . . . .**57 C2**
Putney L Ctr SW15 . .**57 B3**
Putney Park Ave
SW15 . . . .**56 C3**
Putney Park La
SW15 . . . .**57 A2**
Putney Park Sch
SW15 . . . .**57 A3**
Putney Pier SW15 . . .**58 A4**
Putney School of Art
& Design SW15 . . . .**58 A3**
Putney Sta SW15 . . . .**58 A3**
PUTNEY VALE **68 C1**
Putney Wharf Twr
SW15 . . . .**58 A4**
Pylon Trad Est
E16 . . . .**34 C4**
Pymers Mead
SE21 . . . .**75 B3**
Pynfolds SE16 . . . .**40 A4**
Pynnersmead
SE24 . . . .**63 B2**
Pyrford Ho **12**
SW9 . . . .**63 A3**
Pyrland Rd
Richmond TW10 . . . . .**54 B1**
Stoke Newington N5 .**15 C3**
Pyrmont Gr SE27 . . . .**75 A1**
Pyrmont Rd W4 . . . . . .**44 C4**
Pytchley Rd SE22 . . . .**64 A4**

Quadrangle Cl
SE1 . . . .**152 A4**
Quadrangle The
Chelsea SW10 . . . . . .**167 A4**
Fulham SW6 . . . .**154 A1**
Herne Hill SE24 . . . . .**63 B2**
3 North Kensington
W12 . . . .**30 B3**
Paddington W2 . . . .**102 A2**
Quadrant Arc W1 .**119 A3**
Quadrant Bsns Ctr
NW6 . . . .**23 A4**
Quadrant Gr NW5 . .**12 B3**
Quadrant The
4 Kensal Green
NW10 . . . .**22 C2**
Richmond TW9 . . . . . .**54 A3**
Quaker Ct EC1 . . . . . .**97 A2**
Quaker St
E1 . . . .**24 B1 98 C1**
Quality Ct WC2 . . . .**107 B2**
Quantock Ho N16 . . . .**7 B3**
Quantock Mews **3**
SE15 . . . .**49 C1**
Quarrendon St
SW6 . . . .**165 C2**
Quarry Rd SW18 . . . .**59 B1**
Quarterdeck The
E14 . . . .**41 C4**

Quayside Ct 6
SE16 . . . . .32 C1
Quebec & Crown
Wharves E14 . . . .33 B3
Quebec Ind Est
SE16 . . . . .41 A3
Quebec Mews
W1 . . . . .103 A1
Quebec Way SE16 . .41 A4
Quebec Wharf 32
. . . . .24 A4
Quedgeley Ct 3
SE15 . . . . .49 B4
Queen Alexandra
Mans WC1 . . . . . .94 A3
Queen Anne Mews
W1 . . . . .104 B3
Queen Anne Rd
E9 . . . . .17 C2
Queen Anne's Gate
SW1 . . . . .133 B3
Queen Anne's Gdns
Bedford Pk W4 . . . .38 A3
Ealing W5 . . . . . . .36 A4
Queen Anne's Gr
Bedford Pk W4 . . . .38 A3
Ealing W5 . . . . . . .36 A4
Queen Anne St
W1 . . . . .104 A3
Queen Anne Terr 9
E1 . . . . .32 A2
Queen Caroline St
W6 . . . . .39 B1
Queen Charlotte's &
Chelsea Hospl
W12 . . . . .29 C3
Queen Ct WC1 . . . .94 B1
Queen Elizabeth St 5
N1 . . . . .15 C2
Queen Elizabeth Hall
& Purcell Room★
SE1 . . . . .121 A2
Queen Elizabeth Ho
SW12 . . . . .72 C4
Queen Elizabeth II
Con Ctr SW1 . . . .133 C3
Queen Elizabeth II
Jubilee Sch 5
W9 . . . . .23 B1
Queen Elizabeth II
Pier SE10 . . . . . . .35 B1
Queen Elizabeth's Cl
N16 . . . . .6 C2
Queen Elizabeth's Coll
15 SE10 . . . . .52 B3
Queen Elizabeth St
SE1 . . . . .138 C4
Queen Elizabeth Wlk
N16 . . . . .6 C2
Queen Elizabeth Wlk
SW13 . . . . .47 A2
Queenhithe EC4 . .123 A4
Queen Margaret Flats
22 E2 . . . . .25 A2
Queen Margarets Ct
N1 . . . . .16 A3
Queen Margaret's Gr
N1 . . . . .16 A3
Queen Mary's Gdns★
NW1 . . . . .91 B3
Queen Mary's Univ
Hospl SW15 . . . . .56 C1
Queen Mary, Univ of
London E1 . . . . . . .26 A1

Queen Mother Sp Ctr
SW1 . . . . .146 C4
Queen of Denmark Ct
SE16 . . . . .41 B3
Queen St Pl EC4 . .123 A4
Queensberry Mews W
SW7 . . . . .143 B4
Queensberry Pl
SW7 . . . . .143 B4
Queensberry Way
SW7 . . . . .143 B4
Queensborough Mews
W2 . . . . .114 C4
Queensborough Pas
W2 . . . . .114 C4
Queensborough Terr
W2 . . . . .114 B4
Queensbridge Ct 1
E2 . . . . .24 B3
Queensbridge Inf Sch
18 E8 . . . . .16 B1
Queensbridge Rd
Dalston E8 . . . . . . .16 B1
Shoreditch E2, E8 . .24 B4
Queensbury St 22
N1 . . . . .15 B1
Queen's CE Prim Sch
The TW9 . . . . .44 C2
Queen's Cir SW11 .160 A1
Queen's Club Gdns
W14 . . . . .154 B4
Queen's Club The
W14 . . . . .140 B1
Queen's Coll W1 . .104 A3
Queen's Coll Prep Sch
W1 . . . . .104 A3
Queens Cres TW10 . .54 B2
Queen's Cres NW5 . .12 C2
Queen's Ct
Battersea SW11 . . .170 A4
Camberwell SE5 . . .49 A1
4 Limehouse E14 . . .33 B2
Queen's Ct
Barnes SW13 . . . . . .56 C4
Kensington W2 . . . .114 B3
3 Richmond TW10 . .54 B1
Queensdale W11 . . .30 C1
Queensdale Cres
W11 . . . . .30 C1
Queensdale Pl
W11 . . . . . . .31 A1 112 A1
Queensdale Rd
Notting Hill W11 . . . .30 C1
Notting Hill
W11 . . . . . . .31 A1 112 A1
Queensdale Wlk
W11 . . . . . . .31 A1 112 A1
Queensdown Rd
E5 . . . . .17 A4
Queen's Dr N4 . . . . .6 A2
Queen's Elm Par
SW3 . . . . .143 C2
Queen's Elm Sq
SW3 . . . . .143 C1
Queen's Gallery★
SW1 . . . . .132 B3
Queen's Gate
SW7 . . . . .129 A1
Queensgate Gdns
SW15 . . . . .57 A3
Queen's Gate Gdns
SW7 . . . . .143 A4
Queensgate Ho 34
E3 . . . . .26 B3

Queen's Gate Jun Sch
SW7 . . . . .143 B4
Queen's Gate Mews
SW7 . . . . .129 A2
Queensgate Pl 10
NW6 . . . . .10 C1
Queen's Gate Pl
SW7 . . . . .129 A1
Queen's Gate Pl Mews
SW7 . . . . .129 A1
Queen's Gate Terr
SW7 . . . . .129 A2
Queens Gate Villas
E9 . . . . .18 A1
Queen's Gdns W2 .114 C4
Queen's Gr NW8 . . .79 C3
Queen's Head Pas
EC2 . . . . .108 C2
Queen's Head St
N1 . . . . .86 B3
Queen's Head Yd
SE1 . . . . .123 B1
Queens Ho 1
SE17 . . . . .48 C4
Queen's House The★
SE10 . . . . .52 C4
Queensland Rd
N7 . . . . .14 C4
Queens Manor Sch
SW6 . . . . .47 C3
Queens Mans
NW6 . . . . .11 A3
Queen's Mans W6 . .39 C2
Queensmead NW8 . .79 C4
Queensmere Cl
SW19 . . . . .69 C2
Queensmere Ct
SW13 . . . . .46 C4
Queensmere Rd
SW19 . . . . .69 C2
Queens Mews
W2 . . . . .114 A4
Queensmill Rd
SW6 . . . . .47 C3
Queensmill Sch
SW6 . . . . .165 C1
Queens Par Com Sch
NW6 . . . . .9 C1
Queens Park Ct 5
W10 . . . . .22 C2
Queen's Park Prim
Sch 20 W10 . . . . . .23 A1
Queen's Park Sta
NW6 . . . . .23 B3
Queen's Quay EC4 .123 A4
Queen's Rd
Mortlake SW14 . . . .55 C4
New Cross Gate SE14,
SE15 . . . . .50 B2
Richmond TW10 . . . .54 B2
Queen's Ride
SW13 . . . . .57 A4
Queen's Rise
TW10 . . . . .54 B1
Queen's Road Sta
SE15 . . . . .50 B2
Queen's Row SE17 . .48 C4
Queen St
City of London
EC4 . . . . .123 A4
Mayfair W1 . . . . . .118 A2
Queens Terr NW8 . . .79 B2
Queenstown Mews
SW8 . . . . .170 A3

Queenstown Rd
SW8 . . . . .160 A2
Queenstown Road
(Battersea) Sta
SW8 . . . . .170 B4
Queensville Rd SW12,
SW4 . . . . .73 C4
Queensway W2 . . .114 B4
Queensway Sta
W2 . . . . .114 B3
Queen's Wlk SW1 .118 C1
Queenswood Ct 7
SW4 . . . . .62 A2
Queenswood Gdns
E11 . . . . .19 C4
Queen's Yd E9 . . . . .18 C2
Queen's Yd W1 . . . .93 A1
Queen Victoria
Meml★ SW1 . . . .132 C4
Queen Victoria St
EC4 . . . . .122 C4
Queen Victoria Terr
12 E1 . . . . .32 A2
Quelch Ho 2 N19 . .13 C3
Quemerford Rd
N7 . . . . .14 B3
Quendon Ho 9
W10 . . . . .22 B1
Quenington Ct 5
SE15 . . . . .49 B4
Quennel Ho 7
SW12 . . . . .73 B4
Querrin St SW6 . . .166 C1
Quested Ct 27 E8 . . .17 A3
Quex Mews NW6 . . .23 C4
Quex Rd NW6 . . . . .23 C4
Quick Rd W4 . . . . . .38 A1
Quick St N1 . . . . . . .86 B1
Quick Street Mews
N1 . . . . .86 A1
Quickswood NW3 . .12 A1
Quill La SW15 . . . . .57 C3
Quill St N4 . . . . .5 C1
Quilp St SE1 . . . . .136 C4
Quilter St
E2 . . . . .24 C2 99 B4
Quilting Ct 26
SE16 . . . . .40 C4
Quince Rd SE13 . . . .52 A1
Quintin Ct W4 . . . . .45 B3
Quintin Kynaston Sch
NW8 . . . . .79 B3
Quintock Ho 2
TW9 . . . . .44 C2
Quinton Ho SW8 . .162 A2
Quinton St SW18 . . .71 B2
Quixley St E14 . . . . .34 C2
Quorn Rd SE22 . . . .64 A4

R

Rabbit Row
W8 . . . . . . .31 C1 113 C2
Raby St E14 . . . . . . .33 A3
Racine 18 SE5 . . . . .49 A2
Racton Rd SW6 . . . .155 B3
Radbourne Cl E5 . . .17 C4
Radbourne Ct
SW12 . . . . .73 C3
Radcliff Bldg EC1 . .107 B4
Radcliffe Ave
NW10 . . . . .21 C3
Radcliffe Coll
Marylebone W1 . . .104 C1
Soho W1 . . . . .105 B2

Radcliffe Ho 10
. . . . .40 A2
Radcliffe Path 8
SW8 . . . . .170 B1
Radcliffe Rd SE1 . .138 B2
Radcliffe Sq SW15 . .57 C1
Radcot St SE11 . . . .149 C1
Raddington Rd
W10 . . . . .31 A4
Radford Ho
8 Bow Comm E14 . . .34 A4
Islington N7 . . . . . . .14 B3
Radford Rd SE13 . . .67 B1
Radipole Rd SW6 . .164 C4
Radland Rd E16 . . . .35 C3
Radlett Pl NW8 . . . . .80 A4
Radley Ct 28 SE16 . . .40 C4
Radley Ho NW1 . . . .90 C2
Radley Lo 30
SW19 . . . . .69 C3
Radley Mews W8 . .127 C1
Radley Terr 1
E16 . . . . .35 B4
Radnor Lo 2 . . . . . .101 C1
Radnor Mews W2 . .101 C1
Radnor Pl W2 . . . . .102 A1
Radnor Rd
Kensal Rise NW6 . . .23 A4
Peckham SE15 . . . . .49 C3
Radnor St EC1 . . . . .97 A3
Radnor Terr W14 . .140 C4
Radnor Way NW10 . .20 A1
Radnor Wlk
Chelsea SW3 . . . . .144 C1
21 Millwall E14 . . . .41 C2
Radstock St
SW11 . . . . .158 A1
Radway Ho 30 W2 . .31 C4
Radwell Ho SW2 . . .62 C2
Raeburn Ct 6
SW16 . . . . .74 A1
Raeburn St SW2 . . . .62 A3
Ragged School Mus★
E3 . . . .
Raglan Ct SW9 . . . . .62 C4
Raglan St NW5 . . . . .13 A2
Ragley Cl W3 . . . . . .37 B4
Rahere Ho EC1 . . . . .96 C4
Railey Mews NW5 . .13 B3
Railton Rd SE24 . . . .63 A2
Railway App SE1 . . .123 C2
Railway Ave SE16 . . .40 B4
Railway Cotts W6 . . .39 B4
Railway Gr SE14 . . . .51 B3
Railway Rise SE22 . .64 A3
Railway Side
SW13 . . . . .56 A4
Railway St N1 . . . . . .84 B1
Railway Terr 13
SE13 . . . . .67 A2
Rainbow Ave E14 . . .42 A1
Rainbow Ct 3
SE14 . . . . .51 A4
Rainbow Montessori
Sch NW6 . . . . . . .11 A1
Rainbow Quay
SE16 . . . . .41 A3
Rainbow Sch 6
SW17 . . . . .72 B2
Rainbow St SE5 . . . .49 A3
Raines Ct N16 . . . . . .7 B2
Raine's Foundation
Lower Sch 32 E2 . .25 A2
Raine's Foundation
Sch 24 E2 . . . . . . .25 B3
Raine St E1 . . . . .32 A1
Rainford Ho 9 N7 . . .5 B2

Rainham Cl SW11 ....60 A1
Rainham Ho NW1 ....83 A3
Rainham Rd NW10 .22 B2
Rainhill Way E3 ....26 C2
Rainsborough Ave
SE8 ....41 A2
Rainsford Ct
NW10 ....20 A3
Rainsford Ho 14
SW2 ....62 B2
Rainsford Ho
NW10 ....20 A3
Rainsford St W2 ..102 A2
Rainton Rd SE7 ....43 C1
Rainville Rd W6 ...47 B4
Raleigh Ct
7 Hammersmith
W12 ....39 A4
2 Rotherhithe
SE16 ....32 C1
Raleigh Gdns SW2..62 B1
Raleigh Ho
30 Clapham SW8 .171 B2
Isle of Dogs E14.....42 A4
Raleigh Mews N1 ..86 B3
Raleigh St N1 ......86 B3
Ralph Ct 8 W2 ....100 B2
Ralston St SW3 ....44 C1
Ramar Ho 11 E1 ..111 B4
Ramillies Cl SW2...62 A1
Ramillies Ho N1 ..105 A1
Ramillies Pl W1 ..104 C1
Ramillies Rd W4...37 C3
Ramillies St W1 ..104 C1
Rampart St E1 ....32 A3
Rampayne St
SW1 ....147 B2
Ramsay Ho NW8...80 A2
Ramsay Rd W3 ....37 B4
Ramsdean Ho 1
SW15 ....69 A3
Ramsden Rd
SW12 ....72 C4
Ramsey Ct
Putney SW15 .....57 B1
6 Upper Holloway
N19 ....4 C2
Ramsey Ho
5 Battersea
SW11 ....59 C3
14 Kennington
SW9 ....163 C1
Ramsey St
E2 ......24 C1 99 C2
Ramsey Wlk N1 ...15 C2
Ramsfort Ho 4
SE16 ....40 A2
Ramsgate St E8 ..16 B2
Ram St SW18.......59 A2
Randal Cremer JMI
Sch 16 E2 ....24 B3
Randall Cl SW11..168 A4
Randall Pl SE10 ....52 B3
Randall Rd SE11..148 C3
Randall Row SE11 148 C3
Randell's Rd N1 ...84 B4
Randolf Ct
Paddington NW6 ..78 A1
St John's Wood
NW8 ....78 C3
Randolph Ave W9 ..88 C3
Randolph Cres W9 ..88 C2
Randolph Gdns
NW6 ....78 A1

Randolph Mews
W9 ....89 A1
Randolph Rd W9 ...89 A1
Randolph St NW1 ..13 B1
Ranelagh Ave
Barnes SW13 .....46 C1
Fulham SW6 ......58 B4
Ranelagh Gardens
Mans SW6 ....58 A4
Ranelagh Gardens
(site of Chelsea
Flower Show)*
SW1 ....145 C1
Ranelagh Gdns
3 Bedford Pk W6 ..38 B3
Chiswick W4 ......45 B3
Fulham SW6 ......58 B4
Ranelagh Gr SW1 ..145 C2
Ranelagh Ho SW3 ..144 C2
Ranelagh Mans 4
SW6 ....165 A2
Ranelagh Rd
Dagenham NW10 ...21 B3
Pimlico SW1 .....147 A1
Rangdon St E1 ....110 C1
Ranger's House (The
Wernher
Collection)*
SE10 ....52 C2
Rangers Sq SE10 ..52 C2
Rangoon Ho 9
N16 ....15 C4
Rankine Ho SE1 ..136 C1
Ranmere St SW12 ..73 A3
Rann Ho 1 SW14 ..55 C4
Rannoch Rd W6 ....47 C4
Raphael Ct 9
SE16 ....40 A1
Raphael St SW7 ..130 C3
Rapley Ho 9
E2 ......24 C2 99 B3
Rashleigh Ct 8
SW8 ....61 A4
Rashleigh Ho WC1 ..94 A3
Rastell Ave SW2 ..73 C3
RATCLIFF 32 C2
Ratcliffe Cross St
E1 ....32 C3
Ratcliffe Ho 10
E14 ....33 A3
Ratcliffe La 16
E14 ....33 A3
Ratcliffe Orch 3
E1 ....32 C2
Rathbone Ho
5 Canning Town
E16 ....35 B3
Kilburn NW6 ......23 C4
Rathbone Pl W1 ..105 B2
Rathbone St
Canning Town E16 ..35 B3
Fitzrovia W1 .....105 A3
Rathgar Rd SW9 ...63 A4
Rathmell Dr SW4 ..61 C1
Rattray Rd SW2 ....62 C2
Raul Rd SE15 .....49 C2

Raveley St NW5 ...13 B4
Ravenet Ct
Battersea SW11 ...170 A3
Clapham SW4.....61 A2
Ravenet St 1
SW11 ....170 A3
Ravenfield Rd
SW17 ....72 B1
Raven Ho 10 SE16 ..40 C2
Ravenna Rd SW15 ..57 C2
Raven Row E1.....32 A4
Ravensbourne Ho
NW8 ....102 A4
Ravensbourne Mans
9 SE8 ....51 C4
Ravensbourne Pl
SE13 ....52 A1
Ravensbury Rd
SW18 ....71 A2
Ravensbury Terr
SW18 ....71 A2
Ravenscar NW1 ....82 C3
Ravenscourt 1
N16 ....7 C1
Ravenscourt Ave
W6 ....38 C2
Ravenscourt Gdns
W6 ....38 C2
Ravenscourt Ho 13
SE16 ....39 A2
Ravenscourt Park
Mans 6 W6 ......39 A3
Ravenscourt Park
Prep Sch W6 .....38 C2
Ravenscourt Park Sta
W6 ....39 A2
Ravenscourt Pk
W6 ....38 C2
Ravenscourt Pl
W6 ....39 A2
Ravenscourt Rd
W6 ....39 A2
Ravenscourt Sq
W6 ....38 C3
Ravenscourt Theatre
Sch 14 W6 ....39 A2
Ravenscroft Ave
NW11 ....1 B4
Ravenscroft Cl 4
E16 ....35 C4
Ravenscroft Ct
NW11 ....1 B4
Ravenscroft Point 29
E9 ....17 C2
Ravenscroft Rd
Acton W4 ....37 B2
Newham E16 .....35 C4
Ravenscroft St
E2 ......24 B2 99 A4
Ravensdon St
SE11 ....149 C1
Ravenshaw St
NW6 ....10 B3
Ravenslea Rd SW11,
SW12 ....72 B4
Ravensmede Way
W4 ....38 B2
Ravenstone SE17 ..152 B1
Ravenstone Prim Sch
SW12 ....72 C2
Ravenstone St
SW12 ....72 C3
Ravenswood Rd
SW12 ....73 A4
Ravensworth Ct
SW6 ....155 B1

Ravensworth Rd
NW10 ....22 A2
Raven Wharf SE1 ..138 C4
Ravey St
EC2 ....24 A1 98 A2
Rav Pinter Cl N16 ..7 A4
Rawlings St SW3 ..144 C4
Rawlinson Ho
SE13 ....67 C3
Rawlinson Point 8
E16 ......35 B4 A4
Rawreth Wlk N1 ...87 A4
Rawson Ct SW11 ..169 C3
Rawson St SW11 ..170 A3
Rawstone Pl EC1 ..96 A4
Rawstorne St EC1 ..96 A4
Rayburne Ct W14 ..126 A2
Raydon St N19 ....4 A2
Ray Ho
7 North Kensington
W10 ....30 C3
Shoreditch N1 ....87 C3
Raymede Twr 2
W10 ....30 C4
Raymond Bldgs
WC1 ....107 A4
Raymouth Rd
SE16 ....40 A2
Raynald Ho 15
SW16 ....74 A1
Rayne Ct SE1 ....138 C4
Rayne Ho
1 Balham SW12 ...60 C1
Paddington W2 ...88 A2
Rayner Ct 10 W12 ..39 B4
Rayner's Rd SW15 ..58 A2
Raynes Ct NW2 ...10 A4
Raynham W2 ......102 A2
Raynham Ho 1
E1 ....25 C1
Raynor Pl
23 Canonbury N1 ..15 B1
N1 ....87 A4
Ray St EC1 ......95 C1
Ray Wlk N7 ......5 B2
Reachview Ct 17
NW1 ....13 B1
Reade Ct 8 W3 ....37 B3
Reade Ho
W10 ....8 A1
Read Ho 4 SE11 ..163 B4
Reading Ho
Paddington W2 ...100 C1
Peckham SE15 ...49 C4
Reading La E8.....17 A2
Reapers Cl NW1 ...83 B4
Reardon Ho 5 E1 ..32 A1
Reardon Path 31
E1 ....32 A1
Reardon St E1.....32 A1
Reaston St SE14 ..50 C3
Reay Prim Sch
SW9 ....163 A1
Reckitt Rd W4 ....38 A1
Record St SE16 ...50 B4
Rector St N1 ......86 C3
Rectory Gdns 8
SW4 ....61 B4
Rectory Gr SW4 ...61 B4
Rectory Rd
Barnes SW13 .....46 C1
1 London W3 .....28 B1
Shacklewell N16 ...7 B1
Rectory Road Sta
N16 ....7 B1

Rectory Sq E1.....32 C4
Reculver Ho 2
SE15 ....50 B4
Reculver Rd SE16..40 C1
Red Anchor Cl
SW3 ....158 A3
Redan Pl W2 .....100 A1
Redan St W14 ....39 C3
Redan Terr SE5 ...48 A1
Redbourne Ho 7
E14 ....33 B3
Redbourn Ho 10
W10 ....22 B1
Redbridge Gdns
SE5 ....49 A3
Redburn St SW3...158 C4
Redcar St SE5 ....48 B3
Redcastle Cl E1 ...32 B2
Redchurch St
E2 ......24 B1 98 C2
Redcliffe Cl 5
SW5 ....142 A1
Redcliffe Gdns
Chiswick W4 .....45 A3
Fulham SW10 ....156 B4
Redcliffe Mews
SW10 ....142 B1
Redcliffe Pl SW10 ..156 C3
Redcliffe Rd
SW10 ....157 A4
Redcliffe Sch
SW10 ....156 C4
Redcliffe Sq
SW10 ....142 B1
Redcliffe St SW10 ..156 B4
Redclyf Ho 13 E1 ...25 B1
Redcroft 5 NW6 ...11 A2
Red Cotts
SE1 ....137 A4
Redcross Way
SE1 ....123 A1
Reddins Rd SE15...49 C4
Rede Pl
W2 ......31 C2 113 C4
Redesdale St
SW3 ....158 C4
Redfern Rd NW10 ..8 A1
Redfield La SW5 ..142 A4
Redfield Mews
SW5 ....141 C4
Redfiff Est SE16 ...41 B3
Redford Wlk N1 ...86 C4
Redgate Terr
SW15 ....57 C1
Redgrave Rd
SW15 ....57 C4
Redhill Ct SW2 ...74 C2
Redhill St NW1 ....92 B4
Red House Sq 20
N1 ....15 B1
Redington Gdns
NW3 ....11 A4
Redington Ho N1 ..85 A2
Redington Rd
NW3 ....11 A4
Redlands Prim Sch 35
E1 ....32 B4
Redlands Way
SW2 ....74 B4
Red Lion Cl 5
SE17 ....48 C4
Red Lion Ct EC4 ..107 C1
Red Lion Row
SE17 ....48 B4
Red Lion Sq WC1 ..106 C3

Red Lion St WC1 . . 106 C3
Red Lion Yd W1 . . 117 C2
Redlynch Ct W14 . . 126 B3
Redlynch Ho **27**
  SW9 . . . . 173 C4
Redriff Prim Sch
  SE16 . . . . 41 A4
Redriff Rd SE16 . . . . 41 A3
Red Rover SW11 . . 56 C4
Redrup Ho **21**
  SE14 . . . . 50 C4
Redruth Rd E9 . . . . 25 B4
Red Sq The N16 . . . . 6 C1
Redstart Cl SE14 . . 51 A3
Redvers St
  E2 . . . . 24 A2 98 B4
Redwald Rd E5 . . . . 17 C4
Redwood Cl
  4 Bow E3 . . . . 26 C3
  Rotherhithe SE16 . . 33 A1
Redwood Ct
  Brondesbury NW6 . . 10 A1
  Crouch End N19 . . . . 4 C4
Redwood Mews **2**
  SW4 . . . . 61 A4
Redwoods SW15 . . 68 C3
Reece Mews SW7 143 B4
Reed Cl E16 . . . . . . 35 C4
Reedham St SE15 . . 64 C4
Reed Ho SW15 . . . . 56 C1
Reedholm Villas
  N16 . . . . 15 C4
Reed PI
  Battersea SW11 . . . . 60 A3
  Clapham SW4 . . . . . . 61 C3
Reed's PI NW1 . . . . 13 B1
Reedworth St
  SE11 . . . . 149 C3
Reef Ho E14 . . . . . . 42 B3
Rees St N1 . . . . 87 A3
Reeves Ho
  Lambeth SE1 . . . . 135 B3
  Mayfair W1 . . . . . . 117 B3
Reeves Mews W1 117 C3
Reeves Rd E3 . . . . . . 27 A1
Reflection Ho **9**
  E2 . . . . 24 C1 99 B2
Reform St SW11 . . 169 A2
Regal CI E1 . . . . . . 111 C4
Regal La NW1 . . . . . . 81 C3
Regal PI
  6 Tower Hamlets
  E3 . . . . 26 B2
  Walham Green
  SW6 . . . . 156 B1
Regan Way N1 . . . . 24 A3
Regatta Point
  TW8 . . . . 44 B4
Regency Ct
  5 Bow E3 . . . . 26 B3
  14 South Hackney
  E9 . . . . 25 B4

Regency Ho NW1 . . . 92 B2
Regency Lo NW3 . . 11 C1
Regency Mews
  Camberwell SW9 . . 48 A3
  1 Willesden NW10 . . 8 C2
Regency PI SW1 . . 147 C4
Regency St SW1 . . 147 C3
Regency Terr
  SW7 . . . . 143 B2
Regency Wlk **8**
  TW10 . . . . 54 A2
Regeneration Rd
  SE16 . . . . 40 C1
Regent Ct
  Lisson Gr NW8 . . . . 90 A3
  1 Stamford Hill N16 . . 7 C4
Regent Ho W14 . . 140 A4
Regent PI W11 . . . 119 A4
Regent Rd SE24 . . . . 63 A2
Regents Bridge Gdns
  SW8 . . . . 162 B2
Regents Canal Ho **19**
  E14 . . . . 33 B3
Regent's Coll NW1 91 B2
Regent's Ct E8 . . . . 24 C4
Regents Gate Ho **20**
  E14 . . . . 33 A2
Regents Lo **9**
  SW2 . . . . 74 B3
Regents Mews
  NW8 . . . . 79 A2
REGENT'S PARK . . 92 A4
Regent's Park★
  NW1 . . . . 81 B1
Regent's Park
  Barracks NW1 . . . . 82 B3
Regent's Park Rd
  Camden Town
  NW1 . . . . 81 B4
  Primrose Hill NW3 . . 12 C1
Regent's Park Sta
  NW1 . . . . 92 A1
Regent's Park Terr
  NW1 . . . . 82 A4
Regents PI SE3 . . . 53 C1
Regents Plaza **2**
  NW6 . . . . 78 A2
Regent Sq
  3 Bromley E3 . . . . 27 A2
  St Pancras WC1 . . . . 94 B3
Regent's Row E8 . . 24 C4
Regent St
  Brentford W4 . . . . . . 36 C1
  7 Kensal Green
  NW10 . . . . 22 C2
  Mayfair W1 . . . . . . 118 C4
Regina Rd N4 . . . . . . 5 B3
Regnart Bldgs
  NW1 . . . . 93 A3
Reginald Rd SE8 . . 51 C3
Reginald Sq SE8 . . 51 C3
Regina Point SE16 . . 40 B3
Regis Ct NW1 . . . . 102 C4
Regis PI **17** SW2 . . 62 B3
Regis Rd NW5 . . . . . 13 A3

Reliance Sq
  E2 . . . . 24 A1 98 B2
Relton Ct W3 . . . . . . 36 C4
Relton Mews
  SW7 . . . . 130 B2
Rembrandt Cl E14 . . 42 C3
Rembrandt Ct **10**
  SE16 . . . . 40 A1
Rembrant St NW5 . . 86 B1
Remington St N1 . . 86 B1
Remnant St WC2 . 106 C2
Remsted Ho **7**
  NW6 . . . . 78 A3
Remus Rd E3 . . . . . . 18 C1
Renaissance Wlk **4**
  SE10 . . . . 43 B3
Renbold Ho **5**
  SE10 . . . . 52 B2
Rendlesham Ho **3** E5,
  N16 . . . . 7 C1
Rendlesham Rd E5 . . 7 C1
Renforth St SE16 . . 40 B4
Renfrew Ho NW6 . . 78 A1
Renfrew Rd SE11 . 150 A3
Rennell Ho **18** E9 . . 17 C2
Rennell St SE13 . . . . 67 B4
Rennie Cotts **29**
  E1 . . . . 25 B1
Rennie Ct SE1 . . . 122 A2
Rennie Ho SE1 . . . 136 C1
Rennie St SE1 . . . . 122 A2
Renoir Ct **7** SE16 . . 40 A1
Renton Cl SW2 . . . . 62 B1
Rephidim St SE1 . . 138 A1
Replingham Rd
  SW18 . . . . 70 C3
Reporton Rd SW6 . 154 B1
Repton Ho SW1 . . 147 A3
Repton St E14 . . . . . . 33 A3
Reservoir Rd SE4 . . 51 A1
Reservoir Studios **14**
  E1 . . . . 32 C3
Resolution Way **7**
  SE8 . . . . 51 C3
Restell Cl SE3 . . . . 53 A4
Reston Pl SW7 . . . 128 C3
Restoration Sq
  SW11 . . . . 167 C3
Retcar PI N19 . . . . . . 4 A2
Retford St E2 . . . . . . 24 A3
Retreat Ho **9** E9 . . 17 B2
Retreat PI E9 . . . . . . 17 B2
Retreat The SW14 . . 56 A4
Reunion Row E1 . . 32 A2
Reveley Sq SE16 . . 41 A4
Revelon Rd SE4 . . . . 66 A4
Revelstoke Rd SW18,
  SW19 . . . . 70 C2
Reverdy Rd SE1 . . 153 B3
Rewell St SW6 . . . 156 C1
Rex PI W1 . . . . 117 C2
Reynard Cl SE4 . . . . 66 A4
Reynard PI SE14 . . 51 A4
Reynolds Cl NW11 . . 2 A4
Reynolds Ho
  Finsbury Pk N4 . . . . 5 A3
  18 South Hackney
  E2 . . . . 25 B3
  St John's Wood
  NW8 . . . . 79 C1
  Westminster SW1 . 147 C3
Reynolds PI **12**
  TW10 . . . . 54 B1
Reynolds Rd
  Acton Green W4 . . 37 B3
  Nunhead SE15 . . . . 65 B3

Reynolds Sp Ctr
  W3 . . . . 36 C4
Rffra Rd Ret Pk
  SW2 . . . . 62 C2
Rheidol Mews N1 . . 86 C3
Rheidol Terr N1 . . . . 86 C3
Rhizotron & Xstrata
  Treetop Walkway★
  TW9 . . . . 44 A4
Rhoda St E2 . . 24 B1 99 A2
Rhodes Ho
  Shepherd's Bush
  W12 . . . . 30 A1
  Shoreditch N1 . . . . . 97 B4
Rhodesia Rd SW9 172 B1
Rhodes St N7 . . . . . . 14 B3
Rhodeswell Rd
  E14 . . . . 33 C4
Rhondda Gr E3 . . . . 26 B2
Rhyl Prim Sch **21**
  NW5 . . . . 12 C2
Rhyl St NW5 . . . . . . 12 C2
Ribblesdale Ho **11**
  NW6 . . . . 23 C4
Ribbon Dance Mews
  SE5 . . . . 48 C2
Ribstone Ho **2** E9 . . 17 C2
Ricardo St E14 . . . . 34 A3
Riceyman Ho WC1 . . 95 B3
Richard Anderson Ct
  4 SE14 . . . . 50 C3
Richard Atkins Prim
  Sch **22** SW2 . . . . . . 74 A4
Richard Burbidge
  Mans SW13 . . . . . . 47 B4
Richard Cloudesley
  Sch (Prim Dept)
  EC1 . . . . 97 A1
Richard Cloudesley
  Sch (Secondary
  Dept) EC1 . . . . 96 C1
Richard Cobden Prim
  Sch NW1 . . . . 83 A3
Richard Fox Ho N4 . . 6 B1
Richard Ho **10**
  SE16 . . . . 40 B2
Richard Knight Ho
  SW6 . . . . 165 C4
Richard Neale Ho **2**
  E1 . . . . 32 A2
Richardson Cl **10**
  E8 . . . . 24 B4
Richardson Ct **20**
  SW4 . . . . 172 B2
Richardson Ho **10**
  E14 . . . . 33 C4
Richardson's Mews
  W1 . . . . 92 C1
Richard's PI SW3 . 144 B4
Richard St **20** E1 . . 32 A3
Richbell WC1 . . . . . 106 B4
Richbell PI WC1 . . 106 C4
Richborne Terr
  SW8 . . . . 163 A2
Richborough Ho
  10 Deptford SE15 . . 50 B4
  14 Hackney E5 . . . . 17 A4
Richborough Rd
  NW2 . . . . 10 A3
Richbourne Ct
  W1 . . . . 102 B2
Richford Gate W6 . . 39 B3
Richford St W6 . . . . 39 B3
Rich Ind Est SE15 . . 50 A4
Rich La SW5 . . . . . 142 A2

Richland Ho **4**
  SE15 . . . . 49 C2
Richman Ho **10**
  SE8 . . . . 41 B1
RICHMOND 54 B3
Richmond Ave
  Islington N1 . . . . . . 85 A4
  Willesden NW10 . . . . 9 B2
Richmond Bldgs
  W1 . . . . 105 B1
Richmond Circus
  TW9 . . . . 54 A3
Richmond Coll
  W8 . . . . 128 B2
Richmond Cres N1 . . 85 B4
Richmond Ct
  SW1 . . . . 131 A3
Richmond Gr N1 . . 15 A1
Richmond Healthcare
  Hamlet Hospl
  TW9 . . . . 54 A4
RICHMOND HILL . . 54 A1
Richmond Hill
  TW10 . . . . 54 A1
Richmond Hill Ct **5**
  TW10 . . . . 54 A1
Richmond Ho
  12 Forest Hill
  SE26 . . . . 76 C1
  Regent's Pk NW1 . . 82 B1
  Walworth SE17 . . . . 151 B2
Richmond
  International Bsns
  Ctr **9** TW9 . . . . . . 54 B3
Richmond Mans
  Earl's Ct SW5 . . . . 142 A2
  Putney SW15 . . . . . . 58 A4
Richmond Mews
  W1 . . . . 105 B1
Richmond Park Rd
  SW14 . . . . 55 C3
Richmond Rd
  Dalston E8 . . . . 16 C1
  Ealing W5 . . . . 36 A4
Richmond Sta
  TW9 . . . . 54 A3
Richmond Terr
  SW1 . . . . 134 A4
Richmond Way W12,
  W14 . . . . 39 C4
Rich St E14 . . . . 33 B2
Rickard Cl SW2 . . . . 74 C3
Rickett St SW6 . . . 155 C4
Rickman Ho **22** E2 . . 25 B1
Rickman St **21** E1 . . 25 B1
Rick Roberts Way
  E15 . . . . 27 C3
Rickthorne Rd **7**
  N19 . . . . 5 A2
Riddell Ct SE1 . . . . 152 C2
Ridgdale St E3 . . . . 27 A3
Ridge Hill NW11 . . . . 1 A3
Ridge Rd NW2 . . . . . . 1 B1
Ridgeway **11**
  TW10 . . . . 54 A1
Ridgeway Dr W3 . . 36 C3
Ridgeway Gdns N6 . . 4 B4
Ridgeway The
  Acton W3 . . . . 36 C3
  Golders Green NW11 . . 1 B3
Ridgewell Cl N1 . . . . 87 A4
Ridgmount Gdns
  WC1 . . . . 105 B4
Ridgmount PI
  WC1 . . . . 105 B4

Ridgmount Rd
SW18 . . . . .59 A2
Ridgmount St
WC1 . . . . 105 B4
Ridgway Rd SW9 . . .63 A4
Riding House St
W1 . . . . 104 C3
Ridings Cl N6 . . . . . . 4 B4
Riding The NW11 . . . 1 B4
Ridley Ho 4
SW11 . . . . .60 A4
Ridley Rd
Dalston E8 . . . . . . .16 B3
Willesden Green
NW10 . . . . .21 C3
Ridley Road Mkt★
E8 . . . . .16 B3
Riffel Rd NW2 . . . . . .9 B3
Rifle Cl SE11 . . . . . 163 C4
Rifle Pl W11 . . . . . . .30 C1
Rifle St E14 . . . . . . .34 A4
Riga Ho 11 E1 . . . . . .32 C4
Rigault Rd SW6 . . . 164 B1
Rigden St E14 . . . . . .34 A3
Rigeley Rd NW10 . . .21 C2
Rigge Pl SW4 . . . . . .61 C3
Rigg Ho 2 SW4 . . . . .74 A4
Rignold Ho 6 SE5 . .49 A1
Riley Ho
1 Bow E3 . . . . .26 C1
Chelsea SW10 . . . . 157 B3
1 Streatham SW4 . .73 C4
Riley St SW10 . . . . . 157 B2
Rill Ho 16 SE5 . . . . . .49 A3
Rimini Ct SW12 . . . . .72 B3
Rinaldo Rd SW12 . . .73 A4
Ringcroft St N7 . . . . .14 C3
Ringford Ho SW18 . .58 B2
Ringford Rd SW18 . .58 C1
Ring Ho 18 E1 . . . . . .32 B2
Ringmer Ave SW6 . . 164 B3
Ringmer Gdns 3
N19 . . . . .5 A2
Ringmer Ho 18
SE22 . . . . .64 A4
Ring Rd W12 . . . . . . .30 B1
Ringsfield Ho
SE17 . . . . 151 A1
Ringwood Gdns
17 Millwall E14 . . . .41 C2
Roehampton SW15 . .68 C3
Ripley Gdns SW14 . . .55 C4
Ripley Ho
Mortlake SW14 . . . . .56 A4
Nine Elms SW11 . . 165 A4
Ripley's Believe It or
Not!★ SW1 . . . . . . 119 B3
Riplington Ct
SW15 . . . . .69 A4
Ripplevale Gr N1 . . . .14 B1
Risborough SE17 . . 150 C4
Risborough Ho
NW8 . . . . .90 B2
Risborough St
SE1 . . . . 136 B4
Risdon Ho 22 SE16 . .40 B4
Risdon St 27 SE16 . . .40 B4
Riseholme Ct E9 . . . .18 B2
Riseholme Ho 14
SE22 . . . . .64 A4
Riseldine Rd SE23 . . .66 A1
Risinghill St N1 . . . . .85 B2
Rising Sun Ct EC1 . . 108 B3
Risley Ho 7 E9 . . . . .17 C2
Rita Rd SW8 . . . . . . 162 C2

Ritchie Ho
Crouch End N19 . . . . 4 C4
5 Rotherhithe
SE16 . . . . .40 B3
15 South Bromley
E14 . . . . .34 C3
Ritchie St N1 . . . . . . .85 C2
Ritherdon Rd
SW17 . . . . .73 A2
Ritson Ho N1 . . . . . . .84 C3
Ritson Rd E8 . . . . . . .16 C2
Rivaz Pl E9 . . . . .17 B2
Riven Ct 10 W2 . . . . 100 B1
Riverains The
SW11 . . . . 167 B3
River Barge Cl
E14 . . . . .42 B4
Rivercourt Rd W6 . . .39 A1
River Ct SE1 . . . . . . 122 A3
Riverdale Dr
SW18 . . . . .71 A3
Riverfleet WC1 . . . . .94 B4
River Ho SW13 . . . . .46 A1
River House
Montessori Sch
E14 . . . . .42 A4
Rivermead Ct SW6 . .58 B4
Rivermead Ho E9 . . .18 A3
River Pl N1 . . . . .15 B1
River Plate Ho
EC2 . . . . 109 C3
Riversdale Prim Sch
SW18 . . . . .70 C3
Riversdale Rd N5 . . . . 6 B1
Riversdene N5 . . . . . . 6 B1
Rivers Ho 10 TW8 . . .36 C1
Riverside
Battersea SW11 . . . 158 B2
11 Rotherhithe
SE16 . . . . .40 B4
St Pancras N1 . . . . .84 B4
SW18 . . . . .71 A3
Riverside Ct SW8 . . 161 C4
Riverside Dr W4 . . . .46 A2
Riverside Gdns
W6 . . . . .39 A1
Riverside Health &
Racquets Club
Chiswick W4 . . . . . .46 A2
Riverside Ho 14
N1 . . . . .15 B1
Riverside Mans 4
E1 . . . . .32 B1
Riverside Prim Sch 87
SE16 . . . . 139 C3
Riverside Rd
Mill Meads E15 . . . .27 B3
Wandsworth SW17,
SW19 . . . . .71 B1
Riverside Wlk Mkt★
WC2 . . . . 121 A2
Riverside Workshops
SE1 . . . . 123 A2
River St EC1 . . . . . . .95 B4
River Terr
London W6 . . . . . . .39 B1
St James SW1 . . . . 120 C3
Riverton Cl W9 . . . . .23 B2
Riverview Gdns
SW13 . . . . .47 A4
Riverview Gr W4 . . . .45 A4
Riverview Rd W4 . . . .45 A4
River Way SE10 . . . . .43 B3

Rivet Ho SE1 . . . . . . 153 A2
Rivington Ct
NW10 . . . . .21 C4
Rivington Pl
EC2 . . . . .24 A2 98 B3
Rivington St
EC2 . . . . .24 A2 98 A3
Rivington Wlk 4
E8 . . . . .24 C4
Rixon Ho 4 SE17 . . 151 B2
Rixon St N7 . . . . 5 C1
Roach Rd E3 . . . . . . .18 C1
Roads Pl N19 . . . . 5 A2
Roan St SE10 . . . . . . .52 B4
Robert Adam St
W1 . . . . 103 B2
Roberta St
E2 . . . . .24 C2 99 C3
Robert Bell Ho 2
SE16 . . . . 153 B4
Robert Blair Prim Sch
N7 . . . . .14 A2
Robert Browning
Prim Sch SE17 . . . 151 B2
Robert Cl W9 . . . . . . .89 A1
Robert Dashwood
Way SE17 . . . . 150 C3
Robert Gentry Ho
W14 . . . . 140 B1
Robert Jones Ho 3
SE16 . . . . 153 B4
Robert Keen Cl 18
SE15 . . . . .49 C2
Robert Lowe Cl
SE14 . . . . .50 C3
Robert Owen Ho
Fulham SW6 . . . . . .47 C2
6 Spitalfields
E2 . . . . .24 B2 99 A4
Robert Owen Lo 4
E5 . . . . .17 A4
Roberts Ct
Islington N1 . . . . . . .86 B3
5 Willesden NW10 . . 8 A1
Roberts Ho 6
SE27 . . . . .75 A1
Roberts Mews
SW1 . . . . 131 B1
Robertson Ho 11
SE10 . . . . .52 B2
Robertson St
SW8 . . . . 170 B1
Robert's Pl EC1 . . . . .95 C2
Robert St
Regent's Pk NW1 . . .92 B3
Strand WC2 . . . . . . 120 B3
Robert Sutton Ho 25
E1 . . . . .32 B3
Robeson St 7 E3 . . .33 B4
Robin Ct 15 E14 . . . .42 B3
Robin Gr
Dartmouth Pk N6 . . . 3 C2
Highgate N6 . . . . 3 C2
Robin Ho NW8 . . . . .80 A1
Robin Hood SW15 . . .68 A1
Robin Hood Gdns 12
E14 . . . . .34 B2
Robin Hood La
E14 . . . . .34 B2
Robinscroft Mews 18
SE10 . . . . .52 A2
Robins Ct TW10 . . . .54 A1
Robin's Ct SW4 . . . . .62 A1
Robinsfield Inf Sch
NW8 . . . . .80 A2
Robinson Ct
Islington N1 . . . . . . .86 B4

Robinson Ct continued
4 Richmond TW9 . . .54 B3
Robinson Ho
4 North Kensington
W10 . . . . .30 C3
12 Tower Hamlets
E14 . . . . .33 C4
Robinson Rd E2 . . . . .25 B3
Robinson St SW3 . . 158 C4
Robinswood Mews 4
N5 . . . . .15 A3
Robsart St SW9 . . . . 173 B2
Robson Ave NW10 . . . 8 C1
Robson Rd SE21 . . . .75 B1
Roby Ho EC1 . . . . . . .96 C2
Rochdale Way 4
SE8 . . . . .51 C3
Roche Ho 13 E14 . . .33 B2
Rochelle Cl SW11 . . .59 C3
Rochelle Ct 4 E1 . . .32 B3
Rochelle St 81
E2 . . . . .24 B2 98 C3
Rochemont Wlk 2
E8 . . . . .24 C4
Roche Sch The 15
SW18 . . . . .58 C2
Rochester Ct
1 Bethnal Green
E2 . . . . .25 A1
9 Camden Town
NW1 . . . . .13 B1
Rochester Ho
Bermondsey SE1 . . 137 C3
18 Deptford SE15 . .50 B4
Rochester Mews
NW1 . . . . .13 B1
Rochester Pl NW1 . . .13 B1
Rochester Rd
NW1 . . . . .13 B2
Rochester Row
SW1 . . . . 147 A4
Rochester Sq NW1 . .13 B1
Rochester St SW1 . . 133 B1
Rochester Terr
NW1 . . . . .13 B2
Rochford Wlk 8
E8 . . . . .16 C1
Rochfort Ho 4
SE8 . . . . .41 B1
Rock Ave 13 SW14 . .55 C4
Rockell's Pl SE22 . . . .65 A1
Rockfield Ho SE10 . .52 B4
Rock Grove Way
SE16 . . . . 153 C4
Rockhall Rd NW2 . . . . 9 C4
Rockingham Cl
SW15 . . . . .56 B3
Rockingham St
SE1 . . . . 136 C2
Rockland Rd
SW15 . . . . .58 A3
Rockley Ct 9
W14 . . . . .39 C4
Rockley Rd W14 . . . .39 C4
Rocks La SW13 . . . . .56 C4
Rock St N4 . . . . 5 C2
Rockstraw Ho 5
NW3 . . . . .12 B1
Rockwood Ct N16 . . . 7 C4
Rocliffe St N1 . . . . . . .86 B1
Rocque Ho SW6 . . . 154 C2
Rodborough Rd
NW11 . . . . 1 C3

Rid–Rok 261

Rodenhurst Ct
SW4 . . . . .61 C2
Rodenhurst Rd
SW4 . . . . .61 C1
Roden St N7 . . . . 5 B1
Roderick Ho 3
SE16 . . . . .40 B2
Roderick Rd NW3 . . .12 B4
Rodgers Ho 4
SW4 . . . . .73 C4
Rodin Ct N1 . . . . .86 A3
Roding Ct 6 W12 . . .38 A4
Roding Ho N1 . . . . . .85 B3
Roding Mews E1 . . . 125 C2
Roding Rd E5 . . . . . . .18 A3
Rodmarton St W1 . . 103 A3
Rodmell WC1 . . . . . . .94 B3
Rodmere St SE10 . . .43 A1
Rodney Ct NW8 . . . . .89 A2
Rodney Ho
4 Cubitt Town
E14 . . . . .42 A2
Islington N1 . . . . . . .85 A1
Notting Hill
W11 . . . . .31 C2 113 B4
Rodney Pl SE17 . . . . 151 A4
Rodney Rd SE17 . . . 151 B3
Rodney St N1 . . . . . . .85 A1
Rodway Rd SW15 . . .68 C4
Rodwell Rd SE22 . . .64 B1
Roedean Cres
SW15 . . . . .56 A2
ROEHAMPTON 68 A4
Roehampton Church
SW15 . . . . .69 A4
Roehampton Cl
SW15 . . . . .56 C3
Roehampton Ct
SW15 . . . . .56 C3
Roehampton Gate
SW15 . . . . .56 A1
Roehampton High St
SW15 . . . . .68 C4
Roehampton La
Putney SW15 . . . . . .56 C1
Roehampton SW15 . .69 A3
Roehampton Univ
(Digby Stuart Coll)
SW15 . . . . .56 C3
Roehampton Univ
(Froebel Coll)
SW15 . . . . .56 B1
Roehampton Univ
(Southlands Coll)
SW15 . . . . .56 C2
Roehampton Univ
(Whitelands Coll)
SW15 . . . . .68 C4
Roehampton Vale
SW15 . . . . .68 B2
Roffey St E14 . . . . . . .42 B4
Rogate Ho E5 . . . . 7 C1
Roger Dowley Ct 8
E2 . . . . .25 B3
Roger's Almshouses
2 SW9 . . . . .62 B3
Rogers Est 28 E2 . . .25 B2
Rogers Ho SW1 . . . . 147 C4
Rogers Rd E16 . . . . . .35 B3
Roger St WC1 . . . . . . .95 A1
Rokeby Ho
8 Balham SW12 . . . .73 A4
Bloomsbury WC1 . . . .94 C1

Rokeby Rd SE4 . . . . . 51 B1
Rokeby Sch E15 . . . . 19 C1
Rokeland Ho SE4 . . . 66 A3
Roland Ho SW7 . . . . 143 A2
Roland Mews **1**
E1 . . . . 32 C4
Roland Way
South Kensington
SW7 . . . . 143 A2
Walworth SE17 . . . . 151 C1
Rollins St SE15 . . . . 50 B4
Rollit Ho N7 . . . . . . 14 C3
Rollit St N7 . . . . . . 14 C3
Rolls Ct SW11 . . . . 170 A3
Rolls Bldgs EC4 . . . 107 C2
Rollscourt Ave
SE24 . . . . 63 B2
Rolls Pas EC4 . . . . 107 B2
Rolls Rd SE1 . . . . . 153 A2
Rolt St SE8 . . . . . . 51 A4
Roman Cl W3 . . . . . 37 A4
Roman Ct **4** N7 . . . 14 B2
Romanfield Rd
SW2 . . . . 74 B4
Roman Rd
Chiswick W4 . . . . . . 38 B2
Globe Town E2, E3 . . 25 C3
2 Old Ford E3 . . . . 26 B4
Roman Road Mkt★ **1**
E3 . . . . 26 B3
Roman Way
Barnsbury N7 . . . . . 14 B2
4 Deptford SE15 . . 50 B4
Roma Read Cl
SW15 . . . . 69 A4
Romayne Ho SW4 . . 61 C4
Romberg Rd
SW17 . . . . 72 C1
Romborough Gdns
SE13 . . . . 67 B2
Romborough Way
SE13 . . . . 67 B2
Romer Ho **9** SW2 . . 62 B2
Romero Cl SW9 . . . 62 B4
Romeyn Rd SW16 . . 74 B1
Romford Ho 1
N1 . . . . 15 C2
Romford St E1 . . . . 32 A4
Romilly Rd N4 . . . . . 6 A2
Romilly St W1 . . . . 119 C4
Romily Ct **3** SW6 . 164 B2
Romney Cl
7 Deptford SE14 . . 50 B3
North End NW11 . . . . 2 B3
Romney Ct
9 Hammersmith
W12 . . . . 39 B4
9 Hampstead NW3 . 12 A2
Romney Ho 2
E14 . . . . 34 C2
Romney Mews
W1 . . . . 103 B4
Romney Rd SE10 . . . 52 C4
Romney St SW1 . . . 134 A1
Romola Rd SE24,
SW2 . . . . 75 A3
Ronald Ross Prim Sch
6 SW19 . . . . 70 A4
Ronaldsway N4 . . . . 5 C3
Ronalds Rd N5 . . . . 14 C3
Ronald St E1 . . . . . 32 B3
Rona Rd NW3 . . . . . 12 C4
Rona Wlk **20** N1 . . . 15 C2

Rondu Rd NW2 . . . . . 10 A3
Rood La EC3 . . . . . 124 A4
Rookery Rd SW4 . . . 61 B3
Rooke Way SE10 . . . 43 B1
Roosevelt Ct **15**
SW19 . . . . 70 A3
Rootes Dr W10 . . . . 30 C4
Ropemaker Rd
SE16 . . . . 41 A3
Ropemaker's Fields **7**
E14 . . . . 33 B2
Ropemaker St
EC2 . . . . 109 B4
Roper La SE1 . . . . 138 B3
Roper's Orch
SW3 . . . . 158 A3
Ropers Wlk **13**
SE24 . . . . 74 C4
Ropery St E3 . . . . . 26 B1
Rope St SE16 . . . . . 41 A3
Ropewalk Gdns 18
E1 . . . . 111 C2
Ropley St **8** E2 . . . 24 C3
Rosa Alba Mews
N5 . . . . 15 B4
Rosalind Ho **25** N1 . 24 A3
Rosaline Rd SW6 . . 154 B1
Rosaline Terr
SW6 . . . . 154 B1
Rosa Parks Ho **8**
SW9 . . . . 172 C1
Rosary Ct **17** E1 . . . 32 C4
Rosary Gdns SW7 . 143 A3
Rosary RC Prim Sch
NW3 . . . . 12 B1
Rosaville Rd SW6 . . 154 C1
Rosbury SW15 . . . . 58 A1
Roscastle Rd SE4 . . 66 A2
Roscoe St EC1 . . . . 97 A1
Roscommon Ho 2
NW3 . . . . 11 C3
Rose Alley
Borough The SE1 . . 123 A2
Broadgate EC2 . . . 110 B3
Rosebank
2 Dagenham W3 . . 28 C3
Fulham SW6 . . . . . . 47 B3
Rosebank Gdns
Bow E3 . . . . 26 B3
1 Dagenham W3 . . 28 C3
Rosebank Way
W3 . . . . 28 C3
Rosebank Wlk
NW1 . . . . 13 C1
Rosebay Ho **20** E3 . . 33 C4
Roseberry PI E8 . . . 16 B2
Roseberry St SE16 . . 40 A2
Rosebery Ave EC1 . . 95 C3
Rosebery Ct
Holborn EC1 . . . . . . 95 B2
Mayfair W1 . . . . . . 118 A2
Rosebery Ho 21
E2 . . . . 25 B3
Rosebery Rd SW2 . . 62 A1
Rosebery Sq EC1 . . . 95 B1
Rose Bush Ct NW3 . . 12 B3
Rosecroft Ave NW3 . . 1 C1
Rose & Crown Ct
EC2 . . . . 108 C2
Rose & Crown Yd
SW1 . . . . 119 A1
Rose Ct
7 Dalston E8 . . . . 16 B1
Islington N1 . . . . . . 86 A3

Rose Ct continued
Spitalfields E1 . . . . 111 A3
Rosedale Ct N5 . . . . 15 A4
Rosedale Ho N16 . . . . 6 C3
Rosedale Rd TW9 . . 54 A3
Rosedale Terr **6**
W6 . . . . 39 A3
Rosedene Ave
SW16 . . . . 74 B1
Rosedene NW6 . . . . 10 C4
Rosedew Rd W6 . . . 47 C4
Rosefield Gdns
E14 . . . . 33 C2
Roseford Ct **18**
W12 . . . . 39 C4
Rosegate Ho **32**
E3 . . . . 26 B3
Rosehart Mews 7
W11 . . . . 31 C3
Rosehill Rd SW18 . . 59 B2
Rose Joan Mews
NW6 . . . . 10 C4
Roseland Ho SW6 . . 58 A4
Roseleigh Ave N5 . . 15 A4
Rosemary Branch
Bridge N1 . . . . 87 C4
Rosemary Ct **35**
SE8 . . . . 51 B4
Rosemary Dr **18**
E14 . . . . 34 C3
Rosemary Gdns
SW14 . . . . 55 B4
Rosemary Ho
Shoreditch N1 . . . . . 87 C3
Willesden NW10 . . . 22 A4
Rosemary La
SW14 . . . . 55 B4
Rosemary Rd
Camberwell SE15 . . . 49 B3
Wandsworth SW17 . . 71 B1
Rosemary St N1 . . . 87 C4
Rosemary Works Sch
N1 . . . . 87 C3
Rosemead Prep Sch
SE27 . . . . 75 B2
Rosemont Mans 11
NW3 . . . . 11 A2
Rosemont Rd
Acton W3 . . . . 28 A2
Hampstead NW3 . . . 11 C2
South Hampstead
NW3 . . . . 11 B2
Rosemoor St
SW3 . . . . 144 C3
Rosemount Ct **2**
W3 . . . . 28 A1
Rosemount Lo W3 . . 28 A2
Rosenau Cres
SW11 . . . . 168 C3
Rosenau Rd
SW11 . . . . 168 C4
Rosendale Prim Sch
SE21 . . . . 75 B4
Rosendale Rd SE21,
SE24 . . . . 75 B3
Roseneath Rd
SW11 . . . . 60 C1
Rosenthal Ho SE6 . . 67 A1
Rosenthal Rd SE6 . . 67 B1
Rosenthorpe Rd
SE15 . . . . 65 C2
Roserton St E14 . . . 42 B4
Rose Sq SW7 . . . . 143 C2
Rose St
Holborn EC4 . . . . . 108 B2
Strand WC2 . . . . . 120 A4
Rose Theatre SE1 . . 122 C2

Rosethorn Cl
SW12 . . . . 73 C4
Rosetta Cl SW8 . . . 162 B1
Roseway SE21 . . . . 63 C1
Rosewood Ct **2**
E11 . . . . 19 C4
Rosewood Gdns
SE13 . . . . 52 B1
Rosewood Ho 3
NW3 . . . . 11 A2
Rosewood Sq
W12 . . . . 29 C3
Rosher Cl E15 . . . . 19 C1
Rosina St E9 . . . . . 17 C2
Roskell Rd SW15 . . . 57 C4
Roslin Ho **2** E1 . . . 32 C2
Roslin Rd W3 . . . . . 37 A3
Rosmead Rd
W11 . . . . 31 A2 112 B4
Rosoman PI EC1 . . . 95 C2
Rosoman St EC1 . . . 95 C3
Ross Ct
1 Hackney E5 . . . . 17 A4
4 Putney SW15 . . . 69 C4
Rossdale Rd SW15 . . 57 B3
Rosse Gdns SE13 . . 67 C1
Rossendale Way
NW1 . . . . 83 A4
Rossetti Ct WC1 . . . 105 B4
Rossetti Gdns Mans
SW3 . . . . 158 C4
Rossetti Ho **1** SW1 147 C3
Rossetti Mews
NW8 . . . . 79 C3
Rossetti Rd SE16 . . 40 A1
Rossetti Studios
SW3 . . . . 158 A3
Ross Ho **6** E1 . . . . 32 A1
Rossington St E5 . . . 7 C2
Rossiter Rd SW12 . . 73 A3
Rosslyn Ave SW13 . . 56 B4
Rosslyn Ct NW3 . . . 12 A3
Rosslyn Hill NW3 . . 11 C3
Rosslyn Ho 7
TW9 . . . . 44 B2
Rosslyn Mans
7 Hampstead
NW3 . . . . 11 B2
South Hampstead
NW6 . . . . 11 B2
Rosslyn Mews 7
NW3 . . . . 11 C4
Rosslyn Park Mews
NW3 . . . . 11 C3
Rossmore Ct NW1 . . 90 C2
Rossmore Rd NW1 . . 90 B2
Rostrevor Mans
SW6 . . . . 164 C4
Rostrevor Mews
SW6 . . . . 164 C3
Rostrevor Rd
SW6 . . . . 164 C4
Rotary Lo **12** SE27 . 75 A1
Rotary St SE1 . . . . 136 B2
Rothay NW1 . . . . . . 92 B4
Rothbury Rd E9 . . . 18 C1
Rotheley Ho **9** E9 . . 17 B1
Rotherfield Ct
De Beauvoir Town
N1 . . . . 15 C1
Shoreditch N1 . . . . . 87 B4
Rotherfield Prim Sch
N1 . . . . 87 A4
Rotherfield St
Islington N1 . . . . . . 15 B1
Shoreditch N1 . . . . . 87 A4

Rotherham Wlk
SE1 . . . . 122 A1
ROTHERHITHE 40 C3
Rotherhithe Bsns Est
8 SE16 . . . . 40 B2
Rotherhithe New Rd
SE16 . . . . 40 A1
Rotherhithe Old Rd
SE16 . . . . 40 C2
Rotherhithe Prim Sch
25 SE16 . . . . 40 C2
Rotherhithe St
SE16 . . . . 40 B4
Rotherhithe Sta
SE16 . . . . 40 B4
Rotherhithe Tunnel
SE16 . . . . 32 C1
Rother Ho SE15 . . . 65 A3
Rotherwick Rd
NW11 . . . . 1 C4
Rotherwood Rd
SW15 . . . . 57 C4
Rothery St N1 . . . . . 86 B4
Rothesay Ave SW14,
TW10 . . . . 55 A3
Rothesay Ct 13
SE11 . . . . 163 B3
Rothley Ct NW8 . . . 89 B2
Rothsay St SE1 . . . 138 A1
Rothsay Wlk **19**
E14 . . . . 41 C2
Rothschild Rd W4 . . 37 B3
Rothwell St
1 Hampstead
NW1 . . . . 12 B1
Primrose Hill NW1 . . 81 A4
Roth Wlk N7 . . . . . . 5 B2
Rotten Row SW1 . . 130 C4
Rotterdam Dr E14 . . 42 B3
Rouel Rd
Bermondsey SE16 . . 153 B4
Bermondsey SE16 . . 139 B1
Roundacre SW19 . . 69 C2
Roundel Cl SE4 . . . . 66 B3
Roundwood Rd
NW10 . . . . 8 B1
Rounton Rd E3 . . . . 26 C1
Roupell Rd SW2 . . . 74 B3
Roupell St SE1 . . . . 121 C1
Rousden St NW1 . . . 13 B1
Routh Rd SW18 . . . 72 A4
Rover Ho **20** N1 . . . 24 A4
Rowallan Rd SW6 . . 154 A1
Rowan Cl W5 . . . . . 36 A4
Rowan Ct
15 Camberwell
SE15 . . . . 49 B3
Wandsworth SW11 . . 60 B1
Rowan Ho
8 Bow E3 . . . . . . 26 B4
Dagenham NW10 . . . 21 A1
5 Maitland Pk
NW3 . . . . 12 B2
Rowan Rd W6 . . . . . 39 C2
Rowan Terr W6 . . . . 39 C2
Rowan Wlk
7 Dartmouth Pk
N19 . . . . 4 B2
Kensal Town W10 . . 23 A1
Rowberry Cl SW6 . . 47 B3
Rowcross St SE1 . . 153 A2
Rowditch La
SW11 . . . . 169 B2
Rowdon Ave NW10 . . 9 A1
Rowe Ho E9 . . . . . . 17 B2
Rowe La E9 . . . . . . 17 B3

Rowena Cres
SW11 . . . . **168** B1

Rowfant Rd SW12,
SW17 . . . .**72** C2

Rowhill Mans **11**
E5 . . . . .17 A4

Rowhill Rd E5 . . . . . . .17 A4

Rowington Cl W2 **100** A4

Rowland Hill Ho
SE1 . . . .**136** A4

Rowland Hill St
NW3 . . . . .12 B3

Rowley Gdns N4. . . . . .6 B4

Rowley Ho SE8 . . . . . .51 C4

Rowley Ind Pk W3 . . . .37 A3

Rowley Way NW8 . .**78** C4

Rowntree Cl NW6 . .**10** C2

Rowse Cl E15 . . . . . . .27 B4

Rowstock **11** NW5 . .13 C2

Rowstock Gdns
N7 . . . . .13 C3

Roxby Pl SW6 . . . . **155** C4

Roxford Ho **2** E3 . . .27 A1

Roxley Rd SE13. . . . . .67 A1

Roxwell **10** NW1 . . . .13 A2

Roxwell Rd W12. . . . .38 C4

Royal Academy of
Dramatic Art★
WC1 . . . .**105** B4

Royal Acad of Arts★
W1 . . . .**118** C3

Royal Acad of Dance
SW11 . . . .**167** C3

Royal Acad of Music
NW1 . . . .**91** C1

Royal Albert Hall★
SW7 . . . .**129** B3

Royal Arc W1 . . . . . **118** C3

Royal Armouries
The★ E1 . . . .**124** C3

Royal Ave SW3 . . . .**144** C2

Royal Avenue Ho
SW3 . . . .**144** C2

Royal Ballet Upper
Sch The WC2 . . . . .**106** B1

Royal Brompton Hospl
Chelsea SW3 . . . . .**143** B2
Chelsea SW3 . . . . .**144** A2

Royal Cir SE27. . . . . .75 A1

Royal Cl
Deptford SE8 . . . . . .51 B4
Putney SW15 . . . . . .69 C2
Stamford Hill N16. . . .7 A3

Royal College of
Physicians Liby
NW1 . . . .**92** B2

Royal College St
NW1 . . . .**83** A4

Royal Coll of
Anaesthetists
WC1 . . . .**106** C3

Royal Coll of Art
SW7 . . . .**129** B3

Royal Coll of Art
Sculpture Sch
SW11 . . . .**158** A1

Royal Coll of
Midwives W1. . . .**104** A3

Royal Coll of Music
SW7 . . . .**129** B2

Royal Coll of
Obstetricians &
Gynaecologists
NW1 . . . .**90** C3

Royal Coll of
Ophthalmologists
NW1 . . . .**91** B1

Royal Coll of
Paediatrics & Child
Health W1 . . . . . .**107** A4

Royal Coll of
Pathologists
SW1 . . . .**119** B1

Royal Coll of
Physicians NW1 . .**92** B2

Royal Coll of
Radiologists W1. .**104** B4

Royal Coll of Science
SW7 . . . .**129** B2

Royal Coll of Speech
Language Therapists
SE1 . . . .**123** B1

Royal Coll of
Surgeons WC2 . . .**107** A2

Royal Coll of
Veterinary Surgeons
SW1 . . . .**134** A1

Royal Courts of
Justice WC2 . . . . .**107** B1

Royal Cres
W11 . . . . . .**31** A1 **112** A1

Royal Crescent Mews
W11 . . . . .30 C1

Royal Ct
City of London
EC3 . . . .**109** C1
Rotherhithe SE16. . .**41** B3

Royal Duchess Mews
11 SW12 . . . . .73 A4

Royal Exchange★
EC3 . . . .**109** C1

Royal Exchange Bldgs
EC3 . . . .**109** C1

Royal Festival Hall★
SE1 . . . .**121** A1

Royal Free Hospl
NW3 . . . . .12 A3

Royal Fusiliers Mus★
E1 . . . .**124** C3

Royal Geographical
Society SW7 . . . .**129** C3

Royal Hill SE10 . . . .**52** B3

Royal Hill Ct **2**
SE10 . . . . .52 B3

Royal Horticultural
Society (Lawrence
Hall & Conf Ctr)
SW1 . . . .**133** B1

Royal Horticultural
Society (Lindley
Hall) SW1 . . . . . .**147** B4

Royal Hospital
Chelsea The★
SW1 . . . .**145** B1

Royal Hospital Rd
SW3 . . . .**145** A1

Royal Hospl for Neuro-
Disability The
SW15 . . . . .58 A1

Royal Hospl Mus★
SW3 . . . .**145** A1

Royal Institute of
British Architects
W1 . . . .**104** B4

Royal Institution Mus
The★ SW1 . . . . . .**118** C3

Royal Langford
Apartments **3**
NW6 . . . .**78** A2

Royal London Est The
NW10 . . . . .20 C1

Royal London
Homeopathic Hospl
WC1 . . . .**106** B4

Royal London Hospl
Mus★ 32 A4

Royal London Hospl
(Whitechapel) The
E1 . . . . .32 A4

Royal Marsden Hospl
SW3 . . . .**143** C2

Royal Mews The★
SW1 . . . .**132** B2

Royal Mint Pl **6**
E1 . . . .**125** B4

Royal Mint St E1 . .**125** A4

Royal National
Orthopaedic Hospl
W1 . . . .**92** B1

Royal National TNE
Hospl The TN1 . . .**94** C4

Royal Naval Pl
SE14 . . . . .51 B3

Royal Oak Ct **1**
N1 . . . .**24** A2 **98** A4

Royal Oak Pl SE22 . .65 A1

Royal Oak Rd **5**
E8 . . . . .17 A2

Royal Oak Sta W2 **100** B3

Royal Oak Yd SE1 **138** A3

Royal Observatory
The★ SE10 . . . . . . .52 C3

Royal Opera Arc
SW1 . . . .**119** B2

Royal Orchard Cl
SW18 . . . . .70 A4

Royal Par
Blackheath Vale
SE3 . . . . .53 B1
Fulham SW6 . . . . .**154** A2
12 Richmond TW9 . . . .44 C2

Royal Pl **11** SE10 . .**52** B3

Royal Rd SE17 . . . . .48 A4

Royal Sch Hampstead
The **8** NW3 . . . . .11 C4

Royal St SE1 . . . . . .**135** A2

Royalty Ho W1 . . . .**105** B1

Royalty Mews W1 . .**105** B1

Royalty Studios
W11 . . . . .31 A3

Royal United Services
Mus★ SW1 . . . . . .**120** A1

Royal Veterinary Coll
NW1 . . . .**83** B3

Royal Victoria Sta
E16 . . . . .35 C2

Royal Victor Pl E3 . .25 C3

Roycroft Cl SW2 . . . .74 C3

Roydon Cl **7**
SW11 . . . .**168** C2

Roy Ridley Ho **6**
SW4 . . . . .61 C4

Roy Sq E14 . . . . .33 A2

Royston Ct
New Cross SE14 . . . .51 B1
1 Richmond TW9 . . .44 B2

Royston Ho **14**
SE15 . . . . .49 C4

Royston Rd TW10 . . .54 A2

Royston St **2** E2 . . .25 B3

Rozel Ct **3** N1. . . . .24 A4

Rozel Rd SW4 . . . . . .61 B4

Ruby St SE15 . . . . . .50 A4

Ruby Triangle
SE15 . . . . .50 A4

Ruckholt Rd E9,
E10 . . . . .18 C4

Rucklidge Ave
NW10 . . . . .21 C3

Rudall Cres NW3 . . . .11 C4

Rudbeck Ho **11**
SE15 . . . . .49 C3

Ruddington Cl E5 . . .18 A4

Rudge Ho **1**
SE16 . . . .**139** C2

Rudgwick Terr
NW8 . . . .**80** B3

Rudhall Ho **4**
SW2 . . . . .62 C1

Rudloe Rd SW12 . . . .73 B4

Rudolf Pl SW8 . . . .**162** B3

Rudolph Rd NW6 . . .**23** C3

Rudstone Ho **10**
E3 . . . . .27 A2

Rudyard Ct SE1. . . .**137** C3

Rufford St N1 . . . . . .**84** B4

Rufford Street Mews
N1. . . . .**14** A1

Rufford Twr **5**
W3 . . . . .28 A1

Rufus Bsns Ctr
SW18 . . . . .71 A2

Rufus Ho SE1 . . . . .**139** A2

Rufus St N1 . . .24 A2 **98** A3

Rugby Mans W14. **140** B4

Rugby Rd W4. . . . . . .38 A4

Rugby St WC1 . . . . .**94** C1

Rugg St E14. . . . . . . .33 C2

Rugless Ho **2** E14. .42 B4

Rugmere **4** NW1. .12 C1

Rumball Ho **14**
SE5 . . . . .49 A2

Rumbold Rd SW6. **156** B1

Rum Cl E1 . . . . .32 B2

Rumford Ho SE1. . .**136** C1

Rumsey Rd SW9 . . . .62 B4

Runacres Ct SE17 **150** C1

Runcorn Pl
W11 . . . . .31 A2 **112** A4

Rundell Twr SW8 . .**172** C4

Running Horse Yd **12**
TW8 . . . . .44 A4

Runnymede Ct
SW15 . . . . .68 C3

Runnymede Ho
Hackney E9. . . . . . . .18 A4
Richmond TW10 . . . .54 C2

Rupack St **3** SE16 . .40 B4

Rupert Ct W1 . . . . .**119** B4

Rupert Gdns SW9 . . .48 A1

Rupert Ho
SE11 . . . .**149** C3
8 Upper Holloway
N19. . . . . .4 C1

Rupert Rd
Bedford Pk W4 . . . . .38 A3
Paddington NW6 . . .23 B3
Upper Holloway N19 . .4 C2

Rupert St W1. . . . . .**119** B4

Rusbridge Cl E8 . . . .16 C3

Ruscoe Rd E16 . . . . .35 B3

Rusham Rd SW12. . . .72 B4

Rushbrook Ho **2**
SW8 . . . .**171** B2

Rushby Ct SW4 . . . .**172** A3

Rush Common Mews
15 SW2 . . . . .74 B4

Rushcroft Rd SW2,
SW9 . . . . .62 C3

Rushcutters Ct **18**
SE16 . . . . .41 A2

Rushey Mead SE4 . .**66** C2

Rushford Rd SE4 . . .**66** B1

Rush Hill Mews **3**
SW11 . . . . .60 C4

Rush Hill Rd SW11. .60 C4

Rushlake Ho **3**
SW11 . . . .**169** B2

Rushmead **5**
E2 . . . . .25 A2

Rushmere Ho **4**
SW15 . . . . .68 C3

Rushmore Cres **9**
E5 . . . . .17 C4

Rushmore Ho
8 Kentish Town
NW5 . . . . .13 C3
W14 . . . .**126** B1

Rushmore Prim Sch
13 E5 . . . . .17 C4

Rushmore Rd
Clapton Pk E5 . . . . . .17 C4
Hackney E5. . . . . . . .18 A4

Rusholme Rd
SW15 . . . . .58 A1

Rushton Ho **26**
SW8 . . . .**171** B1

Rushton St N1 . . . . .**87** C2

Rushworth St SE1 **136** B3

Ruskin Ave TW9 . . . .44 C3

Ruskin Cl SE5 . . . . . .63 C4

Ruskin Ho SW1. . . .**147** C3

Ruskin Park Ho
SE5 . . . . .63 C4

Ruskin Wlk SE24 . . .63 B2

Rusper Cl SW9 . . . .**172** B1

Russell Cl W4 . . . . . .46 B4

Russell Ct
Battersea SW11 . . .**169** C3
Bloomsbury WC1 . . . .94 A1
5 Peckham SE15 . . . .50 A1
St James SW1 . . . .**119** A1

Russell Gdns W14 **126** A2

Russell Gdns Mews
W14 . . . .**126** A2

Russell Gr **33**
SW9 . . . .**173** C4

Russell Ho
21 Poplar E14 . . . . . .33 C3
SW1 . . . .**146** C2

Russell Kerr Cl
W4 . . . . .45 B3

Russell Lo SE1 . . . .**137** B2

Russell Mans
WC1 . . . .**106** B4

Russell Pickering Ho
2 SW4 . . . . .62 A4

Russell Pl
Hampstead NW3 . . . .12 A3
Rotherhithe SE16. . . .41 A3

Russell Rd W14. . . .**126** B1

Russell Sq WC1 . . . .**94** A1

Russell Square Ho
WC1 . . . . .94 A1

Russell Square Mans
WC1 . . . .**106** B4

Russell Square Sta
WC1 . . . . .94 A1

Russell St WC2 . . . .**120** B4

Russell's Wharf **2**
W9 . . . . .23 B1

Russell Wlk **2**
TW10 . . . . .54 B1

Russett Yd SW15. . . .58 A3

Russet Cres N7. . . . .14 B3

Russett Way SE13 . .52 A1

Russia Dock Rd
SE16 . . . .**33** A1
Russia La E2 . . . .**25** B3
Russia Row EC2 . . .**109** A1
Rusthall Ave W4 . . . .**37** C3
Rusthall Mans 3
W4 . . . .**37** C2
Ruston Mews W11. .**31** A3
Ruston St E3 . . . .**26** B4
Rust Sq SE5 . . . .**48** C3
Ruth Ct 16 E3 . . . . . .**26** A3
Rutherford Ho 12
E1 . . . .**25** A1
Rutherford St
SW1 . . . .**147** B4
Ruth Ho W10 . . . .**23** A1
Ruthin Rd SE3 . . . . . .**53** C4
Ruthven St E9 . . . . . .**25** C4
Rutland Cl SW14 . . . .**55** B4
Rutland Ct
Herne Hill SE5 . . . . . .**63** C3
SW7 . . . .**130** B3
Rutland Gate
SW7 . . . .**130** B3
Rutland Gate Mews
SW7 . . . .**130** A3
Rutland Gdns
SW7 . . . .**130** B3
Rutland Gdns Mews
SW7 . . . .**130** B3
Rutland Gr W6 . . . . . .**39** A1
Rutland Ho
10 Putney SW15 . . . .**69** B4
W8 . . . .**128** A1
Rutland Mews 21
NW8 . . . .**78** B3
Rutland Mews E
SW7 . . . .**130** B2
Rutland Mews S
SW7 . . . .**130** A2
Rutland Mews W
SW7 . . . .**130** A2
Rutland Park Gdns 1
NW2 . . . .**9** B2
Rutland Park Mans 2
NW2 . . . .**9** B2
Rutland Pk NW2 . . . . .**9** B2
Rutland Pl EC1 . . . . .**108** B4
Rutland Rd E9 . . . . . .**25** C4
Rutland St SW7 . . . .**130** B2
Rutland Studios
NW10 . . . .**21** C2
Rutley Cl SE11 . . . . . .**48** A4
Rutt's Terr SE14 . . . .**50** C2
Ruvigny Gdns
SW15 . . . .**57** C4
Ruvigny Mans 7
SW15 . . . .**57** C4
Rycott Path SE22 . . .**76** C4
Rycuiff Sq SE3 . . . . . .**53** B1
Rydal Ho 9 SW8 . . .**171** B1
Rydal Water NW1 . . .**92** C3
Ryde Ho 1 NW6 . . . .**23** C4
Ryder Ct SW1 . . . . . .**119** A2
Ryder Dr SE16 . . . . . .**40** A1
Ryder Ho 5 E1 . . . . . .**25** B1
Ryder St SW1 . . . . . .**119** A2
Ryder's Terr NW8 . . . .**78** C2
Ryder St SW1 . . . . . .**119** A2
Ryde Vale Rd
SW12 . . . .**73** B2
Rydon St N1 . . . .**87** A4
Rydston Cl 2 N7 . . . .**14** B1

Ryecotes Mead
SE21 . . . .**76** A3
Ryecroft Rd SE13 . . . .**67** B2
Ryecroft St SW6 . . .**166** A3
Ryedale SE22 . . . .**65** A1
Ryefield Path 7
SW15 . . . .**68** C3
Ryegates 2 SE15 . . . .**50** A1
Rye Hill Pk SE15 . . . .**65** B3
Rye Ho 17 SE16 . . . . . .**40** B4
Rye La SE15 . . . .**49** C1
Rye Lane Mkt★
SE15 . . . .**49** C1
Rye Oak Sch 3
SE15 . . . .**65** A4
Rye Rd SE15 . . . .**65** C3
Rye Wlk SW15. . . . . . .**57** C2
Ryfold Rd SW19 . . . .**70** C1
Ryland Rd NW5 . . . . .**13** A2
Rylett Cres W12 . . . .**38** B3
Rylett Rd W12 . . . . . .**38** B3
Rylston Rd SW6 . . . .**154** C3
Rymer St SE24 . . . . . .**63** A1
Rysbrack St SW1 . . .**130** C2

S

Saatchi Gallery Duke
of York's HQ★
SW3 . . . .**145** A2
Sabbarton St 9
E16 . . . .**35** B3
Sabella Ct E3 . . . .**26** B3
Sabine Rd SW11 . . . .**60** C4
Sable St N1 . . . .**15** A1
Sacketts Ho 2
SW9 . . . .**173** C4
Sackville Ho 16
SW16 . . . .**74** A1
Sackville St W1 . . . .**119** A3
Sacred Heart High
Sch 8 W6 . . . .**39** B2
Sacred Heart Prim
Sch, Battersea
SW11 . . . .**168** B1
Sacred Heart RC Prim
Sch SW15 . . . .**56** C2
Sacred Heart RC Sec
Sch 10 SE5 . . . .**48** B2
Sacred Heart Sch
N7 . . . .**14** B3
Saddlers Mews
SW8 . . . .**172** B4
Sadler Ho
17 Bromley E3 . . . . . .**27** A2
EC1 . . . .**96** A4
Saffron Ave E14 . . . .**34** C2
Saffron Ct 10 N1 . . . .**15** C2
Saffron Hill EC1 . . . .**107** C4
Saffron Wharf
SE1 . . . .**139** A4
Sage Mews SE22 . . . .**64** B2
Sage St E1 . . . .**32** B2
Sage Way WC1 . . . . . .**94** C3
Sailacre Ho 10
SE10 . . . .**43** B1
Sail Ct 18 E14 . . . . . .**34** C2
Sailmakers Ct
SW6 . . . .**59** B4
Sail St SE11 . . . .**149** A4
Sainfoin Rd SW17 . . .**72** C2
St Agnes Cl E9 . . . . . .**25** B4

St Agnes Pl SE11 . . . .**48** A4
St Agnes RC Prim Sch
15 E3 . . . .**27** A2
London NW2 . . . .**1** A1
St Aidan's Prim Sch
N4 . . . .**5** C4
St Aidan's Rd SE22 . .**65** A2
St Albans Ave W4 . . . .**37** C3
St Alban's CE Prim
Sch EC1 . . . .**107** B4
St Alban's Cl NW11 . . .**1** C3
St Alban's Gr W8 . . .**128** B2
St Albans La NW11 . . .**1** C3
St Albans Mans
W8 . . . .**128** B2
St Alban's Pl N1 . . . . .**86** A3
St Alban's Rd
Dagenham NW10 . . . .**21** A4
Dartmouth Pk NW5 . . . .**4** A1
St Alban's St SW1 . .**119** B3
St Alban's Studios
W8 . . . .**128** B2
St Albans Terr
W6 . . . .**154** A4
St Alban's Villas
NW5 . . . .**3** C1
St Alfege Pas
SE10 . . . .**52** B4
St Alfege with St
Peter's CE Prim Sch
SE10 . . . .**52** B4
St Aloysius Convent
NW1 . . . .**93** B4
St Aloysius RC Coll 10
N19 . . . .**4** B3
St Aloysius RC Jun
Sch NW1 . . . .**83** B1
St Alphage Gdn
EC2 . . . .**109** A3
St Alphage Highwalk
EC2 . . . .**109** A3
St Alphonsus Rd
SW4 . . . .**61** C3
St Andrew & St
Francis CE Prim Sch
6 NW2 . . . .**8** C2
St Andrew's
(Barnsbury) Prim
Sch N1 . . . .**85** A4
St Andrews Chambers
W1 . . . .**105** A2
St Andrews Ct 4
SE16 . . . .**40** A1
St Andrews Ct W4 . . .**45** B2
St Andrew's Ct 2
SW18 . . . .**71** B2
St Andrew's Gr N16 . .**6** C3
St Andrew's Greek
Sch NW1 . . . .**13** B2
St Andrew's Hill
EC4 . . . .**108** B1
St Andrews Ho 11
SE16 . . . .**40** A3
St Andrews Mans 9
E5 . . . .**17** A4
St Andrew's Mans
W1 . . . .**103** B3
St Andrews Mews
Greenwich SE3 . . . . . .**53** C3
8 Streatham SW12 . .**73** C3
St Andrew's Mews
N16 . . . .**7** A3
St Andrew's Pl
NW1 . . . .**92** B2

St Andrew's Prim Sch
82 SW9 . . . .**172** B1
St Andrews Rd
W3 . . . .**29** A3
St Andrew's Rd
W14 . . . .**154** B4
Willesden NW2 . . . .**9** A2
St Andrew's Sq
W11 . . . .**31** A3
St Andrew St EC4 . .**107** C3
St Andrews Way
E3 . . . .**27** B1
St Andrew's Wharf
SE1 . . . .**139** A4
St Anne RC Prim Sch
E1 . . . .**24** C1 **99** B1
St Anne's CE Prim Sch
6 SW18 . . . .**59** A2
St Anne's Cl N6 . . . . . .**3** C1
St Anne's Ct
Kensal Rise NW6 . . . . .**23** A4
W1 . . . .**105** B1
St Anne's Flats
NW1 . . . .**93** B4
St Anne's Pas E14 . . .**33** B3
St Anne's RC Prim Sch
SE11 . . . .**162** C4
St Anne's Row E14 . .**33** B3
St Anne St E14 . . . . . .**33** B3
St Anne's Trad Est 23
E14 . . . .**33** B3
St Ann's Cres
SW18 . . . .**59** B1
St Ann's Gdns
NW5 . . . .**12** C2
St Ann's Hill SW18. . .**59** B1
St Ann's Ho WC1 . . . .**95** B3
St Ann's La SW1 . . . .**133** C1
St Ann's Park Rd
SW18 . . . .**59** B1
St Ann's Rd
Barnes SW13 . . . .**46** B2
Shepherd's Bush
W11 . . . .**30** C2
St Ann's St SW1 . . . .**133** C2
St Ann's Terr NW8 . . .**79** C2
St Ann's Villas
W11 . . . .**31** A1 **112** A1
St Anselm's 3
W1 . . . .**118** A4
St Anselm's RC Prim
Sch SW17 . . . .**72** C1
St Anthonys Cl 5
E1 . . . .**125** B2
Hackney Wick E9. . . . .**18** B2
St Anthony's Ct
1 Balham SW12 . . . . .**60** C1
Upper Tooting
SW17 . . . .**72** C2
St Anthony's Flats
NW1 . . . .**83** B1
St Anthony's RC Prim
Sch SE22 . . . .**64** C1
St Anthony's Sch 8
NW3 . . . .**11** C3
St Asaph Ct SE4 . . . . .**65** C4
St Asaph Rd SE4 . . . .**65** C4
St Aubins Ct N1 . . . . .**87** C4
St Augustine's CE
High Sch 15 NW6 . .**23** C3
St Augustine's Ho
NW1 . . . .**93** B4
St Augustine's Prim
Sch 5 NW6 . . . .**78** A2

St Augustine's RC
Prim Sch W6 . . . . .**154** B3
St Augustine's Rd
NW1 . . . .**13** C1
St Austell Rd SE13 . . .**52** C1
St Barnabas CE Prim
Sch SW1 . . . .**145** C2
St Barnabas Cl 1
SE22 . . . .**64** A2
St Barnabas St
Philip CE Prim Sch
W8 . . . .**127** B1
St Barnabas St
SW1 . . . .**145** C2
St Barnabas Terr
E9 . . . .**17** C3
St Barnabas Villas
SW8 . . . .**172** B4
St Bartholomew's
Hospl EC1 . . . .**108** B3
St Bartholomew's
Mus★ EC1 . . . .**108** B3
St Bede's RC Inf Sch
SW12 . . . .**73** C3
St Benets Cl 1
SW17 . . . .**72** A2
St Benet's Pl EC3 . . .**123** C4
St Bernadette RC Jun
Sch 9 SW12 . . . .**73** B4
St Bernard Ho 6
E14 . . . .**42** B3
St Botolph St E1,
EC3 . . . .**110** C2
St Brelades Ct N1 . . .**87** C4
St Bride's EC4. . . . . .**108** A1
St Bride's Ave
EC4 . . . .**108** A1
St Bride's Pas
EC4 . . . .**108** A1
St Bride St EC4 . . . . .**108** A2
St Catherines Cl 7
SW17 . . . .**72** A2
St Catherine's Ct 8
W4 . . . .**38** A3
St Catherine's Dr
SE14 . . . .**50** C1
St Catherines Mews
SW3 . . . .**144** C4
St Cecilia's CE Sch
SW18 . . . .**70** B3
St Chad's Pl WC1 . . . .**94** C4
St Chad's St WC1 . . . .**94** B4
St Charles' Hospl
W10 . . . .**30** C4
St Charles Ho W10 . .**31** A4
St Charles RC Prim
Sch 7 W10 . . . .**30** C4
St Charles RC Sixth
Form Coll 8
W10 . . . .**30** C4
St Charles Sq W10. . .**30** C4
St Christina's RC Prep
Sch NW8 . . . .**80** B2
St Christophers Ct 13
N19 . . . .**4** B1
St Christopher's Ho
NW1 . . . .**83** B1
St Christopher's Pl
W1 . . . .**103** C2
St Clair Ho 17 E3 . . . .**26** B2
St Clare St EC3 . . . . .**110** C1
St Clement Danes CE
Prim Sch WC2. . . . . .**106** C1

St Clement & St
James CE Prim Sch
W11 . . . . . 31 A1 112 A2
St Clements Ct
Barnsbury N7 . . . . . . 14 B2
7 SE14 . . . . 50 C4
8 Shepherd's Bush
W11 . . . . 30 C2
St Clement's Ct
EC3 . . . . 123 C4
St Clements Ho
E1 . . . . 110 C3
St Clement's La
WC2 . . . . 107 A1
St Clements Mans 3
SW6 . . . . 47 C4
St Clements St N7 . . 14 C1
St Columb's Ho 11
W10 . . . . 31 A4
St Crispins Cl
NW3 . . . . 12 A4
St Cross St EC1 . . . 107 C4
St Cuthbert's Rd
NW2 . . . . 10 B2
St Cuthbert with St
Matthias CE Prim
Sch SW5 . . . . 142 A2
St Davids Cl 27
SE16 . . . . 40 A1
St David's Sq E14 . . 42 A1
St Dionis Rd SW6 165 A2
St Dominic RC Prim
Sch 14 NW5 . . . . . . 12 B3
St Dominics RC Prim
Sch 23 E9 . . . . 18 A2
St Donatt's Rd
London SE14 . . . . . 51 B2
New Cross Gate SE4 . 51 B1
St Dunstan Ave
W3 . . . . 28 C2
St Dunstan Gdns
W3 . . . . 28 C2
St Dunstan's Ct
EC4 . . . . 107 C1
St Dunstan's Hill
EC3 . . . . 124 A3
St Dunstan's La
EC3 . . . . 124 A3
St Dunstan's Rd
W6 . . . . 39 C1
St Edmunds Cl 3
SW17 . . . . 72 A2
St Edmund's Cl
NW8 . . . . 80 C3
St Edmund's Ct
NW8 . . . . 80 C3
St Edmunds RC Prim
Sch E14 . . . . 41 C2
St Edmund's Sq
SW13 . . . . 47 B4
St Edmund's Terr
NW8 . . . . 80 C3
St Edward's RC Prim
Sch NW1 . . . . 90 B1
St Elizabeth RC Prim
Sch 33 E2 . . . . 25 B3
St Elizabeth's RC Prim
Sch TW10 . . . . 54 B1
St Elmo Rd W12 . . . 38 B4
St Elmos Rd SE16 . . 41 A4
St Ermin's Hill
SW1 . . . . 133 B2
St Ervan's Rd W10 . . 31 B4

St Eugene de
Mazenod RC Prim
Sch 12 NW6 . . . . . . 10 C1
St Faith's CE Prim Sch
17 SW18 . . . . 59 B2
St Faith's Rd SE24 . . 75 A3
St Francesca Cabrini
RC Prim Sch
SE23 . . . . 65 B1
St Francis' Ho
NW1 . . . . 83 B1
St Francis of Assisi
Prim Sch 11 W11 . . 30 C2
St Francis Pl
SW12 . . . . 61 A1
St Francis RC Prim
Sch 23 SE15 . . . . . 49 C3
St Francis Rd
SE22 . . . . 64 A3
St Francis Xavier Coll
SW12 . . . . 61 A1
St Frideswides Mews
5 E14 . . . . 34 B3
St Gabriel's CE Prim
Sch SW1 . . . . 146 C1
St Gabriels Cl 3
E14 . . . . 34 A4
St Gabriel's Rd
NW2 . . . . 9 C3
St George Ho
SW11 . . . . 169 C3
ST GEORGE IN THE
EAST 32 A2
St George's Ave
N7 . . . . 13 C4
St George's Bldgs
SE11 . . . . 136 B1
St George's Cath
NW1 . . . . 92 B4
St George's Cath RC
Prim Sch SE1 . . . . 136 B2
St George's CE Prim
Sch
18 SE5 . . . . 49 A3
SW8 . . . . 161 A1
St George's Circ
SE1 . . . . 136 A2
St Georges Cl
SW8 . . . . 171 A4
St Georges Ct
SW15 . . . . 58 B3
St George's Ct
Brompton SW3 . . . . 144 A4
Kensington SW7 . . . 128 C1
Newington SE1 . . . . 136 A1
St George's Dr
SW1 . . . . 146 C2
St George's Field
W2 . . . . 102 B1
St George's Gr
SW17 . . . . 71 C1
St George Hanover
Sq Sch W1 . . . . . . 117 C3
St George's Ho
NW1 . . . . 83 B2
St George's La
EC3 . . . . 124 A4
St Georges Mews 11
W11 . . . . 31 B3
St George's Mews
8 Rotherhithe
SE8 . . . . 41 B2
SE1 . . . . 135 C2
St Georges Pl N7 . . 13 C4

St George's Pools
E1 . . . . 32 A2
St George's RC Cath
SE1 . . . . 135 C2
St George's RC Sec
Sch W9 . . . . 78 B1
St Georges Rd W4 . . 37 C4
St George's Rd
Newington SE1 . . . . 136 A1
Richmond TW9 . . . . . 54 B4
St George's
Residences 4
SW2 . . . . 62 C2
St George's Sq
E14 . . . . 108 A2
St George's Sq
Rotherhithe SE8 . . . . 41 A2
SW1 . . . . 147 B1
St George's Square
Mews SW1 . . . . . . 147 B1
St George St W1 . . 118 B4
St Georges Terr
Hampstead NW1 . . . 12 B1
NW1 . . . . 81 A4
St George's Way
SE15 . . . . 49 A4
St George the Martyr
CE Prim Sch WC1 . . 95 A1
St George Wharf
SW8 . . . . 162 A4
St Gerards Cl SW4 . 61 B2
St German's Pl
SE3 . . . . 53 C2
St Gildas' RC Jun Sch
18 N8 . . . . 5 A4
ST GILES 106 A2
St Giles Cir WC1 . . 105 C2
St Giles Coll 11 . . 106 B4
St Giles Ct WC2 . . 106 A2
St Giles High St
WC2 . . . . 105 C2
St Giles Ho SW16 . . 74 A1
St Giles Pas WC2 . 105 C1
St Giles Rd SE5 . . . 49 A2
St Giles Terr EC1 . . 109 A3
St Giles Twr 3
SE5 . . . . 49 A2
St Gilles Ho 15 E2 . 25 C3
St Helena Ho WC1 . . 95 B3
St Helena Rd SE16 . 40 C2
St Helena St WC1 . . 95 B3
St Helens Gdns
W10 . . . . 30 C3
St Helen's Pl EC3 . 110 A2
St Helen's RC Sch 17
SW9 . . . . 62 C4
St Helier Ct 4 N1 . . 24 A4
St Hildas Cl 2
SW17 . . . . 72 A2
St Hilda's Cl 11 NW6 . 9 C1
St Hilda's Rd
SW13 . . . . 47 A4
St Hilda Wharf
E1 . . . . 32 B1
St Hubert's Ho 2
E14 . . . . 41 C3
St Hughes Cl 4
SW17 . . . . 72 A2
St Ives Ct NW2 . . . . 10 A2
ST JAMES 119 B2
St James Ct
26 Bethnal Green
E2 . . . . 24 C2 99 C3
5 Brentford W4 . . . . 36 C1

St James' Ct
Bedford Pk W4 . . . . 37 C3
SW1 . . . . 133 A2
St James Ho N5 . . . 14 C3
St James Independent
Schs W14 . . . . . . 140 B4
St James Ind Mews 2
SE1 . . . . 153 C1
St James Mans
NW6 . . . . 10 C1
St James Mews
E14 . . . . 42 B3
St James's SE14 . . . 51 A2
St James & St
Michael's CE Prim
Sch W2 . . . . 115 A4
St James's App
EC2 . . . . 24 A1 98 A1
St James's Ave E2 . . 25 B3
St James's Ct
Sch SE14 . . . . 51 A2
St James School Flats
5 N7 . . . . 14 C3
St James's Cl
NW8 . . . . 80 C3
Upper Tooting
SW17 . . . . 72 B2
St James's Cloisters
2 SE22 . . . . 64 B3
St James's Cres
SW9 . . . . 62 C4
St James's Dr
Balham SW12,
SW17 . . . . 72 B4
Upper Tooting
SW17 . . . . 72 B3
St James's Gdns
W11 . . . . . 31 A1 112 A2
St James's Gr
SW11 . . . . 169 A2
St James's Market
SW1 . . . . 119 B3
St James's Pal★
SW1 . . . . 119 A1
St James's Park Sta
SW1 . . . . 133 B2
St James's Pas
EC3 . . . . 110 B1
St James's Pk★
SW1 . . . . 133 B4
St James's Pl
SW1 . . . . 118 C1
St James's Rd
Bermondsey SE1,
SE16 . . . . 153 C4
Peckham SE1 . . . . . 49 C4
St James's Sq
SW1 . . . . 119 A2
St James's St
SW1 . . . . 118 C2
St James St W6 . . . 39 B1
St James's Terr
NW8 . . . . 80 C4
2 Upper Tooting
SW12 . . . . 72 C3
St James's Terrace
Mews NW8 . . . . . . 80 C3
St James The Great
RC Prim Sch 17
SE15 . . . . 49 B2
St James Wlk EC1 . . 96 A2
St Joan of Arc RC
Prim Sch N5 . . . . . 15 B4
St John of Jerusalem
CE Prim Sch 42
E9 . . . . 17 B1

ST JOHN'S 51 C1
St John & St James
CE Prim Sch 1
E9 . . . . 17 B3
St John's Angell Town
CE Prim Sch 28
SW9 . . . . 173 B1
St John's Ave
Dagenham NW10 . . . 21 B4
Putney SW15 . . . . . 57 C2
St John's CE Prim Sch
25 E2 . . . . 25 B3
St John's CE Walham
Green Prim Sch
SW6 . . . . 164 B4
St John's Church Rd
E9 . . . . 17 B3
St John's Cl SW6 . 155 B2
St John's Concert
Hall★ SW1 . . . . . . 134 A1
St John's Cres
SW9 . . . . 62 C4
St Johns Ct 30 EC1 . 32 A1
St John's Ct
Finsbury Pk N4 . . . . . 6 A2
Hammersmith W6 . . 39 A2
Lewisham SE13 . . . . 52 B1
5 South Hampstead
NW3 . . . . 11 B2
Saint John's Ct N5 . 15 A3
St John's Dr SW18 . 71 A3
St John's Est SE1 . 138 C3
St John's Gdns
W11 . . . . . 31 B2 112 C3
3 Barnes SW13 . . . 46 B1
1 Richmond TW9 . . 54 A3
Upper Holloway N19 . . 4 C2
St John's Highbury
Vale CE Prim Sch
N5 . . . . 6 A1
St John's Hill
SW11 . . . . 59 C3
St John's Hill Gr
SW11 . . . . 59 C3
St Johns Ho 5
SE17 . . . . 48 C4
St John's Ho 1
E14 . . . . 42 B2
St John's La EC1 . . 108 B4
St John's Lodge 8
SE8 . . . . 51 C2
St John's Mans 11
N19 . . . . 4 C1
St John's Path EC1 . 96 A1
St John's Pk SE3 . . 53 C3
St John's Pl EC1 . . . 96 A1
St John's RC Prim Sch
SE16 . . . . 41 A4
St John's Rd
Battersea SW11 . . . 60 A3
Canning Town E16 . . 35 C3
Richmond TW9 . . . . . 54 A3
St John's &
St Clements CE Jun &
Inf Sch 42 SE15 . . . 64 C4
St John's Sq EC1 . . 96 A1
St John's Sta SE8 . . 51 C1
St John St EC1 . . . . 96 A2
St John's Terr
W10 . . . . 22 C1
St John's Therapy Ctr
SW11 . . . . 59 C3

St John's Upper
Holloway CE Prim
Sch **7** N19..........4 C2
St John's Vale SE8..**51** C1
St John's Villas
Upper Holloway N19 ..4 C2
W8 ....**128** B1
St John's Walworth
CE Prim Sch
SE17 ....**151** A3
St John's Way N19 ..4 C3
ST JOHN'S WOOD .79 B1
St John's Wood Cl
NW8 ....**89** C3
St John's Wood High
St NW8 ....**80** A1
St John's Wood Park
NW8 ....**79** B4
St John's Wood Pre-
Prep Sch NW8.....**90** A4
St John's Wood Rd
NW8 ....**89** C3
St John's Wood Sta
NW8 ....**79** B2
St John's Wood Terr
NW8 ....**80** A2
St John the Baptist
VA CE Prim Sch
N1................**87** C1
St John the Divine CE
Jun & Inf Sch
SE5.................48 A3
St John the Evangelist
RC Prim Sch N1...**86** A2
St Joseph's Cl
W10 ....31 A4
St Josephes Ct **3**
NW10 ....21 B3
St Joseph's Flats
NW1 ....**93** B4
St Joseph's Ho
W6 ....39 C2
St Joseph's Hospice
E9, E8.............25 A4
St Joseph's RC Inf &
Jun Schs **53** SE5...48 B3
St Joseph's RC Prim
Sch
Chelsea SW3 .....**144** C3
10 Deptford SE8....**51** C3
11 Greenwich SE10 ..43 A1
Paddington W9 ....**88** C3
Rotherhithe SE16 ..40 B3
St Giles WC2......**106** B2
Upper Holloway N19 ..4 A3
16 Wandsworth
SW18 ....**58** C2
6 Willesden NW10...8 A1
St Joseph's St
SW8 ....**170** B4
St Joseph's Ho
SE3................**67** C4
St Jude & St Paul's CE
Prim Sch **17** N1 ..16 A2
St Jude's CE Prim Sch
4 London SE24......63 A2
SE1...............**136** A1
St Judes Ho **6**
W10 ....23 B2
St Jude's Rd E2.....25 A3
St Jude St N16 .....16 A3
St Julian's Rd
NW6 ....23 C4

St Katharine's Ho
N1................85 B2
St Katharine's Prec
NW1 ....82 A2
St Katharine's Way
E1...............125 A2
St Katharine's Row
EC3 ....110 B1
St Katharine's Wlk **1**
N1................30 C1
St Kilda's Rd N16....7 A3
St Laurence's Cl
NW6 ....22 C4
St Lawrence Ct N1 87 C4
St Lawrence Ho
SE1..............138 B2
St Lawrence St
E14 ....34 B1
St Lawrence Terr
W10 ....31 A4
St Lawrence Way
SW9 ....173 C2
St Leonards Ct
N1................55 B4
St Leonard's Ct N1 97 C4
St Leonard's Hospl
N1................24 A3
St Leonards Rd
SW14 ....55 B4
Becontree NW10....20 C1
South Bromley E14..34 B4
St Leonard's Sq
NW5 ....12 C2
St Leonard's St **3**
E3 ....27 A2
St Leonard's Terr
SW3 ....145 A1
St Loo Ave SW3 ..158 B4
St Loo Ct SW3 ....158 C4
St Luke Prim CE Sch
5 E16 ....35 B3
ST LUKE'S.........97 A2
St Luke's Ave SW4..61 C3
St Luke's CE Prim Sch
7 Cubitt Town
E14 ....42 C2
Paddington W9.....23 B2
Shoreditch EC1....97 A3
St Luke's Cl EC1....97 A2
St Luke's Ct W11 ..31 B3
St Luke's Mews
W11 ....31 B3
St Luke's Rd W11...31 B4
St Luke's Sq E16 ..35 B3
St Luke's St SW3 .144 B2
St Margaret's Cres
SW15 ....57 A2
St Margaret's Ct
Putney SW15 ......57 A3
SE1..............123 B1
St Margaret's La
W8 ....128 A1
St Margaret's Lo
W3 ....37 A4
St Margaret's Rd
Brockley SE4......66 B3
Kensal Green NW10..22 B2
St Margaret's Sch
NW3 ....11 A4
St Margaret St
SW1 ....134 A3
St Mark's CE Prim Sch
SE11.............163 A4
St Marks Cl **5**
SE10 ....52 B3

St Mark's Cres
NW1 ....81 C4
St Marks Gate E9...18 B1
St Mark's Gr
SW10 ....156 B2
St Marks Ho **6**
SE17 ....48 C4
St Mark's Mans **14**
N4................14 C1
St Mark's Pl W11...31 A3
St Mark's Prim Sch **11**
N19................5 A2
St Marks Rd
8 North Kensington
W10 ....30 C3
North Kensington
W10 ....30 C4
St Mark's Rd W11..31 A3
St Mark's Rise E8..16 B3
St Mark's Sq NW1..81 C3
St Mark St E1.....111 A1
St Martin-in-the-
Fields High Sch **2**
SW2...............74 C3
St Martin's
Almshouses NW1 82 C4
St Martin's Cl NW1 82 C4
St Martins Ct N1 ...24 A4
St Martin's Ct
WC2 ....120 A4
West Norwood
SE27..............75 A2
St Martin's La
WC2 ....120 A3
St Martin's Le Grand
EC1 ....108 C2
St Martin's Pl
WC2 ....120 A3
St Martin's Rd
SW9 ....172 C2
St Martin's St
WC2 ....119 C3
St Martin's Way
SW17 ....71 B1
St Mary Abbots CE
Prim Sch W8.....128 A3
St Mary Abbot's Ct
W14 ....126 C1
St Mary Abbot's Pl
W8 ....127 A1
St Mary Abbots Terr
W14 ....127 A1
St Mary at Hill
EC3 ....124 A3
St Mary Axe EC3...110 B2
St Marychurch St
SE16 ....40 B4
St Mary Graces Ct
E1...............125 A3
St Marylebone CE Sch
The W1...........103 C4
St Mary le Bow
Church* EC2......109 A1
St Mary- le-Park Ct
SW11 ....158 B3
St Mary Magdalene
Acad N7 ....14 C2
St Mary Magdalene
CE Prim Sch
Paddington
W2...............100 A4
5 Peckham SE15 ...50 A1
St Mary Magdalene's
RC Prim Sch
Brockley SE4......66 A3
14 Mortlake SW14...55 C4

St Mary Magdalen's
RC Jun Sch **1**
NW2 ....9 A2
St Mary Newington Cl
SE17.............152 B2
St Mary of the Angels
RC Prim Sch **2**
W2................31 C3
St Mary RC Prim Sch
22 W10.............23 A3
St Mary & St Michael
Prim Sch **27** E1....32 B3
St Mary & St Pancras
CE Prim Sch **8** N1 83 B1
St Mary's Bryanston
Square CE Sch
W1...............102 C4
St Mary's CE Prim Sch
Islington N1 ......86 B4
London SE13......67 A2
Putney SW15 ......57 C4
Willesden NW10....8 A3
St Mary's CE Sch W6 39 C3
St Mary's Est **2**
SE16 ....40 B4
St Mary's Flats
NW1 ....93 B4
St Mary's Gate
W8 ....128 A1
St Mary's Gdns
SE11.............149 C4
St Mary's Gr
Barnes SW13......57 A4
Chiswick W4.......45 A4
Islington N1.......15 A2
Richmond TW10,
TW9 ....54 B3
St Mary's Ho N1....86 B4
St Mary's Hospl
W2...............101 C2
St Mary's Hospl
Medical Sch W2 101 C2
St Mary's Kilburn CE
Prim Sch **18** NW6..23 C4
St Mary's Mans
Dagenham NW10 ...21 A4
Paddington W2.....101 B4
St Mary's Mews
NW6 ....11 A1
St Mary's Path N1..86 B4
St Mary's Pl W8 ..128 A1
St Mary's RC Prim Sch
Chiswick W4.......46 A4
10 Clapham Pk SW4 .61 B2
Clapham SW8......170 B4
Hammersmith W14 ..39 C3
Paddington NW6 ...23 C3
St Mary's Rd
Golders Green
NW11 ....1 A4
Harlesden NW10 ...21 A4
Nunhead SE15.....50 B1
St Mary's Sch
Hampstead NW3 ...11 B4
St Mary's Sq W2...101 B4
St Mary's Stoke
Newington CE Prim
Sch **2** N16........7 A2
St Mary's Terr
St Mary's Twr EC1..97 A1
St Mary's Wlk
SE11.............149 C4
St Matthews CE Sch
SW1 ....133 C2

St Matthews Ct
SE1..............136 C1
St Matthew's Ho **8**
SE17 ....48 C4
St Matthew's Lo
NW1 ....83 A2
St Matthew's Rd
SW2...............62 B2
St Matthew's Row
E2 ....24 C1 99 B2
St Matthew St
SW1 ....133 B1
St Matthias CE Prim
Sch E2........24 B1 99 A2
St Matthias CE Prim
Sch **3** N16......16 A4
St Mauritius Ho
SE13 ....67 B2
St Maur Rd SW6...165 A3
St Michael & All
Angels CE Acad **35**
SE5................48 A3
St Michael's Alley
EC3 ....109 C1
St Michael's CE Prim
Sch
Camden Town NW1..82 C4
Highgate N6........3 C4
Wandsworth SW18 ..70 B4
St Michaels Ct **2**
E14 ....34 B4
St Michael's Ct
NW11 ....1 B4
St Michael's Flats
NW1 ....83 B1
St Michael's Gdns
W10 ....31 A4
St Michael's Rd
Cricklewood NW2....9 B4
Stockwell SW9 ...172 C2
St Michael's St
W2...............102 A2
St Michael Steiner
Sch The SW18 ....58 C2
St Mildred's Ct
EC2 ....109 B1
St Monica's RC Prim
Sch **2** N1...24 A2 98 B4
St Nicholas' Flats
NW1 ....83 B1
St Nicholas Ho
SE8................51 C4
St Nicholas Mans
SW17 ....72 B2
St Nicholas St SE8..51 C2
St Norbert Gn SE4..66 A3
St Norbert Rd SE4..66 A3
St Olaf's Rd SW6..154 B1
St Olaves Ct W2 ..114 A3
St Olave's Est SE1 138 B4
St Olave's Gdns
SE11.............149 B4
St Olave's Mans
SE11.............149 B4
St Olav's Sq **32**
SE16 ....40 B4
St Osmund's RC Prim
Sch SW13.........46 B2
St Oswald's Pl
SE11.............148 C1
St Oswald St SW1 147 C3
St Owen Ho SE1...138 B2
ST PANCRAS 94 B4

St Pancras Almshouses 13
NW5 . . . . 12 B3

St Pancras Commercial Ctr
NW1 . . . . 83 A4

St Pancras Hospl
NW1 . . . . 83 B3

St Pancras International Sta
WC1 . . . . 94 A4

St Pancras Way
NW1 . . . . 83 B4

St Patrick's Coll
W1 . . . . 105 B2

St Patrick's RC Prim Sch NW5 . . . . . 13 A3

St Paul's Ave
Rotherhithe SE16 . . . 32 C1
Willesden NW2 . . . . . 9 B2

St Paul's Cath *
EC4 . . . . 108 C1

St Paul's Cath Sch
EC4 . . . . 108 C1

St Paul's CE Prim Sch
25 Hammersmith
W6 . . . . 39 B1
Hampstead NW3 . . . 12 B3
SE17 . . . . 150 C2

St Paul's Church Yd
EC4 . . . . 108 C1

St Pauls Cl W5 . . . 36 B4
St Pauls Cres
NW1 . . . . 13 C1

St Paul's Ct
Clapham SW4 . . . . . 61 C3
6 Upper Holloway
N19 . . . . 5 A2

St Paul's Dr E15 . . 19 C3
St Pauls Mews
NW1 . . . . 13 C1

St Pauls Pl N1 . . . 15 C2
St Pauls Rd TW9 . . 54 B4
St Paul's Rd N1 . . 15 B2
St Paul's Sch
SW13 . . . . 38 C1
St Pauls Sta EC2 . 108 C2
St Pauls Steiner Sch
25 N1 . . . . 87 A3
St Paul St N1 . . . . 87 A2
St Paul's Terr
SE17 . . . . 48 A4
St Pauls View WC1 . 95 B3
St Paul's Way E3 . . 33 C4
St Paul's Way Com Sch 23 E3 . . . . . 33 C4
St Paul's with St Michael's Prim Sch
24 E8 . . . . 24 C4
St Paul with St Luke CE Prim Sch 10
E3 . . . . 33 B4
St Peter & St Paul RC Prim Sch E3 . . . . . 96 B2
St Peter's Alley
EC3 . . . . 109 C1
St Peter's Ave 27
E2 . . . . 24 C3
St Petersburgh Mews
W2 . . . . 114 A4
St Petersburgh Pl
W2 . . . . 114 A3

St Peter's CE Prim Sch
15 Chiswick W6 . . . . 38 C1
6 E1 . . . . 32 B1
8 Paddington W9 . . . 23 C1
SE17 . . . . 151 B1
SW1 . . . . 132 B1

St Peter's Church Ct
N1 . . . . 86 B3

St Peters Cl 1
N1 . . . . 24 A3
St Peter's Cl E2 . . 24 C3
St Peters Ct
New Cross SE4 . . . . 51 B1
2 Stepney E1 . . . . . 25 B1

St Peter's Gdns
SE27 . . . . 74 C1
St Peter's Gr W6 . . 38 C2
St Peters Ho WC1 . 94 B3
St Peter's Ho
4 SE17 . . . . 48 C4
Stamford Hill N16 . . . 7 A4
St Peter's Pl W9 . . 88 A1
St Peter's Rd W6 . . 38 C1
St Peter's Sq
Chiswick W6 . . . . . . 38 B1
Hackney E2 . . . . . . 24 C3
St Peter's St N1 . . 86 B3
St Peter's Street Mews N1 . . . . 86 B2
St Peter's Terr
SW6 . . . . 154 B1
St Peter's Villas 5
W6 . . . . 38 C2
St Peter's Way N1 . 16 A1
St Peter's Wharf 6
W6 . . . . 38 C1
St Philip Ho WC1 . . 95 B3
St Philip Sq 1
SW8 . . . . 170 A1
St Philip's Rd E8 . . 16 C2
St Philip's Sch
SW7 . . . . 143 A3
St Philip St SW8 . . 170 A1
St Philip's Way N1 . 87 A3
St Quentin Ho
SW18 . . . . 59 C1
St Quintin Ave
W10 . . . . 30 C4
St Quintin Gdns 21
W10 . . . . 30 B4
St Regis Hts NW3 . . 2 A1
St Richard's Ho
NW1 . . . . 93 B4
St Rule St SW8 . . 170 C1
St Saviours SW4 . . 61 A3
St Saviour & St Olaves CE Sch SE1 . . . 137 C1
St Saviour's CE Prim Sch
8 Bow Comm E14 . . 34 B4
Camberwell SE24 . . 63 B4
20 Paddington W9 . . 88 B1
St Saviours Ho 55
SE1 . . . . 139 B3
St Saviour's RC Prim Sch SE13 . . . . . 67 B3
St Saviour's Rd
SW2 . . . . 62 B2
St Saviour's Wharf
SE1 . . . . 139 A4
St Scholastica's RC Prim Sch 5 E5 . . . 7 C1
St Silas Pl NW5 . . . 12 C2
St Simon's Ave
SW15 . . . . 57 B2

St Stephen's Ave
W12 . . . . 39 A4
St Stephen's CE Prim Sch
Paddington W2 . . . . 31 C4
7 Shepherd's Bush
W12 . . . . 39 B4
2 St Johns SE8 . . . . 51 C1
SW8 . . . . 162 C2
St Stephen's Cl
Maitland Pk NW5 . . . 12 B3
NW8 . . . . 80 B3
St Stephen's Cres
W2 . . . . 31 C3
St Stephen's Gdns
Notting Hill W2 . . . . 31 C3
4 Putney SW15 . . . . 58 B2
St Stephen's Gr
SE13 . . . . 67 B4
St Stephens Ho 7
SE17 . . . . 48 C4
St Stephen's Mews 34
W2 . . . . 31 C4
St Stephen's Rd
E3 . . . . 26 B3
St Stephen's Row
EC4 . . . . 109 B1
St Stephen's Terr
SW8 . . . . 162 C1
St Stephen's Wlk
SW7 . . . . 142 C4
St Swithin's La
EC4 . . . . 123 B4
St Swithun's Rd
SE13 . . . . 67 C2
St Thomas' CE Prim Sch 25 W10 . . . . 23 A1
St Thomas Ct 14
NW1 . . . . 13 B1
St Thomas Ho 2
E1 . . . . 32 C3
St Thomas More Language Coll
SW3 . . . . 144 C3
St Thomas of Canterbury RC Prim Sch SW6 . . . . 154 C2
St Thomas Rd E16 . 35 C3
St Thomas' Rd W4 . 45 B4
St Thomas's Gdns
NW5 . . . . 12 C2
St Thomas's Hospl
SE1 . . . . 134 C2
St Thomas's Pl 20
E9 . . . . 17 B1
St Thomas's Rd
Dagenham NW10 . . . 21 A4
Highbury N4, N5 . . . . 5 C1
St Thomas's Sq E9 . 17 B1
St Thomas St SE1 . 123 C1
St Thomas's Way
SW6 . . . . 155 A2
St Thomas the Apostle Coll SE15 . 50 B2
St Ursula's Convent Sch SE10 . . . . . . 52 C3
St Vincent De Paul Ho
2 E1 . . . . 32 B4
St Vincent De Paul RC Prim Sch SW1 . . 133 A2
St Vincent Ho
SE1 . . . . 138 C2
St Vincent's RC Prim Sch
Acton W3 . . . . 28 A2

St Vincent's RC Prim Sch *continued*
Marylebone W1 . . . 103 C3
St Vincent St W1 . 103 C3
Salamanca Pl SE1 . 148 C3
Salamanca St SE1,
SE11 . . . . 148 C3
Salcombe Gdns
SW4 . . . . 61 A3
Salcombe Lo NW5 . 12 C4
Salcombe Rd 23
N16 . . . . 16 A3
Salcombe Villas 13
TW10 . . . . 54 A2
Salcot W1 . . . . 5 B2
Salcott Rd SW11 . . 60 B2
Salehurst Rd SE4 . . 66 B1
Salem Ho 13 E9 . . 17 C2
Salem Rd W2 . . . 114 B4
Sale Pl W2 . . . . . 102 A2
Salesian Coll
SW11 . . . . 168 A3
Sale St E2 . . . . 24 C1
Salford Ho 5 E14 . . 42 B2
Salford Rd SW12,
SW2 . . . . 73 B3
Salisbury Cl SE17 . 151 B4
Salisbury Ct
15 Bermondsey
SE16 . . . . 139 C1
Chiswick W4 . . . . . . 38 A2
EC4 . . . . 108 A1
Hackney E9 . . . . . . 18 A3
Salisbury Ho
2 Islington N1 . . . . . 15 A2
Islington N1 . . . . . . 86 A4
3 Poplar E14 . . . . . 34 A3
Westminster SW1 . . 147 C2
Wimbledon SW19 . . 69 C1
Salisbury Mews
SW6 . . . . 154 C1
Salisbury Pl
Camberwell SW9 . . . 48 A3
Marylebone W1 . . . 102 C4
Salisbury Rd TW9 . 54 A3
Salisbury Sq EC4 . 107 C1
Salisbury St
10 Acton W3 . . . . . . 37 B4
NW8 . . . . 90 A1
Salisbury Terr
SE15 . . . . 65 B4
Salisbury Wlk N19 . . 4 B2
Salmon La E14 . . . 33 A3
Salmon St 14 E14 . 33 B3
Saltcoats Rd W4 . . 38 A4
Saltdene N4 . . . . . . 5 B3
Salter Rd
Rotherhithe SE16 . . 32 C1
SE16 . . . . 33 A1
Salters' Hall Ct
EC4 . . . . 123 B4
Salters Rd W10 . . . 22 C1
Salter St
College N5 NW11 . . 21 C2
10 Poplar E14 . . . . 33 C2
Salterton Rd N7 . . . 5 B1
Saltoun Rd SW2,
SW9 . . . . 62 C3
Saltram Cres W9 . . 23 C2
Saltwell St E14 . . . 33 C2
Saltwood Gr SE17 . 151 B1
Saltwood Ho 16
SE15 . . . . 50 B4
Salusbury Prim Sch
NW6 . . . . 23 B4
Salusbury Rd NW6 . 23 B4

Salutation Rd
SE10 . . . . 43 A2
Salvin Rd SW15 . . . 57 C4
Salway Rd E15 . . . 19 C2
Salween Ho 2
N16 . . . . 15 C4
Sambrook Ho 25
E1 . . . . 32 B4
Samels Ct W6 . . . . 38 C1
Samford Ho N1 . . . 85 B3
Samford St NW8 . . 90 A1
Sam Manners Ho 7
SE10 . . . . 43 A1
Sam March Ho 5
E14 . . . . 34 C3
Sampson St E1 . . 125 C1
Samuel Cl
SE14 . . . . 50 C4
Shoreditch E8 . . . . . 24 B4
Samuel Ct
N1 . . . . 24 A2 98 A3
Samuel Ho 18 E8 . . 24 B4
Samuel Jones Ind Est
7 SE15 . . . . 49 A3
Samuel Lewis Bldgs
N1 . . . . 14 C2
Samuel Lewis Trust Dwellings
6 Camberwell
SE5 . . . . 48 B2
Chelsea SW3 . . . . . 144 A3
Walham Green
SW6 . . . . 155 C2
West Kensington
W14 . . . . 140 B4
Samuel Rhodes Sch
N1 . . . . 85 B4
Samuel Richardson Ho W14 . . . . . . 140 C3
Samuel St 2 W6 . . 39 B2
Sancroft Ct SW11 . 168 B4
Sancroft Ho SE11 . 149 B2
Sancroft St SE11 . 149 B2
Sanctuary Mews 18
E8 . . . . 16 B2
Sanctuary St SE1 . 137 A4
Sanctuary The
13 Wapping E1L . . . 32 A1
Westminster SW1 . . 133 C2
Sandale Cl N16 . . . . 6 C1
Sandall Ho 7 E3 . . 26 A3
Sandall Rd NW5 . . . 13 B2
Sandalwood Cl 11
E1 . . . . 26 A1
Sandalwood Ho 6
NW3 . . . . 11 A2
Sandbourne
4 Kensington
W11 . . . . 31 C3
14 Paddington NW8 . 78 B4
Sandbourne Rd
SE4 . . . . 51 A1
Sandbrook Rd N16 . 7 A1
Sandby Ho
11 Camberwell
SE5 . . . . 49 A2
6 Kilburn NW6 . . . . 23 C4
Sandell St SE1 . . . 135 B4
Sanderling Ct 20
SE8 . . . . 51 B4
Sanders Ho WC1 . . 95 B4
Sanderson Cl
NW5 . . . . 13 A4

Sanderson Ho **7**
SE8 . . . . 41 B1
Sandersted Ave
NW2 . . . . 1 A2
Sandersted Cl
SW12 . . . . 73 B4
Sanders Way **3**
N19 . . . . 4 C3
Sandfield WC1 . . . . 94 B3
Sandford Ct N16 . . . 7 A3
Sandford Row
SE17 . . . . 151 C2
Sandford St SW6 . . 156 B1
Sandgate Ho **10**
E5 . . . . 17 A4
Sandgate La SW17,
SW18 . . . . 72 A3
Sandgate St SE15 . . 50 A4
Sandgate Trad Est
SE15 . . . . 50 A4
Sandham Ct SW4 . 172 B3
Sandhills The
SW10 . . . . 157 A4
Sandhurst Ct SW2 . 62 A3
Sandhurst Ho **12**
E1 . . . . 32 B4
Sandilands Rd
SW6 . . . . 166 A3
Sandison St SE15 . . 64 C4
Sandland St WC1 . 107 A3
Sandlings The SE15 . 50 A1
Sandmere Rd
SW4 . . . . 62 A3
Sandon Ho **5**
SW2 . . . . 74 A4
Sandown Ho **2**
W4 . . . . 37 B1
Sandpiper Cl SE16 . 41 B4
Sandpiper Ct
15 Cubitt Town
E14 . . . . 42 B3
1 SE8 . . . . 51 C3
Sandridge St **3**
N19 . . . . 4 B2
Sandringham Cl **1**
SW19 . . . . 69 C3
Sandringham Ct
Marylebone W1 . . . 105 A1
Putney SW15 . . . . . . 57 C1
6 Rotherhithe
SE16 . . . . 32 C1
St John's Wood W9 . 89 A3
Sandringham Flats
WC2 . . . . 119 C4
Sandringham Ho
Richmond TW10 . . . 54 C2
W14 . . . . 140 A4
Sandringham Rd
Dalston E8 . . . . 16 B3
Golders Green NW11 . 1 A4
Willesden NW2 . . . . . 9 A2
Sandrock Rd SE13 . 66 C4
SANDS END 59 B4
Sands End La
SW6 . . . . 166 B4
Sandstone TW9 . . . 44 C3
Sandstone Pl N19 . . 4 A2
Sandways **6** TW9 . 44 C2
Sandwell Cres **2**
NW6 . . . . 10 C2
Sandwell Mans **3**
NW6 . . . . 10 C2

Sandwich Ho
16 Rotherhithe
SE16 . . . . 40 B4
WC1 . . . . 94 A3
Sandwich St WC1 . . 94 A3
Sandycombe Ctr
TW9 . . . . 54 C4
Sandycombe Rd
TW9 . . . . 44 C1
Sandy Lo N6 . . . . . . 4 B4
Sandy Rd NW3 . . . . 2 A2
Sandy's Row E1 . . 110 B3
Sanford La **3** N16 . . 7 B2
Sanford St SE14,
SE8 . . . . 51 A4
Sanford Terr N16 . . 7 B2
Sanford Wlk
SE14 . . . . 51 A4
4 Stoke Newington
N16 . . . . 7 B2
Sangora Rd **17**
SW11 . . . . 59 C3
San Ho **22** E9 . . . . 17 C2
Sankey Ho **22** E2 . . 25 B3
Sansom St
Camberwell SE5 . . . 48 C2
SE5 . . . . 48 C3
Sans Wlk EC1 . . . . 96 A2
Santley Ho SE1 . . 135 C3
Santley St SW4 . . . 62 B3
Santos Rd SW18 . . 58 C2
Sapcote Trad Ctr
NW10 . . . . 8 B2
Saperton Wlk
SE11 . . . . 149 A4
Sapperton Ct EC1 . 96 C2
Sapphire Ct **13**
E1 . . . . 125 B4
Sapphire Rd SE8 . . 41 A2
Saracen's Head Yd
EC2 . . . . 110 B1
Saracen St E14 . . . 33 C3
Sarah Ho
Roehampton SW15 . 56 B3
8 Stepney E1 . . . . 32 A3
Sarah Swift Ho
SE1 . . . . 137 C4
Sara Lane Ct **31**
N1 . . . . 24 A3
Saratoga Rd E5 . . . 17 B4
Sardinia Ho WC2 . 106 C1
Sardinia St WC2 . . 106 C2
Sarjant Path SW19 . 69 C2
Sark Ho **23** N1 . . . . 15 B2
Sarnesfield Ho
SE15 . . . . 50 A4
Sarratt Ho **9** W10 . 30 B4
Sarre Rd NW2 . . . . 10 B3
Sarsden Bldgs
W1 . . . . 103 C1
Sarsfeld Rd SW12,
SW17 . . . . 72 B3
Sartor Rd SE15 . . . 65 C3
Sarum Hall Sch
NW3 . . . . 12 A1
Sarum Ho
W11 . . . . . . 31 B2 113 A3
Sassoon Ho SE15 . . 50 B2
Satchwell Rd **17**
E2 . . . . 24 C2 99 B3
Saturn Ho **43** E3 . . 26 C4
Saul Ct **2** SE15 . . . 49 B4
Saunders Cl **16**
E14 . . . . 33 B2
Saunders Ho **11**
SW2 . . . . 74 C3

Saunders Ness Rd
E14 . . . . 42 C2
Saunders St SE11 . 149 B4
Savage Gdns EC3 . 124 B4
Savana N16 . . . . . . 7 A2
Savannah Cl **9**
SE15 . . . . 49 B3
Savernake Ho N4 . . 6 C4
Savernake Rd
NW3 . . . . 12 B4
Saville Rd W4 . . . . 37 C3
Saville Row W1 . . 118 C4
Savill Ho **2** SW4 . . 61 C1
Savona St SW8 . . . 160 C1
Savoy Circus W3 . . 29 B2
Savoy Ct
Earl's Ct SW5 . . . . 141 C4
Strand WC2 . . . . . 120 B3
Savoy Hill WC2 . . 120 C3
Savoy Mews SW9 . . 62 A4
Savoy Pier WC2 . . 120 C3
Savoy Row WC2 . . 120 C3
Savoy St WC2 . . . 120 C3
Savoy Stps WC2 . . 120 C3
Savoy Way WC2 . . 120 C3
Sawkins Cl SW19 . . 70 A2
Sawley Rd W12 . . . 29 C1
Sawmill Yd E3 . . . . 26 A4
Sawyer St SE1 . . . 136 C4
Saxby Rd SW2 . . . . 74 A4
Saxonbury Ct
6 Kentish Town
N7 . . . . 13 C3
2 Lower Holloway
N7 . . . . 14 A3
Saxoncroft Ho
SW16 . . . . 73 C1
Saxon Dr W3 . . . . . 28 A4
Saxon Ho **4** SW4 . . 74 B4
Saxon Hall W2 . . . 114 A3
Saxon Ho **4** SW4 . . 61 C3
Saxon Rd E3 . . . . . 26 B3
Saxton Cl SE13 . . . 67 C4
Sayer Ho SE4 . . . . 66 A3
Sayes Court St
SE8 . . . . 51 B4
Sayes Ct SE8 . . . . . 51 B4
Scafell NW1 . . . . . . 92 C4
Scala St W1 . . . . . 105 A4
Scampston Mews **5**
W10 . . . . 30 C3
Scandrett St **38**
E1 . . . . 32 A1
Scarba Wlk N1 . . . 15 C2
Scarborough Rd N4 . 5 C3
Scarborough St
E1 . . . . 111 A1
Scarlette Manor Wlk
10 SE24 . . . . 63 B2
Scarsbrook Ho **2**
SW2 . . . . 62 C1
Scarsdale Pl W8 . . 128 A2
Scarsdale Villas
W8 . . . . 127 C1
Scarth Rd SW13 . . 56 B4
Scawen Rd SE8 . . . 41 A1
Scawfell St E2 . . . . 24 B3
Sceptre Ho **16** E1 . . 25 B1
Sceptre Rd E2 . . . . 25 B2
Schiller International
Univ SE1 . . . . 121 B1
Schofield Wlk SE3 . 53 C3
Sch of Pharmacy
WC1 . . . . 94 B2

Sch of the Islamic
Republic of Iran The
6 NW6 . . . . 23 C3
Scholars Ct **5** N19 . 4 C3
Scholars Rd SW12 . 73 B3
Scholefield Rd N19 . 4 C2
Scholey Ho SW11 . . 60 A4
Schomberg Ho
SW1 . . . . 147 C3
Schonfeld Sq N16 . . 6 C3
School App **21**
E2 . . . . 24 A2 98 B4
Schoolbank Rd
SE10 . . . . 43 B2
School Bell Cloisters
17 E3 . . . . 26 A3
Schoolbell Mews **10**
E3 . . . . 26 A3
School Flats SW8 . 172 A3
School Ho SE1 . . . 152 A4
Schoolhouse La
E1 . . . . 32 C2
School Rd NW10 . . 20 C1
School Sq SE10 . . . 43 B3
Schooner Cl
Cubitt Town E14 . . . 42 C3
1 Rotherhithe
SE16 . . . . 40 C4
Schubert Rd SW15 . 58 B2
Science Mus ∗
SW7 . . . . 129 B1
Sclater St
E1 . . . . 24 B1 99 A2
Scoles Cres SW2 . . 74 C3
Scoresby St SE1 . . 122 A1
Scorton Ho **2** N1 . . 24 A3
Scotch Ho SW1 . . 130 C3
Scoter Ct **23** SE8 . . 51 B4
Scotia Bldg **16** E1 . 32 C2
Scotia Ct **3** SE16 . . 40 B3
Scotia Rd **2** SW2 . . 74 C4
Scotland Pl SW1 . . 120 A1
Scotney Ho **7** E9 . . 17 B2
Scotson Ho SE11 . . 149 B3
Scotswood St EC1 . 95 C2
Scott Ave SW15,
SW18 . . . . 58 A1
Scott Ct
Acton W4 . . . . 37 C4
4 Clapham SW11 . 170 B1
7 Stoke Newington
N16 . . . . 7 A1
Scott Ellis Gdns
NW8 . . . . 89 B3
Scott Ho
2 Barnsbury N7 . . 14 B2
Islington N1 . . . . . . 87 B4
Lisson Gr NW8 . . . . 90 A1
7 Millwall E14 . . . 41 C2
Scott Lidgett Cres
SE16 . . . . 139 C3
Scotts Ct **8** W12 . . 39 A4
Scott's Rd W12 . . . 39 A4
Scott's Sufferance
Wharf SE1 . . . . . . 139 A3
Scott's Yd EC4 . . . 123 B4
Scouler Ho **12**
SE24 . . . . 41 C3
Scoulding Rd E16 . . 35 C3
Scouler St E14 . . . 34 C2
Scout App NW10 . . . 8 A4
Scout La SW4 . . . . 61 B4
Scovell Cres SE1 . . 136 C3
Scovell Rd SE1 . . . 136 C3
Scriven Ct **2** E8 . . . 24 B4
Scriven St E8 . . . . 24 B4

Scriven St E8 . . . . 24 B4
Scrooby St SE6 . . . 67 A1
Scrope Bldg EC1 . . 107 B4
Scrubs La NW10, W10,
W12 . . . . 22 A1
Scrutton Cl SW12 . 73 C4
Scrutton St
EC2 . . . . 24 A1 98 A1
Scutari Rd SE22 . . 65 B2
Scylla Rd SE15 . . . 65 A4
Seabright St **27**
E2 . . . . 25 A2
Seacole Cl W3 . . . . 28 C4
Seacon Twr **8**
E14 . . . . 41 C4
Seaford Ho **13**
SE16 . . . . 40 B4
Seaford St WC1 . . . 94 B3
Seaforth Cres N5 . . 15 B3
Seaforth Lo **2**
SW13 . . . . 46 B1
Seagrave Lo SW6 . 155 C4
Seagrave Rd SW6 . 155 C4
Seagrove Cl E1 . . . 32 C4
Seagull La E16 . . . 35 C2
Seal Ho SE1 . . . . . 137 C2
Sea Life London
Aquarium ∗ SE1 . . 134 C3
Seal St E8 . . . . 16 B4
Searle Pl N4 . . . . . 5 B3
Searles Cl SW11 . . 158 B1
Searles Rd SE1 . . . 151 C4
Searson Ho SE17 . . 150 B3
Sears St SE5 . . . . . 48 C3
Seasalter Ho **10**
SW9 . . . . 173 B4
Seaton Cl SW15 . . . 69 A4
Seaton Point E5 . . 16 C4
Seavington Ho **3**
SE5 . . . . 64 A4
Sebastian Ho **22**
N1 . . . . 24 A3
Sebastian St EC1 . . 96 B3
Sebbon St N1 . . . . 15 A1
Sebright Ho **22** E2 . 24 C3
Sebright Pas **2**
E2 . . . . 24 C3
Sebright Sch **58**
E2 . . . . 24 C3
Secker Ho SW9 . . . 48 A1
Secker St SE1 . . . . 121 B1
Second Ave
East Acton W3 . . . . 29 B1
Kensal Town W10 . . 23 A1
Mortlake SW14 . . . 56 A4
Sedan Way SE17 . . 152 A2
Sedding St SW1 . . 145 B4
Seddon Ho EC2 . . . 108 C4
Seddon St WC1 . . . 95 A3
Sedgeford Rd
W12 . . . . 29 B1
Sedgewick Ho
SW19 . . . . 69 C2
Sedley Ho SE11 . . . 149 A2
Sedley Pl W1 . . . . 104 A1
Seething La EC3 . . 124 B4
Sefton St SW15 . . . 57 B4
Sekforde St EC1 . . 96 A2
Selbie Ave NW10 . . 8 B3

Selborne **2** SW11 . . . .60 C4
Selborne Ho SE1 . .**137** B3
Selborne Rd **1**
SE5 . . . . .48 C1
Selby Ho **10** SW4 . .61 B1
Selby Rd SE20 . . . . .91 A2
Selby St E1 . . . .24 C1 99 C1
Selden Ho **8** SE15 . .50 B1
Selden Rd SE15 . . . .50 B1
Selden Wlk N7 . . . . . .5 B2
Seldon Ho
Nine Elms SW8 . . . .**160** C1
Pimlico SW1 . . . . . .**146** C1
Selhurst Cl SW19 . . .69 C3
Selina Ho NW8 . . . . .89 C2
Selkirk Ho
N1 . . . . .84 C4
4 Stoke Newington
N16 . . . . .7 A1
Sellons Ave NW10 . . .21 B4
Selma Ho **9** W12 . . .30 A3
Selman Ho **3** E9 . . .18 A2
Selsdon Way E14 . . . .42 A3
Selsea St E14 . . . . . .16 A3
Selsey St E14 . . . . . .33 C4
Selway Ho SW8 . . . .**172** B4
Selwood Ho **1** N4 . . .6 C4
Selwood Pl SW7 . .**143** B2
Selwood Terr
SW7 . . . .**143** B2
Selworthy Ho
SW11 . . . .**167** C4
Selwyn Ave TW9 . . . .54 B4
Selwyn Ct **8**
TW10 . . . . .54 B2
Selwyn Ho **3**
SW15 . . . . .57 C1
Selwyn Rd
Bow E3 . . . . .26 B3
Willesden NW10 . . . . .8 A1
Semley Gate E9 . . . .18 B2
Semley Ho SW1 . . .**146** A3
Semley Pl SW1 . . . .**146** A3
Senate St SE15 . . . . .50 B1
Senators Ln **51** E3 . .26 A3
Sendall St **12**
SW11 . . . . .59 C4
Senior St W2 . . . .**100** A4
Senrab St E1 . . . . . . .32 C3
Seraph Ct EC1 . . . . .96 C4
Serenaders Rd **20**
SW9 . . . .**173** B1
Sergeant Ind Est The
SW18 . . . . .59 A1
Serica Ct **14** SE10 . .52 B3
Serjeants' Inn
EC4 . . . .**107** C1
Serlby Ct W14 . . . .**126** C2
Serle St WC2 . . . . .**107** A2
Sermon La EC4 . . . .**108** C1
Serpentine Ct **11**
SE16 . . . . .40 C4
Serpentine Gallery*
W2 . . . .**129** C4
Serpentine Rd
W2 . . . .**116** B1
Serpentine The*
W2 . . . .**116** B1
Service Route No 1
E15 . . . . .19 C1
Service Route No 2 **1**
E15 . . . . .19 C1
Service Route No 3 **2**
E15 . . . . .19 C1
Servite Ho SE13 . . . .52 A2

Servite RC Prim Sch
SW10 . . . .**156** C4
Setchell Rd SE1 . . .**152** C4
Setchell Way SE1 . .**152** C4
Seth St **16** SE16 . . . .40 B4
Settlers Ct **11** E14 . .34 C2
Settles St E1 . . . . . .**111** C2
Settrington Rd
SW6 . . . .**166** A1
Seven Dials WC2 . .**106** A1
Seven Islands L Ctr
SE16 . . . . .40 B3
Seven Mills Prim Sch
E14 . . . . .41 C4
Sevenoaks Rd SE4 . .66 B1
Seven Sisters Rd
Finsbury Pk N4 . . . . . .6 A2
Stoke Newington N4, N7,
N16 . . . . .7 A3
Seven Stars Cnr
SW15 . . . . .38 C3
Seven Stars Yd
E1 . . . .**111** A4
Severnake Cl E14 . . .41 C2
Severn Ave **2**
W10 . . . . .23 A2
Severn Way NW10 . . . .8 B3
Severus Rd SW11 . . .60 A3
Seville Ho **10** E1 . .**125** C1
Seville Mews N1 . . . .16 A1
Seville St SW1 . . . .**131** A3
Sevington St W9 . . . .88 A1
Seward St EC1 . . . . .96 C3
Sewardstone Rd
E2 . . . . .25 B3
Sewell Ho **9** N16 . . .16 A3
Sextant Ave E14 . . . .42 C2
Sexton Ct **7** E14 . . .34 C2
Sexton's Ho **5**
SE13 . . . . .52 B4
Seymour Ct
Putney SW15 . . . . . .57 A3
Upper Clapton N16 . . . .7 C3
Seymour Gdns
SE4 . . . . .66 A4
Seymour Ho
Bloomsbury WC1 . . .**94** A2
1 Clapham SW8 . .**171** A2
Somers Town NW1 . . .**93** C4
Seymour Mews
W1 . . . .**103** B2
Seymour Pl W1 . . .**102** C2
Seymour Rd
Acton W4 . . . . .37 B2
Wandsworth SW18 . . .58 B1
Wimbledon SW19 . . . .69 C1
Seymour St W1 . . .**103** A1
Seymour Wlk
SW10 . . . .**156** C4
Seyssel St E14 . . . . .42 B2
Shaa Rd W3 . . . . . . .28 C2
Shabana Ct **3**
W12 . . . . .30 B1
Shackleton Ct
3 Dulwich SE21 . . .75 C2
2 Isle of Dogs E14 . .41 C1
4 Shepherd's Bush
W12 . . . . .39 A4
Shackleton Ho **5**
E1 . . . . .32 B1
SHACKLEWELL 16 B4
Shacklewell Ho **6**
E8 . . . . .16 B4
Shacklewell La E8 . . .16 B3
Shacklewell Prim Sch
5 E8 . . . . .16 B4

Shacklewell Rd
N16 . . . . .16 B4
Shacklewell Row
E8 . . . . .16 B4
Shacklewell St **9**
E2 . . . . .24 B2 99 A3
Shad Thames SE1 . .**139** A4
SHADWELL 32 B2
Shadwell Gdns E1 . . .32 B2
Shadwell Pierhead
E1 . . . . .32 B2
Shadwell Pl **1** E1 . .32 B2
Shadwell Sta E1 . . . .32 A2
Shaftesbury Ave
W1 . . . .**119** C4
Shaftesbury Ct
Borough The SE1 . . .**137** B2
1 Herne Hill SE5 . . .63 C3
Shoreditch N1 . . . . .87 B1
Streatham SW16 . . . .73 C1
Shaftesbury Ctr
NW10 . . . . .22 C1
Shaftesbury Gdns
NW10 . . . . .21 A1
Shaftesbury Ho
1 Canning Town
E16 . . . . .35 B3
2 Stoke Newington
N16 . . . . .7 A1
W2 . . . .**114** B4
Shaftesbury Lo **9**
E14 . . . . .34 A3
Shaftesbury Mews
2 Clapham Pk
SW4 . . . . .61 B2
W8 . . . .**127** C1
Shaftesbury Park
Chambers **1**
SW11 . . . . .60 C4
Shaftesbury Rd
Finsbury Pk N4, N19 . . .5 A3
Richmond TW9 . . . . .54 A4
Shaftesbury St N1 . . .87 B1
Shaftesworld Ct
SW17 . . . . .72 B1
Shafto Mews
SW1 . . . .**131** A1
Shafton Rd E9 . . . . .25 C4
Shaftsbury Park Prim
Sch **10** SW11 . . . . .60 C4
Shafts Ct EC3 . . . .**110** A1
Shahjalal Ho **18**
E2 . . . . .24 C3
Shakespeare Ho **7**
NW10 . . . . .20 C4
Shakespeare Rd
Acton W3 . . . . .28 B1
Brixton SE24 . . . . . .63 A3
Stonebridge NW10 . . .20 C4
Shakespeare's Globe
Theatre (site of)*
SE1 . . . .**123** A2
Shakespeare Twr
EC2 . . . .**109** A4
Shakspeare Mews **4**
N16 . . . . .16 A4
Shakspeare Wlk
N16 . . . . .16 A4
Shalbourne Sq E9 . . .18 B2
Shalcomb St
SW10 . . . .**157** A3
Shalden Ho SW15 . . .56 B1
Shalfleet Dr W10 . . . .30 C2
Shalford NW10 . . . .**21** C4

Shalford Ct N1 . . . . .**86** A2
Shalford Ho SE1 . . .**137** C2
Shalimar Gdns W3 . .28 B2
Shalimar Lo W3 . . . .28 B2
Shalimar Rd W3 . . . .28 B2
Shalstone Rd SW14,
SW15 . . . . .55 A4
Shamrock St SW4 . . .61 C4
Shandon Ct SE4 . . . .51 A1
Shandon Rd SW4 . . .61 B1
Shand St SE1 . . . . .**138** B4
Shandy St E1 . . . . . .25 C1
Sha Ho WC1 . . . . . . .94 C1
Shannon Ct
11 Peckham SE15 . .49 B3
2 Stoke Newington
N16 . . . . .7 A1
Willesden NW10 . . . .21 A4
Shannon Gr SW9 . . .62 B3
Shannon Pl NW8 . . .80 B2
Shanti Ct SW18 . . . .70 C3
Shapla Prim Sch **2**
E1 . . . .**125** C3
Shardcroft Ave
SE24 . . . . .63 A2
Shardeloes Rd
SE14 . . . . .51 B1
Shard's Sq SE15 . . . .49 C4
Sharebourne Ho
SW2 . . . . .62 C2
Sharman Ho **13**
E14 . . . . .34 B3
Sharnbrook Ho
W6 . . . .**155** B4
Sharon Gdns E9 . . . .25 B4
Sharon Rd W4 . . . . .37 C1
Sharp Ho SW8 . . . . .61 A4
Sharples Hall St **1**
NW1 . . . . .12 B1
Sharpness Ct **2**
SE15 . . . . .49 B3
Sharratt St SE15 . . . .50 B4
Sharsted St SE17 . .**150** A1
Sharwood Rd N1 . . . .85 A1
Shaver's Pl SW1 . . .**119** B3
Shawford Ct **3**
SW15 . . . . .68 C4
Shaw Rd SE22 . . . . .64 A3
Shearling Way N7 . . .14 A2
Shearsmith Ho **1**
E1 . . . .**125** C4
Shearwater Ct **24**
SE8 . . . . .51 B4
Sheba Pl E1 . . .24 B1 99 A1
Sheen Common Dr
SW14, TW10 . . . . . .54 C2
Sheen Court Rd
TW10 . . . . .54 C3
Sheen Ct TW10 . . . . .54 C3
Sheendale Rd
TW9 . . . . .54 B3
Sheen Gate Gdns
SW14 . . . . .55 B3
Sheengate Mans
SW14 . . . . .55 C3
Sheen Gr N1 . . . . . . .85 B4
Sheen La SW14 . . . . .55 B3

Sheen Mount Prim
Sch SW14 . . . . .55 A2
Sheen Pk TW10,
TW9 . . . . .54 A3
Sheen Rd TW10,
TW9 . . . . .54 B3
Sheen Wood
SW14 . . . . .55 A2
Sheepcote La
SW11 . . . .**169** A1
Sheep La E8 . . . . . . .25 A4
Sheffield Ho **18**
SE15 . . . . .49 B2
Sheffield Sq **3** E3 . .26 B2
Sheffield St WC2 . . .**106** C1
Sheffield Terr
W8 . . . . .31 C1 **113** C1
Shelbourne Ho **20**
N19 . . . . .4 C4
Shelburne Ct
SW15 . . . . .57 C2
Shelburne Rd N7 . . . .14 B4
Shelbury Rd SE22 . . .65 A2
Sheldon Ct SW8 . .**162** A1
Sheldon Ho **9** E9 . .17 C2
Sheldon Pl E2 . . . . .25 A3
Sheldon Rd NW2 . . . .9 C4
Sheldon Sq W2 . . . .**101** A3
Sheldrake Ho **18**
SE16 . . . . .40 C2
Sheldrake Pl W8 . .**127** B4
Shelduck Ct **37**
SE8 . . . . .51 B4
Shelford Pl N16 . . . . .6 C1
Shelgate Rd SW11 . .60 B2
Shell Ctr SE1 . . . . .**121** A1
Shelley Cl SE15 . . . .50 A1
Shelley Ct
Finsbury Pk N4 . . . . . .5 B3
SW3 . . . .**159** A4
Shelley Ho
21 Bethnal Green
E2 . . . . .25 B2
Chelsea SW1 . . . . .**160** C4
9 Stoke Newington
N16 . . . . .16 A4
Walworth SE17 . . . .**151** A2
Shelley Rd NW10 . . .20 C4
Shellgrove Rd **11**
N16 . . . . .16 A3
Shellness Rd E5 . . . .17 A3
Shell Rd SE13 . . . . . .67 A4
Shellwood Rd
SW11 . . . .**168** C1
Shelmerdine Cl
E3 . . . . .33 C4
Shelton St WC2 . . .**106** A1
Shene Bldg EC1 . . .**107** B4
Shene Sch SW14 . . . .56 A3
Shenfield St N1 . . . . .24 A3
Shenley Rd SE5 . . . .49 A2
Shepard Ho
SW11 . . . . .59 C4
Sheperdess Pl N1 . . .97 A4
Shepherd Cl W1 . . .**117** B4
Shepherdess Wlk
N1 . . . . .87 A1
Shepherd Ho
Barnsbury N7 . . . . . .14 A2
10 Poplar E14 . . . .34 A3
Shepherd Mkt
W1 . . . .**118** A1
SHEPHERD'S
BUSH 30 A1

Shepherd's Bush Gn
W12 . . . . **39** B4
Shepherd's Bush
Market W12 . . . . **39** B4
Shepherd's Bush Mkt
Sta W12 . . . . **30** B1
Shepherd's Bush
Overground Sta
W12 . . . . **39** C4
Shepherd's Bush Pl
W12 . . . . **39** C4
Shepherd's Bush Rd
W6 . . . . **39** B3
Shepherd's Bush Sta
W12 . . . . **39** C4
Shepherds Ct B
W12 . . . . **39** C4
Shepherd's La E9 . . **17** C2
Shepherds Pl W1 . . **117** B4
Shepherd St W1 . . **118** A1
Shepherd's Wlk
NW3 . . . . **11** C4
Sheppard Dr SE16 . **40** A1
Sheppard Ho
31 Hackney E2 . . . . . **24** C3
8 Streatham SW2 . . **74** C3
Shepperton Rd N1 **87** B4
Sheppey Ho 15 E5 . . **17** A4
Shepton Ct SW1 **167** C4
Shepton Hos 11
E2 . . . . **25** B2
Sherard Ct N19 . . . . **5** A1
Sherard Ho 29 E9 . . **17** B1
Sheraton Ho SW1 **160** B4
Sheraton St W1 . . **105** B1
Sherborne Ho
Pimlico SW1 . . . . . **146** B2
South Lambeth
SW8 . . . . **162** C1
Sherborne La EC4 **123** C4
Sherborne St N1 . . **87** B4
Sherbourne Ct
SW5 . . . . **142** A4
Sherbrooke Ho 9
E2 . . . . **25** B3
Sherbrooke Rd
SW6 . . . . **154** B1
Sherbrooke Terr
SW6 . . . . **154** B1
Shere Ho SE1 . . . . **137** B2
Sherfield Gdns
SW15 . . . . **56** B1
Sheridan Bldgs
WC2 . . . . **106** B1
Sheridan Ct
Earl's Ct SW5 . . . . **142** A3
South Hampstead
NW6 . . . . **11** B1
South Lambeth
SW9 . . . . **173** A3
Sheridan Ho
SE11 . . . . **149** C3
7 Stoke Newington
N16 . . . . **7** A1
Sheridan Pl SW13 . **56** B4
Sheridan St 3 E1 . . **32** A3
Sheringdale Prim Sch
SW18 . . . . **70** B3
Sheringham NW8 . . **79** C4
Sheringham Ho
NW1 . . . . **102** B4
Sheringham Mews 4
SW18 . . . . **71** B2

Sheringham Rd
N7 . . . . **14** C2
Sherlock Ct NW8 . . **79** B4
Sherlock Holmes
Mus* NW1 . . . . **91** A1
Sherlock Mews
W1 . . . . **103** B4
Sherren Ho 81 E1 . . **25** B1
Sherrick Green Rd
NW10 . . . . **9** A3
Sherriff Ct NW6 . . . **10** C2
Sherriff Rd NW6 . . . **10** C2
Sherrin Rd E10 . . . . **19** A4
Sherston Ct
Finsbury WC1 . . . . . **95** B3
Newington SE1 . . **150** B4
Sherwin Ho 1
SE11 . . . . **163** B4
Sherwin Rd SE14 . . **50** C2
Sherwood NW6 . . . **10** A1
Sherwood Cl
SW13 . . . . **57** A4
Sherwood Ct
1 Battersea
SW11 . . . . **59** B4
St Johns SE13 . . . . . **52** A1
W1 . . . . **102** C3
Sherwood Gdns
Bermondsey SE16 . . **40** A1
Millwall E14 . . . . **41** C2
Sherwood Ho N4 . . . **6** B4
Sherwood St W1 . . **119** A4
Shetland Rd E3 . . . . **26** B3
Shillaker Ct SW3 . . **29** B1
Shillibeer Pl W1 . . **102** B3
Shillingford Ho 10
E3 . . . . **27** A2
Shillingford St 23
N1 . . . . **15** A1
Shillingstone Ho
W14 . . . . **126** B1
Shinfield St W12 . . **30** B3
Shipka Rd SW12 . . . **73** A3
Ship La SW14 . . . . . **45** B1
Shiplake Ho 49
E2 . . . . **24** B2 **98** C3
Shipley Ho 27
SW8 . . . . **171** B1
Ship & Mermaid Row
SE1 . . . . **138** A4
Ship St SE8 . . . . **51** C2
Shipton Street Pas
EC3 . . . . **124** A4
Shipton Ho
7 Camden Town
NW5 . . . . **12** C2
10 Haggerston E2 . . **24** B3
Shipton St
E2 . . . . **24** B2 **99** A4
Shipwright Rd
SE16 . . . . **41** A4
Shipwright Yd
SE1 . . . . **124** A1
Shirbutt St E14 . . . . **34** A2
Shire Pl SW18 . . . . . **71** B4
Shirland Mews
W9 . . . . **23** B2
Shirland Rd W9 . . . . **23** C1
Shirley Gr SW11 . . . **60** C4
Shirley Ho 15 SE5 . . **48** C3
Shirley Rd W4 . . . . . **37** C4
Shirley St E16 . . . . . **35** B3
Shirlock Rd NW3 . . . **12** B4
Shoe La EC4 . . . . . **107** C2
Shooters Hill Rd SE3,
SE10 . . . . **53** A2

Shoot-Up Hill
NW2 . . . . **10** A2
Shopstop SW11 . . . **60** A3
Shore Bsns Ctr 51
E9 . . . . **17** B1
SHOREDITCH **87** C1
Shoreditch Ct 6
E8 . . . . **16** B1
Shoreditch High St
Sta E2 . . . . **24** B1
Shoreditch High St
E2 . . . . . . **24** A1 **98** B2
Shoreditch Ho N1 . . **97** C3
Shoreham Cl
SW18 . . . . **59** A2
Shore Ho SW8 . . . . . **61** A4
Shore Mews 25 E9 . **17** B1
Shore Pl E9 . . . . **17** B1
Shore Rd E9 . . . . **17** B1
Shorncliffe Rd
SE1 . . . . **152** C2
Shorrolds Rd
SW6 . . . . **155** A2
Shortcroft Mead Ct
NW10 . . . . **8** C3
Shorter St SE13 . . . **124** C4
Shortlands W6 . . . . . **39** C2
Short Rd W4 . . . . **46** A4
Shorts Gdns WC2 **106** A1
Short St SE1 . . . . . . **135** C4
Shottendane Rd
SW6 . . . . **165** B4
Shottfield Ave
SW14 . . . . **56** A3
Shottsford 6 W11 . . **31** C3
Shoulder of Mutton
Alley **10** E14 . . . . **33** A2
Shouldham St
W1 . . . . **102** B3
Shreveport Ho 23
N19 . . . . **4** C4
Shrewsbury Ave
SW14 . . . . **55** C3
Shrewsbury Cres
NW10 . . . . **20** C4
Shrewsbury Ho
Chelsea SW3 . . . . . **158** A3
Kennington SE11 . . **163** A3
Shrewsbury Mews 33
W2 . . . . **31** C4
Shrewsbury Rd
W2 . . . . **31** C3
Shrewsbury St
W10 . . . . **22** B1
Shropshire Ho
WC1 . . . . **93** A1
Shroton St NW1 . . **102** B4
Shrubbery Cl N1 . . . **87** A3
Shrubland Rd E8 . . . **24** C4
Shrubs Ho SW1 . . **147** C3
Shurland Gdns
SE15 . . . . **49** B3
Shuters Sq W14 . . **140** C1
Shuttle St
E1 . . . . **24** C1 **99** B1
Shuttleworth Rd
SW11 . . . . **168** A2
Sibella Rd SW4 . . . **171** C1
Sicilian Ave WC1 . . **106** B3
Sidbury St SW6 . . . **164** A4
Siddons Ct WC2 . . **106** C1
Siddons Ho 8
NW3 . . . . **11** B2
Siddons La NW1 . . . **91** A1
Sidford Ho SE1 . . . **135** A1
Sidford Pl SE1 . . . **135** A1

Sidgwick Ho 26
SW9 . . . . **172** B1
Sidings Mews N7 . . . **14** C4
Sidlaw Ho N16 . . . . . . **7** B3
Sidmouth Ho
18 Camberwell
SE15 . . . . **49** C3
Marylebone W1 . . **102** B3
20 Streatham SW2 . **74** C4
Sidmouth Mews
WC1 . . . . **94** C3
Sidmouth Par NW2 . **9** B1
Sidmouth Rd NW2 . . **9** B1
Sidmouth St WC1 . . **94** C3
Sidney Boyd Ct
NW6 . . . . **10** C1
Sidney Godley (VC)
Ho 11 E2 . . . . **25** B2
Sidney Gr EC1 . . . . . **86** A1
Sidney Ho 4 E2 . . . . **25** B3
Sidney Miller Ct 8
W3 . . . . **28** A1
Sidney Rd SW9 . . . **173** A1
Sidney Sq E1 . . . . . . **32** B4
Sidney St E1 . . . . **32** B4
Sidworth St 6 E8 . . . **17** A1
Siebert Rd SE3 . . . . **53** C4
Siege Ho 14 E1 . . . . **32** A3
Sigdon Rd E8 . . . . . . **16** C3
Signal Ho
9 London E8 . . . . . . **17** A1
SE1 . . . . **136** C3
Signmakers Yd
NW1 . . . . **82** B3
Silbury Ho 8
SE26 . . . . **76** C1
Silbury St N1 . . . . . . **97** B4
Silchester Rd W10 . . **30** C3
Silesia Bldgs E8 . . . **17** A1
Silex St SE1 . . . . . . **136** B3
Silkin Mews 24
SE15 . . . . **49** C3
Silk Mews SE11 . . **149** C1
Silk Mills Path
SE13 . . . . **67** B4
Silk Mills Sq E9 . . . . **18** B2
Silk St EC2 . . . . . . **109** A4
Sillitoe Ho N1 . . . . . **87** C3
Silsoe Ho NW1 . . . . . **82** B1
Silverbirch Wlk 1
NW3 . . . . **12** C2
Silverburn Ho 4
SW9 . . . . **173** C4
Silver Cl SE14 . . . . . **51** A3
Silver Cres W4 . . . . . **37** A2
Silver Ct N19 . . . . **4** B1
Silverdale NW1 . . . . **92** C4
Silverdale Ct EC1 . . **96** B2
Silvermere Rd SE6 . . **67** A1
Silver Pl W1 . . . . . . **119** A4
Silver Rd
Shepherd's Bush
W12 . . . . **30** C2
St Johns SE13 . . . . . **67** A4
Silverthorn 17
NW8 . . . . **78** B3
Silverthorne Rd
SW8 . . . . **170** B1
Silverton Rd W6 . . . . **47** C4
Silvertown Way
E16 . . . . **35** C1
Silver Wlk SE16 . . . . **33** B1
Silvester Ho
27 Bethnal Green
E2 . . . . **25** B2
1 Notting Hill W11 . . **31** C3

Silvester Ho continued
6 Stepney E1 . . . . . **32** A3
Silvester Rd SE22 . . **64** B2
Silvester St SE1 . . **137** B3
Silwex Ho
E1 . . . . **24** B1 **98** C1
Silwood St SE16 . . . . **40** B1
Simla Ho SE1 . . . . **137** C3
Simmonds Ct
SW5 . . . . **142** A3
Simmons Ho
20 Bethnal Green
E2 . . . . **24** C2 **99** B3
Finsbury Pk N7 . . . . . **5** B2
Simms Ct SW6 . . . . . **58** A4
Simms Rd SE1 . . . . **153** C3
Simon Cl
W11 . . . . **31** B2 **113** A4
Simon Ct W9 . . . . . . **23** C2
Simon Lo 81 SW19 . **69** C3
Simon Marks Jewish
Prim Sch **8** N16 . . . **7** B2
Simons Wlk E15 . . . . **19** C3
Simpson Dr W3 . . . . **28** C3
Simpson Ho
Lisson Gr NW8 . . . . . **90** A3
Vauxhall SE11 . . . . **148** C1
Simpson's Rd E14 . . **34** A2
Simpson St SW11 **168** A1
Sinclair Ct N5 . . . . . **15** B2
Sinclair Gdns W14 . . **39** C4
Sinclair Ho 1
SW12 . . . . **73** C3
Sinclair Mans 13
W12 . . . . **39** C4
Sinclair Pl SE4 . . . . . **66** C1
Sinclair Rd W14 . . . **126** A2
Sinclairs Ho 19 E3 . . **26** B3
Singer St EC2 . . . . . **97** C3
Sion Ho SE13 . . . . . **67** B3
Sion-Manning RC Sch
for Girls
10 Kensal Town
W10 . . . . **31** A4
8 North Kensington
W10 . . . . **30** C4
Sir Abraham Dawes
Cotts SW15 . . . . . . **58** A3
Sir Alexander Cl
W3 . . . . **29** B1
Sir Alexander Rd
W3 . . . . **29** B1
Sirdar Rd
W11 . . . . **31** A2 **112** A3
Sir Francis Drake
Prim Sch **1** SE8 . . **41** A1
Sirinham Point
SW8 . . . . **163** A3
Sirius Bldg 12 E1 . . **32** C2
Sir James Barrie Prim
Sch SW8 . . . . **171** A3
Sir John Cass
Foundation &
Redcoat CE Sec Sch
10 E1 . . . . **32** C4
Sir John Cass's
Foundation Prim Sch
EC3 . . . . **110** B1
Sir John Kirk Cl 83
SE5 . . . . **48** B3
Sir John Lillie Prim
Sch SW6 . . . . **154** B3
Sir John Soane's
Mus* WC2 . . . . . . **106** C2

Sir Oswald Stoll
Foundation The
SW6 .... 156 A2
Sir Thomas Abney
Prim Sch N16 .... 6 C3
Sir Thomas More Est
SW3 .... 157 C3
Sir William Burrough
Prim Sch E14 ... 33 B3
Sir William Powell's
Almshos SW6 .... 58 A4
Sise La EC4 .... 109 B1
Siskin Ho E14 ... 16 C2
Sispara Gdns
SW18 .... 58 B1
Sissinghurst Ho 10
SE15 .... 50 B4
Sister Mabel's Way 15
SE15 .... 49 C3
Sisters Ave SW11 .. 60 B3
Sisters of
Marcellina Sch 34
NW3 .... 11 B4
Sistova Rd SW12 .. 73 A3
Sisulu Pl SW9 .... 62 C4
Sitarey Ct 4 W12 .. 30 A1
Site of Changing of
the Guard★ SW1 132 C3
Sivill Ho 9
E2 .... 24 B2 99 A4
Siward Rd SW17 ... 71 B1
Six Bridges Ind Est 16
SE1 .... 153 C1
Sixth Ave W10 ... 23 A2
Skardu Rd NW2 ... 10 A3
Skeena Hill SW18,
SW19 .... 70 A4
Skeggs Ho 5 E14 .. 42 B3
Skegness Ho 3
N7 .... 14 B1
Skelbrook St
SW18 .... 71 B2
Skelgill Rd SW15 .. 58 B3
Skelton Cl 7 E8 ... 16 B2
Skelton Ho N16 ... 16 A3
Skelwith Rd W6 ... 47 B4
Skenfrith Ho SE15 . 50 A4
Sketchley Gdns
SE16 .... 40 C1
Skiffington Cl
SW2 .... 74 C3
Skinner Pl SW1 ... 145 B3
Skinners Company
Sch (Upper) 10
N16 .... 7 B4
Skinners La EC4 .. 123 A4
Skinner St EC1 .... 95 C2
Skipsea Ho SW18 .. 59 C1
Skipton Ho SE4 ... 66 A3
Skipwith Bldg
EC1 .... 107 B4
Skipworth Rd E9 .. 25 B4
Skua Ct 23 SE8 ... 51 B4
Skyline Ct SE1 ... 138 C1
Skyline Plaza Bldg 10
E1 .... 111 C2
Skylines E14 ..... 42 B4
Slade Ct NW2 .... 10 A3
Sladen Pl 3 E5 ... 17 A4
Slagrove Pl SE13 .. 67 A2
Slaidburn St
SW10 .... 157 A3
Slaithwaite Rd
SE13 .... 67 B3
Slaney Ct NW10 ... 9 B1
Slaney Pl 1 N7 ... 14 C3

Sleaford Ho 10 E3 .26 C1
Sleaford Ind Est
SW8 .... 161 A3
Sleaford St SW8 .. 161 A1
Sleat Ho 11 E3 ... 26 B3
Slievemore Cl 8
SW4 .... 61 C4
Sligo Ho 8 E1 ... 25 C1
Slingsby Pl WC2 .. 120 A4
Slippers Pl SE16 ... 40 A3
Slipway Ho 1 E14 . 42 A1
Sloane Ave SW3 .. 144 B3
Sloane Avenue Mans
SW3 .... 144 C3
Sloane Ct E SW3 .. 145 B2
Sloane Ct W SW3 .. 145 B2
Sloane Gate Mans
SW1 .... 145 B4
Sloane Gdns SW1 . 145 B3
Sloane Ho 2 E9 .. 17 B1
Sloane Sq SW1 ... 145 A3
Sloane Square Sta
SW1 .... 145 B3
Sloane St SW1 .... 131 A1
Sloane Terr SW1 .. 145 B4
Sloane Terr Mans
SW1 .... 145 B4
Sly St 17 E1 ..... 32 A3
Smallbrook Mews
W2 .... 101 B1
Smalley Cl N16 ... 7 B1
Smart's Pl WC1,
WC2 .... 106 B2
Smart St E2 ..... 25 C2
Smeaton Ct SE1 .. 136 C1
Smeaton Rd SW18 . 70 C4
Smeaton St E1 ... 32 A1
Smedley St SW4 .. 171 C2
Smeed Rd E3 .... 18 C1
Smiles Pl SE13 ... 52 B1
Smith Cl SE16 ... 32 C1
Smithfield Mkt★
EC1 .... 108 B3
Smithfield St EC1 108 A3
Smith's Ct W1 ... 119 B4
Smith's Yd SW18 .. 71 B2
Smith Terr SW3 .. 144 C1
Smithwood Cl
SW19 .... 70 A2
Smithy St E1 .... 32 B4
Smithy Street Sch 34
E1 .... 32 B4
Smugglers Way
SW18 .... 59 A3
Smyrk's Rd SE17 . 152 B1
Smyrna Mans 8
NW6 .... 10 C1
Smyrna Rd NW6 .. 10 C1
Smythe St E14 ... 34 A2
Snarsgate St W10 .30 B4
Sneath Ave NW11 .. 1 B4
Sneyd Rd NW2 ... 9 B4
Snowberry Cl E11 .19 C4
Snowbury Rd 6
SW6 .... 166 B1
Snowden St
EC2 .... 24 A1 98 A1
Snowe Ho SE22 .. 75 A1
Snow Hill EC1 ... 108 A3
Snowman Ho NW6 78 B4
Snowsfields SE1 .. 137 C4
Snowsfields Prim Sch
SE1 .... 138 A4
Soames St SE15 .. 64 B4

Soane Ct 10 NW1 .13 B1
Soane Ho SE17 .. 151 C1
Soaphouse La
TW8 .... 44 A3
Sobell L Ctr N7 .... 5 B1
SOHO 105 B1
Soho★ W1 .... 105 B2
Soho Parish CE Prim
Sch W1 .... 119 B4
Soho Sq W1 ..... 105 B2
Soho St W1 ..... 105 B2
Sojourner-Truth Cl 11
E8 .... 17 A2
Solander Gdns
15 Shadwell E1 .. 32 B2
Stepney E1 ...... 32 C3
Soldene Ct N7 ... 14 B2
Solebay St E1 ... 26 A1
Solent Ho 6 E1 ... 33 A4
Solent Rd NW6 ... 10 C3
Soley Mews WC1 .. 95 B4
Solidarity Ho 1
NW10 .... 9 A2
Solna Ave SW15 .. 57 B2
Solomon's Pas
SE15 .... 65 A3
Solon New Rd
SW4 .... 62 A3
Solon Rd SW2 ... 62 A3
Solway Ho 2 E1 .. 25 C1
Solway Rd SE22 .. 64 C3
Somali Rd NW2 ... 10 B3
Somborne Ho 11
SW15 .... 68 C4
Sombrook Ho
SE11 .... 149 B3
Somer Ct SW6 ... 155 B3
Somerfield Rd N4 .. 6 A2
Somerfield St
SE16 .... 40 C1
Somerford Gr N16 .16 B4
Somerford Grove Est
N16 .... 16 B4
Somerford St E1 .. 25 A1
Somerford Way
SE16 .... 41 A4
Somerleyton Rd
SW9 .... 62 C3
Somers Cl NW1 ... 83 A2
Somers Cres W2 .. 102 A1
SOMERS TOWN .. 93 C4
Somers Town Est
NW1 .... 83 A1
Somerton Ave
TW9 .... 55 A4
Somerton Rd
Cricklewood NW2 .. 1 A1
Nunhead SE15 ... 65 A3
Somerville Ave
SW13 .... 47 B4

Somerville Cl
SW9 .... 173 A2
Somerville Ho 10
SW15 .... 57 C1
Somerville Point
SE16 .... 41 B4
Sonderburg Rd 13
N7 .... 5 B2
Sondes St SE17 .. 48 C4
Sonia Gdns NW10 . 8 B4
Sonning Ho 28
E2 .... 24 B2 98 C3
Sophia Cl N7 ... 14 B2
Sophia Ho 10 W6 . 39 B1
Sophia Sq 16 SE16 .33 A2
Sopwith Way
SW8 .... 160 A2
Sorrel La 7 E14 ... 34 C3
Sorrell Cl
6 Brixton SW9 .. 173 C2
4 Deptford SE14 .51 A3
Soseki Mus★ SW4 61 A4
Sotheby Rd N5 ... 15 B4
Sotheran Cl E8 ... 24 C4
Sotheron Pl SW6 . 156 B1
Soudan Rd SW11 . 168 C3
Souldern Rd 10
W14 .... 39 C3
SOUTH ACTON .. 37 A3
South Acton Sta W3,
W4 .... 37 B3
South Africa Rd
W12 .... 30 A2
Southall Pl SE1 .. 137 B3
Southam Ho 9
W10 .... 23 A1
Southampton Bldgs
WC2 .... 107 B3
Southampton Pl
WC1 .... 106 B3
Southampton Rd
NW5 .... 12 B3
Southampton Row
WC1 .... 106 B4
Southampton St
WC2 .... 120 B4
Southampton Way
SE5 .... 49 A3
Southam St W10 .. 23 A1
South Audley St
W1 .... 117 C2
South Ave TW9 ... 44 C1
SOUTH BANK ... 120 C1
South Bank Bsns Ctr
SW8 .... 161 C3
Southbank
International Sch 14
SW7 .... 11 B2
Southbank
International Sch
(Westminster
Campus) W1 .... 104 A4
South Bank Int Sch
W11 .... 31 C2 113 B3
South Bank Univ
SW8 .... 171 C4
South Bank University
(Erlang House)
SE1 .... 136 A3
South Bermondsey
Sta SE16 .... 40 B1
South Black Lion La
6 W6 .... 38 C1
South Block 20 E1 .32 B2

South Bolton Gdns
SW10 .... 142 B2
Southborough Ho
SE17 .... 152 B2
Southborough Rd
E9 .... 25 C4
SOUTH BROMLEY .35 A4
South Building★
SE10 .... 52 C3
Southbury NW8 ... 79 A4
South Camden Com
Sch NW1 .... 83 B2
South Carriage Dr
SW1, SW7 ..... 130 C4
South Chelsea Coll
SW9 .... 62 B3
South Colonnade The
E14 .... 34 A1
Southcombe St
W14 .... 140 A4
Southcote Rd N19 . 13 B4
Southcott Ho
31 Bromley E3 .. 27 A2
W9 .... 89 A1
South Cres
Newham E16 ..... 27 C1
WC1 .... 105 B3
Southcroft Rd
NW10 .... 20 C4
South Ct 7 SW15 . 57 C1
Southdean Gdns
SW19 .... 70 B2
Southdown N7 ... 14 A2
Southdown N7 ..... 5 B1
South Eaton Pl
SW1 .... 145 C4
South Edwardes Sq
W8 .... 127 B1
South End NW3 .. 128 B2
South End Cl NW3 .12 A4
South End Gn
NW3 .... 12 A4
South End Rd
NW3 .... 12 A4
South End Row
W8 .... 128 B2
Southerngate Way
SE14 .... 51 A3
Southern Gr E3 ... 26 B1
Southern Row
W10 .... 23 A1
Southern St N1 ... 84 C2
Southern Way
SE10 .... 43 B3
Southerton Rd W6 .39 B2
Southey Ho SE17 . 151 A2
Southey Mews
E16 .... 35 C1
Southey Rd SW9 . 173 B4
Southfield Lo W4 . 37 C4
Southfield Prim Sch
W4 .... 38 A3
Southfield Rd W4 . 37 C4
SOUTHFIELDS ... 71 A3
Southfields Com Coll
SW18 .... 70 C4
Southfields Rd
SW18 .... 58 C1
Southfields Sta
SW18 .... 70 B3
Southgate Ct N1 .. 15 C1
Southgate Gr N1 .. 15 C1
Southgate Rd N1 .. 87 C3

South Gr N6 . . . . 3 C3
South Grove Ho N6 . . 3 C3
SOUTH HACKNEY . . 25 B4
SOUTH HAMPSTEAD 11 B1
South Hampstead High Sch NW3 . . 11 C2
South Hampstead Sta NW8 . . . . 11 B1
South Hill Pk NW3 . . 12 A4
South Hill Pk Gdns NW3 . . . . 12 A4
Southill St E14 . . . . . . 34 A3
South Island Pl SW9 . . . . 163 B1
SOUTH KENSINGTON 143 A3
South Kensington Sta SW7 . . . . 143 C4
South Kensington Station Arc SW7 143 C4
SOUTH LAMBETH 172 B3
South Lambeth Pl SW8 . . . . 162 A4
South Lambeth Rd SW8 . . . . 162 A4
Southlands Dr SW19 . . . . 69 C2
South Lo NW8 . . . . . 89 B4
South London Gall* SE5 . . . . 49 A2
South London Montessori Sch SW11 . . . . 168 A3
Southmead Prim Sch SW19 . . . . 70 A3
Southmoor Way E9 . . . . 18 B3
South Molton St W11 . . . . 170 B3
South Par W4 . . . . . . 37 C2
South Parade SW3 . . . . 143 C2
South Park Mews SW6 . . . . 59 A4
South Pl EC2 . . . . . . 109 C3
South Pl Mews EC2 . . . . 109 C3
South Quay Plaza E14 . . . . 42 A4
South Quay Sta E14 . . . . 42 A4
South Rise W2 . . . . . 116 B4
South Row SE3 . . . . . 53 B1
South Sea St SE16 . . 41 B3
Southside N7 . . . . . . 13 C4
South Side W6 . . . . . 38 B3
Southside Ind Est SW8 . . . . 170 C4
Southside Quarter SW11 . . . . 168 C2
Southside Sh Ctr SW18 . . . . 59 A1
South Sq WC1 . . . . . 107 B3
South St W1 . . . . . . 117 C2

South Tenter St E1 . . . . 111 A1
South Terr SW7 . . . . 144 A4
South Thames Coll (Putney Ctr) **12** SW15 . . . . 57 C2
South Thames Coll (Roehampton Ctr) SW15 . . . . 56 C1
South Thames Coll (Wandsworth Ctr) **7** SW18 . . . . 59 A2
Southvale Rd SE3 . . 53 A1
Southview Ave NW10 . . . . 8 B3
South Villas NW1 . . 13 C2
Southville SW8 . . . . 171 C3
South Lambeth SOUTHWARK **8** SE1 . . . . 123 A1
Southwark Bridge SE1, EC4 . . . . 123 A3
Southwark Bridge Rd SE1 . . . . 136 A4
Southwark Cath* SE1 . . . . 123 B2
Southwark Coll (Blackfriars Ctr) SE1 . . . . 122 A1
Southwark Coll (Camberwell Ctr) **7** SE5 . . . . 49 A3
Southwark Coll (Grange Ctr) SE1 . . . . 138 B1
Southwark Coll (Surrey Docks Ctr) **12** SE16 . . . . 40 B3
Southwark Park Est **11** SE16 . . . . 40 A2
Southwark Park Prim Sch **15** SE16 . . . 40 A3
Southwark Park Rd SE16 . . . . 153 B4
Southwark Pk Sports Complex SE16 . . . 40 B2
Southwark Sta SE1 . . . . 122 C1
Southwater Cl **8** E14 . . . . 33 B3
Southway Cl **9** W12 . . . . 39 A4
Southwell Gdns SW7 . . . . 142 C3
Southwell Ho **18** Bermondsey SE16 . . . . 40 A2
13 Stoke Newington N16 . . . . 16 A3
Southwell Rd SE5 . . 63 B4
South Wharf Rd W2 . . . . 101 C2
Southwick Mews W2 . . . . 101 C2
Southwick Pl W2 . . 102 A1
Southwick St W2 . . 102 A2
Southwick Yd W2 . . 102 A1
Southwold Mans W9 . . . . 23 C2
Southwood Ave N6 . . 4 A4
Southwood Ct EC1 . . 96 A3

Southwood Ho W11 . . . . 31 A2 112 A4
Southwood Hts N6 . . 4 A4
Southwood La N6 . . . 3 C4
Southwood Lawn Rd N6 . . . . 3 C4
Southwood Park N6 . . . . 3 C4
Southwood Smith Ho **4** E2 . . . . 25 A2
Southwood Smith St N1 . . . . 86 A3
South Worple Ave SW14 . . . . 56 A4
Southwyck Ho SW9 . . . . 62 C3
South Yd EC1 . . . . . 109 B4
Sovereign Cl E1 . . . . 32 A2
Sovereign Cres SE16 . . . . 33 A2
Sovereign Ct **3** Richmond TW9 . . 54 B3
18 Stepney E1 . . . . 32 A2
Sovereign Ho **23** E2 . . . . 25 A3
Sovereign Mews **6** E2 . . . . 24 B3
Sovereign Pk NW10 . . . . 20 A1
Space Bsns Pk NW10 . . . . 20 A2
Spa Ct **12** SE16 . . . 139 B1
Spafield St EC1 . . . . 95 B2
Spalding Ho SE4 . . . 66 A2
Spanby Rd E3 . . . . . 26 C1
Spaniards Cl NW11 . . 2 C3
Spaniards End NW3 . . 2 C3
Spaniards Rd NW3 . . 2 B3
Spanish Billingual Sch
Spanish Pl W1 . . . . 103 C2
Spanish Rd SW18 . . 59 B2
Spa Rd SE16 . . . . . . 139 A1
Sparke Terr **2** E16 . . . . 35 B3
Sparkford Ho SW11 . . . . 167 C4
Sparks Cl W3 . . . . . . 28 C3
Sparsholt Rd N19 . . . 5 B3
Sparta St SE10 . . . . 52 B2
Spa Sch SE1 . . . . . . 153 B4
Spa View **6** SW16 . . 74 B1
Speakers' Corner* W1 . . . . 117 A3
Speakman Ho SE4 . . 66 A4
Spear Mews SW5 . . 141 C3
Spears Rd N19 . . . . . 5 A3
Spectrum Ho NW5 . . 12 C4
Spedan Cl NW3 . . . . 2 B1
Speechly Mews E8 . . . . 16 B3
Speed Ho EC2 . . . . 109 B4
Speedwell St **8** SE8 . . . . 51 C3
Speedy Pl WC1 . . . . 94 A3
Speldhurst Rd Bedford Pk W4 . . . . 37 C3
Homerton E9 . . . . . . 17 C1
Spellbrook Wlk N1 . . 87 A4
Spelman Ho **18** E1 . . . . 111 B3
Spelman St E1 . . . . 111 B4
Spence Cl SE16 . . . . 41 B4
Spencer Gdns SW14 . . . . 55 B2

Spencer Ho **31** Clapham SW8 . . 171 B1
24 Putney SW19 . . . 69 C3
Vale of Health NW3 . . 2 C1
Wimbledon SW19 . . . 69 C1
Spencer House Mus* SW1 . . . . 118 C1
Spencer Mews Fulham W6 . . . . . . 154 A4
South Lambeth SW9 . . . . 172 C3
Spencer Park Ct SW18 . . . . 59 C2
Spencer Pk SW18 . . 59 C2
Spencer Pl **18** Islington N1 . . . 15 A1
SW1 . . . . 133 A1
Spencer Rd Acton W3 . . . . 28 B1
Chiswick W4 . . . . . . 45 B3
Wandsworth SW18 . . 59 C2
Spencer Rise NW5 . . 4 A1
Spencer St EC1 . . . . 96 A3
Spencer Way **55** E1 . . . . 32 A3
Spencer Wlk **23** Hampstead NW3 . . . . 11 B4
Putney SW15 . . . . . . 57 C3
Spencer Yd SE3 . . . 53 B1
Spenlow Ho **2** SE16 . . . . 139 C2
Spenser Gr N16 . . . . 16 A4
Spenser Mews SE21 . . . . 75 C3
Spenser Rd SE24 . . 63 A2
Spenser St SW1 . . . 133 A2
Spens Ho WC1 . . . . . 94 C1
Spensley Wlk N16 . . 6 C1
Spert St E14 . . . . . . 33 A2
Spey St E14 . . . . 34 B4
Spezia Rd NW10 . . . 21 C3
Spice Ct **10** Battersea SW11 . . . . 59 B4
2 St George in t East E1 . . . . 125 C2
Spice Quay Htss SE1 . . . . 125 A1
Spicer Cl SE5, SW9 . . 48 A1
Spicer Ho E2 . . . . 24 C2 99 B3
Spindrift Ave E14 . . 42 A2
Spinnaker Ho **21** E14 . . . . 41 C4
Spinney The Barnes SW13 . . . . 47 A4
Streatham SW16 . . . 73 C1
Spire Ct **10** TW10 . . 54 A1
Spirit Ho W2 . . . . . 115 A4
Spirit Quay E1 . . . . . 32 A1
SPITALFIELDS 111 A4
Spital Sq E1 . . . . . . 110 B4
Spital St E1 . . . . 111 B4
Spital Yd E1 . . . . . . 110 B4
Splendour Wlk SE16 . . . . 135 B1
Spode Ho SE11 . . . . 135 B3
Sporle Ct **5** SW11 . . 59 C4
Sprewell SW15 . . . . 58 A1
Spriggs Ho **10** N1 . . 15 A1
Sprimont Pl SW3 . . 144 C2
Springall St **9** SE15 . . . . 50 A3

Springalls Wharf **2** SE16 . . . . 139 B4
Spring Mews W1 . . . . 103 C1
Spring Cott **10** W12 . . . . 38 C4
Spring Ct NW2 . . . . 10 B2
Springdale Rd N16 . . . . 15 C4
Springett Ho **15** SW2 . . . . 62 B2
Springfield Ct **7** Dagenham W3 . . 28 B3
Hampstead NW3 . . . 12 A1
Springfield Ho Acton W3 . . . . 29 B3
1 Camberwell SE5 . . 49 A1
13 Dalston E8 . . . . 16 B1
Springfield La NW6 . . . . 78 A3
Springfield Rd NW8 . . . . 79 A3
Springfield University Hospl SW17 . . . . . 72 A1
Springfield Wlk NW6 . . . . 78 A3
Spring Gdns Islington N5 . . . . . . 15 B3
SW1 . . . . 120 A2
Spring Gr W4 . . . . . . 44 C4
Spring Grove Rd TW10 . . . . 54 B2
Springhill Cl SE5 . . 63 C4
Springhill Cl SE5 . . 63 C4
Spring Ho WC1 . . . . 95 B3
Spring Mews W1 . . 103 A4
Springpark Dr N4 . . . 6 B3
Spring Pl NW5 . . . . . 13 A3
Springrice Rd SE13 . . . . 67 C1
Spring St W2 . . . . . 101 B1
Spring Terr TW10 . . . 54 A2
Springtide Cl **10** SE15 . . . . 49 C2
Springvale Ave TW8 . . . . 36 A1
Springvale Terr **5** W14 . . . . 39 C3
Springwater WC1 . . 106 C4
Springwell Ave NW10 . . . . 21 B4
Spring Wlk E1 . . . . 111 C4
Springwood Cl **8** E3 . . . . 26 C3
Spruce Ct W5 . . . . . 36 A3
Spruce Ho **15** SE16 . . . . 40 C4
Sprules Rd SE4 . . . . 51 A1
Spurgeon St SE1 . . 137 B2
Spurling Rd SE22 . . 64 B3
Spur Rd SE1 . . . . . . 135 B4
Spurstowe Rd E8 . . . 17 A2
Spurstowe Terr E8 . . . . 17 A3
Square Rigger Row **7** SW11 . . . . 59 B4
Square The Hammersmith W6 . . 39 B1
Shacklewell 165 B3
Squarey St SW17 . . 71 B1
Squire Gdns NW8 . . 89 B3
Squires Ct SW4 . . . 172 B3
Squire's Mount NW3 . . . . 2 C1
Squirrels The SE13 . . . . 67 C4

Squirries St
E2 . . . . 24 C2
Stable Ho **5** SE16 . . . 40 B4
Stables Way SE11 . . 149 B2
Stable Way W10 . . . . 30 B3
Stable Yd Rd
SW1 . . . . 133 A4
Stacey St
Highbury N7 . . . . 5 C1
Soho WC2 . . . . 105 C1
Stack Ho SW1 . . . . 130 C2
Stackhouse St
SW1 . . . . 130 C2
Stacy Path **15** SE5 . . 49 A3
Stadium SW10 . . . . 157 A1
Stafford Cl N4 . . . . . . 5 C4
Stafford Cripps Ho
30 Bethnal Green
E2 . . . . 25 B2
SW6 . . . . 155 A3
Stafford Ct
Kensington W8 . . . 127 C2
South Lambeth
SW8 . . . . 172 A4
Stafford Ho SE1 . . . 153 A2
Stafford Mans
13 Hammersmith
W14 . . . . 39 C3
14 Stockwell SW4 . . 62 A3
SW11 . . . . 158 C1
Stafford PI SW1 . . . 132 C2
Stafford Rd
Bow E3 . . . . 26 B3
Maida Vale NW6 . . . 23 C2
Staffordshire St
Peckham SE15 . . . . 49 C2
Peckham SE15 . . . . 50 A2
Stafford St W1 . . . . 118 C2
Stafford Terr W8 . . . 127 B2
Stag La SW15 . . . . . . 68 B2
Stagshaw Ho **12**
SE22 . . . . 64 A4
Stainer St SE1 . . . . 123 C1
Staining La EC2 . . . . 109 A2
Stainsbury St **25**
E2 . . . . 25 B3
Stainsby Rd E14 . . . . 33 C3
Stalbridge Flats
W1 . . . . 103 C1
Stalbridge Ho
NW1 . . . . 82 C1
Stalbridge St
NW1 . . . . 102 B4
Stalham St SE16 . . . . 40 A3
Stambourne Ho
SW8 . . . . 172 B4
Stamford Bridge
Stadium (Chelsea
FC) SW6 . . . . . . 156 A2
Stamford Brook Ave
W6 . . . . 38 B3
Stamford Brook Gdns
1 W6 . . . . 38 B3
Stamford Brook Mans
2 W6 . . . . 38 B3
Stamford Brook Rd
W6 . . . . 38 B3
Stamford Ct **2**
NW3 . . . . 2 B1
Stamford Cotts
SW10 . . . . 156 B2
Stamford Ct W6 . . . . 38 C2
Stamford Gr E **1**
N16 . . . . 7 C3

Stamford Gr W **4**
N16 . . . . 7 C3
STAMFORD HILL 7 A3
Stamford Hill N16 . . . . 7 B3
Stamford Hill Mans **1**
N16 . . . . 7 A4
Stamford Hill Sta
N16 . . . . 7 A4
Stamford Lo **2** N16 . . 7 B4
Stamford Mans **2**
N16 . . . . 7 B4
Stamford Rd N1 . . . . 16 A2
Stamford St SE1 . . . 121 C2
Stamp PI E2 . . . . 24 B2 99 A4
Stanard Ct N16 . . . . . 7 A4
Stanborough Ho **5**
E3 . . . . 27 A1
Stanborough Pas
E8 . . . . 16 B2
Stanbridge Mans
SW15 . . . . 57 B4
Stanbridge Rd
SW15 . . . . 57 B4
Stanbrook Ct W1 . . . 118 C2
Stanbury Ct **18**
NW3 . . . . 12 B2
Stanbury Rd
Nunhead SE15 . . . . 50 B1
Peckham SE15 . . . . 50 A1
Standard Ho
NW10 . . . . 20 C1
Standen **1** SW15 . . . 70 C4
Standish Ho **6**
W6 . . . . 38 C2
Standish Rd W6 . . . . 38 C2
Stanesgate Ho **20**
SE15 . . . . 49 C3
Stanfield Ho NW8 . . . 89 C2
Stanfield Rd **14** E3 . . 26 A3
Stanford Ct
Kensington W8 . . . 128 B1
Walham Green
SW6 . . . . 166 B3
Stanford PI SE1 . . . . 152 A3
Stanford Rd W8 . . . 128 B2
Stanford St SW1 . . . 147 B3
Stangate SE1 . . . . . 135 A2
Stanhope Cl **23**
SE16 . . . . 40 C4
Stanhope Gate
W1 . . . . 117 C2
Stanhope Gdns
SW7 . . . . 143 A4
Stanhope Ho
4 Putney SW15 . . 57 B2
SW8 . . . . 51 B1
Stanhope Mews E
SW7 . . . . 143 A4
Stanhope Mews S
SW7 . . . . 143 A3
Stanhope Mews W
SW7 . . . . 143 A4
Stanhope Par NW1 . . 92 C4
Stanhope PI W2 . . . 102 C1
Stanhope Rd N6 . . . . 4 B4
Stanhope Row
W1 . . . . 118 A1
Stanhope St NW1 . . . 92 C4
Stanhope Terr
W2 . . . . 115 C4
Stanier CI SW5 . . . . 141 A1
Stanlake Mews **7**
W12 . . . . 30 B1
Stanlake Rd W12 . . . 30 B1

Stanlake Villas **8**
W12 . . . . 30 B1
Stanley CI SW8 . . . . 162 C3
Stanley Cohen Ho
EC1 . . . . 96 C1
Stanley Cres
W11 . . . . 31 B2 112 C4
Stanley Gdns
Bedford Pk W3 . . . . 38 A4
Cricklewood NW2 . . . 9 B3
W11 . . . . 31 B2 112 C4
Stanley Gr SW11 . . . 169 C1
Stanley Ho
5 Clapham SW8 . . 171 B1
22 Poplar E14 . . . . . 33 C3
Stanley Holloway Ct
E16 . . . . 35 C3
Stanley Mans
SW10 . . . . 157 A4
Upper Tooting
SW17 . . . . 72 B2
Stanley Rd
Acton Green W3 . . . 37 B3
Mill Meads E15 . . . . 27 C4
Mortlake SW14 . . . . 55 B3
Stanley St SE14,
SE8 . . . . 51 B3
Stanley Studios
SW10 . . . . 157 A4
Stanley Terr **8** N19 . . 5 A2
Stanliff Ho **8** E14 . . . 41 C3
Stanmer St SW11 . . 168 B2
Stanmore Gdns
TW9 . . . . 54 B4
Stanmore Ho **21**
SW8 . . . . 171 C2
Stanmore PI NW1 . . . 82 B4
Stanmore Rd TW9 . . . 54 B4
Stanmore St N1 . . . . 84 C4
Stannard Cotts **7**
E1 . . . . 25 B1
Stannard Mews
E8 . . . . 16 C2
Stannard Rd E8 . . . . 16 C2
Stannary PI SE11 . . 149 C1
Stannary St SE11 . . 149 C1
Stansbury Sq **3**
W10 . . . . 23 A2
Stansfield Rd SW9 . . 62 B3
Stanstead Ho E3 . . . 27 B1
Stansted Express
Terminal EC2 . . . . 110 A4
Stanswood Gdns
SE5 . . . . 49 A3
Stanton Ct N16 . . . . . 6 C4
Stanton Ho **9**
SE10 . . . . 52 B4
Stanton Rd SW13 . . . 46 B1
Stanway Ct **23** N1 . . 24 A3
Stanway St N1 . . . . . 24 A3
Stanwick Rd W14 . . 140 C3
Stanworth St SE1 . . 139 A3
Staplefield CI **3**
SW2 . . . . 74 A3
Stapleford CI
SW19 . . . . 70 A4
Staplehurst Ct **1**
N1 . . . . 60 B1
Staplehurst Ho **18**
E5 . . . . 17 A3
Staple Inn WC1 . . . 107 B3
Staple Inn Bldgs
WC2 . . . . 107 B3
Staples CI SE16 . . . . 33 A1
Staple St SE1 . . . . . 137 C3

Stapleton Hall N4 . . . 5 B4
Stapleton Hall Rd
N4 . . . . 5 B4
Stapleton Ho **19**
E2 . . . . 25 A2
Stapleton Rd
SW17 . . . . 72 C1
Star Alley EC3 . . . . 124 B4
Starboard Way
E14 . . . . 41 C3
Starcross St NW1 . . . 93 A3
Stardome * NW1 . . . 91 B1
Starfield Rd W12 . . . 38 C4
Star & Garter Mans **3**
SW15 . . . . 57 C4
Starliner Ct N7 . . . . . 14 C2
Starling Ho NW8 . . . 80 A2
Star PI E1 . . . . 125 A3
Star Rd W14 . . . . . 140 C1
Star St W2 . . . . . . 102 A2
Star Works NW10 . . . 21 C2
Star Yd WC2 . . . . . 107 B2
Statham Ct N7 . . . . . 5 A1
Statham Gr N16 . . . . 6 C1
Statham Ho SW8 . . 170 C4
Station App
Dagenham NW10 . . . 21 B2
Fulham SW6 . . . . . 164 B1
Richmond TW9 . . . . 44 C2
Station Approach Rd
W4 . . . . 45 B3
Station Ave
1 Brixton SW9 . . . 63 A4
14 Richmond TW9 . . 44 C2
Station Cres SE3 . . . 43 C1
Station Ct **5** SE15 . . 50 B1
Stationers Hall Ct
EC4 . . . . 108 B1
Station Gdns W4 . . . 45 B3
Station Mews Terr
SE3 . . . . 43 C1
Station Par
Cricklewood NW2 . . . 9 B2
Richmond TW9 . . . . 44 C2
4 Upper Tooting
SW12 . . . . 72 C3
Station Pas SE15 . . . 50 B2
Station PI N4 . . . . . . 5 C2
Station Rd
Barnes SW13 . . . . . 46 B1
Camden Town N19 . . 4 B1
Harlesden NW10 . . . 21 B3
Lewisham SE13 . . . . 67 B4
Station Rise SE27 . . . 75 A2
Station St E15 . . . . . 19 C1
Station Terr
Camberwell SE5 . . . 48 B2
Kensal Rise NW10 . . 22 C3
Staunton Ho SE17 . . 152 A3
Staunton St SE8 . . . 51 B4
Staveley NW1 . . . . . 92 C4
Staveley CI
Hackney E9 . . . . . . 17 B3
Lower Holloway N7 . . 14 A4
New Cross Gate
SE15 . . . . 50 B2
8 Peckham SE15 . . 50 A2
Staveley Gdns W4 . . 45 C2
Staveley Ho SE5 . . . 64 A2
Staveley Rd W4 . . . . 45 C3
Stavers Ho **31** E3 . . . 26 B3
Staverton Rd NW2 . . . 9 B1
Stave Yard Rd
SE16 . . . . 33 A1
Stavordale Lo
W14 . . . . 127 A2

Stavordale Rd N5 . . . 15 A4
Stayner's Rd E1 . . . . 25 C1
Steadman Ct EC1 . . . 97 A2
Stead St SE17 . . . . 151 B3
Stean St E8 . . . . . . 24 B4
Stebbing Ho **8**
W11 . . . . 30 C1
Stebondale St E14 . . 42 B2
Stebon Prim Sch *
E14 . . . . 33 C4
Stedham PI WC1 . . . 106 A2
Steedman St
SE17 . . . . 150 C3
Steele Rd
Acton Green W4 . . . 37 B3
Becontree NW10 . . . 20 B2
Steele's Mews N
NW3 . . . . 12 B2
Steele's Mews S
NW3 . . . . 12 B2
Steele's Rd NW3 . . . 12 B2
Steel's La **22** E1 . . . . 32 B3
Steen Way **7**
SE22 . . . . 64 A2
Steep Hill SW16 . . . . 73 C1
Steeple Cl SW6 . . . 164 B1
Steeple Ct **16** E1 . . . 25 A1
Steeple Wlk N1 . . . . 87 A4
Steerforth St
SW18 . . . . 71 B2
Steers Way SE16 . . . 41 A4
Stelfax Ho WC1 . . . . 95 A4
Stellman CI E5 . . . . . 7 C1
Stephan CI E8 . . . . . 24 C4
Stephen Ct **18**
SW19 . . . . 69 C3
Stephendale Rd
SW6 . . . . 166 C2
Stephen Fox Ho **7**
W4 . . . . 38 A1
Stephen Hawking Sch
2 E14 . . . . 33 A3
Stephen Mews
W1 . . . . 105 B3
Stephen St **8** W1 . . . 61 B4
Stephen Saunders Ct
SW11 . . . . 60 A2
Stephens Ct SE4 . . . 66 A4
Stephenson Ho
2 Gospel Oak
NW5 . . . . 13 A4
6 Maitland Pk
NW1 . . . . 12 B3
Newington SE1 . . . 136 C2
Stephenson St
Dagenham NW10 . . 21 B2
Newham E16 . . . . . 35 A4
Stephenson Way
NW1 . . . . 93 A2
Stephen St W1 . . . . 105 B3
STEPNEY 32 C4
Stepney City E1 . . . . 32 B4
Stepney Cswy E1 . . . 32 C3
Stepney Gn E1 . . . . 32 C4
Stepney Greencoat CE
Prim Sch The **28**
E14 . . . . 33 B3
Stepney Green Ct **4**
E1 . . . . 32 C4
Stepney Green Mans
& Computing Coll **18**
E1 . . . . 32 C4
Stepney Green Sta
E1 . . . . 25 C1

Stepney High St
E1 . . . . .32 C4
Stepney Way E1 . . . .32 B4
Stepping Stones
Farm★ E1 . . . . .32 C4
Sterling Cl NW10 . . . .8 C1
Sterling Gdns
SE14 . . . . .51 A4
Sterling Pl W5 . . . . . .36 A2
Sterling St SW7 . . . .130 B2
Sterndale Rd W14 . . .39 C3
Sterne St W12 . . . . . .39 C4
Sternhall La SE15 . . .64 C4
Sternhold Ave SW12,
SW2 . . . . .73 C2
Sterry St SE1 . . . . . .137 B3
Steve Biko Ct W10 . . .22 C1
Steve Biko Rd N7 . . . .5 C1
Stevedore St 1
E1 . . . . .32 A1
Stevenage Rd
SW6 . . . . .47 C2
Stevens Ave E9 . . . . .17 B2
Stevenson Cres
SE16 . . . . .40 A1
Stevenson Ho
1 Battersea
SW11 . . . . .168 C1
6 Clapham Pk SW2 . .62 A2
NW8 . . . . .78 C4
Stevens St SE1 . . . . .138 B2
Steventon Rd W12 . . .29 B2
Stewart Headlam
Prim Sch 28 E1 . . . . .25 A1
Stewart Ho SE1 . . . .138 A1
Stewart Rd E15 . . . . .19 C4
Stewart's Gr SW3 . . .144 A2
Stewart's Rd SW8 . . .170 C4
Stewart St E14 . . . . .42 B4
Stew La EC4 . . . . . . .122 C4
Steyne Ho
16 Acton W3 . . . . . . .28 A1
11 Acton W3 . . . . . . .28 B1
Steyne Rd W3 . . . . . .28 A1
Stifford Ho E1 . . . . . .32 B4
Stile Hall Gdns
W4 . . . . .36 C1
Stile Hall Par 8
W4 . . . . .36 C1
Stileman Ho 4 E3 . . .33 B4
Stillingfleet Rd
SW13 . . . . .46 C4
Stillington St
SW1 . . . . .147 A4
Stillness Jun & Inf
Schs SE23 . . . . .66 A1
Stillness Rd SE23 . . . .66 B1
Stirling Ct
Clerkenwell EC1 . . . . .96 A2
Strand WC2 . . . . . . .106 C1
Stirling Mans NW6 . .11 B2
Stirling Rd
South Acton W3 . . . . .37 A4
Stockwell SW9 . . . . .172 B1
Stoatley Ho 10
SW15 . . . . .68 C3
Stockbeck NW1 . . . . .83 A1
Stockfield Rd
SW16 . . . . .74 B1
Stockholm Ho E1 . . .125 C4
Stockholm Rd
SE16 . . . . .40 B1
Stockholm Way
E1 . . . . .125 B2

Stockhurst Cl
SW15 . . . . .47 C1
Stockleigh Hall
NW8 . . . . .80 B2
Stock Orchard Cres
N7 . . . . .14 B3
Stock Orchard St
N7 . . . . .14 B3
Stocks Ct 6 E1 . . . . .25 C1
Stocks Pl 8 E14 . . . . .33 B2
Stockton Ho 10 E2 . . .25 A2
STOCKWELL 62 A4
Stockwell Ave
SW9 . . . . .62 B4
Stockwell Gdns
SW9 . . . . .172 C2
Stockwell Gn
SW9 . . . . .172 C1
Stockwell Park Cres
SW9 . . . . .173 A2
Stockwell Park Rd
SW9 . . . . .173 A3
Stockwell Park Sch
SW9 . . . . .172 C4
Stockwell Park Wlk
SW9 . . . . .62 C4
Stockwell Prim Sch 6
SW9 . . . . .62 B4
Stockwell St SE10 . . .52 B4
Stockwell Sta
SW4 . . . . .172 B2
Stockwell Terr
SW9 . . . . .172 C3
Stoddart Ho SW8 . . .163 A3
Stodmarsh Ho 28
SW9 . . . . .173 C4
Stokenchurch St
SW6 . . . . .166 A3
STOKE
NEWINGTON 7 A2
Stoke Newington
Church St N16 . . . . . . .7 A2
Stoke Newington
Comm N16 . . . . .7 B2
Stoke Newington
High St N16 . . . . .7 B1
Stoke Newington Rd
N16 . . . . .16 B4
Stoke Newington Sch
N16 . . . . .7 A2
Stoke Newington Sta
N16 . . . . .7 B2
Stoke Pl NW10 . . . . .21 B2
Stokesley St W12 . . . .29 B3
Stondon Pk SE23 . . . .66 A1
Stone Bldgs WC2 . . .107 A3
STONEBRIDGE 20 B4
Stonebridge Ctr 6
NW10 . . . . .20 C4
Stonebridge Prim Sch
NW10 . . . . .20 B4
Stonecutter St
EC4 . . . . .108 A2
Stonefield N4 . . . . . . .5 B2
Stonefield Mans
N1 . . . . .85 B3
Stonefield St N1 . . . . .85 C4
Stonegate 8 NW5 . . .12 C2
Stonehill Cl SW14 . . .55 C2
Stonehill Ho
Brentford W4 . . . . . . .36 C1
Mortlake SW14 . . . . . .55 C2

Stonehills Ct SE21 . . .76 A1
Stonehill's Mans 3
SW16 . . . . .74 A2
Stonehouse NW1 . . . .83 A3
Stonehouse Ct
EC2 . . . . .110 B2
Stonehouse Ho 7
W2 . . . . .31 C4
Stoneleigh Lo 13
TW9 . . . . .44 B2
Stoneleigh Mews 15
E3 . . . . .26 A3
Stoneleigh Pl W11 . . .30 C2
Stoneleigh St W11 . . .30 C2
Stoneleigh Terr
N19 . . . . .4 A2
Stonell's Rd SW11 . . .60 B2
Stonenest St N4 . . . . .5 B3
Stones End St
SE1 . . . . .136 C3
Stoneyard La E14 . . . .34 A2
Stoney La EC3 . . . . .110 B2
Stoney St SE1 . . . . . .123 B2
Stonhouse St SW4 . . .61 C3
Stonor Rd W14 . . . . .140 C3
Stopes St SE15 . . . . . .49 B3
Stopford Rd SE17 . . .150 B1
Stopher Ho SE1 . . . .136 B3
Storace Ho 6
SW4 . . . . .62 A3
Storers Quay E14 . . . .42 C2
Store St
Bloomsbury WC1 . . . .105 B4
Stratford New Town
E15 . . . . .19 C3
Storey Ct NW8 . . . . . .89 B3
Storey Ho 8 E14 . . . . .34 A2
Storey's Gate
SW1 . . . . .133 C3
Stories Rd SE5 . . . . . .64 A4
Storks Rd SE16 . . . . .139 C1
Stormont House Sch
E5 . . . . .17 A4
Stormont Rd
Clapham SW11 . . . . . .60 C3
Highgate N6 . . . . .3 B4
Storrington WC1 . . . . .94 B3
Story St N1 . . . . .14 B1
Stothard Ho 28 E1 . . .25 B1
Stothard Pl E2 . . . . .110 B4
Stothard St 12 E1 . . . .25 B1
Stott Cl SW18 . . . . . . .59 C1
Stoughton Cl
Roehampton SW15 . . . .68 C3
SE11 . . . . .149 A3
Stourcliffe Cl W1 . . . .102 C2
Stourcliffe St W1 . . . .102 C1
Stourhead Cl 6
SW19 . . . . .69 C4
Stowage SE8 . . . . .52 A4
Stowe Ho 11 N16 . . . .6 C2
Stowe Rd W12 . . . . . .39 A4
Stracey Rd NW10 . . . .20 C4
Stradbroke Rd N5 . . . .15 B4
Stradella Rd SE24 . . . .63 B1
Stralanz . . . .
N3 . . . . .12 A2
Strafford Ho 9
SE8 . . . . .41 B1
Strafford Rd W3 . . . . .37 B4
Strafford St E14 . . . . .41 C4
Strahan Rd E3 . . . . . .26 A2
Straightsmouth
SE10 . . . . .52 B3
Straker's Rd SE15 . . .65 A3

Strale Ho 17 N1 . . . . .24 A4
STRAND 120 C4
Strand
Strand WC2 . . . . . . .120 C4
Strand WC2 . . . . . . .107 A1
Strand Dr TW9 . . . . . .45 A3
Strand La WC2 . . . . .121 A4
STRAND ON THE
GREEN 44 C4
Strand-on-the-Green
Schs 5 W4 . . . . .44 C4
Strang Ho N1 . . . . . . .86 C3
Strangways Terr
W14 . . . . .126 C1
Stranraer Way N1 . . .14 A1
Strasburg Rd
SW11 . . . . .170 A3
Stratford Bus Sta
E15 . . . . .19 B2
Stratford Coll
(Newham 6th Form
Coll) E15 . . . . .19 C2
Stratford Gr SW15 . . .57 C3
Stratford
International Sta
E15 . . . . .19 B2
STRATFORD
MARSH 27 A4
STRATFORD NEW
TOWN 19 B3
Stratford Pl W1 . . . . .104 A1
Stratford Rd W8 . . . .127 C1
E15 . . . . .19 C1
Stratford Sh Ctr
E15 . . . . .19 C1
Stratford Sta E15 . . . .19 C1
Stratford Studios
W8 . . . . .128 A1
Stratford Villas
NW1 . . . . .13 C1
Stratford Workshops
E15 . . . . .19 C1
Strathan Cl SE18 . . . .58 A1
Strathblaine Rd
SW11 . . . . .59 C3
Strathdon Dr
SW17 . . . . .71 C1
Strathearn Ho
W2 . . . . .116 A4
Strathearn Pl W2 . . .116 A4
Stratheden Par
SE3 . . . . .53 C3
Stratheden Rd
SE3 . . . . .53 C3
Strathleven Rd
SW2 . . . . .62 A2
Strathmore Ct
NW8 . . . . .90 A4
Strathmore Gdns
W8 . . . . .31 C1 113 C2
Strathmore Rd
SW19 . . . . .70 C1
Strathnairn St
SE1 . . . . .153 C3
Strathray Gdns
NW3 . . . . .12 A2
Strath Terr SW11 . . . .60 A3
Strathville Rd
SW18 . . . . .71 A2
Stratton Cl 4 N1 . . . .16 A1
Strattondale St
E14 . . . . .42 B3
Stratton St W1 . . . . .118 B2
Strauss Rd W4 . . . . . .37 C4

Streamline Mews
SE22 . . . . .76 C3
Streatham Cl
SW16 . . . . .74 A2
Streatham & Clapham
High Sch SW16 . . . . .73 C1
Streatham Ct
SW16 . . . . .74 A1
STREATHAM HILL . . .74 A3
Streatham Hill
SW2 . . . . .74 A4
Streatham Hill &
Clapham High Sch 14
SW2 . . . . .74 B3
Streatham Hill Sta
SW2 . . . . .74 A4
Streatham Pl SW2 . . .74 A4
Streatham St
WC1 . . . . .106 A2
Streathbourne Rd
SW17 . . . . .72 C1
Streatley Pl
27 Hampstead
NW3 . . . . .11 B4
Hampstead NW3 . . . . .11 C4
Streatley Rd NW6 . . .10 B1
Streimer Rd E15 . . . . .27 B3
Strelley Way W3 . . . . .29 A2
Stretton Mans 16
SE8 . . . . .51 C4
Strickland Ct SE15 . . .64 C4
Strickland Ho 9
E2 . . . . .24 B2 99 A3
Strickland Row
SW18 . . . . .71 C4
Strickland St SE8 . . . .51 C2
Stringer Hos 10
N1 . . . . .24 A4
Strode Ho 8 SW2 . . . .74 C3
Strode Rd
SW6 . . . . .154 A2
Willesden NW10 . . . . . .8 C2
Strome Ho NW6 . . . . .78 A1
Stronsa Rd W12 . . . . .38 B4
Strood Ho SE1 . . . . .137 C3
Stroud Cres SW15 . . .68 C1
Stroud Green Prim
Sch N4 . . . . .5 C3
Stroud Green Rd
N4 . . . . .5 C3
Stroudley Ho
SW8 . . . . .171 A4
Stroudley Wlk E3 . . . .27 A2
Stroud Rd SW19 . . . . .70 C1
Strout's Pl 2 E2 . . . . .
E2 . . . . .24 B2 98 C4
Strudwick Ct
SW4 . . . . .172 B3
Strutton Ground
SW1 . . . . .133 B1
Strype St E1 . . . . . . .110 C3
Stuart Ave W5 . . . . . .36 A4
Stuart Ho
Hammersmith W6 . . . .39 B3
1 Homerton E9 . . . . .17 B1
5 Stockwell SW4 . . . .62 A3
W14 . . . . .140 A4
Stuart Mill Ho N1 . . .84 C1
Stuart Rd
Acton W3 . . . . .28 B1
Maida Vale NW6 . . . . .23 C2
Nunhead SE15 . . . . . .65 B3

Stuart Rd continued
Wimbledon SW19 . . . . . .70 C1
Stubbs Ho SE16 . . . . . .40 A1
Stubbs Ho
Finsbury Pk N4 . . . . . .5 B3
1 Globe Town E2 . . .25 C2
Stucley Pl **19** NW1 . .13 A1
Studdridge St
SW6 . . . . .165 C2
Studd St N1 . . . . .86 A4
Studholme Ct
NW3 . . . . .10 C4
Studholme St
SE15 . . . . .50 A3
Studio Pl SW1 . . . . . .131 A3
Studios NW8 . . . . .78 C2
Studios The
4 Clapham SW4 . . . .61 B3
SW8 . . . . .171 C3
Studland Cl **1** SE1 . . .82 C2
Studland Ho E14 . . . . .33 A3
Studland St 39 A2
Studley Cl E5 . . . . .18 A3
Studley Ct **13** E14 . . .34 C2
Studley Rd SW4 . . . . .172 B2
Stukeley St WC2 . . . . .106 B2
Stunell Ho **23**
SE14 . . . . .50 C4
Sturdee Ho **2** E2 . . . .24 C3
Sturdy Ho **28** E3 . . . .26 A3
Sturdy Rd SE15 . . . . . .50 A1
Sturgeon Rd SE17 . . .150 C1
Sturge St SE1 . . . . . . .136 C4
Sturmer Way N7 . . . . .14 B3
Sturminster Ho
SW8 . . . . .163 A1
Sturry St E14 . . . . .34 A3
Sturt St N1 . . . . .87 A1
Stutfield St E1 . . . . . . .111 C1
Stuttle Ho **14**
E1 . . . . .24 C1 99 B1
Styles Gdns SW9 . . . . .63 A4
Styles Ho SE1 . . . . . . .122 A1
Stylus Apartments **25**
E1 . . . . .32 B3
Sudbourne Prim Sch
18 SW2 . . . . .62 B2
Sudbourne Rd
SW2 . . . . .62 B2
Sudbrooke Rd
SW12 . . . . .60 C1
Sudbury Ct SW8 . . . . .171 C4
Sudbury Ho SW18 . . . .59 A2
Sudeley St N1 . . . . .86 B1
Sudlow Rd SW18 . . . . .58 C2
Sudrey St SE1 . . . . . . .136 C3
Suffield Ho SE17 . . . . .150 B2
Suffolk Ho **6** NW5 . . . .4 B1
Suffolk La EC4 . . . . . . .123 B4
Suffolk Pl SW1 . . . . . .119 C2
Suffolk Rd
Barnes SW13 . . . . . . .46 C3
Willesden NW10 . . . . . .8 A1
Suffolk St SW1 . . . . . .119 C2
Sugar House La
E15 . . . . .27 B3
Sugar Loaf Wlk **6**
E2 . . . . .25 B2
Sugden Rd SW11 . . . . .60 C3
Sulby Ho SE4 . . . . .66 A3
Sulgrave Gdns **11**
W6 . . . . .39 C3
Sulgrave Rd W6 . . . . . .39 B3
Sulina Rd SW2 . . . . . . .74 A4
Sulivan Ct SW6 . . . . . .165 B1

Sulivan Ent Ctr
SW6 . . . . .58 C4
Sulivan Prim Sch
SW6 . . . . .165 B1
Sulivan Rd SW6 . . . . . .58 C4
Sulkin Ho **11** E2 . . . .25 C2
Sullivan Cl SW11 . . . . .60 A4
Sullivan Ct
Stamford Hill N16 . . . . .7 B3
SW5 . . . . .141 C4
Sullivan Ho
Chelsea SW1 . . . . . . .160 B4
Vauxhall SE11 . . . . . . .149 A3
Sullivan Rd SE11 . . . .149 C4
Sultan St SE5 . . . . .48 B3
Sumatra Rd NW6 . . . . .10 C2
Sumburgh Rd
SW12 . . . . .60 C1
Summercourt Rd
E1 . . . . .32 B3
Summerfield Ave
NW6 . . . . .23 A3
Summer Ho SE13 . . . . .67 C3
Summerhouse Rd
N16 . . . . .7 A2
Summerlands Ave
W3 . . . . .28 B2
Summerley St
SW18 . . . . .71 A2
Summers St EC1 . . . . . .95 B1
SUMMERSTOWN 71 B1
Summit Ct NW2 . . . . . .10 A3
Summit Est N16 . . . . . .7 C4
Sumner Ave SE15 . . . . .49 B2
Sumner Bldgs
SE1 . . . . .122 C2
Sumner Ho **1** E3 . . . .34 A4
Sumner Pl SW7 . . . . . .143 C3
Sumner Place Mews
SW7 . . . . .143 C3
Sumner Rd SE15 . . . . .49 B3
Sumner St SE1 . . . . . .122 C2
Sumpter Cl NW3 . . . . .11 B2
Sun Alley **6** W9 . . . . .54 A3
Sun Alliance Ho
WC2 . . . . .107 B2
Sunbeam Cres
W10 . . . . .20 C1
Sunbeam Rd
NW10 . . . . .20 C1
Sunbury Ave
SW14 . . . . .55 C3
Sunbury Ct **3**
SE14 . . . . .50 C4
Sunbury Ho **5**
E2 . . . . .24 B2 98 C3
Sunbury Workshops
5 E2 . . . . . .24 B2 98 C3
Sun Ct EC3 . . . . .109 C1
Sunderland Ct
SE22 . . . . .76 C4
Sunderland Ho **26**
W2 . . . . .31 C4
Sunderland Terr
W2 . . . . .100 A2
Sundew Ave W12 . . . . .29 C2
Sundra Wlk **22** E1 . . .25 C1
Sundridge Ho **4**
E9 . . . . .17 C1
Sunley Ho E1 . . . . .111 A3
Sunlight Sq **20** E2 . . .25 A2
Sunningdale Ave
W3 . . . . .29 A1

Sunningdale Cl **22**
SE16 . . . . .40 A1
Sunningdale Gdns
W8 . . . . .127 C1
Sunninghill Ct **9**
W3 . . . . .37 B4
Sunninghill Rd
SE13 . . . . .52 A1
Sunnyhill Cl E5 . . . . . . .18 A4
Sunnymead Rd
SW15 . . . . .57 A2
Sunnyside **4** NW2 . . .1 B1
Sunnyside Ho **4**
NW2 . . . . .1 B1
Sunnyside Rd N19 . . . . .4 C4
Sun Pas **5** SE16 . . . .139 B2
Sunray Ave SE5,
SE24 . . . . .63 C3
Sun Rd W14 . . . . .140 C1
Sun St Pas EC2 . . . . . .110 A3
Sunset Rd SE5 . . . . . . .63 C3
Sun St EC2 . . . . .109 C4
Sunwell Cl SE15 . . . . . .50 A2
Surcot Ho **2**
SW1 . . . . .147 C3
Surma Cl E1 . .24 C1 99 C1
Surrendale Pl W9 . . . . .23 C1
Surrey Canal Rd SE14,
SE8 . . . . .125 B1
Surrey Cres **1**
W4 . . . . .36 C1
Surrey Docks Farm*
SE16 . . . . .41 B4
Surrey Docks
Watersports Ctr
SE8 . . . . .41 B2
Surrey Gr SE17 . . . . . .152 A1
Surrey Ho **8** SE16 . . .32 C1
Surrey La SW11 . . . . . .168 B3
Surrey Quays Rd
SE16 . . . . .40 C3
Surrey Quays Sh Ctr
SE16 . . . . .40 C3
Surrey Quays Sta
SE16 . . . . .40 C3
Surrey Rd SE15 . . . . . .65 C2
Surrey Row SE1 . . . . . .136 B4
Surrey Sq SE17 . . . . . .152 B2
Surrey Square Inf &
Jun Sch SE17 . . . . .152 B2
Surrey St WC2 . . . . . . .121 A4
Surrey Terr SE17 . . . . .152 B2
Surrey Water Rd
SE16 . . . . .32 C1
Surrey Wharf SE1 . . . . .49 C4
Surridge Ct **15**
SW9 . . . . .172 B2
Surr St N7 . . . . .14 A3
Susan Constant Ct **3**
E14 . . . . .34 C2
Susannah St E14 . . . . .34 B3
Sussex Cl N19 . . . . .5 A3
Sussex Ct
4 Barnes SW13 . . . .46 B1
Greenwich SE10 . . . . . .52 B4
Paddington W2 . . . . . .101 B1
Sussex Gdns W2 . . . . .101 B1
Sussex Ho
Hampstead NW3 . . . . .12 A2
Sussex House Sch
SW3 . . . . .144 C4
Sussex Lo **22** 101 C1

Sussex Mans
South Kensington
SW7 . . . . .143 B3
Strand WC2 . . . . .120 B4
Sussex Mews E
W2 . . . . .101 C1
Sussex Mews W
W2 . . . . .115 C4
Sussex Pl
22 Hammersmith
W6 . . . . .39 B1
Lisson Gr NW1 . . . . . . .90 C2
Paddington W2 . . . . . .101 C1
Sussex Sq W2 . . . . . . .115 C4
Sussex St SW1 . . . . . .146 B2
Sussex Way
Upper Holloway N7 . . . .5 B1
Upper Holloway N7,
N19 . . . . .5 A2
Upper Holloway N19 . . .4 C2
Sutherland Ave
W9 . . . . .88 C2
Sutherland Ct
3 Paddington W9 . . .23 C1
Stoke Newington N16 . .6 C1
Sutherland Gdns
SW14 . . . . .56 A4
Sutherland Gr SW18,
SW19 . . . . .70 B4
Sutherland Ho
Kensington W8 . . . . . .128 A1
7 Putney SW15 . . . .69 B4
5 South Hampstead
NW6 . . . . .11 B1
Sutherland Pl W2 . . . . .31 C3
Sutherland Rd W4 . . . .45 B4
Sutherland Row
SW1 . . . . .146 B2
Sutherland Sq
SE17 . . . . .150 C1
Sutherland St
SW1 . . . . .146 B2
Sutherland Wlk
SE17 . . . . .151 A1
Sutterton St N7 . . . . . .14 B2
Sutton Court Mans
W4 . . . . .45 B4
Sutton Court Rd
W4 . . . . .45 B4
Sutton Ct
Chiswick W4 . . . . .45 B4
6 Hackney E5 . . . . .17 A4
Sutton Est SW3 . . . . . .144 B2
Sutton Est The **8**
W10 . . . . .30 B4
Sutton House* E9 . . . . .17 B3
Sutton La EC1 . . . . .96 B1
Sutton La N W4 . . . . . .45 B3
Sutton La S W4 . . . . . .45 B4
Sutton Pl E9 . . . . .17 B3
Sutton Row W1 . . . . . .105 C2
Sutton Sq E9 . . . . .17 B3
Sutton St E1 . . . . .32 B3
Suttons Way EC1 . . . . .97 A1
Sutton Way W10 . . . . . .30 B4
Sutton Wlk SE1 . . . . . .121 A1
Swaby Rd SW17,
SW18 . . . . .71 B2
Swaffield Prim Sch
SW18 . . . . .71 B4
Swaffield Rd
SW18 . . . . .71 B4
Swain's La N6 . . . . .4 A2
Swainson Ho N7 . . . . . .14 C4
Swainson Rd W3 . . . . .38 B4
Swain St NW8 . . . . .90 A2

Swallow Cl SE14 . . . . . .50 C2
Swallow Ct **4** W9 . . . .31 C4
Swallowfield NW1 . . . .92 B3
Swallow Ho **4** NW8 . .80 A2
Swallow Pl
24 Poplar E14 . . . . .33 B3
W1 . . . . .104 B1
Swallow St W1 . . . . . .119 A3
Swanage Ho SW8 . . . .162 C1
Swanage Rd SW18 . . . .59 B1
Swanbourne SE17 . . .150 C3
Swanbourne Ho
NW8 . . . . .90 A2
Swan Bsns Ctr **8**
W4 . . . . .37 C2
Swan Ct
Chelsea SW3 . . . . . . .144 B1
Parsons Green
SW6 . . . . .155 B1
Poplar E14 . . . . .33 C3
Swan Ctr SW17 . . . . . .71 B1
Swandon Way
SW18 . . . . .59 A3
Swanfield St
E2 . . . . .24 B2 99 A3
Swan Ho N1 . . . . .15 C1
Swan La EC4 . . . . .123 C3
Swan Lane Pier
EC4 . . . . .123 B3
Swanlea Sch E1 . . . . . .25 A1
Swanley Ho SE17 . . . .152 B2
Swan Mead **1** SE1 . .138 A1
Swan Mews
Stockwell SW9 . . . . . .172 C2
SW6 . . . . .165 B4
Swanmore Ct
SW18 . . . . .59 B1
Swanne Ho **12**
SE10 . . . . .52 B3
Swan Pas **5** E1 . . . . .125 B3
Swan Rd SE16 . . . . . . .40 B4
Swanscombe Ho **11**
W11 . . . . .30 C1
Swanscombe Point **7**
E16 . . . . .35 B4
Swanscombe Rd
5 Chiswick W4 . . . .38 A1
Shepherd's Bush
W11 . . . . .30 C1
Swan St SE1 . . . . .137 A3
Swanton Gdns
SW19 . . . . .69 C3
Swanwick Cl
SW15 . . . . .68 B4
Swan Wlk SW3 . . . . . .158 C4
Swan Yd N1 . . . . .15 A2
Swaton Rd E3 . . . . .26 C1
Swaythling Ho
SW15 . . . . .56 B1
Swedenborg Gdns
E1 . . . . .125 C4
Sweden Gate SE16 . . . .41 A2
Swedish Quays
SE16 . . . . .41 A3
Swedish Sch The
SW13 . . . . .46 C4
Sweeney Cres
SE1 . . . . .139 A3
Sweyn Pl SE3 . . . . .53 C1
Swift Ho
18 Stepney E1 . . . .32 B3

Swift Ho *continued*
15 Stoke Newington
  N16 . . . . 7 A1
1 SW9 . . . . 163 C2
Swift St SW6 . . . . . . 164 C4
Swinbrook Rd
  W10 . . . . 31 A4
Swinburne Ct **4**
  SE5 . . . . 63 C3
Swinburne Ho **15**
  E2 . . . . 25 B2
Swinburne Rd
  SW15 . . . . 56 C3
Swindon St W12 . . . . 30 B1
Swinford Gdns
  SW9 . . . . 63 A4
Swingfield Ho **3**
  E9 . . . . 25 B4
Swinley Ho NW1 . . . . 92 B4
Swinnerton St E9 . . . . 18 A3
Swinton Ho **7**
  E2 . . . . 24 C2 99 B3
Swinton Pl WC1 . . . . 94 C4
Swinton St WC1 . . . . 94 C4
Swiss Cottage
  NW3 . . . . 11 C1
Swiss Cottage L Ctr
  NW3 . . . . 11 C1
Swiss Cottage Sch
14 South Hampstead
  NW3 . . . . 11 C1
St John's Wood
  NW8 . . . . 79 C4
Swiss Cottage Sta
  NW3 . . . . 11 C1
Swiss Ct SW1 . . . . 119 C3
Swiss Re Building*
  EC2 . . . . 110 B2
Swiss Terr **7**
  NW3 . . . . 11 C1
Switch Ho **4** E14 . . 34 C2
Sybil Phoenix Cl
  SE8 . . . . 40 C1
Sybil Thorndike
  Casson Ho SW5 141 C1
Sybil Thorndike Ho **12**
  N1 . . . . 15 B2
Sycamore Ave E3 . . . . 26 B4
Sycamore Cl W3 . . . . 29 A1
Sycamore Ct
  Kilburn NW6 . . . . . . 23 C4
  Tufnell Pk N19 . . . . . . 4 C1
Sycamore Gdns W6,
  W12 . . . . 39 A3
Sycamore Gr SE6 . . . . 67 B1
Sycamore Ho
10 Maitland Pk
  NW3 . . . . 12 B2
17 Rotherhithe
  SE16 . . . . 40 C4
3 Shepherd's Bush
  W6 . . . . 39 A4
2 Stoke Newington
  N16 . . . . 6 C2
Sycamore Lo
  SW15 . . . . 57 A4
Sycamore Mews **4**
  SW4 . . . . 61 B4
Sycamore St EC1 . . . . 96 C1
Sycamore Wlk **3**
  W10 . . . . 23 A1
Sydcote SE21 . . . . . . 75 B3

Sydenham Hill SE21,
  SE22, SE23, SE26,
  SE19 . . . . 76 C4
Sydenham Hill Sta
  SE21 . . . . 76 B1
Sydenham Hill Wood
  Nature Reserve
  SE26 . . . . 76 C1
Sydner Mews N16 . . 16 B4
Sydner Rd N16 . . . . . . 16 B4
Sydney Cl SW3 . . . . 143 C3
Sydney Ho **4** W4 . . 38 A2
Sydney Mews
  SW3 . . . . 143 C3
Sydney Pl SW7 . . . . 144 A3
Sydney Rd TW10,
  TW9 . . . . 54 A3
Sydney St SW3 . . . . 144 A2
Sylva Cotts **3** SE8 . . 51 C2
Sylva Ct **3** SW15 . . 69 C4
Sylvan Ct **1** NW6 . . 78 A4
Sylvan Gr
  Hampstead NW2 . . . . 9 C4
  SE15 . . . . 50 A4
Sylvester Ho **7**
  E8 . . . . 17 A2
Sylvester Path **8**
  E8 . . . . 17 A2
Sylvia Ct N1 . . . . 87 B1
Sylvia Pankhurst Ho
14 E2 . . . . 25 C3
Sylvia Young Theatre
  Sch NW1 . . . . 90 B1
Symes Mews NW1 . . 82 C2
Symington Ho
  SE1 . . . . 137 B1
Symington Mews
  E9 . . . . 17 C3
Symister Mews
  N1 . . . . 24 A2 98 A3
25 Shoreditch
Symons Cl **6**
  SE15 . . . . 50 B1
Symons St SW3 . . . . 145 A3
Symphony Mews **13**
  W10 . . . . 23 A2
Syracuse Univ
  W11 . . . . 31 B2 112 C5
Syringa Ho SE4 . . . . 66 B4

T

Tabard Ct **6** E14 . . 34 B3
Tabard Ho SE1 . . . . 137 C2
Tabard St SE1 . . . . . 137 B2
Tabernacle St EC2 . . 97 C2
Tableer Ave SW4 . . . . 61 C2
Tabley Rd N7 . . . . . . 14 A4
Tabor Rd W6 . . . . . . 39 A3
Tachbrook Est
  SW1 . . . . 147 C1
Tachbrook Mews
  SW1 . . . . 146 C4
Tachbrook St
  SW1 . . . . 147 A3
Tack Mews SE4 . . . . 66 C4
Tadema Ho NW8 . . 89 C1
Tadema Rd SW10 . . 157 A1
Tadmor St W12 . . . . 30 C1
Tadworth Ho SE1 . . 136 A3
Taeping St E14 . . . . 42 A2
Taffrail Ho **2** E14 . . 42 A1
Taft Way **44** E3 . . . . 27 A2

Tailsworth St **18**
  E1 . . . . 111 B3
Tait Ct
13 Old Ford E3 . . . . 26 B4
  SW8 . . . . 171 C4
Tait Ho
  SE1 . . . . 121 C1
2 Tufnell Pk N19 . . 13 B4
Takhar Mews
  SW11 . . . . 168 B1
Talacre Com Sp Ctr
  NW5 . . . . 12 A2
Talacre Rd NW5 . . . . 12 C2
Talbot Ct EC3 . . . . . 123 C4
Talbot Grove Ho **10**
  W11 . . . . 31 A3
Talbot Ho
  Highbury N7 . . . . 5 C1
  Poplar E14 . . . . 34 A3
Talbot Rd
  Camberwell SE22 . . 64 A3
  Notting Hill W11 . . . . 31 C3
  Notting Hill W11 . . . . 31 B3
Talbot Sq W2 . . . . . 101 B1
Talbot Wlk
  Notting Hill W11 . . . . 31 A3
  Willesden NW10 . . . . 8 A2
Talbot Yd SE1 . . . . . 123 B1
Talcott Path **12**
  SW2 . . . . 74 C3
Talfourd Pl SE15 . . . . 49 B2
Talfourd Rd SE15 . . 49 B2
Talgarth Rd
  Hammersmith W6 . . 39 B1
  W14 . . . . 140 B2
Talia Ho E14 . . . . . . 42 B3
Talleyrand Ho SE5 . . 48 B1
Tallis St EC4 . . . . . . 121 C4
Talma Rd SW2 . . . . 62 C3
Talmud Torah
  Machzikei Hadass
  Sch E5 . . . . 7 C4
Talmud Torah Tiferes
  Shlomo **1** NW11 . . 1 A4
Talmud-Torah Yetev-
  Lev **6** N16 . . . . 7 C3
Talwin St E3 . . . . . . 27 A2
Tamar Cl E3 . . . . . . 26 B4
Tamar Ho
10 Cubitt Town
  E14 . . . . 42 B4
  SE11 . . . . 149 C2
Tamarind Ct **8**
  W3 . . . . 28 B3
Tamarind Ho **4**
  SE15 . . . . 49 C3
Tamarind Sq **5**
  E1 . . . . 125 C2
Tamarisk Sq W12 . . 29 B2
Tamworth N7 . . . . . . 14 A2
Tamworth St
  SW6 . . . . 155 B3
Tangier Rd TW10 . . 55 A4
Tangley Gr SW15 . . 68 B4
Tangmere WC1 . . . . 94 C3
Tankerton St WC1 . . 94 B3
Tanner Ho SE1 . . . . 138 B3
Tanner's Hill SE8 . . 51 C2
Tanners Mews
  SE8 . . . . 51 B2
Tanner St SE1 . . . . 138 B3
Tanners Yd **33** E2 . . 25 A3
Tannery Ho **22** E1 111 B4

Tannington Terr
  N5 . . . . 5 C1
Tansley Cl N7 . . . . . 13 C3
Tanswell St SE1 . . . 135 B3
Tantallon Rd
  SW12 . . . . 72 C3
Tant Ave E16 . . . . . . 35 B3
Tanza Rd NW3 . . . . 12 B4
Tapley Ho **11** SE1 . 139 B3
Taplow NW3 . . . . . . 11 C1
Taplow Ho **38**
  E2 . . . . 24 B2 98 C3
Taplow St N1 . . . . . . 87 A1
Tappesfield Rd
  SE15 . . . . 65 B4
Tapp St E1 . . . . 25 A1
Taranto Ho **14** E1 . . 32 C4
Tarbert Rd SE22 . . . . 64 A2
Tarbert Wlk E1 . . . . 32 B2
Tarling Rd E16 . . . . 35 B3
Tarling St E1 . . . . . . 32 B3
Tarnbrook Ct
  SW1 . . . . 145 B3
Tarn St SE1 . . . . . . 136 C1
Tarns The NW1 . . . . 92 C4
Tarplett Ho **22**
  SE14 . . . . 50 C4
Tarragon Cl SE14 . . 51 A3
Tarranbrae NW6 . . . . 10 A1
Tarrant Ho E2 . . . . . . 25 B2
Tarrant Pl W1 . . . . . 102 C3
Tarrantt Ho W14 . . 126 A2
Tarriff Cres SE8 . . . . 41 B2
Tarrington Cl
  SW16 . . . . 73 C1
Tartan Ho **12** E14 . . 34 B3
Tarver Rd SE17 . . . . 150 B2
Tarves Way SE10 . . 52 A3
Tasker Ho **17** E14 . . 33 C4
Tasker Lo W8 . . . . . 127 B4
Tasker Rd NW3 . . . . 12 B3
Tasman Ct **3** E14 . . 42 A2
Tasman Ho **17** E1 . . 32 A1
Tasman Rd SW9 . . . . 62 A4
Tasso Rd W6 . . . . . 154 A4
Tasso Yd W6 . . . . . . 154 A3
Tatchbury Ho
  SW15 . . . . 56 B1
Tate Britain* SW1 . 148 A3
Tate Ho **8** E2 . . . . 25 C3
Tate Modern*
  EC4 . . . . 122 B2
Tatham Pl NW8 . . . . 79 C2
Tatnell Rd SE23 . . . . 66 A1
Tatton Cres E5, N16 . . 7 B4
Tatum St SE17 . . . . 151 C3
Tauheed Cl N4 . . . . . . 6 B2
Taunton Ho W2 . . . 100 C1
Taunton Mews
  NW1 . . . . 90 C1
Taunton Pl NW1 . . . . 90 C2
Tavern Cl SE1 . . . . . 137 A1
Taverner Ho N16 . . . . 6 C1
Taverners Cl
  W11 . . . . . . 31 A1 112 A1
Taverner Sq **4** N5 . . 15 B4
Tavern La SW9 . . . . 173 C2
Tavistock Cl N16 . . 16 A3
Tavistock Cres
  W11 . . . . 31 B4
Tavistock Ct WC1 . . 93 C2
Tavistock Ho **3**
  W11 . . . . 31 B3
Tavistock Mews **3**
  W11 . . . . 31 B3

Tavistock Pl WC1 . . 94 A3
Tavistock Rd
  Dagenham NW10 . . 21 B3
  Notting Hill W11 . . . . 31 B4
Tavistock Sq WC1 . . 93 C2
Tavistock Sq WC2 120 B4
Tavistock Terr N19 . . 4 C1
Tavistock Twr
  SE16 . . . . 41 A3
Taviton St WC1 . . . . 93 B2
Tavy Cl SE11 . . . . . 149 C2
Tawhid Boys Sch
  N16 . . . . 7 A3
Tawny Way SE16 . . 40 C2
Taybridge Rd
  SW11 . . . . 60 C3
Tayburn Cl E14 . . . . 34 B3
Tay Ho **10** E3 . . . . 26 B3
Tayler Ct NW8 . . . . 79 B4
Taylor Ave TW9 . . . . 45 A1
Taylor Cl SE8 . . . . . . 51 B4
Taylor Ho **10** SW2 . . 74 C3
Taylor's Gn W3 . . . . 29 A3
Taylor's La NW10 . . 8 A1
Tayport Cl N1 . . . . . 14 A1
Tayside Ct **6** SE5 . . 63 C3
Teak Cl SE16 . . . . . 33 A1
Tealby Ct N7 . . . . . . 14 B2
Teal Ct **38** SE8 . . . . 51 B4
Teale St E2 . . . . 24 C3
Teal St **1** SE10 . . . . 43 B3
Teather St **12** SE5 . . 49 A3
Tebbs Ho **2** SW2 . . 74 C4
Tedman Ct SE13 . . 67 B3
Ted Roberts Ho **25**
  E2 . . . . 25 A3
Tedworth Gdns
  SW3 . . . . 144 C1
Tedworth Sq SW3 144 C1
Teesdale Cl E2 . . . . 25 A3
Teesdale St E2 . . . . 25 A3
Teesdale Yd **34** E2 . . 25 A3
Tee The W3 . . . . 29 A3
Teignmouth Cl **6**
  SW4 . . . . 61 C3
Teignmouth Rd
  NW2 . . . . 9 C2
Telegraph Hill NW3 . . 2 A1
Telegraph Pl E14 . . 42 A2
Telegraph Rd
  SW15 . . . . 69 B4
Telegraph St EC2 . . 109 B2
Telephone Pl
  SW6 . . . . 155 A4
Telfer Cl **4** W3 . . . . 37 B4
Telfer Ho EC1 . . . . . 96 B3
Telferscot Prim Sch
5 SW12 . . . . 73 C3
Telferscot Rd
  SW12 . . . . 73 C3
Telford Ave SW12,
  SW2 . . . . 74 A3
Telford Avenue Mans
7 SW2 . . . . 74 A3
Telford Ho
8 Kensal Town
  W10 . . . . 31 A4
  SE1 . . . . 136 C2
Telford Parade Mans
8 SW2 . . . . 74 A3
Telford Rd W10 . . . . 31 A4
Telford Terr SW1 . . 160 C4
Telford Way W3 . . . . 29 A4
Tell Gr SE22 . . . . . . 64 B3
Telscombe Ho
  SW11 . . . . 169 B3

Temair Ho 🔢
SE10 . . . . .52 B3
Temeraire Pl TW8 . .36 B1
Temeraire St SE16 . .40 B4
Temperley Rd
SW12 . . . . .72 C4
Templar Ho NW2 . . .10 B2
Templar St SE5 . . . .48 A1
Temple Ave EC4 . . .121 C4
Temple Bar ★ EC4 108 B1

Templecombe Rd
E9 . . . . .25 B4
Temple Ct
Stepney E1 . . . . .32 C4
SW8 . . . . .162 A1
Temple Dwellings 🔢
E2 . . . . .25 A3
Temple Gr Hatcham
Sch SE14 . . . . .50 C1
Temple Ho
🔢 Battersea
SW11 . . . . .60 A4
🔢 Finsbury Pk N7 . . . .4 B1
Temple La EC4 . . . .107 C1
Templemead Cl
W3 . . . . .29 A3
Templemead Ho
E9 . . . . .18 A4
TEMPLE MILLS 19 B3
Temple Mills La
London E10, E15 . . . .19 A4
Stratford E15 . . . . . . .19 A4
Temple Mills Rd
E9 . . . . .18 A4
Temple Pl WC2 . . .121 A4
Temple Rd
Acton Green W4 . . . .37 B3
Richmond TW9 . . . . . .54 B4
Temple Sheen
SW14 . . . . .55 B2
Temple Sheen Rd
SW14 . . . . .55 B3
Temple St E2 . . . . .25 A3
Temple Sta WC2 . . .121 B4
Templeton Cl 🔢
N16 . . . . .16 A3
Templeton Pl
SW5 . . . . .141 C3
Temple West Mews
SE11 . . . . .136 A1
Templewood Ave
NW3 . . . . .2 A1
Templewood Gdns
NW3 . . . . .2 A1
Templewood Point
NW2 . . . . .1 B2
Tenbury Ct SW12 . .73 C3
Tenby Ho
Islington N7 . . . . . . .14 C4
W2 . . . . .100 C1
Tench St E1 . . . . . . .32 A1
Tenda Rd SE16 . . . .40 A2
Tendring Ho SW2 . .62 C1
Tenham Ave SW2 . .73 C2
Tenison Ct W1 . . . .118 C4
Tenison Way SE1 . .121 B1
Tenniel Cl W2 . . . .114 B4
Tennis St SE1 . . . .137 B4
Tennyson Ho
SE17 . . . . .151 A2
Tennyson Rd NW6 . .23 B4
Tennyson St SW8 . .170 A1
Tensing Ho N1 . . . . .15 A2
Tenterden Ho
SE17 . . . . .152 B2
Tenterden St W1 . .104 B1

Tenter Ground
E1 . . . . .110 C3
Tent St E1 . . . . .25 A1
Tequila Wharf E14 . .33 A3
Terborch Way 🔢
SE22 . . . . .64 A2
Tercelet Terr NW3 . .11 B4
Teredo St SE16 . . . .40 C3
Terling Ho 🔢 W10 . .30 B4
Terling Wlk N1 . . . . .86 C4
Terminus Pl SW1 . .132 B1
Tern Ho 🔢 SE15 . . . .49 B2
Terrace Gdns
SW13 . . . . .46 B1
Terrace La TW10 . . .54 A1
Terrace Rd E9 . . . . .17 B1
Terrace The
Barnes SW13,
SW14 . . . . .46 A1
EC4 . . . . .107 C1
Kilburn NW6 . . . . . . .23 C4
🔢 Rotherhithe SE8 . .41 B2
Terrapin Ct SW17 . .73 A1
Terrapin Rd SW17 . .73 A1
Terrick St W12 . . . . .30 A3
Territorial Ho
SE11 . . . . .149 C3
Terry Ho SW2 . . . . .74 C3
Tersha St TW9 . . . . .54 B3
Tessa Sanderson Pl
🔢 SW8 . . . . .61 A4
Testerton Wlk 🔢
W11 . . . . .30 C2
Tetcott Rd SW10 . .156 C1
Teversham La
SW8 . . . . .172 B4
Teviot St E14 . . . . . .34 B4
Teyham Ct 🔢
SW11 . . . . .60 B1
Thackeray Ct
Chelsea SW3 . . . . . .144 C2
West Kensington
W14 . . . . .126 A1
Thackeray Ho
College Pk NW10 . . . .21 C2
N16 . . . . .16 C4
W14 . . . . .94 A2
Thackeray Mews 🔢
E8 . . . . .16 C2
Thackeray Rd
SW8 . . . . .170 B1
Thackeray's
Almshouses SE6 . .67 A1
Thackeray St W8 . .128 B2
Thalia Cl SE10 . . . . .52 C4
Tham Cl 🔢 SE24 . . .63 A4
Thame Rd SE16 . . . .40 C4
Thames Ave
SW10 . . . . .167 A4
Thames Bank
SW14 . . . . .45 B1
Thames Christian Coll
🔢 SW11 . . . . .59 C4
Thames Circ E14 . . .41 C2
Thames Cres W4 . . .46 A3
Thames Ct 🔢
SE15 . . . . .49 B3
Thames Hts SE1 . . .138 C4
Thames Link Ho 🔢
TW9 . . . . .54 A3
Thames Pl SW15 . . .57 C4
Thames Quay
Millwall E14 . . . . . . .42 A4

Thames Quay continued
SW10 . . . . .167 A3
Thames Rd W4 . . . . .45 A4
Thames Reach W6 . .47 B4
Thames Row TW9 . .44 B4
Thames St SE10 . . . .52 A4
Thames Village
W4 . . . . .45 B2
Thames Wlk
SW11 . . . . .158 A2
Thane Mans N7 . . . . .5 B1
Thanet Ho
🔢 West Norwood
SE27 . . . . .75 A1
Thanet Lo NW2 . . . .10 A2
Thanet St WC1 . . . .94 A3
Thane Villas N7 . . . . .5 B1
Thane Works N7 . . . .5 B1
Thavies Inn EC4 . . .107 C2
Thaxted Ct N1 . . . . .87 C1
Thaxted Ho SE16 . . .40 B2
Thaxton Rd W14 . . .155 A4
Thayer St W1 . . . . .103 C2
Theatre Royal ★
E10 . . . . .19 C2
Theatre Sq E15 . . . .19 C2
Theatre St SW11 . . .60 B4
Theberton St N1 . . .86 A4
Theed St SE1 . . . . .121 C1
Thelbridge Ho 🔢
E3 . . . . .27 A2
Theobalds Ct N4 . . . .6 B2
Theobald's Rd
WC1 . . . . .106 C4
Theobald St SE1 . . .137 B1
Theodore St SE13 . .67 C1
Theodore Ho 🔢
SW15 . . . . .56 B3
Theodore Rd SE13 . .67 C1
Therapia Rd SE22 . .65 B1
Theresa Rd W6 . . . . .38 C2
Therfield Ct N4 . . . . .6 B2
Thermopylae Gate
E14 . . . . .42 A2
Theseus Ho 🔢
E14 . . . . .34 C3
Theseus Wlk N1 . . . .86 B1
Thessaly Ho SW8 . .160 C1
Thessaly Rd SW8 . .171 A4
Thetford Ho SE1 . . .138 C2
Thetis Terr TW9 . . . .44 C4
Third Ave
East Acton W3 . . . . . .29 A3
West Kilburn W10 . . .23 A2
Thirleby Rd SW1 . . .133 A1
Thirlmere NW1 . . . . .92 B4
Thirlmere Ho
🔢 16 C4
Thirsk Rd SW11 . . . .60 C3
Thistle Gr SW7 . . . .143 A1
Thistle Ho E14 . . . . .34 B3
Thistlewood Cl 🔢
N7 . . . . .5 B2
Thistly Ct SE8 . . . . .52 A4
Thomas Baines Rd
SW11 . . . . .59 C4
Thomas Burt Ho 🔢
E2 . . . . .25 A2
Thomas Buxton Jun &
Inf Sch 🔢
E1 . . . . .24 C1 99 C1
Thomas Crowell Ct 🔢
N1 . . . . .16 A3
Thomas Doyle St
SE1 . . . . .136 B2

Thomas Fairchild
Com Sch N1 . . . . . .87 A2
Thomas Ho
🔢 Hackney E9 . . . . . .17 B2
🔢 Stockwell SW4 . . . .62 A3
Thomas Hollywood
Ho 🔢 E2 . . . . .25 B3
Thomas Jones Prim
Sch 🔢 W11 . . . . . . .31 A3
Thomas London Ind
Day Sch W8 . . . . . .128 B2
Thomas Milner Ho 🔢
SE15 . . . . .49 C3
Thomas More Ho
EC2 . . . . .108 C3
Thomas More Sq
E1 . . . . .125 B3
Thomas More St
E1 . . . . .125 B2
Thomas Neal's Ctr
WC1 . . . . .106 A1
Thomas North Terr 🔢
E16 . . . . .35 B4
Thomas Pl W8 . . . . .128 A1
Thomas Rd E14 . . . . .33 B4
Thomas Road Ind Est
🔢 E14 . . . . .33 C4
Thomas's Prep Sch
Clapham SW11 . . . . .60 B2
Thomas's Prep Schs
SW11 . . . . .167 C3
Thompson Ave
Richmond TW9 . . . . .54 C4
🔢 SE5 . . . . .48 B3
Thompson Ho
🔢 Kensal Town
W10 . . . . .23 A1
SE14 . . . . .50 C4
Thompson Rd
SE22 . . . . .64 B1
Thomson Ct 🔢 E8 . .16 C2
Thomson Ho
Pimlico SW1 . . . . . .147 C1
Walworth SE17 . . . . .152 A3
Thorburn Ho SW1 . .131 B3
Thorburn Sq SE1 . . .153 B3
Thoresby Ho N16 . . . .6 C1
Thoresby St N1 . . . . .97 A4
Thornaby Ho 🔢
E2 . . . . .25 A2
Thornbill Ho 🔢
SE15 . . . . .49 C3
Thornbury Cl N16 . . .16 A3
Thornbury Ct
W11 . . . . .31 C2 113 B4
Thornbury Ho N6 . . . .4 B3
Thornbury Rd
SW2 . . . . .62 A1
Thornbury Sq N6 . . . .4 B3
Thorncliffe Ct
SW2 . . . . .62 A1
Thorncliffe Rd
SW2 . . . . .62 A1
Thorncombe Rd
SE22 . . . . .64 A2
Thorncroft St
SW8 . . . . .162 A1
Thorndale Ho 🔢
N16 . . . . .7 A3
Thorndean St
SW18 . . . . .71 B2
Thorndike Cl
SW10 . . . . .156 C2
Thorndike Ho
SW1 . . . . .147 B2

Thorndike Rd 🔢
N1 . . . . .15 C2
Thorndike St
SW1 . . . . .147 B3
Thorne Cl E16 . . . . . .35 C3
Thorne Ho
🔢 Bethnal Green
E2 . . . . .25 B2
🔢 Cubitt Town E14 . .42 B3
Thorne Pas 🔢
SW13 . . . . .46 B1
Thorne Rd SW8 . . . .162 B1
Thorness Rd SW18 . .59 B1
Thorne St SW13,
SW14 . . . . .56 A4
Thornewill Ho 🔢
E1 . . . . .32 B2
Thorney Cres
SW11 . . . . .157 C1
Thorney Ct W8 . . . . .128 C3
Thorney Ct W8 . . . . .128 C3
Thorney Hedge Rd
W4 . . . . .37 A2
Thorney St SW1 . . .148 A4
Thornfield Ho 🔢
E14 . . . . .33 C2
Thornfield Rd
W12 . . . . .39 A4
Thornford Rd
SE13 . . . . .67 B2
Thorngate Rd W9 . . .23 C1
Thornham Gr E15 . . .19 C3
Thorn Ham Ho
SE1 . . . . .137 C2
Thornham St SE10 . .52 A4
Thornhaugh St
WC1 . . . . .93 C1
Thornhill Bridge
Wharf N1 . . . . .84 C3
Thornhill Cres N1 . . .14 B1
Thornhill Gr N1 . . . . .14 C1
Thornhill Ho
🔢 Chiswick W4 . . . . .38 A1
Islington N1 . . . . .14 C1
Thornhill Mews
SW15 . . . . .58 B3
Thornhill Prim Sch 🔢
N1 . . . . .14 C1
Thornhill Rd N1 . . . .85 B4
Thornhill Sq N1 . . . .14 B1
Thornicroft Ho 🔢
SW9 . . . . .173 A1
Thornley Pl 🔢
SE10 . . . . .43 A1
Thornsett Rd
SW18 . . . . .71 A3
Thornton Ave
Chiswick W4 . . . . . . .38 A2
Streatham SW2 . . . . .73 C3
Thornton Ct N7 . . . . .14 A3
Thornton Gdns
SW12 . . . . .73 C3
Thornton Ho
SE17 . . . . .152 A3
Thornton Pl W1 . . . .103 A4
Thornton Rd
Mortlake SW14 . . . . .55 C4
Streatham SW12,
SW2 . . . . .73 C3
Thornton St SW9 . . .173 B2
Thornville St SE8 . . .51 C2
Thornwood Gdns
W8 . . . . .127 B4

Thornwood Lo
W8 . . . . **127** B4
Thornycroft Ct
TW9 . . . . .44 B1
Thorold Ho
SE1 . . . . **136** C4
 6 Streatham SW2 . .74 A4
Thorparch Rd
SW8 . . . . **161** C1
Thorpebank Rd
W12 . . . . .29 C1
Thorpe Cl W10 . . . . .31 A3
Thorpedale Rd N4 . . . .5 B3
Thorpe Ho N1 . . . . . .85 A3
Thorverton Rd NW2 . .1 A1
Thoydon Rd E3 . . . . .26 A3
Thrale St SE1 . . . . . **123** A1
Thrasher Cl 20 E8 . . .24 B4
Thrawl St E1 . . . . . . **111** A3
Thrayle Ho 2
SW9 . . . . .62 B4
Threadgold Ho 8
N1 . . . . .15 C2
Threadneedle St EC2,
EC3 . . . . **109** C1
Three Colts La E2 . . .25 A1
Three Colt St E14 . . .33 B2
Three Cups Yd
WC1 . . . . **107** A3
Three Kings Yd
W1 . . . . **118** A4
Three Mill La E3 . . . .27 B2
Three Mills Studios★
E14 . . . . .27 C2
Three Nun Ct EC2 **109** A2
Three Oak La SE1 **138** C4
Threshers Pl
W11 . . . . . . .31 A2 **112** A4
Thring Ho 2
SW9 . . . . **172** C2
Throgmorton Ave
EC2 . . . . **109** C2
Throgmorton St
EC2 . . . . **109** C2
Thrush St SE17 . . . **150** C2
Thurland Ho 5
SE16 . . . . .40 A2
Thurland Rd SE16 **139** B2
Thurleigh Ave
SW12 . . . . .60 C1
Thurleigh Ct
SW12 . . . . .60 C1
Thurleigh Rd
SW12 . . . . .60 C1
Thurloe Cl SW7 . . . **144** A4
Thurloe Ct SW3 . . . **144** A3
Thurloe Pl SW7 . . . **143** C4
Thurloe Place Mews
SW7 . . . . **143** C4
Thurloe Sq SW7 . . . **144** A4
Thurloe St SW7 . . . **143** C4
Thurlow Hill SE21 . . .75 B2
Thurlow Ho 17
SW16 . . . . .74 A1
Thurlow Park Rd SE21,
SE24 . . . . .75 B2
Thurlow Rd NW3 . . . .11 C3
Thurlow St SE17 . . . **152** A1
Thurlow Terr NW5 . .12 C3
Thurlow Twrs
SE27 . . . . .74 C1
Thurlow Wlk
SE17 . . . . **152** A1
Thurnscoe NW1 . . . .82 C3

Thursley Gdns
SW19 . . . . .69 C2
Thursley Ho 10
SW2 . . . . .74 B4
Thurso Ho NW6 . . . .78 A1
Thurston Ind Est
SE13 . . . . .67 A4
Thurston Rd SE8,
SE13 . . . . .52 A1
Thurtle Rd E2 . . . . . .24 B3
Tibbatt's Rd E3 . . . . .27 A1
Tibberton Sq N1 . . . .86 C4
Tibbets Cl SW19 . . . .69 C3
Tibbet's Corner
SW19 . . . . .69 C4
Tibbet's Ride
SW19 . . . . .69 C4
Tiber Cl 10 E3 . . . . . .26 C4
Tiber Gdns N1 . . . . .84 B3
Tickford Ho NW8 . . .90 A3
Tidal Basin Rd
E16 . . . . .35 B2
Tidbury Ct SW8 . . . **160** C1
Tidemill Prim Sch 20
SE8 . . . . .51 C3
Tideswell 16 NW5 . . .13 A4
Tideswell Rd
SW15 . . . . .57 B3
Tideway Ct 9
SE16 . . . . .32 C1
Tideway Ho E14 . . . .41 C4
Tideway Ind Est
SW8 . . . . **161** A3
Tideway Wharf
SW13 . . . . .46 A1
Tideway Yd SW13 . . .46 A1
Tidey St E3 . . . . .33 C4
Tidworth Ho 18
SE22 . . . . .64 A4
Tidworth Rd E3 . . . . .26 C1
Tierney Rd SW2 . . . .74 A3
Tierney Terr SW2 . . .74 A3
Tiger Ho WC1 . . . . . .93 C3
Tiger Way E5 . . . . . . .17 A4
Tignel Ct W3 . . . . . . .36 C4
Tilbury Cl 14 SE15 . .49 B3
Tilbury Ho 4
SE14 . . . . .50 C4
Tildesley Rd SW15 . .57 B1
Tilehurst NW1 . . . . . .92 B3
Tilehurst Rd SW17,
SW18 . . . . .71 C3
Tile Kiln La N6 . . . . . .4 B3
Tileyard Rd N7 . . . . .14 A1
Tilford Gdns SW19 . .69 C3
Tilford Ho 5 SW2 . . .74 B4
Tilia Rd E5 . . . . .17 A4
Tilia Wlk 2 SW9 . . . .63 A3
Tiller Ho 22 N1 . . . . .24 A4
Tiller L Ctr E14 . . . . .41 C3
Tiller Rd E14 . . . . . . .41 C3
Tilney St SE16 . . . . . .41 A4
Tillet Way 6
E2 . . . . .24 C2 **99** B4
Tilling Ho 1 SE15 . . .65 A4
Tillman Ho 3
SW2 . . . . .74 B3
Tillman St E1 . . . . . . .32 A3
Tilloch St 9 N1 . . . . .14 B1
Tillotson Ct SW8 . . **161** C1
Tilney Ct EC1 . . . . . . .97 A2
Tilney Gdns 12 N1 . .15 C2
Tilney St W1 . . . . . . **117** C2
Tilson Cl 2 SE5 . . . . .49 A3
Tilson Ho SW2,
SW4 . . . . .74 A4

Tilton Ho SW2 . . . . .74 A4
Tilton St SW6 . . . . **154** B3
Tiltwood The W3 . . .28 B2
Timberland Cl 16
SE15 . . . . .49 C3
Timberland Rd E1 . .32 A3
Timber Mill Way
SW4 . . . . .61 C4
Timber Pond Rd
SE16 . . . . .40 C4
Timber St EC1 . . . . . .96 C2
Time Sq E8 . . . . .16 B3
Timothy Cl 1
SW4 . . . . .61 B2
Timsbury Wlk 5
SW15 . . . . .68 C3
Tina Ct SW16 . . . . . .74 C1
Tindal St SW9 . . . . . .48 A2
Tinniswood Cl N5 . . .14 C3
Tinsley Rd E1 . . . . . .32 B4
Tintagel Cres
SE22 . . . . .64 B3
Tintagel Ct EC1 . . . .96 A2
Tintern Cl SW15 . . . .58 A2
Tintern Ho
Belgravia SW1 . . . **146** A3
Regent's Pk NW1 . .82 B1
Tintern St SW4 . . . . .62 A3
Tinworth St SE11 . . **148** B2
Tipthorpe Rd
SW11 . . . . .60 C4
Tiptree 7 NW1 . . . . .13 A1
Tisbury Ct W1 . . . . **119** B4
Tisdall Pl SE17 . . . . **151** C3
Tissington Ct 4
SE16 . . . . .40 C2
Titan Bsns Est 3
SE8 . . . . .51 C3
Titan Ct TW8 . . . . . . .36 B1
Titchborne Row
W2 . . . . **102** B1
Titchfield Rd NW8 **80** C4
Titchwell Rd
SW18 . . . . .71 C3
Tite St SW3 . . . . . . **158** C4
Titmuss St W12 . . . .39 B4
Tiverton Rd NW6,
NW10 . . . . .22 C4
Tiverton St SE1 . . . **136** C1
Tivoli Ct SE16 . . . . . .33 B1
Tobago St 12 E14 . .41 C4
Tobin Cl NW3 . . . . . .12 A1
Toby La E1 . . . . .26 A1
Todber Ho W14 . . . **126** A2
Todds Wlk N7 . . . . . . .5 B2
Tokenhouse Yd
EC2 . . . . **109** B2
Token Yd SW15 . . . . .58 A3
Toland Sq SW15 . . . .56 C2
Tolchurch 2 W11 . . .31 C3
Toldos Sch N16 . . . . .7 A3
Tolhurst Dr 4
W10 . . . . .23 A2
Tollbridge Cl W10 . . .23 A1
Tollet St E1 . . . . .25 C1
Tollgate Dr SE21 . . . .76 A2
Tollgate Ho 1
NW6 . . . . .78 A2
Tollgate Rd E6 . . . . . .25 A1
Tollington Ct N4 . . . . .5 B2
Tollington Ho 4
N19 . . . . .5 A2
Tollington Pk N4 . . . . .5 B2
Tollington Pl N4 . . . . .5 B2
Tollington Rd N7 . . .14 B4
Tollington Way N7 . . .5 A1

Tolmers Sq NW1 . . . .93 A2
Tolpaide Ho SE11 . **149** B3
Tolpuddle St N1 . . . .85 B2
Tolsford Rd E5 . . . . .17 A3
Tom Blau Gallery★
SE1 . . . . **134** C4
Tom Groves Cl
E15 . . . . .19 C1
Tom Hood Cl E15 . . .19 C3
Tom Jenkinson Rd 5
E16 . . . . .35 C1
Tomkyns Ho SE11 . **149** B3
Tomlin Ho SE1 . . . **122** C1
Tomlin's Gr E3 . . . . .26 C2
Tomlinson Cl
 5 Gunnersbury
 . . . . .37 A1
Spitalfields
 E2 . . . . .24 B2 **99** A3
Tomlin's Terr E14 . . .33 A3
Tomlins Wlk 4 N7 . . .5 B2
Tompion Ho EC1 . . . .96 B2
Tompion St EC1 . . . .96 B3
Tom Smith Cl
SE10 . . . . .53 A4
Tomson Ho SE1 . . . **138** C2
Tom Williams Ho
SW6 . . . . **154** C3
Tonbridge Ho
SE11 . . . . .94 A3
Tonbridge St WC1 . .94 A3
Tonbrough 10
NW8 . . . . .78 B3
Tonsley Hill SW18 . .59 A2
Tonsley Pl SW18 . . .59 A2
Tonsley Rd SW18 . .59 A2
Tonsley St SW18 . . .59 A2
Took's Ct EC4 . . . . . **107** B2
Tooley St SE1 . . . . **124** A1
Tooting Bec Sta
SW17 . . . . .72 C1
Topham Ho 3
SE10 . . . . .52 B3
Topham St EC1 . . . . .95 B2
Topmast Point 23
E14 . . . . .41 C4
Torah Vodaas
NW11 . . . . .1 B3
Tora Temimah Prim
Sch NW2 . . . . .9 A4
Torbay Ct 13 NW1 . .13 A1
Torbay Mans NW6 . .23 B4
Torbay Rd NW6 . . . .10 B1
Torbay St 16 NW1 . .13 A1
Tor Ct W8 . . . . **127** C4
Tor Gdns W8 . . . . . **127** B4
Tornay Ho
Hackney E9 . . . . . . .17 B1
N1 . . . . .84 C2
Torquay St W2 . . . **100** A3
Torrence Ho 6
N19 . . . . .4 B2
Torrens Ct SE5 . . . . .63 C4
Torrens Rd SW2 . . . .62 B2
Torrens St EC1 . . . . .86 A1
Torres Sq E14 . . . . . .41 C1
Torriano Ave NW5 . .13 C3
Torriano Cotts
NW5 . . . . .13 B3
Torriano Jun & Inf
Schs 24 NW5 . . . . . .13 C3
Torriano Mews
NW5 . . . . .13 B3
Torridge Gdns
SE15 . . . . .65 B3

Torridon Ho NW6 . . .78 A1
Torrington Pl
Bloomsbury WC1 . **105** B4
St George in t East
 E1 . . . . **125** C2
Torrington Sq
WC1 . . . . .93 C1
Tortington Ho 1
SE15 . . . . .50 A3
Torwood Rd SW15 . .56 C2
Tothill Ho SW1 . . . **147** C4
Tothill St SW1 . . . . **133** C3
Totland Ho SW18 . . .59 A1
Tottan Terr E1 . . . . . .32 C3
Tottenhall 5 NW1 . . .12 C1
Tottenham Court Rd
W1 . . . . **105** A4
Tottenham Court
Road Sta W1 . . . . **105** C2
Tottenham Mews
W1 . . . . **105** A4
Tottenham Rd N1 . . .16 A2
Tottenham St W1 . **105** A4
Totteridge Ho
SW11 . . . . **167** C2
Touchard Ho N1 . . . .97 C3
Toulmin St SE1 . . . **136** C3
Toulon St SE5 . . . . . .48 B3
Toulouse Ct 2
SE16 . . . . .40 A1
Tounson Ct SW1 . . **147** C3
Tournay Rd SW6 . . **155** A2
Toussaint Wlk 18
SE16 . . . . **139** C2
Tovy Ho 6 SE1 . . . **153** B1
Towcester Rd E3 . . .27 B1
Tower 42★ EC2 . . . **110** A2
Tower Bldgs 22
E1 . . . . .32 A1
Tower Br App E1,
EC3 . . . . **124** C3
Tower Bridge★ E1, EC3,
SE1 . . . . **124** C2
Tower Bridge Bsns
Complex SE16 . . . . . .40 A3
Tower Bridge Bsns
SE1 . . . . **138** C4
Tower Bridge Ex★
SE1 . . . . **124** C3
Tower Bridge Piazza
SE1 . . . . **124** C1
Tower Bridge Prim
Sch SE1 . . . . **138** C4
Tower Bridge Rd
SE1 . . . . **138** A1
Tower Bridge Sq
SE1 . . . . **138** C4
Tower Ct NW3 . . . . .11 C3
Tower Ct
Brockley SE4 . . . . . .66 A3
Stamford Hill E5 . . . .7 B4
St Giles WC2 . . . . **106** A1
St John's Wood
 NW8 . . . . .80 B2
Towergate SE1 . . . **152** A4
Towergate Ho 35
E3 . . . . .26 B3
Tower Gateway Sta
EC3 . . . . **124** C4
TOWER HAMLETS 33 B4
Tower Hamlets Coll
 22 Poplar E14 . . . .34 A3
 21 Poplar E14 . . . .34 A4
 18 Stepney E1 . . . .32 C3
Tower Hill EC3 . . . **125** A3

Tower Hill Sta
EC3 . . . . 124 C4
Tower House Sch
SW14 . . . . 55 B3
Tower Mews SE1 . . 138 C1
Tower Mews E5 . . . 18 A3
Tower Millennium
Pier EC3 . . . . 124 B2
Tower Mill Rd
7 Camberwell
SE15 . . . . 49 A4
1 SE15 . . . . 49 A4
Tower Pl E EC3 . . . 124 B3
Tower Pl W EC3 . . . 124 B3
Tower Rd NW10 . . . 8 C1
Tower Rise TW9 . . . 54 A4
Tower Royal EC4 . 123 B4
Towers Pl TW10 . . . 54 A2
Tower St WC2 . . . . 106 A1
Towers The
Dartmouth Pk NW5 . 4 A1
1 Richmond TW9 . . 54 B3
Tower Terr SE4 . . . . 66 A3
Tower The★ EC3 . . 124 C3
Towerview SE13 . . . 66 C2
Tower Wharf SE1 138 C4
Tower Wlk SE1 . . . 152 A4
Towncourt Path N4 . 6 B3
Townhall Ave 3
W4 . . . . 37 C1
Town Hall Rd
SW11 . . . . 60 B4
Townley Rd SE22 . . 64 B2
Townley St SE17 . 151 B2
Townmead Bsns Ctr
SW6 . . . . 59 B4
Townmead Rd
Richmond TW9 . . . . 45 A1
Sands End SW6 . . . 166 C1
Townsend Ho 14
SE1 . . . . 153 C3
Townsend Ind Est
NW10 . . . . 20 B3
Townsend Mews 3
SW18 . . . . 71 B2
Townsend Prim Sch
SE17 . . . . 152 A4
Townsend Rd NW8 . 80 B2
Townsend St SE1,
SE17 . . . . 152 A4
Townsend Yd N6 . . . 4 A3
Townshend Ct
NW8 . . . . 80 B2
Townshend Est
NW8 . . . . 80 A2
Townshend Rd
Primrose Hill NW8 . 80 A3
Richmond TW9 . . . . 54 B3
Townshend Terr
TW9 . . . . 54 B3
Towns Ho 8 SW4 . 61 C4
Towpath Wlk E9 . . . 18 B3
Towton Rd SE27 . . . 75 B2
Toxteth Ho N4 . . . . . 6 B4
Toynbee St E1 . . . 110 C3
Toynbee Studios★
E1 . . . . 111 A3
Tracey Ave NW2 . . . 9 B3
Tracy Ho 15 E3 . . . 26 B2
Tradescant Ho 18
E3 . . . . 26 B2
Tradescant Rd
SW8 . . . . 162 B1
Trade Twr 8
SW11 . . . . 59 B4

Trade Winds Ct 1
E1 . . . . 125 C2
Trading Estate Rd
NW10 . . . . 20 B1
Traemore Ct
SW16 . . . . 74 C1
Trafalgar Ave
SE15 . . . . 49 B4
Trafalgar Cl 1
SE16 . . . . 41 A2
Trafalgar Gdns
Stepney E1 . . . . . . 32 C4
W8 . . . . 128 B2
Trafalgar Ho
SE17 . . . . 151 A2
Trafalgar Mews
E9 . . . . 18 B2
Trafalgar Point 2
N1 . . . . 15 C1
Trafalgar Rd SE10 . 43 A1
Trafalgar Sq★
SW1 . . . . 119 C2
Trafalgar St SE17 151 C2
Trafalgar Way E14 . 34 B1
Trafford Ho N1 . . . . 87 C2
Tragail SW15 . . . . . 58 A2
Trahorn Cl E1 . . . . . 25 A1
Traitors Gate★
EC3 . . . . 124 C3
Tralee Ct 5 SE16 . . 40 A1
Tramway Ave E15 . . 19 C1
Trance Way W3 . . . 36 C3
Tranmere Ho 7
N7 . . . . 14 C3
Tranmere Rd SW17,
SW18 . . . . 71 B2
Tranquil Pas SE3 . . 53 B1
Tranquil Vale SE3 . . 53 A1
Transept St NW1 . 102 B3
Transom Cl SE16 . . 41 A2
Transom Sq E14 . . . 42 A1
Tranton Rd SE16 . . 40 A3
Trappes Ho 2
SE16 . . . . 40 A2
Travers Ho 8
SE10 . . . . 52 C4
Travers Rd N7 . . . . . 5 C1
Travis Ho SE10 . . . 52 B2
Treadgold Ho 7
W11 . . . . 30 C2
Treadgold St W11 . 30 C2
Treadway St E2 . . . 25 A3
Treasury Bldgs
SW1 . . . . 134 A4
Treaty St N1 . . . . . . 84 C3
Trebeck St W1 . . . 118 A1
Treborough Ho
W1 . . . . 103 B4
Trebovir Rd SW5 . 141 C3
Treby St E3 . . . . 26 B1
Trecastle Way 7
N7 . . . . 13 C4
Tredegar Mews 10
E3 . . . . 26 B2
Tredegar Rd E3 . . . 26 B3
Tredegar Sq E3 . . . 26 B2
Tredegar Terr E3 . . 26 B2
Trederwen Rd E8 . . 24 C4
Treen Ave SW13 . . . 56 B4
Trees The N16 . . . . . 6 C4
Trefil Wlk N7 . . . . . 14 A4
Trefoil Rd SW18 . . . 59 B2
Tregarvon Rd
SW11 . . . . 60 C3
Trego Rd E9 . . . . . . 18 C1

Tregothnan Rd
SW9 . . . . 62 A4
Tregunter Rd
SW10 . . . . 142 C1
Treherne Ct SW9 . . 48 A2
Trehern Rd 12
SW14 . . . . 55 C4
Trehurst St E5 . . . . 18 A3
Trelawney Est E9 . . 17 B2
Trelawney Ho
SE1 . . . . 136 C4
Trelawn Rd SW2 . . 62 C2
Trellis Sq 1 E3 . . . . 26 B2
Tremadoc Rd SW4 . 61 C3
Tremaine Cl SE4 . . . 51 C1
Tremlett Gr N19 . . . 4 B1
Tremlett Ho
SE11 . . . . 149 C2
Tremlett Mews 17
N19 . . . . 4 B1
Trenchard St SE10 . 42 C1
Trenchold St
SW8 . . . . 162 A3
Trendell Ho 8
E14 . . . . 33 C3
Trenmar Gdns
NW10 . . . . 22 A2
Trentham Ct W3 . . . 28 C4
Trentham St SW18 . 70 C3
Trent Ho SE15 . . . . 65 B3
Trent Rd SW2 . . . . . 62 B2
Treport St SW18 . . . 71 A4
Tresco Ho SE11 . . . 149 B2
Tresco Rd SE15 . . . 65 A3
Tresham Cres
NW8 . . . . 90 A2
Tresham Wlk E9 . . . 17 B3
Tresidder Ho 10
SW4 . . . . 73 C4
Tressel Cl 20 N1 . . . 15 A1
Tressillian Cres
SE4 . . . . 66 C4
Tressillian Rd SE4 . 66 C4
Trevanion Rd
W14 . . . . 140 B2
Trevelyan Gdns
NW10 . . . . 22 B4
Trevelyan Ho
10 Globe Town E2 . 25 C2
SE5 . . . . 48 A3
Treveris St SE1 . . . 122 B1
Treverton St W10 . 22 C1
Treverton Twr 1
W10 . . . . 30 C4
Treves Ho
E1 . . . . 24 C1 99 C1
Treville St SW15 . . . 69 A4
Trevithick Ho
13 Bermondsey
SE16 . . . . 40 A2
3 Gospel Oak NW5 . 13 A4
SW8 . . . . 171 B4
Trevithick St SE8 . . 51 C4
Trevor Pl SW7 . . . 130 B3
Trevor Roberts Sch
NW8 . . . . 11 C1
Trevor Sq SW7 . . . 130 B3
Trevor St SW7 . . . 130 B3
Trevose Ho SE11 . 149 A2
Trewint St SW18 . . 71 B2
Triangle Cl E1 . . . 123 A1
Triangle Est The
SE11 . . . . 149 B1
Triangle Ho SE1 . . 138 C4
Triangle Pl SW4 . . . 61 C3
Triangle Rd 7 E8 . . 25 A4

Triangle The
Crouch End N19 . . . 4 C4
EC1 . . . . 96 B2
16 Hackney E8 . . . . 25 A4
Trident Ho 14 E14 . 34 B3
Trident St SE16 . . . 40 C2
Trieste Ct SW12 . . . 72 B3
Trig La EC4 . . . . . 122 C4
Trigon Rd SW8 . . . 163 A2
Trillington Ho
W12 . . . . 29 C1
Trimdon NW1 . . . . . 83 A3
Trimmer Wlk 7
TW8 . . . . 44 A4
Trim St SE8 . . . . . . 51 B4
Trinder Gdns N19 . . 5 A3
Trinder Rd N4, N19 . 5 A3
Trinidad Ho 17
E14 . . . . 33 B2
Trinidad St E14 . . . 33 B2
Trinity Church Rd
SW13 . . . . 47 A4
Trinity Church Sq
SE1 . . . . 137 A2
Trinity Cl
3 Clapham SW4 . . . 61 B3
Lewisham SE13 . . . 67 C3
Trinity Coll London
SE1 . . . . 148 B1
Trinity Coll of Music
SE10 . . . . 52 B4
Trinity Cotts TW9 . . 54 B4
Trinity Cres SW17 . 72 C2
Trinity Ct
Finsbury WC1 . . . . 94 C2
2 Hoxton N1 . . . . . . 24 A4
Rotherhithe SE16 . . 41 A4
Willesden NW2 . . . . 9 B3
Trinity Gdns
E16 . . . . 35 B4
Stockwell SW2,
SW9 . . . . 62 B3
Trinity Gn 1 E1 . . . . 32 B4
Trinity Gr 2 SE10 . . 52 B2
Trinity Ho SE1 . . . 137 A2
Trinity Homes 14
SW2 . . . . 62 B3
Trinity Mews
SW18 . . . . 70 C3
Trinity Pl EC3 . . . 124 C3
Trinity Rd
Richmond TW9 . . . . 54 B4
Wandsworth SW17,
SW18 . . . . 72 A4
Trinity Rise SE24,
SW2 . . . . 75 A4
Trinity St Mary's Prim
Sch 8 SW12 . . . . . 72 C3
Trinity Sq EC3 . . . 124 C3
Trinity St
Newham E16 . . . . . 35 C4
SE1 . . . . 137 B2
Trinity Way W3 . . . . 29 B2
Trio Pl SE1 . . . . . . 137 B2
Tristan Ct 24 SE8 . . 51 B4
Triton Ct EC2 . . . . . 97 C2
Triton Ho 2 E14 . . . 42 A2
Tritton Rd SE21,
SE27 . . . . 75 C1
Trocette Mans
SE1 . . . . 138 B2
Trojan Ct NW6 . . . . 10 A1
Trojan Ind Est
NW10 . . . . 8 B2
Troon Cl 34 SE16 . . 40 A1
Troon Ho 9 E14 . . . 33 A3

Troon St E1 . . . . . . 33 A3
Tropical Ct 2
W10 . . . . 22 C2
Trossachs Rd
SE22 . . . . 64 A2
Trothy Rd SE1 . . . 153 C3
Trotman Ho 1
E14 . . . . 50 B2
Trott St SW11 . . . 168 A3
Trotwood Ho 3
SE16 . . . . 40 A4
Troubridge Ct 4
W10 . . . . 37 B1
Troutbeck NW1 . . . 92 B3
Troutbeck Rd
SE14 . . . . 51 A2
Trouville Rd SW4 . . 61 B1
Trowbridge Est 6
E15 . . . . 18 B2
Trowbridge Rd E9 . 18 B2
Trower Ho 6 E9 . . . 18 A2
Troy Ct 1 W8 . . . . 127 B2
Troyes Ho NW3 . . . 12 B3
Troy Town SE15 . . . 64 C4
Troy Town Flats
SE15 . . . . 64 C4
Truman's Rd 24
N16 . . . . 16 A3
Trump St EC2 . . . . 109 A1
Trundle St SE1 . . . 136 C4
Trundleys Rd SE8 . 51 A4
Trundleys Terr
SE8 . . . . 40 C2
Truro Ho 25 W2 . . . 31 C4
Truro St NW5 . . . . . 12 C2
Trussley Rd W6 . . . 39 B3
Trust Wlk SE21 . . . 75 A3
Tryon Cres E9 . . . . 25 B4
Tryon St SW3 . . . . 144 C2
Tubbs Rd NW10 . . . 21 B3
Tudor Cl
Crouch End N6 . . . . 4 B4
Hampstead NW3 . . . 12 A2
Tulse Hill SW2 . . . . 62 B1
Tudor Coll WC1 . . . 94 A3
Tudor Ct
Kingsland N1 . . . . . 16 A2
5 Rotherhithe
SE16 . . . . 32 C1
South Acton W5 . . . 36 C4
Tudor Est NW10 . . . 20 A3
Tudor Gdns SW14 . 56 A4
Tudor Gr E9 . . . . . . 17 B1
Tudor Ho
Brook Green W14 . . 39 C2
34 Hackney E9 . . . . 17 B1
Tudor Mews 2
W10 . . . . 8 C2
Tudor Rd E9 . . . . . . 25 A4
Tudor St EC4 . . . . 121 C4
Tudor Way W3 . . . . 36 C4
Tufnell Ct 13 E3 . . . 26 B4
Tufnell Mans 7
N7 . . . . 13 C4
TUFNELL PARK 5 A1
Tufnell Park Mans 2
N7 . . . . 5 A1
Tufnell Park Prim Sch
N7 . . . . 13 C4
Tufnell Park Rd N19,
N7 . . . . 13 C4
Tufnell Park Sta
N19 . . . . 13 B4

Tufton Ct SW1..... **134** A1
Tufton St SW1..... **134** A1
Tuke Sch SE15.......50 A2
Tullis Ho **10** E9......17 B1
TULSE HILL..........75 A4
Tulse Ho
 Tulse Hill SW2 ....74 C4
 Tulse Hill SW27 ......75 A2
Tulse Hill Sta
 SE27..................75 A2
Tulse Ho SW2.......62 C1
Tunbridge Ct **1**
 SE26..................76 C1
Tunbridge Ho EC1.. **96** A4
Tunis Rd W12 ....30 A1
Tunley Gn **12** E14....33 B4
Tunley Rd
 Dagenham NW10......21 A4
 Upper Tooting SW12,
 SW17..................72 C2
Tunnel Avenue Trad
 Est SE10 ....42 C4
Tunnel Rd SE16......40 B4
Tunstall Ct **14**
 TW9 ....44 B2
Tunstall Rd SW9....62 B3
Tunstall Wlk **10**
 TW8 ....44 A4
Tunworth Cres
 SW15 ....56 B1
Tun Yd SW8 ....61 A4
Tupman Ho **26**
 SE16 .... **139** B3
Turberville Ho **1**
 SW9 ....62 B4
Turenne Cl SW18....59 B3
Turin St E22........24 C2 99 B3
Turk's Head Yd
 EC1................. **108** A4
Turks Row SW3 .... **145** A2
Turle Rd N4..........5 B2
Turlewray Cl N4.....5 B3
Turnagain La EC4 **108** A2
Turnberry Cl **24**
 SE16 ....40 A1
Turnberry Quay **1**
 E14 ....42 A3
Turnbull Ho N1......86 B4
Turnchapel Mews **3**
 SW4 ....61 A4
Turner Ct **7** SW9...48 A2
Turner Ct
 1 Herne Hill SE5....63 C3
 2 Rotherhithe
 ....40 B4
Turner Ho
 Finsbury Pk N4........5 B3
 2 Millwall E14.....41 C4
 St John's Wood
 NW8 .... **80** A2
 Strand WC2 .... **120** B3
 Westminster SW1 . **147** C3
Turner Lo **10**
 SW19 ....69 C3
Turner Pl SW11......60 A2
Turners Ct E15 ......19 B4
Turney Rd **2** E3 ....33 B4
Turner St
 Canning Town E16 ...35 B3
 Stepney E1 ....32 A4
Turneville Rd
 W14 .... **154** C4

Turney Rd SE21.....75 C4
Turney Sch SE21....75 B4
Turnham Green Sta
 W4 ....38 A2
Turnham Green Terr
 W4 ....38 A2
Turnham Ho SE4....66 A3
Turnham Prim Sch **1**
 SE4 ....66 A3
Turnham Rd SE4....66 A3
Turnmill Ho **8**
 SW2 ....62 C2
Turnmill St EC1.... **108** A4
Turnour Ho **5** E1 ...32 A3
Turnpike Cl SE8 .....51 B3
Turnpike Ho EC1.... **96** B3
Turnpin La **3**
 SE10 ....52 B4
Turpentine La
 SW1 .... **146** B1
Turpin Ho SW11.... **170** A4
Turpin Way N19 ......4 C3
Turquand St SE17 . **151** A3
Turret Gr SW4.......61 B4
Turville Ho NW8.... **90** A2
Turville St
 E2................24 B1 **98** C2
Tuscan Ho **39** E2....25 B2
Tuskar St SE10.......43 A1
Tuttle Ho NW1..... **147** C1
Tweed Ho E14 ....27 B1
Tweezer's Alley
 WC2 .... **121** B4
Twelvetrees Bsns Pk
 E16 ....27 C1
Twelvetrees Cres
 E3 ....27 B1
Twig Folly Cl **21**
 E2 ....25 C3
Twilley St SW18 .....71 A4
Twine Ct E1..........32 B2
Twinings Mus★
 WC2 .... **107** B1
Twisden Rd NW5....13 A4
Twycross Mews
 SE10 ....43 A2
Twyford CE High Sch
 W3 ....28 A1
Twyford Sp Ctr
 W3 ....28 A1
Twyford St N1...... **84** C4
Twynholm Mans
 SW6 .... **154** A2
Tyburn Tree (site
 of)★ W2 .... **116** C3
Tyburn Way **1** W1 ... **117** A4
Tyer's Est SE1 ..... **138** A4
Tyers Gate SE1 ... **138** A3
Tyers St SE11..... **148** C2
Tyers Terr SE11 ... **149** A1
Tyler Cl E2.......... **24** B3
Tyler Ho SE3 ....52 C1
Tyler St
 Greenwich SE10.....43 A1
 SE10 ....43 A1
Tylney Ho **10** E1....32 A3
Tymperley Ct
 SW19 ....70 A3
Tyndale La N1 ....15 A1
Tyndale Mans N1...15 A1
Tyndale Terr **13**
 N1.....................15 A1
Tyneham Cl **10**
 SW11 ....60 C4
Tyneham Rd SW11..60 C4

Tynemouth St
 SW6 .... **166** C2
Tyne St E1........ **111** A2
Tynsdale Rd NW10...8 A2
Tynte Ct E9..........18 A3
Tyrawnal Ho **14**
 SE26..................76 C1
Type St E2...........25 C3
Tyrawley Rd SW6 . **166** A4
Tyrells Ct **3** SE15...65 A4
Tyrrel Ho **1** SW1 . **161** A4
Tyrrel Rd SE22......64 C3
Tyrwhitt Rd SE4....66 C4
Tysoe St EC1........95 C3
Tyssen Com Prim Sch
 N16.....................7 B1
Tyssen Rd N16.......7 B1
Tyssen St
 Dalston E8...........16 B2
 Hoxton N1...........24 A3
Tysson Ho E9........18 A1
Tytherton **22** E2...25 B3
Tytherton Rd N19...4 C1

U

Uamvar St E14.......34 A4
Udall St SW1...... **147** A3
Udimore Ho **11**
 W10....................30 B4
Uffington Rd
 NW10.................22 A4
Ufford St SE1..... **135** C4
Ufton Gr N1.........15 C1
Ufton Rd N1.........16 A1
Uhura Sq **10** N16....7 A1
Ujima Ct N19.........5 A3
Ullin St E14...........34 B4
Ullswater SW15 ... **57** C1
Ullswater Ho SE15..50 B4
Ullswater Rd
 Barnes SW13........46 C3
 West Norwood SE27,
 SW16.................75 A2
Ulster Pl NW1..... **92** A1
Ulster Terr NW1... **92** A2
Ulundi Rd SE3......53 A4
Ulva Rd SW15.......57 C3
Ulverscroft Rd
 SE22..................64 C2
Ulverstone Rd
 SE27..................75 A2
Ulysses Rd NW6....10 B3
Umberston St E1....32 A3
Umbria St SW15....56 C1
Una Ho **7** NW5....13 A2
Undercliff SE10......52 B2
Undercliff Rd
 SE13..................67 A4
Underhill Ho **7**
 E14 ....33 C4
Underhill Pas NW1 **82** B4
Underhill St NW1.. **82** B3
Undershaft EC3 ... **110** A1
Underwood Ho
 W6 ....39 A3
Underwood Rd
 E1................24 C1 **99** C1
Underwood Row
 N1.................... **97** A4
Underwood St N1.. **97** A4
Undine Rd E14 ......42 A2
Unicorn Bldg **14**
 E1 ....32 C2
Unicorn Sch TW9...44 B2

Union Cl E11........19 C4
Union Ct
 45 Paddington W2... **31** C4
 2 Richmond TW10...54 A2
 South Lambeth
 SW4 .... **172** A1
 Whitechapel E2.. **110** A2
Union Dr E1..........26 A1
Union Gr SW8..... **171** C2
Union Mews **32**
 SW9 .... **172** A1
Union Pk **8** SE10...43 B1
Union Rd SW8..... **171** C1
Union Sq N1........ **87** A3
Union St
 Mill Meads E15.....27 C4
 SE1 .... **122** C1
Union Wharf N1... **87** A2
Union Wlk
 E2...............24 A2 **98** B4
Union Yd W1...... **104** B1
United International
 Coll W1............ **104** B3
Unity Cl NW10.......8 C2
Unity Mews NW1 . **83** B2
Univ Coll Jun Sch **53**
 ....11 B4
Univ Coll London
 Bloomsbury WC1 .... **93** B2
 Bloomsbury WC1 .... **94** B2
Univ Coll London
 (Windeyer Inst)
 W1................... **105** A4
Univ Coll London
 (Wolfson Ho)
 NW1 .... **93** A3
University Coll Hospl
 WC1 .... **93** A2
University Coll Sch
 NW3 ....11 B3
University Mans **9**
 SW15 ....57 C4
University St WC1 . **93** A1
Univ of California
 WC1 .... **105** C3
Univ of East London
 (Duncan Ho) **7**
 E15 ....27 C4
Univ of Greenwich
 SE10 ....52 C4
Univ of London
 WC1 .... **93** C1
Univ of London
 (King's Coll Hall)
 SE5 ....63 C4
Univ of London
 (Queen Mary &
 Westfield Coll)
 E1 ....26 A1
Univ of Notre Dame
 SW1 .... **119** C2
Univ of Notre Dame
 SW1 .... **119** C2
Univ of Westminster
 (Cavendish Campus)
 W1................... **104** C4
Univ of Westminster
 (Marylebone
 Campus) W1...... **103** B4
Univ of Westminster
 (Regent Campus)
 W1................... **104** C3
Univ of Westminster
 (Regent Campus,
 Univ HQ) W1..... **104** B3

Univ of Westminster
 (Wigram House Halls
 of Residence)
 SW1 .... **133** A1
Unwin Cl SE15.......49 C4
Unwin Rd SW7.... **129** C2
Upbrook Mews
 W2 .... **101** A1
Upcerne Rd SW10 **157** A1
Upcott Ho
 33 Bromley E3......27 A2
 6 Hackney E9.......17 B1
Upgrove Manor Way
 12 SE24 ....74 C4
Upham Park Rd
 W4 ....38 A2
Upland Rd SE22....64 C1
Uplands Cl SW14...55 A2
Upnall Ho **6** SE5...50 B4
Upnor Way SE17... **152** B2
Upper Addison Gdns
 W14 .... **126** A3
Upper Bank St
 E14 ....34 A1
Upper Bardsey Wlk **2**
 N1.....................15 B2
Upper Belgrave St
 SW1 .... **131** C2
Upper Berkeley St
 W1................... **103** A1
Upper Brockley Rd
 SE4 ....51 B1
Upper Brook St
 W1................... **117** B4
Upper Caldy Wlk **18**
 N1.....................15 B2
Upper Camelford Wlk
 14 W10...............31 A3
Upper Cheyne Row
 SW3 .... **158** A4
Upper Clarendon Wlk
 12 W11...............31 A3
Upper Dengie Wlk
 N1..................... **86** C4
Upper Grosvenor St
 W1................... **117** B3
Upper Ground
 SE1 .... **121** B2
Upper Gulland Wlk **23**
 26 N1.................15 B2
Upper Hampstead Wlk
 28 NW3 ....11 B4
Upper Handa Wlk **2**
 N1.....................15 B2
Upper Harley St
 NW1 .... **91** B1
Upper Hawkwell Wlk
 N1..................... **87** A4
UPPER
 HOLLOWAY........4 C2
Upper Holloway Sta
 N19.....................4 C2
Upper James St
 W1................... **119** A4
Upper John St
 W1................... **119** A4
Upper Lismore Wlk **8**
 N1.....................15 B2
Upper Mall W6......39 A1
Upper Marsh SE1 **135** A2
Upper Montague St
 W1................... **102** C3
Upper North St E3,
 E14 ....33 C4
Upper Park Rd
 NW3 ....12 B3

Upper Phillimore
Gdns W8 . . . . 127 B3
Upper Ramsey Wlk 19
N1 . . . . 15 C2
Upper Rawreth Wlk
N1 . . . . 87 A4
Upper Richmond Rd
SW15 . . . . 57 B3
Upper Richmond Rd
W TW10, SW14,
SW15 . . . . 55 B3
Upper St Martin's La
WC2 . . . . 120 A4
Upper St N1 . . . . . . 86 A3
Upper Tachbrook St
SW1 . . . . 147 A4
Upper Talbot Wlk 3
W10 . . . . 31 A3
Upper Terr NW3 . . . 2 B1
Upper Thames St
EC4 . . . . 123 A4
Upper Tollington Pk
N4 . . . . 5 C3
UPPER TOOTING . . 72 B1
Upper Tooting Park
Mans 1 SW17 . . . 72 C2
Upper Tooting Pk
SW17 . . . . 72 B2
Upper Tooting Rd
SW17 . . . . 72 B1
Upper Tulse Hill
SW2 . . . . 74 B3
Upper Wimpole St
W1 . . . . 103 C4
Upper Woburn Pl NW1,
WC1 . . . . 93 C3
Upstall St SE5 . . . . 48 A2
Upton Cl NW2 . . . . . 1 A1
Urban Mews N4 . . . 6 A4
Urlwin St SE5 . . . . . 48 B4
Urlwin Wlk SW9 . . . 48 A2
Urmston Dr SW19 . . 70 A3
Urmston Ho 4
E14 . . . . 42 B2
Ursula Mews N4 . . . 6 B3
Ursula St SW11 . . . 168 A3
Urswick Rd E5, E9 . 17 B3
Usborne Mews
SW8 . . . . 163 A2
Usher Rd E3 . . . . . . 26 B3
Usk Rd SW11 . . . . . 59 B3
Usk St E2 . . . . 25 C2
Utah Bldg 3 SE13 . 52 A2
Utopia Ho 3 NW2 . 9 C2
Utopia Village
NW1 . . . . 81 B4
Uverdale Rd
SW10 . . . . 157 A1
Uxbridge Rd W12 . . 30 A1
Uxbridge St
W8 . . . . 31 C1 113 B2

V

Vadnie Bish Ho
NW5 . . . . 13 B2
Vaine Ho 4 E9 . . . . 18 A2
Vale Cl W9 . . . . 88 C3
Vale Ct
East Acton W3 . . . . 29 B1
St John's Wood W9 . 88 C3
Vale End SE22 . . . . 64 B3
Vale Est The W3 . . . 29 A1
Vale Gr
Acton W3 . . . . 28 C1

Vale Gr continued
Stoke Newington N4 . 6 B4
Valens Ho 1 SW2 . 74 C3
Valentia Pl SW9 . . . 62 C3
Valentine Ho
1 Clapham Pk
SW4 . . . . 61 B1
26 Old Ford E3 . . . . 26 B4
Valentine Pl SE1 . . 136 A4
Valentine Rd E9 . . . 17 C2
Valentine Row
SE1 . . . . 136 A3
VALE OF HEALTH . . 2 C1
Vale of Health NW3 . 2 C1
Vale Rise NW11 . . . 1 B3
Vale Row N5 . . . . . . 6 A1
Vale Royal N7 . . . . 14 A1
Vale Sch The
SW7 . . . . 128 C1
Vale The
Cricklewood NW11 . 1 A2
East Acton W3 . . . . 29 A1
Chelsea SW3 . . . . 157 C4
Valette Ho E9 . . . . 17 B2
Valette St E8 . . . . . 17 A2
Valiant Ho
6 Cubitt Town
E14 . . . . 42 B4
SW11 . . . . 167 C3
Vallance Rd
E1, E2 . . . . 24 C1 99 C1
Valliere Rd NW10 . . 21 C2
Val McKenzie Ave
N7 . . . . 5 C1
Valmar Rd SE5 . . . 48 B2
Valmar Trad Est
SE5 . . . . 48 B2
Valonia Gdns
SW18 . . . . 58 B1
Vanbern Ho NW5 . . 12 C2
Vanbrugh Ct SE11 . 149 C3
Vanbrugh Fields
SE3 . . . . 53 B3
Vanbrugh Hill SE10,
SE3 . . . . 53 B4
Vanbrugh Ho 3
E9 . . . . 17 B1
Vanbrugh Park Rd
SE3 . . . . 53 B3
Vanbrugh Park Rd W
SE3 . . . . 53 B3
Vanbrugh Pk SE3 . . 53 B3
Vanbrugh Rd W4 . . 37 C3
Vanbrugh Terr
SE3 . . . . 53 B2
Vanburgh Ho 1
E1 . . . . 110 C4
Vancover Ho 33
E1 . . . . 32 A1
Vanderbilt Rd
SW18 . . . . 71 B3
Vanderbilt Villas 5
W12 . . . . 39 C4
Vandon Pas SW1 . . 133 A2
Vandon St SW1 . . . 133 A2
Vandyke Cl SW15 . . 57 C1
Vandy St
EC2 . . . . 24 A1 98 A1
Vange Ho 10 W10 . . 30 B4
Van Gogh Ct E14 . . 42 C3

Vanguard Bldg 6
E14 . . . . 41 C4
Vanguard Ho 11
E8 . . . . 17 A1
Vanguard St SE8 . . 51 C2
Vanneck Sq SW15 . 56 C2
Vanner Point 7
E9 . . . . 17 C2
Vansittart St 7
SE14 . . . . 51 A3
Vanston Pl SW6 . . . 155 C2
Vantage Mews 7
E14 . . . . 34 B1
Vantage Pl W8 . . . 127 C1
Vantrey Ho SE11 . . 149 B3
Varcoe Rd SE16 . . . 40 B1
Vardens Rd SW11 . 59 C3
Varden St E1 . . . . . 32 A3
Vardon Cl W3 . . . . 28 C3
Vardon Ho SE10 . . . 52 B2
Varley Ho 5 NW6 . 23 C4
Varley Ho 8 NW6 . 23 C4
Varma Ct SE3 . . . . . 53 C2
Varna Rd SW6 . . . . 154 C1
Varndell St NW1 . . 92 C4
Varnishers Yard
N1 . . . . 84 B1
Varsity Row SW14 . 45 B1
Vascroft Est NW10 . 20 A1
Vassall Ho 3 E3 . . . 26 A2
Vassall Rd SW9 . . . 163 C1
Vat Ho SW8 . . . . . . 162 B2
Vauban Est SE16 . . 139 A1
Vauban St SE16 . . . 139 A1
Vaudeville Ct N4 . . 5 C2
Vaughan Ave W6 . . 38 B2
Vaughan Est 3
E2 . . . . 24 B2 98 C4
Vaughan Ho SE1 . . 136 A4
Vaughan Rd SE5 . . 48 B1
Vaughan St SE16 . . 41 B4
Vaughan Way E1 . . 125 C2
Vaughan Williams Cl
SE8 . . . . 51 C3
VAUXHALL 148 B1
Vauxhall Bridge Rd
SW1 . . . . 147 A3
Vauxhall City Farm*
SE11 . . . . 148 C2
Vauxhall Cross SE1,
SW8 . . . . 148 B1
Vauxhall Gr SW8 . . 162 C4
Vauxhall Prim Sch
SE11 . . . . 149 A2
Vauxhall St SE11 . . 149 A2
Vauxhall Sta SE11 . 148 B1
Vauxhall Wlk
SE11 . . . . 148 C2
Vawdrey Cl E1 . . . . 25 B1
Vaynor Ho N7 . . . . 14 A4
Vectis Ct SW18 . . . 59 A1
Veda Rd SE13 . . . . 66 C3
Velde Way 1
SE22 . . . . 64 A2
Vellacott Ho 3
W12 . . . . 30 A3
Velletri Ho 17 E2 . . 25 C3
Venables St NW8 . . 101 C4
Vencourt Pl W6 . . . 38 C2
Venetian Rd SE5 . . 48 B1
Venice Ct 3 SE5 . . 48 B3
Venn Ho N1 . . . . . . 85 A3
Venn St SW4 . . . . . 61 B3
Ventnor Rd SE14 . . 50 C3
Ventura Ho 12
SW2 . . . . 62 A3

Venue St E14 . . . . . 34 B4
Venus Ho
7 Millwall E14 . . . . 41 C2
8 Old Ford E3 . . . . 26 C4
Vera Ct W3 . . . . . . 38 A4
Vera Rd SW6 . . . . 164 B4
Verbena Gdns 4
W6 . . . . 38 C1
Verdun Rd SW13 . . 46 C3
Vere Bank SW19 . . 70 B3
Vereker Rd W14 . . 140 B1
Vere St W1 . . . . . . 104 A1
Verity Cl W11 . . . . . 31 A3
Verity Ho 8 E3 . . . . 26 B2
Vermeer Ct E14 . . . 42 C3
Vermont Rd SW18 . 59 A1
Verne Ct 3 W3 . . . 37 B3
Verneer Gdns
SE15 . . . . 65 B3
Verney Ho
Lisson Gr NW8 . . . . 90 A2
South Kensington
SW10 . . . . 156 C4
Verney Rd SE16 . . . 40 A1
Verney Way SE16 . . 40 A1
Vernon Ct NW2 . . . 1 B1
Vernon Ho SE11 . . 149 A1
Vernon Mews
W14 . . . . 140 B3
Vernon Pl WC1 . . . 106 B3
Vernon Rd
Bow E3 . . . . 26 B3
Mortlake SW14 . . . 55 C4
Vernon Rise WC1 . . 95 A4
Vernon Sq WC1 . . . 95 A4
Vernon St W14 . . . 140 B3
Vernon Yd
W11 . . . . 31 B2 112 C4
Verona Ct
Chiswick W4 . . . . . 38 A1
10 SE14 . . . . 50 C4
Veronica Ho
Brockley SE4 . . . . . 66 B4
28 Bromley E3 . . . . 27 A2
Veronica Rd SW17 . 73 A2
Verran Rd SW12 . . 73 A4
Verulam Bldgs
WC1 . . . . 107 A4
Verulam Ho 6
W6 . . . . 39 B4
Verulam St EC1 . . . 107 B4
Vervain Ho 2
SE15 . . . . 49 C3
Verwood Ho SW8 . 163 A1
Verwood Lo 1
E14 . . . . 42 C2
Vesage Ct EC1 . . . 107 C3
Vesey Path 15 E14 . 34 A3
Vespan Rd W12 . . . 38 C4
Vesta Ct SE1 . . . . 138 A3
Vesta Ho 3 E3 . . . . 26 C4
Vesta Rd SE4, SE14 . 51 A1
Vestry Mews 12
SE5 . . . . 49 A2
Vestry Rd SE5 . . . . 49 A2
Vestry St N1 . . . . . 97 B4
Viaduct Pl 2 E2 . . . 25 A2
Viaduct St E2 . . . . 25 A2
Vian St SE13 . . . . . 67 A4
Vibart Gdns SW2 . . 74 B4
Vibart Wlk N1 . . . . 84 B4
Vicarage Ave SE3 . 53 C3
Vicarage Cres
SW11 . . . . 167 B3
Vicarage Ct
7 Putney SW15 . . . 68 C4

Upp–Vic 281

Vicarage Ct continued
W8 . . . . 128 A4
Vicarage Dr SW14 . 55 C2
Vicarage Gate
W8 . . . . 114 A1
Vicarage Gdns
Mortlake SW14 . . . 55 C2
W8 . . . . 31 C1 113 C1
Vicarage Gr SE5 . . 48 C2
Vicarage Rd SW14 . 55 C2
Vicarage Wlk
SW11 . . . . 167 C4
Vicar's Cl E9 . . . . . 25 B4
Vicars Hill SE13 . . . 67 A3
Vicar's Rd NW5 . . . 12 C3
Viceroy Ct NW8 . . . 80 B2
Vic Johnson Ho 21
E3 . . . . 26 B4
Vickery Ct EC1 . . . . 97 A2
Vickery Ho 13
SW4 . . . . 62 A3
Vickery's Wharf 8
E14 . . . . 33 C3
Victor Cazalet Ho
N1 . . . . 86 A4
Victoria & Albert
Mus* SW7 . . . . . 129 C1
Victoria Arc SW1 . . 132 B1
Victoria Ave EC2 . . 110 B3
Victoria Bldgs 18
E8 . . . . 25 A4
Victoria Chambers
EC2 . . . . 24 A1 98 A2
Victoria Coach Sta
SW1 . . . . 146 A3
Victoria Coll Wc2 . 107 B2
Victoria Cotts
7 Richmond TW9 . . 44 C2
6 Spitalfields E1 . . 111 B4
Victoria Ct
6 Clapham Pk
SW4 . . . . 61 C1
South Acton W3 . . . 36 C4
4 St George in t East
E1 . . . . 125 B3
Victoria Dr SW19 . . 69 C3
Victoria Emb
WC2 . . . . 121 B3
Victoria Gdns
W11 . . . . 31 C1 113 B2
Victoria Gr W8 . . . 128 C2
Victoria Gr Mews
W2 . . . . 114 A3
Victoria Hall 16
E16 . . . . 35 C1
Victoria Ho
5 Clapham Pk
SW4 . . . . 61 C1
2 Shepherd's Bush
W12 . . . . 38 C4
SW1 . . . . 146 A2
Victoria Ind Est
W3 . . . . 29 A4
Victoria Mans
8 Islington N7 . . . . 14 C3
Willesden NW10 . . . 9 A1
Victoria Mews
Kilburn NW6 . . . . . 23 C4
Wandsworth SW18 . 71 B3
Victoria Mills 1
E15 . . . . 27 C4
Victorian Gr N16 . . 7 A1
Victorian Rd N16 . . 7 B1

Victoria Park Ct 🇮🇮
E9 . . . . **17** B1
Victoria Park Ind Ctr
E9 . . . . **18** B1
Victoria Park Lofts
E9 . . . . **25** C4
Victoria Park Rd
E9 . . . . **17** C1
Victoria Park Sq
E2 . . . . **25** B2
Victoria Pas NW8 . . **89** B2
Victoria Place Sh Ctr
SW1 . . . . **146** B4
Victoria Rd
Finsbury Pk N4 . . . . . . **5** C3
Kensington W8 . . **128** C2
Kilburn NW6 . . . . **23** B4
Mortlake SW14 . . . . . . **55** C4
North Acton NW10 . . **21** A1
Victoria Rise SW4 . . **61** A4
Victoria Sq SW1 . . **132** B2
Victoria St SW1 . . **133** A1
Victoria St SW1 . . **146** B4
Victoria Terr
Dagenham NW10 . . . . **21** A1
Finsbury Pk N4 . . . . . . **5** C3
Victoria
(Underground)
SW1 . . . . **132** B1
Victoria Villas
TW9 . . . . **54** B3
Victoria Wharf
E14 . . . . **33** A2
Victoria Yd 🇮🇮 E1 **111** C1
Victor Rd NW10 . . . . **22** A2
Victory Pl
🇮🇮 Limehouse E14 . . **33** A2
SE17 . . . . **151** B4
Victory Prim Sch
SE17 . . . . **151** A4
Victory Way SE16 . . **41** A4
Victory Wlk SE8 . . . . **51** C2
Video Ct N4 . . . . **5** A4
View Ct N6 . . . . **3** B4
Viewfield Rd
SW18 . . . . **58** B1
Viewpoint 🇮🇮 N5 . . **15** A3
Vigo St W1 . . . . . . **118** C3
Viking Ho 🇮🇮 SE5 . . **26** A3
Viking Ho 🇮🇮 SE5 . . **48** B1
Village Cl NW3 . . . . . . **11** C3
Village Mount 🇮🇮
NW3 . . . . **11** B4
Village Sch The
NW3 . . . . **12** B2
Village The SW11 . . **60** B4
Village Way SE21 . . **63** C1
Villa Rd SW9 . . . . . . **62** C4
Villas On The Heath
NW3 . . . . **2** B1
Villa St SE17 . . . . **151** C1
Villiers Ct SW11 . . **168** B4
Villiers Rd NW2 . . . . **8** C2
Villiers St WC2 . . **120** B2
Vince Ct N1 . . . . . . **97** C3
Vincent Ct
Finsbury Pk N4 . . . . . . **5** A3
Marylebone W1 . . **102** C2
South Lambeth
SW9 . . . . **173** A3
Vincent Mews 🇮🇮
E3 . . . . **26** C3
Vincent Rd W3 . . . . **37** B3
Vincents Cl SE16 . . **41** A4

Vincent Sq SW1 . . **147** B4
Vincent St
Canning Town E16 . . **35** B4
Westminster SW1 . . **147** C4
Vincent Terr N1 . . . . **86** B2
Vince St EC1 . . . . . . **97** C3
Vine Ct E1 . . . . **16** C4
Vine Ct E1 . . . . **111** C3
Vinegar St E1 . . . . . . **32** A1
Vinegar Yd SE1 . . **138** A4
Vine Hill EC1 . . . . . . **95** B1
Vine La SE1 . . . . . . **124** B1
Vine Rd SW13 . . . . . . **56** B4
Vine St Bridge EC1 **95** C1
Vine Sq W14 . . . . . . **141** A1
Vine St
W1 . . . . **119** A3
Whitechapel EC3 . . **110** C1
Vineyard Path
SW14 . . . . **55** C4
Vineyard Prim Sch
The TW10 . . . . **54** A1
Vineyard The
TW10 . . . . **54** A2
Vineyard Wlk EC1 . . **95** B2
Viney Ct 🇮🇮 SW4 . . **61** C1
Viney Yd SE1 . . . . . . **137** A4
Viney Rd SE13 . . . . . . **67** A4
Vining St
SW2 . . . . **62** C3
Vinson Ho N1 . . . . . . **87** C1
Vinters Ct SE4 . . . . **123** A4
Viola Sq W12 . . . . . . **29** B2
Violet Cl 🇮🇮 SE8 . . . . **51** B4
Violet Hill NW8 . . . . **78** C1
Violet Hill Ho NW8 **78** C1
Violet Rd E3 . . . . **27** A1
Violet St E2 . . . . **25** A1
Virgil Pl W1 . . . . . . **102** C3
Virgil St SE1 . . . . . . **135** A2
Virginia Ct 🇮🇮
SE16 . . . . **40** C4
Virginia Ho 🇮🇮 E14 **34** B2
Virginia Prim Sch
E2 . . . . **24** B2 98 C3
Virginia Rd 🇮🇮
E2 . . . . **24** B2 98 C3
Virginia St E1 . . . . **125** C3
Virginia Wlk SW2 . . **62** B1
Viscount Ct 🇮🇮
W11 . . . . **31** C3
Viscount St EC1 . . **108** C4
Vision Coll of
Theology E9 . . . . **18** A2
Vista Bldgs 🇮🇮 E3 **26** B2
Vitae Apartments 🇮🇮
W6 . . . . **38** C3
Vittoria Ho N1 . . . . . . **85** A3
Vittoria Prim Sch
N1 . . . . **85** B2
Vivian Comma Cl 🇮🇮
N4 . . . . **6** A1
Vivian Ct NW6 . . . . . . **78** A2
Vivian Ho N4 . . . . **6** C4
Vivian Rd E3 . . . . **26** A3
Vivian Sq SE15 . . . . **65** A4
Vogans Mill SE1 . . **139** A4
Vogler Ho 🇮🇮 E1 . . . . **32** B2
Vollasky Ho 🇮🇮 E1 **111** B4
Voltaire
🇮🇮 Camberwell
SE5 . . . . **48** B3
🇮🇮 Richmond TW9 . . **44** B2
Voltaire Ct 🇮🇮
SW11 . . . . **169** C2
Voltaire Rd SW4 . . **61** C4

Volt Ave NW10 . . . . . . **21** A2
Vorley Rd N19 . . . . **4** B2
Voss St E2 . . . . **24** C2 99 C3
Voyager Bsns Est 🇮🇮
SE16 . . . . **40** A4
Vulcan Rd SE4 . . . . . . **51** B1
Vulcan Sq E14 . . . . . . **41** C2
Vulcan Terr SE4 . . . . **51** B1
Vulcan Way N7 . . . . . . **14** B2
Vyner Ct E5 . . . . **17** A3
Vyner Rd W3 . . . . **28** C2
Vyner St E2 . . . . **25** A4

W

Wadcroft Ct SE4 . . . . **66** B4
Wadding St SE17 **151** B3
Waddington Rd
E15 . . . . **19** C2
Waddington St
E15 . . . . **19** C2
Wade Ho 🇮🇮 SE1 . . **139** B3
Wadeson St E2 . . . . . . **25** A3
Wade's Pl E14 . . . . . . **34** A2
Wadham Gdns
NW3 . . . . **80** A4
Wadham Rd SW15 **58** A3
Wadhurst Rd W4 . . . . **37** C4
Wager St E3 . . . . **26** B1
Waghorn St SE15 . . **64** C4
Wagner St SE15 . . . . **50** B3
Wainford Cl SW19 . . **69** C3
Wainwright Ho 🇮🇮
E1 . . . . **32** B1
Waite St SE15 . . . . . . **49** B4
Waithman St EC4 . . **108** A1
Wakefield Ho 🇮🇮
SE15 . . . . **49** C2
Wakefield Mews
WC1 . . . . **94** B3
Wakefield St WC1 . . **94** B3
Wakeford Cl SW4 . . **61** B2
Wakeham St 🇮🇮
N1 . . . . **15** C2
Wakehurst Rd
SW11 . . . . **60** B2
Wakeling Ho 🇮🇮
SE27 . . . . **75** A1
Wakeling St 🇮🇮
E14 . . . . **33** A3
Wakelin Ho 🇮🇮 N1 . . **15** A1
Wakeman Rd
NW10 . . . . **22** C2
Wakley St EC1 . . . . . . **96** A4
Walberswick St
SW8 . . . . **162** B1
Walbrook EC4 . . . . **123** B4
Walbrook Ct 🇮🇮
N1 . . . . **24** A3
Walbrook Wharf
EC4 . . . . **123** B4
Walburgh St E1 . . . . **32** A3
Walcorde Ave
SE17 . . . . **151** A3
Walcot Gdns
SE11 . . . . **149** B4
Walcot Ho 🇮🇮
SE22 . . . . **64** A4
Walcot Sq SE11 . . **149** C4
Walcott St SW1 . . **147** A4
Waldeck Gr SE27 . . **75** A1
Waldeck Rd
Brentford W4 . . . . . . **44** C4
Mortlake SW14 . . . . . . **55** B4

Waldeck Terr
SW14 . . . . **55** B4
Waldegrave Ho 🇮🇮
SW15 . . . . **57** B2
Waldemar Ave
SW6 . . . . **164** B2
Waldemar Avenue
Mans SW6 . . . . . . **164** A3
Walden Ct SW8 . . **171** C4
Walden Ho
🇮🇮 Clapham
SW11 . . . . **169** B2
SW1 . . . . **145** C3
Walden St E1 . . . . . . **32** A3
Waldo Cl SW4 . . . . . . **61** B2
Waldo Rd NW10 . . . . **22** A2
Waldorf Sch of S W
London SW16 . . . . . . **73** C2
Waldron Ho 🇮🇮
SW2 . . . . **62** B2
Waldron Mews
SW3 . . . . **157** C4
Waldron Rd SW18 . . **71** B1
Walerand Rd SE13 . . **52** B1
Waleran Flats
SE1 . . . . **152** A4
Wales Cl SE15 . . . . . . **50** A4
Wales Farm Rd
W3 . . . . **28** C4
Waley St 🇮🇮 E1 . . . . . . **33** A4
Walford Ho 🇮🇮 E1 . . **32** A3
Walford Rd N16 . . . . **16** A4
Walham Ct 🇮🇮
NW3 . . . . **12** B2
Walham Gr SW6 . . **155** B2
WALHAM
GREEN **155** B1
Walham Green Arc
SW6 . . . . **155** C2
Walham Yd SW6 . . **155** B2
Walker Ho N1 . . . . . . **83** B1
Walker Mews 🇮🇮
SW2 . . . . **62** C2
Walkerscroft Mead
SE21 . . . . **75** B3
Walker's Ct W1 . . **119** B4
Walkers Lo 🇮🇮 E14 . . **42** B4
Walker's Pl SW15 . . **58** A3
Walkinshaw Ct 🇮🇮
N1 . . . . **15** B1
Walkynscroft 🇮🇮
SE15 . . . . **50** A1
Wallace Collection★
W1 . . . . **103** B3
Wallace Ct NW1 . . **102** B3
Wallace Ho N7 . . . . . . **14** B2
Wallace Lo N4 . . . . **5** C3
Wallace Rd N1, N5 . . **15** B2
Wallbutton Rd
SE4 . . . . **51** A1
Wall Ct N4 . . . . **5** B3
Waller Rd SE14 . . . . . . **50** C1
Wallett Ct 🇮🇮 NW1 . . **13** B1
Wallflower St W12 . . **29** B2
Wallgrave Rd
SW5 . . . . **142** A3
Wallingford Ave
W10 . . . . **30** C3
Wallis Alley SE1 . . **137** A4
Wallis Cl SW11 . . . . . . **59** C4
Wallis Ho 🇮🇮 SE14 . . **51** A2
Wallis Rd E9 . . . . **18** C2
Wallorton Gdns
SW14 . . . . **55** C3
Wallside EC2 . . . . . . **109** A3
Wall St N1 . . . . **15** C2

Wallwood St E14 . . . . **33** B4
Walmer Ho 🇮🇮
W10 . . . . **30** C3
Walmer Pl W1 . . . . **102** C4
Walmer Rd
North Kensington
W10 . . . . **30** B3
W11 . . . . **31** A2 112 A3
Walm La NW2 . . . . **9** B2
Walney Wlk 🇮🇮 N1 . . **15** B2
Walnut Cl SE8 . . . . . . **51** B4
Walnut Ho 🇮🇮 E3 . . . . **26** B4
Walnut Tree Cl
SW13 . . . . **46** B2
Walnut Tree Ho
SW10 . . . . **156** B4
Walnut Tree Rd
Brentford TW8 . . . . . . **44** A4
Greenwich SE10 . . . . **43** A1
Walnut Tree Walk
Prim Sch SE11 . . **149** B4
Walnut Tree Wlk
SE11 . . . . **149** B4
Walpole Ave TW9 . . **44** B1
Walpole Ct
🇮🇮 Hammersmith
W14 . . . . **39** C3
South Hampstead
NW6 . . . . **11** B1
Walpole Gdns W4 . . **37** B1
Walpole Mews
NW8 . . . . **79** B3
Walpole St SW3 . . **145** A2
Walsham Cl N16 . . . . . **7** C3
Walsham Ho
New Cross Gate
SE14 . . . . **50** C1
SE17 . . . . **151** B2
Walsham Rd SE14 . . **50** C1
Walsingham NW8 . . **79** C4
Walsingham Lo
SW13 . . . . **46** C2
Walsingham Mans
SW6 . . . . **156** B2
Walsingham Pl SW4,
SW11 . . . . **60** C1
Walter Besant Ho 🇮🇮
E1 . . . . **25** C2
Walter Ct 🇮🇮 W3 . . . . **28** B3
Walter Green Ho
SE15 . . . . **50** B2
Walter Ho SW10 . . **157** B2
Walter Northcott Ho
🇮🇮 NW6 . . . . **10** C3
Walters Cl SE17 . . **151** A3
Walters Ho
🇮🇮 Camberwell
SE5 . . . . **49** A1
Islington N1 . . . . **86** B4
🇮🇮 Kennington SE17 . . **48** A4
Walter Sickert Hall
🇮🇮 N1 . . . . **86** C1
Walter St E2 . . . . **25** C2
Walters Way SE23 . . **65** C1
Walter Taylor Ct
SE4 . . . . **66** B3
Walter Terr E1 . . . . . . **32** C3
Walterton Rd W9 . . **23** C1
Waltham Green Ct
SW6 . . . . **156** A1
Waltham Ho
NW8 . . . . **78** C4
🇮🇮 Stockwell SW9 **173** A1
Walton Cl SW8 . . . . **162** B2
Walton Gdns W3 . . **28** A4

Walton Ho
E2 . . . . .24 B1 99 A2
Upper Holloway N7 . . 5 B1
Wandsworth SW18 . . 58 C1
Walton Pl SW3 . . . . 130 C2
Walton St SW3 . . . . 130 B1
Walton Way W3 . . . . 28 A4
Walt Whitman Cl 6
SE24 . . . . 63 A3
WALWORTH 151 C2
Walworth Acad
(Lower School)
SE17 . . . . 151 C2
Walworth Acad
(Upper School)
SE17 . . . . 152 B1
Walworth Pl SE17 151 A1
Walworth Rd
SE17 . . . . 151 A2
Wanborough Dr
SW15 . . . . 69 A3
Wandle Ct 4 W12 . . 38 A4
Wandle Ho
NW8 . . . . 102 A4
Wandsworth SW18 . . 71 A4
Wandle Rd SW17 . . . 72 A2
Wandle Way SW18 . . 71 A3
Wandon Rd SW6 . . . 156 B1
WANDSWORTH 58 C1
Wandsworth Bridge
Rd SW6 . . . . 166 A3
Wandsworth Common
Sta SW12 . . . . 72 B4
Wandsworth Common
West Side SW18 . . . 59 B2
Wandsworth Gyory
SW18 . . . . 59 A2
Wandsworth High St
SW18 . . . . 59 A2
Wandsworth Plain
SW18 . . . . 59 A2
Wandsworth Rd
SW8 . . . . 162 A1
Wandsworth Road Sta
SW4 . . . . 171 A1
Wandsworth Town
Sta SW18 . . . . 59 A2
Wangford Ho 13
SW9 . . . . 63 A3
Wanless Rd SE24 . . . 63 B3
Wanley Rd SE5 . . . . 63 C3
Wansbeck Rd E3,
E9 . . . . 18 B1
Wansdown Pl
SW6 . . . . 156 A2
Wandsworth
Riverside Quarter
Pier SW6 . . . . 58 C4
Wansey St SE17 . . . 151 A3
WAPPING 32 A1
Wapping Dock St 13
E1 . . . . 32 A1
Wapping High St
E1 . . . . 32 A1
Wapping La E1 . . . . . 32 A1
Wapping Sta E1 . . . . 32 B1
Wapping Wall E1 . . . 32 B1
Warbeck Rd W12 . . . 39 A4
Warburg Ho
E2 . . . . .24 C2 99 B3
Warburton Cl 6
N1 . . . . 16 A2
Warburton Ho 5
E8 . . . . 25 A4

Warburton Rd 8
E8 . . . . 25 A4
Warburton St 6
E8 . . . . 25 A4
Wardalls Ho 12
SE8 . . . . 51 B4
Wardell Ho 7
SE10 . . . . 52 B4
Warden Rd NW5 . . . 12 C2
Wardens Gr SE1 . . . 122 C1
Wardle St E9 . . . . . . 17 C3
Wardley St SW18 . . . 71 A4
Wardlow 8 NW5 . . . 13 A4
Wardo Ave SW6 . . . 164 A4
Ward Rd
Camden Town N19 . . 4 B1
Mill Meads E15 . . . . 27 C4
Wardrobe Pl EC4 . . 108 B1
Wardrobe Terr
EC4 . . . . 122 B4
Wareham Ct 2
N1 . . . . 16 A1
Wareham Ho
SW8 . . . . 162 C2
Warfield Rd NW10 . . 22 C2
Warfield Yd 6
NW10 . . . . 22 C2
Wargrave Ho 46
E2 . . . . .24 B2 98 C3
Warham St SE5 . . . . 48 A3
Waring Ho 22
E2 . . . . .24 C2 99 C3
Warley Ho N1 . . . . . 15 C2
Warley St E2 . . . . . . 25 C2
Warlock Rd W9 . . . . 23 C1
Warlters Cl N7 . . . . . 14 A4
Warlters Rd N7 . . . . 14 A4
Warltersville Mans
N19 . . . . 5 A4
Warltersville Rd N4, N8,
N19 . . . . 5 A4
War Meml Homes
W4 . . . . 45 C3
Warmington Rd
SE24 . . . . 63 B1
Warmsworth NW1 . 82 C4
Warndon St SE16 . . 40 B2
Warneford St E9 . . . 25 A4
Warner Ho
4 Homerton E9 . . . . 17 C2
Lewisham SE13 . . . . 52 A1
NW8 . . . . 88 C4
Warner Pl
E2 . . . . .24 C2 99 C4
Warner Rd SE5 . . . . 48 B2
Warner St EC1 . . . . . 95 B1
Warner Yd EC1 . . . . 95 B1
Warnford Ho
SW15 . . . . 56 A1
Warnham WC1 . . . . 94 C3
Warnham Ho 6
SW2 . . . . 74 B4
Warple Mews W3 . . 38 A4
Warple Way W3,
W12 . . . . 38 A4
Warren Ave SW14,
TW10 . . . . 55 A3
Warren Cl SE21 . . . 75 B4
Warren Ct N1 . . . . . 85 B2
Warrender Rd N19 . . 13 B4
Warren Gdns E15 . . 19 C3
Warren Ho 21 E3 . . 27 A2

Warren Mews W1 . . 92 C1
Warren St W1 . . . . . 92 C1
Warren Street Sta
NW1 . . . . 93 A2
Warriner Gdns
SW11 . . . . 169 B3
Warrington Cres
W9 . . . . 88 C2
Warrington Gdns
W9 . . . . 88 C1
Warspite Ho 3
E14 . . . . 41 C2
Warton Rd E15 . . . . 27 B4
Warwick W14 . . . . 141 A3
Warwick Ave W9 . . 88 C1
Warwick Avenue Sta
W9 . . . . 88 C1
Warwick Bldg
SW8 . . . . 160 A3
Warwick Chambers
W8 . . . . 127 B2
Warwick Cres W2 . . 100 C4
Warwick Ct WC1 . . 107 A3
Warwick Dr SW15 . . 57 A4
Warwick Gdns
W14 . . . . 141 A4
Warwick Ho
10 Brixton SW9 . . 173 B1
6 Putney SW15 . . . . 69 B4
Stoke Newington N4 . . 6 B3
Warwick House St
SW1 . . . . 119 C2
Warwick La EC4 . . . 108 B1
Warwick Lo NW2 . . 10 A3
Warwick Mans
SW5 . . . . 141 B4
Warwick Pas EC4 . . 108 B2
Warwick Pl W9 . . . 100 C4
Warwick Pl N
SW1 . . . . 146 C3
Warwick Rd W14,
SW5 . . . . 141 A4
Warwick Row
SW1 . . . . 132 B2
Warwickshire Path
SE8 . . . . 51 B3
Warwick Sq
Holborn EC4 . . . . . 108 B2
Pimlico SW1 . . . . . 146 C2
Warwick Sq Mews
SW1 . . . . 146 C3
Warwick St W1 . . . 119 A4
Warwick Way
SW1 . . . . 146 B4
Warwick Yd EC1 . . . 97 A1
Wasdale NW1 . . . . . 92 B3
Washbrook Ho
SW2 . . . . 62 C1
Washington Bldg 1
SE13 . . . . 52 A2
Washington Cl 49
E3 . . . . 27 A2
Washington Ho
SW1 . . . . 130 C3
Washington Rd
SW13 . . . . 46 C3
Watchfield Ct 7
W4 . . . . 37 B1
Watcombe Cotts
TW9 . . . . 44 C4
Watercress Pl 12
N1 . . . . 16 A1
Waterford Rd
SW6 . . . . 156 A1
Waterford Way
NW10 . . . . 8 C3

Water Gardens The
W2 . . . . 102 B2
Watergate EC4 . . . . 122 A4
Watergate St SE8 . . . 51 C4
Watergate Wlk
WC2 . . . . 120 B2
Waterhead Ho 4
E2 . . . . .25 C3 99 A2
Waterhouse Cl
Hammersmith W6 . . 39 C1
Hampstead NW3 . . . 11 C3
Waterhouse Sq
EC1 . . . . 107 B3
Wateridge Cl E14 . . 41 C3
Water La
26 Camden Town
NW1 . . . . 13 A1
SE14 . . . . 50 B3
Waterloo Bridge SE1,
WC2 . . . . 121 A3
Waterloo Cl E9 . . . . 17 B3
Waterloo East Sta
SE1 . . . . 121 C1
Waterloo Gdns
20 Islington N1 . . . . 15 A1
South Hackney E2 . . 25 B3
Waterloo Millennium
Pier SE1 . . . . 134 C4
Waterloo Pl
Kew TW9 . . . . 44 C4
3 Richmond TW9 . . 54 A3
SW1 . . . . 119 B2
Waterloo Rd SE1 . . 135 C4
Waterloo Sta SE1 . . 135 B4
Waterloo Terr N1 . . 15 A1
Waterlow Ct NW11 . . 2 A4
Waterlow Rd N19 . . . 4 B3
Waterman Bldg 2
E14 . . . . 41 C4
Watermans Arts Ctr*
TW8 . . . . 44 A4
Watermans Ct 2
TW8 . . . . 44 A4
Waterman St
SW15 . . . . 57 C4
Waterman Way 31 E1 . . 32 A1
Watermead Ho E9 . . 18 B3
Watermeadow La
SW6 . . . . 166 C1
Water Mews SE15 . . 65 B3
Watermill Ct SE13 . . 67 A4
Watermint Quay
N16 . . . . 7 C4
Water's Edge SW6 . . 47 B2
Waterside Cl
3 Bermondsey
SE1 . . . . 139 C3
Old Ford E3 . . . . . . 26 B4
Waterside Ct SE13 . . 67 B3
Waterside Pl NW1 . . 81 C4
Waterside Point
SW11 . . . . 158 B2
Waterson St
E2 . . . . .24 B2 98 C4
Waters Pl SW15 . . . 47 B1
Water St WC2 . . . . 121 B4
Water Tower Pl
N1 . . . . 86 A3
Waterview Ho 15
E14 . . . . 33 A4
Waterway Ave 2
SE13 . . . . 67 A4
Waterworks Rd
SW2 . . . . 62 B1
Watford Cl SW11 . . 168 B4
Watford Rd E16 . . . 35 C4

Watkins Ho 11 E14 . 42 B4
Watkinson Rd N7 . . 14 B2
Watling Ct EC4 . . . 109 A1
Watling Gdns
NW2 . . . . 10 A2
Watling St
4 Camberwell
SE15 . . . . 49 A4
City of London EC4 109 A1
Watney Cotts
SW14 . . . . 55 B4
Watney Mkt* E1 . . 32 A3
Watney Rd SW14 . . . 55 B4
Watney St E1 . . . . . 32 A3
Watson Cl N16 . . . . 15 C3
Watson Ho 3
SW2 . . . . 74 A4
Watsons Mews
W1 . . . . 102 B3
Watson's St SE8 . . . 51 C3
Watts Gr E3 . . . . . . 34 A4
Watts Ho 6 W10 . . . 31 A4
Watts St
SE15 . . . . 49 B2
Wapping E1 . . . . . . 32 A1
Wat Tyler Rd SE10 . . 52 C2
Wavel Ct
7 Streatham
SW16 . . . . 74 A1
2 Wapping E1 . . . . 32 B1
Wavel Mews NW6 . . 11 A1
Wavendon Ave
W4 . . . . 37 C1
Waveney Ave
SE15 . . . . 65 B3
Waveney Cl 20 E1 . 125 C2
Waveney Ho SE15 . . 65 B3
Waverley Ct
5 Brondesbury
NW6 . . . . 10 A1
Hackney W1 . . . . . 103 C4
Waverley Pl
Finsbury Pk N4 . . . . 6 A3
St John's Wood
NW8 . . . . 79 B2
Waverley Rd N8 . . . 5 A4
Waverly Ct NW3 . . 12 B3
Waverton Ho 2
E3 . . . . 26 B4
Waverton Rd
SW18 . . . . 71 B4
Waverton St W1 . . 118 A2
Wavertree Ct 3
SW2 . . . . 74 A3
Wavertree Rd
SW2 . . . . 74 B3
Waxham NW5 . . . . 12 B3
Waxlow Rd NW10 . . 20 C3
Wayford St SW11 . . 168 B1
Wayland Ave E8 . . . 16 C3
Wayland Ho 12
SW9 . . . . 173 B2
Waylett Ho SE11 . . 149 B1
Waylett Pl SE27 . . . 75 A1
Wayman Ct E8 . . . . 17 A2
Waynflete Sq
18 North Kensington
W10 . . . . 30 C2
18 Shepherd's Bush
W10 . . . . 30 C2
Waynflete St
SW18 . . . . 71 B2

Wayside
Golders Green
NW11 . . . . 1 A3
Mortlake SW14 . . . . 55 B2
Weald Cl 14 SE16 . . 40 A1
Weardale Ho N4 . . . 6 B4
Weardale Rd SE13 . . 67 C3
Wearmouth Ho 1
E3 . . . . 33 B4
Wear Pl 13 E2 . . . . 25 A2
Wearside Rd SE13 . . 67 A3
Weatherbury 6
W2 . . . . 31 C3
Weatherbury Ho 3
N19 . . . . 4 C1
Weatherley Cl E3 . . 33 B4
Weaver Ct 2 E2 . . 25 A1
Weaver Ho 12
E1 . . . . 24 C1 99 B1
Weaver's La SE1 . . 124 B1
Weaver St
E1 . . . . 24 C1 99 B1
Weavers Way
8 Camden Town
NW1 . . . . 13 C1
NW1 . . . . 83 B4
Webb Cl NW10 . . . . 22 B1
Webb Ct W3 . . . . . 37 A4
Webber Row SE1 . . 136 A3
Webber St SE1 . . . . 136 A3
Webb Est E5 . . . . . . 7 C4
Webb Ho SW8 . . . 161 C1
Webb Pl NW10 . . . . 21 C2
Webb Rd SE3 . . . . . 53 B4
Webb's Rd SW11 . . 60 B2
Webb St SE1 . . . . . 138 A1
Webheath 6 NW6 . . 10 A1
Webster Ho 18
N16 . . . . 16 A3
Webster Rd SE16 . . 139 C1
Weddell Ho 2 E1 . . 25 C1
Wedderburn Rd
NW3 . . . . 11 C3
Wedgewood Ho
SW1 . . . . 146 C1
Wedgewood Mews
W1 . . . . 105 C1
Wedgewood Wlk
NW3 . . . . 11 A3
Wedgwood Ho
17 Globe Town E2 . . 25 C2
SE11 . . . . 135 B1
Wedlake St W10 . . 23 A1
Wedmore Gdns
N19 . . . . 4 C2
Wedmore Mews
N19 . . . . 4 C1
Wedmore St N19 . . 4 C1
Weech Rd NW6 . . . . 10 C4
Weedington Rd
NW5 . . . . 12 C3
Weedon Ho W12 . . . 29 C3
Weekley Sq SW11 . . 59 C4
Weighhouse St
W1 . . . . 103 C1
Weimar St SW15 . . 58 A4
Weir Ho 8 SW12 . . 73 B4
Weir Rd
Streatham SW12 . . 73 B4
Wimbledon SW19,
SW19 . . . . 71 A1
Weiss Rd SW15 . . . 57 C4
Welbeck Ct W14 . . 140 C4

Welbeck Mans 10
NW6 . . . . 10 C3
Welbeck St W1 . . . 104 A2
Welbeck Way W1 . . 104 A2
Welbury Ct E8 . . . . 16 A1
Welby Ho N19 . . . . . 4 C4
Welby St SE5 . . . . . 48 A2
Weldon Ct SE8 . . . . 51 C1
Welford Ct
12 Camden Town
NW1 . . . . 13 A1
7 Clapham SW8 . . 170 C1
Welland Ho SE15 . . 65 B3
Welland Mews 21
E1 . . . . 125 C2
Welland St SE10 . . 52 B4
Wellclose Sq E1 . . 125 C4
Wellclose St 4
E1 . . . . 125 C3
Wellday Ho 2 E9 . . 18 A2
Welldon Ct 1
SE21 . . . . 75 C2
Weller Ho 23
SE16 . . . . 139 B3
Weller St SE1 . . . . 136 C4
Welles Ct 15 E14 . . 33 C2
Wellesley Ave W6 . . 39 A3
Wellesley Ct W9 . . . 88 C4
Wellesley Ho NW1 . . 93 B3
Wellesley Pl
Camden Town
NW5 . . . . 12 C3
NW1 . . . . 93 B3
Wellesley Rd
Gospel Oak NW5 . . 12 C3
Gunnersbury W4 . . 37 A1
Wellesley St E1 . . . 32 C4
Wellesley Terr N1 . . 97 A4
Wellfit St 8 SE24 . . 63 A4
Wellgarth Rd NW11 . 2 A3
Wellington Arch★
SW1 . . . . 131 C4
Wellington Bldgs
16 Bow E3 . . . . 26 C2
SW1 . . . . 145 C1
Wellington Cl
Kensington W11 . . . 31 C3
New Cross Gate
SE14 . . . . 50 C2
Wellington Ct
Knightsbridge
SW1 . . . . 130 C3
St John's Wood
NW8 . . . . 79 C1
Strand WC2 . . . . . 120 A4
Wandsworth SW18 . 60 A2
Wellington Gr
SE10 . . . . 52 C3
Wellington Ho 18
NW3 . . . . 12 B2
Wellington Hospl 18
NW8 . . . . 79 C1
Wellington Mans
N16 . . . . 16 B4
Wellington Mews
East Dulwich SE22 . 64 C3
1 Islington N7 . . . . 14 B2
Streatham SW16 . . 73 C1
Wellington Pl NW8 . 80 A1
Wellington Prim Sch
E3 . . . . 26 C2
Wellington Rd
Kensal Green
NW10 . . . . 22 C2

Wellington Rd
continued
St John's Wood
NW8 . . . . 79 C1
Wimbledon SW19 . . 70 C2
Wellington Row
E2 . . . . 24 C2 99 B4
Wellington Sq
Islington N1 . . . . . . 84 B4
SW3 . . . . 144 C2
Wellington St
WC2 . . . . 120 C4
Wellington Terr 2
E1 . . . . 32 A1
Wellington Way
E3 . . . . 26 C2
Well La SW14 . . . . . 55 B2
Well Rd NW3 . . . . . . 2 C1
Wells Ct
21 Hampstead
NW3 . . . . 11 B4
1 Paddington NW6 . 23 C3
Stoke Newington N1 16 A3
Wells Ho
Finsbury Pk N7 . . . . 5 B2
Wells Ho 1
Kensal Town
W10 . . . . 23 A1
New Cross Gate
SE4 . . . . 51 A1
9 Rotherhithe
SE16 . . . . 40 B3
Wells Ho The 2
NW10 . . . . 29 A4
Wellside Gdns
SW14 . . . . 55 B2
Wells Mews W1 . . . 105 A2
Wells Pl SW18 . . . . 71 B4
Wells Rd W12 . . . . . 39 B4
Wells Rise NW8 . . . 80 C3
Wells Sq WC1 . . . . . 95 A3
Wells St W1 . . . . . 105 A2
Wells Terr N4 . . . . . . 5 C2
Wells Way
Brompton SW7 . . . 129 B2
Camberwell SE5 . . . 49 A4
Well Wlk NW3 . . . . . 2 C1
Wellwood Ct
SW15 . . . . 57 B3
Welmar Works
SW4 . . . . 61 C3
Welsford St SE1 . . 153 B3
Welsh Ho 14 E1 . . . 32 A1
Welshpool Ho 22
E8 . . . . 24 C4
Welshpool St 1
E8 . . . . 25 A4
Welstead Ho 25
E1 . . . . 32 A3
Welstead Way W4 . . 38 B2
Weltje Rd W6 . . . . . 38 C1
Welton Ct SE5 . . . . 49 A2
Welton Ho E1 . . . . . 32 C4
Welwyn St E2 . . . . . 25 B2
Wembury Mews N6 . 4 B4
Wembury Rd N6 . . . . 4 A4
Wemyss Rd SE3 . . . 53 B1
Wendell Park Prim
Sch W12 . . . . 38 B4
Wendell Rd W12 . . . 38 B4
Wendle Ct SW8 . . . 162 A3
Wendling NW5 . . . . 12 B3
Wendon St E3 . . . . . 26 B4
Wendover SE17 . . . 152 A1

Wendover Ct
Acton W3 . . . . 20 A1
Becontree SW2 . . . . 20 B1
4 Child's Hill NW2 . . 1 C1
W1 . . . . 103 B3
Wendover Ho W1 . . 103 B3
Wendover Rd
NW10 . . . . 21 B3
Wengham Ho W12 . . 29 C2
Wenham Ho SW8 . 160 C1
Wenlake Ho EC1 . . 96 C2
Wenlock Ct N1 . . . . 87 C1
Wenlock Rd N1 . . . . 87 A1
Wenlock St N1 . . . . 87 B1
Wennington Rd
E3 . . . . 25 C3
Wensdale Ho E5 . . . . 7 C2
Wensleydale Ho 8
N4 . . . . 6 B4
Wentworth Cres
SE15 . . . . 49 C3
Wentworth Ct
W6 . . . . 154 A3
Wandsworth SW18 . 59 A1
Wentworth Dwellings
E1 . . . . 110 C2
Wentworth Ho 2
SE3 . . . . 53 B3
Wentworth Mews
E3 . . . . 26 B2
Wentworth St E1 . . 111 A3
Werrington St
NW1 . . . . 83 A1
Werter Rd SW15 . . . 58 A3
Wesleyan Pl NW5 . . 13 A4
Wesley Ave NW10 . . 20 C2
Wesley Cl
Finsbury Pk N7 . . . . 5 B2
SE17 . . . . 150 B3
Wesley Ct W1 . . . . 103 C3
Wesley Rd SE17 . . . 64 C1
Wesley Rd NW10 . . 20 B4
Wesley Sq W11 . . . . 31 A3
Wesley St W1 . . . . 103 C3
Wessex Ct SW15 . . . 57 C2
Wessex Gardens Prim
Sch NW11 . . . . . . 1 A3
Wessex Gdns NW11 . 1 A3
Wessex Ho
SE1 . . . . 153 A1
4 Tufnell Pk N19 . . . 4 C1
Wessex St E2 . . . . . 25 B2
Wessex Way NW11 . 1 A3
West 12 Sh Ctr
W12 . . . . 39 C4
Westacott Cl N19 . . 4 C3
West Acton Prim Sch
W3 . . . . 28 A3
West Arbour St
E1 . . . . 32 C3
West Bank N16 . . . . . 7 A4
West Barnes Rd NW2 10 A3
West Block 18 EL . . 32 B2
Westbourne Ave
W3 . . . . 28 C3
Westbourne Cres
W2 . . . . 115 B4
Westbourne Ct
W2 . . . . 100 C2
Westbourne Gdns
W2 . . . . 100 A2
Westbourne Gr
Notting Hill W2,
W11 . . . . 31 C3
W11 . . . . 31 B2 113 A4

WESTBOURNE
GREEN 88 A2
Westbourne Gr Mews
7 W11 . . . . 31 C3
Westbourne Gr Terr
W2 . . . . 100 A1
Westbourne Ho
SW1 . . . . 146 A2
Westbourne Park Rd
Notting Hill W11 . . . 31 C3
W11 . . . . 31 B3
Westbourne Park Sta
W11 . . . . 31 B4
Westbourne Park
Villas W2 . . . . . . 100 A3
Westbourne Rd
N7 . . . . 14 B2
Westbourne St
W2 . . . . 115 B4
Westbourne Terr
W2 . . . . 101 A2
Westbourne Terrace
Mews W2 . . . . . . 100 C2
Westbourne Terrace
Rd W2 . . . . 100 C3
Westbridge Cl
W12 . . . . 29 C1
Westbridge Prim Sch
SW11 . . . . 168 A4
Westbridge Rd
SW11 . . . . 168 A4
WEST
BROMPTON 156 A4
West Brompton Sta
SW5 . . . . 141 C1
Westbrook Ho
E2 . . . . 25 B2
6 Clapham Pk SW4 . 61 B2
Westbury Ct SW4 . . 61 A1
Westbury Ho 6
NW10 . . . . 8 A1
Westbush Ct 1
W12 . . . . 39 A4
West Carriage Dr
W2 . . . . 116 A2
West Central St
WC1 . . . . 106 A2
Westchester Ho
W2 . . . . 102 C2
Westcliff Ho 13
N1 . . . . 15 C2
Westcombe Ct 1
SE3 . . . . 53 B3
Westcombe Hill SE3,
SE10 . . . . 53 C4
Westcombe Park Rd
SE3 . . . . 53 B3
Westcombe Park Sta
SE3 . . . . 43 C1
Westcott Ho 14
E14 . . . . 34 A2
Westcott Rd SE17 . . 48 A4
West Cotts NW6 . . . 10 C3
Westcroft Cl NW2 . . 10 A4
Westcroft Ct 3
W6 . . . . 38 C2
Westcroft Sq W6 . . . 38 C2
Westcroft Way
NW2 . . . . 10 A4
West Cromwell Rd
W14 . . . . 141 A2
West Cross Route W10,
W11 . . . . 30 C2
Westdean Cl
SW18 . . . . 59 A1

Westdown Rd E15 . . .19 B4
WEST DULWICH . . .75 B2
West Dulwich Sta
  SE21 . . . . .75 C3
West Eaton Pl
  SW1 . . . . .145 B4
West Eaton Pl Mews
  SW1 . . . . .145 B4
West Ella Rd NW10 . .8 A1
West End Ct NW6 . . .11 A1
West End La NW6 . . .11 A2
Westerdale Ct N5 . . .15 A4
Westerdale Rd 2
  SE10 . . . . .43 B2
Westerham NW1 . . .82 C3
Westerham Ho
  SE1 . . . . .137 C2
West Ferry Rd W3 . . .28 C3
Western Avenue Bsns
  Pk W3 . . . . .20 A1
Western Beach Apts
  E16 . . . . .35 C1
Western Ct
  4 Dagenham W3 . .28 C3
  5 Kilburn W9 . . . . .23 B3
Western Eye Hospl
  The NW1 . . . . .102 C4
Western Gateway
  E16 . . . . .35 C2
Western Ho 5
  W9 . . . . .23 B1
Western La SW12 . . .72 C4
Western Mews
  W9 . . . . .23 B1
Western Pl 18
  SE16 . . . . .40 B4
Western Rd
  Becontree NW10 . . .20 B1
  Brixton SW9 . . . . . .62 C4
Westferry Sta 33 C2
Westfield Cl
  SW10 . . . . .156 C1
Westfield Ct 1
  W10 . . . . .22 C2
Westfield Ho 6
  SE16 . . . . .40 C2
Westfield London Shop
  Ctr W12 . . . . .30 C1
Westfields SW13 . . .56 B4
Westfields Ave
  SW13 . . . . .56 A4
Westfields Rd W3 . . .28 A4
Westfield Way E1 . . .26 A1
West Garden Pl
  W2 . . . . .102 B1
Westgate Bsns Ctr
  2 Kensal Town
  W10 . . . . .23 A1
  North Kensington
  W10 . . . . .22 C2
Westgate Ct 15
  SW9 . . . . .62 C4
Westgate St E8 . . . .25 A4
Westgate Terr
  SW10 . . . . .156 B4
West Gdns E1 . . . . . .32 A2
West Halkin St
  SW1 . . . . .131 B2
West Hall Rd TW9 . .45 A2
WEST
  HAMPSTEAD 10 C4
West Hampstead
  Mews NW6 . . . . . . .11 A2
West Hampstead Sta
  NW6 . . . . .10 C2
West Hampstead
  Thameslink Sta
  NW6 . . . . .10 C2
West Harding St
  EC4 . . . . .107 C2
Westhay Gdns
  SW14 . . . . .55 A2
West Heath Ave
  NW11 . . . . .1 C4
West Heath Cl NW3 . .1 C1
West Heath Ct
  NW11 . . . . .1 C3
West Heath Dr
  NW11 . . . . .1 C4
West Heath Gdns
  NW3 . . . . .1 C1
West Heath Rd
  NW3 . . . . .2 A1
WEST HILL 58 B1
West Hill SW15 . . . .58 A1
Westhill Ct
  W11 . . . . .31 B2 113 A4
West Hill Ct N6 . . . . .3 C1
Westhill Pk
  Dartmouth Pk N6 . . . .3 C2
  Highgate N6 . . . . .3 B2
West Hill Prim Sch 17
  SW18 . . . . .58 C2
West Hill Rd SW18 . .58 B1
West Ho 19 SW12 . . .73 B4
Westhope Ho 29
  E2 . . . . .24 C2 99 C3
Westhorpe Rd
  SW15 . . . . .57 B4
West House Cl
  SW19 . . . . .70 A3
West India Ave
  E14 . . . . .33 C1
West India Dock Rd
  E14 . . . . .33 C2
West India Ho 1
  E14 . . . . .33 C2
West India Quay Sta
  E14 . . . . .33 C2
WEST
  KENSINGTON . . .140 B3
West Kensington Ct
  W14 . . . . .140 C2
West Kensington
  Mans W14 . . . . . . .140 C2
West Kensington Sta
  W14 . . . . .140 C2
Westmore Ct
  SW15 . . . . .58 A2
Westmoreland Ho
  NW10 . . . . .21 C2
Westmoreland Pl
  SW1 . . . . .146 B1
Westmoreland Rd
  Barnes SW13 . . . . .46 C2
  Camberwell SE17 . .48 C4
Westmoreland St
  W1 . . . . .103 C3
Westmoreland Terr
  SW1 . . . . .146 B1
WEST NORWOOD . .75 B1
West Norwood Sta
  SE27 . . . . .75 A1
Westonbirt Ct 6
  SE15 . . . . .49 B4
Weston Ct N4 . . . . . .6 B1
West One Ho W1 . .104 C3
West One Sh Ctr
  W1 . . . . .104 A1
Weston Ho
  3 Brondesbury
  NW6 . . . . .10 A1
  8 South Hackney
  E9 . . . . .25 B4
Weston Rd W4 . . . . .37 B3
Weston Rise N1,
  WC1 . . . . .95 A4
Weston St SE1 . . . .137 C4
Weston Wlk 8 E8,
  E9 . . . . .17 A1
Westover Hill NW3 . .1 C2
Westover Rd
  SW18 . . . . .59 B1
West Park Ave
  TW9 . . . . .45 A2
West Park Rd
  TW9 . . . . .44 C2
West Parkside
  Greenwich SE10 . . . .43 B3
  Greenwich SE10 . . . .43 C2
West Plaza E14 . . . .42 A1
Westpoint SW15 . . .57 C1
West Point 2
  SE1 . . . . .153 B2
Westpoint Trad Est
  W3 . . . . .28 A4
Westpott St E1 . . . . .61 C2
West Poultry Ave
  EC1 . . . . .108 A3
West Quarters
  W12 . . . . .29 C3
West Rd
  Chelsea SW3 . . . . .159 A4
  Clapham Pk SW4 . . .61 C2
Westrow SW15 . . . . .57 B1
West Row NW10 . . . .23 A1
West Sheen Vale
  TW9 . . . . .54 B3
Westside 11 W6 . . . .38 C2
Westside Ct 1
  W9 . . . . .23 C1
West Silvertown Sta
  E16 . . . . .35 C1
West Smithfield
  EC1 . . . . .108 B3
West Sq SE11 . . . . .136 A1
West St
  50 Bethnal Green
  E2 . . . . .25 A3
  Soho WC2 . . . . . . .105 C1
West Temple Sheen
  SW14 . . . . .55 A2
West Tenter St
  E1 . . . . .111 A1
Westvale Mews
  W3 . . . . .38 A4
Westview Cl
  North Kensington
  W10 . . . . .30 B3
  Willesden NW10 . . . .8 B3
Westville Rd W12 . . .38 C4
West Warwick Pl
  SW1 . . . . .146 C3
Westway W10,
  W12 . . . . .29 C2
Westway (Elevated
  Rd) W10 . . . . .31 B4
Westway Lo 18
  W2 . . . . .31 C4
Westwell NW5 . . . . .12 C2
Westwick Gdns
  W14 . . . . .39 C4
Westwood Ho
  NW10 . . . . .21 A1
Westwood Gdns
  SW13 . . . . .56 B4
Westwood Ho
  6 Shepherd's Bush
  W12 . . . . .30 B1
  5 Stoke Newington
  N4 . . . . .6 C4
Westwood Park Trad
  Est W3 . . . . .20 A1
Westwood Rd
  SW13 . . . . .56 B4
Wetherby Gdns
  SW5 . . . . .142 C3
Wetherby Mans
  SW5 . . . . .142 A2
Wetherby Mews
  SW5 . . . . .142 B2
Wetherby Pl SW7 . .143 A3
Wetherby Prep Sch
  SW12 . . . . . . .22 C2 113 B4
Wetherell Rd E9 . . . .25 C4
Wevco Wharf
  SE15 . . . . .50 A4
Wexford Ho 11 E1 . .32 B4
Wexford Rd SW12 . .72 B4
Weybourne St
  SW18 . . . . .71 B2
Weybridge Ct 19
  SE16 . . . . .40 A1
Weybridge Ho N4 . . .6 B4
Weybridge Point 11
  SW11 . . . . .169 A2
Weydown Cl SW19 . .70 A3
Weyhill Ho 26 SE5 . .48 B1
Weyhill Rd 11 E1 . . .111 C2
Wey Ho NW8 . . . . . .89 C1
Weymouth Ct
  2 Haggerston E2 . . .24 B3
  15 Streatham SW2 . .74 B4
Weymouth Ho
  Fitzrovia W1 . . . . . .104 B4
  South Lambeth
  SW8 . . . . .162 C2
Weymouth Mews
  W1 . . . . .104 A4
Weymouth St W1 . .104 A4
Weymouth Terr
  E2 . . . . .24 B3
Whadcoat St N4 . . . .5 C2
Whaddon Ho
  10 Camberwell
  SE5 . . . . .64 A4
  SW1 . . . . .131 A3
Wharfdale Rd N1 . . .84 B2
Wharfedale Ct 5
  E5 . . . . .17 C4
Wharfedale St
  SW10 . . . . .142 A1
Wharf La 13 E14 . . . .33 B3
Wharf Pl E2 . . . . . . .25 A4
Wharf Rd
  King's Cross NW1 . . .83 C3
  Shoreditch N1 . . . . . .86 C1
Wharf Road E15 . . . .27 C4
Wharfside Rd E16 . . .35 A4
Wharf St E16 . . . . . .35 A4

West Mall
  W11 . . . . . . .31 C1 113 C2
Westmark Point 18
  SW15 . . . . .69 A3

Westmead SW15 . . .57 A1
West Mews SW1 . . .146 C3
Westmill Ct N4 . . . . .6 B2
WESTMINSTER . . .133 A1
Westminster Abbey*
  SW1 . . . . .134 A2
Westminster Abbey
  Choir Sch SW1 . . . .133 C2
Westminster Acad
  W2 . . . . .31 C4
Westminster Acad
  (Sch of English)
  W1 . . . . .105 A2
Westminster Boating
  Base SW1 . . . . .161 B4
Westminster Bridge
  SE1, SW1 . . . . .134 B3
Westminster Bridge
  Rd SE1 . . . . .134 C3
Westminster Cath*
  SW1 . . . . .132 C1
Westminster Cath
  Choir Sch SW1 . . . .147 A4
Westminster Cath RC
  Prim Sch SW1 . . . .147 C2
Westminster City Hall
  SW1 . . . . .133 A2
Westminster City Sch
  SW1 . . . . .133 A1
Westminster Coll
  W1 . . . . .119 B4
Westminster Ct
  22 Rotherhithe
  SE16 . . . . .32 C1
  5 Wandsworth
  SW18 . . . . .58 C2
Westminster
  Dragons Mus*
  SW6 . . . . .58 A4
Westminster Gdns
  SW1 . . . . .148 A4
Westminster
  Kingsway Coll (King's
  Cross Centre)
  WC1 . . . . .94 C3
Westminster
  Kingsway Coll
  (Regent's Park Ctr)
  NW1 . . . . .92 C2
Westminster
  Kingsway Coll
  (Victoria Centre)
  SW1 . . . . .147 B4
Westminster Pier
  SW1 . . . . .134 B3
Westminster Sch
  SW1 . . . . .134 A2
Westminster Under
  Sch SW1 . . . . .147 B4
Westmore Ct

Wharf View Ct 🔞
E14 . . . . .34 B3
Wharncliffe Ho �
SW15 . . . . .57 B2
Wharton Cl NW10 . . .8 A2
Wharton Ho SE1 . . .138 C2
Wharton St WC1 . . . .95 A3
Whateley Rd SE22 . . .64 B2
Whatman Ho 🔟
E14 . . . . .33 B3
Wheatland Ho 🔟
SE22 . . . . .64 A4
Wheatlands Rd
SW17 . . . . .72 C1
Wheatley Ho
Gospel Oak NW5 . . . .13 A4
🔳 Putney SW15 . . . .68 C4
Wheatley St W1 . . .103 C3
Wheat Sheaf Cl
E14 . . . . .42 A2
Wheatsheaf La
Fulham SW6 . . . . . . .47 B3
SW8 . . . . .162 B2
Wheatsheaf Terr
SW6 . . . . .155 A1
Wheatstone Ho 🔟
W10 . . . . .31 A4
Wheatstone Rd
W10 . . . . .31 A4
Wheeler Ct 🔳
SW11 . . . . .59 C4
Wheeler Gdns N1 . . .84 C4
Wheeler La E1 . . . .110 C4
Wheelhouse The 🔳
E14 . . . . .42 A1
Wheelwright St
N7 . . . . .14 B1
Wheldon Ct SE1 . . .138 C4
Wheler Ho
E1 . . . . .24 B1 98 C1
Wheler St
E1 . . . . .24 B1 98 C1
Whellock Rd W4 . . . .38 A3
Whetstone Park
WC2 . . . . .106 C2
Whewell Rd N19 . . . .5 A2
Whichcote St SE1 . .121 B1
Whidborne Bldgs
WC1 . . . . .94 A3
Whidborne Cl SE8 . .51 C1
Whidborne St WC1 . .94 B3
Whippingham Ho 🔞
E3 . . . . .26 B2
Whiskin St EC1 . . . .96 A3
Whistler Mews 🔞
SE15 . . . . .49 B3
Whistlers Ave
SW11 . . . . .157 C1
Whistler St N5 . . . . .15 A3
Whistler Twr
SW10 . . . . .156 C1
Whistler Wlk
SW10 . . . . .157 A2
Whiston Ho 🔟 N1 . .15 A1
Whiston Rd E2 . . . . .24 C4
Whitbread Ctr EC1 . .97 B1
Whitbread Rd SE4 . .66 B3
Whitburn Rd SE13 . .67 B3
Whitby Ave NW10 . .20 A2
Whitby Ct 🔳 N7 . . . .14 A4
Whitby Ho NW8 . . . .78 C3
Whitby St
E1 . . . . .24 B1 98 C2
Whitcher Cl SE14 . . .51 A4

Whitcher Pl NW1 . . . .13 B2
Whitchurch Ho 🔞
W10 . . . . .30 C3
Whitchurch Rd
W11 . . . . .30 C2
Whitcomb Ct W1 . . .119 C3
Whitcomb St
WC2 . . . . .119 C3
Whitcome Mews
TW9 . . . . .45 A2
Whiteacre Mews
SE11 . . . . .149 C1
Whiteadder Way
E14 . . . . .42 A2
Whitear Wlk E15 . . .19 C2
Whitebeam Cl
SW9 . . . . .163 A1
Whitebeam Ho 🔳
NW3 . . . . .12 B2
White Bear Pl 🔳
NW3 . . . . .11 C4
White Bear Yd EC1 . .95 B1
WHITECHAPEL . .110 C1
Whitechapel Gall ★
E1 . . . . .111 A2
Whitechapel High St
E1 . . . . .111 A2
Whitechapel Mkt★
E1 . . . . .111 C3
Whitechapel Rd
E1 . . . . .32 A4
Whitechapel Sta
E1 . . . . .32 A4
Whitechurch La 🔳
E1 . . . . .111 B2
Whitechurch Pas 🔳
E1 . . . . .111 B2
White City W10 . . . .30 B3
White City Cl W12 . .30 B2
White City Est
W12 . . . . .30 A2
White City Rd
W12 . . . . .30 B2
White City Sta
W12 . . . . .30 B2
Whitecliff Ho
SW18 . . . . .59 A1
White Conduit St
N1 . . . . .85 C2
Whitecross Pl
EC2 . . . . .109 C4
Whitecross St EC1 . .97 A1
*White Cube The, Art
Gallery*★
N1 . . . . .24 A2 98 A3
Whitefield Cl
SW15 . . . . .58 A1
Whitefriars St
EC4 . . . . .107 C1
Whitehall SW1 . . . .134 A4
Whitehall Ct SW1 . .120 B1
Whitehall Gdns
Chiswick W4 . . . . . . .45 A4
SW1 . . . . .120 A1
Whitehall Mews 🔳
N19 . . . . .4 B3
Whitehall Park Rd
W4 . . . . .45 A4
Whitehall Pk N19 . . . .4 B3
Whitehall Pl WC2,
SW1 . . . . .120 A1
White Hart Ct
EC2 . . . . .110 A3
White Hart La
Mortlake SW13 . . . . .56 A4
Willesden NW10 . . . .8 B2

White Hart St
Holborn EC4 . . . . . . .108 B2
Kennington SE11 . . . .149 C2
White Hart Yd
SE1 . . . . .123 B1
Whitehaven St
NW8 . . . . .90 A1
Whitehead Cl
SW18 . . . . .71 B4
Whitehead Ho 🔳
SW15 . . . . .57 C2
Whitehead's Gr
SW3 . . . . .144 B3
White Ho 🔳
🔳 Battersea
SW11 . . . . .167 C2
🔳 Streatham SW4 . .73 C4
Whitehorn Ho 🔳
E1 . . . . .32 B1
White Horse La
E1 . . . . .32 C4
Whitehorse Mews
SE1 . . . . .136 A2
Whitehorse Rd E1 . .33 A4
White Horse Rd
E1 . . . . .33 A3
White Horse St
W1 . . . . .118 B1
White Horse Yd
EC2 . . . . .109 B2
White Ho The
NW1 . . . . .92 B2
**White House Prep
Sch** SW12 . . . . . . .73 C3
White Kennett St
E1 . . . . .110 B2
Whitelands Cres
SW18 . . . . .70 A4
Whitelands Ho
SW3 . . . . .145 A2
Whiteley Ho 🔳
SW4 . . . . .73 C4
Whiteleys Ctr 🔞
W2 . . . . .100 B1
White Lion Ct
EC3 . . . . .110 A1
White Lion Hill
EC4 . . . . .122 B4
White Lion St N1 . . .85 C1
White Lo NW11 . . . . .1 B3
Whitelock Ho 🔳
E9 . . . . .17 C2
White Lyon Ct
EC2 . . . . .108 C4
Whiteness Ho 🔞
SW9 . . . . .173 B4
White Post La E9 . . .18 C2
White Post St SE14,
SE15 . . . . .50 B3
White Rd EC2 . . . . .110 A3
White's Grounds
SE1 . . . . .138 B4
White's Grounds Est
SE1 . . . . .138 B4
White's Row E1 . . . .110 C3
White's Sq SW4 . . . .61 C3
Whitestone La NW3 . .2 B1
Whitestone Wlk
NW3 . . . . .2 B1
Whitethorn St E3 . . .33 C4
White Twr Way E1 . .33 A4
Whitfield Ct SW4 . . .172 A3
Whitfield Gdns
W1 . . . . .105 A4
Whitfield Ho NW8 . . .90 A1
Whitfield Pl W1 . . . . .93 A1

Whitfield St W1 . . . .105 A4
Whitgift Ho
Battersea SW11 . . . .168 A4
Lambeth SE11 . . . . .148 C4
Whitgift St SE11 . . .148 C4
Whitington Ave
EC3 . . . . .110 A1
Whitley Ho SW1 . . .161 A4
Whitlock Dr SW19 . .70 A3
Whitman Ho 🔞 E2 . .25 B2
Whitman Rd E3 . . . .26 A1
Whitmore Gdns
NW10 . . . . .22 B3
Whitmore Ho 🔞
E1 . . . . .24 A4
Whitmore Prim Sch
N1 . . . . .87 C3
Whitmore Rd N1 . . . .24 A4
Whitnell Ct 🔳
SW15 . . . . .57 C2
Whitnell Way
SW15 . . . . .57 C2
Whitney Ho 🔲
SE22 . . . . .64 A4
Whitstable Ho 🔢
W10 . . . . .30 C3
Whittaker Ct SW4 . .172 B3
Whittaker St SW1 . .145 B3
Whittaker Way 🔟
SE1 . . . . .153 C4
Whittingham Ct
W4 . . . . .46 A3
Whittingstall Mans
SW6 . . . . .165 A3
Whittingstall Rd
SW6 . . . . .165 A3
Whittington Hospl
The N19 . . . . .4 B2
Whittlebury Ho N4 . .6 B4
Whittlesey St SE1 . .121 C1
Whitton NW3 . . . . . .12 B1
Whitton Wlk E3 . . . .26 C2
Whitworth Ho
SE1 . . . . .137 A1
Whitworth St
SE10 . . . . .43 A1
Whorlton Rd SE15 . .65 A4
Whytlaw Ho 🔟 E3 . .33 B4
Wicker St 🔢 E1 . . . .32 A3
Wickfield Ho 🔟
SE16 . . . . .139 C3
Wickford Ho 🔳
E1 . . . . .25 B1
Wickford St E1 . . . . .25 B1
Wickham Cl E1 . . . . .32 B4
Wickham Gdns
SE4 . . . . .66 B4
Wickham Ho
SW15 . . . . .57 C1
Wickham Mews
SE4 . . . . .51 B1
Wickham Rd SE4 . . .66 B3
Wickham St SE11 . .148 C2
Wick La
Hackney E3 . . . . .18 B1
Stratford Marsh E3 . .26 C4
Wicklow Ho N16 . . . . .7 B3
Wicklow St WC1 . . . .94 C4
Wick Rd
Hackney E9 . . . . .17 C2
Hackney E9 . . . . .18 A2
Wickstead Ho
TW8 . . . . .36 B1
Wicksteed Ho
SE1 . . . . .137 A1

Wick Village 🔳
E15 . . . . .18 B3
Wickway Ct 🔳
SE15 . . . . .49 B4
Wickwood St SE5 . . .48 A1
Widdenham Rd
N7 . . . . .14 B4
Widecombe Ho 🔞
SE5 . . . . .48 B1
Widegate St E1 . . . .110 B3
Widford 🔳 NW1 . . . .13 A2
Widford Ho N1 . . . . .86 A1
Widley Rd W9 . . . . . .23 C1
Widnes Ho 🔟 N7 . . .14 C3
Wigmore Hall★
W1 . . . . .104 A2
Wigmore Pl W1 . . . .104 A2
Wigmore Rd W1 . . . .103 C2
Wigram Ct SW11 . . .168 A4
Wigram Ho 🔟 E14 . .34 A2
Wigton Pl SE11 . . . .149 C1
Wilberforce Ho 🔳
SW11 . . . . .59 C4
Wilberforce Mews 🔳
SW4 . . . . .61 C3
Wilberforce Prim Sch
W10 . . . . .23 A2
Wilbraham Ho
SW8 . . . . .162 A1
Wilbraham Pl
SW1 . . . . .145 B4
Wilby Mews
W11 . . . . . .31 B1 113 A2
Wilcox Cl SW8 . . . . .162 B2
Wilcox Ho 🔳 E3 . . . .33 B4
Wilcox Pl SW1 . . . .133 A1
Wilcox Rd SW8 . . . .162 A2
Wildcroft Manor
SW15 . . . . .69 B4
Wildcroft Rd
SW15 . . . . .69 B4
Wild Ct WC2 . . . . . .106 C2
Wilde Cl E8 . . . . .24 C4
Wilde Pl SW18 . . . . .71 C4
Wilderness Mews
SW4 . . . . .61 A3
Wilderton Rd N16 . . . .7 A4
Wild Goose Dr
SE14 . . . . .50 B2
Wilding Ho 🔟 E9 . . .17 C2
Wild's Rents SE1 . . .138 A2
Wild St WC2 . . . . . .106 C1
Wildwood Gr NW3 . . .2 B3
Wildwood Rd NW11 . .2 B4
Wildwood Rise
NW11 . . . . .2 B3
Wildwood Terr NW3,
NW11 . . . . .2 B3
Wilfred Fienburgh Ho
N7 . . . . .13 C4
Wilfred St SW1 . . . .132 C2
Wilfrid Gdns W3 . . . .28 B4
Wilkes Rd 🔢 TW8 . . .44 A4
Wilkes St E1 . . . . . .111 A4
Wilkie Ho SW1 . . . . .147 C2
Wilkin St Mews
NW1 . . . . .13 A2
Wilkins Ho SW1 . . . .160 C4
Wilkinson Ho N1 . . . .87 C1
Wilkinson St SW8 . .162 C1
Wilkinson Way
W4 . . . . .37 C2
Wilkin St NW5 . . . . .13 A2

Wilks Pl N1 . . . . .24 A3
Willan Wall E16 . . . . . .35 B2
Willard St SW8 . . . . . . .61 A4
Willbury Ho **4** N7 . .13 C3
Willcott Rd W3 . . . . . . .28 A1
Willenfield Rd
  NW10 . . . . .20 B3
WILLESDEN **8** B1
Willesden Community
  Hospl The NW10 . . . .8 C1
WILLESDEN
  GREEN **22** A4
Willesden Green Sta
  NW2 . . . . .9 B2
Willesden Junction
  Sta NW10 . . . . .21 B2
Willesden La NW2,
  NW6 . . . . .9 C2
Willesden Sports Ctr
  W10 . . . . .22 A2
Willes Rd NW5 . . . . . .13 A2
Willett Ho SW9 . . . . . .62 A4
William Banfield Ho
  10 SW6 . . . . .164 C2
William Blake Ho **8**
  SE1 . . . . .49 C1
William Bonney Est **10**
  SW4 . . . . .61 C3
William Booth Meml
  Training Coll SE5 . .48 C1
William Brown Ct
  SE27 . . . . .75 A2
William Caslon Ho **28**
  E2 . . . . .25 A3
William Channing Ho
  6 E2 . . . . .25 A2
William Cl SE13 . . . .67 B4
William Davis Prim
  Sch **2** E2 . . . . .24 C1 99 B2
William Dromey Ct
  NW6 . . . . .10 B1
William Dunbar Ho
  NW6 . . . . .23 B3
William Ellis Sch
  NW5 . . . . .3 C1
William Ellis Way **18**
  SE16 . . . . .153 C4
William Evans Ho **2**
  SE8 . . . . .40 C2
William Gdns
  SW15 . . . . .57 A2
William Guy Gdns **17**
  E3 . . . . .27 A2
William Harvey Ho **1**
  SW19 . . . . .70 A3
William Hogarth Sch
  The **15** W4 . . . . . . .38 A1
William Hunt Mans
  SW13 . . . . .47 B4
William IV St
  WC2 . . . . .120 A3
William Margrie Cl **1**
  SE15 . . . . .49 C1
William Mews
  SW1 . . . . .131 A3
William Morris Acad
  W6 . . . . .39 C1
William Morris Ho
  W6 . . . . .47 C4
William Morris Way
  SW6 . . . . .166 C1
William Patten Prim
  Sch **3** N16 . . . . .7 B2
William Pl **1** E3 . . . .26 B3
William Rathbone Ho
  8 E2 . . . . .25 A2

Willan Rd NW1 . . . . . .92 C3
William Rushbrooke
  Ho **4** SE16 . . . . . .153 B4
William Saville Ho **2**
  NW6 . . . . .23 B3
William's Bldgs **1**
  E2 . . . . .25 B1
Williams Cl SW6 . . . .154 B2
Williams Coll EC1 . .107 C3
Williams Ho
  11 Bow E3 . . . . . . .26 C2
  9 Hackney E9 . . . .25 A4
  14 Streatham SW2 .74 A3
Williams La SW14 . . .45 B1
Williamson Cl
  SE10 . . . . .43 B1
Williamson St
  SE17 . . . . .150 C1
William St SW7 . . . .14 A4
William Sq **18**
  SE16 . . . . .33 A2
William St SW1 . . . .131 A3
Willingham Cl **2**
  NW5 . . . . .13 B3
Willingham Terr
  NW5 . . . . .13 B3
Willington Rd
  SW9 . . . . .62 A4
Willis Ho **8** E14 . . . . .34 A2
Willis St E14 . . . . .34 A2
Willoughby Ho
  EC2 . . . . .109 B3
  24 Wapping E1 . . .32 A1
Willoughby Rd
  NW3 . . . . .11 C4
Willoughby St
  WC1 . . . . .106 A3
Willoughbys The
  SW14 . . . . .56 A3
Willow Ave SW13 . . . .46 B1
Willowbank SW6 . . . .58 A4
Willowbank Rd
  SE15 . . . . .49 B4
Willow Bridge Rd
  N1 . . . . .15 B2
Willow Cotts TW9 . . .44 C4
Willow Ct
  Brixton SW9 . . . . .173 B3
  Chiswick W4 . . . . .46 A3
  EC2 . . . . .24 A1 98 A2
  Islington N7 . . . . .14 B3
  40 Paddington W2 . .31 C4
  5 Streatham SW16 .74 B1
Willowdene
  Highgate N6 . . . . .3 C3
  1 Peckham SE15 . . .50 A2
  5 SE15 . . . . .50 A3
Willow Farm La
  SW15 . . . . .57 A4
Willow Hall NW3 . . . .11 C4
Willow Ho
  4 Maitland Pk
    NW3 . . . . .12 B2
  North Kensington
    W10 . . . . .22 C1
Willow Lo
  Fulham SW6 . . . . .47 C2
  Putney SW15 . . . . .57 A4
Willow Lodge **10**
  SW8 . . . . .61 A4
Willowmere SE13 . . .67 A2
Willow Pl SW1 . . . .147 A4

Willow Rd
  Ealing W5 . . . . .36 A4
  Hampstead NW3 . . . .11 C4
Willow St
  EC2 . . . . .24 A1 98 A2
Willows Terr
  NW10 . . . . .21 B3
Willow Tree Cl
  14 Old Ford E3 . . . .26 B4
  Wandsworth SW18 .71 A3
Willow Vale W12 . . . .29 C1
Willow Way **9**
  W11 . . . . .30 C2
Willow Wlk SE1 . . . .152 B4
Willsbridge Ct **1**
  SE15 . . . . .49 B4
Wilman Gr E8 . . . . . . .16 C1
Wilmcote Ho W2 . . . .100 A4
Wilmer Gdns **22**
  N1 . . . . .24 A4
Wilmer Ho **3** E3 . . . .26 A3
Wilmer Lea Cl E15 . .19 C1
Wilmer Pl N16 . . . . .7 B2
Wilmers Ct **5**
  NW10 . . . . .20 C4
Wilmington Ave
  W4 . . . . .45 C3
Wilmington Sq
  WC1 . . . . .95 B3
Wilmington St
  WC1 . . . . .95 B3
Wilmot Cl SE15 . . . . .49 C3
Wilmot Pl NW1 . . . . .13 B1
Wilmot St E2 . . . . .25 A1
Wilna Rd SW18 . . . . . .71 B4
Wilsham St
  W11 . . . . . .31 A1 112 A2
Wilshaw St SE14 . . . .51 C2
Wilson Gr SE16 . . . . .40 A4
Wilson Ho
  30 Clapham SW8 . .171 B1
  South Hampstead
    NW6 . . . . .11 B1
Wilson Rd SE5 . . . . . .49 A2
Wilson's Pl E14 . . . . .33 B3
Wilson's Rd W6 . . . . .39 C1
Wilson St EC2 . . . . . .109 C4
Wiltern Ct NW2 . . . . .10 A2
Wilton Ave W4 . . . . . .38 A1
Wilton Cres SW1 . . .131 B3
Wilton Ct
  7 Richmond
    TW10 . . . . .54 A2
  7 Stepney E1 . . . . .32 A3
Wilton Est E8 . . . . .16 C2
Wilton Ho **3** SE22 . .64 A4
Wilton Mews
  SW1 . . . . .131 C2
Wilton Pl SW1 . . . . .131 B3
Wilton Rd SW1 . . . .146 C4
Wilton Row SW1 . . .131 B3
Wilton Sq N1 . . . . .87 B4
Wilton St SW1 . . . . .132 A2
Wilton Terr SW1 . . . .131 B3
Wilton Villas N1 . . . . .87 B3
Wilton Way E8 . . . . . .16 C2
Wiltshire Cl SW3 . . .144 C3
Wiltshire Ct **2** N4 . . .5 B3
Wiltshire Rd SW9 . . .62 C4
Wiltshire Row N1 . . . .87 C3
Wimbart Rd SW2 . . . .74 B4
Wimbledon Lawn
  Tennis Mus *
  SW19 . . . . .70 A1

Wimbledon Park Ct
  SW19 . . . . .70 B3
Wimbledon Park
  Montessori Sch
  SW18 . . . . .70 C2
Wimbledon Park Prim
  Sch SW19 . . . . .71 A2
Wimbledon Park Rd
  SW18, SW19 . . . . .70 B3
Wimbledon Park Side
  SW19 . . . . .69 C3
Wimbledon Park Sta
  SW19 . . . . .71 C1
Wimbledon Stadium
  Bsns Ctr SW17 . . . . . .71 A1
Wimbledon Windmill
  Mus * SW19 . . . . .69 B1
Wimbolt St
  E2 . . . . .24 C2 99 B4
Wimborne Ho
  Canning Town E16 . . .35 B2
  Marylebone NW1 . . . . .90 B1
  South Lambeth
    SW8 . . . . .163 A1
  Upper Tooting
    SW12 . . . . .73 B1
Wimbourne Ct N1 . . .87 B2
Wimbourne St N1 . . .87 B2
Wimpole Mews
  W1 . . . . .104 A3
Wimpole St W1 . . . .104 A2
Winans Wlk SW9 . . .173 B1
Winant Ho **19** E14 . .34 A2
Wincanton Rd
  SW18 . . . . .70 B4
Winchelsea Cl
  SW15 . . . . .57 C2
Winchelsea Ho **16**
  SE16 . . . . .40 B4
Winchelsea Rd
  NW10 . . . . .20 C4
Winchendon Rd
  SW6 . . . . .165 A4
Winchester Ave
  NW6 . . . . .10 A1
Winchester Cl
  SE17 . . . . .150 B3
Winchester Ct
  Richmond TW9 . . . . . .54 B4
  W8 . . . . .128 A4
Winchester Ho
  Bayswater W2 . . . . . .100 C1
  Chelsea SW3 . . . . . . .157 C3
  24 Tower Hamlets
    E3 . . . . .26 B2
  Winchester Pal *
    SE1 . . . . .123 B2
Winchester Pl
  8 Dalston E8 . . . . . .16 B3
  Highgate N6 . . . . .4 A3
Winchester Rd
  Highgate N6 . . . . .4 A3
  South Hampstead
    NW3 . . . . .11 C1
Winchester Sq
  SE1 . . . . .123 B2
Winchester St
  Acton W3 . . . . .37 B4
  SW1 . . . . .146 B2
Winchester Wlk
  SE1 . . . . .123 B2
Winchfield Ho
  SW15 . . . . .56 B1
Winch Ho
  Isle of Dogs E14 . . . . .42 A3
  SW10 . . . . .157 A2

Winchilsea Ho
  NW8 . . . . .89 C3
Wincott St SE11 . . .149 C3
Windermere
  NW1 . . . . .92 B4
  12 Putney SW15 . . .57 C1
Windermere Ave
  NW6 . . . . .23 A4
Windermere Ct
  SW13 . . . . .46 B4
Windermere Ho
  E3 . . . . .26 B1
Windermere Point **3**
  SE15 . . . . .50 B3
Windermere Rd
  N19 . . . . .4 B2
Winders Rd SW11 . . .168 A2
Windham Rd TW9 . . .54 B4
Windlass Pl SE8 . . . .41 A2
Windlesham Gr
  SW19 . . . . .69 C3
Windmill WC1 . . . . .106 C3
Windmill Alley **7**
  W4 . . . . .38 A2
Windmill Cl
  12 Bermondsey
    SE1 . . . . .153 C4
  4 Lewisham SE13 .52 B1
Windmill Ct NW2 . . . .10 A2
Windmill Dr
  Clapham SW4 . . . . . . .61 A2
  Cricklewood NW2 . . . .1 A1
Windmill Gdns
  SW2 . . . . .62 B1
Windmill Hill
  1 Hampstead
    NW3 . . . . .11 B4
  Hampstead NW3 . . . . .2 B1
Windmill Ho
  4 Millwall E14 . . . .41 C2
  SE1 . . . . .121 C2
Windmill La E15 . . . .19 C2
Windmill Pas **10**
  W4 . . . . .38 A2
Windmill Rd
  Chiswick W4 . . . . .38 A2
  Roehampton SW19 . . .69 A1
  Wandsworth SW18 . . .71 A1
Windmill Row
  SE11 . . . . .149 B1
Windmill St W1 . . . .105 B3
Windmill Wlk SE1 . .135 C4
Windrose Cl SE16 . . .40 C4
Windrush Cl
  Battersea SW11 . . . . .59 C3
  Chiswick W4 . . . . .45 B3
  4 Hackney E8 . . . . .16 C1
Windrush Ho
  NW8 . . . . .101 C4
Windrush Rd
  NW10 . . . . .20 C4
Windrush Sq SW9 . . .62 C3
Windsock Cl **1**
  SE16 . . . . .41 B2
Windsor Ct
  Battersea SW11 . . . . .167 C2
  Bayswater W2 . . . . . .114 A4
  Chelsea SW3 . . . . . . .144 B2
  2 Clapham SW4 . . .61 B3
  Fulham SW6 . . . . .58 A4
  26 Rotherhithe
    SE16 . . . . .32 C1
  4 Wandsworth
    SW18 . . . . .58 C2

Windsor Ct continued
West Hampstead
NW3 . . . .**10** C4
Windsor Gdns W9 . .**23** C1
Windsor Ho
4 Acton Green
W4 . . . .**37** B1
Brondesbury NW2 . . .**10** A2
4 Globe Town E2 . . .**25** C2
Regent's Pk NW1 . . . .**92** B4
Shoreditch N1 . . . . . .**87** A2
Stoke Newington N4 . .**6** B3
Windsor Pl SW1 . . .**147** A4
Windsor Rd
Richmond TW9 . . . . . .**44** B1
Upper Holloway N7 . . .**5** A1
Willesden NW2 . . . .**9** A2
Windsor St N1 . . . . .**86** B4
Windsor Terr N1 . . . .**97** A4
Windsor Way
W14 . . . .**140** A4
Windsor Wharf E9 . .**18** B3
Windsor Wlk SE5 . . .**48** C1
Windspoint Dr
SE15 . . . .**50** A4
Windus Rd N16 . . . . . .**7** B3
Windus Wlk N16 . . . . .**7** B3
Wine Cl E1 . . . .**32** B2
Wine Office Ct
EC4 . . . .**107** C2
Winfield Ho 3
SW11 . . . .**167** C2
Winford Ct 18
SE15 . . . .**49** C2
Winford Ho E3 . . . . . .**26** B4
Winforton St SE10 . .**52** B2
Winfrith Rd SW18 . .**71** B3
Wingate Ho
2 Bromley E3 . . . . . .**27** A2
8 Stoke Newington
N16 . . . .**7** A3
Wingate Rd W6 . . . .**39** A3
Wingfield Ct 5
E14 . . . .**34** C2
Wingfield Ho
Paddington NW6 . . . .**78** A2
8 Spitalfields
E2 . . . .**24** B2 **98** C3
Wingfield Mews
SE15 . . . .**64** C4
Wingfield St SE15 . . .**64** C4
Wingford Rd SW2 . .**62** A1
Wingham 3 NW5 . . . .**12** C2
Wingmore Rd
SE24 . . . .**63** B4
Wingrad Ho 18 E1 . . .**32** B4
Wingrave SE17 . . . . .**151** B3
Wingrave Rd W6 . . . .**47** B4
Wingreen 15 NW8 . . . .**78** B4
Winicotte Ho W2 . .**101** C4
Winifrede Paul Ho 7
N19 . . . .**13** A4
Winkley St 5 E2 . . . .**25** A3
Winkworth Cotts 14
E1 . . . .**25** A1
Winnett St W1 . . . .**119** B4
Winnington Ho
19 Kensal Town
W10 . . . .**23** A1
8 SE5 . . . .**48** B3
Winscombe St N19 . .**4** A2
Winsham Gr SW11 . .**60** C2
Winsham Ho NW1 . . .**93** C4
Winslade Rd SW2 . . .**62** A2

Winsland Mews
W2 . . . .**101** B3
Winsland St W2 . . .**101** B3
Winsley St W1 . . . .**105** A2
Winslow SE17 . . . . .**152** A1
Winslow Rd W6 . . . .**47** B4
Winstanley Rd
SW11 . . . .**59** C4
Winston Churchill
Britain at War
Experience★
SE1 . . . .**124** A1
Winston Ho WC1 . . . .**93** C2
Winston Rd N16 . . . .**15** C4
Winston Wlk 2
W4 . . . .**37** C2
Winterbourne Ho
W11 . . . .**31** A2 **112** A3
Winter Box Wlk
TW10 . . . .**54** B2
Winterbrook Rd
SE24 . . . .**63** B1
Winterfold Cl
SW19 . . . .**70** A2
Winterleys 7
NW6 . . . .**23** B3
Winter Lo 17
SE16 . . . .**153** C1
Winterslow Ho 20
SE5 . . . .**48** B1
Winterton Ho 15
E1 . . . .**32** B3
Winterton Pl
SW10 . . . .**157** A4
Winterwell Rd
SW2 . . . .**62** A2
Winthorpe Rd
SW15 . . . .**58** A3
Winthrop Ho 10
W12 . . . .**30** A2
Winthrop St 1 E1 . . .**32** A4
Winton Prim Sch
N1 . . . .**84** C1
Wirrall Ho 18
SE26 . . . .**76** C1
Wisbech 3 N4 . . . . . .**5** B3
Wisden Ho SW8 . . .**163** A3
Wise Rd E15 . . . .**27** C4
Wiseton Rd SW17 . . .**72** B3
Wisley Ho SW1 . . . .**147** B2
Wisley Rd SW11 . . . .**60** C2
Wisteria Ho SE4 . . . .**66** A4
Wisteria Rd SE13 . . .**67** C3
Wistow Ho 14 E2 . . .**24** C4
Witanhurst La N6 . . . .**3** C3
Witan St E2 . . . .**25** A2
Witchwood Ho 10
SW9 . . . .**62** C4
Witcombe Point 14
SE15 . . . .**49** C2
Witechapel Sp Ctr
E1 . . . .
Witham Ct SW17 . . . .**72** B1
Witham Ho 54 SE5 . . .**48** B1
Witherington Rd
N5 . . . .**14** C3
Withers Pl EC1 . . . . .**97** A2
Withycombe Rd
SW19 . . . .**69** C4
Withy Ho 4 E1 . . . . .**25** C1
Witley Ct WC1 . . . . . .**94** A1
Witley Ho 2 SW2 . . .**74** B4
Witley Point 8
SW15 . . . .**69** A3
Witley Rd N19 . . . . . .**4** B2

Wittering Ho 9
SW11 . . . .**169** A2
Wivenhoe Cl SE15 . . .**65** A4
Wix Prim Sch
SW4 . . . .**61** A3
Wix's La SW4 . . . .**61** A3
Woburn Ct
23 Bermondsey
SE16 . . . .**40** A1
Richmond TW9 . . . . . .**54** B4
Woburn Pl WC1 . . . . .**94** A1
Woburn Sq WC1 . . . .**93** C1
Woburn Wlk WC1 . . .**93** C3
Wodeham Gdns 3
E1 . . . .**32** A4
Wodehouse Ave
SE5 . . . .**49** B2
Woking Cl SW15 . . . .**56** B3
Wolcot Ho NW1 . . . .**83** A1
Wolfe Cres 34
SE16 . . . .**40** C4
Wolfe Ho 19 W12 . . . .**30** B2
Wolfson Ct
Golders Green
NW11 . . . .**1** A4
Wollaston Cl SE1 . . .**150** C4
Wollotan Ho N1 . . . .**85** C2
Wolseley Ave SW18,
SW19 . . . .**70** C2
Wolseley Gdns
W4 . . . .**45** A4
Wolseley Rd W4 . . . .**37** B2
Wolseley St SE1 . . .**139** A3
Wolsey Ct NW6 . . . . .**11** B1
Wolsey Ho 3
NW5 . . . .**13** C2
Wolsey Mews
NW5 . . . .**13** B2
Wolsey Rd N1 . . . . . .**15** C3
Wolsey St E1 . . . .**32** B4
Wolverley St E2 . . . .**25** A2
Wolverton SE17 . . . .**152** A2
Wolverton Gdns
W6 . . . .**39** C2
Woman's Lby The★
EC2 . . . .**110** C2
Wontner Cl 3 N1 . . . .**15** B1
Wontner Rd SW12,
SW17 . . . .**72** B2
Woodall Cl 13 E14 . . .**34** A2
Woodberry Down
N4 . . . .**6** B4
Woodberry Down
Com Prim Sch N4 . . . .**6** B4
Woodberry Gr N4 . . . .**6** B4
Woodbine Terr E9 . . .**17** B2
Woodborough Rd
SW15 . . . .**57** A3
Woodbourne Ave
SW16 . . . .**73** C1
Woodbourne Cl
SW16 . . . .**74** A1
Woodbridge Cl 10
N7 . . . .**5** B2
Woodbridge Ct N16 . .**6** C1
Woodbridge St
EC1 . . . .**96** A2
Woodchester Sq
W2 . . . .**100** A4
Woodchurch Ho 16
SW9 . . . .**173** B4

Woodchurch Rd
NW6 . . . .**11** A1
Wood Cl E2 . .**24** C1 **99** B2
Woodcock Ho 4
E14 . . . .**33** C4
Woodcote Ho 4
SE8 . . . .**51** B4
Woodcott Ho 1
SW15 . . . .**68** C4
Woodcroft Mews
SE8 . . . .**41** A2
Wood Dene 6
SE15 . . . .**50** A2
Woodfall Rd N4 . . . . .**5** C2
Woodfall St SW3 . . .**144** C1
Woodfarrs SE5 . . . . .**63** C3
Wood Field NW3 . . . .**12** B3
Woodfield Ave
SW16 . . . .**73** C1
Woodfield Gr
SW16 . . . .**73** C1
Woodfield Gr
SW16 . . . .**73** C1
Woodfield La
SW16 . . . .**73** C1
Woodfield Pl W9 . . . .**23** B1
Woodfield Rd W9 . . . .**23** B1
Woodford Ct 18
W12 . . . .**39** C4
Woodger Rd W12 . . . .**39** B4
Woodhall NW1 . . . . .**92** C3
Woodhall Ave
SE21 . . . .**76** B1
Woodhall Dr SE21 . . .**76** B1
Woodhall Ho
SW18 . . . .**59** C1
Woodheyes Rd
NW10 . . . .**8** A3
Wood Ho
6 Clapham SW4 . . .**171** C2
6 Paddington NW6 . . .**23** B3
Woodhurst Rd W3 . . .**28** B2
Woodison St E3 . . . . .**26** A1
Wood La W12 . . . .**30** B2
Woodland Cres
2 Rotherhithe
SE16 . . . .**40** C4
SE10 . . . .**52** C3
Woodland Gr SE10 . . .**43** A1
Woodland Hts SE3 . . .**53** A4
Woodland Mews
SW16 . . . .**74** A1
Woodlands SW4 . . . .**61** A3
Woodlands Ave
W3 . . . .**28** A1
Woodlands Ct
NW10 . . . .**22** C4
Woodlands Gt
SW15 . . . .**58** B2
Woodlands Park Rd
SE10 . . . .**53** A4
Woodlands Rd
SW13 . . . .**56** B4
Woodland St 2
E8 . . . .**16** B2
Woodlands The
Highbury N5 . . . .**15** B4
12 Hornsey N8 . . . . . .**5** A4
Woodlands Way
SW15 . . . .**58** B2
Woodland Wlk
9 Greenwich
SE10 . . . .**43** A1
Hampstead NW3 . . . . .**12** A3
Wood Lane High Sch
W12 . . . .**30** A3

Wood Lane Sta
W12 . . . .**30** B2
Wood La Sta N12 . . . .**30** B2
Woodlawn Cl
SW15 . . . .**58** B2
Woodlawn Rd
SW6 . . . .**47** C2
Woodlea Rd N16 . . . . .**7** A1
Woodleigh Gdns
SW16 . . . .**74** A1
Woodman Mews
TW9 . . . .**45** A2
Woodmans Gr
NW10 . . . .**8** B3
Woodmans Mews
W12 . . . .**30** A4
Woodmere Cl 11
SW11 . . . .**60** C4
Woodpecker Mews
SE13 . . . .**67** C3
Woodpecker Rd 6
SE14 . . . .**51** A4
Wood Point 8
E16 . . . .**35** C4
Woodquest Ave
SE24 . . . .**63** B2
Woodruff Ho 12
SW2 . . . .**62** C1
Woodrush Cl 4
SE14 . . . .**51** A3
Woodseer St E1 . . . .**111** B4
Woodsford SE17 . . . .**151** B1
Woodsford Sq
W14 . . . .**126** B4
Wood's Ho SW8 . . . . .**17** C4
Wood's Mews W1 . . .**117** B4
Woodsome Rd NW5 . . .**4** A1
Wood's Pl SE1 . . . . .**138** B1
Woodspring Rd
SW19 . . . .**70** A2
Wood's Rd SE15 . . . .**50** A2
Wood St
Chiswick W4 . . . .**38** A1
City of London EC2 . .**109** A2
Woodstar Ho 3
SE15 . . . .**49** C3
Woodstock Ave
NW11 . . . .**1** A4
Woodstock Ct
SE11 . . . .**149** A2
Woodstock Gr
W12 . . . .**39** C4
Woodstock Ho 2
N5 . . . .**15** B4
Woodstock Mews
W1 . . . .**103** C3
Woodstock Rd
Bedford Pk W4 . . . . . .**38** A3
Finsbury Pk N4 . . . .**5** C3
Golders Green NW11 . .**1** B3
Woodstock St W1 . . .**104** A1
Woodstock Studios 17
W12 . . . .**39** C4
Woodstock Terr
E14 . . . .**34** A2
Woodthorpe Rd
SW15 . . . .**57** A3
Woodview Cl N4 . . . . .**6** A4
Woodville Cl 3
SE10 . . . .**52** B4
Woodville Ho SE1 . .**138** C2
Woodville Rd
Golders Green
NW11 . . . .**1** A4
Paddington NW6 . . . . .**23** B3

Woodville Rd continued
Stoke Newington
N16 . . . . 16 A3
Woodwarde Rd
SE22 . . . . 64 A1
Woodwell St
SW18 . . . . 59 B2
Wood Wharf SE10 . . 52 B4
Woodyard Cl NW5 . . 12 C3
Woodyard La SE21 . . 76 A4
Woolcombes Ct 🟦
SE16 . . . . 32 C1
Wooler St SE17 . . . . 151 C2
Woolf Ct 🟦 W3 . . . . 37 B3
Woolf Mews NW1 . . 94 A2
Woolley Ho NW9 . . . 63 A4
Woollon Ho 🟦 E1 . . 32 B3
Woolmore Prim Sch
🟦 E14 . . . . 34 B2
Woolmore St E14 . . 34 B2
Woolneigh St
SW6 . . . . 166 A1
Woolpack Ho 🟦
E9 . . . . 17 B2
Woolridge Way E9 . . 17 B1
Woolstaplers Way
SE16 . . . . 153 B4
Woolstone Ho 🟦
E2 . . . . 24 C4
Woolven Ho SE3 . . . 53 B4
Wooster Gdns E14 . . 34 C3
Wooster Pl SE1 . . . 151 C4
Wootton St SE1 . . . 121 C1
Worcester Ct 🟦
W2 . . . . 31 C4
Worcester Dr W4 . . 38 A4
Worcester Gdns
SW11 . . . . 60 B2
Worcester Ho
Bayswater W2 . . . . . 100 C1
🟦 Islington N1 . . . . 15 B1
Lambeth SE11 . . . . . 135 B1
🟦 Putney SW15 . . . . 69 B4
Worcester Mews 🟦
NW6 . . . . 11 A2
Wordsworth Ho
NW6 . . . . 23 C2
Wordsworth Pl 🟦
NW5 . . . . 12 B3
Wordsworth Rd
Bermondsey SE1 . . . 153 A3
Stoke Newington
N16 . . . . 16 A4
Worfield St SW11 . . 158 B1
Worgan St
Rotherhithe SE16 . . . 40 C2
SE11 . . . . 148 C2
Working Men's Coll
The NW1 . . . . 83 A2
World's End Pas
SW10 . . . . 157 B2
World's End Pl 🟦
SW10 . . . . 157 A2
World Trade Ctr
London E14 . . . . 42 A4
Worlidge St W6 . . . . 39 B1
Worlingham Rd
SE22 . . . . 64 B3
Wormholt Park Prim
Sch W12 . . . . 29 C2
Wormholt Rd W12 . . 29 C1
Wormwood St
EC2 . . . . 110 A2

Wornington Rd
W10 . . . . 31 A4
Woronzow Rd
NW8 . . . . 80 A3
Worple St SW14 . . . 55 C4
Worple Way TW10 . . 54 A3
Worship St
EC2 . . . . 24 A1 98 A1
Worsley Gr E5 . . . . . 16 C4
Worsopp Dr SW4 . . . 61 B2
Worth Gr SE17 . . . . 151 B1
Worthington Ho
EC1 . . . . 95 C4
🟦 Streatham SW2 . . 74 C4
Wotton Ct 🟦 E14 . . 34 C2
Wotton Rd 🟦 SE8 . . 51 B4
Wouldham Rd E16 . . 35 B3
Wrayburn Ho 🟦
SE16 . . . . 139 C3
Wray Cres N4 . . . . . . 5 B2
Wray Ct N4 . . . . 5 B2
Wray Ho 🟦 SW2 . . . 74 A3
Wren Ave NW2 . . . . . 9 B4
Wren Cl E16 . . . . 35 B3
Wren Ho
🟦 Bow E3 . . . . 26 A3
SW1 . . . . 147 B1
Wren Landing E14 . . 33 C1
Wrenn Ho SW13 . . . 47 B4
Wren Rd SE5 . . . . . . 48 C2
Wren St WC1 . . . . . . 95 A2
Wrentham Ave
NW10 . . . . 22 C3
Wren View N6 . . . . . . 4 B3
Wrestlers Ct EC3 . . 110 A2
Wrexham Rd E3 . . . . 26 C3
Wrigglesworth St
SE14 . . . . 50 C3
Wright Cl SE13 . . . . 67 C3
Wright Ho SW15 . . . 57 A2
Wright's Gn SW4 . . . 61 C3
Wright's La W8 . . . 128 A2
Wright's Rd E3 . . . . 26 B3
Wrights Wlk SW14 . . 55 C4
Wrotham Ho SE1 . . 137 C2
Wrotham Rd 🟦
NW1 . . . . 83 A3
Wrottesley Rd
NW10 . . . . 21 C3
Wroughton Rd
SW11 . . . . 60 B1
Wroxton Rd SE15 . . 50 B1
Wulfstan St W12 . . . 29 B3
Wyatt Cl SE16 . . . . . 41 B4
Wyatt Dr SW13 . . . . 47 A3
Wyatt Ho
Blackheath Vale
SE3 . . . . 53 B1
NW8 . . . . 89 C1
Wyatt Park Mans 🟦
SW2 . . . . 74 A2
Wyatt Park Rd
SW2 . . . . 74 B2
Wyatt Rd N5 . . . . 6 B1
Wybert St NW1 . . . . 92 C2
Wycherley Cl SE3 . . 53 B3
Wychwood End N6 . . 4 B4
Wychwood Ho N4 . . . 6 B4
Wyclif Ct EC1 . . . . . 96 A3
Wycliffe Ho 🟦
N16 . . . . 16 A4
Wyclif St EC1 . . . . . 96 A3
Wycombe Gdns SE3 . 53 C3

Wycombe Gdns
NW11 . . . . 1 C2
Wycombe Ho NW8 . . 90 A2
Wycombe Pl SW18 . . 59 B1
Wycombe Sq
W8 . . . . 31 C1 113 B1
Wyersdale Ho N4 . . . 6 B4
Wye St SW11 . . . . . 167 C1
Wyfold Rd SW6 . . . 154 A1
Wyke Rd E3 . . . . 18 C1
Wyldes Cl NW11 . . . . 2 B3
Wyllen Cl E1 . . . . . . 25 B1
Wymering Mans 🟦
W9 . . . . 23 C2
Wymering Rd W9 . . . 23 C2
Wymondham Ct
NW8 . . . . 79 C4
Wymond St SW15 . . 57 B4
Wynan Rd E14 . . . . . 42 A1
Wyndham Deedes Ho
🟦 E2 . . . . 24 C3
Wyndham Ho
SW1 . . . . 145 B3
Wyndham Mews
W1 . . . . 102 C3
Wyndham Pl W1 . . . 102 C3
Wyndham Rd SE5 . . 48 B3
Wyndham St W1 . . . 102 C4
Wyndham Yd W1 . . . 102 C3
Wyneham Rd SE24 . . 63 C2
Wynford Rd N1 . . . . 85 A2
Wynne Ho SE14 . . . . 50 C2
Wynne Rd SW9 . . . . 173 B1
Wynnstay Gdns
W8 . . . . 127 C2
Wynter Ho 🟦
SW9 . . . . 173 A1
Wynter St SW11 . . . 59 B3
Wynton Pl W3 . . . . . 28 A3
Wynyard Ho SE11 . . 149 A2
Wynyard Terr
SE11 . . . . 149 A2
Wynyatt Ho EC1 . . . 96 A4
Wynyatt St EC1 . . . . 96 A4
Wytham Ho NW8 . . . 89 C1
Wythburn Ct W1 . . . 102 C2
Wythburn Pl W1 . . . 102 C2
Wyvil Prim Sch
SW8 . . . . 162 B2
Wyvil Rd SW8 . . . . . 162 A2
Wyvis St E14 . . . . . . 34 A4

Y

Yabsley St E14 . . . . 34 B1
Yaldam Ho SE1 . . . 152 A3
Yalding Ho 🟦 E5 . . 17 A3
Yalding Rd SE16 . . . 153 B4
Yale Ct NW6 . . . . . . 11 A3
Yardley St WC1 . . . . 95 B3
Yard The N1 . . . . . . 84 B1
Yarmouth Pl W1 . . . 118 A1
Yarnfield Sq 🟦
SE15 . . . . 49 C2
Yarrow Ho
🟦 Cubitt Town
E14 . . . . 42 B3
🟦 North Kensington
W10 . . . . 30 B4
Yatesbury Ct E5 . . . 18 A3

Yates Ct NW2 . . . . . . 9 C2
Yates Ho 🟦
E2 . . . . 24 C2 99 C4
Yatton Ho 🟦 W10 . . 30 B4
Yeadon Ho 🟦
W10 . . . . 30 B4
Yearby Ho W10 . . . . 22 B1
Yeate St N1 . . . . 15 C1
Yeats Cl NW10 . . . . . 8 A3
Yeldham Ho W6 . . . . 39 C1
Yeldham Rd W6 . . . . 39 C1
Yelverton Rd
SW11 . . . . 167 C1
Yeoman Cl SE27 . . . 75 A1
Yeoman's Row
SW3 . . . . 130 B1
Yeoman St SE8 . . . . 41 A2
Yeoman's Yd E1 . . . 125 A4
Yeo St E3 . . . . 34 A4
Yeovil Ho
Finsbury Pk N7 . . . . . 5 B2
North Kensington
W10 . . . . 22 B1
Yerbury Prim Sch
N19 . . . . 4 C1
Yerbury Rd N19 . . . . 4 C1
Yeshivo Horomo
Talmudical Coll
. . . . 6 C3
Yesodey Hatorah Jun
Sch for Girls 🟦
N16 . . . . 7 B4
Yesodey Hatorah Sec
Sch for Girls 🟦
N16 . . . . 7 B4
Yet Lev Ct E5 . . . . . . 7 C3
Yewfield Rd NW10 . . 8 B2
Yew Gr NW2 . . . . 9 C4
Yew Ho SE14 . . . . . . 51 B1
Yew Tree Cl 🟦
SE13 . . . . 67 B4
Yew Tree Ct 🟦 N16 . 6 C2
Yew Tree Rd W12 . . . 29 B2
Yoakley Rd N16 . . . . . 7 A2
Yoke Cl N7 . . . . 14 A2
Yonge Pk N4, N7 . . . . 5 C1
York Ave
Mortlake SW14 . . . . . 55 B2
Walworth SE17 . . . . 151 A2
York Bldgs WC2 . . . 120 B3
York Cl 🟦 SE5 . . . . 48 B1
York Gate NW1 . . . . 91 C1
York Gr SE15 . . . . . . 50 B2
York Hall L Ctr E2 . . 25 B3
York Hill SE27,
SW16 . . . . 75 A1
York Ho
Acton W3 . . . . 28 B2
Chelsea SW3 . . . . . . 145 A2
Islington N5 . . . . 14 C3
Kensington W8 . . . . 128 A4
🟦 Kentish Town N7 . . 13 C2
Kew TW9 . . . . 44 C3
Lambeth SE1 . . . . . . 135 A1
Marylebone W1 . . . . 102 C4
Pentonville N1 . . . . . 84 C1
Richmond TW10 . . . . 54 C2
York House Pl
W8 . . . . 128 A4

Woo–Zof 289

York Mans
Battersea SW11 . . . 169 C4
Marylebone W1 . . . . 103 B4
Walworth SE17 . . . . 151 A2
York Mews NW5 . . . 13 A3
York Pl
Battersea SW11 . . . . 59 C4
WC2 . . . . 120 B3
York Place Mans
NW1 . . . . 103 A4
York Rd
Battersea SW11,
SW18 . . . . 59 C4
Dagenham W3 . . . . . 28 C3
🟦 Richmond TW10 . . 54 B2
SE1 . . . . 135 A4
York Rise NW5 . . . . . 4 A1
York Road Bsns Ctr
SW11 . . . . 167 B1
York St Chambers
W1 . . . . 102 C4
Yorkshire Cl N16 . . . 7 A1
Yorkshire Grey 🟦
NW3 . . . . 11 B4
Yorkshire Grey Yd
WC1 . . . . 106 C3
Yorkshire Rd E14 . . 33 A3
York Sq 🟦 E14 . . . . 33 A3
York St W1 . . . . 103 A4
York Terr E NW1 . . . 91 C1
York Terr W NW1 . . . 91 B1
Yorkton St E2 . . . . . 24 C3
York Way
Barnsbury N1, N7,
N1 . . . . 14 A1
N1 . . . . 84 B3
York Way Ct
Islington N1 . . . . 84 C3
Islington N1 . . . . 84 B3
York Wr Gate *
SW1 . . . . 120 B2
Young's Bldgs EC1 . . 97 A2
Youngs Brewery
Visitor Ctr *
SW18 . . . . 59 A2
Youngs Ct SW11 . . . 169 C3
Young St W8 . . . . . . 128 A3
Yoxall Ho 🟦 W10 . . 22 B1
Yukon Rd SW12 . . . . 73 A4

Z

Zampa Rd SE16 . . . . 40 B1
Zander Ct
E2 . . . . 24 C2 99 C4
Zangwill Ho NW6 . . 23 B3
Zealand Ho 🟦 SE5 . 48 B1
Zealand Rd E3 . . . . . 26 A3
Zennor Rd SW12 . . . 73 B3
Zenoria St SE22 . . . 64 B3
Zetland Ho W8 . . . . 128 A2
Zetland St E14 . . . . 34 B4
Zeus Ho N1 . . . . 97 A4
Zion Ho 🟦 E1 . . . . 32 B3
Zoar St SE1 . . . . . . 122 C2
Zodiac Ho 🟦 E3 . . . 26 C1
Zoffany St N19 . . . . . 4 C2

List of numbered locations

This atlas shows thousands more place names than any other London street atlas. In some busy areas it is impossible to fit the name of every place.

Where not all names will fit, some smaller places are shown by a number. If you wish to find out the name associated with a number, use this listing.

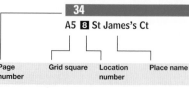

34

A5 **8** St James's Ct

| Page number | Grid square | Location number | Place name |

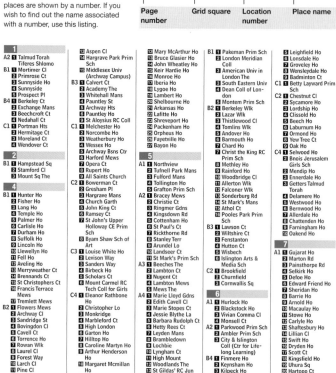

1

A2 **1** Talmud Torah Tiferes Shlomo
B1 **1** Mortimer Cl
2 Primrose Ct
3 Sunnyside Ho
4 Sunnyside
5 Prospect Pl
B4 **1** Berkeley Ct
2 Exchange Mans
3 Beechcroft Ct
4 Nedahall Ct
C1 **1** Portman Hts
2 Hermitage Ct
3 Moreland Ct
4 Wendover Ct

2

B1 **1** Hampstead Sq
2 Stamford Cl
3 Mount Sq The

4

B1 **1** Hunter Ho
2 Fisher Ho
3 Lang Ho
4 Temple Ho
5 Palmer Ho
6 Carlisle Ho
7 Durham Ho
8 Suffolk Ho
9 Lincoln Ho
10 Llewellyn Ho
11 Fell Ho
12 Aveling Ho
13 Merryweather Ct
14 Brennands Ct
15 St Christophers Ct
16 Francis Terrace Mews
17 Tremlett Mews
B2 **1** Flowers Mews
2 Archway Cl
3 Sandridge St
4 Bovingdon Cl
5 Cavell Ct
6 Torrence Ho
7 Rowan Wlk
8 Laurel Ct
9 Forest Way
10 Larch Cl
11 Pine Cl
12 Alder Mews

13 Aspen Cl
14 Hargrave Park Prim Sch
15 Middlesex Univ (Archway Campus)
B3 **1** Calvert Ct
2 Academy The
3 Whitehall Mans
4 Pauntley St
5 Archway Hts
6 Pauntley Ho
7 St Aloysius RC Coll
C1 **1** Melchester Ho
2 Norcombe Ho
3 Weatherbury Ho
4 Wessex Ho
5 Archway Bsns Ctr
6 Harford Mews
7 Opera Ct
8 Rupert Ho
9 All Saints Church
C2 **1** Bowerman Ct
2 Gresham Pl
3 Hargrave Mans
4 Church Garth
5 John King Ct
6 Ramsey Ct
7 St John's Upper Holloway CE Prim Sch
8 Byam Shaw Sch of Art
C3 **1** Louise White Ho
2 Levison Way
3 Sanders Way
4 Birbeck Ho
5 Scholars Ct
6 Mount Carmel RC Tech Coll for Girls
C4 **1** Eleanor Rathbone Ho
2 Christopher Lo
3 Monkridge
4 Marbleford Ct
5 High London
6 Garton Ho
7 Hilltop
8 Caroline Martyn Ho
9 Arthur Henderson Ho
10 Margaret Mcmillan Ho
11 Enid Stacy Ho

12 Mary McArthur Ho
13 Bruce Glasier Ho
14 John Wheatley Ho
15 Keir Hardie Ho
16 Monroe Ho
17 Iberia Ho
18 Lygoe Ho
19 Lambert Ho
20 Shelbourne Ho
21 Arkansas Ho
22 Lafitte Ho
23 Shreveport Ho
24 Packenham Ho
25 Orpheus Ho
26 Fayetville Ho
27 Bayon Ho

5

A1 **1** Northview
2 Tufnell Park Mans
3 Fulford Mans
4 Tollington Ho
5 Grafton Prim Sch
A2 **1** Bracey Mews
2 Christie Ct
3 Ringmer Mans
4 Kingsdown Rd
5 Cottenham Ho
6 St Paul's Ct
7 Rickthorne Rd
8 Stanley Terr
9 Arundel Lo
10 Landseer Ct
11 St Mark's Prim Sch
A3 **1** Beeches The
2 Lambton Ct
3 Nugent Ct
4 Lambton Mews
5 Mews The
A4 **1** Marie Lloyd Gdns
2 Edith Cavell Cl
3 Marie Stopes Ct
4 Jessie Blythe La
5 Barbara Rudolph Ct
6 Hetty Rees Ct
7 Leyden Mans
8 Brambledown
9 Lochbie
10 Lyngham Ct
11 High Mount
12 Woodlands The
13 St Gildas' RC Jun Sch

B1 **1** Pakeman Prim Sch
2 London Meridian Coll
3 American Univ in London The
4 South Eastern Univ London The
5 Dean Coll of London
6 Montem Prim Sch
B2 **1** Berkeley Wlk
2 Lazar Wlk
3 Thistlewood Cl
4 Tomlins Wlk
5 Andover Ho
6 Barmouth Ho
7 Chard Ho
8 Christ the King RC Prim Sch
9 Methley Ho
10 Rainford Ho
11 Woodbridge Cl
12 Allerton Wlk
13 Falconer Wlk
14 Sonderburg Rd
15 St Mark's Mans
16 Athol Ct
17 Pooles Park Prim Sch
B3 **1** Lawson Ct
2 Wiltshire Ct
3 Fenstanton
4 Hutton Ct
5 Islington Arts & Media Sch
C2 **1** Brookfield
2 Churnfield
3 Cornwallis Sq

6

A1 **1** Hurlock Ho
2 Blackstock Ho
3 Vivian Comma Cl
4 Monsell Ct
A2 **1** Parkwood Prim Sch
2 Ambler Prim Sch
3 City & Islington Coll (Ctr for Life-long Learning)
B4 **1** Finmere Ho
2 Keynsham Ho
3 Kilpeck Ho
4 Knaresborough Ho

5 Leighfield Ho
6 Lonsdale Ho
7 Wensleydale Ho
8 Badminton Ct
C1 **1** Betty Layward Prim Sch
C2 **1** Chestnut Cl
2 Sycamore Ho
3 Lordship Ho
4 Clissold Ho
5 Beech Ho
6 Laburnam Ho
7 Ormond Ho
8 Yew Tree Ct
9 Oak Ho
C4 **1** Selwood Ho
2 Bnois Jerusalem Girls Sch
3 Mendip Ho
4 Ennerdale Ho
5 Getters Talmud Torah
6 Delamere Ho
7 Westwood Ho
8 Bernwood Ho
9 Allerdale Ho
10 Chattenden Ho
11 Farningham Ho
12 Oakend Ho

7

A1 **1** Gujarat Ho
2 Marton Rd
3 Painsthorpe Rd
4 Selkirk Ho
5 Defoe Ho
6 Edward Friend Ho
7 Sheridan Ho
8 Barrie Ho
9 Arnold Ho
10 Macaulay Ho
11 Stowe Ho
12 Carlyle Ho
13 Shaftesbury Ho
14 Lillian Cl
15 Swift Ho
16 Dryden Ho
17 Scott Ct
18 Kingsfield Ho
19 Uhura Sq
20 Hartopp Ct
A2 **1** Denman Ho

2 St Mary's Stoke Newington CE Prim Sch
A3 1 Godstone Ct
2 Farnham Ct
3 Milford Ct
4 Cranleigh Ct
5 Haslemere Ct
6 Belmont Ct
7 Hockworth Ho
8 Garratt Ho
9 Fairburn Ho
10 Thorndale Ho
11 Oakdene Ho
12 Briardale Ho
A4 1 Beis Rochel d'Satmar Girls Sch
2 Our Lady's Convent RC High Sch
B1 1 Lawrence Bldgs
2 Cottage Wlk
3 Batley Pl
B2 1 Garnham St
2 Garnham Cl
3 Sanford La
4 Sanford Wlk
5 Abney Gdns
6 Fleet Wood
7 Simon Marks Jewish Prim Sch
8 William Patten Prim Sch
B3 1 Stamford Hill Mans
2 Montefiore Ct
3 Berwyn Ho
4 Clent Ho
5 Chiltern Ho
6 Laindon Ho
7 Pentland Ho
B4 1 Regent Ct
2 Stamford Lo
3 Holmwood Ct
4 Bobov Foundation Sch
5 Yesodey Hatorah Sec Sch for Girls
6 Lubavitch Boys Prim Sch
7 Yesodey Hatorah Jun Sch for Girls
8 Lubavitch Girls Prim Sch
9 Lubavitch House Sch (Jun Boys)
10 Skinners Company Sch (Upper)
C1 1 Ravenscourt
2 Mellington Ct
3 Rendlesham Ho
4 Carroll Ct
5 St Scholastica's RC Prim Sch
C2 1 Cazenove Mans
2 Chedworth Ho
3 Aldergrove Ho
4 Abbotstone Ho
5 Briggeford Cl
6 Inglethorpe Ho
7 Ashdown Ho
8 Epping Ho
9 Cypress Cl
C3 1 Stamford Gr E
2 Stamford Mans
3 Grove Mans
4 Stamford Gr W
5 Talmud-Torah Yetev-Lev

8

A1 1 Beveridge Rd
2 Purcell Mews
3 George Lansbury Ho
4 Charles Hobson Ho
5 Reade Wlk
6 Westbury Ho
7 Bridge Ct
8 St Joseph's RC Prim Sch
9 Dixon Way
10 Armstrong Rd
11 Brittage Rd
A4 1 Grange Ct
2 Green Ct
C2 1 Regency Mews
2 Tudor Mews
3 Utopia Ho
4 Bell Flats
5 Angel Ct
6 St Andrew & St Francis CE Prim Sch

9

A2 1 St Mary Magdelen's RC Jun Sch
2 Islamic Coll for Advanced Studies
B2 1 Rutland Park Gdns
2 Rutland Park Mans
3 Queens Par
4 Harcourt Ho
5 Solidarity Ho
6 Electra Ct
7 Cassandra Ct
8 Carlton Ct
9 Convent of Jesus & Mary RC Inf Sch
C4 1 Oaklands Mews
2 Acer Ct
3 Maple Ct
4 Argyle Mans

10

A1 1 Christ Church Ct
2 Paul Daisley Ct
3 Fountain Ho
4 Kingston Ho
5 Waverley Ct
6 Weston Ho
7 Mapes Ho
8 Athelstan Gdns
9 Leff Ho
10 Brondesbury Coll for Boys
B1 1 Alma Birk Ho
2 Brooklands Ct
3 Brooklands Court Apartments
4 Cleveland Mans
5 Buckley Ct
6 Webheath
C1 1 Linstead St
2 Embassy Ho
3 Acol Ct
4 Kings Wood Ct
5 Douglas Ct
6 King's Gdns
7 Carlton Mans
8 Smyrna Mans
9 New Priory Ct
10 Queensgate Pl
11 Brondesbury Mews
12 St Eugene de Mazenod RC Prim Sch

C2 1 Dene Mans
2 Sandwell Cres
3 Sandwell Mans
4 Hampstead West
5 Redcroft
C3 1 Orestes Mews
2 Walter Northcott Ho
3 Polperro Mans
4 Lyncroft Mans
5 Marlborough Mans
6 Alexandra Mans
7 Cumberland Mans
8 Cavendish Mans
9 Ambassador Ct
10 Welbeck Mans
11 Inglewood Mans
12 Dennington Park Mansions
C4 1 Parsifal Coll

11

A2 1 Beswick Mews
2 Worcester Mews
3 Minton Mews
4 Doulton Mews
5 Laurel Ho
6 Sandalwood Ho
7 Iroko Ho
8 Banyan Ho
9 Rosewood Ho
10 Ebony Ho
11 Rosemont Mans
12 Exeter Mews
B1 1 Harrold Ho
2 Glover Ho
3 Byron Ct
4 Nalton Ho
5 Petros Gdns
6 Heath Ct
7 Imperial Twrs
8 Fairhurst
9 St John's Ct
10 New College Ct
11 Chalford
12 Rosslyn Mans
13 Sutherland Ho
14 Holy Trinity CE Prim Sch
15 Phoenix Sch The
16 North Bridge House Sch
17 Southbank International Sch
B3 1 Arkwright Mans
2 Hatstone Ct
3 Hampstead High Sch
B4 1 Windmill Hill
2 Highgrove Point
3 Gainsborough Ho
4 Holly Bush Hill
5 Heath Mans
6 Holly Bush Steps
7 Pavilion Ct
8 Holly Berry La
9 New Campden Ct
10 Holly Bush Vale
11 Benham's Pl
12 Prospect Pl
13 Yorkshire Grey Pl
14 Gardnor Mans
15 Ellerdale Cl
16 Monro Ho
17 Prince Arthur Mews
18 Prince Arthur Ct

19 Village Mount
20 Perrin's Ct
21 Wells Ct
22 Bakers Pas
23 Spencer Wlk
24 Bird In Hand Yd
25 Kings Well
26 New Ct
27 Streatley Pl
28 Mansfield Pl
29 Upper Hampstead Wlk
30 Hampstead Parochial CE Prim Sch
31 Univ Coll Jun Sch
32 Heathside Prep Sch
33 New End Prim Sch
34 Sisters of St Marcellina Sch
C1 1 New College Par
2 Northways Par
3 Noel Ho
4 Campden Ho
5 Centre Hts
6 Hickes Ho
7 Swiss Terr
8 Leitch Ho
9 Jevons Ho
10 Langhorne Ct
11 Park Lo
12 Avenue Lo
13 Frank Barnes Sch
14 Swiss Cottage Sch
C2 1 Belsize Park Mews
2 Baynes Mews
3 McCrone Mews
4 South Hampstead High Sch
C3 1 Belsize Court Garages
2 Roscommon Ho
3 Akenside Ct
4 Fitzjohns Prim Sch
5 St Christopher's Sch
6 St Anthony's Sch
C4 1 White Bear Pl
2 Wells Ho The
3 Boades Mews
4 Flask Cotts
5 Coach House Yd
6 Pilgrim's Pl
7 Rosslyn Mews
8 Royal Sch Hampstead The
9 Academy Sch The

12

A2 1 Banff Ho
2 Glenloch Ct
3 Havercourt
4 Holmefield Ct
5 Gilling Ct
6 Howitt Cl
7 Manor Mans
8 Straffan Lo
9 Romney Ct
10 Lancaster Stables
11 Eton Garages
12 Hampstead Coll of Fine Arts & Humanities
A3 1 Hampstead Hill Sch
B1 1 Hancock Nunn Ho
2 Higginson Ho
3 Duncan Ho
4 Mary Wharrie Ho

5 Rockstraw Ho
6 Cleaver Ho
7 Chamberlain St
8 Sharples Hall St
9 Primrose Mews
10 Rothwell St
11 St Georges Mews
B2 1 Alder Ho
2 Hornbeam Ho
3 Whitebeam Ho
4 Aspen Ho
5 Rowan Ho
6 Beech Ho
7 Chestnut Ho
8 Oak Ho
9 Willow Ho
10 Sycamore Ho
11 Maple Ho
12 Hazel Ho
13 Elaine Ct
14 Faircourt
15 Walham Ct
16 Stanbury Ct
17 Priory Mans
18 Wellington Ho
19 Grange The
B3 1 Cayford Ho
2 Du Maurier Ho
3 Isokon Flats
4 Palgrave Ho
5 Garnett Ho
6 Stephenson Ho
7 Park Dwellings
8 Siddons Ho
9 Mall Studios
10 Park Hill Wlk
11 Wordsworth Pl
12 Fraser Regnart Ct
13 St Pancras Almshouses
14 St Dominic RC Prim Sch
15 Fleet Prim Sch
C1 1 Bridge Ho
2 Hardington
3 Mead Cl
4 Rugmere
5 Tottenhall
6 Beauvale
7 Broomfield
8 Camden Coll of English
C2 1 Silverbirch Wlk
2 Penshurst
3 Wingham
4 Westwell
5 Chislet
6 Burmarsh
7 Shipton Ho
8 Stonegate
9 Leysdown
10 Headcorn
11 Lenham
12 Halstow
13 Fordcombe
14 Cannington
15 Langridge
16 Athlone Ho
17 Hawkridge
18 Beckington
19 Hawkridge
20 Kilgerton
21 Rhyl Prim Sch
22 Haverstock Sch

13

A1
1 Ferdinand Ho
2 Harmood Ho
3 Hawley Rd
4 Hawley Mews
5 Leybourne St
6 Barling
7 Tiptree
8 Havering
9 Candida Ct
10 Lorraine Ct
11 Donnington Ct
12 Welford Ct
13 Torbay Ct
14 Bradfield Ct
15 Torbay St
16 Water La
17 Leybourne Rd
18 Haven St
19 Stucley Pl
20 Lawrence Ho
21 Chalcot Sch
22 Holy Trinity & Saint
Silas CE Prim Sch
23 Hawley Inf Sch

A2
1 Ashington
2 Priestley Ho
3 Leonard Day Ho
4 Old Dairy Mews
5 Monmouth Ct
6 Alpha Ct
7 Una Ho
8 Widford
9 Heybridge
10 Roxwell
11 Hamstead Gates
12 Kingsway Coll

A4
1 Denyer Ho
2 Stephenson Ho
3 Trevithick Ho
4 Brunel Ho
5 Newcomen Ho
6 Faraday Ho
7 Winifrede Paul Ho
8 Wardlow
9 Fletcher Ct
10 Tideswell
11 Grangemill
12 Hambrook Ct
13 Calver

B1
1 Cherry Tree Ct
2 Chichester Ct
3 Durdans Ho
4 Philia Ho
5 Bernard Shaw Ct
6 Foster Ct
7 Bessemer Ct
8 Hogarth Ct
9 Rochester Ct
10 Soane Ct
11 Wallett Ct
12 Inwood Ct
13 Wrotham Rd
14 St Thomas Ct
15 Caulfield Ct
16 Bruges Pl
17 Reachview Cl
18 Lawfords Wharf

B3
1 Eleanor Ho
2 Falkland Pl
3 Kensington Ct
4 Willingham Cl
5 Kenbrook Ho
6 Aborfield

7 Great Field
8 Appleford
9 Forties The
10 Maud Wilkes Cl
11 Dunne Mews
12 Dowdeny Cl
13 Kentish Town CE
Prim Sch

B4
1 Benson Ct
2 Tait Ho
3 Manorfield Cl
4 Greatfield Cl
5 Longley Ho
6 Lampson Ho
7 Davidson Ho
8 Palmer Ho
9 Lambourn Cl
10 Morris Ho
11 Owen Ho
12 Eleanor Palmer
Prim Sch

C1
1 Hillier Ho
2 Gairloch Ho
3 Cobham Mews
4 Bergholt Mews
5 Blakeney Cl
6 Weavers Way
7 Allensbury Pl

C2
1 Rowstock
2 Peckwater Ho
3 Wolsey Ho
4 Pandian Way
5 Busby Mews
6 Caledonian Sq
7 Canal Bvd
8 Northpoint Sq
9 Lock Mews
10 Carters Cl
11 York Ho
12 Hungerford Rd
13 Cliff Road Studios
14 Cliff Ct
15 Camelot Ho
16 Church Studios
17 Camden Terr
18 Brecknock Prim
Sch
19 Hungerford Prim
Sch

C3
1 Blake Ho
2 Quelch Ho
3 Lee Ho
4 Willbury Ho
5 Howell Ho
6 Holmsbury Ho
7 Leith Ho
8 Betchworth Ho
9 Rushmore Ho
10 Dugdale Ho
11 Horsendon Ho
12 Colley Ho
13 Coombe Ho
14 Ivinghoe Ho
15 Buckhurst Ho
16 Saxonbury Ct
17 Charlton Ct
18 Apollo Studios
19 Barn Cl
20 Long Meadow
21 Landleys Field
22 Margaret Bondfield
Ho
23 Haywood Lo
24 Torriano Jun & Inf
Schs

C4
1 Fairlie Ct
2 Trecastle Way

3 Dalmeny Avenue
Est
4 Hyndman Ho
5 Carpenter Ho
6 Graham Ho
7 Tufnell Mans

14

A2
1 Clock Tower Pl
2 Clock View Cres
3 Jim Veal Dr
4 Gower Sch The

A3
1 Kimble Ho
2 Saxonbury Ct
3 Poynder Ct
4 Pangbourne Ho
5 Moulsford Ho

A4
1 Arcade The
2 Macready Pl
3 Cardwell Ho
4 Mcmorran Ho
5 Crayford Ho
6 Whitby Ct
7 Prospect Pl
8 City & Islington
Coll (Ctr for Bsns,
Arts & Technology)

B1
1 Kerwick Cl
2 Rydston Cl
3 Skegness Ho
4 Frederica St
5 Ponder St
6 Kings Ct
7 Freeling St
8 Coatbridge Ho
9 Tilloch St

B2
1 Burns Ho
2 Scott Ho
3 Wellington Mews
4 Roman Ct
5 Piccadilly Ct
6 Knowledge Point
Sch

B3
1 Culverin Ct
2 Garand Ct
3 Mount Carmel

B4
1 Buckmaster Ho
2 Loreburn Ho
3 Cairns Ho
4 Halsbury Ho
5 Chelmsford Ho
6 Cranworth Ho
7 City & Islington
Coll (Ctr for Health,
Social & Child
Care)

C1
1 Mountfort Terr
2 Avon Ho
3 Buckland Ho
4 Dovey Lo
5 Carfree Cl
6 Mitchell Ho
7 New College Mews
8 Lofting Ho
9 Brooksby Ho
10 Cara Ho
11 Thornhill Prim Sch
12 North London Sci-
ence Ctr

C2
1 London Metropo-
litan Univ (Spring
Ho)
2 Slaney Pl
3 Eastwood Cl
4 Milton Pl
5 Hartnoll Ho

5 St James School
Flats
6 Widnes Ho
7 Tranmere Ho
8 Victoria Mans
9 Formby Ct
10 Mersey Ho
11 Birkenhead Ho
12 Drayton Park Mews
13 Drayton Park Prim
Sch

15

A1
1 Islington Park
Mews
2 Evelyn Denington
Ct
3 Bassingbourn Ho
4 Cadmore Ho
5 Adstock Ho
6 Garston Ho
7 Flitton Ho
8 Datchworth Ho
9 Battishill St
10 Almeida St
11 Edward's Cotts
12 Hyde's Pl
13 Tyndale Terr
14 Spriggs Ho
15 Barratt Ho
16 Spencer Pl
17 Chadston Ho
18 Whiston Ho
19 Wakelin Ho
20 Tressel Cl
21 Canonbury Ct
22 Halton Ho
23 Shillingford St
24 Highbury Mans
25 Premier Ho
26 Waterloo Gdns
27 William Tyndale
Prim Sch

A2
1 Hampton Ct
2 Salisbury Ho
3 Canonbury Prim
Sch

A3
1 De Barowe Mews
2 Fieldview Ct
3 Viewpoint
4 Ashurst Lo
5 Highbury Fields
Sch
6 London Metropoli-
tan Univ (Ladbroke
Ho)
7 Robinswood Mews

A4
1 Chestnuts The
2 Bowen Ct
3 Peckett Sq
4 De Barowe Mews

B1
1 Astey's Row
2 Lincoln Ho
3 Worcester Ho
4 Melville Pl
5 Wontner Cl
6 Hedingham Cl
7 Laundry La
8 Base Apartments
9 Walkinshaw Ct
10 New Bentham Ct
11 Bentham Ct
12 Haslam Ho
13 Horsfield Ho
14 Riverside Ho
15 Eric Fletcher Ct

16 Annette Cres
17 Ashby Ho
18 Lindsey Mews
19 Cardigan Wlk
20 Red House Sq
21 Orchard Cl
22 Queensbury St
23 Raynor Pl

B2
1 Crowline Wlk
2 Upper Handa Wlk
3 Handa Wlk
4 Lismore Wlk
5 Bardsey Wlk
6 Walney Wlk
7 Upper Bardsey Wlk
8 Upper Lismore Wlk
9 Sark Ho
10 Guernsey Ho
11 Guernsey Rd
12 Sybil Thorndike Ho
13 Clephane Rd
14 Florence Nightin-
gale Ho
15 Jersey Ho
16 Jethou Ho
17 Islay Wlk
18 Upper Caldy Wlk
19 Caldy Wlk
20 Alderney Ho
21 Gulland Wlk
22 Nightingale Rd
23 Upper Gulland Wlk
24 Church Rd
25 Oransay Rd
26 Canonbury Yd E

B3
1 Pearfield Ho
2 Larchfield Ho
3 Beresford Terr
4 Pondfield Ho
5 Ashfield Ho
6 Elmfield Ho
7 Highbury Grove
Sch

B4
1 Fountain Mews
2 Woodstock Ho
3 Henson Ct
4 Taverner Sq

C1
1 Downham Ct
2 Trafalgar Point

C2
1 John Kennedy Ct
2 John Kennedy Lo
3 Ball's Pond Pl
4 Haliday Wlk
5 Queen Elizabeth Ct
6 Canonbury Hts
7 Pinnacle The
8 Threadgold Ho
9 Wakeham St
10 Saffron Ct
11 Callaby Terr
12 Tilney Gdns
13 Westcliff Ho
14 Ilford Ho
15 Ongar Ho
16 Greenhills Terr
17 Romford Ho
18 Bute Wlk
19 Upper Ramsey Wlk
20 Rona Wlk
21 Thorndike Rd
22 St Pauls Steiner
Sch

C3
1 Newington Green
Prim Sch

C4
1 Ledo Ho
2 Salween Ho
3 Prome Ho

4 Arakan Ho
5 Rangoon Ho
6 Mandalay Ho
7 Karen Ho
8 Wingate Ho
9 Jubet Ho
10 Orde Ho
11 Chindit Ho
12 Mabel Thornton Ho
13 Crawshay Ho
14 Avon Ho
15 Connaught Mans
16 Jonson Ho
17 Herrick Ho
18 Donne Ho
19 Thirlmere Ho
20 Grasmere Ho

16
A1 1 Dorchester Ct
2 Wareham Ct
3 Dorset Ct
4 Stratton Ct
5 Swanage Ct
6 Blandford Ct
7 Portland Ct
8 Oscar Faber Pl
9 Metropolitan Bsns Ctr
10 Lancaster Cl
11 Palazzo Apartments
12 Watercress Pl
A2 1 Kingsland Gn
2 Kingsland Pas
3 Metropolitan Benefit Societies Almshouses
4 Nimrod Pas
5 De Beauvoir Pl
6 Warburton Ct
7 Buckingham Mews
8 Aztec Ct
10 Kerridge Ct
11 Isabella Mews
12 St Jude & St Paul's CE Prim Sch
13 De Beauvoir Prim Sch
14 Our Lady & St Joseph RC Prim Sch
15 Childrens House Upper Sch
A3 1 Hewling Ho
2 Matthias Ho
3 Port Royal Pl
4 Cressington Cl
5 King Henry's Yd
6 Bronte Ho
7 Sewell Ho
8 Lydgate Ho
9 Patmore Ho
10 Congreve Ho
11 Elton St
12 Conrad Ho
13 Southwell Ho
14 Neptune Ho
15 Campion Ho
16 Webster Ho
17 Meredith Ho
18 Beckford Ho
19 Ashley Ct
20 Hayling Cl
21 Millard Cl
22 Lydford Cl
23 Salcombe Rd

24 Truman's Rd
25 Templeton Cl
26 John Campbell Rd
27 Gillett Pl
28 Bradbury St
29 Thomas Crowell Ct
A4 1 Londesborough Ho
2 Knebworth Ho
3 Knebworth Rd
4 Bransby Ct
5 Imperial Ave
6 Leonard Pl
7 Shakspeare Mews
8 Binyon Ho
9 Shelley Ho
10 Browning Ho
11 Burns Ho
12 Andrew Marvell Ho
13 Wycliffe Ho
14 Blake Ho
15 Marlowe Ho
16 Fletcher Ho
17 Chaucer Ct
St Matthias's CE Prim Sch
B1 1 Hindrup Rd
2 Shoreditch Ct
3 Evergreen Sq
4 Wyndhams Ct
5 Festival Ct
6 Fortune Ct
7 Rose Ct
8 Ability Plaza
9 Briar Ct
10 Lomas Dr
11 Queensbridge Inf Sch
B2 1 Prospect Ho
2 Woodland St
3 Crosby Wlk
4 Kirkland Wlk
5 Bowness Cl
6 Carlisle Wlk
7 Skelton Cl
8 Camerton Cl
9 Buttermere Wlk
10 Houghton Cl
11 Hayton Cl
12 Kingsland Sh Ctr
13 Springfield Ho
14 Parton Lo
15 Sanctuary Mews
16 Fenton Cl
B3 1 Miller's Terr
2 Chow Sq
3 Drysdale Flats
4 Gateway Mews
5 Birkbeck Mews
6 Winchester Pl
B4 1 Coronation Ave
2 Morris Blitz Ct
3 Shacklewell Ho
4 Alexandra Ct
5 Shacklewell Prim Sch
6 Princess May Prim Sch
C1 1 Aldington Ct
2 Bayton Ct
3 Rochford Wlk
4 Windrush Cl
5 Gayhurst Prim Sch
C2 1 Burdon Ct
2 Thomson Ct
3 Bruno Ct
4 Thackeray Mews

7 Madinah Rd
C3 1 Kingsdown Ho
2 Glendown Ho
3 Moredown Ho
4 Blakeney Cl
5 Beeston Cl
6 Benabo Ct
7 David Devine Ho
8 Kreedman Wlk
9 Hermitage Row
10 Grafton Ct
11 Lushington Terr
12 Aspen Ct
13 Pykewell Lo
14 Albion Works Studios

17
A1 1 Fortescue Ave
2 Pemberton Pl
3 Weston Wlk
4 Bayford St Ind Ctr
5 Bayford St
6 Sidworth St
7 Helmsley St
8 Cyntra Pl
9 Signal Ho
10 All Nations Ho
11 Vanguard Ho
12 Hacon Sq
A2 1 Bohemia Pl
2 Graham Mans
3 Marvin St
4 Boscobel Ho
5 Royal Oak Rd
6 Colonnades The
7 Sylvester Ho
8 Sylvester Path
9 Doctor Spurstowe Almshouses
10 Great Eastern Bldgs
11 Sojourner-Truth Cl
A3 1 Birchington Ho
2 Bicknor Ho
3 Boxley Ho
4 Adisham Ho
5 Cranbrook Ho
6 Marden Ho
7 Broome Ho
8 Crandale Ho
9 Cheriton Ho
10 Ditton Ho
11 Langley Ho
12 Dymchurch Ho
13 Elham Ho
14 Davina Ho
15 Pembury Pl
16 Downs Ct
17 Perrywood Ho
18 Staplehurst Ho
19 Pegwell Ho
20 Yalding Ho
21 Northbourne Ho
22 Monkton Ho
23 Milsted Ho
24 Athlone Ct
25 Clarence Pl
26 Gould Terr
27 Quested Ct
28 Brett Pas
29 Marcon Ct
30 Appleton Ct
31 Institute Pl
A4 1 Ross Ct
2 Downs La
3 Gaviller Pl
4 Robert Owen Lo

5 Apprentice Way
6 Arrowe Ct
7 Gilwell Ct
8 Sutton Ct
9 St Andrews Mans
10 Kinnoull Mans
11 Rowhill Mans
12 Sladen Pl
13 Mothers Sq The
14 Richborough Ho
15 Sandgate Ho
16 Sheppey Ho
B1 1 Pitcairn Ho
2 Lyme Grove Ho
3 Shakespeare Ho
4 Upcott Ho
5 Loddiges Ho
6 Parkinson Ho
7 Sloane Ho
8 Vanbrugh Ho
9 Cambridge Pas
10 Lyttleton Ho
11 Victoria Park Ct
12 Tullis Ho
13 Fairchild Ho
14 Forsyth Ho
15 Tradescant Ho
16 Mason Ho
17 Capel Ho
18 Cordwainers Ct
19 Bridgeman Ho
20 St Thomas's Pl
21 Barclay Ho
22 Clayton Ho
23 Danby Ho
24 Sherard Ho
25 Catesby Ho
26 Petiver Cl
27 Leander Ct
28 Philip Turner Est
29 Grendon Ho
30 Shore Mews
31 Shore Bsns Ctr
32 Kendal Ho
33 Classic Mans
34 Tudor Ho
35 Park Ho
36 Enterprise Ho
37 Alpine Gr
38 Clarendon Cl
39 Rotheley Ho
40 Bernie Grant Ho
41 Orchard Prim Sch
42 St John of Jerusalem CE Prim Sch
B2 1 Woolpack Ho
2 Elvin Ho
3 Thomas Ho
4 Hockley Ho
5 Retreat Ho
6 Butfield Ho
7 Brooksbank Ho
8 Cresset Ho
9 Brooksbank St
10 Lennox Ho
11 Milborne Ho
12 Collent Ho
13 Middlesex Pl
14 Elsdale Ho
15 Devonshire Hall
16 Brent Ho
17 Morningside Prim Sch
18 Hackney Free & Parochial CE Sec Sch

B3 1 St John & St James CE Prim Sch
C1 1 Stuart Ho
2 Gascoyne Ho
3 Chelsfield Point
4 Sundridge Ho
5 Banbury Ho
6 Lauriston Ho
C2 1 Musgrove Ho
2 Cheyney Ho
3 Haynes Ho
4 Warner Ho
5 Gilby Ho
6 Gadsden Ho
7 Risley Ho
8 Baycliffe Ho
9 Sheldon Ho
10 Offley Ho
11 Latimer Ho
12 Ribstone Ho
13 Salem Ho
14 Fieldwick Ho
15 Lever Ct
16 Matson Ho
17 Wilding Ho
18 Rennell Ho
19 Dycer Ho
20 Granard Ho
21 Whitelock Ho
22 Harrowgate Ho
23 Cass Ho
24 Lofts on the Park
25 Heathcote Point
26 Ravenscroft Point
27 Vanner Point
28 Hensley Point
29 San Ho
30 Berger Prim Sch
C4 1 Cromford Path
2 Longford Ct
3 Overbury Ho
4 Heanor Ct
5 Wharfedale Ct
6 Ladybower Ct
7 Ilkeston Ct
8 Derby Ct
9 Rushmore Cres
10 Blackwell Cl
11 Belper Ct
12 Rushmore Prim Sch

18
A2 1 Chigwell Ct
2 Wellday Ho
3 Selman Ho
4 Vaine Ho
5 Trower Ho
6 St Dominics RC Prim Sch
B2 1 Mallard Cl
2 Merriam Ave
3 Gainsborough St
4 Palace Cl
5 St Anthony's Cl
6 Trowbridge Est
B3 1 Wick Village

19
C1 1 Service Route No 2
2 Service Route No 3
3 Newham Sixth Form Coll (Stratford Ctr)

294 19 C4

C4
1 Mulberry Ct
2 Rosewood Ct
3 Gean Ct
4 Blackthorn Ct
5 Cypress Ct

20
C4
1 Carlyle Rd
2 Bernard Shaw Ho
3 Longlents Ho
4 Mordaunt Ho
5 Wilmers Ct
6 Stonebridge Ct
7 Shakespeare Ave
8 Southcroft
9 Brent Adult Comm Education Service Coll

21
A3
1 Futters Ct
2 Barrett Ct
3 Elms The
4 Fairlight Ct
B3
1 New Crescent Yd
2 Harlesden Plaza
3 St Josephs Ct
4 Jubilee Cl
5 Ellery Cl

22
B1
1 Princess Alice Ho
2 Yoxall Ho
3 Yorkley Ho
4 Northaw Ho
5 Oakham Ho
6 Markyate Ho
7 Letchmore Ho
8 Pagham Ho
9 Quendon Ho
10 Redbourn Ho
11 Ketton Ho
12 Hillman Dr
C2
1 Westfield Ct
2 Tropical Ct
3 Chamberlayne Mans
4 Quadrant The
5 Queens Park Ct
6 Warfield Yd
7 Regent St
8 Cherrytree Ho
9 Artisan Mews
10 Artisan Quarter

23
A1
1 Sycamore Wlk
2 Westgate Bsns Ctr
3 Buspace Studios
4 Bosworth Ho
5 Golborne Gdns
6 Appleford Ho
7 Adair Twr
8 Gadsden Ho
9 Southam Ho
10 Norman Butler Ho
11 Thompson Ho
12 Wells Ho
13 Paul Ho
14 Olive Blythe Ho
15 Katherine Ho
16 Breakwell Ct
17 Pepler Ho
18 Edward Kennedy Ho
19 Winnington Ho
20 Queen's Park Prim Sch
21 Middle Row Prim Sch
22 St Mary RC Prim Sch
23 St Thomas' CE Prim Sch
A2
1 Selby Sq
2 Severn Ave
3 Stansbury Sq
4 Tolhurst Dr
5 John Fearon Wlk
6 Mundy Ho
7 Macfarren Ho
8 Bantock Ho
9 Banister Ho
10 Batten Ho
11 Croft Ho
12 Courtville Ho
13 Mounsey Ho
14 Bliss Mews
15 Symphony Mews
B1
1 Octavia Mews
2 Russell's Wharf
3 Western Ho
4 Kelly Mews
5 Queen Elizabeth II Jubilee Sch
B2
1 Boyce Ho
2 Farnaby Ho
3 Danby Ho
4 Purday Ho
5 Naylor Ho
6 St Judes Ho
7 Leeve Ho
8 Longhurst Ho
9 Harrington Ct
10 Mulberry Ct
11 Kilburn Ho
12 Carlton Vale Inf Sch
B3
1 Claremont Ct
2 William Saville Ho
3 Western Ct
4 Bond Ho
5 Crone Ct
6 Wood Ho
7 Winterleys
8 Carlton Ho
9 Fiona Ct
10 Kilburn Park Sch
C1
1 Westside Ct
2 Byron Mews
3 Sutherland Ct
4 Fleming Cl
5 Hermes Ct
6 St Peter's CE Prim Sch
7 Paddington Acad
C2
1 Pentland Rd
2 Nelson Cl
3 Pavilion Ct
4 Masefield Ho
5 Austen Ho
6 Fielding Ho
7 Argo Bsns Ctr
8 John Ratcliffe Ho
9 Wymering Mans
10 City of Westminster Coll, Queens Park Ctr
11 Essendine Prim Sch
C3
1 Wells Ct
2 Cambridge Ct
3 Ely Ct
4 Durham Ct
5 St Augustine's CE High Sch
6 Sch of the Islamic Republic of Iran The
C4
1 Ryde Ho
2 Glengall Pass
3 Leith Yd
4 Daynor Ho
5 Varley Ho
6 Sandby Ho
7 Colas Mews
8 Bishopsdale Ho
9 Lorton Ho
10 Marshwood Ho
11 Ribblesdale Ho
12 Holmesdale Ho
13 Kilburn Vale Est
14 Kilburn Bridge
15 Coll of NW London
16 St Mary's Kilburn CE Prim Sch

24
A2
1 Pimlico Wlk
2 Aske Ho
3 Hathaway Ho
4 Haberdasher Pl
5 Fairchild Ho
6 Burtt Ho
7 Enfield Cloisters
8 McGregor Ct
9 Royal Oak Ct
10 Hoxton Mkt
11 Bath Pl
12 Chapel Pl
13 Standard Pl
14 Cleeve Workshops
15 Cleeve Ho
16 Printing House Yd
17 Perseverance Works
18 Crooked Billet Yd
19 Drysdale Ho
20 Castlefrank Ho
21 School App
22 Basing House Yd
23 Mail Coach Yd
24 St Monica's RC Prim Sch
25 Symister Mews
26 Hackney Com Coll
A3
1 Bracer Ho
2 Scorton Ho
3 Fern Cl
4 Macbeth Ho
5 Oberon Ho
6 Buckland Ct
7 Crondall Ct
8 Osric Path
9 Caliban Twr
10 Celia Ho
11 Juliet Ho
12 Bacchus Wlk
13 Malcolm Ho
14 Homefield St
15 Crondall Pl
16 Blanca Ho
17 Miranda Ho
18 Falstaff Ho
19 Charmian Ho
20 Myrtle Wlk
21 Arden Ho
22 Sebastian Ho
23 Stanway Ct
24 Jerrold St
25 Rosalind Ho
26 Cordelia Ho
27 Monteagle Ct
28 John Parry Ct
29 James Anderson Ct
30 Ben Jonson Ct
31 Sara Lane Ct
32 Walbrook Ct
33 Burbage Sch
A4
1 Portelet Ct
2 Trinity Ct
3 Rozel Ct
4 St Helier Ct
5 Corbiere Ho
6 Kenning Ho
7 Higgins Ho
8 Cavell Ho
9 Girling Ho
10 Fulcher Ho
11 Francis Ho
12 Norris Ho
13 Kempton Ho
14 Nesham Ho
15 Crossbow Ho
16 Catherine Ho
17 Strale Ho
18 Horner Hos
19 Stringer Hos
20 Whitmore Ho
21 Nightingale Ho
22 Wilmer Gdns
23 Arrow Ho
24 Archer Ho
25 Meriden Ho
26 Rover Ho
27 Bowyer Ho
28 Tiller Ho
29 Canalside Studios
30 Kleine Wharf
31 Benyon Wharf
32 Quebec Wharf
33 Belvedere Ct
34 Portfleet Pl
B2
1 Gorsuch Pl
2 Strout's Pl
3 Vaughan Est
4 George Loveless Ho
5 Baroness Rd
6 James Brine Ho
7 Arthur Wade Ho
8 Robert Owen Ho
9 Sivill Ho
10 Georgina Gdns
11 Old Market Sq
12 Cuff Point
13 Bakers Rents
14 Leopold Bldgs
15 Dunmore Point
16 Wingfield Ho
17 Gascoigne Pl
18 Mandela Ho
19 Virginia Rd
20 Briggs Ho
21 Packenham Ho
22 Gowan Ho
23 Kirton Gdns
24 Chambord Ho
25 Ducal St
26 Strickland Ho
27 Alliston Ho
28 Gibraltar Wlk
29 Equity Sq
30 Shacklewell St
31 Rochelle St
32 Sonning Ho
33 Culham Ho
34 Hurley Ho
35 Palissy St
36 Taplow Ho
37 Chertsey Ho
38 Sunbury Ho
39 Sunbury Workshops
40 Datchett Ho
41 Hocker St
42 Coll Sharp Ct
43 Marlow Studio Workshops
44 Marlow Ho
45 Shiplake Ho
46 Wargrave Ho
47 Iffley Ho
48 Virginia Prim Sch
49 Bethnal Green Tech Coll
B3
1 Queensbridge Ct
2 Godwin Ho
3 Kent Ct
4 Brunswick Ho
5 Weymouth Ct
6 Sovereign Mews
7 Dunloe Ct
8 Cremer Bsns Ctr
9 James Hammett Ho
10 Allgood St
11 Horatio St
12 Cadell Ho
13 Horatio Ho
14 Shipton Ho
15 Haggerston Sch
16 Randal Cremer JMI Sch
B4
1 Hilborough Ct
2 Scriven Ct
3 Livermere Ct
4 Angrave Ct
5 Angrave Pas
6 Benfleet Ct
7 Belford Ho
8 Orme Ho
9 Clemson Ho
10 Longman Ho
11 Lowther Ho
12 Lovelace Ho
13 Harlowe Ho
14 Pamela Ho
15 Samuel Ho
16 Acton Ho
17 Loanda Ct
18 Phoenix Cl
19 Richardson Cl
20 Thrasher Cl
21 Mary Secole Cl
22 Canal Path
23 Pear Tree Cl
24 Hebden Ct
25 Charlton Ct
26 Laburnum Ct
27 Mansfield Ct
28 Garden Pl
29 Amber Wharf
30 Haggerston Studios
C1
1 Bentworth Ct
2 Hawksmoor Pl
3 Kerbela St
4 Fuller Cl
5 Kinsham Ho
6 Menotti St
7 Barwell Ho
8 Grimsby St
9 Reflection Ho

10 Fleet Street Hill
11 Bratley St
12 Weaver Ho
13 Cornerstone Ct
14 Stuttle Ho
15 McGlashon Ho
16 John Pritchard Ho
17 Thomas Buxton Jun & Inf Sch
18 St Anne RC Prim Sch
19 William Davis Prim Sch

C2 1 Providence Yd
2 Lygon Ho
3 Brabner Ho
4 Delta St
5 Delta Point
6 Tillet Way
7 Mullet Gdns
8 Lampern Sq
9 Kite Pl
10 Elver Gdns
11 Cobden Ho
12 Eversley Ho
13 Lorden Wlk
14 Rapley Ho
15 Dence Ho
16 McKinnon Wood Ho
17 Satchwell Rd
18 Dickinson Ho
19 Hutton Ho
20 Simmons Ho
21 Swinton Ho
22 Yates Ho
23 Johnson Ho
24 Jeremy Bentham Ho
25 Waring Ho
26 St James Ct
27 Ebony Ho
28 Azure Ho
29 Westhope Ho
30 Hague St
31 Elizabeth Selby Inf Sch
32 Lawdale Jun Sch

C3 1 London Terr
2 Sturdee Ho
3 Maude Ho
4 Haig Ho
5 Jellicoe Ho
6 Ropley St
7 Guinness Trust Bldgs
8 Ion Ct
9 Columbia Rd
10 Moye Cl
11 Morrel Cl
12 Courtauld Ho
13 Drummond Ho
14 Gurney Ho
15 Atkinson Ho
16 Halley Ho
17 Goldsmith's Sq
18 Shajjalal Ho
19 Ken Wilson Ho
20 April Ct
21 Crofts Ho
22 Sebright Ho
23 Beechwood Ho
24 Gillman Ho
25 Cheverell Ho
26 Besford Ho
27 Dinmont Ho
28 Elizabeth Mews

20 Sebright Pas
30 Wyndham Deedes Ho
31 Sheppard Ho
32 Mary James Ho
33 Hadrian Est
34 George Vale Ho
35 Lion Mills
36 St Peter's Ave
37 Pritchard Ho
38 Sebright Sch

C4 1 Broke Wlk
2 Rochemont Wlk
3 Marlborough Ave
4 Rivington Wlk
5 Magnin Cl
6 Gloucester Sq
7 Woolstone Ho
8 Marsworth Ho
9 Cheddington Ho
10 Linslade Ho
11 Cosgrove Ho
12 Blisworth Ho
13 Eleanor Ct
14 Wistow Ho
15 Muscott Ho
16 Boxmoor Ho
17 Linford Ho
18 Pendley Ho
19 Northchurch Ho
20 Debdale Ho
21 Broadway Market Mews
22 Welshpool Ho
23 Ada Ho
24 St Paul's with St Michael's Prim Sch

25
A1 1 Rochester Ct
2 Weaver Ct
3 Greenheath Bsns Ctr
4 Glass St
5 Herald St
6 Northesk Ho
7 Codrington Ho
8 Heathpool Ct
9 Mocatta Ho
10 Harvey Ho
11 Blackwood Ho
12 Rutherford Ho
13 Bullen Ho
14 Fremantle Ho
15 Pellew Ho
16 Ashington Ho
17 Dinnington Ho
18 Bartholomew Sq
19 Steeple Ct
20 Orion Ho
21 Fellbrigg St
22 Hague Prim Sch
23 Eagle Ho
24 Sovereign Ho
25 Redmill Ho
26 Berry Ho
27 Grindall Ho
28 Collingwood Ho
29 Stewart Headlam Prim Sch

A2 1 Charles Dickens Ho
2 Adrian Bolt Ho
3 William Rathbone Ho
4 Southwood Smith Ho

5 Rushmead
6 William Channing Ho
7 John Cartwright Ho
8 Charles Darwin Ho
9 Thomas Burt Ho
10 John Fielden Ho
11 Gwilym Maries Ho
12 Joseph Priestley Ho
13 Wear Pl
14 John Nettleford Ho
15 Thornaby Ho
16 Stockton Ho
17 Barnard Ho
18 Gainford Ho
19 Stapleton Ho
20 James Middleton Ho
21 Kedleston Wlk
22 Queen Margaret Flats
23 Hollybush Ho
24 Horwood Ho
25 Norden Ho
26 Newcourt Ho
27 Seabright St
28 Viaduct Pl
29 Sunlight Sq
30 Providence Row Cl
31 Oaklands Sec Sch
32 Raine's Foundation Lower Sch
33 Beatrice Tate Sch

A3 1 Dinmont St
2 Marian St
3 Claredale Ho
4 Keeling Ho
5 Maple St
6 Winkley St
7 Temple Dwellings
8 Argos Ho
9 Helen Ho
10 Lysander Ho
11 Antenor Ho
12 Paris Ho
13 Nestor Ho
14 Hector Ho
15 Ajax Ho
16 Achilles Ho
17 Priam Ho
18 Peabody Est
19 Felix St
20 Cambridge Cres
21 Peterley Bsns Ctr
22 Beckwith Ho
23 Brookfield Ho
24 Parminter Ind Est
25 Ted Roberts Ho
26 Cambridge Ct
27 Millennium Dr
28 William Caslon Ho
29 Hugh Platt Ho
30 West St
31 Mayfield Ho
32 Apollo Ho
33 Tanners Yd
34 Teesdale Yd

A4 1 Welshpool St
2 Broadway Ho
3 Regents Wharf
4 London Wharf
5 Warburton Ho
6 Warburton St
7 Triangle Rd
8 Warburton Rd
9 Williams Ho

10 Booth Cl
11 Albert Cl
12 King Edward Mans
13 Victoria Bldgs
14 Andrews Wharf
15 London Fields Prim Sch
16 Triangle The
17 Com Coll Hackney The

B1 1 William's Bldgs
2 Donegal Ho
3 Pelican Pas
4 Frederick Charrington Ho
5 Wickford Ho
6 Braintree Ho
7 Doveton Ho
8 Doveton St
9 Cephas Ho
10 Sceptre Ho
11 Bancroft Ho
12 Stothard Ho
13 Redclyf Ho
14 Winkworth Cotts
15 Amiel St
16 Hadleigh Ho
17 Hadleigh Cl
18 Ryder Ho
19 Kenton Ho
20 Colebert Ho
21 Ibbott St
22 Rickman Ho
23 Rickman St
24 Stothard Ho
25 Barbanel Ho
26 Stannard Cotts
27 St Peters Ct
28 Rennie Cotts
29 Pemell Cl
30 Pemell Ho
31 Leatherdale St
32 Gouldman Ho
33 Lamplighter Cl
34 Sherren Ho
35 Marlborough Lo
36 Hamilton Lo
37 Montgomery Lo
38 Cleveland Gr
39 Cromwell Lo
40 Bardsey Pl
41 Charrington Ho
42 Hayfield Yd
43 Allport Mews
44 Colin Winter Ho
45 John Scurr Prim Sch

B2 1 Mulberry Ho
2 Gretton Ho
3 Merceron Ho
4 Montfort Ho
5 Westbrook Ho
6 Sugar Loaf Wlk
7 Museum Ho
8 Burnham Est
9 Globe Terr
10 Moravian St
11 Shepton Hos
12 Mendip Hos
13 Academy Ct
14 Pepys Ho
15 Swinburne Ho
16 Moore Ho
17 Morris Ho
18 Burns Ho
19 Milton Ho
20 Whitman Ho

25 B4   295
21 Shelley Ho
22 Keats Ho
23 Dawson Ho
24 Bradheer Ho
25 Forber Ho
26 Hughes Ho
27 Silvester Ho
28 Rogers Est
29 Pavan Ct
30 Stafford Cripps Ho
31 Sidney Godley (VC) Ho
32 Butler Ho
33 Butler St
34 Thorne Ho
35 Bevin Ho
36 Tuscan Ho
37 Globe Prim Sch
38 Bangabandhu Prim Sch
39 Bonner Prim Sch

B3 1 Evesham Ho
2 James Campbell Ho
3 Thomas Hollywood Ho
4 James Docherty Ho
5 Ebenezer Mussel Ho
6 Jameson Ct
7 Edinburgh Cl
8 Roger Dowley Ct
9 Sherbrooke Ho
10 Calcraft Ho
11 Burrard Ho
12 Dundas Ho
13 Ponsonby Ho
14 Barnes Ho
15 Paget Ho
16 Maitland Ho
17 Chesil Ct
18 Reynolds Ho
19 Cleland Ho
20 Goodrich Ho
21 Rosebery Ho
22 Sankey Ho
23 Cyprus Pl
24 Royston St
25 Stainsbury St
26 Hunslett St
27 Baildon
28 Brockweir
29 Tytherton
30 Malmesbury
31 Kingswood
32 Colville Ho
33 St Elizabeth RC Prim Sch
34 Raine's Foundation Sch
35 St John's CE Prim Sch
36 Mowlem Prim Sch

B4 1 Halkett Ho
2 Christchurch Sq
3 Helena Pl
4 Swingfield Ho
5 Greenham Ho
6 Dinmore Ho
7 Anstey Ho
8 Weston Ho
9 Carbroke Ho
10 Bluebell Cl
11 Cherry Tree Cl

2 Hallings Wharf Studios
3 Poland Ho
4 Peter Heathfield Ho
5 Burford Rd
6 John F Kennedy Specl Sch
7 Univ of East London (Duncan Ho)

28

A1 **1** Lantry Ct
2 Rosemount Ct
3 Moreton Terr
4 Acton Central Ind Est
5 Rufford Twr
6 Narrow St
7 Mount Pl
8 Sidney Miller Ct
9 Mill Hill Terr
10 Cheltenham Pl
11 Mill Hill Gr
12 Benjamin Ho
13 Arlington Ct
14 Lombard Ct
15 Steyne Ho
16 Acton & West London Coll

B1 **1** Rectory Rd
2 Derwentwater Mans
3 Market Pl
4 Hooper's Mews
5 Cromwell Pl
6 Locarno Rd
7 Edgecote Cl
8 Harleyford Manor
9 Coopers Ct
10 Avingdor Ct
11 Steyne Ho

B3 **1** Avon Ct
2 Bromley Lo
3 Walter Ct
4 Lynton Terr
5 Acton Ho
6 Fells Haugh
7 Springfield Ct
8 Tamarind Ct
9 Lynton Ct
10 Aspen Ct
11 Pegasus Ct
12 Friary Park Ct

C3 **1** Rosebank Gdns
2 Rosebank
3 Edinburgh Ho
4 Western Ct
5 Kilronan

30

A1 **1** Arlington Ho
2 Lugard Ho
3 Shabana Ct
4 Sitarey Ct
5 Oaklands Ct
6 Davenport Mews

A2 **1** Abercrombie Ho
2 Bathurst Ho
3 Brisbane Ho
4 Bentinck Ho
5 Ellenborough Ho
6 Lawrence Cl
7 Mackenzie Cl
8 Carteret Ho
9 Calvert Ho
10 Winthrop Ho
11 Auckland Ho

12 Blaxland Ho
13 Havelock Cl
14 Hargraves Ho
15 Hudson Cl
16 Phipps Ho
17 Lawson Ho
18 Hastings Ho
19 Wolfe Ho
20 Malabar Ct
21 Charnock Ho
22 Canning Ho
23 Cornwallis Ho
24 Commonwealth Ave
25 Champlain Ho
26 Grey Ho
27 Durban Ho
28 Baird Ho
29 Campbell Ho
30 Mitchell Ho
31 Denham Ho
32 Mackay Ho
33 Evans Ho
34 Davis Ho

A3 **1** Holborn Ho
2 Clement Danes Ho
3 Vellacott Ho
4 O'Driscoll Ho
5 King Ho
6 Daley Ho
7 Selma Ho
8 Garrett Ho

B1 **1** Linden Ct
2 Frithville Ct
3 Blomfield Mans
4 Poplar Mews
5 Hopgood St
6 Westwood Ho
7 Stanlake Mews
8 Stanlake Villas
9 Alexandra Mans

B3 **1** Latimer Ind Est
2 Pankhurst Ho
3 Quadrangle The
4 Nightingale Ho
5 Gordon Ct
6 Ducane Ct
7 Browning Ho
8 Pavilion Terr
9 Ivebury Ct
10 Olympic Ho

B4 **1** Galleywood Ho
2 Edgcott Ho
3 Cuffley Ho
4 Addlestone Ho
5 Hockliffe Ho
6 Sarratt Ho
7 Firle Ho
8 Sutton Est The
9 Terling Ho
10 Danes Ho
11 Udimore Ho
12 Vange Ho
13 Binbrook Ho
14 Yeadon Ho
15 Yatton Ho
16 Yarrow Ho
17 Clement Ho
18 Danebury
19 Coronation Ct
20 Calderon Pl
21 St Quintin Gdns

C1 **1** St Katherine's Wlk
2 Dorrit Ho
3 Pickwick Ho
4 Dombey Ho

5 Caraday Villas
6 Mortimer Ho
7 Nickleby Ho
8 Stebbing Ho
9 Boxmoor Ho
10 Poynter Ho
11 Swanscombe Ho
12 Darnley Terr
13 Norland Ho
14 Hume Ho
15 Boundary Ho
16 Norland Rd
17 Helix Ct

C2 **1** Frinstead Ho
2 Hurstway Wlk
3 Testerton Wlk
4 Grenfell Wlk
5 Grenfell Twr
6 Barandon Wlk
7 Treadgold Ho
8 St Clements Ct
9 Willow Way
10 Florence Ho
11 Dora Ho
12 Carton Ho
13 Agnes Ho
14 Marley Ho
15 Estella Ho
16 Waynflete Sq
17 Pippin Ho
18 Baseline Business Studios
19 St Francis of Assisi Prim Sch
20 Nicholas Rd

C3 **1** Kelfield Ct
2 Downing Ho
3 Crosfield Ct
4 Robinson Ho
5 Scampston Mews
6 Girton Villas
7 Ray Ho
8 Walmer Ho
9 Goodrich Ct
10 Arthur Ct
11 Whitstable Ho
12 Kingsnorth Ho
13 Bridge Cl
14 Prospect Ho
15 St Marks Rd
16 Whitchurch Ho
17 Blechynden Ho
18 Waynflete Sq
19 Bramley Ho
20 Dixon Ho
21 Oxford Gardens Prim Sch
22 Bassett House Sch

C4 **1** Treverton Twr
2 Raymede Twr
3 Bruce Ho
4 Balfour Ho
5 Burleigh Ho
6 Sion-Manning RC Sch for Girls
7 St Charles RC Prim Sch
8 St Charles RC Sixth Form Coll

31

A3 **1** Malton Mews
2 Lancaster Lo
3 Manning Ho
4 Galsworthy Ho
5 Hudson Ho
6 Cambourne Mews

7 Upper Talbot Wlk
8 Kingsdown Cl
9 Lower Clarendon Wlk
10 Talbot Grove Ho
11 Clarendon Wlk
12 Upper Clarendon Wlk
13 Camelford Wlk
14 Upper Camelford Wlk
15 Camelford Ct
16 Thomas Jones Prim Sch
17 Notting Hill Prep Sch

A4 **1** Murchison Ho
2 Macaulay Ho
3 Chesterton Ho
4 Chiltern Ho
5 Lionel Ho
6 Watts Ho
7 Wheatstone Ho
8 Telford Ho
9 Golborne Mews
10 Millwood St
11 St Columb's Ho
12 Norfolk Mews
13 Lionel Mews
14 Kensington & Chelsea Coll
15 Bevington Prim Sch
16 Sion-Manning RC Sch for Girls
17 Lloyd Williamson Sch

B3 **1** Silvester Ho
2 Golden Cross Mews
3 Tavistock Mews
4 Clydesdale Ho
5 Colville Prim Sch
6 Melchester
7 Pinehurst Ct
8 Denbigh Ho

B4 **1** Blagrove Rd
2 All Saints Ho
3 Tavistock Ho
4 Leamington Ho

C3 **1** Shottsford
2 Tolchurch
3 Casterbridge
4 Sandbourne
5 Anglebury
6 Weatherbury
7 Westbourne Gr Mews
8 Rosehart Mews
9 Viscount Ct
10 Hereford Mans
11 Hereford Mews
12 St Mary of the Angels RC Prim Sch

C4 **1** Ascot Ho
2 Ashgrove Ct
3 Lockbridge Ct
4 Swallow Ct
5 Nightingale Lo
6 Hammond Lo
7 Penfield Lo
8 Harvey Lo
9 Hunter Lo
10 Barnard Lo
11 Falcon Lo
12 Johnson Lo
13 Livingstone Lo
14 Nuffield Lo

32 A1 **297**

15 Finch Lo
16 Polesworth Ho
17 Oversley Ho
18 Derrycombe Ho
19 Buckshead Ho
20 Combe Ho
21 Culham Ho
22 Dainton Ho
23 Devonport Ho
24 Honwell Ho
25 Truro Ho
26 Sunderland Ho
27 Stonehouse Ho
28 Riverford Ho
29 Portishead Ho
30 Mickleton Ho
31 Keyham Ho
32 Moulsford Ho
33 Shrewsbury Mews
34 St Stephen's Mews
35 Westway Lo
36 Langley Ho
37 Brindley Ho
38 Radway Ho
39 Astley Ho
40 Willow Ct
41 Larch Ct
42 Elm Ct
43 Beech Ct
44 Worcester Ct
45 Union Ct
46 Leicester Ct
47 Kennet Ct
48 Oxford Ct
49 Fazerley Ct

32

A1 **1** China Ct
2 Wellington Terr
3 Stevedore St
4 Portland Sq
5 Reardon Ho
6 Lowder Ho
7 Meeting House Alley
8 Farthing Fields
9 Oswell Ho
10 Park Lo
11 Doughty Ct
12 Inglefield Sq
13 Chopin's Ct
14 Welsh Ho
15 Hilliard Ho
16 Clegg St
17 Tasman Ho
18 Ross Ho
19 Wapping Dock St
20 Bridewell Pl
21 New Tower Bldgs
22 Tower Bldgs
23 Chimney Ct
24 Jackman Ho
25 Fenner Ho
26 Franklin Ho
27 Frobisher Ho
28 Flinders Ho
29 Chancellor Ho
30 Beechey Ho
31 Reardon Path
32 Parry Ho
33 Vancover Ho
34 Willoughby Ho
35 Sanctuary The
36 Dundee Ct

22 Grosvenor Ct
23 Lime House Ct
24 Swallow Pl
25 St Anne's Trad Est
26 Stepney Greencoat CE Prim Sch The
27 Sir William Burrough Prim Sch
28 Our Lady RC Prim Sch

B4 1 Wearmouth Ho
2 Elmslie Point
3 Grindley Ho
4 Stileman Ho
5 Wilcox Ho
6 Huddart St
7 Robeson St
8 Couzens Ho
9 Perley Ho
10 Whytlaw Ho
11 Booker Cl
12 Tunley Gn
13 Callingham Cl
14 Bowry Ho
15 Perkins Ho
16 Printon Ho
17 Tasker Ho
18 St Paul with St Luke CE Prim Sch

C2 1 West India Ho
2 Berber Pl
3 Birchfield Ho
4 Elderfield Ho
5 Thornfield Ho
6 Gorsefield Ho
7 Arborfield Ho
8 Colborne Ho
9 East India Bldgs
10 Compass Point
11 Salter St
12 Garland Ct
13 Bogart Ct
14 Fonda Ct
15 Welles Ct
16 Rogers Ct
17 Premier Pl
18 Kelly Ct
19 Flynn Ct
20 Mary Jones Ho
21 Cannon Dr
22 Horizon Bldg
23 Holy Family RC Prim Sch

C3 1 Landin Ho
2 Thomas Road Ind Est
3 Vickery's Wharf
4 Abbotts Wharf
5 Limehouse Ct
6 Charlesworth Ho
7 Gurdon Ho
8 Trendell Ho
9 Menteath Ho
10 Minchin Ho
11 Donne Ho
12 Old School Sq
13 Anglesey Ho
14 Gough Wlk
15 Baring Ho
16 Gladstone Ho
17 Hopkins Ho
18 Granville Ho
19 Overstone Ho
20 Pusey Ho
21 Russell Ho
22 Stanley Ho

C4 1 Bredel Ho

2 Linton Ho
3 Matthews Ho
4 Woodcock Ho
5 Limborough Ho
6 Maydwell Ho
7 Underhill Ho
8 Meyrick Ho
9 Ambrose Ho
10 Carpenter Ho
11 Robinson Ho
12 Bellmaker Ct
13 Lime Tree Ct
14 Bracken Ho
15 Bramble Ho
16 Berberis Ho
17 Bilberry Ho
18 Ladyfern Ho
19 Rosebay Ho
20 Invicta Cl
21 Phoenix Bsns Ctr
22 Metropolitan Cl
23 Busbridge Ho
24 St Paul's Way Com Sch
25 Stebon Prim Sch

34

A2 1 Westcott Ho
2 Corry Ho
3 Malam Gdns
4 Blomfield Ho
5 Devitt Ho
6 Leyland Ho
7 Wigram Ho
8 Willis Ho
9 Balsam Ho
10 Finch's Ct
11 Poplar Bath St
12 Lawless St
13 Storey Ho
14 Abbot Ho
15 Woodall Cl
16 Landon Wlk
17 Goodhope Ho
18 Goodfaith Ho
19 Winant Ho
20 Goodspeed Ho
21 Lubbock Ho
22 Goodwill Ho
23 Martindale Ho
24 Holmsdale Ho
25 Norwood Ho
26 Constant Ho
27 Tower Hamlets Coll

A3 1 Colebrook Ho
2 Essex Ho
3 Salisbury Ho
4 Maidstone Ho
5 Osterley Ho
6 Norwich Ho
7 Clarissa Ho
8 Elgin Ho
9 Shaftesbury Lo
10 Shepherd Ho
11 Jeremiah St
12 Elizabeth Cl
13 Chilcot Cl
14 Fitzgerald Ho
15 Vesey Path
16 Ennis Ho
17 Kilmore Ho
18 Cygnet House N
19 Cygnet House S
20 Lansbury Lawrence Prim Sch
21 Bygrove Prim Sch

2 Mayflower Prim Sch
3 Tower Hamlets Coll

A4 1 Sumner Ho
2 David Hewitt Ho
3 St Gabriels Cl
4 Limehouse Cut
5 Colmans Wharf
6 Foundary Ho
7 Radford Ho
8 Manorfield Prim Sch
9 St Saviour's CE Prim Sch
10 Pioneer Cl

B1 1 Lumina Bldg
2 Nova Ct W
3 Nova Ct E
4 Aurora Bldg
5 Arran Ho
6 Kintyre Ho
7 Vantage Mews
8 Managers St
9 Horatio Pl
10 Concordia Wharf

B2 1 Discovery Ho
2 Mountague Pl
3 Virginia Ho
4 Collins Ho
5 Lawless Ho
6 Carmichael Ho
7 Commodore Ho
8 Mermaid Ho
9 Bullivant St
10 Anderson Ho
11 Mackrow Wlk
12 Robin Hood Gdns
13 Prestage Way
14 Woolmore Prim Sch

B3 1 Glenkerry Ho
2 Carradale Ho
3 Langdon Ho
4 Balfron Twr
5 St Frideswides Mews
6 Tabard Ct
7 Delta Bldg
8 Findhorn St
9 Kilbrennan Ho
10 Thistle Ho
11 Heather Ho
12 Tartan Ho
13 Sharman Ho
14 Trident Ho
15 Wharf View Ct
16 Culloden Prim Sch

B4 1 Mills Gr
2 St Michaels Ct
3 Duncan Ct

C2 1 Quixley St
2 Romney Ho
3 Pumping Ho
4 Switch Ho
5 Wingfield Ct
6 Explorers Ct
7 Sexton Ct
8 Keel Ct
9 Bridge Ct
10 Sail Ct
11 Settlers Ct
12 Pilgrims Mews
13 Studley Ct
14 Wotton Ct
15 Cape Henry Ct
16 Bartholomew Ct
17 Adventurers Ct

18 Susan Constant Ct
19 Atlantic Ct

C3 1 Lansbury Gdns
2 Theseus Ho
3 Adams Ho
4 Jones Ho
5 Sam March Ho
6 Arapiles Ho
7 Athenia Ho
8 Julius Ho
9 Jervis Bay Ho
10 Helen Mackay Ho
11 Gaze Ho
12 Ritchie Ho
13 Blairgowrie Ct
14 Circle Ho
15 Dunkeld Ho
16 Rosemary Dr
17 Sorrel La
18 East India Dock Road Tunnel

35

B3 1 Newton Point
2 Sparke Terr
3 Montesquieu Terr
4 Crawford Point
5 Rathbone Ho
6 George St
7 Emily St
8 Fendt Cl
9 Sabbarton St
10 St Luke Prim CE Sch
11 Briary Ct
12 Shaftesbury Ho

B4 1 Radley Terr
2 Bernard Cassidy St
3 Rathbone Mkt
4 Thomas North Terr
5 Mary St
6 Hughes Terr
7 Swanscombe Point
8 Rawlinson Point
9 Kennedy Cox Ho
10 Cooper St

C1 1 Capulet Mews
2 Pepys Cres
3 De Quincey Mews
4 Hardy Ave
5 Tom Jenkinson Rd
6 Kennacraig Cl
7 Charles Flemwell Mews
8 Gatcombe Rd
9 Badminton Mews
10 Holyrood Mews
11 Britannia Gate
12 Dalemain Mews
13 Bowes-Lyon Hall
14 Lancaster hall
15 Victoria Hall

C2 1 Clements Ave
2 Martindale Ave
3 Balearic Apts
4 Marmara Apts
5 Baltic Apts
6 Coral Apts
7 Aegean Apts
8 Capital East Apts

C4 1 Odeon Ct
2 Edward Ct
3 Newhaven La
4 Ravenscroft Cl
5 Douglas Rd
6 Ferrier Point
7 Harvey Point

8 Wood Point
9 Trinity St
10 Pattinson Point
11 Clinch Ct
12 Mint Bsns Pk
13 Keir Hardy Prim Sch

36

A1 1 Burford Ho
2 Hope Cl
3 Centaur Ct
4 Phoenix Ct

C1 1 Surrey Cres
2 Forbes Ho
3 Haining Cl
4 Melville Ct
5 London Stile
6 Stile Hall Par
7 Priory Lo
8 Meadowcroft
9 St James Ct
10 Rivers Ho

37

A1 1 Churchdale Ct
2 Cromwell Cl
3 Cambridge Rd S
4 Oxbridge Ct
5 Tomlinson Cl
6 Gunnersbury Mews
7 Grange The
8 Gunnersbury Cl
9 Bellgrave Lo

A2 12 Orchard House Sch

A4 1 Cheltenham Pl
2 Beaumaris Twr
3 Arundel Ho
4 Pevensey Ct
5 Jerome Twr
6 Anstey Ct
7 Bennett Ct
8 Gunnersbury Ave
9 Barrington Ct
10 Hope Gdns
11 Park Road E

B1 1 Arlington Park Mans
2 Sandown Ho
3 Goodwood Ho
4 Windsor Ho
5 Lingfield Ho
6 Ascot Ho
7 Watchfield Ct
8 Belgrave Ct
9 Beverley Ct
10 Beaumont Ct
11 Harvard Rd
12 Troubridge Ct
13 Branden Lo
14 Fromow's Cnr
15 Heathfield House Sch

B2 1 Chiswick Green Studios
2 Bell Ind Est
3 Fairlawn Ct
4 Dukes Gate
5 Dewsbury Ct
6 Chiswick Terr
7 Mortlake Ho

B3 1 Blackmore Twr
2 Bollo Ct
3 Kipling Twr

4 Lawrence Ct
5 Maugham Ct
6 Reade Ct
7 Woolf Ct
8 Shaw Ct
9 Verne Ct
10 Wodehouse Ct
11 Greenock Rd
12 Garden Ct
13 Barons Gate
14 Cleveland Rd
15 Carver Cl
16 Chapter Cl
17 Beauchamp Cl
18 Holmes Ct
19 Copper Mews
B4 1 Belgrave Ct
2 Buckland Wlk
3 Frampton Ct
4 Telfer Cl
5 Harlech Twr
6 Corfe Twr
7 Barwick Ho
8 Charles Hocking Ho
9 Sunninghill Ct
10 Salisbury St
11 Jameson Pl
12 Castle Cl
C1 1 Chatsworth Lo
2 Prospect Pl
3 Townhall Ave
4 Devonhurst Pl
5 Heathfield Ct
6 Horticultural Pl
7 Merlin Ho
8 Autumn Rise
C2 1 Disraeli Ct
2 Winston Wlk
3 Rusthall Mans
4 Bedford Park Mans
5 Essex Place Sq
6 Holly Rd
7 Homecross Ho
8 Swan Bsns Ctr
9 Jessop Ho
10 Belmont Prim Sch

38
A1 1 Glebe Ct
2 Devonshire Mews
3 Binns Terr
4 Ingress St
5 Swanscombe Rd
6 Brackley Terr
7 Stephen Fox Ho
8 Manor Gdns
9 Coram Ho
10 Flaxman Ho
11 Thorneycroft Ho
12 Thornhill Ho
13 Kent Ho
14 Oldfield Ho
15 William Hogarth Sch The
A2 1 Chestnut Ho
2 Bedford Ho
3 Bedford Cnr
4 Sydney Ho
5 Bedford Park Cnr
6 Priory Gdns
7 Windmill Alley
8 Castle Pl

9 Jonathan Ct
10 Windmill Pas
11 Chardin Rd
12 Gable Ho
13 Chiswick & Bedford Park Prep Sch
14 Arts Educational Sch The
A3 1 Fleet Ct
2 Ember Ct
3 Emlyn Gdns
4 Clone Ct
5 Brent Ct
6 Abbey Ct
7 Ormsby Lo
8 St Catherine's Ct
9 Lodge The
A4 1 Longford Ct
2 Mole Ct
3 Lea Ct
4 Wandle Ct
5 Beverley Ct
6 Roding Ct
7 Crane Ct
B1 1 Miller's Ct
2 British Grove Pas
3 British Grove S
4 Berestede Rd
5 North Eyot Gdns
B2 1 Flanders Mans
2 Stamford Brook Mans
3 Linkenholt Mans
4 Prebend Mans
5 Middlesex Ct
B3 1 Stamford Brook Gdns
2 Hauteville Court Gdns
3 Ranelagh Gdns
C1 1 Chisholm Ct
2 North Verbena Gdns
3 Western Terr
4 Verbena Gdns
5 Montrose Villas
6 Hammersmith Terr
7 South Black Lion La
8 St Peter's Wharf
9 Eden High Sch
10 St Peter's CE Prim Sch
C2 1 Hamlet Ct
2 Derwent Ct
3 Westcroft Ct
4 Black Lion Mews
5 St Peter's Villas
6 Standish Ho
7 Chambon Pl
8 Court Mans
9 Longthorpe Ct
10 Charlotte Ct
11 Westside
12 Park Ct
13 London Ho
14 Latymer Upper Sch
15 Polish Univ Abroad
C3 1 Elizabeth Finn Ho
2 Ashchurch Ct
3 King's Par
4 Inver Ct
5 Ariel Ct
6 Pocklington Ct
7 Vitae Apartments
C4 1 Becklow Gdns
2 Victoria Ho

3 Lycett Pl
4 Kylemore Ct
5 Alexandra Ct
6 Lytten Ct
7 Becklow Mews
8 Northcroft Ct
9 Bailey Ct
10 Spring Cott
11 Landor Wlk
12 Laurence Mews
13 Hadyn Park Ct
14 Askew Mans
15 Malvern Ct

39
A1 1 Prince's Mews
2 Aspen Gdns
3 Hampshire Hog La
4 Blades Ct
A2 1 Albion Gdns
2 Flora Gdns
3 Lamington St
4 Felgate Mews
5 Galena Ho
6 Albion Mews
7 Albion Ct
8 King Street Cloisters
9 Dimes Pl
10 Clarence Ct
11 Hampshire Hog La
12 Marryat Ct
13 Ravenscourt Ho
14 Ravenscourt Theatre Sch
15 Cambridge Sch
16 Godolphin & Latymer Sch
17 Flora Gardens Prim Sch
A3 1 Ravenscourt Park Mans
2 Paddenswick Ct
3 Ashbridge Ct
4 Brackenbury Prim Sch
A4 1 Westbush Ct
2 Goldhawk Mews
3 Sycamore Ho
4 Shackleton Ct
5 Drake Ct
6 Scotts Ct
7 Raleigh Ct
8 Melville Court Flats
9 Southway Ct
B1 1 Bridge Avenue Mans
2 Bridgeview
3 College Ct
4 Beatrice Ho
5 Amelia Ho
6 Edith Ho
7 Joanna Ho
8 Mary Ho
9 Adela Ho
10 Sophia Ho
11 Henrietta Ho
12 Charlotte Ho
13 Alexandra Ho
14 Bath Pl
15 Elizabeth Ho
16 Margaret Ho
17 Peabody Est
18 Eleanor Ho
19 Isabella Ho
20 Caroline Ho
21 Chancellors Wharf

22 Sussex Pl
23 St Paul's CE Prim Sch
B2 1 Phoenix Lodge Mans
2 Samuel's Cl
3 Broadway Arc
4 Brook Ho
5 Hammersmith Broadway
6 Broadway Ctr The
7 Cambridge Ct
8 Ashcroft Sq
9 Sacred Heart High Sch
10 King Street Coll
B4 1 Verulam Ho
2 Grove Mans
3 Frobisher Ct
4 Library Mans
5 Pennard Mans
6 New Shepherd's Bush Mkt
7 Kerrington Ct
8 Granville Mans
9 Romney Ct
10 Rayner Ct
11 Sulgrave Gdns
12 Bamborough Gdns
13 Hillary Ct
14 Market Studios
15 Lanark Mans
16 Miles Coverdale Prim Sch
17 St Stephen's CE Prim Sch
18 London Coll of Fashion (Lime Grove)
C2 1 St Paul's Girls' Sch
2 Bute House Prep Sch
3 Jacques Prevert Sch
4 Larmenier & Sacred Heart RC Prim Sch
C3 1 Grosvenor Residences
2 Blythe Mews
3 Burnand Ho
4 Bradford Ho
5 Springvale Terr
6 Ceylon Rd
7 Walpole Ct
8 Bronte Ct
9 Boswell Ct
10 Souldern Rd
11 Brook Green Flats
12 Haarlem Rd
13 Stafford Mans
14 Lionel Mans
15 Barradell Ho
C4 1 Vanderbilt Villas
2 Bodington Ct
3 Kingham Cl
4 Clearwater Terr
5 Lorne Gdns
6 Cameret Ct
7 Bush Ct
8 Shepherds Ct
9 Rockley Ct
10 Grampians The
11 Charcroft Ct
12 Addison Park Mans
13 Sinclair Mans
14 Fountain Ct

15 Woodford Ct
16 Roseford Ct
17 Woodstock Studios

40
A1 1 Hockney Ct
2 Toulouse Ct
3 Lowry Ct
4 Barry Ho
5 Lewis Ct
6 Gainsborough Ct
7 Renoir Ct
8 Blake Ct
9 Raphael Ct
10 Rembrandt Ct
11 Constable Ct
12 Da Vinci Ct
13 Gauguin Ct
14 Michelangelo Ct
15 Monet Ct
16 Weald Cl
17 Jasmin Lo
18 Birchmere Lo
19 Weybridge Ct
20 Florence Ho
21 Gleneagles Cl
22 Sunningdale Cl
23 Muirfield Cl
24 Turnberry Cl
25 St Andrews Cl
26 Kingsdown Cl
27 St Davids Cl
28 Galway Cl
29 Edenbridge Cl
30 Birkdale Cl
31 Tralee Ct
32 Woburn Ct
33 Belfry Cl
34 Troon Cl
35 Holywell Cl
A2 1 Market Pl
2 Trappes Ho
3 Thurland Ho
4 Ramsfort Ho
5 Hambley Ho
6 Holford Ho
7 Pope Ho
8 Southwell Ho
9 Mortain Ho
10 Radcliffe Ho
11 Southwark Park Est
12 Galleywall Road Trad Est
13 Trevithick Ho
14 Barlow Ho
15 Donkin Ho
16 Landmann Ho
17 Fitzmaurice Ho
18 Dodd Ho
A3 1 Perryn Rd
2 Chalfont Ho
3 Prestwood Ho
4 Farmer Ho
5 Gataker Ho
6 Gataker St
7 Cornick Ho
8 Glebe Ho
9 Matson Ho
10 Hickling Ho
11 St Andrews Ho
12 Southwark Coll (Surrey Docks Ctr)
13 Southwark Park Prim Sch
A4 1 Butterfield Cl
2 Janeway Ct
3 Trotwood Ho

302 43 C1

4 Station Mews Terr
5 Halstow Prim Sch
6 Holyrood Mews

44
A4 1 Ferry Sq
2 Watermans Ct
3 Wilkes Rd
4 Albany Par
5 Charlton Ho
6 Albany Ho
7 Alma Ho
8 Griffin Ct
9 Cressage Ho
10 Tunstall Wlk
11 Trimmer Wlk
12 Running Horse Yd
13 Mission Sq
14 Distillery Wlk
B2 1 Primrose Ho
2 Lawman Ct
3 Royston Ct
4 Garden Ct
5 Capel Lo
6 Devonshire Ct
7 Celia Ct
8 Rosslyn Ho
9 Branstone Ct
10 Lamerton Lo
11 Kew Lo
12 Dunraven Ho
13 Stoneleigh Lo
14 Tunstall Ct
15 Voltaire
C2 1 Clarendon Ct
2 Quintock Ho
3 Broome Ct
4 Lonsdale Mews
5 Elizabeth Cotts
6 Sandvays
7 Victoria Cotts
8 North Ave
9 Grovewood
10 Hamilton Ho
11 Melvin Ct
12 Royal Par
13 Power Ho
14 Station Ave
15 Blake Mews
C4 1 Strand-on-the-Green Schs

45
A2 1 Terrano Ho
2 Oak Ho
3 Aura Ho
4 Maple Ho
5 Cedar Ho
6 Saffron Ho
7 Lime Ho
8 Lavender Ho
9 Juniper Ho
A4 1 Falcons Pre Prep Sch The

46
B1 1 Melrose Rd
2 Seaforth Lo
3 St John's Gr
4 Sussex Ct
5 Carmichael Ct
6 Hampshire Ct
7 Thorne Pas
8 Brunel Ct

9 Beverley Path

47
C4 1 Cobb's Hall
2 Dorset Mans
3 St Clements Mans
4 Bothwell St
5 Hawksmoor St
6 Melcombe Prim Sch

48
A1 1 Langport Ho
2 Iveagh Ho
3 Newark Ho
4 Edgehill Ho
5 Hopton Ho
6 Ashby Ho
7 Nevil Ho
A2 1 Fairbairn Gn
2 Hammelton Gn
3 Foxley Sq
4 Silverburn Ho
5 Butler Ho
6 Dalkeith Ho
7 Turner Cl
8 Bathgate Ho
9 Black Roof Ho
10 Charles Edward Brooke Sch (Dennen Site)
11 Charles Edward Brooke Sch
A3 55 St Michael & All Angels CE Acad
A4 1 Faunce Ho
2 Garbett Ho
3 Harvard Ho
4 Doddington Pl
5 Kean Ho
6 Jephson Ho
7 Cornish Ho
8 Bateman Ho
9 Molesworth Ho
10 Walters Ho
11 Cruden Ho
12 Brawne Ho
13 Prescott Ho
14 Chalmer's Wlk
15 Copley Cl
16 King Charles Ct
B1 1 Bergen Ho
2 Oslo Ho
3 Viking Ho
4 Jutland Ho
5 Norvic Ho
6 Odin Ho
7 Baltic Ho
8 Nobel Ho
9 Mercia Ho
10 Kenbury Gdns
11 Zealand Ho
12 Elsinore Ho
13 Norse Ho
14 Denmark Mans
15 Dane Ho
16 Canterbury Ct
17 York Cl
18 Kenbury Mans
19 Parade Mans
20 Winterslow Ho
21 Lilford Ho
22 Bartholomew Ho
23 Guildford Ho
24 Boston Ho
25 Hereford Ho
26 Weyhill Ho

27 Lichfield Ho
28 Lansdown Ho
29 Honiton Ho
30 Pinner Ho
31 Baldock Ho
32 Widecombe Ho
33 Nottingham Ho
34 Witham Ho
35 Barnet Ho
36 Empress Mews
B2 1 Bertha Neubergh Ho
2 Mornington Mews
3 Badsworth Rd
4 Pearson Cl
5 Elm Tree Ct
6 Samuel Lewis Trust Dwellings
7 Milkwell Yd
8 Keswick Ho
9 Mitcham Ho
10 Sacred Heart RC Sec Sch
B3 1 Boundary Ho
2 Day Ho
3 Burgess Ho
4 Carlyle Ho
5 Myers Ho
6 Thompson Ave
7 Palgrave Ho
8 Winnington Ho
9 Brantwood Ho
10 Lowell Ho
11 Jessie Duffett Ho
12 Otterburn Ho
13 Crossmount Ho
14 Venice Ct
15 Bowyer St
16 Livingstone Ho
17 Gothic Ct
18 Coniston Ho
19 Harlynwood
20 Carey Ct
21 Finley Ct
22 Grainger Ct
23 Hayes Ct
24 Moffat Ho
25 Marinel Ho
26 Hodister Cl
27 Arnot Ho
28 Lamb Ho
29 Kipling Ho
30 Keats Ho
31 Kenyon Ho
32 New Church Rd
33 Sir John Kirk Cl
34 Comber Grove Prim Sch
35 St Joseph's RC Inf & Jun Schs
C1 1 Selborne Rd
2 Hascombe Terr
C2 1 Joiners Arms Yd
2 Butterfly Wlk
3 Cuthill Wlk
4 Colonades
5 Artichoke Mews
6 Peabody Bldgs
7 Brighton Ho
8 Park Ho
9 Peabody Ct
10 Lomond Ho
11 Lamb Ho
12 Kimpton Ct
13 Belham Wlk
14 Datchelor Pl
15 Harvey Rd

C3 1 Masterman Ho
2 Milton Ho
3 Pope Ho
4 Chester Ct
5 Marvel Ho
6 Flecker Ho
7 Landor Ho
8 Leslie Prince Ct
9 Evelina Mans
10 Langland Ho
11 Drinkwater Ho
12 Procter Ho
13 Shirley Ho
14 Drayton Ho
15 Bridges Ho
16 Cunningham Ho
17 Hood Ho
18 Herrick Ho
19 Dekker Ho
20 Houseman Way
21 Coleby Path
22 Brunswick Park Prim Sch
C4 1 Queens Ho
2 Arnside Ho
3 Horsley St
4 St Peter's Ho
5 St Johns Ho
6 St Marks Ho
7 St Stephens Ho
8 St Matthew's Ho
9 Red Lion Cl
10 Boyson Rd
11 Bradenham

49
A1 1 Springfield Ho
2 Craston Ho
3 Walters Ho
4 Edgecombe Ho
5 Fowler Ho
6 Rignold Ho
7 Chatham Ho
A2 1 Barnwell Ho
2 Brunswick Villas
3 St Giles Twr
4 Bentley Ho
5 Dawson Ho
6 Dryden Ho
7 Mayward Ho
8 Longleigh Ho
9 Fairwall Ho
10 Bodeney Ho
11 Sandby Ho
12 Vestry Mews
13 Netley
14 Lakanal
15 Racine
16 Camberwell Coll of Arts
A3 1 Tower Mill Rd
2 Tilson Cl
3 Granville Sq
4 Edgar Wallace Cl
5 Potters Cl
6 Dorton Cl
7 Samuel Jones Ind Est
8 Dibden Ho
9 Marchwood Cl
10 Pilgrims Cloisters
11 Beacon Ho
12 Teather St
13 Stacy Path
14 Rumball Ho
15 Ballow Cl
16 Rill Ho

17 Southwark Coll (Camberwell Ctr)
18 St George's CE Prim Sch
A4 1 Downend Ct
2 Andoversford Ct
3 Pearse St
4 Watling St
5 Gandolfi St
6 Comfort St
7 Tower Mill Rd
B2 1 Colbert
2 Voltaire
3 Finch Mews
4 Charles Coveney Rd
5 Bamber Rd
6 Crane St
7 Curlew Ho
8 Mallard Ho
9 Tern Ho
10 Crane Ho
11 Falcon Ho
12 Bryanston Ho
13 Basing Ct
14 Marcus Ho
15 Sheffield Ho
16 Highshore Sch
17 St James The Great RC Prim Sch
18 Oliver Goldsmith Prim Sch
B3 1 Painswick Ct
2 Sharpness Ct
3 Mattingly Way
4 Hordle Prom N
5 Burcher Gale Gr
6 Calypso Cres
7 Hordle Prom S
8 Cinnamon Cl
9 Savannah Cl
10 Thames Cl
11 Shannon Ct
12 Amstel Cl
13 Danube Ct
14 Tilbury Cl
15 Hordle Prom E
16 Indus Ct
17 Oakcourt
18 Palm Ct
19 Rowan Ct
20 Blackthorn Ct
21 Pear Ct
22 Lidgate Rd
23 Whistler Mews
24 Boathouse Wlk
25 Camberwell Coll of Arts
B4 1 Willsbridge Ct
2 Cam Ct
3 Quedgeley Ct
4 Saul Ct
5 Quenington Ct
6 Westonbirt Ct
7 Wickway Ct
C1 1 William Margrie Cl
2 William Blake Ho
3 Quantock Mews
4 Choumert Sq
5 Parkstone Rd
6 Atwell Rd
C2 1 Canal Head Public Sq
2 Angelina Ho
3 Jarvis Ho
4 Richland Ho
5 Honeywood Ho
6 Wakefield Ho

7 Primrose Ho
8 Hardcastle Ho
9 Dunstall Ho
10 Springtide Cl
11 Purdon Ho
12 Flamborough Ho
13 Lambrook Ho
14 Witcombe Point
15 Yarnfield Sq
16 Winford Ct
17 Portbury Cl
18 Robert Keen Cl
C3 1 Thornbill Ho
2 Vervain Ho
3 Woodstar Ho
4 Tamarind Ho
5 Hereford Retreat
6 Haymerle Ho
7 Furley Ho
8 Thomas Milner Ho
9 Applegarth Ho
10 Freda Corbett Cl
11 Rudbeck Ho
12 Henslow Ho
13 Lindley Ho
14 Collinson Ho
15 Sister Mabel's Way
16 Timberland Cl
17 Hastings Cl
18 Sidmouth Ho
19 Budleigh Ho
20 Stanesgate Ho
21 Breamore Ho
22 Ely Ho
23 Gisburn Ho
24 Silkin Mews
25 Peckham Park Prim Sch
26 St Francis RC Prim Sch
C4 1 Bowles Rd
2 Western Wharf
3 Northfield Ho
4 Millbrook Ho
5 Denstone Ho
6 Deerhurst Ho
7 Caversham Ho
8 Battle Ho
9 Cardiff Ho
10 Bridgnorth Ho
11 Exeter Ho
12 Grantham Ho
13 Aylesbury Ho
14 Royston Ho
15 Haymerle Sch

50
A1 1 Walkynscroft
2 Ryegates
3 Hathorne Cl
4 Pilkington Rd
5 Russell Ct
6 Heaton Ho
7 Magdalene Cl
8 Iris Ct
10 St Mary Magdalene CE Prim Sch
A2 1 Willowdene
2 Pinedene
3 Oakdene
4 Beechdene
5 Hollydene
6 Wood Dene
7 Staveley Cl
8 Carnicot Ho
10 Martock Ct
11 Cherry Tree Ct

12 Kendrick Ct
13 John Donne Prim Sch
A3 1 Tortington Ho
2 Credenhill Ho
3 Bromyard Ho
4 Hoyland Ct
5 Willowdene
6 Ashdene
7 Acorn Par
8 Havelock Ct
9 Springall St
10 Harry Lambourn Ho
11 Grenier Apartments
B1 1 Honiton Gdns
2 Selden Ho
3 Hathway Ho
4 Hathway St
5 Station Ct
6 Symons Cl
7 Hollydale Prim Sch
B2 1 Trotman Ho
2 Boddington Ho
3 Heydon Ho
4 Boulter Ho
5 Astbury Bsns Pk
B3 1 Ambleside Point
2 Grasmere Point
3 Windermere Point
4 Roman Way
5 Laburnum Cl
6 Juniper Ho
7 Romney Cl
8 Hammersley Ho
9 Hutchinson Ho
10 Hammond Ho
11 Fir Tree Ho
12 Glastonbury Ct
13 Highbridge Ct
14 Filton Ct
15 Chiltern Ct
16 Cheviot Ct
B4 1 Penshurst Ho
2 Reculver Ho
3 Mereworth Ho
4 Camber Ho
5 Chiham Ho
6 Otford Ho
7 Olive Tree Ho
8 Aspen Ho
9 Lewis Silkin Ho
10 Richborough Ho
11 Dover Ho
12 Eynsford Ho
13 Horton Ho
14 Lamberhurst Ho
15 Canterbury Ind Pk
16 Upnall Ho
17 Sissinghurst Ho
18 Rochester Ho
19 Saltwood Ho
20 Leybourne Ho
21 Lullingstone Ho
22 Pilgrims Way Prim Sch
C3 1 Richard Anderson Ct
2 Palm Tree Ho
3 Edward Robinson Ho
4 Antony Ho
5 Gerrard Ho
6 Palmer Ho
7 Pankhurst Cl
C4 1 Harrisons Ct
2 Grantley Ho
3 Sunbury Ct

4 Tilbury Ho
5 Graham Ct
6 Connell Ct
7 St Clements Ct
8 Henderson Ct
9 Jennotts Ct
10 Verona Ct
11 Heywood Ho
12 Francis Ct
13 Hind Ho
14 Donne Ho
15 Carew Ct
16 Burbage Ho
17 Newland Ho
18 Dobson Ho
19 Greene Ct
20 Redrup Ho
21 Tarplett Ho
22 Stunell Ho
23 Gasson Ho
24 Bryce Ho
25 Barnes Ho
26 Barkwith Ho
27 Bannister Ho
28 Apollo Ind Bsns Ctr

51
A2 1 Archer Ho
2 Browning Ho
3 Hardcastle Ho
4 Brooke Ho
5 Wallis Ho
A3 1 Batavia Ho
2 Marlowe Bsns Ctr
3 Batavia Mews
4 Woodrush Cl
5 Alexandra St
6 Primrose Wlk
7 Vansittart St
8 Granville Ct
9 Cottesbrook St
10 Ewen Henderson Ct
11 Fordham Ho
12 Deptford Green Sch (Annex)
A4 1 Portland Ct
2 Phoenix Ct
3 Rainbow Ct
4 Hawke Twr
5 Woodpecker Rd
6 Hercules Ct
B3 1 Austin Ho
2 Exeter Way
3 Crossleigh Ct
4 Mornington Pl
5 Maple Ho
B4 1 Chester Ho
2 Lynch Wlk
3 Arlington Ho
4 Woodcote Ho
5 Cornbury Ho
6 Prospect Pl
7 Akintaro Ho
8 Mulberry Ho
9 Laurel Ho
10 Linden Ho
11 Ashford Ho
12 Wardalls Ho
13 Magnolia Ho
14 Howard Ho
15 Larch Cl
16 Ibis Ct
17 Merganser Ct
18 Wotton Rd
19 Kingfisher Sq

20 Sanderling Ct
21 Dolphin Twr
22 Mermaid Twr
23 Scoter Ct
24 Shearwater Ct
25 Brambling Ct
26 Kittiwake Ct
27 Diana Cl
28 Guillemot Ct
29 Marine Twr
30 Teal Ct
31 Lapwing Twr
32 Violet Cl
33 Skua Ct
34 Tristan Ct
35 Rosemary Ct
36 Cormorant Ct
37 Shelduck Ct
38 Eider Ct
39 Pintail Ct
40 Fulcher Ct
41 Grinling Gibbons Prim Sch
C1 1 Ashmead Mews
2 St Stephen's CE Prim Sch
C2 1 Admiralty Cl
2 Harton Lodge
3 Sylva Cotts
4 Pitman Ho
5 Heston Ho
6 Mereton Mans
7 Indiana Bldg
8 St John's Lodge
9 Dean's Gateway
10 Lucas Vale Prim Sch
11 Addey & Stanhope Sch
12 Lewisham Coll (Deptford Campus)
C3 1 Sandpiper Ct
2 Flamingo Ct
3 Titan Bsns Est
4 Rochdale Way
5 Speedwell St
6 Reginald Pl
7 Fletcher Path
8 Frankham Ho
9 Cremer Ho
10 Wilshaw Ho
11 Castell Ho
12 Holden Ho
13 Browne Ho
14 Resolution Way
15 Lady Florence Ctyd
16 Covell Ct
17 Albion Ho
18 Maritime Greenwich Coll
19 St Joseph's RC Prim Sch
20 Tidemill Prim Sch
C4 1 Dryfield Wlk
2 Blake Ho
3 Hawkins Ho
4 Grenville Ho
5 Langford Ho
6 Mandarin Ct
7 Bittern Ct
8 Lamerton St
9 Ravensbourne Mans
10 Armada St
11 Armada Ct
12 Benbow Ho
13 Oxenham Ho

14 Caravel Mews
15 Hughes Ho
16 Stretton Mans

52
A1 1 Morden Mount Prim Sch
A2 1 Washington Bldg
2 California Bldg
3 Utah Bldg
4 Montana Bldg
5 Oregon Bldg
6 Dakota bldg
7 Idaho Bldg
8 Atlanta Bldg
9 Colorado Bldg
10 Arizona Bldg
11 Nebraska Bldg
12 Alaska Bldg
13 Ohio Bldg
14 Charter Bldgs
15 Flamsteed Ct
16 Friendly Pl
17 Dover Ct
18 Robinscroft Mews
19 Doleman Ho
20 Plymouth Ho
A3 1 Finch Ho
2 Jubilee The
3 Maitland Cl
4 Ashburnham Retreat
B1 1 Ellison Ho
2 Pitmaston Ho
3 Aster Ho
4 Windmill Cl
5 Hertmitage The
6 Burnett Ho
7 Lacey Ho
8 Darwin Ho
9 Pearmain Ho
B2 1 Penn Almshouses
2 Jervis Ct
3 Woodville Ct
4 Darnall Ho
5 Renbold Ho
6 Lindsell St
7 Plumbridge Ct
8 Trinity Gr
9 Hollymount Cl
10 Cade Tyler Ho
11 Robertson Ho
B3 1 Temair Ho
2 Royal Hill Ct
3 Prince of Orange La
4 Lambard Ho
5 St Marks Cl
6 Ada Kennedy Ct
7 Arlington Pl
8 Topham Ho
9 Darnell Ho
10 Hawks Mews
11 Royal Pl
12 Swanne Ho
13 Maribor
14 Serica Ct
15 Queen Elizabeth's Coll
16 James Wolfe Prim Sch
17 Greenwich Coll
B4 1 Crescent Arc
2 Greenwich Mkt

304 52 B4

B1
- 3 Turnpin La
- 4 Durnford St
- 5 Sexton's Ho
- 6 Bardsley Ho
- 7 Wardell Ho
- 8 Clavell St
- 9 Stanton Ho
- 10 Macey Ho
- 11 Boreman Ho
- 12 Clipper Appts

C4
- 1 Frobisher Ct
- 2 Hardy Cotts
- 3 Palliser Ho
- 4 Bernard Angell Ho
- 5 Corvette Sq
- 6 Travers Ho
- 7 Maze Hill Lodge
- 8 Park Place Ho
- 9 Meridian Prim Sch

53

B1
- 1 Heath House Prep Sch

B3
- 1 Westcombe Ct
- 2 Kleffens Ct
- 3 Ferndale Ct
- 4 Combe Mews
- 5 Mandeville Cl
- 6 Pinelands Cl

C3
- 1 Mary Lawrenson Pl
- 2 Bradbury Ct
- 3 Dunstable Ct
- 4 Wentworth Ho

C4
- 1 Nethercombe Ho
- 2 Holywell Cl

54

A1
- 1 Lancaster Cotts
- 2 Lancaster Mews
- 3 Bromwich Ho
- 4 Priors Lo
- 5 Richmond Hill Ct
- 6 Glenmore Ho
- 7 Hillbrow
- 8 Heathshott
- 9 Friars Stile Pl
- 10 Spire Ct
- 11 Ridgeway
- 12 Matthias Ct
- 13 Old Vicarage Sch

A2
- 1 Lichfield Terr
- 2 Union Ct
- 3 Carrington Lo
- 4 Wilton Ct
- 5 Egerton Ct
- 6 Beverley Lo
- 7 Bishop Duppa's Almshouses
- 8 Regency Wlk
- 9 Clear Water Ho
- 10 Onslow Avenue Mans
- 11 Michels Almshouses
- 12 Albany Pas
- 13 Salcombe Villas

A3
- 1 St John's Gr
- 2 Michel's Row
- 3 Michelsdale Dr
- 4 Blue Anchor Alley
- 5 Clarence St
- 6 Sun Alley
- 7 Thames Link Ho
- 8 Benns Wlk

B1
- 9 Waterloo Pl
- 10 Northumbria Ct

B1
- 1 Chester Ct
- 2 Evesham Ct
- 3 Queen's Ct
- 4 Russell Wlk
- 5 Charlotte Sq
- 6 Jones Wlk
- 7 Hilditch Ho
- 8 Isabella Ct
- 9 Damer Ho
- 10 Eliot Ho
- 11 Fitzherbert Ho
- 12 Reynolds Pl
- 13 Chisholm Rd

B2
- 1 Alberta Ct
- 2 Beatrice Rd
- 3 Lorne Rd
- 4 York Rd
- 5 Connaught Rd
- 6 Albany Terr
- 7 Kingswood Ct
- 8 Selwyn Ct
- 9 Broadhurst Cl

B3
- 1 Towers The
- 2 Longs Ct
- 3 Sovereign Ct
- 4 Robinson Ct
- 5 Calvert Ct
- 6 Bedford Ct
- 7 Hickey's Almshouses
- 8 Church Estate Almshouses
- 9 Richmond International Bsns Ctr
- 10 Abercorn Mews

55

A3
- 1 Hershell Ct
- 2 Deanhill Ct
- 3 Park Sheen
- 4 Furness Lo
- 5 Merricks Ct

C4
- 1 Rann Ho
- 2 Craven Ho
- 3 John Dee Ho
- 4 Kindell Ho
- 5 Montgomery Ho
- 6 Avondale Ho
- 7 Addington Ho
- 8 Dovecote Gdns
- 9 Firmston Ho
- 10 Glendower Gdns
- 11 Chestnut Ave
- 12 Trehern Rd
- 13 Rock Ave
- 14 St Mary Magdalen's RC Prim Sch

56

C2
- 1 Theodore Ho
- 2 Nicholas Ho
- 3 Bonner Ho
- 4 Downing Ho
- 5 Jansen Ho
- 6 Fairfax Ho
- 7 Devereux Ho
- 8 David Ho
- 9 Leigh Ho
- 10 Clipstone Ho
- 11 Mallet Ho
- 12 Arton Wilson Ho

57

B2
- 1 Inglis Ho
- 2 Ducie Ho

B1
- 3 Wharncliffe Ho
- 4 Stanhope Ho
- 5 Waldegrave Ho
- 6 Mildmay Ho
- 7 Mullens Ho

C1
- 1 Balmoral Cl
- 2 Glenalmond Ho
- 3 Selwyn Ho
- 4 Keble Ho
- 5 Bede Ho
- 6 Gonville Ho
- 7 Magdalene Ho
- 8 Armstrong Ho
- 9 Newnham Ho
- 10 Somerville Ho
- 11 Balliol Ho
- 12 Windermere
- 13 Little Combe Cl
- 14 Classinghall Ho
- 15 Chalford Ct
- 16 Garden Royal
- 17 South Ct
- 18 Anne Kerr Ct
- 19 Ewhurst

C2
- 1 Geneva Ct
- 2 Laurel Ct
- 3 Cambalt Ho
- 4 Langham Ct
- 5 Lower Pk
- 6 King's Keep
- 7 Whitnell Ct
- 8 Whitehead Ho
- 9 Halford Ho
- 10 Humphry Ho
- 11 Jellicoe Ho
- 12 South Thames Coll (Putney Ctr)

C3
- 1 Olivette St
- 2 Mascotte Rd
- 3 Glegg Pl
- 4 Crown Ct
- 5 Charlwood Terr
- 6 Percy Laurie Ho
- 7 Our Lady of Victories RC Prim Sch

C4
- 1 Griffin Gate
- 2 Darfur St
- 3 John Keall Ho
- 4 Henry Jackson Ho
- 5 Felsham Ho
- 6 Ardshiel Cl
- 7 Ruvigny Mans
- 8 Star & Garter Mans
- 9 University Mans
- 10 Lockyer Ho
- 11 Phelps Ho
- 12 Princeton Ct
- 13 Kingsmere Cl
- 14 Felsham Mews
- 15 St Mary's CE Prim Sch

58

A2
- 1 Claremont
- 2 Downside
- 3 Cavendish Cl
- 4 Ashcombe Ct
- 5 Carltons The
- 6 Espirit Ho
- 7 Millbrooke Ct
- 8 Coysh Ct
- 9 Keswick Hts
- 10 Avon Ct
- 11 Merlin Sch The

B2
- 1 Keswick Broadway
- 2 Burlington Mews
- 3 Cambria Ho

B1
- 4 St Stephen's Gdns
- 5 Atlantic Ho
- 6 Burton Lo
- 7 Manfred Ct
- 8 Meadow Bank
- 9 Hooper Ho
- 10 Aspire Bld

C2
- 1 Pembridge Pl
- 2 Adelaide Rd
- 3 London Ct
- 4 Windsor Ct
- 5 Westminster Ct
- 6 Fullers Ho
- 7 Bridge Pk
- 8 Lambeth Ct
- 9 Milton Ct
- 10 Norfolk Mans
- 11 Francis Snary Lo
- 12 Bush Cotts
- 13 Downbury Mews
- 14 Newton's Yd
- 15 Roche Sch The
- 16 St Joseph's RC Prim Sch
- 17 West Hill Prim Sch
- 18 St Michael Steiner Sch The

59

A2
- 1 Fairfield Ct
- 2 Blackmore Ho
- 3 Lancaster Mews
- 4 Cricketers Mews
- 5 College Mews
- 6 Arndale Wlk
- 7 St Anne's CE Prim Sch
- 8 South Thames Coll (Wandsworth Ctr)

B2
- 1 St Faith's CE Prim Sch

B4
- 1 Molasses Ho
- 2 Molasses Row
- 3 Cinnamon Row
- 4 Calico Ho
- 5 Calico Row
- 6 Port Ho
- 7 Square Rigger Row
- 8 Trade Twr
- 9 Ivory Ho
- 10 Spice Ct
- 11 Sherwood Ct
- 12 Mendip Ct
- 13 Chalmers Ho
- 14 Coral Row
- 15 Ivory Sq
- 16 Kingfisher Ho

C3
- 1 Burke Ho
- 2 High View Prim Sch
- 3 Centre Acad
- 4 Fox Ho
- 5 Buxton Ho
- 6 Pitt Ho
- 7 Ramsey Ho
- 8 Beverley Cl
- 9 Florence Ho
- 10 Linden Ct
- 11 Dorcas Ct
- 12 Johnson Ct
- 13 Agnes Ct
- 14 Hilltop Ct
- 15 Courtyard The
- 16 Old Laundry The
- 17 Oberstein Rd
- 18 Fineran Ct
- 19 Sangora Rd
- 20 Harvard Mans

60

A4
- 1 Kiloh Ct
- 2 Lanner Ho
- 3 Griffon Ho
- 4 Kestrel Ho
- 5 Kite Ho
- 6 Peregrine Ho
- 7 Hawk Ho
- 8 Inkster Ho
- 9 Harrier Ho
- 10 Eagle Hts
- 11 Kingfisher Ct
- 12 Lavender Terr
- 13 Temple Ho
- 14 Ridley Ho
- 15 Eden Ho
- 16 Hertford Ct
- 17 Nepaul Rd

B1
- 1 Staplehurst Ct
- 2 Teyham Ct
- 3 Honeywell Jun & Inf Schs

B2
- 1 Clapham Computer & Secretarial Coll

C1
- 1 Rayne Ho
- 2 St Anthony's Ct
- 3 Earlsthorpe Mews
- 4 Nightingale Mans

C4
- 1 Shaftesbury Park Chambers
- 2 Selborne
- 3 Rush Hill Mews
- 4 Marmion Mews
- 5 Crosland Pl
- 6 Craven Mews
- 7 Garfield Mews
- 8 Audley Cl
- 9 Basnett Rd
- 10 Tyneham Cl
- 11 Woodmere Cl

D1
- 5 Broomwood Hall (Lower Sch)

61

A1
- 1 Oliver House Prep Sch

A4
- 1 Turnchapel Mews

C4
- 1 Milner Ho
- 2 McManus Ho
- 3 Wilberforce Ho
- 4 Wheeler Ct
- 5 Sporle Ct
- 6 Holliday Sq
- 7 John Parker Sq
- 8 Carmichael Cl
- 9 Fenner Sq
- 10 Clark Lawrence Ct
- 11 Shaw Ct
- 12 Sendall Ct
- 13 Livingstone Rd
- 14 Farrant Ho
- 15 Jackson Ho
- 16 Darien Ho
- 17 Shepard Ho
- 18 Ganley Ct
- 19 Arthur Newton Ho
- 20 Chesterton Ho
- 21 John Kirk Ho
- 22 Mantua St
- 23 Heaver Rd
- 24 Candlemakers
- 25 Thames Christian Coll
- 26 Falconbrook Prim Sch

C4
- 19 Plough Mews

2 Redwood Mews
3 Phil Brown Pl
4 Bev Callender Cl
5 Keith Connor Cl
6 Tessa Sanderson Pl
7 Daley Thompson Way
8 Rashleigh Ct
9 Abberley Mews
10 Willow Lodge
11 Beaufry Rd
B1 **1** Joseph Powell Cl
2 Cavendish Mans
3 Westlands Terr
4 Cubitt Ho
5 Hawkesworth Ho
6 Normanton Ho
7 Eastman Ho
8 Couchman Ho
9 Poynders Ct
10 Selby Ho
11 Valentine Ho
12 Gorham Ho
13 Deauville Mans
14 Deauville Ct
B2 **1** Timothy Cl
2 Shaftesbury Mews
3 Brook Ho
4 Grover Ho
5 Westbrook Ho
6 Hewer Ho
7 Batten Ho
8 Mandeville Ho
9 George Beare Lo
10 St Mary's RC Prim Sch
B3 **1** Polygon The
2 Windsor Ct
3 Trinity Cl
4 Studios The
5 Bourne Ho
B4 **1** Clapham Manor Ct
2 Clarke Ho
3 Gables The
4 Sycamore Mews
5 Maritime Ho
6 Rectory Gdns
7 Floris Pl
8 Clapham Manor Prim Sch
C1 **1** Parrington Ho
2 Savill Ho
3 Blackwell Ho
4 Bruce Ho
5 Victoria Ct
6 Victoria Ho
7 Belvedere Ct
8 Ingram Lo
9 Viney Ct
10 Bloomsbury Ho
11 Belgravia Ho
12 Barnsbury Ho
C3 **1** Kendoa Rd
2 Felmersham Cl
3 Abbeville Mews
4 Saxon Ho
5 Gifford Ho
6 Teignmouth Cl
7 Holwood
8 Oaklands Pl
9 Wilberforce Mews
10 William Bonney Est
11 London Coll of Bsns & Computer Studies
C4 **1** Chelsham Ho
2 Lynde Ho

3 Greener Ho
4 Towns Ho
5 Hugh Morgan Ho
6 Roy Ridley Ho
7 Lendal Terr
8 Slievemore Cl
9 Cadmus Cl
10 Clapham North Bsns Ctr

62
A2 **1** King's Mews
2 Clapham Court Terr
3 Clapham Ct
4 Clapham Park Terr
5 Pembroke Ho
6 Stevenson Ho
7 Queenswood Ct
8 Oak Tree Ct
9 Park Lofts
10 Ashby Mews
A3 **1** Morris Ho
2 Gye Ho
3 Clowes Ho
4 Thomas Ho
5 Stuart Ho
6 Storace Ho
7 Bedford Ho
8 Ascot Ct
9 Ascot Par
10 Ashmere Ho
11 Ashmere Gr
12 Ventura Ho
13 Vickery Ho
14 Stafford Mans
15 Beresford Ho
A4 **1** Callingham Ho
2 Russell Pickering Ho
3 Ormerod Ho
4 Lopez Ho
5 Coachmaker Mews
6 Brixton Day Coll
B2 **1** Beatrice Ho
2 Florence Ho
3 Evelyn Ho
4 Diana Ho
5 Brixton Hill Ct
6 Austin Ho
7 Manor Ct
8 Camsey Ho
9 Romer Ho
10 Gale Ho
11 Byrne Ho
12 Farnfield Ho
13 Marchant Ho
14 Rainsford Ho
15 Springett Ho
16 Mannering Ho
17 Waldron Ho
18 Sudbourne Prim Sch
19 Corpus Christi RC Prim Sch
B3 **1** Freemens Hos
2 Roger's Almshouses
3 Gresham Almshouses
4 Exbury Ho
5 Glasbury Ho
6 Dalbury Ho
7 Fosbury Ho
8 Chalbury Ho
9 Neilson-Terry Ct
10 Pavilion Mans
11 Daisy Dormer Ct

12 George Lashwood Ct
13 Marie Lloyd Ct
14 Trinity Homes
15 Lethaby Ho
16 Edmundsbury Ct Est
17 Regis Pl
18 Marlborough Mews
19 Alpha Ho
20 Beta Pl
21 Cedars Ho
22 South Chelsea Coll
B4 **1** Turberville Ho
2 Thrayle Ho
3 Percheron Ct
4 Draymans Ct
5 Lansdowne Sch
6 Stockwell Prim Sch
C1 **1** Eccleston Ho
2 Scarsbrook Ho
3 Purser Ho
4 Rudhall Ho
5 Hardham Ho
6 Heywood Ho
7 Haworth Ho
8 Birch Ho
9 Lansdell Ho
10 Lomley Ho
11 Laughton Ho
12 Woodruff Ho
13 Bascome St
14 Dudley Mews
15 Herbert Mews
16 Blades Lo
17 Dick Shepherd Ct
18 Charman Ho
19 Morden Ho
20 Bishop Ct
21 Blackburn Ct
22 Leigh Ct
23 John Conwey Ho
24 Bristowe Ct
C2 **1** Crownstone Ct
2 Brockwell Ct
3 Nevena Ct
4 St George's Residences
5 Hanover Mans
6 Fleet Ho
7 Langbourne Ho
8 Turnmill Ho
9 Walker Mews
10 Cossar Mews
11 Carter Ho
12 Arungford Mews
C3 **1** Electric Mans
2 Electric La
3 Connaught Mans
4 Clifton Mans
5 Hereford Ho
6 Chaplin Ho
7 Brixton Oval
8 Lord David Pitt Ho
9 Marcus Garvey Way
10 Montego Cl
11 Bob Marley Way
12 Leeson Rd
C4 **1** Buckmaster Ho
2 Albemarle Ho
3 Goodwood Mans
4 Angell Park Gdns
5 Fyfield Rd
6 Howard Ho
7 Harris Ho
8 Broadoak Ct
9 Burgate Ct

10 Witchwood Ho
11 Blacktree Mews
12 Chartham Ct
13 Chilham Ct
14 Northgate Ct
15 Westgate Ct
16 Dover Mans
17 St Helen's RC Sch
18 Dorrell Pl

63
A2 **3** Poets Mews
6 St Jude's CE Prim Sch
A3 **1** Mahatma Gandhi Ind Est
2 Dylan Rd
3 Bessemer Park Ind Est
4 Pablo Neruda Cl
5 Langston Hughes Cl
6 Walt Whitman Cl
7 James Joyce Wlk
8 Alice Walker Cl
9 Louise Bennett Cl
10 Chadacre Ho
11 Burwood Ho
12 Pyrford Ho
13 Wangford Ho
14 Ashford Ho
15 Kenwood Ho
16 Moyne Ho
17 Elveden Ho
18 Carrara Cl
19 Broughton Dr
20 Angela Davis Ind Est
21 Tilia Wlk
22 County Ho
23 Hill Mead Prim Sch
A4 **1** Mallams Mews
2 Amberley Ct
3 Harper Ho
4 Leicester Ho
5 Station Ave
6 Wellfit St
7 Loughborough Ct
8 Belinda Rd
9 Higgs Ind Est
10 Tham Cl
C3 **1** Shaftesbury Ct
2 Mayhew Ct
3 Morris Ct
4 Swinburne Ct
5 Perth Ct
6 Tayside Ct
7 Matlock Ct
8 Hunter Ct
9 Turner Ct

64
A2 **1** Velde Way
2 Delft Way
3 Arnhem Way
4 Isel Way
5 Kempis Way
6 Terborch Way
7 Steen Way
8 Deventer Cres
9 Nimegen Way
10 Hilversum Cres
11 St Barnabas Sq
12 James Allen's Girls' Sch
13 James Allen's Prep Sch

67 C1 **305**

A4 **1** Harfield Gdns
2 Karen Ct
3 Seavington Ho
4 Appleshaw Ho
5 Birdsall Ho
6 Whitney Ho
7 Wheatland Ho
8 Wilton Ho
9 Walcot Ho
10 Whaddon Ho
11 Melbreak Ho
12 Ledbury Ho
13 Tidworth Ho
14 Riseholme Ho
15 Ringmer Ho
16 Petworth Ho
17 Stagshaw Ho
18 Ivybridge Ho
19 Inwood Ho
20 Gatcombe Ho
21 Felbridge Ho
22 Cowdray Ho
23 Dog Kennel Hill Sch
B3 **1** Dulwich Mews
2 New Hope Christian Sch
3 St James's Cloisters
C2 **1** Dorothy Charrington Ho
2 Keswick Ct
3 Kendall Ct
4 Halliwell Ct
C4 **4** St John's & St Clements CE Jun & Inf Sch
5 Bellenden Prim Sch

65
A4 **1** Tilling Ho
2 Goodwin Ho
3 Tyrells Ct
4 Citron Terr
5 Basswood Ct
6 Cheam St
7 Rye Oak Sch
C3 **1** Laxton Path
2 Barlings Ho
3 Bayfield Ho
4 Coston Wlk
5 Coverham Ho
6 Gateley Ho
7 Dereham Ho
8 Greenwood Ho
9 Hilton Ho
10 Goodall Ho
11 Horsley Ho
12 Jordan Ho

66
A3 **1** Turnham Prim Sch

67
A4 **1** Pine Tree Way
2 Waterway Ave
3 Lewisham Bridge Prim Sch
B4 **1** Bankside Ave
2 Elder Wlk
3 Yew Tree Cl
4 Mill Ho
C1 **1** Park Piazza
2 Birdwood Ave

C4 1 Our Lady of Lourdes RC Prim Sch

68

C3 1 Farnborough Ho
2 Rushmere Ho
3 Horndean Cl
4 Highcross Way
5 Timsbury Wlk
6 Foxcombe Rd
7 Ryefield Path
8 Greatham Wlk
9 Gosport Ho
10 Stoatley Ho
11 Milland Ho
12 Clanfield Ho
13 Fareham Ho
14 Grayswood Point

C4 1 Woodcott Ho
2 Lyndhurst Ho
3 Wheatley Ho
4 Allbrook Ho
5 Bordon Wlk
6 Chilcombe Ho
7 Vicarage Ct
8 Shawford Ct
9 Eastleigh Wlk
10 Kings Ct
11 Somborne Ho

69

A3 1 Ramsdean Ho
2 Purbrook Ho
3 Portsea Ho
4 Blendworth Point
5 Eashing Point
6 Hindhead Point
7 Hilsea Point
8 Witley Point
9 Buriton Ho
10 Grateley Ho
11 Hascombe Ho
12 Dunhill Point
13 Westmark Point
14 Longmoor Point
15 Cadnam Point

B4 1 Cumberland Ho
2 Devonshire Ho
3 Cornwall Ho
4 Norfolk Ho
5 Leicester Ho
6 Warwick Ho
7 Sutherland Ho
8 Carmarthen Ho
9 Worcester Ho
10 Rutland Ho
11 Paddock Way
12 Putney Hill

C3 1 Sandringham Cl
2 Eastwick Ct
3 Oatlands Ct
4 Banning Ho
5 Grantley Ho
6 Caryl Ho
7 Duncombe Ho
8 Chilworth Ct
9 Kent Lo
10 Turner Lo
11 Marlborough
12 Parkland Gdns
13 Lewesdon Cl
14 Pines Ct
15 Ashtead Ct
16 Mynterne Ct

17 Arden
18 Stephen Ct
19 Marsham Ct
20 Doradus Ct
21 Acorns The
22 Heritage Ho
23 Conifer Ct
24 Spencer Ho
25 Chartwell
26 Blenheim
27 Chivelston
28 Greenfield Ho
29 Oakman Ho
30 Radley Lo
31 Simon Lo
32 Admirals Ct
33 Augustus Rd

C4 1 Brett Ho
2 Brett House Cl
3 Sylva Ct
4 Ross Ct
5 Potterne Cl
6 Stourhead Ct
7 Fleur Gates
8 Greenwood
9 John Paul II Sch
10 Our Lady Queen of Heaven RC Prim Sch
11 Prospect House Sch

70

A3 1 William Harvey Ho
2 Highview Ct
3 Cameron Ct
4 Galgate Cl
5 Green Ho The
6 King Charles Wlk
7 Florys Ct
8 Augustus Ct
9 Albert Ct
10 Hertford Lo
11 Mortimer Lo
12 Allenswood
13 Ambleside
14 Hansler Ct
15 Roosevelt Ct
16 Southmead Prim Sch

A4 1 Douglas Gracey Ho
2 Aman Dalvi Ho
3 Andrew Reed Ho
4 Stoford Cl
5 Ronald Ross Prim Sch

71

B2 1 Bremans Row
2 St Andrew's Ct
3 Townsend Mews
4 Sheringham Mews
5 Rainbow Sch
6 Garratt Park Sec Specl Sch

72

A2 1 St Peters Cl
2 St Hildas Cl
3 St Edmunds Cl
4 St Hughes Cl
5 St Anthonys Cl
6 St Benets Cl
7 St Catherines Cl
8 Elsley Sch

C2 1 Upper Tooting Park Mans

2 Cecil Mans
3 Marius Mans
4 Boulevard The
5 Elmfield Mans
6 Holderness Rd
7 Lumiere Ct

C3 1 Heslop Ct
2 St James's Terr
3 Boundaries Mans
4 Station Par
5 Old Dairy Mews
6 Chestnut Grove Sch
7 Hornsby House Sch
8 Trinity St Mary's Prim Sch

C4 1 Hollies Way
2 Endlesham Ct
3 Broomwood Hall Sch (Upper Sch)
4 Holy Ghost RC Prim Sch

73

A3 1 Holbeach Mews
2 Hildreth Street Mews
3 Coalbrook Mans
4 Hub Buildings The
5 Metropolis Apartments
6 Hildreth St

A4 1 Meyer Ho
2 Faraday Ho
3 Hales Ho
4 Frankland Ho
5 Graham Ho
6 Gibbs Ho
7 Dalton Ho
8 Ainslie Wlk
9 Rokeby Ho
10 Caistor Ho
11 Ivanhoe Ho
12 Catherine Baird Ct
13 Marmion Ho
14 Devonshire Ct
15 Blueprint Apartments
16 Royal Duchess Mews
17 Alderbrook Prim Sch

B3 2 Henry Cavendish Prim Sch
3 Margaret Rutherford Pl

B4 1 Limerick Ct
2 Homewoods
3 Jewell Ho
4 Glanville Ho
5 Dan Bryant Ho
6 Olding Ho
7 Quennel Ho
8 Weir Ho
9 West Ho
10 Neville Ct
11 Friday Grove Mews
12 St Bernadette RC Jun Sch

C3 1 Sinclair Ho
2 MacGregor Ho
3 Ingle Ho
4 St Andrews Mews
5 Telferscot Prim Sch

C4 1 Riley Ho
2 Bennett Ho
3 White Ho
4 Rodgers Ho

5 Dumphreys Ho
6 Homan Ho
7 Prendergast Ho
8 Hutchins Ho
9 Whiteley Ho
10 Tresidder Ho
11 Primrose Ct
12 Angus Ho
13 Currie Ho

74

A1 1 De Montfort Ct
2 Leigham Hall Par
3 Leigham Hall
4 Endsleigh Mans
5 John Kirk Ho
6 Raeburn Ct
7 Wavel Ct
8 Homeleigh Ct
9 Howland Ho
10 Beauclerk Ho
11 Bertrand Ho
12 Drew Ho
13 Dowes Ho
14 Dunton Ho
15 Raynald Ho
16 Sackville Ho
17 Thurlow Ho
18 Astoria Mans

A2 1 Wyatt Park Mans
2 Broadlands Mans
3 Stonehill's Mans
4 Streatleigh Par
5 Dorchester Ct
6 Picture Ho

A3 1 Beaumont Ho
2 Christchurch Ho
3 Staplefield Cl
4 Chipstead Ho
5 Coulsdon Ho
6 Conway Ho
7 Telford Avenue Mans
8 Telford Parade Mans
9 Wavertree Ct
10 Hartswood Ho
11 Wray Ho

A4 1 Picton Ho
2 Rigg Ho
3 Watson Ho
4 MacArthur Ho
5 Sandon Ho
6 Thorold Ho
7 Pearce Ho
8 Mudie Ho
9 Miller Ho
10 Lycett Ho
11 Lafone Ho
12 Lucraft Ho
13 Freeman Ho
14 New Park Par
15 Argyll Ct
16 Dumbarton Ct
17 Kintyre Ct
18 Cotton Ho
19 Crossman Hos
20 Cameford Ct
21 Parsons Ho
22 Brindley Ho
23 Arkwright Ho
24 Perry Ho
25 Brunel Ho
26 New Park Ct
27 Tanhurst Ho
28 Hawkshaw Cl

29 Richard Atkins Prim Sch

B1 1 Carisbrooke Ct
2 Pembroke Lo
3 Willow Ct
4 Poplar Ct
5 Leigham Cl
6 Mountview
7 Spa View

B3 1 Charlwood Ho
2 Earlswood Ho
3 Balcombe Ho
4 Claremont Ct
5 Holbrook Ho
6 Gwynne Ho
7 Kynaston Ho
8 Tillman Ho
9 Regents Lo
10 Hazelmere Ct
11 Dykes Ct
12 Hartwell Ct
13 Christ Church Streatham CE Prim Sch
14 Streatham Hill & Clapham High Sch

B4 1 Archbishop's Pl
2 Witley Ho
3 Outwood Ho
4 Dunsfold Ho
5 Deepdene Lo
6 Warnham Ho
7 Albury Lo
8 Tilford Ho
9 Elstead Ho
10 Thursley Ho
11 Brockham Ho
12 Capel Lo
13 Leith Ho
14 Fairview Ho
15 Weymouth Ct
16 Ascalon Ct
17 China Mews
18 Rush Common Mews

C3 1 Valens Ho
2 Loveday Ho
3 Strode Ho
4 Ethelworth Ct
5 Harbin Ho
6 Brooks Ho
7 Godolphin Ho
8 Sheppard Ho
9 McCormick Ho
10 Taylor Ho
11 Saunders Ho
12 Talcott Path
13 Derrick Ho
14 Williams Ho
15 Baldwin Ho
16 Churston Cl
17 Neil Wates Cres
18 Burnell Ho
19 Portland Ho
20 Fenstanton Prim Sch
21 St Martin-in-the-Fields High Sch

C4 1 Ellacombe Ho
2 Booth Ho
3 Hathersley Ho
4 Brereton Ho
5 Holdsworth Ho
6 Dearmer Ho
7 Cherry Cl
8 Greenleaf Cl
9 Longford Wlk

www.philips-maps.co.uk

First published in 2001 by
Philip's, a division of
Octopus Publishing Group Ltd
www.octopusbooks.co.uk
Endeavour House,
189 Shaftesbury Avenue
London WC2H 8JG
An Hachette UK Company
www.hachette.co.uk

Fourth edition 2010
First impression 2010
LONDA

© Philip's 2010

Spiral-bound
ISBN 978-1-84907-062-1

Perfect-bound
ISBN 978-1-84907-063-8

Hardback (red)
ISBN 978-1-84907-105-5

Hardback (blue snake)
ISBN 978-1-84907-106-2

Hardback (red reptile)
ISBN 978-1-84907-107-9

This product includes mapping data licensed
from Ordnance Survey® with the permission
of the Controller of Her Majesty's Stationery
Office. © Crown copyright 2010. All rights
reserved. Licence number 100011710.

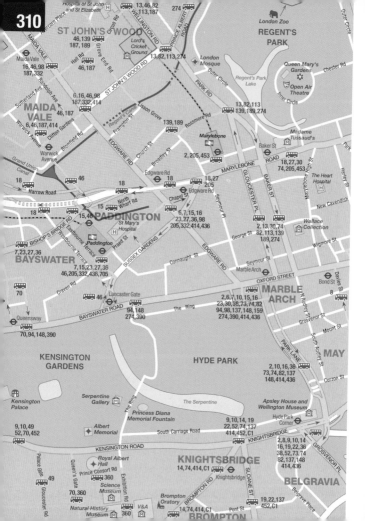

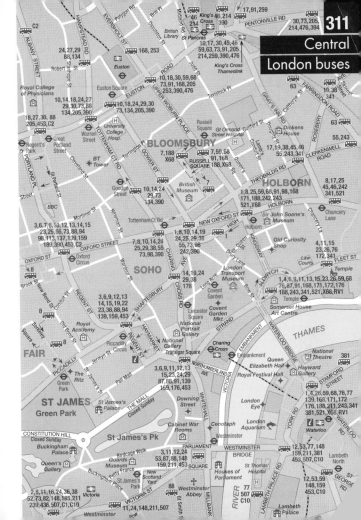

MAYOR OF LONDON

© Transport for London

Reg. user No. 09/1596/P

Website
tfl.gov.uk

24 hour travel information
020 7222 1234

Improvement works may affect your journey, please check before you travel

Transport for London

Version A TfL 12.09
Correct at time of going to print

West End theatres and cinemas

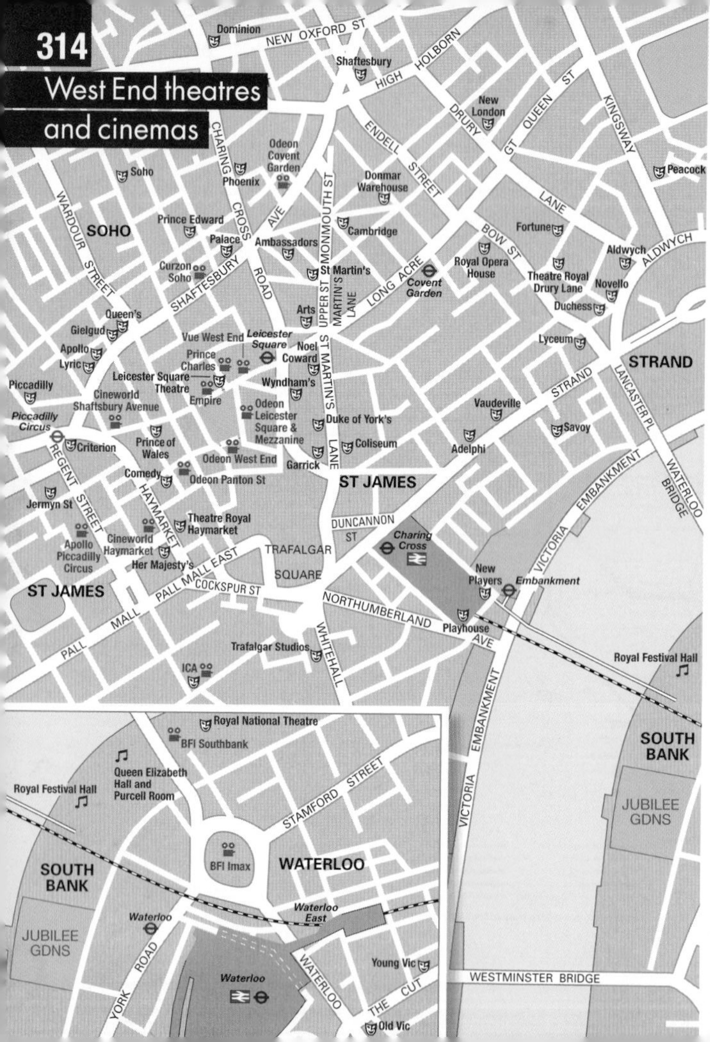

NEW OXFORD ST

Dominion

Shaftesbury

HIGH HOLBORN

New London

GT QUEEN ST

KINGSWAY

DRURY

ENDELL STREET

Peacock

WARDOUR STREET

Soho

CHARING CROSS ROAD

Odeon Covent Garden

Phoenix

Donmar Warehouse

UPPER ST MONMOUTH ST

SOHO

Prince Edward

Palace

Cambridge

BOW ST

Fortune

ALDWYCH

Ambassadors

LANE

Royal Opera House

Aldwych

Curzon Soho

SHAFTESBURY

St Martin's

Theatre Royal Drury Lane

Novello

Queen's

Arts

LONG ACRE

Covent Garden

Duchess

Gielgud

Leicester Square

ST MARTIN'S LANE

Lyceum

STRAND

Apollo

Lyric

Vue West End

Noel Coward

Piccadilly

Prince Charles

Leicester Square Theatre

Wyndham's

STRAND

Piccadilly Circus

Cineworld Shaftesbury Avenue

Empire

Odeon Leicester Square & Mezzanine

Duke of York's

Vaudeville

LANCASTER PL

Savoy

WATERLOO BRIDGE

Criterion

Prince of Wales

Garrick

Coliseum

Adelphi

REGENT STREET

Comedy

Odeon West End

ST JAMES

Jermyn St

Odeon Panton St

HAYMARKET

DUNCANNON ST

Charing Cross

Apollo Piccadilly Circus

Theatre Royal Haymarket

VICTORIA EMBANKMENT

Cineworld Haymarket

TRAFALGAR SQUARE

New Players

Embankment

ST JAMES

Her Majesty's

PALL MALL EAST

COCKSPUR ST

NORTHUMBERLAND

Playhouse

AVE

Royal Festival Hall

PALL MALL

WHITEHALL

Trafalgar Studios

ICA

Royal National Theatre

BFI Southbank

STAMFORD STREET

SOUTH BANK

Queen Elizabeth Hall and Purcell Room

Royal Festival Hall

SOUTH BANK

WATERLOO

JUBILEE GDNS

BFI Imax

Waterloo

Waterloo East

YORK ROAD

JUBILEE GDNS

Waterloo

WATERLOO

THE CUT

Young Vic

WESTMINSTER BRIDGE

VICTORIA EMBANKMENT

Old Vic